In Association with
American Heritage

The PRENTICE HALL
American Nation

We the People

Davidson ★ Castillo ★ Stoff

Prentice
Hall

Upper Saddle River, New Jersey
Glenview, Illinois
Needham, Massachusetts

Authors

James West Davidson is coauthor of *After the Fact: The Art of Historical Detection* and *Nation of Nations: A Narrative History of the American Republic*. Dr. Davidson has taught at both the college and high school levels. He has also consulted on curriculum design for American history courses. Dr. Davidson is an avid canoeist and hiker. His published works on these subjects include *Great Heart,* the true story of a 1903 canoe trip in the Canadian wilderness.

Pedro Castillo teaches American history at the University of California, Santa Cruz, where he also co-directs the Chicano-Latino Research Center. He has earned a Rockefeller Foundation Research Fellowship and two Senior Fulbright-Hayes Lectureships in Latin America. Dr. Castillo's published works on American history and Chicano Latino history include *Mexico en Los Angeles* and *An Illustrated History of Mexican Los Angeles.*

Michael B. Stoff teaches history at the University of Texas at Austin, where he also directs the graduate program in history. He is the author of *Oil, War, and American Security: The Search for a National Policy on Foreign Oil, 1941–1947*, coauthor of *Nation of Nations: A Narrative History of the American Republic*, and co-editor of *The Manhattan Project: A Documentary Introduction to the Atomic Age*. Dr. Stoff has won numerous grants and fellowships.

AmericanHeritage® *American Heritage* magazine was founded in 1954, and it quickly rose to the position it occupies today: the country's preeminent magazine of history and culture. Dedicated to presenting the past in incisive, entertaining narratives underpinned by scrupulous scholarship, *American Heritage* today goes to more than 300,000 subscribers and counts the country's very best writers and historians among its contributors. Its innovative use of historical illustration and its wide variety of subject matter have gained the publication scores of honors across more than forty years, among them the National Magazine Awards.

Acknowledgments and Illustration Credits begin on page 936.

ISBN 0-13-052953-2

1 2 3 4 5 6 7 8 9 10   04 03 02 01 00

Program Reviewers

▲ *Anasazi pottery*

▲ *West African mask*

▲ *Statue of a New England Puritan*

UNIT 2   A Nation Is Born   128

▲ *Colonial powderhorn*

▲ *Early American flag*

▼ *Quill and inkwell used at the Constitutional Convention*

★ **v**

▲ *Thomas Jefferson*

▲ *Women factory workers*

The Louisiana Purchase ➤

▲ *Conestoga wagon*

▲ *Elias Howe sewing machine*

▲ *African American preacher*

UNIT 5 Division and Reunion 420

History Through Literature

▲ Civil War army caps

▲ Emancipation Proclamation

◄ Confederate soldiers roll up their flag for the last time.

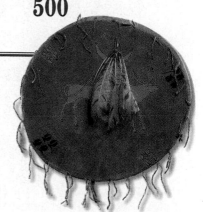

▲ *American Federation of Labor emblem*

UNIT 7 A New Role for the Nation 584

▲ *Statue of a women's rights worker*

▲ *Wilson campaign button*

▲ *American soldiers wounded in World War I, in a painting by John Singer Sargent*

x ★

UNIT 8 Prosperity, Depression, and War 670

▲ *Magazine cover from the 1920s*

▲ *General Douglas MacArthur*

Battle of the ➤
Coral Sea

▲ Dogtags of an American soldier in the Korean War

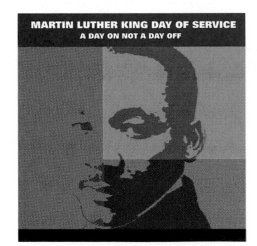

MARTIN LUTHER KING DAY OF SERVICE
A DAY ON NOT A DAY OFF

▲ Poster honoring Martin Luther King Day

Reference Section

Special Features

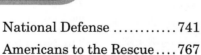

★ *With the editors of* American Heritage *magazine as your guides, you see and read about special sites where American history happened.*

HISTORY HAPPENED HERE

▲ *The Erie Canal*

Linking ...

★ *The Linking features use engaging visuals to make historical connections.*

Linking Past and Present

Linking History and Technology

Linking United States and the World

▲ *Because heroes of the past can be models for today*

▲ *Because you can learn about helping others*

★ *Learn and practice valuable skills that you will be able to use throughout your life.*

▲ *Using the Internet*

Critical Thinking

Managing Information

Communication

Maps, Charts, and Graphs

Charts, Graphs, and Time Lines

Continued ➤

Charts, Graphs, and Time Lines (continued)

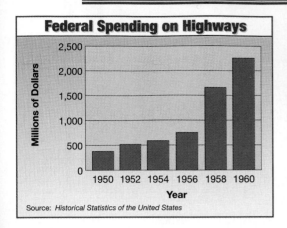

Federal Spending on Highways

Source: *Historical Statistics of the United States*

Graphic Organizers

Maps and Geography Activities

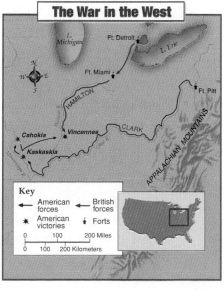

The War in the West

L. Michigan — Ft. Detroit — *L. Erie* — Ft. Miami — Ft. Pitt — HAMILTON — CLARK — Cahokia — Vincennes — Kaskaskia — APPALACHIAN MOUNTAINS

Key
← American forces ← British forces
★ American victories ⚓ Forts
0   100   200 Miles
0 100 200 Kilometers

About This Book

The American Nation is organized into 9 units and 30 chapters. The Table of Contents lists units, chapters, sections, and special features.

IN EACH UNIT

- **Unit Opener** a two-page introduction to the contents and major theme of the unit.
- **History Through Literature** a two-page excerpt from a work of American literature.

IN EACH CHAPTER

- **Chapter Opener** a two-page introduction that includes a time line and chapter summary.
- **As You Read** an introduction to each section, including questions to guide your reading and lists of vocabulary terms and people.
- **Section Reviews** questions and activities that test your understanding of each section.
- **Skills for Life** a lesson that helps you to learn, practice, and apply a useful skill.
- **Linking...** Past and Present, or United States and the World, or History and Technology is a visual feature that shows interesting connections.
- **Biographies** portraits of and information about key people in American history.
- **Interdisciplinary Connections** footnotes that give connections to Geography, Economics, Civics, Arts, or Science.
- **Maps, Graphs, and Charts** visual tools that help you understand history and practice important skills.
- **Chapter Review and Activities** two pages to help you review key terms and ideas and practice valuable skills, with these special features:

  - *Using Primary Sources,* a primary source excerpt with questions that help you recognize different points of view.

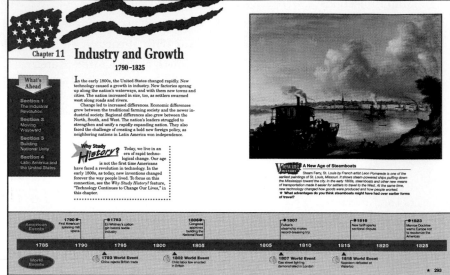

  - *Activity Bank,* includes Interdisciplinary, Career Skills, Citizenship, and Internet activities.

  - *Eyewitness Journal,* writing activity that lets you take on different historical roles.

  - *Critical Thinking and Writing,* questions and exercises that go beyond simple recall.

SPECIAL FEATURES

- **Why Study History?** This feature demonstrates the relevance of historical ideas and events to American life today and to your life in particular.

- **AmericanHeritage® Magazine History Happened Here** The editors of *American Heritage* magazine are your guides to interesting historic sites throughout the nation.

REFERENCE SECTION

- Includes an Atlas, a Gazetteer, a Glossary, the Declaration of Independence, the Constitution of the United States, documents, information about the fifty states, information about the Presidents of the United States, and an Index.

Researching on the Internet

THE INTERNET

The **Internet** includes millions of business, governmental, educational, and individual computers on the World Wide Web. Using programs called browsers, Internet users can find out what sites are available on the Web and then access those sites.

SEARCHING THE INTERNET

There are two basic ways to find information on the Internet. The first is to go directly to the Net site that contains the information you want. Each site has an address, called a **URL**, or Universal Resource Locator. (For example, http://www.phschool.com is the URL of the Prentice Hall Web site.) Of course, this method works only if you know the appropriate URL.

The second way is to use a **search engine**, such as Infoseek or Yahoo! Type the key words representing the topic you want to research. The search engine will then scan the Internet and list sites that pertain to your topic.

Whichever method you choose, you will encounter sites containing **hyperlinks.** These appear as colored or underlined text or as icons. Hyperlinks act as doorways to other documents at the same Web site or others. When you click your mouse on hyperlinked text or graphics, an entirely new document appears on your screen.

Pay careful attention to the source of the information you find. Is the source a government agency, or a university, or a private company, or an individual? Not all sources are equally accurate or reliable in what they present.

See us on the Internet

http://www.phschool.com

At Prentice Hall's Web site, you will find current event updates, social studies links, and other resources to help you learn about American history.

TIPS FOR SUCCESSFUL SEARCHES

Focus your search. Because the Internet contains so much, it is easy to "wander off" into other parts of the Internet and forget about the information that you are trying to locate. To avoid this problem, establish a specific research goal before you begin.

Make bookmarks for useful Web sites. A bookmark is a note to your computer to "remember" the location of a Web site. Later, you can reach any bookmarked site with a simple click of your mouse.

Use specific key words. If your key words are too general, your search might turn up thousands of Net sites. Make your key words specific. Many search engines have useful tips on searching with key words.

Seek guidance from teachers and parents. Ask a teacher, parent, or librarian for help in evaluating whether Web sites and information are reliable and appropriate to your research.

Early Heritage of the Americas

Viewing UNIT THEMES — A Meeting of Different Cultures

George Catlin, an American artist of the 1800s, painted LaSalle Claiming Louisiana for France, April 9, 1682. *As Native Americans watch, newly arrived French explorers gather around a flag and a cross. Encounters and exchanges between Europeans and Native Americans helped form the roots of American society.* ★ **In addition to Europeans and Native Americans, what other people have helped shape American society?**

Unit Theme Origins

Over thousands of years, Native Americans formed diverse societies throughout North America. In the 1500s and 1600s, Europeans and Africans began to arrive in the Americas. The blending and clashing of these three cultures helped shape the nature of modern American life.

Along the Atlantic coast of North America, settlers from England established 13 colonies. English political traditions would form the basis for the American government today.

How did people of the time view American origins? They can tell you in their own words.

★ ★

VIEWPOINTS ON AMERICAN ORIGINS

❝ Roots have spread out from the Tree of the Great Peace, one to the north, one to the east, one to the south, and one to the west. ❞
Treaty forming an alliance among Iroquois nations (1500s)

❝ The people are a collection of diverse nations in Europe as French, Dutch, Germans, Swedes, Danes, Finns, Scotch, Irish, and English. ❞
William Penn, founder of Pennsylvania (1685)

❝ A democracy...is when...power is lodged in a council consisting of all the members and where every member has the privilege of a vote. ...Every man has the privilege freely to deliver his opinion concerning the common affairs. ❞
John Wise, Massachusetts minister (1717)

★ ★

Activity Writing to Learn The peoples who first settled in North America came from many different backgrounds. Think about your school and your community. Then, make a list of the things that can help different people to live together without conflict.

Chapter 1

Focus on Geography
Prehistory–Present

The United States of America is blessed with a beautiful, diverse, and valuable natural environment. In this chapter, you will study geography in general and the geography of our nation in particular. You will learn about the landforms, physical regions, natural resources, and climates of the United States.

Several tools will aid you in your study. Geographers have developed five themes to help you understand the relationship between geography and history. Various kinds of maps will also prove useful.

Why Study History?

In the months ahead, you will see how geography has influenced the history, the government, and the economy of the United States. You will also study how people's actions affect the natural environment. You can learn about the vital importance of one natural resource and how you can help preserve it by reading this chapter's *Why Study History?* feature, "We All Need Water."

American Events			
	1500s Early encounters between Europeans and Native Americans		**1600s** Growing numbers of enslaved Africans in the Americas
Prehistory	1500	1600	1700

1500s World Event
Europeans explore the Americas

World Events

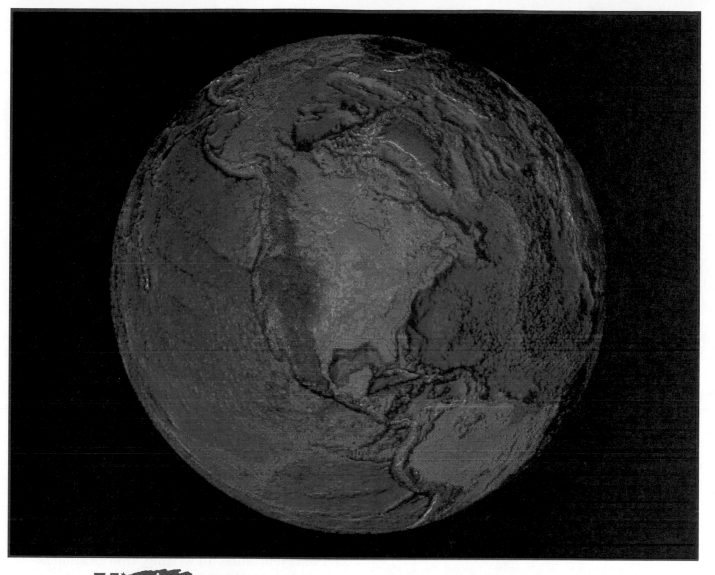

Viewing HISTORY

The View From Space

This picture was taken by a satellite in orbit around the Earth. You are looking directly at North America. The colors are enhanced to highlight the Earth's physical features. Green represents lowlands and orange represents highlands.

★ **What other continents are visible in this satellite photograph?**

1700	1800	1900	Present

1800s ●
Migration to the Pacific Coast increases

1900s ●
Industrialization affects the natural environment

Present ●
Efforts to protect the environment increase

▲ **1700s World Event**
European states struggle for control of North America

▲ **1800s World Event**
Millions of immigrants move to the United States

★ 3

Five Themes of Geography

As You Read

Explore These Questions
- What are the five themes of geography?
- How do people and their natural environment interact?
- What are some causes and effects of the movement of people?

Define
- geography
- history
- latitude
- longitude
- irrigate

SETTING the Scene If you read almost any newspaper, you will find stories about the land around you. One story might argue that building a dam will be harmful to a river. Another might announce the discovery of oil. To understand these and other issues, we need to understand geography.

Geography and History

Geography is the study of people, their environments, and their resources. Geographers ask how the natural environment affects the way we live and how we, in turn, affect the environment. By showing how people and the land are related, geography helps to explain both the past and the present.

Geography is closely linked to history. **History** is an account of what has happened in the lives of different peoples. Both historians and geographers want to understand how the characteristics of a place affect people and events.

To help show the connection between geography and history, geographers have developed five themes. The themes are location, place, interaction between people and their environment, movement, and region.

Location

Where did this event happen? Where is this place? Both historians and geographers often ask such questions. Finding the answers involves the geographic theme of location.

Exact location

As you study American history, you will sometimes need to know the absolute, or exact, location of a place. For example, where, exactly, is Washington, D.C., the nation's capital?

To describe the exact location of Washington, D.C., geographers use a grid of numbered lines on a map or globe that measure latitude and longitude. Lines of **latitude** measure distance north and south from the Equator. Lines of **longitude** measure distance east and west from the Prime Meridian, which runs through Greenwich (GREHN ihch), England.

The exact location of Washington, D.C., is 39 degrees (°) north latitude and 77 degrees (°) west longitude. In writing, this location is often shortened to 39°N/77°W. The Gazetteer in the Reference Section of this book provides the exact location of many important places in American history.

Relative location

Sometimes it is more useful to know the relative location of a place, or its location in relation to some other place. Is Washington, D.C., on the east or west coast of the United States? Is it north or south of Richmond, Virginia? These questions involve relative location.

Knowing relative locations will help you see the relationship between places. Is a place located near a lake, river, or other source of water and transportation? Is it inland or on the coast? Answers to such ques-

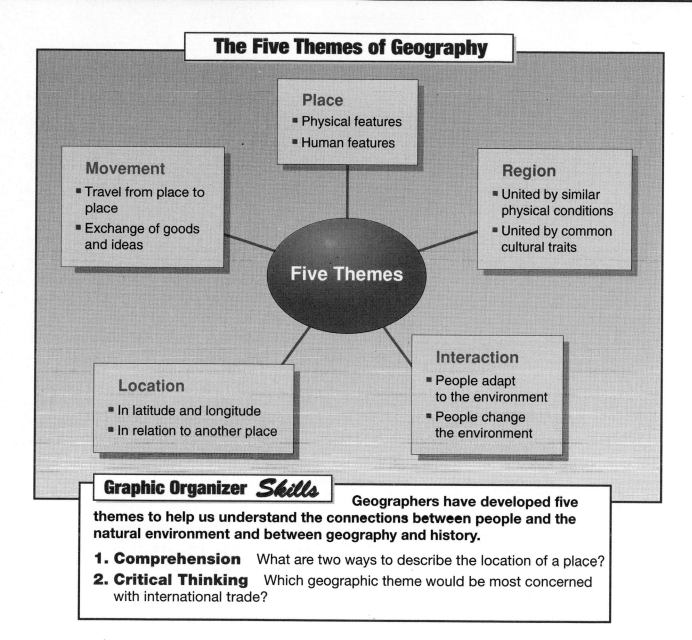

The Five Themes of Geography

Place
- Physical features
- Human features

Movement
- Travel from place to place
- Exchange of goods and ideas

Region
- United by similar physical conditions
- United by common cultural traits

Five Themes

Location
- In latitude and longitude
- In relation to another place

Interaction
- People adapt to the environment
- People change the environment

Graphic Organizer Skills Geographers have developed five themes to help us understand the connections between people and the natural environment and between geography and history.

1. Comprehension What are two ways to describe the location of a place?

2. Critical Thinking Which geographic theme would be most concerned with international trade?

tions help explain why cities grew where they did. Chicago, Illinois, for instance, developed at the center of water, road, and railroad transportation in the Midwest.

Place

A second geography theme is place. Geographers generally describe a place in terms of both physical and human features.

The physical features of a place include climate, soil, plant life, animal life, and bodies of water. For example, New England has a hilly terrain, a rocky coast, and many deep harbors. Because of these physical features,

early Native Americans of the region turned to fishing for a living.

People help to shape the character of a place through their ideas and actions. The human features of a place include the kinds of houses people build as well as their means of transportation, ways of earning a living, languages, and religions.

Think of the human features of the American frontier. In the forests of the frontier, early settlers built log cabins. On the grassy plains, where trees were scarce, some settlers built their homes out of sod, clumps of earth, and grass.

Chicago is one of several major cities that dot the shores of Lake Michigan. Before people interacted with the natural environment, only dense forests encircled the lake. Notice how Chicago has extended into Lake Michigan through the construction of large piers. ★ **How might lakeshore cities like Chicago have a negative impact on the natural environment?**

Interaction

Interaction between people and their environment is a third theme of geography. Throughout history, people have adapted to and changed their natural environment.

For example, ancient hunters in the Americas learned to plant seeds and grow food crops. This adaptation greatly affected their lives. No longer did they have to move from place to place in search of food.

Connections With Geography

Agriculture was impossible in the arid Imperial Valley of southeastern California until irrigation canals were built in the 1900s. The canals bring water from the Colorado River. Today, the Imperial Valley is a very productive farming region.

Later, Native Americans in the Southwest found ways to **irrigate,** or bring water to, the desert. They dug ditches that channeled water from the Salt and Gila rivers. In this way, they were able to change arid, unproductive land into farmland.

In the 1860s, railroad builders in the United States changed the natural environment in order to improve transportation. They wanted to link the Atlantic and Pacific coasts. The railroad workers blasted through mountains and built bridges across rivers. When the project was completed, a railroad line stretched across the nation, linking the eastern and western parts of the United States.

Today, advanced technology allows people to alter their environment dramatically. People have invented ways to take oil from beneath the ocean floor. They have cut down forests to build communities. They have wiped out pests that destroy crops. Such changes have brought great benefits. They have also created new problems, such as air and water pollution.

Movement

A fourth geographic theme involves the movement of people, goods, and ideas. Movement occurs because people and resources are scattered unevenly around the globe. To get what they need or want, people travel from place to place. As they meet other people, they exchange ideas and technology as well as goods.

History provides many examples of the movement of people and ideas. The first people who came to the Americas were hunters following animal herds. Much later, people from all over the world moved to the United States in search of political and religious freedom. They brought with them customs and beliefs that have helped shape American life.

Today, the movement of goods links the United States with all parts of the world. For example, American producers ship goods such as grain and computers to Europe and Africa. Meanwhile, we rely on materials such as oil and tin from other parts of the world.

Region

Geographers study regions. A region is an area of the world that has similar, unifying characteristics. The characteristics of a region may be physical, such as its climate or landforms. For example, the Great Plains is considered a region because it has fairly level land, very hot summers, very cold winters, and little rainfall. The Pacific Coast region, meanwhile, is known for its rugged mountains, dense forests, and scenic ocean shore.

A region's characteristics may also be human and cultural. San Francisco's Chinatown is a region because Chinese Americans there have preserved their language and culture. In New York City, Broadway is a theater district where many plays are performed. In Chicago, the Loop is a downtown area where there are office buildings and museums.

A region can be any size. It can be as large as the United States or as small as a neighborhood. Within one city, there could be several regions. For example, there may be a parkland area known for its natural beauty. There may be a residential area where people live in homes and apartments. There also may be a business district, occupied mostly by office buildings and stores.

★ Section 1 Review ★

Recall

1. **Define** **(a)** geography, **(b)** history, **(c)** latitude, **(d)** longitude, **(e)** irrigate.

Comprehension

2. Briefly describe the five themes of geography.
3. **(a)** Describe two examples of how the natural environment can affect the way people live. **(b)** Give two examples of problems that can result when people change the natural environment.

4. How has the movement of people helped shape American life?

Critical Thinking and Writing

5. **Synthesizing Information** How does the picture of the New England coast on page 17 illustrate the theme of place?
6. **Understanding Causes and Effects** How does modern technology affect the movement of people, goods, and ideas?

Activity **Using Geographic Themes** Use the five themes of geography to describe the neighborhood, community, or state in which you live. Develop your description by writing one or two sentences for each of the five themes.

Maps and Mapmaking

Explore These Questions

- What different types of maps do people use?
- How do latitude and longitude help us to locate places?
- Why are today's maps more accurate than maps of the past?

Define

- globe
- cartographer
- map projection
- hemisphere
- standard time zone

Identify

- Equator
- Prime Meridian

SETTING the Scene In a tiny Indian fishing village in the early 1600s, a small group gathered around Samuel de Champlain. They watched closely as the French explorer pointed to the shore and then drew a sweeping line on a deerskin spread out on the ground. The line represented the coastline where they stood. Quickly, the Native American chief drew other lines on the informal map. A young man added piles of rocks to represent the village and nearby settlements.

Champlain and the Native Americans he met on Cape Ann in Massachusetts did not understand each other's languages. Yet they found a way to communicate. Together, they created a map of the local area. Champlain later used the map to aid him in exploring the Massachusetts coast. People today use maps, too, to help them locate places, judge distances, and follow routes.

Maps and Globes

To locate places, geographers use maps and globes. A map is a drawing of the Earth's surface. A **globe** is a sphere with a map of the Earth printed on it. Because a globe is the same shape as the Earth, it shows sizes and shapes accurately.

Geographers often use flat maps rather than globes.

Unlike a globe, a flat map of the world allows you to see all of the Earth's surface at one time. It is easier to handle and can show more detail. Still, a flat map has the disadvantage that it distorts, or misrepresents, some parts of the Earth.

Map Projections

Mapmakers, or **cartographers,** have developed dozens of different map projections. **Map projections** are ways of drawing the Earth on a flat surface.

Each map projection has benefits and disadvantages. Some projections show the sizes of landmasses correctly but distort their shapes. Others give continents their true shapes but distort their sizes. Still other projections distort direction or distances.

Mercator projection

In 1569, Gerardus Mercator developed the Mercator projection, the best map of its day. For hundreds of years, sailors depended on the Mercator map. Mercator himself boasted of his map:

66 If you wish to sail from one port to another, here is a chart, and a straight line on it, and if you follow this line carefully you will certainly arrive at your destination. 99

A globe is a map of the world.

A Mercator map shows the true shapes of landmasses, but it distorts size, especially for places that are far from the Equator. On a Mercator map, for example, Greenland appears as big as all of South America, even though South America is more than eight times larger!

Robinson projection

Today, many geographers use the Robinson projection. It shows the correct sizes and shapes of landmasses for most parts of the world. The Robinson projection also gives a fairly accurate view of the relationship between landmasses and water.

Kinds of Maps

Maps are part of our daily lives. You have probably read road or bus maps. On television, you have seen weather maps and maps of places in the news.

As you study history, you will use various maps. Examine the Geographic Atlas in the Reference Section of this book. There, you will find maps showing national and state boundaries as well as the physical features and natural resources of the United States.

Each kind of map serves a specific purpose. A political map shows boundaries that people have set up to divide the world into countries and states. A physical map shows natural features, such as mountains and rivers. A population map lets you see how many people live in a particular area. An economic map shows how people of a certain region make a living. A natural resource map helps you see links between the resources of an area and the way people use the land.

Still other kinds of maps include election maps, product maps, and battle maps. These maps also help you to see the connections between geography and history.

Map Projections

Mercator Projection

Robinson Projection

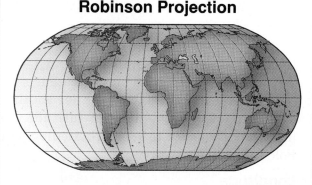
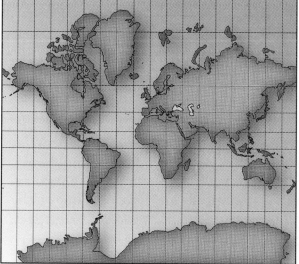

Geography Skills

Map projections make it possible for mapmakers to show a round world on a flat map.

1. Location   Use the map on page 10 to locate: **(a)** North America, **(b)** Africa, **(c)** Asia.

2. Place   How does North America appear differently on the two projections?

3. Critical Thinking   On the Mercator map, which areas are most distorted?

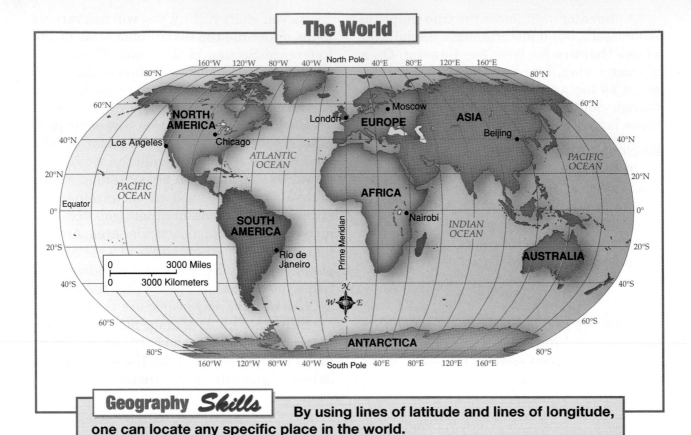

The World

Geography *Skills* By using lines of latitude and lines of longitude, one can locate any specific place in the world.

1. Location   On the map, locate: **(a)** Atlantic Ocean, **(b)** Pacific Ocean, **(c)** Europe, **(d)** North America, **(e)** Africa.

2. Location   Which city is located at about 55°N/35°E?

3. Critical Thinking   Which continents lie entirely in the Northern Hemisphere?

Latitude and Longitude

Most maps and globes include lines of latitude and lines of longitude. The lines form a grid, making it possible to locate places exactly. Each latitude and longitude line on the grid is measured in degrees (°).

Latitude

Look at the map of the world, above. Notice that lines of latitude run east and west. As you have read, lines of latitude measure distances north and south from the Equator.

The **Equator** is an imaginary line that lies at 0° latitude. It divides the Earth into two halves, called **hemispheres.**

The Northern Hemisphere lies north of the Equator. In the Northern Hemisphere, lines of latitude are numbered from 1°N to 90°N, where the North Pole is located.

The Southern Hemisphere lies south of the Equator. There, lines of latitude are numbered from 1°S to 90°S, where the South Pole is located.

Longitude

Lines of longitude on a map or globe run north and south between the two poles. They measure distances east and west from the **Prime Meridian,** which lies at 0º longitude and runs through the Royal Observatory in Greenwich, England. Unlike lines of latitude, lines of longitude are not parallel to each other. They converge at the North Pole and South Pole. The distance between longitude lines is greatest at the Equator. The distance

Skills FOR LIFE

Reading a Map

How Will I Use This Skill?

Maps are not used just to study history and geography. They can also help you plan a trip, understand current events, or find out about the weather. Knowing how to read a map can keep you from getting lost, or help you find your way again.

LEARN the Skill

You can read a map by following these three steps:

❶ Identify the topic of the map. The **title** will tell you the subject of the map. The **key** explains the meanings of the map's symbols and colors.

❷ Look at a map's **scale** to determine distances between places. The scale shows you how many inches on the map equal how many actual miles or kilometers.

❸ Study the **directional arrow** to identify north, south, east, and west on a map.

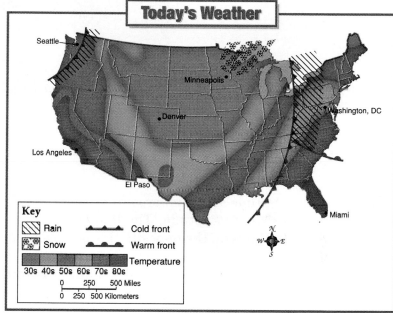

Today's Weather

PRACTICE the Skill

Use the steps above and the map on this page to answer the following questions.

❶ (a) What is the title of the map? (b) How is a cold front shown on the map? (c) According to the color key, what is today's temperature in Los Angeles? In Denver?

❷ (a) On the scale, how many miles are represented by 3/4 of an inch?

(b) What is the approximate distance from Washington, DC, to Miami in miles? In kilometers?

❸ (a) What is the northernmost city shown on the map? (b) What direction would you travel from El Paso to reach a place where it is snowing?

APPLY the Skill

With a group of classmates, create a map of your classroom. Include a title, plus a key that explains what symbols represent doors, windows, desks, and other features. Use a compass or the sun to determine north, south, east, and west. Use a tape measure to measure the room and create a scale.

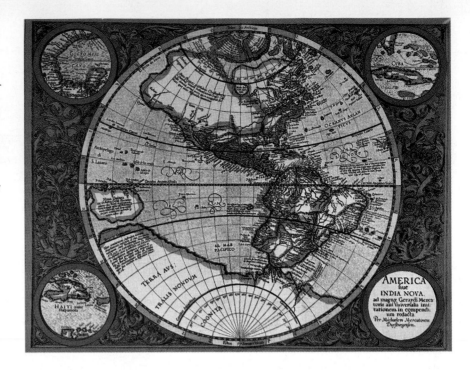

Viewing HISTORY — Early Map of the Americas

This 1595 map distorts the true shapes of North America and South America. Gerardus Mercator, the map's creator, refers to the Americas as New India. Maps of the 1500s may not have been totally accurate, but they were very artistic. ★ **Why are today's maps much more accurate than those of several centuries ago?**

between the lines decreases as they approach and finally meet at the poles.

Lines of longitude are numbered from 1° to 179° east or west longitude. The line of longitude at 180° lies on the opposite side of the world from the Prime Meridian.

The circle formed by the Prime Meridian and 180° divides the Earth into the Eastern and Western hemispheres. The Eastern Hemisphere includes most of Europe, Africa, and Asia. The Western Hemisphere includes North America and South America.

Locating places

To locate places, you must combine latitude and longitude. Look at the map on page 10. Chicago is located north of the Equator at about 42°N latitude. It lies west of the Prime Meridian at about 88°W longitude. Its location is 42°N/88°W. Use the United States map in the Reference Section to find the exact location of your state capital.

Time Zones

Lines of longitude are also used to help us know what time it is around the world. When it is 11 A.M. in Miami, Florida, it is 8 A.M. in Portland, Oregon. In Lagos, Nigeria, it is 5 P.M.

Why does time differ from place to place? The answer is that the Earth rotates on its axis. As the Earth moves, the sun appears to rise in some places and to set in others. Throughout the world, people determine time by this rising and setting of the sun.

To make it easier to tell time around the world, a system of **standard time zones** was set up in 1884. Under this system, the world was divided into 24 times zones. Standard time is measured from the Prime Meridian, which runs through Greenwich, England.

When it is noon in Greenwich, it is before noon (A.M.) in places west of Greenwich. It is after noon (P.M.) in places east of Greenwich.

$ Connections With Economics

In the United States, the Daylight Saving Time system provides people with more usable hours of daylight. From April to October, clocks are set ahead one hour. The total amount of daylight remains the same, but more daylight hours are available for outdoor activities in the late afternoon and evening.

If you travel east from Greenwich across Europe, Africa, or Asia, you add one hour as you move through each time zone.

Making Accurate Maps

The oldest surviving map in the world today was created by an ancient cartographer on a clay tablet sometime around 2300 B.C. Ever since, geographers have worked to make maps more accurate.

Early mapmaking

Early cartographers relied on information from sailors and travelers as well as legends to create their maps. As a result, their maps included many errors. Six hundred years ago, European mapmakers did not even know that North America and South America existed!

Since the 1500s, mapmaking has improved greatly. Daring sailors gained information about uncharted lands. Explorers studied ocean currents and wind patterns around the world. Scientists learned more about the Earth itself.

Using satellites

Today, mapmakers depend on computers and satellites. By taking photographs from space, satellites provide information that no one on the ground can furnish. As a result, maps are more accurate than ever before.

Launched in 1972, Landsat 1 was the first satellite specially designed to study the Earth's surface from space. The unmanned spacecraft took pictures from about 570 miles (900 km) above the Earth. Each photo showed a land area that an airplane would need 1,000 pictures to depict. Within two years, Landsat photographed more than 80 percent of the Earth's surface.

Images from Landsat 1 and later satellites provided extraordinary help to mapmakers. They revealed uncharted islands. They enabled scientists to see entire mountain ranges and drainage basins at a single glance. They allowed surveys of remote areas, such as the polar regions and oceans. Based on these images, cartographers corrected old maps and mapped some places for the first time.

Today, geographers rely on satellites for more and more information about the Earth. Geographers can use satellite information to chart changes in population density and economic activity. They can also learn more about weather patterns, vegetation, pollution, and mineral resources.

★ Section 2 Review ★

Recall

1. **Locate** (a) North America, (b) South America, (c) Asia, (d) Arctic Ocean.
2. **Identify** (a) Equator, (b) Prime Meridian.
3. **Define** (a) globe, (b) cartographer, (c) map projection, (d) hemisphere, (e) standard time zone.

Comprehension

4. Why does a globe show the Earth more accurately than a flat map?

5. How can we use latitude and longitude to find the exact location of a place?
6. How have satellites made maps more accurate than ever before?

Critical Thinking and Writing

7. **Applying Information** Describe some of the special features of a road map.
8. **Understanding Causes and Effects** Before the 1500s, why were European maps of the world very inaccurate?

★ ★

Activity Making a Weather Map You are the meteorologist for a local television news program. Make a map of your region, showing your forecast for tomorrow's weather conditions. You may wish to use the map on page 11 as a model.

American Lands and Climates

As You Read

Explore These Questions
- What are the eight physical regions of the United States?
- How are rivers and lakes important to the United States?
- What are the major climates of North America?

Define
- isthmus
- mountain
- elevation
- hill
- plain
- plateau
- tributary
- weather
- climate
- precipitation
- altitude
- El Niño

SETTING the Scene North America is the world's third largest continent. As the World map in the Reference Section shows, the Atlantic Ocean washes the eastern shore of North America. The Pacific Ocean laps at its western shore. To the north lies the icy Arctic Ocean. To the south, an **isthmus** (IHS muhs), or narrow strip of land, links North America to South America.

North America has many different features. For example, one of the world's highest mountains, Mount McKinley, is in Alaska. Yet one of the lowest points on the Earth is in Death Valley, California. You will find many examples of contrast as you read more about the American land.

Types of Landforms

North America has many landforms, or natural features. There are high mountains, rolling hills, and long rivers. There are grassy plains, dense forests, and barren deserts. Within these different landscapes are four basic landforms: mountains, hills, plains, and plateaus (pla TOHZ).

Mountains are high, steep, rugged land. They rise to an **elevation,** or height, of at least 1,000 feet (300 m) above the surrounding land. Few people live on steep mountainsides. Yet people often settle in valleys between mountains.

Hills are areas of raised land that are lower and more rounded than mountains. Farming is often possible on hilly land. Therefore, more people live in hilly areas than on mountains.

Plains are broad areas of fairly level land. Few plains are totally flat. Most are gently rolling. Plains do not usually rise much above sea level. People often settle on plains because it is easy to build farms, roads, and cities on the level land.

Plateaus are plains that range from a few hundred to many thousand feet above sea level. With enough rain, plateaus can be good for farming. Mountains surround some plateaus. Such plateaus are often very dry because the mountains cut off rainfall.

Mountains, hills, plains, and plateaus are only a few of the special words that geographers use. For definitions of other geographic terms, you may refer to the Dictionary of Geographic Terms on pages 24–25.

Physical Regions of North America

The landforms of North America form seven major physical regions. The United States also includes an eighth region, the Hawaiian Islands in the Pacific Ocean. (See the map on page 19.)

The seven physical regions of North America offer great

The red fox is native to North America.

contrasts. In some regions, the land is fertile. There, farmers plant crops and reap rich harvests. Other regions have natural resources such as coal and oil.

Pacific Coast

The westernmost region of North America is the Pacific Coast. It includes high mountain ranges that stretch from Alaska to Mexico. In the United States, some of these western ranges hug the Pacific Ocean. The Cascades and Sierra Nevada* stand a bit farther inland. Some important cities of the Pacific Coast are Seattle, Portland, San Francisco, and Los Angeles.

An important feature of the Pacific Coast region is the San Andreas Fault. This is a

600-mile (970 km) fracture in the Earth's crust. It runs through California from northwest to southeast. Movement of the Earth's crust along this fault causes earthquakes.

In 1906, a powerful earthquake shook the city of San Francisco. The tremors and fires that followed destroyed thousands of buildings and killed some 700 people. In 1994, another strong earthquake caused significant damage and loss of life in Los Angeles.

Intermountain region

East of the coast ranges is the Intermountain region. It is a very rugged region of mountain peaks, high plateaus, deep canyons, and deserts. The Grand Canyon, which is more than 1 mile (1.6 km) deep, and the Great Salt Lake are natural features of this region. Salt Lake City and Phoenix are among the few major cities of the Intermountain region.

---

*Sierra (see EHR uh) is the Spanish word for mountain range. Nevada is Spanish for snowy. Spanish explorers were the first to see these snow-covered mountains.

Viewing HISTORY **Mount Rainier**

The beauty of the Cascade Mountains can be seen at Mount Rainier National Park in the state of Washington. In spring, colorful wildflowers and evergreen trees contrast sharply with Mount Rainier's snowcap. ★ **In what physical region are the Cascades located?**

Rocky Mountains

The Rocky Mountains stretch from Alaska through Canada into the United States. They include the Bitterroot Range in Idaho and Montana, the Big Horn Mountains in Wyoming, and the Sangre de Cristo Mountains in Colorado and New Mexico. In Mexico, the Rocky Mountains become the Sierra Madre (MAH dray), or mother range.

The Rockies include some of the highest peaks in North America. Many peaks are more than 14,000 feet (4,200 m) high. Throughout history, people have described the mountains' rugged beauty and grandeur.

The Rockies, however, were a serious barrier to settlement of the United States. When settlers moved west in the 1800s, crossing the Rockies posed great hardships. Some people decided to stay and live in the Rockies. Today, Denver is a major city in the region.

Interior Plains

Between the Rockies in the West and the Appalachian Mountains in the East is a large lowland area called the Interior Plains. The dry western part of the Interior Plains is called the Great Plains. The eastern part is called the Central Plains.

According to scientists, a great inland sea once covered the Interior Plains. Today, some parts are rich in coal and petroleum.* Other parts offer fertile soil for farming and grassland for raising cattle. Chicago and Dallas are major cities on the Interior Plains.

Appalachian Mountains

The Appalachian Mountains run along the eastern part of North America. They stretch from Canada in the North to Georgia and Mississippi in the South. The Appalachians have different names in different places. For example, the Green Mountains, Alleghenies, and Great Smokies are all part of the Appalachian Mountains.

The Appalachians are lower and less rugged than the Rockies. The highest Appalachian peak is Mt. Mitchell in North Carolina, which is 6,684 feet (2,037 m) high. Still, early European settlers had a hard time crossing these heavily forested mountains.

Canadian Shield

The Canadian Shield is a lowland area that lies mostly in eastern Canada. The

---

*The Natural Resources map in the Reference Section shows where natural resources are located.

Viewing HISTORY — **Interior Plains**

Plains cover much of the central United States. They stretch from the Mississippi River to the Rocky Mountains and from Texas (shown at right) to Montana. The region is ideal for raising cattle. ★ **Why is this region ideal for raising cattle?**

▼ *Texas longhorn*

southern part extends into the United States. The region was once an area of high mountains. The mountains were worn away to low hills and plains. The Canadian Shield lacks topsoil for farming, but it is rich in minerals.

Coastal Plains

The region called the Coastal Plains is a fairly flat, lowland area that includes the Atlantic Plain and the Gulf Plain. The Atlantic Plain lies between the Atlantic Ocean and the foothills of the Appalachians. The Atlantic Plain is narrow in the North, where Boston and New York City are located. It broadens in the South to include all of Florida.

Another part of the Coastal Plains is the Gulf Plain, which lies along the Gulf of Mexico. The Gulf Plain has large deposits of petroleum. New Orleans and Houston are major cities of the Gulf Plain.

Hawaiian Islands

The Hawaiian Islands lie far out in the Pacific, about 2,400 miles (3,860 km) west of California. There are eight large islands and many small islands.

The islands are the visible tops of volcanoes that erupted through the floor of the Pacific Ocean. Some volcanoes are still active. Mauna Loa, on the island of Hawaii, is an active volcano that rises 13,680 feet (4,170 m) above sea level.

Rivers and Lakes

Great river systems crisscross North America. They collect runoff water from rains and melting snows and carry it into the oceans.

The mighty Mississippi

The Mississippi and Missouri rivers make up the longest and most important river system in the United States. This river system carries water through the Interior Plains into the Gulf of Mexico.

Many **tributaries,** or streams and smaller rivers, flow into the Mississippi-Missouri river system. Among these tributaries are the Ohio, Tennessee, Arkansas, and Platte rivers. These and other rivers provide water for the rich farmlands of the Interior Plains.

The Mississippi River also serves as a means of transportation. Today, barges carry freight up and down the river. As in the past, people travel by boat on the river.

Biography — Ansel Adams

Ansel Adams (1902–1984) is well known for his sharply focused black-and-white photographs of American landscapes. In 1946, the native Californian founded the California School of Fine Arts in San Francisco. From 1936 to 1973, he served as director of the Sierra Club, a group devoted to conservation of the natural environment. ★ **Why do you think Adams was so interested in conservation of the environment?**

◄ *Ansel Adams took this photo of the Grand Canyon.*

The mighty Mississippi has inspired many admiring descriptions. Among them is this one from the 1937 film *The River:*

❝ The Mississippi River runs to the
　Gulf.
Carrying every drop of water, that
　flows down two thirds of the
　continent,
Carrying every brook and rill,
　rivulet and creek,
Carrying all the rivers that run
　down two thirds of the continent.
The Mississippi runs to the Gulf of
　Mexico. ❞

The Colorado River

The Colorado River is another important river. It begins in the Rocky Mountains and flows through Colorado, Utah, Arizona, and Nevada. It forms the border between California and Arizona as it flows toward the Gulf of California. Smaller rivers feed into the Colorado. These include the Green River and the San Juan River.

The Colorado River created the Grand Canyon in Arizona. For millions of years, the river rushed over layers of rock, carving a deeper and deeper channel. Today, the Grand Canyon is one mile (1.6 km) deep and 18 miles (29 km) wide in some places.

There are several dams along the course of the Colorado River. These dams hold back the flow of the river. They help provide water and electricity to the people of the Southwest.

International borders

The Rio Grande and the St. Lawrence River serve as political boundaries. The Rio Grande is part of the border between the United States and Mexico. The St. Lawrence is part of the border with Canada.

Five large lakes, called the Great Lakes, also form part of the border between the United States and Canada. The Great Lakes are Superior, Michigan, Huron, Erie, and Ontario. Today, canals connect the Great Lakes, forming a major inland waterway that is important for commerce.

Weather and Climate

North America has a variety of weather patterns and climates. **Weather** is the condition of the Earth's atmosphere at any given time and place. It may be hot or cold, rainy or dry, or something in between.

Climate is the average weather of a place over a period of 20 to 30 years. Two main aspects of climate are temperature and **precipitation** (pree sihp uh TAY shuhn), or water that falls in the form of rain, sleet, hail, or snow.

Several factors affect climate. One factor is distance from the Equator. Lands near the Equator usually are hot and wet all year. Lands near the North and South poles are cold all year. **Altitude,** or height above sea

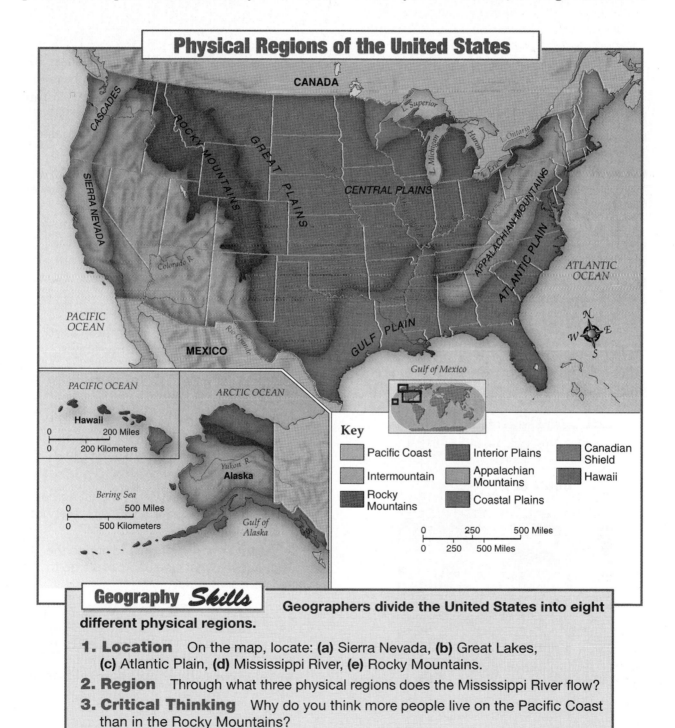

Physical Regions of the United States

Key

- Pacific Coast
- Intermountain
- Rocky Mountains
- Interior Plains
- Appalachian Mountains
- Coastal Plains
- Canadian Shield
- Hawaii

Geography Skills   Geographers divide the United States into eight different physical regions.

1. **Location**   On the map, locate: **(a)** Sierra Nevada, **(b)** Great Lakes, **(c)** Atlantic Plain, **(d)** Mississippi River, **(e)** Rocky Mountains.
2. **Region**   Through what three physical regions does the Mississippi River flow?
3. **Critical Thinking**   Why do you think more people live on the Pacific Coast than in the Rocky Mountains?

Why Study History?

Because We All Need Water

* *

Historical Background

In the past century, the demand for water has risen greatly. More and more water is diverted from rivers to serve people's needs. As a result, some major rivers throughout the world have begun to run dry.

Connections to Today

The Colorado River is one of those rivers. (See page 18.) Today, the Colorado rarely empties into the Pacific Ocean. Instead, it gradually shrinks until its last traces evaporate in the desert heat of Mexico.

Today, the demand for Colorado River water is greater than the supply. In 1922, an agreement divided the river's water among seven western states. Other agreements guaranteed water rights to Native Americans and Mexico. Now, more than 20 million people rely on the Colorado River.

Colorado River water disputes are often settled in court. Large cities such as Los Angeles and San Diego frequently accuse farmers of wasting water through old-fashioned irrigation methods. The farmers reply that cities are overbuilding and drawing too much water.

According to California Congressman George Miller, "The heart of the West is water. . . . It will be the most important commodity in dictating the future."

Connections to You

We all need water. You can help save water by taking these and other steps.

- Take short showers.
- Fix leaky faucets.
- Do only full loads in the dishwasher and clothes washer.
- Wash automobiles and water lawns infrequently.

1. **Comprehension**   Why do past agreements on sharing Colorado River water not meet today's needs?
2. **Critical Thinking**   In addition to the ideas above, what else can people do to help conserve water?

 **Debating**   Work with a partner to stage a debate on the issue of water rights in the West. One of you should present a farmer's viewpoint. The other should present a city official's viewpoint.

In California, this poster urges young people to conserve water.

The Philippines

United States

Weather Connections

Conditions around the world can affect your weather. Mount Pinatubo (above, left), a volcano in the Philippines, erupted in 1991. Gases and dust blocked some of the sun's rays and lowered temperatures in much of the world. In North America, though, the eruption led to a milder than average winter. ★ **What is the average winter like in the area where you live?**

level, also affects climate. In general, highlands are cooler than lowlands. Other factors that influence climate include ocean currents, wind currents, and mountains.

In the Pacific Ocean, wind and ocean currents interact to create the cyclical phenomenon called the **El Niño** (ehl NEEN yoh) Southern Oscillation. The temperature of Pacific Ocean water plays a major role in the phenomenon. During an El Niño period, the surface water of the eastern Pacific Ocean warms. During a La Niña (lah NEEN yah) period, ocean surface temperatures cool.

The Southern Oscillation affects weather patterns in nearly three quarters of the world. In the United States, for example, the warm ocean water of an El Niño helps to cause frequent and powerful storms in California and the Southwest. In Northeastern states, meanwhile, El Niño usually contributes to milder than normal winters.

North American Climates

The United States has 10 major climates. Look at the map on page 22 to see the locations of these climates.

Marine

The strip of land from southern Alaska to northern California is sometimes called the Pacific Northwest. This region has a mild, moist marine climate, with warm summers and cool winters. Moist winds from the Pacific Ocean bring mild temperatures and moisture that condenses and falls as rain or snow. The Pacific Northwest has many forests. This makes it the center of the lumber industry.

Mediterranean

Much of California has a Mediterranean climate. Winters are mild and wet. Summers are hot and dry. Farmers and fruit growers

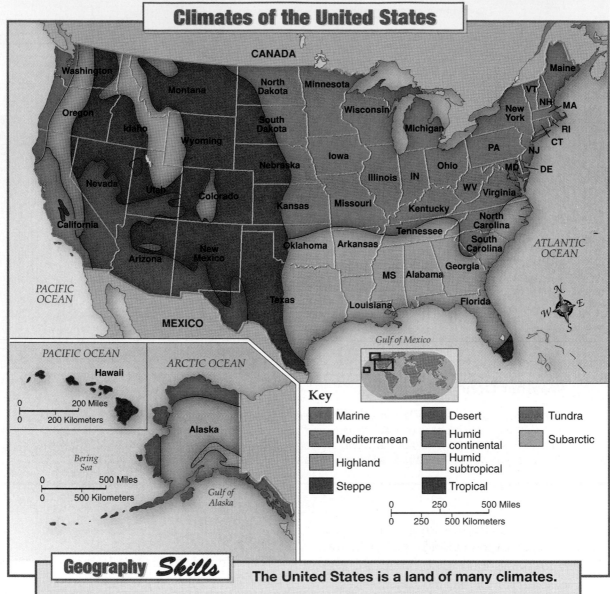

Climates of the United States

CANADA

Washington, Montana, North Dakota, Minnesota, Maine

Oregon, Idaho, Wyoming, South Dakota, Wisconsin, Michigan, New York, VT, NH, MA, RI, CT, PA, NJ

Nevada, Utah, Colorado, Nebraska, Iowa, Illinois, IN, Ohio, WV, MD, DE, Virginia

California, Kansas, Missouri, Kentucky, North Carolina

Arizona, New Mexico, Oklahoma, Arkansas, Tennessee, South Carolina, Georgia

MS, Alabama

PACIFIC OCEAN

Texas, Louisiana, Florida

MEXICO

Gulf of Mexico

ATLANTIC OCEAN

PACIFIC OCEAN

Hawaii

0 200 Miles
0 200 Kilometers

ARCTIC OCEAN

Alaska

Bering Sea

0 500 Miles
0 500 Kilometers

Gulf of Alaska

Key

- Marine
- Mediterranean
- Highland
- Steppe
- Desert
- Humid continental
- Humid subtropical
- Tropical
- Tundra
- Subarctic

0 250 500 Miles
0 250 500 Kilometers

Geography *Skills*

The United States is a land of many climates.

1. **Location** On the map, locate: **(a)** New York, **(b)** Ohio, **(c)** Arizona.
2. **Place** What states have three or more different climates?
3. **Critical Thinking** **(a)** Identify a state or part of a state where water is probably scarce. **(b)** Why is water in such short supply there?

must often irrigate the land. Because of the climate, this region produces crops that cannot be grown anywhere else in the country. For example, it produces almost all the nation's almonds, walnuts, olives, apricots, dates, and figs.

Highland

In the Cascades, Sierra Nevada, and Rocky Mountains, a highland climate brings cooler temperatures. Conditions in a high-

land climate vary according to altitude. For example, Mount Rainier in the state of Washington, at over 14,000 feet (4,200 m) above sea level, is snow-capped all year. During the spring and summer, runoff from melting snows provides water to the major rivers of the West. Many people vacation in the mountains so they can participate in winter sports. In summer, vacationers come to the mountains to escape the heat and enjoy the cool highland temperatures.

Desert and steppe

Much of the southwestern United States has a desert climate, with hot days and cold nights. This dry region stretches as far east as the Rockies. In the deserts of Nevada, Arizona, and southeastern California, there is almost no rainfall. In many areas, people irrigate the land so that they can grow crops.

East of the Rockies are the Great Plains. They have a steppe climate with limited rainfall. Summers are hot and winters are cold. Huge herds of buffaloes once grazed on the short grasses of the Great Plains. In the 1800s, settlers brought cattle to graze on the plains.

Humid continental

The Central Plains and the northeastern United States have a humid continental climate. This climate, with mild summers and cold winters, has more precipitation than the steppe. Tall prairie grasses once covered the Central Plains. Today, American farmers raise much of the world's food in this region.

At one time, the humid continental climate supported forests that covered much of the northeastern United States. Early European settlers cleared forests to build settlements and to grow crops. However, many forests remain, and the lumber industry thrives in some areas.

Tropical and humid subtropical

Southern Florida and Hawaii, located near the Equator, have tropical climates. The hot, humid conditions make these regions good for growing such crops as pineapples and citrus fruits. The warm tropical temperatures are also ideal for the tourism industry.

The southeastern United States has a humid subtropical climate. Warm temperatures and regular rainfall make this region ideal for growing crops such as cotton, soybeans, and peanuts.

Tundra and subarctic

Northern and western coastal regions of Alaska have a tundra climate. It is cold all year round. The rest of Alaska and northern Canada have a subarctic climate with long, cold winters and short summers. Farming is limited to a small fertile valley in southern Alaska. Almost one third of Alaska is covered by forest. Therefore, logging and the production of paper pulp are important industries.

★ Section 3 Review ★

Recall

1. **Locate** (a) North America, (b) Pacific Coast, (c) Intermountain region, (d) Rocky Mountains, (e) Interior Plains, (f) Appalachian Mountains, (g) Mississippi River, (h) Great Lakes.
2. **Define** (a) isthmus, (b) mountain, (c) elevation, (d) hill, (e) plain, (f) plateau, (g) tributary, (h) weather, (i) climate, (j) precipitation, (k) altitude, (l) El Niño.

Comprehension

3. Name the eight physical regions of the United States and describe one feature of each region.

4. How do rivers and lakes benefit the economy of the United States?
5. Describe the climate of the region where you live.

Critical Thinking and Writing

6. **Drawing Conclusions** Do you think more people live in the Appalachian Mountains or in the Rocky Mountains? Why?
7. **Making Decisions** If you could live anywhere in the United States, which physical region and climate would you choose? Explain.

★ ★

History AND YOU

Activity **Making a Chart** You are the graphic designer for a popular vacation and travel magazine. Create a chart that lists and describes the 10 major climates of the United States.

Dictionary of Geographic Terms

The list below includes important geographic terms and their definitions. Sometimes, the definition of a term includes an example in parentheses. An asterisk (*) indicates that the term is illustrated above.

altitude   height above sea level.

*archipelago   chain of islands. (Hawaiian Islands)

basin   low-lying land area that is surrounded by land of higher elevation; land area that is drained by a river system. (Great Basin)

*bay   part of a body of water that is partly enclosed by land. (San Francisco Bay)

canal   waterway made by people that is used to drain or irrigate land or to connect two bodies of water. (Erie Canal)

*canyon   deep, narrow valley with high, steep sides. (Grand Canyon)

*cape   narrow point of land that extends into a body of water. (Cape Cod)

climate   pattern of weather in a particular place over a period of 20 to 30 years.

*coast   land that borders the sea. (Pacific Coast)

coastal plain   lowland area lying along the ocean. (Gulf Plain)

continent   any of seven large landmasses on the Earth's surface. (Africa, Antarctica, Asia, Australia, Europe, North America, South America)

continental divide   mountain ridge that separates river systems flowing toward opposite sides of a continent.

*delta   land area formed by soil that is deposited at the mouth of a river. (Mississippi Delta)

desert   area that has little or no moisture or vegetation. (Painted Desert)

directional arrow   arrow on a map that always points north.

downstream   in the direction of a river's flow; toward a river's mouth.

elevation   the height above sea level.

fall line   place where rivers drop from a plateau or foothills to a coastal plain, usually marked by many waterfalls.

foothills   low hills at the base of a mountain range.

*gulf   arm of an ocean or sea that is partly enclosed by land, usually larger than a bay. (Gulf of Mexico)

hemisphere   half of the Earth. (Western Hemisphere)

*hill   area of raised land that is lower and more rounded than a mountain. (San Juan Hill)

*island   land area that is surrounded by water. (Puerto Rico)

Map labels: source of a river, plain, canyon, plateau, river, tributary, delta, mouth of a river, coast, isthmus, peninsula, bay, sea, valley, mountain

*isthmus narrow strip of land joining two large land areas or joining a peninsula to a mainland. (Isthmus of Panama)

*lake body of water surrounded entirely by land. (Lake Superior)

latitude the distance in degrees north and south from the Equator.

longitude the distance in degrees east or west from the Prime Meridian.

marsh lowland with moist soils and tall grasses.

*mountain high, steep, rugged land that rises sharply above the surrounding land. (Mount McKinley)

mountain range chain of connected mountains. (Allegheny Mountains)

*mouth of a river place where a river or stream empties into a large body of water.

ocean any of the four largest bodies of salt water on the Earth's surface. (Arctic, Atlantic, Indian, and Pacific Oceans)

*peninsula piece of land that is surrounded by water on three sides. (Delmarva Peninsula)

piedmont rolling land along the base of a mountain range.

*plain broad area of fairly level land that is generally close to sea level.

*plateau large area of high, flat, or gently rolling land.

prairie large area of natural grassland with few or no trees or hills.

*river large stream of water that empties into an ocean or lake or another river. (Pecos River)

*sea large body of salt water that is smaller than an ocean. (Caribbean Sea)

sea level average level of the ocean's surface from which the height of land or depth of the ocean is measured.

*source of a river place where a river begins.

steppe flat, treeless land with limited moisture.

*strait narrow channel that connects two larger bodies of water. (Straits of Florida)

*tributary stream or small river that flows into a larger stream or river.

upstream in the direction that is against a river's flow; toward a river's source.

*valley land that lies between hills or mountains. (Shenandoah Valley)

*volcano cone-shaped mountain formed by an outpouring of lava—hot, liquid rock—from a crack in the Earth's surface. (Mount St. Helens or Mauna Loa)

weather condition of the air at any given time and place.

Chapter 1 Review and Activities

★ Sum It Up ★

Section 1 Five Themes of Geography
▶ Geography is the study of people, their environments, and their resources.
▶ The five themes of geography help show the connection between geography and history.
▶ The five themes of geography are location, place, interaction, movement, and region.

Section 2 Maps and Mapmaking
▶ Each type of map projection has advantages and disadvantages.
▶ Latitude and longitude lines on maps enable us to locate places exactly.
▶ The use of computers and satellites has made modern mapmaking more accurate than the mapmaking of centuries ago.

Section 3 American Lands and Climates
▶ Mountains, plains, and many other types of landforms can be found in North America.
▶ There are eight major physical regions in the United States.
▶ Rivers and lakes provide many benefits to the people of the United States.
▶ A variety of factors interact to produce weather and climate conditions.
▶ The United States has 10 major climates.
▶ The climate of a region helps to determine some of the economic activities that take place in the region.

CD-ROM Review For additional review of the major ideas of Chapter 1, see **Guide to the Essentials of American History** or **Interactive Student Tutorial CD-ROM,** which contains interactive review activities, graphic organizers, and practice tests.

🗂 Reviewing the Chapter

Define These Terms
Match each term with the correct definition.

Column 1
1. history
2. latitude
3. longitude
4. cartographer
5. precipitation

Column 2
a. lines measuring distance east and west from the Prime Meridian
b. a mapmaker
c. lines measuring distance north and south from the Equator
d. an account of what has happened in people's lives
e. water that falls as rain, sleet, or snow

Explore the Main Ideas
1. How do geographers generally describe place?
2. How do people interact with their environment?
3. Why do all flat maps distort the shapes of continents and oceans?
4. Locate and describe three physical regions of the United States.
5. Why is the Mississippi River such an important waterway?
6. Locate and describe three climates found in the United States.

🗂 Geography Activity

Match the letters on the map with the following places:
1. North America, **2.** South America, **3.** Atlantic Ocean, **4.** Pacific Ocean, **5.** Isthmus of Panama, **6.** Great Lakes.
Location What ocean lies to the east of North America?

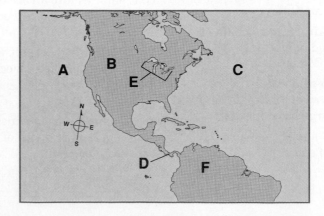

☐ Critical Thinking and Writing

1. **Applying Information** Using the themes of geography, **(a)** describe the special geographic characteristics of the place where you live, **(b)** describe an example of how people in your community have adapted to or changed the natural environment.
2. **Evaluating Information** Which is more reliable: a map of North America from the 1500s or a map of North America from the 1900s? Explain the reasons for your choice.
3. **Synthesizing Information** Look at the picture of Mount Rainier that appears in Section 3 of this chapter. **(a)** Describe the physical region in which Mount Rainier is located. **(b)** Describe the climate of that region.
4. **Exploring Unit Themes** Origins How can the climate of a region affect people's economic activities in that region?

☐ Using Primary Sources

In 1845, Lansford W. Hastings wrote a guide for people traveling to the West. In it he made the following predictions:

> ❝ The time is not distant, when those wild forests, trackless plains, untrodden valleys . . . will present one grand scene of continuous improvements . . . when those vast forests shall have disappeared before the hardy pioneer; those extensive plains shall abound with innumerable herds of domestic animals; those fertile valleys shall groan under the weight of their abundant products. ❞

Source: *The Emigrants' Guide to Oregon and California,* Lansford W. Hastings, 1845.

Recognizing Points of View **(a)** What changes did Hastings expect from human interaction with the environment? **(b)** How did he feel about the predicted changes?

ACTIVITY BANK

▶ Interdisciplinary Activity

Exploring the Arts Do research to find a song or poem about an American river. Read or sing the composition to the class. Then lead a group discussion on what the song or poem says about the river.

▶ Career Skills Activity

Cartographers On a large sheet of paper, create a map of the United States. On the map, draw and label the 50 states. Then label the major physical regions and landforms of the United States.

▶ Citizenship Activity

Using a Political Map Find a map that shows the Congressional districts in your state. Identify the district in which you live. Through research, find out the name of your district's representative in Congress. If an issue or question concerns you, you can write about it to your Congressperson and ask for a response.

Internet Activity

Use the Internet to find the official site of NASA (National Aeronautics and Space Administration). There you will find images of the Earth taken by satellites orbiting the Earth. Select a picture that interests you and, if possible, print it out. In a written report, describe what the picture shows and explain why the picture might be useful to a cartographer.

EYEWITNESS Journal

You are traveling across the United States from somewhere on the Atlantic Coast to somewhere on the Pacific Coast. List all the states that you are traveling through. Also, list and describe all the physical regions that you are crossing.

The First Americans
Prehistory–1600

Thousands of years ago, hunters from Asia followed herds of wild animals to the Americas. As the hunters gradually spread through North and South America, they developed a variety of cultures. The economic activities, religious beliefs, and societies of these first Americans reflected the environments in which they lived, from the icy north to the dry desert of the Southwest. Farther south, in Mexico and Central and South America, several great civilizations arose.

The world of these first Americans changed dramatically after Europeans reached American shores. At the same time, aspects of Native American culture spread to other parts of the globe.

Why Study History?

European settlers adapted many Native American customs. These included sports, such as lacrosse. Today, as in the past, sports play a role in society that goes far beyond just having fun. To focus on this connection, see this chapter's *Why Study History?* feature, "Sports Are Important in Our Culture."

American Events

300–900
Mayan cities flourish in Mexico and Central America

1100–1200
Anasazis build cliff dwellings in Southwest

Prehistory — 1000 — 1200

World Events

30,000–15,000 Years Ago World Event
Hunters from Asia cross land bridge to the Americas

1013 World Event
Danish Vikings conquer England

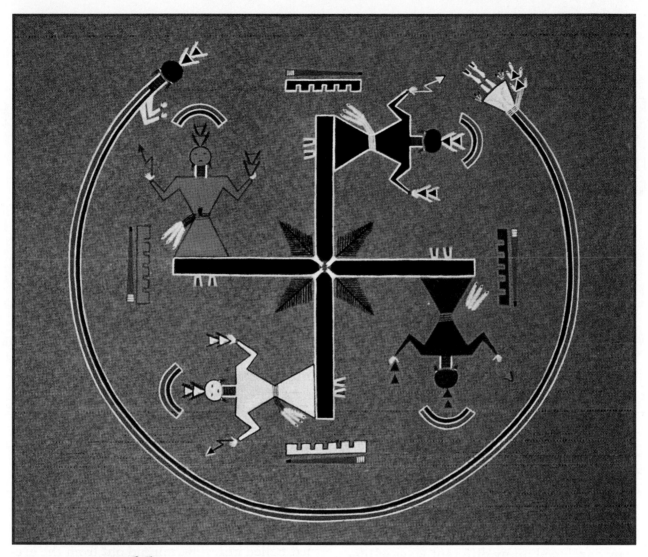

Viewing HISTORY — Native American Art

The Navajos used sand paintings in healing and religious ceremonies. This painting shows a whirlwind, or tornado, as people on spinning logs. Navajo culture arose in the American Southwest. Dozens of other Native American cultures emerged in the varied environments of North and South America. ★ **How does this painting reflect the desert environment of the Navajos?**

1400s ●
Aztecs build powerful empire in Mexico

Early 1500s ●
Incas control the largest empire in the Americas

●**1570s**
Peoples of the Eastern Woodlands form the Iroquois League to promote peace

1200   **1400**   **1600**

1300s World Event
West African kingdom of Mali reaches its height

1492 World Event
Columbus reaches the Americas

Early People and Cultures

As You Read

Explore These Questions
- Where did the first Americans come from?
- How do archaeologists learn about the past?
- How did early people adapt to the desert Southwest?

Define
- glacier
- artifact
- archaeology
- culture
- adobe
- pueblo
- drought

Identify
- Native American
- Mound Builder
- Hohokam
- Anasazi

SETTING the Scene Crouched low, the small band of hunters crept slowly forward. Ahead, a herd of bison grazed at the edge of a swamp. At a signal, the hunters leaped up, shouting loudly. The startled herd stampeded into the swamp. As the bison struggled in the deep mud, the hunters hurled their spears.

Scenes much like this one took place on the Great Plains more than 10,000 years ago. Tracking herds of bison or woolly mammoths, skillful hunters were among the first people to settle the Americas. Over many thousands of years, their descendants spread out across two continents. In the process, they developed many different ways of life.

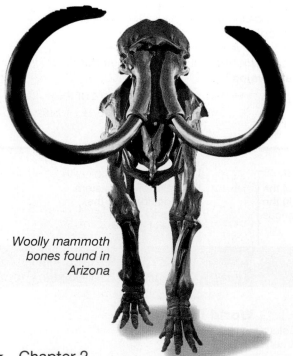

Woolly mammoth bones found in Arizona

The First Americans Migrate From Asia

Like other early people, the first Americans left no written records to tell us where they came from or when they arrived. However, scientists have found evidence to suggest that the first people reached the Americas sometime during the last ice age.

The last ice age

According to geologists, the Earth has gone through four ice ages. The last one took place between 100,000 and 10,000 years ago.

During the last ice age, thick sheets of ice, called **glaciers,** spread out from the arctic regions. Almost one third of the Earth was buried under these sheets of ice. In North America, glaciers stretched across Canada and reached as far south as Kentucky.

As they moved, glaciers changed the lands they covered. They pushed soil, rocks, and huge boulders across the land. They created islands such as Long Island, New York, as well as Nantucket and Martha's Vineyard off the coast of Massachusetts. Water from melting glaciers drained into channels, creating rivers such as the Missouri.

Crossing the land bridge

Because glaciers locked up water from the oceans, sea levels fell. As a result, land that had been under water was uncovered. In the far north, a land bridge joined Siberia in northeastern Asia to Alaska in North

America. Today, this land bridge is under the Bering Strait.

Scientists think that the first Americans were probably hunters. Traveling in small bands, they followed herds of woolly mammoth, bison, and other game across the land bridge. Some groups may have wandered along the southern coast of the land bridge, catching fish and sea mammals.

Experts date the arrival of these first Americans anywhere from 30,000 to 15,000 years ago. Once they reached the Americas, the continuing search for better hunting grounds led the newcomers across the land. Over thousands of years, they spread out through North America, Central America, and South America.

Adapting to new conditions

About 12,000 years ago, the ice age ended. Temperatures rose around the globe. Glaciers melted, and the ocean once more covered the land bridge. At about the same time, the woolly mammoths and mastodons died out.

The people of the Americas adapted to the new conditions. They hunted smaller animals, gathered wild berries and grains, and caught fish.

Then, about 5,000 years ago, some people learned to grow crops such as corn, beans, and squash. Farming changed those people's lives. People who farmed no longer had to move constantly in search of food. Instead, they built the first permanent villages in the Americas. As farming methods improved, villagers produced more food. In turn, the increased food supply allowed populations to grow.

Studying the First Americans

Today, experts in many fields are working to develop a clearer picture of the first Americans. Some are studying the remains of ancient people of northeast Asia. They hope to learn how these Asian people might be related to the first Americans.

Other experts are analyzing the languages of Native American groups today. **Native Americans** are the descendants of the

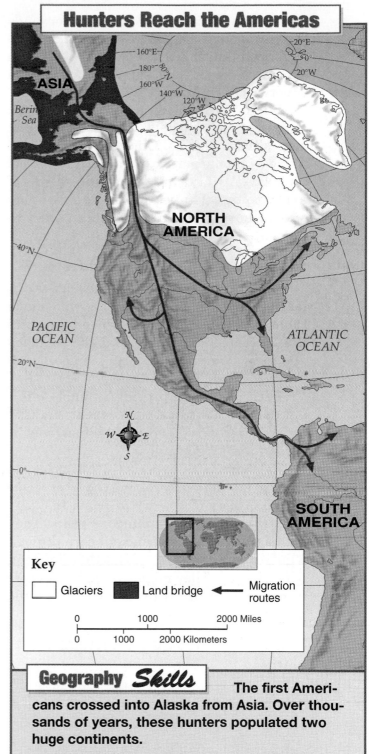

Hunters Reach the Americas

ASIA
NORTH AMERICA
PACIFIC OCEAN
ATLANTIC OCEAN
SOUTH AMERICA

Key

☐ Glaciers   ■ Land bridge   ← Migration routes

0   1000   2000 Miles
0   1000   2000 Kilometers

Geography Skills   The first Americans crossed into Alaska from Asia. Over thousands of years, these hunters populated two huge continents.

1. **Location**   On the map, locate: **(a)** Asia, **(b)** Bering Sea, **(c)** North America, **(d)** South America.

2. **Movement**   In which direction did early hunters travel from Asia to reach North America?

3. **Critical Thinking**   Why do you think many of the first Americans continued to travel southward after crossing the land bridge?

first people to reach the Americas thousands of years ago. Through the study of Native American languages, scholars are trying to trace how these people spread out across the Americas.

Still other scholars are examining stone tools, weapons, baskets, and carvings found across the Americas. Objects such as these made by humans are called **artifacts** (AHRT uh faktz). Artifacts are the building blocks of **archaeology** (ahr kee AHL uh jee), the study of evidence left by early people in order to find out about their way of life.

Artifacts provide valuable clues

By studying artifacts, archaeologists can learn much about the people who made them. A finely carved arrowhead suggests that a people knew how to make weapons and hunt. Woven plant fibers suggest that they were skilled basket makers.

Each object can provide valuable information. At the same time, each new find raises questions such as, "When was it made?" and "Who made it?"

In laboratories, experts use technology to analyze new finds. By testing the level of carbon in a piece of pottery or bone, they can date it to within a few hundred years. They might study kernels of ancient corn through a microscope to find out about the climate in which it grew. They might compare clay pots from different areas to find out about the people who made them.

Forming theories about ancient cultures

From artifacts and other evidence, archaeologists form theories about the cultures of ancient people. A **culture** is the entire way of life that a people has developed. It includes their homes, clothing, economy, arts, and government. It also includes the customs, ideas, beliefs, and skills that they pass on from generation to generation.

Often, very little evidence survives about an ancient people. Sometimes, archaeologists find evidence in unexpected places, through sheer luck. A flood might wash away a river bank and uncover ancient bones. A bulldozer clearing land might dig up a buried campsite. Each new find or new method of studying ancient artifacts helps to fill in the story of early Americans.

In their search for evidence about the past, archaeologists often dig up ancient sites. In recent years, however, they have grown more aware of the need to respect Native American landmarks and traditions. Government officials, too, have become more respectful of Native American concerns. Some laws have been passed to protect Native American burial grounds.

The Mound Builders

Among the artifacts that archaeologists have found in North America are thousands of earthen mounds. The mounds are scattered across a region stretching from the Appalachian Mountains to the Mississippi Valley and from Wisconsin to Florida. Scholars call the people who built these earthworks **Mound Builders.** The Mound Builders lived at various times from about 3,000 years ago until the 1700s. The two main groups were the Hopewells and the Mississippians.

Purpose of the mounds

The mounds served different purposes. The first mounds were burial grounds, probably for important leaders. Inside the mounds, archaeologists have found carved pipes, stone sculptures, and copper weapons, tools, and ornaments. They have also found shells from the Gulf of Mexico and turquoise from the Southwest. This evidence shows that the Mound Builders traded with people from other parts of North America.

Some mounds were used for religious ceremonies. They are shaped like pyramids

Connections With Geography

In the southwestern United States, geography has helped archaeologists study early cultures. The dry climate has preserved baskets, bags, sandals, nets, and other items dating back approximately 2,000 years. In a damper climate, many of these items might have rotted away.

The ancient Americans known as the Mound Builders left behind thousands of mounds. One of the largest is the Great Serpent Mound, shown here. It twists across the Ohio landscape for more than 1,200 feet (365 m). ★ **Why do you think present-day archaeologists are eager to examine early burial mounds?**

▲ *Flints found at Great Serpent Mound*

with flat tops. On the flat surfaces, the people built temples and homes for the ruling class.

More than 2,000 years ago, Hopewell builders created the twisting Great Serpent Mound in present-day Ohio. From above, it looks like a snake with a coiled tail. The meaning of this and other animal-shaped mounds remains a mystery.

Monk's Mound

Some time between 700 and 1500, the Mississippians built a large city at Cahokia (kah HOH kee ah), in present-day Illinois. As many as 30,000 people may have lived there at one time. Over the years, the Cahokians moved tons of soil, basketload by basketload, to build Monk's Mound. This vast platform mound covers 16 acres—equal to 14½ football fields! Hundreds of other smaller mounds stand nearby.

The Mississippians built a wooden fence around Cahokia. Beyond this fence, they placed circles of evenly spaced posts. Some archaeologists think the posts served as a kind of calendar. From the top of Monk's Mound, rulers could see the shadows cast by the posts. Shorter shadows announced the

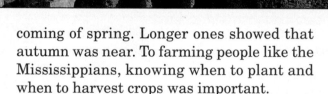

HISTORY HAPPENED HERE

Mesa Verde National Park

The cliff dwellings at Mesa Verde were abandoned more than 700 years ago. Yet these spectacular buildings still stand. They remind us of the skill of Native Americans who carved entire villages out of the canyons and cliffs of southwest Colorado. Cliff Palace (left) is the largest complex at Mesa Verde. It contains more than 200 rooms, with sections up to four stories tall. The park also has a museum where you can see many Anasazi artifacts.

★ **To learn more about this historic site, write:** *Superintendent, Mesa Verde National Park, Colorado 81330.*

◄ Clay cup from Mesa Verde

coming of spring. Longer ones showed that autumn was near. To farming people like the Mississippians, knowing when to plant and when to harvest crops was important.

Early Cultures of the Southwest

Through careful study, archaeologists have also learned much about the early people of the American Southwest. This desert region may seem like a poor place to farm. Annual rainfall is only 5 to 10 inches (13 to 25 cm). In the daytime, temperatures can soar above 100° Fahrenheit (38°C). Cactus and sagebrush cover the desert floor.

Still, at least 3,000 years ago, people in the Southwest learned to grow crops such as corn. In time, several major farming societies, including the Hohokams (hoh HOH kahmz) and Anasazis (ah nuh SAH zeez), made their homes there.

The **Hohokams** lived in present-day southern Arizona. About 2,000 years ago,

they developed ways to turn the dry desert into fertile farmland. They dug a vast system of irrigation ditches to bring water to dry land. The irrigation ditches channeled water from the Salt and Gila rivers into fields that then produced corn, squash, and beans.

In the late 1800s, archaeologists began to study thousands of abandoned stone buildings that dotted the Southwest. Most were built between 750 and 1300.

Who built these structures? Archaeologists asked the Navajos, the Native Americans who live in the region today. The Navajos replied that the mounds were built by the Anasazis. In the Navajo language, Anasazi means "ancient one."

Anasazi pueblos

As the Hohokams did, the **Anasazis** farmed the desert by using irrigation. The Anasazis built large, multistoried houses.

Walls were made of stone and sun-dried bricks, called **adobe.** When the Spanish explored the Southwest in the early 1500s, they called these houses **pueblos** (PWEHB lohz), or villages. Similar in some ways to modern apartment buildings, pueblos could shelter hundreds of families.

Anasazi pottery

At Pueblo Bonito, in New Mexico's Chaco Canyon, a giant house was once home to 1,000 people. Its 800 rooms are tiny, but the Anasazis spent much of their time in sunny, outdoor courtyards. The house has no stairways or hallways. To reach rooms on the upper floors, people climbed steep ladders.

Cliff dwellings

Sometime between 1,000 and 800 years ago, some Anasazis sought protection from warlike neighbors. To make their villages harder to attack, they built adobe houses along the cliffs that dotted the region. Toeholds cut into the rock let the Anasazis climb up and down the cliff walls. On top of the cliffs, they planted corn and other crops.

A network of roads connected Anasazi villages. Along these roads, traders carried cotton, sandals made from yucca leaves, and blankets woven from turkey feathers. Some Anasazi traders headed into present-day Mexico to trade with people there.

In the late 1200s, the Anasazis abandoned most of their villages. Archaeologists think that a **drought,** or long dry spell, hit the region. One legend speaks of such a disaster:

66 Snow ceased in the north and the west; rain ceased in the south and the east; the mists of the mountains above were drunk up; the waters of the valleys below were dried up.... Our ancients who dwelt in the cliffs fled ... when the rain stopped long, long ago. 99

Later, some of the Anasazis may have gone back to their homes. Most, however, became part of other cultures. Today, descendants of these early people preserve traditions of the ancient Anasazi culture.

★ Section 1 Review ★

Recall

1. **Identify** (a) Native American, (b) Mound Builder, (c) Hohokam, (d) Anasazi.
2. **Define** (a) glacier, (b) artifact, (c) archaeology, (d) culture, (e) adobe, (f) pueblo, (g) drought.

Comprehension

3. How did ancient people first arrive in the Americas?
4. Describe three kinds of evidence that archaeologists study.

5. (a) How did the Hohokams farm the desert? (b) Why did the Anasazis abandon their villages?

Critical Thinking and Writing

6. **Applying Information** Review the subsection The First Americans Migrate From Asia on page 30. How does the information in this subsection support the idea that geography affects history?
7. **Recognizing Points of View** Why have archaeologists and Native Americans sometimes clashed over the digging up of burial grounds?

★ ★

Activity **Writing a Survival Plan** Unplug that computer! Circumstances have forced you to live for a year in the desert Southwest. Write a plan explaining how you might adapt to your environment, as early Native Americans did. Consider all your options!

People of North America

As You Read

Explore These Questions

- Why did many different cultures develop in North America?
- What ways of life did Native Americans develop?
- What role did religion play in the lives of Native Americans?

Define

- culture area
- tribe
- igloo
- kayak
- potlatch
- kiva
- hogan
- travois
- tepee
- long house
- clan
- sachem

Identify

- Inuit
- Pueblo
- kachina
- Apache
- Navajo
- Natchez
- Iroquois
- League of the Iroquois

SETTING the Scene When Italian explorer Christopher Columbus reached the Americas in 1492, he thought he had reached the East Indies, a group of islands off the coast of Asia. He called the people he met "los Indios," or "the Indians." Soon, all Europeans were calling the people of the Americas Indians. By the time they realized Columbus's error, they were used to the term.

The name Indian is misleading for another, more important, reason. Native Americans do not belong to a single group. In Columbus's time, as now, Native Americans included many different people with many distinct cultures. In North America alone, Native Americans spoke hundreds of languages. Their cultures also varied greatly, from simple to highly complex.

Culture Areas and Tribes

The map on page 39 shows the 10 major culture areas of North America, north of Mexico. A **culture area** is a region in which people share a similar way of life.

Within each culture area, there were many different tribes. A **tribe** is a group of villages or settlements that shares common customs, language, and rituals. Members of a tribe saw themselves as a distinct people who shared the same origin. Throughout history, tribal organizations have played an important role in Indian life.

The tribe felt a strong bond with the land, plants, and animals in the region where they lived. As they hunted animals or raised crops or gathered wild plants, members of the tribe tried to keep a balance with the forces of the natural world. Their religious ceremonies and daily customs were designed to help them maintain that balance.

People of the Far North

Two culture areas, the Arctic and Subarctic, stretched across the far northern part of North America. In both regions, people adapted to harsh climates. In the Arctic, winter temperatures drop to −30° Fahrenheit (−34° C). Snow stays on the ground much of the year.

Arctic

Frozen seas and icy, treeless plains made up the world of the **Inuits,** the people of the Arctic.* The Inuits used all the limited re-

---

*Inuit, meaning "humans," was the Arctic people's name for themselves. Neighboring people, the Crees, called the Inuits "Eskimos," or "Eaters of Raw Meat."

sources of their environment in order to survive. In summer, they collected driftwood from the ocean shores to make tools and shelters. In winter, they built **igloos,** or houses of snow and ice. Lamps filled with seal oil kept the igloos warm even in the most bitter cold. Inuit women made warm clothing out of furs and waterproof boots out of sealskins.

Because food was scarce, the Inuits could not live in the same place all year round. In winter, large bands set up camp at a favorite spot near the sea. There on the thick sea ice, they hunted for seals. In spring, they paddled **kayaks** (KI aks), or small skin boats, to spear seals, whales, or walruses. When the summer came, they moved inland in smaller bands to hunt caribou or to fish in inland rivers and lakes.

Inuit religious beliefs reflected their close ties to the natural world. Inuits believed that each animal had a spirit. Before the hunt, they offered gifts to the animal they hoped to catch. After a successful hunt, they sang songs of praise and thanks to the animals.

Subarctic

Like their Arctic neighbors, the people of the Subarctic faced a severe environment. They, too, moved from place to place, hunting moose and caribou or fishing in rivers and

Viewing HISTORY In the Frozen Arctic

In the Arctic region, Inuit hunters moved across an icy landscape in search of food. Inuit carvings reflect the importance of the seals, walruses, and polar bears they depended on for survival. ★ **How did Inuits find shelter during the Arctic winter?**

Inuit carving of a walrus

oceans. They fashioned caribou and rabbit skins into robes and leggings. When Europeans arrived, many Subarctic peoples supplied furs to traders.

People of the Northwest Coast

The people of the Northwest Coast enjoyed a favorable climate and abundant food supplies. They gathered rich harvests of fish from the sea. Sea creatures provided more than just food. In some areas, people caught shellfish, called dentalia, to use as money. The longer the string of dentalia shells, the greater was the value.

In autumn, the rivers were full of salmon. To show their gratitude, the people returned salmon skeletons to the water. They believed that the Salmon Beings would grow new bodies and continue to provide food. The fishers of one Northwest Coast group, the Kwakiutls (kwah kee OOT 'lz), chanted this prayer of thanks when they caught their first fish of the year:

> **66** We have come to meet alive, Swimmer,
> do not feel wrong about what I have done to you,
> friend Swimmer,
> for that is the reason why you came,
> that I may spear you,
> that I may eat you,
> Supernatural One, you, Long-Life-Giver, you Swimmer.
> Now protect us, me and my wife. **99**

The Northwest Coast people also benefited from nearby forests. They cut down tall cedar trees and floated the timber by water to their villages. There, they split the tree trunks into planks for houses and canoes. From the soft inner bark, they made rope, baskets, and clothes. The forests also were home to deer, moose, and bears that the people hunted for meat and hides.

With plenty of food, the people of the Pacific Northwest could stay in one place. They built permanent villages and prospered from trade with nearby groups.

Within a village, families gained status according to how much they owned. Families sometimes competed for rank. To improve their standing, they held a **potlatch,** or ceremonial dinner, to show off their wealth. The family invited many guests and gave everyone presents. The more the family gave away, the more respect it earned. At one potlatch, which took years for the family to prepare, gifts included 8 canoes, 54 elk skins, 2,000 silver bracelets, 7,000 brass bracelets, and 33,000 blankets!

Other People of the West

Climates and resources varied in other parts of the West. As people adapted to these environments, they developed very different cultures.

Great Basin

The Great Basin lies in the dry Intermountain region of the United States. With little water, few plants or animals survived. As a result, Great Basin people like the Utes (yootz) and Shoshones (shoh SHOH neez) had to spend most of their time looking for food. They hunted rabbits or dug for roots in the desert soil.

Because the land offered so little, only a few related families traveled together in search of food. They had few possessions beyond digging sticks, baskets, and other tools or weapons needed for hunting. When they camped, they built temporary shelters out of willow poles and reeds.

Plateau

The people of the Plateau lived between two mountain ranges: the Rocky Mountains to the east and the Cascades to the west. Their main source of food was fish from rivers, like the Columbia and Fraser, or from smaller streams. They also hunted and gathered roots, nuts, and berries. In winter, they lived in earth houses that were partly underground. In summer, they set up lodges, temporary shelters made by placing rush mats over cottonwood frames.

Some groups traded with the Northwest Coast people and were influenced by their way of life. Others, like the Nez Percés (NEHZ PER sihz), adopted customs from the peoples of the Great Plains.

Native American Cultural Areas

Geography Skills Historians group the Native Americans who lived north of Mexico into 10 major culture areas.

1. **Location** On the map, locate the areas inhabited by the following groups: **(a)** Iroquois, **(b)** Inuit, **(c)** Pomo, **(d)** Hopi, **(e)** Shoshone.
2. **Place** Name two groups that lived in the coldest regions of North America.
3. **Critical Thinking** In which culture areas could Native Americans probably depend on the sea for food? Explain.

California

Differences in climate and resources helped create diverse cultures in California. Coastal people fished in the ocean and rivers. In the northern valleys, people hunted deer, rabbits, and elk or collected berries and nuts. In the southeast desert, small bands lived much like the people of the Great Basin.

For many Californians, like the Pomos, acorns were the basic food. Women harvested the nuts in autumn and later pounded them into flour. Both women and men among the Pomos were skilled at weaving baskets, which they decorated with fine designs.

People of the Southwest

The **Pueblos,** the Spanish name for people of the Southwest, were descended from the Anasazis. They included such groups as the Hopis, Acomas, Zuñis, and Lagunas. By

Skills FOR LIFE

Critical Thinking	Managing Information	Communication	Maps, Charts, and Graphs

Listening

How Will I Use This Skill?

Listening is not as easy as it sounds. Statistics show that most people miss much of what they hear. Listening clearly will help you follow directions, get along with people, and do better in school and on the job.

LEARN the Skill

Use these steps to practice listening skills:

❶ Listen to the opening words to determine the main topic.

❷ Notice how changes in the speaker's voice emphasize certain ideas.

❸ Look for facial expressions and gestures that stress important ideas.

❹ Listen for closing remarks that summarize the main point.

PRACTICE the Skill

Native American groups passed along tales like the one at right. Work with a partner. One partner reads the tale aloud, while the other listens and answers the following questions.

❶ What is the main topic of the story?

❷ What changes in voice helped you understand the story?

❸ Did the speaker use any gestures?

❹ How do the closing words summarize the story?

APPLY the Skill

Select a partner. Give each other brief descriptions of yourselves. Then, introduce your partner to the class. See how accurate you are.

> 66 *Listen, and learn why the rabbit has long ears. When the world was new, the rabbit had short ears. Back then, many, many moons ago, the rabbit and the eagle argued a lot. One day, in anger, the eagle grabbed the rabbit and flew it to her nest high in the trees. She gave the rabbit to her baby eagles as a toy.*
>
> *The baby eagles enjoyed chasing and tugging at the rabbit. One time, the rabbit got hurt. In a fit of rage, he killed all the baby eagles. The rabbit became frightened. He knew the mother eagle would look for him. He tried to disguise himself by taking feathers from the tiny eagles and stuffing them in his ears, stretching them very long. He then ran away and tried to hide himself in a hole of a fallen birch tree.*
>
> *When the eagle saw what happened, she searched for the rabbit for revenge. She saw the ears showing out of the tree and was ready to attack when she remembered an old tradition of covering the dead with birch bark. She thought the rabbit was dead, and so she flew away.*
>
> *Later, the eagle realized her mistake. To this day, the eagle still hunts the rabbit. Now you know why the rabbit has long ears and hides from the eagle.* 99

Kachina Dolls

To the Hopis of the Southwest, kachina dolls represented the spirits of the natural world. To create figures like these required great skill and care. For example, the kachina on the left is made of wood, cotton, fur, horsehair, feathers, shell, horn, and stone. ★ **Why do you think Hopi craftworkers took such care to create kachina dolls?**

1500, only the Hopis still farmed on clifftops as the Anasazis had done. Other groups lived in villages along the Rio Grande and its tributaries.

Pueblo way of life

Like their ancestors, the Pueblos built adobe houses and grew corn, beans, and squash. Their religious beliefs reflected the importance of farming. Most Pueblo villages had a **kiva,** or underground chamber, where men held religious ceremonies. Through prayers and other rituals, they tried to please the spirits of nature, such as wind, rain, and thunder.

At planting or harvest time, the Hopis and Zuñis held ceremonies to ensure rainfall and good crops. In the villages, cries rang out: "The kachinas are coming!" **Kachinas,** or masked dancers, represented the spirits. If the dance was pleasing to the spirits, they would return as rain to water the next season's crops.

The Pueblos traced their family lines through their mothers. This custom gave women special importance. When a man married, he went to live with his wife's family. Also, Pueblo wives owned most of the family property.

Navajos and Apaches

About 1500, two new groups reached the Southwest: the **Apaches** and the **Navajos.** Both groups lived as hunters, but they often raided Pueblo fields for food.

In time, the Navajos accepted many Pueblo ways. They began to farm and to build **hogans,** or houses made of mud plaster over a framework of wooden poles. The Apaches, however, continued to follow herds of buffalo and the other game they hunted. They traded dried buffalo meat and animal skins to the Pueblos in exchange for corn and woven cloth.

People of the Great Plains

Centuries ago, vast grasslands extended across the Great Plains from the Rocky Mountains to the Mississippi River. Because there were few trees, Plains people built their homes of sod, chunks of thickly matted grass.

Farming and hunting

Some Plains people farmed along river banks. In spring, women broke up the soft ground using hoes made from animal bones. They then planted corn, beans, squash, and sunflowers.

Large herds of animals grazed on the Plains, including buffalo, antelope, elk, deer, and bighorn sheep. Plains people hunted the animals on foot. In winter, men hunted near the village. In summer, however, they often traveled for miles in search of buffalo and other animals. They carried their belongings with them on a **travois** (truh VOY), or sled, pulled by dogs.

Each village had a ruling council that included the best hunters. The chief was respected by other council members because he spoke well and judged wisely.

Viewing HISTORY — Clothing From the Great Plains

On the Great Plains, Comanche hunters followed herds of deer and antelope. They ate the deer meat and used the hides to make clothing, like this woman's buckskin dress. ★ **In what other way did Plains people make use of the animals they hunted?**

A new way of life

During the 1700s, the way of life of the Plains people changed. They began to catch and tame wild horses that appeared on the Plains. These horses descended from animals brought to the Southwest by Spanish settlers some 200 years earlier. Until then, there had been no horses in North America. A Blackfoot tale describes their reaction to seeing horses for the first time:

> 66 After a time, a woman said, 'Let's put a travois on one of them just like we do on our small dogs.' They made a larger travois and attached it to one of the gentler horses. It didn't kick or jump. They led the horse around with the travois attached. Finally, a woman mounted the horse and rode it. 99

Soon, Plains people became skillful riders. Because they could travel farther and faster than before, they raised fewer crops. They hunted more, moving often to follow huge herds of buffalo that roamed the plains. They also began to live in **tepees,** cone-shaped tents made of buffalo hides that could be carried easily on a travois.

People of the Southeast

The Southeast was home to more Native Americans than any other region. A warm climate, fertile soil, and plentiful rain helped Southeast people produce good crops.

Most people lived in villages and farmed nearby land. They built their homes from saplings, or young trees. They split the trees into strips and wove them to make a frame for walls. Then, they plastered the walls with a mixture of clay and dry grass.

Farming and religion

Men and women had clearly defined roles in the community. Men cleared the land and hunted deer and other animals. Women planted, weeded, and harvested the crops. Among rows of corn, they planted beans that climbed up the cornstalks. They also grew squash, pumpkins, and sunflowers.

Most religious ceremonies were linked to farming. The most important, the Green Corn Ceremony, took place in midsummer, when the corn ripened. It marked the end of the year. Celebrations lasted several days. The highlight, on the last day, was the lighting of the sacred fire followed by a dance around its flames. With this event, the new year began.

Natchez society

One Southeast group, the **Natchez** (NACH ihz), hunted, fished, and farmed along the fertile coast of the Gulf of Mexico. They divided the year into 13 months. Each month

Connections With Civics

While warrior chiefs led most Plains Indian societies, the Cheyennes had a complex civil, or nonmilitary, government. The ruling council included representatives from the 10 main Cheyenne bands. Any warrior chief sent to the council had to resign his military power.

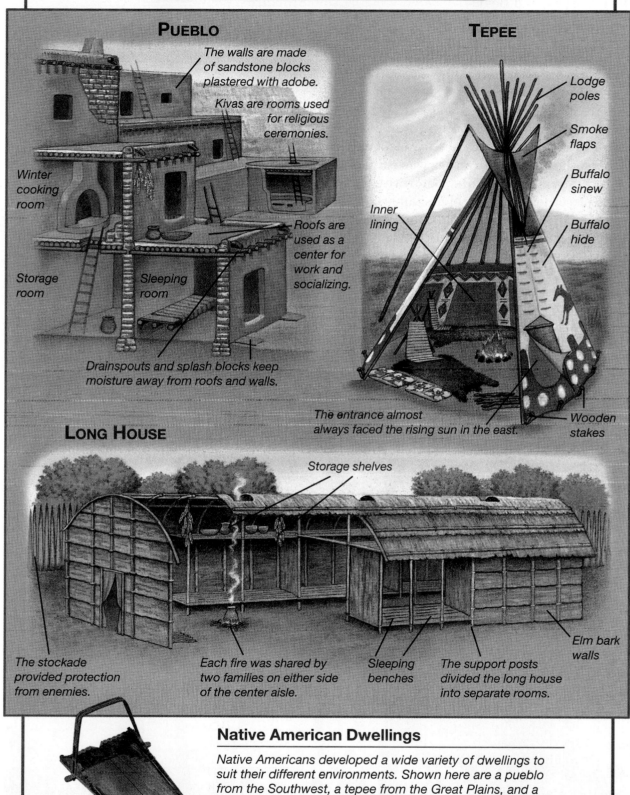

PUEBLO

The walls are made of sandstone blocks plastered with adobe.

Kivas are rooms used for religious ceremonies.

Winter cooking room

Storage room

Sleeping room

Roofs are used as a center for work and socializing.

Drainspouts and splash blocks keep moisture away from roofs and walls.

TEPEE

Lodge poles

Smoke flaps

Buffalo sinew

Buffalo hide

Inner lining

The entrance almost always faced the rising sun in the east.

Wooden stakes

LONG HOUSE

Storage shelves

The stockade provided protection from enemies.

Each fire was shared by two families on either side of the center aisle.

Sleeping benches

The support posts divided the long house into separate rooms.

Elm bark walls

Iroquois ▶ cradleboard

Native American Dwellings

Native Americans developed a wide variety of dwellings to suit their different environments. Shown here are a pueblo from the Southwest, a tepee from the Great Plains, and a long house from the Eastern Woodlands. ★ **Describe one way each type of dwelling reflects the local environment.**

was named after a food or animal that the Natchez harvested or hunted. Months included Strawberry, Little Corn, Mulberry, Deer, Turkey, and Bear.

Natchez religious beliefs centered on worship of the sun. Priests kept a fire going day and night in a temple dedicated to the sun. The Natchez believed that fire came from the sun.

The Natchez ruler, the Great Sun, was worshipped as a god. He lived atop a giant pyramid mound. The Great Sun's feet never touched the ground. He either was carried in a litter or walked on mats. Below the Great Sun were other members of his family, called Little Suns. Next came Nobles, then Honored People, and finally Stinkards, or commoners, who were the majority of the people.

Marriage laws ensured that membership in each class kept changing. By law, noble men and women had to marry Stinkards. Even the Great Sun chose a Stinkard as a wife. In this way, no one family could hold the position of Great Sun forever. In time, even descendants of a Great Sun became Stinkards.

People of the Eastern Woodlands

Many groups lived in the Eastern Woodlands. In the forests and open lands, they hunted deer, moose, and other game. They also planted crops of corn, pumpkins, and squash.

The Iroquois: a complex society

The most powerful people of this region were the **Iroquois** (IHR uh kwoi). They lived in present-day New York State.

The Iroquois called themselves House Builders. They built **long houses** out of wood poles sided with bark. A typical long house was about 150 feet (46 m) long and 20 feet (7 m) wide. A hallway, with small rooms

Viewing HISTORY — Iroquois Women at Work

In several Native American cultures, including the Iroquois, women were responsible for growing and gathering food. Here, Iroquois women collect sap to make maple sugar. ★ **In what culture region did the Iroquois live?**

on either side, ran the length of the long house. Each room was home to one family. Families living across from each other shared a fireplace in the hallway.

Women had a special place in Iroquois society. They owned all household property and were in charge of planting and harvesting. Like a Pueblo man, an Iroquois man moved in with his wife's family when he married. Iroquois women also shared in political power because they chose clan leaders. A **clan** was a group of two or more related families. If a clan leader did not do his job well, the women could remove him from his position.

League of the Iroquois

The Iroquois included five nations: the Mohawk, Seneca, Onondaga (ahn uhn DAW guh), Oneida (oh NI duh), and Cayuga (kay YOO guh). Each nation had its own ruling council.

Constant warfare disrupted the Iroquois nations. Around 1570, the nations formed an alliance to end the fighting. According to legend, a religious leader named Dekanawida (deh kan ah WEE dah) inspired Hiawatha, a Mohawk, to organize the alliance. It became known as the **League of the Iroquois.** According to Iroquois tradition, the founders of the League of the Iroquois made this promise:

> 66 We bind ourselves together by taking hold of each other's hands.... Our strength shall be in union, our way the way of reason, righteousness, and peace.... Be of strong mind, O chiefs. Carry no anger and hold no grudges. 99

Later, a sixth nation, the Tuscarora (tuhs kuh ROR uh), joined the League.

A council of 50 **sachems,** or specially chosen tribal leaders, met once a year to make decisions for the League. Again, Iroquois women chose the sachems. At meetings, the council discussed problems and voted on ways to solve them. Each nation had one vote. The council could take action only if all of the nations agreed. The League helped end warfare among the Iroquois nations, and gave them a united defense against their enemies.

★ Section 2 Review ★

Recall

1. **Identify** (a) Inuit, (b) Pueblo, (c) kachina, (d) Apache, (e) Navajo, (f) Natchez, (g) Iroquois, (h) League of the Iroquois.

2. **Define** (a) culture area, (b) tribe, (c) igloo, (d) kayak, (e) potlatch, (f) kiva, (g) hogan, (h) travois, (i) tepee, (j) long house, (k) clan, (l) sachem.

Comprehension

3. (a) Name two Native American cultures that developed in North America. (b) Explain how each adapted to its environment.

4. How did cultures that relied on farming for food differ from those that were mainly hunters?

5. How did religion play a major role in the everyday life of most Native American cultures?

Critical Thinking and Writing

6. **Synthesizing Information** Review the feature Linking History and Technology on page 43. (a) Which of the three kinds of home shown here would you expect to find in a culture that relied on hunting for its way of life? Explain. (b) Which would be most suited to a settled farming community? Explain.

7. **Linking Past and Present** The Iroquois League helped settle disputes and keep the peace. What institutions perform this role in American society today?

★ ★

Activity **Writing a Chant** Write a chant celebrating your links with the natural world. For example, you could express gratitude for the foods you eat, or for the type of weather you most enjoy. For one example of a chant, see the Kwakiutl chant on page 38.

3 ⭐ Great Civilizations in the Americas

As You Read

Explore These Questions
- Where did the Mayan, Aztec, and Incan civilizations flourish?
- What were the main achievements of these civilizations?
- How were religion and learning linked in Aztec society?

Define
- civilization
- hieroglyphics
- causeway
- chinampas
- absolute power
- terrace
- aqueduct
- surplus

Identify
- Maya
- Olmec
- Aztec
- Tenochtitlán
- Inca
- Cuzco

SETTING the Scene Some 1,500 years ago, large oceangoing canoes sped along the Caribbean coast of Mexico. Cutting swiftly through the blue waters of the Caribbean Sea, the canoes made an impressive sight. Even more impressive were the riches inside the canoes. Traders carried jade statues, turquoise jewelry, parrot feathers, cocoa beans, and other valuable goods across a wide area.

The canoes belonged to the **Mayas,** a people who flourished in Mexico and Central America. The Mayas were one of several Native American people who built great, complex societies in the ancient Americas.

The Earliest American Civilizations

A **civilization** is an advanced culture. Historians identify several basic features of early civilizations. Perhaps the most important is the building of cities. Other features include a well-organized government, a system of social classes, specialized jobs, a complex religion, and some method of keeping records.

The earliest known American civilization was that of the **Olmecs.** The Olmecs emerged in the forests along the Gulf of Mexico, around 3,500 years ago. Archaeologists know very little about the Olmecs. However, rich tombs and temples suggest a powerful class of priests and nobles stood at the top of Olmec society.

The most dramatic Olmec artifacts are the giant carved stone heads found near a religious center. Without the use of pack animals or wheeled vehicles, the Olmecs moved these colossal stones from distant quarries. Olmec temples were decorated with designs of grinning snakes and dragons. Similar designs in later buildings suggest that the Olmec civilization influenced the later, more advanced Mayan civilization.

Vase showing a Mayan king

Mayan Civilization

Mayan civilization emerged about 3,000 years ago. It grew up in the rain forests of present-day Mexico and Guatemala. The rain forests were difficult and dangerous places to live. Poisonous snakes hung from trees. Jaguars and other wild animals prowled the forest floor. Disease-carrying insects infested the swamps.

From earlier people, the Mayas learned to grow corn and to build stone structures. With much work, they cleared the jungle and drained the swamps.

On the cleared land, they grew corn to feed a growing population. They lived in simple homes with mud walls and thatched roofs.

Great cities

In time, the Mayas built great cities in many parts of Mexico and Central America. Two of these cities were Tikal and Copán. Each city had its own ruler. Although rival cities sometimes fought, they also enjoyed times of peaceful trade. Roads that cut through the jungle linked inland cities to the coast.

Towering above the cities were huge stone pyramids. Atop each pyramid stood a temple. There, priests performed ceremonies to please the Mayan gods.

Social classes

Priests were at the top of Mayan society. Only priests had the knowledge to perform the ceremonies that the Mayas believed were necessary to guarantee good harvests and victory in battle.

Nobles, government officials, and warriors also enjoyed high rank. A visitor to a Mayan city could easily spot priests and nobles. They wore gold jewelry, fine headdresses, and colorful cotton garments. While most rulers were men, Mayan records and carvings indicate that sometimes women governed on their own or in the name of young sons.

Near the bottom of Mayan society was a large class of peasant farmers. Lowest of all were slaves. Slaves were generally prisoners of war.

Advances in learning

Mayan priests paid careful attention to the passage of time and to the pattern of daily events. By studying the sun and the stars, they tried to predict the future. In that way, they could honor the gods who controlled events, including harvests, trade, and hunts.

Concern with time and the seasons led the Mayas to explore astronomy and mathematics. With the knowledge they gained, they created an accurate 365-day calendar. They also developed an advanced number system that included the concept of zero.

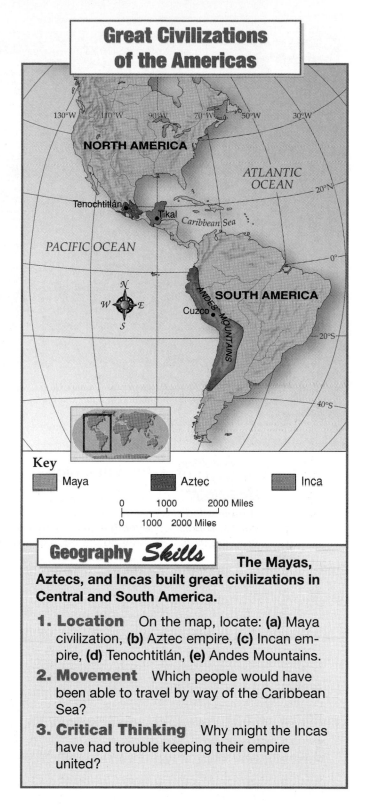

Great Civilizations of the Americas

Key

Maya   Aztec   Inca

| 0 | 1000 | 2000 Miles |
| 0 | 1000 | 2000 Miles |

Geography Skills The Mayas, Aztecs, and Incas built great civilizations in Central and South America.

1. **Location** On the map, locate: **(a)** Maya civilization, **(b)** Aztec empire, **(c)** Incan empire, **(d)** Tenochtitlán, **(e)** Andes Mountains.
2. **Movement** Which people would have been able to travel by way of the Caribbean Sea?
3. **Critical Thinking** Why might the Incas have had trouble keeping their empire united?

To record their findings, Mayan priests invented a system of **hieroglyphics,** or writing that uses pictures to represent words and ideas. Not until recent years have scholars deciphered Mayan hieroglyphics. The Mayas carved records on stone columns or painted them on paper made from bark.

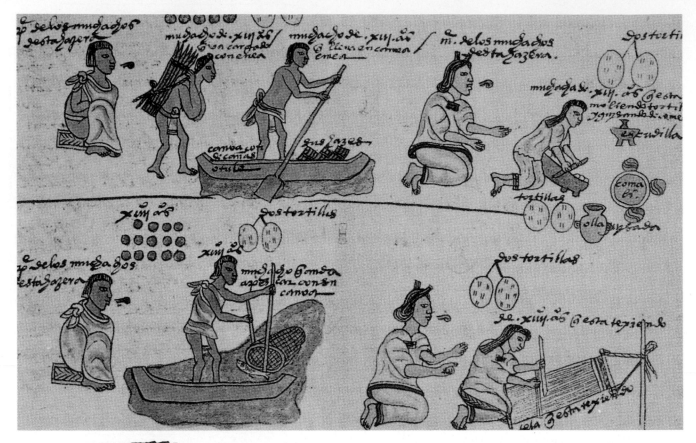

Viewing HISTORY — Aztec Education

Pictures in an Aztec book show how Aztec parents taught their children needed skills. At left, a father teaches his son how to gather firewood, paddle a canoe, and fish. The mother, at right, instructs her daughter in grinding grain and weaving cloth. ★ **How do we pass on important skills to young people today?**

Decline of the Mayas

About 850, the Mayas abandoned their cities, and the forests once more took over the land. For centuries, these "lost cities" of the Mayas remained hidden in the thick rain forests of Central America.

We are unsure why the cities were left to decay. Perhaps peasants rebelled against heavy taxes imposed by their rulers. Maybe farming wore out the soil. Even though their cities declined, the Mayan people survived. Today, more than 2 million people in southern Mexico and Guatemala speak Mayan languages.

Aztec Civilization

To the north of the Mayan cities, the **Aztecs** built a powerful empire. Until the 1300s, the Aztecs were wanderers, moving from place to place in search of food. Then,

according to legend, a god told the Aztecs to look for a sign. They were to search for an eagle perched on a cactus with a snake in its beak.* On that spot, the god instructed, the Aztecs should build their capital. After more wandering, the Aztecs found the eagle in swampy Lake Texcoco (tay SKOH koh), in central Mexico.

Tenochtitlán

The Aztecs built their capital, **Tenochtitlán** (tay noch tee TLAHN), on an island in the middle of Lake Texcoco. Aztec engineers built **causeways,** or raised roads, out of packed earth. Aztec causeways connected the island to the mainland.

Farmers learned to grow crops on the swampland. They dug canals and filled in

---

*Today, the eagle, snake, and cactus remain symbols of Mexico and appear on the Mexican flag.

parts of the lake. With long stakes, they attached reed mats to the swampy lake bottom. Then, they piled mud onto the mats and planted their crops. Aztec farmers harvested as many as seven crops a year on these **chinampas,** or floating gardens.

In the 1400s, the Aztecs expanded their power by conquering neighboring people. They adopted many beliefs and ideas from these defeated people.

Riches from trade and conquest turned Tenochtitlán into a large, bustling city. City marketplaces offered an abundance of goods. "There are daily more than 60,000 people bartering and selling," wrote a Spanish visitor in the 1500s.

Canoes darted up the canals that crisscrossed the city. Soldiers and merchants traveled the causeways between Tenochtitlán and the mainland. Drawbridges on the roads could be raised in case of attack.

Religion

Religion was central to Aztec life. Young men and women attended special schools where they trained to become priests and priestesses. Like the Mayas, Aztec priests studied the heavens and developed advanced calendars. They used these calendars to determine when to plant or harvest and to predict future events. The priests divided the year into 18 months. Each month was governed by its own god. Aztec books contained knowledge about the gods as well as special prayers and hymns.

The sun god was especially important. Each day, the Aztecs believed, the sun battled its way across the heavens. They compared the sun's battles to their own, calling themselves "warriors of the sun." To ensure a successful journey across the sky, the sun required human sacrifices. The Aztecs sacrificed tens of thousands of prisoners of war each year to please their gods.

A powerful empire

By 1500, the Aztecs ruled millions of people from the Gulf of Mexico to the Pacific Ocean. The emperor had **absolute power,** that is, he had total authority over the people he ruled. The Aztec emperor was treated

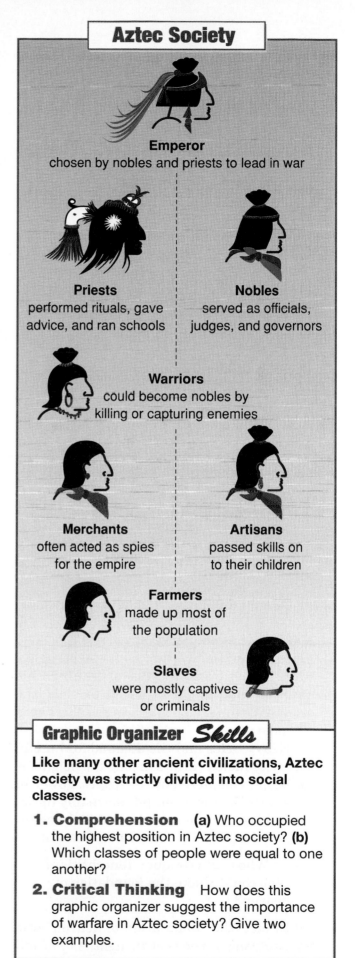

Aztec Society

Emperor
chosen by nobles and priests to lead in war

Priests
performed rituals, gave advice, and ran schools

Nobles
served as officials, judges, and governors

Warriors
could become nobles by killing or capturing enemies

Merchants
often acted as spies for the empire

Artisans
passed skills on to their children

Farmers
made up most of the population

Slaves
were mostly captives or criminals

Graphic Organizer *Skills*

Like many other ancient civilizations, Aztec society was strictly divided into social classes.

1. **Comprehension** **(a)** Who occupied the highest position in Aztec society? **(b)** Which classes of people were equal to one another?

2. **Critical Thinking** How does this graphic organizer suggest the importance of warfare in Aztec society? Give two examples.

In 1438, Pachacuti rallied Incan forces to drive off an invasion. The Incas soon made him their leader. As founder of the Incan empire, Pachacuti devoted himself to uniting all the lands and people of Peru. He demanded that conquered people all speak one language, Quechua. He also turned the city of Cuzco into a magnificent capital. ★ **Why would Pachacuti think that one language would help unite his empire?**

almost like a god. Servants carried him from place to place on a litter. If the emperor did walk, nobles scattered flower petals in his path so that his feet never touched the ground. Ordinary people lowered their eyes when he passed.

Heavy taxes and the demand for human sacrifices fueled revolts among the neighboring people conquered by the Aztecs. Powerful Aztec armies, however, put down any uprising, taking even more prisoners to be sacrificed to the gods. One Aztec poet boasted:

❝ Who could conquer Tenochtitlán? Who could shake the foundation of heaven? ❞

In fact, the "foundation of heaven" was not as strong as the poet thought. As you will read in Chapter 3, in the 1520s, enemies of the Aztecs would help to destroy Tenochtitlán and end the Aztec empire.

Incan Civilization

Far to the south of the Aztec empire, the **Incas** united the largest empire in the Americas. By 1492, the Incan empire stretched for almost 3,000 miles (4,800 km) along the western coast of South America. (See the map on page 47.)

The Incan capital at **Cuzco** (KOOS koh) was high in the Andes Mountains. From there, the Incas ruled more than 10 million people living in coastal deserts, lowland jungles, and high mountains.

Farming

Like the Mayas and Aztecs, the Incas adapted customs and ideas from earlier cultures. Among them were the Moche, who lived along the Pacific coast of South America between about 250 and 700, and the Chimu people, who came after them.

Expanding on farming methods of these earlier Andean peoples, the Incas carved **terraces,** land shaped like wide steps, into the steep mountainsides. Sturdy stone walls kept the rains from washing the soil off the terraces. Stone **aqueducts,** or raised channels, carried water to the terraces from distant rivers. Most gardens produced two crops a year, including more than 100 varieties of potatoes.

The emperor, known as the Sapa Inca, controlled all the land and riches of the empire. Officials kept records of what each family in the empire produced. The government stored their **surplus,** or extra, crops in warehouses owned by the emperor. Incan officials used much of the food in these warehouses to feed the sick or victims of famine.

Engineering and medicine

The Incas perfected highly advanced building techniques. Their huge stone temples and forts showed their expert engineering skills. With only human labor, ropes, and wooden rollers, the Incas moved into place massive stones that weighed as much as 200 tons.

Stonemasons chiseled each block so that it fit tightly to the next without any kind of cement. Even a knife blade could not fit between blocks. Incan buildings survived hundreds of earthquakes. Some remain standing today.

To unite and control their sprawling empire, the Incas built a complex network of roads. Between 10,000 and 20,000 miles of roads linked all parts of the empire. Incan engineers carved roads through rock mountains and stretched rope bridges across deep gorges.

Teams of runners carried royal commands and news quickly across the empire. A runner from Cuzco, for example, would carry a message to a nearby village. From there, another runner would race to the next relay station. This system helped the emperor to control his people. If a runner brought news of a revolt, Incan armies could move swiftly along the network of roads to crush it.

Besides their success as farmers and engineers, the Incas made several important advances in medicine. They used quinine to treat malaria, performed successful brain surgery, and also discovered medicines to lessen pain.

Incan gold earrings

Religious beliefs

Like the Aztecs, the Incas worshipped the sun. The emperor, they believed, was descended from the sun god. A specially trained class of "chosen women of the sun" attended the emperor and performed religious rituals. To honor the sun, the Incas lined the walls of palaces and temples with sheets of gold. They called gold "the sweat of the gods." Nobles and priests adorned themselves with golden ornaments.

Very little Incan gold has survived. In the 1530s, as you will read, the Spanish rode up Incan highways to the golden city of Cuzco. The Incas, weakened by civil war and disease, were unable to fight off the invaders. The newcomers melted down the golden treasures of the Incan empire and sent them to Europe.

★ Section 3 Review ★

Recall

1. **Locate** (a) Mexico, (b) Guatemala, (c) Tikal, (d) Aztec empire, (e) Andes Mountains, (f) Incan empire.

2. **Identify** (a) Maya, (b) Olmec, (c) Aztec, (d) Tenochtitlán, (e) Inca, (f) Cuzco.

3. **Define** (a) civilization, (b) hieroglyphics, (c) causeway, (d) chinampas, (e) absolute power, (f) terrace, (g) aqueduct, (h) surplus.

Comprehension

4. (a) What civilizations emerged in present-day Mexico? (b) Where did the Incas build their civilization?

5. Describe one achievement of each of the following: (a) Mayas, (b) Aztecs, (c) Incas.

6. How was religion central to Aztec life?

Critical Thinking and Writing

7. **Synthesizing Information** Review the definition of a civilization on page 46. Then, choose one of the groups discussed in this section and explain why it should be considered a civilization.

8. **Comparing** Compare the major features of two of the civilizations discussed in the section. How are they similar? How are they different?

★ ★

Activity **Writing a Travel Plan** Next stop—Tenochtitlán! You are planning a trip through time to the Aztec capital. Write a list of the sights you want to see and the things you most want to do.

After 1492

As You Read

Explore These Questions
- How did the 1492 encounter with Europeans affect Native Americans?
- What is the Columbian Exchange?
- What elements of Native American culture did Europeans adopt?

Identify
- Viking
- Leif Erickson
- Vinland
- Christopher Columbus
- Taíno
- Columbian Exchange

 Approximately 1,000 years ago, a group of seafaring men and women sailed across the Atlantic Ocean to settle on an island they called Vinland. There, they met local traders, who carried packs made of fur and skins. A witness wrote:

Figurehead of a Viking ship

66 Neither party could understand the other's language.... The Skraelings unslung their bales, untied them, and proffered their wares, and above all wanted weapons in exchange. 99

This meeting was one of the earliest encounters between Native Americans and Europeans. The "Skraelings" were Inuits. The settlers were **Vikings,** seafaring people from Scandinavia in Northern Europe.

The Viking settlement was brief and had no long-term effect on Native Americans. Then, in 1492, an expedition from Spain sailed into the Caribbean Sea. This time, the arrival of Europeans would have a dramatic impact on people throughout the Americas.

Early Contacts

For thousands of years, Native Americans had little knowledge of the world beyond their shores. Early contacts with outsiders were limited.

In 1001, Viking sailors led by **Leif Erickson** reached the northern tip of North America. They settled for a brief time in a flat, wooded territory they called **Vinland.** Today, many archaeologists believe that the Viking settlement was located in present-day Newfoundland, in Canada. The Vikings did not stay in Vinland long. No one is sure why they left. Viking stories, however, describe fierce battles with the Inuits.

There are also many stories about seafaring people from Asia reaching the Americas. Most experts agree that such voyages were very rare, if they occurred at all. Still, some believe that even after the last ice age ended, people continued to cross the Bering Sea from Asia into North America. Others claim that fishing boats from China and Japan blew off course and landed on the western coast of South America.

Encounter in 1492

If these early contacts did in fact take place, they had little impact either on Native Americans or the rest of the world. The encounter in 1492, however, changed history. Italian-born sailor **Christopher Columbus** led a Spanish fleet into the Caribbean. The voyage set off a chain of events whose effects are still felt throughout the world today. (You will read more about Christopher Columbus and other Europeans in Chapter 3.)

Columbus first landed in the Americas on a small Caribbean island. Friendly relations with the **Taínos** (TI nohz), the Native Americans he met there, did not last. Columbus and the Europeans who followed him were convinced that their culture was superior to that of the Indians. They claimed Taíno lands for themselves. They forced Taínos to work in gold mines, on ranches, or in Spanish households. Many Taínos died from harsh conditions. Others died from European diseases. Within 100 years of Columbus's arrival, the entire Taíno population had been destroyed.

The Taínos' experience with Europeans set a tragic pattern for Native Americans. That pattern was repeated again and again throughout the Americas.

Cultural Exchange

The 1492 encounter between Native Americans and Europeans had other effects. It started a worldwide exchange of goods and ideas that transformed people's lives around the globe. Because it began with Columbus, this transfer is known as the **Columbian Exchange.** It covered a wide range of areas, including food, medicine, government, technology, the arts, and language.

The exchange went in both directions. Europeans learned much from Native Americans. At the same time, Europeans contributed in many ways to the culture of the Americas. They introduced domestic animals such as chickens and horses. They also taught Native Americans how to use metals to make copper pots and iron knives.

Tragically, Europeans also brought new diseases to the Americas. Millions of Native Americans died of smallpox and other diseases to which they had no resistance.

Native American Influences

For their part, Native Americans introduced Europeans to new customs and ideas. Beginning with the encounter in 1492, elements of Native American culture gradually spread around the world.

Food and farming

Over thousands of years, Native Americans had learned to grow a variety of crops.

After 1492, they introduced Europeans to valuable food crops such as corn, potatoes, beans, tomatoes, manioc (a root vegetable), squash, peanuts, pineapples, and blueberries. Today, almost half the world's food crops come from plants that were first grown in the Americas.

Europeans carried the new foods with them as they sailed around the world. Everywhere, people's diets changed and populations increased. In South Asia, people used American hot peppers and chilies to spice their curries, or stews. Millions of Chinese peasants began growing sweet potatoes. Italians made sauces from tomatoes. People in West Africa grew manioc and maize.

 **Potato Farming in South America**

Farmers in the Andes first raised potatoes about 2,000 years ago. As a result of the Columbian Exchange, the potato has become an important part of people's diets around the world. ★ **Identify two other food crops that were first grown in the Americas.**

Why Study History?

Because Sports Are Important in Our Culture

★ ★

Historical Background

The athletes lined the playing field—nearly 1,000 young men in all. Each held a long pole topped with a web of leather netting. As the game began, they rushed up and down the mile-long field, trying to pass a ball over the other team's goal. Play was fast, dangerous, and exhausting. It might last well into the next day!

The players were Iroquois. They called the game baggataway. You know it by its French name: lacrosse.

The game was more than fun. The game taught young men agility, quick thinking, and teamwork—skills they would need as hunters or warriors. In fact, some called the game "the little brother of war." Each boy was assigned to a team at birth. The night before a match, villages held ceremonies with music, dancing, and speeches to cheer their team to victory.

Connections to Today

Today, lacrosse is popular in many American schools. Other sports we enjoy today were played by Native Americans. Field hockey and ice hockey developed partly from a sport known as the shinny game. Like Native Americans, we also compete in kayaking, canoeing, archery, swimming, wrestling, and foot races.

Connections to You

For us, as for Native Americans, sports are more than just fun. Athletics can improve your health and physical fitness.

Modern lacrosse player

School pep rallies, like the pregame ceremonies of the Iroquois, encourage a sense of pride and community. Sports can also teach skills that you will use later in life. Today's sports emphasize teamwork, responsibility, and fair play.

1. **Comprehension** **(a)** Why did the Iroquois consider baggataway important? **(b)** How did they make sure each new generation learned the game?

2. **Critical Thinking** Choose a sport that is popular at your school. What kind of skills can that sport teach?

 **Reporting on Sports** Research the modern rules of lacrosse or one of the other sports mentioned above. Report on how that sport is played and why you think it has remained so popular today.

Language

Native American influences also show up in language. Europeans adopted words for clothing (poncho, moccasin, parka), trees (pecan, hickory), and inventions (toboggan, hammock). In an essay titled "The Indian All Around Us," historian Bernard DeVoto noted:

66 Depending on what part of the country you are in, you may see a chipmunk, muskrat, woodchuck, or coyote. The names of all these animals are Indian words.... Twenty-six of our states have Indian names. 99

Massachusetts, Alabama, Texas, Michigan, and Missouri are all Native American words. Many rivers bear Native American names, including the Mississippi, the Potomac, and the Monongahela.

Technology and medicine

Native Americans helped European settlers survive in North America. Besides showing the newcomers how to grow foods such as corn, Indians taught them hunting skills suitable to the American land. They led explorers on foot along Indian trails and paddled them up rivers in Indian canoes.

In the North, Indians showed Europeans how to use snowshoes and trap fur-bearing animals. Europeans also learned to respect Native American medical knowledge. Indians often treated the newcomers with medicines unknown to Europeans.

Other influences

As time went on, Native American cultures influenced the arts, sports, and even government. Today, Indian designs in pottery and leather work are highly prized. Americans play versions of such Indian games as lacrosse.

Some early leaders of the United States studied Native American political structures. Benjamin Franklin saw the League of the Iroquois as a model and urged Americans to unite in a similar way.

In time, all Native Americans felt the effects of European conquest. Still, despite attacks on their culture, Native Americans survived throughout the two continents. They preserved many traditions, including a respect for nature. Native Americans sought to live in harmony with the natural world. If that harmony was disrupted, they believed, misfortune would result. Today, many people have come to admire and share this concern for nature.

★ Section 4 Review ★

Recall

1. **Identify** **(a)** Viking, **(b)** Leif Erickson, **(c)** Vinland, **(d)** Christopher Columbus, **(e)** Taíno, **(f)** Columbian Exchange.

Comprehension

2. How did the arrival of Columbus affect the Taínos?

3. Describe two effects of the Columbian Exchange on Native Americans.

4. Name three ways that Native Americans influenced our culture today.

Critical Thinking and Writing

5. **Analyzing Information** Some historians think that Asians explored the Americas years before Columbus arrived. What kinds of evidence might prove that these historians are correct?

6. **Defending a Position** Do you think that the world was harmed or enriched by the Columbian Exchange? Defend your position.

★ ★

History AND YOU

Activity Examining Exchange List three items or activities in your life that were part of the Columbian Exchange. Write one or two sentences explaining how your life would be different without each item or activity.

Chapter 2 — Review and Activities

★ Sum It Up ★

Section 1   Early People and Cultures
► The first Americans crossed a land bridge from Asia between 30,000 and 15,000 years ago.
► The first Americans adapted to the desert Southwest by learning to grow crops under dry conditions and building adobe houses.

Section 2   People of North America
► Native American cultures varied widely depending on geography.
► The religious beliefs of Native Americans reflected their close ties with the natural world.
► In the Eastern Woodlands, the five Iroquois nations formed a league to end warfare.

Section 3   Great Civilizations in the Americas
► The Mayan civilization boasted skill in astronomy, mathematics, and writing.
► The Aztecs of Mexico ruled a huge empire with millions of people.
► In South America, the Incas perfected advanced building techniques and built roads and bridges to unite their empire.

Section 4   After 1492
► Contact with Europeans had tragic consequences for Native Americans, as millions died of European diseases.
► The Columbian Exchange brought new products, technology, and ideas both to the Americas and to the rest of the world.

For additional review of the major ideas of Chapter 2, see *Guide to the Essentials of American History* or *Interactive Student Tutorial CD-ROM,* which contains interactive review activities, graphic organizers, and practice tests.

📖 Reviewing the Chapter

Define These Terms

Match each term with the correct definition.

Column 1
1. culture
2. tribe
3. civilization
4. hieroglyphics
5. artifact

Column 2
a. group of villages or settlements that share common customs
b. advanced culture
c. object made by humans
d. complete way of life
e. writing that uses pictures

Explore the Main Ideas

1. What evidence suggests that early Native Americans traded with one another?
2. What was one important purpose of the religious ceremonies of Native Americans?
3. What role did women play in Iroquois society?
4. How did the Aztecs treat people captured in warfare?
5. **(a)** Describe one skill Native Americans learned from Europeans. **(b)** Identify two American products that Europeans adopted.

📖 Geography Activity

Match the letters on the map with the following places:
1. Mayan civilization, **2.** Aztec empire, **3.** Incan empire, **4.** Tenochtitlán, **5.** Tikal, **6.** Cuzco. **Interaction** How were the Aztecs able to grow crops on swampland?

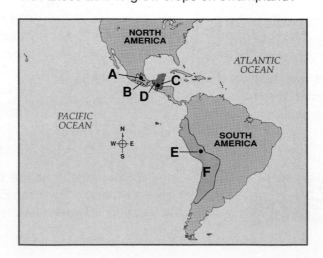

📋 Critical Thinking and Writing

1. **Understanding Chronology** **(a)** Place the following in correct chronological order: the height of the Mayan culture; the arrival of Columbus; the crossing of the land bridge; the founding of the League of the Iroquois. **(b)** How do you know that Columbus never ate tomato sauce when he was a boy?

2. **Linking Past and Present** Compare the communication technology of the Incas with our communication technology today.

3. **Analyzing Ideas** Review what you have read about Natchez society. **(a)** What was one advantage of the Natchez rule regarding marriage? **(b)** What was one disadvantage?

4. **Exploring Unit Themes** **Origins** Is it valuable for Americans to study early American cultures? Support your answer by citing examples from this chapter.

📋 Using Primary Sources

Alvar Nuñez Cabeza de Vaca was an early Spanish explorer. He described the Yguazes people of the Gulf Coast region in this way:

> 66 These Indians are so accustomed to running that without rest or fatigue they follow a deer from morning to night. In this way they kill many. They pursue them until [the deer are] tired down, and sometimes overtake them in the race. Their houses are of matting, placed upon four hoops. They carry them on the back, and [move] every two or three days in search of food.... They are a merry people, considering the hunger they suffer; for they never cease, notwithstanding, to observe their festivities. 99

Source: *Original Narratives of Early American History: Spanish Explorers in the Southern United States*, 1959.

Recognizing Points of View **(a)** How did the Yguazes catch deer? **(b)** What does the writer think is interesting or surprising about the Yguazes?

ACTIVITY BANK

▶ Interdisciplinary Activity

Exploring the Arts Do research on traditional Native American designs from your region of the country. Then, use one of these designs in your own work of art.

▶ Career Skills Activity

Engineers Do research on Incan engineering. Make a model or draw a diagram of an Incan bridge. Prepare a report in which you compare the bridge with a modern bridge.

▶ Citizenship Activity

Forming a League Forming the League of the Iroquois required cooperation, organization, and commitment. Sketch out a plan for a league that would meet a need in your school. Suggest what kind of body would make decisions and what groups would need to be represented.

Internet Activity

Use the Internet to find sites dealing with Native Americans in your state. Save the information you have found as a text file. Work with other members of your class to print out and bind the text files in an attractive format.

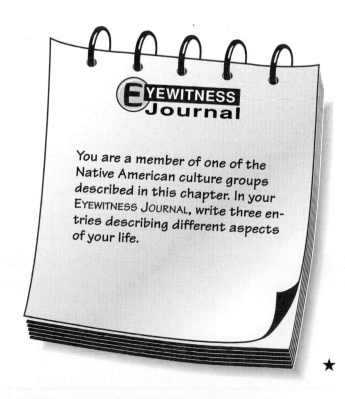

EYEWITNESS Journal

You are a member of one of the Native American culture groups described in this chapter. In your EYEWITNESS JOURNAL, write three entries describing different aspects of your life.

Chapter 3

A Meeting of Different Worlds 1100–1700

In the late 1400s, Europeans in search of trade sailed across the Atlantic and made contact with Native Americans. Soon, Spain and other nations established settlements in the Americas. The Europeans also began to bring enslaved Africans there. Gradually, Native American, European, and African peoples and cultures interacted to form a new way of life.

By the early 1600s, the nations of Europe were competing eagerly for wealth in the Americas. The Spanish built a large empire that spread over both North and South America. The French, Dutch, and English sought territory in North America. The English who settled at Jamestown and Plymouth brought with them traditions of political rights and freedoms.

Why Study History?

Today, we take contact among different parts of the world for granted.

You can look at African art in European museums, or eat tacos in Japan. In the modern world, the pace of global exchange is much faster than it was 500 years ago. To focus on this connection, see this chapter's *Why Study History?* feature, "You Live in a Shrinking World."

American Events

1493 Columbus founds Spanish colony on Hispaniola

1521 Aztec empire falls to the Spanish

1100   **1400**   **1500**

World Events

 1100–1300s World Event
Christians go on Crusades to Holy Land

 1400s World Event
Prince Henry encourages exploration by sea

Viewing HISTORY Crossing the Atlantic

This illustration by Johann Theodor de Bry shows Portuguese ships in an ocean filled with flying fish and sea monsters. Beginning in the late 1400s, European explorers and conquerors set sail across the Atlantic Ocean. Their voyages had a lasting impact, not only on Europe and the Americas, but on West Africa as well.

★ **How do you think illustrations like this affected European sailors as they sailed out into the Atlantic Ocean?**

1535
Incan empire is controlled by the Spanish

1607
Jamestown is founded by British colonists

1620
Pilgrims arrive at Plymouth

1673
French explore the Mississippi River

1500   **1600**   **1700**

1500s World Event
Protestant Reformation causes religious conflicts

1600s World Event
British East India Company trades in India

1 Europeans Reach the Americas

As You Read

Explore These Questions
- How did the Crusades and the Renaissance change Europe?
- Why did Europeans look for new sea routes to Asia?
- What were the effects of Columbus's voyages?

Define
- monarch
- feudalism
- manor
- serf
- magnetic compass
- astrolabe
- caravel
- colony

Identify
- Middle Ages
- Crusades
- Renaissance
- Johannes Gutenberg
- Prince Henry
- Bartholomeu Dias
- Vasco da Gama
- Christopher Columbus

SETTING the Scene During the **Middle Ages,** the period in European history from about 500 to 1350, many Europeans thought of the world as a disk floating on a great ocean. The disk was made up of only three continents: Europe, Africa, and Asia.

Most Europeans knew little about the lands beyond their small villages. Even mapmakers called the waters bordering Europe the Sea of Darkness. Sailors who strayed into these waters often returned with tales of fearsome creatures: "One of these sea monsters," swore one sailor, "has horns, flames, and huge eyes 16 or 20 feet across."

Were such tales true? The few who wondered had no way of finding out. Most Europeans were not interested in the outside world because daily life was hard and their main concern was survival.

The Middle Ages

During the Middle Ages, weak European **monarchs,** or kings and queens, divided their lands among nobles. These nobles, or lords, had their own armies and courts but owed loyalty to a monarch. This system of rule by lords who owe loyalty to a monarch is called **feudalism** (FYOOD 'l ihz uhm).

Feudal life revolved around the manors of these powerful lords. The **manor** included the lord's castle, peasants' huts, and surrounding villages or fields. Most people on the manor were **serfs,** or peasants who worked for the lord and could not leave the manor without the lord's permission.

On the manor, people had to produce for themselves nearly everything they needed. There were few merchants and traders. Few roads or towns existed.

During the Middle Ages, all Christians in Western Europe belonged to the Roman Catholic Church. As a result, the Church had great influence.

A Changing Europe

Toward the end of the Middle Ages, conditions began to change. Religious wars led to increased trade with people in Asia and Africa. There was also a revival of learning in Europe.

The Crusades

To Christians, the city of Jerusalem in the Middle East was sacred because Jesus had lived and taught there. They referred to the city and other places in Palestine as the Holy Land. Jerusalem was also a holy place to Jews and Muslims.

From about 1100 to 1300, Christians and Muslims fought a series of religious wars for control of the Holy Land. Thousands of Christians from all over Europe joined in these wars, known as the **Crusades.** In the end, however, the Europeans failed to win control of the Holy Land.

Still, the Crusades had lasting effects for the Europeans. For the first time, large numbers of Europeans had traveled beyond the small towns of their birth. In the Middle East, they ate exotic foods, such as rice, oranges, and dates. They tasted ginger, pepper, and other spices that both improved the taste of food and helped preserve it. They bought shimmering silks and colorful rugs from Arab traders.

Italian merchants quickly realized that Europeans would pay handsome prices for these foreign goods. They therefore began a lively trade with Arab merchants in the Middle East.

The increase in trade led to an increase in knowledge. From the Arabs, Italian merchants learned about new instruments that made it easier to sail across large bodies of water. The **magnetic compass,** with a needle that always pointed north, helped ship captains sail a straight course. Another useful instrument was the **astrolabe** (AS troh layb). This tool made it possible for sailors to determine the positions of stars and figure out latitude at sea. Both the magnetic compass and the astrolabe helped make sailing less frightening.

A revival of learning

Increased trade and travel made Europeans curious about the wider world. Scholars translated ancient Greek, Roman, and Arab works. They then made discoveries of their own in fields such as art, medicine, astronomy, and chemistry. This burst of learning was called the **Renaissance** (REHN uh sahns), a French word meaning rebirth. It lasted from the late 1300s to about 1600.

The invention of the printing press helped to spread the Renaissance spirit. It was invented during the mid-1400s by German printer **Johannes Gutenberg** (GOOT uhn berg). Before Gutenberg's invention, there were few books because people had to copy them by hand. With the printing press, however, large numbers of books could be printed at low cost. As books became more available, more people learned to read. As reading increased, people learned more about the world around them.

Search for New Trade Routes

As trade brought new prosperity to Europe, kings and queens fought to increase their power. In England and France, rulers established greater authority over feudal lords. In Portugal and Spain, Christian monarchs drove out Arab Muslims who had conquered much of the area.

The rulers of England, France, Portugal, and Spain also looked for ways to increase their wealth. Huge profits could be made by trading with China and other Asian lands. However, Arab and Italian merchants controlled the trade routes across the Mediterranean Sea. Western European rulers would have to find another route to Asia.

Portugal led the way. In the early 1400s, **Prince Henry,** known as the Navigator, encouraged sea captains to sail south along the coast of West Africa. He founded an informal school to help sailors in their explorations.

Viewing HISTORY Wealth and Knowledge

In his painting The Moneylender and His Wife, *Renaissance painter Quentin Metsys captured the spirit that was changing Europe in the 1400s and 1500s. Europeans wanted new wealth and knowledge. This spirit encouraged overseas trade and voyages of exploration.*
★ **How did Metsys communicate the ideas of wealth and knowledge in this painting?**

Columbus Reaches the Americas

The Spanish watched the Portuguese with envy because they, too, wanted a share of the rich Asian spice trade. In 1492, King Ferdinand and Queen Isabella agreed to finance a voyage of exploration by an Italian sea captain named **Christopher Columbus.** Columbus planned to reach the East Indies by sailing west across the Atlantic.

Across the Atlantic

In August 1492, Columbus set sail with three ships and a crew of about 90 sailors. As captain, he commanded the largest vessel, the *Santa María.* The other ships were the *Niña* and the *Pinta.*

After stopping briefly at the Canary Islands, the little fleet continued west into unknown territory. Fair winds sped them along, but a month passed without the sight of land. Some sailors began to grumble. They had never been beyond the sight of land for so long. Still, Columbus sailed on.

On October 7, sailors saw flocks of birds flying southwest. Columbus changed course to follow the birds. A few days later, crew members spotted tree branches and flowers floating in the water. At 2 A.M. on October 12, the lookout on the *Pinta* spotted white cliffs shining in the moonlight. *"Tierra! Tierra!"* he shouted. "Land! Land!"

At dawn, Columbus rowed ashore and planted the banner of Spain. Columbus called the local people Indians because he was convinced that he had reached the East Indies, in Asia. In fact, as you read in Chapter 2, he had reached the island home of the Taínos, in what are now called the West Indies. The West Indies lie off the coasts of North and South America. At the time, these continents were unknown to Europeans.

Riches for Spain

For three months, Columbus explored the West Indies. To his delight, he found signs of gold on the islands. Eager to report his success, he returned home to Spain.

Columbus gave King Ferdinand and Queen Isabella gifts of pink pearls and brilliantly colored parrots. The two Spanish

▲ *Astrolabe*

Biography Christopher Columbus

Christopher Columbus grew up in Genoa, one of the busiest seaports in Italy. As a young sailor, he heard how Portuguese sea captains were trying to reach the Indies and other parts of Asia by sailing around Africa. After studying Portuguese charts, Columbus formed his own idea. He would reach the Indies not by sailing south and east, but by sailing west. ★ **Was Columbus correct in thinking that he could reach Asia by sailing west? Explain.**

Under Henry's guidance, the Portuguese designed a new type of ship, the **caravel** (KAR uh vehl). With triangular sails and a steering rudder, the caravel enabled captains to sail against the wind.

Portuguese sailors gradually established a new route from Western Europe to Asia. In 1488, **Bartholomeu Dias** reached the southern tip of Africa. Then, in 1498, **Vasco da Gama** sailed around southern Africa and continued to India. (See the map on page 75.) Gradually, Portuguese ships pressed on to the East Indies, an island chain off the southeastern coast of Asia. This was the source of the trade in spices.

Why Study History?

Because You Live in a Shrinking World

★ ★

Historical Background

Among the Aztecs in Mexico 600 years ago, a typical meal included corn porridge, beans, tortillas, and tomato or pepper sauce. In Europe, meanwhile, most people ate dark bread, cheese, and cabbage or turnip soup.

Then in the 1500s, contacts grew between the Americas and the rest of the world. Europeans got their first taste of potatoes, corn, and cocoa from the Americas. Native Americans began eating wheat bread, bananas, and citrus fruit from Europe, Africa, and Asia.

Connections to Today

Our world continues to get smaller. Today, people around the world watch American movies and television shows. They wear American styles of clothing and listen to American forms of music. At the same time, new ideas and goods travel from other lands to become part of American culture. New dance styles have come from Latin America, new clothing fashions from France, and new advances in communication from Japan. Due to modern communication and transportation, exchanges take place more quickly than ever before.

Connections to You

You can see—and taste—examples of cultural exchange in the international foods aisle of your local supermarket. The chart above lists some foods from other lands that have become popular in the United States.

Food	Description	Place of Origin
borscht	Cold beet soup	Russia, Ukraine
chutney	Sauce or relish made of fruits, herbs, and spices	India
couscous	Tiny grains of wheat cooked until fluffy	North Africa
feta cheese	White, crumbly cheese	Greece
gazpacho	Chilled tomato soup	Spain
hummus	Spread made from chickpeas	Middle East
salsa	Hot sauce made from tomatoes, chilies, peppers, herbs, and spices	Mexico
egg rolls	Shredded vegetables in fried dough wrapper	China
sushi	Raw fish and rice, often wrapped in seaweed	Japan

Plate of tacos ➤

1. **Comprehension**
   (a) Name two foods that Native Americans introduced to Europeans.
   (b) Name two Mexican foods that are popular in the United States today.

2. **Critical Thinking** How do you think communication via the Internet affects cultural exchange today?

 **★Activity** **Planning a Food Festival** Working with other students, plan a festival of popular international foods. For ideas on what foods to include, visit your local supermarket or consult an international cookbook.

monarchs listened intently to his descriptions of tobacco, pineapples, and hammocks used for sleeping. Columbus also described the natives of the islands he had visited:

> 66 [They were] of a very acute intelligence...[but had] no iron or steel weapons....Should your majesties command it, all the inhabitants could be made slaves. 99

The Spanish monarchs were impressed. They gave Columbus the title of Admiral of the Ocean Sea. They also agreed to finance his future voyages.

Columbus made three more voyages to the West Indies. In 1493, on an island he called Hispaniola (present-day Haiti and the Dominican Republic), he founded the first Spanish colony in the Americas. A **colony** is a group of people who settle in a distant land and are ruled by the government of their native land. Columbus also explored Cuba and Jamaica and sailed along the coasts of Central America and northern South America. Wherever he went, he claimed the lands for Spain.

Columbus's lasting impact

For years, Columbus has been remembered as the bold sea captain who "discovered America." In at least one sense, he deserves that honor. Europeans knew nothing of the Americas before Columbus brought them news about this "new world." Today, however, we also recognize that other people "discovered" America long before Columbus. Still, his daring voyages initiated lasting contact among the peoples of Europe, Africa, and the Americas.

For Native Americans, though, the contact begun by Columbus resulted in tragedy. Columbus and other Europeans who came after him seized Indian lands. They forced native people to work in mines or on farms. Over the next 50 years, hundreds of thousands of Caribbean Indians died from harsh working conditions and European diseases.

For better or for worse, the voyages of Columbus signaled a new era for the Americas. Curious Europeans wanted to explore the lands across the Atlantic. They saw the Americas as a place where they could settle, trade, and grow rich.

★ Section 1 Review ★

Recall

1. **Locate** (a) Europe, (b) Middle East, (c) Asia, (d) Mediterranean Sea, (e) East Indies, (f) West Indies.
2. **Identify** (a) Middle Ages, (b) Crusades, (c) Renaissance, (d) Johannes Gutenberg, (e) Prince Henry, (f) Bartholomeu Dias, (g) Vasco da Gama, (h) Christopher Columbus.
3. **Define** (a) monarch, (b) feudalism, (c) manor, (d) serf, (e) magnetic compass, (f) astrolabe, (g) caravel, (h) colony.

Comprehension

4. Describe how each of the following changed life in Europe: (a) the Crusades, (b) the Renaissance.

5. Why did Western European rulers want to find new routes to Asia?
6. How did Columbus's voyages affect (a) Europeans, (b) Native Americans?

Critical Thinking and Writing

7. **Drawing Conclusions** In what way were the Crusades both a success and a failure?
8. **Recognizing Points of View** For many years, American schoolchildren were taught that Columbus "discovered America." In what way is this an accurate statement? In what way is the statement inaccurate?

★ ★

Activity **Writing a Contract** You are a legal expert in service to King Ferdinand and Queen Isabella. Draw up a contract explaining what your monarchs will provide to Christopher Columbus and what they expect from him in return.

Spain Builds an Empire

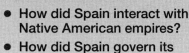

As You Read

Explore These Questions
- How did Spain interact with Native American empires?
- How did Spain govern its lands in the Americas?
- Why was life difficult for the Native Americans who lived under Spanish rule?

Define
- conquistador
- pueblo
- presidio
- mission
- peninsulare
- creole
- mestizo
- encomienda
- plantation

Identify
- Vasco Núñez de Balboa
- Ferdinand Magellan
- Montezuma
- Hernando Cortés
- Francisco Pizarro
- Spanish borderlands
- Laws of the Indies
- Juan de Oñate
- Eusebio Francisco Kino
- Bartolomé de Las Casas

SETTING the Scene "What a troublesome thing it is to discover new lands. The risks we took, it is hardly possible to exaggerate." Thus said Bernal Díaz del Castillo, one of the many Spanish **conquistadors** (kahn KEES tuh dorz), or conquerors, who marched into the Americas in the 1500s. When asked why they traveled to the Americas, Díaz responded, "We came here to serve God and the king and also to get rich."

In their search for glory and gold, the conquistadors made Spain one of the richest nations in Europe. Soon, Spanish colonists followed the conquistadors and created a vast new empire in the Americas. However, the building of Spain's empire meant suffering and even death for Aztecs, Incas, and other Native Americans.

Early Explorations

After Columbus reached the West Indies, the Spanish explored and settled other islands in the Caribbean Sea. By 1511, they had conquered Puerto Rico, Jamaica, and Cuba. They also explored the eastern coasts of North America and South America. Like Columbus, these explorers were searching for a western route to Asia.

Then, in 1513, an adventurer named **Vasco Núñez de Balboa** (bal BOH uh) plunged into the jungles of the Isthmus of Panama. Native Americans had told him that a large body of water lay to the west. With a party of Spanish and Indians, Balboa reached the Pacific Ocean after about 25 days. He stood in the crashing surf and claimed the ocean for Spain.

The Spanish had no idea how wide the Pacific was until a sea captain named **Ferdinand Magellan** (muh JEHL uhn) sailed across it. The expedition left Spain in 1519. After much hardship, it rounded the very stormy southern tip of South America and entered the Pacific Ocean. Crossing the Pacific, the sailors were forced to eat rats and sawdust when they ran out of food. Magellan himself was killed in a battle with the local people of the Philippine Islands off the coast of Asia.

Of five ships and about 250 crew members, only one ship and 18 sailors returned to Spain in 1522, three years after they set out.

Spanish sailing ship of the 1400s

This illustration depicts one episode in the Spanish conquest of the Aztecs. In 1520, a unit of Spanish soldiers attacked a group of Aztecs as they were participating in a religious celebration. Unprepared for battle, the Aztecs suffered heavy losses. ★ **How did the military equipment of the Spaniards differ from the equipment used by the Aztecs?**

◄ *Steel breast plate of a conquistador*

These survivors were the first men to circumnavigate, or sail around, the world. In doing so, they had found an all-water western route to Asia. Their voyage made Europeans aware of the true size of the Earth.

Spanish Conquistadors

Meanwhile, Spanish colonists in the Caribbean heard rumors of gold and other riches in nearby Mexico. Spanish conquistadors began to dream of new conquests. The rulers of Spain gave conquistadors permission to establish settlements in the Americas. In return, conquistadors agreed to give Spain one fifth of any gold or treasure they captured.

Cortés conquers the Aztecs

In 1519, messengers brought disturbing news to **Montezuma** (mahn tuh ZYOO muh), the Aztec emperor who ruled over much of Mexico. They said that they had seen a large house floating on the sea. It was filled with white men with long, thick beards.

Montezuma thought that these strangers might be messengers of gods. Aztec sacred writings predicted that a powerful white-skinned god would come from the east to rule the Aztecs. The white strangers did come from the east, and they were certainly powerful. They wore metal armor and had weapons that spit fire. As the strangers neared Tenochtitlán (tay nawch tee TLAHN), the capital of the Aztec empire, Montezuma decided to welcome them as his guests.

The Spanish leader, **Hernando Cortés** (kor TEHZ), took advantage of Montezuma's invitation. Like other conquistadors, Cortés wanted power and riches. An Indian woman the Spanish called Doña Marina had told him about Aztec gold. With only about 600 soldiers and 16 horses, Cortés set out to seize the Aztecs' gold. On November 8, 1519, Cortés marched into Tenochtitlán. For the next six months, he held Montezuma prisoner.

Finally, the Aztecs attacked and drove out the Spanish, but the victory was brief. Aided by people whom the Aztecs had conquered, Cortés recaptured Tenochtitlán. In the end, the Spanish killed Montezuma and destroyed Tenochtitlán. The mighty Aztec empire had fallen.

Pizarro conquers the Incas

Another bold conquistador, **Francisco Pizarro** (pee ZAR oh), heard about the fabulous Incan empire while marching with Balboa across Panama. Pizarro decided to sail down the Pacific coast of South America with fewer than 200 Spanish soldiers. In 1532, he captured the Incan emperor Atahualpa (at ah WAHL pa) and much of his army. An Incan historian described the surprise attack:

66 The Spaniards killed them all— with horses, with swords, with guns.... From more than 10,000 men, there did not escape 200. 99

Later, the Spanish executed Atahualpa. The following year, Pizarro's army attacked

Cuzco, the Incan capital in present-day Peru. Without the leadership of Atahualpa, Incan resistance collapsed. By 1535, Pizarro controlled much of the Incan empire.

Reasons for Spanish victories

With only a handful of soldiers, the Spanish had conquered two great empires. There were several major reasons for the remarkable success that the Spanish enjoyed.

First, the Spanish had superior military equipment. They were protected by steel armor and had guns. Meanwhile, the Aztecs and Incas relied on clubs, bows and arrows, and spears. Also, the Native Americans had never seen horses. As a result, they were frightened by mounted Spanish soldiers.

Another factor was that the Native Americans offered weak resistance. The Aztecs were slow to fight because they thought the Spanish might be gods. The Incas were weak from fighting among themselves over control of their government.

Finally, the Indians fell victim to European diseases. Large numbers of Indians died from chicken pox, measles, and influenza. Some historians believe that disease alone would have ensured Spanish victory over the Indians.

Seeking Riches in the North

The Spanish search for treasure extended beyond the lands of the Aztecs and Incas. Moving north, conquistadors explored the area known as the **Spanish borderlands.** The borderlands spanned the present-day United States from Florida to California.

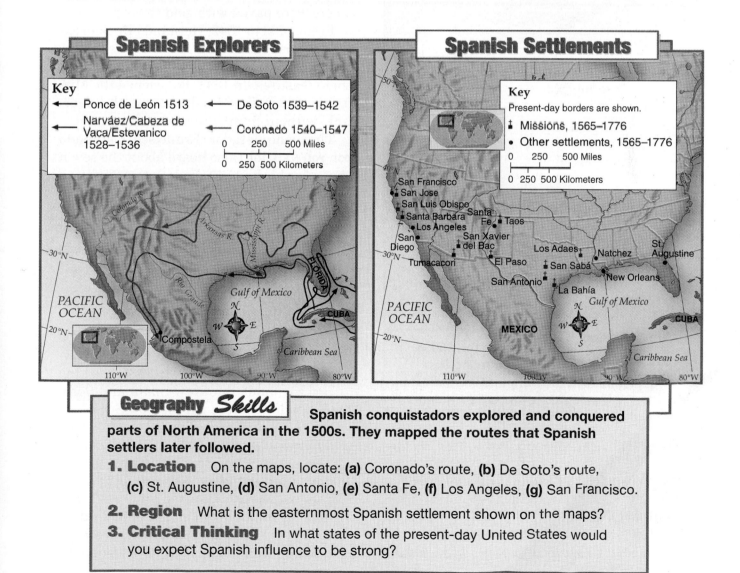

Geography Skills   Spanish conquistadors explored and conquered parts of North America in the 1500s. They mapped the routes that Spanish settlers later followed.

1. Location   On the maps, locate: **(a)** Coronado's route, **(b)** De Soto's route, **(c)** St. Augustine, **(d)** San Antonio, **(e)** Santa Fe, **(f)** Los Angeles, **(g)** San Francisco.

2. Region   What is the easternmost Spanish settlement shown on the maps?

3. Critical Thinking   In what states of the present-day United States would you expect Spanish influence to be strong?

Juan Ponce de León (PAWN suh day lay AWN) traveled through parts of Florida in 1513, looking for a legendary fountain of youth. Indians claimed that anyone who bathed in its magical water would remain young forever. Ponce de León found no such fountain.

Spain in the Americas

(See the map on page 67.)

Geography Skills

In the 1500s, Spain established a system for ruling its American colonies. The colonies were divided into the Viceroyalty of New Spain and the Viceroyalty of Peru.

1. Location On the map, locate: **(a)** Brazil, **(b)** West Indies, **(c)** Mexico City, **(d)** Lima.

2. Region Which viceroyalty included Mexico and Florida?

3. Critical Thinking Why was control of the Caribbean Sea important to Spain?

In 1528, Panfilo Narváez (nar VAH ehs) led an expedition that ended in disaster. A storm struck his fleet in the Gulf of Mexico. Narváez and many others were lost at sea. The rest landed on an island near present-day Texas. Native Americans captured the few survivors and held them prisoner. Álvar Núñez Cabeza de Vaca assumed leadership of the group, which included an enslaved African named Estevanico.

In 1533, Cabeza de Vaca, Estevanico, and two others finally escaped their captors. The four went searching for a Spanish settlement. Their astonishing journey did not end until 1536, when they reached a town in Mexico. They had traveled by foot more than 1,000 miles through the Southwest. (See the map on page 67.) They learned much about Native American ways. They also heard amazing tales about seven cities whose streets were paved with gold.

From 1539 to 1542, Hernando De Soto explored Florida and other parts of the Southeast. He was looking for the cities of gold and other treasures. In 1541, he reached the Mississippi River. De Soto died along the riverbank, without finding the riches he sought.

The conquistador Francisco Coronado (koh roh NAH doh) also heard about the seven cities of gold. In 1540, he led an expedition into the southwestern borderlands. He traveled through Mexico to present-day Arizona and New Mexico. Some of his party went as far as the Grand Canyon. Still, the Zuñi villages he visited had no golden streets.

Governing New Spain

The Spanish king decided to set up a strong system of government to rule his growing empire in the Americas. In 1535, the king divided his lands into New Spain and Peru. The borderlands were part of New Spain. He put a viceroy in charge of each region to rule in his name.

The viceroys enforced the **Laws of the Indies,** a code of laws that stated how the colonies should be organized and ruled. The Laws of the Indies provided for three kinds of settlements in New Spain: pueblos, presidios (prih SIHD ee ohz), and missions. Sometimes,

Juan Ponce de León (PAWN suh day lay AWN) traveled through parts of Florida in 1513, looking for a legendary fountain of youth. Indians claimed that anyone who bathed in its magical water would remain young forever. Ponce de León found no such fountain.

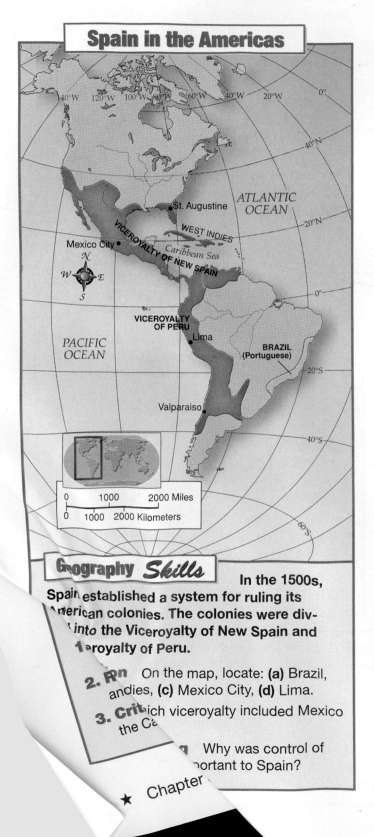

Spain in the Americas

Geography Skills In the 1500s, Spain established a system for ruling its American colonies. The colonies were divided into the Viceroyalty of New Spain and Viceroyalty of Peru.

2. **Rn** On the map, locate: **(a)** Brazil, andies, **(c)** Mexico City, **(d)** Lima.

3. **Crit**ich viceroyalty included Mexico the Ca

Why was control of ortant to Spain?

Chapter

In 1528, Panfilo Narváez (nar VAH ehs) led an expedition that ended in disaster. A storm struck his fleet in the Gulf of Mexico. Narváez and many others were lost at sea. The rest landed on an island near present-day Texas. Native Americans captured the few survivors and held them prisoner. Álvar Núñez Cabeza de Vaca assumed leadership of the group, which included an enslaved African named Estevanico.

In 1533, Cabeza de Vaca, Estevanico, and two others finally escaped their captors. The four went searching for a Spanish settlement. Their astonishing journey did not end until 1536, when they reached a town in Mexico. They had traveled by foot more than 1,000 miles through the Southwest. (See the map on page 67.) They learned much about Native American ways. They also heard amazing tales about seven cities whose streets were paved with gold.

From 1539 to 1542, Hernando De Soto explored Florida and other parts of the Southeast. He was looking for the cities of gold and other treasures. In 1541, he reached the Mississippi River. De Soto died along the riverbank, without finding the riches he sought.

The conquistador Francisco Coronado (koh roh NAH doh) also heard about the seven cities of gold. In 1540, he led an expedition into the southwestern borderlands. He traveled through Mexico to present-day Arizona and New Mexico. Some of his party went as far as the Grand Canyon. Still, the Zuñi villages he visited had no golden streets.

Governing New Spain

The Spanish king decided to set up a strong system of government to rule his growing empire in the Americas. In 1535, the king divided his lands into New Spain and Peru. The borderlands were part of New Spain. He put a viceroy in charge of each region to rule in his name.

The viceroys enforced the **Laws of the Indies,** a code of laws that stated how the colonies should be organized and ruled. The Laws of the Indies provided for three kinds of settlements in New Spain: pueblos, presidios (prih SIHD ee ohz), and missions. Sometimes,

American Heritage
M A G A Z I N E

Castillo de San Marcos

Castillo de San Marcos was the tenth fort built to protect the town of St. Augustine. The first nine were built of wood. The Spanish decided to build a stone fortress after a pirate attack in 1668. The fort was completed in 1695 and survived its first major test in 1702 when it was attacked by the British. Today, you can cross a moat to Castillo de San Marcos and stand atop the stone walls that defended Spanish settlers some 300 years ago.

★ **To learn more about this historic site, write:** Castillo de San Marcos National Monument, 1 South Castillo Drive, St. Augustine, FL 32084.

Cannon at Castillo de San Marcos ➤

a large community included all three types of settlements.

Pueblos, or towns, were centers of farming and trade. In the middle of the town was a plaza, or public square. Here, townspeople and farmers gathered on important occasions. They also came to worship at the church. Shops and homes lined the four sides of the plaza.

Spanish rulers took control of Indian pueblos and built new towns as well. In 1598, **Juan de Oñate** (oh NYAH tay) founded the colony of New Mexico among the adobe villages of the Pueblo Indians. He used brutal force to conquer the Native Americans of the region. In 1609, Don Pedro de Paralta founded Santa Fé as the Spanish capital of New Mexico.

Presidios were forts where soldiers lived. Inside the high, thick walls of a presidio were shops, stables for horses, and storehouses for food. Most soldiers lived in large barracks. Soldiers protected the farmers who settled around the presidios. The first presidio in the borderlands was built in 1565 at St. Augustine, Florida. (See History Happened Here above.)

Missions were religious settlements run by Catholic priests and friars. Like other Europeans in the Americas, the Spanish believed they had a duty to convert Indians to Christianity. They often forced Indians to live and work on the missions.

Missionaries gradually moved into various parts of the Spanish borderlands. The first mission in Texas was founded at El Paso in 1659. In 1691, Father **Eusebio Francisco Kino** (KEE noh) crossed into present-day Arizona. He eventually set up 24 missions in the area. Missionaries also moved into California. By the late 1700s, a string of missions dotted the California coast from San Diego to San Francisco. (See the map on page 67.)

Biography — Sor Juana

Juana Inés de la Cruz was one of the most talented poets of New Spain. Because she was a girl, she was refused admission to the university in Mexico City. She entered a convent at age 16 and devoted herself to studying and writing poetry. She also wrote a spirited defense of women's right to an education. ★ **Besides women, what other people in New Spain were denied equal rights?**

Society in New Spain

The Laws of the Indies divided the people in Spanish colonies into four social classes: peninsulares (puh nihn suh LAH rayz), creoles (KREE ohlz), mestizos (mehs TEE zohz), and Indians.

Four social classes

At the top of the social scale were the **peninsulares.** Born in Spain, the peninsulares held the highest jobs in the colonial government and the Catholic Church. They also owned large tracts of land as well as rich gold and silver mines.

Below the peninsulares were the **creoles.** Creoles were people born in the Americas to Spanish parents. Many creoles were wealthy and well educated. They owned farms and ranches, taught at universities, and practiced law. However, they could not hold the jobs that were reserved for peninsulares.

Below the creoles were the **mestizos,** people of mixed Spanish and Indian background. Mestizos worked on farms and ranches owned by peninsulares and creoles. In the cities, they worked as carpenters, shoemakers, tailors, and bakers.

The lowest class in the colonies was the Indians. The Spanish treated them as a conquered people. Under New Spain's strict social system, Indians were kept in poverty for hundreds of years.

A blending of cultures

By the mid-1500s, a new way of life had begun to take shape in New Spain. It blended Spanish and Indian ways.

Spanish settlers brought their own culture to the colonies. They introduced their language, laws, religion, and learning. In 1539, a printer in Mexico City produced the first European book in the Americas. In 1551, the Spanish founded the University of Mexico.

Native Americans also influenced the culture of New Spain. As you have read in Chapter 2, colonists adopted items of Indian clothing, such as the poncho and moccasins. Indians also introduced Spanish colonists to new foods, including potatoes, corn, tomatoes, and chocolate.

With the help of Indian workers, Spanish settlers built many fine libraries, theaters, and churches. The Indians used materials they knew well, such as adobe bricks. Sometimes, Spanish priests allowed Indian artists to decorate the church walls with paintings of harvests and local traditions.

Harsh Life for Indians

The colonists who came to the Americas needed workers for their ranches, farms, and mines. To help them, the Spanish government gave settlers **encomiendas** (ehn koh mee EHN dahz), or the right to demand labor or taxes from Native Americans living on the land.

Working in mines and plantations

During the 1500s, mines in Mexico, Peru, and other areas of the Americas made Spain

Skills FOR LIFE

Critical Thinking | Managing Information | Communication | Maps, Charts, and Graphs

Reading a Line Graph

How Will I Use This Skill?

Graphs present statistics, or number facts, in a visual way. A line graph can show you at a glance how statistics change over time—from the population of the world to your batting average.

LEARN the Skill

You can read a line graph by following these four steps:

❶ Use the title to identify the subject of the graph. The source line will tell you where the information was found.

❷ Study the labels on the graph. The horizontal (or side-to-side) axis usually tells you the time period covered by the graph. The vertical (or up-and-down) axis tells you what is being measured.

❸ Practice reading the Information on the graph. Line up the points on the graph with the horizontal and vertical axes to determine how much or how many of something there was at a given time.

❹ Draw conclusions about the information presented on the graph.

PRACTICE the Skill

Use the line graph on this page to answer the following questions.

❶ (a) What is the subject of the line graph? (b) What is the source of the information?

❷ (a) What time period is covered by the graph? (b) What is being measured?

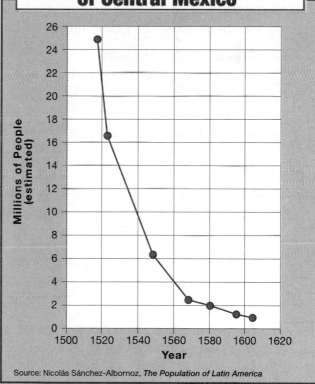

Native American Population of Central Mexico

Millions of People (estimated) vs. Year

Source: Nicolás Sánchez-Albornoz, *The Population of Latin America*

❸ About how many Native Americans lived in central Mexico before 1520? In 1580?

❹ Using the information on the graph, make a generalization about the Indian population of central Mexico.

APPLY the Skill

For the next week, keep track of the number of hours you spend each day performing a certain activity. Use your statistics to make a line graph.

rich. Spanish treasure ships laden with thousands of tons of gold and silver sailed regularly across the Atlantic.

The Spanish forced Native Americans to work in the gold and silver mines. In flickering darkness, Indians labored in narrow tunnels where they hacked out rich ores. Many died when tunnels caved in.

Meanwhile, on the islands of the West Indies, large numbers of Indians worked on **plantations,** or large estates farmed by many workers. They grew sugar cane and tobacco, which plantation owners sold in Spain at a huge profit.

Thousands of Native Americans died from overwork in mines and on plantations. As you have read, European diseases killed millions more. (See the graph on page 71.)

Las Casas seeks reform

These harsh conditions led one priest, **Bartolomé de Las Casas** (day lahs KAH sahs), to seek reform. Traveling through New Spain, Las Casas witnessed firsthand the deaths of Indians due to hunger, disease, and mistreatment. He was horrified by the terrible conditions that he saw:

66 The Indians were totally deprived of their freedom.... Even beasts enjoy more freedom when they are allowed to graze in the field. 99

Las Casas journeyed to Spain and asked the king to protect the Indians. In the 1540s, the royal government did pass laws prohibiting the enslavement of Native Americans. The laws also allowed Indians to own cattle and grow crops. However, few officials in New Spain enforced the new laws.

As the death toll among Native Americans rose, the Spanish looked for a new source of labor. Las Casas, still seeking to help the Indians, suggested that Africans be brought as slaves to replace Indian laborers. Unlike Indians, Africans did not catch European diseases, he said. Besides, they were used to doing hard farm work in their homelands. In the years ahead, Las Casas would regret the results of his suggestion.

★ Section 2 Review ★

Recall

1. **Locate** (a) Pacific Ocean, (b) Gulf of Mexico, (c) Florida, (d) New Spain.

2. **Identify** (a) Vasco Núñez de Balboa, (b) Ferdinand Magellan, (c) Montezuma, (d) Hernando Cortés, (e) Francisco Pizarro, (f) Spanish borderlands, (g) Laws of the Indies, (h) Juan de Oñate, (i) Eusebio Francisco Kino, (j) Bartolomé de Las Casas.

3. **Define** (a) conquistador, (b) pueblo, (c) presidio, (d) mission, (e) peninsulare, (f) creole, (g) mestizo, (h) encomienda, (i) plantation.

Comprehension

4. Why were a handful of Spanish soldiers able to conquer the empires of the Aztecs and Incas?

5. How did the Laws of the Indies regulate life in New Spain?

6. (a) In what ways was life harsh for Native Americans under Spanish rule? (b) How did Bartolomé de Las Casas try to help Indians?

Critical Thinking and Writing

7. **Making Generalizations** Based on what you have read in this section, make a generalization about the way Spain governed its colonies in the Americas.

8. **Recognizing Points of View** Why do you think the Spanish felt they had the right to force the Indians to work for them?

★ ★

Activity **Creating a Chart** One of your friends has asked you for help understanding the social classes of Spain's American colonies. Help your friend by creating a chart that accurately illustrates the social structure that existed in New Spain.

3 ★ Africans Come to the Americas

Explore These Questions
- Why were African states prosperous?
- How did the African slave trade change in the 1500s?
- What was the Middle Passage?

Define
- city-state
- kinship network
- Middle Passage

Identify
- Swahili
- Mansa Musa
- Affonso

SETTING the Scene In the late afternoon, the distant sound of a horn, blown repeatedly, interrupted the peace of a small West African village. Children ran toward the sound. *"Batafo! Batafo!"* they cried. "Traders!"

Soon the caravan arrived. The long line of porters and camels carried precious goods. Some brought sacks of salt or fish. Others had gold, fine fabrics, or jewelry. Some pushed slaves toward the village.

Trade had long played a vital role in African life. Complex trade routes across the Sahara, a vast desert, linked African villages and kingdoms. At first, Europeans played little or no role in this trade. After the 1400s, however, new trading patterns developed. They drew Africa into closer contact with both Europe and the Americas.

African States

Africa is a vast continent, the second largest on Earth. Across the continent, a wide variety of societies and cultures developed. By the 1400s, there were prosperous trading states in both East Africa and West Africa.

East Africa

On the coast of East Africa, where there were natural harbors, small villages grew

West African ivory carving, showing Portuguese traders

into busy trading centers. Gold from Zimbabwe, a powerful inland state, made its way to coastal cities such as Mogadishu, Kilwa, and Sofala. From the coastal cities, ships carried the gold and other valuable products up the African coast as well as to India. (See the map on p. 75.)

The profits from trade helped local rulers build strong city-states in East Africa. A **city-state** is a large town that has its own independent government.

As East Africans mingled with merchants from other lands, a rich variety of cultures developed. From Arab traders, many East Africans adopted the religion of Islam. The blend of cultures also gave rise to **Swahili,** a new language that used both Arab and African words.

West Africa

Several major trading states also emerged south of the Sahara in West Africa. Of these, two of the most important were Mali and Songhai.

Between 1200 and 1400, the kingdom of Mali reached its height. Its most famous ruler was the emperor **Mansa Musa.** In 1324, Mansa Musa journeyed from Mali across North Africa to Egypt and the Middle East. His wealth dazzled the Egyptians, who spread tales of his splendor as far as Europe. A Spanish map of the period shows a powerful Mansa Musa on his throne. The

Past

Present

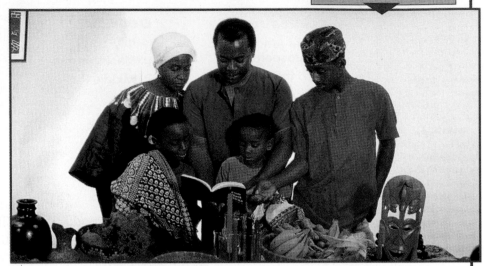

African Art

In many African societies, elaborate masks were used in political, religious, and social ceremonies. At left is a mask of a West African king, carved by African artists several hundred years ago. At right, a similar mask is present during an American family's celebration of Kwanzaa. ★ **How else does this American family show pride in its African roots?**

mapmaker praised Mansa Musa's great wealth by writing these words on the map:

> 66 So abundant is the gold in his country that he is the richest and most noble king in all the land. 99

Later, in the 1400s, Songhai (SAWNG hi) became the most powerful kingdom in West Africa. Timbuktu, located on the Niger River, was one of Songhai's thriving cities. Timbuktu boasted over 100 schools, including a university.

$ Connections With Economics

Captain Theodore Canot, a European slave trader, witnessed the busy economy of the West African town of Timbo: "They weave cotton, work in leather, fabricate iron, . . . engage diligently in agriculture, and, whenever not laboriously employed, devote themselves to reading and writing."

Village and Family Life

Throughout Africa, most people lived in small villages and made a living by herding or farming. Many farmers worked the same land as their parents and grandparents before them. In rain forests close to the coast, farmers grew yams and other crops. In the grasslands, they raised millet, rice, and other grains. During the 1500s, Africans also began to grow corn, which had been introduced from the Americas.

Family relations played an important part in African life. Children had duties not only to their parents but also to aunts, uncles, and cousins. Grandparents received special respect. These kinds of close family ties are called a **kinship network.** Kinship ties encouraged a strong sense of community and cooperation.

African religions helped to stress the importance of kinship. Religious ceremonies honored ancestors and the spirits of the Earth. Farmers believed that by farming the land properly, they brought honor to their families.

The African Slave Trade

In Africa, as elsewhere around the world, slavery had been part of the social and economic system since ancient times. Most slaves in Africa were people who had been captured in war. African traders often transported and sold slaves as laborers. Muslim merchants also carried African slaves into Europe and the Middle East.

In many African societies, slaves were part of the community. They were treated as servants rather than property. According to a saying of the Ashanti people, "A slave who knows how to serve inherits his master's property." In time, slaves or their children might become full members of the society.

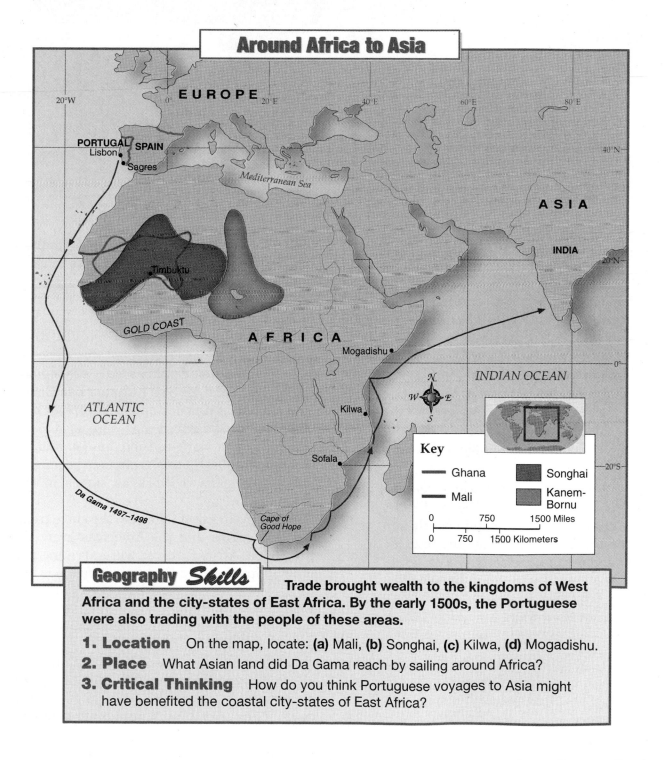

Around Africa to Asia

Geography Skills Trade brought wealth to the kingdoms of West Africa and the city-states of East Africa. By the early 1500s, the Portuguese were also trading with the people of these areas.

1. Location On the map, locate: **(a)** Mali, **(b)** Songhai, **(c)** Kilwa, **(d)** Mogadishu.
2. Place What Asian land did Da Gama reach by sailing around Africa?
3. Critical Thinking How do you think Portuguese voyages to Asia might have benefited the coastal city-states of East Africa?

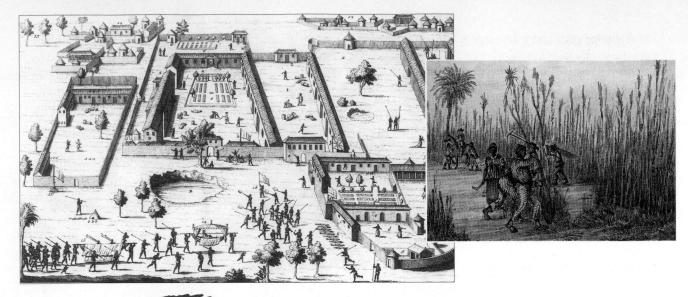

Viewing HISTORY — The African Slave Trade

Along the coast of West Africa, the Portuguese, French, Dutch, and English built forts from which they could participate in the profitable slave trade. African traders became wealthy by selling captives to the Europeans. The inset picture shows enslaved Africans in the West Indies, doing the backbreaking work of harvesting sugar cane. ★ **How did the plantation system in the Americas affect the African slave trade?**

Europeans participate

During the 1400s, the slave trade took a dramatic new turn. It was at this time that the Portuguese started trading with communities along the African coast. At first, they were primarily interested in gold, ivory and other trade goods. However, by 1500, the Portuguese were also buying as many as 2,500 enslaved Africans each year.

Some African leaders protested the growing slave trade. **Affonso,** a Christian king of the Central African kingdom of Kongo, wrote to the king of Portugal:

f Merchants are taking every day our natives, sons of the land and sons of our nobles and vassals and our relatives, because the thieves and men of bad conscience...grab them and get them to be sold. ™

Such protests, however, could not stop the rapid spread of the slave trade.

Slavery in the Americas

Meanwhile, as you have learned, Spain was building a great empire in the Americas. Portugal too had established a colony—in the present-day country of Brazil in South America. For a while, Spanish and Portuguese colonists forced Native Americans to work in mines and on plantations. Before long, however, thousands of Indians were dying from mistreatment and disease.

As you have read (see page 72), Bartolomé de Las Casas suggested that Africans be brought to New Spain as slaves to replace Indian laborers. Unlike Indians, Las Casas said, Africans did not catch European diseases. He also said that they were used to doing hard farm work in their homelands. In the early 1500s, Spanish colonists began importing Africans to work as slaves in the Americas.

In the years that followed, the slave trade between Africa and the Americas grew. By the 1600s, African slaves were arriving not only in Spanish and Portuguese colonies but in Dutch, English, and French colonies as well. Over a period of less than 400 years, millions of Africans were enslaved and sent across the Atlantic Ocean.

Slave traders from Spain, Portugal, Britain, France, and other western European nations set up posts along the West African coast. They offered guns and other goods in exchange for slaves. As the demand for slaves increased, Africans who lived along the coast made raids into the interior, seeking captives to sell to the Europeans. They marched their captives to the coast. There, the slaves were loaded aboard European ships headed for the Americas.

Some scholars today estimate that more than 10 million enslaved Africans were transported to the Americas between the 1500s and 1800s. The vast majority came from West Africa and most were sent to Brazil or the Caribbean. However, a total of more than 500,000 enslaved Africans would eventually arrive in the British colonies of North America. (You will read about the English colonies in Chapter 4.)

The Middle Passage

In the 1700s, English sailors began referring to the passage of slave ships west across the Atlantic Ocean as the **Middle Passage.** Below the decks of the slave ships, slaves were crammed tightly together on shelves. One observer noted that they were "rammed like [fish] in a barrel." They were "chained to each other hand and foot, and stowed so close, that they were not allowed above a foot and a half for each in breadth." The captives were allowed above deck to eat and exercise in the fresh air only once or twice a day.

Many enslaved Africans resisted, but only a few escaped. Some fought for their freedom during the trip. Others refused to eat or even jumped overboard to avoid a life of slavery. Olaudah Equiano (oh LAW dah ehk wee AH noh), an enslaved African, recalled an incident from his Middle Passage:

66 One day... two of my wearied countrymen who were chained together... jumped into the sea; immediately another... followed their example.... Two of the wretches were drowned, but [the ship's crew] got the other, and afterwards flogged him unmercifully for thus attempting to prefer death to slavery. 99

Records of slave ships show that about 10 percent of Africans loaded aboard ship for passage to the Americas died during the voyage. Many died of illnesses that spread rapidly in the filthy, crowded conditions inside a ship's hold. Others died of mistreatment. The Atlantic slave trade would last about 400 years. During that time, it may have caused the deaths of as many as 2 or 3 million Africans.

★ Section 3 Review ★

Recall

1. **Locate** (a) Mogadishu, (b) Kilwa, (c) Mali, (d) Songhai, (e) Timbuktu.
2. **Identify** (a) Swahili, (b) Mansa Musa, (c) Affonso.
3. **Define** (a) city-state, (b) kinship network, (c) Middle Passage.

Comprehension

4. **(a)** How did trade affect the culture of East Africa? **(b)** What were some of the achievements of Songhai?

5. How did the slave trade change after Europeans arrived in Africa?
6. Describe conditions on the Middle Passage.

Critical Thinking and Writing

7. **Comparing** How do traditional African kinship networks compare to American family ties today?
8. **Drawing Conclusions** Why do you think the antislavery protests of King Affonso and others were ignored by both Africans and Europeans?

Activity Writing a Short Story Write a short story about a young African who is captured by slavers and transported across the Atlantic to the Americas. In your story, also describe the life that the African was forced to leave behind.

Colonizing North America

As You Read

Explore These Questions
- How did competition grow among European nations?
- How did trappers and missionaries help New France grow?
- How did the arrival of Europeans affect Native Americans in North America?

Define
- northwest passage
- Protestant Reformation
- missionary

Identify
- Jacques Cartier
- Henry Hudson
- Samuel de Champlain
- coureur de bois
- Jacques Marquette
- Robert de La Salle
- Peter Minuit
- New Netherland
- Algonquin

SETTING the Scene In August 1497, the court of King Henry VII of England buzzed with excitement. Italian sea captain Giovanni Caboto and a crew of sailors from England had just returned from a 79-day Atlantic voyage. Caboto, called John Cabot by the English, reported that he had reached a "new-found island" in Asia where fish were plentiful.

Cabot was one of many Europeans who explored North America in the late 1400s and early 1500s. England, France, and the Netherlands all envied Spain's new empire. They wanted American colonies of their own.

Search for a Northwest Passage

Throughout the 1500s, European nations continued looking for new ways to reach the riches of Asia. They felt that Magellan's route around South America was too long. They wanted to discover a shorter **northwest passage,** or waterway through or around North America. (See the map on page 79.)

As you read above, John Cabot was confident he had found such a passage in 1497. He was mistaken. His "new-found island" off the Asian coast in fact lay off the shore of North America. Today, it is called Newfoundland and is the easternmost province of Canada.

In 1524, the French sent Giovanni da Verrazano (vehr rah TSAH noh), another Italian captain, in search of a northwest passage. Verrazano journeyed along the North American coast from the Carolinas to Canada. During the 1530s, **Jacques Cartier** (KAR tee YAY), also sailing for the French, sailed a good distance up the river that is now known as the St. Lawrence.

In 1609, the English sailor **Henry Hudson** sailed for the Dutch. His ship, the *Half Moon,* entered what is today New York harbor. Hudson continued some 150 miles (240 km) up the river that now bears his name.

The following year, Hudson made a voyage into the far north—this time for the English. After spending a harsh winter in what is now called Hudson Bay, Hudson's crew rebelled. They put Hudson, his son, and seven loyal sailors into a small boat and set it adrift. The boat and its crew were never seen again.

All these explorers failed to find a northwest passage to Asia. However, they succeeded in mapping and exploring many parts of North America. The rulers of western Europe began thinking about how to profit from the region's rich resources.

European Rivalries

As European nations began to compete for riches around the world, religious differences also heightened their rivalry. Until the 1500s, the Roman Catholic Church was the only church in western Europe. After that, however, a major religious reform movement split the Catholic Church and sharply divided Christians.

Catholics and Protestants

In 1517, a German monk named Martin Luther challenged many practices of the Catholic Church. Luther believed that the Church had become too worldly and greedy. He opposed the power of popes. He also objected to the Catholic teaching that believers needed to perform good works to gain eternal life. Luther argued that people could be saved only by their faith in God.

Luther's supporters became known as Protestants because of their protests against the Church. The **Protestant Reformation,** as the new movement was known, divided Europe. Soon, the Protestants themselves split, forming many different Protestant churches.

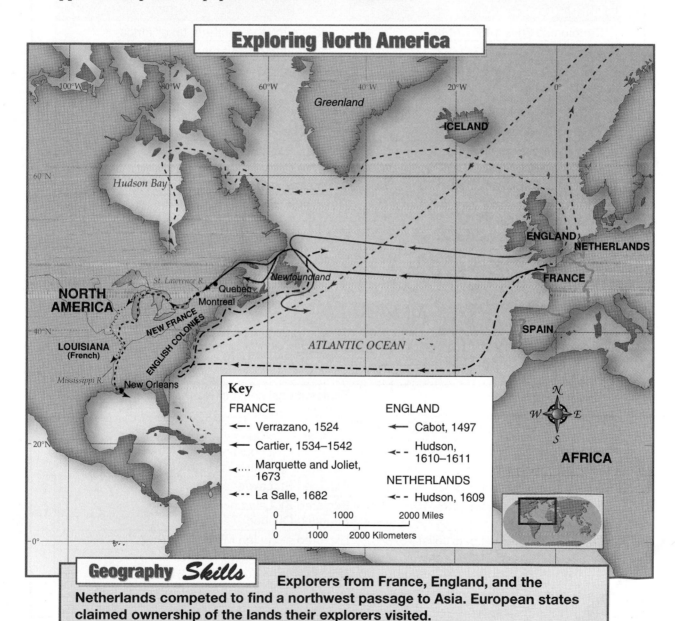

Exploring North America

Key

FRANCE
←-- Verrazano, 1524
←— Cartier, 1534–1542
←.... Marquette and Joliet, 1673
←--- La Salle, 1682

ENGLAND
←— Cabot, 1497
←-- Hudson, 1610–1611

NETHERLANDS
←- - Hudson, 1609

0   1000   2000 Miles
0   1000   2000 Kilometers

Geography Skills   Explorers from France, England, and the Netherlands competed to find a northwest passage to Asia. European states claimed ownership of the lands their explorers visited.

1. Location   On the map, locate: **(a)** English Colonies, **(b)** New France.

2. Region   What waterway was most important for travel through Louisiana?

3. Critical Thinking   Why might you expect conflict between the French and English in North America?

As a result, religion divided the states of western Europe. In the late 1500s, Roman Catholic monarchs ruled Spain and France. Elizabeth I, a Protestant queen, ruled England. In the Netherlands, the Dutch people were mostly Protestant.

Rivalries in the Americas

As Europeans spread to the Americas, they brought their religious conflicts with them. Queen Elizabeth encouraged English adventurers to raid Spanish colonies and capture the treasure fleets of Catholic Spain.

European Explorers

Explorer	Achievements
For Portugal	
Bartolomeu Dias 1487–1488	Sailed around the southern tip of Africa
Vasco da Gama 1497–1498	Sailed around Africa to India
Pedro Álvares Cabral 1500	Reached Brazil
For Spain	
Christopher Columbus 1492–1504	Explored the West Indies and the Caribbean
Vasco Núñez de Balboa 1513	Sighted the Pacific Ocean
Juan Ponce de León 1508–1509, 1513	Explored Puerto Rico Explored Florida
Ferdinand Magellan 1519–1522	Led first expedition to sail around the world
Pánfilo de Narváez/Cabeza de Vaca/ Estevanico 1528–1536	Traveled in the Spanish borderlands
Francisco Coronado 1540–1542	Explored southwestern North America
Hernando De Soto 1516–1520, 1539–1542	Explored Central America Led expedition to the Mississippi River
Juan Cabrillo 1542–1543	Explored west coast of North America
For England	
John Cabot 1497–1501(?)	Explored east coast of North America
Henry Hudson 1610–1611	Explored Hudson Bay
For the Netherlands	
Henry Hudson 1609	Explored east coast of North America and the Hudson River
For France	
Giovanni da Verrazano 1524	Explored east coast of North America, including present-day New York harbor
Jacques Cartier 1534–1542	Explored St. Lawrence River
Samuel de Champlain 1603–1615	Explored St. Lawrence River valley Founded Quebec
Jacques Marquette/Louis Joliet 1673	Explored along the Mississippi River
Robert de La Salle 1679–1682	Explored Great Lakes Reached the mouth of the Mississippi River

Chart Skills

Starting in the late 1400s, western European nations sent explorers to find new trades and to establish new colonies.

1. **Comprehension** (a) Name two explorers who worked for England. (b) What Frenchman explored the Great Lakes?

2. **Critical Thinking** What theory can you offer to explain why Henry Hudson sailed for two different countries?

Protestant England also competed with Catholic France for lands in North America.

Not all rivalries were religious, however. The Netherlands and England struggled against each other even though both were Protestant. They competed for control of land in North America and for economic markets all over the world.

New France

The first permanent French settlements, in what became known as New France, were founded by **Samuel de Champlain** (sham PLAYN). The first colony took root at Port Royal, Nova Scotia, in 1605. Three years later, Champlain led another group of settlers along the route Cartier had pioneered. On a rocky cliff high above the St. Lawrence River, Champlain built a trading post known as Quebec (kwi BEHK).

Economy of New France

Unlike Spain's empire in the Americas, the French empire had little gold or silver. Instead, the French profited from fishing, trapping, and trading.

Most French colonists were traders and trappers. Those who lived and worked in the woods became known as **coureurs de bois** (koo RYOOR duh BWAH), or runners of the woods. The French brought knives, kettles, cloth, and other items for trade with Native Americans. In return, the Native Americans gave them beaver skins and other furs that sold for high prices in Europe.

Coureurs de bois established friendly relations with the Native Americans. Many married Indian women. They learned trapping and survival skills from Native Americans. For example, Indians taught them how to make valuable tools such as snowshoes and canoes.

Missionary work

Catholic **missionaries** often came from Europe and traveled with the fur traders. The missionaries were determined to convert Native Americans to Christianity. They set up missions, drew maps, and wrote about the lands they explored. Life was difficult, espe-

Viewing HISTORY "Runner of the Woods"

To be a successful hunter and trapper in New France, a coureur de bois, or "runner of the woods," often relied on Native American skills and technology. For example, the snowshoes that Indians invented made it easier to travel through deep snow. ★ **What other skills did coureurs de bois learn from Indians?**

cially in winter. One priest recalled traveling through deep snow using Indian snowshoes:

66 If a thaw came, dear Lord, what pain!...I was marching on an icy path that broke with every step I took; as the snow softened...we often sunk in it up to our...waist. 99

Expansion to the Mississippi

French trappers followed the St. Lawrence deep into the heart of North America. Led by Indian guides, they reached the Great Lakes. Here, Indians spoke of a mighty river, which they called Mississippi, or "Father of the Waters."

In 1673, a French missionary, Father **Jacques Marquette** (mar KEHT), and a fur trader, Louis Joliet (JOH lee eht), set out with

NOVI BELGII
NOVÆQUE ANGLIÆ NEC NON
PARTIS
VIRGINIÆ TABULA
multis in locis emendata
per Nicolaum Visscher
Nunc apud Petr. Schenk Iun.

NIEUW AMSTERDAM
of t Eylant Manhattans

Viewing History — A View of Manhattan

The Dutch built New Amsterdam on the southern tip of Manhattan Island. From a small town of fewer than 30 houses, the settlement grew into a busy port visited by ships from around the world. This painting shows New Amsterdam as it appeared in the 1600s. ★ **What does Manhattan Island look like today?**

Indian guides to reach the Mississippi. They followed the river for more than 700 miles (1,100 km) before turning back. In 1682, another explorer, **Robert de La Salle,** completed the journey to the Gulf of Mexico. La Salle named the region Louisiana in honor of the French king, Louis XIV.

To keep Spain and England out of Louisiana, the French built forts along the Mississippi. One fort, at the mouth of the river, was named New Orleans. New Orleans soon grew into a busy trading center. The French also built forts in the north along the Great Lakes. Among them was Fort Detroit, built by Antoine Cadillac near Lake Erie.

Government of New France

New France was governed much like New Spain. The French king controlled the government directly, and people had little freedom. A council appointed by the king made all decisions.

King Louis XIV was concerned that too few French were moving to the territories of New France. In the 1660s, therefore, he sent about a thousand farmers to the colony. The newcomers included many young women.

Despite Louis's efforts to increase the population of New France, the colony grew slowly. By 1680, only about 10,000 settlers lived in the colony. Of those, one third lived on farms along the St. Lawrence. Many more chose the life of the coureurs de bois, who lived largely free of government control.

New Netherland

Like the French, the Dutch hoped to profit from their discoveries in the Americas. In 1626, **Peter Minuit** (MIHN yoo wiht) led a group of Dutch settlers to the mouth of the Hudson River. There, he bought Manhattan Island from local Indians. Minuit called his settlement New Amsterdam. Other Dutch colonists settled farther up the Hudson River. The entire colony was known as **New Netherland.**

By the mid-1600s, New Amsterdam grew into a busy port. The Dutch welcomed people of many nations and religions to their colony. One Dutch governor boasted that more than 15 languages could be heard in the streets of New Amsterdam.

In 1655, the Dutch enlarged New Netherland by taking over the colony of New Sweden. The Swedes had established New Sweden along the Delaware River some 15 years earlier.

Rivalry over furs

Dutch traders sent furs to the Netherlands. The packing list for the first shipment included "the skins of 7,246 beaver, 853 otter, 81 mink, 36 cat lynx, and 34 small rats."

The Dutch and French became rivals in the fur trade. In this rivalry, the French were helped by the **Algonquin** (al GAHN kwihn) Indians. The Dutch made friends with the Iroquois. For many years, fighting raged among the Europeans and their Indian allies.

Dutch ways in North America

The Dutch brought many of their customs to New Netherland. They liked to ice-skate, and in winter the frozen rivers and ponds filled with skaters. Every year on Saint Nicholas's birthday, children put out their shoes to be filled with all sorts of presents. Later, "Saint Nick" came to be called Santa Claus.

Some Dutch words entered the English language. A Dutch master was a "boss." The people of New Amsterdam sailed in "yachts." Dutch children munched on "cookies" and went for rides through the snow on "sleighs."

Impact on Native Americans

The coming of Europeans to North America brought major changes for Native Americans. Once again, as in New Spain, European diseases killed millions of Indians. Rivalry over the fur trade increased Indian warfare because European settlers encouraged their Indian allies to attack one another. The scramble for furs also led to overtrapping. By 1640, trappers had almost wiped out the beavers on Iroquois lands in upstate New York.

The arrival of European settlers affected Native Americans in other ways. Missionaries tried to convert Indians to Christianity. Indians eagerly adopted European trade goods, such as copper kettles and knives, as well as muskets and gunpowder for hunting. Alcohol sold by European traders had a harsh effect on Native American life.

The French, Dutch, and English all waged warfare to seize Indian lands. As Indians were forced off their lands, they moved westward onto lands of other Indians. The conflict between Native Americans and Europeans would continue for many years.

★ Section 4 Review ★

Recall

1. **Locate** (a) Newfoundland, (b) St. Lawrence River, (c) Hudson Bay, (d) Quebec, (e) Mississippi River, (f) Louisiana.
2. **Identify** (a) Jacques Cartier, (b) Henry Hudson, (c) Samuel de Champlain, (d) coureur de bois, (e) Jacques Marquette, (f) Robert de La Salle, (g) Peter Minuit, (h) New Netherland, (i) Algonquin.
3. **Define** (a) northwest passage, (b) Protestant Reformation, (c) missionary.

Comprehension

4. Why did European nations compete for control of lands in North America?

5. (a) How did French trappers get along with Native Americans? (b) Why did missionaries often travel with the coureurs de bois?
6. How did competition between the French and Dutch affect the Algonquins and Iroquois?

Critical Thinking and Writing

7. **Comparing** (a) Describe one way in which New France was similar to New Spain. (b) Describe one way in which they were different.
8. **Inferring** How did missionaries help New France expand?

Activity Making a Map Suppose you can send a map back through time to French explorers of the 1600s. On your map, show how they can travel by land and water from Newfoundland through New France to the mouth of the Mississippi.

The First English Colonies

As You Read

Explore These Questions
- How did representative government take root in Virginia?
- Why did the Pilgrims start a colony in North America?
- How did Native Americans help the Plymouth Colony to survive?

Define
- charter
- representative government
- Magna Carta
- Parliament
- Mayflower Compact

Identify
- Sir Walter Raleigh
- John Smith
- Powhatan
- Pocahontas
- House of Burgesses
- Pilgrims
- Squanto

SETTING the Scene

❝ If England possesses these places in America, Her Majesty will have good harbors, plenty of excellent trees for masts, good timber to build ships . . . all things needed for a royal navy, and all for no price. ❞

Richard Hakluyt wrote these words to persuade Queen Elizabeth I of England to set up colonies in North America. Hakluyt explained a total of more than 30 arguments in favor of settlement. "We shall," Hakluyt concluded, "[stop] the Spanish king from flowing over all the face . . . of America."

Hakluyt's pamphlet, written in 1584, appealed to English pride. England's rival, Spain, had built a great empire in the Americas. England was determined to win a place there, too.

Settlement at Roanoke

The man who encouraged Hakluyt to write his pamphlet was **Sir Walter Raleigh,** a favorite of Queen Elizabeth. With the queen's permission, Raleigh raised money to outfit a colony in North America. In 1585, seven ships and about 100 men set sail across the Atlantic.

The colonists landed on Roanoke (ROH uh nohk), an island off the coast of present-day North Carolina. Within a year, the colonists ran short of food and quarreled with neigh-

boring Native Americans. When an English ship stopped in the harbor, the weary settlers climbed aboard and sailed home.

In 1587, Raleigh asked John White, one of the original colonists, to return to Roanoke with a new group of settlers. This time, women and children went along, too. In Roanoke, one of the women gave birth to a baby girl named Virginia Dare. She was the first English child born in North America.

When supplies ran low, White returned to England, leaving behind 117 colonists. White planned to return in a few months. In England, however, he found the whole nation preparing for war with Spain. It was three years before he returned to Roanoke.

When White did reach Roanoke, he found the settlement strangely quiet. Houses stood empty. Vines twined through the windows and pumpkins sprouted from the earthen floors. White found the word CROATOAN, the name of a nearby island, carved on a tree.

⚛ Connections *With* Science

In 1998, researchers from the University of Arkansas and the College of William and Mary theorized that the Roanoke settlers were victims of the region's worst drought in eight centuries. Their theory was based on the study of moisture-sensitive tree rings from 800-year-old cypress trees.

White was eager to investigate, but a storm was blowing up and his crew refused to make the trip. The next day, White stood sadly on board as the captain set sail for England. To this day, the fate of Roanoke's settlers remains a mystery.

Jamestown Colony

Nearly 20 years passed before England tried again to plant a colony. Then, in 1606, the Virginia Company of London received a charter from King James I. A **charter** is a legal document giving certain rights to a person or company. The charter gave the Virginia Company the right to settle lands to the north of Roanoke, between North Carolina and the Potomac River. The land was called Virginia. The charter guaranteed colonists of Virginia the same rights as English citizens.

A difficult start

In the spring of 1607, 105 colonists arrived in Virginia. They sailed into Chesapeake Bay and began building homes along the James River. They named their tiny outpost Jamestown, after their king, James I.

The colonists soon discovered that Jamestown was located in a swampy area. The water was unhealthy, and mosquitoes spread malaria. Many settlers suffered or died from disease.

Governing the colony also proved difficult. The Virginia Company had chosen a council of 13 men to rule the settlement. Members of the council quarreled with one another and did little to plan for the colony's future. By the summer of 1608, the Jamestown colony was near failure.

Starvation and recovery

Another major problem was starvation. Captain **John Smith,** a 27-year-old soldier and explorer, observed that the colonists were not planting enough crops. He complained that people wanted only to "dig gold, wash gold, refine gold, load gold." As they searched in vain for gold, the colony ran out of food.

Smith helped to save the colony. He set up stern rules that forced colonists to work if

Etatis suæ 21. A. 1616.

Biography　Pocahontas

Pocahontas, daughter of Powhatan, brought food to starving colonists at Jamestown. According to John Smith, she also saved him from an execution that her father had ordered. Later, Pocahontas converted to Christianity, married colonist John Rolfe, and moved to England. There, an artist painted this portrait of her in English dress.
★ **Why do you think the story of Pocahontas remains so popular today?**

they wished to eat. He also visited nearby Indian villages to trade for food. **Powhatan** (pow uh TAN), the most powerful chief in the area, agreed to sell corn to the English.

Peaceful relations between the English and Native Americans of the region were short-lived, however. Whenever the Indians did not agree to supply food voluntarily, the colonists used force to seize what they needed. On one occasion John Smith aimed a gun at Powhatan's brother until the Indians provided corn to buy his freedom. Incidents such as these led to frequent and bloody warfare. Peace was restored, for a brief time only, when the colonist John Rolfe married **Pocahontas,** daughter of Powhatan.

While the English were enjoying the peace, their economic difficulties resumed.

Viewing HISTORY **Representative Government**

Virginia's House of Burgesses, shown at left, first met in 1619. It consisted of 22 representatives elected by "freemen" of the colony. In their first session, the burgesses passed laws against drunkenness and gambling and required colonists to attend church each Sunday. ★ **What people in Virginia could not elect burgesses?**

Problems arose soon after John Smith returned to England in 1609. For the next few years, the colony suffered terribly. Desperate settlers cooked "dogs, cats, snakes, [and] toadstools" to survive. To keep warm, they broke up houses to burn as firewood.

Tobacco and economic success

The Jamestown economy finally got on a firm footing after 1612, when colonists began growing tobacco. Europeans had learned about tobacco and pipe smoking from Native Americans. Although King James I considered smoking "a vile custom," the new fad caught on quickly. By 1620, England was importing more than 30,000 pounds (13,500 kg) of tobacco a year. At last, Virginians had found a way to make their colony succeed.

Representative Government

With Jamestown's economy improving, the Virginia Company took steps to establish a stable government in Virginia. In 1619, it sent a governor with orders to consult settlers on all important matters. Male settlers were allowed to elect burgesses, or representatives. The burgesses met in an assembly called the **House of Burgesses.** Together with the governor, they made laws for the colony.

The House of Burgesses marked the beginning of **representative government** in the English colonies. A representative government is one in which voters elect representatives to make laws for them.

The idea that people had political rights was deeply rooted in English history. In 1215, English nobles had forced King John to sign the **Magna Carta,** or Great Charter. This document said that the king could not raise taxes without first consulting the Great Council of nobles and church leaders. The Magna Carta established the principle, or basic idea, that English monarchs had to obey the laws of the land.

Over time, the rights won by nobles were extended to other English people. The Great Council grew into a representative assembly, called **Parliament.** By the 1600s, Parliament was divided into the House of Lords, made up of nobles, and an elected House of Commons. Only a few rich men had the right to vote. Still, the English had established that their king or queen must consult Parliament on money matters and must respect the law.

At first, free Virginians had even greater rights than citizens in England. They did not have to own property in order to vote. In 1670, however, the colony restricted the vote to free, male property owners.

Despite these limits, representative government remained important in Virginia. The idea took root that settlers should have a say in the affairs of the colony.

 **Colonial Life in Needlework**

In England's North American colonies, women skilled at needle-work recorded details of their daily life. This sampler shows wealthy Bostonians in the mid-1700s. By this time, different ways of life had developed across the 13 English colonies. ★ **Do you think this sampler gives an accurate picture of colonial life? Why or why not?**

1700s
Plantations in the Southern Colonies rely on slave labor

1730s
Religious movement, known as the Great Awakening, sweeps through the colonies

1732
Georgia is founded as refuge for people jailed for debt

| 1690 | 1710 | 1730 | 1750 |

 1700s World Event
Age of Enlightenment begins

1725 World Event
British Quakers speak out against slavery

The New England Colonies

Explore These Questions
- Why did the Puritans set up the Massachusetts Bay Colony?
- Who founded the colonies of Connecticut and Rhode Island?
- What was life like in the New England colonies?

Define
- toleration
- common
- Sabbath
- town meeting

Identify
- John Winthrop
- Puritans
- General Court
- Great Migration
- Thomas Hooker
- Fundamental Orders of Connecticut
- Roger Williams
- Anne Hutchinson
- Metacom

 April and May 1630 were cold, stormy months in the North Atlantic. Huddled below deck, colonists aboard the ship *Arbella* wondered if they had been foolish to sail to a new land. Their leader, however, had no doubts. **John Winthrop,** a lawyer and a devout Christian, assured them that their new colony would set an example to the world:

> 66 The Lord will make our name a praise and glory, so that men shall say of succeeding [colonies]: 'The Lord make it like that of New England.' For we must consider that we shall be like a City upon a Hill. The eyes of all people are on us. 99

The passengers on the *Arbella* were among more than 1,000 people who left England in 1630 to settle in North America. They set up their colony on Massachusetts Bay, north of Plymouth. Over the next 100 years, English settlers would build towns and farms throughout New England.

Puritans in Massachusetts

John Winthrop and his followers were part of a religious group known as **Puritans.** Unlike the Pilgrims, the Puritans did not want to separate entirely from the Church of England. Instead, they hoped to reform the church by introducing simpler forms of worship. They wanted to do away with many practices inherited from the Roman Catholic church, such as organ music, finely decorated houses of worship, and special clothing for priests.

Leaving England

The Puritans were a powerful group in England. Many were well-educated and successful merchants or landowners. Some sat in the House of Commons.

Charles I, who became king in 1625, disapproved of the Puritans and their ideas. He canceled Puritan business charters and had Puritans expelled from universities. He even had a few Puritans jailed.

By 1629, some Puritan leaders were convinced that England had fallen on "evil and declining times." They persuaded royal officials to grant them a charter to form the Massachusetts Bay Company. The company's bold plan was to build a new society in New England. They vowed to base their new society on biblical laws and teachings. Far from the watchful eye of the king, Puritans would run their colony as they pleased.

Some settlers joined the Massachusetts colonists for economic rather than religious reasons. In wealthy English families, the oldest son usually inherited his father's estate. With little hope of owning land, younger sons sought opportunity elsewhere. They were attracted to Massachusetts Bay because it offered cheap land or a chance to start a business.

Governing the colony

In 1629, the Puritans sent a small advance party to North America. John Winthrop and his larger party arrived the following year. Winthrop was chosen first governor of the Massachusetts Bay Colony, as the Puritan settlement was called.

Once ashore, Winthrop set an example for others. Although he was governor, he worked hard to build a home, clear land, and plant crops. One colonist wrote, "He so encouraged us that there was not an idle person to be found in the whole colony."

Under the charter, only stockholders who had invested money in the Massachusetts Bay Company had the right to vote. Most settlers, however, were not stockholders. They resented taxes and laws passed by a government in which they had no say.

Winthrop and other stockholders quickly realized that the colony would run more smoothly if a greater number of settlers could take part. At the same time, Puritan leaders sought to keep non-Puritans out of government. As a result, they granted the right to vote for governor to all men who were church members. Later, male church members also elected representatives to an assembly called the **General Court.**

Under the firm leadership of Winthrop and other Puritans, the Massachusetts Bay Colony grew and prospered. Between 1629 and 1640, some 15,000 men, women, and children made the journey from England to Massachusetts. This movement of people is known as the **Great Migration.** Many of the newcomers settled in Boston, which grew into the colony's largest town.

Settling Connecticut

In May 1636, a Puritan minister named **Thomas Hooker** led about 100 settlers out

Viewing HISTORY   **The New England Puritan**

Augustus Saint-Gaudens, a leading American sculptor of the 1800s, captured the Puritan spirit in his bronze statue The Puritan, *below. The meetinghouse was the center of the Puritan community. Here, families attended services several times a week and all day on Sunday. The meetinghouse at left has been in use since 1681.* ★ **How does the architecture of this meetinghouse reflect what you have learned about Puritan beliefs?**

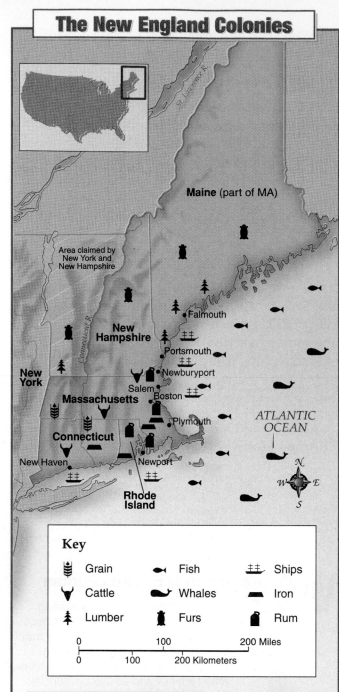

The New England Colonies

Maine (part of MA)

Area claimed by New York and New Hampshire

Falmouth

New Hampshire

Portsmouth

Newburyport

New York

Salem

Boston

Massachusetts

Plymouth

ATLANTIC OCEAN

Connecticut

New Haven

Newport

Rhode Island

Key

- 🌾 Grain
- 🐟 Fish
- ‡‡ Ships
- 🐂 Cattle
- 🐋 Whales
- ▬ Iron
- 🌲 Lumber
- Furs
- Rum

0   100   200 Miles
0   100   200 Kilometers

Geography Skills

The New England colonies were among the first English settlements in North America. Major economic activities in the region included shipbuilding, fishing, and fur trapping.

1. **Location** On the map, locate: **(a)** Massachusetts, **(b)** Connecticut, **(c)** Rhode Island, **(d)** New Hampshire, **(e)** Boston, **(f)** Plymouth.

2. **Interaction** In which colonies did settlers mine iron ore?

3. **Critical Thinking** How did New England's geography encourage the growth of shipbuilding?

---

of Massachusetts Bay. Pushing west, they drove their cattle, goats, and pigs along Indian trails that cut through the forests. When they reached the Connecticut River, they built a town, which they called Hartford.

Hooker left Massachusetts Bay because he believed that the governor and other officials had too much power. He wanted to set up a colony in Connecticut with strict limits on government.

In 1639, the settlers wrote a plan of government called the **Fundamental Orders of Connecticut.** It created a government much like that of Massachusetts. There were, however, two important differences. First, the Fundamental Orders gave the vote to all men who were property owners, including those who were not church members. Second, the Fundamental Orders limited the governor's power. In this way, the Fundamental Orders expanded the idea of representative government in the English colonies.

In 1662, Connecticut became a separate colony, with a new charter granted by the king of England. By then, 15 towns were thriving along the Connecticut River.

Settling Rhode Island

Another Puritan who challenged the leaders of Massachusetts Bay was **Roger Williams.** A young minister in the village of Salem, Williams was gentle and good-natured. Most people, including Governor Winthrop, liked him. Williams's ideas, however, alarmed Puritan leaders.

Williams believed that the Puritan church had too much power in Massachusetts. In Williams's view, the business of church and state should be completely separate. The role of the state, said Williams, was to maintain order and peace. It should not support a particular church.

Williams also believed in religious toleration. **Toleration** means a willingness to let others practice their own beliefs. In Puritan Massachusetts, non-Puritans were not permitted to worship freely.

Puritan leaders viewed Williams as a dangerous troublemaker. In 1635, the General Court ordered him to leave Massachusetts. Fearing that the court would send him back to England, Williams fled to Narragansett Bay, where he spent the winter with Indians. In the spring, the Indians sold him land for a settlement. After a few years, it became the English colony of Rhode Island.

In Rhode Island, Williams put into practice his ideas about toleration. He allowed complete freedom of religion for all Protestants, Jews, and Catholics. He did not set up a state church or require settlers to attend church services. He also gave all white men the right to vote. Before long, settlers who disliked the strict Puritan rule of Massachusetts flocked to Providence and other towns in Rhode Island.*

Anne Hutchinson

Among those who fled to Rhode Island was **Anne Hutchinson.** A devout Puritan, Hutchinson regularly attended church services. After church, she and her friends gathered at her home to discuss the minister's sermon. At first, Hutchinson merely related what the minister had said. Later, she began to express her own views. Often, she seemed to criticize the minister's teachings.

Puritan leaders grew angry. They believed that Hutchinson's opinions were full of religious errors. Even worse, they said, a woman did not have the right to explain God's law. In November 1637, Hutchinson was ordered to appear before the General Court.

At her trial, Hutchinson answered all the questions put to her by General Winthrop and other members of the court. Time after time, she revealed weaknesses in their arguments. They could not prove that she had broken any Puritan laws or disobeyed any religious teachings.

Then, after two days of questioning, Hutchinson made a serious mistake. She told the court that God spoke directly to her, "By the voice of His own spirit to my soul." Members of the court were shocked. Puritans be-

*In 1763, Jewish settlers in Rhode Island built Touro Synagogue, the first Jewish house of worship in North America. It still stands today.

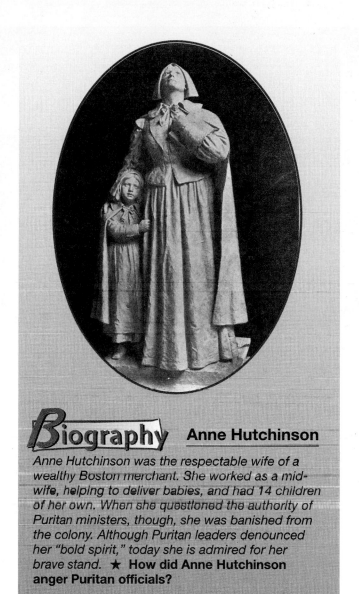

Biography — Anne Hutchinson

Anne Hutchinson was the respectable wife of a wealthy Boston merchant. She worked as a midwife, helping to deliver babies, and had 14 children of her own. When she questioned the authority of Puritan ministers, though, she was banished from the colony. Although Puritan leaders denounced her "bold spirit," today she is admired for her brave stand. ★ **How did Anne Hutchinson anger Puritan officials?**

lieved that God spoke only through the Bible, not directly to individuals. The court declared that Hutchinson was "deluded by the Devil" and ordered her out of the colony.

In 1638, Hutchinson, along with her family and some friends, went to Rhode Island. The Puritan leaders had won their case. For later Americans, however, Hutchinson became an important symbol of the struggle for religious freedom.

Conflict With Native Americans

From Massachusetts Bay, settlers fanned out across New England. Some built trading and fishing villages along the coast north of

This engraving shows a street near Boston harbor in the 1660s. By this time, fishing was already a vital part of the New England economy. The cod was so important that it even appeared in home decoration. ★ **Identify two other ways the sea played an important role in the economy of New England.**

▲ *Wooden cod from a Massachusetts home*

Boston. In 1680, the king made these coastal settlements into a separate colony called New Hampshire.

As more colonists settled in New England, they took over Native American lands. As a result, fighting broke out between white settlers and Indian nations of the region.

The largest conflict came in 1675. Wampanoag Indians, led by their chief, **Metacom,** attacked villages throughout New England. Other Indian groups soon allied themselves with the Wampanoags. Fighting lasted 14 months. Metacom and his allies destroyed 12 towns and killed more than 600 European settlers.

In the end, however, Metacom was captured and killed. The English sold his family and about 1,000 other Indians into slavery in the West Indies. Other Indians were forced from their homelands. Many of them died of starvation.

The pattern of English expansion followed by war between colonists and Indians was repeated throughout the colonies. It would continue for many years to come.

Life in New England

Puritans believed that people should worship and tend to local matters as a community. As a result, New England became a land of tightly knit towns and villages.

At the center of each village was the **common,** an open field where cattle grazed. Nearby stood the meetinghouse, where Puritans worshipped and held town meetings. Wooden houses with steep roofs lined the town's narrow streets.

Religion and family

The Puritans took their **Sabbath,** or holy day of rest, very seriously. On Sundays, no one was allowed to play games or visit taverns to joke, talk, and drink. The law required all citizens to attend church services, which on Sunday lasted all day.

During the 1600s, women sat on one side of the church and men on the other. Blacks and Indians stood in a balcony at the back. Children had separate pews, where an adult watched over them. If they "sported and played," they were punished.

The Puritans taught that children were a blessing of God. The average family had seven or eight children. The healthy climate allowed New Englanders to live long lives. Many reached the age of 70. As a result, children often grew up knowing both their parents and their grandparents.

Government

At **town meetings,** settlers discussed and voted on many issues. What roads should be built? How much should the schoolmaster be paid? Town meetings gave New Englanders a chance to speak their minds. This early experience encouraged the growth of democratic ideas in New England.

Puritan laws were strict. About 15 crimes carried the death penalty. One crime punishable by death was witchcraft. In 1692, Puritans in Salem Village executed 20 men and women as witches.

Economy

New England was a difficult land for colonists. The Puritans, though, believed that daily labor honored God as much as prayer. With hard work, they built a thriving way of life.

New England's rocky soil was poor for farming. After a time, however, settlers learned to grow many Native American crops, such as Indian corn, pumpkins, squash, and beans.

Although the soil was poor, the forests were full of riches. Settlers hunted wild turkey and deer, as well as hogs that they let roam free in the woods. In the spring, colonists collected sweet sap from sugar maple trees. Settlers also cut down trees and floated them to sawmills near ports such as Boston, Massachusetts, or Portsmouth, New Hampshire. These cities grew into major shipbuilding centers.

Other New Englanders fished the coastal waters for cod and halibut. When the fish were running, fishers worked tirelessly, seldom taking time to eat or sleep. Shellfish in New England were especially large. Oysters sometimes grew to be a foot long. Lobsters stretched up to 6 feet!

In the 1600s, New Englanders also began to hunt whales. Whales supplied oil for lamps, as well as ivory and other products. In the 1700s and 1800s, whaling grew into a big business.

Decline of the Puritans

During the 1700s, the Puritan tradition declined. Fewer families left England for religious reasons. Ministers had less influence on the way colonies were governed. Even so, the Puritans stamped New England with their distinctive customs and their dream of a religious society.

★ Section 1 Review ★

Recall

1. **Locate** (a) Massachusetts, (b) Connecticut, (c) Rhode Island, (d) New Hampshire.
2. **Identify** (a) John Winthrop, (b) Puritans, (c) General Court, (d) Great Migration, (e) Thomas Hooker, (f) Fundamental Orders of Connecticut, (g) Roger Williams, (h) Anne Hutchinson, (i) Metacom.
3. **Define** (a) toleration, (b) common, (c) Sabbath, (d) town meeting.

Comprehension

4. How did the Puritans govern the Massachusetts Bay Colony?

5. Explain why each of the following left the Massachusetts Bay Colony: (a) Thomas Hooker, (b) Roger Williams, (c) Anne Hutchinson.
6. How did the New England colonists make a living?

Critical Thinking and Writing

7. **Making Generalizations** Make a generalization about the role of religion in the Massachusetts Bay Colony. Give two examples to support your generalization.
8. **Making Inferences** Why do you think the Puritan leaders felt threatened by settlers who voiced opposing views?

★ ★

Activity **Writing a Letter** Go back in time! You are a young person living in Puritan New England about 1650. Write a letter to a friend in England, explaining what you like and what you do not like about life in New England.

The Middle Colonies

As You Read

Explore These Questions
- Why did William Penn start a colony in North America?
- Why were the Middle Colonies known as the Breadbasket Colonies?
- What was life like in the backcountry?

Define
- patroon
- proprietary colony
- proprietor
- royal colony
- cash crop
- backcountry

Identify
- Peter Stuyvesant
- William Penn
- Quakers
- Pennsylvania Dutch
- Breadbasket Colonies
- Great Wagon Road

SETTING the Scene In the summer of 1744, a doctor from the colony of Maryland traveled north to Philadelphia. Doctor Hamilton was amazed at the wide variety of people he met during his stay in that city. He wrote:

> 66 I dined at a tavern with a very mixed company of different nations and religions. There were Scots, English, Dutch, Germans, and Irish. There were Roman Catholics, Church [of England] men, Presbyterians, Quakers,...Moravians,...and one Jew. 99

By 1700, England had four colonies in the region directly south of New England. These colonies became known as the Middle Colonies because they were located between New England and the Southern Colonies. As Doctor Hamilton observed, the Middle Colonies had a much greater mix of people than either New England or the Southern Colonies.

New Netherland Becomes New York

As you read, the Dutch set up the colony of New Netherland along the Hudson River. In the colony's early years, settlers traded with Indians for

Dutch-style writing desk from colonial New York

furs and built the settlement of New Amsterdam into a thriving port.

To encourage farming in New Netherland, Dutch officials granted large parcels of land to a few rich families. A single land grant could stretch for miles. Indeed, one grant was as big as Rhode Island! Owners of these huge estates were called **patroons.** In return for the grant, each patroon promised to settle at least 50 European farm families on the land. Few farmers wanted to work for the patroons, however. Patroons had great power and could charge whatever rents they pleased.

Most settlers lived in the trading center of New Amsterdam. They came from all over Europe. Many were attracted by the chance to practice their religion freely.

Dutch colonists were mainly Protestants who belonged to the Dutch Reformed Church. Still, they permitted members of other religions—including Roman Catholics, French Protestants, and Jews—to buy land. "People do not seem concerned what religion their neighbor is," wrote a shocked visitor from Virginia. "Indeed, they do not seem to care if he has any religion at all."

By 1664, the rivalry between England and the Netherlands for trade and colonies was at its height. In August of that year, English warships entered New Amsterdam's harbor. **Peter Stuyvesant** (STI vuh sehnt), the governor of New Netherland, swore to defend the city. However, he had few weapons and little gunpowder. Also, Stuyvesant had made himself so unpopular with his harsh rule and heavy taxes that the colonists refused to help him. In the end, he surrendered without firing a shot.

King Charles II of England then gave New Netherland to his brother, the Duke of York. He renamed the colony New York in the duke's honor.

New Jersey

At the time of the English takeover, New York stretched as far south as the Delaware River. The Duke of York realized that it was too big to govern easily. He gave some of the land to friends, Lord Berkeley and Sir George Carteret. They set up a proprietary (proh PRI uh tuhr ee) colony, which they called New Jersey.

In setting up a **proprietary colony,** the king gave land to one or more people. These **proprietors** were free to divide the land and rent it to others. They made laws for the colony but had to respect the rights of colonists under English law.

Like New York, New Jersey attracted people from many lands. English Puritans mingled with French Protestants, Scots, Irish, Swedes, and Finns.

In 1702, New Jersey became a **royal colony,** that is, a colony under control of the English crown. The colony's charter protected religious freedom and the rights of an assembly that voted on local matters.

Pennsylvania

South of New Jersey, **William Penn** founded the colony of Pennsylvania in 1682. Penn came from a wealthy English family. King Charles II was a personal friend. At age 22, however, Penn shocked family and friends by joining the **Quakers,** one of the most despised religious groups in England.

The Quakers

Like Pilgrims and Puritans, Quakers were Protestant reformers. Their reforms went further than those of other groups, however. Quakers believed that all people—men and women, nobles and commoners—were equal in God's sight. They allowed women to preach in public and refused to bow or remove their hats in the presence of the nobility. Quakers spoke out against war and refused to serve in the army.

To most English people, Quaker beliefs seemed wicked. In both England and New England, Quakers were arrested, fined, or even hanged for their ideas. Penn became convinced that the Quakers must leave England. He turned to the king for help.

Charles II made Penn proprietor of a large tract of land in North America. The king named the new colony Pennsylvania, or Penn's woodlands.

 **Peter Stuyvesant**

Peter Stuyvesant lost a leg fighting in the Caribbean. He fought just as hard when he became governor of New Netherland. Given almost total power, he imposed heavy taxes and punished lawbreakers with public whippings. When colonists demanded a voice in government, he replied that his authority came "from God." Still, Stuyvesant was powerless to stop England from taking over the colony. ★ **What are some advantages and disadvantages of having a strong ruler like Stuyvesant?**

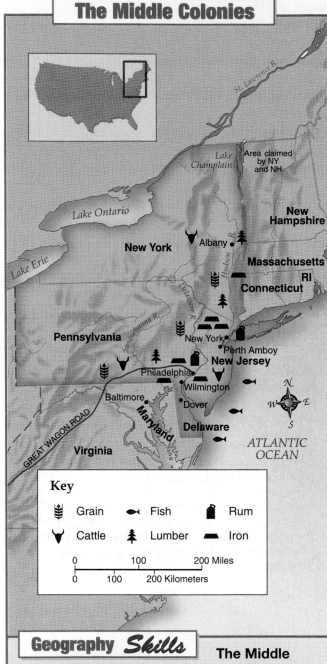

Key

🌾 Grain   🐟 Fish   🍶 Rum

🐂 Cattle   🌲 Lumber   ⬛ Iron

0   100   200 Miles

0   100   200 Kilometers

Geography Skills

The Middle Colonies were located to the south and west of New England and north of the Southern Colonies.

1. **Location** On the map, locate: **(a)** New York, **(b)** New Jersey, **(c)** Pennsylvania, **(d)** Delaware, **(e)** Hudson River, **(f)** Philadelphia, **(g)** Great Wagon Road.

2. **Movement** Identify two ways settlers could have traveled inland from the Atlantic Coast.

3. **Critical Thinking** Based on the map, why do you think Philadelphia would become a major trading center?

A policy of fairness

Penn thought of his colony as a "holy experiment." He wanted it to be a model of religious freedom, peace, and Christian living. Protestants, Catholics, and Jews went to Pennsylvania to escape persecution. Later, English officials forced Penn to turn away Catholic and Jewish settlers.

Penn's Quaker beliefs led him to speak out for fair treatment of Native Americans. Penn believed that the land belonged to the Indians. He said that settlers should pay for the land. Native Americans respected Penn for this policy. As a result, colonists in Pennsylvania enjoyed many years of peace with their Indian neighbors. One settler later remarked:

> 66 And as [Penn] treated the Indians with extraordinary humanity, they became very civil and loving to us.... As in other countries, the Indians were [angered] by hard treatment, which hath been the [cause] of much bloodshed, so the [opposite] treatment here hath produced love and affection. 99

The colony grows

Penn sent pamphlets describing his colony all over Europe. Soon, settlers from England, Scotland, Wales, the Netherlands, France, and Germany began to cross the Atlantic Ocean to Pennsylvania.

Among the new arrivals were large numbers of German-speaking Protestants. They became known as **Pennsylvania Dutch** because people could not pronounce the word Deutsch (DOICH), which means German.

Penn carefully planned a capital city along the Delaware River. He named it Philadelphia, a Greek word meaning "brotherly love." Philadelphia grew quickly. By 1710, a visitor wrote that it was "the most noble, large, and well-built city I have seen."

Delaware

For a time, Pennsylvania included some lands along the lower Delaware River. The region was known as Pennsylvania's Lower Counties.

Past	Present

A Simple Country Life

Today, in certain parts of Pennsylvania, horses and buggies are still a common sight, as they were in colonial days. The Amish, a Christian sect, came to Pennsylvania in the 1700s. Today, Amish families farm the land, use horses, and dress as plainly as their ancestors did.
★ **Why do you think the Amish chose Pennsylvania as their home?**

Settlers in the Lower Counties did not want to send delegates to a faraway assembly in Philadelphia. In 1701, Penn allowed them to elect their own assembly. Later, the Lower Counties broke away to form the colony of Delaware.

Life in the Middle Colonies

Farmers found more favorable conditions in the Middle Colonies than in New England. The broad Hudson and Delaware river valleys were rich and fertile. Winters were milder than in New England, and the growing season lasted longer.

A thriving economy

On such promising land, farmers in the Middle Colonies produced surpluses of wheat, barley, and rye. These were **cash crops,** or crops that are sold for money at market. In fact, the Middle Colonies exported so much grain that they became known as the **Breadbasket Colonies.**

Farmers of the Middle Colonies also raised herds of cattle and pigs. Every year, they sent tons of beef, pork, and butter to the ports of New York and Philadelphia. From there, the goods went by ship to New England and the South or to the West Indies, England, and other parts of Europe.

Encouraged by William Penn, skilled German craftsworkers set up shop in Pennsylvania. In time, the colony became a center of manufacturing and crafts. One visitor reported that workshops turned out "hardware, clocks, watches, locks, guns, flints, glass, stoneware, nails, [and] paper."

Settlers in the Delaware River valley profited from the region's rich deposits of iron ore. Heating the ore in furnaces, they purified it and then hammered it into nails, tools, and parts for guns.

Middle Colony homes

Farms in the Middle Colonies were generally larger than those in New England.

Skills FOR LIFE

Critical Thinking	Managing Information	Communication	Maps, Charts, and Graphs

Reading a Pie Graph

How Will I Use This Skill?
When you read textbooks, newspapers, or magazines, you will often find important statistics presented as part of a pie graph. A pie graph is in the shape of a circle that represents 100% of the group you are examining. Pie graphs present statistics in wedges, like pieces of a pie. The wedges represent percentages of the whole, helping you better compare the groups.

LEARN the Skill
You can learn to understand pie graphs by using the steps below.

❶ Identify the topic of the pie graph. Remember that the circle represents 100% of the group you are examining.

❷ Identify which groups are represented by the various wedges of the pie. Some groups which are few in number or not easily identified may be shown as "others."

❸ Compare the sizes of the various groups. The largest wedge will correspond to the largest group.

PRACTICE the Skill
Use the steps below to read the pie graph. The graph does not include Indians.

❶ (a) What is the topic of this graph? (b) What entire group does the circle as a whole represent?

❷ (a) List the population groups represented by the wedges. (b) Are all groups identified individually on the graph?

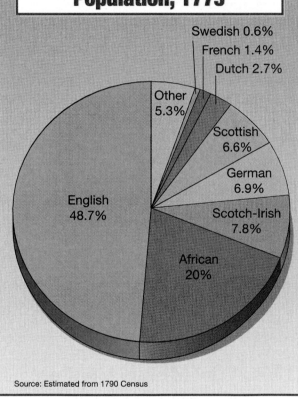

Ethnic Division of Colonial Population, 1775

Swedish 0.6%
French 1.4%
Dutch 2.7%
Other 5.3%
Scottish 6.6%
German 6.9%
Scotch-Irish 7.8%
English 48.7%
African 20%

Source: Estimated from 1790 Census

❸ (a) Which group made up the largest percentage of the colonial population? (b) What percentage of the population had Swedish roots? (c) What was the largest non-European group shown here?

APPLY the Skill
Take a poll to determine in which month each member of your class was born. Turn the numbers into percentages and show the information on a pie graph. To figure out percentages, divide the number in each group by the total number of the class.

Because houses tended to be far apart in the Middle Colonies, towns were less important. Counties, rather than villages, became centers of local government.

The different groups who settled the Middle Colonies had their own favorite ways of building. Swedish settlers introduced log cabins to the Americas. The Dutch used red bricks to build narrow, high-walled houses. German settlers developed a wood-burning stove that heated a home better than a fireplace, which let blasts of cold air leak down the chimney.

The Backcountry

In the 1700s, thousands of German and Scotch-Irish settlers arrived in Philadelphia. From there, they traveled west into the **backcountry,** the area of land along the eastern slopes of the Appalachian Mountains. Settlers followed an old Iroquois trail that became known as the **Great Wagon Road.**

To farm the backcountry, settlers had to clear thick forests. From Indians, settlers learned how to use knots from pine trees as candles to light their homes. They made wooden dishes from logs, gathered honey from hollows in trees, and hunted wild animals for food. German gunsmiths developed a lightweight rifle for use in forests. Sharpshooters boasted that the "Pennsylvania rifle" could hit a rattlesnake between the eyes at 100 yards.

Many of the settlers who arrived in the backcountry moved onto Indian lands. "The Indians...are alarmed at the swarm of strangers," one Pennsylvania official reported. "We are afraid of a [fight] between them for the [colonists] are very rough to them." On more than one occasion, disputes between settlers and Indians resulted in violence.

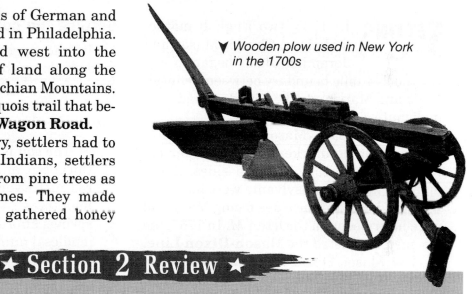
▼ *Wooden plow used in New York in the 1700s*

★ Section 2 Review ★

Recall

1. **Locate** (a) New York, (b) New Jersey, (c) Pennsylvania, (d) Philadelphia, (e) Delaware.
2. **Identify** (a) Peter Stuyvesant, (b) William Penn, (c) Quakers, (d) Pennsylvania Dutch, (e) Breadbasket Colonies, (f) Great Wagon Road.
3. **Define** (a) patroon, (b) proprietary colony, (c) proprietor, (d) royal colony, (e) cash crop, (f) backcountry.

Comprehension

4. What policies did William Penn follow in the Pennsylvania colony?

5. How did the land and climate help Middle Colonies farmers to prosper?
6. What did settlers have to do in order to farm the backcountry?

Critical Thinking and Writing

7. **Comparing** (a) How was Penn's "holy experiment" like the Puritan idea of a "city upon a hill"? (b) How was it different?
8. **Understanding Causes and Effects** Why do you think many settlers moved westward into the backcountry?

Activity Creating a Pamphlet Did you ever think about a career in advertising? Make up a pamphlet advertising the settlement of Pennsylvania like the ones that Penn sent to countries all over Europe. Encourage people to move to Pennsylvania by describing its economy and society.

3 The Southern Colonies

As You Read

Explore These Questions
- Why were the Southern Colonies founded?
- What two ways of life developed in the Southern Colonies?
- Why did slavery become important in the South?

Define
- indigo
- debtor
- buffer
- plantation
- slave code
- racism

Identify
- Mason-Dixon Line
- Lord Baltimore
- Act of Toleration
- Bacon's Rebellion
- James Oglethorpe
- Mary Musgrove
- Tidewater

 SETTING the Scene In 1763, two English mathematicians, Charles Mason and Jeremiah Dixon, began to survey the 244-mile boundary between Pennsylvania and Maryland. The boundary had been in dispute since 1681.

For four years, Mason and Dixon carefully laid stone markers on the border between the two colonies. The sides of the markers facing Pennsylvania were inscribed with the letter *P*. The sides facing Maryland were inscribed with the letter *M*. In 1767, the two men completed the **Mason-Dixon Line.**

The Mason-Dixon Line was more than just the boundary between Pennsylvania and Maryland. It also divided the Middle Colonies from the Southern Colonies. Below the Mason-Dixon Line, the Southern Colonies developed a way of life different in many ways from that of the other English colonies.

Maryland

In 1632, Sir George Calvert persuaded King Charles I to grant him land for a colony in the Americas. Calvert had ruined his career in Protestant England by becoming a Roman Catholic. Now, he planned to build a colony where Catholics could practice their religion freely. He named the colony Maryland in honor of Queen Henrietta Maria, the king's wife.

Calvert died before his colony could get underway. His son Cecil, **Lord Baltimore,** pushed on with the project.

Settling the colony

In the spring of 1634, 200 colonists landed along the upper Chesapeake Bay, across from England's first southern colony, Virginia. The land was rich and beautiful. In the words of one settler:

66 The soil is dark and soft, a foot in thickness, and rests upon a rich and red clay. Every where there are very high trees.... An abundance of springs afford water.... There is an [endless] number of birds.... There is [nothing] wanting to the region. 99

Maryland was truly a land of plenty. Chesapeake Bay was full of fish, oysters, and crabs. Across the bay, Virginians were already growing tobacco for profit. Maryland's new settlers hoped to do the same.

Remembering the early problems at Jamestown, the newcomers avoided the swampy lowlands. They built their first town, St. Mary's, in a healthful location.

As proprietor of the colony, Lord Baltimore appointed a governor and a council of advisers. He gave colonists a role in government by creating an elected assembly. Eager to attract settlers to Maryland, Lord Baltimore made generous land grants to anyone who brought over servants, women, and children.

A few women took advantage of Lord Baltimore's offer of land. Two sisters, Margaret and Mary Brent, arrived in Maryland in

1638 with nine male servants. In time, they set up two plantations of 1,000 acres each. Later, Margaret Brent helped prevent a rebellion among the governor's soldiers. The Maryland assembly praised her efforts, saying that "the colony's safety at any time [was better] in her hands than in any man's."

Religious toleration

To ensure Maryland's continued growth, Lord Baltimore welcomed Protestants as well as Catholics to the colony.

Later, Lord Baltimore came to fear that Protestants might try to deprive Catholics of their right to worship freely. In 1649, he asked the assembly to pass an **Act of Toleration.** The act provided religious freedom for all Christians. As in many colonies, this freedom did not extend to Jews.

Bacon's Rebellion

Meanwhile, settlers continued to arrive in Virginia, lured by the promise of profits from tobacco. Wealthy planters, however, controlled the best lands near the coast. Newcomers had to push farther inland, onto Indian lands.

As in New England, conflict over land led to fighting between settlers and Indians. After several bloody clashes, settlers called on the governor to take action against Native Americans. The governor refused. He was unwilling to act, in part because he profited from his own fur trade with Indians. Frontier settlers were furious.

Finally, in 1676, Nathaniel Bacon, an ambitious young planter, organized angry men and women on the frontier. He raided Native American villages. Then, he led his followers to Jamestown and burned the capital.

The uprising, known as **Bacon's Rebellion,** lasted only a short time. When Bacon died suddenly, the revolt fell apart. The governor hanged 23 of Bacon's followers. Still, he could not stop English settlers from moving onto Indian lands along the frontier.

The Carolinas

South of Virginia and Maryland, English colonists settled in a region which they called

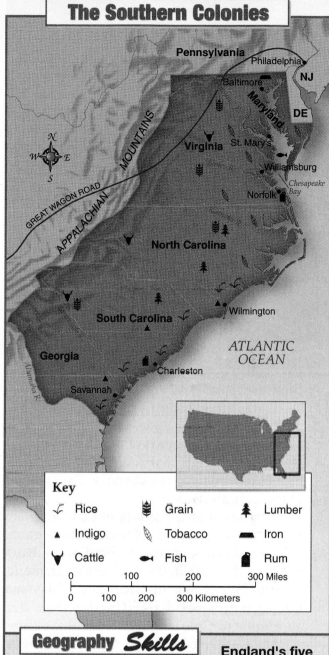

The Southern Colonies

Key

Rice	Grain	Lumber
Indigo	Tobacco	Iron
Cattle	Fish	Rum

0 100 200 300 Miles

0 100 200 300 Kilometers

Geography Skills England's five Southern Colonies stretched along the Atlantic coast from Maryland to Georgia. Farm products and lumber were important to the economy of the region.

1. **Location** On the map, locate: **(a)** Maryland, **(b)** Virginia, **(c)** North Carolina, **(d)** South Carolina, **(e)** Georgia, **(f)** Chesapeake Bay, **(g)** Charleston.

2. **Place** Describe the area where cattle herding took place.

3. **Critical Thinking** Compare this map to the maps on pages 96 and 102. **(a)** What crops were grown only in the Southern Colonies? **(b)** Why do you think such products were not grown farther north?

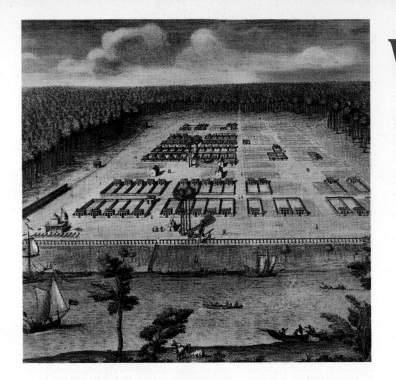

Viewing HISTORY · **Settling Georgia**

This engraving from 1734 is the earliest known picture of Savannah, Georgia. English colonists carved the settlement out of a forest on the banks of the Savannah River. ★ **Based on this picture, how can you tell that building Savannah was hard work?**

caped into the forests. Planters then turned to slaves from Africa. By 1700, the majority of people coming to Charleston were African men and women brought there against their will.

The northern area of Carolina had fewer slaves. Differences between the two areas led to division of the colony into North Carolina and South Carolina in 1712.

Georgia

The last of England's 13 colonies was carved out of the southern part of South Carolina. **James Oglethorpe,** a respected English soldier and energetic reformer, founded Georgia in 1732. He wanted the new colony to be a place where **debtors,** or people who owed money they could not pay back, could make a new start.

A haven for debtors

Under English law, the government could imprison debtors until they paid what they owed. If they ever got out of jail, debtors often had no money and no place to live. Oglethorpe offered to pay for debtors and other poor people to travel to Georgia. "In America," he said, "there are enough fertile lands to feed all the poor of England."

In 1733, Oglethorpe and 120 colonists built the colony's first settlement at Savan-

the Carolinas. Settlement took place in two separate areas, one in the north and the other in the south.

In the northern part of the Carolinas, settlers were mostly poor tobacco farmers who had drifted south from Virginia. They tended to have small farms.

Farther south, a group of eight English nobles set up a larger colony. As proprietors, they received a grant of land from King Charles II in 1663. The largest settlement, Charles Town, grew up where the Ashley and Cooper rivers met. Later, Charles Town was shortened to Charleston.

Most early settlers in Charleston were English people who had been living in Barbados, a British colony in the Caribbean. Later, other immigrants arrived, including Germans, Swiss, French Protestants, and Spanish Jews.

Around 1685, a few planters discovered that rice grew well in the swampy lowlands along the coast. Before long, Carolina rice was a valuable crop traded around the world. Settlers in southern Carolina later learned to raise **indigo,** a plant used to make a valuable blue dye.

Carolina planters needed large numbers of workers to grow rice. At first, they tried to enslave local Indians. Many Indians died of disease or mistreatment, however. Others es-

Connections With Geography

Indigo was first grown in South Carolina by 17-year-old Eliza Lucas. She ran the family plantation while her father, an army colonel, served overseas. While away, Colonel Lucas sent his daughter seeds from all over the world. Eliza Lucas found that the West Indian indigo plant grew well in land that was bad for planting rice.

nah, above the Savannah River. Oglethorpe set strict rules for the colony. Farms could be no bigger than 500 acres, and slavery was forbidden.

At first, Georgia grew slowly. Later, however, Oglethorpe changed the rules to allow large plantations and slave labor. After that, the colony grew more quickly.

Rivalry with Spain

England hoped that Georgia would act as a buffer between the Carolinas and Spanish Florida. A **buffer** is a land located between two larger lands that reduces the possibility of conflict between them. Spain and England both claimed the land between South Carolina and Florida. Spain, aided by Creek allies, tried to force the English out. Oglethorpe and the Georgians held their ground.

A woman known as **Mary Musgrove** greatly helped Oglethorpe during this time. The daughter of a Creek mother and an English father, Musgrove spoke both Creek and English. She helped to keep peace between the Creeks and the settlers in Georgia. Musgrove's efforts did much to allow the colony of Georgia to develop in peace.

Two Ways of Life

Today, we often think of the colonial South as a land where wealthy planters lived in elegant homes, with large numbers of enslaved African Americans toiling in the fields. In fact, this picture is only partly true. As the Southern colonies grew, two distinct and different ways of life emerged—one along the Atlantic coast and another in the backcountry.

Tidewater plantations

The Southern Colonies enjoyed warmer weather and a longer growing season than the colonies to the north. Virginia, Maryland, and parts of North Carolina all became major tobacco-growing areas. Settlers in South Carolina and Georgia raised rice and indigo.

Colonists soon found that it was most profitable to raise tobacco and rice on large plantations. As you recall, a **plantation** is a large estate farmed by many workers. On these southern plantations, anywhere from 20 to 100 slaves did most of the work. Most slaves worked in the fields. Some were skilled workers, such as carpenters, barrel

Viewing HISTORY — Two Ways of Life

These pictures from the 1700s show two vastly different ways of life in the Southern Colonies. At left, wealthy planters enjoy a life of elegant leisure. At right, a woman in the backcountry fetches water for her daily chores. ★ **Who do you think fetched the water for the wealthy planters shown here?**

Viewing History — Slavery in the South

As the poster shows, colonial law permitted Africans to be bought and sold as property. The growth of slavery allowed southern colonists to work large plantations. The painting at right shows rows of slave cabins on a plantation in the Southern Colonies. ★ **Where did the slaves advertised on the poster come from? Where would they end up?**

makers, or blacksmiths. Still other slaves worked in the main house as cooks, servants, or housekeepers.

The earliest plantations were located along rivers and creeks of the coastal plain. Because the land was washed by ocean tides, the region was known as the **Tidewater.** The Tidewater's gentle slopes and rivers offered rich farmland for plantations.

Farther inland, planters settled along rivers. Rivers provided an easy way to move goods to market. Planters loaded crops onto ships bound for the West Indies and Europe. On the return trip, the ships carried English manufactured goods and other luxuries for planters and their families.

Most Tidewater plantations had their own docks, and merchant ships picked up crops and delivered goods directly to them. For this reason, few large seaport cities developed in the Southern Colonies.

Only a small percentage of white southerners owned large plantations. Yet, planters set the style of life in the South. Life centered around the Great House, where the planter's family lived. The grandest homes had elegant quarters for the family, a parlor for visitors, a dining room, and guest bedrooms.

In the growing season, planters decided which fields to plant, what crops to grow, and when to harvest the crops and take them to market. Planters' wives kept the household running smoothly. They directed house slaves and made sure daily tasks were done, such as milking cows.

The backcountry South

West of the Tidewater, life was very different. Here, at the base of the Appalachians, rolling hills and thick forests covered the land. As in the Middle Colonies, this inland area was called the backcountry. Attracted by rich soil, settlers followed the Great Wagon Road into the backcountry of Maryland, Virginia, and the Carolinas.

The backcountry was more democratic than the Tidewater. Settlers there were more likely to treat one another as equals. Men tended smaller fields of tobacco or corn or hunted game. Women cooked meals and fashioned simple, rugged clothing out of wool or deerskins.

The hardships of backcountry life brought settlers closer together. Families gathered to husk corn or help one another build barns. Spread out along the edge of the Appalachians, these hardy settlers felled trees, grew crops, and changed the face of the land.

Growth of Slavery

In the early years, Africans in the English colonies included free people and servants as well as slaves. Indeed, during the 1600s, even those Africans who were enslaved enjoyed some freedom. In South Carolina, for example, some enslaved Africans worked without supervision as cowboys, herding cattle to market.

Planters rely on slavery

On plantations throughout the Southern Colonies, enslaved Africans used farming skills they had brought from West Africa. They showed English settlers how to grow rice. They also knew how to use wild plants

unfamiliar to the English. They made water buckets out of gourds, and they used palmetto leaves to make fans, brooms, and baskets.

By 1700, plantations in the Southern Colonies had come to rely on slave labor. Slaves cleared the land, worked the crops, and tended the livestock.

Limiting rights

As the importance of slavery increased, greater limits were placed on the rights of slaves. Colonists passed laws that set out rules for slaves' behavior and denied slaves their basic rights. These **slave codes** treated enslaved Africans not as human beings but as property.

Most English colonists did not question the justice of owning slaves. They believed that black Africans were inferior to white Europeans. The belief that one race is superior to another is called **racism.** Some colonists claimed that they were helping slaves by introducing them to Christianity.

A handful of colonists saw the evils of slavery. In 1688, Quakers in Germantown, Pennsylvania, became the first group of colonists to call for an end to slavery.

★ Section 3 Review ★

Recall

1. **Locate** (a) Maryland, (b) Virginia, (c) North Carolina, (d) South Carolina, (e) Georgia.
2. **Identify** (a) Mason-Dixon Line, (b) Lord Baltimore, (c) Act of Toleration, (d) Bacon's Rebellion, (e) James Oglethorpe, (f) Mary Musgrove, (g) Tidewater.
3. **Define** (a) indigo, (b) debtor, (c) buffer, (d) plantation, (e) slave code, (f) racism.

Comprehension

4. Why did their founders set up the colonies of (a) Maryland, and (b) Georgia?

5. How was life in the Tidewater different from life in the backcountry South?
6. What role did slaves play in the economy of the Southern Colonies by 1700?

Critical Thinking and Writing

7. **Applying Information** Review the definition of religious toleration. Did Maryland's Act of Toleration provide true religious toleration? Explain.
8. **Analyzing Ideas** How did the passage of slave codes in the colonies reflect racism?

★ ★

Activity Creating Flashcards Do you get confused about the 13 English colonies? Use the text, including the maps and charts, to create 13 flashcards. On one side, write the name of a colony. On the other, write three facts about that colony. You may later use these cards for review.

Governing the Colonies

As You Read

Explore These Questions
- Why did England pass the Navigation Acts?
- What were colonial governments like?
- What rights did English colonists enjoy?

Define
- mercantilism
- import
- export
- triangular trade
- legislature
- bill of rights

Identify
- Navigation Acts
- Yankee
- Glorious Revolution
- English Bill of Rights

SETTING the Scene Philadelphia bustled with activity in 1750. Young farmers drove cattle, pigs, and sheep to market along narrow cobblestone streets. On the docks, sailors unloaded barrels of molasses from the West Indies, wines from Spain and Portugal, Dutch and English cloth, as well as spices, leather goods, tea, and coffee.

Philadelphia was the largest and busiest seaport in the colonies. Yet, by the 1700s, trade flourished all along the Atlantic coast. As trade increased, England began to take a new interest in its colonies.

England Regulates Trade

Like other European nations at the time, England believed that colonies existed for the benefit of the home country. This belief was part of an economic theory known as **mercantilism** (MER kuhn tihl ihz uhm). According to this theory, a nation became strong by building up its gold supply and expanding trade.

Because exports help a country earn money, mercantilists thought that a country should export more than it imports. **Imports** are goods brought into a country. **Exports** are goods sent to markets outside a country.

Beginning in the 1650s, the English Parliament passed a series of **Navigation Acts** that regulated trade between England and its colonies. The purpose of these laws was to ensure that only England benefited from colonial trade.

Under the new laws, only colonial or English ships could carry goods to and from the colonies. The Navigation Acts also listed certain products, such as tobacco and cotton, that colonial merchants could ship only to England. In this way, Parliament created jobs for English workers who cut and rolled tobacco or spun cotton into cloth.

The Navigation Acts helped the colonies as well as England. For example, the law encouraged colonists to build their own ships. As a result, New England became a prosperous shipbuilding center. Also, because of the acts, colonial merchants did not have to compete with foreign merchants because they were sure of having a market for their goods in England.

Still, many colonists resented the Navigation Acts. In their view, the laws favored English merchants. Colonial merchants often ignored the Navigation Acts or found ways to get around them.

Trading in Rum and Slaves

The colonies produced a wide variety of goods, and ships moved up and down the Atlantic coast in an active trade. Merchants from New England dominated colonial trade. They were known as **Yankees,** a nickname that implied they were clever and hard-working. Yankee traders earned a reputation for profiting from any deal.

Colonial merchants developed many trade routes. One route was known as the **triangular trade** because the three legs of the route formed a triangle. On the first leg, ships from New England carried fish, lumber, and other goods to the West Indies. There, Yankee traders bought sugar and molasses, a dark-brown syrup made from sugar cane. The ships then sailed back to New England, where colonists used the molasses and sugar to make rum.

On the second leg of the journey, ships carried rum, guns, gunpowder, cloth, and tools from New England to West Africa. In Africa, merchants traded these goods for slaves. On the final leg, ships carried enslaved Africans to the West Indies. With the profits from selling the enslaved Africans, traders bought more molasses.

Many New England merchants grew wealthy from the triangular trade. In doing so, they often disobeyed the Navigation Acts. Traders were supposed to buy sugar and molasses only from English colonies in the West Indies. However, the demand for molasses

The 13 English Colonies

Colony / Date Founded	Leader	Reasons Founded
New England Colonies		
▪ Massachusetts 　Plymouth / 1620 　Massachusetts Bay / 1630	William Bradford John Winthrop	Religious freedom Religious freedom
▪ New Hampshire / 1622	Ferdinando Gorges John Mason	Profit from trade and fishing
▪ Connecticut / 1636	Thomas Hooker	Expand trade; religious and political freedom
▪ Rhode Island / 1636	Roger Williams	Religious freedom
Middle Colonies		
▪ New York / 1624	Peter Minuit	Expand trade
▪ Delaware / 1638	Swedish settlers	Expand trade
▪ New Jersey / 1664	John Berkeley George Carteret	Expand trade; religious and political freedom
▪ Pennsylvania / 1682	William Penn	Profit from land sales; religious and political freedom
Southern Colonies		
▪ Virginia / 1607	John Smith	Trade and farming
▪ Maryland / 1632	Lord Baltimore	Profit from land sales; religious and political freedom
▪ The Carolinas / 1663 　North Carolina / 1712 　South Carolina / 1712	Group of eight proprietors	Trade and farming; religious freedom
▪ Georgia / 1732	James Oglethorpe	Profit; home for debtors; buffer against Spanish Florida

Chart Skills
English settlers founded 13 separate colonies along the Atlantic coast of North America.

1. **Comprehension** (a) Identify two colonies founded by people seeking religious freedom. (b) Identify two colonies founded to expand trade.
2. **Critical Thinking** How long did it take for England to establish its American colonies?

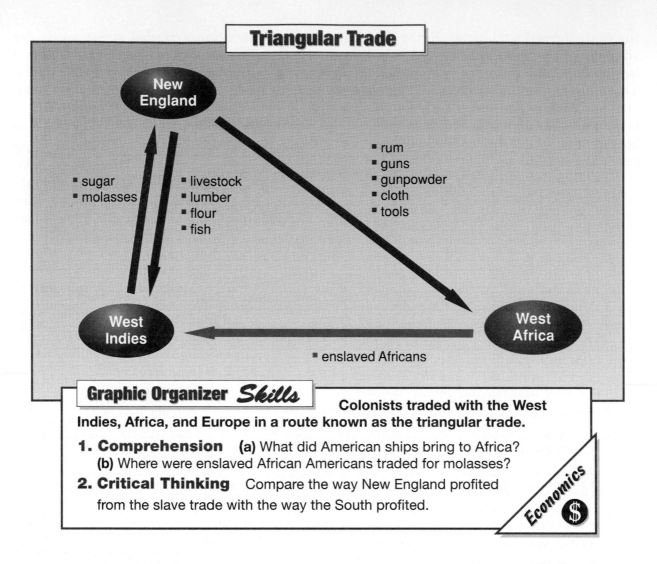

Triangular Trade

- sugar
- molasses

- livestock
- lumber
- flour
- fish

- rum
- guns
- gunpowder
- cloth
- tools

New England

West Indies

West Africa

- enslaved Africans

Graphic Organizer *Skills*

Colonists traded with the West Indies, Africa, and Europe in a route known as the triangular trade.

1. **Comprehension** (a) What did American ships bring to Africa? (b) Where were enslaved African Americans traded for molasses?
2. **Critical Thinking** Compare the way New England profited from the slave trade with the way the South profited.

Economics $

---

was so high that New Englanders smuggled in cargoes from the Dutch, French, and Spanish West Indies, too. Bribes made customs officials look the other way.

Political Life

Although each colony developed its own government, the governments had much in common. A governor directed the colony's affairs and enforced the laws. Most governors were appointed, either by the king or by the colony's proprietor. In Rhode Island and Connecticut, however, colonists elected their own governors.

Elected assemblies

Each colony also had a legislature. A **legislature** is a group of people who have the power to make laws. In most colonies, the legislature had an upper house and a lower house. The upper house was made up of advisers appointed by the governor.

The lower house was an elected assembly. It approved laws and protected the rights of citizens. Just as important, it had the right to approve any taxes the governor asked for. This "power of the purse," or right to raise or spend money, was an important check on the governor's power. Any governor who ignored the assembly risked losing his salary.

The right to vote

Each colony had its own rules about who could vote. By the 1720s, however, all the colonies had laws that restricted the right to vote to white Christian men over the age of 21. In some colonies, only Protestants or members of a particular church could vote. All voters had to own property. Colonial leaders believed that only property owners knew what was best for a colony.

Why Study History?

Because You Have a Say in Government

★ ★

Historical Background

In 1295, King Edward I of England needed money for a war with France. To get the funds, he summoned Parliament, including representatives of the "common people," lords, and clergy. "What touches all should be approved by all," the king said. Over the years, the power of Parliament grew.

The idea of representative government passed on to England's American colonies. In 1619, King James I gave the Virginia colonists the right to form the House of Burgesses. Other colonies developed their own legislatures. Finally, the colonies became the United States of America. The English tradition of electing officials to make laws became the basis of American democracy.

Connections to Today

Today, Americans participate in government at many levels. On the national level, citizens elect representatives to Congress. Each state has its own legislature. In counties, cities, and towns, residents elect councils and boards to pass laws and make regulations. In some small towns, especially in New England, citizens still come together at town meetings to make their own laws.

Connections to You

Representative government affects you in a direct way. Do you attend a public school? If so, an elected school board probably governs your school district. School boards make decisions that affect everything from the books you use to your school's dress code and code of conduct.

You may also participate in representative government right now, by electing or serving on the student council. A student council may seem a long way from the English Parliament. Yet they are part of the same proud tradition.

1. **Comprehension** **(a)** How did the English tradition of representative government come to the colonies? **(b)** List two types of representative government in the United States today.

2. **Critical Thinking** "What touches all should be approved by all," said King Edward I. How do the king's words reflect one basic idea behind representative government?

★**Activity** **Writing a Speech** You have decided to run for a seat on your school's student council. Write a campaign speech. Describe what policies you would support. Explain why other students should elect you to be their representative.

Representative government begins early.

On election day, voters and their families gathered in towns and villages. Smiling candidates shook hands with voters and slapped them heartily on the back. In some areas, they offered to buy them drinks. When things quieted down, the sheriff called the voters together. One by one, he read out their names. Each man announced his vote aloud:

> **66** *Sheriff:* Mr. Blair, whom do you vote for?
> *Mr. Blair:* John Marshall.
> *Mr. Marshall:* Your vote is appreciated, Mr. Blair. **99**

A bill of rights

Colonists took great pride in their elected assemblies. They also valued the rights the Magna Carta gave them as English subjects. (See page 86.)

Colonists won still more rights as a result of the **Glorious Revolution** of 1688. Parliament removed King James II from the throne and asked William and Mary of the Netherlands to rule. In return for Parliament's support, William and Mary signed the **English Bill of Rights** in 1689. A **bill of rights** is a written list of freedoms the government promises to protect.

The English Bill of Rights protected the rights of individuals and gave anyone accused of a crime the right to a trial by jury. Just as important, the English Bill of Rights said that a ruler could not raise taxes or an army without the approval of Parliament.

Limits on liberties

In many ways, English colonists in the Americas enjoyed more freedoms than the English themselves. More ordinary men could vote. Over time, colonial legislatures increased their power.

Still, the rights of English citizens did not extend to everyone in the colonies. Women had more rights in the colonies than in Europe, but far fewer rights than did free white males. A woman's father or husband was supposed to protect her. A married woman could not start her own business or sign a contract unless her husband approved it.

In most colonies, unmarried women and widows had more rights than married women. They could make contracts and sue in court. In Maryland and the Carolinas, women settlers who headed families could buy land on the same terms as men.

Africans and Native Americans in the colonies had almost no rights. Sadly, slavery existed side by side with the English liberties so many colonists held dear. The conflict between liberty and slavery would not be resolved until the 1860s.

★ Section 4 Review ★

Recall

1. **Identify** (a) Navigation Acts, (b) Yankee, (c) Glorious Revolution, (d) English Bill of Rights.
2. **Define** (a) mercantilism, (b) import, (c) export, (d) triangular trade, (e) legislature, (f) bill of rights.

Comprehension

3. List two ways that the Navigation Acts benefited (a) England, and (b) the colonies.

4. How were colonial governments organized?
5. Which colonists had the right to vote?

Critical Thinking and Writing

6. **Predicting Consequences** How do you think the Navigation Acts might affect future relations between England and the colonies? Explain.
7. **Analyzing Ideas** How did colonial legislatures reflect the tradition of self-rule?

Activity **Making a Decision** The time is 1750. You are a young person in Britain looking for success and freedom, so you plan to move to the American colonies. Write a letter to your parents explaining the reasons for your decision.

5 A Changing Colonial Culture

As You Read

Explore These Questions
- What was the Great Awakening?
- How did colonists educate their children?
- How did new ideas spread through the colonies?

Define
- gentry
- middle class
- indentured servant
- public school
- tutor
- apprentice
- dame school
- libel

Identify
- Gullah
- Great Awakening
- Jonathan Edwards
- George Whitefield
- Enlightenment
- Benjamin Franklin
- John Peter Zenger

SETTING the Scene Benjamin Franklin of Philadelphia was a writer, scientist, businessman, and community leader. In 1743, he called on his fellow colonists to expand their cultural horizons:

66 The first drudgery of settling new colonies ... is now pretty well over, and there are many in every province ... [who have time] to cultivate the finer arts, and improve the common stock of knowledge. 99

Franklin invited colonists to join a society to promote "USEFUL KNOWLEDGE." Thus, the American Philosophical Society was born.

Franklin's new society was only one sign that the colonies were coming of age. By the mid-1700s, they had developed a culture that was truly new and American.

Social Classes

For the most part, colonists enjoyed more social equality than people in England did. Still, class differences existed. Like Europeans, colonial Americans thought it was only natural that some people ranked more highly than others.

Powdered wigs like this were the fashion for men of the gentry.

The gentry and the middle class

At the top of society stood the **gentry.** The gentry included wealthy planters, merchants, ministers, successful lawyers, and royal officials. They could afford to dress elegantly in the latest fashions from London.

Below the gentry were the **middle class.** The middle class included farmers who worked their own land, skilled craftsworkers, and some tradespeople. Nearly three quarters of all white colonists belonged to the middle class. They prospered because land in the colonies was plentiful and easy to buy. Also, laborers were in demand, and skilled workers received good wages.

Indentured servants

The lowest social class included hired farmhands, indentured servants, and slaves. **Indentured servants** signed contracts to work without wages for four to seven years for anyone who would pay their ocean passage to the Americas. When their term of service was completed, indentured servants received "freedom dues": a set of clothes, tools, and 50 acres of land. Because there were so few European women in the colonies, female indentured servants often shortened their terms of service by marrying.

New England Mother and Child

Throughout the colonies, women had major household responsibilities such as spinning, preparing meals, and raising children. This 1674 painting shows a mother and daughter in Boston. Generally, the clothing worn by colonial children was just a miniature version of what their parents wore. ★ **What additional duties might a farm woman have?**

◄ *Colonial spinning wheel*

Thousands of men, women, and children came to North America as indentured servants. After completing their terms, some became successful and rose into the middle class.

Women's Work in the Colonies

From New Hampshire to Georgia, colonial women did many of the same tasks. A wife took care of her household, husband, and family. By the kitchen fire, she baked the family's meals. She milked cows, watched the children, and made clothing.

In the backcountry, wives and husbands often worked side by side in the fields at harvest time. With so much to be done, no one worried whether harvesting was proper "woman's work." A visitor described a backcountry woman's activities:

66 She will carry a gunn in the woods and kill deer, turkeys &c., shoot down wild cattle, catch and tye hoggs, knock down [cattle] with an ax, and perform the most manfull Exercises as well as most men. 99

In cities, women sometimes worked outside the home. A young single woman from a poorer family might work as a maid, a cook, or a nurse for one of the gentry. Other women were midwives, delivering babies. Still others sewed fine hats or dresses to be sold to women who could afford them. Learning such skills required many years of training.

Some women learned trades from their fathers, brothers, or husbands. They worked as butchers, shoemakers, or silversmiths. Quite a few women became printers. A woman might take over her husband's business when he died.

African Cultural Influences

By the mid-1700s, the culture of Africans in the colonies varied greatly. On rice plantations in South Carolina, slaves saw few white colonists. As a result, African customs

$ Connections With Economics

In 1733, some women in New York cited their economic achievements in a newspaper notice: "We are house keepers, pay our taxes, carry on trade and most of us are she merchants, and as we . . . contribute to the support of the government, we ought to be entitled to some of the sweets of it."

remained strong. For example, parents often chose African names for their children, such as Quosh or Juba or Cuff. In some coastal areas, African Americans spoke a distinctive combination of English and West African languages, known as **Gullah.**

In Charleston and other South Carolina port towns, more than half the population had African roots. Many of them worked along the docks, making rope or barrels or helping to build ships. Skilled craftsworkers made fine wooden cabinets or silver plates and utensils. Many of their designs reflected African artistic styles. Although most Africans in these towns were enslaved, many opened their own shops or stalls in the market. Some used their earnings to buy their own and their family's freedom.

In Virginia and Maryland, African traditions were weaker. Africans in the Chesapeake region were less isolated from white farmers and planters. Also, by the 1750s, the number of new slaves arriving in the region each year had begun to decline. Even so, many old customs survived. One traveler observed an African-style funeral. Mourners took part in a ceremony to speed a dead man's spirit to his home, which they believed was in Africa.

Fewer Africans lived in the Middle Colonies and New England. Most lived in such cities as Philadelphia, New York, and Newport. Often, the men outnumbered the women. As a result, the number of African families remained small.

The Great Awakening

In the 1730s and 1740s, a religious movement known as the **Great Awakening** swept through the colonies. Its drama and emotion touched women and men of all backgrounds and classes.

Powerful preachers

A New England preacher, **Jonathan Edwards,** set off the Great Awakening. In powerful sermons, Edwards called on colonists, especially young people, to examine their lives. He preached of the sweetness and beauty of God. At the same time, he warned listeners to heed the Bible's teachings. Otherwise, they would be "sinners in the hands of an angry God," headed for the fiery torments of hell. Edwards thundered:

> **66** O sinner! Consider the fearful danger you are in: it is a great furnace of wrath [anger], a wide and bottomless pit.... You hang by a slender thread, with the flames of divine wrath flashing about it, and ready every moment to singe it, and burn it asunder. **99**

In 1739, when an English minister named **George Whitefield** arrived in the colonies, the movement spread like wildfire. Whitefield drew huge crowds to outdoor meetings from Massachusetts to Georgia. His voice rang with feeling as he called on sinners to repent. After hearing Whitefield speak, Jonathan Edwards's wife reported, "I have seen upwards of a thousand people hang on his words with breathless silence, broken only by an occasional half-suppressed sob."

Viewing HISTORY **Preserving African Culture**

In the colonies, African craftsworkers created much fine wooden furniture. Many of their works, such as this detail from a fireplace, were inspired by traditional African designs.
★ **In what colonies did African influences remain strongest?**

Biography — George Whitefield

George Whitefield's preaching drew huge crowds throughout the colonies. One witness reported, "He looked as if he was clothed with authority from the great God, and my hearing him preach gave me a heart wound." Whitefield also encouraged the building of American colleges such as Princeton.

★ **Why did some Americans oppose preachers like Whitefield?**

Impact of the Awakening

The Great Awakening aroused bitter debate. People who supported the movement often split away from their old churches to form new ones. Opponents warned that the movement was too emotional. Still, the growth of so many new churches forced colonists to become more tolerant of people with different beliefs.

The Great Awakening contributed in another way to the spread of democratic feelings in the colonies. Many of the new preachers were not as well educated as most ministers. They argued that book learning was less important than a heart filled with the holy spirit. Such teachings encouraged a spirit of independence. Many believers felt more free to challenge authority when their liberties were at stake. In years to come, many of the same colonists were willing to challenge the authority of British officials.

A Tradition of Education

Among the colonists, New Englanders were the most concerned about education. Puritans taught that all people had a duty to study the Bible. If colonists did not learn to read, how would they fulfill this duty?

New England

In 1647, the Massachusetts assembly passed a law ordering all parents to teach their children "to read and understand the principles of religion." They also required all towns with 50 or more families to hire a schoolteacher. Towns with 100 families or more also had to set up a grammar school to prepare boys for college.

In this way, Massachusetts set up the first **public schools,** or schools supported by taxes. Public schools allowed both rich and poor children to receive an education.

The first New England schools had only one room for students of all ages. Parents paid the schoolteacher with corn, peas, or other foods. Each child was expected to bring a share of wood to burn in the stove. Students who forgot would find themselves seated in the coldest corner of the room!

Middle and Southern Colonies

In the Middle Colonies, churches and individual families set up private schools. Because pupils paid to attend, only wealthy families could afford to educate their children.

In the Southern Colonies, people lived too far from one another to bring children together in one school building. Some planters engaged **tutors,** or private teachers. The wealthiest planters sent their sons to school in England. As a rule, slaves were denied education of any kind.

Apprentices and dame schools

Boys whose parents wished them to learn a trade or craft served as apprentices (uh PREHN tihs ehz). An **apprentice** worked for a master to learn a trade or a craft. For example, when a boy reached age 12 or 13, his parents might apprentice him to a master glassmaker. The young apprentice lived in the glassmaker's home for six or seven years. The glassmaker gave him food and clothing. He was also supposed to teach the boy how to read and write and provide him with religious training.

In return, the apprentice worked without pay in the glassmaker's shop and learned the skills he needed to set up his own shop. Boys were apprenticed in many trades, including papermaking, printing, and tanning.

In New England, some girls attended **dame schools,** or private schools run by women in their own homes. Most schools in the colonies accepted only boys, however. Girls learned skills from their mothers, who taught them to spin wool, weave, and embroider. A few learned to read and write.

An Age of Reason

During the 1600s, European scientists tried to use reason and logic to understand the world. They developed theories and then performed experiments to test them. In doing so, they discovered many laws of nature. The English scientist Isaac Newton, for example, explained the law of gravity.

The Enlightenment spreads

European thinkers of the late 1600s and 1700s believed that reason and scientific methods could be applied to the study of society. They tried to discover the natural laws that governed human behavior. Because these thinkers believed in the light of human reason, the movement that they started is known as the **Enlightenment.**

In the 13 colonies, the Enlightenment spread among better educated colonists. They included wealthy merchants, lawyers, ministers, and others who had the leisure to read the latest books from Europe.

Benjamin Franklin

The best example of the Enlightenment spirit in the 13 colonies was **Benjamin Franklin.** Franklin was born in 1706, the son of a poor Boston soap and candle maker. Although he had only two years of formal schooling, he used his spare time to study literature, mathematics, and foreign languages.

At age 17, Franklin made his way to Philadelphia. There, he built up a successful printing business. His most popular publication was *Poor Richard's Almanac.* Published yearly, it contained useful information and clever quotes, such as "Early to bed, early to rise, makes a man healthy, wealthy, and wise."

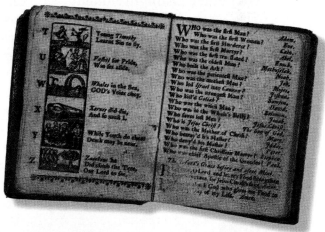

Viewing **HISTORY** **Education in the Colonies**

Education and values were closely linked in the colonies. The picture at left shows apprentices learning beekeeping and carpentry. The writing around the picture praises the value of work. The New England primer, above, taught Bible tales and moral lessons along with the alphabet.

★ **Examine the page from the primer. What moral lesson is taught with the letter Y? What does this suggest about the Puritan attitude toward childhood?**

Colonial Williamsburg

In the 1700s, Williamsburg was one of the most important cities in Virginia. Today, it is one of the state's most popular attractions. As you walk down the restored streets, you can watch people bake bread, print newspapers, or make shoes as they did in colonial times.

★ **To learn more about this historic site, write:** Colonial Williamsburg Foundation, P.O. Box 627, Williamsburg, VA 23187.

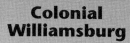

◄ *A wigmaker in Colonial Williamsburg demonstrates her trade.*

Like other Enlightenment thinkers, Franklin wanted to use reason to improve the world around him. He invented practical devices such as a lightning rod, a smokeless fireplace, and bifocal glasses. As a community leader, Franklin persuaded Philadelphia officials to pave streets, organize a fire company, and set up the first lending library in the Americas. Franklin's inventions and his public service earned him worldwide fame.

Colonial Cities and the Spread of Ideas

While most colonists lived on farms, towns and cities strongly influenced colonial life. Through the great ports of Philadelphia, New York, Boston, and Charleston, merchants shipped products overseas. Towns and cities also served as the center of a busy trade between the coast and the growing backcountry.

Culture flourished in the cities. By the mid-1700s, all major colonial cities had their own theaters. City dwellers found entertainment at singing societies, traveling circuses, carnivals, and horse races.

Communication and the growth of newspapers

The growth of colonial cities helped new ideas to spread. The newest ideas from Europe appeared first in city drawing rooms and taverns. In 1704, John Campbell founded the *Boston News-Letter,* the first regular weekly newspaper in the English colonies. Within 50 years, each of the colonies except New Jersey and Delaware had at least one weekly paper.

The growth of colonial newspapers led to a dispute over freedom of the press. **John Peter Zenger** published the *Weekly Journal* in New York City. In 1734, he was arrested for publishing stories that criticized the governor. Zenger was put on trial for **libel,** the act of publishing a statement that may unjustly damage a person's reputation. Zenger's lawyer argued that, since the stories were true, his client had not committed libel. He told the jury:

66 By your verdict, you will have laid a noble foundation for securing to ourselves, our descendants, and our neighbors, the liberty both of exposing and opposing tyrannical power by speaking and writing truth. 99

The jury agreed and freed Zenger. Freedom of the press would later become recognized as a basic American right.

Improved travel

Newspapers often took several months to travel from one colony to another. Travel was often slow and difficult. Roads were rough and muddy, and there were few bridges over streams and rivers. Worst of all, there were no road signs. Most colonists stayed close to home.

Colonists set up a postal system, but it was slow. In 1717, it took one month for a letter to travel from Boston to Williamsburg, Virginia. In the winter, delivery could take twice as long.

As the colonies grew, roads and mail service improved. Families built taverns along main roads and in towns and cities. Travelers stopped to rest and to exchange news and gossip with local people.

Along with the growth of cities, improved travel and communication created an active colonial culture. In cities, large numbers of people exchanged news and ideas that eventually spread throughout the colonies. In the years ahead, these ideas would help shape a revolution.

▲ *Connecticut tavern sign*

★ Section 5 Review ★

Recall

1. **Identify** (a) Gullah, (b) Great Awakening, (c) Jonathan Edwards, (d) George Whitefield, (e) Enlightenment, (f) Benjamin Franklin, (g) John Peter Zenger.
2. **Define** (a) gentry, (b) middle class, (c) indentured servant, (d) public school, (e) tutor, (f) apprentice, (g) dame school, (h) libel.

Comprehension

3. How did the Great Awakening contribute to the spread of democratic feelings in the colonies?

4. Why did the Puritans support public education?
5. In what ways was Benjamin Franklin an example of the Enlightenment spirit?

Critical Thinking and Writing

6. **Making Inferences** Why do you think there was greater social equality in the colonies than in England?
7. **Linking Past and Present** How did New England public schools compare with public schools today?

Activity **Delivering an Editorial** You are a television reporter with a time machine. You have gone back to 1734 to report on the trial of John Peter Zenger. Write and deliver a one-minute editorial explaining why you think he should or should not be found guilty.

★ Sum It Up ★

Section 1 The New England Colonies
▶ The Puritans went to New England to form a society where they could practice their religious beliefs.
▶ Life in New England was based on farming, hunting, and fishing.

Section 2 The Middle Colonies
▶ The Middle Colonies had a diverse mix of people, in part because they offered settlers religious freedom.
▶ The economy of the Middle Colonies was based on farming, but grew to include manufacturing as well.

Section 3 The Southern Colonies
▶ Two distinct ways of life emerged on Tidewater plantations and backcountry farms.
▶ As a plantation economy grew, slavery became firmly established in the Southern Colonies.

Section 4 Governing the Colonies
▶ The British passed laws to control colonial trade.
▶ Democratic traditions grew in the colonies, including representative government and protection of individual rights.

Section 5 A Changing Colonial Culture
▶ The Great Awakening inspired religious feeling and beliefs about equality.
▶ New England offered public education, while schools in the Middle and Southern colonies were usually private.

For additional review of the major ideas of Chapter 4, see *Guide to the Essentials of American History* or *Interactive Student Tutorial CD-ROM,* which contains interactive review activities, graphic organizers, and practice tests.

📖 Reviewing the Chapter

Define These Terms
Match each term with the correct definition.

Column 1
1. toleration
2. patroon
3. debtor
4. mercantilism
5. indentured servant

Column 2
a. owner of a huge estate in New Netherland
b. theory that a nation becomes strong by building its gold supply and expanding trade
c. willingness to let others practice their own beliefs
d. someone who promises to work for four to seven years in exchange for passage
e. someone who owes money

Explore the Main Ideas
1. How did the Fundamental Orders of Connecticut differ from the plan of government in Massachusetts?
2. How did a proprietary colony differ from a royal colony?
3. Why did Catholics and debtors want to move to North America?
4. What rights did English colonists have?
5. Describe the main social classes in the colonies.

🗺 Geography Activity

Match the letters on the map with the following places:
1. New England Colonies, **2.** Middle Colonies, **3.** Southern Colonies, **4.** Massachusetts, **5.** Pennsylvania, **6.** Virginia.
Region Name the five Southern Colonies.

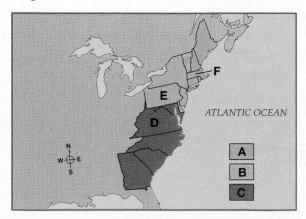

🗂 Critical Thinking and Writing

1. **Analyzing Ideas** "The Puritans came to America in search of religious freedom."
   (a) In what sense is this statement accurate?
   (b) In what sense is this statement inaccurate?

2. **Understanding Chronology (a)** Place the following events in the correct chronological order: Georgia is founded; colonists begin to plant tobacco; Jamestown is founded; Virginia settlers move inland. **(b)** Which of these events was the direct cause of Bacon's Rebellion?

3. **Linking Past and Present** Reread the description of voting in the colonies on page 116. How does it differ from the way Americans vote today?

4. **Exploring Unit Themes Origins** What do you think are the two most important traditions the United States got from England? Explain your reasoning.

🗂 Using Primary Sources

The following notice appeared in Southern newspapers sometime in the 1730s:

> ❝ Ran away some time in June last, from William Pierce of Nansemond County,...a convict servant woman named Winifred Thomas. She is a Welsh woman, short, black-haired and young; marked on the inside of her right arm with gunpowder, W.T., and the date of the year underneath. She knits and spins, and is supposed to be gone into North Carolina by the way of Cureatuck and Roanoke Inlet. Whoever brings her to her master shall be paid a [gold coin] besides what the law allows. ❞

Source: *A Documentary History of American Industrial Society*, 1910.

Recognizing Points of View (a) What is the purpose of this advertisement? **(b)** Based on your reading, was Winifred Thomas a slave or an indentured servant? **(c)** What was Pierce's attitude toward Thomas?

ACTIVITY BANK

▶ Interdisciplinary Activity

Exploring Sciences Do research on the inventions of Benjamin Franklin. Create a display that explains how one of his inventions worked.

▶ Career Skills Activity

Playwrights Read more about the life of women in the British colonies. Write a short play in which a city woman, a backcountry woman, and the mistress of a plantation meet and compare their lives.

▶ Citizenship Activity

Learning About Education In this chapter you read about the beginnings of public education. One of the responsibilities of citizens is being informed about education in the community. Arrange to visit a meeting of a local school board or parent-teacher association. Write a report on your visit.

▶ Internet Activity

Use the Internet to find sites dealing with William Penn. After you have done research to find out more about him, write a letter from Penn to the President of the United States today, advising the President on how to handle some of the challenges facing our nation. Use information from your research in your letter.

EYEWITNESS Journal

You are a Puritan, a Pennsylvania Quaker, a plantation owner, or an enslaved African American. In your EYEWITNESS JOURNAL, describe a visit to another region in the British colonies and compare it with your own. Remember, your own viewpoint will be influenced by the colony in which you live.

History Through Literature

Hiawatha the Unifier

Iroquois Folk Tale

Introduction

People who accomplish heroic deeds often become the subject of legends. The following tale is a legend about Hiawatha. According to Iroquois tradition, Hiawatha helped form the League of the Iroquois around 1570. The following traditional tale appeared in a collection called *American Indian Myths and Legends*.

Vocabulary

Before you read the selection, find the meanings of these words in a dictionary: **untutored, eternal, devastation, tranquil, counselors, orators, recoil, strife, innumerable.**

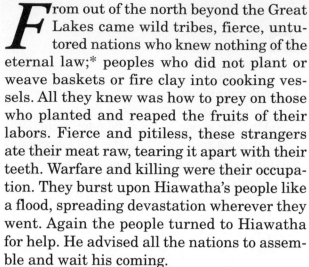

From out of the north beyond the Great Lakes came wild tribes, fierce, untutored nations who knew nothing of the eternal law;* peoples who did not plant or weave baskets or fire clay into cooking vessels. All they knew was how to prey on those who planted and reaped the fruits of their labors. Fierce and pitiless, these strangers ate their meat raw, tearing it apart with their teeth. Warfare and killing were their occupation. They burst upon Hiawatha's people like a flood, spreading devastation wherever they went. Again the people turned to Hiawatha for help. He advised all the nations to assemble and wait his coming.

And so the five tribes came together at the place of the great council fire, by the shores of a large and tranquil lake where the wild men from the north had not yet penetrated. The people waited for Hiawatha one day, two days, three days. On the fourth day his gleaming white magic canoe appeared, floating, gliding above the mist....

When the sachems, elders, and wise men had seated themselves in a circle around the sacred fire, Hiawatha came before them and said:

"My children, war, fear, and disunity have brought you from your villages to this sacred council fire. Facing a common danger, and fearing for the lives of your families, you have yet drifted apart, each tribe thinking and acting only for itself. Remember how I took you from one small band and nursed you up into many nations. You must reunite now and act as one. No tribe alone can withstand our savage enemies, who care nothing about the eternal law, who sweep upon us like the storms of winter, spreading death and destruction everywhere.

"My children, listen well. Remember that you are brothers, that the downfall of one means the downfall of all. You must have one fire, one pipe, one war club....

"Onondagas, you are a tribe of mighty warriors. Your strength is like that of a giant pine tree whose roots spread far and deep so that it can withstand any storm. Be you the protectors. You shall be the first nation.

---

*The eternal law refers to the need to keep a balance between people and nature.

"Oneida, your men are famous for their wisdom. Be you the counselors of the tribes. You shall be the second nation.

"Seneca, you are swift of foot and persuasive in speech. Your men are the greatest orators among the tribes. Be you the spokesmen. You shall be the third people.

"Cayuga, you are the most cunning. You are the most skilled in the building and managing of canoes. Be you the guardians of our rivers. You shall be the fourth nation.

"Mohawk, you are foremost in planting corn and beans and in building longhouses. Be you the nourishers.

"Your tribes must be like the five fingers of a warrior's hand joined in gripping the war club. Unite as one, and then your enemies will recoil before you back into the northern wastes from whence they came. Let my words sink deep into your hearts and minds. Retire now to take counsel among yourselves, and come to me tomorrow to tell me whether you will follow my advice."

On the next morning the sachems and wise men came to Hiawatha with the promise that they would from that day on be as one nation. Hiawatha rejoiced. He gathered up the dazzling white feathers which the great mystery bird of the sky had dropped and gave the plumes to the leaders of the assembled tribes. "By these feathers," he said, "you shall be known as the Ako-no-shu-ne: the Iroquois." Thus with the help of Hiawatha, the Great Unifier, the mighty League of the Five Nations was born and its tribes held sway undisturbed over all the land between the great river of the west and the great sea of the east.

The elders begged Hiawatha to become the chief sachem of the united tribes, but he told them: "This can never be, because I must

Viewing HISTORY **Cap of an Iroquois Leader**
Wooden caps like this one were traditionally worn by important members of the Iroquois League. The six-sided design on the band may symbolize the six nations that belonged to the League after the Tuscarora joined. ★ **What was the chief purpose of the Iroquois League?**

leave you. Friends and brothers, choose the wisest women in your tribes to be the future clan mothers and peacemakers. Let them turn any strife rising among you into friendship. Let your sachems be wise enough to go to such women for advice when there are disputes. Now I have finished speaking. Farewell."

At that moment there came to those assembled the sweet sound like the rush of rustling leaves and the song of innumerable birds. Hiawatha stepped into his white mystery canoe, and instead of gliding away on the waters of the lake, it rose slowly into the sky and disappeared into the clouds. Hiawatha was gone, but his teachings survive in the hearts of the people.

Analyzing Literature

1. Why did the Five Nations seek Hiawatha's help?
2. According to Hiawatha, why was each of the Five Nations important to the League as a whole?
3. **Synthesizing Information** (a) What final advice did Hiawatha give the sachems? (b) Based on your reading, did they follow this advice?

Unit 2 A Nation Is Born

Viewing UNIT THEMES

Freedom of Religion: A Basic American Right

Since colonial days, American women have used the craft of quilt-making to express their values and depict their daily life. This detail from a New England quilt from the late 1700s portrays a church as the center of the community. Americans of the time expected their new government to safeguard freedom of religion. ★ **List two other freedoms that Americans enjoy.**

Unit Theme Rights and Liberties

In 1776, the 13 colonies declared their independence from Britain. One major reason was colonists' belief that Britain had violated their basic rights.

Later, American leaders worked to create a government. Many people in the United States demanded that the new government protect basic liberties, such as freedom of religion, freedom of the press, and the right to trial by jury.

How did Americans of the time feel about basic rights and liberties? They can tell you in their own words.

★ ★

VIEWPOINTS ON RIGHTS AND LIBERTIES

❝ If we separate from Britain, what code of laws will be established? How shall we be governed so as to retain our liberties? ❞
Abigail Adams, wife of John Adams (1775)

❝ By reason of long bondage and hard slavery, we have been deprived of the profits of our labor or the advantage of inheriting estates from our parents as our neighbors the white people do. ❞
Paul Cuffe, African American ship owner (1783)

❝ Were it left to me to decide whether we should have a government without newspapers, or newspapers without a government, I should not hesitate a moment to prefer the latter. ❞
Thomas Jefferson, Virginia political leader (1787)

★ ★

Activity Writing to Learn Turn to the First Amendment in the Reference Section and read the Constitution. List the freedoms guaranteed by the First Amendment. Then, choose one of those freedoms. Write a skit showing what life might be like if that freedom were not protected.

Chapter 5

The Road to Revolution

1745–1775

Between 1754 and 1760, competition for land led to a conflict between England and France that is now known as the French and Indian War. The British, with the help of American colonists and Indian allies, put an end to French power in North America.

After the war, Britain angered colonists by taxing them without giving them representation in Parliament. Over the next years, colonial protests grew stronger. Finally, in April 1775, British troops and colonial farmers clashed at the villages of Lexington and Concord in Massachusetts. The battles marked the start of the American Revolution.

Why Study History?

"Taxation without representation is tyranny!" This protest sparked a revolution in the 13 colonies. Today, American citizens have representation. Still, attempts to raise taxes always stir heated debate. To focus on this connection, look at the *Why Study History?* feature, "You Pay Taxes," in this chapter.

American Events

1740s
Settlers cross
Appalachian
Mountains

1754
French and
Indian War begins

1759
British capture of
French Quebec is
turning point
of war

1745   1750   1755   1760

World Events

1748 World Event
Britain and France fight for
control of trade in India

1756 World Event
Seven Years' War begins
in Europe

 Viewing HISTORY

Protests in the Colonies

This 1774 engraving, The Bostonians Paying the Exciseman, *shows American colonists who have just tarred and feathered a British tax collector. While they force tea down the tax collector's throat, other colonists throw chests of British tea into Boston harbor. Violent protests like this one contributed to a split between Britain and its American colonists.* ★ **Do you think the artist who created this engraving had a favorable view of the Americans? Give reasons for your answer.**

1763
Proclamation
of 1763 closes
western lands to
further settlement

1773
Colonists stage
Boston Tea Party
to protest taxes

1775
Fighting breaks
out at Concord
and Lexington

| 1760 | 1765 | 1770 | 1775 |

1763 World Event
Treaty of Paris ends French
power in North America

1773 World Event
British Parliament passes
Tea Act

Rivalry in North America

As You Read

Explore These Questions
- What European nations competed for land in North America?
- Why did the French build a system of forts?
- Why did Indian nations become involved in the struggle between France and England?

Identify
- Hurons
- Joseph Brant

SETTING the Scene In June 1749, the governor of New France sent a group of men down the Ohio River. The men stopped from time to time to nail an engraved lead plate to a tree or to set one in the ground. These plates proclaimed that the fertile land of the Ohio Valley belonged to France.

About the same time, Christopher Gist, a Virginia fur trader, was also roaming the Ohio Valley. Gist worked for the Ohio Company, a group of English investors. King George II had given the company a huge tract of land in the valley. They sent Gist to find a good spot for settlement.

Gist chose a site where the Ohio and Allegheny rivers meet. On a rock beside the water, he carved these words:

> The Ohio Company
> FEBy 1751
> By Christopher Gist

Clearly, with two great powers claiming the same land, the stage was set for conflict. At stake was more than control of the Ohio River valley. France and England each hoped to drive the other nation out of North America altogether.

Competing Claims

By the mid-1700s, the major powers of Europe were locked in a worldwide struggle for empire. England, France, Spain, and the Netherlands competed for trade and colonies in far-flung corners of the globe. The English colonies in North America soon became caught up in the contest.

By the late 1600s, England had already taken over New York from the Dutch. Its two remaining rivals in North America were Spain and France. The major threat from Spain was in the West Indies and along the border between Georgia and Spanish Florida. England and Spain clashed often in these areas.

Spain also had settlements in present-day New Mexico, Texas, and Arizona. However, these settlements were located far away from England's colonies on the Atlantic coast. As a result, the English paid little attention to them.

The threat from France was much more serious to the English colonies. France claimed a vast area that stretched from the St. Lawrence River westward to the Great Lakes and southward to the Gulf of Mexico. To protect their land claims, the French built an extensive system of forts. (See the map on page 133.)

Connections With Geography

As the French explored and settled North American lands, they gave French names to forts, towns, and natural features. Familiar examples of these French names include *Detroit* (narrow water passage), *Des Moines* (belonging to the monks), *Baton Rouge* (red stick), and *Vermont* (green mountain).

Conflict in the Ohio Valley

At first, most English settlers were content to remain along the Atlantic coast. By the 1740s, however, traders from New York and Pennsylvania were crossing the Appalachian Mountains in search of furs. Pushing into the Ohio Valley, they tried to take over the profitable French trade with the Indians.

France was determined to stop the English from intruding on their territory. The Ohio River was especially important to the French because it provided a vital link between their lands in Canada and the Mississippi River. In 1751, the French government sent the following orders to its officials in New France:

66 Drive from the Ohio River any European foreigners, and do it in a way that will make them lose all taste for trying to return. 99

Native Americans Choose Sides

Native Americans had hunted animals and grown crops in the Ohio Valley for centuries. They did not want to give up the land to European settlers, French or English. One Native American protested to an English trader:

66 You and the French are like the two edges of a pair of shears. And we are the cloth which is to be cut to pieces between them. 99

Still, the growing conflict between England and France was too dangerous to ignore. Some Native Americans decided that the only way to protect their way of life was to take sides in the struggle.

Allies for the French

At the same time, both France and England tried to make Indian allies. The French expected the Indians to side with them. Most French in North America were trappers and traders, not farmers like the English. The French generally did not destroy Indian hunting grounds by clearing forests for

North America in 1753

Geography Skills In 1753, France and Spain claimed land to the north, south, and west of the 13 English colonies.

1. **Location** On the map, locate: **(a)** New France, **(b)** Louisiana, **(c)** Florida, **(d)** Mississippi River, **(e)** Ohio River.

2. **Region** Which nation controlled Florida in 1753?

3. **Critical Thinking** Note the location of the French forts in 1753. Why do you think France built forts at these locations?

farms. Also, many French trappers married Native American women and adopted their ways.

France built strong alliances with several Native American groups. As you read, the French gained the support of the Algonquins. (See page 83.) They also built friendly relations with the **Hurons.** The Hurons often served as negotiators between French traders and other Indian nations.

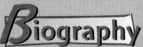 **Joseph Brant**

Known to the British as Joseph Brant, the Mohawk chief Thayendanegea was a valuable ally. He helped persuade the Iroquois nations to side with Britain in their struggle against the French. In later years, Brant became a Christian and helped translate the Bible into the Mohawk language. ★ **How does this painting show that Brant combined Native American and English cultures?**

Allies for the English

In contrast to the French, English settlers were mostly farm families. They ignored Indian rights when they cleared land for crops. Nor did they respect Indian ways. As the English moved onto their lands, the Indians fought back.

Still, in the end, England also found allies among Native Americans. The English won over the powerful Iroquois nations, who were old enemies of the Algonquins and the Hurons.

An English trader and official, William Johnson, helped gain Iroquois support for England. The Iroquois respected Johnson, and they listened carefully when he urged them to side with the English. Johnson was one of the few English settlers who had an Indian wife, Molly Brant. She was the sister of the Mohawk chief Thayendanegea, known to the English as **Joseph Brant.** Brant became a valuable ally for the English.

Some Indians supported the English because they charged lower prices for trade goods than the French did. Many Indians began to buy goods from English rather than French traders. The loss of Indian trade angered the French, who were determined to defend their claims in the Ohio Valley.

★ **Section 1 Review** ★

Recall

1. **Identify** (a) Hurons, (b) Joseph Brant.

Comprehension

2. Who were England's two main rivals in North America?
3. What steps did France take to protect its lands in North America?
4. (a) Why did the French expect Native Americans to side with them? (b) Why did some Indians side with the English?

Critical Thinking and Writing

5. **Applying Information** How did the rivalry among England, France, and Spain in North America reflect their worldwide struggle for power?
6. **Recognizing Points of View** Reread the statement by the Native American to the English trader on page 133. (a) What did the speaker mean by these words? (b) Do you think he felt that Native Americans could hold out against the British and French? Explain.

★ ★

Activity **Writing a Speech** You are William Johnson. Write a speech in which you explain to the Iroquois why they should help the English instead of the French.

The French and Indian War

★ ★

Explore These Questions

As You Read

- Why did the British and French go to war in North America?
- What advantages did each side have in the war?
- How did the Treaty of Paris affect North America?

Identify

- George Washington
- French and Indian War
- Albany Plan of Union
- Edward Braddock
- William Pitt
- James Wolfe
- Marquis de Montcalm
- Plains of Abraham
- Treaty of Paris

SETTING the Scene Captain Joncaire had just sat down to dinner on December 4, 1753, when a tall young man strode into the room. He introduced himself as Major **George Washington.** He said he had a letter from the English lieutenant governor of Virginia, Robert Dinwiddie, to the commander of the French forces in the Ohio Valley.

Joncaire told his visitor where the commander could be found. The captain then politely invited Washington to dine. As they ate, Joncaire boasted that France was determined to take full possession of the Ohio River valley. The remark made Washington pause. He knew that in the letter he was carrying, Dinwiddie warned the French to get out of the Ohio Valley!

For years, tensions had been building between the French and the English. By the 1750s, armed conflict seemed certain. The war that followed would forever change the balance of power in North America.

Fighting Begins

Three times between 1689 and 1748, France and Great Britain* had fought for power in Europe and North America. Each war ended with an uneasy peace.

---

* In 1707, England and Scotland were officially joined into the United Kingdom of Great Britain. After that date, the terms *Great Britain* and *British* were used to describe the country and its people. However, the terms *England* and *English* were still used throughout much of the 1700s.

In 1754, fighting broke out for a fourth time. The struggle that followed lasted until 1760. English settlers called the conflict the **French and Indian War** because it pitted them against France and its Native American allies.

Scuffles between France and Britain in the Ohio River valley triggered the opening shots of the French and Indian War. Young George Washington played a major role in this early phase of the conflict.

George Washington

At the time, George Washington was only 22 years old, but he was an able and brave soldier. Washington had grown up on a plantation in Virginia, the son of wealthy parents. Gifted at mathematics, he began working as a land surveyor at the age of 15. His job took him to frontier lands in western Virginia. In 1753, when Lieutenant Governor Dinwiddie wanted to warn the French out of Ohio, Washington offered to deliver the message. On this dangerous mission, the young officer narrowly escaped death.

After Washington returned, Dinwiddie promoted him to colonel. He also sent the young man west again. At the time, some wealthy Virginians claimed land in the upper Ohio Valley. To protect their claims, they urged the governor of Virginia to build a fort where the Monongahela and Allegheny rivers meet. (See the map on page 138.) Dinwiddie ordered Washington to take a party of 150 men and build the fort.

Conflict at Fort Necessity

In April 1754, Washington and his party headed for Ohio country. Along the way, they heard that the French had just completed Fort Duquesne (doo KAYN) at the fork of the Monongahela and Allegheny rivers. This was the very spot where Dinwiddie had ordered Washington to build a fort.

Determined to carry out his orders, Washington journeyed on. Indian allies revealed that a French scouting party was camped in the woods ahead. Marching quietly through the night, Washington surprised and scattered the French.

Washington's success was short-lived, however. Hearing that the French were plan-ning to counterattack, he and his men quickly built a makeshift stockade. They named it Fort Necessity. A huge force of French and Indians surrounded the fort. Trapped and heavily outnumbered, the Virginians were forced to surrender. Soon after, the French released Washington, and he returned home to Virginia.

Despite Washington's defeat, the British quickly saw the importance of the skirmish. "The volley fired by this young Virginian in the forests of America," a British writer noted, "has set the world in flames."

The Albany Congress

While Washington was defending Fort Necessity, delegates from seven colonies gathered in Albany, New York. The delegates to the Albany Congress met for two reasons. They wanted to persuade the Iroquois to help them against the French. They also wanted to plan a united colonial defense.

The Iroquois refuse

Iroquois leaders listened patiently to the delegates, but they were wary of the request for help. The British and French "are quarreling about lands which belong to us," pointed out Hendrik, a Mohawk chief. "And such a quarrel as this may end in our destruction." In addition, the Iroquois believed that the French were stronger and had more forts than the British.

In the end, the Iroquois left without agreeing to help the British. At the same time, they did not join the French either.

Franklin's plan of union

The delegates in Albany knew that the colonists had to work together to defeat the French. Benjamin Franklin, the delegate from Pennsylvania, proposed the **Albany Plan of Union.** The plan was an attempt to create "one general government" for the 13 colonies. It called for a Grand Council made up of representatives from each colony. The council would make laws, raise taxes, and set up the defense of the colonies.

The delegates voted to accept the Plan of Union. When the plan was submitted to the colonial assemblies, however, not one ap-

*B*iography George Washington

Like many wealthy young Virginians, George Washington enjoyed dancing and horseback riding. At the same time, he worked hard managing the family plantation and later as a surveyor. After his defeats in the French and Indian War, Washington wrote, "I have been on the losing [side] ever since I entered the service." Little did he know that he would one day lead his country to independence.
★ **List two facts you know about Washington.**

proved it. None of the colonies wanted to give up any of its powers to a central council. The largest colony, Virginia, had not even sent a delegation to the Albany Congress! A disappointed Benjamin Franklin expressed his frustration at the failure of his plan:

66 Everyone cries a union is necessary. But when they come to the manner and form of the union, their weak noodles are perfectly distracted. 99

The Two Sides

At the start of the French and Indian War, the French had several advantages over the British. Because the English colonies could not agree on a united defense, 13 separate colonial assemblies had to approve all decisions. New France, on the other hand, had a single government that could act quickly when necessary. Also, the French had the support of many more Indian allies than the British did.

Britain, however, also had strengths. At the time, the population of the English colonies was about 15 times greater than that of New France. The English colonies were clustered along the coast, so they were easier to defend than the widely scattered French settlements. In addition, while most Indians sided with the French, the British did have some Indian allies. Finally, the British navy ruled the seas.

Early English Defeats

In 1755, General **Edward Braddock** led British and colonial troops in an attack against Fort Duquesne. Braddock was a stubborn man, called "Bulldog" behind his back. He knew how to fight a war in the open fields of Europe. However, he knew little about how to fight in the wilderness of North America. Still, the general boasted that he would sweep the French from the Ohio Valley.

Disaster for "Bulldog" Braddock

Braddock's men moved slowly because they had to clear a road through thick forests for their cannons and other heavy gear. George Washington, who went with Braddock, was upset by the slow pace. Indian scouts warned Braddock that he was headed for trouble. He ignored them.

As the British neared Fort Duquesne, the French and their Indian allies launched a surprise attack. Sharpshooters hid in the forest and picked off British soldiers, whose bright-red uniforms made them easy targets. Washington later wrote to his mother:

66 Our [forces] consisted of about 1,300 well-armed troops, chiefly of the English soldiers, who were struck with such a panic that they behaved with more cowardice than it is possible to conceive. The officers behaved gallantly in order to encourage their

JOIN, or DIE.

Viewing HISTORY ▶ A Call for Union

In 1754, Benjamin Franklin printed this famous cartoon in the Pennsylvania Gazette. *That year, Franklin drew up the Albany Plan of Union. However, his hopes for political unity among the 13 colonies did not succeed.*

★ **Summarize the main point of Franklin's cartoon in your own words.**

◀ *Model of Ben Franklin*

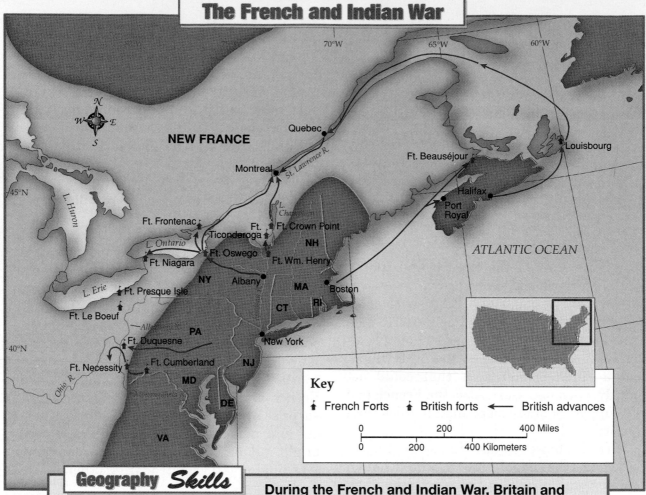

The French and Indian War

NEW FRANCE

L. Huron

Quebec

Ft. Beauséjour

Louisbourg

Montreal

St. Lawrence R.

Halifax

Port Royal

L. Champlain

Ft. Frontenac

Ft. Crown Point

Ft. Ticonderoga

L. Ontario

Ft. Oswego

NH

ATLANTIC OCEAN

Ft. Niagara

Ft. Wm. Henry

L. Erie

NY

Albany

MA

Ft. Presque Isle

CT

RI

Boston

Ft. Le Boeuf

Allegheny

PA

Ft. Duquesne

New York

Ohio R.

Ft. Necessity

Ft. Cumberland

NJ

MD

Monongahela R.

DE

VA

Key

French Forts   British forts   ◄—— British advances

0   200   400 Miles

0   200   400 Kilometers

Geography Skills

During the French and Indian War, Britain and France battled for control of North America. The conflict began in the Ohio River valley.

1. **Location**   On the map, locate: **(a)** Fort Necessity, **(b)** Fort Duquesne, **(c)** Louisbourg, **(d)** Quebec, **(e)** Albany.

2. **Movement**   About how many miles did advancing British forces travel from Louisbourg to Quebec?

3. **Critical Thinking**   Based on the map, do you think naval power was important in fighting the French and Indian War? Explain.

men, for which they suffered greatly, there being nearly 60 killed or wounded—a large proportion out of the number we had! **99**

Braddock himself had five horses shot out from under him before he fell, fatally injured. Washington was luckier. He later reported that he "escaped without a wound, although I had four bullets through my coat."

Almost half the British were killed or wounded. Washington and other survivors returned to Virginia with news of Braddock's defeat. Washington was now put in command of a small force of men. For the rest of the war, he had the almost impossible task of guarding the long Virginia frontier against Indian attack.

Further British setbacks

During the next two years, the war continued to go badly for the British. British attacks against several French forts ended in failure. Meanwhile, the French won important victories, capturing Fort Oswego on Lake Ontario and Fort William Henry on

Skills FOR LIFE

Critical Thinking	Managing Information	Communication	Maps, Charts, and Graphs

Reading a Time Line

How Will I Use This Skill?

A time line is a graphic organizer that lists events in chronological, or time, order. Using a time line can help you understand sequences and see relationships between events. You might find time lines, not only in history books, but also in magazine and newspaper articles about current events.

LEARN the Skill

At the start of each chapter in this book, you will find a two-page horizontal time line. It is organized from left to right, with the earliest date on the left. Some events may take place over several years. This will be indicated on the time line.

Time lines are divided into equal time periods. The total period of time from beginning to end is called the time span. Use the following steps to read a time line:

❶ Look at the first and last dates on the time line to determine the complete time span.

❷ Notice the intervals, or divisions, on the time line.

❸ Look at the specific events and dates listed.

❹ Determine if there is any relationship between events.

PRACTICE the Skill

Use the time line below to answer the following questions.

❶ (a) What is the earliest event shown? (b) What is the latest event? (c) What is the time span of the time line?

❷ How many years are there between dates on the time line?

❸ (a) What took place in 1755? (b) When did the fighting in North America end?

❹ (a) How would you describe the success of the British in the early years of the war? (b) What relation did the events of 1758 have to the events of 1760?

APPLY the Skill

Make a time line of important events in your life. Use your life up to this point as the time span. Include at least six events that you feel made a major difference in your life.

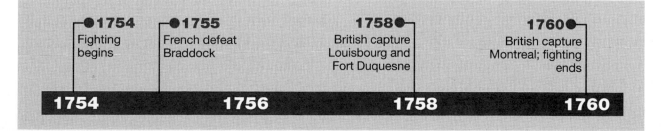

●1754 Fighting begins	●1755 French defeat Braddock	1758● British capture Louisbourg and Fort Duquesne	1760● British capture Montreal; fighting ends
1754	**1756**	**1758**	**1760**

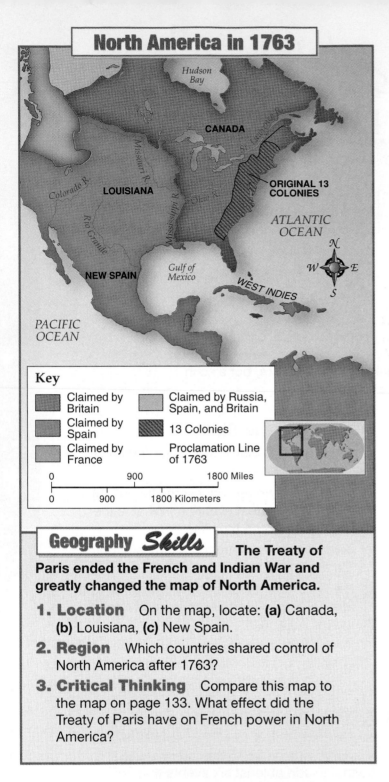

North America in 1763

Key

■ Claimed by Britain
■ Claimed by Spain
□ Claimed by France
■ Claimed by Russia, Spain, and Britain
▨ 13 Colonies
— Proclamation Line of 1763

0   900   1800 Miles
0   900   1800 Kilometers

Geography Skills

The Treaty of Paris ended the French and Indian War and greatly changed the map of North America.

1. **Location** On the map, locate: **(a)** Canada, **(b)** Louisiana, **(c)** New Spain.

2. **Region** Which countries shared control of North America after 1763?

3. **Critical Thinking** Compare this map to the map on page 133. What effect did the Treaty of Paris have on French power in North America?

are the Head, and we are the Tail. . . . What will become of us God only knows. **99**

The Tide of Battle Turns

In 1757, **William Pitt** became the new head of the British government. Pitt was a bold leader. "I believe that I can save this nation and that no one else can," he declared with great confidence.

Pitt set out to win the war in North America. Once that goal was achieved, he argued, the British would be free to focus on victory in other parts of the world.* Pitt sent Britain's best generals to North America. To encourage colonists to support the war, he promised large payments for military services and supplies.

Under Pitt's leadership, the tide of battle turned. In 1758, Major General Jeffrey Amherst captured Louisbourg, the most important fort in French Canada. That year, the British also won more Iroquois support.

The Iroquois persuaded the Delawares at Fort Duquesne to abandon the French. Without the Delawares, the French could no longer hold the fort. Acting quickly, the British seized Fort Duquesne, which they renamed Fort Pitt after the British leader. The city of Pittsburgh later grew up on the site of Fort Pitt.

The Fall of New France

The British enjoyed even greater success in 1759. By summer, they had pushed the French from Fort Niagara, Crown Point, and Fort Ticonderoga (ti kahn duh ROH guh). Now, Pitt sent General **James Wolfe** to take Quebec, capital of New France.

Battle for Quebec

Quebec was vital to the defense of New France. Without Quebec, the French would be unable to supply their forts farther up the St. Lawrence River. Quebec was well de-

Lake George. (See the map on page 138.) To English colonists, the situation looked grim. In the words of Massachusetts minister Jonathan Edwards:

66 God indeed is remarkably frowning upon us every where; our enemies get up above us very high, and we are brought down very low: They

---

* By 1756, fighting between the French and British had broken out in Europe. There, it became known as the Seven Years' War. The British and the French also fought in India. In the early years of the war, the British suffered setbacks on every front.

fended, though. The city sat atop a steep cliff high above the St. Lawrence. An able French general, the **Marquis de Montcalm,** was prepared to fight off any British attack.

General Wolfe devised a bold plan to capture Quebec. He knew that Montcalm had only a few soldiers guarding the cliff because the French thought that it was too steep to climb. Late one night, Wolfe ordered British troops to move quietly in small boats to the foot of the cliff. Under cover of darkness, the soldiers swarmed ashore and scrambled to the top.

The next morning, Montcalm awakened to some shocking news. A force of 4,000 British troops were drawn up on the **Plains of Abraham,** a grassy field just outside the city.

Montcalm quickly marched out his own troops to meet the enemy. A fierce battle followed. When it was over, both Montcalm and Wolfe were dead. Moments before Wolfe died, a soldier gave him the news that the British had won. Wolfe reportedly whispered, "Now, God be praised, I will die in peace." On September 18, 1759, Quebec surrendered to the British.

Treaty of Paris

The fall of Quebec sealed the fate of New France. In 1760, the British took Montreal, and the war in North America ended. Fighting dragged on in Europe for several more years. Finally, in 1763, Britain and France signed the **Treaty of Paris,** officially bringing the long conflict to an end.

The Treaty of Paris marked the end of French power in North America. Under the treaty, Britain gained Canada and all French lands east of the Mississippi River. France was allowed to keep two islands in the Gulf of St. Lawrence, as well as its rich sugar-growing islands in the West Indies. Spain, which had entered the war on the French side in 1762, gave up Florida to Britain. In return, Spain received all French land west of the Mississippi. In addition, Spain gained the vital port city of New Orleans. Spain retained control of its vast empire in Central and South America.

After years of fighting, peace returned to North America. Yet, in a few short years, a new conflict would break out. This time, the struggle would pit Britain against its own 13 colonies.

★ Section 2 Review ★

Recall

1. **Locate** (a) Fort Necessity, (b) Fort Duquesne, (c) Louisbourg, (d) Quebec.
2. **Identify** (a) George Washington, (b) French and Indian War, (c) Albany Plan of Union, (d) Edward Braddock, (e) William Pitt, (f) James Wolfe, (g) Marquis de Montcalm, (h) Plains of Abraham, (i) Treaty of Paris.

Comprehension

3. What were the causes of the French and Indian War?
4. (a) List two strengths of the French in the French and Indian War. (b) List two strengths of the British.
5. (a) What lands did Britain gain under the Treaty of Paris? (b) How did the treaty affect French power in North America?

Critical Thinking and Writing

6. **Analyzing Ideas** (a) How would the Albany Plan of Union have helped the colonies fight the French? (b) Why do you think colonists rejected the Plan of Union?
7. **Linking Past and Present** How might your life be different if France, not England, had won the French and Indian War?

★ ★

Activity **Creating a Battle Plan** You are a British commander at the start of the French and Indian War. You know all of your strengths and weaknesses and those of your enemy. Examine the map on page 138. Then, write up a brief statement explaining why you think you should attack the French fort at Louisbourg.

A Crisis Over Taxes

As
You
Read

**Explore
These Questions**

- What was the goal of the Proclamation of 1763?
- How did colonists protest British taxes?
- What was the Boston Massacre?

Define

- petition
- boycott
- repeal
- writ of assistance
- nonimportation agreement
- committee of correspondence

Identify

- Pontiac's War
- Proclamation of 1763
- Stamp Act
- Townshend Acts
- Sons of Liberty
- Daughters of Liberty
- Samuel Adams
- John Adams
- Mercy Otis Warren
- Patrick Henry
- Boston Massacre

SETTING the Scene As Britain celebrated the victory over France, a few officials expressed concern. Now that the French were no longer a threat, would the 13 colonies become too independent? Might they even unite one day against Britain? Benjamin Franklin scoffed at such an idea. He recalled the failure of the colonies to agree to his Albany Plan of Union:

66 If [the colonies] could not agree to unite for their defense against the French and Indians, . . . can it reasonably be supposed there is any danger of their uniting against their own nation? . . . I will venture to say, a union amongst them for such a purpose is not merely improbable, it is impossible. 99

Franklin was wrong. After the French and Indian War, new British policies toward the colonies aroused angry cries from Massachusetts to Georgia. Despite their differences, colonists began to move toward unity.

New Troubles on the Frontier

By 1760, the British had driven France from the Ohio Valley. Their troubles in the region were not over, however. For many years, fur traders had sent back glowing reports of the land beyond the Appalachian Mountains. With the French gone, English colonists eagerly headed west to claim the lands for themselves.

Clashes with Native Americans

Many Native American nations lived in the Ohio Valley. They included the Senecas, Delawares, Shawnees, Ottawas, Miamis, and Hurons. As British settlers moved into the valley, they often clashed with these Native Americans.

In 1762, the British sent Lord Jeffrey Amherst to the frontier to keep order. French traders had always treated Native Americans as friends, holding feasts for them and giving them presents. Amherst refused to do this. Instead, he raised the price of goods traded to Indians. Also, unlike the French, Amherst allowed English settlers to build farms and forts on Indian lands.

Discontented Native Americans found a leader in Pontiac, an Ottawa chief who had fought on the side of the French. An English trader remarked that Pontiac "commands more respect amongst these nations than any Indian I ever saw." In April 1763, Pontiac spoke out against the British, calling them "dogs dressed in red, who have come to rob [us] of [our] hunting grounds and drive away the game."

Pontiac's War

Soon after, Pontiac led an attack on British troops at Fort Detroit. He then called on other Indians to join the fight. A number of other nations responded. In a few months, they captured most British forts on the frontier. British and colonial troops struck back and regained much of what they had lost.

Pontiac's War, as it came to be called, did not last long. In October 1763, the French informed Pontiac that they had signed the Treaty of Paris. Because the treaty marked the end of French power in North America, the Indians could no longer hope for French aid against the British.

One by one, the Indian nations stopped fighting and returned home. "All my young men have buried their hatchets," Pontiac reportedly observed. By December, the British controlled the frontier.

Proclamation of 1763

Pontiac's War convinced British officials that they should stop British subjects from settling on the western frontier. To do this, the government issued the **Proclamation of 1763.** The proclamation drew an imaginary line along the crest of the Appalachian Mountains. Colonists were forbidden to settle west of the line. All settlers already west of the line were "to remove themselves" at once.

To enforce the law, Britain sent 10,000 troops to the colonies. Few troops went to the frontier, however. Most stayed in cities along the Atlantic coast.

The proclamation angered colonists. Some colonies, including New York, Pennsylvania, and Virginia, claimed lands in the West. Also, colonists had to pay for the additional British troops that had been sent to enforce the law. In the end, many settlers simply ignored the proclamation and moved west anyway.

One colonist who defied the Proclamation of 1763 was Daniel Boone. In 1767, Boone explored Kentucky, west of the Appalachians. Later, he led settlers through the Cumberland Gap along an old Indian path, renamed the Wilderness Road. Boone fought a number of battles against the Indians.

Britain Imposes New Taxes

The French and Indian War had plunged Britain deeply into debt. As a result, the tax bill for citizens in Britain rose sharply. The British prime minister, George Grenville, decided that colonists in North America should help share the burden. After all, he reasoned, it was the colonists who had gained most from the war.

Sugar Act

In 1764, Grenville asked Parliament to approve the Sugar Act, which put a new tax on molasses. Molasses, you will recall, was a valuable item in the triangular trade. (See page 114.)

Viewing HISTORY Pontiac's War

Despite a hard-fought struggle, Indian forces under Pontiac were unable to drive English settlers out of the Ohio Valley. More than 100 years later, Frederic Remington imagined this scene of Pontiac's warriors attacking Fort Detroit. Remington was a painter and sculptor who specialized in scenes of the American West. ★ **Why did Pontiac want to drive out the British?**

The Sugar Act replaced an earlier tax, which had been so high that any merchant who paid it would have been driven out of business. As a result, most colonial merchants simply avoided the tax by smuggling molasses into the colonies. Often, they bribed tax collectors to look the other way. The Sugar Act of 1764 lowered the tax. At the same time, the law made it easier for British officials to bring colonial smugglers to trial. Grenville made it clear that he expected the new tax to be paid.

Stamp Act

Grenville also persuaded Parliament to pass the **Stamp Act** of 1765. The act placed new duties on legal documents such as wills, diplomas, and marriage papers. It also taxed newspapers, almanacs, playing cards, and even dice.

All items named in the law had to carry a stamp showing that the tax had been paid. Stamp taxes were used in Britain and other countries to raise money. However, Britain had never required American colonists to pay such a tax.

"No Taxation Without Representation!"

When British officials tried to enforce the Stamp Act, they met with stormy protests. Riots broke out in Boston, New York City, Newport, and Charleston. Angry colonists threw rocks at agents trying to collect the unpopular tax. Some tarred and feathered the agents. In Boston, a mob burned an effigy, or likeness, of the English tax collector and then destroyed his home. John Adams, a Massachusetts lawyer, wrote:

> 66 Our presses have groaned, our pulpits have thundered, our legislatures have resolved, our towns have voted, the crown officers everywhere trembled. 99

The fury of the colonists shocked the British. After all, Britain had spent a great deal of money to protect the colonies against the French. Besides, people living in Britain were paying much higher taxes than the colonists were. Why, the British asked, were colonists so angry about the Stamp Act?

Colonists replied that the taxes imposed by the Stamp Act were unjust. The taxes, they claimed, went against the principle that there should be no taxation without representation. That principle was rooted in English traditions dating back to the Magna Carta. (See page 86.)

Colonists insisted that only they or their elected representatives had the right to pass taxes. Since the colonists did not elect representatives to Parliament, Parliament had no right to tax them. The colonists were willing to pay taxes—but only if the taxes were passed by their own colonial legislatures.

Moving toward unity

The Stamp Act crisis brought a sense of unity to the colonies. Critics of the law called for delegates from every colony to meet in New York City. There, the delegates would consider actions against the hated Stamp Act.

In October 1765, nine colonies sent delegates to what became known as the Stamp Act Congress. The delegates drew up petitions to King George III and to Parliament. A **petition** is a formal written request to someone in authority, signed by a group of people. In these petitions, the delegates rejected the Stamp Act and asserted that Parliament had no right to tax the colonies. Parliament paid little attention.

The colonists took other steps to change the law. They joined together to boycott British goods. To **boycott** means to refuse to buy certain goods and services. The boycott of British goods took its toll. Trade fell off by 14 percent. British merchants suffered. So, too, did British workers who made goods for the colonies.

Finally, in 1766, Parliament **repealed,** or canceled, the Stamp Act. At the same time, though, it passed a law asserting that Parliament had the right to raise taxes in "all cases whatsoever."

The Townshend Acts

In May 1767, Parliament reopened the debate over taxing the colonies. In a fierce exchange, George Grenville, now a member

▼ British tax stamp

▲ Teapot protesting the Stamp Act

Viewing HISTORY — Protesting the Stamp Act

Tax collectors hoped to make a good living distributing stamps. Instead, they found themselves targets of violence. Here, protesters tie a tax collector to a pole and drive him through the streets on a cart. ★ **Why do you think many Americans were dismayed by the tactics used by tax protesters?**

of Parliament, clashed with Charles Townshend, the official in charge of the British treasury. "You are cowards, you are afraid of the Americans, you dare not tax America!" Grenville shouted.

"Fear? Cowards?" Townshend snapped back. "I dare tax America!"

The next month, Parliament passed the **Townshend Acts,** which taxed goods such as glass, paper, paint, lead, and tea. The taxes were low, but colonists still objected. The principle, they felt, was the same: Parliament did not have the right to tax them without their consent.

The Townshend Acts also set up new ways to collect taxes. Customs officials were sent to American ports with orders to stop smuggling. Using legal documents known as **writs of assistance,** the officers would be allowed to inspect a ship's cargo without giving a reason.

Colonists protested that the writs of assistance violated their rights as British citizens. Under British law, an official could not search a person's property without a good reason for suspecting the owner of a crime.

Arguing against the writs, Massachusetts lawyer James Otis commented:

❝ Now, one of the most essential branches of English liberty is the freedom of one's house. A man's house is his castle; and while he is quiet, he is as well guarded as a prince in his castle. This writ, if it should be declared legal, would totally [destroy] this privilege. Customhouse officers may enter our houses when they please. ❞

Colonial protests widen

Colonists responded swiftly and strongly to the Townshend Acts. From north to south, colonial merchants and planters signed **nonimportation agreements.** In these agreements, they promised to stop importing goods taxed by the Townshend Acts. The colonists hoped that the new boycott would win repeal of the Townshend Acts.

To protest British policies, some angry colonists formed the **Sons of Liberty.** From Boston to Charleston, Sons of Liberty staged

Why Study History?

Because You Pay Taxes

★ ★

Many Americans protest that their taxes are too high.

Historical Background

In the 1760s and 1770s, colonists charged that taxes levied on them by the British government were unfair because Americans did not elect representatives to Parliament. "No taxation without representation!" American patriots cried. In protest, they boycotted British goods and attacked tax collectors. They even tarred and feathered a few agents. The furor over taxes helped cause the American Revolution.

Connections to Today

Fortunately, we no longer tar and feather tax collectors, but many people do still object to taxes. The most frequent complaint is that taxes are too high. In the late 1990s, the average American worked from January to April or May just to pay taxes!

The size of the tax bill is not the only complaint. Some people charge that the tax system is unfair. They say that the poor pay too much while the rich pay too little. Others say that the tax system is too complicated and that the rules are hard to understand. Recently, one sentence in a tax instruction was 436 words long

Taxes pay for essential services, such as fire protection.

—longer than the entire Gettysburg Address. As a result, nearly half of all Americans pay someone else to prepare their taxes.

Connections to You

If your state has a sales tax, you already pay taxes whenever you buy a taxable item. When you get a job, you will pay income taxes. Some day, you may pay property taxes on a home. As a voter, you will help to choose the legislators who decide our nation's tax laws.

Do you think taxes should be drastically reduced? Before you decide, remember that taxes pay for important services. Tax cuts could mean less money for national defense, health care, education, and transportation. There would also be less money for fire and police protection, recreation facilities, and the environment. So when you consider taxes, consider carefully.

1. **Comprehension** Describe three reasons some Americans complain about taxes today.

2. **Critical Thinking** Taxes spread the cost of services across the entire population. What are the benefits of this system? What are the disadvantages?

 **Debating** Organize a classroom debate on taxes. One side should argue in favor of lower tax rates and the benefits to be gained from them. The other side should oppose tax cuts because of the possible negative effects on the community.

mock hangings of cloth or straw effigies dressed like British officials. The hangings were meant to show tax collectors what might happen to them if they tried to collect the unpopular taxes.

Some women joined the **Daughters of Liberty.** They paraded, signed petitions, and organized a boycott of fine British cloth. They urged colonial women to raise more sheep, prepare more wool, and spin and weave their own cloth. A slogan of the Daughters of Liberty declared, "It is better to wear a Homespun coat than to lose our Liberty."

Some Sons and Daughters of Liberty also used other methods to support their cause. They visited merchants and urged them to sign the nonimportation agreements. A few even threatened people who continued to buy British goods.

New Leaders Emerge

As the struggle over taxes continued, new leaders emerged in all the colonies. Men and women in New England and Virginia were especially active in the colonial cause.

In Massachusetts

Samuel Adams of Boston stood firmly against Britain. Sam Adams seemed an unlikely leader. He was a failure in business and a poor public speaker. Still, he loved politics. He was always present at Boston town meetings and Sons of Liberty rallies. Adams's greatest talent was organizing people. He knew how to work behind the scenes, arranging protests and stirring public support.

Sam's cousin John was another important Massachusetts leader. **John Adams** was a skilled lawyer. More cautious than Sam, he weighed evidence carefully before acting. His knowledge of British law earned him much respect.

Mercy Otis Warren also aided the colonial cause. Warren published plays that made fun of British officials. She formed a close friendship with Abigail Adams, the wife of John Adams. The two women used their pens to spur the colonists to action. They also called for greater rights for women in the colonies.

In Virginia

Virginia contributed many leaders to the struggle against taxes. In the House of Burgesses, George Washington joined other Virginians to protest the Townshend Acts.

A young lawyer, **Patrick Henry,** became well known as a violent critic of British policies. His speeches in the House of Burgesses moved listeners to both tears and anger. Once, Henry attacked Britain with such fury that some listeners cried out, "Treason!" Henry boldly replied, "If this be treason, make the most of it!"

Britain Takes Action

Port cities such as Boston and New York were centers of protest. In New York, a dispute arose over the Quartering Act. Under

 **Mercy Otis Warren**

Mercy Otis Warren's anger was inflamed when her brother, James Otis, was struck on the head by an English officer and suffered permanent brain damage. Warren used her pen and sharp wit to stir feelings against the British. In plays like The Blockheads, *she ridiculed British officials. Warren's home in Massachusetts became a meeting place for colonists who opposed British policies.* ★ **How do writers influence public opinion today?**

Viewing HISTORY The Boston Massacre

Paul Revere's engraving of the Boston Massacre helped whip up colonial fury against the British. In fact, the picture is very inaccurate. No British officer ever gave an order to fire, as shown here. The redcoats, faced with an unruly mob, fired on their own. Revere also shows seven American dead, when there were actually five. ★ **Why do you think Revere distorted the event in his engraving?**

that law, colonists had to provide housing, candles, bedding, and beverages to soldiers stationed in the colonies. When the New York assembly refused to obey the law, Britain dismissed the assembly in 1767.

Britain also sent two regiments to Boston to protect customs officers from local citizens. To many Bostonians, the soldiers were a daily reminder that Britain was trying to bully them into paying unjust taxes. When British soldiers walked along the streets of Boston, they risked insults or even beatings. The time was ripe for disaster.

The Boston Massacre

On the night of March 5, 1770, a crowd gathered outside the Boston customs house. Colonists shouted insults at the "lobster-

backs," as they called the redcoated British who guarded the building. Then the Boston crowd began to throw snowballs, oyster shells, and chunks of ice at the soldiers.

The crowd grew larger and rowdier. Suddenly, the soldiers panicked. They fired into the crowd. When the smoke from the musket volley cleared, five people lay dead or dying. Among the first to die was Crispus Attucks, a black sailor who was active in the Sons of Liberty.

Colonists were quick to protest the incident, which they called the **Boston Massacre**. Boston silversmith Paul Revere stirred up anti-British feeling with an engraving that showed British soldiers firing on unarmed colonists. Sam Adams wrote letters to other colonists to build outrage about the shooting.

The soldiers were arrested and tried in court. John Adams agreed to defend them, saying that they deserved a fair trial. He wanted to show the world that the colonists believed in justice, even if the British government did not. At the trial, Adams argued that the crowd had provoked the soldiers. His arguments convinced the jury. In the end, the heaviest punishment any soldier received was a branding on the hand.

Samuel Adams later expanded on the idea of a letter-writing campaign like the one he had used to arouse colonists after the Boston Massacre. Adams formed a **committee of correspondence.** Members of the committee regularly wrote letters and pamphlets reporting on events in Massachusetts. Before long, committees of correspondence became a major tool of protest in every colony.

Samuel Adams

A Temporary Calm

By chance, on the very day of the Boston Massacre, Parliament voted to repeal most of the Townshend Acts. English merchants, harmed by the nonimportation agreements, had pressured Parliament to end the taxes. Still, King George III asked Parliament to retain the tax on tea. "There must always be one tax to keep up the right [to tax]," he argued. Parliament agreed.

News of the repeal delighted the colonists. Most people dismissed the remaining tax on tea as not important and ended their boycott of British goods. For a few years, calm returned. Yet the underlying issue—Britain's power to tax the colonies—remained unsettled. For the first time, the colonists were thinking more clearly about their political rights.

★ Section 3 Review ★

Recall

1. **Identify** (a) Pontiac's War, (b) Proclamation of 1763, (c) Stamp Act, (d) Townshend Acts, (e) Sons of Liberty, (f) Daughters of Liberty, (g) Samuel Adams, (h) John Adams, (i) Mercy Otis Warren, (j) Patrick Henry, (k) Boston Massacre.

2. **Define** (a) petition, (b) boycott, (c) repeal, (d) writ of assistance, (e) nonimportation agreement, (f) committee of correspondence.

Comprehension

3. (a) Why did Britain issue the Proclamation of 1763? (b) How did colonists respond to the Proclamation?

4. (a) What argument did the colonists use against British taxes? (b) How did colonists protest the taxes?

5. Describe the key events leading up to the Boston Massacre.

Critical Thinking and Writing

6. **Understanding Causes and Effects** Why did the French defeat in North America doom Pontiac's efforts to drive English settlers out of the Ohio Valley?

7. **Defending a Position** Do you think Britain had the right to tax the colonies? Defend your position.

★ ★

Activity **Writing a Letter** Spread the word! You are a member of Sam Adams's committee of correspondence. Write a letter to other colonists in which you remind them of the injustice of British taxes and the actions of British officials and troops, and call for further protests.

The Fighting Begins

As You Read

Explore These Questions
- Why did Americans protest the Tea Act?
- How did Britain respond to the Boston Tea Party?
- Why did fighting break out at Lexington and Concord?

Define
- militia
- minuteman

Identify
- British East India Company
- Tea Act
- Boston Tea Party
- Intolerable Acts
- First Continental Congress

SETTING the Scene One night in July 1774, John Adams stopped at a tavern in eastern Massachusetts. After riding for more than 30 miles, he was hot and dusty, and his body ached with fatigue.

Adams asked the innkeeper for a cup of tea. The innkeeper, however, refused his request. She did not serve tea, she informed him. He would have to drink coffee instead.

Adams later praised the innkeeper's conduct. In a letter to his wife, Abigail, he wrote that tea must be given up by all colonists. He promised to break himself of the habit as soon as possible.

Why did colonists like John Adams give up tea? The answer was taxes. When Parliament decided to enforce a tea tax in 1773, a new crisis exploded. This time, colonists began to think the unthinkable. Perhaps the time had come to reject British rule and declare independence.

Uproar Over Tea

Tea was tremendously popular in the colonies. By 1770, at least one million Americans brewed tea twice a day. People "would rather go without their dinners than without a dish of tea," a visitor to the colonies noted.

Parliament passes the Tea Act

Most tea was brought to the colonies by the **British East India Company.** The company bought tea in southern Asia and sold it to colonial tea merchants. The merchants then sold the tea to the colonists. To make a profit, the merchants sold the tea at a higher price than they had paid for it.

In the 1770s, however, the British East India Company found itself in deep financial trouble. More than 15 million pounds of its tea sat unsold in British warehouses. Britain had kept a tax on tea as a symbol of its right to tax the colonies. The tax was a small one, but colonists resented it. They refused to buy English tea.

Parliament tried to help the East India Company by passing the **Tea Act** of 1773. The act let the company bypass the tea merchants and sell directly to colonists. Although colonists would still have to pay the tea tax, they would not have to pay the higher price charged by tea merchants. As a result, the tea itself would cost less than ever before.

To the surprise of Parliament, colonists protested the Tea Act. Tea merchants were angry because they had been cut out of the

Connections With Science

American physicians joined the protest against tea. They spread stories warning about tea's adverse effects on health. One doctor claimed that drinking tea would make one an invalid for life. Another said that tea weakened "the tone of the stomach, and therefore of the whole system, inducing tremors and spasmodic affections."

Disguised as Indians, some 50 or 60 Bostonians attacked British tea ships. A crowd watched silently as the colonists dumped tea into Boston harbor. British officials called the Boston Tea Party "the most wanton and unprovoked insult offered to the civil power that is recorded in history."

★ **Why did colonists attack the tea ships?**

◄ *Colonial tea caddy*

tea trade. If Parliament ruined tea merchants today, they warned, what would prevent it from turning on other businesses tomorrow?

Even tea drinkers, who would have benefited from the law, scorned the Tea Act. They believed that it was a British trick to make them accept Parliament's right to tax the colonies.

A new boycott

Once again, colonists responded to the new tax with a boycott. One colonial newspaper warned:

> 66 Do not suffer yourself to sip the accursed, dutied STUFF. For if you do, the devil will immediately enter into you, and you will instantly become a traitor to your country. 99

Daughters of Liberty and other women led the boycott. They served coffee or made "liberty tea" from raspberry leaves. At some ports, Sons of Liberty enforced the boycott by keeping the British East India Company from unloading cargoes of tea.

Boston Tea Party

Three ships loaded with tea reached Boston harbor in late November 1773. The colonial governor of Massachusetts, Thomas Hutchinson, insisted that they unload their cargo as usual.

Sam Adams and the Sons of Liberty had other plans. On the night of December 16,

they met in Old South Church. They sent a message to the governor, demanding that the ships leave the harbor. When the governor rejected the demand, Adams stood up and declared, "This meeting can do nothing further to save the country."

Adams's words seemed to be a signal. As if on cue, a group of men burst into the meetinghouse. Dressed like Mohawk Indians, they waved hatchets in the air. From the gallery above, voices cried, "Boston harbor a teapot tonight! The Mohawks are come!"

The disguised colonists left the meetinghouse and headed for the harbor. Others joined them on the way. In the cold, crisp night, under a nearly full moon, the men boarded the ships, split open the tea chests, and dumped the tea into the harbor. By 10 P.M., the **Boston Tea Party,** as it was later called, was over. Its effects would be felt for a long time to come.

Britain Strikes Back

Colonists had mixed reactions to the Boston Tea Party. Some cheered the action. Others worried that it would encourage lawlessness in the colonies. Even those who condemned the Boston Tea Party, though, were shocked at Britain's response.

Punishing Massachusetts

The British were outraged by what they saw as Boston's lawless behavior. In 1774, Parliament, encouraged by King George III,

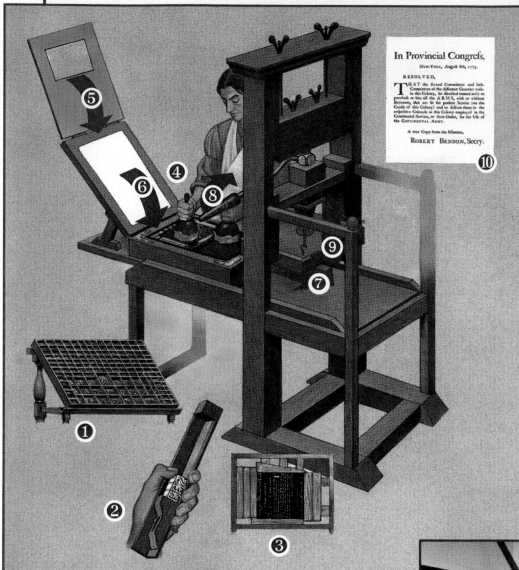

❶ The type case held metal letters.

❷ Letters were placed in a composing stick to create lines of type.

❸ Lines of type were locked in a form to create a sheet of text.

❹ The form was inked with ink balls.

❺ The frisket kept the margins of the paper clean. It folded onto the tympan.

❻ The tympan held the paper. It folded onto the form.

❼ The form was slid under the platen.

❽ The press bar was pulled to lower the platen.

❾ The platen pressed the inked form against the paper.

❿ The printed page was removed and hung on a drying rack.

Colonial Printing Press

Colonial printers played a vital role in uniting colonists against the British. Besides publishing newspapers and magazines, they also printed letters and pamphlets that kept colonists informed of such developments as the Intolerable Acts. The drawing shows how a printing press of the time worked. ★ **Why would printing a document with this press be very time-consuming?**

Printing press owned by ➤ Benjamin Franklin

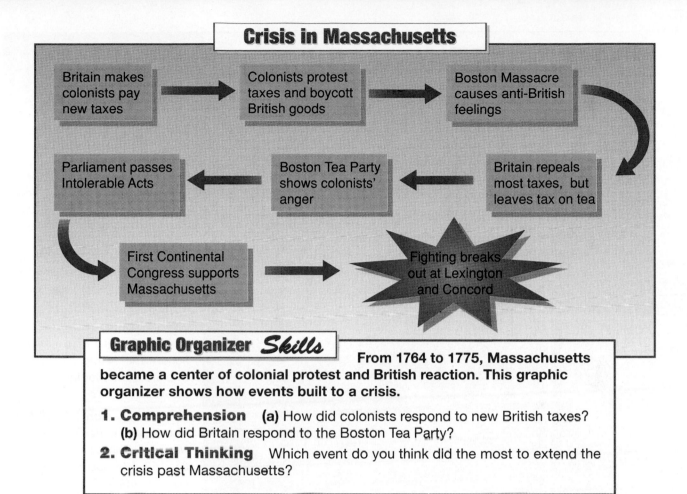

Crisis in Massachusetts

| Britain makes colonists pay new taxes | → | Colonists protest taxes and boycott British goods | → | Boston Massacre causes anti-British feelings |

| Parliament passes Intolerable Acts | ← | Boston Tea Party shows colonists' anger | ← | Britain repeals most taxes, but leaves tax on tea |

First Continental Congress supports Massachusetts → Fighting breaks out at Lexington and Concord

Graphic Organizer *Skills* **From 1764 to 1775, Massachusetts** became a center of colonial protest and British reaction. This graphic organizer shows how events built to a crisis.

1. Comprehension **(a)** How did colonists respond to new British taxes? **(b)** How did Britain respond to the Boston Tea Party?

2. Critical Thinking Which event do you think did the most to extend the crisis past Massachusetts?

acted to punish Massachusetts. Colonists called the four laws they passed the **Intolerable Acts** because they were so harsh.

First, Parliament shut down the port of Boston. No ship could enter or leave the harbor—not even a small boat. The harbor would remain closed until the colonists paid for the tea.

Second, Parliament forbade Massachusetts colonists to hold town meetings more than once a year without the governor's permission. In the past, colonists had called town meetings whenever they wished.

Third, Parliament provided for customs officers and other officials charged with major crimes to be tried in Britain instead of in Massachusetts. Colonists protested that a dishonest official could break the law in the colonies and avoid punishment "by being tried, where no evidence can pursue him."

Fourth, Parliament passed a new Quartering Act. No longer would redcoats camp in tents on Boston Common. Instead, British commanders could force citizens to house troops in their homes.

Other colonies support Boston

The committees of correspondence spread news of the Intolerable Acts. They warned that the people of Boston faced hunger while their port was closed. People from other colonies responded quickly. Carts rolled into the city with rice from South Carolina, corn from Virginia, and flour from Pennsylvania.

In the Virginia assembly, a young lawyer named Thomas Jefferson suggested that a day be set aside to mark the shame of the Intolerable Acts. The royal governor of Virginia rejected the idea and dismissed the assembly. The colonists went ahead anyway. On June 1, 1774, church bells tolled slowly. Merchants closed their shops. Many colonists prayed and fasted all day.

In September 1774, colonial leaders called a meeting in Philadelphia. Delegates from 12 colonies gathered in what became

Concord

The old North Bridge in Concord looks peaceful now. On April 19, 1775, though, this quiet spot was a scene of turmoil and bloodshed. It was here that colonial minutemen met and drove back three companies of redcoats. Today, you can walk across the restored bridge and view the stone monument shown here. Nearby, an 1873 statue by sculptor Daniel Chester French honors the heroic minutemen who fired "the shot heard round the world."

★ **To learn more about this historic site, write:** Minute Man National Historical Park, P.O. Box 160, 174 Liberty Street, Concord, MA 01742.

◄ The Minute Man, *by Daniel Chester French*

known as the **First Continental Congress.** Only Georgia did not send delegates.

After much debate, the delegates passed a resolution backing Massachusetts in its struggle. They agreed to boycott all British goods and to stop exporting goods to Britain until the Intolerable Acts were repealed. The delegates also urged each colony to set up and train its own militia (muh LIHSH uh). A **militia** is an army of citizens who serve as soldiers during an emergency.

Before leaving Philadelphia, the delegates agreed to meet again in May 1775. Little did they know that before then an incident in Massachusetts would change the fate of the colonies forever.

Lexington and Concord

In Massachusetts, newspapers called on citizens to prevent what they called "the Massacre of American Liberty." Volunteers known as **minutemen** trained regularly. Minutemen got their name because they kept their muskets at hand, and were prepared to fight at a minute's notice. Meanwhile, Britain built up its forces. More troops arrived in Boston, bringing the total number in that city to 4,000.

Early in 1775, General Thomas Gage, the British commander, heard a rumor that minutemen had a large store of arms in Concord, a village about 18 miles (29 km) from Boston. Gage planned a surprise march to Concord to seize the arms. (See the map on page 162.)

Sounding the alarm

On April 18, about 700 British troops quietly left Boston under cover of darkness. The Sons of Liberty were watching. As soon as the British set out, the Americans hung two lamps from the Old North Church in Boston. This signal meant that the redcoats were on the move.

Colonists who were waiting across the Charles River saw the signal. Messengers mounted their horses and galloped through the night toward Concord. One midnight rider was Paul Revere. "The redcoats are coming! The redcoats are coming!" shouted Revere as he passed through each sleepy village along the way.

"The shot heard round the world"

At daybreak on April 19, the redcoats reached Lexington, a town near Concord. On the village green, some 70 minutemen were waiting, commanded by Captain John Parker. The British ordered the minutemen to go home.

Outnumbered, the colonists began to leave. Suddenly, a shot rang out through the chill morning air. No one knows who fired it. In the brief struggle that followed, eight colonists were killed and one British soldier was wounded.

The British pushed on to Concord. Finding no arms in the village, they turned back to Boston. On a bridge outside Concord, they met 300 minutemen. Again, fighting broke out. This time, the British were forced to retreat. As they withdrew, colonial sharpshooters took deadly aim at them from the woods and fields. Local women also fired at the British from their windows. By the time they reached Boston, the redcoats had lost 73 men. Another 200 British soldiers were wounded or missing.

News of the battles at Lexington and Concord spread swiftly. To many colonists, the fighting ended all hope of reaching an agreement with Britain. Only war would decide the future of the 13 colonies.

More than 60 years after the battles of Lexington and Concord, a well-known New England poet, Ralph Waldo Emerson, wrote a poem honoring the minutemen. Emerson's "Concord Hymn" begins:

> 66 By the rude bridge that arched the flood,
> Their flag to April's breeze unfurled,
> Here once the embattled farmers stood,
> And fired the shot heard round the world. 99

The "embattled farmers" faced long years of war. At the war's end, though, the 13 colonies would stand strong and free as a new, independent nation.

★ Section 4 Review ★

Recall

1. **Locate** (a) Boston, (b) Concord, (c) Lexington.
2. **Identify** (a) British East India Company, (b) Tea Act, (c) Boston Tea Party, (d) Intolerable Acts, (e) First Continental Congress.
3. **Define** (a) militia, (b) minuteman.

Comprehension

4. (a) Why did Britain pass the Tea Act? (b) Why did the act anger colonists?
5. How did the Intolerable Acts help to unite the colonies?

6. Describe the events that led to the fighting at Lexington.

Critical Thinking and Writing

7. **Making Inferences** Do you think the organizers of the Boston Tea Party would have ended their protests against Britain if Parliament had repealed the tax on tea? Explain.
8. **Identifying Alternatives** (a) Do you think Parliament should have passed the Intolerable Acts in response to the Boston Tea Party? (b) What other actions might Parliament have taken in this situation?

Activity Writing a Poem Today, as in the past, writers like Mercy Otis Warren often use their skills to comment on current events. You are a poet living in colonial Boston. Write a poem in which you tell about the Boston Tea Party, the Intolerable Acts, or the events of April 19, 1775.

★ Sum It Up ★

Section 1 Rivalry in North America
▶ By the mid-1700s, England, France, Spain, and the Netherlands were competing for land and trade in North America.
▶ Native Americans were drawn into the struggle between the French and British in the Ohio Valley.

Section 2 The French and Indian War
▶ In 1754, the French and Indian War pitted the British against the French and their Indian allies.
▶ As a result of the French and Indian War, Britain won control of French land claims in North America.

Section 3 A Crisis Over Taxes
▶ Colonists objected to the Proclamation of 1763 because it forbade them to settle in lands west of the Appalachian Mountains.
▶ American colonists objected to Parliament's attempts to tax them without their consent.
▶ Colonists were outraged when British soldiers shot and killed Americans in the Boston Massacre.

Section 4 The Fighting Begins
▶ Conflict over taxes gradually increased until colonists staged the Boston Tea Party and Britain passed the Intolerable Acts.
▶ In April 1775, fighting between British troops and colonial minutemen marked the start of the American Revolution.

CD-ROM Review For additional review of the major ideas of Chapter 5, see *Guide to the Essentials of American History* or *Interactive Student Tutorial CD-ROM,* which contains interactive review activities, graphic organizers, and practice tests.

🗋 Reviewing the Chapter

Define These Terms
Match each term with the correct definition.

Column 1
1. petition
2. boycott
3. repeal
4. committee of correspondence
5. militia

Column 2
a. refusal to buy certain goods and services
b. formal written request
c. army of citizens who serve as soldiers during an emergency
d. cancel
e. group that wrote letters and pamphlets reporting events in the colonies

Explore the Main Ideas
1. Why was the Ohio River especially important to the French before 1754?
2. Why did Pontiac call for war against British settlers?
3. How did the Daughters of Liberty protest the Tea Act?
4. How did the Intolerable Acts affect the port of Boston?
5. Describe the outcome of the battles of Lexington and Concord.

🗋 Geography Activity

Match the letters on the map with the following locations:
1. Spanish lands in 1763, **2.** British lands in 1763, **3.** Original 13 English colonies, **4.** Mississippi River, **5.** Ohio River.
Location What body of water formed the western boundary of British lands in North America in 1763?

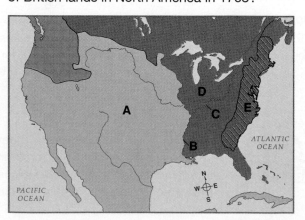

Critical Thinking and Writing

1. **Understanding Chronology** In 1763, Britain banned settlement west of the Appalachian Mountains. Why do you think it did not issue such a proclamation before the French and Indian War?

2. **Linking Past and Present** Why is English the most widely spoken language in the United States and Canada today?

3. **Exploring Unit Themes Origins** The principle that people must give their consent before they pay taxes goes back to ancient British law. How is it reflected in our government today?

4. **Ranking** Which of the Intolerable Acts do you think would have been most alarming to the Americans throughout the colonies? Explain your reasoning.

Using Primary Sources

In August 1765, Francis Bernard, the governor of Massachusetts, reported to England on a Stamp Act riot in Boston:

> 66 Toward evening some boys began to light a bonfire before the Town House, which is a usual signal for a mob. Before it was quite dark a great company of people gather together crying liberty and property, which is the usual notice of their intention to plunder and pull down a house. . . . They went to the house of Mr. Story, . . . broke into it and tore it all to pieces; and took out all the books and papers, among which were all the records of the Court of the Admiralty, and carried them to the bonfire and burned them. 99

Source: *The Annals of America*, Volume 2, 1976.

Recognizing Points of View (a) In the first sentence, what words does Bernard use to describe the protesters? **(b)** How does he view the protesters' use of the word *liberty*? **(c)** How do you think Samuel Adams would have responded to the governor's report?

ACTIVITY BANK

Interdisciplinary Activity

Exploring the Arts List five reasons for the colonists' anger with Britain. Based on your list, write a song of protest against British treatment. You can make up your own melody or write new words to an existing tune. Sing or play your song for the class.

Career Skills Activity

Scriptwriters Write a script dramatizing one of the events you have read about in this chapter. With a small group of students, perform your skit for the class.

Citizenship Activity

Testing Alternative Courses of Action Review the events of the Boston Tea Party. List reasons for citizens of the colonies to support the actions of the protesters. Then, list reasons for citizens to condemn the protesters' actions.

Internet Activity

Use the Internet to find sites dealing with one of the people you have read about in this chapter. Write a mini-biography of the person you have chosen. If possible, illustrate your biography with a picture downloaded from the Web site.

EYEWITNESS Journal

You are one of the following: a Native American in the Ohio Valley in 1750; Major George Washington in the 1750s; a Son or Daughter of Liberty in 1770; a minuteman on April 19, 1775. In your EYEWITNESS JOURNAL, describe the events of the time that have had the greatest effect on you.

Chapter 6

The American Revolution

1775–1783

After Lexington and Concord, representatives of the colonies tried, without success, to find a peaceful solution to the conflict with Britain. In 1776, as the fighting spread, they called for separation from Britain. With the bold words of the Declaration of Independence, the United States became a nation.

The Americans now fought a life-and-death struggle for liberty. From New England, the major operations of the war gradually spread to the Middle States and the South. With help from France and other nations, the Americans defeated the British and won their war for independence.

Why Study History?

On July 4, 1776, Americans declared their independence from British rule. Today, on every Fourth of July, we celebrate the Declaration of Independence and the ideals it proclaims. To learn more about how and why we celebrate, see this chapter's *Why Study History?* feature, "We Celebrate Our Independence."

American Events

●1775
Battle of Bunker Hill

●1776
Declaration of Independence is issued

●1777
American victory at Saratoga is turning point of war

1775 1776 1777 1778 1779

World Events

1778 World Event
France recognizes American independence

Viewing HISTORY

A Nation Wins Its Independence

This painting, Surrender of Lord Cornwallis, *is by John Trumbull, one of the greatest early American artists. It shows British troops surrendering to an American army at Yorktown, Virginia, in 1781. The Battle of Yorktown marked the end of the American Revolution. The six-year struggle freed the 13 colonies from British rule.*
★ **Why do you think Britain was unwilling to give up its colonies?**

1780 ●
Patriots' victory at
King's Mountain
boosts morale

● **1781**
British surrender
at Yorktown

1783 ●
Britain recognizes
American inde-
pendence in the
Treaty of Paris

1779　　**1780**　　**1781**　　**1782**　　**1783**

1779 World Event
Spain enters the war
against Britain

1782 World Event
War between British and
Marāthā people of India ends

Early Battles

As You Read

Explore These Questions
- How did Americans pursue both war and peace in 1775?
- What were the advantages of each side as they entered the war?
- How did the Continental Army gain control of Boston?

Define
- refugee
- blockade
- mercenary

Identify
- Ethan Allen
- Green Mountain Boys
- Continental Army
- Olive Branch Petition
- Patriots
- Loyalists
- Battle of Bunker Hill
- Benedict Arnold

The events of April 19, 1775, left the British stunned. How had a handful of rebels forced 700 redcoats to retreat? That night, British soldiers grew even more uneasy as they watched rebels set up campfires all around Boston.

In the months ahead, the campfires remained. They were a clear sign that the quarrel between Britain and its colonies had blazed into war. Many colonists clung to hopes for a peaceful solution. Others were ready and eager to fight.

War or Peace?

On May 10, 1775, just a few weeks after the battles at Lexington and Concord, delegates from the colonies met at the Second Continental Congress in Philadelphia. Most who attended still hoped to avoid a final break with Britain. However, while they were meeting, the fighting spread.

Rebels take Ticonderoga

Ethan Allen, a blacksmith known for his fierce temper, followed a course of action rather than talk. Allen decided to lead a band of Vermonters, known as the **Green Mountain Boys,** in a surprise attack on Fort Ticonderoga, located at the southern tip of Lake Champlain. (See the map on page 162.) Allen knew that inside the fort were many cannons which the colonies badly needed.

In early May, the Green Mountain Boys crept quietly through the morning mists to Fort Ticonderoga. They quickly overpowered the guard on duty and entered the fort. Allen rushed to the room where the British commander slept. "Come out, you old rat!" he shouted. The commander demanded to know by whose authority Allen acted. "In the name of the Great Jehovah and the Continental Congress!" Allen replied.

The British commander surrendered Ticonderoga. With the fort, the Green Mountain Boys won a valuable supply of cannons and gunpowder. Allen's success also gave the Americans control of a key route into Canada.

Setting up an army

Then, in June, the Second Continental Congress took the bold step of setting up the **Continental Army.** John Adams proposed that George Washington of Virginia be appointed commander:

> 66 I [have] in mind for that important command...a gentleman whose skill and experience as an officer, whose independent fortune, great talents, and excellent universal character would command the [approval] of all America. 99

Tall and dignified, George Washington commanded the respect of all the delegates. They promptly voted to approve him as commander. Without wasting any time, the new general left Philadelphia to take charge of the forces around Boston.

A peace petition

Even though the delegates had created an army, they were not eager for war. After much debate, Congress decided to try to patch up the quarrel with Britain by sending the **Olive Branch Petition,** written by John Dickinson of Pennsylvania. In it, they declared their loyalty to King George and asked him to repeal the Intolerable Acts.

George III was furious when he heard about the petition. The colonists, he raged, were trying to begin a war "for the purpose of establishing an independent empire!" He blamed "wicked and desperate persons" in the colonies for the growing conflict. Rejecting the Olive Branch Petition, the king vowed to bring the rebels to justice.

The Opposing Sides

The rebels that King George III spoke of called themselves **Patriots.** They opposed aspects of British rule that they considered harsh and unjust. Most of the American colonists were Patriots.

In their war with Britain, the Patriots faced a powerful foe. They also had to struggle against a large number of colonists who chose to remain loyal British subjects.

American Patriots

It would take a great effort for the Patriots to overcome their disadvantages. Colonial forces were poorly organized and untrained. They had few cannons, little gunpowder, and no navy.

Yet the Patriots had some important advantages. Many Patriots owned rifles and were good shots. Also, they had a brilliant commander in George Washington. Another strength was that they would fight hard to defend their homes and property. Reuben Stebbins of Massachusetts was typical of many patriotic farmers. When the British approached, he rode off to battle. "We'll see who's goin' t' own this farm!" he cried.

The British

The British were a powerful foe. They had highly trained, experienced troops. Their navy was the best in the world. British ships could move soldiers quickly up and down the Atlantic coast. In addition, many colonists still supported the British.

Still, Britain was not without problems. Britain's armies were 3,000 miles (4,800 km) from home. News and supplies took months to travel from Britain to North America. Also, British soldiers risked attacks by colonists once they marched out of the cities into the countryside.

Viewing History **Rebels Take Ticonderoga**

In May 1775, Ethan Allen and the Green Mountain Boys made a bold attack on Fort Ticonderoga. In this painting, Allen demands that the British commander surrender. ★ **Why was Fort Ticonderoga an important prize?**

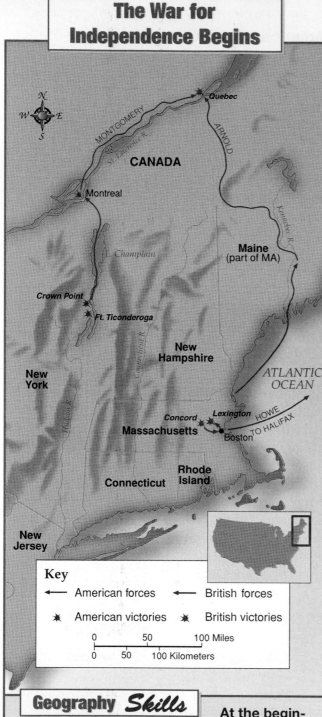

The War for Independence Begins

CANADA

Quebec

Montreal

L. Champlain

Maine
(part of MA)

Crown Point

Ft. Ticonderoga

New
Hampshire

New
York

ATLANTIC
OCEAN

Concord   Lexington   HOWE
Massachusetts   TO HALIFAX
          Boston

Rhode
Island

Connecticut

New
Jersey

Key

← American forces   ← British forces

✴ American victories   ✴ British victories

0   50   100 Miles

0   50   100 Kilometers

Geography Skills

At the beginning of the War for Independence, most of the fighting took place in the northern colonies and in Canada.

1. **Location** On the map, locate: **(a)** Lexington, **(b)** Concord, **(c)** Boston, **(d)** Fort Ticonderoga, **(e)** Quebec.

2. **Movement** **(a)** Describe Arnold's route to Canada. **(b)** Describe Montgomery's route from Crown Point to Quebec.

3. **Critical Thinking** Based on the map, which American commander would have a harder time reaching Quebec? Explain.

American Loyalists

American colonists who remained loyal to Britain were known as **Loyalists** or Tories. It is estimated that they made up about 20 percent of the colonists. They included wealthy merchants and former officials of the royal government. However, some farmers and craftsworkers were also Loyalists. There were more Loyalists in the Middle States and the South than in New England.

Loyalists faced tough times during the American Revolution. Patriots tarred and feathered people known to favor the British. Many Loyalists fled to England or Canada. Others found shelter in cities controlled by the British. Those who fled lost their homes, stores, and farms.

The Fight for Boston

During the first year of conflict, much of the fighting was centered around Boston. About 6,000 British troops were stationed there. Colonial militia surrounded the city and prevented the British from marching out.

Battle of Bunker Hill

Even before Washington reached Boston, the Patriots took action. On June 16, 1775, Colonel William Prescott led 1,200 minutemen up Bunker Hill, across the river from Boston. From there, they could fire on British ships in Boston harbor. Prescott, however, noticed that nearby Breed's Hill was an even better position. He ordered his men to move there and dig defensive trenches.

At sunrise, the British general, William Howe, spotted the Americans. He ferried about 2,400 redcoats across the harbor to attack the rebels' position. Slowly, the British began to climb Breed's Hill. Each soldier carried a heavy pack that weighed about 125 pounds. Many of the British troops were exhausted even before the fighting began.

The Americans waited patiently as the British approached. The Patriots held their fire because they had very little gunpowder. Their commanders warned, "Don't shoot until you see the whites of their eyes!"

When the Americans finally fired, the British were forced to retreat. A second British attack was also turned back. On the

Boston · Charles Town

Viewing History — The Fight for Boston

In this painting of the Battle of Bunker Hill, British ships bombard the village of Charlestown, across the river from Boston. Meanwhile, British troops make the long march up Breed's Hill to attack the waiting Americans. ★ **Why was the Battle of Bunker Hill important to Americans?**

Drum carried ➤
at Bunker Hill

third try, the British succeeded in pushing over the top. They took both Bunker Hill and Breed's Hill, but paid a high price for their victory. More than 1,000 redcoats lay dead or wounded. American losses numbered only about 400.

The **Battle of Bunker Hill** was the first major battle of the Revolution. It proved that the Americans could fight bravely. However, it also showed that the British would not be easy to defeat.

The British leave Boston

Washington finally reached Boston a few weeks after the Battle of Bunker Hill. There, he found about 16,000 troops camped in huts and tents at the edge of the city. Their

weapons ranged from rifles to swords made by local blacksmiths.

General Washington quickly began to turn raw recruits into a trained army. His job was especially difficult because soldiers from different colonies mistrusted one another. "Connecticut wants no Massachusetts men in her corps," he wrote. And "Massachusetts thinks there is no necessity for a Rhode Islander to be introduced into her [ranks]." Slowly, Washington won the loyalty of his troops. They, in turn, learned to take orders and work together.

In January 1776, Washington had a stroke of good fortune. Soldiers arrived outside Boston with cannons they had dragged across the mountains from Fort Ticonderoga.

Washington had the cannons placed on Dorchester Heights, overlooking the harbor.

Once General Howe saw the American cannons in place, he knew that he could not hold Boston. In March 1776, he and his troops sailed from Boston to Halifax, Canada. About 1,000 American Loyalists went with the British. The Loyalists of Boston became **refugees,** people who flee their homes to seek refuge from war, persecution, or other hardships.

Although the British left New England, they had not given up. King George III ordered a **blockade** of all colonial ports. A blockade is the shutting off of a port to keep people or supplies from moving in or out. The king also used Hessian **mercenaries,** or troops for hire, from Germany to help fight the colonists.

March on Canada

While Washington's army was winning control of Boston, other Americans were launching an attack on Canada. The Americans hoped to get help from French Canadians, who were unhappy under British rule.

In the fall of 1775, two American armies moved north into Canada. (See the map on page 162.) Richard Montgomery led one army from Fort Ticonderoga to Montreal. He seized that city in November 1775. He then moved toward Quebec. **Benedict Arnold** led the second army north through Maine. He was supposed to join forces with Montgomery in Quebec.

Arnold and his troops had a terrible journey through the Maine woods in winter. Rainstorms followed by freezing nights coated their clothes with ice. Supplies ran so low that soldiers survived only by eating boiled bark and shoe leather. Finally, Arnold reached Quebec. However, he was disappointed to learn that most French Canadians did not support the Americans.

In a blinding snowstorm on December 31, 1775, the Americans attacked Quebec. Montgomery was killed, and Arnold was wounded. The Americans failed in their attempt to take the city. They stayed outside Quebec until May 1776, when the British landed new forces in Canada. At last, weakened by disease and hunger, the Americans withdrew, leaving Canada to the British.

★ Section 1 Review ★

Recall

1. **Locate** (a) Fort Ticonderoga, (b) Boston, (c) Montreal, (d) Quebec.
2. **Identify** (a) Ethan Allen, (b) Green Mountain Boys, (c) Continental Army, (d) Olive Branch Petition, (e) Patriots, (f) Loyalists, (g) Battle of Bunker Hill, (h) Benedict Arnold.
3. **Define** (a) refugee, (b) blockade, (c) mercenary.

Comprehension

4. (a) How did the Second Continental Congress pursue a peaceful settlement with Britain? (b) What steps did the Congress take to prepare for war with Britain?

5. (a) What advantages did the British have over the Patriots? (b) What advantages did the Patriots have?
6. How did Washington force the British to leave Boston?

Critical Thinking and Writing

7. **Understanding Causes and Effects** Explain two reasons for the American failure to capture Quebec.
8. **Making Inferences** Why did the Boston Loyalists feel that they had to go with the British to Canada?

★ ★

Activity Making a Decision You are an American in 1775. War between the rebels and the British seems certain! Decide whether you will become a Loyalist or a Patriot. Explain the facts and ideas that led to your decision.

Declaring Independence

As You Read

Explore These Questions
- How did *Common Sense* influence the colonists?
- How did American Patriots respond to the Declaration of Independence?
- What are the main ideas of the Declaration of Independence?

Define
- traitor
- preamble
- natural rights

Identify
- *Common Sense*
- Thomas Paine
- Richard Henry Lee
- Thomas Jefferson
- Declaration of Independence

SETTING the Scene Many Americans had come to believe that Parliament did not have the right to make laws for the 13 colonies. After all, they argued, the colonists had their own elected legislatures. At the same time, however, most Americans still felt strong bonds of loyalty to Britain. Especially, they felt they owed allegiance to the king.

Then, in January 1776, a pamphlet titled **Common Sense** appeared on the streets of Philadelphia. "I offer nothing more than simple facts, plain arguments, and common sense," wrote its author, **Thomas Paine.** Though Paine had only recently arrived from England, he strongly supported the colonists in their quarrel with the king. In blunt words, he boldly urged the colonies to declare their independence.

Common Sense

In *Common Sense,* Thomas Paine tried to convince the colonists that they did not owe loyalty to George III or any other monarch. The very idea of setting up kings and queens was wrong, he said.

66 In England a King hath little more to do than to make war and give away [jobs]; which in plain terms, is to impoverish the nation.... Of more worth is one honest man to society and in the sight of God, than all the crowned ruffians that ever lived. 99

Americans did not owe anything to England, either, Paine went on. If the English had helped the colonists, they had done so for their own profit. It could only hurt the Americans to remain under British rule:

66 Everything that is right or reasonable pleads for separation.... 'Tis time to part. 99

Common Sense won many colonists to the idea of independence. In six months, more than 500,000 copies of the pamphlet were printed and sold. "*Common Sense* is working a powerful change in the minds of men," George Washington observed.

Moving Toward Independence

Paine's *Common Sense* affected many members of the Continental Congress. In June 1776, **Richard Henry Lee** of Virginia offered a resolution stating that "these United Colonies are, and of right ought to be, free and independent States."

Delegates faced a difficult decision. There could be no turning back once

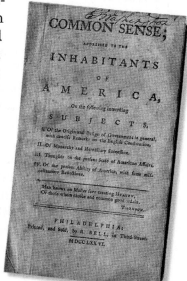

Common Sense *by* ➤ Thomas Paine

Viewing HISTORY Signing the Declaration

Thomas Jefferson labored many hours perfecting the Declaration of Independence. Here, Jefferson and other committee members present the Declaration to the Continental Congress. This painting, like the one on page 159, is by John Trumbull. ★ **What was the purpose of the Declaration of Independence?**

they declared independence. If they fell into British hands, they would be hanged as traitors. A **traitor** is a person who betrays his or her country.

The Congress took a fateful step. They chose a committee to draw up a declaration of independence. The committee included John Adams, Benjamin Franklin, Thomas Jefferson, Robert Livingston, and Roger Sherman. Their job was to tell the world why the colonies were breaking away from Britain.

The committee asked Jefferson to write the document. **Thomas Jefferson** was one of the youngest delegates. A quiet man, he spoke little at formal meetings. Among friends, however, he liked to sprawl in a chair with his long legs stretched out and talk for hours. His ability to write clearly and gracefully had earned him great respect.

The Declaration of Independence

In late June, Jefferson completed the declaration, and it was read to the Congress. On July 2, the Continental Congress voted that the 13 colonies were "free and independent States." Two days later, on July 4, 1776, the delegates accepted Jefferson's **Declaration of Independence,** making only a few minor changes.

John Hancock, president of the Continental Congress, signed the Declaration first. He penned his signature boldly, in large, clear letters. "There," he said, "I guess King George will be able to read that."

Copies of the Declaration were distributed throughout the colonies. Across the colonies, those who were Patriots greeted the

Why Study History?

Because We Celebrate Our Independence

★ ★

Independence Day fireworks over Washington, D.C.

Historical Background

John Adams reacted proudly to the signing of the Declaration of Independence. He declared that the event "ought to be solemnized with pomp and parade, with shows, games, sports, guns, bells, bonfires, and illuminations, from one end of this continent to the other, from this time forward, forevermore."

In 1777, on the first anniversary of the Declaration of Independence, Philadelphia overflowed with excitement. A navy ship on the Delaware River sounded a 13-gun salute. Bells rang all day, bonfires burned in the streets, and fireworks lit up the evening sky. Following a dinner attended by members of Congress, American soldiers paraded through the city's streets.

Connections to Today

Throughout the nation, we celebrate Independence Day in much the same way that people did in 1777. John Adams would feel right at home with our parties, picnics, athletic games, patriotic speeches, and American flags. Today's televised concerts, parades of large, decorated floats, and massive displays of community-sponsored fireworks would have been beyond his imagination, but certainly in keeping with his spirit.

Connections to You

How do you commemorate the Fourth of July? You may celebrate the day at the beach, at the park, or in your own backyard. Yet, no matter how you spend the Fourth of July, the reason for celebration remains the same—to honor the foresight and courage of our founders.

The Declaration of Independence that they issued spoke of equality. It also discussed the rights and freedoms that all people have and the responsibility of government to protect those rights and freedoms. During the Revolutionary War, Americans fought and died for those ideas. Today, you enjoy a democratic way of life based on those ideas.

1. **Comprehension** Describe three things that Philadelphians did in 1777 to commemorate Independence Day.

2. **Critical Thinking** How do the ideas in the Declaration of Independence still live on today?

★ *Activity* It is 1776 and you are a member of the Continental Congress. Review the ideas contained in the Declaration of Independence. Write a short speech explaining to the Congress (your classmates) why they should sign it.

news of independence with joyous celebrations. In New York, Patriots tore down a statue of King George III. In Boston, the sound of cannons could be heard for hours.

The Declaration of Independence consists of a **preamble,** or introduction, followed by three main parts. (The complete Declaration of Independence is printed in the Reference Section.)

Natural rights

The first part of the Declaration stresses the idea of **natural rights,** or rights that belong to all people from birth. In bold, ringing words, Jefferson wrote:

> ❝ We hold these truths to be self-evident, that all men are created equal, that they are endowed by their Creator with certain unalienable rights, that among these are life, liberty, and the pursuit of happiness. ❞

According to the Declaration of Independence, people form governments in order to protect their natural rights and liberties. Governments can exist only if they have the "consent of the governed." If a government fails to protect the rights of its citizens, then it is the people's "right [and] duty, to throw off such government, and provide new guards for their future security."

British wrongs

The second part of the Declaration lists the wrongs committed by Britain. Jefferson condemned King George III for disbanding colonial legislatures and for sending troops to the colonies in times of peace. He complained about limits on trade and about taxes that had been imposed without the consent of the people. Jefferson listed many other wrongs to show why the colonists had the right to rebel. He also pointed out that the colonies had petitioned the King to correct these injustices. Yet they remained.

Independence

The last part of the Declaration announces that the colonies had become the United States of America. All political ties with Britain were cut. As a free and independent nation, the United States had the power to make alliances and trade with other countries.

★ Section 2 Review ★

Recall

1. **Identify** (a) *Common Sense,* (b) Thomas Paine, (c) Richard Henry Lee, (d) Thomas Jefferson, (e) Declaration of Independence.

2. **Define** (a) traitor, (b) preamble, (c) natural rights.

Comprehension

3. What arguments did Thomas Paine offer in favor of independence?

4. How did American Patriots react to the Declaration of Independence?

5. Describe the four parts of the Declaration of Independence.

Critical Thinking and Writing

6. **Analyzing Primary Sources** Review the excerpts from Thomas Paine's *Common Sense* that appear on page 165. Explain the meaning of those excerpts in your own words.

7. **Synthesizing Information** After the Declaration of Independence was issued, enslaved Africans sent petitions to state legislatures asking for freedom. How might they have used the Declaration of Independence to support their demands?

Activity **Writing a Document** You are Thomas Jefferson. Reports are coming in that many people cannot understand the Declaration of Independence because the language is too complex. Try to help them by rewriting the preamble, or first paragraph, in simpler language.

3 Fighting in the Middle States

As You Read

Explore These Questions
- What defeats and hardships did the Americans suffer in the Middle States?
- Why was the Battle of Saratoga a turning point in the war?
- What help did the United States receive from other nations?

Define
- ally
- cavalry

Identify
- Battle of Long Island
- Nathan Hale
- Battle of Trenton
- John Burgoyne
- Battle of Saratoga
- Marquis de Lafayette
- Friedrich von Steuben
- Thaddeus Kosciusko

Continental Army medicine chest

SETTING the Scene It was early one morning in late June of 1776. Daniel McCurtin glanced out his window at New York harbor. He was amazed to see "something resembling a wood of pine trees trimmed." He watched the forest move across the water. Then, he understood. The trees were the masts of ships!

> **66** I could not believe my eyes...the whole bay was full of shipping as ever it could be. I declare that I thought all London was afloat. **99**

Daniel McCurtin had witnessed the arrival of a large British fleet in New York. Aboard the ships were General Howe and his redcoats. Thus began a new stage in the war. Previously, most of the fighting of the American Revolution took place in New England. In mid-1776, the heavy fighting shifted to the Middle States. There, the Continental Army suffered through the worst days of the war.

The British Take New York

Washington, expecting Howe's attack, had led his forces south from Boston to New York City. His army, however, was no match for the British. Howe had about 34,000 troops and 10,000 sailors. He also had ships to ferry them ashore. Washington had fewer than 20,000 poorly trained troops. Worse, he had no navy.

In August, Howe's army landed on Long Island. In the **Battle of Long Island,** more than 1,400 Americans were killed, wounded, or captured. The rest retreated to Manhattan. The British followed. To avoid capture, Washington hurried north.

Throughout the autumn, Washington fought a series of battles with Howe's army. In November, he crossed the Hudson River into New Jersey. Pursued by the British, the Americans retreated across the Delaware River into Pennsylvania.

During the campaign for New York, Washington needed information about Howe's forces. **Nathan Hale,** a young Connecticut officer, slipped behind British lines and returned with the details. Soon after, the British captured Hale. They tried him and condemned him to death. As Hale walked to the gallows, he is said to have declared: "I only regret that I have but one life to lose for my country."

Despair and New Hope

Months of campaigning took a toll on the Continental Army. In December 1776, Washington described his troops as sick, dirty, and "so thinly clad as to be unfit for service." Every day, soldiers deserted. Washington

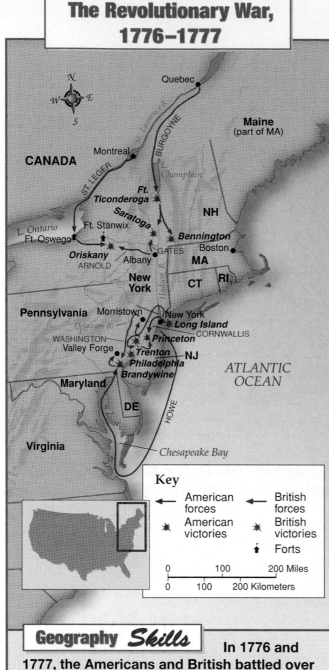

The Revolutionary War, 1776–1777

Geography *Skills*

In 1776 and 1777, the Americans and British battled over a large area. The American victory at Saratoga marked a major turning point of the war.

1. **Location**   On the map, locate: **(a)** Long Island, **(b)** New York City, **(c)** Trenton, **(d)** Hudson River, **(e)** Saratoga, **(f)** Valley Forge.

2. **Movement**   How did the British use sea power to help them capture Philadelphia?

3. **Critical Thinking**   How did Burgoyne and St. Leger use geography to help move their armies quickly toward Albany?

wrote to his brother: "I am wearied to death. I think the game is pretty near up."

The Crisis

Thomas Paine had retreated with the army through New Jersey. Once again, he took up his pen. This time, he wrote *The Crisis,* urging Americans to support the army.

> 66 These are the times that try men's souls. The summer soldier and the sunshine patriot will, in this crisis, shrink from the service of his country; but he that stands it *now* deserves the love and thanks of man and woman. 99

Grateful for Paine's inspiring words, Washington had *The Crisis* read aloud to his troops.

American victories in New Jersey

The Americans needed more than words to help their cause, however. General Washington decided on a bold move—a surprise attack on Trenton.

On Christmas night, Washington secretly led his troops across the icy Delaware River. Soldiers shivered as spray from the river froze on their faces. Once ashore, they marched through swirling snow. "Soldiers, keep by your officers," Washington urged.

Early on December 26, the Americans surprised the Hessian troops guarding Trenton and took most of them prisoner. An American summed up the **Battle of Trenton:** "Hessian population of Trenton at 8 A.M.—1,408 men and 39 officers; Hessian population at 9 A.M.—0."

British General Charles Cornwallis set out at once to retake Trenton and capture Washington. Late on January 2, 1777, he saw the lights of Washington's campfires. "At last we have run down the old fox," he said, "and we will bag him in the morning."

Washington fooled Cornwallis. He left the fires burning and slipped behind British lines to attack Princeton. There, the Continental Army won another victory. From Princeton, Washington moved to Morristown, where the army spent the winter. The victories at Trenton and Princeton gave the Americans new hope.

Victory at Princeton

This painting depicts the battle at Princeton, New Jersey, in January 1777. Victories at Trenton and Princeton boosted American morale. Still, difficult times lay ahead for Washington's troops. ★ **How was Washington able to surprise the British at Princeton?**

Turning Point of the War

In London, British officials were dismayed by the army's failure to crush the rebels. Early in 1777, General **John Burgoyne** (buhr GOIN) presented George III with a new plan for victory. If British troops cut off New England from the other colonies, he argued, the war would soon be over.

Burgoyne wanted three British armies to march on Albany, New York, from different directions. They would crush American forces there. Once they controlled the Hudson River, the British could stop the flow of soldiers and supplies from New England to Washington's army.

Britain's plan fails

Burgoyne's plan called for General Howe to march on Albany from New York City. George III, however, wanted Howe to capture Philadelphia first.

In July 1777, Howe sailed from New York to the Chesapeake Bay. (See the map on page 170.) Despite Washington's efforts to stop him, Howe captured Philadelphia. He then went on to defeat the Americans at the battles of Brandywine and Germantown. Howe then retired to comfortable quarters in Philadelphia for the winter. Washington retreated to Valley Forge, where he set up a makeshift camp.

Meanwhile, two other British armies under Burgoyne and Barry St. Leger (lay ZHAIR) marched from Canada toward Albany. St. Leger tried to take Fort Stanwix. However, Benedict Arnold drove him back with a strong American army.

Victory at Saratoga

Only Burgoyne was left to march on Albany. His army moved slowly because it had many heavy baggage carts to drag through the woods. To slow Burgoyne further, Patriots cut down trees to block the route and dammed up streams to create swampy bogs.

Despite these obstacles, Burgoyne retook Fort Ticonderoga. He then sent troops into Vermont to find food and horses. There, Patriots attacked the redcoats. At the Battle of

Bennington, they wounded or captured nearly 1,000 British.

Burgoyne's troubles grew. The Green Mountain Boys hurried into New York to help other American forces there. At the village of Saratoga, the Americans surrounded the British. When Burgoyne tried to break free, the Americans beat him back. Realizing he was trapped, Burgoyne surrendered his entire army to the Americans on October 17, 1777.

The American victory at the **Battle of Saratoga** was a major turning point in the war. It ended the British threat to New England. It boosted American spirits at a time when Washington's army was suffering defeats. Most important, it convinced France to become an **ally** of the United States. Nations that are allies work together to achieve some common goal.

Help from Europe

The Continental Congress had long hoped for French aid. In 1776, the Congress had sent Benjamin Franklin to Paris. His job was to persuade Louis XVI, the French king, to help the Americans with weapons and other badly needed supplies. The Congress also wanted France to declare war on Britain. France had a strong navy that could stand up to the British.

The French were eager to hurt Britain, but they were also cautious. France and Britain were rivals for power and France was still angry about their defeat by the British in the French and Indian War. However, Louis XVI did not want to help the Americans openly until he was sure they could win.

The American victory at Saratoga convinced France and other nations that the United States could stand up to Britain. In February 1778, France became the first nation to sign a treaty with the United States. In it, Louis XVI recognized the new nation and agreed to provide military aid. Later, the Netherlands and Spain also joined in the war against Britain. France, the Netherlands, and Spain all provided loans to the Americans.

Even before European nations provided aid to the United States, individual volunteers had been coming from Europe to join the American cause. Some became leading officers in the American army.

The **Marquis de Lafayette** (lah fee YEHT), a young French noble, brought trained

Saratoga: A Turning Point

Before
- France gives American rebels money and supplies but stays neutral.
- French king does not want to make commitment unless he is sure Americans will win.

American Victory at Saratoga

After
- Victory proves that Americans can win.
- France becomes official ally of the United States.
- France gives military and naval support.
- France declares war on Britain.

Graphic Organizer *Skills*

The American victory at the Battle of Saratoga was a major turning point in the War for Independence.

1. **Comprehension** (a) How did France help the Americans before Saratoga? (b) How did France help them after Saratoga?
2. **Critical Thinking** What do you think France hoped to gain by helping the Americans win independence?

soldiers to help the Patriot cause. Lafayette, who fought at Brandywine, became one of Washington's most trusted friends.

From the German state of Prussia came **Friedrich von Steuben** (STOO buhn). He helped train Washington's Continental troops to march and drill. Von Steuben had served in the Prussian army, considered the best in Europe.

Two Polish officers also joined the Americans. **Thaddeus Kosciusko** (kahs ee UHS koh), an engineer, helped build forts and other defenses. Casimir Pulaski trained **cavalry,** or troops on horseback.

Harsh Winter at Valley Forge

The victory at Saratoga and the promise of help from Europe did much to boost American morale. Nevertheless, Washington's ragged army still faced hard times. During the long, cold winter of 1777–1778, the Continental Army suffered severe hardships at Valley Forge in Pennsylvania.

The conditions at Valley Forge were terrible. American soldiers shivered in damp, drafty huts. Many slept on the frozen ground. They had little or no warm clothing. Some soldiers stood on guard wrapped only in blankets. Many had no shoes, so they wrapped bits of cloth around their feet. As the bitter winter wore on, soldiers suffered from frostbite and disease. An army surgeon from Connecticut wrote about the suffering:

66 There comes a Soldier, his bare feet are seen thro his worn-out stockings, his Breeches not sufficient to cover his nakedness . . . his whole appearance pictures a person forsaken & discouraged. 99

As news of the suffering at Valley Forge spread, Patriots from around the nation sent help. Women collected food, medicine, warm clothes, and ammunition for the army. Some women, like Martha Washington, wife of the commander, went to Valley Forge to help the sick and wounded.

The arrival of desperately needed supplies was soon followed by warmer weather. By the spring of 1778, the army at Valley Forge was more hopeful. Washington could not know it at the time, but the Patriots' bleakest hour had passed.

★ Section 3 Review ★

Recall

1. **Locate** **(a)** New York City, **(b)** Trenton, **(c)** Princeton, **(d)** Hudson River, **(e)** Albany, **(f)** Saratoga, **(g)** Valley Forge.
2. **Identify** **(a)** Battle of Long Island, **(b)** Nathan Hale, **(c)** Battle of Trenton, **(d)** John Burgoyne, **(e)** Battle of Saratoga, **(f)** Marquis de Lafayette, **(g)** Friedrich von Steuben, **(h)** Thaddeus Kosciusko.
3. **Define** **(a)** ally, **(b)** cavalry.

Comprehension

4. What problems did the Americans face during the campaign in the Middle States?

5. Describe three results of the Battle of Saratoga.
6. Why was help from France and other nations important to the Americans?

Critical Thinking and Writing

7. **Synthesizing Information** Reread the excerpt from *The Crisis* on page 170. **(a)** What did Paine mean by the words, "These are the times that try men's souls"? **(b)** What are "sunshine patriots"? **(c)** Why do you think Washington wanted Paine's words read to the troops?
8. **Drawing Conclusions** Why do you think Burgoyne's plan to cut the colonies in two by seizing Albany ended in failure?

Activity Reporting the News You are a newspaper reporter during the American Revolution. Write a report on a major event or battle that took place in the Middle States. You may need to do some additional research to write an interesting and informative article.

Other Battlefronts

Explore These Questions
- What were the major military events in the West?
- How did the South become the major battlefield of the war?
- How did women and African Americans take part in the war?

Define
- neutral

Identify
- George Rogers Clark
- Bernardo de Gálvez
- John Paul Jones
- Betsy Ross
- Molly Pitcher
- Peter Salem

As You Read

SETTING the Scene Flying Crow, a Seneca chief, looked sternly at the British officers who were seated before him. "If you are so strong, Brother, and they but a weak boy, why ask our assistance?"

Like many Native American leaders, Flying Crow did not want to become involved in a war between the "weak boy"—the United States—and Britain. Yet, Native Americans could not avoid the struggle.

Americans of various backgrounds played significant roles in the Revolution. Also, the American Revolution took place on many fronts. Fighting occurred not only in the North but also in the West and South. The war was also fought at sea.

The War in the West

When the Revolution began, most Indians tried to stay **neutral,** or uninvolved in the war. The British and Patriots, however, both sought Native American aid. In the end,

Connections With Civics

Unlike most other Iroquois, the Oneida Indians allied themselves with the Americans. The Congress thanked them in these words: "You stood forth in the cause of your friends and ventured your lives in our battles. While the sun and moon continue to give light to the world, we shall love and respect you."

the British were more persuasive. They convinced many Native Americans that a Patriot victory would mean more white settlers crossing the Appalachians and taking Indian lands.

Native Americans help the British

In the South, the British gained the support of the Cherokees, Creeks, Choctaws, and Chickasaws. In the summer of 1776, a Cherokee force attacked dozens of settlements on the frontier. Only after hard fighting were Patriot militia able to drive the Native Americans into the mountains. Sporadic fighting continued throughout the war.

Fighting was equally fierce on the northern frontier. In 1778, Iroquois forces led by the Mohawk leader Joseph Brant joined with Loyalists in raiding frontier settlements in Pennsylvania and New York. The next year, Patriots retaliated by invading Iroquois lands. They destroyed dozens of Iroquois villages. They also ruined thousands of acres of crops.

Victory at Vincennes

Further west, in 1778, **George Rogers Clark** led Virginia frontier fighters against the British in the Ohio Valley. With help from Miami Indians, Clark captured the British forts at Kaskaskia and Cahokia.

Clark then plotted a surprise winter attack on the British fort at Vincennes. He led a small band 150 miles (240 km) through heavy rains, swamps, and icy rivers.

When Clark's force reached the fort, they spread out through the woods to make their numbers appear greater than they really were. The British commander thought it was useless to fight so many Americans. He surrendered Vincennes in February 1779.

Spanish aid

On the southwestern frontier, Americans received help from New Spain. In the early years of the war, Spain was neutral. However, **Bernardo de Gálvez,** governor of Spanish Louisiana, favored the Patriots. He secretly supplied medicine, cloth, muskets, and gunpowder to the Americans. He also sent cattle from Texas to feed the Continental Army.

When Spain entered the war against Britain in 1779, Gálvez took a more active role. He seized British forts along the Mississippi River and the Gulf of Mexico. He also drove the British out of West Florida.

The War in the South

Scattered fighting had taken place in the South throughout the Revolution. In February 1776, North Carolina Patriots defeated a Loyalist army at the Battle of Moore's Creek Bridge. This battle is sometimes called the Lexington and Concord of the South.

After the British plan to conquer New York and New England failed, the South became the main battleground of the war. Sir Henry Clinton, the new British commander-in-chief, knew that many Loyalists lived in the southern backcountry. He hoped that if British troops marched through the South, Loyalists would join them.

At first, Clinton's plan seemed to work. In December 1778, the British seized Savannah, Georgia. A year and a half later, they took Charleston, South Carolina. Next, they crushed a Continental force at Camden, South Carolina. (See the map on page 179.) "I have almost ceased to hope," wrote Washington when he learned of the losses.

Fighting at Sea

At sea, the Americans could do little against the powerful British navy. British ships blockaded American ports. From time to time, however, a bold American captain captured a British ship.

The most daring American captain was **John Paul Jones.** In his most famous battle, in September 1779, Jones commanded the *Bonhomme Richard.* He was sailing in the North Sea near Britain when he spotted a large fleet of enemy merchant ships. They were guarded by a single warship, the *Serapis.* Jones attacked the *Serapis,* even though it was larger than the *Bonhomme Richard.*

In a furious battle, cannonballs ripped through the *Bonhomme Richard,* setting it on fire. The British commander called on

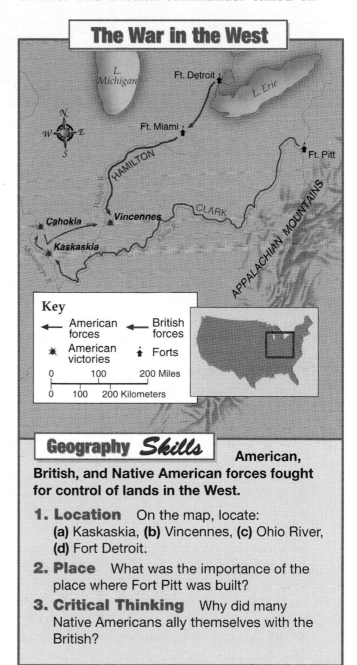

The War in the West

Key

← American forces   ← British forces

★ American victories   ⬆ Forts

0   100   200 Miles

0   100   200 Kilometers

Geography *Skills*   **American, British, and Native American forces fought for control of lands in the West.**

1. **Location**   On the map, locate: (a) Kaskaskia, (b) Vincennes, (c) Ohio River, (d) Fort Detroit.
2. **Place**   What was the importance of the place where Fort Pitt was built?
3. **Critical Thinking**   Why did many Native Americans ally themselves with the British?

Past

Present

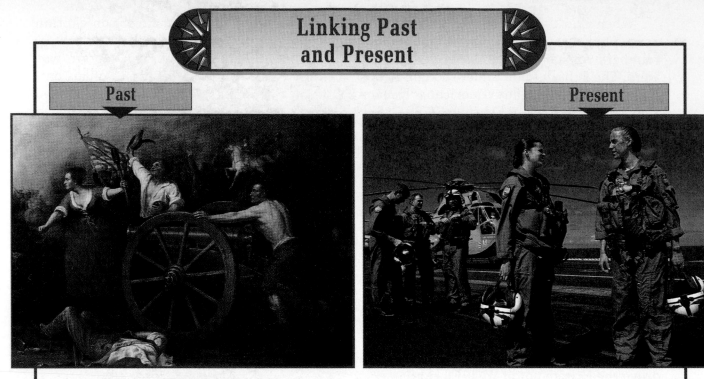

Women in Arms

During the American Revolution, few women took part in battle. Those who did became legendary. At left, Mary Ludwig Hays—known as "Molly Pitcher"—loads and fires a cannon. Today, thousands of American women serve on active duty in the United States military. Shown above are two female pilots aboard the aircraft carrier Eisenhower. ★ **Why do you think so many young women have volunteered to serve in the military?**

Jones to surrender. "I have not yet begun to fight!" Jones replied.

Jones sailed close to the *Serapis* so that his sailors could board the enemy ship. In hand-to-hand combat, the Americans defeated the British. Jones earned a hero's welcome on his return home.

Women in the War

Women also helped in the struggle for independence. When men went off to war, women took on added work. Some planted and harvested the crops. Others made shoes and wove cloth for blankets and uniforms. One woman, called "Handy Betsy the Blacksmith," was known for making cannons and guns for the army.

Many women joined their husbands who were serving in the army. The women cared for the wounded, washed clothes, and cooked. Martha Washington joined her husband whenever she could.

Some women achieved lasting fame for their activities in the war. **Betsy Ross** of Philadelphia sewed flags for Washington's army. Legend claims that she made the first American flag of stars and stripes.

A few women even took part in battle. During the Battle of Monmouth in 1778, Mary Ludwig Hays carried water to her husband and other soldiers. The soldiers called her Moll of the Pitcher or **Molly Pitcher.** When her husband was wounded, she took his place, loading and firing a cannon.

African Americans in the War

By 1776, more than a half million African Americans lived in the colonies. At first, the Continental Congress refused to let African Americans, whether free or enslaved, join the army. The British, however, offered freedom to any male slave who served the king. In response, Washington changed his policy and allowed free African Americans to enlist.

Joining the fight

It is estimated that about 5,000 African Americans fought against the British. At least nine black minutemen saw action at Lexington and Concord. One of them, Prince Estabrook, was wounded. Two others, **Peter Salem** and Salem Poor, went on to fight bravely at Bunker Hill.

Some African Americans formed special regiments. Others served in white regiments as drummers, fifers, spies, and guides. Thousands of black sailors also served on American ships. Whites recognized the courage of their African American comrades, as this eyewitness account shows:

    66 Three times in succession, [African American soldiers] were attacked...by well-disciplined and veteran [British] troops, and three times did they successfully repel the assault, and thus preserve our army from capture. **99**

Enslaved African Americans faced difficult choices. If they tried to flee to the British army to gain freedom, they risked being hanged by angry Patriots. If they joined the American army or continued to work on Patriot plantations, the British might capture and sell them.

Hoping for freedom

Black Patriots hoped that the Revolution would bring an end to slavery. After all, the Declaration of Independence proclaimed that "all men are created equal." In Massachusetts and elsewhere, enslaved African Americans sent petitions to lawmakers asking for freedom.

Some white leaders also hoped the war would end slavery. James Otis wrote that "the colonists are by the law of nature free born, as indeed all men are, white or black." Quakers in particular spoke out strongly against slavery.

By the 1770s, slavery was declining in the North, where a number of free African Americans lived. During the American Revolution, several states moved to make slavery illegal, including Massachusetts, New Hampshire, and Pennsylvania. Other states also began to debate the slavery issue.

★ Section 4 Review ★

Recall

1. **Locate** (a) Kaskaskia, (b) Cahokia, (c) Vincennes.
2. **Identify** (a) George Rogers Clark, (b) Bernardo de Gálvez, (c) John Paul Jones, (d) Betsy Ross, (e) Molly Pitcher, (f) Peter Salem.
3. **Define** neutral.

Comprehension

4. Describe the role that each of the following played in the war in the West: (a) Native Americans, (b) the Spanish.
5. How did the South replace the North as the major battlefield of the Revolution?

6. (a) How did women participate in the war effort? (b) Why did some African Americans join the British army?

Critical Thinking and Writing

7. **Understanding Causes and Effects** Read the following two statements. Then decide which is the cause and which is the effect. Explain your answer. (a) Many Native Americans sided with the British. (b) During the Revolution, settlers continued to push west of the Appalachians.
8. **Drawing Conclusions** How do you think the story of John Paul Jones's victory over the *Serapis* affected the attitudes of American Patriots?

★ ★

Activity **Writing a Tribute** During the American Revolution, you are a member of a special awards committee in the Congress. Choose a person or group mentioned in this section who helped the American cause. Write a tribute praising the individual's or group's accomplishments.

Winning the War

As You Read

Explore These Questions

- How did the Americans begin to win battles in the South?
- How did the Americans and French defeat the British at Yorktown?
- What were the terms of the Treaty of Paris?

Define

- guerrilla
- siege
- ratify

Identify

- Battle of King's Mountain
- Nathanael Greene
- Daniel Morgan
- Francis Marion
- Benedict Arnold
- Comte de Rochambeau
- Admiral de Grasse
- Battle of Yorktown
- Treaty of Paris

Powder horn

SETTING the Scene When he was only 16 years of age, Thomas Young set out with about 900 other Patriots to capture King's Mountain in South Carolina. Although most of the Patriots were barefoot, they moved quickly up the wooded hillside, shouldering their old muskets. They were determined to take the mountain from the Loyalists dug in at the top.

Whooping and shouting, Young and his comrades dashed from tree to tree, dodging bullets as they fired their own weapons. They climbed higher and higher toward the enemy lines. Suddenly, Thomas heard the frantic cry, "Colonel Williams is shot!"

    66 I ran to his assistance for I loved him as a father. . . . He revived, and his first words were, 'For God's sake boys, don't give up the hill!' . . . [I] returned to the field to avenge his fate. **99**

Patriots Rally in the South

The Patriots succeeded in capturing King's Mountain on October 7, 1780. The victory boosted morale and breathed new life into the Patriot cause in the South. Jefferson called the **Battle of King's Mountain** "the turn of the tide."

The American Patriots in the South certainly needed the good news. General Clinton's redcoats had captured both Savannah and Charleston, forcing the American armies into retreat. Throughout the southern countryside, attacks by British troops and Loyalist militia had become especially destructive and brutal. One Loyalist officer boasted how the army was "destroying furniture, breaking windows, taking . . . cattle, horses, mules."

The Patriot victory at King's Mountain was only the first in a string of American victories in the South. In the months ahead, two able American generals helped to turn the tide against Cornwallis and his British army. The American generals were **Nathanael Greene** of Rhode Island and **Daniel Morgan** of Virginia.

Connections With Geography

Geography helped the Patriots win at King's Mountain. To reach the Loyalists atop the ridge, the Patriots climbed through a forest that protected them from enemy fire. The Loyalists had a difficult downhill line of fire. One Patriot recalled how the Loyalists "overshot us altogether, scarce touching a man except those on horseback."

General Greene's ability as a military leader was perhaps second only to Washington's. In 1780, Greene took command of the Continental Army in the South. Making good use of his soldiers' knowledge of the local geography, Greene chose to fight only on ground that put the British at a disadvantage. When he retreated, he followed the easiest routes. He often arranged for boats to be waiting at river crossings. General Cornwallis wore out his soldiers trying to catch Greene's army.

In January 1781, General Morgan won an important battle at Cowpens, South Carolina. Morgan used a clever tactic to defeat the British. Morgan divided his soldiers into a front line and a rear line. He ordered the front line to retreat after firing just two volleys. The British, thinking the Americans were retreating, charged forward—straight into the devastating fire of Morgan's second rank. In this way, the Americans won the Battle of Cowpens.

Greene and Morgan had combined their armies when they fought Cornwallis at Guilford Court House, near present-day Greensboro, North Carolina. The battle was one of the bloodiest of the war. Though the Americans retreated, the British sustained great losses. One Englishman observed that "another such victory would destroy the British army." Cornwallis withdrew to the coastal town of Wilmington to rest and regroup his army.

Francis Marion of South Carolina added to British frustrations. He led a small band of militia, who often slept by day and traveled by night. Marion was known as the Swamp Fox. His soldiers used **guerrilla,** or hit-and-run, tactics to harass the British. They would appear suddenly out of the swamps, quickly attack, and then retreat back into the swamps.

Victory at Yorktown

Finally, Cornwallis gave up on his plan to take the Carolinas. In the spring of 1781, he moved his troops north into Virginia. He planned to conquer Virginia and cut off the Americans' supply routes to the South.

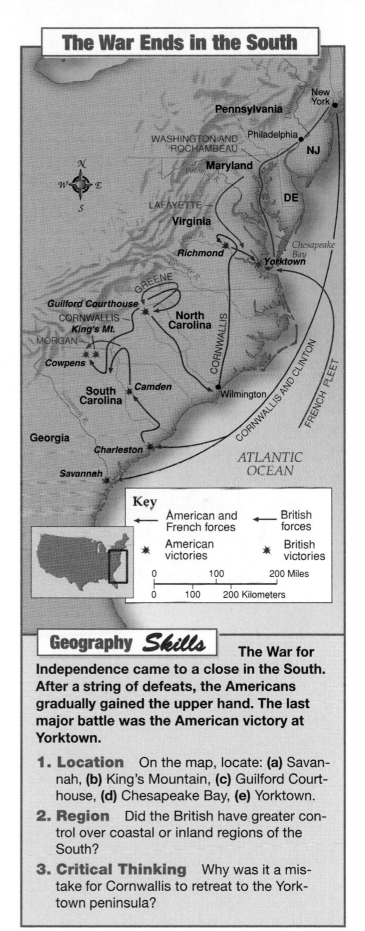

The War Ends in the South

Key

← American and French forces

← British forces

✸ American victories

✸ British victories

0   100   200 Miles

0   100   200 Kilometers

Geography Skills   The War for Independence came to a close in the South. After a string of defeats, the Americans gradually gained the upper hand. The last major battle was the American victory at Yorktown.

1. **Location**   On the map, locate: **(a)** Savannah, **(b)** King's Mountain, **(c)** Guilford Courthouse, **(d)** Chesapeake Bay, **(e)** Yorktown.

2. **Region**   Did the British have greater control over coastal or inland regions of the South?

3. **Critical Thinking**   Why was it a mistake for Cornwallis to retreat to the Yorktown peninsula?

An American traitor

The British had achieved some success in Virginia, even before the arrival of Cornwallis. **Benedict Arnold,** formerly one of the Americans' best generals, was now leading British troops. Arnold captured and burned the capital city of Richmond. His forces raided and burned other towns as well.

Arnold had turned traitor to the American cause in September 1780, while commanding West Point, a key fort in New York. Arnold was resentful because he felt he had not received enough credit for his victories. He also needed money. He secretly agreed to turn over West Point to the British. The plot was uncovered by a Patriot patrol, but Arnold escaped to join the British.

Arnold's act of treachery and his raids on towns in Connecticut and Virginia enraged the Patriots. Thomas Jefferson, governor of Virginia, offered a sizable reward in gold for his capture. Washington wrote orders that Arnold was to be hanged. Despite these efforts, Arnold was never captured.

Cornwallis trapped

Cornwallis hoped to meet with the same kind of success in Virginia that Arnold had. At first, things did go well. Cornwallis sent Loyalist troops to attack Charlottesville, where the Virginia legislature was meeting. Governor Thomas Jefferson and other officials had to flee.

American troops under Lafayette fought back by making raids against the British. Lafayette did not have enough troops to fight a major battle. Still, his strategy kept Cornwallis at bay.

Then, Cornwallis made a mistake. He refused an order from Sir Henry Clinton to send part of his army to New York. Instead, he retreated to Yorktown peninsula, a strip of land jutting into Chesapeake Bay. He felt confident that British ships could supply his army from the sea.

Washington saw an opportunity to trap Cornwallis on the Yorktown peninsula. He marched his Continental troops south from New York. With the Americans were French soldiers under the **Comte de Rochambeau** (roh shahm BOH). The combined army rushed to join Lafayette in Virginia.

Meanwhile, a French fleet under **Admiral de Grasse** was also heading towards Virginia. Once in Chesapeake Bay, De Grasse's fleet closed the trap. Cornwallis was cut off. He could not get supplies. He could not escape by land or by sea.

The British surrender

By the end of September, more than 16,000 American and French troops laid **siege** to Cornwallis's army of fewer than 8,000. A siege is the act of surrounding an enemy position in an attempt to capture it. Day after day, American and French artillery pounded the British.

For several weeks, Cornwallis held out. Finally, with casualties mounting and his

Biography James Armistead

Though enslaved, James Armistead faithfully served the Patriot cause as a spy. Under the direction of Lafayette, Armistead worked as a volunteer in the camps of Benedict Arnold and Lord Cornwallis. The information he gained contributed to the American victory at Yorktown. Later, after winning his freedom, Armistead changed his name to Lafayette. ★ **Why do you think Armistead decided to change his name to Lafayette?**

Skills FOR LIFE

| **Critical Thinking** | **Managing Information** | **Communication** | **Maps, Charts, and Graphs** |

Understanding Causes and Effects

How Will I Use This Skill?

Some causes and effects are easy to see. A frost in Florida causes the price of orange juice to rise. An accident at a busy intersection leads the town to put up a new stop sign. Recognizing the relationship between causes and effects can help you understand what has happened and predict future events.

LEARN the Skill

❶ Identify the primary event or condition that you will examine.

❷ Determine which events had a role in causing the primary event.

❸ Determine which events occurred as a result of the primary event.

❹ Explain the relationship between causes and effects.

PRACTICE the Skill

At right are a list of events and a partially filled-in cause-and-effect chart. After reading this section, answer the following questions:

❶ What primary event is the focus of the chart?

❷ Which events on the list would you include in the chart as causes? Why?

❸ Which events on the list would you include in the chart as effects? Why?

❹ (a) Why was taxation one cause of the American Revolution? (b) Do you think the United States of America could have been formed without the American Revolution?

Cause and Effect

Causes
- Parliament taxes the colonies
- _____
- _____

The American Revolution

Effects
- United States of America is formed
- _____
- _____

George Washington emerges as national leader

Proclamation of 1763 stops colonists from moving west

Intolerable Acts set up harsh rule in Massachusetts

United States borders extend to Florida and Mississippi River

APPLY the Skill

Select an event that affected you. Create a chart that identifies at least two causes and two effects of that event.

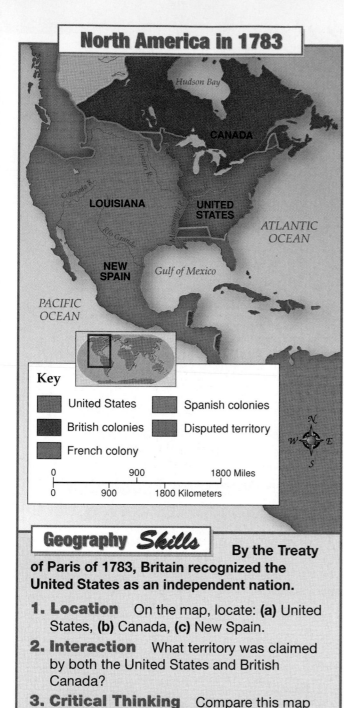

North America in 1783

Hudson Bay

CANADA

LOUISIANA

UNITED STATES

ATLANTIC OCEAN

NEW SPAIN

Gulf of Mexico

PACIFIC OCEAN

Key

- United States
- British colonies
- French colony
- Spanish colonies
- Disputed territory

| 0 | 900 | 1800 Miles |
| 0 | 900 | 1800 Kilometers |

Geography *Skills*
By the Treaty of Paris of 1783, Britain recognized the United States as an independent nation.

1. Location On the map, locate: **(a)** United States, **(b)** Canada, **(c)** New Spain.

2. Interaction What territory was claimed by both the United States and British Canada?

3. Critical Thinking Compare this map with the map on page 140. According to the maps, what was the major difference between North America in 1763 and North America in 1783?

---

marched between the victorious troops, a British army band played the tune "The World Turned Upside Down."

The Peace Treaty

The British thought that they could settle their disputes with the American colonies through a show of massive military strength. They were mistaken. In fact, British efforts to impose their will by force served only to alienate the colonists even more. Americans who suffered at the hands of British troops usually became strong supporters of the Patriots' fight for independence. In London, however, the defeat shocked the British. "It is all over," cried the British prime minister, Lord North. Left with no other choice, he agreed to peace talks.

The talks began in Paris in 1782. Congress sent Benjamin Franklin and John Adams, along with John Jay of New York and Henry Laurens of South Carolina, to work out a treaty. Because Britain was eager to end the war, the Americans got most of what they wanted.

Under the **Treaty of Paris,** the British recognized the United States as an independent nation. The borders of the new nation extended from the Atlantic Ocean to the Mississippi River. The southern border stopped at Florida, which was returned to Spain.

On their part, the Americans agreed to ask state legislatures to pay Loyalists for property they lost in the war. In the end, however, most states ignored Loyalist claims.

On April 15, 1783, Congress **ratified,** or approved, the Treaty of Paris. It was almost eight years to the day since the battles of Lexington and Concord.

Washington's Farewell

In December 1783, General Washington bid farewell to his officers at Fraunces Tavern in New York City. Colonel Benjamin Tallmadge recalled the event:

66 Such a scene of sorrow and weeping I had never before witnessed
....[W]e were then about to part
from the man who had conducted us

---

supplies running low, Cornwallis decided the situation was hopeless. The British had lost the **Battle of Yorktown.**

On October 19, 1781, the British surrendered their weapons to the Americans. The French and the Americans lined up in two facing columns. As the defeated redcoats

through a long and bloody war, and under whose conduct the glory and independence of our country had been achieved. **99**

All along Washington's route home to Virginia, crowds cheered the hero of American independence. The new nation faced difficult days ahead. Americans would call on Washington to lead them once again.

Reasons for the American Victory

Geography had much to do with the American victory in the Revolutionary War. It was difficult for the British to send soldiers and supplies to a war several thousand miles from home. The Patriots they sought to conquer were spread over a very wide area. When the British captured coastal cities, American forces moved inland. The Americans knew

Flag of a new nation

the local geography. They knew the best routes and the best places to fight.

Assistance from other nations also contributed to the American victory. Spanish forces attacked the British along the Gulf of Mexico and in the Mississippi Valley. French money helped pay for supplies. Most important was French military aid. Without French soldiers and warships, the Americans might not have won the Battle of Yorktown.

Victory over the British was also due to the patriotic spirit, determination, and fighting skill of the Patriots. Despite many setbacks in the early years of the war, the Americans battled on. As time passed, their devotion to liberty and their fighting ability both grew. Critically important, too, was the leadership of General Washington. By war's end, Washington's ability as a general was respected by Americans and British alike.

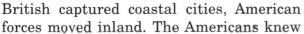

★ Section 5 Review ★

Recall

1. **Locate** (a) King's Mountain, (b) Savannah, (c) Charleston, (d) Cowpens, (e) Guilford Courthouse, (f) Yorktown.

2. **Identify** (a) Battle of King's Mountain, (b) Nathanael Greene, (c) Daniel Morgan, (d) Francis Marion, (e) Benedict Arnold, (f) Comte de Rochambeau, (g) Admiral de Grasse, (h) Battle of Yorktown, (i) Treaty of Paris.

3. **Define** (a) guerrilla, (b) siege, (c) ratify.

Comprehension

4. For each of the American military leaders that follow, describe a tactic that the leader used to defeat the British: (a) Greene, (b) Morgan, (c) Marion.

5. How did the Americans and French achieve victory over the British at Yorktown?

6. Describe the major points of the Treaty of Paris of 1783.

Critical Thinking and Writing

7. **Analyzing Ideas** Why do you think the British played "The World Turned Upside Down" when they surrendered at Yorktown?

8. **Understanding Causes and Effects** Describe three reasons why the Americans were able to defeat the British and win the American Revolution.

★ ★

History AND YOU

Activity **Writing a Song** You are a member of a fife and drum band in the Continental Army. General Washington has asked you to write the words for a lively tune that the soldiers can march to. The General wants the song to praise the daring exploits of American soldiers in the South.

Chapter 6 Review and Activities

★ Sum It Up ★

Section 1 Early Battles
▶ King George III rejected the Second Continental Congress's attempt to solve their conflict peacefully.
▶ The Americans captured Ticonderoga and Boston from the British, but lost a major battle in Canada.

Section 2 Declaring Independence
▶ In his pamphlet *Common Sense,* Thomas Paine argued that colonists did not owe loyalty to the king.
▶ The Continental Congress declared in 1776 that the American colonies had become the independent United States of America.

Section 3 Fighting in the Middle States
▶ The British gained contol of New York City and forced Washington's army into retreat.
▶ The American victory at Saratoga was the major turning point of the war.

Section 4 Other Battlefronts
▶ Fighting took place on many battlefronts, including the West and the high seas.
▶ Women aided the war effort by making needed goods, by caring for the wounded, and, in some cases, by fighting.

Section 5 Winning the War
▶ With help from the French, the Americans defeated the British army at Yorktown.
▶ By the Treaty of Paris, Britain recognized the United States as an independent nation.

 **CD-ROM Review** For additional review of the major ideas of Chapter 6, see *Guide to the Essentials of American History* or *Interactive Student Tutorial CD-ROM,* which contains interactive review activities, graphic organizers, and practice tests.

🗎 Reviewing the Chapter

Define These Terms

Match each term with the correct definition.

Column 1	Column 2
1. traitor	**a.** to approve
2. mercenary	**b.** a friend or supporter
3. ally	**c.** not taking sides in a war
4. neutral	**d.** hired soldier who fights for a foreign country
5. ratify	**e.** person who betrays his or her country

Explore the Main Ideas

1. In 1775, how did American Patriots offer peace, but prepare for war?
2. **(a)** How did *Common Sense* affect American colonists? **(b)** Describe three ideas contained in the Declaration of Independence.
3. Why did Thomas Paine write *The Crisis*?
4. In what ways was the Battle of Saratoga a major turning point of the war?
5. What role did African Americans play during the war?
6. **(a)** What advantages did the British have in the War for Independence? **(b)** Why were Americans able to win the war?

🗎 Geography Activity

Match the letters on the map with the following places:
1. Boston, **2.** Trenton, **3.** Saratoga, **4.** Cowpens, **5.** Savannah, **6.** Yorktown. **Movement** Why was control of the Chesapeake Bay important to Cornwallis at Yorktown?

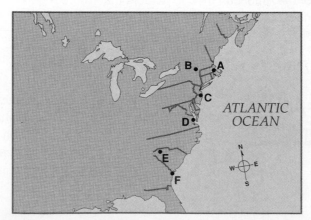

🗒 Critical Thinking and Writing

1. **Ranking** In your opinion, what were the three biggest mistakes that British political and military leaders made between 1775 and 1783? Explain the reasons for your choices.

2. **Exploring Unit Themes** **Rights and Liberties** According to the Declaration of Independence, when do people have a right and duty to rebel against their government?

3. **Understanding Chronology** **(a)** Arrange the following four events in chronological order: (1) British defeat at Yorktown, (2) American victory at Saratoga, (3) French entry into the war against Britain, (4) the signing of the Treaty of Paris. **(b)** Explain how each event helped to cause the next event.

4. **Linking Past and Present** Today, the United States and Britain are close allies. Why do you think the two nations have such close ties?

🗒 Using Primary Sources

In 1776, General George Washington wrote to John Hancock, president of the Continental Congress, about the condition of the army:

> 66 To place any dependance upon Militia, is, assuredly, resting upon a broken staff. Men just dragged from the tender Scenes of domestick life; unaccustomed to the din of Arms; totally unacquainted with every kind of Military skill, which being followed by a want of confidence in themselves, when opposed to Troops regulary train'd, disciplined, and appointed, superior in knowledge, and superior in Arms, makes them timid, and ready to fly from their own shadows. 99

Source: *The Writings of George Washington from the Original Manuscript Sources: 1745–1799.*

Recognizing Points of View **(a)** What was Washington's view of British soldiers? **(b)** What was his opinion of American militia? **(c)** What do you think Washington wanted from Congress?

ACTIVITY BANK

▶ Interdisciplinary Activity

Exploring Sciences Do research to learn about medical treatments provided to sick and wounded soldiers of the American Revolution. Summarize your findings in a report and create illustrations of the medical instruments used at the time.

▶ Career Skills Activity

Graphic Artist In a graphic organizer, show the role that each of the following played in the American Revolution: **(a)** Native Americans, **(b)** French, **(c)** women, **(d)** African Americans, **(e)** Spanish.

▶ Citizenship Activity

Honoring Good Citizenship Create a "Nathan Hale Award" for a citizen of your community who has proudly made a sacrifice for the good of the United States. Working with classmates, hold a ceremony in which you explain why you are giving the award to the citizen you have chosen.

Internet Activity

Use the Internet to learn more about the activities of Nathan Hale, James Armistead Lafayette, or another spy of the Revolution. Based on what you learn, write a short fictional story about espionage in the American Revolution.

EYEWITNESS Journal

It is 1776 and you have just heard about the Declaration of Independence. Choose one of the following roles: Loyalist; Patriot; African American; Native American; British soldier; French government official; a woman whose husband, father, or son is a soldier in the war. In your EYEWITNESS JOURNAL, explain what the Declaration means for you and your future.

Chapter 7

Creating a Republic

1776–1791

After the American Revolution ended, the new nation struggled to create a workable government. At first, the states were knit together only by a loose set of laws. When this central government proved too weak, representatives of 12 states gathered in 1787. They created a new framework for government: the Constitution of the United States.

During nearly four exhausting months of debate, the representatives hammered out a set of laws that would make the nation strong, yet protect the rights of the people. After fiery arguments in each state, the Constitution was finally approved. It lives on as the framework of our government today.

Why Study History?

While the new nation was taking shape, American leaders were also creating many symbols and traditions. Today, as in the past, emblems such as the flag and the eagle bind the American people together. To focus on this connection, see the *Why Study History* feature, "National Symbols Unite Us," in this chapter.

American Events

●1777
Continental Congress completes the Articles of Confederation

1783 ●
Treaty of Paris formally ends the American Revolution

1776   **1780**   **1784**

World Events

 1778 World Event
British Captain Cook becomes first European to reach Hawaii

 1784 World Event
Emperor Joseph II forces Czechs to use German language

Signing the Constitution

In 1787, representatives from 12 states gathered in Philadelphia to create a new national government. The result of their work was the Constitution, which still governs the nation today. This painting by Howard Chandler Christy shows delegates to the Constitutional Convention, including George Washington (standing right) and Benjamin Franklin (seated center). Washington served as the president of the Convention. ★ **Why do you think the representatives chose Washington as their president?**

1787 Northwest Ordinance sets up method to admit new states to the United States

1788 The Constitution is ratified

1791 Bill of Rights guarantees individual rights and freedoms

1784   **1788**   **1792**

 1785 World Event Russians settle in Aleutian Islands off coast of Alaska

 1789 World Event French Revolution begins

★ 187

A Confederation of States

As You Read

Explore These Questions
- What ideas guided the new state governments?
- What problems did the nation face under the Articles of Confederation?
- How did the Northwest Ordinance benefit the nation?

Define
- constitution
- execute
- confederation
- ordinance
- economic depression

Identify
- Articles of Confederation
- Land Ordinance of 1785
- Northwest Ordinance
- Shays' Rebellion

SETTING the Scene In 1776, the Declaration of Independence created a new nation made up of 13 independent states. The former colonies, though, had little experience working together. In the past, Britain had made the major decisions. Now, the Americans set about the business of establishing 13 state governments. Furthermore, they hoped to create a central government that all the states would follow.

State Governments

In forming a government, most states wrote a constitution. A **constitution** is a document that sets out the laws and principles of a government. States created written constitutions for two reasons. First, a written constitution would spell out the rights of all citizens. Second, it would set limits on the power of government.

The new state governments were similar to the colonial governments. The states divided political power between an executive and a legislature. The legislature was elected by the voters to pass the laws. Most legislatures had an upper house, called a senate, and a lower house. All states except Pennsylvania had a governor who **executed,** or carried out, the laws.

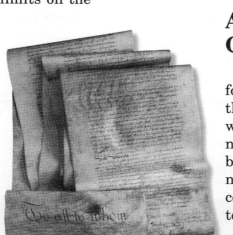

Articles of Confederation

Virginia limited government power by including a bill of rights in its constitution. A bill of rights lists freedoms that the government promises to protect. Virginia's bill of rights protected freedom of religion and freedom of the press. It also guaranteed citizens the right to a trial by jury. Other states followed Virginia's example and included bills of rights in their constitutions.

Under the state constitutions, more people had the right to vote than in colonial times. To vote, a citizen had to be white, male, and over age 21. He had to own a certain amount of property or pay a certain amount of taxes.

For a time, some women in New Jersey could vote. In a few states, free black men could vote. In no state did enslaved African Americans have the right to vote.

A Weak Confederation

In 1776, as citizens were forming state governments, the Continental Congress was drafting a plan for the nation as a whole. Delegates believed that the colonies needed to be united by a central government in order to win independence.

It was difficult to write a constitution that all of the states would approve. They were reluctant to give up power to a national government. In 1776, few Americans saw themselves as citizens of one nation. Instead, they felt loyal to their own states. Also, people were fearful of replacing the "tyranny" of British rule with another strong government. Still, in 1777, after much debate, the Continental Congress completed the **Articles of Confederation**—the first American constitution. It created a **confederation,** or alliance of independent states.

Government under the Articles

Under the Articles of Confederation, the states sent delegates to a Confederation Congress. Each state had one vote in Congress. Congress could declare war, appoint military officers, and coin money. It was also responsible for foreign affairs. However, these powers were few compared with those of the states.

The Articles limited the powers of Congress and preserved the powers of the states. Congress could pass laws, but at least 9 of the 13 states had to approve a law before it could go into effect.

Congress had little economic power. It could not regulate trade between states nor could it regulate trade between states and foreign countries. It could not pass tax laws. To raise money, Congress had to ask the states for it. No state could be forced to contribute funds.

The new confederation government was weak. There was no president to carry out laws. It was up to the states to enforce the laws passed by Congress. There was no system of courts to settle disputes between states. The Articles created a very loose alliance of 13 states.

Dispute over western lands

A dispute arose even before the Articles of Confederation went into effect. Maryland refused to ratify the Articles unless Virginia and other states gave up their claims to lands west of the Appalachian Mountains. Maryland wanted these western lands turned over to Congress. In this way, the "landed" states would not become too powerful.

One by one, the states gave up their western claims. Only Virginia held out. However,

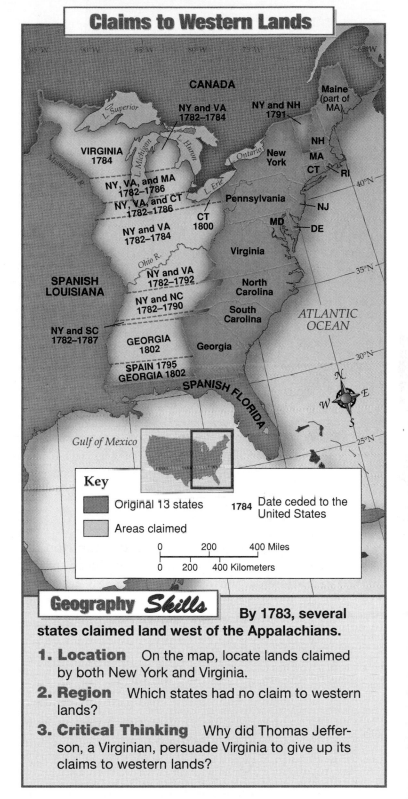

Claims to Western Lands

Geography Skills By 1783, several states claimed land west of the Appalachians.

1. **Location** On the map, locate lands claimed by both New York and Virginia.
2. **Region** Which states had no claim to western lands?
3. **Critical Thinking** Why did Thomas Jefferson, a Virginian, persuade Virginia to give up its claims to western lands?

Thomas Jefferson and other leading Virginians saw a great need for a central government. They persuaded state lawmakers to give up Virginia's claims in the West. At last, in 1781, Maryland ratified the Articles of Confederation, and the first American government went into effect.

State Banknotes

During and after the American Revolution, each state issued its own money. The bills here came from Rhode Island and South Carolina.
★ **What problems might arise due to the fact that each state issued its own money?**

Troubles for the New Nation

By 1783, the United States had won independence. The new nation faced many challenges, however. From 1783 to 1787, Americans had reason to doubt whether their country could survive.

Conflicts between states

Despite its weaknesses, the Articles might have succeeded if the states could have put aside their differences and worked together. Many conflicts arose, however. New Hampshire and New York both claimed Vermont. Most states refused to accept the money of other states.

The Articles did not provide a way for states to settle such disputes. Noah Webster, a teacher from New England, warned:

> 66 So long as any individual state has power to defeat the measures of the other twelve, our pretended union is but a name, and our confederation, a cobweb. 99

Money problems

As a result of borrowing during the Revolution, the United States owed millions of dollars to individuals and foreign nations. Since Congress did not have the power to tax, it had no way to repay these debts. Congress asked the states for money, but the states had the right to refuse. Often, they did.

During the Revolution, the Continental Congress solved the problem of raising funds by printing paper money. However, the money had little value because it was not backed by gold or silver. Before long, Americans began to describe any useless thing as "not worth a Continental."

As Continental dollars became worthless, states printed their own paper money. This caused confusion. How much was a North Carolina dollar worth? Was a Virginia dollar as valuable as a Maryland dollar? As a result, trade became difficult.

Other nations take advantage

Foreign countries took advantage of the confederation's weakness. Britain, for example, refused to withdraw its troops from the Ohio Valley, as it had agreed to do in the Treaty of Paris. Spain closed its port in New Orleans to American farmers. This was a serious blow to western farmers, who depended on the port to ship their products to the East.

Organizing the Northwest Territory

Despite its troubles, Congress did pass important **ordinances,** or laws, concerning the Northwest Territory, the name for lands lying north of the Ohio River and east of the Mississippi. The principles established in these laws were later applied to other areas of settlement.

Townships and sections

The **Land Ordinance of 1785** set up a system for surveying and settling the Northwest Territory. The law called for the territory to be surveyed and then divided into townships.

Each township would have 36 sections. A section was 1 square mile and contained 640 acres. (See the diagram below.) Congress planned to sell sections to settlers for $640 each. One section in every township was set aside to support public schools.

A plan for new states

Another law, passed in 1787, was the **Northwest Ordinance.** It set up a government for the Northwest Territory, guaranteed basic rights to settlers, and outlawed slavery there. It also provided for the vast region to be divided into separate territories in the future.

Once a territory had a population of 60,000 free settlers, it could ask Congress to be admitted as a new state. The newly admitted state would be "on an equal footing with the original states in all respects whatsoever."

The Northwest Ordinance was the finest achievement of the national government under the Articles. It provided a way to admit new states to the nation. It guaranteed that new states would be treated the same as the original 13 states. In time, the states of Ohio, Indiana, Illinois, Michigan, and Wisconsin were created from the Northwest Territory.

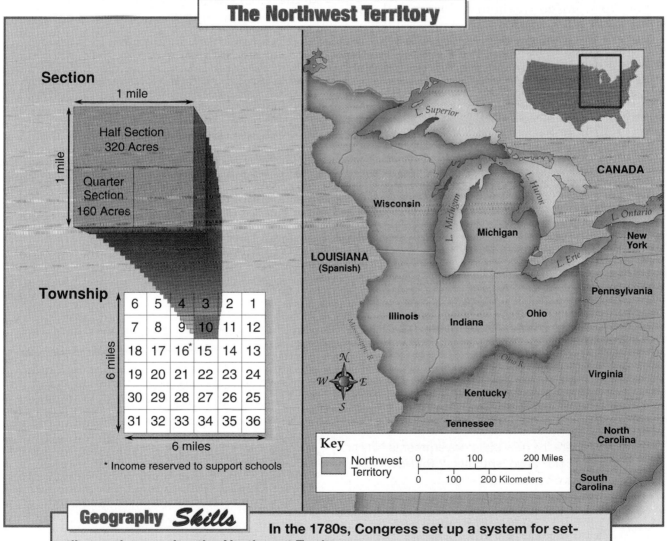

The Northwest Territory

Section

1 mile

Half Section
320 Acres

1 mile

Quarter Section
160 Acres

Township

6	5	4	3	2	1
7	8	9	10	11	12
18	17	16*	15	14	13
19	20	21	22	23	24
30	29	28	27	26	25
31	32	33	34	35	36

6 miles

6 miles

* Income reserved to support schools

Key

Northwest Territory

0   100   200 Miles
0   100   200 Kilometers

Geography *Skills*

In the 1780s, Congress set up a system for settling and governing the Northwest Territory.

1. **Location** On the map, locate: **(a)** Ohio River, **(b)** Mississippi River, **(c)** Michigan, **(d)** Indiana, **(e)** Illinois, **(f)** Wisconsin, **(g)** Ohio.

2. **Place** What was the size of **(a)** a township, **(b)** a section?

3. **Critical Thinking** Did the state of Wisconsin have public education when it joined the Union? Explain.

A Farmers' Revolt

While Congress dealt successfully with the Northwest Territory, it failed to solve its economic problems. After the Revolution, the nation suffered an economic depression. An **economic depression** is a period when business activity slows, prices and wages fall, and unemployment rises.

The depression hit farmers hard. During the Revolution, there had been high demand for farm products. To increase production, farmers had borrowed money for land, seed, animals, and tools. However, when the war ended and soldiers returned home, demand for farm goods weakened. Prices fell, and many farmers could not repay their loans.

In Massachusetts, matters worsened when the state raised taxes. The courts seized the farms of those who could not pay their taxes or loans. Angry farmers felt they were being treated unfairly.

In 1786, Daniel Shays, a Massachusetts farmer who had fought at Bunker Hill and Saratoga, organized an uprising. Nearly 2,000 farmers took part in **Shays' Rebel-lion.** They attacked courthouses and prevented the state from seizing farms. They even tried to capture an arsenal filled with guns. Finally, the Massachusetts legislature sent the militia to drive them off.

A Change Is Needed

Many Americans saw Shays' Rebellion as a sign that the Articles of Confederation did not work. George Washington warned that a terrible crisis was at hand:

66 No day was ever more clouded than the present.... I predict the worst consequences from a half-starved, limping government, always moving upon crutches and tottering at every step. 99

To avoid such a crisis, leaders from several states called for a convention to revise the Articles of Confederation. They decided to meet in Philadelphia in May 1787. In the end, however, this convention would do much more than just revise the Articles. It would change the course of the nation.

★ Section 1 Review ★

Recall

1. **Locate**   Northwest Territory.
2. **Identify**   (a) Articles of Confederation, (b) Land Ordinance of 1785, (c) Northwest Ordinance, (d) Shays' Rebellion.
3. **Define**   (a) constitution, (b) execute, (c) confederation, (d) ordinance, (e) economic depression.

Comprehension

4. (a) How were the new state governments similar to the old colonial governments? (b) How were they different?
5. Describe three problems the nation faced under the Articles of Confederation.

6. How did the Northwest Ordinance affect the future growth of the United States?

Critical Thinking and Writing

7. **Analyzing Ideas**   When Thomas Jefferson heard about Shays' Rebellion, he wrote: "The spirit of resistance to government is so valuable on occasion that I wish it to be always kept alive." Do you think Shays' Rebellion was good for the United States? Explain.
8. **Identifying Main Ideas**   After only 10 years, many Americans agreed that the Articles of Confederation did not work. Why did the Articles fail to serve as a lasting constitution for the United States?

Activity   Drawing a Political Cartoon   You have been asked to create a political cartoon about Shays' Rebellion. The purpose is to help explain to younger students the reasons why farmers like Daniel Shays were angry and what happened as a result of their rebellion.

The Constitutional Convention

As You Read

Explore These Questions
- How did the Virginia Plan and the New Jersey Plan differ?
- How did the Great Compromise satisfy both large and small states?
- What compromises were made on the issue of slavery?

Define
- legislative branch
- executive branch
- judicial branch
- compromise

Identify
- Constitutional Convention
- James Madison
- Virginia Plan
- New Jersey Plan
- Roger Sherman
- Great Compromise
- Three-Fifths Compromise

◄ The Liberty Bell, a symbol of freedom, originally hung in the Pennsylvania State House.

SETTING the Scene An air of mystery hung over the Pennsylvania State House in Philadelphia during the summer of 1787. Philadelphians watched as the nation's greatest leaders passed in and out of the building. Eleven years earlier, some of the same men had signed the Declaration of Independence there. What was going on now? Susannah Dillwyn wrote to her father about the excitement:

66 There is now sitting in this city a grand convention, who are to form some new system of government or mend the old one. I suppose it is a body of great consequence, as they say it depends entirely upon their pleasure whether we shall in the future have a congress. 99

What would this "grand convention" decide? No one knew. For almost four months, Americans waited for an answer.

The Convention Opens

On May 25, 1787, the **Constitutional Convention** opened in Philadelphia. Every state except Rhode Island sent representatives. Their mission was to revise the Articles of Confederation.

The 55 delegates gathered for the convention were a remarkable group. At age 81,

Benjamin Franklin was the oldest delegate. He was wise in the ways of government and human nature. George Washington was a representative from Virginia. Washington was so well respected that the delegates at once elected him president of the Convention.

Perhaps the best-prepared delegate to the Constitutional Convention was young **James Madison** of Virginia. For months, Madison had secluded himself on his father's plantation. There, he read many books on history, politics, and commerce. He arrived in Philadelphia with a case bulging with volumes of research.

Many delegates were young men in their twenties and thirties. Among them was Alexander Hamilton of New York. During the Revolution, Hamilton served for a time as Washington's private secretary. Hamilton despised the Articles of Confederation. "The nation," he wrote, "is sick and wants powerful remedies." The powerful remedy he prescribed was a strong national government.

When the Convention began, the delegates decided to keep their talks secret. They wanted to be able to speak their minds freely. They wished to explore issues and solutions without pressures from outside.

The Virginia Plan

Edmund Randolph and James Madison, both from Virginia, proposed a plan for the new government. This **Virginia Plan** called for a strong national government with three branches. The **legislative branch** would pass the laws. The **executive branch** would carry out the laws. The **judicial branch,** or system of courts, would decide if laws were carried out fairly.

According to the Virginia Plan, the legislative branch would consist of two houses. Seats in both houses would be awarded on the basis of population. Thus, in both houses, larger states would have more representatives than smaller ones. This differed from the Articles of Confederation, which gave every state, regardless of population, one vote in Congress.

The New Jersey Plan

Small states objected strongly to the Virginia Plan. They feared that the large states could easily outvote them in Congress. In response, supporters of the Virginia Plan said that it was only fair for a state with more people to have more representatives.

After two weeks of debate, William Paterson of New Jersey presented a plan that had the support of the small states. Like the Virginia Plan, the **New Jersey Plan** called for three branches of government. However, it provided for a legislature that had only one house. Each state, regardless of its population, would have one vote in the legislature.

The Great Compromise

For a while, no agreement could be reached. With tempers flaring, it seemed that the Convention would fall apart without adopting any plan. Finally, **Roger Sherman** of Connecticut worked out a compromise that he hoped would satisfy both large and small states. A **compromise** is a settlement in which each side gives up some of its demands in order to reach an agreement.

Sherman's compromise called for a two-house legislature. Members of the lower house, known as the House of Representatives, would be elected by popular vote. As

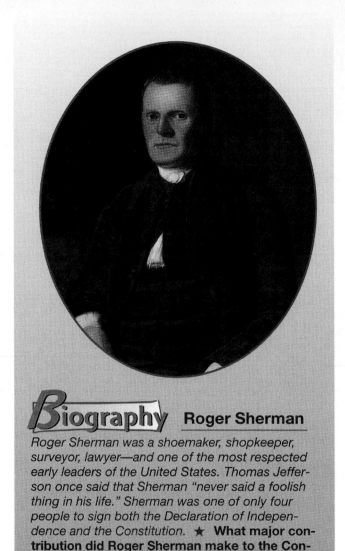

*B*iography   Roger Sherman

Roger Sherman was a shoemaker, shopkeeper, surveyor, lawyer—and one of the most respected early leaders of the United States. Thomas Jefferson once said that Sherman "never said a foolish thing in his life." Sherman was one of only four people to sign both the Declaration of Independence and the Constitution. ★ **What major contribution did Roger Sherman make to the Constitutional Convention?**

To ensure secrecy, guards stood at the door. The windows were left closed to keep passersby from overhearing the debates. The closed windows made the room very hot, however. New Englanders in their woolen suits suffered terribly in the summer heat. Southerners, with clothing more suited to warm temperatures, were less bothered.

Hopelessly Divided

Soon after the meeting began, the delegates decided to do more than revise the Articles of Confederation. They chose instead to write an entirely new constitution for the nation. They disagreed, however, about what form the national government should take.

| Critical Thinking | Managing Information | Communication | Maps, Charts, and Graphs |

Identifying Main Ideas

How Will I Use This Skill?

Every day you get huge quantities of information—from print materials, radio, television, the Internet, and other sources. Sometimes, excessive details make it easy to miss the main point. Learning to identify main ideas saves you time and makes it easier to understand the information you receive.

LEARN the Skill

When dealing with written information, such as in this textbook, use the structure that is provided. Take note of topic headings. In each paragraph, look for the main idea, usually found in a topic sentence at the beginning or end of the paragraph. Details and examples support the topic sentence. To identify main ideas, follow these steps.

❶ Identify main topic headings and subtopic headings.

❷ Identify the topic sentence found in each paragraph.

❸ Identify the supporting details in each paragraph. Determine how each relates to the topic sentence.

❹ Review the topic headings and main ideas of each paragraph to determine the main idea of the entire section or chapter.

PRACTICE the Skill

Review the subsection Hopelessly Divided on page 194.

❶ Identify the two subtopic headings under Hopelessly Divided.

❷ Identify the topic sentence of each of the five paragraphs in this subsection.

❸ Identify two supporting details from the first paragraph. How does each support the main idea?

❹ Review the main ideas of each paragraph. In your own words, restate the main idea of the entire subsection.

APPLY the Skill

Our mailboxes are often stuffed with business letters. Choose a letter from today's mail. Using the skills that you have learned, determine the main idea.

Quill and inkwell used at the Constitutional Convention

Independence Hall

For many, the birthplace of the United States is the old Pennsylvania State House, known today as Independence Hall. Here, the Declaration of Independence was signed, the Articles of Confederation were approved, and the Constitution was adopted. The site is now part of a national park. Visitors to the park can tour the building, learn about the Constitution, and see the Liberty Bell.

★ **To learn more about this historic site, write:** *Independence National Historical Park, 313 Walnut Street, Philadelphia, PA 19106.*

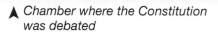

▲ *Chamber where the Constitution was debated*

the larger states wished, seats in the lower house would be awarded to each state according to its population.

Members of the upper house, called the Senate, would be chosen by state legislatures. Each state, no matter what its size, would have two senators. This part of Sherman's compromise appealed to the smaller states.

On July 16, the delegates narrowly approved Sherman's plan. It became known as the **Great Compromise.** Each side gave up some demands to preserve the nation.

Northern and Southern States Compromise

Just as there were disagreements between large and small states, there were also disagreements between northern and southern states. These disagreements concerned the issue of slavery. Would slaves be counted as part of a state's population? Would the slave trade continue to bring enslaved Africans into the United States?

The Three-Fifths Compromise

Southerners wanted to include slaves in the population count even though they would not let slaves vote. If slaves were counted, southern states would have more representatives in the House of Representatives. Northerners argued that since slaves could not vote, they should not be counted.

Once again, the delegates compromised. They agreed that three fifths of the slaves in any state would be counted. In other words, if a state had 5,000 slaves, 3,000 of them would be included in the state's population count. This agreement became known as the **Three-Fifths Compromise.**

The slave trade

There was another disagreement over slavery. By 1787, some northern states had banned the slave trade within their borders. They urged that the slave trade be banned in the entire nation. Southerners warned that such a ban would ruin their economy.

In the end, the two sides compromised once more. Northerners agreed that Congress could not outlaw the slave trade for at least 20 years. After that, Congress could regulate the slave trade if it wished. Northerners also agreed that no state could stop a fugitive slave from being returned to an owner who claimed that slave.

Signing the Constitution

As summer drew to a close, the weary delegates struggled with other difficult questions. How many years should the President, head of the executive branch, serve? How should the courts be organized? Would members of Congress be paid?

Finally, on September 17, 1787, the Constitution was ready. Gathering for the last time, delegates listened quietly as Benjamin Franklin rose to plead that the document be accepted:

> 66 I doubt...whether any other Convention...may be able to make a better Constitution....I cannot help expressing a wish, that every member of the Convention, who may still have objections to it, would with me, on this occasion, doubt a little of his own infallibility, and...put his name to this instrument. 99

One by one, delegates came forward to sign the document. Of the 42 delegates remaining in Philadelphia, 39 signed the document. Edmund Randolph and George Mason of Virginia, along with Elbridge Gerry of Massachusetts, refused to sign. They felt that the new Constitution gave too much power to the national government.

The Constitution required each state to hold a state convention to decide if the plan for the new government should be accepted. Once 9 of the 13 states endorsed it, the Constitution would go into effect. Before that occurred, the new Constitution was discussed and debated in all the states.

★ Section 2 Review ★

Recall

1. **Identify** (a) Constitutional Convention, (b) James Madison, (c) Virginia Plan, (d) New Jersey Plan, (e) Roger Sherman, (f) Great Compromise, (g) Three-Fifths Compromise.
2. **Define** (a) legislative branch, (b) executive branch, (c) judicial branch, (d) compromise.

Comprehension

3. Why did New Jersey and other small states oppose the Virginia Plan?
4. (a) How did the Great Compromise satisfy large states? (b) How did it satisfy small states?
5. What compromise did the North and South reach on the slave trade?

Critical Thinking and Writing

6. **Defending a Position** James Madison said that "no Constitution would ever have been adopted by the Convention if the debates had been made public." Do you agree or disagree? Defend your position.
7. **Predicting Consequences** Some historians refer to the issue of slavery as the Constitutional Convention's "unfinished business." How do you think the issue of slavery would continue to divide North and South in the years after the Convention?

 **Activity** Writing a Letter You are the editor of a Philadelphia newspaper in 1787. Decide whether you agree or disagree with the Convention's decision to keep its talks secret. Explain your viewpoint in a letter to the delegates of the Constitutional Convention.

A More Perfect Union

As You Read

Explore These Questions

- What ideas helped shape the Constitution?
- How did the framers of the Constitution divide power between the national government and the states?
- How did they limit the power of government?

Define

- republic
- separation of powers
- federalism
- electoral college
- checks and balances
- bill
- veto
- override
- impeach

Identify

- Magna Carta
- English Bill of Rights
- House of Burgesses
- Mayflower Compact
- Enlightenment
- John Locke
- Montesquieu

SETTING the Scene Jonathan Smith, a Massachusetts farmer, wanted to learn the results of the Constitutional Convention. During Shays' Rebellion, he had seen how weak government could lead to violence and tyranny. Smith noted:

66 When I saw this Constitution, I found that it was a cure for these disorders. It was just such a thing as we wanted. I got a copy of it and read it over and over. I had been a member of the convention to form our state constitution, and had learnt something of the checks and balances of power; and I found them all here. I formed my own opinion, and I was pleased with this Constitution. 99

The framers of the Constitution had designed a **republic,** a government in which citizens rule themselves through elected representatives. The Constitution outlined a new government that would be strong. At the same time, it protected the people from excessive power in government. As Smith hoped, it also prevented any one branch of government from becoming too powerful.

Origins of the Constitution

The framers of the Constitution were well-educated men. They were familiar with the traditions of British and American government. Many of them had read the latest works of Europe's leading political philosophers. In creating the Constitution, the framers made good use of their rich knowledge and experience.

British government

As you learned in Chapter 3, the **Magna Carta** limited the power of English rulers. The Magna Carta contained two basic ideas that helped to shape both British and American government. First, it stated that English nobles had certain rights—rights that were later extended to other classes of people as well. Second, the Magna Carta made clear that English monarchs themselves had to obey the law.

When King John signed the Magna Carta, he agreed not to raise taxes without first consulting the Great Council of nobles and church officials. Eventually, the Great Council grew into the representative body known as Parliament. Parliament consisted

Connections With Civics

Benjamin Franklin admired the government formed by Indian nations in the Iroquois League. The nations in the League governed their own affairs, but joined together for mutual defense.

of two bodies—the House of Lords and the House of Commons.

In the Magna Carta, King John was also forced to recognize that citizens had legal rights. One of the most important of these was the right to a trial by jury:

> 66 No freeman shall be arrested or imprisoned or dispossessed or... in any way harmed... except by the lawful judgment of his peers or by the law of the land. 99

In 1689, the **English Bill of Rights** went further in limiting the monarchy and protecting the rights of citizens. The document said that parliamentary elections should be held regularly. It reaffirmed the right to a trial by jury, while protecting people from excessive fines and cruel or unjust punishment. It allowed citizens to bear arms. It also affirmed the right of habeas corpus, the idea that no person could be held in prison without first being charged with a specific crime.

The American experience

Americans enjoyed a long tradition of elected representative government. In 1619, the Virginia colonists set up the **House of Burgesses.** Eventually, each of Britain's thirteen American colonies had its own representative legislature.

Another American tradition was having written documents that clearly identified the powers and limits of government. In 1620, the Pilgrim leaders at Plymouth drew up and signed the **Mayflower Compact,** the first document of self-government in North America. They agreed to "combine ourselves together in a civil body politic" in order to establish "just and equal laws." Each of the 13 colonies had a written charter granted by the monarch or Parliament.

The framers of the Constitution also drew on their own experiences. They were very familiar with the workings of the Second Continental Congress, the Articles of Confederation, and their own state governments. Much that went into the Constitution came from either the Articles or from one of the state constitutions.

The Enlightenment

The Constitution was also based on the ideas of the European **Enlightenment.** Enlightenment thinkers believed that people could improve society through the use of reason. Many of the Constitution's framers had read the works of Enlightenment thinkers, such as John Locke and the Baron de Montesquieu (MOHN tehs kyoo).

In 1690, **John Locke** published *Two Treatises on Government.* In it, he stated two important ideas.

First, Locke declared that all people had natural rights to life, liberty, and property. Second, he suggested that government is an agreement between the ruler and the ruled. The ruler must enforce the laws and protect the people. If a ruler violates the people's natural rights, the people have a right to rebel.

*B*iography **Baron de Montesquieu**

Montesquieu studied European, Chinese, and Native American governments. His ideas influenced the framers of the Constitution to divide government power among three separate branches. He said that "government should be set up so that one man need not be afraid of another." ★ **Why do you think the framers of the Constitution did not want to place all power into a single branch of government?**

The Federal System

Powers Delegated to the National Government

- Regulate interstate and foreign trade
- Set standard weights and measures
- Create and maintain armed forces
- Make copyright and patent laws
- Establish postal offices
- Establish foreign policy
- Create federal courts
- Coin money
- Declare war
- Admit new states

Shared Powers

- Provide for public welfare
- Administer criminal justice
- Charter banks
- Raise taxes
- Borrow money

Powers Reserved to the States

- Create corporation laws
- Regulate trade within state
- Establish and maintain schools
- Establish local governments
- Make laws about marriage and divorce
- Conduct elections
- Provide for public safety

Graphic Organizer Skills The system of federalism divides power between the national government and state governments.

1. Comprehension (a) List two powers shared by national and state governments. (b) List two powers reserved to the states.

2. Critical Thinking Why do you think the power to create and maintain armed forces was delegated to the federal government?

Civics

Locke's ideas were popular among Americans. The framers of the Constitution wanted to protect people's natural rights and limit the power of government. They saw the Constitution as a contract between the people and their government.

In 1748, the French thinker Baron de **Montesquieu** published *The Spirit of the Laws.* He urged that the power of government be divided among three separate branches: the legislative, executive, and judicial. This idea, known as the **separation of powers,** was designed to keep any person or group from gaining too much power.

Montesquieu stressed the importance of the rule of law. The powers of government, he said, should be clearly defined. This would prevent individuals or groups from using government power for their own purposes. In the Constitution, the framers set out the basic laws of the nation, defining and limiting the powers of the government.

A Federal System

The framers had to decide how to divide power between the national government and the states. Under the Articles of Confederation, states had more power than Congress. Under the Constitution, states delegated, or gave up, some of their powers to the national government. At the same time, the states reserved, or kept, other powers. This division of power between the states and the national government is called **federalism.**

Federal powers

The Constitution spells out the powers of the federal government. For example, only the federal government can coin money or declare war. The federal government can also regulate trade between the states and with other countries.

State powers

Under the Constitution, states have the power to regulate trade within their borders. They decide who can vote in state elections. They also have power to establish schools and local governments.

In addition, the Constitution says that those powers not clearly given to the federal government belong to the states or the people. This point pleased people who were afraid that the federal government might become too powerful.

Shared powers

The Constitution lists some powers that are to be shared by federal and state governments. Both governments, for example, can build roads and raise taxes.

The framers of the Constitution had to decide how the state governments and the federal government would settle disagreements. They did so by making the Constitution "the supreme law of the land." This means that the Constitution is the final authority in any dispute between the states and the federal government.

Separation of Powers

The framers of the Constitution set up a strong federal government. However, they also took steps to prevent any one branch from becoming too powerful. James Madison said that this was necessary in order to prevent tyranny:

> **66** The accumulation of all powers, legislative, executive, and judiciary, in the same hands, whether one, a few, or many...may justly be pronounced the very definition of tyranny. **99**

To prevent such a tyranny, the framers relied on Montesquieu's idea of separation of powers. In the Constitution, they created three branches of government and then defined the powers of each.

The legislative branch

The legislative branch of government is Congress. Its main function is to make laws. Congress consists of the House of Representatives and the Senate. Members of the House are elected for two-year terms. Senators are elected for six-year terms.

Under the Constitution, voters in each state elect members of the House of Representatives. Delegates to the Constitutional Convention wanted the House to represent the interests of ordinary people.

At first, the Constitution provided for senators to be chosen by state legislatures. In 1913, this was changed. Today, senators are elected in the same way as House members.

Article 1 of the Constitution sets out the powers of Congress. These include the power to collect taxes and to regulate foreign and interstate trade. In foreign affairs, Congress has the power to declare war and to "raise and support armies."

The executive branch

Article 2 of the Constitution sets up the executive branch of government. It is headed by the President. The executive branch also includes the Vice President and any advisers appointed by the President. The President and Vice President serve four-year terms.

The President is responsible for carrying out all laws passed by Congress. The President is also commander in chief of the armed forces and is responsible for directing foreign relations. Over the years, the power of the presidency has greatly increased.

The judicial branch

Article 3 of the Constitution calls for a Supreme Court. The article also allows Congress to set up other federal courts. The Supreme Court and other federal courts hear cases that involve the Constitution or any laws passed by Congress. They also hear cases arising from disputes between two or more states.

Legislative Branch
(Congress)

Passes laws
Can override President's veto
Approves treaties and presidential
   appointments
Can impeach and remove President
   and other high officials
Creates lower federal courts
Appropriates money
Prints and coins money
Raises and supports the armed forces
Can declare war
Regulates foreign and interstate trade

Executive Branch
(President)

Carries out laws
Proposes laws
Can veto laws
Negotiates foreign treaties
Serves as commander in
   chief of the armed forces
Appoints federal judges,
   ambassadors, and other
   high officials
Can grant pardons to federal
   offenders

Judicial Branch
(Supreme Court and
Other Federal Courts)

Interprets laws
Can declare laws
   unconstitutional
Can declare executive
   actions unconstitutional

Chart *Skills*

The Constitution set up three branches of government. Each of the branches has its own powers.

1. **Comprehension** **(a)** Who heads the executive branch? **(b)** What is the role of the legislative branch?

2. **Critical Thinking** Based on this chart, describe the relationship between the judicial branch and the executive branch.

Civics

Electing the President

The framers of the Constitution wanted to ensure that the President would not become too strong. Some feared that a President elected directly by the people might become too independent of Congress and the states.

Others opposed direct election because they worried that voters would not know a candidate from outside their area. In the late 1700s, news traveled slowly. New Englanders would probably know little about a candidate from the South. A candidate from Pennsylvania might be unknown to voters in Vermont or Georgia.

As a result of these concerns, the Constitution calls for an **electoral college.** It is made up of electors from every state. Every four years, the electors vote for the President and Vice President of the United States.

The framers of the Constitution expected that the electors would be well informed and familiar with the national government. They believed that such people would choose a President and Vice President wisely.

Checks and Balances

The Constitution set up a system of **checks and balances.** Under this system, each branch of the federal government has some way to check, or control, the other two branches. The system of checks and balances is another way in which the Constitution limits the power of government. (See the chart on page 220.)

Checks on Congress

To do its work, Congress passes **bills,** or proposed laws. A bill then goes to the President to be signed into law. The President can check the power of Congress by **vetoing,** or rejecting, a bill.

The Supreme Court checks the power of Congress by reviewing laws. If a law violates the Constitution, the Court can declare the law unconstitutional.

Checks on the President

After the President vetoes a bill, Congress can **override,** or overrule the veto. To override a veto, two thirds of both houses of Congress must vote for the bill again. In this way, a bill can become law without the President's signature.

Congress has other checks on the President. The President appoints officials such as ambassadors to foreign countries and federal judges. The Senate must approve these appointments. The President can negotiate treaties with other nations; however, a treaty becomes law only if two thirds of the Senate approve it.

Congress also has the power to remove a President from office if it finds the President guilty of a crime or serious misbehavior. First of all, the House of Representatives must **impeach,** or bring charges against, the President. A trial is then held in the Senate. If two thirds of the senators vote for conviction, the President must leave office.

Checks on the courts

Congress and the President have checks on the courts. The President appoints judges, who must be approved by the Senate. If judges misbehave, Congress may remove them from office. Congress establishes the number of justices in the Supreme Court. Congress can also propose changes to the Constitution to overturn Court decisions.

A Living Document

The Constitution carefully balances power among the three branches of the federal government. It also divides power between the federal government and the states. This balance has helped keep it alive for more than 200 years, longer than any other written constitution in the world. The Constitution has lasted because it is a living document. As you will read, it can be changed to meet new conditions.

★ Section 3 Review ★

Recall

1. **Identify** (a) Magna Carta, (b) English Bill of Rights, (c) House of Burgesses, (d) Mayflower Compact, (e) Enlightenment, (f) John Locke, (g) Montesquieu.
2. **Define** (a) republic, (b) separation of powers, (c) federalism, (d) electoral college, (e) checks and balances, (f) bill, (g) veto, (h) override, (i) impeach.

Comprehension

3. Describe three traditions or ideas that helped to shape the Constitution.

4. Why did the framers of the Constitution set up a system of federalism?
5. Describe one check on each of the following: (a) Congress, (b) the President, (c) the courts.

Critical Thinking and Writing

6. **Analyzing Ideas** On page 200, you read that the framers "...saw the Constitution as a contract between the people and their government." What do you think is meant by this statement?
7. **Comparing** Was the national government stronger under the Articles of Confederation or the Constitution? Explain.

Activity **Summarizing** You have been shipwrecked on a far-off island! The islanders want to set up a government like that of the United States. Write a summary for them in which you explain the basic ideas behind the Constitution.

Ratifying the Constitution

★ ★

As You Read

Explore These Questions
- What arguments did Americans raise for and against the Constitution?
- How can the Constitution be amended?
- What rights does the Bill of Rights protect?

Define
- ratify
- amend
- due process

Identify
- Federalist
- Antifederalist
- *The Federalist Papers*
- Bill of Rights

SETTING the Scene In homes and in town squares across the nation, Americans discussed the new Constitution. Many supported it. Many others did not. Its critics especially worried that the Constitution had no bill of rights. In Virginia, Patrick Henry sounded the alarm:

“ Show me an age and country where the rights and liberties of the people were placed on the sole chance of their rulers being good men, without a consequent loss of liberty! ”

Was a bill of rights needed? Did the Constitution give too much power to the federal government? In the fall of 1787, citizens began to debate the document sentence by sentence. The Convention had done its work. Now the states had to decide whether or not to ratify the new frame of government.

The Constitution Goes to the Nation

The framers of the Constitution sent the document to Congress. With it, they sent a letter from George Washington, as president of the Constitutional Convention. In the letter, Washington described how the framers had struggled to make the Constitution meet the varied needs of the different states. He wrote:

“ In our deliberations, we kept steadily in view... the greatest inter-

ests of every true American. That [the Constitution] will meet the full and entire [approval] of every state is not perhaps to be expected; but each will doubtless consider that had her interest been alone consulted, the consequences might have been... disagreeable or [harmful] to others. ”

Washington warmly endorsed the document and called on Congress to support it. It was his belief, he said, that the Constitution would "promote the lasting welfare of that country so dear to us all, and secure her freedom and happiness."

The framers of the Constitution had set up a process for the states to decide on the new government. At least 9 of the 13 states had to **ratify,** or approve, the Constitution before it could go into effect. In 1787 and 1788, voters in each state elected delegates to special state conventions. These delegates then met to decide whether or not to ratify the Constitution.

⚛ Connections *With* Science

Today, the Constitution is publicly displayed. For protection against damage due to light, insects, and impurities in the air, each page is in a glass case filled with helium. Levels of light and humidity are carefully controlled.

Heated Debate

In every state, heated debates took place. Supporters of the Constitution called themselves **Federalists.** They called people who opposed the Constitution **Antifederalists.**

The Federalist position

The Federalists argued that the Articles of Confederation had produced an excessively weak central government. It had placed the nation in grave danger because it left too much power with the individual states. Disputes among the states, Federalists said, had made it too difficult for the Confederation government to function.

According to the Federalists, the Constitution gave the national government the authority to function effectively. At the same time, it still protected the rights of the individual states.

Among the best-known Federalists were James Madison, Alexander Hamilton, and John Jay. They wrote a series of essays, called *The Federalist Papers*, defending the Constitution. They used pen names, but most people knew who they were. Today, *The Federalist Papers* remains one of the best discussions of the political theory behind the American system of government.

The Antifederalist position

Antifederalists opposed the Constitution for many reasons. They felt that it made the national government too strong and left the states too weak. They thought that the Constitution gave the President too much power. Patrick Henry was among those who voiced such concerns:

> 66 This Constitution is said to have beautiful features, but ... they appear to me horribly frightful.... Your President may become king ... If your American chief be a man of ambition and abilities, how easy is it for him to render himself absolute! 99

Most people expected George Washington to be elected President. Antifederalists admired Washington, but they warned that future Presidents might lack Washington's

Biography — James Madison

Historians call James Madison the "Father of the Constitution" because much of the document was based on his ideas. When the Constitution was being debated, Madison was only in his 30s. He went on to serve the nation as a member of Congress, as Secretary of State, and as the fourth President of the United States . ★ **Was Madison a Federalist or an Antifederalist?**

honor and skill. For this reason, they said, the office should not be too powerful.

Need for a bill of rights

The chief argument used by Antifederalists against the Constitution was that it had no bill of rights. Americans had just fought a revolution to protect their freedoms. They wanted a bill of rights in the Constitution that spelled out basic freedoms such as freedom of speech and freedom of religion.

Federalists replied that the Constitution protected citizens very well without a bill of rights. Anyway, they argued, it was impossible to list all the natural rights of people. Antifederalists responded that if rights were not written into the Constitution, it would be easy to ignore them. Several state conventions refused to ratify the Constitution unless they received a firm promise that a bill of rights would be added.

Viewing HISTORY The Nation Celebrates

When the Constitution was ratified, celebrations were held across the nation. Shown here is a celebration parade in New York City. The three-masted ship on the float represented the "ship of state." ★ **Why do you think Alexander Hamilton's name is displayed so visibly?**

The States Vote to Ratify

One by one, states voted to ratify the Constitution. Delaware was the first, in December 1787. In June 1788, New Hampshire became the ninth state to ratify. The new government could now go into effect.

Still, the future of the United States remained in doubt. It was important that all the states support the Constitution. However, New York and Virginia, two of the largest states, had not yet ratified the plan. In both states, Federalists and Antifederalists were closely matched.

In Virginia, Patrick Henry strongly opposed the Constitution. Henry charged that the document gave the government too much power. "There will be no checks, no real balances in this government," he cried. In the end, however, Washington, Madison, and other Virginia Federalists prevailed. In late June, Virginia approved the Constitution.

In New York, the struggle went on for another month. At last, in July 1788, the state convention voted to ratify. North Carolina ratified in November 1789. Rhode Island was the last state to approve the Constitution, finally doing so in May 1790.

The Nation Celebrates

Throughout the land, Americans celebrated the news that the Constitution was ratified. The city of Philadelphia set its festival for July 4, 1788. At sunrise, church bells rang. In the harbor, the ship *Rising Sun* boomed a salute from its cannons. Horses wore bright ribbons, and bands played popular tunes.

A festive parade filed along Market Street, led by soldiers who had fought in the Revolution. Thousands cheered as six colorfully outfitted horses pulled a blue carriage shaped like an eagle. Thirteen stars and stripes were painted on the front, and the Constitution was raised proudly above it.

That night, even the skies seemed to celebrate. The northern lights, vivid bands of color, lit up the sky above the city. Benjamin Rush, a Philadelphia doctor and strong supporter of the Constitution, wrote to a friend: "'Tis done. We have become a nation."

Adding a Bill of Rights

Americans voted in the first election under the Constitution in January 1789. As

Why Study History?

Because National Symbols Unite Us

★ ★

Historical Background

The Constitution changed a loose alliance of states into a more unified nation. It takes more than a document, however, to create a nation. Shared ideals and symbols also help to bring people together. In 1782, the bald eagle was declared a symbol of the United States by Congress.

The presidential seal

Today, the eagle and other symbols appear on the Great Seal of the United States and on the Seal of the President of the United States. On both seals, the American eagle holds an olive branch representing peace and a bundle of arrows representing military readiness. In its beak, it holds a scroll with the Latin phrase *"E pluribus Unum."* These words, which mean "Out of many, one," are our nation's motto. They refer to the union of states and to the union of the diverse American people.

Connections to Today

Almost 200 years after Congress declared it an American symbol, the American bald eagle was in serious trouble. Only about 400 breeding pairs of eagles remained in the lower 48 states. Hunting, loss of habitat, and pollution were some causes of the decline. In the 1960s, President John F. Kennedy made an urgent appeal. "The fierce beauty and proud independence of this great bird aptly symbolize the strength

and freedom of America," he said, "and we shall have failed a trust if we allow the eagle to disappear."

The nation took action. Congress banned the use of DDT, an insecticide that damaged the birds' eggs. Also, it declared the eagle an endangered species. This step prohibited the hunting of eagles and protected their habitat. By the mid-1990s, the eagle population had recovered.

Connections to You

The bald eagle is only one of the emblems that represent you and all citizens of the United States. The foremost symbol of the nation is the American flag. Others include the Liberty Bell, the Statue of Liberty, and Uncle Sam. Such images have a long and interesting history as symbols of our nation.

1. **Comprehension** **(a)** Why was the bald eagle endangered in the 1960s? **(b)** How did government help the eagle to recover?

2. **Critical Thinking** Why do you think Congress chose the eagle as a symbol of the United States?

Researching and Writing Conduct research to learn about the origins and meaning of the American flag, the Liberty Bell, or other symbols of the United States. Write an essay summarizing your findings.

Linking Past and Present

Past

Present

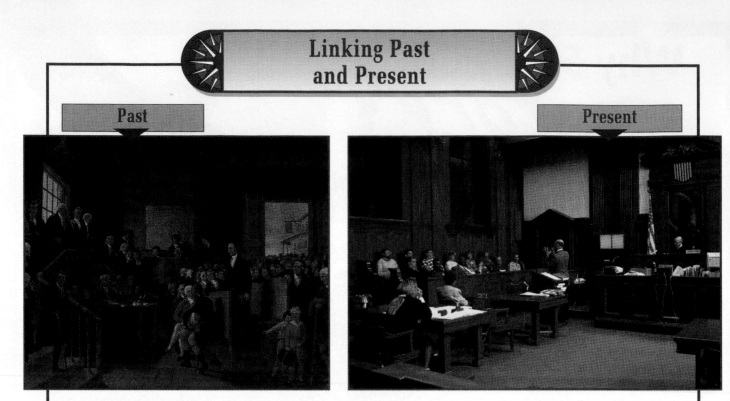

Trial by Jury

Trial by jury is part of the nation's English heritage. Yet in colonial times, British officials sometimes suspended jury trials. Therefore, many Americans wanted the new Constitution to guarantee this right. The members of a jury promise to give an impartial verdict based on evidence. ★ **Turn to the Reference Section and read the Sixth Amendment. List three rights guaranteed to Americans accused of crimes.**

expected, George Washington was elected President, while John Adams was chosen Vice President.

The first Congress was made up of 59 representatives and 22 senators. It met in New York City, which was chosen as the nation's first capital. The first Congress quickly turned its attention to adding a bill of rights to the Constitution.

The amendment process

The framers had set up a way to **amend,** or change, the Constitution. They did not want people to make changes lightly, however. Thus, they made the process of amending the Constitution fairly difficult.

To start the amendment process, an amendment must be proposed. This can be done in two ways. Two thirds of both houses of Congress can vote to propose an amendment, or two thirds of the states can request special conventions to propose amendments.

Next, the amendment must be ratified. Three fourths of the states must approve the amendment before it becomes part of the Constitution.

In the more than 200 years since the Constitution was adopted, only 27 amendments have been approved. Ten of those amendments were added in the first years after the Constitution was ratified.

The first 10 amendments

The first Congress proposed a series of amendments to the Constitution of the United States in 1789. By December 1791, three fourths of the states had ratified 10 amendments. Those 10 amendments became known as the **Bill of Rights.**

James Madison, who wrote the amendments, insisted that the Bill of Rights does not give Americans any rights. People already have the rights listed in the amendments. They are natural rights, said Madison, that belong to all human beings. The Bill of Rights simply prevents the government from taking these rights away.

Protecting individual rights

The 10 amendments that make up the Bill of Rights ensure the basic freedoms of American citizens. The First Amendment guarantees individual liberties, including freedom of religion, freedom of speech, and freedom of the press. It also guarantees the right to assemble peacefully and the right to petition the government.

The next three amendments came out of the colonists' struggle with Britain. The Second Amendment guarantees the right of citizens to keep and bear arms. The Third Amendment was included because the framers remembered Parliament's efforts to make colonists house and feed British soldiers. The amendment prevents Congress from forcing citizens to quarter, or house, troops in their homes. The Fourth Amendment protects citizens from unreasonable searches and seizures. Before the Revolution, you will remember, British customs officials had often searched and seized the property of colonists without their permission.

The Fifth Amendment guarantees due process of law. **Due process** means that the government must follow the same fair rules in all cases brought to trial. Under the Fifth Amendment, the accused must be notified of the charges brought against him or her. The accused must also be given the chance to present a defense in court. Also, the government cannot require self-incriminating testimony nor may it try a defendant twice for the same crime if the defendant has already been acquitted.

Amendments 6 through 8 provide other protections for citizens accused of crimes. The Sixth Amendment guarantees a jury trial in criminal cases and the right to be defended by a lawyer. The Seventh Amendment requires jury trials in civil cases. The Eighth Amendment prevents judges from ordering "excessive bail" or imposing "cruel and unusual punishment" on a convicted criminal.

The Ninth Amendment assures that the rights listed in the Constitution are not the only ones that exist. The Tenth Amendment states that all powers not given to the national government and not denied to the states are reserved for the states or for the people. This assured that the power of the national government would be limited.

With the Bill of Rights in place, the new framework of government was complete. Over time, the Constitution became a living document that grew and changed along with the nation.

★ Section 4 Review ★

Recall

1. **Identify** (a) Federalist, (b) Antifederalist, (c) *The Federalist Papers,* (d) Bill of Rights.
2. **Define** (a) ratify, (b) amend, (c) due process.

Comprehension

3. (a) Why did Federalists favor ratification of the Constitution? (b) Why did Antifederalists oppose it?
4. Describe the process for adding amendments to the Constitution.

5. Describe three specific rights protected by the first 10 amendments to the Constitution.

Critical Thinking and Writing

6. **Defending a Position** Imagine that you are a citizen of the United States in 1789. Would you argue for or against the Constitution? How would you defend your position?
7. **Analyzing Ideas** (a) List five rights protected by the Bill of Rights. (b) Which do you think is most important? Explain.

Activity Making Illustrations You are the illustrator for a handbook on the rights of American citizens. Draw a series of sketches to illustrate the rights that are guaranteed by the First Amendment.

Chapter 7 Review and Activities

★ Sum It Up ★

Section 1 A Confederation of States
▶ During the American Revolution, most states wrote constitutions providing for a governor and legislature.
▶ The Articles of Confederation created a weak alliance of states.
▶ Under the Articles of Confederation, the government set up a system for forming and governing new territories.

Section 2 The Constitutional Convention
▶ The Constitutional Convention met in Philadelphia in 1787 to revise the nation's government.
▶ The delegates created the Constitution by making important compromises on several divisive issues.

Section 3 A More Perfect Union
▶ The framers of the Constitution drew ideas from British government, colonial and state governments, and the Enlightenment.
▶ A federal system divides power between the national and state governments.
▶ The separation of powers prevents any branch of government from becoming too strong.

Section 4 Ratifying the Constitution
▶ After many debates, the separate states approved the Constitution.
▶ The first 10 amendments form a Bill of Rights designed to protect the rights of individuals.

 **CD-ROM Review** For additional review of the major ideas of Chapter 7, see *Guide to the Essentials of American History* or *Interactive Student Tutorial CD-ROM,* which contains interactive review activities, graphic organizers, and practice tests.

🖵 Reviewing the Chapter

Define These Terms

Match each term with the correct definition.

Column 1	Column 2
1. constitution	**a.** system of courts
2. judicial branch	**b.** to bring charges against
3. republic	**c.** nation in which voters elect representatives to govern them
4. legislative branch	**d.** branch that passes laws
5. impeach	**e.** document that sets out the laws and principles of a government

Explore the Main Ideas

1. Describe three reasons for the failure of the Articles of Confederation.
2. **(a)** Why was the Great Compromise necessary? **(b)** Why was the Three-Fifths Compromise necessary?
3. Describe three ideas that shaped the Constitution.
4. What is one benefit of a federal system of government?
5. **(a)** Describe one reason why Federalists favored the Constitution. **(b)** Describe one reason why Antifederalists opposed it.

🖵 Chart Activity

Use the chart below to answer the following questions:
1. Which state was the first to ratify the Constitution?
2. Which state was the last? **Critical Thinking** In which three states was support for the Constitution strongest?

Ratification of the Constitution		
State	**Date**	**Vote**
Delaware	Dec. 7, 1787	30–0
Pennsylvania	Dec. 12, 1787	46–23
New Jersey	Dec. 19, 1787	38–0
Georgia	Jan. 2, 1788	26–0
Connecticut	Jan. 9, 1788	128–40
Massachusetts	Feb. 6, 1788	187–168
Maryland	Apr. 28, 1788	63–11
South Carolina	May 23, 1788	149–73
New Hampshire	June 21, 1788	57–46
Virginia	June 25, 1788	89–79
New York	July 26, 1788	30–27
North Carolina	Nov. 21, 1789	184–77
Rhode Island	May 29, 1790	34–32

📋 Critical Thinking and Writing

1. **Understanding Chronology** Arrange the following documents in chronological order: **(a)** the Constitution, **(b)** Articles of Confederation, **(c)** the First Amendment, **(d)** Magna Carta, **(e)** Mayflower Compact.

2. **Making Inferences** Benjamin Franklin said that Americans had a republic, if they could keep it. Why do you think Franklin was unsure whether the government would last?

3. **Predicting Consequences** What do you think might happen if the government was not required to follow due process?

4. **Exploring Unit Themes** **Rights and Liberties** The nation has changed a great deal since 1787. Does the Bill of Rights still protect individual rights in the United States today? Explain.

📋 Using Primary Sources

During the American Revolution, Johann David Schoepf was a physician for Britain's Hessian troops. After the war, he traveled about the United States, recording his observations. Here, he comments on the government created by the Articles of Confederation:

> 66 The Congress has neither the necessary weight nor the necessary solidity.... It was to be expected of a people so enthusiastic for liberty that they should grant their Congress only a shadow of dignity, and watch its proceedings with a jealous eye. 99

Source: *Travels in the Confederation,* Johann David Schoepf, 1911.

Recognizing Points of View **(a)** Did Schoepf consider the new American Congress to be strong or weak? **(b)** Schoepf wrote that Americans watched Congress "with a jealous eye." What do you think he meant by this? **(c)** How do you think Schoepf's background affected his point of view?

ACTIVITY BANK

▶ Interdisciplinary Activity

Exploring Geography Find out more about the early settlement of one of the five states carved out of the Northwest Territory. Report on how people traveled there, what obstacles they faced, and how they lived. Include a map showing geographic features of the area.

▶ Career Skills Activity

Teachers Every immigrant who wants to become an American citizen has to learn about the Constitution. Suppose you were teaching a citizenship class. With a partner, prepare a presentation on one part of the Constitution. Use visual aids such as diagrams and pictures in your presentation.

▶ Citizenship Activity

Identifying Community Issues The process of amending the Constitution often starts with a petition—a statement signed by many members of a community and presented to lawmakers to show public support for a change. Working with others in your class, choose a problem in your community. Prepare a petition that suggests a solution.

Internet Activity

On the Internet, find information on one of the leading figures at the Constitutional Convention. Write a brief biography of the person, noting especially his role in producing the Constitution.

EYEWITNESS Journal

You are a delegate to the Constitutional Convention. In your EYEWITNESS JOURNAL, describe the debate over the Virginia Plan and the New Jersey Plan. Also, describe the debates that took place over issues of slavery.

★ CIVICS OVERVIEW ★

Chapter 8

The Constitution at Work 1789–Present

The goal of the Constitution is to create a single, united nation with a fair government and system of laws. It ensures peace within the nation, provides for the defense of the country, and guarantees people's rights and liberties. The principles behind the Constitution include the people's right to rule themselves and the careful division of power among three separate branches of the government.

Changing the Constitution is not easy. For this reason, the basic framework of government has grown slowly. One key change over the centuries has been to extend the rights of citizenship to more and more Americans.

Why Study History?

As you study American history, you will see how different people won greater rights. Such rights carry with them responsibilities. Americans meet their responsibilities as citizens in many ways, such as voting or serving in the military. There are also individuals who see a problem in their community and work to solve it. To meet one such person, see this chapter's *Why Study History?* feature, "Citizens Have Responsibilities."

American Events

1788
Constitution of the United States is ratified

1791
Bill of Rights is approved

1700   **1750**   **1800**   **1850**

World Events

1700s World Event
Age of Enlightenment begins

1789 World Event
French Revolution begins

Voting: A Right and a Responsibility

Voting is one of the most important duties of an American citizen. Two hundred years ago, only white male property owners over the age of 21 could vote in most states. Today, as this painting shows, every citizen over the age of 18 has the right to vote. ★ **List three other rights that American citizens enjoy.**

●**1870**
Fifteenth Amendment gives African American men the right to vote

●**1920**
Nineteenth Amendment gives women the right to vote

●**1971**
Twenty-sixth Amendment extends voting rights to Americans 18 to 21 years old

1850　　　　　**1900**　　　　　**1950**　　　　　**2000**

 1893 World Event
New Zealand is first nation to give vote to women

 1948 World Event
United Nations approves Universal Declaration of Human Rights

★ **213**

Goals of the Constitution

Explore These Questions
- How does the national government help to unify the nation?
- What are the benefits of a national system of courts?
- How does the Constitution protect the basic rights of the people?

Define
- federal
- justice
- domestic tranquillity
- general welfare
- liberty

Identify
- Preamble
- Bill of Rights

SETTING the Scene In 1787, Benjamin Franklin was 81 years old. As long ago as the French and Indian War, he had urged the 13 colonies to unite for their mutual interest. Now, he was serving as the oldest delegate to the Constitutional Convention.

At the end of the convention, Franklin commented on the new Constitution. The document, he admitted, was not perfect:

66 When you assemble a number of men, to have the advantage of their joint wisdom, you inevitably assemble with those men all their prejudices, their passions, their errors of opinion, their local interests, and their selfish views.... It therefore astonishes me, Sir, to find this system approaching so near to perfection as it does. 99

Constitution of the United States
▼

He expressed his hope that the Constitution would unite the nation and be "a blessing to the people." The Constitution has lived up to Franklin's hopes. It has remained the framework of our government for more than 200 years. It endures in part because it guarantees people their rights and liberties.

Ensuring liberty is just one of the main goals of the Constitution.

Preamble to the Constitution

The opening statement, of the Constitution is called the **Preamble.** In it the American people proudly announce that they have established the Constitution to achieve certain goals:

66 We the people of the United States, in order to form a more perfect Union, establish justice, ensure domestic tranquillity, provide for the common defense, promote the general welfare, and secure the blessings of liberty to ourselves and our posterity, do ordain and establish this Constitution for the United States of America. 99

As you read about these six goals, think about their importance to you.

"Form a More Perfect Union"

Under the Articles of Confederation, the United States was a loose alliance of independent, quarreling states. Many states acted like separate nations. One of the main goals of the framers of the Constitution was to get the states to work together as part of a single, united nation.*

---

* *E pluribus unum,* the official motto of the United States, also expresses this principle of unity. The Latin phrase means, "Out of many, one."

To achieve this goal of unity, the Constitution gives a broad range of powers to the national government. For example, only Congress—the national legislature—has the power to tax all the people. The President—the national executive—is responsible for carrying out all the laws of the nation. And **federal,** or national, courts enforce one system of law for the entire nation.

"Establish Justice"

A second goal of the Constitution is to establish **justice,** or fairness. Justice requires that the law be applied fairly to every American, regardless of that person's race, religion, gender, country of origin, political beliefs, or financial situation. The Constitution gives this task to a federal system of courts.

Federal courts deal with a broad range of issues. They hear cases involving the Constitution, national laws, treaties, foreign ambassadors, and ships at sea. They also decide disputes between individuals, between individuals and the national government, and between the states.

When federal courts decide cases, they must often interpret, or explain, the law. The Supreme Court, the highest court in the land, can rule that a law passed by Congress or a state legislature is not permitted by the Constitution.

Why is a national system of courts necessary? Without it, state or local courts would interpret national laws. Judges in some states might refuse to enforce national laws they did not like. Disputes about the meaning of certain laws would remain unsettled. Confusion, and even injustice, might result.

"Ensure Domestic Tranquillity"

In 1786, Daniel Shays marched on a Massachusetts courthouse with hundreds of protesters. Upon hearing about Shays' Rebellion, George Washington warned, "We are fast verging to [absence of government] and confusion!" The uprising made it clear that the national government must have the power to ensure **domestic tranquillity,** or peace at home.

Contents of the Constitution

Chart Skills The Constitution of the United States includes a preamble, 7 articles, and 27 amendments.

1. **Comprehension** (a) What is the subject of Article 4? (b) On what pages would you find the Bill of Rights?

2. **Critical Thinking** (a) Identify as many amendments as you can that deal with voting or elections. (b) Why do you think so many amendments are concerned with this issue?

Civics

"Provide for the Common Defense"

After the American Revolution, the United States had no armed forces to defend itself. Without an army, it could not force British troops to leave the western frontier. Without a navy, it could not prevent Spain from closing part of the Mississippi River to American trade.

The framers of the Constitution realized that armed forces are vital to a nation's survival. Military power helps not only to prevent attack by other nations, but also to protect economic and political interests.

The Constitution gives Congress the power to "raise and support Armies" and to "provide and maintain a Navy." Today, the armed forces include the army, navy, air force, marine corps, and coast guard.

At the same time, the Constitution establishes the principle that the military is under civilian, or nonmilitary, control. Article 2 of the Constitution states that the President is Commander in Chief of the armed forces. Thus, even the highest-ranking military officer must answer to an elected official.

"Promote the General Welfare"

The Constitution gives the national government the means to promote the **general welfare,** or well-being of all the people. The national government has the power to collect taxes. It also has the power to set aside money for programs that will benefit the people.

▲ Logo of the FDA

Biography — Frances Kelsey

In the early 1960s, a prescription drug named thalidomide caused birth defects in hundreds of children in Europe and Canada. Thanks to Frances Kelsey (left), the drug was never sold in the United States. As an official at the Food and Drug Administration (FDA), Kelsey refused to approve thalidomide without more tests. For her work, Kelsey received a medal from President John Kennedy (right). ★ **How did Kelsey's work fulfill one of the goals of the Constitution?**

The Constitution gives the national government certain powers that allow it to keep the peace. State and local governments can use their own police to enforce national laws within their borders. When crime crosses state borders, however, national police agencies, such as the Federal Bureau of Investigation (FBI), can step in to help protect life and property.

Have you ever seen a news report about a civil emergency, such as a riot or a flood? If so, you probably saw the National Guard keeping the peace. The President can summon such aid if a state or community cannot or will not respond to the emergency.

$ Connections With Economics

Government spending for defense and the general welfare has grown dramatically. In 1795, government outlays totaled $7.5 million for a population of 4.6 million people — an average of $1.63 per person. In 1999, the government's outlays totaled $1.7 billion for a population of 273 million people — an average of $6.20 per person.

The workplace provides many examples of how the national government—often in cooperation with state governments—has acted to promote the general welfare. Factory owners are required to meet safety standards for work areas. Workers who are disabled or unemployed receive financial support. Thanks to the Social Security system, all workers are entitled to income upon retirement.

Another way in which the national government helps to promote the general welfare is by supporting education. Education helps to prepare people to become responsible citizens. It also provides tools and training for employment.

Support for education takes many forms. The national government pays for school nutrition programs in local school districts. Many students receive money to help pay the costs of a college education.

The national government also supports scientific research and development to improve the quality of life. For example, researchers at the National Institutes of Health lead the fight against many diseases. Scientists at the Department of Agriculture help farmers to improve their crops and develop better livestock.

"Secure the Blessings of Liberty"

Protection of liberty was a major reason that colonists fought the American Revolution. It is no wonder, then, that the framers made securing liberty a major goal of the Constitution. **Liberty** is the freedom to live as you please, as long as you obey the laws and respect the rights of others.

One way that the Constitution ensures liberty is by limiting the powers of government. For example, the **Bill of Rights,** the first 10 amendments to the Constitution, lists basic rights and freedoms that the government may not take away.

The Constitution provides yet another safeguard of liberty—the right to vote. The people select the leaders who make the laws. At the same time, they can remove from office those leaders who abuse their power.

The "blessings of liberty" have been extended to more Americans since the Constitution was written. Changes in the Constitution have been made to ensure that all Americans—no matter what their sex, religion, or race—have the same rights regarding voting, education, housing, employment, and other opportunities in life.

★ Section 1 Review ★

Recall

1. **Identify** (a) Preamble, (b) Bill of Rights.
2. **Define** (a) federal, (b) justice, (c) domestic tranquillity, (d) general welfare, (e) liberty.

Comprehension

3. (a) List two goals of the Constitution. (b) Describe one way that the national government helps to achieve each of these goals.
4. How does the national system of courts help to ensure justice for all Americans?

5. List two ways the Constitution safeguards the people's liberty.

Critical Thinking and Writing

6. **Evaluating Information** Which goal of the Constitution do you think is most important? Explain.
7. **Linking Past and Present** Are the goals of the nation today the same as those set out in the Preamble to the Constitution?

★ ★

Activity **Teaching Through Pictures** A fifth-grader in your school has to recite the Preamble to the Constitution in a speaking contest. When you hear him practice, you realize he doesn't understand what it means. Draw six pictures with captions that will explain the goals of the Constitution for him.

2 ★ Five Principles of the Constitution

As You Read

Explore These Questions
- What are the five basic principles of the Constitution?
- Why do people adopt a system of representative government?
- How did the framers of the Constitution try to strike a balance between too much and too little government?

Define
- popular sovereignty
- representative government
- bill
- veto
- unconstitutional
- override

SETTING the Scene In 1787, when American leaders were struggling to create the new Constitution, every government in Europe was a monarchy. In most cases, a king or queen made, enforced, and interpreted the laws. Many European rulers would have agreed with Louis XIV, an earlier king of France. *"L'état, c'est moi,"* declared Louis. "I am the state."

The framers of the Constitution knew they had to set up a strong government. At the same time, they sought to keep power from falling into the hands of a privileged few. To achieve this delicate balance, they rested the Constitution on five basic principles: popular sovereignty, limited government, federalism, separation of powers, and checks and balances.

The People Rule

The first three words of the Constitution, "We the people," express the principle of **popular sovereignty.** According to this principle, the people hold the final authority in government.

The Constitution is a contract between the American people and their government. In it, the people grant the government the powers it needs to achieve its goals. At the same time, they limit the power of government by spelling out what the government may not do.

Poster urging Americans to vote

In a large society, not all citizens can take part directly in government. Instead, they exercise their ruling power indirectly by electing public officials to make laws and other decisions for them. This system is called **representative government.**

The people elect public officials by voting in free and frequent elections. Americans today have the constitutional right to vote for members of the House of Representatives (Article 1, Section 2) and for members of the Senate (Amendment 17). The people also elect the members of the electoral college, who, in turn, choose the President (Article 2, Section 2).

The right to vote has been gradually expanded over time. When the Constitution was ratified, only white men over age 21 who owned property could vote. Over the years, other Americans have won the right to vote. Today, all citizens are eligible to vote at the age of 18.

Limited Government

The framers of the Constitution had lived under the harsh rule of the British king. They feared tyranny, or cruel and unjust government. However, the failures of the Articles of Confederation made it clear that the national government had to be strong. How could the framers strike a balance between too much government and too little?

The answer was limited government. According to this principle, the government has only the powers that the people grant it. The Constitution clearly states the powers of the national government. It also states what powers the government does not have.

Guarantees of liberty

The most important limits on government are set out in the Bill of Rights. It guarantees that the government may not take away the individual freedoms of the people. These liberties include freedom of speech, freedom of the press, and freedom of religion.

The Ninth Amendment goes beyond these specific guarantees. It states that the people have rights that are not listed in the Constitution. The Tenth Amendment gives the states or the people any powers not formally granted by the Constitution to the national government.

Federalism

The framers of the Constitution created a strong central government. Yet they also wanted the states to retain much of their power. Like most Americans, they believed that state governments would best understand the special needs and concerns of their citizens. As one defender of the Constitution stated in 1788:

❞ The two governments act in different manners, and for different purposes—the general government in great national concerns, in which we are interested in common with other members of the Union; the state legislature in our mere local concerns. ❞

The principle of federalism divides power between the federal government and state governments. The federal government has the power to deal with national issues. The states have the power to meet local needs.

The Constitution delegates, or assigns, certain powers to the national government. Other powers are reserved, or left, to the states. Still other powers, sometimes called concurrent powers, are shared by the federal and state governments. The chart on page 200 shows how government powers are divided under federalism.

Powers of the states

The Constitution does not list the powers of the states. Instead, it says that all powers not specifically granted to the federal government are reserved to the states (Tenth Amendment). At the same time, it makes clear exactly what powers the states do not have (Article 1, Section 10).

In addition to the reserved powers, the Constitution makes several guarantees to the states. All states must be treated equally in matters of trade (Article 1, Section 9). Each state must respect the laws of other states (Article 4, Section 1). Perhaps most important, all states have representation in the national government.

State License Plates

Under federalism, each state makes its own traffic laws and issues its own drivers' licenses and car registrations. At the same time, a driver's license issued by one state is valid in every other state. ★ **Name two other powers reserved to the states.**

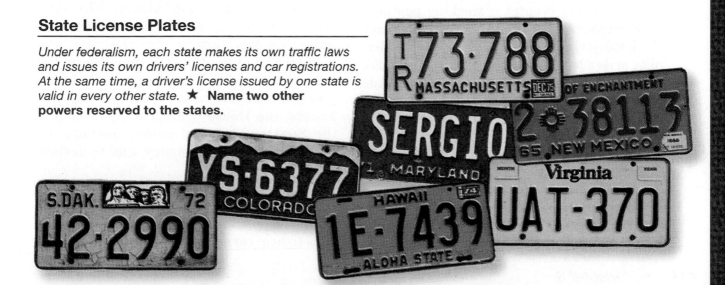

System of Checks and Balances

Executive Branch (President carries out laws) 	**Checks on the Legislative Branch** Can propose laws Can veto laws Can call special sessions of Congress Makes appointments Negotiates foreign treaties	**Checks on the Judicial Branch** Appoints federal judges Can grant pardons to federal offenders
Legislative Branch (Congress makes laws) 	**Checks on the Executive Branch** Can override President's veto Confirms executive appointments Ratifies treaties Can declare war Appropriates money Can impeach and remove President	**Checks on the Judicial Branch** Creates lower federal courts Can impeach and remove judges Can propose amendments to overrule judicial decisions Approves appointments of federal judges
Judicial Branch (Supreme Court interprets laws) 	**Check on the Executive Branch** Can declare executive actions unconstitutional	**Check on the Legislative Branch** Can declare acts of Congress unconstitutional

Chart Skills

Through the system of checks and balances, each branch of government controls the powers of the other two.

1. **Comprehension** (a) Name one check the President has on Congress. (b) How can the Supreme Court check Congress?
2. **Critical Thinking** Why do you think the framers of the Constitution gave Congress so many checks on the power of the President?

Civics

The "law of the land"

Federalism creates a working partnership between the national government and the state governments. However, when a dispute arises between them, there is no doubt where the final authority lies. The Constitution is the "supreme law of the land" (Article 6, Section 2). Only federal courts can settle the dispute.

Separation of Powers

The framers wanted to prevent the abuse of power by one person or group. To do so, the Constitution divides the national government into three branches: the legislative, the exec-utive, and the judicial. Each branch has its own powers and responsibilities. This division of the national government is known as separation of powers.

Article 1 of the Constitution sets up the legislative branch. This branch, called Congress, makes the laws. Congress has two houses: the House of Representatives and the Senate. Its many powers include the power to tax, to coin money, and to declare war.

Article 2 describes the executive branch, which carries out the laws. The President heads the executive branch and appoints officials to help carry out the duties of the office.

Article 3 creates the Supreme Court to head the judicial branch. The Supreme Court interprets and explains laws. Congress may set up lower courts as needed.

Checks and Balances

To prevent one branch of government from gaining too much power, the Constitution sets up a system of checks and balances. Each branch can check, or control, the power of the other two branches. (See the chart on page 220.)

Checks on Congress

Congress has the power to pass **bills,** or proposed laws. However, the President can influence the lawmaking process by proposing new bills or by pushing members of Congress to vote for or against a bill. The President can also check Congress by **vetoing,** or rejecting, a bill. The vetoed bill then goes back to Congress.

The Supreme Court has the power to rule whether a law is **unconstitutional,** or not permitted by the Constitution. The power to declare laws unconstitutional is one check the Supreme Court has on Congress. Any law declared unconstitutional by the Court cannot take effect.

Checks on the President

Congress has several checks on the powers of the President. For example, the President is commander in chief of the armed forces, but only Congress has the power to declare war. In addition, the President has the power to make treaties with foreign nations. However, the Senate must ratify all treaties.

Congress may also check the President by **overriding,** or setting aside, a presidential veto. In this way, a bill can become a law without the President's signature. Two thirds of each house must vote to override a veto. The Supreme Court can also check the President by declaring that an act of the President is unconstitutional.

Checks on the courts

Both the President and Congress have several checks on the power of the judicial branch. The President appoints all federal judges, while the Senate must approve the President's court appointments. In addition, Congress has the power to remove federal judges from office if they are found guilty of wrongdoing. Congress may also propose a constitutional amendment to overrule a judicial decision.

★ Section 2 Review ★

Recall

1. **Define** (a) popular sovereignty, (b) representative government, (c) bill, (d) veto, (e) unconstitutional, (f) override.

Comprehension

2. (a) Identify the five basic principles of the Constitution. (b) Describe two of them.

3. (a) Explain how representative government works. (b) Why do people in a democracy adopt this system?

4. (a) Why did the framers of the Constitution set up three branches of government? (b) How does the Constitution prevent any branch from becoming too powerful?

Critical Thinking and Writing

5. **Synthesizing Information** How are the principles of popular sovereignty and limited government related?

6. **Analyzing Ideas** Explain the following statement: The Constitution sets up a government of laws, not of people.

★ ★

Activity Making a Chart Working with a partner or your class, create a chart that gives examples of ways in which the five basic principles of the Constitution protect you and your community.

3   A Living Document

As You Read

Explore These Questions
- What is the formal process for changing the Constitution?
- What is the purpose of the Bill of Rights?
- What informal changes have been made to the Constitution?

Define
- amendment
- precedent
- Cabinet
- judicial review

Identify
- First Amendment
- Fourth Amendment
- Sixth Amendment
- Elastic Clause
- Commerce Clause

SETTING the Scene The framers of the Constitution realized that the nation would grow and change. With this in mind, they created a living Constitution—one that could be altered and improved to meet new conditions and challenges as they arose. As George Washington commented:

> 66 I do not think we are more inspired, have more wisdom, or possess more virtue than those who will come after us. 99

Formal Changes to the Constitution

The framers spelled out a process for making **amendments,** or formal written changes, to the Constitution. Amending the Constitution is not easy, however. It requires two difficult steps: proposal and ratification. (See the chart on page 223.)

Proposing an amendment

Article 5 describes two methods for proposing amendments. Two thirds of each house of Congress can vote to propose an amendment. Or two thirds of the state legislatures can demand that Congress summon a national "convention for proposing amendments."

So far, only the first method—a vote by Congress—has been used. As experts have pointed out, the Constitution does not give guidelines for a national convention. Who should set the agenda? How should delegates be selected? Such questions probably would cause much delay and confusion.

Ratifying an amendment

Article 5 also outlines two methods of ratifying a proposed amendment. Either three fourths of the state legislatures or three fourths of the states meeting in special conventions must approve the amendment. Congress decides which method of ratification to use.

So far, only the Twenty-first Amendment was ratified by state conventions. All other amendments were ratified by state legislatures. In recent years, Congress has set a time limit for ratification. The limit today is seven years, but it may be extended.

The 27 Amendments

As you can see, the amendment process is a difficult one. Since 1789, more than 9,000 amendments have been introduced in Congress. Yet, only 27 amendments have been ratified!

The Bill of Rights

The original Constitution did not list basic freedoms of the people. In fact, several states refused to ratify the Constitution until they were promised that a bill of rights would be added. Those states wanted to ensure that the national government would not be able to take away people's basic freedoms.

The Bill of Rights, the first 10 amendments to the Constitution, was ratified in 1791. (See the chart on page 215.)

You will recognize many of the freedoms in the Bill of Rights. The **First Amendment** protects your right to worship and speak freely and to hold peaceful meetings. The **Fourth Amendment** protects you from "unreasonable" search and seizure of your home and property. The **Sixth Amendment** guarantees you the right to a trial by jury.

The protections of the Bill of Rights extend into many areas of your life. Suppose that you sent a letter to a newspaper criticizing the governor. Without the First Amendment protection of free speech, the governor might order your arrest. Without the Sixth Amendment, you might even be imprisoned for years without a trial.

Amendments 11 through 27

Only 17 amendments have been ratified since 1791. Several of these amendments reflect changing ideas about equality.

Amendments 13 through 15—the so-called Civil War amendments—were passed to protect the rights of former slaves. The Thirteenth Amendment ended slavery. The Fourteenth Amendment guaranteed citizenship and constitutional rights to African Americans. The Fifteenth Amendment guaranteed African Americans the right to vote.

Equality was also the goal of two later amendments. The Nineteenth Amendment gave women the right to vote. The Twenty-sixth Amendment set age 18 as the minimum voting age. The chart on page 215 lists Amendments 11 through 27. For more information about the amendments, refer to the page numbers shown on the chart.

Informal Changes

The language of the Constitution provides a general outline rather than specific details about the national government. Over time, this flexible language has allowed the government to adapt to the changing needs of the nation.

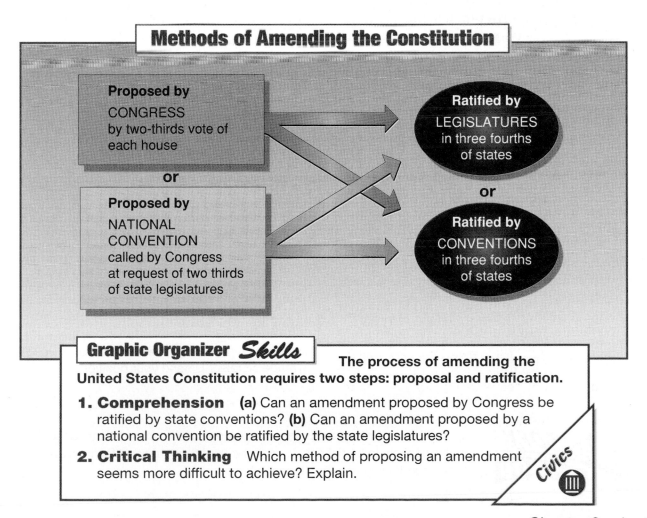

Methods of Amending the Constitution

Proposed by
CONGRESS
by two-thirds vote of
each house

or

Proposed by
NATIONAL
CONVENTION
called by Congress
at request of two thirds
of state legislatures

Ratified by
LEGISLATURES
in three fourths
of states

or

Ratified by
CONVENTIONS
in three fourths
of states

Graphic Organizer *Skills*   The process of amending the
United States Constitution requires two steps: proposal and ratification.

1. **Comprehension** **(a)** Can an amendment proposed by Congress be ratified by state conventions? **(b)** Can an amendment proposed by a national convention be ratified by the state legislatures?

2. **Critical Thinking** Which method of proposing an amendment seems more difficult to achieve? Explain.

Civics

New powers for Congress

The framers knew that they could not foresee the future. To deal with this problem, Article 1, Section 8, Clause 18, gives Congress the power to make all laws that shall be "necessary and proper" to carry out the powers of the national government. This so-called **Elastic Clause** has allowed Congress to stretch its power to pass laws.

Still another clause of the Constitution has allowed Congress to extend its powers. Article 1, Section 8, Clause 3, gives Congress the power to "regulate" trade with other nations and between the states.

Armed with the **Commerce Clause** and the Elastic Clause, Congress has been able to keep pace with change. For example, it has passed laws that regulate the airline industry, television, nuclear energy, and genetic engineering.

A more powerful executive

The Constitution does not describe in detail the powers of the President. Some Presidents, however, have taken actions or made decisions that set a **precedent,** or example, for later Presidents.

George Washington set one such precedent. The Constitution does not state that the President may appoint a **Cabinet,** or group of close advisers. President Washington assumed the power to do so on his own. Every President since then has followed his lead.

In national emergencies, Presidents have expanded their constitutional role. During the Great Depression, President Franklin Roosevelt expanded the size and power of the executive branch to propose and carry out programs that would restore the national economy.

A broader role for the judiciary

The Supreme Court can decide whether acts of a President or laws passed by Congress are unconstitutional. This power is known as **judicial review.**

The Constitution does not list judicial review as a power of the judicial branch. Like the unstated powers of the President, judicial review is implied in the words and structure of the Constitution. Article 3, Section 2, states that the Supreme Court has the right to hear "all cases . . . arising under this Constitution." In the case of *Marbury* v. *Madison,* an early Supreme Court decision interpreted Article 3, Section 2, to mean that the Supreme Court has the right to decide whether any law violates the Constitution.

★ Section 3 Review ★

Recall

1. **Identify** (a) First Amendment, (b) Fourth Amendment, (c) Sixth Amendment, (d) Elastic Clause, (e) Commerce Clause.
2. **Define** (a) amendment, (b) precedent, (c) Cabinet, (d) judicial review.

Comprehension

3. Describe the process for amending the United States Constitution.
4. List four rights protected by the Bill of Rights.

5. (a) How did George Washington expand the powers of the President? (b) How did Franklin Roosevelt expand the President's powers during the Great Depression?

Critical Thinking and Writing

6. **Drawing Conclusions** Why do you think there have been more informal changes than formal changes to the Constitution?
7. **Defending a Position** Do you think the process of amending the Constitution should be made simpler? Defend your position.

★ ★

Activity Writing an Essay Choose one of the amendments described in this section. In a brief essay, describe your thoughts and feelings about that amendment and what it means to you.

4 ★ The National Government at Work

As You Read

Explore These Questions
- What are the roles of Congress?
- What jobs does the President do?
- How is the federal court system organized?

Define
- appropriate
- standing committee
- joint committee
- impeach
- constituent
- executive agreement
- appeal
- opinion
- dissenting opinion

Identify
- House of Representatives
- Senate
- Supreme Court

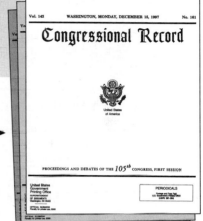

| Vol. 143 | WASHINGTON, MONDAY, DECEMBER 15, 1997 | No. 161 |

Congressional Record

United States
of America

PROCEEDINGS AND DEBATES OF THE 105th CONGRESS, FIRST SESSION

The *Congressional Record reports events in Congress.* ➤

SETTING the Scene On October 10, 1788, the last Congress under the Articles of Confederation transacted its final business. By September of the following year, the Presidential electors had chosen George Washington as the first President of the United States, the first Congress under the Constitution had met in New York City, and the Federal Judiciary Act had provided for the organization of the United States Supreme Court. The government of the United States, as set up by the Constitution, was in place.

More than 200 years later, Americans still live under this three-branched government set up by the Constitution. Each branch has its own clearly defined powers. Together, they provide us with a government of laws.

The Legislative Branch

Congress, the legislative branch of government, is made up of two houses: the House of Representatives and the Senate. Together, the two houses have the power to make the laws that govern all 50 states. At the same time, the states have a say in making those laws.

Two houses of Congress

The larger house, the **House of Representatives,** currently seats 435 members. The number of representatives for each state is determined according to that state's population. The more people who live in a state, the greater its number of representatives. Each state, however, is guaranteed at least one representative.*

Representatives serve for two-year terms. As a result, the entire House is up for election every even-numbered year. Congressional terms are numbered consecutively. The Congress that served from 1789 to 1791 is known as the First Congress. The Congress serving from 2001 to 2003 is the One Hundred Seventh Congress.

The **Senate,** the smaller house, has 100 members. Each state, no matter how large or small its population, has two senators. Senators serve for six-year terms. The terms are staggered, however. As a result, one third of the Senate are up for election every two years.

Powers of Congress

The chief job of Congress is to make the nation's laws. A new law first appears as a

---

*Guam, the Virgin Islands, American Samoa, and Washington, D.C., each elect a delegate to the House, while Puerto Rico elects a resident commissioner. However, these delegates are not voting members of the House.

Federal Officeholders

Office	Number	Term	Selection	Requirements
Representative	At least 1 per state; based on population	2 years	Elected by voters of congressional district	Age 25 or over Citizen for 7 years Resident of state in which elected
Senator	2 per state	6 years	Original Constitution—elected by state legislature Amendment 17—elected by voters	Age 30 or over Citizen for 9 years Resident of state in which elected
President and Vice President	1	4 years	Elected by electoral college	Age 35 or over Natural-born citizen Resident of U.S. for 14 years
Supreme Court Justice	9	Life	Appointed by President	No requirements in Constitution

Chart Skills

The Constitution details the number, length of term, method of selection, and requirements for officeholders in the three branches of government.

1. **Comprehension** (a) At what age can you be elected to the Senate? The House of Representatives? (b) How long may a Supreme Court Justice remain in office?

2. **Critical Thinking** Why do you think the requirements for President and Vice President are the same?

Civics

proposal called a bill. The bill must be passed by both houses of Congress and signed by the President to become law. The chart on page 227 shows the steps a bill must pass through before becoming a law.

Congress has another equally important power. It decides what laws or programs will receive funds. The federal government cannot spend money on any program unless Congress **appropriates** it, or sets it aside for a special purpose. In this way, Congress controls how much money the government spends, whether for military aircraft, national highways, or school lunches.

Congressional committees

During the first session of Congress, 31 bills were proposed by both houses. Today, thousands of bills are introduced every year in Congress. Clearly, it would be impossible

for each member of Congress to study and make recommendations about every bill. This job is reserved for committees.

The House of Representatives and the Senate each have **standing committees.** These are permanent committees assigned to study specific issues such as agriculture, labor, and energy. They are often broken up into subcommittees that examine certain problems in depth.

Congress may sometimes create a **joint committee,** or committees that include both House and Senate members. One of the most important kinds of joint committee is the conference committee. Its task is to settle differences between the House and the Senate versions of the same bill. Members of a conference committee try to find a middle ground and to agree on the language of the bill. Compromise is often difficult.

Skills FOR LIFE

Critical Thinking	Managing Information	Communication	Maps, Charts, and Graphs

Reading a Flowchart

How Will I Use This Skill ?

A flowchart is a type of graphic organizer. It uses boxes and arrows to guide you step by step through a development or process. Learning to read a flowchart can help you understand even the most complicated processes—from programming a VCR to running for public office.

LEARN the Skill

❶ Identify the process described by the flowchart.

❷ Locate the starting point of the process. (This is the box with no arrow leading toward it.) Some flowcharts may have more than one starting point, since more than one part of a process is being tracked to the end point.

❸ Follow the steps of the process by following the arrows to the end point.

PRACTICE the Skill

❶ What process does the flowchart below describe?

❷ (a) Where can a bill be introduced? (b) Why are there two starting points on this flowchart?

❸ (a) What happens to a bill after it is introduced? (b) At what point in the process do the work of the Senate and the House come together? (c) What happens next?

APPLY the Skill

Create a flowchart to describe the steps of a process you know well. You might show how to play a game, how to repair something, or how to prepare a meal. Show your flowchart to some friends. See if they can understand the process by looking at your chart.

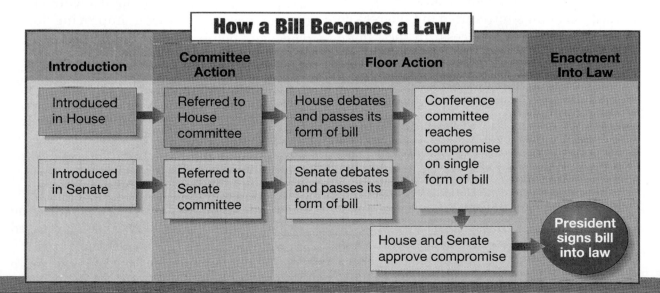

How a Bill Becomes a Law

Introduction	Committee Action	Floor Action	Enactment Into Law
Introduced in House	Referred to House committee	House debates and passes its form of bill	Conference committee reaches compromise on single form of bill
Introduced in Senate	Referred to Senate committee	Senate debates and passes its form of bill	
		House and Senate approve compromise	President signs bill into law

◀ *The Capitol Building in Washington, D.C.*

Passing a bill requires the cooperation of many individuals. For example, a recent trade bill was 1,000 pages long. It required the efforts of 200 members of Congress, working in 17 subcommittees, to get it passed. Most bills introduced in Congress do not meet with such success. In fact, more than 90 percent of all the bills introduced are defeated in committees.

Other roles of Congress

Members of Congress have duties other than serving on committees and making laws. They also guard the public trust. For example, the House of Representatives can **impeach,** or bring a formal charge of wrongdoing against, the President or another federal official. The Senate acts as a court to try the accused. Congress also acts as a "watchdog" by supervising the way the executive branch carries out the laws.

Members of Congress must also respond to the special needs of their states. Responsible representatives and senators must remember their **constituents,** or the people who elected them. They do this by supporting bills that have a direct impact on the people "back home." Such bills might include promoting new post offices, improving highways, and helping to pay for local education programs.

The Executive Branch

The framers created an executive branch to carry out the laws. However, they left out details about the President's powers. They thought that Congress would be the central branch of government except in times of war and other emergencies. Over the years, the powers of the President have been increased or decreased, depending on the needs of the time. Still, Americans expect the President to fill certain roles.

Roles of the President

The main role of the President is to carry out the nation's laws. As chief executive, the President oversees the many departments, agencies, and commissions that help to accomplish this task.

The President directs the nation's foreign policy. Three important powers allow the President to influence relations with other countries. They are the powers to appoint ambassadors, make treaties, and enter into **executive agreements.** Executive agreements are informal agreements with other heads of state, usually dealing with trade. Unlike treaties, they do not require Senate approval.

The President is the highest-ranking officer in the armed forces. As commander in chief, the President can appoint and remove top military commanders. The President may also use the armed forces to deal with crises both at home and abroad. (However, only Congress has the power to declare war on another country.)

As the nation's chief legislator, the President suggests new laws and works for their passage. In this role, the President often meets with members of Congress to win their support. Sometimes, the President campaigns for public support through television or radio speeches and press conferences. The President also can use persuasion to oppose a bill. In this case, however, the President's most powerful weapon is the power to veto a bill.

The President is the living symbol of the nation. In this role, the President represents all American citizens at many occasions. For example, the President welcomes visiting foreign leaders, makes speeches to commemorate national holidays, and gives medals to national heroes. (See the photograph on page 216.)

The American people also see the President as the chief symbol of the condition of the nation, even though this responsibility is shared with Congress and the judiciary. In describing this situation, former President Jimmy Carter declared that "When things go bad you get entirely too much blame," and "when things go good, you get entirely too much credit."

Executive agencies and departments

The nation's laws cover a broad range of concerns—defense, housing, crime, and pollution, to name a few. To carry out these laws and to perform other duties, the President needs the help of millions of government workers and assistants.

Presidents at Work

Under the Constitution, the President commands the armed forces and directs foreign policy. At left, President Bill Clinton meets with Tony Blair, prime minister of Great Britain. Above, President George Bush visits American troops in Saudi Arabia. ★ **Describe two other roles of the President.**

One group of assistants, the Executive Office, includes many agencies and individuals. They range from the Vice President to the Office of Management and Budget, which prepares the total budget of the United States.

The President's Cabinet, called secretaries, are the heads of executive departments. Today, the President relies on 14 executive departments—among them, the Departments of Defense, Commerce, Justice, Labor, and Energy. Each department has many concerns. For example, the Department of Agriculture deals with food quality, crop improvement, and nutrition. The Department of Transportation establishes rules for speed limits, automobile exhaust systems, and highway and vehicle safety.

More than 30 independent executive agencies also help the President carry out duties. For example, the Central Intelligence Agency (CIA) provides the President with secret information about the world's trouble spots. The National Aeronautics and Space Administration (NASA) is in charge of the nation's space program.

Eleven independent regulatory commissions enforce national laws. They establish rules, rates, and standards for trade, business, science, and transportation. For example, the Federal Trade Commission (FTC) enforced the federal law banning "false or misleading advertising" by ruling that cigarettes may not be advertised as "kind" to your throat.

Finally, there are government corporations. There are at least 60 government corporations today. They include the United States Postal Service, the Tennessee Valley Authority, and Amtrak.

The Judicial Branch

Article 3 of the Constitution gives the judicial power of the United States to the Supreme Court and to lower courts that Congress may set up. Under the Judiciary Act of 1789, Congress created the system of federal courts that still operates today.

Lower courts

Most federal cases are first heard in the district courts. These courts are located in more than 90 districts around the country. Cases brought to these courts may involve matters of criminal law, such as kidnapping and murder, or matters of civil law, such as bankruptcy and divorce. In district courts, decisions are made by either a judge or a jury, which is a panel of citizens.

Every citizen has the right to **appeal** a decision, or ask that it be reviewed by a higher court. These higher courts of appeal are called circuit, or appellate, courts. The United States has 13 circuit courts of appeal.

Circuit courts operate differently from district courts. A panel of three judges reviews each case. The judges decide if rules of trial procedure were followed in the original trial. If errors did occur, the circuit court may reverse, or overturn, the original decision. Or it may send back the case to the district court for a new trial.

Supreme Court

The **Supreme Court** is the highest court in the United States. Americans depend upon the Supreme Court to settle disputes, interpret the law, and protect their guaranteed rights. The Court is made up of a Chief Justice and eight Associate Justices. The President appoints the Supreme Court Justices, but Congress must approve the appointments. In about one out of five cases, Congress rejects the President's appointment and a new nomination must be made. Appointments to the Supreme Court are for life.

Only two kinds of cases can begin in the Supreme Court. One kind involves disputes between states. The other involves foreign ambassadors. In other cases, the Supreme Court serves as a final court of appeals. It hears cases that have been tried and appealed as far as law permits in lower courts.

The Supreme Court hears only issues about the Constitution, federal law, or treaties. It selects only about 120 cases from the 4,000 or more requests it receives each year. Most of the cases involve laws written in unclear language. The Court must decide what each law means, whom it affects, and whether it is constitutional.

A Supreme Court decision rests on a simple majority vote of at least five Justices. A member of the majority writes an **opinion,** or official statement of the legal reasons for the Court's decision. Sometimes, a member of the minority strongly disagrees with the majority ruling. That Justice may write a **dissenting opinion,** explaining the reasons for the disagreement. Justice Oliver Wendell Holmes, Jr., wrote so many dissenting opinions that he became known as the "Great Dissenter."

Supreme Court decisions are final. There are no other courts of appeal. If Congress strongly disagrees with a Supreme Court decision, however, it can take other action. It can pass a modified version of the law that will meet the Court's objections. Congress can also propose an amendment to the Constitution.

★ Section 4 Review ★

Recall

1. **Identify** (a) House of Representatives, (b) Senate, (c) Supreme Court.
2. **Define** (a) appropriate, (b) standing committee, (c) joint committee, (d) impeach, (e) constituent, (f) executive agreement, (g) appeal, (h) opinion, (i) dissenting opinion.

Comprehension

3. What are the two most important powers of Congress?
4. (a) How does the President influence legislation?

(b) What three powers enable the President to direct foreign policy?
5. (a) What is the role of circuit courts? (b) What is the role of the Supreme Court?

Critical Thinking and Writing

6. **Ranking** Review the subsection "Roles of the President." List the President's roles. Then rank the roles in order of importance. Be prepared to support your ranking.
7. **Analyzing Ideas** Why is it important for Congress to approve the President's choices for Supreme Court Justices?

★ ★

Activity **Making a Diagram** Make a graphic organizer with three branches. Fill in the chart to show the roles of each branch of government and the smaller parts that make them up.

Good Citizenship

As You Read

Explore These Questions
- How was the Bill of Rights limited?
- How did the Supreme Court use the Fourteenth Amendment to expand citizens' rights?
- What are the rights and responsibilities of citizens?

Define
- due process

Identify
- *Gideon* v. *Wainwright*

Plaque listing ➤ the Bill of Rights

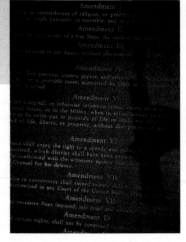

SETTING the Scene Americans first proclaimed their rights in the Declaration of Independence. In it, they declared boldly:

❝ All men are created equal; . . . they are endowed by their Creator with certain unalienable rights, that among these are life, liberty, and the pursuit of happiness. ❞

Since the birth of the nation, Americans have struggled to reach this ideal of basic rights for all. They have learned, however, that along with the rights of citizenship come responsibilities.

Citizens' Rights

The Constitution originally protected some individual rights by limiting government actions. For example, Article 6, Section 3, prevents the government from making religion a requirement for public service. Article 1, Section 9, prohibits Congress from passing a law punishing an act that was not illegal at the time it was committed.

Bill of Rights

Many Americans, however, demanded a more specific list of rights. In response, the first Congress drew up and the states ratified the Bill of Rights.

Still, the Bill of Rights applied only to the federal government. States were free to restrict or deny basic rights of many people, including women, African Americans, and Asian Americans. At times, the federal government also restricted rights through laws and court decisions.

Fourteenth Amendment

An amendment passed in 1868 paved the way for a major expansion of rights. The Fourteenth Amendment states that persons born or naturalized in the United States are citizens of both the nation and their state. No state may limit the rights of citizens or deny citizens **due process,** or a fair hearing or trial. States are also forbidden to deny citizens "equal protection of the laws."

Over the years, the Supreme Court has decided that the Fourteenth Amendment's guarantee of due process and equal protection includes rights listed in the Bill of Rights. States cannot deny citizens the protections of the Bill of Rights.

For example, in the 1960s, the Supreme Court ruled that due process includes the Sixth Amendment right to representation by a lawyer. The case of *Gideon* v. *Wainwright* involved a poor Florida man who had been convicted of breaking and entering. The judge hearing the case had refused the defendant's request for a lawyer. The Supreme Court ruled that a state court must appoint a lawyer for any defendant who cannot afford to hire one.

What are basic rights?

As the Ninth Amendment states, the people have rights beyond those listed in the Constitution. Americans still strive to define these rights. Some people believe that a citizen's basic rights include the opportunity to get a good education and to find a job. Others argue that these rights are not guaranteed by the Constitution.

Citizens' Responsibilities

Like every citizen, you must do your part to safeguard your rights. At the same time, you must accept the civic responsibilities that are a part of living in a free and democratic society.

Know your rights

You cannot protect your rights unless you know what they are. Books, government pamphlets, and groups such as the League of Women Voters, the National Association for the Advancement of Colored People (NAACP), and the Legal Aid Society can give you information about your rights and the law.

You must also know the limits of your rights. A popular saying states, "Your right to swing your fist ends where my nose begins." As part of your civic responsibilities, you must respect the rights of others. After all, your rights are only as safe as your neighbor's. If you abuse or allow abuse of another citizen's rights, your own rights may be at risk someday.

Become involved

Good government depends on good leaders. Therefore, citizens have the responsibility to exercise their right to vote. A good citizen studies the candidates and the issues in order to make responsible choices.

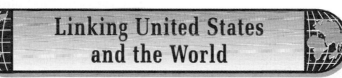

Linking United States and the World

United States

South Africa

Getting Out the Vote

Voting is both a right and a responsibility. Yet, many take this right for granted. In 1996, only 48.8 percent of Americans who were eligible to vote actually voted. In 1994, when South Africa's black majority won the right to vote for the first time (right), 86.9 percent of eligible voters cast their ballots. ★ **Why do you think South Africans were so eager to vote? What point is the cartoon on the left making?**

Why Study History?

Because Citizens Have Responsibilities

★ ★

Historical Background

For many Americans, providing unpaid community service is an important civic responsibility. In the 1770s, cities like Boston and Philadelphia had volunteer fire departments. During the Revolution, thousands of Americans volunteered to serve in state militias. By the mid-1800s, women took a leading role in charitable organizations that cared for the sick and needy.

In April 1997, the Presidents' Summit for America's Future encouraged a national spirit of volunteerism. At the meeting, President Bill Clinton said good citizenship meant that you "serve in your community to help make it a better place."

Connections to Today

Adults are not the only volunteers. Young people can also find ways to serve their community. Consider, for example, the story of David Levitt.

David Levitt was a sixth grader in Florida when he read about Kentucky Harvest. This organization collected leftover food from restaurants and distributed it to people in need. David had an idea. He had seen how much unused food was thrown out in his school cafeteria. Why not start a similar program himself?

David presented his plan to the local school board and got permission to start a food distribution program. His first delivery was cartons of milk and bags of salad. Over the next few years, David sent more than 250,000 pounds of cafeteria leftovers to

David Levitt collects food for the needy.

shelters and food banks all over Florida. While still in middle school, he was invited to the White House and awarded a medal for his volunteer work.

Connections to You

There are many ways for you to volunteer in your community. You can participate in a food or clothing drive. You can help clean up a neighborhood park. Perhaps you would like to tutor a younger child or help at a local hospital or senior citizen center. To learn more about these and other opportunities, look up community organizations in your local telephone directory.

1. **Comprehension** **(a)** How did President Clinton define good citizenship? **(b)** How did David Levitt help his local community?

2. **Critical Thinking** How might volunteering affect the cost of government?

★ *Activity*  **Writing a Proposal** Decide on a volunteer program that might be helpful in your community. Describe the benefits of the program and how it could be set up. Write your plan as a formal written proposal.

The First Amendment guarantees you the freedom to speak, write, sign petitions, and meet with others freely. You can use those freedoms not only to defend your rights but also to take a stand on political and community issues. It is important to remember that such expressions should be truthful and peaceful. Supreme Court Justice Oliver Wendell Holmes, Jr., once warned:

66 The most [strict] protection of free speech would not protect a man in falsely shouting fire in a theater and causing a panic. 99

Responsible citizens keep informed about national and community issues. In addition to reading newspapers, you can attend local meetings. At a town council meeting, for example, you might learn about proposed solutions to local health issues or pollution problems. Groups such as the League of Women Voters may sponsor debates by candidates for political office.

The Bill of Rights guarantees citizens the right to a trial by jury. Every citizen, in turn, has the responsibility to serve on juries when called. Serving on a jury is a serious duty. Jurors must take time out from their work and personal lives. Deciding the guilt or innocence of the accused can be difficult.

Civic Values

Citizens enter into a contract with the government. They give the government the power to make certain laws. In return, they expect government to protect the well-being of society. As part of this contract, the government has the power to set penalties if laws are broken.

Like other citizens, you have a responsibility to obey the laws and respect the rights of others. For example, you should not steal, damage property, or harm someone.

Volunteer

Responsible citizens offer their time and talents to help others and to improve the community. For example, you can join or start a group to clean up parks or to serve food to senior citizens. You can also take part in a walk-a-thon or bike-a-thon to raise money for a worthy cause. Many volunteer fire departments have junior divisions.

Defend the nation

At age 18, all men must report their name, age, and address to the government. In time of war, the government may call them to serve in the armed forces. Many young citizens feel the duty to enlist in the military on their own.

★ Section 5 Review ★

Recall

1. **Identify** *Gideon* v. *Wainwright.*
2. **Define** due process.

Comprehension

3. Why were some states able to ignore the guarantees of the Bill of Rights?
4. **(a)** What does the Fourteenth Amendment guarantee? **(b)** How did the Supreme Court expand the guarantees of this amendment?

5. List three responsibilities of citizenship.

Critical Thinking and Writing

6. **Analyzing Ideas** Reread the words of Justice Holmes, above. How does this statement relate to the need to balance the rights of the individual and civic responsibility?
7. **Solving Problems** Why must a citizen of a democracy learn how to compromise?

★ ★

Activity Making a Poster Help people in your school and community become better citizens. Create a poster that encourages people to do one of the following: know their rights, vote, become involved in government, volunteer in the community, or join the armed services.

Review and Activities

★ Sum It Up ★

Section 1 Goals of the Constitution
▶ The goals of the Constitution include establishing justice, keeping peace at home, and defending the nation.
▶ The Constitution helps guarantee the rights and liberties of American citizens.

Section 2 Five Principles of the Constitution
▶ The five basic principles of the Constitution are popular sovereignty, limited government, federalism, separation of powers, and checks and balances.

Section 3 A Living Document
▶ The process for amending the Constitution was made difficult on purpose.
▶ Flexible language has allowed informal changes to the Constitution.

Section 4 The National Government at Work
▶ Congress, made up of the Senate and House of Representatives, makes the nation's laws.
▶ The duties of the President include carrying out the nation's laws, directing foreign policy, and commanding the armed forces.
▶ The judicial branch, headed by the Supreme Court, interprets the laws.

Section 5 Good Citizenship
▶ Over time, the protections of the Bill of Rights were extended to all Americans.
▶ Citizens have responsibilities, including obeying the law and voting.

 **CD-ROM Review** For additional review of the major ideas of Chapter 8, see **Guide to the Essentials of American History** or **Interactive Student Tutorial CD-ROM,** which contains interactive review activities, graphic organizers, and practice tests.

Reviewing the Chapter

Define These Terms
Match each term with the correct definition.

Column 1	Column 2
1. federal	a. proposed law
2. bill	b. put money aside
3. general welfare	c. set aside a veto
4. appropriate	d. national
5. override	e. well-being of all the people

Explore the Main Ideas
1. How may the government promote the general welfare?
2. Describe how the Constitution is a contract.
3. How does the Elastic Clause allow for informal changes in the Constitution?
4. Give three examples of checks and balances.
5. What rights and responsibilities do citizens have in the justice system?

Chart Activity

Look at the chart and answer the following questions:
1. What percentage of Americans vote in presidential elections? In local elections? **2.** Are people more likely to know the names of their representatives or their senators?
Critical Thinking Why do you think so few Americans attend public meetings? What can happen if citizens do not participate in government?

Political Participation and Awareness

Percentage of Americans who...	
Vote in presidential elections	50%
Vote in congressional elections	35–40
Know name of congressional representative	36
Know names of both U.S. senators	29
Occasionally contact local officials	28
Vote in local elections	10–30
Occasionally attend public meetings	19
Give money to candidate or party	13

Source: Selected polls, including Gallup, *Denver Post* Poll, University of Michigan, and *The New York Times, 1989.*

🔲 Critical Thinking and Writing

1. **Exploring Unit Themes Rights and Liberties** How might our government be different today if there were no Tenth Amendment?

2. **Understanding Chronology (a)** In what order did the following groups win the right to vote: women; people 18 to 21 years old; African American men?
(b) Who could vote for President in 1964 who could not do so in 1960?

3. **Linking Past and Present** The federal government recently adopted rules about a new type of nationwide television broadcasting that will provide sharper, clearer pictures. Explain how the government gets its power to make such rules.

4. **Defending a Position** Why is keeping informed an important responsibility of citizenship? Give reasons and examples.

🔲 Using Primary Sources

Long after the Constitution was ratified, Thomas Jefferson commented:

> 66 As the [human mind] becomes more developed, . . . as new discoveries are made, . . . and manners and opinions changed with the change of circumstances, [constitutions] must advance also, and keep pace with the times. We might as well require a man to wear still the coat which fitted him when a boy, as civilized society to remain ever under the [government] of their . . . ancestors. 99

Source: *Patterns in American History,* ed. Alexander De Conde et al., 1965.

Recognizing Points of View (a) What did Jefferson think happens as time goes on?
(b) How do you think he felt about the process of amending the Constitution? Explain.

ACTIVITY BANK

▶ Interdisciplinary Activity

Exploring the Arts Find out more about the procedure of a courtroom. If possible, visit a courthouse or watch a trial on television. Then, with several classmates, write a script and conduct a mock trial.

▶ Career Skills Activity

Fiction Writer Write a short story about what might happen if people had no political rights. Set the story in the United States or in another country.

▶ Citizenship Activity

Holding a Panel Discussion Organize a panel discussion to consider a proposal for a new constitutional amendment. You might examine the idea of limiting the President to a single six-year term, changing the voting age, or another issue.

Internet Activity

Use the Internet to find sites dealing with the agencies of the United States government. Choose one agency and prepare a report on its activities. Questions you should answer are: When was the agency founded? What does it do? What branch does it serve? How many employees does it have? How much money does it spend every year?

EYEWITNESS Journal

You are the President of the United States. In three EYEWITNESS JOURNAL entries, describe some of the kinds of activities you have to perform and what you think about your job. Use information from the chapter to help think up events.

History Through Literature

Valley Forge

by Maxwell Anderson

Introduction

For 30 years, Maxwell Anderson was one of the most respected American playwrights. Many of his dramas were based on history. His 1934 play *Valley Forge* describes the hardships the Continental Army faced during the winter of 1777–1778. In this scene, George Washington hears some of the complaints of his troops.

Vocabulary

Before you read the selection, find the meanings of these words in a dictionary: **lenient, commissary, savvy, munitions.**

TEAGUE: General Washington!

WASHINGTON: What is it?

TEAGUE: These here new regulations about men going home. Going home without leave. They say it's seventy-five lashes if they catch you now. Why is that?

WASHINGTON: The traditional penalty for desertion is shooting at sunrise. We've been more lenient here.

TEAGUE: But look, General Washington, it don't make sense. It don't stand to reason—

NICK: Do you want to talk your neck into a rope?

WASHINGTON: Let him say what's on his mind.

TEAGUE: Well, here it is: I'm going hungry here and my woman's going hungry at home. You let me go home for the winter, and you won't have to feed me, and that relieves the commissary. I rustle some wild meat for the younguns and the old woman, and they don't starve and I don't starve. More'n that, everybody knows there's two or three thousand men gone home already for that same reason, and if they was here now they'd be chewing the bark off the second-growth birch like so many cottontails. I don't hold it against you and I don't hold it against anybody because I don't know who in thunder to hold it against, but there's nothing to eat here.

ALCOCK: Stow it, will you? The dog ate the stuff, and he isn't dead yet.

TEAGUE: It ain't that I'm afraid of a good fight. A good fight's ham and eggs to me. Me and my boy here, we make for home every winter when the grub gets scarce, and we come back every spring when the fighting starts. We're coming back next spring, and every spring, till we chase the...redcoats clear out of Chesapeake Bay, and across the Atlantic Ocean and right up a lamppost in London town! Fightin's fine, but sitting here and starving down to a hide and buttons—I don't savvy it.

WASHINGTON: What is your name, sir?

TEAGUE: Teague, sir. Teague's my name.

WASHINGTON: Well, Master Teague, if they catch you they'll give you seventy-five

The March to Valley Forge by William B. Trego shows General George Washington on horseback, reviewing his troops. At Valley Forge, Washington had to plead with local merchants and farmers for food supplies. ★ **Why does Trego show one of the soldiers taking off his hat to Washington?**

lashes, and that's a good deal to take and live. On the other hand you're quite right from your own angle, and if I were you I'd feel as you do.—But this you should know, sir: if you go home, and we all go home this winter, you won't need to bother about coming back in the spring. There'll be no fighting to come back to.—General Howe will march out of Philadelphia and take over these states of ours. If he knew now how many have deserted, how many are sick, how many unfit for duty on account of the lack of food and clothes and munitions, he'd come back in force and wring our necks one by one, and the neck of our sickly little revolution along with us.... What are we in this war for? Do we want to quit?

THE MEN: No, sir. No.

WASHINGTON: I can't blame you if you sound a bit half-hearted about it.

TEAGUE: I'm not half-hearted about it! Not me! I'm fighting to keep King George out of my backyard! I moved west three times to get away from his...tax-collectors, and every time they caught up to me! I'm sick of tax-collectors, that's why I'm in it!

WASHINGTON: Then it may be you're here in error, and the sooner you discover it the better. You'll get death and taxes under one government as well as another. But I'll tell you why I'm here, and why I've hoped you were here, and why it's seemed to me worthwhile to stick with it while our guns rust out for lack of powder, and men die around me for lack of food and medicine, and women and children sicken at home for lack of clothing and the little they need to eat.... [W]hat I fight for is your right to do what you please with your government and with yourselves without benefit of kings.—It's for you to decide, Master Teague—you, and your son, and the rest of you.... But if we lose you—if you've lost interest in this cause of ours—we've lost our war, lost it completely, and the men we've left lying on our battlefields died for nothing whatever—for a dream that came too early—and may never come true....

TEAGUE: I guess the old woman'll get along. She's brought in her own bear meat before.

NICK: Well, it's all right with me.

Analyzing Literature

1. What were some of the hardships that Washington's troops faced?
2. Summarize one argument Teague gives in favor of going home.
3. **Critical Thinking   Comparing** How do Washington's reasons for fighting differ from Teague's?

Unit 3 The Nation Takes Shape

Viewing UNIT THEMES — Celebrating the Nation

American artist John Lewis Krimmel painted this election celebration in 1815. This detail shows people of all ages enjoying parades and public debate in the streets of Philadelphia. By this time, Americans had developed strong feelings of pride in their young nation. ★ **Why do you think Americans at this time felt that an election was cause for celebration?**

Unit Theme Nationalism

In the years after winning independence and adopting a new Constitution, the United States grew and prospered. As the nation took shape, so did American nationalism. Nationalism is a feeling of loyalty and devotion to one's country.

Proud Americans sought to identify qualities that set the United States apart from older nations.

How did Americans of the time describe their feelings about their country? They can tell you in their own words.

★ ★

VIEWPOINTS ON AMERICAN NATIONALISM

66 Britain, whose children we are, and whose language we speak, should no longer be *our* standard.... Customs, habits, and language, as well as government, should be national. America should have her *own* distinct from all the world. 99

Noah Webster, scholar and dictionary writer (1789)

66 We have learned to love our country... because the sweat of our fathers' brows has subdued its soil;... because it embraces our fathers and mothers. 99

John Thornton Kirkland, Boston minister (1798)

66 Our country! In her [dealings] with foreign nations, may she always be in the right; but our country, right or wrong. 99

Stephen Decatur, naval hero (1816)

★ ★

Activity Writing to Learn Another word for nationalism is patriotism. Many things might stir patriotic feelings, including holidays like the Fourth of July, symbols like the flag, or songs like "The Star-Spangled Banner." List 5 or 6 other things that may stir patriotic feelings. Then, choose one of the items from your list. Write a paragraph describing what you think it represents.

Chapter 9

The New Republic Begins

1789–1800

In this chapter, you will learn about the early years of the United States. The new nation faced many decisions about how it would govern itself. Everything was a fresh issue, from what the President should be called to how the nation should pay its bills. The young republic also had to meet violent challenges inside its borders and on the high seas.

In these confusing times, leaders clashed over what policies to follow. Some wanted a stronger national government. Others felt the states should have more power. Before long, two political parties formed. Despite powerful feelings on both sides, the nation successfully elected its second President and moved into the 1800s.

Why Study History?

Again and again, as you study American history, you will find people arguing about something called "the tariff." Tariffs may not seem very exciting. However, they can directly affect how much we pay for the things we buy. To focus on a recent issue involving tariffs, see the *Why Study History?* feature, "The Debate Over Tariffs Continues," in this chapter.

 American Events

●1789
George Washington becomes first President of the United States

●1791
Congress creates the Bank of the United States

●1793
Washington issues Neutrality Proclamation to keep the United States out of war

1788	1790	1792	1794

 World Events

 1789 World Event
French Revolution begins

1792 World Event
French assembly votes to end monarchy

 Symbols of a Proud New Nation

In the late 1700s, paper cutouts like this one were a popular form of artwork. This design shows an eagle holding a flag under the word LIBERTY—symbols of the new nation's patriotism. As President George Washington took office in 1789, Americans looked to the future with pride and hope. ★ **If you were an American in 1789, what hopes and worries might you have about the new government?**

1795 ●
Jay's Treaty keeps peace between the United States and Britain

1797 ●
John Adams becomes second President of the United States

●**1798**
Sedition Act makes it a crime to criticize the government

| 1794 | 1796 | 1798 | 1800 |

 1794 World Event
Thaddeus Kosciusko leads Polish uprising

1797 World Event
British sailors mutiny to demand better conditions

 243

Launching the New Government

As You Read

Explore These Questions

- How did George Washington's actions set an example for future Presidents?
- How did Alexander Hamilton plan to strengthen the nation's economy?
- Why did some people oppose Hamilton's economic plan?

Define

- inauguration
- precedent
- Cabinet
- national debt
- bond
- speculator
- tariff
- protective tariff

Identify

- Judiciary Act
- District of Columbia
- Bank of the United States
- Whiskey Rebellion

SETTING the Scene The new Congress met for the first time in the spring of 1789. Vice President John Adams brought up a curious question. How should people address the President?

For three weeks, members of Congress debated the issue. Some favored the simple title "President Washington." Others felt that it lacked dignity. Instead, they suggested titles such as "His Elective Highness" or "His Highness the President of the United States and Protector of the Rights of the Same."

Finally, Washington let Congress know he was content with "President of the United States." By choosing a simple title, Washington showed he was not interested in the kind of power that European monarchs had. In this decision, like many others, Washington set an example for later Presidents.

The New Government

George Washington was inaugurated in New York City on April 30, 1789. A President's **inauguration** is the ceremony at which the President officially takes the oath of office. A witness reported that the new President looked "grave, almost to sadness." Washington no doubt was feeling the awesome responsibility of his office. He knew that Americans were looking to him to make their new government work.

As the first President, Washington had no one to imitate. While the Constitution provided a framework for the new government, it did not explain how the President should govern from day to day. Washington knew he was setting an example for future generations. "There is scarcely any part of my conduct," he said, "which may not hereafter be drawn into precedent." A **precedent** (PREHS uh dehnt) is an act or decision that sets an example for others to follow.

Washington set one important precedent at the end of his second term. In 1796, he decided not to run for a third term. Not until 1940 did any President seek a third term.

The first Cabinet

The Constitution said little about how the executive branch should be organized. It was clear, however, that the President needed talented people to help him carry out his duties.

Connections With Civics

The President who finally broke Washington's two-term precedent was Franklin D. Roosevelt. In 1940, he ran for and won a third term. Four years later, Roosevelt was elected yet again. Today, the Twenty-Second Amendment to the Constitution prohibits any President from being elected more than twice.

The First President

George Washington traveled on horseback to his inauguration in New York City. Along the way, crowds gathered to cheer their new President. Here, women and children scatter flower petals in Washington's path. ★ **How can you tell this painter greatly admired Washington?**

Mug honoring President Washington's inauguration ▶

In 1789, the first Congress created five executive departments. They were the departments of State, Treasury, and War and the offices of Attorney General and Postmaster General. The heads of these departments made up the President's **Cabinet.** Members of the Cabinet gave Washington advice and directed their departments.

Washington set a precedent by carefully choosing well-known leaders to serve in his Cabinet. The two most influential were the Secretary of State, Thomas Jefferson, and the Secretary of the Treasury, Alexander Hamilton.

The federal court system

The Constitution called for a Supreme Court. Congress, however, had to organize the federal court system. In 1789, Congress passed the **Judiciary Act.** It called for the Supreme Court to have one Chief Justice and five Associate Justices.* Washington named John Jay to serve as the first Chief Justice of the United States.

The Judiciary Act also set up a system of district courts and circuit courts across the nation. Decisions made in these lower courts could be appealed to the Supreme Court, the highest court in the land.

Battling the National Debt

As Secretary of the Treasury, Alexander Hamilton wanted to build a strong economy. He faced many major problems, however. Among the most pressing was the large national debt. The **national debt** is the total sum of money a government owes to others.

---

* Today, the Supreme Court has eight Associate Justices.

Biography Alexander Hamilton

Alexander Hamilton was born on the Caribbean island of Nevis in 1755. As a boy, he faced poverty, but he worked his way up in a local trading company. He later came to New York, served as an officer in the American Revolution, and became the first Secretary of the Treasury. This portrait was painted by John Trumbull, one of the most famous early American artists.

★ **How did Alexander Hamilton help strengthen the new nation?**

During the Revolution, both the national government and the individual states needed money to pay soldiers and buy supplies. They borrowed money from foreign countries and ordinary citizens.

Then, as now, governments borrowed money by issuing bonds. A **bond** is a certificate which promises to repay the money loaned plus interest on a certain date. For example, if a person pays $100 for a bond, the government agrees to pay back $100 plus interest in five or ten years.

By 1789, most southern states had paid off their debts from the Revolution. Other states and the federal government had not.

Hamilton insisted that all these debts be repaid. After all, he asked, who would lend money to the United States in the future if the country did not pay its old debts?

Hamilton's Plan

Hamilton developed a two-part plan to repay both the national and state debts. First, he wanted to buy up all the bonds issued by the national and state governments before 1789. He planned to sell new bonds to pay off those old debts. When the economy improved, the government would be able to pay off the new bonds. Second, he wanted the national government to pay off debts owed by the states.

Many people, including bankers and investors, welcomed Hamilton's plan. Others attacked it.

Madison leads the opposition

James Madison led the opposition to Hamilton's plan. Madison argued that the plan was unfair because it would reward speculators. A **speculator** is someone willing to invest in a risky venture in the hope of making a large profit.

During the Revolution, the government had paid soldiers and citizens who supplied goods with bonds. Many of these bondholders needed cash to survive. They sold their bonds to speculators. Speculators paid only 10 or 15 cents for bonds that had an original, or face, value of one dollar.

If the government repaid the bonds at face value, speculators stood to make great fortunes. Madison thought that speculators did not deserve to make such profits.

Hamilton disagreed. The United States had to repay its bonds in full, he said, in order to gain the trust and help of investors. The support of investors, he argued, was crucial for building the new nation's economy. After much debate, Hamilton convinced Congress to accept his plan of repaying the national debt.

As a southerner, James Madison also led the fight against the other part of Hamilton's plan. It called for the federal government to pay state debts. Many southern states had already paid their own debts in full. They thought other states should do the same. As a result, southerners bitterly opposed Hamilton's proposal.

Hamilton's compromise

To win support for his plan, Hamilton suggested a compromise. He knew that many southerners wanted to move the nation's capital to the South. He offered to persuade his northern friends to vote for a capital in the South if southerners supported the repayment of state debts.

Madison and other southerners accepted this compromise. In July 1790, Congress passed bills taking over state debts and providing for a new capital city.

The capital would not be part of any state. Instead, it would be built on land along the Potomac River between Virginia and Maryland. Congress called this area the **District of Columbia.** It is known today as Washington, D.C. Congress hoped that the new capital would be ready by 1800. Meanwhile, the nation's capital was moved from New York to Philadelphia.

Building Up the Economy

Hamilton's compromise with the South had resolved the problem of the national debt. Now he took steps to build up the new nation's economy.

A national bank

Hamilton called on Congress to set up a national bank. In 1791, Congress passed a bill creating the first **Bank of the United States.** The national government deposited the money it collected in taxes in the Bank. The Bank, in turn, issued paper money. The government used the paper money to make loans to farmers and businesses. By making loans to citizens, the Bank encouraged the growth of the economy.

The Bank also used the paper money to pay government bills. The new government had many expenses. It had to pay its employees, build the new capital, and keep up the army and navy.

Protecting American industry

Another part of Hamilton's economic program was designed to give American manu-

facturing a boost. He proposed that Congress pass a **tariff,** or tax, on all foreign goods brought into the country. Hamilton called for a very high tariff. He wanted to make imported goods more expensive to buy than goods made in the United States. Because such a tariff was meant to protect American industry from foreign competition, it was called a **protective tariff.**

In the North, where factories were growing, many people supported Hamilton's plan. Southern farmers, however, bought more imported goods than northerners did. They did not want a protective tariff that would make these goods more expensive.

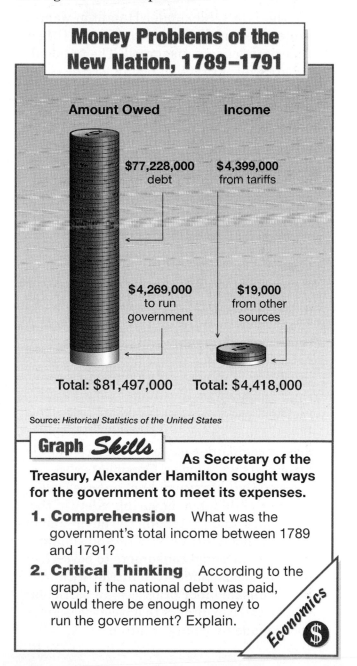

Money Problems of the New Nation, 1789–1791

Amount Owed	Income
$77,228,000 debt	$4,399,000 from tariffs
$4,269,000 to run government	$19,000 from other sources
Total: $81,497,000	Total: $4,418,000

Source: *Historical Statistics of the United States*

Graph Skills As Secretary of the Treasury, Alexander Hamilton sought ways for the government to meet its expenses.

1. **Comprehension** What was the government's total income between 1789 and 1791?
2. **Critical Thinking** According to the graph, if the national debt was paid, would there be enough money to run the government? Explain.

Economics $

Why Study History?

Because the Debate Over Tariffs Continues

★ ★

Historical Background

In the 1790s, Alexander Hamilton wanted protective tariffs placed on imports. Other American leaders disagreed. The national debate over tariffs had begun.

Over the years, supporters have praised tariffs for raising the price of foreign imports and encouraging Americans to buy domestic goods. They say that American businesses and workers prosper as a result. Opponents, however, feel that tariffs limit competition. They want people to be free to buy the least expensive and best-made product, regardless of where it is produced.

Tariffs can increase the cost of the goods you buy.

Connections to Today

By 1993, the United States, Canada, and Mexico formed the North American Free Trade Agreement (NAFTA). The three nations agreed to remove all tariffs and other trade barriers over a period of 15 years.

Public opinion on NAFTA was divided. Supporters cheered when exports to Canada and Mexico increased. Opponents complained that American workers were losing jobs as companies moved to Mexico where labor costs were lower. Opponents also charged that Mexico did not enforce laws banning child labor, ensuring safety in the workplace, and protecting the environment.

The opponents of NAFTA and similar agreements urged consumers to boycott, or not buy, goods made in countries with unfair or unsafe labor practices. In particular, they urged consumers to boycott foreign goods made by young children.

Connections to You

In one case, students in American schools made an impact. Manufacturers in Pakistan were using children to stitch soccer balls. In protest, American and European students threatened a boycott of soccer balls made in Pakistan. As a result, the manufacturers agreed to stop using child labor.

1. **Comprehension** **(a)** Explain one argument in favor of tariffs. **(b)** Explain one argument against tariffs.
2. **Critical Thinking** It can cost less to make some products in Mexico than in the United States. Why do you think this is so?

Debating Work with other students to stage a debate on NAFTA. One group will support the treaty. Another group will oppose it. Do additional research to find information supporting your position.

In the end, Congress did pass a tariff bill. However, its purpose was to raise money for operating the government, rather than protect American industries. For this reason, it was much lower than the protective tariff called for by Hamilton.

The Whiskey Rebellion

Congress also passed a bill that taxed all liquor made and sold in the United States. Hamilton wanted this tax to raise money for the Treasury. Instead, the whiskey tax led to a rebellion that tested the strength of the new government.

A hated tax

Like many other Americans, farmers in the backcountry grew corn. However, corn was bulky to haul over rough backcountry roads. Instead, farmers converted their corn into whiskey, which they could easily ship in barrels to markets in the East.

Backcountry farmers protested the whiskey tax. They compared it to the hated taxes Britain had forced on the colonies in the 1760s. Many farmers refused to pay the tax. A backcountry poet wrote:

66 Some chaps whom freedom's spirit warms
Are threatening hard to take up arms....
Their liberty they will maintain,
They fought for't, and they'll fight again. 99

In 1794, officials in western Pennsylvania tried to collect the tax. Farmers rebelled. Soon, thousands were marching through Pittsburgh. They sang Revolutionary songs and tarred and feathered tax officials.

A show of strength

Washington responded quickly to this challenge to authority. He called up the militia and sent them to Pennsylvania. When the rebels heard that 15,000 troops were marching against them, they scattered. Washington later pardoned the leaders of the rebellion.

The **Whiskey Rebellion** was a critical test of the strength of the new government. Washington had shown those who disagreed with the government that violence would not be tolerated. The President's quick response proved to Americans that their new government would act firmly in times of crisis.

★ Section 1 Review ★

Recall

1. **Identify** (a) Judiciary Act, (b) District of Columbia, (c) Bank of the United States, (d) Whiskey Rebellion.
2. **Define** (a) inauguration, (b) precedent, (c) Cabinet, (d) national debt, (e) bond, (f) speculator, (g) tariff, (h) protective tariff.

Comprehension

3. Describe one precedent that George Washington set for future governments of the United States.
4. (a) Why did Alexander Hamilton think it was important to pay off government bonds?

(b) Why did James Madison oppose Hamilton's repayment plan?
5. Describe two proposals Hamilton made to raise money for the new government.

Critical Thinking and Writing

6. **Linking Past and Present** By the late 1990s, the Cabinet included the heads of 13 separate departments. Why do you think the Cabinet has grown so much since Washington's time?
7. **Forecasting** What do you think might have happened if Washington had not taken strong action to put down the Whiskey Rebellion?

Activity Acting a Scene The year is 1789. Your family owns government bonds, but you are not sure whether the bonds will be repaid at full value. With a partner, act out a scene between two members of the family. Discuss whether you should hold onto the bonds or sell them to a speculator.

A Policy of Neutrality

**Explore
These Questions**

- How did Americans react to the French Revolution?
- What policy did the United States adopt when war broke out in Europe?
- How did Washington's Farewell Address influence American foreign policy?

Define

- foreign policy

Identify

- French Revolution
- Neutrality Proclamation
- Jay's Treaty
- Farewell Address

 Late in 1789, French ships arriving at American seaports brought startling news. On July 14, an angry mob in Paris, France, had destroyed the Bastille (bahs TEEL), a huge fort that was being used as a prison. The attack on the Bastille was one of several events that launched the **French Revolution**.

The French Revolution broke out a few years after Americans won independence. Like the Americans, the French fought for liberty and equality. As the French Revolution grew more violent, however, it ignited political quarrels that had been smoldering in the United States.

Revolution in France

The French had many reasons to rebel against their king, Louis XVI. Peasants and the middle class paid heavy taxes, while nobles paid none. Reformers called for a constitution to limit the power of the king. They also wanted a guarantee of rights like that in the American Constitution.

Americans support the revolution

At first, most Americans supported the French Revolution. Americans knew what it meant to struggle for liberty. Then, too, France had been the first ally of the United States in the war against Great Britain.

Many Americans wanted to rally behind the Marquis de Lafayette, a leading French reformer. They remembered that Lafayette had fought side by side with them in the American Revolution.

In the 1790s, however, the French Revolution entered a very violent stage. A radical group gained power. In 1793, they beheaded Louis XVI and his wife, Queen Marie Antoinette. During a "reign of terror," tens of thousands of French citizens were executed.

Violence divides American opinion

The violence in France divided Americans. Some, like Thomas Jefferson, continued to support the French. He condemned the killings of the king and queen. Still, he felt that the French had the right to use violence to win freedom.

Alexander Hamilton, John Adams, and others disagreed with Jefferson's view. They thought that the French Revolution was doomed to fail. One could no more create democracy through violence, claimed Adams, "than a snowball can exist in the streets of Philadelphia under a burning sun."

Remaining Neutral

The French Revolution shocked rulers and nobles across Europe. They feared the spread of revolutionary ideas to their own

Viewing HISTORY · The French Revolution

At the start of the French Revolution, famine gripped Paris. Thousands of angry women (above) marched on the palace of the king shouting, "Bread! Bread!" The statue at right honored the army of ragged peasants that rose up against long years of injustice. ★ **Why would the French expect Americans to support their revolution?**

lands. Britain, Spain, Prussia, Austria, and the Netherlands sent armies to overpower the revolutionaries in France. Europe was soon plunged into a war that continued on and off for more than 20 years.

A difficult decision

Faced with the war in Europe, Washington had to form a foreign policy for the nation. **Foreign policy** refers to the actions and stands that a nation takes in relation to other nations. An old treaty, signed during the American Revolution, allowed French ships to use American ports. As the war in Europe continued, the French wanted to use American ports to supply their ships and launch attacks on British ships.

"It is the sincere wish of United America," said the President, "to have nothing to do with... the squabbles of European nations." How could the United States honor its treaty with France and still remain neutral?

Divisions in the Cabinet

The issue of the treaty deepened divisions within Washington's Cabinet. Hamilton pointed out that the United States had signed the treaty with Louis XVI. Since the king was dead, he argued, the treaty was no longer valid. Jefferson, however, supported the French cause. He was suspicious of Hamilton, who wanted friendlier relations with Britain, the nation's old enemy.

After much debate, Washington issued the **Neutrality Proclamation** in April 1793. In it, he stated that the United States would not support either side in the war. It also forbade Americans to aid either Britain or France in any way.

Many viewed the Neutrality Proclamation as a defeat for Jefferson. Eventually, this and other conflicts with Hamilton caused Jefferson to leave the Cabinet.

An Unpopular Treaty

Declaring neutrality was easier than enforcing it. American merchants wanted to trade with both Britain and France. However, those warring nations ignored the rights of neutral ships. They seized American cargoes headed for each other's ports.

In 1793, the British captured more than 250 American ships trading in the French

West Indies. Americans clamored for war. Washington, however, knew that the United States was too weak to fight. He sent Chief Justice John Jay to Britain for talks.

Jay worked out a treaty. It called for Britain to pay damages for American ships seized in 1793. At the same time, Americans had to pay debts to British merchants, owed from before the Revolution. Britain agreed to give up forts it still held in the Ohio Valley. However, the treaty did nothing to protect the rights of neutral American ships.

Jay's Treaty sparked a storm of protest. Many Americans felt they were giving up more than Britain was. After a furious debate, the Senate finally approved the treaty in 1795. Washington accepted the treaty because he wanted to avoid war.

Washington Retires

In 1796, George Washington published his **Farewell Address**. In it, he announced he would retire. He urged the United States to remain neutral in its relations with other countries:

> 66 Observe good faith and justice toward all nations.... Nothing is more essential than that permanent, [habitual hatred] against particular nations and passionate attachments for others should be excluded. 99

Washington warned Americans to avoid becoming involved in European affairs. " 'Tis our true policy to steer clear of permanent alliances with any portion of the foreign world," said the retiring President. Such alliances, he felt, would pull the United States into war. That advice guided American foreign policy for many years.

George Washington retired to Mount Vernon, his Virginia home, where he died in 1799.

★ Section 2 Review ★

Recall

1. **Identify** (a) French Revolution, (b) Neutrality Proclamation, (c) Jay's Treaty, (d) Farewell Address.
2. **Define** foreign policy.

Comprehension

3. How did the revolution in France divide Americans?
4. Describe two actions Washington took to avoid war.
5. What advice did Washington give in his Farewell Address?

Critical Thinking and Writing

6. **Recognizing Points of View** Writing about the French Revolution, Thomas Jefferson said he was willing to see "half the earth devastated" in order to win the "liberty of the whole." (a) Restate Jefferson's main idea in your own words. (b) What does this statement tell you about Jefferson's values?
7. **Analyzing Information** How did geographic location help the United States to "steer clear of permanent alliances" with European nations for many years?

★ ★

Activity Giving an Introduction President Washington has chosen to deliver his Farewell Address in your school auditorium. You have been asked to introduce him. Prepare a two-minute introduction naming what you consider to be Washington's greatest achievements.

The Rise of Political Parties

As You Read

Explore These Questions

- How did political differences lead to the rise of two political parties?
- What role did newspapers play in politics?
- How did the election of 1796 increase political tensions?

Define

- faction
- unconstitutional

Identify

- Democratic Republicans
- Federalists

SETTING the Scene When President Washington took office in 1789, the United States had no political parties. In fact, most American leaders opposed the very idea of forming parties. "If I could not go to heaven but with a party," said Thomas Jefferson, "I would not go at all."

Still, deep divisions began to form in the Cabinet and Congress. Jefferson described the unpleasant mood:

66 Men who have been [friends] all their lives cross streets to avoid meeting, and turn their heads another way, lest they should be obliged to touch their hats. 99

By the time Washington left office in 1797, there were two parties competing for power.

A Distrust of Political Parties

Americans had reason to distrust political parties. They had seen how **factions,** or opposing groups within parties, worked in Britain. British factions were made up of a few people who schemed to win favors from the government. Most were more interested in personal gain than in the public good.

Americans also saw political parties as a threat to national unity. They agreed with George Washington, who warned Americans that parties would lead to "jealousies and false alarms."

Despite the President's warning, parties grew up around two members of his Cabinet, Alexander Hamilton and Thomas Jefferson.

The two men differed in background, looks, and personality as well as in politics. Born in the West Indies, Hamilton had worked his way up from poverty. He dressed in fine clothes and spoke forcefully. Energetic, brilliant, and restless, Hamilton enjoyed political debate.

Jefferson was tall and lanky. Although he was a wealthy Virginia planter, he dressed and spoke informally. One senator recalled:

66 His clothes seem too small for him. He sits in a lounging manner, on one hip commonly, and with one of his shoulders elevated much above the other. His face has a sunny aspect. His whole figure has a loose, shackling air.... He spoke almost without ceasing. [His conversation] was loose and rambling; and yet he scattered information wherever he went. 99

Differing Views

Alexander Hamilton did not agree with Thomas Jefferson on many issues. At the root of their quarrels were different views about what was best for the young United States.

Manufacturing or farming

First, Hamilton and Jefferson disagreed about economic policy. Hamilton thought the United States should model itself on Britain. He felt the government should encourage

Viewing HISTORY: Two Views of the Nation

Federalists and Republicans disagreed. Should the new nation build its future mainly on agriculture or on manufacturing? The farmer, above, and the ironworker, right, represent these two viewpoints.
★ **Which of these pictures represents Hamilton's view? Which picture represents Jefferson's view?**

manufacturing and trade. He also favored the growth of cities and the merchant class who helped make cities prosperous.

Jefferson believed that farmers, rather than merchants, were the backbone of the new nation. "Cultivators of the earth," he wrote, "are the most valuable citizens." He feared that a manufacturing economy would corrupt the United States by concentrating power in the hands of a small group of wealthy Americans.

Federal or state governments

Hamilton and Jefferson disagreed about the power of the federal government. Hamilton wanted the federal government to have greater power than state governments. A strong federal government, he argued, could encourage the growth of commerce. It would also have the power needed to restrain unruly mobs, such as the protesters who led the Whiskey Rebellion.

In contrast, Jefferson hoped to make the government as small as possible. Then, citizens would have the freedom to act as they

pleased. Jefferson feared that a strong federal government might take over powers that the Constitution gave to the states.

Strict or loose interpretation of the Constitution

These disagreements led the two leaders to clash over the Bank of the United States. Jefferson worried that a national bank would give too much power to the federal government and the wealthy investors who helped run it.

To oppose Hamilton's proposal, Jefferson argued that the law creating the bank was **unconstitutional,** that is, not permitted by the Constitution. Nowhere did the Constitution give Congress the power to create a Bank, he argued. Jefferson thought that any power not specifically given to the federal government belonged to the states.

Hamilton did not agree with Jefferson's strict interpretation of the Constitution. He preferred a looser interpretation. The Constitution gave Congress the power to make all laws "necessary and proper" to carry out

Skills FOR LIFE

Critical Thinking	Managing Information	Communication	Maps, Charts, and Graphs

Outlining

How Will I Use This Skill?

In school and, later, at work, you may be asked to write a report or give a presentation. You will find the job easier if you prepare an outline. An outline helps you arrange information in logical order. In addition, when you speak in public, an outline can keep you from fumbling for words!

LEARN the Skill

Make an outline by following these four steps.

❶ Use the theme or topic as the title of your outline.

❷ Identify and list the main ideas in order. Label them with Roman numerals.

❸ Identify subtopics for each main idea. Label these with capital letters and list them under the main ideas.

❹ Identify details that support each subtopic. Label and list these with Arabic numerals as shown.

PRACTICE the Skill

The sample at right is a partial outline of the subsection Differing Views. Study the sample. Then, using the steps above, make an outline of the subsection Party Rivalry.

❶ Take notes as you read the subsection.

❷ Using your notes and the headings in the text, write down the main ideas.

❸ Using the topic sentences of the paragraphs in the text, identify the subtopics for your outline.

❹ Find and list supporting details from the text.

APPLY the Skill

Choose a topic that interests you. Make an outline for a short talk on this subject.

The Clash of Jefferson and Hamilton

I. Jefferson's Views
   A. Preferred farm economy
   B. Favored strict interpretation of Constitution
     1. Against Bank of United States
       a. Too much power to federal government
       b. Unconstitutional
     2. Favored state power
   C. Favored France in foreign policy

II. Hamilton's Views
   A. Supported manufacturing economy
   B. Favored loose interpretation of Constitution
     1. Planned Bank of United States
       a. Way to collect taxes
       b. Way to pay government bills
     2. Favored federal power
   C. Supported Britain in foreign policy

Federalists vs. Republicans

FEDERALISTS	REPUBLICANS
① Led by Alexander Hamilton	① Led by Thomas Jefferson
② Wealthy and well educated should lead nation	② People should have political power
③ Strong central government	③ Strong state governments
④ Emphasis on manufacturing, shipping, and trade	④ Emphasis on agriculture
⑤ Loose interpretation of Constitution	⑤ Strict interpretation of the Constitution
⑥ Pro-British	⑥ Pro-French
⑦ Favored national bank	⑦ Opposed national bank
⑧ Favored protective tariff	⑧ Opposed protective tariff

Graphic Organizer *Skills*

By the 1790s, there were two political parties in the United States—the Federalist party and the Republican party.

1. **Comprehension** Describe two ways the Republicans and Federalists differed on economic issues.
2. **Critical Thinking** "The average person is far too ignorant to make wise political decisions." Do you think a Republican or a Federalist would be more likely to agree with this statement? Explain.

Civics

its duties. Hamilton argued that the Bank was necessary for the government to collect taxes and pay its bills.

Britain or France

Finally, the two leaders clashed over foreign policy. Hamilton wanted to form close ties with Britain, an important trading partner. Jefferson favored France, the first ally of the United States and a nation struggling for its own liberty.

Party Rivalry

At first, Hamilton and Jefferson clashed in private. However, when Congress began to pass many of Hamilton's programs, Jefferson and James Madison decided to organize public support for their views.

Madison and Jefferson moved cautiously at first. In 1791, they went to New York, telling people that they were going to study

its wildlife. In fact, Jefferson was interested in nature and did travel far into upstate New York. Their main purpose, though, was to meet with important New York politicians like Governor George Clinton and Aaron Burr, a strong critic of Hamilton. Jefferson asked Clinton and Burr to help defeat Hamilton's program by getting New Yorkers to vote for Jefferson supporters.

Republicans and Federalists

Soon, leaders in other states began organizing to support either Hamilton or Jefferson. Jefferson's supporters called themselves **Democratic Republicans,** often shortened to Republicans.* Republicans included small farmers, craftworkers, and some wealthy planters.

---

*Jefferson's Republican party was not the same as today's Republican party. In fact, his party later grew into the Democratic party.

Hamilton and his supporters were called **Federalists** because they wanted a strong federal government. Federalists drew most of their support from merchants and manufacturers in cities such as Boston and New York. They also gained the backing of some southern planters.

Newspapers take sides

In the late 1700s, the number of American newspapers more than doubled. This growth met a demand for information. A visitor from Europe noted with surprise that so many Americans could read:

66 The common people [in the United States] are on a footing, in point of literature with the middle ranks of Europe. They all read and write, and understand arithmetic; almost every little town now furnishes a circulating library. 99

As party rivalry grew, newspapers took sides. In the *Gazette of the United States*, publisher John Fenno printed articles in favor of Alexander Hamilton and the Federalists. Philip Freneau (frih NOH), a friend of Thomas Jefferson, started a rival paper, the *National Gazette*. Freneau vigorously supported Republicans.

Newspapers had great influence on public opinion. In stinging language, they raged against opponents. Often, articles mixed rumor and opinion with facts. Emotional attacks and counterattacks fanned the flames of party rivalry. Still, newspapers performed a needed service. They kept people informed and helped shape public opinion.

Election of 1796

Political parties played a major role in the election of George Washington's successor. In 1796, Republicans backed Thomas Jefferson for President and Aaron Burr for Vice President. Federalists supported John Adams for President and Thomas Pinckney for Vice President.

The election had an unexpected outcome, which created new tensions. Under the Constitution, the person with the most electoral votes became President. The person with the next highest total was made Vice President. John Adams, a Federalist, won office as President. The leader of the Republicans, Thomas Jefferson, came in second and became Vice President.

With the President and the Vice President from different parties, political tensions remained high. Future events would further increase the distrust between the two men. Meanwhile, John Adams took office in March 1797 as the second President of the United States.

★ Section 3 Review ★

Recall

1. **Identify** (a) Democratic Republicans, (b) Federalists.
2. **Define** (a) faction, (b) unconstitutional.

Comprehension

3. Describe two issues on which Thomas Jefferson and Alexander Hamilton disagreed.
4. How did newspapers contribute to the rivalry between political parties?

5. What role did parties play in the 1796 election?

Critical Thinking and Writing

6. **Drawing Conclusions** Why do you think political parties emerged even though most Americans opposed them?
7. **Ranking** Which of the disagreements between Jefferson and Hamilton do you think was the most serious? Explain.

Activity Writing a Newspaper Headline You are the publisher of either the *Gazette of the United States* or the *National Gazette*. Write three headlines about the election of 1796. Be sure your headlines express the point of view of your own newspaper.

The Second President

As You Read

Explore These Questions

- Why did many Americans favor war with France?
- Why did the Federalist party split in two?
- Why did the Alien and Sedition acts outrage many Americans?

Define

- immigrant
- sedition
- nullify

Identify

- XYZ Affair
- High Federalists
- Napoleon Bonaparte
- Alien and Sedition acts
- Kentucky and Virginia resolutions

 SETTING the Scene Late in his life, John Adams looked back on his career with mixed feelings. He knew that leaders such as Washington and Jefferson were more widely admired than he was. Still, Adams wrote proudly of his life's work:

> **❝** I have done more labor, run through more and greater dangers, and made greater sacrifices than any man ... living or dead, in the service of my country. **❞**

At the same time, Adams found it hard to boast of his achievements. In the end, he concluded: "I am not, never was, and never shall be a great man."

Although he was not a popular hero, like Washington, Adams was an honest and able leader. As President, he tried to act in the best interests of the nation, even when his actions hurt him politically.

Conflict With France

No sooner did Adams take office than he faced a crisis with France. The French objected to Jay's Treaty because they felt that it favored Britain. In 1797, French ships began to seize American ships in the West Indies, as the British had done.

Once again, Americans called for war, this time against France. Adams tried to avoid war by sending diplomats to Paris to discuss the rights of neutral nations.

The XYZ Affair

France's foreign minister, Charles Maurice de Talleyrand, did not deal directly with the Americans. Instead, he sent three secret agents to offer the Americans a deal. Before Talleyrand would begin talks, the agents said, he wanted $250,000 for himself, as well as a loan to France of $10 million. "Not a sixpence!" replied one of the American diplomats angrily.

The diplomats informed Adams about the offer. Adams, in turn, told Congress. He did not reveal the names of the French agents, referring to them only as X, Y, and Z.

Many Americans were outraged when they heard about the **XYZ Affair** in 1798. They took up the slogan, "Millions for defense, but not one cent for tribute!" They were willing to spend money to defend their country, but they refused to pay a bribe to another nation.

Adams avoids war

Despite growing pressure, Adams refused to ask Congress to declare war on France. Still, he could not ignore French attacks on American ships. He moved to strengthen the navy. Shipyards built frigates—fast-sailing ships with many guns.

This show of strength helped convince Talleyrand to stop attacking American ships. He also promised Adams that if American ambassadors came to France, they would be treated with respect.

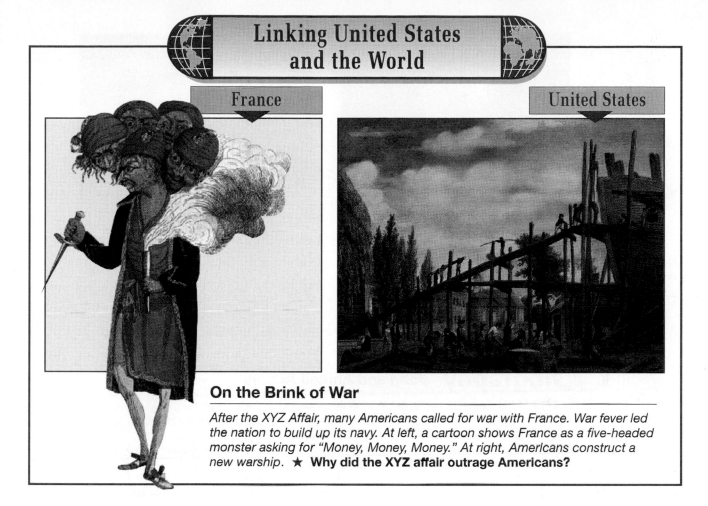

France

United States

On the Brink of War

After the XYZ Affair, many Americans called for war with France. War fever led the nation to build up its navy. At left, a cartoon shows France as a five-headed monster asking for "Money, Money, Money." At right, Americans construct a new warship. ★ **Why did the XYZ affair outrage Americans?**

The Federalist Party Splits

Many Federalists, led by Hamilton, criticized Adams's actions. They hoped a war would weaken the Republicans, supporters of France. War would also force the United States to build up its military. A stronger army and navy would increase federal power, a major Federalist goal.

Although John Adams was a Federalist, he would not give in to Hamilton. Their disagreement created a split in the Federalist party. Hamilton and his supporters were called **High Federalists**.

Over Hamilton's opposition, Adams again sent diplomats to France. When they arrived, they found an ambitious young army officer, **Napoleon Bonaparte**, in charge. Napoleon did not have time for a war with the United States. He signed an agreement to stop seizing American ships.

Like Washington, Adams kept the nation out of war. His success, however, cost him the support of many Federalists.

Alien and Sedition Acts

During the crisis with France, Federalists pushed several laws through Congress. Passed in 1798, the laws were known as the **Alien and Sedition acts**.

The Alien Act allowed the President to expel any alien, or foreigner, thought to be dangerous to the country. Another law made it harder for immigrants to become citizens. An **immigrant** is a person who enters another country in order to settle there. Before, white immigrants could become citizens after living in the United States for 5 years. Under the new law, immigrants had to wait 14 years. This law was meant to keep new settlers, who often supported the Republicans, from voting.

Republican anger grew when Congress passed the Sedition Act. **Sedition** means stirring up rebellion against a government. Under this law, citizens could be fined or jailed if they criticized the government or its officials.

Locket given
by John to
Abigail Adams

Biography   John and Abigail Adams

Throughout 54 years of marriage, John Adams valued the advice and support of his wife, Abigail. A brilliant woman and fine writer, Abigail Adams supported greater rights for women. They were the first President and First Lady to live in the White House. Their son, John Quincy Adams, also became President. ★ **Why would it have been hard for Abigail Adams to pursue her own political career?**

Republicans protested that the Sedition Act violated the Constitution. After all, they argued, the First Amendment protected freedom of speech and freedom of the press. Jefferson warned that the new laws threatened American liberties:

66 If this goes down, we shall immediately see attempted another act of Congress, declaring that the President shall continue in office during life, and after that other laws giving both the President and the Congress life terms in office. 99

Under the Sedition Act, several Republican newspaper editors, and even members of Congress, were fined and jailed for expressing their opinions.

The Rights of States

Outraged, Jefferson urged the states to take strong action against the Alien and Sedition acts. He argued that the states had the right to **nullify,** or cancel, a law passed by the federal government. In this way, states could resist the power of the federal government.

With the help of Jefferson and Madison, Kentucky and Virginia passed resolutions in 1798 and 1799. The **Kentucky and Virginia resolutions** claimed that each state "has an equal right to judge for itself" whether a law is constitutional. If a state decides a law is unconstitutional, said the resolutions, it has the power to nullify that law within its borders.

Connections With Arts

The picture of Abigail Adams, above, is by Gilbert Stuart, one of the greatest American portrait painters. In fact, you may have a Gilbert Stuart painting in your pocket right now. His portrait of George Washington appears on the one dollar bill.

The Kentucky and Virginia resolutions raised a difficult question. Did a state have the right to decide on its own that a law was unconstitutional?

The question remained unanswered in Jefferson's lifetime. Before long, the Alien and Sedition acts were changed or dropped. Still, the issue of a state's right to nullify federal laws would come up again.

Election of 1800

By 1800, the cry for war against France was fading. As the election approached, the Republicans hoped to sweep the Federalists from office. Republicans focused on two issues. First, they attacked the Federalists for raising taxes to prepare for war. Second, they opposed the unpopular Alien and Sedition acts.

Republicans supported Thomas Jefferson for President and Aaron Burr for Vice President. Despite the bitter split in the Federalist party, John Adams was again named the Federalist candidate.

A deadlock

In the race for President, the Republicans won the popular vote. However, when the electoral college voted, Jefferson and Burr each received 73 votes. At the time, the electoral college did not vote separately for President and Vice President. Each Republican elector cast one vote for Jefferson and one vote for Burr.

Under the Constitution, if no candidate wins the electoral vote, the House of Representatives decides the election. The House vote, however, was also evenly split between Jefferson and Burr. After four days, and 36 votes, the tie was finally broken. The House chose Jefferson as President. Burr became Vice President.

Congress afterward passed the Twelfth Amendment. It required electors to vote separately for President and Vice President. The states ratified the amendment in 1804.

End of the Federalist era

The Republican victory set an important precedent for the nation. To this day, power continues to pass peacefully from one party to another.

After 1800, the Federalist party began to decline. Federalists won fewer seats in Congress. In 1804, the Federalist party was further weakened when their leader, Alexander Hamilton, was killed in a duel with Aaron Burr. Despite their decline, the Federalist party had helped shape the new nation. Republican Presidents eventually kept most of Hamilton's economic programs.

★ Section 4 Review ★

Recall

1. **Identify** (a) XYZ Affair, (b) High Federalists, (c) Napoleon Bonaparte, (d) Alien and Sedition acts, (e) Kentucky and Virginia resolutions.
2. **Define** (a) immigrant, (b) sedition, (c) nullify.

Comprehension

3. Why did many Americans want to declare war on France?
4. Why did John Adams lose the support of many Federalists?

5. (a) Why did Federalists favor the Alien and Sedition acts? (b) Why did Republicans oppose these laws?

Critical Thinking and Writing

6. **Applying Information** How did the Kentucky and Virginia resolutions reflect Jefferson's view of government?
7. **Analyzing Information** How did the Twelfth Amendment help prevent deadlocks like the one that took place in the election of 1800?

Activity Drawing a Political Cartoon Suppose that the Sedition Act of 1798 were passed by Congress today. Draw a political cartoon expressing your opinion of the law.

Chapter 9 Review and Activities

★ Sum It Up ★

Section 1 Launching the New Government
▶ George Washington set many precedents that determined how future Presidents would govern the nation.
▶ Alexander Hamilton formed a plan to improve the nation's finances.
▶ A rebellion against the national government quickly melted away when President Washington responded forcefully.

Section 2 A Policy of Neutrality
▶ Americans were sharply divided in their reaction to the French Revolution.
▶ Washington responded to war between Britain and France by declaring that the United States would remain neutral.

Section 3 The Rise of Political Parties
▶ Because of widely differing views on national issues, two major political parties soon formed in the new republic.
▶ Federalists supported a strong federal government, while Republicans opposed policies that made the national government too strong.

Section 4 The Second President
▶ Despite pressure, President John Adams avoided war with France.
▶ The unpopular Alien and Sedition acts led the states to consider ways to take power back from the federal government.
▶ In the election of 1800, power passed from the Federalists to the Republicans.

CD-ROM Review For additional review of the major ideas of Chapter 9, see *Guide to the Essentials of American History* or *Interactive Student Tutorial CD-ROM,* which contains interactive review activities, graphic organizers, and practice tests.

🗋 Reviewing the Chapter

Define These Terms
Match each term with the correct definition.

Column 1	Column 2
1. national debt	**a.** stirring up rebellion
2. tariff	**b.** type of tax
3. speculator	**c.** person who enters a country in order to settle there
4. sedition	**d.** someone who invests in a risky venture to make a profit
5. immigrant	**e.** total a government owes

Explore the Main Ideas
1. Why did many southerners oppose Hamilton's plan to settle state debts?
2. How did Britain and France make Washington's neutrality policy difficult to enforce?
3. Describe the people who supported: **(a)** the Federalist party; **(b)** the Republican party.
4. How did President Adams avoid war?
5. How was the Sedition Act used to silence Republicans?

🗋 Graph Activity

Look at the graph below and answer the following questions:
1. How many people served in the navy in 1798? **2.** What had happened to the navy by 1800? **Critical Thinking** Why did the size of the navy change?

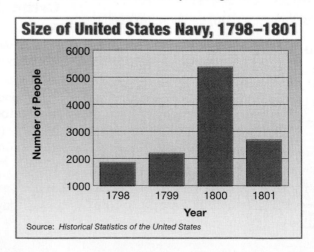

Size of United States Navy, 1798–1801

Source: *Historical Statistics of the United States*

Critical Thinking and Writing

1. **Exploring Unit Themes   Nationalism** How did each of the following strengthen the nation: **(a)** the presidency of Washington; **(b)** Hamilton's plan to pay off state debts; **(c)** Washington's response to the Whiskey Rebellion?

2. **Linking Past and Present**   Washington urged the United States never to take sides in the world's wars. Do you think this policy would make sense in today's world? Explain.

3. **Defending a Position**   Do you think the Constitution should be interpreted strictly or loosely? Give reasons for your position.

4. **Understanding Chronology**   **(a)** Place the following events in chronological order: XYZ Affair; Neutrality Proclamation; French Revolution begins; Adams builds up American navy; Washington's Farewell Address. **(b)** Describe the relationship between two of these events.

Using Primary Sources

In its early years, Washington, D.C., was little more than a clearing in the wilderness. First Lady Abigail Adams described its location in a letter to a friend in 1800:

> **66** Woods are all you see, from Baltimore until you reach the city. ... Here and there is a small [hut], without a glass window, [all alone] amongst the forests, through which you travel miles without seeing any human being.... But, surrounded with forests, can you believe that [fire]wood is not to be had, because people cannot be found to cut and cart it! **99**

Source: *Letters of Mrs. Adams,* edited by Charles Francis Adams, 1840.

Recognizing Points of View   **(a)** Why was Abigail Adams unable to get firewood? **(b)** Why did she consider this surprising? **(c)** Do you think Abigail Adams approved of the new city? Explain.

ACTIVITY BANK

Interdisciplinary Activity

Exploring Economics   Use library resources to locate information on our current national debt in newspapers or magazines. Prepare a three-minute presentation in which you explain what economic problems may arise because of the national debt.

Career Skills Activity

Reporters   Early newspapers often mixed rumor and opinion with facts. Today, reporters have to keep facts and opinions apart. Practice this skill by writing a brief account of the election of 1796 as it might have appeared in a paper of the time. Then, write another account based only on facts.

Citizenship Activity

Researching Political Parties   Learn about the political organizations in your area. Most groups will be glad to tell you about the rights and responsibilities of membership. Prepare a one-page data sheet covering at least two political parties. Describe their views and some of their recent or planned activities.

Internet Activity

Today, as in the 1790s, the United States has a special government bank. Use the Internet to find information about the Federal Reserve Bank. Then, write a reaction to the Federal Reserve Bank from the point of view of a Federalist or of a Democratic Republican.

EYEWITNESS Journal

You are a Federalist ship owner in 1797 or a Democratic Republican newspaper editor in 1798. In your EYEWITNESS JOURNAL, write an exciting account of how your life was affected by the events of your times.

Chapter 10

The Age of Jefferson
1801–1816

Republican Presidents in the early 1800s tried to serve the needs of ordinary Americans while limiting the role of government. During this time, events that affected France and Britain reached beyond their borders. As a result, the United States had the opportunity to double its size by purchasing the Louisiana territory from France. The young nation also faced war with Britain again. Although there was no clear winner in the war, many Americans became more proud of their growing nation.

Why Study History?

During the early 1800s, each branch of the new government was learning its responsibilities and limits. It was at this time that the power and importance of the Supreme Court began to emerge. To learn more about the powerful influence of the "highest court in the land," see this chapter's *Why Study History?* feature, "Supreme Court Decisions Affect You."

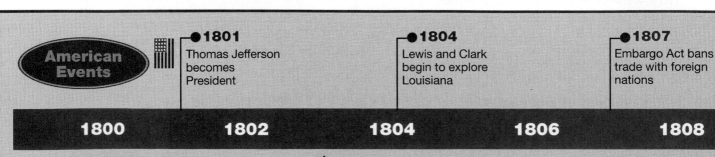

American Events

1801
Thomas Jefferson becomes President

1804
Lewis and Clark begin to explore Louisiana

1807
Embargo Act bans trade with foreign nations

| 1800 | 1802 | 1804 | 1806 | 1808 |

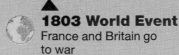

World Events

1803 World Event
France and Britain go to war

Viewing HISTORY   Lewis and Clark on the Lower Columbia

In 1803, President Thomas Jefferson doubled the size of the United States by purchasing the Louisiana territory. He sent Meriwether Lewis and William Clark to explore the land and establish friendship with Native Americans. In this painting by Charles M. Russell, Lewis (right) stands by the Native American Sacajawea as she addresses Chinook Indians. ★ **Do you think Native Americans welcomed Lewis and Clark? Explain.**

1811
Harrison fights
Native Americans
at Tippecanoe

1812
War begins between
United States and
Britain

1815
Jackson defeats
British at New Orleans

| 1808 | 1810 | 1812 | 1814 | 1816 |

1810 World Event
Simón Bolívar leads revolt
against Spanish rule in
South America

Republicans in Power

As You Read

Explore These Questions
- What were Jefferson's ideas about government?
- How did he reduce the power of government?
- Why was *Marbury* v. *Madison* important?

Define
- democratic
- laissez faire
- judicial review

Identify
- John Marshall
- *Marbury* v. *Madison*

SETTING the Scene When Thomas Jefferson became President of the United States in 1801, nearly nine out of ten Americans were farmers. This fact gave Jefferson confidence in the nation's future. Even though Jefferson came from a wealthy family, he believed in the importance of ordinary people, especially farmers. In a letter to James Madison, he expressed his faith in the American people:

66 Educate and inform the whole mass of the people. Enable them to see that it is their interest to preserve peace and order, and they will preserve them....They are the only [ones to rely on] for the preservation of our liberty. 99

A More Democratic Style

As President, Jefferson tried to protect and expand the rights of ordinary citizens. He felt that the Federalists promoted the interests of the wealthy few, but neglected the needs of others. Jefferson was determined to make the government more democratic. **Democratic** means ensuring that all people have the same rights.

Jefferson's personal style matched his democratic beliefs. The new President preferred quiet dinners to the formal parties that Washington and Adams had given. He wore casual clothes and greeted people by shaking hands instead of bowing. With his informal manner, Jefferson showed that the President was an ordinary citizen.

Some Federalists worried about Jefferson's democratic beliefs. They knew that he supported the French Revolution and they feared that he might bring revolutionary change to the United States. They were also afraid that he might punish Federalists who had used the Alien and Sedition acts to jail Republicans.

In his inaugural address, Jefferson tried to quiet Federalists' fears. Though a minority, Federalists "possess their equal rights, which equal laws must protect," he told the nation. He called for an end to the political disputes of past years. "We are all Republicans, we are all Federalists," the President said. Jefferson was determined to unite the country, not divide it further.

Reduced Role of Government

Jefferson had no plan to punish Federalists. He did, however, want to change their policies. In his view, the Federalists had made the national government too large and too powerful. Jefferson wanted to reduce government power by cutting the federal budget and by reducing the federal debt.

Connections With Civics

When Jefferson became President in 1801, there were fewer than 1,000 federal employees. Today, the United States government employs more than 2 million people—not counting those in the military.

Jefferson believed in an idea known as **laissez faire** (lehs ay FAYR), from the French term for "let alone." According to laissez faire, government should play as small a role as possible in economic affairs. Laissez faire was very different from the Federalist idea of government. Alexander Hamilton, you recall, wanted government to promote trade and manufacturing.

President Jefferson tried to reduce the role of government in people's lives. He decreased the size of government departments and cut the federal budget. With the approval of Congress, he reduced the size of the army and navy. He also asked Congress to repeal the unpopular whiskey tax.

The Sedition Act expired the day before Jefferson took office. Jefferson hated the law, and he pardoned those who were in jail because of it. He also asked Congress to restore the law allowing foreign-born people to become citizens after only a five-year waiting period. Jefferson acted to change other Federalist policies as well.

Jefferson did not discard all Federalist programs, however. He kept the Bank of the United States, which he had once opposed. The federal government also continued to pay off state debts that it had taken over when Washington was President. In addition, Jefferson let many Federalists keep their government jobs.

A Stronger Supreme Court

The election of 1800 gave Republicans control of Congress. Federalists, however, remained powerful in the courts.

Several months passed between Jefferson's election and his inauguration on March 4, 1801. During that time, Federalists in the old Congress passed a law increasing the number of federal judges. President Adams then appointed Federalists to fill these new judicial positions.

One of the judges that Adams appointed was **John Marshall,** the Chief Justice of the Supreme Court. Like Jefferson, Marshall

Biography Thomas Jefferson

Jefferson, author of the Declaration of Independence and third President of the United States, was a man of many talents. A skilled architect, he designed his own home, Monticello, in the classical style of ancient Greece and Rome. Jefferson felt that it was important for citizens in a democracy to be well educated. ★ **Why do you think Jefferson placed so much value on education?**

◀ *Monticello, home of Thomas Jefferson*

Why Study History?

Because Supreme Court Decisions Affect You

★ ★

Historical Background

In the early 1800s, the Supreme Court was not as respected as it is today. In fact, for a while, the justices met in the basement of the Capitol because the designers of Washington, D.C., had not provided a meeting place for the Court. However, under the strong leadership of Chief Justice John Marshall, the Supreme Court gained respect and power.

Connections to Today

Today, the Supreme Court is very important as the final authority on cases involving the Constitution. By exercising its power of judicial review (see page 269), the Supreme Court decides whether or not laws are constitutional. Supreme Court justices interpret the Constitution and define and limit our constitutional rights.

Connections to You

Supreme Court cases often involve young people like you. One recent example is the case of *Veronia School District* v. *Acton*.

In 1991, a seventh grader in Oregon wanted to join his school football team. The school required that he submit to a drug test. The student refused, and the school did not allow him to play on the team. The boy's parents sued, arguing that the school had violated the Fourth Amendment's protection against unreasonable searches. The case eventually went to the Supreme Court.

In a 6–3 decision, the Court agreed with the school. It ruled that schools can require athletes to undergo drug tests, just as they require physical examinations and vaccinations. The Court said that schools have a special responsibility to prevent drug abuse and to protect students' health.

This 1995 decision did not affect just one student in one school. The Court's ruling applied to student athletes across the nation. Indirectly, it also had an impact on other issues regarding the rights of students in American schools.

1. **Comprehension** **(a)** How did *Veronia School District* v. *Acton* involve the Constitution? **(b)** Why did the Supreme Court agree with the Oregon school's policy?

2. **Critical Thinking** How do you think the decision affected sports programs in other schools?

Researching Use library or Internet sources to research a recent Supreme Court case. Report to the class on the issue, the Court's decision, and possible effects of the decision.

was a rich Virginia planter with a brilliant mind. Unlike Jefferson, however, Marshall was a Federalist. He wanted to make the federal government stronger.

The framers of the Constitution expected the courts to balance the powers of the President and Congress. However, John Marshall found the courts to be very weak. In his view, it was not clear what powers the federal courts had.

Marbury v. Madison

In 1803, Marshall decided a case that increased the power of the Supreme Court. The case involved William Marbury, another one of the judges appointed by Adams. Adams made the appointment on his last night as President.

The Republicans refused to accept this "midnight judge." They accused Federalists of using unfair tactics to keep control of the courts. Jefferson ordered Secretary of State James Madison not to deliver the official papers confirming Marbury's appointment.

Marbury sued Madison. According to the Judiciary Act of 1789, only the Supreme Court could decide a case that was brought against a federal official. Therefore, the case of *Marbury* v. *Madison* was tried before the Supreme Court.

An important precedent

In its decision, the Supreme Court ruled against Marbury. Chief Justice Marshall wrote the decision, stating that the Judiciary Act was unconstitutional. The Constitution, Marshall argued, did not give the Supreme Court the right to decide cases brought against federal officials. Therefore, Congress could not give the Court that power.

The Supreme Court's decision in *Marbury* v. *Madison* set an important precedent. It gave the Supreme Court the power to decide whether laws passed by Congress were constitutional and to reject laws that it considered to be unconstitutional. This power of the Court is called **judicial review**.

Jefferson was displeased that the decision gave more power to the Supreme Court. He felt that the decision upset the balance of power that existed among the three branches of government. Even so, the President and Congress accepted the right of the Court to overturn laws. Today, judicial review remains one of the most important powers of the Supreme Court.

★ Section 1 Review ★

Recall

1. **Identify** (a) John Marshall, (b) *Marbury* v. *Madison*.
2. **Define** (a) democratic, (b) laissez faire, (c) judicial review.

Comprehension

3. Explain how Jefferson's ideas on government differed from Federalist ideas.
4. Describe three steps Jefferson took to reduce the power of government.
5. (a) What precedent did *Marbury* v. *Madison* set?

(b) How did the precedent affect the balance of power in American government?

Critical Thinking and Writing

6. **Analyzing a Primary Source** "We are all Republicans, we are all Federalists." (a) What did Jefferson mean by these words? (b) Why did he need to make such a statement?
7. **Drawing Conclusions** Today, the federal government protects consumers by regulating the quality of certain goods. Would a laissez-faire economist agree with this policy? Why or why not?

★ ★

Activity Writing a Letter Welcome to the United States! You are a newly arrived immigrant from Europe. Write a letter to your friends in Europe describing your feelings about President Jefferson and the Republican government.

The Louisiana Purchase

As You Read

Explore These Questions

- Why was control of the Mississippi River important to western farmers?
- How did the United States gain Louisiana?
- What did the Lewis and Clark expedition achieve?

Define

- expedition
- Continental Divide

Identify

- Pinckney Treaty
- Toussaint L'Ouverture
- Louisiana Purchase
- Lewis and Clark
- Sacajawea
- Zebulon Pike

◄ *William Clark's journal*

SETTING the Scene One day, President Jefferson received several packages. Inside, he found hides and skeletons of animals, horns of a mountain ram, and a tin box full of insects. There were also cages of live birds and squirrels, as well as gifts from the Mandan and Sioux Indians.

All of these packages were from Meriwether Lewis and William Clark. Jefferson had sent the two to explore the land west of the Mississippi River. Almost two years before, President Jefferson had purchased the territory for the United States. The packages confirmed his belief that the new lands were a valuable addition to the nation.

Control of the Mississippi

By 1800, almost one million Americans lived between the Appalachian Mountains and the Mississippi. Most were farmers.

With few roads west of the Appalachians, western farmers relied on the Mississippi to ship their wheat and corn. First, they sent their produce down the river to New Orleans. From there, oceangoing ships carried the produce to ports along the Atlantic coast.

Threats from Spain and France

Spain sometimes threatened to close the port of New Orleans to Americans. In 1795, President Washington sent Thomas Pinckney to find a way to keep the vital port open. In the **Pinckney Treaty**, Spain agreed to let Americans ship their goods down the Mississippi and store them in New Orleans. The treaty also settled a dispute over the northern border of Spanish Florida.

For a time, Americans sent their goods to New Orleans without a problem. Then, however, Spain signed a treaty with Napoleon Bonaparte, the ruler of France. The treaty gave Louisiana back to France. President Jefferson was alarmed. Napoleon had already set out to conquer Europe. Jefferson feared that Napoleon might now try to build an empire in North America.

Revolt in Haiti

President Jefferson had good reason to worry. Napoleon wanted to grow food in Louisiana and ship it to French islands in the West Indies. However, events in Haiti soon ruined Napoleon's plan.

Haiti was the richest French colony in the Caribbean. There, enslaved Africans worked sugar plantations that made French planters wealthy. Inspired by the French Revolution, the African slaves in Haiti decided to fight for their liberty. **Toussaint L'Ouverture** (too SAN loo vehr TYOOR) led the revolt. By 1801, Toussaint and his followers had nearly forced the French out of Haiti.

Napoleon sent troops to retake Haiti. Although the French captured Toussaint, they did not regain control of the island. In 1804, Haitians declared their independence. Napoleon's dream of an empire in the Americas ended with the loss of Haiti.

Buying Louisiana

Meanwhile, President Jefferson decided to try to buy the city of New Orleans from Napoleon. Jefferson wanted to be sure that American farmers would always be able to ship their goods through the port. The President sent Robert Livingston and James Monroe to buy New Orleans and West Florida from the French. Jefferson said they could offer as much as $10 million.

A surprising deal

Livingston and Monroe negotiated with Talleyrand, the French foreign minister. At first, Talleyrand showed little interest in their offer. However, changing conditions in Haiti and in Europe were causing Napoleon to alter his plans for the future.

After losing Haiti, Napoleon had abandoned his plan for an empire in the Americas. He also needed money to pay for his very costly wars in Europe. Suddenly Talleyrand asked Livingston if the United States wanted to buy all of Louisiana, not just New Orleans.

Livingston and Monroe carefully debated the matter. They had no authority to buy all of Louisiana. However, they knew that Jefferson wanted control of the Mississippi. They agreed to pay the French $15 million for Louisiana. When he signed the treaty with France, Livingston proudly declared,

66 We have lived long, but this is the noblest work of our whole lives.... From this day the United States take their place among the powers of the first rank. 99

Viewing HISTORY A View of New Orleans

New Orleans, shown here in an 1803 painting by John L. Boqueta de Woiseri, grew prosperous by controlling trade on the Mississippi River. The city's strategic location near the Gulf of Mexico was one reason for the Louisiana Purchase.
★ **How does this 1803 painting show the prosperity of New Orleans?**

UNDER MY WINGS EVERY THING PROSPERS

Was the purchase constitutional?

Jefferson was pleased by the news from France, but he was not sure that he in fact had the constitutional power to purchase Louisiana. He had always insisted that the federal government had only those powers spelled out in the Constitution. The document said nothing about a President's power to buy land.

After giving it much thought, Jefferson decided that he did have the authority to buy Louisiana. The Constitution, he reasoned, allowed the President to make treaties. At his request, the Senate quickly approved a treaty making the **Louisiana Purchase.** In 1803, the United States took control of the vast lands west of the Mississippi.

Jefferson Plans an Expedition

The United States owned Louisiana now, but few Americans knew anything about the territory. In 1803, Congress provided money for a team of explorers to study the new lands. Jefferson chose Meriwether Lewis, his private secretary, to head the expedition. An **expedition** is a long journey or voyage of exploration. Lewis asked William Clark, another Virginian, to go with him. About 50 men made up the original band.

Jefferson gave Lewis and Clark careful instructions. He asked them to map a route to the Pacific Ocean. He also told them to study the climate, wildlife, and mineral resources of the new lands. The President requested a detailed report on the following:

66 Climate as characterized by the thermometer, by the proportion of rainy, cloudy, and clear days, by lightning, hail, snow, ice... by the winds prevailing at different seasons, the dates at which particular plants put forth or lose their flower, or leaf, times of appearance of particular birds, reptiles or insects. 99

Jefferson also instructed Lewis and Clark to learn about the Indian nations who lived in the Louisiana Purchase. For decades, these Native Americans had carried on a very busy trade with English, French, and Spanish merchants. Jefferson hoped that the Indians might trade with American merchants instead. Therefore, he urged Lewis and Clark to tell the Indians of "our wish to be neighborly, friendly, and useful to them."

The Lewis and Clark Expedition

In May 1804, **Lewis and Clark** started up the Missouri River from St. Louis. In time, their trip would take them to the Pacific Ocean. (Follow their route on the map on page 273.)

Across the plains

At first, the expedition's boats made slow progress against the Missouri's swift current. One night, the current tore away the riverbank where they were camping. The party had to scramble into the boats to avoid being swept downstream.

Lewis and Clark kept journals on their travels. They marveled at the broad, grassy plains that stretched "as far as the eye can reach." Everywhere, they saw "immense herds of buffalo, deer, elk, and antelopes."

As they traveled across the plains, the expedition met people of various Indian nations. Lewis and Clark had brought many gifts for Native Americans. They carried medals stamped with the United States seal. They also brought mirrors, beads, knives, blankets, and thousands of sewing needles and fishhooks.

During the first winter, Lewis and Clark stayed with the Mandans in present-day North Dakota. The explorers planned to continue up the Missouri in the spring. However, they worried about how they would cross the steep Rocky Mountains.

✳ Connections With Science

Acting as botanist for the expedition, Meriwether Lewis collected and preserved many plants. He carefully dried and pressed each specimen. Of the more than 200 specimens Lewis brought back, 39 still remain at the Academy of Natural Sciences in Philadelphia.

| Critical Thinking | Managing Information | Communication | Maps, Charts, and Graphs |

Following Map Routes

How Will I Use This Skill?

You can use map routes to find your way through a school or office building. With a road map, you can chart a route from home to other places. You can also give directions to others.

LEARN the Skill

You can follow a map route by using the steps below.

❶ Identify the map's subject and symbols that indicate routes.

❷ Use the directional arrow that identifies N, S, E, and W to determine in what direction a route goes. Recognize other directions, such as northeast (NE), the direction between N and E. Other directions are southeast (SE), southwest (SW), and northwest (NW).

❸ Use the scale of miles to determine the distance of a route.

❹ Choose the map route you will follow and describe it in terms of direction and distance.

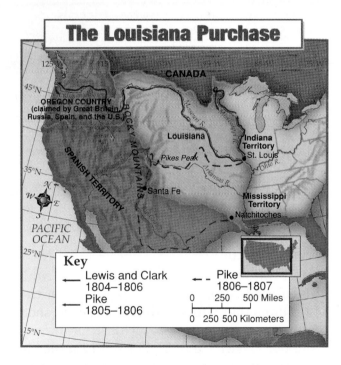

The Louisiana Purchase

Key
← Lewis and Clark 1804–1806
← Pike 1805–1806
← - Pike 1806–1807
0   250   500 Miles
0   250 500 Kilometers

PRACTICE the Skill

Using the steps and the map above, answer the following questions.

❶ What does the map show? What symbols represent routes?

❷ In what general direction did Lewis and Clark travel from St. Louis?

❸ About how many miles did Lewis and Clark travel in order to reach the Pacific Ocean?

❹ Describe Pike's route from St. Louis to Natchitoches.

APPLY the Skill

Using a map of your community, describe the route that you follow to travel from home to school or to any other destination, such as a library or a park.

Antelope

Viewing HISTORY **The Way West**

In this painting, Lewis, Clark, and Sacajawea stand at the Great Falls of the Missouri River in 1804. Accompanying them is York, an enslaved African American in the service of Clark. After serving as a valuable member of the Lewis and Clark expedition, York was freed. He returned to the West to live with the Native Americans.
★ Why did Lewis and Clark include Sacajawea in the expedition?

Over the Rockies

A Shoshone woman, **Sacajawea** (sahk uh juh WEE uh), was also staying with the Mandans that winter. The Shoshones (shoh SHOH neez) lived in the Rockies. Sacajawea and her French Canadian husband agreed to accompany Lewis and Clark and serve as translators.

In early spring, the party set out. In the foothills of the Rockies, the landscape and wildlife changed. Bighorn sheep ran along the high hills. The thorns of prickly pear cactus jabbed the explorers' moccasins. One day, a grizzly bear chased Lewis while he was exploring alone.

Sacajawea contributed greatly to the success of the expedition. She gathered wild vegetables and advised the men where to fish and hunt. She knew about the healing qualities of plants and herbs, so the expedition relied on her for medical help.

In the mountains, Sacajawea recognized the lands of her people. One day, Lewis met some Shoshone leaders and invited them back to camp. Sacajawea began to "dance and show every mark of the most extravagant joy." One of the men, she explained, was her brother. The Shoshone people supplied the expedition with food and horses. The Shoshones also advised Lewis and Clark about the best route to take over the Rockies.

In the Rocky Mountains, Lewis and Clark crossed the **Continental Divide.** A continental divide is a mountain ridge that separates river systems flowing toward opposite sides of a continent. In North America, some rivers flow east from the Rockies into the Mississippi, which drains into the Gulf of Mexico. Other rivers flow west from the Rockies and empty into the Pacific Ocean.

To the Pacific

After building canoes, Lewis and Clark's party floated toward the Columbia River. It carried them into the Pacific Northwest.

On November 7, 1805, Lewis and Clark finally reached their goal. Lewis wrote in his journal: "Great joy in camp. We are in view of the ocean, this great Pacific Ocean which we have been so long anxious to see." On a nearby tree, Clark carved, "By Land from the U. States in 1804 & 5."

The return trip to St. Louis took another year. In 1806, Americans celebrated the return of Lewis and Clark. The explorers brought back much useful information about the Louisiana Purchase.

Pike Explores the West

Before Lewis and Clark returned, another explorer set out from St. Louis. From 1805 to 1807, **Zebulon Pike** explored the upper Mississippi River, the Arkansas River, and parts of present-day Colorado and New Mexico. In November 1806, Pike viewed a mountain peak rising above the Colorado plains. Today, this mountain is known as Pikes Peak.

Continuing further westward into the Rocky Mountains, Pike came upon a small river. It was the Rio Grande. Pike had entered into Spanish territory. Spanish troops soon arrested Pike and his men and took them into Mexico.

After being questioned and detained for a while, the Americans were escorted through Texas back into the United States. Pike's maps and journals had been confiscated by the Spanish. Still, Pike was able to remember enough to write a report. The report greatly expanded Americans' knowledge about the Southwest.

The journeys of Zebulon Pike and Lewis and Clark excited Americans. It was a number of years, however, before settlers moved into the rugged western lands. As you will read, they first settled the region closest to the Mississippi River. Soon, the territory around New Orleans had a large enough white population for the settlers to apply for statehood. In 1812, this territory entered the Union as the state of Louisiana.

★ Section 2 Review ★

Recall

1. **Locate** (a) Mississippi River, (b) St. Louis, (c) Missouri River, (d) Rocky Mountains, (e) Columbia River, (f) Pikes Peak.

2. **Identify** (a) Pinckney Treaty, (b) Toussaint L'Ouverture, (c) Louisiana Purchase, (d) Lewis and Clark, (e) Sacajawea, (f) Zebulon Pike.

3. **Define** (a) expedition, (b) Continental Divide.

Comprehension

4. Why did western farmers oppose Spanish and French control of New Orleans?

5. Why was the United States able to buy Louisiana at a very low price?

6. Did Lewis and Clark accomplish what President Jefferson had asked them to do? Explain.

Critical Thinking and Writing

7. **Drawing Conclusions** Was Jefferson's purchase of Louisiana based on a strict or loose interpretation of the Constitution? Explain.

8. **Making Decisions** If you had been a Native American leader of the time, would you have welcomed Lewis and Clark in friendship? Explain the reasons for your decision.

★ ★

Activity **Writing a Diary** Westward Ho! You are with Lewis and Clark as they travel to the Pacific. Write several diary entries describing what you see and feel as you explore Louisiana and meet the Native Americans who live there.

New Threats From Overseas

★ ★

As You Read

Explore These Questions
- How did overseas trade grow in the late 1700s?
- How did war in Europe hurt American trade?
- Why was the Embargo Act a failure?

Define
- impressment
- embargo
- smuggler

Identify
- Barbary States
- Stephen Decatur
- Embargo Act
- Nonintercourse Act

SETTING the Scene James Brown, a young American sailor, wrote a letter. It was smuggled from a British ship and carried to the United States. The message described a desperate situation:

66 Being on shore one day in Lisbon, Portugal, I was [seized] by a gang and brought on board the [British ship] *Conqueror,* where I am still confined. Never have I been allowed to put my foot on shore since I was brought on board, which is now three years. 99

Brown's situation was not unusual. In the early 1800s, the British navy forced thousands of American sailors to serve on their ships. This was only one of many dangers that Americans faced as their sea trade began to thrive.

The British navy seized American sailors.

Trading Around the World

After the Revolution, American overseas trade grew rapidly. Ships sailed from New England ports on voyages that sometimes lasted three years. Everywhere they went, Yankee captains kept a sharp lookout for new goods to trade and new markets in which to sell. One clever trader sawed up the winter ice from New England ponds, packed it deep in sawdust for insulation, and carried it to India. There, he traded the ice for silk and spices.

In 1784, the *Empress of China* became the first American ship to trade with China. Before long, New England merchants built up a profitable trade with China. Yankee traders took ginseng, a plant that grew wild in New England, and exchanged it for Chinese silks and tea. The Chinese used the roots of the ginseng plant for medicines.

Yankee merchants sailed up the Pacific coast of North America in the 1790s. In fact, Yankee traders visited the Columbia River more than 10 years before Lewis and Clark. So many traders from Boston visited the Pacific Northwest that Native Americans called every white man "Boston." Traders bought furs from Native Americans. Then they sold the furs for large profits in China.

War With Tripoli

American traders ran great risks, especially in the Mediterranean Sea. For many years, pirates from nations along the coast of

North Africa attacked vessels from Europe and the United States. The North African nations were called the **Barbary States.** To protect American ships, the United States paid a yearly tribute, or bribe, to the rulers of the Barbary States.

In the early 1800s, Tripoli, one of the Barbary States, demanded a larger bribe than usual. When President Jefferson refused to pay, Tripoli declared war on the United States. In response, Jefferson ordered the navy to blockade the port of Tripoli.

During the blockade, the American ship *Philadelphia* ran aground near Tripoli. Pirates boarded the ship and hauled the crew to prison. The pirates planned to use the *Philadelphia* to attack other ships.

Then, **Stephen Decatur,** a United States Navy officer, took action. Very late one night, Decatur and his crew quietly sailed a ship into Tripoli harbor. When they reached the captured American ship, they set it on fire so that the pirates could not use it.

In the meantime, American marines landed on the coast of North Africa. They then marched 500 miles (805 km) to launch a surprise attack on Tripoli. The war with Tripoli lasted until 1805. In the end, the ruler of Tripoli signed a treaty promising not to interfere with American ships.

American Neutrality Is Violated

During the early 1800s, American ships faced another problem. In 1803, Britain and France went to war again. At first, Americans profited from the war. British and French ships were too busy fighting to engage in trade. American merchants took advantage of the war to trade with both sides. As trade increased, American shipbuilders hurried to build new ships.

Of course, neither Britain nor France wanted the United States to sell supplies to its enemy. As in the 1790s, they ignored American claims of neutrality. Each nation tried to stop American trade with the other. Napoleon seized American ships bound for England, and the British stopped Yankee traders on their way to France. Between

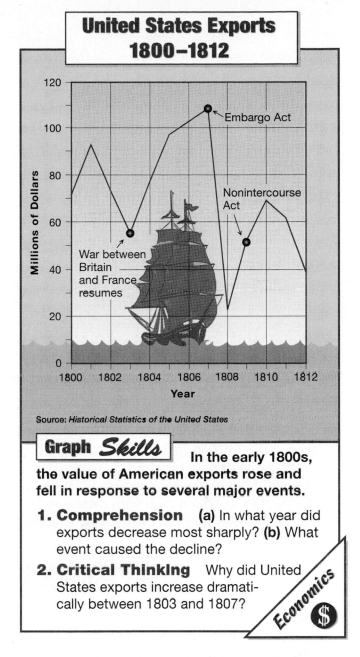

United States Exports 1800–1812

Source: *Historical Statistics of the United States*

Graph Skills In the early 1800s, the value of American exports rose and fell in response to several major events.

1. **Comprehension** (a) In what year did exports decrease most sharply? (b) What event caused the decline?
2. **Critical Thinking** Why did United States exports increase dramatically between 1803 and 1807?

Economics $

1805 and 1807, hundreds of American ships were captured.

The British navy also seized American sailors and forced them to serve on British ships. This practice of forcing people into service, called **impressment,** was common in Britain. For centuries, impressment gangs had raided villages and forced young men to serve in the navy.

Because the British navy needed more men to fight France, British ships stopped and searched American vessels. British officers seized all British sailors serving on American ships. They also impressed thousands of American sailors.

Limits on Trade

Americans were furious with the British for attacking their ships and impressing their sailors. Many wanted to declare war on Britain. Still, like Washington and Adams, President Jefferson hoped to avoid war. He knew that the small American fleet was no match for the powerful British navy.

A total ban

Jefferson persuaded Congress to pass the Embargo Act in 1807. An **embargo** is a ban on trade with another country. The **Embargo Act** forbade Americans to export or import goods. Jefferson hoped that the embargo would hurt France and Britain by cutting off needed supplies. "Our trade is the most powerful weapon we can use in our defense," one Republican newspaper wrote.

The embargo hurt Britain and France, but it hurt the United States even more. Americans were unable to get imports such as sugar, tea, and molasses. Exports dropped from $108 million in 1807 to $22 million in 1808. American sailors had no work. Farmers could not ship wheat overseas. Docks in the South were piled high with cotton and tobacco. The Embargo Act hurt New England merchants most of all.

Merchants from New England and other parts of the country protested loudly against the embargo. Some went a step further and became smugglers. A **smuggler** is a person who violates trade laws by illegally sneaking goods into or out of a country.

To stop defiance of the law, President Jefferson began using the navy and federal troops to enforce the embargo. On the border between New York and Canada, smugglers fought back. Some engaged in skirmishes with federal troops. Others, disguised as Indians, fired on federal ships.

A limited ban

After more than a year, Jefferson admitted that the Embargo Act had failed. In 1809, Congress replaced it with the less severe **Nonintercourse Act**. It allowed Americans to carry on trade with all nations except Britain and France.

The embargo was the most unpopular measure of Jefferson's years in office. Still, the Republicans remained strong. In 1808, Jefferson followed the precedent set by Washington and refused to run for a third term. James Madison, his fellow Republican, easily won the presidential election. Madison hoped that Britain and France would soon agree to stop violating American neutrality.

★ Section 3 Review ★

Recall

1. **Identify** (a) Barbary States, (b) Stephen Decatur, (c) Embargo Act, (d) Nonintercourse Act.
2. **Define** (a) impressment, (b) embargo, (c) smuggler.

Comprehension

3. How did American merchants expand their trading operations in the 1780s and 1790s?
4. How did war in Europe affect American overseas trade?

5. (a) What was the purpose of the Embargo Act? (b) Why did it fail?

Critical Thinking and Writing

6. **Making Generalizations** How can war both benefit and hurt the economy of a neutral nation? Explain.
7. **Predicting Consequences** What do you think the United States will do if Britain and France continue to violate American neutrality after 1809?

Activity **Drawing a Cartoon** Suppose the United States were under a limited or total embargo today. Draw a cartoon showing how such an embargo might affect you.

The Road to War

As You Read

Explore These Questions
- Why did the Prophet and Tecumseh unite Native Americans?
- How did fighting on the frontier lead to war with Britain?
- Why did War Hawks want war with Britain?

Define
- neutral
- nationalism

Identify
- Treaty of Greenville
- Tecumseh
- the Prophet
- William Henry Harrison
- Battle of Tippecanoe
- War Hawks
- Henry Clay

In the 1790s, U.S. infantry ➤ soldiers wore coats such as the one shown here.

SETTING the Scene James Madison was a quiet, scholarly man. He had helped to write the Constitution and to pass the Bill of Rights. As President, he hoped to keep the United States out of war.

Many Americans, however, felt that Madison's approach was too timid. They argued that the United States must stand up to Native Americans and foreign countries. How could the nation grow if Native Americans stood in the way? How could the nation win respect if it allowed the British and French navies to seize American ships? The cost of war might be great, said one member of Congress. Yet, he continued, who would count in money "the slavery of our impressed seamen"?

This kind of talk aroused the nation. In the early 1800s, the United States went to war with several Native American nations. By 1812, many Americans were also calling for war with Britain.

Conflict With Native Americans

Thousands of white settlers had moved into the Northwest Territory in the 1790s. The large number of newcomers caused problems for Native Americans. The settlers ignored treaties the United States had signed with Indian nations of the region. They built farms on Indian lands. They hunted the animals that Indians depended on for food.

Fighting often broke out between the Native Americans and settlers. Isolated acts of violence led to larger acts of revenge. As a result, both sides killed innocent people who had not taken part in acts of violence. In this way, warfare spread and minor conflicts grew into larger ones.

In 1791, the Miamis of Ohio joined with other Indian nations. Little Turtle, a skilled fighter, led the Miami nation. Armed with muskets and gunpowder supplied by the British, the Miamis drove white settlers from the area.

In 1794, President Washington sent General Anthony Wayne with a well-trained army into Miami territory. The Native American forces gathered at a place called Fallen Timbers. They thought that Wayne would have trouble fighting there because fallen trees covered the land. However, Wayne's army pushed through the tangle of logs and defeated the Indians.

In 1795, leaders of the Miamis and a number of other Indian nations signed the **Treaty of Greenville.** They gave up land that would later become part of Ohio. In return, they received $20,000 and the promise of more money if they kept the peace.

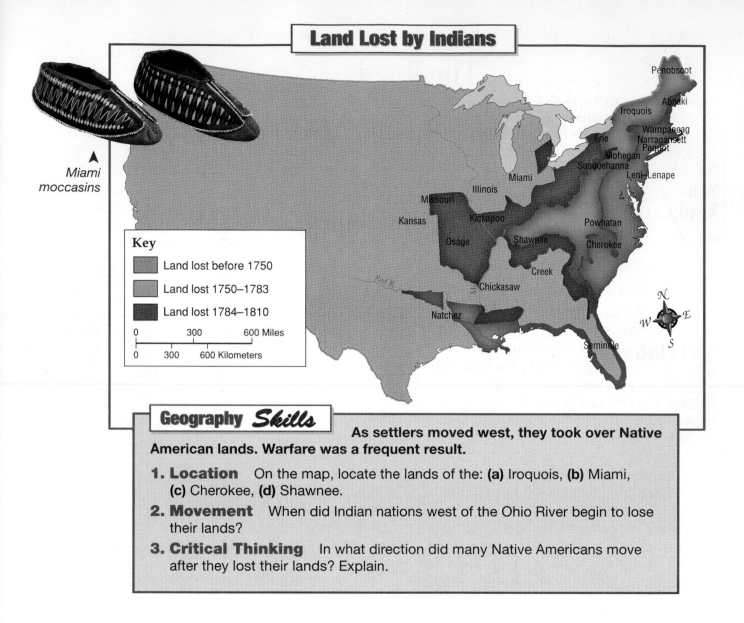

Land Lost by Indians

Miami moccasins

Key
- Land lost before 1750
- Land lost 1750–1783
- Land lost 1784–1810

0   300   600 Miles

0   300   600 Kilometers

Penobscot
Abnaki
Iroquois
Wampanoag
Erie
Narragansett
Pequot
Mohegan
Susquehanna
Leni–Lenape
Miami
Illinois
Missouri
Kansas
Kickapoo
Powhatan
Osage
Shawnee
Cherokee
Creek
Red R.
Chickasaw
Natchez
Seminole

N E W S

Geography *Skills*

As settlers moved west, they took over Native American lands. Warfare was a frequent result.

1. **Location**   On the map, locate the lands of the: **(a)** Iroquois, **(b)** Miami, **(c)** Cherokee, **(d)** Shawnee.

2. **Movement**   When did Indian nations west of the Ohio River begin to lose their lands?

3. **Critical Thinking**   In what direction did many Native Americans move after they lost their lands? Explain.

Tecumseh's Confederation

Ohio joined the Union in 1803. By then, white settlers were pushing beyond Ohio into Indiana Territory. Many Native Americans grew angry. They wanted to keep settlers from taking more Indian land. Among those who felt this way were two Shawnee leaders: **Tecumseh** (tih KUHM suh) and his brother, called **the Prophet**.

Unity and the Old Ways

The Prophet said that he had journeyed to the spirit world. There, he learned the path that Indians must take if they were to live happily. Both the Prophet and Tecumseh said that white customs corrupted the Native American way of life. They said that many Indians depended on white trade goods, such as muskets, cloth, cooking pots, and whiskey. They believed that by returning to the old ways, Indians could gain the power to resist white invaders.

In 1808, the Prophet built a village for his followers along Tippecanoe Creek in Indiana Territory. Indians traveled from lands as far away as Missouri, Iowa, and Minnesota to hear his message. His teachings brought hope to many.

In the early 1800s, Tecumseh and the Prophet organized many Native American nations into a confederation, or league. The Prophet was the spiritual leader of the confederation and Tecumseh was its spokesperson. Tecumseh and the Prophet persuaded Native Americans to unite against white settlers:

66 The whites have driven us from the great salt water, forced us over the mountains.... The way...to check and stop this evil is for all red men to unite in claiming a common equal right in the land. 99

Tecumseh also impressed white leaders. **William Henry Harrison,** governor of Indiana Territory, grudgingly admitted, "He is one of those uncommon geniuses which spring up occasionally to produce revolutions and overturn the established order of things."

Showdown at Tippecanoe

Rivalries among Native American nations kept Tecumseh from uniting all Indians east of the Mississippi River. Still, white settlers were alarmed at his success.

In 1811, Governor Harrison marched 1,000 soldiers against Tecumseh's town on the Tippecanoe Creek. The Prophet was in charge because Tecumseh was away organizing Indians in the South. The Prophet led a surprise night attack on Harrison's troops. Neither side won a clear victory in the battle that followed. Still, whites celebrated the **Battle of Tippecanoe** as a major victory.

Growing Conflict With Britain

The fighting with Native Americans caused relations between the United States and Britain to worsen. The British were supplying guns and ammunition to the Native Americans on the frontier. They were also encouraging Indians to attack United States' settlements.

Meanwhile, the United States and Britain also continued to disagree over trade. When the embargo against Britain and France was set to expire in 1810, the United States made a very daring offer. If either the British or French would stop seizing

 **Tecumseh and the Prophet**

Tecumseh (left) and the Prophet (right) felt that no Indian nation could sell land unless all other Indian nations agreed. Tecumseh said, "Sell a country! Why not sell the air, the great sea, as well as the earth?" ★ **Why did Tecumseh and the Prophet dislike the Treaty of Greenville?**

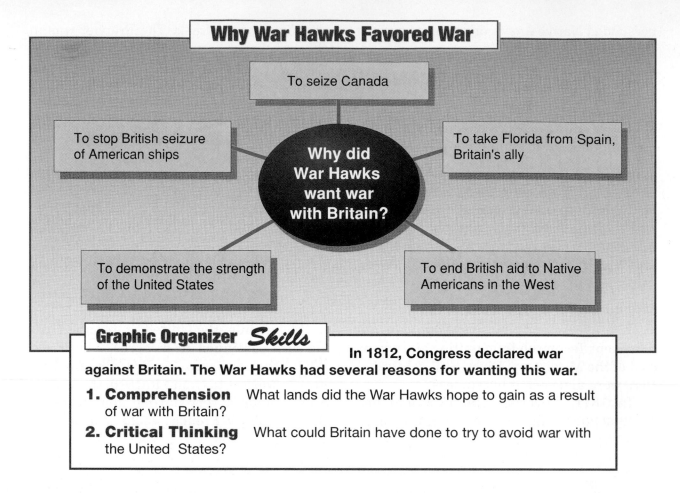

Why War Hawks Favored War

To seize Canada

To stop British seizure of American ships

Why did War Hawks want war with Britain?

To take Florida from Spain, Britain's ally

To demonstrate the strength of the United States

To end British aid to Native Americans in the West

Graphic Organizer Skills In 1812, Congress declared war against Britain. The War Hawks had several reasons for wanting this war.

1. **Comprehension** What lands did the War Hawks hope to gain as a result of war with Britain?
2. **Critical Thinking** What could Britain have done to try to avoid war with the United States?

American ships, the United States would halt trade with the other nation.

Seizing the chance, Napoleon quickly announced that France would respect the United States' policy of staying **neutral,** or uninvolved in the war between Britain and France. As promised, the United States continued trade with France, but stopped all shipments to Britain.

The War Hawks

While President Madison did not want war, other Americans were not as cautious. Except in New England, where many merchants wanted to restore trade with Britain, anti-British feeling ran strong. Members of Congress from the South and the West called for war with Britain. They were known as **War Hawks**.

War Hawks had a strong sense of nationalism. **Nationalism** is pride in or devotion to one's country. War Hawks felt that Britain was treating the United States as if it were still a British colony. They were willing to fight a war to defend American rights.

Arguments for war

Henry Clay of Kentucky was the most outspoken War Hawk. Clay wanted war for two reasons. He wanted revenge on Britain for seizing American ships. He also wanted to conquer Canada. "The militia of Kentucky are alone [able] to place Montreal and Upper Canada at your feet," Clay boasted to Congress. Canadians, Clay believed, would be happy to leave the British empire and join the United States.

War Hawks saw other advantages of war with Britain. South of the United States, Florida belonged to Spain, Britain's ally. If Americans went to war with Britain, War Hawks said, the United States could seize Florida from Spain.

War Hawks had yet another reason to fight Britain. They pointed out that Britain was arming Native Americans on the frontier and encouraging them to attack settlers. The War Hawks felt that winning a war against Britain would bring lasting peace and safety to American settlers on the frontier.

Congress Declares War

In 1811, the United States and Britain drifted closer to war. To prevent Americans from trading with France, British warships blockaded some American ports. The British continued to board American ships and impress American seamen. In May 1811, near New York Harbor, a brief battle broke out between an American frigate and a British warship. The Americans crippled the British ship and left 32 British dead or wounded.

The War Hawks urged that Congress prepare for a war against Britain. One of the most radical and outspoken of the War Hawks was Felix Grundy, a Congressman from Tennessee. In December 1811, he gave a very emotional speech describing what he saw as the benefits of war:

66 This war... will have its advantages. We shall drive the British from our continent—they will no longer have an opportunity of intriguing with our Indian neighbors. 99

Grundy hoped that a war with Britain would achieve other more ambitious goals. Like most War Hawks, he dreamed of winning additional land for the United States. He closed his speech with these words: "I therefore feel anxious not only to add the Floridas to the South, but the Canadas to the North of this empire."

Others in Congress opposed the strong views of the War Hawks. John Randolph of Virginia warned that the people of the United States would "not submit to be taxed for this war of conquest and dominion." Representatives of New England were especially concerned. They feared that the British navy would attack New England seaports.

President Madison at last gave in to war fever. In June 1812, he asked Congress to declare war on Britain. The House voted 79 to 49 in favor of war. The Senate vote was 19 to 13. Americans soon discovered, however, that winning the war would not be as easy as declaring it.

Cannon used ➤ in the war against Britain

★ Section 4 Review ★

Recall

1. **Locate** Native American lands lost **(a)** from 1750 to 1783, **(b)** from 1784 to 1810.
2. **Identify** **(a)** Treaty of Greenville, **(b)** Tecumseh, **(c)** the Prophet, **(d)** William Henry Harrison, **(e)** Battle of Tippecanoe, **(f)** War Hawks, **(g)** Henry Clay.
3. **Define** **(a)** neutral, **(b)** nationalism.

Comprehension

4. Why was there conflict between Native Americans and white settlers?

5. How did the Battle of Tippecanoe help lead to war between Britain and the United States?
6. What did the War Hawks hope to gain from a war with Britain?

Critical Thinking and Writing

7. **Identifying Main Ideas** What ideas did the Prophet and Tecumseh use to unite many Native Americans?
8. **Defending a Position** In 1812, would you have favored or opposed war with Britain? Explain the reasons for your position.

Activity **Writing a Speech** You are a Native American leader of the early 1800s. Write a speech explaining why you are against white settlement and what you think Native Americans can do to stop it. Deliver your speech to the class.

The War of 1812

As You Read

Explore These Questions

- How was the United States unready for war with Britain?
- What were the major turning points of the war in the West?
- What were the results of the war?

Identify

- Oliver Hazard Perry
- Battle of Lake Erie
- Andrew Jackson
- Battle of Horseshoe Bend
- Dolley Madison
- Battle of New Orleans
- Richard Allen
- Hartford Convention
- Treaty of Ghent

SETTING the Scene Many Americans welcomed the news of war with Britain. In some cities, they fired cannons and guns and danced in the streets. One New Jersey man wrote a song calling for a swift attack on Canada:

66 On to Quebec's embattled halls! Who will pause, when glory calls? Charge, soldiers, charge, its lofty walls. And storm its strong artillery. 99

Other Americans were less enthusiastic. New Englanders, especially, talked scornfully of "Mr. Madison's war." In fact, before the war ended, some New Englanders would threaten to leave the Union and make a separate peace with Britain.

Unready for War

The American declaration of war took the British by surprise. They were locked in a bitter struggle with Napoleon, and could not spare troops to fight the United States. As the war began, however, the United States faced difficulties of its own.

Because Jefferson believed in a small federal government and had reduced spending on defense, the United States was not ready for war. The navy had only 16 ships to fight against the huge British fleet. The army was small and ill equipped. Moreover, many of the officers knew little about the military. "The state of the Army," commented a member of Congress, "is enough to make any man

who has the smallest love of country wish to get rid of it."

Since there were few regular troops, the government relied on volunteers to fight the war. Congress voted to give them $124 and 360 acres of land for their service. The money was high pay at the time—equal to a year's salary for most workers.

Attracted by money and the chance to own their own farm, young men eagerly enlisted. They were poorly trained, however, and did not know how to be good soldiers. Many deserted after a few months.

Fighting at Sea

The British navy blockaded American ports to stop Americans from trading with other countries. The small American navy was unable to break the blockade. Still, several sea captains won stunning victories.

One famous battle took place early in the war, in August 1812. As he was sailing near Newfoundland, Isaac Hull, captain of the *Constitution*, spotted the British ship *Guerrière* (gai ree AIR). For nearly an hour, the two ships jockeyed for position.

At last, the guns of the *Constitution* roared into action. They tore holes in the sides of the *Guerrière* and shot off both masts. When the smoke cleared, Hull asked the British captain if he had "struck" his flag—that is, lowered his flag in surrender. "Well, I don't know," replied the stunned British captain. "Our mizzenmast is gone, our mainmast

HISTORY HAPPENED HERE

The USS Constitution

The USS Constitution *became known as "Old Ironsides" because British cannonballs often bounced off her thick wooden hull. In 1905, the ship was docked in Boston and opened to the public. In 1997, the ship underwent major restoration. Today, the United States Navy invites you to come aboard and tour "Old Ironsides." In the nearby museum, you can relive history by commanding a ship, hoisting a sail, or firing a cannon.*

★ *To learn more about this historic ship, write:* USS Constitution *Museum, Charlestown Navy Yard, Charlestown, MA 02129.*

is gone. And, upon the whole, you may say we *have* struck our flag."

American sea captains won other victories at sea. These victories cheered Americans, but did little to win the war.

War in the West

One goal of the War Hawks was to conquer Canada. They were convinced that Canadians would welcome the chance to throw off British rule and join the United States. The United States planned to invade Canada at three different points: Detroit, the Niagara River, and Montreal.

Invasion of Canada

General William Hull moved American troops into Canada from Detroit. The Canadians had only a few untrained troops to ward off the invasion. However, they were led by a clever and skillful British leader, General Isaac Brock.

Brock paraded his soldiers in red coats to make it appear that experienced British troops were helping the Canadians. He also let a message with false information fall into American hands. It exaggerated the number of Indians who were fighting with the Canadians. Brock's scare tactics worked. Hull retreated from Canada.

Other attempts to invade Canada also failed. Americans were wrong in thinking that the Canadians would welcome them as liberators from British rule. Instead, the Canadians fought fiercely and forced the Americans into retreat.

Battle of Lake Erie

In 1813, the Americans set out to win control of Lake Erie. Captain **Oliver Hazard Perry** had no fleet, so he designed and built his own ships. In September 1813, he sailed his tiny fleet against the British.

During the **Battle of Lake Erie**, the British battered Perry's own ship and left it

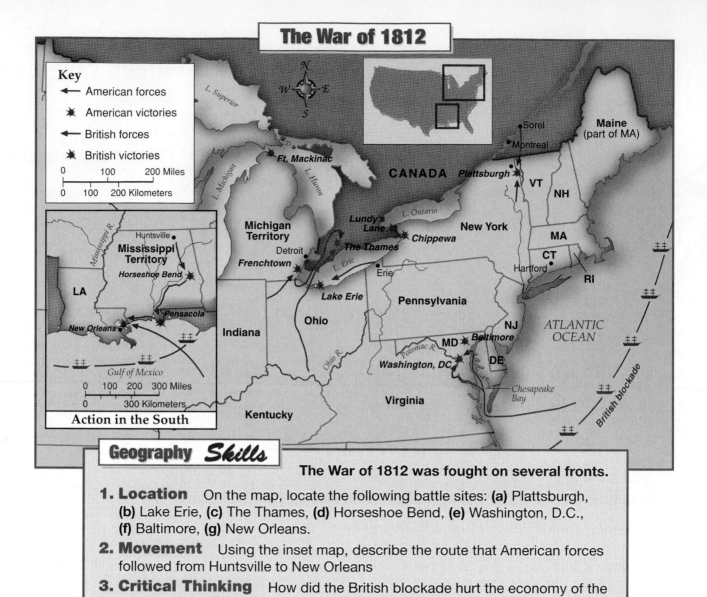

The War of 1812

Key
← American forces
✳ American victories
← British forces
✳ British victories

0   100   200 Miles
0   100   200 Kilometers

Action in the South

Huntsville
Mississippi Territory
Horseshoe Bend
LA
Pensacola
New Orleans
Gulf of Mexico
0   100   200   300 Miles
0   300 Kilometers
Mississippi R.

L. Superior
Ft. Mackinac
L. Michigan
L. Huron
Michigan Territory
Detroit
Frenchtown
Indiana
Ohio
Kentucky
Lake Erie
L. Erie
Erie
Ohio R.
CANADA
Lundy's Lane
Chippewa
The Thames
L. Ontario
Sorel
Montreal
Plattsburgh
VT
NH
Maine (part of MA)
New York
MA
CT
Hartford
RI
Pennsylvania
NJ
MD
Baltimore
Washington, DC
DE
Virginia
Potomac R.
Chesapeake Bay
ATLANTIC OCEAN
British blockade

Geography *Skills*

The War of 1812 was fought on several fronts.

1. **Location**   On the map, locate the following battle sites: **(a)** Plattsburgh, **(b)** Lake Erie, **(c)** The Thames, **(d)** Horseshoe Bend, **(e)** Washington, D.C., **(f)** Baltimore, **(g)** New Orleans.

2. **Movement**   Using the inset map, describe the route that American forces followed from Huntsville to New Orleans

3. **Critical Thinking**   How did the British blockade hurt the economy of the United States?

helpless. Perry took his flag down and rowed over to another American ship. There, he raised the colors again and continued to fight. Finally, the Americans won the battle. Captain Perry wrote his message of victory on the back of an envelope: "We have met the enemy and they are ours."

Native American losses

After losing control of Lake Erie, the British and their ally Tecumseh retreated from Detroit into Canada. General William Henry Harrison, veteran of Tippecanoe, pursued them. The Americans won a decisive victory at the Battle of the Thames. Tecumseh died in the fighting. Without Tecumseh's leadership, the Indian confederation soon fell apart.

Still, the Creeks, Tecumseh's allies in the South, continued their fight against the settlers. **Andrew Jackson,** a Tennessee officer, took command of American troops in the Creek War. In 1814, with the help of the Cherokees, Jackson won a crushing victory at the **Battle of Horseshoe Bend.** The leader of the Creeks walked alone into Jackson's camp to surrender:

❝ I am in your power. Do unto me as you please.... If I had an army I would yet fight, and contend to the last.... But your people have destroyed my nation. ❞

For the time being, the fighting ended. Once again, Native Americans had to give up land to whites.

Final Battles

In 1814, Britain and its allies defeated France. With the war in Europe over, Britain could send more troops and ships against the United States.

The British burn Washington

In the summer of 1814, British ships sailed into Chesapeake Bay and landed an invasion force about 30 miles (48 km) from Washington, D.C. American troops met the British at Bladensburg, Maryland. President Madison himself watched the battle. To his dismay, the battle-hardened British quickly scattered the untrained Americans. The British met little further resistance as they continued their march to the capital.

In the White House, **Dolley Madison** waited for her husband to return. Hastily, she scrawled a note to her sister:

66 Will you believe it, my sister? We have had a battle or skirmish near Bladensburg and here I am still within sound of the cannon! Mr. Madison comes not. May God protect us. Two messengers covered with dust come bid me fly. But here I mean to wait for him. 99

Soon after, British troops marched into the capital. Dolley Madison gathered up important papers of the President and a portrait of George Washington. Then, she fled south. She was not there to see the British burn the White House and other buildings.

From Washington, the British marched north toward the city of Baltimore. The key to Baltimore's defense was Fort McHenry.

Linking Past and Present

Past

Present

The White House

After capturing Washington in August 1814, the British burned the White House. Margaret Smith, a resident of the city, recalled the sad scene: "Who would have thought that this mass so solid, so magnificent, so grand . . . [should] be thus irreparably destroyed." In fact, the White House was not destroyed. A torrential thunderstorm put out the flames and saved the structure. Today, the White House continues to serve as the official residence of Presidents of the United States. ★ **How do you think the burning of the White House affected American morale?**

In this engraving, Andrew Jackson stands atop the American defense works as he spurs his troops to victory. The Battle of New Orleans was the bloodiest engagement of the War of 1812. Neither side knew that the war had ended two weeks earlier. ★ **Why did it take so long for the news of war's end to reach New Orleans?**

From evening on September 13 until dawn on September 14, British rockets bombarded the harbor.

When the early morning fog lifted, the "broad stripes and bright stars" of the American flag still waved over Fort McHenry. The British withdrew. Francis Scott Key, who witnessed the battle, wrote a poem about the bombardment. Later, "The Star-Spangled Banner" was set to music and adopted as the national anthem of the United States.

Battle of New Orleans

In late 1814, the British prepared to attack New Orleans. From there, they hoped to sail up the Mississippi. However, Andrew Jackson was waiting for the British. Jackson had turned his frontier fighters into a strong army. He took Pensacola in Spanish Florida to keep the British from using it as a base. He then marched through Mobile and set up camp in New Orleans.

Jackson's force included thousands of frontiersmen. Many of them were expert riflemen. In addition, citizens of New Orleans joined the army to defend their city from the approaching British. Among the volunteers were hundreds of African Americans.

The American soldiers dug trenches to defend themselves. On January 8, 1815, the British attacked. Again and again, British soldiers marched toward the American trenches. More than 2,000 British fell under the deadly fire of American sharpshooters and cannons. Only seven Americans died.

All over the United States, Americans cheered the victory at the **Battle of New Orleans**. Andrew Jackson became a national hero. His fame did not dim even when Americans later learned that the battle could have been avoided. It took place two weeks after the United States and Britain had signed a treaty in Europe ending the war.

African Americans in the War

African Americans served alongside other Americans in the fight against the British. African American soldiers helped win the Battle of New Orleans. Following the British attacks on Washington and Baltimore, African American volunteers helped defend Philadelphia against a possible attack. Bishop **Richard Allen** and the Reverend Absalom Jones recruited more than 2,000 men to help build Philadelphia's fortifications. The state of New York, meanwhile, organized two regiments of black volunteers to serve in the army.

African Americans also served with distinction in the United States Navy. They helped win the Battle of Lake Erie as well as other naval battles. Commander Nathaniel Shaler praised one particular black sailor who was killed in battle: "When America has such [sailors], she has little to fear from the tyrants of the ocean."

Peace at Last

In the early 1800s, news took weeks to cross the Atlantic Ocean. By late 1814, Americans knew that peace talks had begun, but they did not know how they were progressing or how long they would last. As Jackson was preparing to fight the British at New Orleans, New Englanders were meeting to protest "Mr. Madison's war."

New Englanders protest

The British blockade had hurt New England's sea trade. Also, many New Englanders feared that the United States might win land in Florida and Canada. If new states were carved out of these lands, the South and the West would become more influential than New England.

Delegates from around New England met in Hartford, Connecticut, in December 1814. Most were Federalists. They disliked the Republican President and the war. The delegates to the **Hartford Convention** threatened to leave the Union if the war continued.

Then, while the delegates debated what to do, news of the peace treaty arrived. The Hartford Convention ended quickly. With the war over, the protest was meaningless.

"Nothing was settled"

The **Treaty of Ghent** was signed in the city of Ghent, Belgium, on December 24, 1814. John Quincy Adams, one of the Americans at Ghent, summed up the treaty in one sentence: "Nothing was adjusted, nothing was settled."

Britain and the United States agreed to restore prewar conditions. The treaty said nothing about impressment or neutrality. These issues had faded due to the end of the Napoleonic Wars in Europe. Other issues were settled later. In 1818, for example, the two nations settled a dispute over the border between Canada and the United States.

Looking back, some Americans felt that the War of 1812 had been a mistake. Others argued that Europe would now treat the young republic with more respect. The victories of heroes like Oliver Hazard Perry and Andrew Jackson gave Americans new pride in their country. As one Republican leader remarked, "The people are now more American. They feel and act more as a nation."

★ Section 5 Review ★

Recall

1. **Locate** (a) Lake Erie, (b) Detroit, (c) Chesapeake Bay, (d) Washington, D.C., (e) Baltimore, (f) New Orleans.
2. **Identify** (a) Oliver Hazard Perry, (b) Battle of Lake Erie, (c) Andrew Jackson, (d) Battle of Horseshoe Bend, (e) Dolley Madison, (f) Battle of New Orleans, (g) Richard Allen, (h) Hartford Convention, (i) Treaty of Ghent.

Comprehension

3. What military problems did the United States face as the War of 1812 began?

4. How did the death of Tecumseh affect the war in the West?
5. What were the results of the War of 1812?

Critical Thinking and Writing

6. **Understanding Causes and Effects** How do you think the War of 1812 helped Andrew Jackson to later become the President of the United States?
7. **Applying Information** Why did the results of the War of 1812 please some Americans, but disappoint others?

Activity Writing a Song Keep your head down! You are in the trenches at the Battle of New Orleans. Write a song describing what you see, hear, and feel as you help Andrew Jackson defeat the British and save New Orleans.

Review and Activities

★ Sum It Up ★

Section 1   Republicans in Power
▶ President Jefferson tried to help ordinary citizens and limit government power.
▶ The Supreme Court established its power to decide if laws are constitutional.

Section 2   The Louisiana Purchase
▶ In 1803, the United States bought the vast western territory of Louisiana from France.
▶ Lewis and Clark explored Louisiana and tried to establish friendly relations with Native Americans.

Section 3   New Threats From Overseas
▶ American trade increased but was threatened by France and Britain.
▶ The Embargo Act hurt the United States more than Britain and France.

Section 4   The Road to War
▶ Native Americans fought to preserve their lands and culture.
▶ War Hawks wanted war with Britain to protect American trade and to gain new lands.

Section 5   The War of 1812
▶ Though poorly prepared, American forces defeated the British in key battles.
▶ Not all Americans supported the war. For many, however, the war brought a new sense of national pride.

 For additional review of the major ideas of Chapter 10, see **Guide to the Essentials of American History** or **Interactive Student Tutorial CD-ROM,** which contains interactive review activities, graphic organizers, and practice tests.

🖾 Reviewing the Chapter

Define These Terms
Match each term with the correct definition.

Column 1	Column 2
1. laissez faire	**a.** forcing people into naval service
2. judicial review	**b.** ban on trade with another country
3. impressment	**c.** government should play a very limited role in economic affairs
4. embargo	
5. nationalism	**d.** pride in one's country
	e. Supreme Court's power to decide if laws are constitutional

Explore the Main Ideas
1. Describe two of President Jefferson's ideas about the proper role of government.
2. Why did the United States buy Louisiana from France?
3. What were the goals of the Lewis and Clark expedition?
4. How did war between Britain and France affect the United States?
5. Why did many Native Americans unite under Tecumseh and the Prophet?
6. **(a)** Describe one major turning point in the War of 1812. **(b)** Explain one result of the war.

🖾 Geography Skills

Match the letters on the map with the following places:
1. Canada, **2.** Battle of the Thames, **3.** Battle of Horseshoe Bend, **4.** Battle of New Orleans, **5.** Baltimore, **6.** British blockade.

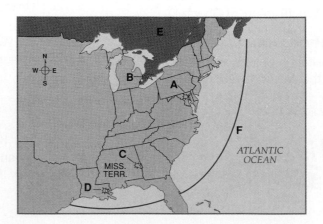

◻ Critical Thinking and Writing

1. **Defending a Position** Do you agree or disagree with Jefferson's idea that federal power should be limited? Explain the reasons for your position.

2. **Understanding Chronology** How did a British-French war help lead to a British-American war?

3. **Solving Problems** Describe a treaty that might have satisfied both Native Americans and white settlers in the early 1800s.

4. **Exploring Unit Themes** **Nationalism** Describe two events or developments that caused many Americans to become more nationalistic during the Age of Jefferson.

◻ Using Primary Sources

Soon after passage of the Embargo Act, President Jefferson received this letter from Jonathan Hall, a resident of New Hampshire:

❝ Sir: I have respected your laws and your government for the United States of America and I wish to have you continue your laws and government and keep the embargo on till you see fit to take it off, though it is very trying to the people in this country about their debts.... I have a father and a mother and they can't take care of themselves and as times are I can't pay for their place so...I hope that...your [honor] will do a little for me, Jonathan Hall. ❞

Source: *Jefferson Papers.* "Capt. Jonathan Hall to Jefferson." August 12, 1808.

Recognizing Points of View **(a)** Did Hall approve of the Embargo Act? **(b)** How did the embargo affect Hall? **(c)** Explain how the embargo might have caused this effect.

ACTIVITY BANK

▶ Interdisciplinary Activity

Exploring Civics Create a chart comparing the different ideas of the Federalists and Republicans during the Age of Jefferson. Include categories such as ideas about democracy, economic policy, military policy, and foreign policy.

▶ Career Skills Activity

Political Leaders Write a persuasive speech supporting or opposing war with Britain in 1812. The purpose of the speech is to persuade listeners to agree with your point of view. Deliver your speech to the class. Then, invite students to express their own views. If there is disagreement, you might wish to debate the issue.

▶ Citizenship Activity

Creating a Poster "We are all Republicans, we are all Federalists," said President Jefferson. Create a poster describing and illustrating four goals you think all Americans should agree on, regardless of their political party.

Internet Activity
Use the Internet to find information about current or recent embargoes. In a written report, describe two of these modern embargoes and the reason for each. Explain whether or not each has been successful.

EYEWITNESS Journal

You are a War Hawk in Congress, or a Native American at the Battle of Horseshoe Bend, or a British soldier attacking Washington, D.C., or an American soldier at New Orleans. In your EYEWITNESS JOURNAL, record your participation in and feelings about the War of 1812.

Chapter 11 Industry and Growth

1790–1825

In the early 1800s, the United States changed rapidly. New technology caused a growth in industry. New factories sprang up along the nation's waterways, and with them new towns and cities. The nation increased in size, too, as settlers swarmed west along roads and rivers.

Change led to increased differences. Economic differences grew between the traditional farming society and the newer industrial society. Regional differences also grew between the North, South, and West. The nation's leaders struggled to strengthen and unify a rapidly expanding nation. They also faced the challenge of creating a bold new foreign policy, as neighboring nations in Latin America won independence.

Why Study History?

Today, we live in an era of rapid technological change. Our age is not the first time Americans have faced a revolution in technology. In the early 1800s, as today, new inventions changed forever the way people lived. To focus on this connection, see the *Why Study History?* feature, "Technology Continues to Change Our Lives," in this chapter.

American Events

1790
First American spinning mill opens

1793
Eli Whitney's cotton gin boosts textile industry

1806
Congress approves building the National Road

| 1785 | 1790 | 1795 | 1800 | 1805 |

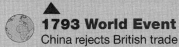

1793 World Event
China rejects British trade

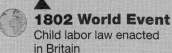

1802 World Event
Child labor law enacted in Britain

World Events

 A New Age of Steamboats

Steam Ferry, St. Louis by French artist Leon Pomarede is one of the earliest paintings of St. Louis, Missouri. It shows steam-powered ships puffing down the Mississippi toward the city. In the early 1800s, steamboats and other new means of transportation made it easier for settlers to travel to the West. At the same time, new technology changed how goods were produced and how people worked.

★ **What advantages do you think steamboats might have had over earlier forms of travel?**

●1807
Fulton's
steamship makes
record-breaking trip

●1816
New tariff sparks
sectional dispute

●1823
Monroe Doctrine
warns Europe not
to recolonize the
Americas

| 1805 | 1810 | 1815 | 1820 | 1825 |

 1807 World Event
Gas street lighting
demonstrated in London

1815 World Event
Napoleon defeated at
Waterloo

The Industrial Revolution

Explore These Questions
- What were the effects of the Industrial Revolution?
- How did the Industrial Revolution come to the United States?
- What was life like in early factories?

Define
- spinning jenny
- capitalist
- factory system
- interchangeable parts
- urbanization

Identify
- Industrial Revolution
- Samuel Slater
- Moses Brown
- Francis Cabot Lowell
- Boston Associates
- "Lowell girls"
- Eli Whitney

SETTING the Scene At dawn, the factory bell woke 11-year-old Lucy Larcom. Rising quickly, she ate her breakfast, and hurried to her job at a spinning mill in Lowell, Massachusetts. Years later, Larcom described her workplace:

66 I never cared much for machinery. The buzzing and hissing and whizzing of pulleys and rollers and spindles and flyers around me often grew tiresome.... I could look across the room and see girls moving backward and forward among the spinning frames, sometimes stooping, sometimes reaching up their arms, as their work required. 99

Factories and machinery were part of a revolution that reached the United States in the early 1800s. Unlike the American Revolution, this one had no battles or fixed dates. The new **Industrial Revolution** was a long, slow process which completely changed the way goods were produced.

The Industrial Revolution Begins

Before the 1800s, most people were farmers and most goods were produced by hand. As a result of the Industrial Revolution, this situation gradually began to change. Machines replaced hand tools. New sources of power, such as steam, replaced human and animal power. While most Americans contin-

ued to farm for a living, the economy began a gradual shift toward manufacturing.

New technology

The Industrial Revolution started in Britain in the mid-1700s. British inventors developed new technologies that transformed the textile industry.

Since early times, workers used spinning wheels to make thread. A spinning wheel, however, could spin only one thread at a time. In 1764, James Hargreaves developed the **spinning jenny,** a machine that could spin several threads at once. Later, Richard Arkwright invented a machine that could hold 100 spindles of thread. It was called the water frame because it required water power to turn its wheels.

Other inventions speeded up the process of weaving thread into cloth. In the 1780s, Edmund Cartwright built a loom powered by water. It allowed a worker to produce 200 times more cloth in a day than was possible before.

The factory system

New inventions led to a new method of production. Before the Industrial Revolution, most spinning and weaving took place in the home. Machines like the water frame, however, had to be housed in large mills near rivers. Water flowing downstream or over a waterfall turned a wheel that produced the power to run the machines.

To set up and operate a spinning mill required large amounts of capital, or money.

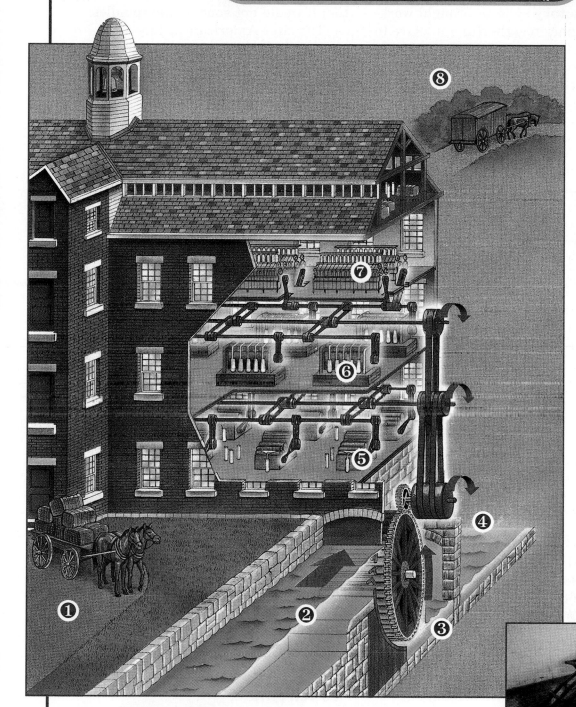

❶ Wagons bring raw cotton to the mill to be spun into thread.

❷ Fast-moving water causes the water wheel to turn.

❸ The turning water wheel powers the mill's main shaft.

❹ The main shaft drives pulleys, which turn belts that drive the mill machinery.

❺ Carding machines comb the raw cotton fiber.

❻ Drawing machines pull the combed cotton fibers into ropelike strands.

❼ Spinning frames twist combed and drawn cotton strands into thread and wind them onto a bobbin.

❽ Wagons carry spun thread to weavers who use it to make cloth.

Spinning Mill

New technology in the textile industry sparked the Industrial Revolution. As shown here, rapidly moving water turned a water wheel, like the one above. The wheel produced the power to run the machines. ★ **Would your town or community have been a suitable place for a spinning mill like this one? Why or why not?**

Main shaft of a spinning mill

Capitalists supplied this money. A **capitalist** is a person who invests in a business in order to make a profit. Capitalists built factories and hired workers to run the machines.

The new **factory system** brought workers and machinery together in one place to produce goods. Factory workers earned daily or weekly wages. They had to work a set number of hours each day.

A Revolution Crosses the Atlantic

Britain wanted to keep its new technology secret. It did not want rival nations to copy the new machines. The British Parliament passed a law forbidding anyone to take plans of Arkwright's water frame out of the country. It also tried to prevent factory workers from leaving Britain.

Slater breaks the law

Samuel Slater soon showed that the law could not be enforced. Slater was a skilled mechanic in one of Arkwright's mills. When he heard that Americans were offering large rewards for plans of British factories, he decided to leave England.

In 1789, Slater boarded a ship bound for New York City. He knew that British officials searched the baggage of passengers sailing to the United States. Carrying any sketches of the factory would be dangerous. To avoid getting caught, he memorized the design of the machines in Arkwright's mill.

In New York, Slater learned that **Moses Brown**, a Quaker merchant, wanted to build a spinning mill in Rhode Island. Slater wrote confidently to Brown:

> 66 If I do not make as good yarn as they do in England, I will have nothing for my services, but will throw the whole of what I have attempted over the bridge. 99

Brown replied at once: "If thou canst do what thou sayest, I invite thee to come to Rhode Island."

The first American mill

In 1790, Slater and Brown opened their first mill in Pawtucket, Rhode Island. In the following years, Slater continued to work on improvements. His wife, Hannah Slater, also contributed to the success of the mill. She discovered how to make thread stronger so that it would not snap on the spindles.

The first American factory was a huge success. Before long, other American manufacturers began to build mills using Slater's ideas.

Lowell, Massachusetts: A Model Factory Town

The War of 1812 provided a boost to American industries. The British blockade cut Americans off from their supply of foreign goods. As a result, they had to produce more goods themselves.

Francis Cabot Lowell

During the war, **Francis Cabot Lowell,** a Boston merchant, found a way to improve on British textile mills. In Britain, one factory spun thread while a second factory wove it into cloth. Why not, Lowell wondered, combine spinning and weaving under one roof?

To finance his project, Lowell joined with several partners in 1813 to form the **Boston Associates.** They built a textile factory in Waltham, Massachusetts. The new mill had all the machines needed to turn raw cotton into finished cloth.

After Lowell's death, the Boston Associates took on a more ambitious project. They built an entire factory town and named it after him. In 1821, Lowell, Massachusetts, was a village of five farm families. By 1836, it boasted more than 10,000 people. Visitors to Lowell described it as a model community made up of "small wooden houses, painted white, with green blinds, very neat, very snug, very nicely carpeted."

"Lowell girls"

To work in their new mills, the Boston Associates hired young women from nearby farms. The **"Lowell girls,"** as they came to be called, usually worked for a few years in the mills before returning home to marry. Most sent their wages home to their families. Some saved part of their wages to help set up their own homes.

At Work in the Lowell Mills

The town of Lowell, Massachusetts, became a model for American industry. This label was attached to a bolt of cloth produced at a Lowell mill. As the label shows, much of the machinery in the Lowell factories was operated by women. ★ How does this label express pride in American industry?

◀ *Cloth from a Lowell factory*

At first, parents hesitated to let their daughters work in the mills. To reassure parents, the Boston Associates built boarding houses for their workers. The company also built a church and made rules to protect the young women.

Factory work was often tedious and hard. However, many women valued the economic freedom they got from working in the mills. The *Lowell Offering*, a magazine by and for workers in the Lowell mills, printed a song that began:

❝ Despite of toil we all agree
Out of the mills, or in,
Dependent on others we ne'er will be
So long as we're able to spin. ❞

Impact on Daily Life

In Lowell and elsewhere, mill owners mostly hired women and children. They did this because they could pay women and children half of what they would have had to pay men.

Child labor

Boys and girls as young as seven years of age worked in factories. Small children were especially useful in textile mills because they could squeeze around the large machines to change spindles. "I can see myself now," recalled a woman who had worked in a mill as a child, "carrying in front of me a [spindle] bigger than I was."

Today, most Americans look upon child labor as cruel. Yet in the 1800s, farm children also worked hard from an early age. Most people did not see much difference between children working in a factory or on a farm. Often, a child's wages were needed to help support the family.

Long hours

Working hours in the mills were long—12 hours a day, 6 days a week. True, farmers also put in long hours. However, farmers worked shorter hours in winter. Mill workers, by contrast, worked nearly the same hours all year round.

In the early 1800s, conditions in American mills were generally much better than in most factories in Europe. As industries grew, however, competition increased and employers took less interest in the welfare of their workers. In later chapters, you will read how working conditions grew worse.

Why Study History?

Because Technology Continues to Change Our Lives

★ ★

Historical Background

Inventors like James Hargreaves and Richard Arkwright were not trying to change the world. They just wanted a better way to spin thread. (See page 294.) In the end, though, the Industrial Revolution changed forever how people worked, where they lived, and even how they spent their leisure time. Later inventions, such as the telephone and the automobile, have also transformed the world we live in.

Connections to Today

Not long before you were born, another revolution in technology began: the computer revolution. The earliest computers were not the kind you could have in your bedroom. One early model weighed 30 tons and filled an entire room!

Slowly, computers got smaller and spread out—to schools, businesses, hospitals, arcades, homes. Computers can help keep records, diagnose illnesses, or take people into outer space.

Connections to You

You already know some of the advantages of computers. You can research a report online and revise it on screen. You can enjoy a video game or create your own greeting cards. You can chat with people living in Sweden or Korea or Egypt.

Not every change is positive, though. Sitting at a computer screen for hours may cause severe headaches or hand injuries.

Some critics even fear that computers may lead to isolation. People can work, shop, and even make friends without leaving their homes. You may spend more time chatting with someone halfway around the world than going bowling with friends in your own neighborhood.

1. **Comprehension** (a) Name one result of the Industrial Revolution. (b) Name two results of the computer revolution.
2. **Critical Thinking** Do you think computers will lead to greater or less contact between people? Explain.

★ **Activity** **Making a Concept Web** Make a concept web to show some of the ways that computers affect you. Then, review your web and decide whether each effect is positive, negative, or both.

What point is this cartoon making about the impact of computers?

Changes in home life

The Industrial Revolution had a great impact on home life. On farms or in home workshops, families worked together as a unit. As the factory system spread, more family members left the home to earn a living.

These changes affected ideas about the role of women. In poorer families, women often had to go out to work. In wealthier families, husbands supported the family while women stayed at home. For many husbands, having a wife who stayed at home became a sign of a success.

Interchangeable Parts

Manufacturers benefited from the pioneering work of American inventor **Eli Whitney**. Earlier, skilled workers made goods by hand. For example, a gunsmith spent days making the barrel, stock, and trigger for a single musket. Because the parts were handmade, each musket differed a bit from the next. If a part broke, a gunsmith had to fashion a new part to fit that gun.

Whitney wanted to speed up gunmaking by having machines manufacture each part. Machine-made parts would all be alike—for example, one trigger would be identical to another. **Interchangeable parts** would save time and money.

Because the government bought many guns, Whitney went to Washington, D.C., to demonstrate his method. At first, officials laughed at his plan. Whitney paid them no attention. Carefully, he sorted parts for 10 muskets into separate piles. He then asked an official to choose one part from each pile. In minutes, the first musket was assembled. Whitney repeated the process until 10 muskets were complete.

The idea of interchangeable parts spread rapidly. Inventors designed machines to produce interchangeable parts for clocks, locks, and many other goods. With such machines, small workshops grew into factories.

Growing Cities

Since colonial times, cities played an important role in American life. The vast majority of people lived in rural areas. However, farmers often sent crops to cities for sale or shipment. Cities were also centers of finance and manufacturing.

During the Industrial Revolution, many people left farms to work in factories. Older

Cause and Effect

Causes

- British ideas of a spinning mill and powerloom reach the United States
- War of 1812 prompts Americans to make their own goods
- Eli Whitney introduces the idea of interchangeable parts

The Industrial Revolution in the United States

Effects

- Factory system spreads
- Young women and children from nearby farms work in mills
- Growing cities face problems of fire, sewage, garbage, and disease

Effects Today

- United States becomes leader in industrialized world
- Oil is a highly valued natural resource

Graphic Organizer *Skills*

The Industrial Revolution brought with it many immediate and long-term changes.

1. **Comprehension** What inventions and ideas contributed to the spread of the Industrial Revolution?
2. **Critical Thinking** Do you think the impact of the Industrial Revolution was positive or negative? Give reasons.

Economics $

cities expanded rapidly, while new cities sprang up around factories. This movement of the population from farms to cities is called **urbanization**.

Urbanization was a steady but gradual process. In 1800, only 6 percent of the nation's population lived in urban areas. By 1850, the number had risen to 15 percent. Not until 1920 did more Americans live in cities than on farms.

By today's standards, these early cities were small. A person could walk from one end of any American city to the other in 30 minutes. Buildings were only a few stories tall. As the factory system spread, the nation's cities grew.

Hazards

Growing cities had many problems. Dirt and gravel streets turned into mudholes when it rained. Cities had no sewers, and people threw garbage into the streets. A visitor to New York reported:

66 The streets are filthy, and the stranger is not a little surprised to meet the hogs walking about in them, for the purpose of devouring the vegetables and trash thrown into the gutter. 99

In these dirty, crowded conditions, disease spread easily. Epidemics of yellow fever or cholera (KAHL er uh) raged through cities, killing hundreds.

Fire posed another threat to safety. If a sooty chimney caught fire, the flames quickly spread from one wooden house to the next. Rival volunteer companies often competed to get to a blaze first. Sometimes, they fought each other instead of the fire!

Attractions

Cities had attractions, too. Theaters, museums, and circuses created an air of excitement. In New York City, P. T. Barnum exhibited rare animals at his American Museum.

In rural areas, people depended on door-to-door peddlers for ready-made goods. In cities, people could shop in fine stores that sold the latest fashions from Europe. Some offered modern "ready-to-wear" clothing. One store in New York City advertised that "gentlemen can rely upon being as well fitted from the shelves as if their measures were taken."

Most women continued to sew their own clothes. However, they enjoyed visiting hat shops, china shops, shoe stores, and "fancy-goods" stores.

★ Section 1 Review ★

Recall

1. **Identify** (a) Industrial Revolution, (b) Samuel Slater, (c) Moses Brown, (d) Francis Cabot Lowell, (e) Boston Associates, (f) "Lowell girls," (g) Eli Whitney.
2. **Define** (a) spinning jenny, (b) capitalist, (c) factory system, (d) interchangeable parts, (e) urbanization.

Comprehension

3. Describe three ways the Industrial Revolution changed life.

4. How did industry move from Britain to the United States?
5. What were conditions like in the Lowell mills?

Critical Thinking and Writing

6. **Drawing Conclusions** Why were both inventors and capitalists needed to bring about the Industrial Revolution?
7. **Understanding Causes and Effects** How did the building of factories encourage the growth of cities?

★ ★

Activity Writing a Letter The time is 160 years ago. You are the same age you are now, but instead of being in school, you are working in the Lowell mills. Write a letter home describing how you feel about working in a factory to help support your family.

Moving Westward

As You Read

Explore These Questions
- How did settlers travel westward in the early 1800s?
- What steps did Americans take to improve roads?
- How did steamboats and canals affect transportation?

Define
- turnpike
- corduroy road
- canal

Identify
- Lancaster Turnpike
- National Road
- John Fitch
- Robert Fulton
- *Clermont*
- Henry Shreve
- Erie Canal
- DeWitt Clinton

 SETTING the Scene An Irish visitor to the United States described a stagecoach trip through Maryland:

66 The driver frequently had to call to the passengers in the stage, to lean out of the carriage first at one side, then at the other, to prevent it from oversetting in the deep ruts with which the road abounds: 'Now gentlemen, to the right,' ... 'Now gentlemen, to the left,' and so on. 99

In the 1790s, travel was as difficult as it had been in colonial times. Most roads were mud tracks. River travel could be difficult, too, when boats had to push their way upstream against the current. As the young nation grew westward, Americans saw the need to improve transportation.

To the Mississippi

Settlers had been moving steadily westward since the 1600s. By the early 1800s, "the West" referred to the land between the Appalachians and the Mississippi.

In the early 1800s, the stream of pioneers turned into a flood. By 1820, so many people had moved west that the population in some of the original 13 states had actually declined!

Western routes

Settlers took a number of routes west. One well-traveled path was the Great Wagon Road across Pennsylvania. It dated back to colonial days. Some settlers continued south and west along the trail opened by Daniel Boone before the Revolution. Known as the Wilderness Road, it led through the Cumberland Gap into Kentucky. (See the map on page 303.)

Other settlers pushed west to Pittsburgh. There, they loaded their animals and wagons onto flatboats and journeyed down the Ohio River into Indiana, Kentucky, and Illinois. Flatboats were well suited to the shallow waters of the Ohio. Even when carrying heavy cargoes, these raftlike barges rode high in the water.

Pioneers from Georgia and South Carolina followed other trails west to Alabama and Mississippi. Enslaved African Americans

Many settlers headed west in covered wagons, such as this Conestoga wagon.

Viewing HISTORY **A Need for Better Roads**

This painting, by a visitor from Russia, shows a stagecoach on its run between Philadelphia, Pennsylvania, and Trenton, New Jersey. Passengers traveling on rocky, muddy, unpaved roads could expect to be "crushed, shaken, thrown about...and bumped." ★ **What details in this painting suggest that these passengers were having a rough ride?**

helped to carve plantations in the rich, fertile soil of these territories.

People from New England, New York, and Pennsylvania pushed into the Northwest Territory. Some settlers traveled west from Albany, New York, along the Mohawk River and across the Appalachians. Some settlers then followed Indian trails around Lake Erie. Others sailed across the lake into Ohio.

New states

Before long, some western territories had populations large enough to apply for statehood. Between 1792 and 1819, eight states joined the Union: Kentucky (1792), Tennessee (1796), Ohio (1803), Louisiana (1812), Indiana (1816), Mississippi (1817), Illinois (1818), and Alabama (1819).

Better Roads

Settlers faced a difficult journey. Many roads were narrow trails, barely wide enough for a single wagon. One pioneer wrote of "rotten banks down which horses plunged" and streams that "almost drowned them." Tree stumps stuck up through the road and often broke the axles on the wagons of careless travelers. The nation badly needed better roads.

Turnpikes and bridges

In the United States, as in Europe, private companies built gravel and stone roads. To pay for these roads, the companies collected tolls from travelers. At various points along the road, a pike, or pole, blocked the road. After a wagon driver paid a toll, the pike keeper turned the pole aside to let the wagon pass. As a result, these toll roads were called **turnpikes.**

Probably the best road in the United States was the **Lancaster Turnpike**. Built in the 1790s by a private company, the road linked Philadelphia and Lancaster, Pennsylvania. Because the road was set on a bed of gravel, water drained off quickly. It was topped with smooth, flat stones.

In swampy areas, roads were made of logs. These roads were known as **corduroy roads** because the lines of logs looked like corduroy cloth. Corduroy roads kept wagons from sinking into the mud, but they made for a bumpy ride.

Bridges carried travelers across streams and rivers. Stone bridges were costly to build, but wooden ones rotted quickly. A clever Massachusetts carpenter designed a wooden bridge with a roof to protect it from the weather. Covered bridges lasted much longer than open ones.

The National Road

Some states set aside money to build or improve roads. In 1806, for the first time, Congress approved funds for a national road-building project. The **National Road** was to run from Cumberland, Maryland, to Wheeling, in western Virginia.

Work on the National Road began in 1811 and was completed in 1818. Later, the road was extended into Illinois. As each new section of road was built, settlers eagerly used it to drive their wagons west.

Steam Transport

Whenever possible, travelers and freight haulers used river transportation. Floating downstream on a flatboat was both faster and more comfortable than bumping along rutted roads. It also cost less.

Yet, river travel had its own problems. Moving upstream was difficult. People used paddles or long poles to push boats against the current. Sometimes, they hauled boats from the shore with ropes. Both methods were slow. A boat could travel downstream from Pittsburgh to New Orleans in about six weeks. The return trip upstream took at least 17 weeks!

Fitch and Fulton

A new invention, the steam engine, improved river travel. **John Fitch** improved on steam engines that had been built in Britain.

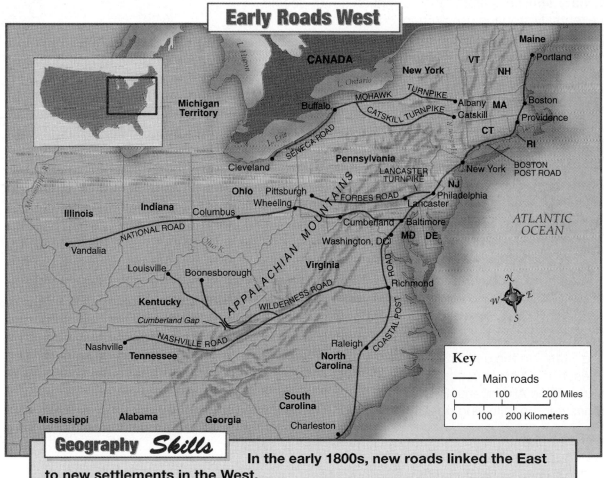

Early Roads West

Geography Skills

In the early 1800s, new roads linked the East to new settlements in the West.

1. **Location** On the map, locate: **(a)** Appalachian Mountains, **(b)** Cumberland Gap, **(c)** Wilderness Road, **(d)** Lancaster Turnpike, **(e)** National Road.

2. **Movement** What major roads would settlers use to travel from Boston, Massachussetts, to Nashville, Tennessee?

3. **Critical Thinking** Based on this map, what effect do you think roadbuilding had on cities like Philadelphia, Baltimore, and Richmond?

Skills
FOR LIFE

| Critical Thinking | Managing Information | Communication | Maps, Charts, and Graphs |

Analyzing a Primary Source

How Will I Use This Skill?

A **primary source** is firsthand information about people and events. Historians use primary sources to learn about the past. You, too, use primary sources—when you watch an interview on television, or listen to two friends tell their sides of something that happened. Learning to analyze primary sources helps you determine the reliability of the information that you get.

LEARN the Skill

❶ Identify the source of the account. Decide if he or she has firsthand knowledge of the event.

❷ Determine which words indicate facts. Are there enough facts to make the speaker reliable?

❸ Recognize how emotions, points of view, and opinions affect the telling of the story.

❹ Judge how reliable the source is.

PRACTICE the Skill

Fanny Kemble, an English actress, visited the United States in the early 1800s. In her journal, she described a stagecoach ride with her father and some Americans. Read the excerpt, then answer the following questions:

❶ Explain why this journal is a primary source.

❷ (a) What facts does Kemble include about stagecoach travel? (b) What facts does she include about American rural life?

❸ What effect do you think Kemble's nationality and her discomfort may have had on her account?

❹ Would you consider this journal a reliable source of information? Explain.

"Bones of me! what a road! Even my father's solid proportions...were jerked up to the roof and down again every three minutes. Our companions... laughed and talked [constantly], the young ladies, at the very top of their voices, and with the national nasal twang....The few cottages and farm-houses which we passed reminded me of similar dwellings in France and Ireland; yet the peasantry here have not the same excuse for disorder and [ruin] as either the Irish or French....The farms had the same desolate, untidy, untended look; the gates broken, the fences carelessly put up."

Excerpt from Journal by Frances Anne Kemble Butler

APPLY the Skill

Watch or read an interview given by an eyewitness to an event. Using the steps above, decide whether you think the interview is a reliable source of information.

The Erie Canal

The opening of the Erie Canal in 1825 launched an age of canal building. Today, at the Erie Canal Village in Rome, New York, you can relive life along the old Erie Canal. Here, passengers ride atop a canal boat, pulled along by a team of mules, just as they did 150 years ago. Riding up top could be risky, though. When the boatmen yelled "Low bridge!" passengers who did not duck could bump their heads.

★ *To learn more about this historic site, write: Erie Canal Village, 5789 New London Road, Rome, NY 13440.*

◀ *Canal boat lantern*

In 1787, he showed members of the Constitutional Convention how a steam engine could power a boat. He then opened a ferry service on the Delaware River. However, few people used the ferry, and Fitch went out of business.

Inventor **Robert Fulton** may have seen Fitch's steamboat in Philadelphia. In 1807, Fulton launched his own steamboat, the *Clermont,* on the Hudson River. On its first run, the *Clermont* carried passengers from New York City to Albany and back. The 300-mile (480-km) trip took just 62 hours—a record at the time.

The age of steamboats

Fulton's success ushered in the age of steamboats. Soon, steamboats were ferrying passengers up and down the Atlantic coast. More important, they revolutionized travel in the West. Besides carrying people, steamboats on the Mississippi, Ohio, and Missouri rivers gave farmers and merchants a cheap means of moving goods.

Because western rivers were shallow, **Henry Shreve** designed a flat-bottomed steamboat. It could carry heavy loads without getting stuck on sandbars.

Still, steamboat travel could be dangerous. Sparks from smokestacks could cause fires. As steamboat captains raced each other along the river, high-pressure boilers sometimes exploded. Between 1811 and 1851, 44 steamboats collided, 166 burned, and more than 200 exploded.

The Canal Boom

Steamboats and improved roads did not help western farmers get their goods directly to markets in the East. To meet this need, Americans dug canals. A **canal** is an artificial channel filled with water that allows boats to cross a stretch of land.

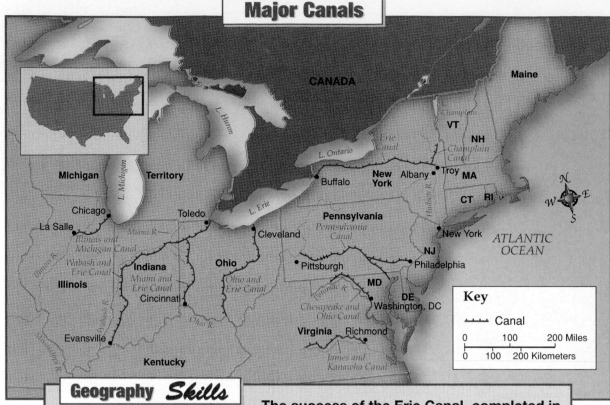

Major Canals

Geography Skills

The success of the Erie Canal, completed in 1825, set off an age of canal building.

1. **Location** On the map, locate: **(a)** New York City, **(b)** Troy, **(c)** Buffalo, **(d)** Lake Erie, **(e)** Erie Canal.
2. **Movement** What two bodies of water were linked by the Illinois and Michigan Canal?
3. **Critical Thinking** Use the map to describe an all-water route from Evansville, Indiana, to New York City.

The earliest American canals were no more than a few miles long. Some provided routes around waterfalls on a river. Other canals linked a river to a nearby lake. By the early 1800s, however, Americans were building longer canals.

Building the Erie Canal

Some New Yorkers had a bold idea. They wanted to build a canal linking the Great Lakes with the Mohawk and Hudson rivers. The **Erie Canal** would let western farmers ship their goods to the port of New York. It would also bring business to towns along the route.

To many people, the idea of such a canal seemed farfetched. When Thomas Jefferson heard of the plan, he exclaimed:

66 Why, sir, you talk of making a canal 350 miles through the wilderness—it is little short of madness to think of it at this day! 99

New York governor **DeWitt Clinton** ignored such criticism. He persuaded state lawmakers to provide money for the Erie Canal. Scoffers referred to the project as "Clinton's Ditch."

Work on the Erie Canal began in 1817. At first, workers dug the waterway by hand. To speed up progress, inventors developed new equipment. One machine, a stump-puller, could pull out nearly 40 tree stumps a day. In two places, workers had to find ways to build stone bridges to carry the canal over other rivers along the way.

An instant success

By 1825, the immense job was finished. On opening day of the Erie Canal, a cannon fired a volley in Buffalo, New York. When the sound got to the next town along the route, it, too, fired a cannon. Town after town fired their cannons—all the way to New York City. The thunderous salute took 80 minutes to complete.

The Erie Canal was an instant success. It reduced travel time. The cost of shipping goods dropped to about 1/20 of what it was before the canal was built. The canal also helped to make New York City a center of commerce.

The success of the Erie Canal led other states to build canals. (See the map on the opposite page.) These canals created vital economic links between western farms and eastern cities.

Transportation Builds Prosperity

In 1831, a young Frenchman, Alexis de Tocqueville (TOHK vihl), made a nine-month tour of the United States. In his writings, Tocqueville described what he admired about the young nation. One of the things that impressed him most was the American transportation system.

"Of all the countries in the world," Tocqueville wrote, "America is that in which the spread of ideas and of human industry is most continual and most rapid." Tocqueville was amazed by "immense canals" and roads built in the middle of the wilderness. He also praised the American postal system:

66 In America one of the first things done in a new state is to make the post go there. In the forests of Michigan there is no cabin so isolated, no valley so wild but that letters and newspapers arrive at least once a week. 99

Tocqueville noted that Americans could easily ship goods from the western frontier to any part of the country. (By contrast, in his native France—a much smaller country—many large towns could not be reached by road at all!) Faster, easier transportation thus contributed to the growing prosperity of the United States.

★ Section 2 Review ★

Recall

1. **Locate** (a) Kentucky, (b) Tennessee, (c) Ohio, (d) Louisiana, (e) Indiana, (f) Mississippi, (g) Illinois, (h) Alabama.
2. **Identify** (a) Lancaster Turnpike, (b) National Road, (c) John Fitch, (d) Robert Fulton, (e) *Clermont,* (f) Henry Shreve, (g) Erie Canal, (h) DeWitt Clinton.
3. **Define** (a) turnpike, (b) corduroy road, (c) canal.

Comprehension

4. What means of transportation did settlers take to the West in the early 1800s?

5. (a) Why did the nation need better transportation in the early 1800s? (b) Describe two ways that travel improved.

Critical Thinking and Writing

6. **Linking Past and Present** Today, airplanes provide a faster means of travel than land transportation. Why do you think roads are still important to the nation?
7. **Identifying Alternatives** Examine the maps in this section. Then, describe two alternate ways a farmer might have shipped a cargo of grain from Cleveland, Ohio, to New York City.

Activity Designing a Monument You have been asked to design a monument honoring the two-hundredth anniversary of the Erie Canal. Draw a rough sketch of the monument, showing what design you would use. You may also include an inscription describing the importance of the canal.

Building National Unity

Explore These Questions

- How did Congress try to strengthen the national economy?
- What were the goals of Henry Clay's American System?
- How did the Supreme Court strengthen national unity?

Define

- dumping
- sectionalism
- interstate commerce

Identify

- James Monroe
- John C. Calhoun
- Daniel Webster
- Henry Clay
- American System
- *McCulloch* v. *Maryland*
- *Gibbon* v. *Ogden*

SETTING the Scene After his visit to the United States, Alexis de Tocqueville described what he saw as the character of the American people. He wrote:

66 The American...is less afraid than any other inhabitant of the globe to risk what he has gained in the hope of a better future.... There is not a country in the world where man more confidently takes charge of the future, or where he feels with more pride that he can fashion the universe to please himself. 99

Tocqueville echoed the confidence Americans felt in themselves. After the War of 1812, the country grew rapidly. New lands opened to settlers with improved transportation. New industries appeared. In Congress, a new generation of political leaders sought to direct this expansion.

An Era of Good Feelings

In 1816, the Republican candidate for President, **James Monroe**, easily defeated the Federalist, Rufus King. Once in office, Monroe spoke of creating a new sense of national unity.

Monroe was the last of three Presidents in a row to come from Virginia. He was also the last Revolutionary War officer to become President.

In 1817, Monroe made a goodwill tour of the country. Not since George Washington had a President made such a tour. In Boston, crowds cheered Monroe. Boston newspapers expressed surprise at this warm welcome for a Republican from Virginia. After all, Boston had been a Federalist stronghold. One newspaper wrote that the United States was entering an "Era of Good Feelings."

By the time Monroe ran for a second term in 1820, no candidate opposed him. The Federalist party had disappeared.

Three Sectional Leaders

While conflict between political parties declined, disputes between different sections of the nation sharpened. In Congress, three ambitious young men took center stage. All three played key roles in Congress for more than 30 years, as well as serving in other offices. Each represented a different section of the country.

Calhoun of the South

John C. Calhoun spoke for the South. He had grown up on a frontier farm in South Carolina. Later, he went to Yale College in Connecticut. Calhoun's immense energy and striking features earned him the nickname "young Hercules." His intense way of speaking sometimes made people uncomfortable in his presence.

Calhoun had supported the War of 1812. Like many southerners, though, he generally opposed policies that would strengthen the power of the federal government.

Webster of the North

Daniel Webster of New Hampshire was perhaps the most skillful public speaker of his time. With eyes flashing and shoulders thrown back, Webster was an impressive sight when he stood up to speak in Congress. An observer described him as a "great cannon loaded to the lips."

Like many New Englanders, Webster had opposed the War of 1812. He even refused to vote for taxes to pay for the war effort. After the war, he wanted the federal government to take a larger role in building the nation's economy.

Clay of the West

Henry Clay spoke for the West. You have already met Clay as a leader of the War Hawks who pushed for war against Britain in 1812.

Clay was born in Virginia. When he was 20, he traveled across the Cumberland Gap into Kentucky. As a young lawyer, he was once fined for brawling with an opponent. Usually, however, he charmed both friends and rivals. Supporters called him "Gallant Harry of the West." Like Webster, Clay strongly favored a more active role for the central government.

A New National Bank

After the War of 1812, leaders like Calhoun, Webster, and Clay had to deal with the nation's economic weakness. The problem was due in part to the lack of a national bank.

The charter for the Bank of the United States ran out in 1811. Without the Bank to lend money and regulate the nation's money supply, the economy suffered. State banks made loans and issued money. Often, they put too much money into circulation. With so much money available to spend, prices rose rapidly.

In the nation's early years, Republicans like Jefferson and Madison had opposed a national bank. By 1816, however, many Republicans believed that a bank was needed. They supported a law to charter the second Bank of the United States. By lending money and restoring order to the nation's money supply, the Bank helped American businesses grow.

Protection From Foreign Competition

Another economic problem facing the nation was foreign competition, especially from

CLAY

Viewing History — Three Sectional Leaders

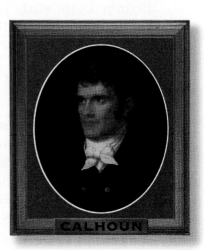

Henry Clay, left, was the first major political leader to emerge from the new states of the West. Along with Daniel Webster and John C. Calhoun, below, Clay played a major role in government for more than 30 years. ★ **What role did sectional politics play in the rise of Webster, Calhoun, and Clay?**

WEBSTER

CALHOUN

Effect of a Protective Tariff

In the United States

American-made cloth sells for $6 per roll

In Britain

British-made cloth sells for $5 per roll

Shipped to the United States

Add 25% tariff of $1.25 per roll

In the United States

British-made cloth sells for $6.25 per roll

Chart *Skills*

In 1816, Congress passed a protective tariff to help American factory owners.

1. **Comprehension** According to this chart, how much would 100 rolls of British cloth cost before the tariff? How much would they cost after the tariff?

2. **Critical Thinking** Why did southerners object to the tariff?

Economics $

Britain. In the early 1800s, the Embargo Act and then the War of 1812 kept most British goods out of the United States. In response, ambitious American business leaders like Francis Cabot Lowell set up their own mills and factories.

A flood of British goods

In 1815, British goods again poured into the United States. The British could make and sell goods more cheaply than Americans. Most British factories and machines were older and had already been paid for. By con-

trast, Americans still had to pay for building their new factories.

Sometimes, British manufacturers sold cloth in the United States for less than it cost to make. The practice of selling goods in another country at very low prices is today called **dumping.** Through dumping, British manufacturers hoped to put American rivals out of business.

Congress passes a protective tariff

Dumping caused dozens of New England businesses to fail. Angry owners asked Congress to place a protective tariff on all goods imported from Europe. As you recall, the purpose of a protective tariff is to protect a country's industries from foreign competition.

Congress responded by passing the Tariff of 1816. It greatly raised tariffs on imports. This increase made imported goods far more expensive than similar American-made goods. In 1818 and 1824, Congress passed even higher tariffs.

Higher tariffs led to angry protests, especially from southerners. Southerners had built few factories. As a result, they did not benefit from the tariff. Also, southerners bought many British goods. The new tariff drove up the price of British-made goods. Southerners complained that the tariff made northern manufacturers rich at the expense of the South.

Clay's American System

The bitter dispute over tariffs reflected the growth of sectionalism. **Sectionalism** is loyalty to one's state or section rather than to the nation as a whole. Americans identified themselves as southerners, northerners, or westerners. In Congress, representatives from different sections often clashed.

Henry Clay wanted to promote economic growth for all sections. He set out a program that became known as the **American System.** It called for high tariffs on imports, which would help northern factories. With wealth from industry, northerners would buy farm products from the West and the South. High tariffs would also reduce American dependence on foreign goods. Clay argued:

66 Every nation should...be able to feed and clothe and defend itself. If it rely upon a foreign supply that may be cut off...it cannot be independent. 99

Clay also urged Congress to use money from tariffs to build roads, bridges, and canals. A better transportation system, he believed, would make it easier and cheaper for farmers in the West and the South to ship goods to city markets.

Clay's American System never went fully into effect. Tariffs did remain high. However, Congress spent little on internal improvements. Southerners in particular disliked Clay's plan. The South had many fine rivers to transport goods. Many southerners opposed paying for roads and canals that brought them no direct benefits.

The Supreme Court Expands Federal Power

Under Chief Justice John Marshall, the Supreme Court strengthened the power of the federal government to promote economic growth. After Congress chartered the second Bank of the United States, Maryland tried to tax the bank in order to drive it out of the state. James McCulloch, the bank cashier, refused to pay the tax.

In the case of **McCulloch v. Maryland** (1819), the Court ruled that states had no right to interfere with federal institutions within their borders. "The power to tax involves the power to destroy," warned Marshall. The ruling strengthened federal power. It also allowed the National Bank to continue, which helped the economy to expand.

In another case, **Gibbon v. Ogden** (1824), the Supreme Court upheld the power of the federal government to regulate commerce. The Court struck down a New York law that tried to control steamboat travel between New York and New Jersey. The Court ruled that a state could only regulate trade within its own borders. Only the federal government had the power to regulate **interstate commerce,** or trade between different states. This decision helped the national economy by making it easier for the government to regulate trade.

★ Section 3 Review ★

Recall

1. **Identify** (a) James Monroe, (b) John C. Calhoun, (c) Daniel Webster, (d) Henry Clay, (e) American System, (f) *McCulloch* v. *Maryland,* (g) *Gibbon* v. *Ogden.*
2. **Define** (a) dumping, (b) sectionalism, (c) interstate commerce.

Comprehension

3. How did Congress try to solve each of the following problems: (a) the money supply, (b) foreign competition?
4. Describe Clay's program to promote economic growth.

5. Describe one way the Supreme Court upheld the authority of the federal government.

Critical Thinking and Writing

6. **Analyzing a Primary Source** In 1816, a member of Congress said, "I will buy where I can get [manufactured goods] cheapest....It is unjust to aggravate the burdens of the people for the purpose of favoring the manufacturers." Do you think this speaker favored or opposed the Tariff of 1816? Explain.
7. **Drawing Conclusions** Based on your reading, do you think sectional differences were a serious threat to national unity? Give examples to support your conclusion.

★ ★

Activity Conducting an Interview You are a political reporter assigned to interview a Congressional leader around 1820. Choose either Clay, Calhoun, or Webster. List three or four questions you would ask about the issues facing the nation.

As You Read

Explore These Questions
- How did Latin American nations win independence?
- How did the United States gain Florida?
- What was the purpose of the Monroe Doctrine?

Define
- creole
- intervention

Identify
- Miguel Hidalgo
- Simón Bolívar
- José de San Martín
- "black Seminoles"
- John Quincy Adams
- Adams-Onís Treaty
- Monroe Doctrine

SETTING the Scene On a quiet Sunday in September 1810, the church bell rang in the Mexican village of Dolores. In the square, people found their priest, **Miguel Hidalgo** (mee GEHL ee DAHL goh), making a stirring speech. No one knows the exact words, but Mexicans remembered and passed along his message:

> ❝ My children.... Will you be free? Will you recover the lands stolen 300 years ago from your forefathers by the hated Spaniards? We must act at once! ❞

Thousands of Mexicans rallied to Father Hidalgo's call for freedom.

South of the United States, Spanish colonies in Latin America* fought wars for independence in the early 1800s. As new nations emerged, President Monroe formed a bold new foreign policy.

Revolution in Latin America

By 1810, many people in Spain's American colonies were eager for independence. They had many reasons for discontent. Most people, even wealthy creoles, had little or no say in government. **Creoles** were people born in Latin America to Spanish parents. Harsh laws ruled Indians and the poor. The

---

*Latin America refers to the region of the Western Hemisphere where Latin-based languages such as Spanish, French, and Portuguese are spoken. It includes Mexico, Central and South America, and the West Indies.

French and American revolutions inspired colonists to seek self-rule.

Mexican independence

As you read, Miguel Hidalgo sounded the call for Mexican independence. Rebel forces won control of several provinces before Father Hidalgo was captured. In 1811, he was executed.

Another priest, José Morelos (hoh ZAY moh RAY lohs), took up the fight. Because he called for a program to give land to peasants, wealthy creoles opposed him. Before long, Morelos, too, was captured and killed by the Spanish.

Slowly, creoles began to support the revolution. In 1821, creole forces won control of Mexico. A few years later, Mexico became a republic with its own constitution.

The Liberator

In South America, too, a series of revolutions freed colonies from Spanish rule. The best-known revolutionary leader was **Simón Bolívar** (see MOHN boh LEE vahr). He became known as the Liberator for his role in the Latin American wars of independence.

Bolívar came from a wealthy creole family in Venezuela. As a young man, he took up the cause of Venezuelan independence. Bolívar promised, "I will never allow my hands to be idle, nor my soul to rest until I have broken the shackles which chain us to Spain."

Bolívar rose to become a leader of the rebel forces. In a bold move, he led an army

Biography   Simón Bolívar

As a young man, Simón Bolívar enjoyed a life of wealth and privilege. He studied the republican form of government of the United States. He also admired the military genius of Napoleon. Later, Bolívar's democratic ideals and military skills helped him free several South American nations from Spanish rule.

★ **Which nations did Bolívar help to liberate?**

Crown given to Bolívar by ➤
South American Indians

from Venezuela over the high Andes Mountains into Colombia. There, Bolívar took the Spanish forces by surprise and defeated them in 1819.

Soon after, Bolívar became president of the independent Republic of Great Colombia. It included the present-day nations of Venezuela, Colombia, Ecuador, and Panama.

Other new nations

Other independent nations emerged in Latin America. **José de San Martín** (san mahr TEEN) led Argentina to freedom in 1816. He then helped the people of Chile, Peru, and Ecuador win independence.

In 1821, the peoples of Central America declared independence from Spain. Two years later, they formed the United Provinces of Central America. It included the present-day nations of Nicaragua, Costa Rica, El Salvador, Honduras, and Guatemala. By 1825, Spain had lost all its colonies in Latin America except Puerto Rico and Cuba.

The Portuguese colony of Brazil won independence peacefully. Prince Pedro, son of the Portuguese king, ruled the colony. The king advised his son, "If Brazil demands independence, proclaim it yourself and put the crown on your own head." In 1822, Pedro became emperor of the new independent nation of Brazil.

The New Republics

Spain's former colonies modeled their constitutions on that of the United States. Yet their experience after independence was very different from that of their neighbor to the north.

Unlike the people of the 13 British colonies, the peoples of Latin America did not unite into a single country. In part, geography made unity difficult. Latin America covered a much larger area than the English colonies. Mountains like the high, rugged Andes acted as a barrier to travel and communication.

The new republics had a hard time setting up stable governments. Under Spanish rule, the colonists had little or no experience in self-government. Economic problems and deep divisions between social classes increased discontent. Powerful leaders took advantage of the turmoil to seize control. As a result, the new nations were often unable to achieve democratic rule.

Connections With Civics

Like the United States, new Latin American nations created national flags. Venezuela's flag of yellow, blue, and red symbolized the gold of the Americas separated from Spain by the blue ocean. Argentina's blue-white-blue flag was the same flag flown by pirates who attacked Spanish ports and ships along the coasts of South and Central America.

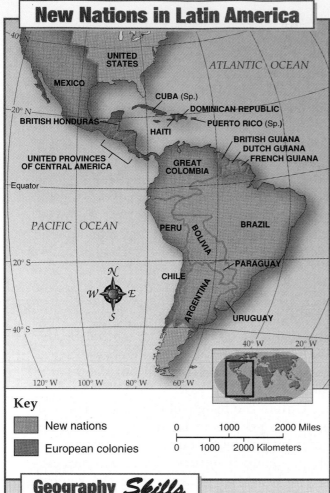

New Nations in Latin America

Key

■ New nations

■ European colonies

0   1000   2000 Miles

0 1000 2000 Kilometers

Geography Skills Wars of independence led to the creation of many new countries in Latin America.

1. **Location** On the map, locate: **(a)** Mexico, **(b)** Great Colombia, **(c)** United Provinces of Central America, **(d)** Brazil, **(e)** Argentina, **(f)** Chile, **(g)** Bolivia.

2. **Region** What parts of Latin America remained European colonies?

3. **Critical Thinking** Use the world map in the Reference Section to identify the modern nations that were eventually carved out of the United Provinces of Central America.

The United States Gains Florida

Spain lost another one of its colonies, Florida—not to independence, but to the United States. Many Americans wanted to gain possession of Florida. As early as 1810, President Madison tried to claim West Florida for the United States.

Concern over Florida grew, especially among Southerners. Creek and Seminole Indians in Florida sometimes raided settlements in Georgia. Also, Florida was a refuge for many enslaved African Americans.

"Black Seminoles"

Since the 1700s, Spanish officials had protected slaves who fled from plantations in Georgia and South Carolina. Seminole Indians allowed African Americans to live near their villages. In return, these **"black Seminoles"** gave the Indians a share of the crops they raised every year. The black Seminoles adopted many Indian customs. In addition, some African Americans married Seminoles.

After the War of 1812, African Americans occupied a fort on the Apalachicola River. They invited runaway slaves to settle nearby. Soon, some 1,000 African Americans farmed on the banks of the Apalachicola, protected by the "Negro Fort."

American gunboats attack

General Andrew Jackson demanded that Spain demolish the Negro Fort. The Spanish governor refused. In 1816, Jackson's gunboats invaded Spanish territory and sailed up the Apalachicola.

Inside the Negro Fort, a force of free African Americans waited, cannons ready. They knew that the Americans had come to return them to slavery. After a spirited fight, the gunboats destroyed the fort. Black settlers along the Apalachicola were forced to flee. Many joined nearby Seminoles. Together, they continued to resist American raids into Florida.

Spain gives up Florida

In 1818, Jackson headed to Florida again with a force of over 3,000 soldiers. Spain protested, but it was busy fighting rebels in Latin America. It could not risk war with the United States.

In the end, Spain agreed to peace talks. Secretary of State **John Quincy Adams** worked out a treaty with Spain. In it, Spain agreed to give Florida to the United States in exchange for $5 million. The **Adams-Onís Treaty** took effect in 1821.

The Monroe Doctrine

Americans cheered as Latin American nations won independence. The actions of European powers, however, worried American officials. Prussia, France, Russia, and Austria seemed ready to help Spain regain its colonies in Latin America. In addition, Russia claimed lands on the Pacific coast of North America.

The British, too, were concerned about European nations meddling in the Western Hemisphere. They suggested issuing a joint statement with the United States. It would guarantee the freedom of the new nations.

Monroe decided to act independently of Britain. In a message to Congress in 1823, he made a bold foreign policy statement, known as the **Monroe Doctrine.** Monroe declared that the United States would not interfere in the affairs of European nations or colonies. At the same time, he warned European nations not to interfere with newly independent nations of Latin America:

66 The American continents ... are henceforth not to be considered as subjects for future colonization by any European powers. . . . We should consider any attempt on their part to extend their system to any portion of this hemisphere as dangerous to our peace and safety. 99

The Monroe Doctrine also stated that the United States would oppose any attempt to build new colonies in the Americas. Monroe's message showed that the United States was determined to keep European powers out of the Western Hemisphere.

The United States did not have the military power to enforce the Monroe Doctrine. Britain, however, supported the statement. With its strong navy, it could stop Europeans from interfering in the Americas.

As the United States became stronger, the Monroe Doctrine grew in importance. On several occasions, the United States successfully challenged European **intervention,** or direct involvement, in Latin America. In the early 1900s, Presidents also used the Monroe Doctrine to justify sending troops to Caribbean nations. Thus, Monroe's bold statement helped shape United States foreign policy for more than 100 years.

★ Section 4 Review ★

Recall

1. **Locate** (a) Mexico, (b) Great Colombia, (c) Argentina, (d) United Provinces of Central America, (e) Brazil.
2. **Identify** (a) Miguel Hidalgo, (b) Simón Bolívar, (c) José de San Martín, (d) "black Seminoles," (e) John Quincy Adams, (f) Adams-Onís Treaty, (g) Monroe Doctrine.
3. **Define** (a) creole, (b) intervention.

Comprehension

4. (a) Why did Latin American nations seek independence in the early 1800s? (b) What problems did the new republics face?

5. Why did many Americans want to gain control of Florida?
6. Why did President Monroe issue the Monroe Doctrine?

Critical Thinking and Writing

7. **Making Inferences** How do you think the defenders of the Negro Fort in Florida might have inspired enslaved African Americans in the United States?
8. **Predicting Consequences** What do you think might have happened if Spain had sent an army to regain control of Mexico in the late 1820s?

Activity **Designing a Poster** Your school is participating in a "Know Your Neighbors" fair. The goal is to promote friendly relations with Latin American nations. Design a poster honoring how one neighboring nation gained independence.

Chapter 11 Review and Activities

★ Sum It Up ★

Section 1   The Industrial Revolution
▶ The Industrial Revolution spread to the United States from Britain in the late 1700s.
▶ Though factory work was hard, many people moved from farms to work in factories in cities and towns.

Section 2   Moving Westward
▶ Westward movement was so heavy that eight new states joined the nation between 1789 and 1819.
▶ Improved roads, steamboats, and canals reduced travel time and lowered the cost of moving goods and people.

Section 3   Building National Unity
▶ As disputes between different sections of the nation grew more intense, great sectional leaders emerged.
▶ Political leaders tried to use their power to make the United States stronger economically.

Section 4   Latin America and the United States
▶ In the early 1800s, almost all of Spain's Latin American colonies won their independence.
▶ The Monroe Doctrine stated that the United States would oppose European efforts to create new colonies in the Western Hemisphere.

CD-ROM Review For additional review of the major ideas of Chapter 11, see *Guide to the Essentials of American History* or *Interactive Student Tutorial CD-ROM,* which contains interactive review activities, graphic organizers, and practice tests.

🔲 Reviewing the Chapter

Define These Terms

Match each term with the correct definition.

Column 1
1. capitalist
2. urbanization
3. turnpike
4. canal
5. dumping

Column 2
a. channel that allows boats to cross a stretch of land
b. person who invests in a business to make a profit
c. practice of selling goods in another country at low prices
d. movement of populations from farms to cities
e. toll road

Explore the Main Ideas

1. Describe the factory system.
2. Why was river travel better than travel by road?
3. Identify the great leader who spoke for each of the three sections of the United States.
4. Why did Congress pass the Tariff of 1816?
5. What two important points did Monroe make in the Monroe Doctrine?

🔲 Geography Activity

Match the letters on the map with the following places:
1. Wheeling, Virginia, **2.** New York City, **3.** Cumberland Gap, **4.** Lancaster Turnpike, **5.** National Road, **6.** Erie Canal.
Interaction What obstacles did Americans overcome in building the Erie Canal?

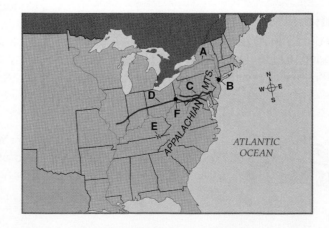

◻ Critical Thinking and Writing

1. **Understanding Chronology** **(a)** Did the War of 1812 begin before or after the formation of the Boston Associates? **(b)** How were these two events linked?

2. **Linking Past and Present** Do cities today have the same kinds of problems as cities in the early 1800s? Explain.

3. **Evaluating Information** What information do you have that suggests that "The Era of Good Feelings" did not last?

4. **Exploring Unit Themes** **Nationalism** Henry Clay has been called the "most nationalistic" of the great congressional leaders. What facts support this opinion?

◻ Using Primary Sources

Davy Crockett was a Tennessee settler who became a representative in Congress. He toured the city of Lowell in 1834 and gave this description:

> 66 The dinner bells were ringing, and the folks pouring out of the [work] houses like bees out of a gum [tree]. I looked at them as they passed, all well dressed, lively, genteel in their appearance.... I went in among the young girls, and talked with many of them. No one expressed herself as tired of her employment, or oppressed with work: all talked well, and looked healthy. 99

Source: *An Account of Col. Crockett's Tour to the North and Down East,* Davy Crockett, 1835.

Recognizing Points of View **(a)** What was the condition of the workers at Lowell, according to Crockett? **(b)** Why do you think a representative from Tennessee would have been interested in conditions at mills in Massachusetts?

ACTIVITY BANK

▶ Interdisciplinary Activity

Exploring the Arts With a partner, create a skit, dance, or song about the difficulties of travel in the early 1800s.

▶ Career Skills Activity

Engineers Draw a diagram or prepare a demonstration to show how early factories harnessed the force of water to create power to run machines.

▶ Citizenship Activity

Understanding Regional Politics Sectional politics is still an issue in the United States. Prepare a report in which you describe the needs of your own region. Consider such questions as: Does your region have special resource or energy needs? How do the needs of your region compare with the needs of other regions? What policies would benefit your region?

Internet Activity
Use the Internet to find sites dealing with the National Road, now called Route 40. Using your Web research, create a tourist map of the road showing the towns it passes through, nearby hotels and restaurants, and historic or interesting information about it.

ⒺYEWITNESS Journal

Take one of the following roles: a young woman working at the Lowell mills; a mayor of a frontier town; a settler living in the New York wilderness near the route of the Erie Canal; a black Seminole in Florida. In your EYEWITNESS JOURNAL, record three events that affected your life between 1800 and 1825.

History Through *Literature*

Rip Van Winkle

by Washington Irving

Introduction

Washington Irving (1783–1859) was the first American to make a living as a popular writer. "Rip Van Winkle" is Irving's best-loved tale. The story is a humorous fantasy about a lazy farmer in a small New York village. One night in the early 1770s, Rip Van Winkle wanders up into the Catskill Mountains, falls asleep—and does not wake up for 20 years! In the selection below, Rip returns to his old village after his long nap.

Vocabulary

Before you read the selection, find the meaning of these words in a dictionary: **yore, assemblage, incomprehensible, metamorphosed, buff, disputatious, tranquillity, haranguing, vehemently.**

*H*e had now entered the skirts of the village. A troop of strange children ran at his heels, hooting after him and pointing at his gray beard. The dogs, too, not one of which he recognized for an old acquaintance, barked at him as he passed. The very village was altered; it was larger and more populous. There were rows of houses which he had never seen before, and those which had been his familiar haunts had disappeared....

He now hurried forth and hastened to his old retreat, the village inn—but it too was gone. A large, rickety, wooden building stood in its place, with great gaping windows, some of them broken and mended with old hats and petticoats, and over the door was painted, "the Union Hotel, by Jonathan Doolittle." Instead of the great tree that used to shelter the quiet little Dutch town of yore, there now was reared a tall, naked pole, with something on the top that looked like a red nightcap,* and from it was fluttering a flag, on which was a singular assemblage of stars and stripes—all this was strange and incomprehensible. He recognized on the sign, however, the ruby face of King George...but even this was singularly metamorphosed. The red coat was changed for one of blue and buff, a sword was held in the hand instead of a scepter, the head was decorated with a cocked hat, and underneath was painted in large characters, GENERAL WASHINGTON.

There was, as usual, a crowd of folk about the door, but none that Rip recollected. The very character of the people seemed changed. There was a busy, bustling, disputatious tone about it, instead of the accustomed...drowsy tranquillity. He looked in vain for the sage Nicholas Vedder, with his broad face, double chin, and fair long pipe...or Van Bummel, the schoolmaster, doling forth the contents of an ancient newspaper. In place of these, a lean... fellow, with his pockets full of handbills, was haranguing vehemently about rights of citizens—elections—members of congress—liberty—Bunker's Hill—heroes of seventy-six—and other words, which were [strange] to the bewildered Van Winkle.

---

*"Liberty poles" and "liberty caps" were popular symbols of both the American and French revolutions.

Painter John Quidor was a personal friend of Washington Irving. His painting, Return of Rip Van Winkle *(detail), shows Rip coming home to his village. Rip's long white beard and tattered clothing show the effects of his 20-year nap.*

★ **Identify two objects in this picture that confused Rip when he returned home. Why were they unfamiliar to him?**

The appearance of Rip, with his long, grizzled beard . . . and an army of women and children at his heels, soon attracted the attention of the tavern politicians. They crowded around him, eyeing him from head to foot with great curiosity. The orator bustled up to him and, drawing him partly aside, inquired "on which side he voted?" Rip stared in vacant stupidity. Another short but busy little fellow pulled him by the arm and, rising on tiptoe, inquired in his ear, "whether he was Federal or Democrat?" Rip was equally at a loss to comprehend the question. . . . "Alas! Gentlemen," cried Rip, somewhat dismayed, "I am a poor, quiet man, a native of this place, and a loyal subject of the king, God bless him!"

Here a general shout burst from the bystanders. "A tory! A tory! A spy! A refugee! Hustle him! Away with him!" It was with great difficulty that [a] self-important man in [a] cocked hat restored order; and . . . demanded again of the unknown culprit what he came there for and whom he was seeking. The poor man humbly assured him that he meant no harm, but merely came there in search of some of his neighbors, who used to keep about the tavern.

"Well—who are they? Name them."

Rip bethought himself a moment, and inquired . . . "Where's Brom Dutcher?"

"Oh, he went off to the army at the beginning of the war; some say he was killed at the storming of Stony Point—others say he was drowned in a squall at the foot of Antony's Nose. I don't know—he never came back again."

"Where's Van Bummel, the schoolmaster?"

"He went off to the wars, too, was a great militia general, and is now in congress."

Rip's heart died away at hearing of these sad changes in his home and friends, and finding himself thus alone in the world. Every answer puzzled him, too, by treating of such enormous lapses of time and of matter which he could not understand: war—congress—Stony Point. He had no courage to ask after any more friends, but cried out in despair, "Does nobody here know Rip Van Winkle?"

Analyzing Literature

1. Describe three changes Rip Van Winkle sees when he returns to his village.

2. Why does Rip get into trouble with the men gathered outside the tavern?

3. **Critical Thinking Making Inferences** According to the story, the very nature of the people seemed different to Rip. **(a)** How does Rip think the people changed? **(b)** What do you think may have caused this change?

Unit 4

The Nation Expands

Viewing UNIT THEMES

Wagon Trains to the West

William Henry Jackson, who later became a famous photographer, painted this dramatic scene. It shows long lines of wagons carrying settlers westward across Nebraska toward Oregon. In the mid-1800s, wagon trains like this carried thousands of American families from the East to newly acquired territories in the West. ★ **Based on this painting, jot down four words or phrases that you would use to describe a journey to the West by wagon train.**

Unit Theme Expansion

From 1820 to 1860, the United States grew in several ways. The most dramatic growth was in the size of the nation. It gained vast western territories, including California, Texas, Oregon, and New Mexico. For the first time, an American could travel by land from the Atlantic Ocean to the Pacific without leaving the country.

How did people of the time feel about westward expansion? They can tell you in their own words.

★ ★

VIEWPOINTS ON WESTWARD EXPANSION

66 Our population is rolling toward the shores of the Pacific.... It will soon...reach the Rocky Mountains and be ready to pour into the Oregon territory. 99
John C. Calhoun, South Carolina senator (1843)

66 We traveled till 11 o'clock with the hope of finding water for the weary cattle. The sun was excessively oppressive. 99
Susan Shelby Magoffin, New Mexico pioneer (1846)

66 The white man comes and cuts down the trees, building houses and fences and the buffaloes get frightened and leave and never come back, and the Indians are left to starve. 99
Muguara, Chief of the Penateka Comanche Indians (1840s)

★ ★

Activity Writing to Learn Thousands of families left their homes in the East to make the long journey westward. What if your family was thinking of moving to another part of the country? List what you might gain by moving. Then, make another list of what you might lose. Use your lists to decide whether you want to move.

Chapter 12

Democracy in the Age of Jackson   1824–1840

In this chapter, you will learn that the Age of Jackson was a time of expanding democracy and political conflict. As more and more white males gained the right to vote, two political parties, the Whigs and Democrats, competed for their support. Nominating conventions and heated election campaigns became part of American politics. Not all, however, shared in democracy's growth. Women, Native Americans, African Americans, and others had to wait for political and social equality.

Why Study History?

Soon, you will have a right and a responsibility of all American citizens—voting. Learning more about how politics worked in past elections may help you make wise voting decisions in the future. To learn more about politics and your right to vote, see this chapter's *Why Study History?* feature, "You Will Choose Our Nation's Leaders."

American Events	**●1820s** Right to vote extended to most white men
	●1828 Andrew Jackson is elected President
	●1830 Indian Removal Act forces Native Americans to move west of the Mississippi

1824	1826	1828	1830	1832

World Events

 1824 World Event
Simón Bolívar becomes president of Peru

 1829 World Event
Swiss adopt universal male suffrage

Viewing HISTORY — Election Day

The Age of Jackson was a time of expanding democracy. During the 1820s and 1830s, more and more Americans gained the right to vote. In his painting County Election, *George Caleb Bingham shows that Election Day was a time for voting, socializing, and celebrating.* ★ **How does this painting suggest that women were not allowed to participate fully in American democracy?**

1832
President Jackson vetoes charter of the Bank of the United States

1835
Seminole War begins

1840
William Henry Harrison is elected President

1832 — 1834 — 1836 — 1838 — 1840

 1832 World Event
Reform Act doubles number of eligible voters in Britain

 1837 World Event
Canadian colonists revolt, demanding democratic reform

★ 323

A New Era in Politics

As You Read

Explore These Questions
- Why was John Quincy Adams an unpopular President?
- How did voting rights change in the 1820s and 1830s?
- How did political parties become more democratic?

Define
- majority
- suffrage
- caucus
- nominating convention

Identify
- John Quincy Adams
- Whigs
- Democrats
- Alexis de Tocqueville

 SETTING the Scene Harry Ward, a New England teacher, made a visit to Cincinnati, Ohio, during the 1824 presidential election campaign. Writing to a friend, he described how Ohioans felt about Andrew Jackson, who was running for President. "Strange! Wild! Infatuated! All for Jackson!" he observed.

On election day, more people voted for Andrew Jackson than for any of the other candidates. Oddly enough, Jackson did not become President that year.

The Disputed Election of 1824

There were four candidates for President in 1824. All four were members of the old Republican party. However, each had support in different parts of the country. **John Quincy Adams** was strong in New England. Henry Clay and Andrew Jackson had support in the West. William Crawford was favored in the South but became too ill to campaign.

The candidates

John Quincy Adams of Massachusetts was the son of Abigail and John Adams, the second President. The younger Adams was a graduate of Harvard University. He had served as Secretary of State and had helped end the War of 1812. People admired Adams for his intelligence and high morals. Adams, however, was uncomfortable campaigning among the common people.

Henry Clay, by contrast, was charming. A Kentuckian, Clay was a shrewd politician who had become Speaker of the House of Representatives. In Congress, Clay was a skillful negotiator. He worked out several important compromises. Despite his abilities, Clay was less popular than the other candidate from the West, Andrew Jackson.

Most Americans knew Andrew Jackson for his military victories in the War of 1812. He was the "Hero of New Orleans." Though he was a landowner and a slave owner, many saw him as a man of the people. Jackson was born in a log cabin and his parents were poor farmers. He was admired by small farmers and others who felt left out of the growing economy in the United States.

The "corrupt bargain"

No clear winner emerged from the election of 1824. Jackson won the popular vote, but no candidate won a **majority,** or more than half, of the electoral votes. As a result, the House of Representatives had to choose the President from among the top three candidates. Because he finished fourth, Clay was out of the running. As Speaker of the House, though, he was able to influence the results.

Clay urged members of the House to vote for Adams. After Adams became President, he made Clay his Secretary of State. Jackson and his backers were furious. They accused Adams and Clay of making a "corrupt bargain" and stealing the election from Jackson. As Jackson was riding home to Tennessee, he met an old friend. "Well, General," said the friend, "we did all we could for you here, but the rascals at Washington cheated you out of it."

"Indeed, my old friend," replied Jackson, "there was *cheating* and *corruption,* and *bribery,* too." In fact, such charges were not true. The election had been decided as the Constitution stated. Still, the anger of Jackson and his supporters seriously hampered President Adams's efforts to unify the nation.

An Unpopular President

Adams knew that the election had angered many Americans. To "bring the whole people together," he pushed for a program of economic growth through internal improvements. His plan backfired, however, and opposition to him grew.

Promoting economic growth

Similar to Alexander Hamilton and Henry Clay, Adams thought that the federal government should promote economic growth. He called for the government to pay for new roads and canals. These internal improvements would help farmers to transport goods to market.

Adams also favored projects to promote the arts and the sciences, as governments in Europe did. He suggested building a national university and an observatory from which astronomers could study the stars.

Most Americans objected to spending money on such programs. They feared that the federal government would become too powerful. Congress approved money for a national road and some canals, but turned down most of Adams's other programs.

A bitter campaign

In 1828, Adams faced an uphill battle for reelection. This time, Andrew Jackson was Adams's only opponent.

The campaign was a bitter contest. Jackson supporters renewed charges that Adams had made a "corrupt bargain" after the 1824 election. They attacked Adams as an aristocrat, or member of the upper class. Adams

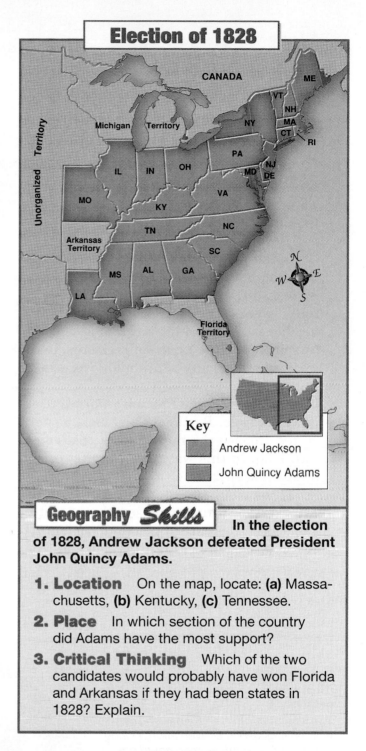

Election of 1828

Key
Andrew Jackson
John Quincy Adams

Geography *Skills* In the election of 1828, Andrew Jackson defeated President John Quincy Adams.

1. **Location** On the map, locate: **(a)** Massachusetts, **(b)** Kentucky, **(c)** Tennessee.
2. **Place** In which section of the country did Adams have the most support?
3. **Critical Thinking** Which of the two candidates would probably have won Florida and Arkansas if they had been states in 1828? Explain.

supporters replied with similar attacks. They called Jackson a dangerous "military chieftain." If Jackson became President, they warned, he could become a dictator like Napoleon Bonaparte of France.

Jackson won the election easily. His supporters cheered the outcome as a victory for common people. By common people, they meant farmers in the West and South and city workers in the East.

More Voters

During the 1820s, more people gained **suffrage,** or the right to vote. Others, however, were denied full participation in the growing democracy.

Expanding suffrage

The United States was growing rapidly. New states were joining the Union and there were many new voters. Many of them lived in western states between the Appalachians and the Mississippi.

In the West, many frontier people began life poor, but prospered through hard work. As a result, westerners commonly believed that it was possible to achieve success by being honest and working hard. This democratic spirit was reflected in suffrage laws. In the western states, any white man over age 21 could vote.

Reformers in the East also worked to expand suffrage. By the 1830s, most eastern states dropped the requirement that voters own land. In this way, many craftsworkers and shopkeepers won the right to vote.

Throughout the country, growing numbers of Americans exercised their right to vote. Before 1828, the turnout of eligible voters was never more than 27 percent. That low percentage rose to nearly 58 percent in the election of 1828. By 1840, voter turnout was nearly 80 percent.

Limits on suffrage

Despite the growing democratic spirit, many Americans did not have the right to vote. They included women, Native Americans, and most African Americans. Slaves had no political rights.

In fact, as more white men were winning suffrage, free African Americans were losing it. In the early years of the nation, most northern states had allowed free African American men to vote. In the 1820s, many of these states took away that right. By 1830, only a few New England states permitted African American men to vote on equal terms with white men. In New York, African American men had to own property in order to vote. White men did not.

New Political Practices

By 1820, the disappearance of the Federalist party temporarily ended party differences. In the 1830s, new political parties took shape. They grew out of the conflict between John Quincy Adams and Andrew Jackson.

Two new parties

People who supported Adams and his programs for national growth called themselves National Republicans. In 1834, they became known as **Whigs.** Whigs wanted the federal government to spur the economy. Whigs included eastern business people, some south-

Viewing HISTORY — **Limits on Suffrage**

The watercolor painting Two Women *by Eunice Pinney shows two women engaged in conversation. During the Age of Jackson, women could not vote in a single state. Most men of the time thought that women should take care of household responsibilities.*
★ **How do you think women were able to influence the outcome of elections?**

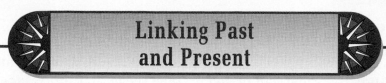

Past

Present

The People and the Presidency

In 1829, President Jackson held a party at the White House to celebrate his inauguration. Cheerful guests helped themselves to slices of a huge cheese. Today, Presidents invite Americans into their home for tours or special events. One example is the Easter egg roll, held each year on the White House lawn. ★ **Why did some people criticize Jackson for opening the White House to the common people?**

ern planters, and former Federalists. Jackson and his supporters called themselves **Democrats.** Today's Democratic party traces its roots to Andrew Jackson's time. Democrats included frontier farmers, as well as factory workers in the East.

New ways to choose candidates

The two new political parties developed more democratic ways to choose candidates for President. In the past, powerful members of each party held a **caucus,** or private meeting. There, they chose their candidate. Critics called the caucus system undemocratic because only a few powerful people were able to take part in it.

In the 1830s, each party began to hold a **nominating convention,** where delegates from all the states chose the party's candidate for President. Nominating conventions gave people a more direct voice in choosing future leaders. Party leaders might still dom-

inate a particular convention, but the nominating process was becoming subject to the will of the people. Today, the major political parties still hold conventions.

Growing Spirit of Equality

The spirit of democracy affected American ideas about social classes. Most Americans did not feel that the rich deserved special respect. "Does a man become wiser, stronger or more virtuous and patriotic because he has a fine house?" asked a Democrat.

Wealthy European visitors to the United States were surprised that American servants expected to be treated as equals. Others were amazed that butlers and maids refused to be summoned with bells, as in Europe. **Alexis de Tocqueville** (tohk VEEL), a visitor from France, became especially well known for his observations on American democracy.

Alexis de Tocqueville

In 1831, Alexis de Tocqueville arrived in the United States. The French government had sent him to study the American prison system. Over a period of several months, Tocqueville toured much of the United States. He observed much more than prisons. He observed a society that was becoming more and more democratic.

After his return to France, Tocqueville recorded his experiences and observations in a book titled *Democracy in America*. In it, he admired the American democratic spirit and its goals of equality and freedom.

66 Although the revolution that is taking place in the social condition, laws, ideas, and feelings of men is still far from coming to an end, yet its results are already incomparably greater than anything which has taken place in the world before. 99

Jacksonian democracy

Andrew Jackson's inauguration in 1829 reflected the spirit of Jacksonian democracy. As Jackson traveled to Washington, large crowds cheered him along the way. For the first time, thousands of ordinary people flooded the capital to watch the President take the oath of office.

After Jackson was sworn in, the crowd followed the new President to a reception at the White House. The appearance and behavior of the "common people" shocked an onlooker:

66 A rabble, a mob, of boys, negros, women, children, scrambling, fighting, romping. What a pity, what a pity! No arrangements had been made, no police officers on duty, and the whole house had been [filled] by the rabble mob. 99

The President, he continued, was "almost suffocated and torn to pieces by the people in their eagerness to shake hands."

Jackson's critics said the scene showed that "King Mob" was ruling the nation. Amos Kendall, a loyal Jackson supporter, viewed the inauguration celebration in a more positive way: "It was a proud day for the people. General Jackson is *their own* President."

★ Section 1 Review ★

Recall

1. **Locate** (a) Massachusetts, (b) Kentucky, (c) Tennessee.
2. **Identify** (a) John Quincy Adams, (b) Whigs, (c) Democrats, (d) Alexis de Tocqueville.
3. **Define** (a) majority, (b) suffrage, (c) caucus, (d) nominating convention.

Comprehension

4. Why did voters not reelect John Quincy Adams to the Presidency in 1828?
5. (a) How did suffrage expand in the 1820s and 1830s? (b) What Americans were denied suffrage?

6. How were nominating conventions more democratic than the caucus system?

Critical Thinking and Writing

7. **Applying Information** Based on what you learned about the election of 1824, if no candidate won a majority of electoral votes in the next presidential election, how would the President be chosen?
8. **Defending a Position** Do you agree or disagree with John Quincy Adams's position that the government should spend money to support the arts and sciences? Explain the reasons for your position.

★ ★

Activity Writing an Advertisement Suffrage has expanded greatly since the Age of Jackson. Still, many Americans do not exercise their right to vote. Write a radio or television advertisement urging people to get out and vote next Election Day.

Jackson in the White House

As You Read

Explore These Questions
- What qualities helped Jackson succeed?
- Why did Jackson replace many office-holders?
- Why did Jackson fight against the Bank of the United States?

Define
- spoils system
- pet bank

Identify
- Old Hickory
- kitchen cabinet
- Nicholas Biddle

SETTING the Scene During the 1828 election campaign, many stories about Andrew Jackson spread. Like the one that follows, they often showed Jackson's courage and determination.

Years before he ran for President, Jackson was a judge in Tennessee. One day, a disorderly lawbreaker, Russell Bean, refused to appear before the court. The story tells how Jackson strutted out of the courthouse. "Surrender, you infernal villain," he roared, "or I'll blow you through." Bean looked into Jackson's blazing eyes and quietly surrendered. The iron will that made Russell Bean surrender also made Jackson a powerful President.

Andrew Jackson

Like many who admired him, Jackson was born in a log cabin on the frontier. His parents had left Ireland to settle on the Carolina frontier. Both died before Jackson was 15. Young Andrew had to grow up quickly.

A tough fighter

Like many other boys who grew up on the frontier, young Andrew Jackson was a determined fighter. Even though he had a slight

A young Andrew Jackson

build, he was strong and determined. A friend who wrestled with him recalled, "I could throw him three times out of four, but he would never stay throwed."

Jackson showed his toughness during the American Revolution. At age 13, he joined the Patriots but was captured by the British. When a British officer ordered the young prisoner to clean his boots, Jackson refused. The officer took a sword and slashed the boy's hand and face. The memory of that attack stayed with Jackson for the rest of his life.

A self-made man

After the Revolution, Jackson studied law in North Carolina. Later, he moved to Tennessee and set up a successful law practice. He became very wealthy by buying and selling land in Georgia and Alabama. While still in his twenties, he was elected to Congress.

Jackson won national fame for his achievements during the War of 1812. He commanded the American forces to a major victory over the British at the Battle of New Orleans. He also defeated the Creek Indians and forced them to give up vast amounts of land in Georgia and Alabama.

A man of many qualities

Andrew Jackson was a man of many qualities. He had led a violent and adventurous life. He was no stranger to brawls, gambling, and duels. He was quick to lose his temper and he dealt with his enemies harshly.

Jackson's supporters admired his ability to inspire and lead others. They considered him a man of his word and a champion of the common people. The soldiers who served under Jackson called him **Old Hickory.** To them, he was as tough as the wood of a hickory tree.

To the Creek Indians, however, Jackson was an enemy who showed no mercy. After defeating them, Jackson had threatened to kill their leaders if they did not give up lands that earlier treaties had guaranteed them. As a result, the Creeks had no affection for Jackson. Their name for him was Sharp Knife.

The Spoils System

In 1828, President Jackson knew that Americans wanted change. "The people expected reform," he said. "This was the cry from Maine to Louisiana."

Reward for victory

After taking office, Jackson fired many government employees. He replaced them with his own supporters. Most other Presidents had done the same, but Jackson did it on a larger scale.

Critics accused Jackson of rewarding Democrats who had helped elect him instead of choosing qualified men. Jackson replied that he was serving democracy by letting more citizens take part in government. He felt that ordinary Americans could fill government jobs. "The duties of all public officers are ...so plain and simple that men of intelligence may readily qualify themselves for their performance," he said.

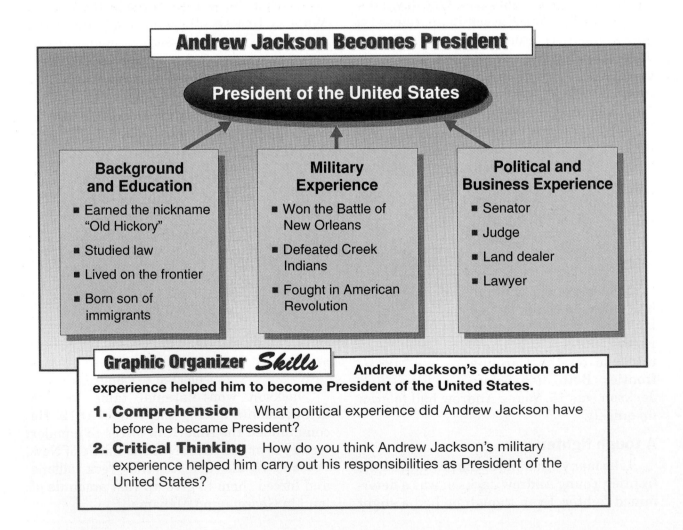

Andrew Jackson Becomes President

President of the United States

Background and Education
- Earned the nickname "Old Hickory"
- Studied law
- Lived on the frontier
- Born son of immigrants

Military Experience
- Won the Battle of New Orleans
- Defeated Creek Indians
- Fought in American Revolution

Political and Business Experience
- Senator
- Judge
- Land dealer
- Lawyer

Graphic Organizer *Skills*   Andrew Jackson's education and experience helped him to become President of the United States.

1. **Comprehension**   What political experience did Andrew Jackson have before he became President?
2. **Critical Thinking**   How do you think Andrew Jackson's military experience helped him carry out his responsibilities as President of the United States?

Viewing HISTORY **A Kitchen Cabinet Dispute**

President Jackson often asked for advice from an unofficial group of advisers. This cartoon presents one artist's view of Jackson's "kitchen cabinet." ★ **What was the cartoonist's opinion of the kitchen cabinet? Explain.**

A Jackson supporter explained the system another way. "To the victor belong the spoils," he declared. Spoils are profits or benefits. From then on, the practice of rewarding supporters with government jobs became known as the **spoils system.**

The kitchen cabinet

Jackson rewarded a number of his supporters with Cabinet jobs. Only Secretary of State Martin Van Buren was truly qualified for his position.

As a result, Jackson seldom met with his official Cabinet. Instead, he relied on a group of unofficial advisers. They included Democratic leaders and newspaper editors. These men had a good sense of the nation's mood. Because Jackson met with them in the White House kitchen, the group became known as the **kitchen cabinet.**

The Bank War

President Jackson waged war on the Bank of the United States. Like many westerners, he thought that it was too powerful.

Mr. Biddle's bank

From the first, the Bank of the United States had been a subject of dispute. (See page 247.) The Bank had great power because it controlled loans made by state banks. When the Bank's directors thought that state banks were making too many loans, they limited the amount these banks could lend. The cutbacks angered farmers and merchants who borrowed money to buy land or finance new businesses.

President Jackson and other leading Democrats saw the Bank as undemocratic. Although Congress had created the Bank, it was run by private bankers. Jackson condemned these men as agents of "special privilege" who grew rich with public funds. He especially disliked **Nicholas Biddle,** president of the Bank since 1823.

Biddle came from a wealthy Philadelphia family. He was well qualified to run the bank, but he was also arrogant and vain. Jackson felt that Biddle used the Bank to benefit only the rich. He also resented Biddle's influence over certain members of Congress.

$ Connections With Economics

Today, the Federal Reserve Board supervises a national system of banks and has much influence over the economy. It can tighten the money supply and reduce inflation by raising interest rates. By lowering interest rates on loans, it can encourage economic growth.

The war begins

Biddle and other Whigs worried that the President might try to destroy the Bank. Two Whig senators, Henry Clay and Daniel Webster, thought of a way to save the Bank and defeat Jackson at the same time.

The Bank's charter was not due for renewal by Congress until 1836. However, Clay and Webster wanted to make the Bank an issue in the 1832 election. They persuaded Biddle to apply for renewal early.

The Whigs believed that most Americans supported the Bank of the United States. If Jackson vetoed the bill to renew the charter, they felt sure that he would anger voters and lose the election. Clay pushed the charter renewal bill through Congress in 1832. Jackson was sick in bed when he heard that Congress had renewed the Bank's charter. "The Bank . . . is trying to kill me," Jackson fumed, "but I will kill it!"

Jackson's veto

In an angry message to Congress, Jackson vetoed the Bank bill. He gave two reasons for his veto. First, he declared the Bank unconstitutional, even though the Supreme Court had ruled in the Bank's favor. Jackson believed that only states, not the federal government, had the right to charter banks. Second, Jackson felt that the Bank helped aristocrats at the expense of the common people. He warned:

66 When the laws undertake . . . to make the rich richer and the potent more powerful, the humble members of society—the farmers, mechanics, and laborers— . . . have a right to complain of the injustice of their government. 99

As planned, the Whigs made the Bank a major issue in the election of 1832. They chose Henry Clay as their candidate to run against Andrew Jackson. When the votes were counted, Jackson won a stunning election victory. The common people had supported Jackson and rejected the Bank of the United States.

The Bank closes

Without a new charter, the Bank would have to close in 1836. Jackson refused to wait. He ordered Secretary of the Treasury Roger Taney to stop putting government money in the Bank. Instead, Taney deposited federal money in state banks. They became known as **pet banks** because Taney and his friends controlled many of them.

The loss of federal money crippled the Bank of the United States. Its closing in 1836 contributed to an economic crisis.

★ Section 2 Review ★

Recall

1. **Identify** (a) Old Hickory, (b) kitchen cabinet, (c) Nicholas Biddle.
2. **Define** (a) spoils system, (b) pet bank.

Comprehension

3. How did Andrew Jackson's education and experience help prepare him for the Presidency of the United States?
4. Why did critics object to the spoils system?

5. Why did many farmers and merchants dislike the Bank of the United States?

Critical Thinking and Writing

6. **Understanding Causes and Effects** How did the spoils system lead to the creation of the kitchen cabinet?
7. **Analyzing Information** What do you think the Creeks were saying about Jackson when they called him Sharp Knife?

★ ★

Activity Writing a Script Write the script for a television drama in which Andrew Jackson and Nicholas Biddle discuss the Bank of the United States and pet banks.

3 ★ Struggles Over States' Rights

Explore These Questions

- How did John C. Calhoun and Daniel Webster disagree on states' rights?
- How did Jackson deal with the Nullification Crisis?
- Why did Native Americans of the Southeast have to leave their lands?

Define

- nullification
- states' rights
- secede

Identify

- Tariff of Abominations
- Nullification Crisis
- Sequoyah
- Indian Removal Act
- Trail of Tears
- Osceola
- Seminole War

SETTING the Scene As President, Andrew Jackson had to deal with a tariff crisis that threatened to split the nation. He also played a major role in deciding the future of many Native Americans. At the heart of both cases was a question that challenged the nation. Did states or the federal government have greater authority?

A Crisis Over Tariffs

In 1828, Congress passed the highest tariff in the nation's history. Southerners called it the **Tariff of Abominations.** An abomination is something that is hated.

Just like earlier tariffs, the new law protected manufacturers from foreign competition. Most manufacturers lived in the North. Southern planters, however, were hurt by the tariff. They sold their cotton in Europe and bought European goods in return. The high tariff meant that southerners had to pay more for these imports.

Calhoun vs. Webster

A leader in the South's fight against the tariff was Vice President John C. Calhoun. He used an argument that Thomas Jefferson had made in the Kentucky and Virginia resolutions. (See page 260.) Like Jefferson, Calhoun claimed that a state

A tariff collector used this stencil to mark goods.

had the right to nullify, or cancel, a federal law that it considered to be unconstitutional. This idea is called **nullification.**

Calhoun supported **states' rights,** the right of states to limit the power of the federal government. He argued that the states had final authority because the states had created the national government.

Daniel Webster disagreed. In 1830, he made a speech in the Senate attacking the idea of nullification. The Constitution, he said, united the American people, not just the states. If states had the right to nullify federal laws, the nation would fall apart. Webster ended his speech with stirring words: "Liberty and Union, now and forever, one and inseparable."

Calhoun resigns

Southerners and westerners strongly supported states' rights. They expected Jackson, who had been born in the South and lived in the West, to support their view.

The President's position soon became clear. Jackson and Calhoun attended a political dinner in 1830. Several guests made toasts in favor of states' rights. Finally, Jackson rose. The room fell silent. Old Hickory

Skills FOR LIFE

| Critical Thinking | Managing Information | Communication | Maps, Charts, and Graphs |

Reaching a Compromise

How Will I Use This Skill?

When individuals or groups disagree, they can solve the problem and avoid conflict by reaching a compromise. In a compromise, the opposing sides give up some of their demands in order to forge an agreement that both can accept. Knowing how to reach a compromise will help you settle disagreements, solve problems, and get along with others.

LEARN the Skill

You can reach a compromise by following these four steps:

❶ Understand the positions of the opposing sides.

❷ Recognize the probable effects of not reaching compromise.

❸ Determine what each side might give up or concede in order to reach an agreement.

❹ Negotiate a deal by discussing the conflicting issues and offering possible concessions. Compromise is reached when an agreement is acceptable to both sides.

PRACTICE the Skill

Using the steps above, review the compromise concerning the Tariff of Abominations and the Nullification Crisis in this section.

❶ Explain the positions of northern manufacturers and southern planters on the two issues.

❷ What did each side threaten to do if a compromise was not reached?

A compromise is often sealed by a handshake.

❸ What did each side give up in order to reach an agreement?

❹ With a partner, reenact a negotiation as it might have occurred between representatives of the North and South.

APPLY the Skill

Working with a partner, role-play a dispute that might occur today between an employer and an employee. Identify various issues that they might disagree on. Then, apply what you have learned in order to reach a compromise.

raised his glass, looked straight at the Vice President, and proclaimed, "Our Federal Union—it must be preserved!"

The drama continued. Calhoun raised his glass and answered the President's challenge: "The Union—next to our liberty, most dear." To him, the liberty of a state was more important than the Union.

Because Calhoun strongly disagreed with Jackson, he resigned from the office of Vice President. He was then elected senator from South Carolina. The debate over states' rights would rage for years.

The Nullification Crisis

Anger against the tariff increased in the South. In 1832, Congress passed a new tariff that lowered the rate slightly. South Carolina was not satisfied. It passed the Nullification Act, declaring the new tariff illegal. It also threatened to **secede,** or withdraw, from the Union if challenged.

Jackson was furious. He knew that nullification could lead to civil war. In private, he raged:

66 If one drop of blood be shed there in defiance of the laws of the United States, I will hang the first man of them I can get my hands on to the first tree I can find. 99

Publicly the President supported a lower compromise tariff proposed by Henry Clay. Jackson also asked Congress to pass the Force Bill. It allowed him to use the army, if necessary, to enforce the tariff.

Faced with Jackson's firm stand, no other state chose to support South Carolina. Calhoun supported the compromise tariff that Clay had proposed. South Carolina repealed the Nullification Act and the **Nullification Crisis** passed. However, sectional tensions between the North and South would increase in the years ahead.

Tragedy for Native Americans

Jackson took a firm stand on another key issue. It affected the fate of Native Americans. Since the early colonial era, white settlers had forced Native Americans off their

Biography Sequoyah

Sequoyah adapted Greek, Hebrew, and English letters to create the 86 symbols of his Cherokee alphabet. The Cherokees used Sequoyah's alphabet to write a constitution. ★ **Why would the lack of a written language be a disadvantage to a society?**

land. Indian leaders like Pontiac and Tecumseh had failed to stop the invasion of white settlers.

Indian nations in the Southeast

The Creek, Choctaw, Chickasaw, Cherokee, and Seminole nations lived in the Southeast. Many hoped to live in peace with their white neighbors. Their fertile land, however, was ideal for growing cotton. Settlers wanted the land for themselves.

Like earlier Presidents, Jackson sided with the white settlers. At his urging, the government set aside lands beyond the Mississippi River and then persuaded or forced Indians to move there. Jackson believed that this policy would provide land for white settlers as well as protect Native Americans from destruction.

Few Indians wanted to move. Some, like the Cherokee nation, had adopted customs of

Removal of Native Americans, 1820–1840

Key
- Indian homelands
- Indian Territory
- ◄•••• Cherokee Trail of Tears
- ◄— Other Indian removals
- — Boundaries in 1838

0   150   300 Miles
0   150   300 Kilometers

Geography Skills   In the 1830s, the United States government forced thousands of Native Americans to leave their homelands and to resettle in western lands.

1. **Location**   On the map, locate: **(a)** Georgia, **(b)** Cherokee homeland, **(c)** Indian Territory, **(d)** Seminole homeland.

2. **Movement**   What five southeastern nations moved to Indian Territory?

3. **Critical Thinking**   Why were many Americans willing to give Native Americans lands west of the Mississippi?

white settlers. The Cherokees lived in farming villages. They had a constitution that set up a republican form of government.

In 1821, **Sequoyah** (sih KWOI uh) created a written alphabet for his people. Using Sequoyah's letters, Cherokee children learned to read and write. The Cherokees also published a newspaper.

A legal battle

In 1828, Georgia claimed the right to make laws for the Cherokee nation. The Cherokees went to court to defend their rights. They pointed to treaties with the federal government that protected their rights and property. The Cherokee case reached the Supreme Court. In the 1832 case of *Worcester* v. *Georgia,* Chief Justice John Marshall ruled in favor of the Cherokees. The Court declared Georgia's action unconstitutional and stated that Native Americans were protected by the United States Constitution.

However, President Jackson refused to enforce the Court's decision. In the Nullification Crisis, Jackson defended the power of the federal government. In the Cherokee case, he backed states' rights. He said that the federal government could not stop Georgia from extending its authority over Cherokee lands. "John Marshall has made his decision," Jackson reportedly said. "Now let him enforce it."

Forced to Leave

In 1830, Jackson supporters in Congress pushed through the **Indian Removal Act.** It forced many Native Americans to move west of the Mississippi. Whites did not mind turning this land over to Indians because they thought the region was a vast desert. During the 1830s, thousands of southeastern Indians were driven from their homes and forced to march to Indian Territory, west of the Mississippi.

A tragic march

In 1838, the United States Army drove more than 15,000 Cherokees westward to a land they had never seen. The Cherokees trekked hundreds of miles over a period of several months. They had little food or shelter. Thousands perished during the march, mostly children and the elderly. In all, about one fourth of the Indians died.

The Cherokees' long, sorrowful journey west became known as the **Trail of Tears.** An eyewitness described the suffering:

❝ The Cherokees are nearly all prisoners. They had been dragged from their homes and encamped at the forts and military places, all over the nation. In Georgia especially, multitudes were allowed no time to take anything with them except the clothes they had on. ❞

The Seminoles resist

In Florida, the Seminole Indians resisted removal. Led by Chief **Osceola** (ahs ee OH luh), they fought the United States Army. The **Seminole War** lasted from 1835 to 1842. It was the costliest war waged by the government to gain Indian lands. More than 1,500 soldiers died in the war and about 20 million dollars were spent in the war effort.

In the end, the Seminoles were defeated. The government forced the Seminole leaders and most of their people to leave Florida. By 1844, only a few thousand Native Americans remained east of the Mississippi River.

★ Section 3 Review ★

Recall

1. **Locate** (a) South Carolina, (b) Georgia, (c) Cherokee homeland, (d) Indian Territory, (e) Seminole homeland.
2. **Identify** (a) Tariff of Abominations, (b) Nullification Crisis, (c) Sequoyah, (d) Indian Removal Act, (e) Trail of Tears, (f) Osceola, (g) Seminole War.
3. **Define** (a) nullification, (b) states' rights, (c) secede.

Comprehension

4. Why did northerners and southerners disagree on the tariff issue?

5. How did Andrew Jackson respond to South Carolina's Nullification Act?
6. Why did Jackson support the policy of using force to move Native Americans beyond the Mississippi River?

Critical Thinking and Writing

7. **Forecasting** What do you think might have happened if other southern states supported South Carolina in the Nullification Crisis?
8. **Drawing Conclusions** Why do you think Andrew Jackson supported states' rights in the Cherokee case but not in the Nullification Crisis?

Activity Writing a Protest Letter You are a Cherokee on the Trail of Tears. Write a protest letter to President Jackson explaining why you consider his policy of Indian removal to be unjust.

4 ★ The Presidency After Jackson

As You Read

Explore These Questions
- What economic problems did Martin Van Buren face?
- How did Whigs and Democrats compete for the Presidency in 1840?
- Why did John Tyler have little success as President?

Define
- speculator
- depression
- laissez faire
- mudslinging

Identify
- Martin Van Buren
- Panic of 1837
- William Henry Harrison
- John Tyler

SETTING the Scene Andrew Jackson retired from office after two terms. Americans then elected **Martin Van Buren** to the Presidency. Van Buren had served as Vice President during Jackson's second term.

As Van Buren took the oath of office in March 1837, Jackson stood at his side. Onlookers watched the outgoing President, not Van Buren. As Old Hickory left the platform, a rousing cheer rose from the crowd. In that moment, the people expressed their loyalty and respect for Andrew Jackson, the "Hero of New Orleans."

Van Buren and Hard Times

Martin Van Buren was very different from Andrew Jackson. He was a politician, not a war hero. Davy Crockett, a Congressman from Tennessee, once described Van Buren as "an artful, cunning, intriguing, selfish, speculating lawyer." As President, however, Van Buren needed more than sharp political instincts.

The Panic of 1837

Two months after taking office, Van Buren faced the worst economic crisis the nation had known. It was called the **Panic of 1837.** The panic had several causes. During the 1830s, the government sold millions of acres of public land in the West. Farmers bought some land, but **speculators** bought even more, hoping that their risky investment would earn them huge profits. To pay for the land, speculators borrowed money from state banks. After the Bank of the United States closed, the state banks could lend money without limit.

To meet the demand for loans, state banks printed more and more paper money. Often, the paper money was not backed by gold or silver. Paper money had value only if people trusted the banks that issued it.

Before leaving office, Jackson had grown alarmed at the wild speculation in land. To slow it down, he ordered that anyone buying public land had to pay for it with gold or silver. Speculators and others rushed to state banks to exchange their paper money for gold and silver. Many banks did not have enough gold and silver and had to close.

Economic depression

The panic worsened when cotton prices went down because of an oversupply. Cotton planters often borrowed money, which they repaid when they sold their crop. Low cotton prices meant that planters could not repay their loans. As a result, more banks failed.

The nation plunged into a deep economic **depression,** a period when business declines and many people lose their jobs. The depression lasted three years. In the worst days, 90 percent of the nation's factories were closed. Thousands of people were out of work. In some cities, hungry crowds broke into warehouses and stole food.

Van Buren's response

It was easy for people to blame President Van Buren for the country's economic depression. Van Buren took little action because he believed in **laissez faire**—the idea that government should play as small a role as possible in the nation's economic affairs. "The less the government interferes with private pursuits," he said, "the better for the general prosperity."

Van Buren's limited actions did little to help the economy. He tried to set up a more stable banking system. He also cut back on government expenses. For example, when he entertained visitors at the White House, they were served simple dinners. Still, the depression wore on. As a result, criticism of Van Buren increased.

Campaigns of 1840

Even though Van Buren had lost support, the Democrats chose him to run for reelection in 1840. The Whigs, learning from the Democrats, chose a candidate who would appeal to the common people. He was **William Henry Harrison** of Ohio. Harrison was known as the hero of the Battle of Tippecanoe. (See page 281.) To run for Vice President, the Whigs chose John Tyler.

Log cabin campaign

Most Americans knew very little about Harrison's stand on the issues. To appeal to voters, the Whigs focused on his war record. "Tippecanoe and Tyler too" became their campaign slogan.

The Whigs created an image for Harrison as a "man of the people." They presented him as a humble farmer who had been born in a log cabin. Harrison was actually a wealthy, educated man who lived in a large mansion. Still, the Whigs made the log cabin their campaign symbol. In a typical Whig cartoon, Harrison stands outside a log cabin, greeting Van Buren and his aides:

> 66 Gentlemen, . . . If you will accept the [simple food] of a log cabin, with a western farmer's cheer, you are welcome. I have no champagne but can give you a mug of good cider, with some ham and eggs, and good clean beds. I am a plain backwoodsman. I have cleared some land, killed some Indians, and made the Red Coats fly in my time. 99

A new sort of politics

The campaigns of 1840 reflected a new sort of politics. Harrison traveled across the land, making speeches and greeting voters. Both parties competed for votes with rallies, banquets, and entertainment. Ordinary citizens participated by giving speeches and singing campaign songs like this one:

> 66 The times are bad, and want curing;
> They are getting past all enduring:
> So let's turn out Martin Van Buren
> And put in old Tippecanoe! 99

![Viewing History] **Log Cabin Campaign**

Harrison's log cabin symbol swept the nation in 1840. Marchers in parades often carried miniature cabins such as the one shown here. The cabin was attached to a pole and raised aloft for all to see. ★ **Why was the log cabin image appealing to many voters?**

Why Study History?

Because You Will Choose Our Nation's Leaders

★ ★

Historical Background

In the political campaigns of 1840, Democrats and Whigs showed little concern for the key issues of the day. Instead, they organized parades, chanted slogans, offered free cider, and participated in name-calling. Candidates also used newspapers, posters, and even whisky jugs to carry their political messages. In 1840, the Whigs' log cabin campaign was a success and William Henry Harrison was elected President. (See page 339.)

Connections to Today

When election day draws near today, politicians flood the radio, television, Internet, and various other media with campaign sound bites. Like politicians of the 1840s, some candidates try to avoid the issues. Some candidates may even use questionable or inappropriate campaign tactics to win votes.

Responsible voters are familiar with the workings of political campaigns. They make their voting decisions based on a clear understanding of the candidates' past performance and stand on the issues. They want to vote for the most qualified candidate. Other voters, however, may be swayed more by clever campaign tactics and political advertisements.

Connections to You

Right now, you may participate in school elections. In a few years, you will have the right and responsibility of voting for our nation's leaders. You will help to choose leaders of your nation, state, and community. Politicians of today, like those of the 1840s, will sometimes use aggressive campaign tactics to try to win your vote. Learning about politics during the Age of Jackson and during other eras of American history can help you to become a knowledgeable and responsible voter.

1. Comprehension
(a) What campaign tactics did the Whigs use in the election of 1840?

(b) What role does advertising play in political campaigns today?

2. Critical Thinking
How can you learn more about a candidate's past performance and stand on major issues?

 **Interviewing** Write several questions to help you learn how people make their voting decisions. Then, use your questions to interview people you know who voted in a recent election. Keep a written or taped record of their responses. What conclusions can you draw from your interviews?

Along the campaign trail, Whigs organized colorful parades in both small towns and big cities. At every stop, they served plenty of free cider. The log cabin symbol appeared on banners, quilts, and even packages of shaving soap.

Name-calling, half-truths, and lies

In their campaigns, both Whigs and Democrats engaged in **mudslinging,** or the use of insults to attack an opponent's reputation. They used name-calling, half-truths, and lies to win votes.

The Whigs attacked the President. One newspaper falsely reported that Van Buren spent thousands of dollars to install a bathtub in the White House. They blamed "Martin Van Ruin" for the depression. Daniel Webster charged that the Democrats had replaced "Old Hickory" Jackson with "Slippery Elm" Van Buren.

The Democrats responded with their own attacks and name-calling. They revealed that "Granny Harrison, the Petticoat General," had resigned from the army before the War of 1812 ended. They accused "General Mum" of not speaking on the issues. "Should Harrison be elected?" they asked voters. "Read his name spelled backwards," they advised. "No sirrah."

Whigs in the White House

Harrison won the election of 1840 easily. As a result, a Whig was in the White House for the first time in 12 years. "We have taught them how to conquer us!" complained one Democrat.

The Whigs had a clear-cut program. They wanted to create a new Bank of the United States and improve roads and canals. Also, they wanted a high tariff.

However, Whig hopes soon crashed. Just weeks after taking office, President Harrison died of pneumonia. **John Tyler** became the first Vice President to succeed a President who died in office.

President Tyler failed to live up to Whig expectations. A former Democrat, he opposed some Whig plans for developing the economy. When the Whigs in Congress passed a bill to recharter the Bank of the United States, Tyler vetoed it.

In response, most of Tyler's Cabinet resigned and the Whigs threw Tyler out of their party. Democrats welcomed the squabbling. "Tyler is heartily despised by everyone," reported an observer. "He has no influence at all." With few friends in either the Whig or Democratic party, Tyler could do little during his term in office.

★ Section 4 Review ★

Recall

1. **Identify** (a) Martin Van Buren, (b) Panic of 1837, (c) William Henry Harrison, (d) John Tyler.
2. **Define** (a) speculator, (b) depression, (c) laissez faire, (d) mudslinging.

Comprehension

3. Describe the economic depression that occurred after the Panic of 1837.
4. Describe some of the campaign tactics Democrats and Whigs used in the election of 1840.

5. Why did the Whigs throw President Tyler out of their party?

Critical Thinking and Writing

6. **Solving Problems** What do you think President Van Buren could have done to ease the economic crisis of the 1830s?
7. **Comparing** How do campaign tactics of today compare with those of 1840?

Activity Researching If you had money in a bank that failed today, would you lose your money just as people did in the 1830s? To find the answer, conduct research on the Federal Deposit Insurance Corporation, also known as the FDIC.

Review and Activities

★ Sum It Up ★

Section 1 A New Era in Politics
▶ The 1828 election of Andrew Jackson for President was seen as a victory for the common people.
▶ In the 1820s, democracy expanded as more and more white males gained the right to vote.
▶ Women and African Americans did not share in the growth of democracy.

Section 2 Jackson in the White House
▶ Jackson rewarded his supporters with government jobs and relied on the advice of his unofficial kitchen cabinet.
▶ Jackson fought against the national bank, which he saw as a tool of the wealthy.

Section 3 Struggles Over States' Rights
▶ In his second term, Jackson used compromise and strong leadership to end a crisis over tariffs and states' rights.
▶ Jackson's Indian removal policy forced thousands of Native Americans to leave their homelands and move west.

Section 4 The Presidency After Jackson
▶ The Panic of 1837 brought an economic depression that caused President Van Buren to lose popular support.
▶ In 1840, Whigs used new political campaign tactics to get William Henry Harrison elected President.

CD-ROM Review For additional review of the major ideas of Chapter 12, see *Guide to the Essentials of American History* or *Interactive Student Tutorial CD-ROM,* which contains interactive review activities, graphic organizers, and practice tests.

📖 Reviewing the Chapter

Define These Terms
Match each term with the correct definition.

Column 1	Column 2
1. suffrage	a. private meeting to choose candidates
2. caucus	
3. nominating convention	b. right to vote
4. spoils system	c. practice of rewarding supporters with government jobs
5. kitchen cabinet	d. meeting where state delegates choose candidates
	e. Jackson's group of unofficial advisers

Explore the Main Ideas
1. Why were there more voters in 1828 than in 1824?
2. What role did each of the following play in the struggle over the Bank: **(a)** Nicholas Biddle, **(b)** Henry Clay, **(c)** Andrew Jackson.
3. Why did South Carolina want to nullify the tariffs of 1828 and 1832?
4. Describe President Jackson's Indian removal policy.
5. What were the causes of the Panic of 1837?

📖 Geography Activity

Match the letters on the map with the following places:
1. Indian Territory, **2.** Chickasaw, **3.** Choctaw, **4.** Creek, **5.** Cherokee, **6.** Seminole. **Place** Why did settlers want Cherokee lands in the Southeast?

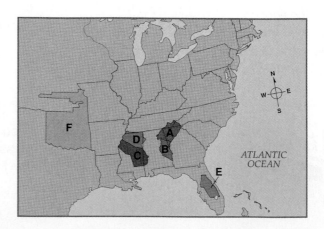

Critical Thinking and Writing

1. **Defending a Position**   Do you think more Americans should have supported John Quincy Adams's plans to promote economic growth? Why or why not?

2. **Understanding Chronology**   Place these events in chronological order: **(a)** Jackson becomes President, **(b)** the Cherokees are ordered off their land, **(c)** the Seminole War begins.

3. **Linking Past and Present**   How are today's political tactics similar to those of the Jackson era? How are the tactics different?

4. **Exploring Unit Themes**   **Expansion**   We often think of the Age of Jackson as a time of expanding democracy. In what ways did American democracy expand during the Age of Jackson?

Using Primary Sources

President Jackson wanted to move all Native Americans west of the Mississippi River. In 1835, when it seemed that the Seminoles would resist, Jackson wrote a forceful letter to them.

> **❝** My Children—
>   I am sorry to have heard that you have been listening to bad counsel. . . . I have ordered a large military force to be sent among you. . . . If you listen to the voice of friendship and truth, you will go quietly and voluntarily. But should you listen to the bad birds that are always flying about you and refuse to move, I have then directed the commanding officer to remove you by force. This will be done. I pray the Great Spirit, therefore, to incline you to do what is right.
>
> Your friend,
> A. Jackson **❞**

Source: "President Andrew Jackson's Letter to the Seminoles" in *History of the Indian Wars*, ed. Henry Trumbull, 1841.

Recognizing Points of View (a) How did President Jackson suggest that he was a friend of the Seminoles? **(b)** How do you think the Seminoles felt about Jackson after reading this letter?

ACTIVITY BANK

▶ Interdisciplinary Activity

Exploring Economics Review the Tariff of Abominations. Then do research to learn about the North American Free Trade Agreement of the 1990s. In an oral report, explain the differences between these two national economic policies.

▶ Career Skills Activity

Artists Select an issue or incident related to Andrew Jackson's presidency. Then create a political cartoon based on your selection. Remember that political cartoonists represent a point of view by using various symbols. Be prepared to explain your cartoon and its symbolism.

▶ Citizenship Activity

Running a Food Drive Thousands of Cherokees died of starvation on the Trail of Tears. Today, in many communities, some people do not have enough food to eat. Form a student group to plan and run a food drive. Work with a charitable organization to deliver food to those in need.

Internet Activity

Search the Internet to find sites dealing with Cherokee culture and history. Continue exploring until you find Cherokee viewpoints on the Indian Removal and the Trail of Tears. Use the Cherokee viewpoints to write a poem about how people suffered on the Trail of Tears.

EYEWITNESS Journal

You are a frontier settler, a Whig politician, a Southern planter, an enslaved African American, or a Seminole. In your EYEWITNESS JOURNAL, record how key events and issues of the Jackson era affect your life.

Chapter 13 Westward Expansion

1820–1860

By the mid-1800s, Americans began to dream of extending their territory to the Pacific Ocean. In this chapter, you will see how that dream came true.

First, the United States secured the Pacific Northwest by signing a treaty with Britain. Next, after American settlers declared independence from Mexico, the United States brought Texas into the Union. Americans then won California and the Southwest by fighting a war with Mexico. As settlers poured into the Southwest, a new culture developed that blended American, Mexican, and Indian cultures.

Why Study History?

Every year, millions of Americans visit historic memorials, from battlefields to the homes of famous people. To many Texans, for example, the best-loved historic site is a San Antonio mission called the Alamo. Why do so many Americans work to preserve the places where history happened? To explore this question, see this chapter's *Why Study History?* feature, "History Is All Around You."

American Events

●1821
First white American traders arrive in Santa Fe, New Mexico

●1836
Republic of Texas is formed

1820	1825	1830	1835	1840

World Events

 1833 World Event
Santa Anna comes to power in Mexico

West Side Main Plaza San Antonio Texas 1849   W.J.M. Samuel

Viewing HISTORY

A Growing Texas City

This painting by William G. Samuel shows a street in San Antonio, Texas, in 1849. Texas had joined the Union a few years before, after winning independence from Mexico. In the mid-1800s, the United States gained vast western territories, including Texas, California, Oregon, and New Mexico. As a result, the nation stretched from the Atlantic Ocean to the Pacific. ★ **How does this painting show the Mexican roots of the Southwest?**

1845
James K. Polk becomes President

1846
Americans in northern California declare independence from Mexico

1859
Oregon is admitted to the Union

| 1840 | 1845 | 1850 | 1855 | 1860 |

1840 World Event
Britain recognizes Texas as an independent nation

1854 World Event
Japan and United States sign trade agreement

★ **345**

Oregon Country

As You Read

Explore These Questions
- How did rival claims to Oregon Country develop?
- How did fur trappers and missionaries help open up the Far West?
- What hardships did settlers face?

Define
- mountain man
- rendezvous

Identify
- John Jacob Astor
- James Beckwourth
- Marie Dorion
- Marcus and Narcissa Whitman

SETTING the Scene In 1851, Horace Greeley, a New York newspaper editor, published an article titled "To Aspiring Young Men." In it, Greeley offered the following advice:

> 66 If you have no family or friends to aid you, . . . turn your face to the great West and there build up your home and fortune. 99

The public soon came to know Greeley's message as a simple, four-word phrase: "Go West, young man." His advice exactly suited the spirit of the times. Thousands of young men—and women—rallied to the cry "Westward Ho!"

The Lure of Oregon

By the 1820s, white settlers had occupied much of the land between the Appalachians and the Mississippi River. Families in search of good farmland continued to move west. Few, however, settled on the Great Plains between the Mississippi and the Rockies. Instead, they went onward to lands in the Far West.

Americans first heard about the area known as Oregon Country in the early 1800s. Oregon Country was the huge area beyond the Rocky Mountains. Today, this land includes Oregon, Washington, Idaho, and parts of Wyoming, Montana, and Canada.

The varied geography of Oregon Country attracted both farmers and trappers. Along the Pacific coast, the soil is fertile. Temperatures are mild all year round and rainfall is plentiful. Early white settlers found fine farmland in the Willamette River valley and the lowlands around Puget Sound.

Farther inland, dense forests covered a coastal mountain range. Beaver and other fur-bearing animals roamed these forests, as well as the Rocky Mountains on the eastern boundary. As a result, trappers flocked to Oregon Country.

Between the coastal mountains and the Rockies is a high plateau. This intermountain region is much drier than the coast and has some desert areas. This region of Oregon had little to attract early settlers.

Competing Claims

In the early 1800s, four countries had claims to Oregon. These countries were the United States, Great Britain, Spain, and Russia. Of course, several Native American groups had lived in Oregon for thousands of years. The land rightfully belonged to them. However, the United States and competing European nations gave little thought to Indian rights.

The United States based its claim to Oregon on several expeditions to the area. For example, Lewis and Clark had journeyed through the area in 1805 and 1806.

The British claim to Oregon dated back to a visit by the English explorer Sir Francis Drake in 1579. Also, Fort Vancouver, built by the British, was the only permanent outpost in Oregon Country.

In 1818, the United States and Britain reached an agreement. The two countries would occupy Oregon jointly. Citizens of each nation would have equal rights in Oregon. Spain and Russia had few settlers in the area and agreed to drop their claims.

Fur Trappers in the Far West

At first, the few Europeans or Americans who traveled to Oregon Country were mostly fur traders. Since furs could be sold at tremendous profits in China, merchants from New England stopped along the Oregon coast before crossing the Pacific. In fact, so many Yankee traders came to Oregon that, in some areas, the Indian name for a white man was "Boston."

Only a few hardy trappers actually settled in Oregon. These adventurous men hiked through Oregon's vast forests, trapping animals and living off the land. They were known as **mountain men.**

Mountain men won admiration as rugged individualists, people who follow their own independent course in life. Even their colorful appearance set them apart from ordinary society. They wore shirts and trousers made of animal hides and decorated with porcupine quills. Their hair reached to their shoulders. Pistols and tomahawks hung from their belts.

Lives filled with danger

Mountain men could make a small fortune trapping beaver in Rocky Mountain streams. They led dangerous lives, however. The long, cold mountain winters demanded special survival skills. In the thick forests, trappers had to be on the lookout for attacks by bears, wildcats, or other animals.

During the harsh winters, game was scarce. Facing starvation, trappers would eat almost anything. "I have held my hands in an anthill until they were covered with ants, then greedily licked them off," one mountain man recalled.

Trappers often spent winters in Native American villages. They learned many trapping skills from Indians. Many mountain men married Indian women who taught the newcomers how to find their way and survive in the mountains.

Relations with Native Americans were not always friendly, however. Indians, like the Blackfeet, sometimes attacked mountain men who trapped on Indian hunting grounds without permission.

Trading furs

During the fall and spring, mountain men tended their traps. Then in July, they

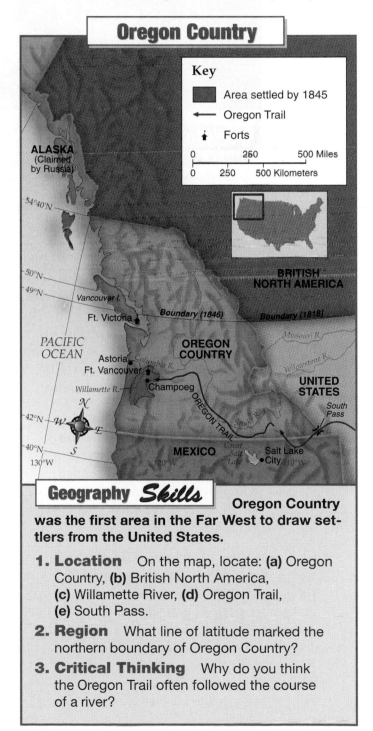

Oregon Country

Key
- Area settled by 1845
- Oregon Trail
- Forts

0 250 500 Miles
0 250 500 Kilometers

ALASKA (Claimed by Russia)

54°40'N

50°N
49°N

Vancouver I.

Ft. Victoria

Boundary (1846)   Boundary (1818)

PACIFIC OCEAN

BRITISH NORTH AMERICA

Missouri R.

OREGON COUNTRY

Astoria   Columbia R.
Ft. Vancouver

Willamette R.   Champoeg

Yellowstone R.

UNITED STATES

42°N

South Pass

40°N
130°W

MEXICO   Great Salt Lake   Salt Lake City

110°W

Geography Skills

Oregon Country was the first area in the Far West to draw settlers from the United States.

1. **Location** On the map, locate: **(a)** Oregon Country, **(b)** British North America, **(c)** Willamette River, **(d)** Oregon Trail, **(e)** South Pass.

2. **Region** What line of latitude marked the northern boundary of Oregon Country?

3. **Critical Thinking** Why do you think the Oregon Trail often followed the course of a river?

Viewing HISTORY   **The Fur Trade**

Alfred Miller painted this watercolor, Fort Laramie, *in 1837. Located in present-day Wyoming, Fort Laramie was originally built as a fur-trading post. Once a year, mountain men and Indian trappers gathered at trading posts like this one to sell their furs and have fun.* ★ **How did Native Americans help fur trappers?**

tramped out of the wilderness, ready to meet the fur traders. They headed to a place chosen the year before, called the **rendezvous** (RAHN day voo). Rendezvous is a French word meaning get-together.

For trappers, the first day of the rendezvous was a time to have fun. A visitor to one rendezvous captured the excitement:

❝ [They] engaged in contests of skill at running, jumping, wrestling, shooting with the rifle, and running horses.... They sang, they laughed, they whooped; they tried to out-brag and out-lie each other in stories of their adventures. ❞

Soon, though, trappers and traders settled down to bargain. Because beaver hats were in demand in the East and in Europe, mountain men got a good price for their furs. Trading companies did even better. **John Jacob Astor,** a New Yorker, founded the American Fur Company. He made so much money in the fur trade that he became the richest man in the United States.

By the late 1830s, the fur trade was dying out. Trappers had killed so many beavers that the animals had grown scarce. Also, beaver hats went out of style. Even so, the mountain men's skills were still in demand. Some began leading settlers across the rugged trails into Oregon.

Exploring New Lands

In their search for furs, mountain men explored much new territory in the West. They followed Indian trails across the Rockies and through mountain passes. Later, they showed these trails to settlers moving west.

Jedediah Smith led white settlers across the Rockies through South Pass, in present-day Wyoming. Manuel Lisa, a Spanish American fur trader, led a trip up the Missouri River in 1807. He founded Fort Manuel, the first outpost on the upper Missouri.

James Beckwourth, an African American, headed west from Virginia to escape slavery. He was accepted as a chief by the Crow Indians. As a guide, Beckwourth discovered a mountain pass through the

Sierra Nevadas that later became a major route to California.

At least one mountain "man" was a woman. **Marie Dorion,** an Iowa Indian, first went to Oregon with fur traders in 1811. She won fame for her survival skills.

Missionaries in Oregon

The first white Americans to build permanent homes in Oregon Country were missionaries. Among them were **Marcus and Narcissa Whitman**. The couple married in 1836 and set out for Oregon, where they planned to convert local Native Americans to Christianity.

The Whitmans built their mission near the Columbia River and began to work with Cayuse (KI oos) Indians. They set up a mission school. Soon, other missionaries and settlers joined the Whitmans. As more settlers arrived and took over Cayuse lands, conflicts arose. Even worse, the newcomers brought diseases that often killed the Indians.

In 1847, tragedy struck. An outbreak of measles among the settlers spread to the Cayuses. Many Cayuse children died. Blaming the settlers, a band of angry Indians attacked the mission, killing the Whitmans and 12 others.

Wagon Trains West

Despite the killing of the Whitmans, other bold pioneers set out on the long trek to Oregon. Missionaries sent back glowing reports about the land. Farmers back East marveled at tales of wheat that grew taller than a man and turnips five feet around. Stories like these touched off an outbreak of "Oregon fever."

Oregon fever spread quickly. Soon, pioneers clogged the trails west. Beginning in 1843, wagon trains left every spring for Oregon. They followed a route called the Oregon Trail. (See the map on page 347.)

Families planning to go west met at Independence, Missouri, in the early spring. When enough families had gathered, they formed a wagon train. Each group elected leaders to make decisions along the way.

The Oregon-bound pioneers hurried to leave Independence in May. Timing was important. Travelers had to reach Oregon by early October, before snow began to fall in the mountains. This meant that pioneers had to cover 2,000 miles (3,200 km) on foot in five months!

Life on the trail

Once on the trail, pioneer families woke to a bugle blast at dawn. Each person had a job to do. Young girls helped their mothers prepare breakfast. Men and boys harnessed the horses and oxen. By 6 A.M., the cry of "Wagons Ho!" rang out across the plains.

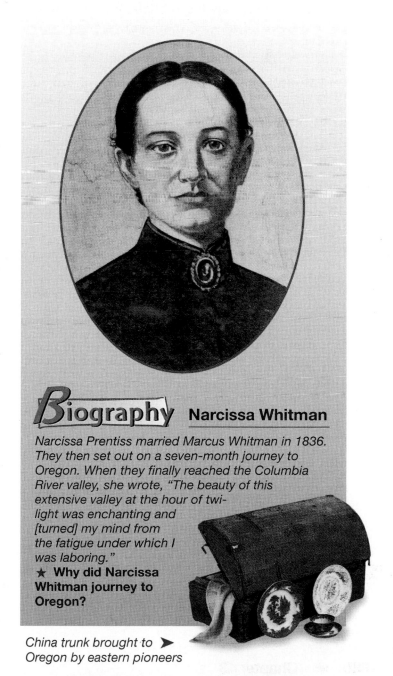

Biography Narcissa Whitman

Narcissa Prentiss married Marcus Whitman in 1836. They then set out on a seven-month journey to Oregon. When they finally reached the Columbia River valley, she wrote, "The beauty of this extensive valley at the hour of twilight was enchanting and [turned] my mind from the fatigue under which I was laboring."
★ **Why did Narcissa Whitman journey to Oregon?**

China trunk brought to ➤
Oregon by eastern pioneers

Wagon trains stopped for a brief meal at noon. Then it was back on the trail until 6 or 7 P.M. At night, wagons were drawn up in a circle to keep the cattle from wandering.

Most pioneer families set out on the journey west with a lot of heavy gear. When it came time to cross rivers and scale mountains, however, many possessions were left behind to lighten the load. One traveler found the Oregon Trail littered with objects such as "blacksmiths' anvils, ploughs, large grindstones, baking ovens, kegs, barrels, harness [and] clothing."

The long trek west held many dangers. During spring rains, travelers risked their lives floating wagons across swollen rivers. In summer, they faced blistering heat on the treeless plains. Early snowstorms often blocked passes through the mountains.

The biggest threat was sickness. Cholera and other diseases could wipe out whole wagon trains. Because the travelers lived so close together, germs spread quickly.

Trading with Native Americans

As they moved west toward the Rockies, pioneers often saw Indians. The Indians seldom attacked the whites trespassing on their land. A guidebook published in 1845 warned that pioneers had more to fear from their own guns than from Indians: "We very frequently hear of emigrants being killed from the accidental discharge of firearms; but we very seldom hear of their being killed by Indians."

Many Native Americans traded with the wagon trains. Hungry pioneers were grateful for food the Indians sold. A traveler noted:

66 Whenever we camp near any Indian village, we are no sooner stopped than a whole crowd may be seen coming galloping into our camp. The [women] do all the swapping. 99

Oregon at last!

Despite the many hardships, more than 50,000 people reached Oregon between 1840 and 1860. Their wagon wheels cut so deeply into the plains that the ruts can still be seen today.

By the 1840s, Americans greatly outnumbered the British in parts of Oregon. As you have read, the two nations agreed to occupy Oregon jointly in 1818. Now, many Americans began to feel that Oregon should belong to the United States alone.

★ Section 1 Review ★

Recall

1. **Locate** (a) Oregon Country, (b) Willamette River, (c) South Pass, (d) Oregon Trail.
2. **Identify** (a) John Jacob Astor, (b) James Beckwourth, (c) Marie Dorion, (d) Marcus and Narcissa Whitman.
3. **Define** (a) mountain man, (b) rendezvous.

Comprehension

4. How did the United States and Britain settle their claims to Oregon Country?
5. (a) Why did mountain men first go to Oregon? (b) How did they contribute to later settlement?

6. (a) Why did settlers flock to Oregon after the 1840s? (b) Describe two difficulties along the way.

Critical Thinking and Writing

7. **Linking Past and Present** (a) What qualities helped the mountain men survive in the wilderness? (b) Do you think such qualities are still important today? Explain.
8. **Analyzing Ideas** Economists talk about the "law of supply and demand." It states that when people want a product that is hard to get, the price goes up. How does the Oregon fur trade illustrate the idea of supply and demand?

★ ★

Activity Writing a Letter to the Editor You are one of the young people Horace Greeley told to "go West." You took his advice. Now, write him a letter and tell him what it was like traveling to the West!

Texas Wins Independence

As You Read

Explore These Questions
- Why did many Americans settle in Texas?
- How did Texas become an independent nation?
- What challenges did the new Republic of Texas face?

Define
- siege
- annex

Identify
- Stephen Austin
- Antonio López de Santa Anna
- Tejanos
- Sam Houston
- Alamo
- William Travis
- Battle of San Jacinto
- Lone Star Republic

SETTING the Scene In late 1835, the word spread: Americans in Texas had rebelled against Mexico! Joseph Barnard, a young doctor, recalled:

66 I was at Chicago, Illinois, practicing medicine, when the news of the Texan revolt from Mexico reached our ears.... They were in arms for a cause that I had always been taught to consider sacred, ... Republican principles and popular institutions. 99

Along with hundreds of other Americans, Dr. Barnard made his way to Texas. Their fight led to the creation of a new nation.

Americans in Mexican Texas

Since the early 1800s, American farmers, especially from the South, had looked eagerly at the vast region called Texas. At the time, Texas was part of the Spanish colony of Mexico.

At first, Spain refused to let Americans move into the region. Then in 1821, Spain gave Moses Austin a land grant in Texas. Austin died before he could set up a colony. His son Stephen took over the project.

This seal from Mexican Texas shows an eagle, serpent, and cactus—symbols of Mexico.

Meanwhile, Mexico won its independence from Spain. The new nation let **Stephen Austin** lead settlers into Texas. Only about 4,000 Mexicans lived there. Mexico hoped that the Americans would help develop the area and control Indian attacks.

Mexico gave each settler a large grant of land. In 1821, Austin and 300 families moved to Texas. Many of these newcomers were slaveowners who brought their slaves with them. Under Austin's leadership, the colony grew rapidly. By 1830, about 20,000 Americans had resettled in Texas.

Conflict With Mexico

In return for land, Austin and the original settlers agreed to become citizens of Mexico and worship in the Roman Catholic Church. However, later American settlers felt no loyalty to Mexico. They spoke only a few words of Spanish. Also, most of the Americans were Protestants. Conflict soon erupted with the Mexican government.

Mexico enforces its laws

In 1830, Mexico forbade any more Americans to move to Texas. Mexico feared that the Americans wanted to make Texas part of

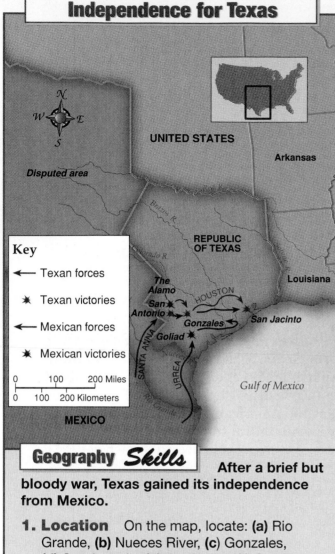

laws and the Mexican troops who came north to enforce them.

In 1833, General **Antonio López de Santa Anna** came to power in Mexico. Two years later, he threw out the Mexican constitution. Rumors spread that Santa Anna intended to drive all Americans out of Texas.

Texans take action

Texans felt that the time had come for action. In this, they had the support of many **Tejanos** (teh HAH nohs), Mexicans who lived in Texas. Tejanos did not necessarily want independence from Mexico. However, they did want to be rid of Santa Anna, who ruled as a military dictator.

In October 1835, Texans in the town of Gonzales (gahn ZAH lehs) clashed with Mexican troops. The Texans forced the Mexicans to withdraw. Inspired by the victory, Stephen Austin vowed to "see Texas forever free from Mexican domination." Two months later, Texans stormed and took San Antonio. Determined to stamp out the rebellion, Santa Anna marched north with a large army.

While Santa Anna tried to regain San Antonio, Texans declared independence on March 2, 1836. They set up a new nation called the Republic of Texas and appointed **Sam Houston** commander of the army. Volunteers of many nationalities, as well as African Americans and Tejanos, joined the fight for Texan independence from Mexico.

Siege at the Alamo

By the time Santa Anna arrived in San Antonio, many of the Texans who had taken the city had drifted away. Fewer than 200 Texans remained as defenders.

In spite of the tremendous odds against them, the Texans refused to give up. Instead, they retired to an old Spanish mission called the **Alamo.**

Against tremendous odds

Texans who gathered in the Alamo in the winter of 1835–1836 were poorly equipped for a battle. Supplies of ammunition and medicine were low. Food consisted of some beef and corn, and access to water was limited. Worst of all, there were only about 150

the United States. Mexico had some reason for this fear. The United States had already tried twice to buy Texas.

Mexico also decided to make Texans obey Mexican laws that they had ignored for years. One was the law requiring Texans to worship in the Catholic Church. Another law banned slavery in Texas. Texans resented the

Why Study History?

Because History Is All Around You

★ ★

Historical Background

Did you know that we almost lost the Alamo? After 1836, it was used as an army supply depot, a warehouse, and a general store. For a time, its neighbors included a beer garden and a meat market. In 1903, there was even talk that it might be turned into a hotel.

Then, the Daughters of the Republic of Texas stepped in. They urged the state government to save the Alamo from destruction. Adina De Zavala gained public attention by barricading herself inside the old mission. In 1905, the state of Texas entrusted the Alamo to the Daughters of the Republic.

The Alamo

Connections to Today

Each year, thousands of tourists visit the Alamo. They walk the same ground where Texans fought for independence.

Throughout the nation, government and citizens work to save and restore important historic sites. Federal laws protect a variety of places, including ruins of Native American towns, homes of famous Americans, and even old factories. The National Trust for Historic Preservation, a nonprofit educational group, helps people to acquire and preserve historic properties.

Today, ordinary people are restoring and living in historic buildings. Some have transformed old train stations, schools, or factories into restaurants, shops, or apartment buildings. Several cities have revitalized old run-down neighborhoods and warehouse districts. These historic areas attract new businesses and residents.

Connections to You

History is all around you. It is there for you to visit and explore. Check out the *National Register of Historic Places* in your local library. It lists thousands of places and structures that have played a role in your nation's history. To find out how you can help preserve American history, contact your local historical society or the National Trust for Historic Preservation.

1. **Comprehension** What have ordinary citizens and local government done to save important historic sites?

2. **Critical Thinking** How can visiting an historic site be more interesting and informative than reading about it?

 **Visiting an Historic Site** Visit a nearby historic site. In a brief presentation, explain the site's importance and describe how it has been preserved and restored.

▲ Republic of Texas flag

Viewing History

Winning Texas Independence

Sam Houston was wounded in the leg during the Battle of San Jacinto. Despite tremendous pain and a boot full of blood, Houston fought on to victory. This painting shows Houston accepting the surrender of Mexican commander Santa Anna.
★ **Why was San Jacinto a turning point in Texas history?**

Texans to defend the Alamo against 6,000 Mexican troops!

Young **William Travis** commanded the Texans inside the mission. Among the volunteers were the famous frontiersmen Jim Bowie and Davy Crockett. Several Tejano families, two Texan women, and two young male slaves were also present.

"Victory or Death!"

On February 23, 1836, Mexican troops began a siege of the Alamo. In a **siege**, enemy forces try to capture a city or fort, usually by surrounding and bombarding it. The Texan defenders fought bravely. Still, Travis knew that unless he received help, he and his troops were doomed. He sent a mes-

Connections With Geography

Santa Anna crossed the Rio Grande on February 16, 1836, in the middle of a harsh Texas winter. Many of the army's cattle died from the brutal cold and inadequate grazing land. For the final thirty days before reaching the Alamo, soldiers ate only eight ounces of corn cake per day.

senger through the Mexican lines with a letter addressed "to the People of Texas and all the Americans in the World":

66 The enemy have demanded a surrender....I have answered the demand with a cannon shot and our flag still waves proudly from the walls.
I shall never surrender or retreat.
I call on you in the name of Liberty, of patriotism, and of everything dear to the American character to come to our aid with all dispatch.... *Victory or Death!* 99

Travis also sent scouts to seek additional soldiers and provisions. About 40 men were able to sneak through enemy lines and join the fighters in the Alamo. However, no large force ever arrived.

For 12 days, the defenders held off Mexican bombardment. Then, at dawn on March 6, Mexican cannon fire broke through the Alamo walls. Thousands of Mexican soldiers poured into the mission. When the bodies were counted, 183 Texans and almost 1,500 Mexicans lay dead. The Texan survivors, including Davy Crockett, were executed.

Texan Independence

The fall of the Alamo set off cries for revenge. The fury of the Texans grew even stronger three weeks later, when Mexican forces killed several hundred Texan soldiers at Goliad after they had surrendered. Volunteers flooded into Sam Houston's army. Men from the United States also raced south to help the Texan cause.

On April 21, 1836, Houston decided that the moment had come to attack. Santa Anna was camped with his army near the San Jacinto (jah SEEN toh) River. With cries of "Remember the Alamo!" the Texans charged the surprised Mexicans.

The **Battle of San Jacinto** lasted only 18 minutes. Although they were outnumbered, Texans killed 630 Mexicans and captured 700 more. The following day, Texans captured Santa Anna himself. They forced the general to sign a treaty granting Texas its independence.

The Lone Star Republic

In battle, Texans had carried a flag with a single white star. After winning independence, they nicknamed their nation the **Lone Star Republic.** They drew up a constitution based on the Constitution of the United States and elected Sam Houston as their president.

The new country faced several problems. First, Mexico refused to accept the treaty signed by Santa Anna. Mexicans still claimed Texas as part of their country. Second, Texas was nearly bankrupt. Most Texans thought that the best way to solve both problems was for Texas to become part of the United States.

In the United States, Americans were divided about whether to **annex**, or add on, Texas. Most white southerners were in favor of the idea. Many northerners, however, were against it. At issue was slavery.

In the 1830s, antislavery feelings were growing in the North. Because many Texans owned slaves, northerners did not want to allow Texas to join the Union. President Andrew Jackson also worried that annexing Texas would lead to war with Mexico. As a result, Congress refused to annex Texas.

Over the next 10 years, the Lone Star Republic prospered under Houston's leadership. During the Panic of 1837, thousands of Americans moved to Texas to find land and start businesses. Settlers from Germany and Switzerland also swelled the population. By the 1840s, there were about 140,000 people in Texas, including many Mexicans and African Americans.

★ Section 2 Review ★

Recall

1. **Locate** (a) Mexico, (b) Gonzales, (c) Goliad, (d) Republic of Texas.
2. **Identify** (a) Stephen Austin, (b) Antonio López de Santa Anna, (c) Tejanos, (d) Sam Houston, (e) Alamo, (f) William Travis, (g) Battle of San Jacinto, (h) Lone Star Republic.
3. **Define** (a) siege, (b) annex.

Comprehension

4. Why did Mexico encourage Americans to move to Texas?

5. (a) Why did Texans seek independence from Mexico? (b) How did they finally achieve their goal?
6. Why did northerners and southerners disagree about annexing Texas?

Critical Thinking and Writing

7. **Drawing Conclusions** Why was the fall of the Alamo both a defeat and a victory for Texans?
8. **Solving Problems** Why do you think many Texans believed that annexation by the United States would help them solve their problems?

★ ★

Activity Writing an Appeal You are trapped in the Alamo with the rebel Texans and Tejanos. Write an appeal to people in the United States to come help you—make it quick!

California and the Southwest

As You Read

Explore These Questions
- What brought the first white settlers to New Mexico?
- What was life like for Native Americans in California?
- Why did Americans want to expand to the Pacific Ocean?

Identify
- New Mexico Territory
- William Becknell
- Santa Fe Trail
- Junípero Serra
- Manifest Destiny
- James K. Polk

SETTING the Scene In 1819, John Quincy Adams made a bold claim. The world, he said, would have to accept the fact that the United States would one day possess all of North America:

> 66 From the time we became an independent nation, it was as much a law of nature that this would become our claim as that the Mississippi should flow to the sea. 99

By the 1840s, many Americans agreed. They, too, believed that it was the mission of the United States to expand all the way to the Pacific Ocean. Americans began to look with interest to the vast, rich lands of California and the Southwest.

New Mexico Territory

The entire Southwest belonged to Mexico in the 1840s. This huge region was called **New Mexico Territory.** It included most of the present-day states of Arizona and New Mexico, all of Nevada and Utah, and parts of Colorado.

Much of the Southwest is hot and dry. In some areas, thick grasses grow. There are also desert and mountain areas. Before the Spanish arrived, Zuñi Indians irrigated and farmed the land. Other Native Americans, such as the Apaches, lived by hunting.

A Spanish explorer, Juan de Oñate, had claimed the territory of New Mexico for Spain in 1598. In the early 1600s, the Spanish built Santa Fe as the capital of the territory. Under the Spanish, Santa Fe grew into a busy trading town. However, Spain refused to let Americans settle in New Mexico. Only after Mexico won its independence in 1821 were Americans welcome in Santa Fe.

William Becknell, a merchant and adventurer, was the first American to head for Santa Fe. In 1821, Becknell led a group of traders from Franklin, Missouri, across the plains. When they reached Santa Fe, they found Mexicans eager to buy their cloth and other goods. Other Americans soon followed Becknell's route. It became known as the **Santa Fe Trail.** (See the map on page 366.)

Early Years in California

California, too, belonged to Mexico in the early 1840s. Spain had claimed the region 65 years before English colonists settled in Jamestown. In the years that followed, Spanish and Native American cultures shaped life in California.

Land and climate

California is a land of dramatic contrasts. Two tall mountain ranges slice through the region. One range hugs the coast. The other sits inland on the border of Nevada and Arizona. Between these two ranges is California's fertile Central Valley.

Northern California receives plenty of rain. In the south, though, water is scarce and much of the land is desert. California enjoys mild temperatures all year, except for areas high in the mountains.

Mission San Juan Capistrano

In 1776, Father Junípero Serra founded Mission San Juan Capistrano in southern California. Today, you can still walk among its adobe walls, enjoy its peaceful gardens, and listen to its old bells. These mission bells told the priests and Native Americans who lived there when to wake up, when to eat, when to pray, when to work, and when to go to bed.

★ **To learn more about this historic site, write:** Mission San Juan Capistrano, P.O. Box 697, San Juan Capistrano, CA 92693.

◄ *Mission bells*

A string of missions

As you have read, Spanish soldiers and priests built the first European settlements in California. In 1769, Captain Gaspar de Portolá led a group of soldiers and missionaries up the Pacific coast. The chief missionary was Father **Junípero Serra** (hoo NEE peh roh SEHR rah). Father Serra built his first mission at San Diego. He went on to build eight others.

Eventually, there were 21 Spanish missions along the California coast. Each mission claimed the surrounding land and soon was able to take care of all its own needs. Spanish soldiers built forts near the missions. The missions supplied meat, grain, and other foods to the forts.

Mission life for Native Americans

California Indians lived in small, scattered groups rather than large, organized nations. As a result, they were not able to offer much organized resistance to soldiers who forced them to work for the missions.

Native Americans herded sheep and cattle and raised crops for the missions. In return, they lived at the missions and learned about the Roman Catholic religion. Many Spanish missionaries were truly concerned with converting the Indians to Christianity. However, mission life was hard. Thousands of Native Americans died from overwork and diseases.

Sometimes, Indians did resist mission life. Many were baptized as Christians but continued to follow their traditional beliefs. Others simply ran away. Still, most continued to live and labor at the missions.

After Mexico won its independence, conditions for Native Americans in California grew even worse. The new Mexican government offered mission land to ranchers. On some ranches, Indians faced cruel mistreatment. If they tried to run away, the ranchers hunted them down. An American observer reported that California Indians lived in a state "even more degrading, and more oppressive than that of our slaves in the South."

Skills

FOR LIFE

Critical Thinking

Managing Information

Communication

Maps, Charts, and Graphs

Distinguishing Fact From Opinion

How Will I Use This Skill?

A fact is a statement that can be observed or proven. An opinion is a judgment that reflects a person's beliefs or feelings. To get a true picture of events, even in everyday conversation, you must be able to distinguish between facts and personal opinions.

LEARN the Skill

To tell fact from opinion, follow these steps:

❶ Identify facts. Look at each phrase or sentence and ask, "Can this be observed or proven?"

❷ Identify words that express the writer's opinion. Some opinions are clearly indicated with phrases like "I think," or "In my opinion." Others are not so easy to identify. Watch for words that express or inspire emotion.

❸ Decide whether the facts can support the writer's opinions. (Remember, this does not mean that you must *agree* with the opinion.)

PRACTICE the Skill

The excerpt to the right is from an 1846 newspaper article urging the United States to gain possession of California.

❶ List three facts that are included in this article. What makes them facts?

❷ (a) What words show that the first sentence is an opinion? (b) Identify two other opinions expressed in this excerpt.

❸ How do the facts presented by the writer support his opinion about gaining California? Give two examples.

> We do regard it as extremely desirable that California—a part, at least, of the province known by that name—should become the property of the United States. Lower California, embracing the long, narrow peninsula between the Gulf and the Pacific, stretching from the 21° to 33° latitude, a distance of about 800 miles, is universally represented by travelers as sterile and hopelessly desolate. It consists, indeed, of a chain of volcanic, treeless, barren mountains of rock, broken only by still more dreary plains of sand. It may well, therefore, be left to Mexico.
>
> The remaining part of Upper California—that which lies nearest the Pacific coast—is not only by far the best portion of the province but one of the most beautiful regions on the face of the earth. Among the highlands which enclose this valley are vast forests filled with the loftiest and finest cedars and pines in the world, with every variety of soil, freshwater lakes, and every element of unbounded agricultural wealth, except a good climate.

Source:
Adapted from the *American Review,*
January 1846.

APPLY the Skill

Choose an article in your local newspaper that includes opinions. Circle facts and underline opinions. Write a paragraph stating whether you think the facts in the article support the opinion.

These harsh conditions had a deadly effect. From 1770 to 1850, the Native American population of California declined from about 310,000 to 100,000.

Expansion: A Right and a Duty

As late as the mid-1840s, only about 700 people from the United States lived in California. Every year, however, more and more Americans began to look toward the West. The United States government even tried to buy California from Mexico several times. Officials were especially interested in gaining the fine ports at San Francisco and San Diego.

The nation's destiny

Many Americans saw the culture and the democratic government of the United States as the best in the world. They believed that the United States had the right and the duty to spread its rule all the way to the Pacific Ocean.

In the 1840s, a newspaper in New York coined a phrase for this belief. The phrase was **Manifest Destiny.** Manifest means clear or obvious. Destiny means something that is sure to happen. Americans who believed in Manifest Destiny thought that the United States was clearly meant to expand to the Pacific.

Manifest Destiny had another side, too. Many Americans believed that they were superior to Native Americans and Mexicans. For these Americans, racism justified taking over lands belonging to Indians and Mexicans.

Election of 1844

Manifest Destiny played an important part in the election of 1844. The Whigs nominated Henry Clay for President. Clay was a famous and respected national leader. The Democrats chose a little-known candidate, **James K. Polk**.

Voters soon came to know Polk as the candidate who favored expansion. Polk demanded that Texas and Oregon be added to the United States. Clay, on the other hand, opposed the annexation of Texas.

The Democrats made Oregon a special campaign issue. As you read, Britain and the United States held Oregon jointly. Polk demanded the whole region all the way to its northern border at latitude 54°40′N. "Fifty-four forty or fight!" became the Democrats' campaign cry. On election day, Americans showed their support for expansion by choosing Polk as President.

★ Section 3 Review ★

Recall

1. **Locate** (a) Sante Fe, (b) Santa Fe Trail, (c) California, (d) San Diego, (e) San Francisco.
2. **Identify** (a) New Mexico Territory, (b) William Becknell, (c) Santa Fe Trail, (d) Junípero Serra, (e) Manifest Destiny, (f) James K. Polk.

Comprehension

3. Describe how American settlers first went to New Mexico.
4. How did mission life affect Native Americans?
5. How did belief in Manifest Destiny affect the election of 1844?

Critical Thinking and Writing

6. **Making Inferences** How do you think missionaries justified forcing Indians to live and work on missions?
7. **Analyzing Ideas** "The irresistible army of [American settlers] has begun to pour down upon [California], armed with the plough and the rifle, and marking its trail with schools and colleges, courts and representative halls, mills and meetinghouses." What does this quotation show you about people's belief in the idea of Manifest Destiny?

Activity Drawing a Political Cartoon Draw a political cartoon from the point of view of Native Americans about conditions on California missions or ranches before 1845.

War With Mexico

As You Read

Explore These Questions
- How did the United States gain Oregon?
- What were the causes and results of the Mexican War?
- How did cultures blend in the new American territories?

Define
- cede

Identify
- Zachary Taylor
- Mexican War
- Winfield Scott
- Stephen Kearny
- Bear Flag Republic
- John C. Frémont
- Chapultepec
- Mexican Cession
- Gadsden Purchase

SETTING the Scene American troops marched off to war with Mexico in 1846. Many Americans were eager to fight. Soldiers proudly sang new words to the popular tune "Yankee Doodle":

> 66 They attacked our men upon our land,
> And crossed our river too, sir.
> Now show them all with sword in hand
> What yankee boys can do, sir. 99

Not all Americans supported the war against Mexico. Some even accused President Polk of provoking the war himself in order to win Texas.

The bloody Mexican War lasted 20 months. In the end, it helped the United States achieve its dream of Manifest Destiny.

Dividing Oregon

James K. Polk took office in March 1845. Acting on his campaign promise, he moved to gain control of Oregon. War with Britain threatened.

Polk did not really want a war with Britain. In 1846, he agreed to a compromise. Oregon was divided at latitude 49°N. Britain got the lands north of the line, and the United States got the lands south of the line. The United States named its portion the Oregon Territory. Later, the states of Oregon

(1859), Washington (1889), and Idaho (1890) were carved out of the Oregon Territory.

Annexing Texas

Texas proved a more dangerous problem. As you read, the United States at first refused to annex Texas. In 1844, Sam Houston, president of Texas, signed a treaty of annexation with the United States. The Senate again refused to ratify the treaty. Senators feared that annexing Texas would cause a war with Mexico.

Sam Houston would not give up. To persuade the Americans to annex Texas, he pretended that Texas might become an ally of Britain. Houston's trick worked. Americans did not want Europe's greatest power to gain a foothold on their western border. In 1845, Congress passed a joint resolution admitting Texas to the Union.

Sam Houston

Conflict With Mexico

The annexation of Texas made Mexicans furious. They had never accepted the independence of Texas. They also were concerned that the example set by Texas would encourage Americans in California and New Mexico to rebel.

At the same time, Americans resented Mexico. President Polk offered to pay Mexico $30 million for California and New Mexico. However, Mexico strongly opposed any further loss of territory and refused the offer. Many Americans felt that Mexico stood in the way of Manifest Destiny.

The war begins

A border dispute finally sparked war. The United States claimed that the southern border of Texas was the Rio Grande. Mexico argued that it was the Nueces (noo AY says) River, some 200 miles (320 km) to the north. Both nations claimed the land between the two rivers.

In January 1846, Polk ordered General **Zachary Taylor** to cross the Nueces River and set up posts in the disputed area along the Rio Grande. (See the map below.) Polk knew that the move might lead to war. In April 1846, Mexican troops crossed the Rio

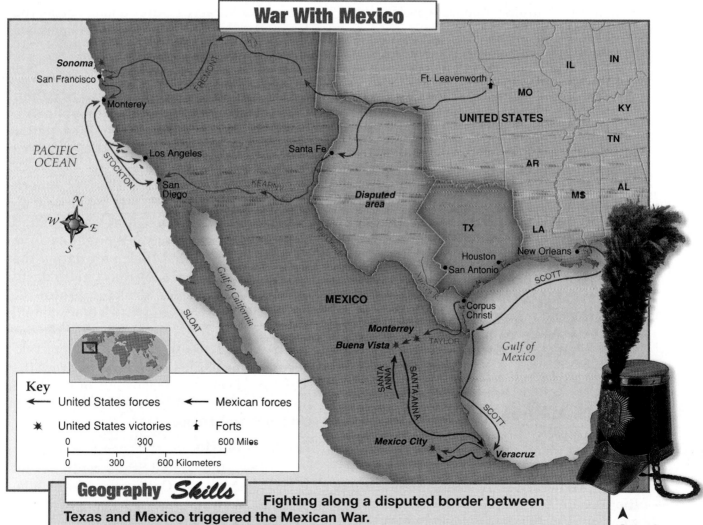

War With Mexico

Key

← United States forces   ← Mexican forces

✳ United States victories   ⬧ Forts

0   300   600 Miles

0   300   600 Kilometers

Geography *Skills*

Fighting along a disputed border between Texas and Mexico triggered the Mexican War.

1. Location   On the map, locate: **(a)** Rio Grande, **(b)** Nueces River, **(c)** Buena Vista, **(d)** Veracruz, **(e)** Mexico City.

2. Movement   Describe the movements of each of the following American commanders: **(a)** Winfield Scott, **(b)** Stephen Kearny, **(c)** John Frémont.

3. Critical Thinking   Based on the map, was sea power important to the United States in the Mexican War? Explain.

▲
Cap of a United States soldier in the Mexican War

Grande and fought briefly with the Americans. Soldiers on both sides were killed.

President Polk was already considering going to war with Mexico. When he heard about the fighting at the Rio Grande, he asked Congress to issue a declaration of war. Polk told Congress:

> 66 Mexico has passed the boundary of the United States, has invaded our territory, and shed American blood upon American soil. 99

Not everyone supported Polk's request. Abraham Lincoln, a young Whig Congressman, disputed Polk's claim that the fighting actually took place "upon American soil." Still, at Polk's urging, Congress declared war on Mexico.

Americans respond

Americans were divided over the war. Many people in the South and West wanted more land and so were eager to fight. Many northerners, however, opposed the war. They saw it as a southern plot to add slave states to the Union. "Fresh markets of human beings are to be established," claimed Charles Sumner, a Massachusetts opponent of slavery. "Further opportunities for this hateful traffic are to be opened."

Still, many Americans joined the war effort. Since the nation's standing army was small, thousands of volunteers were needed. When the call for recruits went out, the response was overwhelming, especially in the South and West.

Fighting in Mexico

As the **Mexican War** began, the United States attacked on several fronts at the same time. President Polk hoped this strategy would allow American forces to win a quick victory. General Zachary Taylor crossed the Rio Grande into northern Mexico. There, he won several battles against the Mexican army. In February 1847, Taylor met Santa Anna at the Battle of Buena Vista. The Mexican troops greatly outnumbered the American forces, but the Americans were better armed and led. After fierce fighting, Santa Anna retreated. A major in Taylor's army later recalled feeding wounded Mexican soldiers after the battle:

> 66 We collected the wounded, who were suffering awfully from hunger and thirst as well as their wounds, and sent them to hospitals in town.... When coffee and biscuit were placed before them, they showed even in their famished state some signs of surprise and gratitude. This was the greatest victory of all, a victory unstained by blood.... 99

Meanwhile, General **Winfield Scott** had landed another American army at the Mexican port of Veracruz. After a long battle, the Americans took the city. Scott then marched west toward the capital, Mexico City.

Rebellion in California

A third army, led by General **Stephen Kearny**, captured Santa Fe without firing a shot. Kearny hurried on to San Diego. After several battles, he took control of southern California early in 1847.

Even before hearing of the war, Americans in northern California had risen up against Mexican rule. The rebels declared California an independent republic on June 14, 1846. They called their new nation the **Bear Flag Republic.** At that time, a dashing young American explorer, **John C. Frémont,** was traveling in California on a scientific expedition for the army. Frémont quickly rushed to support the rebellion. Taking command of the rebel forces, he drove the Mexican governor's troops out of northern California. Frémont later joined forces with United States troops.

The final battle

By 1847, the United States controlled all of New Mexico and California. Meanwhile, General Scott had reached the outskirts of Mexico City.

Before they could take the Mexican capital, Scott's troops faced a fierce battle. Mexican soldiers made a heroic last stand at **Chapultepec** (chah POOL tuh pehk), a fort just outside Mexico City. Like the Texans who died at the Alamo, the Mexicans at Cha-

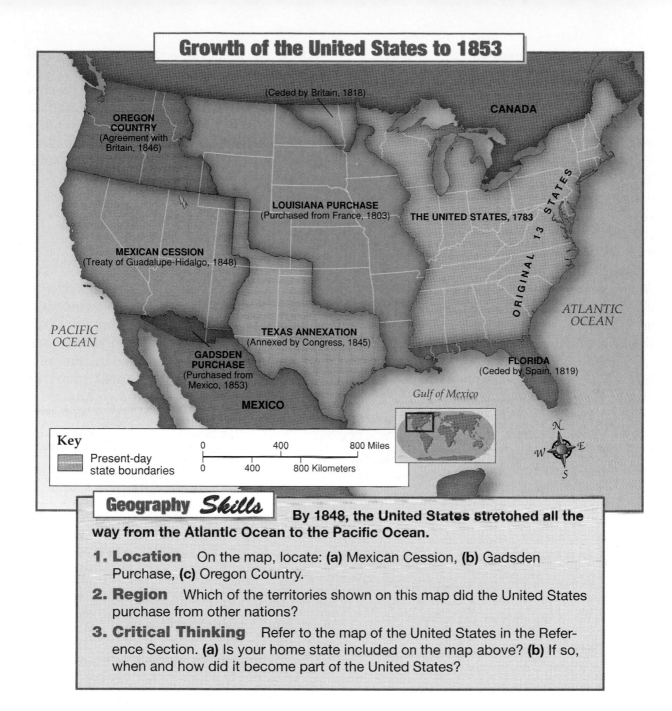

Growth of the United States to 1853

(Ceded by Britain, 1818)

CANADA

OREGON
COUNTRY
(Agreement with
Britain, 1846)

LOUISIANA PURCHASE
(Purchased from France, 1803)

THE UNITED STATES, 1783

ORIGINAL 13 STATES

MEXICAN CESSION
(Treaty of Guadalupe-Hidalgo, 1848)

ATLANTIC
OCEAN

PACIFIC
OCEAN

TEXAS ANNEXATION
(Annexed by Congress, 1845)

GADSDEN
PURCHASE
(Purchased from
Mexico, 1853)

FLORIDA
(Ceded by Spain, 1819)

MEXICO

Gulf of Mexico

Key

Present-day
state boundaries

0   400   800 Miles

0   400   800 Kilometers

N W E S

Geography *Skills*

By 1848, the United States stretched all the way from the Atlantic Ocean to the Pacific Ocean.

1. **Location** On the map, locate: **(a)** Mexican Cession, **(b)** Gadsden Purchase, **(c)** Oregon Country.

2. **Region** Which of the territories shown on this map did the United States purchase from other nations?

3. **Critical Thinking** Refer to the map of the United States in the Reference Section. **(a)** Is your home state included on the map above? **(b)** If so, when and how did it become part of the United States?

pultepec fought to the last man. Today, Mexicans honor these young soldiers as heroes.

Achieving Manifest Destiny

With their capital in American hands, the Mexican government had no choice but to make peace. In 1848, Mexico signed the Treaty of Guadalupe-Hidalgo (gwah duh LOOP ay-ih DAHL goh). The treaty forced Mexico to **cede,** or give, all of California and New Mexico to the United States. These lands were called the **Mexican Cession.** (See the map above.)

In return, the United States paid Mexico $15 million. Americans also agreed to respect the rights of Spanish-speaking people in the Mexican Cession.

A few years after the end of the Mexican War, the United States completed its expansion across the continent. In 1853, it agreed to pay Mexico $10 million for a strip of land in present-day Arizona and New Mexico. The Americans needed this land to complete the building of a railroad. The land was called the **Gadsden Purchase.** The dream of Manifest Destiny was now complete.

A Mix of Cultures in the Southwest

English-speaking settlers poured into the Southwest. They brought their own culture with them, including their ideas about democratic government. The newcomers also learned a great deal from the older residents of the region. Mexican Americans taught the newcomers how to mine silver and irrigate the soil for growing crops. Many Spanish and Native American words—such as stampede, buffalo, tortilla, soda, and tornado—became part of the English language.

The new settlers often treated Mexican Americans and Native Americans poorly. The earlier residents struggled to protect their traditions and rights. However, when Mexican Americans went to court to de-

Many Mexican homes in the Southwest contained religious statuettes like this one.

fend their property, judges rarely upheld their claims. The family of Mariano Guadalupe Vallejo (vah YAY hoh) had lived in California for decades before the English-speaking settlers arrived. Vallejo, a wealthy landowner, noted how some new settlers were able to gain control of much of the land:

66 In their dealings with the rancheros, [Americans] took advantage of laws which they understood, but which were new to the Spaniards. 99

At the same time, Americans in the Southwest kept some Mexican laws. One of these laws said that a husband and wife owned property together. In the rest of the United States, married women could not own any property. Another Mexican law said that landowners could not cut off water to their neighbors. This law was important in the Southwest, where water was scarce.

★ Section 4 Review ★

Recall

1. **Locate** (a) Rio Grande, (b) Nueces River, (c) Buena Vista, (d) Veracruz, (e) Mexico City.
2. **Identify** (a) Zachary Taylor, (b) Mexican War, (c) Winfield Scott, (d) Stephen Kearny, (e) Bear Flag Republic, (f) John C. Frémont, (g) Chapultepec, (h) Mexican Cession, (i) Gadsden Purchase.
3. **Define** cede.

Comprehension

4. How did President Polk avoid war with Britain over Oregon?
5. (a) What event sparked the beginning of the Mexican War? (b) What were the final results of the war?

6. (a) Name two things that English-speaking settlers learned from Mexican Americans in the Southwest. (b) Name one tradition that settlers brought with them.

Critical Thinking and Writing

7. **Identifying Alternatives** Do you think the United States could have avoided going to war with Mexico in 1846? Explain.
8. **Recognizing Points of View** Frederick Douglass, an African American who fought to end slavery, wrote of the Mexican War that Americans "ought [to] blush and hang our heads for shame." (a) Why do you think Douglass opposed the war? (b) Who might have agreed with his statement? Who might have disagreed?

Activity **Roleplaying** With your classmates, choose among the following roles: a citizen of Mexico; a white American living in Texas; a Mexican living in Texas; an American Californian; a northerner; a southerner; President Polk. Hold a debate about whether the United States should go to war with Mexico.

A Rush to the West

As You Read

Explore These Questions
- How did the Mormons settle Utah?
- How did the discovery of gold affect life in California?
- Why did California have a diverse population?

Define
- forty-niner
- vigilante

Identify
- Mormons
- Joseph Smith
- Brigham Young
- Sutter's Mill

SETTING the Scene In 1848, exciting news reached Toishan, a district in southern China. Mountains of gold had been discovered across the Pacific Ocean, in a place called California. It was there just for the digging!

The penalty for trying to leave China was harsh and sure—a swift beheading. Still, tens of thousands of Chinese risked the executioner's axe to cross the Pacific. Like other prospectors from Europe to Boston to South America, they were eager to join the California Gold Rush.

Gold was not the only thing that attracted settlers to the West in the mid-1800s. California, New Mexico, Oregon, and Texas were all now part of the United States. Restless pioneers, always eager to try something new, headed into these lands to build homes and a new way of life.

A Refuge for the Mormons

The largest group of settlers to move into the Mexican Cession were the **Mormons.** Mormons belonged to the Church of Jesus Christ of Latter-day Saints. The church was founded by **Joseph Smith** in 1830. Smith, a farmer who lived in upstate New York, attracted many followers.

Troubles with neighbors

Smith was an energetic and popular man. His teachings, however, angered many non-Mormons. For example, Mormons at first be-lieved that property should be owned in common. Smith also said that a man could have more than one wife. Angry neighbors forced the Mormons to leave New York for Ohio. From Ohio, they were forced to move to Missouri, and from there to Illinois. In the 1840s, the Mormons built a community called Nauvoo on the banks of the Mississippi River in Illinois.

Before long, the Mormons again clashed with their neighbors. In 1844, an angry mob killed Joseph Smith. The Mormons chose **Brigham Young** as their new leader.

Brigham Young realized that the Mormons needed to find a home where they would be safe. He had read about a valley between the Rocky Mountains and the Great Salt Lake in Utah. Young decided that the isolated valley would make a good home for the Mormons.

A difficult journey

To move 15,000 men, women, and children from Illinois to Utah in the 1840s was an awesome challenge. Relying on religious faith and careful planning, Brigham Young achieved his goal.

In 1847, Young led an advance party into the Great Salt Lake valley. Wave after wave of Mormons followed. For the next few years, Mormon wagon trains struggled across the plains and over the Rockies to Utah. When they ran short of wagons and oxen, thousands made the long trip pulling their gear in handcarts.

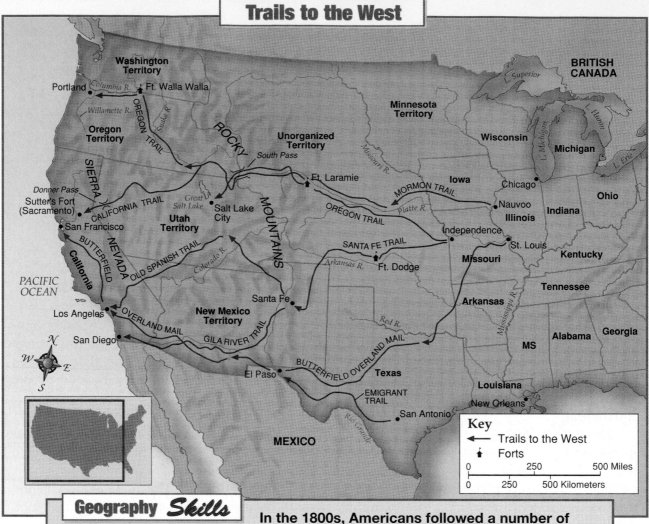

Trails to the West

Geography *Skills* In the 1800s, Americans followed a number of different trails to the West. Mountain passes allowed settlers to cross the Rockies and Sierra Nevada.

1. Location On the map, locate: **(a)** Santa Fe, **(b)** Santa Fe Trail, **(c)** Sierra Nevada, **(d)** Rocky Mountains, **(e)** San Diego, **(f)** San Francisco, **(g)** Salt Lake City.

2. Movement Which trails ended in cities in California?

3. Critical Thinking **(a)** What would be the best route for a pioneer family to take from Independence, Missouri, to Sutter's Fort, California? **(b)** What mountains would they have to cross? **(c)** In which town might they seek shelter along the way?

Prospering in the desert

In Utah, the Mormons had to survive in a harsh desert climate. Still, Young was convinced that, for the Mormons, Utah was Zion, or the promised land:

66 We will raise our wheat, build our houses, fence our farms, plant our vineyards and orchards, and produce everything that will make our bodies comfortable and happy and in this manner we intend to build up Zion on the earth. 99

To meet his goals, Young planned an irrigation system to bring water to farms. He also drew up plans for a large city, called Salt Lake City, to be built in the desert.

The Mormon settlement in Utah grew quickly. Like other whites, Mormons took over thousands of acres of Native American land, usually paying nothing for it.

Congress recognized Brigham Young as governor of the Utah Territory in 1850. Trouble later broke out when non-Mormons moved to the area. In the end, peace was restored, and Utah became a state in 1896.

California Gold Rush

While the Mormons trekked to Utah, thousands of other Americans were racing to California. These adventurous men and women all had a single objective: Gold!

Sutter's Mill

In 1848, John Sutter was building a sawmill on the American River, north of Sacramento, California. James Marshall was in charge of the job. On the morning of January 24, Marshall set out to inspect a ditch his crew was digging. He later told a friend what he saw that day:

66 It was a clear, cold morning; I shall never forget that morning. As I was taking my usual walk, ... my eye was caught with the glimpse of something shining in the bottom of the ditch. There was about a foot of water running then. I reached my hand down and picked it up; it made my heart thump, for I was certain it was gold. 99

In a few days, word of the gold strike at **Sutter's Mill** spread to San Francisco. Carpenters threw down their saws. Bakers left bread in their ovens. Schools emptied as teachers and students joined the rush to the gold fields.

From San Francisco, the news spread across the United States and to the rest of the world. Thousands of Americans caught gold fever. People from Europe, China, Australia, and South America joined the rush as well. More than 80,000 people made the long journey to California in 1849. They became known as **forty-niners.**

In the gold fields

The first miners needed little skill. Because the gold was near the surface of the Earth, they could dig it out with knives. Later, the miners found a better way. They loaded sand and gravel from the riverbed into a washing pan. Then, they held the pan under water and swirled it gently. The water washed away lighter gravel, leaving the heavier gold in the pan. This process was known as "panning for gold."

Cause and Effect

Causes

- Oregon has fertile land
- Texas is ideal for raising cattle and growing cotton
- Many Americans believe in Manifest Destiny
- Mormons seek a safe home
- Gold is discovered in California

Westward Movement

Effects

- Texas wins war for independence
- United States annexes Texas
- Britain and United States divide Oregon
- United States defeats Mexico in war
- Cotton Kingdom spreads

Effects Today

- United States stretches from sea to sea
- California and Texas are the most populous states
- Mexican American culture enriches the United States

Graphic Organizer *Skills*

Westward movement increased at a tremendous rate in the mid-1800s.

1. **Comprehension** List two attractions that drew Americans to the West.
2. **Critical Thinking** According to this chart, was Manifest Destiny successful? Explain.

Economics $

Only a few miners actually struck it rich. Most went broke trying to make their fortunes. Still, although many miners left the gold fields, they stayed in California.

China

United States

From China to the Golden Mountain

Some 25,000 Chinese left their ordered society for the rough-and-tumble world of the California gold fields. Few struck it rich, but their knowledge of farming helped the territory prosper. At left, Chinese peasants tend a rice field. At right, Chinese miners work at a gold claim. ★ **What qualities did the Chinese and other forty-niners need to succeed?**

Women joined the gold rush. Some staked claims and mined for gold. Others took advantage of economic opportunities in the mining camps. Women ran boarding houses, took in laundry, sewed, and ran bakeries.

A new state

The Gold Rush changed life in California. Almost overnight, San Francisco grew from a sleepy town to a bustling city.

Greed led some forty-niners to become criminals. Murders and robberies plagued many mining camps. To fight crime, miners formed vigilance committees. **Vigilantes** (vihj uh LAN teez), self-appointed law enforcers, dealt out punishment even though they had no legal power to do so. Sometimes an accused criminal was lynched, that is, hanged without a legal trial.

Californians realized they needed a government to stop the lawlessness. In 1849, they drafted a state constitution. They then asked to be admitted to the Union. Their request caused an uproar in the United States. Americans wondered whether the new state would allow slavery. As you will read, after a heated debate, California was admitted to the Union in 1850 as a free state.

California's Unique Culture

Most mining camps in California included a mix of peoples. A visitor to a mining town might meet runaway slaves from the South, Native Americans, and New Englanders. There were also people from Hawaii, China, Peru, Chile, France, Germany, Italy, Ireland, and Australia.

Connections With Arts

The California Gold Rush provided the background for the still-popular folk song "My Darling Clementine." The song begins: "In a canyon, in a cavern / Excavating for a mine / Lived a miner, forty-niner / And his daughter Clementine."

Most of the miners, however, were white Americans. During the wild days of the Gold Rush, they often ignored the rights of other Californians.

Mexican Americans and Indians

California included many Mexicans and Native Americans who had lived there long before the Gold Rush. In many instances, Mexican Americans lost land they had owned for generations. Still, they fought to preserve the customs of their people. José Carrillo (cah REE yoh) was from one of the oldest families in California. In part through his efforts, the state's first constitution was written in both Spanish and English.

Indians fared worst of all. Many Native Americans were driven off their lands and later died of starvation or diseases. Others were murdered. In 1850, about 100,000 Indians lived in California. By the 1870s, there were only 17,000 Indians left in the state.

Chinese Americans

Attracted by the tales of a "mountain of gold," thousands of Chinese began arriving in California in 1848. Because California needed workers, the Chinese were welcomed at first. When the Chinese staked claims in the gold fields, however, white miners often drove them off.

Discrimination against Chinese Americans and, later, other Asians would continue in California for many decades. Still, many Chinese Americans stayed in California and helped the state to grow. They farmed, irrigated, and reclaimed vast stretches of land.

African Americans

Free blacks, too, rushed to the California gold fields hoping to strike it rich. Some did become wealthy. By the 1850s, in fact, California had the richest African American population of any state. Yet African Americans were also denied certain rights. For example, California law denied blacks and other minorities the right to testify against whites in court. After a long struggle, blacks gained this right in 1863.

In spite of these problems, California thrived and grew. Settlers continued to arrive in the state. By 1860, it had 100,000 citizens. The mix of peoples in California gave it a unique culture.

★ Section 5 Review ★

Recall

1. **Locate** (a) Nauvoo, (b) Salt Lake City, (c) Sacramento, (d) San Francisco.
2. **Identify** (a) Mormons, (b) Joseph Smith, (c) Brigham Young, (d) Sutter's Mill.
3. **Define** (a) forty-niner, (b) vigilante.

Comprehension

4. Why did Brigham Young lead the Mormons to Utah?
5. Describe two effects of the Gold Rush on California.
6. Explain the problems that each of the following faced in California: (a) Mexican Americans, (b) Native Americans, (c) Chinese Americans, (d) African Americans.

Critical Thinking and Writing

7. **Comparing** Compare the settling of Utah with the settling of California. How were they similar? How were they different?
8. **Linking Past and Present** In the 1990s, almost 30 percent of immigrants to the United States settled in California. The largest group were from Asia. (a) Why do you think California still attracts many immigrants? (b) Why do so many Asian immigrants come to California?

★ ★

Activity **Writing a Speech** There's trouble ahead! You and your friend went to California in the Gold Rush. Now, vigilantes are accusing your friend of a crime he didn't commit—stealing a horse. Write a speech in which you declare his innocence and call upon the vigilantes to wait until your friend can receive a legal trial.

Chapter 13 Review and Activities

★ Sum It Up ★

Section 1 Oregon Country
▶ The first white people to live in Oregon Country were hardy fur trappers.
▶ Settlers traveling by wagon train braved great dangers to reach Oregon Country.

Section 2 Texas Wins Independence
▶ Americans living in Texas, as well as Tejanos, rebelled against the Mexican government in 1835.
▶ After winning several battles, Texans set up an independent republic.

Section 3 California and the Southwest
▶ In the early years of white settlement, California was dotted with Spanish missions, forts, and ranches.
▶ In the 1840s, many Americans came to believe that the United States was destined to expand to the Pacific.

Section 4 War With Mexico
▶ The United States made Texas a part of the Union, and then went to war with Mexico in a border dispute.
▶ After defeating Mexico, the United States gained the Southwest and California.

Section 5 A Rush to the West
▶ Seeking religious freedom, the Mormons built a community in the Utah desert.
▶ A gold rush in California drew many newcomers to that region.

For additional review of the major ideas of Chapter 13, see **Guide to the Essentials of American History** or **Interactive Student Tutorial CD-ROM,** which contains interactive review activities, graphic organizers, and practice tests.

🗒 Reviewing the Chapter

Define These Terms

Match each term with the correct definition.

Column 1	Column 2
1. rendezvous	a. get-together for trappers
2. annex	b. person who joined the California Gold Rush
3. cede	c. to give something up
4. forty-niner	d. to add something on
5. vigilante	e. self-appointed law enforcer

Explore the Main Ideas

1. Describe the way of life of the mountain men in Oregon Country.
2. How did Texans force Santa Anna to grant them independence?
3. What role did the Catholic Church play in the settlement of California?
4. Describe one cause and one effect of the Mexican War.
5. Name the groups that made up the mixed culture of California in the mid-1800s.

🗒 Geography Activity

Match the letters on the map with the following places:
1. Louisiana Purchase, **2.** Gadsden Purchase, **3.** Oregon Country, **4.** Florida, **5.** The United States in 1783, **6.** Texas Annexation, **7.** Mexican Cession. **Location** At what latitude did the United States and Britain agree to divide Oregon?

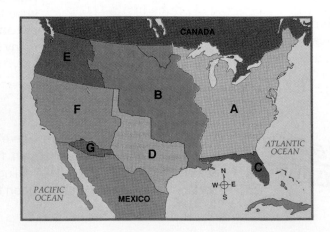

🔲 Critical Thinking and Writing

1. **Linking Past and Present** If you were Horace Greeley today, what advice would you give to young people seeking opportunity?

2. **Understanding Chronology** (a) List the following events in their correct order: Mexican War; annexation of Texas; founding of the Lone Star Republic; Battle of San Jacinto; Treaty of Guadalupe-Hidalgo. (b) Why was it unlikely that the United States would go to war with Mexico *before* Texas joined the Union?

3. **Understanding Causes and Effects** (a) What was the immediate cause of the war with Mexico? (b) Identify two long-range causes.

4. **Exploring Unit Themes Expansion** (a) Describe the idea of Manifest Destiny. (b) Explain how the nation achieved this goal. (c) What do you think were some of the positive and negative effects of Manifest Destiny?

🔲 Using Primary Sources

In a letter written in 1844, Henry Clay explained his thoughts about the annexation of Texas:

> 66 Annexation and war with Mexico are identical. Now, for one, I certainly am not willing to involve this country in a foreign war for the object of acquiring Texas. I know there are those who regard such a war... as a trifling affair, on account of the weakness of Mexico.... But I do not look upon it thus lightly. I regard all wars as great calamities, to be avoided, if possible, and honorable peace as the wisest and truest policy of this country. 99

Source: *National Intelligencer*, April, 17, 1844.

Recognizing Points of View (a) What did Clay predict would happen if the United States annexed Texas? (b) Why did he oppose the idea? (c) How do you think Sam Houston would have responded to Clay's letter?

ACTIVITY BANK

▶ Interdisciplinary Activity

Exploring Science Working with a partner, give a presentation on how a geologic feature of the West influenced history. For example, you might choose the Rio Grande, the Great Salt Lake, the Rocky Mountains, the Central Valley of California, or the gold in California.

▶ Career Skills Activity

City Planner You are a city official of San Francisco in 1849. You know that thousands of people will be moving to your city over the next few years. Write a report in which you propose a plan for growth.

▶ Citizenship Activity

Exploring Immigration Like Californians, most Americans today are immigrants or descended from immigrants. Do you know when any of your ancestors first came to this country? If so, prepare a chart tracing your ancestors back to the first people in your family to come to the United States.

Internet Activity

Use the Internet to find sites dealing with the early history of the Mormons. Take notes on what you find and use them to compose a two-paragraph report on early Mormon history.

EYEWITNESS Journal

You are a mountain man or a missionary in Oregon; an American or Tejano in Texas; an American or Mexican in California; a Mormon in Utah; or a forty-niner. In your EYEWITNESS JOURNAL, describe your participation in whatever was, for you, the single most important event of the years 1820–1860.

Chapter 14

The Worlds of North and South 1820–1860

As the 1800s progressed, the North and the South continued to develop differently. In many ways, the two regions were like separate worlds. The North based its economy largely on industry. The South, meanwhile, developed an agricultural system that relied primarily on cotton. The industry of the North depended on paid workers. These workers struggled to make a living and endured hard working conditions. Still, they were free. In contrast, cotton production in the South depended on the labor of enslaved African Americans. These enslaved people had no rights or freedoms.

Why Study History?

In the mid-1800s, many Americans could trace their roots to one of the British Isles, to Spain, or to a particular region of Africa. New immigrants were arriving from Germany, Ireland, and other European nations. Americans of all backgrounds were proud of their rich heritage. To learn about cultural influences that helped to shape several styles of American music, see this chapter's *Why Study History?* feature, "Music Is Part of Our Culture."

American Events	**1820s** Skilled workers begin to organize unions		**1830s** Railroads allow goods to be shipped quickly and cheaply		
1820	**1825**		**1830**	**1835**	**1840**

World Events

1829 World Event
Steam-powered locomotive travels 30 miles per hour in England

Viewing History

Different Worlds

By the mid-1800s, the North and South had different economies. The North developed a variety of industries based on the labor of free workers. The South depended largely on agriculture and the labor of enslaved African Americans. A typical southern scene appears in William Aiken Walker's painting Plantation Economy in the Old South, *shown above.* ★ **What other economic differences between North and South do the pictures above suggest?**

●**1840s**
Cotton boom in South leads to spread of slavery

●**1844**
Morse receives patent for telegraph

●**1850s**
Millions of Irish and German immigrants settle in the United States

1840 | **1845** | **1850** | **1855** | **1860**

▲ **1840 World Event**
World Anti-Slavery Convention held in Great Britain

▲ **1848 World Event**
Revolutions in Germany

Industry in the North

As You Read

Explore These Questions
- How did new inventions change manufacturing and farming in the North?
- How did new means of communication and transportation benefit business?
- How did steam power help industry grow?

Define
- telegraph
- locomotive
- clipper ship

Identify
- Elias Howe
- John Deere
- Cyrus McCormick
- Samuel F. B. Morse
- John Griffiths

Elias Howe sewing machine

SETTING the Scene In 1834, a young French engineer, Michel Chevalier, toured the North. He was most impressed by the burst of industry there—the textile factories, shipyards, and iron mills. He wrote:

> 66 Everywhere is heard the noise of hammers, of spindles, of bells calling the hands to their work, or dismissing them from their tasks.... It is the peaceful hum of an industrious population, whose movements are regulated like clockwork. 99

Northern industry grew steadily in the mid-1800s. Most northerners still lived on farms. However, more and more of the northern economy centered on manufacturing and trade.

New Machines

The 1800s brought a flood of new inventions in the North. "In Massachusetts and Connecticut," a European visitor exclaimed, "there is not a laborer who has not invented a machine or a tool."

In 1846, **Elias Howe** patented a sewing machine. A few years later, Isaac Singer improved on Howe's machine. Soon, clothing makers bought hundreds of the new sewing machines. Workers could now make dozens of shirts in the time it took a tailor to sew one by hand.

Some new inventions made work easier for farmers. **John Deere** invented a lightweight steel plow. Earlier plows made of heavy iron or wood had to be pulled by slow-moving oxen. A horse could pull a steel plow through a field more quickly.

In 1847, **Cyrus McCormick** opened a factory in Chicago that produced mechanical reapers. The reaper was a horse-drawn machine that mowed wheat and other grains. McCormick's reaper could do the work of five people using hand tools.

The reaper and the steel plow helped farmers raise more grain with fewer hands. As a result, thousands of farm workers left the countryside. Some went west to start farms of their own. Others found jobs in new factories in northern cities.

$ Connections With Economics

Cyrus McCormick used a new business practice to help struggling farmers buy a reaper. He let farmers put some money down and pay the rest in installments. This practice is known as the installment plan or buying on credit.

The Telegraph

In 1844, **Samuel F. B. Morse** received a patent for a "talking wire," or telegraph. The **telegraph** was a device that sent electrical signals along a wire. The signals were based on a code of dots, dashes, and spaces. Later, this system of dots and dashes became known as the Morse code.

Congress gave Morse funds to run wire from Washington, D.C., to Baltimore. On May 24, 1844, Morse set up his telegraph in the Supreme Court chamber in Washington. As a crowd of onlookers watched, Morse tapped out a short message: "What hath God wrought!" A few seconds later, the operator in Baltimore tapped back the same message. The telegraph worked!

Morse's invention was an instant success. Telegraph companies sprang up everywhere. Thousands of miles of wire soon stretched across the country. As a result of the telegraph, news could now travel long distances in a matter of minutes.

The telegraph helped many businesses to thrive. Merchants and farmers could have quick access to information about supply, demand, and prices of goods in different areas of the country. For example, western farmers might learn of a wheat shortage in New York and ship their grain east to meet the demand.

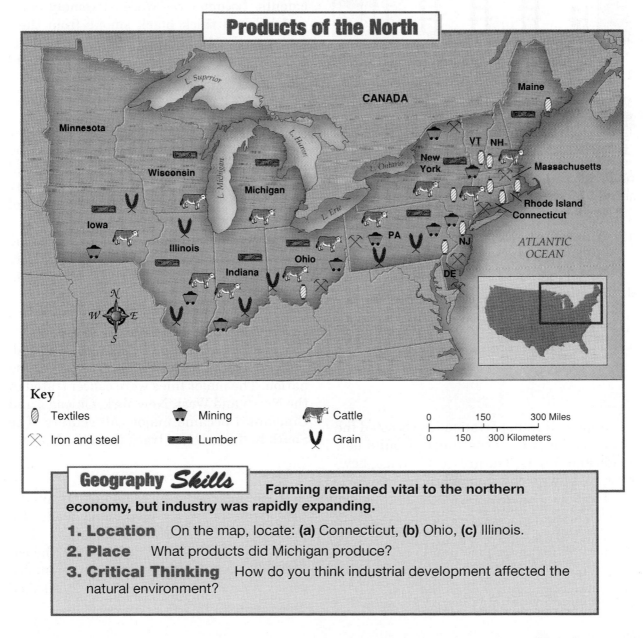

Products of the North

Key

◍ Textiles ⛏ Mining 🐄 Cattle
✕ Iron and steel ▭ Lumber Ⅴ Grain

0   150   300 Miles
0 150 300 Kilometers

Geography *Skills*   Farming remained vital to the northern economy, but industry was rapidly expanding.

1. Location   On the map, locate: **(a)** Connecticut, **(b)** Ohio, **(c)** Illinois.

2. Place   What products did Michigan produce?

3. Critical Thinking   How do you think industrial development affected the natural environment?

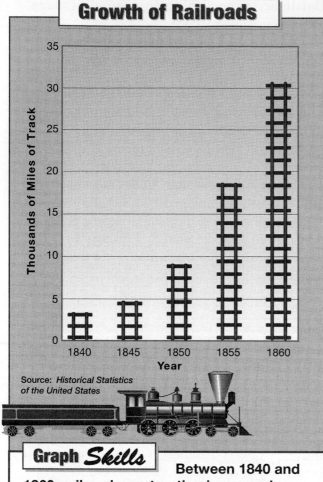

Growth of Railroads

Thousands of Miles of Track (y-axis: 0, 5, 10, 15, 20, 25, 30, 35)

Year (x-axis: 1840, 1845, 1850, 1855, 1860)

Source: *Historical Statistics of the United States*

Graph Skills Between 1840 and 1860, railroad construction increased greatly. More railroad lines were built in the North than in the South.

1. **Comprehension** Approximately how many miles of track were laid between 1855 and 1860?
2. **Critical Thinking** What raw materials were needed to build and run the railroads?

Economics $

Early difficulties

In the United States, there was some initial opposition to railroads. Farmers did not want railroads running through their fields. Teamsters who moved freight on horse-drawn wagons feared that they would lose their jobs. Likewise, people who invested in canals worried that competition from the railroads might cause them to lose their investments. Some states protected the canals by placing limits on railroads. One such limit was that railroads could carry freight only when canals were frozen.

Another problem for the railroads was concern over reliability and safety. Early steam locomotives often broke down. Soft roadbeds and weak bridges contributed to accidents. Locomotives were extremely noisy and belched thick black smoke from their smokestacks. Hot embers from smokestacks sometimes burned holes in passengers' clothing or set nearby buildings on fire.

A railroad boom

Despite these problems, promoters believed in the future of train travel. One boasted that the railroads were "unrivaled for speed, cleanliness, civility of officers and servants, and admirable accommodations of every kind."

Gradually, railroad builders overcame problems and removed obstacles. Engineers learned to build sturdier bridges and solid roadbeds. They replaced wooden rails with iron rails. Such improvements made railroad travel safer and faster. Meanwhile, legal restrictions on railroad building were removed.

By the 1850s, railroads crisscrossed the nation. The major lines were concentrated in the North and West. New York, Chicago, and Cincinnati became major rail centers. The South had much less track than the North.

Yankee Clippers

Railroads increased commerce within the United States. At the same time, trade also increased between the United States and other nations. At seaports in the Northeast, captains loaded their ships with cotton, fur, wheat, lumber, and tobacco. Then they sailed to the four corners of the world.

The First Railroads

Improved transportation also boosted the economy. Americans continued to build new roads and canals. The greatest change, however, came with the railroads.

The first railroads were built in the early 1800s. Horses or mules pulled cars along wooden rails covered with strips of iron. Then, in 1829, an English family developed a steam-powered **locomotive** engine to pull rail cars. The engine, called the *Rocket,* barreled along at 30 miles (48 km) per hour.

Speed was the key to successful trade at sea. In 1845, an American named **John Griffiths** launched the *Rainbow,* the first of the **clipper ships.** These sleek vessels had tall masts and huge sails that caught every gust of wind. Their narrow hulls clipped swiftly through the water.

In the 1840s, American clipper ships broke every speed record. One clipper sped from New York to Hong Kong in 81 days, flying past older ships that took five months to reach China. The speed of the clippers helped the United States win a large share of the world's sea trade in the 1840s and 1850s.

The golden age of the clipper ship was brief. In the 1850s, Britain launched the first oceangoing iron steamships. These sturdy vessels carried more cargo and traveled even faster than clippers.

The Northern Economy Expands

By the 1830s, factories began to use steam power instead of water power. Machines that were driven by steam were powerful and cheap to run. Also, factories that used steam power could be built almost anywhere, not just along the banks of swift-flowing rivers. As a result, American industry expanded rapidly.

At the same time, new machines made it possible to produce more goods at a lower cost. These more affordable goods attracted eager buyers. Families no longer had to make clothing and other goods in their homes. Instead, they could buy factory-made products.

Railroads allowed factory owners to transport large amounts of raw materials and finished goods cheaply and quickly. Also, as railroads stretched across the nation, they linked distant towns with cities and factories. These towns became new markets for factory goods.

The growth of railroads also affected northern farming. Railroads brought cheap grain and other foods from the West to New England. New England farmers could not compete with this new source of cheap foods. Many left their farms to find new jobs as factory workers, store clerks, and sailors. More and more, New Englanders turned to manufacturing and trade.

★ Section 1 Review ★

Recall

1. **Identify** (a) Elias Howe, (b) John Deere, (c) Cyrus McCormick, (d) Samuel F. B. Morse, (e) John Griffiths.
2. **Define** (a) telegraph, (b) locomotive, (c) clipper ship.

Comprehension

3. What new inventions made work easier for farmers?
4. Explain how each of the following helped industry grow: (a) telegraph, (b) railroads, (c) clipper ships.

5. How did steam power and new machines change northern industry?

Critical Thinking and Writing

6. **Linking Past and Present** What technology of today helps businesses in the same way that the telegraph helped businesses in the 1800s?
7. **Understanding Causes and Effects** How did the building of railroads cause many New Englanders to abandon farming?

★ ★

Activity **Creating an Advertisement** It is the mid-1800s and you are working at an advertising agency. Create an advertisement poster urging people to buy or use one of the new inventions of the period. Use both words and pictures to make your advertisement persuasive.

Life in the North

As You Read

Explore These Questions
- What conditions caused northern workers to organize?
- Why did many Europeans move to the United States in the mid-1800s?
- What was life like for African Americans in the North?

Define
- artisan
- trade union
- strike
- famine
- nativist
- discrimination

Identify
- Sarah Bagley
- Know-Nothing party
- Henry Boyd
- Macon Allen
- John Russworm

SETTING the Scene Alzina Parsons never forgot her thirteenth birthday. The day began as usual, with work in the local spinning mill. Suddenly, Alzina cried out. She had caught her hand in the spinning machine, badly mangling her fingers. The foreman summoned the factory doctor. He cut off one of the injured fingers and sent the girl back to work.

In the early 1800s, such an incident probably would not have happened. Factory work was hard, but mill owners treated workers like human beings. By the 1840s, however, there was an oversupply of workers. Many factory owners now treated workers like machines.

Factory Conditions Worsen

Factories of the 1840s and 1850s were very different from the mills of the early 1800s. The factories were larger, and they used steam-powered machines. More laborers worked longer hours for lower wages. Workers lived in dark, dingy houses in the shadow of the factory.

Families in factories

As the need for workers increased, entire families labored in factories. In some cases, a family agreed to work for one year. If even one family member broke the contract, the entire family might be fired.

The factory day began when a whistle sounded at 4 A.M. Father, mother, and children dressed in the dark and headed off to work. At 7:30 A.M. and at noon, the whistle sounded again to announce breakfast and lunch breaks. The workday did not end until 7:30 P.M., when a final whistle sent the workers home.

Hazards at work

During their long day, factory workers faced discomfort and danger. Few factories had windows or heating systems. In summer, the heat and humidity inside the factory were stifling. In winter, the extreme cold chilled workers' bones and contributed to frequent sickness.

Factory machines had no safety devices, and accidents were common. Owners ignored the hazards. There were no laws regulating factory conditions. Injured workers often lost their jobs.

In 1855, a visitor to a textile mill in Fall River, Massachusetts, asked the manager of the mill how he treated his workers. In his reply, the manager was harsh but honest. He described his feelings about the workers.

❝ I regard people just as I regard my machinery. So long as they can do my work for what I choose to pay them, I keep them, getting out of them all I can. ❞

Workers Join Together

Poor working conditions and low wages led workers to organize. The first to do so were **artisans.** Artisans are workers who have learned a trade, such as carpentry or shoemaking.

Trade unions and strikes

In the 1820s and 1830s, artisans in each trade united to form **trade unions**. The unions called for a shorter workday, higher wages, and better working conditions. Sometimes, unions went on strike to gain their demands. In a **strike**, union workers refuse to do their jobs.

At the time, strikes were illegal in many parts of the United States. Strikers faced fines or jail sentences. Employers often fired strike leaders.

Progress for artisans

Slowly, however, workers made progress. In 1840, President Van Buren approved a 10-hour workday for government employees. Other workers pressed their demands until they won the same hours as government workers. Workers celebrated another victory in 1842 when a Massachusetts court declared that they had the right to strike.

Artisans won better pay because factory owners needed their skills. Unskilled workers, however, were unable to bargain for better wages. Unskilled workers held jobs that required little or no training. Because these workers were easy to replace, employers did not listen to their demands.

Women Workers Organize

The success of trade unions encouraged other workers to organize. Workers in New England textile mills especially were eager to protest cuts in wages and unfair work rules. Many of these workers were women.

Women workers faced special problems. First, they had always earned less money than men did. Second, most union leaders did not want women in their ranks. Like many people at the time, they believed that women should not work outside the home. In fact, the goal of many unions was to raise men's wages so that their wives could leave their factory jobs.

Viewing HISTORY Working in a Factory

Factory employees faced crowded and dangerous working conditions. Many were injured on the job. The workers in this scene are making McCormick reapers. ★ **What kinds of accidents could occur in a factory such as this?**

▼ *A worker's lunch pail*

Skills
FOR LIFE

Critical Thinking	Managing Information	**Communication**	Maps, Charts, and Graphs

Teaching Others

How Will I Use This Skill?

You already use it. You may teach others how to do school work, how to make something, how to play a sport, or how to use a computer program. In the future, you may teach job skills to co-workers. If you become a parent, you will teach your child. We are all teachers.

LEARN the Skill

You can teach others by following these four steps:

❶ Make sure you know the material you will teach.

❷ Prepare a teaching plan that is interesting, informative, and at the proper level of difficulty.

❸ Present your lesson. Encourage your students to participate and to ask questions.

❹ Check that your students have learned the material and reteach if necessary.

PRACTICE the Skill

Using the steps above, teach some classmates about the immigrants who came to the United States in the mid-1800s.

❶ Study and take notes on the material in this section under the heading Millions of New Americans.

Teaching and learning

❷ Prepare the teaching plan that you will use for your lesson. You might make an outline or chart or write a skit. You might use additional books or videotapes.

❸ Present your lesson. Keep your students involved! Ask interesting questions and encourage your students to participate.

❹ Provide a quiz or activity to check for student understanding. If your students did not learn the lesson well enough, use a different method and try again.

APPLY the Skill

You can apply this skill by volunteering to tutor a classmate or younger student who is having difficulty with reading, mathematics, or another school subject. You might also teach a friend about a hobby or game that interests you.

Despite these problems, women workers organized. They staged several strikes at Lowell, Massachusetts, in the 1830s. In the 1840s, **Sarah Bagley** organized the Lowell Female Labor Reform Association. The group petitioned the state legislature for a 10-hour workday.

Millions of New Americans

By the late 1840s, many factory workers in the North were immigrants. An immigrant is a person who enters a new country in order to settle there. In the 1840s and 1850s, about 4 million immigrants arrived in the United States.

From Ireland and Germany

In the 1840s, a disease destroyed the potato crop across Europe. The loss of the crop caused a **famine**, or severe food shortage, especially in Ireland. Between 1845 and 1860, over 1.5 million Irish fled to the United States.

Most Irish immigrants were too poor to buy farmland. They settled in the cities where their ships landed. In New York and Boston, thousands of Irish crowded into poor neighborhoods.

In the 1850s, nearly one million German immigrants arrived in the United States. In 1848, revolutions had broken out in several parts of Germany. The rebels fought for democratic reforms. When the revolts failed, thousands had to flee.

Many other German immigrants came to the United States simply to make a better life for themselves.

Enriching the nation

Immigrants supplied much of the labor that helped the nation's economy to grow. Many Irish immigrants worked in northern factories because they did not have enough money to buy farmland. Other Irish workers helped build the canals and railroads that were crisscrossing the nation.

Immigrants from Germany often had enough money to move west and buy good farmland. Many of them were artisans and merchants. Towns of the Midwest often had German grocers, butchers, and bakers.

A Reaction Against Immigrants

Not everyone welcomed the flood of immigrants. One group of Americans, called **nativists**, wanted to preserve the country for native-born, white citizens. Using the slogan "Americans must rule America," they called for laws to limit immigration. They also wanted to keep immigrants from voting until they had lived in the United States for 21 years. At the time, newcomers could vote after only 5 years in the country.

Some nativists protested that newcomers "stole" jobs from native-born Americans by working for lower pay. Others blamed immigrants for crime in the growing cities. Still others mistrusted Irish and German newcomers because many of them were Catholics. Until the 1840s, the majority of immigrants from Europe were Protestants.

In the 1850s, nativists formed a new political party. It was known as the **Know-Nothing party** because members answered, "I know nothing," when asked about the party. Many meetings and rituals of the party were kept secret. In 1856, the Know-Nothing candidate for President won 21 percent of the popular vote. Soon after, however, the party died out. Still, many Americans continued to blame the nation's problems on immigrants.

African Americans in the North

During the nation's early years, slavery was legal in the North. By the early 1800s, however, all the northern states had outlawed slavery. As a result, thousands of free African Americans lived in the North.

Denied equal rights

Free African Americans in the North faced discrimination. **Discrimination** is a policy or an attitude that denies equal rights to certain groups of people. As one writer pointed out, African Americans were denied "the ballot-box, the jury box, the halls of the legislature, the army, the public lands, the school, and the church."

Biography John Jones

In the 1840s, John Jones ran a profitable tailoring business in Chicago. He helped runaway slaves and opposed Illinois laws that discriminated against African Americans. In the 1870s, he would help to integrate Chicago's public schools.

★ **What obstacles did Jones probably have to overcome?**

Even skilled African Americans had trouble finding good jobs. One black carpenter was turned away by every furniture maker in Cincinnati. At last, a shop owner hired him. However, when he entered the shop, the other carpenters dropped their tools. Either he must leave or they would, they declared. Similar experiences occurred throughout the North.

Some success

Despite the obstacles in their way, some African Americans achieved notable success in business. William Whipper grew wealthy as the owner of a lumber yard in Pennsylvania. He devoted much of his time and money to help bring an end to slavery. **Henry Boyd** operated a profitable furniture company in Cincinnati.

African Americans made strides in other areas as well. Henry Blair invented a corn planter and a cotton seed planter. In 1845, **Macon Allen** became the first African American licensed to practice law in the United States. After graduating from Bowdoin College in Maine, **John Russworm** became one of the editors of *Freedom's Journal*, the first African American newspaper.

★ Section 2 Review ★

Recall

1. **Identify** **(a)** Sarah Bagley, **(b)** Know-Nothing party, **(c)** Henry Boyd, **(d)** Macon Allen, **(e)** John Russworm.

2. **Define** **(a)** artisan, **(b)** trade union, **(c)** strike, **(d)** famine, **(e)** nativist, **(f)** discrimination.

Comprehension

3. How did working conditions in factories worsen in the 1840s and 1850s?

4. In the mid-1800s, why did so many immigrants to the United States come from Ireland and Germany?

5. How did discrimination affect free African Americans in the North?

Critical Thinking and Writing

6. **Making Inferences** Who do you think were the strongest supporters of laws that made strikes illegal? Explain.

7. **Recognizing Points of View** Make a graphic organizer that identifies the reasons for the nativist point of view.

★ ★

Activity **Writing a Petition** You are a female mill worker of the 1840s. You are unhappy about the harsh working conditions in the mills. Write a petition to the state legislature listing your complaints and asking for better working conditions.

Cotton Kingdom in the South

As You Read

Explore These Questions

- Why did cotton planters begin to move westward?
- How did the cotton gin affect slavery in the South?
- Why did the South have less industry than the North?

Identify

- Eli Whitney
- Cotton Kingdom
- William Gregg

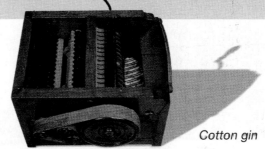

Cotton gin

SETTING the Scene In 1827, an Englishman, Basil Hall, traveled through much of the South aboard a riverboat. He complained that the southerners he met were interested in only one thing—cotton:

> 66 All day and almost all night long, the captain, pilot, crew and passengers were talking of nothing else; and sometimes our ears were so wearied with the sound of cotton! cotton! cotton! that we gladly hailed fresh...company in hopes of some change—but alas!...'What's cotton at?' was the first eager inquiry. 99

Cotton became even more important to the South in the years after Hall's visit. Even though southerners grew other crops, cotton was the region's leading export. Cotton plantations—and the slave system on which they depended—shaped the way of life in the South.

Cotton Gin, Cotton Boom

The Industrial Revolution greatly increased the demand for southern cotton. Textile mills in the North and in Britain needed more and more cotton to make cloth. At first, southern planters could not meet the demand. They could grow plenty of cotton because the South's soil and climate were ideal. However, removing the seeds from the cotton by hand was a slow process. Planters needed a better way to clean cotton.

Eli Whitney's invention

In 1793, **Eli Whitney**, a young Connecticut schoolteacher, was traveling to Georgia. He was going to be a tutor on a plantation. When Whitney learned of the planters' problem, he decided to build a machine to clean cotton.

In only 10 days, Whitney came up with a model. His cotton engine, or gin, had two rollers with thin wire teeth. When cotton was swept between the rollers, the teeth separated the seeds from the fibers. (See Linking History and Technology on page 384.)

The cotton gin was simple, but its effects were enormous. A worker using a gin could do the work of 50 people cleaning cotton by hand. Because of the gin, planters could now grow cotton at a huge profit.

Connections With Science

Technology thieves stole Eli Whitney's first cotton gin. Before Whitney could build another, someone filed a patent for a machine that copied his invention. To receive the profits that were due to him, Whitney went to court. He filed more than 50 lawsuits.

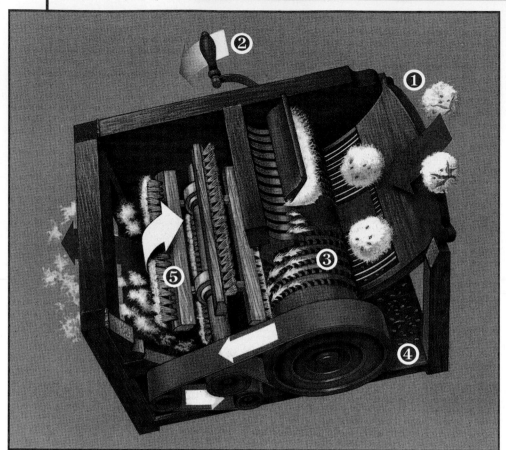

❶ Cotton bolls, made up of fiber and seeds, are fed into the cotton gin. The red arrows show the path of the cotton through the gin.

❷ As the handle is turned, the cylinder and brushes rotate.

❸ Wire teeth catch the cotton bolls and pull them through narrow wire slots.

❹ The seeds are too large to pass through the slots. They fall to the bottom of the gin.

❺ Rotating brushes pull cleaned cotton fiber from the wire teeth and sweep it out of the gin.

The Cotton Gin

The cotton gin separated unwanted seeds from cotton fiber. With the help of a gin, a worker was able to process as much as 50 pounds of cotton in a single day. As a result, cotton production became a very profitable business.
★ **How did the gin separate the seeds from the fiber?**

▲ *A cotton boll*

Cotton Kingdom and slavery

The cotton gin led to a boom in cotton production. In 1792, planters grew only 6,000 bales of cotton a year. By 1850, the figure was over 2 million bales.

Planters soon learned that soil wore out if planted with cotton year after year. They needed new land to cultivate. After the War of 1812, cotton planters began to move west.

By the 1850s, there were cotton plantations extending in a wide band from South Carolina through Alabama and Mississippi to Texas. (See the map on page 386.) This area of the South became known as the **Cotton Kingdom**.

Tragically, as the Cotton Kingdom spread, so did slavery. Even though cotton could now be cleaned by machine, it still had to be planted and picked by hand. The result was a cruel cycle. The work of slaves brought profits to planters. Planters used the profits to buy more land and more slaves.

An Agricultural Economy

Cotton was the South's most profitable cash crop. However, the best conditions for growing cotton could be found mostly in the southernmost portion of the South. In other areas of the South, rice, sugar cane, and tobacco were major crops. In addition, Southerners raised much of the nation's livestock.

Rice was an important crop along the coasts of South Carolina and Georgia. Sugar cane was important in Louisiana and Texas. Growing rice and sugar cane required expensive irrigation and drainage systems. Cane growers also needed costly machinery to grind their harvest. Small-scale farmers could not afford such expensive equipment, however. As a result, the plantation system dominated areas of sugar and rice production just as it did areas of cotton production.

Tobacco had been an export of the South since 1619, and it continued to be planted in Virginia, North Carolina, and Kentucky. However, in the early 1800s, the large tobacco plantations of colonial days had given way to small tobacco farms. On these farms, a few field hands tended five or six acres of tobacco.

In addition to the major cash crops of cotton, rice, sugar, and tobacco, the South also led the nation in livestock production. Southern livestock owners profited from hogs, oxen, horses, mules, and beef cattle. Much of this livestock was raised in areas that were unsuitable for growing crops, such as the pine woods of North Carolina.

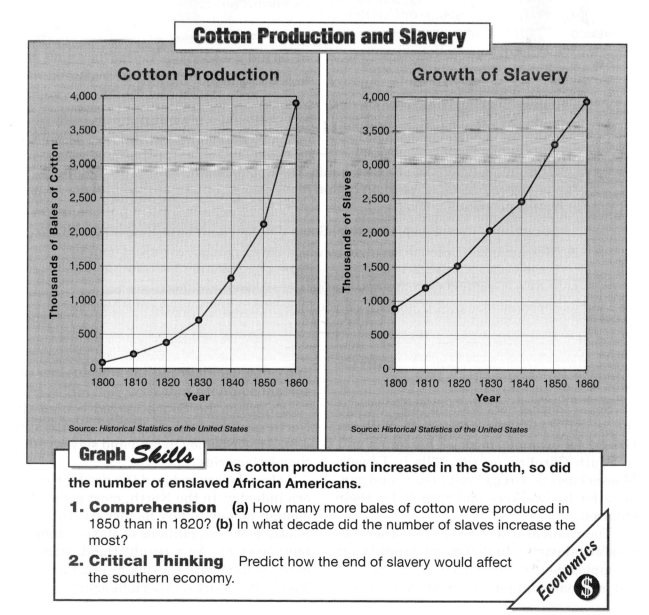

Cotton Production and Slavery

Cotton Production

Thousands of Bales of Cotton vs. Year (1800–1860)

Source: *Historical Statistics of the United States*

Growth of Slavery

Thousands of Slaves vs. Year (1800–1860)

Source: *Historical Statistics of the United States*

Graph *Skills* As cotton production increased in the South, so did the number of enslaved African Americans.

1. **Comprehension** (a) How many more bales of cotton were produced in 1850 than in 1820? (b) In what decade did the number of slaves increase the most?

2. **Critical Thinking** Predict how the end of slavery would affect the southern economy.

Economics $

Life in the South

As You Read

Explore These Questions
- What five groups made up society in the South?
- How did African Americans suffer under slavery?
- How did African Americans struggle against slavery?

Define
- slave code
- extended family

Identify
- "cottonocracy"
- Norbert Rillieux
- Henry Blair
- Denmark Vesey
- Nat Turner

SETTING the Scene ❝I was born in 1844.... First [thing] I remember was my ma and us [children] being sold off the [auction] block to Mistress Payne. When I was...too little to work in the field, I stayed at the big house most of the time and helped Mistress Payne feed the chickens, make scarecrows to keep the hawks away and put wood on the fires. After I got big enough to hoe, I went to the field same as the other[s].❞

In this excerpt, Jack Payne recalls his life as an enslaved person in Texas. Payne was only one of millions of African Americans throughout the South who suffered the anguish of slavery. Toiling from dawn till dusk, they had neither freedom nor rights.

White Southerners

The Old South is often pictured as a land of vast plantations worked by hundreds of slaves. Such grand estates did exist in the South. However, most white southerners were not rich planters. In fact, most whites owned no slaves at all.

The "cottonocracy"

A planter was someone who owned at least 20 slaves. In 1860, only one white southerner in 30 belonged to a planter family. An even smaller number—less than 1 percent—

owned 50 or more slaves. These wealthy families were called the **"cottonocracy"** because they made huge amounts of money from cotton. Though few in number, their views and way of life dominated the South.

The richest planters built elegant homes and filled them with expensive furniture from Europe. They entertained lavishly. They tried to dress and behave like European nobility.

Planters had responsibilities, too. Because of their wealth and influence, many planters became political leaders. They devoted many hours to local, state, and national politics. Planters hired overseers to run day-to-day affairs on their plantations and to manage the work of slaves.

Small farmers

About 75 percent of southern whites were small farmers. These "plain folk" owned the

In later years, both literature and film gave a false view of plantation life. Writers and film producers focused on the "gentility" of the planters and largely ignored the injustices of slavery. The most successful of these fictional works is the 1939 film *Gone With the Wind*. Based on Margaret Mitchell's novel, the film won 10 Academy Awards, including Best Picture.

Rosedown Plantation

Rosedown Plantation, built in 1835, is located in St. Francisville, Louisiana. It was owned by the wealthy cotton planter, Daniel Turnbull, and his wife Martha. The Turnbulls filled their mansion with beautiful furniture and art from Europe. They surrounded their home with avenues of trees and formal gardens. Today, visitors can tour Rosedown, its gardens, and its many outbuildings. You can even stay overnight and recall the luxurious lifestyle of the southern aristocracy.

★ *To learn more about this historic site, write: Rosedown Plantation, 12501 Highway 10, St. Francisville, LA 70775.*

Original bedroom furniture at Rosedown

land they farmed. They might also own one or two slaves. Unlike planters, plain folk worked with their slaves in the fields.

Among small farmers, helping each other was an important duty. "People who lived miles apart counted themselves as neighbors," wrote a farmer in Mississippi. "And in case of sorrow or sickness, there was no limit to the service neighbors provided."

Poor whites

Lower on the social ladder was a small group of poor whites. They did not own the land they farmed. Instead, they rented it, often paying the owner with part of their crop. Many barely made a living.

Poor whites often lived in the hilly, wooded areas of the South. They planted crops such as corn, potatoes, and other vegetables. They also herded cattle and pigs. Poor whites had hard lives, but they enjoyed rights denied to all African Americans, enslaved or free.

African American Southerners

Both free and enslaved African Americans lived in the South. Although free under the law, free African Americans faced harsh discrimination. Enslaved African Americans had no rights at all.

Free African Americans

Most free African Americans were descendants of slaves freed during and after the American Revolution. Others had bought their freedom. In 1860, over 200,000 free blacks lived in the South. Most lived in Maryland and Delaware, where slavery was

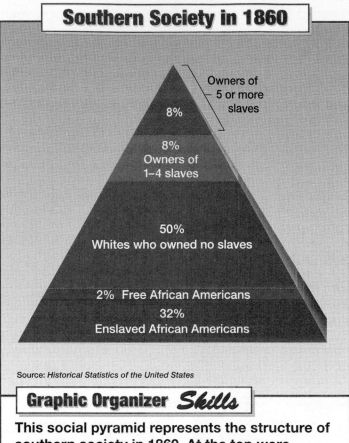

Southern Society in 1860

Owners of 5 or more slaves
8%

8%
Owners of
1–4 slaves

50%
Whites who owned no slaves

2% Free African Americans

32%
Enslaved African Americans

Source: *Historical Statistics of the United States*

Graphic Organizer *Skills*

This social pyramid represents the structure of southern society in 1860. At the top were wealthy and powerful planters. At the bottom were millions of enslaved African Americans.

1. **Comprehension** Which group in southern society was most numerous?
2. **Critical Thinking** Many white southerners owned no slaves but still supported the institution of slavery. Why do you think they did so?

in decline. Others lived in cities such as New Orleans, Richmond, and Charleston.

Slave owners did not like free African Americans living in the South. They feared that free African Americans set a bad example, encouraging slaves to rebel. Also, slave owners justified slavery by claiming that African Americans could not take care of themselves. Free African American workers proved this idea wrong.

To discourage free African Americans, southern states passed laws that made life even harder for them. Free African Americans were not allowed to vote or travel. In some southern states, they either had to move out of the state or allow themselves to be enslaved.

Despite these limits, free African Americans made valuable contributions to southern life. For example, **Norbert Rillieux** (RIHL yoo) invented a machine that revolutionized the way sugar was made. Another inventor, **Henry Blair,** patented a seed planter.

Enslaved African Americans

By 1860, enslaved African Americans made up one third of the South's population. Most worked as field hands on cotton plantations. Both men and women cleared new land and planted and harvested crops. Children helped by pulling weeds, collecting wood, and carrying water to the field hands. By the time they were teenagers, they too worked between 12 and 14 hours a day.

On large plantations, some African Americans became skilled workers, such as carpenters and blacksmiths. A few worked in cities and lived almost as if they were free. Their earnings, however, belonged to their owners.

Life Without Freedom

The life of enslaved African Americans was determined by strict laws and the practices of individual slave owners. Conditions varied from plantation to plantation. Some owners made sure their slaves had clean cabins, decent food, and warm clothes. Other planters spent as little as possible on their slaves.

Slave codes

Southern states passed laws known as **slave codes** to keep slaves from either running away or rebelling. Under the codes, enslaved African Americans were forbidden to gather in groups of more than three. They could not leave their owner's land without a written pass. They were not allowed to own guns.

Slave codes also made it a crime for slaves to learn how to read and write. Owners hoped that this law would make it hard for African Americans to escape slavery. They reasoned that uneducated runaway slaves would not be able to use maps or read train schedules. They would not be able to find their way north.

Why Study History?

Because Music Is Part of Our Culture

★ ★

Historical Background

From the colonial era on, southerners of diverse backgrounds shared their music with one another. As a result, a variety of rich musical traditions developed in the American South.

African Americans built on the musical heritage of their ancestral homelands. One common technique was the "call and response" in which a soloist sang a line and the group responded. African American music stressed varied rhythms and improvisation, the spontaneous creation of new lyrics and melodies. In the 1800s, these qualities were typical of African American work songs, religious songs, and folk songs.

The early musical traditions of most white southerners were rooted in the tunes and melodies of the British Isles. German, Mexican, Cajun, and other traditions also enriched Southern folk music. The sounds of fiddles and banjos often celebrated house raisings, harvest feasts, and other major events.

Connections to Today

Several American music styles of today are firmly rooted in the South. Blues, jazz, and gospel music emerged from the traditions of African American southerners. Country music and rock-and-roll developed from the folk music of both white and black southerners. In fact, most early rock performers of the 1950s came from the South.

Connections to You

The sounds of jazz, country, and rock are all around you. The next time you pop in your favorite CD, consider the roots of the music

▲ Gospel singers

▲ Country music singer

you hear. When you watch a television show, note its theme music. When you go to the movies, listen to the soundtrack. You will discover that American music owes much to the rich and diverse traditions of the American South.

1. **Comprehension**   What music styles of today can be traced to traditions in the American South?
2. **Critical Thinking**   Why do you think jazz and blues music developed in the South rather than in the North?

 **Activity**   **Planning a Documentary**
Research the history of a music style discussed here. Then, outline a television documentary on that style. List the topics and pictures that will appear in your documentary.

African American Community

The painting Plantation Burial *by John Antrobus is unusual for providing a realistic portrait of life on a southern plantation. The central figures are African Americans. To the right, a white couple keeps a respectful distance from the religious ceremony.* ★ **What role did religion play in the life of enslaved African Americans?**

Some laws were meant to protect slaves, but only from the worst forms of abuse. However, enslaved African Americans did not have the right to testify in court. As a result, they were not able to bring charges against owners who abused them.

Enslaved African Americans had only one real protection against mistreatment. Owners looked on their slaves as valuable property. Most slave owners wanted to keep this human property healthy and productive.

Hard work

Even the kindest owners insisted that their slaves work long, hard days. Slaves worked from "can see to can't see," or from dawn to dusk, up to 16 hours a day. Frederick Douglass, who escaped slavery, recalled his life under one harsh master:

66 We were worked in all weathers. It was never too hot or too cold; it could never rain, blow, hail, or snow too hard for us to work in the field. Work, work, work.... The longest days were too short for him and the shortest nights too long for him. 99

Some owners and overseers whipped slaves to get a full day's work. However, the worst part of slavery was not the beatings. It was the complete loss of freedom.

Family life

It was hard for enslaved African Americans to keep their families together. Southern laws did not recognize slave marriages or slave families. As a result, owners could sell a husband and wife to different buyers. Children were often taken from their parents and sold.

On large plantations, many enslaved families did manage to stay together. For those African Americans, the family was a source of strength, pride, and love. Grandparents, parents, children, aunts, uncles, and cousins formed a close-knit group. This idea of an **extended family** had its roots in Africa.

Enslaved African Americans preserved other traditions as well. Parents taught their children traditional African stories and songs. They used folk tales to pass on African history and moral beliefs.

Religion offers hope

By the 1800s, many enslaved African Americans were devout Christians. Planters often allowed white ministers to preach to their slaves. African Americans also had their own preachers and beliefs.

Religion helped African Americans cope with the harshness of slave life. Bible stories about how the ancient Hebrews had escaped from slavery inspired many spiritual songs. As they worked in the fields, slaves sang about a coming day of freedom. One spiritual, "Go Down, Moses," includes these lines:

66 We need not always weep and
   moan,
   Let my people go.
And wear these slavery chains
   forlorn,
   Let my people go. 99

Resistance Against Slavery

Enslaved African Americans struck back against the system that denied them both freedom and wages. Some broke tools, destroyed crops, and stole food.

Many enslaved African Americans tried to escape to the North. Because the journey was long and dangerous, very few made it to freedom. Every county had slave patrols and sheriffs ready to question an unknown black person.

A few African Americans used violence to resist the brutal slave system. **Denmark Vesey**, a free African American, planned a revolt in 1822. Vesey was betrayed before the revolt began. He and 35 other people were executed.

In 1831, an African American preacher named **Nat Turner** led a major revolt. Turner led his followers through Virginia, killing more than 57 whites. Terrified whites hunted the countryside for Turner. They killed many innocent African Americans before catching and hanging him.

Nat Turner's revolt increased southern fears of an uprising of enslaved African Americans. Revolts were rare, however. Since whites were cautious and well armed, a revolt by African Americans had almost no chance of success.

★ Section 4 Review ★

Recall

1. **Identify** (a) "cottonocracy," (b) Norbert Rillieux, (c) Henry Blair, (d) Denmark Vesey, (e) Nat Turner.
2. **Define** (a) slave code, (b) extended family.

Comprehension

3. How did the "cottonocracy" dominate economics and politics in the South?
4. Describe three ways that African Americans suffered under slavery.

5. How did African Americans struggle against the slave system?

Critical Thinking and Writing

6. **Applying Information** How were successful free African Americans a threat to the slave system?
7. **Making Decisions** If you had been an enslaved African American, would you have decided to live under slavery, to try to escape, or to rebel? Explain the reasons for your decision.

★ ★

Activity **Writing a Speech** You are an enslaved African American living in the South in the 1850s. Write a speech encouraging people to resist slavery and explaining ways in which they can do it.

★ Sum It Up ★

Section 1   Industry in the North
▶ During the mid-1800s, new inventions helped industry grow in the North.
▶ Railroads linked the Northeast with Chicago and other midwestern cities.
▶ With produce coming in from western farms, agriculture declined in the Northeast.

Section 2   Life in the North
▶ Northern factory workers endured long hours, dangerous conditions, and low pay.
▶ As millions of immigrants arrived in the United States, nativist fears grew.
▶ Free African Americans faced discrimination. Still, some became very successful.

Section 3   Cotton Kingdom in the South
▶ Due to the invention of the cotton gin, growing cotton became very profitable.
▶ As the Cotton Kingdom spread from the Atlantic coast to Texas, so did slavery.
▶ As planters invested in land and slaves, the South developed an agricultural economy rather than an industrial one.

Section 4   Life in the South
▶ Southern society consisted of rich planters, small farmers, poor whites, and free and enslaved African Americans.
▶ Enslaved people lacked freedoms and rights and were forced to work for no pay.
▶ Some enslaved African Americans resisted slavery by rebelling or running away.

 For additional review of the major ideas of Chapter 14, see *Guide to the Essentials of American History* or *Interactive Student Tutorial CD-ROM,* which contains interactive review activities, graphic organizers, and practice tests.

🗔 Reviewing the Chapter

Define These Terms
Match each term with the correct definition.

Column 1
1. clipper
2. nativist
3. discrimination
4. skilled worker

Column 2
a. a policy or attitude that denies equal rights to certain groups
b. a swift ship with tall masts, huge sails, and a narrow hull
c. a person who has learned a trade
d. someone who favors native-born citizens

Explore the Main Ideas
1. Describe three developments that caused the North's economy to expand.
2. **(a)** Why did workers form unions in the early and mid-1800s? **(b)** Describe two reasons for immigration to the United States in the 1840s and 1850s.
3. How did the cotton gin change life in the South?
4. Describe two ways that slaves resisted slavery.
5. What were two key differences between the North's economy and the South's economy?

🗔 Graph Activity

Use the graph below to answer the following questions: **1.** In what year did Irish immigration to the United States double? **2.** How many Irish immigrants came to the United States in 1851? **Critical Thinking** Why did increasing immigration alarm some Americans?

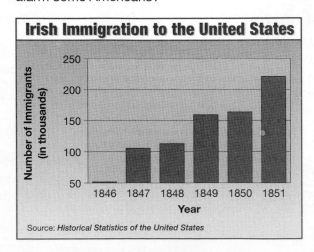

Irish Immigration to the United States

Source: *Historical Statistics of the United States*

📋 Critical Thinking and Writing

1. **Using Chronology** Place these events in chronological order: **(a)** over 1.5 million Irish enter the United States, **(b)** the Know-Nothing party forms, **(c)** famine breaks out in Ireland.

2. **Ranking** In your opinion, what two inventions had the greatest impact on American life in the early and mid-1800s? Explain.

3. **Making Decisions** If you were directing a nation's economy, would you develop agriculture more than industry or industry more than agriculture? Explain.

4. **Exploring Unit Themes   Expansion** **(a)** Why did slavery spread west during the early 1800s? **(b)** How did economic differences between the North and South grow?

📋 Using Primary Sources

Solomon Northrup was a free African American until he was kidnapped and sold as a slave in 1845. For the next twelve years, he worked on a cotton plantation in Louisiana. Below, he describes the start of a typical workday.

> **66** [My bed]...was a plank twelve inches wide and ten feet long. My pillow was a stick of wood. The bedding was a coarse blanket....The cabin is constructed of logs, without floor or window....In stormy weather, the rain drives through [spaces between the logs]....An hour before daylight the horn is blown. Then the slaves arouse, prepare their breakfast...and hurry to the field again. It is an offense invariably followed by a flogging, to be found at the quarters after daybreak. **99**

Source: *Twelve Years a Slave* by Solomon Northrup, 1853.

Recognizing Points of View **(a)** How does Northrup show his home to be uncomfortable? **(b)** How does he feel about the start of each day? Explain.

ACTIVITY BANK

▶ Interdisciplinary Activity

Exploring Science It is fairly easy to make a telegraph. In your school or local library, find a science book with information on how to build one. Working with other students, create your own telegraph and transmit a message using Morse code.

▶ Career Skills Activity

Musicians Learn a spiritual sung by enslaved people in the South in the 1800s. Possible songs are "Go Down, Moses," "Deep River," and "Swing Low, Sweet Chariot." Perform the spiritual for the class and then explain the meaning of the song.

▶ Citizenship Activity

Protecting Religious Freedom Nativists of the mid-1800s discriminated against Catholics even though Americans are guaranteed religious freedom. Create a poster encouraging citizens to respect the religious beliefs of all Americans.

Internet Activity

Use the Internet to find primary sources on enslaved African Americans in the 1800s. Use the Information you find to write a short story about a typical day in the life of an enslaved African American.

EYEWITNESS Journal

In the early 1800s, you are a northern manufacturer or farmer, or a southern planter or enslaved person. In your EYEWITNESS JOURNAL, describe how new inventions are changing your life.

Chapter 15

An Era of Reform

1820–1860

In the mid-1800s, dedicated reformers sought to better American society. Many of these reformers acted out of political ideals. They wanted the nation to live up to its promise of "liberty and equality for all." Religious feeling also spurred many reformers.

Reform took many directions. Two of the most sweeping goals were equal rights for women and the abolition of slavery. Reformers often faced opposition, criticism, and even threats. Yet, they continued to struggle and slowly gained support. In this chapter, you will read about the individuals who contributed to this era of reform.

Why Study History?

Today, as in the 1800s, the reforming impulse is strong in the United States. Americans still work to correct many types of social problems. To learn more about one reform movement that has attracted many Americans, young and old, see the *Why Study History?* feature, "The Fight Against Alcohol Abuse Continues," in this chapter.

American Events			
1826 James Fenimore Cooper publishes *The Last of the Mohicans*	**1831** William Lloyd Garrison begins antislavery newspaper	**1837** Horace Mann begins educational reforms in Massachusetts	

1820	1825	1830	1835	1840

World Events		
1822 World Event Liberia is established in Western Africa	**1837 World Event** First kindergarten opens in Germany	

Viewing History   Spirit of Religion

This painted tray honors Lemuel Haynes, a famous African American preacher. From the nation's earliest years, religion was a powerful influence in the United States. In the early 1800s, a religious revival movement fed a new spirit of reform. ★ **Why would religious feelings lead some people to try to find ways to improve society?**

1848 ●
Women's Rights
Convention is held
at Seneca Falls

● **1851**
Maine bans the
sale of alcohol

| 1840 | 1845 | 1850 | 1855 | 1860 |

1843 World Event
Charles Dickens publishes
A Christmas Carol

1848 World Event
First women's college in
Great Britain opens

The Spirit of Reform

As You Read

Explore These Questions
- What were the political and religious roots of reform?
- What goals did social reformers pursue?
- How did Americans improve public education in the mid-1800s?

Define
- social reform
- predestination
- revival
- penal system
- temperance movement

Identify
- Second Great Awakening
- Charles Grandison Finney
- Dorothea Dix
- Horace Mann
- Prudence Crandall
- Thomas Gallaudet
- Samuel Gridley Howe
- Laura Bridgman

SETTING the Scene In 1840, New England philosopher Ralph Waldo Emerson wrote about Americans' growing passion for improving society:

66 We are all a little wild here with numberless projects for social reform. But what is man born for but to be a Reformer... a restorer of truth and good? 99

Many idealistic Americans shared Emerson's beliefs. Between 1820 and 1860, a wide variety of reform movements sprang up to cure the nation's ills.

The Reforming Impulse

Social reform is an organized attempt to improve what is unjust or imperfect in society. The reforming impulse had both political and religious roots. The political roots went back to the ideals of liberty and equality expressed in the Declaration of Independence. The religious reform involved new teachings about salvation and the individual.

Political ideals

The election of Andrew Jackson in 1828 unleashed a wave of democratic change in the nation. More people could vote and take part in government than ever before.

Still, some critics argued that "Jacksonian democracy" was far from democratic. Many said that a true democracy would not allow slavery. Others questioned why women had fewer rights than men. Reformers hoped that by changing such injustices, they might move the nation closer to its political ideals.

A new religious movement

Many early American Protestants believed that God decided in advance which people would gain salvation in heaven. This idea is known as **predestination.** Belief in predestination led many people to think that society could not be changed. In fact, they felt it was sinful to want to improve the world.

In the early 1800s, a dynamic religious movement, known as the **Second Great Awakening,** swept the nation. Its leaders stressed free will rather than predestination. They taught that individuals could choose by their own actions to save their own souls.

Throughout the nation, preachers held huge outdoor meetings. The goal of these **revivals** was to stir religious feelings. Revivals often lasted for days and attracted thousands of people. A witness described the excitement of a revival in Kentucky:

66 The vast sea of human beings seemed to be agitated as if by storm. I counted seven ministers all preaching at once.... Some of the people were singing, others praying, some crying for mercy. 99

Deeply affected, converts vowed to reform their lives.

One of the leaders of the Second Great Awakening was a Presbyterian minister named **Charles Grandison Finney.** A powerful speaker, Finney wrote articles giving tips on effective preaching. He also taught that individual salvation was the first step toward improving society. He told followers that their goal was "the complete reformation of the whole world." Through teachings like these, the Second Great Awakening encouraged the growing spirit of reform.

Helping the Mentally Ill

Some reformers turned their attention to what one minister called the "outsiders" in society—criminals and the mentally ill. One of the most vigorous of these reformers was a Boston schoolteacher named **Dorothea Dix.**

One day in 1841, Dix visited a jail for women near Boston. She was shocked to discover that some of the prisoners had committed no crime. These women were in jail because they were mentally ill.

The jailer locked the mentally ill prisoners in small, dark, unheated cells. The women were half frozen. Dix demanded to know why these women were treated so cruelly. The jailer replied that "lunatics" did not feel the cold.

That moment changed Dix's life forever. During the next 18 months, Dix visited every jail, poorhouse, and hospital in Massachusetts. Her report shocked state legislators:

66 I proceed, gentlemen, briefly to call your attention to the present state of Insane Persons confined . . . in cages, closets, cellars, stalls, pens! Chained, naked, beaten with rods, and lashed into obedience. **99**

Eventually, legislators agreed to fund a new mental hospital. Dix then went on to inspect jails in states as far away as Louisiana and Illinois. In nearly every state, her reports persuaded legislatures to treat the mentally ill as patients, not criminals.

Reforming Prisons

Dix also joined others in trying to reform the **penal system,** or system of prisons.

Biography Dorothea Dix

Dorothea Dix was shocked by the sight of "harmless lunatics" shackled in dark cells. When she was told that "nothing" could be done, Dix replied, "I know no such word." Largely through her efforts, more than 15 states established special hospitals for the care of the mentally ill by 1860. ★ **How did Dix go about achieving reform?**

Prisons were at the time fairly new to the United States. In colonial days, states generally imposed the death penalty for serious offenses. People who committed minor offenses received some form of physical punishment, such as a public whipping.

In the early 1800s, imprisonment gradually replaced physical punishment. In the early prisons, men, women, and children were often crammed together in cold, damp rooms. When food supplies were low, prisoners might go hungry—unless they had money to buy meals from jailers. Some jailers even made extra money selling rum to prisoners.

Five out of six people in northern jails were in jail because they could not pay their debts. While behind bars, debtors had no way to earn money to pay back their debts.

Why Study History?

Because the Fight Against Alcohol Abuse Continues

★ ★

Historical Background

Americans in the early 1800s consumed more alcohol per person than at any other time in American history. Some American reformers grew concerned about the impact of alcohol on society. The temperance movement that began in the 1820s hoped to end alcohol abuse.

In the late 1800s, the temperance movement grew. Groups like the Women's Christian Temperance Union attracted many followers. Finally, in 1919, the states ratified the Eighteenth Amendment, prohibiting the production and sale of alcoholic drinks. However, law enforcement officials found it nearly impossible to enforce Prohibition. It was repealed in 1933 by the Twenty-first Amendment.

Connections to Today

Reformers now focus on the problems of underage and excessive drinking. Today, the legal drinking age in every state is 21 years. A variety of organizations and programs exist to help people who suffer from alcoholism. Still, as many as 40 million Americans are problem drinkers—people whose drinking causes harm to themselves or their family and friends.

One of the most destructive forms of alcohol abuse is drinking and driving. In the late 1990s, more than 15,000 Americans died each year in accidents involving drunk drivers. Young people were often the victims. In fact, alcohol-related accidents were the number-one killer of teenagers.

Students organize to warn about the dangers of alcohol.

Connections to You

If you or someone you know has a problem with alcohol, there are several things you can do. You can seek support from your parents or other family members. You can get information from school counselors or a family physician. Also, your school may participate in the Students Against Drunk Driving (SADD) program. Students who belong to SADD promise to call their parents if they cannot get a safe ride with a sober driver.

1. **Comprehension** Name and describe the two constitutional amendments related to the use of alcohol in the United States.
2. **Critical Thinking** Why do you think some people make the irresponsible decision to drink and drive?

★ *Activity* **Making a Poster** Construct a poster that warns people about the dangers of underage drinking, excessive drinking, or drinking and driving.

As a result, many debtors remained in prison for years.

Dorothea Dix and others called for changes in the penal system. Some states built prisons with only one or two inmates to a cell. Cruel punishments were banned, and people convicted of minor crimes received shorter sentences. Slowly, states stopped treating debtors as criminals.

Battling "Demon Rum"

Alcohol abuse was widespread in the early 1800s. At political rallies, weddings, and funerals, men, women, and sometimes even children drank heavily. Men could buy whiskey in candy stores or barber shops as easily as at taverns.

During the late 1820s, reformers began the **temperance movement,** a campaign against alcohol abuse. Women often took a leading role in the temperance movement. They knew that "demon rum" could lead to wife beating, child abuse, and the breakup of families.

Some temperance groups urged people to drink less. Others sought to wipe out all drinking of alcohol. They won a major victory in the 1850s, when Maine banned the sale of alcohol. Eight other states passed "Maine laws." Although most states later repealed the laws, temperance crusaders pressed on. They gained new strength in the late 1800s.

Improving Education

In 1816, Thomas Jefferson wrote, "If a nation expects to be ignorant and free, it expects what never was and never will be."

▲ Pages from McGuffey's First Eclectic Reader

◄ Mug to reward good performance

V iewing HISTORY A Better Education

The painting Homework by Winslow Homer shows an elementary school student of the mid-1800s. This boy may be reading a lesson from one of William McGuffey's Eclectic Readers. First published in 1836, McGuffey's popular textbooks used rhymes and stories to teach spelling, grammar, and good behavior. ★ **What methods are used today to teach children to read?**

He knew that a republic needed educated citizens. As more men won the right to vote, reformers acted to improve education.

Before the 1820s, few American children attended school. Public schools were rare. Those that did exist were usually old and run-down. Teachers were poorly trained and ill paid. Students of all ages crowded together in a single room.

Growth of public schools

New York State took the lead in improving public education. In the 1820s, the state ordered every town to build a grade school. Before long, other northern states required towns to support public schools.

$ Connections With Economics

The temperance movement got a lot of support from factory owners. They thought workers would be more productive if they did not drink. Today, many businesses pay for programs to combat alcohol and drug abuse among their employees. In what ways do you think drug or alcohol abuse can hurt the economy?

In Massachusetts, **Horace Mann** led the fight for better schools. Mann became head of the state board of education in 1837. He hounded legislators to provide more money for education. Under his leadership, Massachusetts built new schools, extended the school year, and raised teacher pay. The state also opened three colleges to train teachers.

Reformers in other states urged their legislatures to follow the lead of Massachusetts and New York. By the 1850s, most northern states had set up free tax-supported elementary schools. Schools in the South improved more slowly. In both the North and South, schooling usually ended in the eighth grade. There were few public high schools.

Education for African Americans

In most areas, African Americans had little chance to attend school. A few cities, like Boston and New York, set up separate schools for black students. However, these schools received less money than schools for white students did.

Some attempts to educate African Americans met with great hostility. In the 1830s, **Prudence Crandall,** a Connecticut Quaker, began a school for African American girls. The community was outraged. Crandall continued to teach even when rocks crashed through the classroom window. She was jailed three times. Finally, a band of men broke in one night and destroyed the school.

Despite such obstacles, some free African Americans attended private colleges such as Harvard, Dartmouth, and Oberlin. In the 1850s, several colleges for African Americans opened in the North. The first was Lincoln University, in Pennsylvania.

Meeting special needs

Some reformers took steps to improve education for people with disabilities. In 1817, **Thomas Gallaudet** (gal uh DEHT) set up a school for the deaf in Hartford, Connecticut.

A few years later, **Samuel Gridley Howe** became director of the first American school for blind students. Howe created a system of raised letters that allowed blind students to read with their fingers. One of Howe's pupils, **Laura Bridgman,** was the first deaf and blind student to receive a formal education. She later assisted Howe in teaching other blind students.

★ Section 1 Review ★

Recall

1. **Identify** **(a)** Second Great Awakening, **(b)** Charles Grandison Finney, **(c)** Dorothea Dix, **(d)** Horace Mann, **(e)** Prudence Crandall, **(f)** Thomas Gallaudet, **(g)** Samuel Gridley Howe, **(h)** Laura Bridgman.
2. **Define** **(a)** social reform, **(b)** predestination, **(c)** revival, **(d)** penal system, **(e)** temperance movement.

Comprehension

3. Describe two reasons the reforming spirit grew in the mid-1800s.

4. What were the goals of **(a)** prison reformers, and **(b)** leaders of the temperance movement?
5. What improvements were made in public education after the 1820s?

Critical Thinking and Writing

6. **Linking Past and Present** Do churches and religious leaders still take an active role in promoting social reform today? Give examples.
7. **Understanding Causes and Effects** How would lack of educational opportunities for African Americans contribute to prejudice against them?

★ ★

Activity **Acting a Scene** The year is 1843. You are a legislator. You are unwilling to raise taxes to improve conditions for prisoners while tax money is needed to improve conditions for law-abiding citizens. With a partner, act out a scene between you and Dorothea Dix. For each argument for prison reform given by Dix, present an opposing argument.

The Fight Against Slavery

As You Read

Explore These Questions
- How did reformers try to end slavery?
- How did the underground railroad work?
- How did Americans react to the antislavery movement?

Define
- abolitionist
- underground railroad

Identify
- American Colonization Society
- David Walker
- Maria Stewart
- Frederick Douglass
- William Lloyd Garrison
- Angelina and Sarah Grimké
- Harriet Tubman

SETTING the Scene In 1848, a group of reformers met to listen to a minister named Henry Highland Garnet. Garnet had once escaped slavery himself. He told the crowd:

66 America is my home, my country. . . . I mourn because the accursed shade of slavery rest[s] upon it. I love my country's flag, and I hope that soon it will be cleansed of its stains, and be hailed by all nations as the emblem of freedom and independence. 99

This medallion was a popular emblem of the antislavery movement.

A growing number of Americans—black and white—spoke out against slavery. Only by ending slavery, they believed, could the United States become truly democratic.

Roots of the Antislavery Movement

In the Declaration of Independence, Thomas Jefferson wrote that "all men are created equal." Yet, many white Americans, including Jefferson, did not think the statement applied to enslaved African Americans. In the 1800s, many reformers disagreed.

Religious beliefs led some Americans to speak out against slavery. Since colonial times, Quakers had said that it was a sin for one human being to own another. They preached that all men and women were equal in the eyes of God. Later, ministers like Charles Grandison Finney called on other Christians to join a crusade to stamp out slavery.

In the North, slavery came to an early end. By 1804, all states from Pennsylvania to New England had promised to free their slaves. Still, there were only 50,000 slaves in the North in 1800, compared to nearly one million in the South.

A Colony in Africa

Some Americans proposed to end slavery by setting up an independent colony in Africa for freed slaves. Supporters of colonization founded the **American Colonization Society** in 1817. Five years later, President Monroe helped the society found the nation of Liberia in western Africa. The name Liberia comes from the Latin word for free.

Many white southerners supported the colonization movement because it did not call for an end to slavery. The society promised to pay slave owners who freed their slaves.

Some African Americans also favored colonization. They felt they would never have equal rights in the United States. Most African Americans, however, opposed the movement. Nearly all, enslaved or free, were born in the United States. They wanted to stay in their homeland. In the end, only a few thousand Americans settled in Liberia.

African Americans gave generously to anti-slavery efforts. In the 1820s, Samuel Cornish and John Russwurm set up an abolitionist newspaper, *Freedom's Journal.* They hoped to turn public opinion against slavery by printing stories about the brutal treatment of enslaved African Americans.

David Walker called for stronger measures. In 1829, he published *Appeal to the Colored Citizens of the World.* He encouraged enslaved African Americans to free themselves by any means necessary. Walker's friend **Maria Stewart** also spoke out against slavery. Stewart was the first American woman to make public political speeches.

Douglass speaks out

The best known African American abolitionist was **Frederick Douglass.** Douglass was born into slavery in Maryland. As a child, he defied the slave codes and taught himself to read.

In 1838, Douglass escaped and made his way to Boston. One day at an antislavery meeting, he felt a powerful urge to speak. Rising to his feet, he talked about the sorrows of slavery and the meaning of freedom. The audience was moved to tears. Soon, Douglass was lecturing across the United States and Britain. In 1847, he began publishing an antislavery newspaper, the *North Star.*

Garrison and *The Liberator*

The most outspoken white abolitionist was a fiery, young man named **William Lloyd Garrison.** Garrison launched his antislavery paper, *The Liberator,* in 1831. In it, he proclaimed that slavery was an evil to be ended immediately. On the very first page of the first issue, Garrison revealed his commitment:

> ❝ I will be as harsh as truth, and as uncompromising as justice...I am in earnest...I will not excuse—I will not retreat a single inch—and I WILL BE HEARD. ❞

Biography
William Lloyd Garrison

To William Lloyd Garrison, slavery was a disease that threatened the whole nation. He once even burned a copy of the Constitution because the document permitted slavery. Garrison refused to back down even after a mob in Boston almost killed him. ★ **How did Garrison spread his antislavery message?**

W.L.G.

▲
Garrison's vow

A Call to End Slavery

Supporters of colonization did not attack slavery directly. Another group of Americans, known as **abolitionists,** wanted to end slavery in the United States completely.

Some abolitionists favored a gradual end to slavery. They expected slavery to die out if it were kept out of the western territories. Other abolitionists demanded that slavery end everywhere, at once.

African American abolitionists

African Americans played an important part in the abolitionist movement. Some tried to end slavery through lawsuits and petitions. James Forten and other wealthy

A year later, Garrison helped to found the New England Anti-Slavery Society. Members included Theodore Weld, a young minister connected with Charles Grandison Finney. Weld brought the energy of a religious revival to antislavery meetings.

The Grimké sisters

Women also played an important role in the abolitionist cause. **Angelina and Sarah Grimké** were the daughters of a wealthy slaveholder in South Carolina. They came to hate slavery and moved to Philadelphia to work for abolition. Their lectures drew large crowds.

Some people, including other abolitionists, objected to women speaking out in public. Sarah Grimké replied that "whatsoever it is morally right for a man to do, it is morally right for a woman to do." As you will see, this belief led the Grimkés and others to crusade for women's rights.

The Underground Railroad

Some abolitionists, black and white, risked prison and death to help African Americans escape slavery. These bold men and women formed the **underground railroad.** It was not a real railroad, but a network of abolitionists who secretly helped slaves reach freedom in the North or Canada.

"Conductors" guided runaways to "stations" where they could spend the night. Some stations were homes of abolitionists. Others were churches, or even caves. Conductors sometimes hid runaways under loads of hay in wagons with false bottoms.

One daring conductor, **Harriet Tubman,** had escaped slavery herself. Risking her freedom and her life, Tubman returned to the South 19 times. She led more than 300 slaves, including her parents, to freedom.

Admirers called Tubman the "Black Moses," after the ancient Hebrew leader who

V̄iewing HISTORY : Conductor on the Underground Railroad

"There was one of two things I had a right to," declared Harriet Tubman, "liberty or death. If I could not have the one, I would have the other." After escaping slavery, Tubman became a fearless conductor on the underground railroad. Here, Tubman (left) poses with some of the hundreds of people she led to freedom.
★ **Why was Tubman called the "Black Moses"?**

Skills FOR LIFE

Analyzing Visual Evidence

How Will I Use This Skill?

Today, newspapers and television present us with a world full of images. A photograph of a bombing victim or a sketch of a courtroom can have a powerful impact. Still, artists and photographers can be influenced by their own viewpoints. We must analyze visual evidence to determine the reliability of what we see.

LEARN the Skill

❶ Identify the subject matter of the drawing, painting, or photograph.

❷ Note the details of the picture. Pay attention to facial expressions, actions, objects, and clothing.

❸ What is the artist's point of view? How does the artist use details to stir sympathy or anger?

❹ Determine the reliability of the visual evidence. Is it an accurate picture of what is shown? What may have been left out?

PRACTICE the Skill

The painting at right depicts a scene of the underground railroad. Look at the picture and answer the following questions.

❶ (a) Where do you think this scene is taking place? (b) Who are the two people in the center of the picture? (c) Describe what is happening in this scene.

❷ (a) What is the man holding in his right hand? What does this tell you about him? (b) What does the expression on the woman's face tell you about her? (c) Why is there a hay wagon in the background?

❸ Do you think the artist was sympathetic toward the underground railroad? How can you tell?

❹ Based on your reading, do you think this picture is reliable? Explain.

APPLY the Skill

Analyze a news photograph that had an emotional impact on you. List the details of the photograph that added to the emotional effect.

led the Israelites out of slavery in Egypt. Slave owners offered a $40,000 reward for Tubman's capture.

Reaction in the North

Abolitionists like Douglass and Garrison made enemies in both the North and the South. Northern mill owners, bankers, and merchants depended on cotton from the South. They saw attacks on slavery as a threat to their livelihood. Some northern workers also opposed abolition. They feared that African Americans might come north and take their jobs by working for low pay.

In New York and other northern cities, mobs sometimes broke up antislavery meetings or attacked homes of abolitionists. At times, the attacks backfired and won support for the abolitionists. One night, a Boston mob dragged William Lloyd Garrison through the streets at the end of a rope. A witness wrote, "I am an abolitionist from this very moment."

Reaction in the South

Not all white southerners favored slavery. Some bravely spoke out against it. Others, such as the Grimké sisters, moved north rather than live in a slaveholding state.

Most white southerners, however, were disturbed by the growing abolitionist movement. They accused abolitionists of preaching violence. Many southerners blamed Nat Turner's revolt on William Lloyd Garrison. (See page 393.) Garrison had founded *The Liberator* in 1831, only a few months before Turner's rebellion. David Walker's call for a slave revolt seemed to confirm the worst fears of southerners.

Many slave owners reacted to the abolitionist crusade by defending slavery even more. One slave owner wrote that if slaves were treated well, they would "love their master and serve him...faithfully." Other owners argued that slaves were better off than northern workers who labored long hours in dusty, airless factories.

Even some southerners who owned no slaves defended slavery. To them, slavery was essential to the southern economy. Many southerners believed northern support for the antislavery movement was greater than it really was. They began to fear that northerners wanted to destroy their way of life.

★ Section 2 Review ★

Recall

1. **Locate** Liberia.
2. **Identify** (a) American Colonization Society, (b) David Walker, (c) Maria Stewart, (d) Frederick Douglass, (e) William Lloyd Garrison, (f) Angelina and Sarah Grimké, (g) Harriet Tubman.
3. **Define** (a) abolitionist, (b) underground railroad.

Comprehension

4. Choose two abolitionists. Describe how each contributed to the antislavery movement.

5. (a) Why did some northerners oppose abolition? (b) Describe two effects of the abolitionist movement in the South.

Critical Thinking and Writing

6. **Drawing Conclusions** Why do you think slavery ended more easily in the North than in the South?
7. **Defending a Position** (a) Why do you think some abolitionists favored a gradual end to slavery? (b) How do you think William Lloyd Garrison or Frederick Douglass would have replied?

Activity **Writing a Letter** You are a conductor on the underground railroad. You have a cousin in New Jersey whom you need to hide runaway slaves. Write a letter to the cousin describing who will be coming, what signals they will use to gain entry, and how they can be helped. (You might want to disguise your message in case it gets into the wrong hands.)

3 ★ Struggle for Women's Rights

As You Read

Explore These Questions
- What rights did women lack in the early 1800s?
- What were the goals of the Seneca Falls Convention?
- How did opportunities for women improve in the mid-1800s?

Define
- women's rights movement

Identify
- Sojourner Truth
- Lucretia Mott
- Elizabeth Cady Stanton
- Seneca Falls Convention
- Susan B. Anthony
- Emma Willard
- Mary Lyon
- Elizabeth Blackwell

SETTING the Scene As you have read, Sarah and Angelina Grimké became powerful speakers against slavery. However, the boldness of their activities shocked many people. Some New England ministers even scolded the sisters in a newspaper. "When [a woman] assumes the place and tone of a man as a public reformer," they wrote, "her character becomes unnatural."

Unmoved by such criticism, Angelina Grimké asked, "What then can woman do for the slave, when she herself is under the feet of man and shamed into silence?" More determined than ever, the Grimkés continued their crusade. Now, however, they had a second topic to lecture about—women's rights.

Seeking Equal Rights

Women had few political or legal rights in the mid-1800s. They could not vote or hold office. When a woman married, her husband became owner of all her property. If a woman worked outside the home, her wages belonged to her husband. A husband also had the right to hit his wife as long as he did not seriously injure her.

Many women, like the Grimkés, had joined the abolitionist movement. As these women worked to end slavery, they became aware that they lacked full social and political rights themselves. Both black and white abolitionists joined the struggle for women's rights.

Truth speaks out

One of the most effective women's rights leaders was born into slavery in New York. Her original name was Isabella Baumfree. After gaining her freedom, she came to believe that God wanted her to crusade against slavery. Vowing to sojourn, or travel, across the land speaking the truth, Baumfree took the name **Sojourner Truth.**

Truth was a spellbinding speaker. Her exact words were rarely written down. However, her powerful message spread by word of mouth. According to one witness, Truth ridiculed the idea that women were inferior to men by nature:

> ❝ I have as much muscle as any man, and can do as much work as any man. I have plowed and reaped and husked and chopped and mowed, and can any man do more than that? ❞

In the mid-1800s, women wore tightly laced corsets to make the waist as tiny as possible. Doctors warned that these "tightlacers" caused fainting, squeezed the internal organs, and could even crush the rib cage. Instead, reformers supported a looser, trouserlike garment known as bloomers.

Mott and Stanton

Other abolitionists also turned to the cause of women's rights. The two most influential were Lucretia Mott and Elizabeth Cady Stanton.

Lucretia Mott was a Quaker and the mother of five children. A quiet speaker, she won the respect of many listeners with her persuasive logic. Mott also used her organizing skills to set up petition drives across the North.

Elizabeth Cady Stanton was the daughter of a New York judge. As a child, she was an excellent student as well as an athlete. However, her father gave his gifted daughter little encouragement. Stanton later remarked that her "father would have felt a proper pride had I been a man." In addition, clerks in her father's law office used to tease her by reading laws that denied basic rights to women. Such experiences made her a lifelong foe of inequality.

In 1840, Stanton and Mott joined a group of Americans at a World Antislavery Convention in London. However, convention officials refused to let women take an active part in the proceedings. Female delegates were even forced to sit behind a curtain, hidden from view. After returning home, Mott and Stanton took up the cause of women's rights with new energy.

A Historic Meeting

While they were still in London, Mott and Stanton decided to hold a convention to draw attention to the problems women faced. "The men...had [shown] a great need for some education on that question," Stanton later recalled.

Eight years later, in 1848, in Seneca Falls, New York, the meeting finally took place. About 200 women and 40 men attended the **Seneca Falls Convention.**

 **Elizabeth Cady Stanton and Sojourner Truth**

Elizabeth Cady Stanton (left) was born into a well-to-do, middle-class family and raised her own children in comfort. Sojourner Truth (right) was born into slavery and saw at least one of her children sold. Despite their vastly different backgrounds, the two women became allies in the fight for women's rights. ★ **Both Truth and Stanton were abolitionists. How was abolition linked to the movement for women's rights?**

The Spirit of Reform

Reform Movements

Social Reform	Antislavery Movement	Women's Rights Movement
▪ Humane treatment for mentally ill	▪ End of slavery in the North	▪ Seneca Falls Convention
▪ Prison reform	▪ Establishment of Liberia	▪ Schools for women
▪ Temperance movement against alcohol	▪ Abolitionist speeches, books, and newspapers	▪ New legal rights in some states
▪ Improvements in education	▪ Underground railroad	▪ New work opportunities

Graphic Organizer Skills The spirit of reform of the 1800s motivated some people to try to improve American society.

1. Comprehension What were two types of social reform addressed by reformers in the mid-1800s?

2. Critical Thinking What did the reforms shown in this graphic organizer have in common?

Civics

"Women are created equal"

At the meeting, leaders of the women's rights movement presented a Declaration of Sentiments. Modeled on the Declaration of Independence, it proclaimed, "We hold these truths to be self-evident: that all men and women are created equal."

The women and men at Seneca Falls voted for resolutions that demanded equality for women at work, at school, and in church. Only one resolution met any opposition at the convention. It demanded that women be allowed to vote. Even the bold women at Seneca Falls hesitated to take this step. In the end, the resolution narrowly passed.

A long struggle

The Seneca Falls Convention marked the start of an organized campaign for equal rights, or **women's rights movement.** Other leaders took up the struggle. **Susan B. Anthony** built a close-working partnership with Elizabeth Cady Stanton. While Stanton usually had to stay at home with her seven children, Anthony was free to travel across the country. Anthony was a tireless speaker. Even when audiences heckled her and threw eggs, she always finished her speech.

In the years after 1848, women worked for change in many areas. They won additional legal rights in some states. For example, New York passed laws allowing married women to keep their own property and wages. Still, many men and women opposed the women's rights movement. The struggle for equal rights would last many years.

New Opportunities

In the early 1800s, women from poor families had little hope of learning even to read. Middle-class girls who went to school learned dancing and drawing rather than science or mathematics. After all, people argued, women were expected to care for their families. Why did they need an education?

The women at Seneca Falls believed that education was a key to equality. Elizabeth Cady Stanton said:

66 The girl must be allowed to romp and play, climb, skate, and swim. Her clothes must be more like those of the boy—strong, loose-fitting garments, thick boots.... Like the boy, she must be taught to look forward to a life of self-dependence and to prepare herself early for some trade profession. 99

The American Medical Women's Association gives this annual medal in honor of Elizabeth Blackwell.

Schools for women

Reformers worked to improve education for women. **Emma Willard** opened a high school for girls in Troy, New York. Here, young women studied "men's" subjects, such as mathematics and physics.

Mary Lyon opened Mount Holyoke Female Seminary in Massachusetts in 1837. She did not call the school a college because many people thought it was wrong for women to attend college. In fact, Mount Holyoke was the first women's college in the United States.

New careers

At about this time, a few men's colleges began to admit women. As their education improved, women found jobs teaching, especially in grade schools.

A few women entered fields such as medicine. **Elizabeth Blackwell** attended medical school at Geneva College in New York. To the surprise of school officials, she graduated first in her class. Women had provided medical care since colonial times, but Blackwell was the first woman in the United States to earn a medical degree. She later set up the nation's first medical school for women.

Women made their mark in other fields as well. Maria Mitchell became a noted astronomer. In the 1850s, Antoinette Blackwell was the first American woman to be ordained as a minister. She also campaigned for abolitionism, temperance, and women's right to vote.

★ Section 3 Review ★

Recall

1. **Identify** **(a)** Sojourner Truth, **(b)** Lucretia Mott, **(c)** Elizabeth Cady Stanton, **(d)** Seneca Falls Convention, **(e)** Susan B. Anthony, **(f)** Emma Willard, **(g)** Mary Lyon, **(h)** Elizabeth Blackwell.
2. **Define** women's rights movement.

Comprehension

3. Describe three ways that laws discriminated against women in the early 1800s.
4. What resolutions did the delegates at Seneca Falls make?

5. **(a)** What type of education did most women receive in the mid-1800s? **(b)** How did reformers change women's education?

Critical Thinking and Writing

6. **Understanding Causes and Effects** How was the women's rights movement a long-term effect of the antislavery movement?
7. **Predicting Consequences** How do you think the growth of educational opportunities affected the future of the women's rights movement?

Activity **Designing a T-shirt** It is four weeks before the Seneca Falls Convention. You have been asked to create a T-shirt for all the attendees. Draw a clever and attractive design that expresses the feelings and demands of the women's rights movement.

As You Read

Explore These Questions
- What themes did American novelists and poets explore?
- What ideas did Emerson and Thoreau express?
- How did American painters create their own styles?

Define
- transcendentalism

Identify
- Washington Irving
- James Fenimore Cooper
- Ralph Waldo Emerson
- Henry David Thoreau
- Walt Whitman
- Emily Dickinson
- Hudson River School

 SETTING the Scene In 1820, a Scottish minister named Sydney Smith blasted what he saw as a lack of culture in the United States:

> ❝ In the four quarters of the globe, who reads an American book? Or goes to an American play? Or looks at an American picture or statue? What does the world yet owe to Americans? ❞

Even as Smith wrote these words, American writers and artists were breaking free of European traditions. These men and women created a voice and a vision that were truly American.

American Storytellers

Until the early 1800s, most American writers depended on Europe for their ideas and inspiration. In the 1820s, however, a new crop of writers began to write stories with American themes.

Two early writers

One of the most popular American writers was **Washington Irving,** a New Yorker. Irving first became known for *The Sketch Book,* a collection of tales published in 1820. Two of the best-loved tales are "Rip Van Winkle" and "The Legend of Sleepy Hollow." (See page 318.)

Irving's stories gave Americans a sense of the richness of their past. His appeal went beyond the United States, however. Irving was the first American writer to also enjoy fame in Europe.

James Fenimore Cooper also published novels set in the past. In *The Deerslayer* and *The Last of the Mohicans,* Cooper created the character Natty Bumppo, a heroic model of a strong, silent, solitary frontiersman. The novels also gave an idealized view of relations between whites and Native Americans on the frontier. The stories were so exciting, however, that few readers cared if they were true to life.

Later writers

Nathaniel Hawthorne drew on the history of Puritan New England to create his novels and short stories. Hawthorne was fascinated by Puritan notions of sin and guilt. His best-known novel, *The Scarlet Letter,* was published in 1850.

In 1851, Herman Melville published *Moby-Dick.* The novel tells the story of Ahab, the crazed captain of a whaling ship. Ahab vows revenge against the white whale that years earlier bit off his leg. *Moby-Dick* had only limited success when it was first published. Today, however, critics rank it among the finest American novels.

Edgar Allan Poe became famous for his many tales of horror. His short story "The Tell-Tale Heart" tells of a murderer, driven mad by guilt, who imagines he can hear his victim's heartbeat. Poe is also called the "father of the detective story" for his mystery stories, such as "The Murders in the Rue Morgue."

William Wells Brown published *Clotel,* a novel about slave life, in 1853. Brown was the first African American to earn his living as a writer.

Women writers

Many best-selling novels of the period were written by women. Some novels told about young women who gained wealth and happiness through honesty and self-sacrifice. Others showed the hardships faced by widows and orphans.

Few of these novels are read today. However, writers like Catherine Sedgwick and Fanny Fern earned far more than Hawthorne or Melville. Hawthorne complained about the success of a "mob of scribbling women."

The "Inner Light"

In New England, a small group of writers and thinkers, known as Transcendentalists,

emerged. **Transcendentalism** was the belief that the most important truths in life transcended, or went beyond, human reason. Transcendentalists stressed emotions over reason. They believed that each individual had control over his or her life. This belief influenced many transcendentalists to support social reform.

One Transcendentalist, Margaret Fuller, wrote *Woman in the Nineteenth Century.* The book strongly influenced the movement for women's rights.

Emerson

The leading Transcendentalist was **Ralph Waldo Emerson.** Emerson was the most popular essayist and lecturer of his day. Audiences flocked to hear him talk on subjects such as self-reliance and character. Emerson believed that the human spirit was reflected in nature. Civilization might provide material wealth, he said, but nature held higher values that came from God.

Linking Past and Present

Past

Present

An Enduring American Tale

In 1826, James Fenimore Cooper's frontier tale The Last of the Mohicans *(left) was a best-seller. In 1992, a film version of Cooper's novel (right) was one of the year's most popular movies. The works of other early American writers, such as Hawthorne and Melville, have also been turned into movies or television miniseries.* ★ **Why do you think modern audiences would still enjoy a movie version of** *The Last of the Mohicans?*

Thomas Cole wrote that "it is of the greatest importance for a painter always to have his mind upon Nature." In paintings like Kaaterskill Falls, left, Cole captured the beauty and power of New York's Hudson River valley.
★ **What kinds of emotion might a painting like this stir?**

Thoreau's "different drummer" told him that slavery was wrong. He was a fierce abolitionist and served as a conductor on the underground railroad.

Poetic Voices

Henry Wadsworth Longfellow was the favorite poet of Americans in the mid-1800s. Longfellow based many poems on events from the past. "Paul Revere's Ride" honored the Revolutionary War hero. "The Song of Hiawatha" idealized Native American life.

Other poets spoke out on social issues. John Greenleaf Whittier, a Quaker from Massachusetts, and Frances Watkins Harper, an African American woman from Maryland, used their pens to make readers aware of the evils of slavery.

Walt Whitman published only one book of poems, *Leaves of Grass*. However, he added to it over a period of 27 years. Whitman had great faith in the common people. His poetry celebrated democracy and the diverse people who made the nation great. He wrote proudly of being part of a "Nation of many nations":

In his essays and lectures, Emerson stressed the importance of the individual. Each person, Emerson said, has an "inner light." He urged people to use this inner light to guide their lives and improve society.

Thoreau

Henry David Thoreau (thuh ROW), Emerson's friend and neighbor, believed that the growth of industry and the rise of cities were ruining the nation. He urged people to live as simply as possible. In *Walden,* his best-known work, Thoreau describes spending a year alone in a cabin on Walden Pond in Massachusetts.

Like Emerson, Thoreau believed that each individual must decide what is right or wrong. He wrote:

> 66 If a man does not keep pace with his companions, perhaps it is because he hears a different drummer. Let him step to the music he hears. 99

Connections With Civics

In his essay *Civil Disobedience,* Thoreau argued that people had a right to disobey unjust laws if their consciences demanded it. He once went to jail for refusing to pay taxes to support the Mexican War, which he felt promoted slavery. Thoreau's ideas on nonviolent protest later influenced Mohandas Gandhi and Martin Luther King, Jr.

> 66 A Southerner soon as a
>   Northerner...
> At home on the hills of Vermont or
>   in the woods of Maine, or the
>   Texan ranch,
> Comrade of Californians, comrade of
>   free North-Westerners....
> Of every hue and caste am I, of
>   every rank and religion,
> A farmer, mechanic, artist, gentle-
>   man, sailor, quaker,
> Prisoner, fancy-man, rowdy, lawyer,
>   physician, priest. 99

Today, critics consider **Emily Dickinson** one of the nation's greatest poets. Yet, only seven of her more than 1,700 poems were published in her lifetime. A shy woman who rarely left her home, Dickinson called her poetry "my letter to the world / That never wrote to me."

American Painters

Before the 1800s, most American painters studied in Europe. In 1772, Benjamin West of Philadelphia was appointed historical painter to King George III. Many American painters journeyed to London to study with West, including Charles Willson Peale and Gilbert Stuart. Both Peale and Stuart painted famous portraits of George Washington.

By the mid-1800s, American artists began to develop their own style. The first group to do so became known as the **Hudson River School** because they painted landscapes of New York's Hudson River region. Two of the best-known painters of the Hudson River School were Thomas Cole and Asher B. Durand. African American artist Robert S. Duncanson also reflected the style of the Hudson River School.

Other American artists painted scenes of hardworking country people. George Caleb Bingham was inspired by his native Missouri. His paintings show frontier life along the rivers that feed the great Mississippi.

Several painters tried to capture the culture of Native Americans on canvas. George Catlin and Alfred Jacob Miller traveled to the Far West. Their paintings record the daily life of Indians on the Great Plains and in the Rockies.

★ Section 4 Review ★

Recall

1. **Identify** (a) Washington Irving, (b) James Fenimore Cooper, (c) Ralph Waldo Emerson, (d) Henry David Thoreau, (e) Walt Whitman, (f) Emily Dickinson, (g) Hudson River School.
2. **Define** Transcendentalism.

Comprehension

3. Describe the subjects explored by each of the following writers: (a) Nathaniel Hawthorne, (b) Edgar Allan Poe, (c) William Wells Brown, (d) Henry Wadsworth Longfellow.
4. What did Emerson and Thoreau think about the importance of the individual?

5. (a) Where did early American painters get their inspiration? (b) How did this situation change in the mid-1800s?

Critical Thinking and Writing

6. **Drawing Conclusions** Why do you think writers and artists did not develop a unique American style until the mid-1800s?
7. **Linking Past and Present** (a) What do you think Walt Whitman meant when he called the United States a "Nation of many nations"? (b) Do you think these words can still be used to describe the nation today? Explain.

Activity Creating a Chart Henry David Thoreau is returning to look at today's society. He will spend a week in your community. Make a two-column chart. In the left column, list things, places, and activities he will probably criticize. On the right, list things, places, and activities he will appreciate.

Chapter 15 Review and Activities

★ Sum It Up ★

Section 1 The Spirit of Reform
▶ Political and religious ideals encouraged a spirit of reform.
▶ Reformers worked for many goals, including temperance, improved education, and better treatment for the mentally ill.

Section 2 The Fight Against Slavery
▶ Abolitionists fought to end slavery in many ways, including publishing newspapers, lecturing, and helping runaway slaves escape on the underground railroad.
▶ Slavery was defended by northerners who depended on cotton for their livelihood and by Southerners who felt their economy depended on slavery.

Section 3 Struggle for Women's Rights
▶ Many women joined the struggle for women's rights after fighting for abolition of slavery.
▶ The Seneca Falls Convention in 1848 marked the beginning of an organized women's rights movement.

Section 4 American Literature and Art
▶ In the 1820s, American writers began to explore American themes in their stories and poems.
▶ American artists gradually broke away from European models and developed their own styles.

For additional review of the major ideas of Chapter 15, see **Guide to the Essentials of American History** or **Interactive Student Tutorial CD-ROM,** which contains interactive review activities, graphic organizers, and practice tests.

🗔 Reviewing the Chapter

Define These Terms
Match each term with the correct definition.

Column 1
1. revival
2. temperance movement
3. abolitionist
4. underground railroad
5. penal system

Column 2
a. system of prisons
b. network of people who helped runaway slaves reach freedom
c. campaign against drinking
d. person who wanted to end slavery
e. huge outdoor religious meeting

Explore the Main Ideas
1. What were two goals of the Second Great Awakening?
2. What goals did Dorothea Dix pursue?
3. Why was Harriet Tubman called the "Black Moses"?
4. Why did supporters of the women's rights movement seek better education for women?
5. Name two writers in the 1800s who wrote about American experiences.

🗔 Graph Activity

Look at the graph below and answer the following questions:
1. About how many students were enrolled in American schools in 1840? In 1860? **2.** How much did school enrollment increase between 1850 and 1870? **Critical Thinking** Based on what you have read, why did school enrollment increase steadily in the mid-1800s?

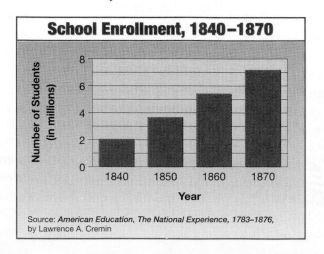

School Enrollment, 1840–1870

Source: *American Education, The National Experience, 1783–1876,* by Lawrence A. Cremin

☐ Critical Thinking and Writing

1. **Linking Past and Present** **(a)** How did reformers in the 1800s try to gain public support? **(b)** What methods do people use to win public support today?

2. **Analyzing Ideas** In his *Appeal to the Colored Citizens of the World,* David Walker wrote that "all men are created equal; that they are endowed by their Creator with certain inalienable rights." **(a)** From which document did Walker borrow this idea? **(b)** What point do you think he was making by including these words?

3. **Ranking** In the mid-1800s, women like Sojourner Truth, the Grimké sisters, Lucretia Mott, and Elizabeth Cady Stanton organized to fight for abolition and women's rights. Make a list of the demands of these women. Then rank the demands from most important to least important. Give reasons for this ranking.

4. **Exploring Unit Themes** **Expansion** How do you think westward expansion increased concerns about slavery?

☐ Using Primary Sources

Frederick Douglass denounced the slave trade in the South:

> **66** Fellow citizens, this murderous traffic is, today, in active operation in this boasted republic. I see the bleeding footsteps; I hear the doleful wail of [chained] humanity on the way to the slave markets where the victims are to be sold like horse, sheep, and swine.... My soul sickens at the sight. **99**

Source: Frederick Douglass, speech to New York abolitionist society, 1852.

Recognizing Points of View **(a)** What words did Douglass use to stir up anger against the slave trade? **(b)** What did he mean when he called the United States a "boasted republic"? **(c)** How did Douglass's background make him an effective speaker on the subject of slavery?

ACTIVITY BANK

► Interdisciplinary Activity

Exploring the Arts Do research on one of the American painters discussed in this chapter. Then, prepare a guidebook for a museum exhibit of that painter's work. Include a brief biographical note and descriptions of two or three paintings.

► Career Skills Activity

Musicians Write and perform a marching song to be used at one of the following events: a temperance rally; an abolitionist meeting; the Seneca Falls Convention. You may work alone or with a group.

► Citizenship Activity

Creating a Campaign Today, as in the past, communities are concerned with making sure all students get a good education. Plan a campaign designed to encourage students to stay in school. Your campaign may include posters, speeches, or other public events.

Internet Activity

Use the Internet to find information on any five of the following women: Antoinette Blackwell, Emily Blackwell, Amelia Bloomer, Myra Bradwell, Margaret Fuller, Matilda Joslyn Gage, Maria Mitchell, Lucy Stone. Write a one-sentence summary of the contribution each woman made to the women's rights movement.

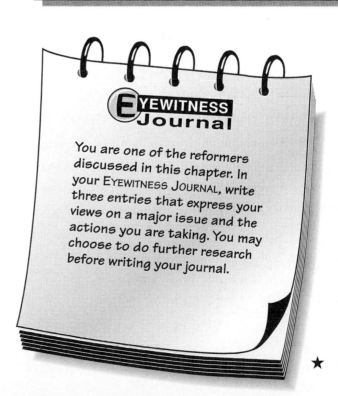

EYEWITNESS Journal

You are one of the reformers discussed in this chapter. In your EYEWITNESS JOURNAL, write three entries that express your views on a major issue and the actions you are taking. You may choose to do further research before writing your journal.

History Through Literature

Nightjohn

by Gary Paulsen

Introduction

Nightjohn, set in the 1850s, is told by Sarny, a 12-year-old slave on a southern plantation. When John comes to live there, Sarny's life is changed forever. John had escaped to the North. Yet, he came back—to teach others to read. As this excerpt begins, Sarny is talking to John late at night in the slave quarters. She is deciding whether to let John teach her some letters.

I knew about reading. It was something that the people in the white house did from paper. They could read words on paper. But we weren't allowed to be reading. We weren't allowed to understand or read nothing but once I saw some funny lines on the side of a feed sack. It said:

100 lbs.

I wrote them down in the dirt with a stick and mammy gave me a smack on the back of the head that like to drove me into the ground.

"Don't you take to that, take to writing," she said.

"I wasn't doing it. I was just copying something I saw on a feed sack."

"Don't. They catch you doing that and they'll think you're learning to read. You learn to read and they'll whip you.... Or cut your thumb off. Stay away from writing and reading."

So I did. But I remembered how it had looked, the drawings on the sack and in the dirt, and it still puzzled me....

[Sarny then speaks to John.]
"You saying you can read?"

He nodded.

"I give you something to read, you can read it? Just like that?"

"I can."...

"Way it works," he said, "is you got to learn all the letters and numbers before you can learn to read. You got to learn the alphabet."

"Alphabet?"

He nodded. "There be lots of letters, and each one means something different. You got to learn each one."

...Then he made a drawing with his thumb.

A

"Tonight we just do *A.*" He sat back on his heels and pointed. "There it be."...

"What does it mean?"

"It means *A*—just like I said. It's the first letter in the alphabet. And when you see it you make a sound like this: *ayyy,* or *ahhh.*"

Learning to Read—In Secret

This illustration from the novel Nightjohn *shows John teaching Sarny to read. By the mid-1800s, many southern states had made it illegal for enslaved African Americans to learn to read and write. Yet many slaves risked severe punishment to learn anyway.*

★ **Why do you think enslaved African Americans valued education so highly?**

"That's reading? To make that sound?" He nodded. "When you see that letter on paper or a sack or in the dirt you make one of those sounds. That's reading."

"Well, that ain't hard at all."

He laughed. That same low roll. Made me think of thunder long ways off, moving in a summer sky. "There's more to it. Other letters. But that's it."

"Why they be cutting our thumbs off if we learn to read—if that's all it is?"

"'Cause to know things, for us to know things, is bad for them. We get to wanting and when we get to wanting it's bad for them. They thinks we want what they got.... That's why they don't want us reading." He sighed. "I got to rest now. They run me ten miles in a day and worked me into the ground. I need some sleep."

He moved back to the corner and settled down and I curled up to mammy in amongst the young ones again.

A, I thought, *ayyy, ahhhh.* There it is. I be reading.

"Hey there in the corner," I whispered.

"What?"

"What's your name?"

"I be John."

"I be Sarny."

"Go to sleep, Sarny."

But I didn't. I snuggled into mammy and pulled a couple of the young ones in for heat and kept my eyes open so I wouldn't sleep and thought:

A.

Analyzing Literature

1. Why did Sarny's mother tell her to stay away from reading and writing?

2. According to John, why did the slave owners want to keep the slaves from learning to read and write?

3. **Critical Thinking   Making Inferences** Based on this excerpt, what are some of John's qualities? How can you tell?

Unit 5 Division and Reunion

Viewing UNIT THEMES — War Divides the Nation

In 1861, conflict between the North and the South erupted into war. Winslow Homer, one of the country's greatest artists, painted Prisoners From the Front. *It shows a northern officer (right) inspecting captured southern troops (left). The opposing soldiers look on each other with pride and hostility.* ★ **Based on what you have learned in earlier units, identify two differences between the North and South.**

Unit Theme Sectionalism

Sectionalism is loyalty to a state or region rather than to the country as a whole. From colonial days, Americans felt strong loyalties to the regions where they lived. By the mid-1800s, several issues increased sectional differences between the North and South. The most dramatic of these issues was slavery. Extreme sectionalism eventually led to war.

How did people of the time feel about sectional divisions? They can tell you in their own words.

★ ★

VIEWPOINTS ON SECTIONAL DIVISIONS

66 We have always been taught to look upon the people of New England as a selfish, cunning set of fellows. **99**

Davy Crockett, Tennessee member of Congress (1835)

66 I have heard something said about allegiance to the South. I know no South, no North, no East, no West, to which I owe any allegiance.... The Union, sir, is my country. **99**

Henry Clay, senator from Kentucky (1848)

66 Union! I can more easily conceive of the Lion and Lambs lying down together, than of a union of the North and South. **99**

Sarah Chase, Massachusetts teacher in the South (1866)

★ ★

Activity Writing to Learn Today, the United States is often divided into these geographic regions: the Northeast; the Midatlantic; the Southeast; the Midwest; the Rocky Mountain states; the Southwest; the Pacific Coast states. List three features, other than location, that make the region you live in special. Then, write a paragraph explaining whether you feel more loyal to your region or to the United States as a whole.

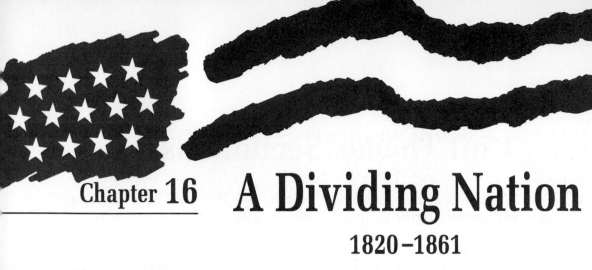

Chapter 16

A Dividing Nation

1820–1861

Between 1820 and 1861, the nation grew increasingly divided as it struggled to answer difficult questions concerning slavery. Should slavery be allowed to spread to the West? Should slavery be abolished throughout the nation? For a time, northerners and southerners settled their differences through compromises. Gradually, however, violence became more and more common. In 1860, voters elected Abraham Lincoln, a member of the anti-slavery Republican party, to be the next President of the United States. In response, southern states withdrew from the Union. The North and the South then prepared for war.

Why Study History?

Many consider Abraham Lincoln to be one of the greatest leaders in American history. Some call him an American hero. Frequently, therefore, he is held as a role model for others to imitate. Could Lincoln be a role model for you? To answer this question, see this chapter's *Why Study History?* feature, "Heroes of the Past Can Be Models for Today."

American Events

●1820
Missouri Compromise allows slavery in some western territories

●1850
Fugitive Slave Law requires citizens to help catch runaway slaves

●1852
Uncle Tom's Cabin increases support for abolitionism

1820   1848   1850   1852   1854

World Events

1833 World Event
Slavery is abolished in British empire

1850 World Event
Taiping Rebellion begins civil war in China

 iewing
HISTORY **From Slavery to Freedom**

In the painting On to Liberty *by Theodor Kaufmann, fugitive slave families try to reach the North and freedom. In the 1850s, many northerners protested against a law requiring all citizens to help return runaway slaves. Disagreement over slavery heightened the growing division between North and South.* ★ **How do you think enslaved African Americans felt as they tried to escape to the North?**

●**1854**
Kansas-Nebraska Act
leads to violence

●**1857**
Supreme Court
says Congress
cannot outlaw
slavery in territories

1861●
Abraham Lincoln
becomes
President

1854   **1856**   **1858**   **1860**   **1862**

▲
 1857 World Event
New constitution in
Mexico prohibits slavery

The Slavery Issue in the West

Explore These Questions
- What were the various views on slavery in the West?
- What was the goal of the Free Soil party?
- What were the results of the Compromise of 1850?

Define
- sectionalism
- popular sovereignty
- secede
- fugitive
- civil war

Identify
- Missouri Compromise
- Wilmot Proviso
- Free Soil party
- Zachary Taylor
- Stephen Douglas
- Compromise of 1850
- Fugitive Slave Law of 1850

SETTING the Scene In 1820, Thomas Jefferson was in his seventies. The former President had vowed "never to write, talk, or even think of politics." Still, he voiced alarm when he heard about a fierce debate going on in Congress:

> **66** In the gloomiest moment of the revolutionary war, I never had any [fears] equal to what I feel from this source.... We have a wolf by the ears, and we can neither hold him nor safely let him go. **99**

Jefferson feared that the "wolf," or the issue of slavery, would tear the North and South apart. He was correct. As settlers continued to move west, tension over slavery worsened. Again and again, Congress faced an agonizing decision. Should it prohibit slavery in the territories and later admit them to the Union as free states? Or should it permit slavery in the territories and later admit them as slave states?

The Missouri Compromise

When Missouri asked to join the Union as a slave state, a crisis erupted. The admission of Missouri would upset the balance of power in the Senate. In 1819, there were 11 free states and 11 slave states. (See the graph on page 427.) Missouri's admission would give the South a majority in the Senate. Determined not to lose power, northerners opposed letting Missouri enter as a slave state.

The argument over Missouri lasted many months. Finally, Senator Henry Clay proposed a compromise. During the long debate, Maine had also applied for statehood. Clay suggested admitting Missouri as a slave state and Maine as a free state. His plan, called the **Missouri Compromise,** kept the number of slave and free states equal.

As part of the Missouri Compromise, Congress drew an imaginary line across the southern border of Missouri at latitude 36° 30´ N. Slavery was permitted in the part of the Louisiana Purchase south of that line. It was banned north of the line. The only exception to this was Missouri. (See the map on page 431.)

New Western Lands

The Missouri Compromise applied only to the Louisiana Purchase. In 1848, the Mexican War added a vast stretch of western land to the United States. (See the map on page 363.) Once again, the question of slavery in the territories arose.

The Wilmot Proviso

Many northerners feared that the South would extend slavery into the West. David Wilmot, a Congressman from Pennsylvania, called for a law to ban slavery in any lands won from Mexico. Southern leaders angrily opposed the **Wilmot Proviso.** They said that Congress had no right to ban slavery in the western territories.

United States

Russia

Forced Labor

In the painting at left, enslaved African Americans await the results of a slave auction. At the same time in Russia, millions of workers were serfs. Serfs were bound to the land and had to work for wealthy nobles. One Russian observer sadly reported "of men and women torn from their families and their villages, and sold . . . of children taken from their parents and sold to cruel masters." ★ **How was slavery in the United States similar to serfdom in Russia?**

In 1846, the House passed the Wilmot Proviso, but the Senate defeated it. As a result, Americans continued to argue about slavery in the West even while their army fought in Mexico.

Opposing views

The Mexican War strengthened feelings of **sectionalism** in the North and South. Sectionalism is loyalty to a state or section, rather than to the country as a whole. Many southerners were united by their support for slavery. They saw the North as a growing threat to their way of life. Many northerners saw the South as a foreign country, where American rights and liberties did not exist.

As the debate over slavery heated up, people found it hard not to take sides. Northern abolitionists demanded that slavery be banned throughout the country. They insisted that slavery was morally wrong. By the late 1840s, many northerners agreed.

Southern slaveholders thought that slavery should be allowed in any territory. They also demanded that slaves who escaped to the North be returned to them. Even white southerners who did not own slaves generally agreed with these ideas.

Between these two extreme views were more moderate positions. Some moderates argued that the Missouri Compromise line should be extended across the Mexican Cession to the Pacific Ocean. Any new state north of the line would be a free state. Any new state south of the line could allow slavery.

$ Connections With Economics

In response to the Wilmot Proviso, some southern states proposed cutting off all trade with the North. Another economic threat was that southerners would stop payments on debts owed to northern banks and businesses.

Other moderates supported the idea of **popular sovereignty,** or control by the people. In other words, voters in a new territory would decide for themselves whether or not to allow slavery in the territory. Slaves, of course, could not vote.

The Free Soil Party

The debate over slavery led to the birth of a new political party. By 1848, many northerners in both the Democratic party and the Whig party opposed the spread of slavery. However, the leaders of both parties refused to take a stand on the question. They did not want to give up their chance of winning votes in the South. Some also feared that the slavery issue would split the nation.

In 1848, antislavery members of both parties met in Buffalo, New York. There, they founded the **Free Soil party.** Their slogan was "Free soil, free speech, free labor, and free men." The main goal of the Free Soil party was to keep slavery out of the western territories. Only a few Free Soilers were abolitionists who wanted to end slavery in the South.

In the 1848 presidential campaign, Free Soilers named former President Martin Van Buren as their candidate. Democrats chose Lewis Cass of Michigan. The Whigs selected **Zachary Taylor,** a hero of the Mexican War.

For the first time, slavery was an important election issue. Van Buren called for a ban on slavery in the Mexican Cession. Cass supported popular sovereignty. Because Taylor was a slave owner from Louisiana, many southern voters assumed that he supported slavery.

Zachary Taylor won the election, but Van Buren took 10 percent of the popular vote. Thirteen other Free Soil candidates won seats in Congress. The success of the new Free Soil party showed that slavery had become a national issue.

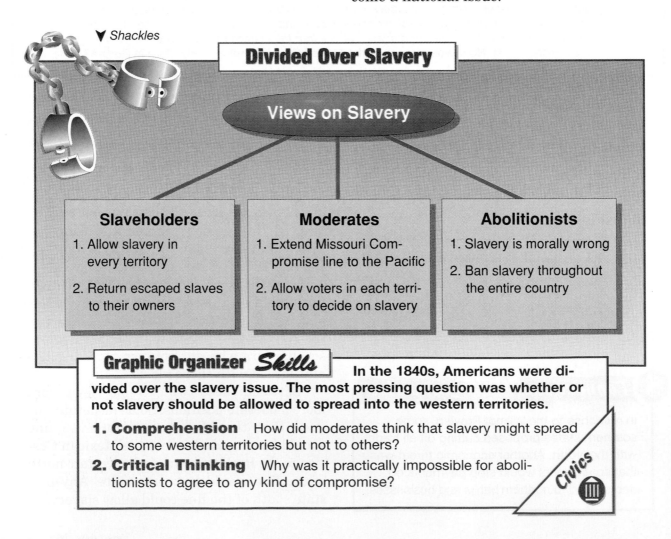

▼ Shackles

Divided Over Slavery

Views on Slavery

Slaveholders	Moderates	Abolitionists
1. Allow slavery in every territory	1. Extend Missouri Compromise line to the Pacific	1. Slavery is morally wrong
2. Return escaped slaves to their owners	2. Allow voters in each territory to decide on slavery	2. Ban slavery throughout the entire country

Graphic Organizer *Skills*   In the 1840s, Americans were divided over the slavery issue. The most pressing question was whether or not slavery should be allowed to spread into the western territories.

1. **Comprehension** How did moderates think that slavery might spread to some western territories but not to others?
2. **Critical Thinking** Why was it practically impossible for abolitionists to agree to any kind of compromise?

Civics

Need for a New Compromise

For a time after the Missouri Compromise, both slave and free states entered the Union peacefully. However, when California requested admission to the Union as a free state in 1850, the balance of power in the Senate was once again threatened. (See the graph to the right.)

California's impact

In 1849, there were 15 slave states and 15 free states in the nation. If California entered the union as a free state, the balance of power would be broken. Furthermore, it seemed quite possible that Oregon, Utah, and New Mexico might also join the Union as free states.

Many Southerners feared that the South would be hopelessly outvoted in the Senate. Some even suggested that southern states might want to **secede,** or remove themselves, from the United States. Northern congressmen, meanwhile, argued that California should enter the Union as a free state because most of the territory lay north of the Missouri Compromise line.

As Congress tried to reach a new compromise, tempers raged. One frightening incident involved Senators Thomas Hart Benton of Missouri and Henry Foote of Mississippi. Benton supported California's entry as a free state even though he himself was a slave owner. He denounced Foote for opposing California's admission. In response, Foote rose angrily from his seat and aimed a pistol at Benton. As other senators watched in horror, Benton roared, "Let him fire. Stand out of the way and let the assassin fire!"

No blood was shed in the Senate that day. However, it was clear that the nation faced a crisis. Many in Congress looked to Senator Henry Clay for a solution.

Clay vs. Calhoun

Clay had won the nickname "the Great Compromiser" for working out the Missouri Compromise. Now, nearly 30 years later, the 73-year-old Clay was frail and ill. Still, he pleaded for the North and South to reach an agreement. If they failed to do so, Clay warned, the nation could break apart.

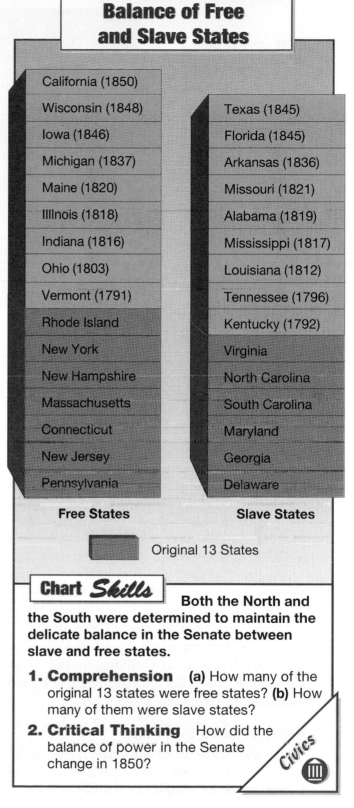

Balance of Free and Slave States

Free States	Slave States
California (1850)	
Wisconsin (1848)	Texas (1845)
Iowa (1846)	Florida (1845)
Michigan (1837)	Arkansas (1836)
Maine (1820)	Missouri (1821)
Illinois (1818)	Alabama (1819)
Indiana (1816)	Mississippi (1817)
Ohio (1803)	Louisiana (1812)
Vermont (1791)	Tennessee (1796)
Rhode Island	Kentucky (1792)
New York	Virginia
New Hampshire	North Carolina
Massachusetts	South Carolina
Connecticut	Maryland
New Jersey	Georgia
Pennsylvania	Delaware

▮ Original 13 States

Chart Skills Both the North and the South were determined to maintain the delicate balance in the Senate between slave and free states.

1. **Comprehension** (a) How many of the original 13 states were free states? (b) How many of them were slave states?

2. **Critical Thinking** How did the balance of power in the Senate change in 1850?

Civics

Senator John C. Calhoun of South Carolina prepared the South's reply to Clay. Calhoun was dying of tuberculosis and could not speak loudly enough to address the Senate. He stared defiantly at his northern foes while Senator James Mason of Virginia read his speech.

Protest!

In 1854, a Boston court ordered that fugitive slaves Anthony Burns and Thomas Sims be returned to their owners in the South. Public outcry against the decision was so great that United States marines and artillery were sent into Boston. Angry protesters lined the streets as the two were led to the ship that would return them to slavery.

★ **Do you think the court made the right decision in this case? Explain.**

ANTI-SLAVE-CATCHERS'
MASS
CONVENTION!

YOUNGS' HALL,
THURSDAY, APRIL 13th.

Calhoun refused to compromise. He insisted that slavery be allowed in the western territories. Calhoun also demanded that **fugitive,** or runaway, slaves be returned to their owners in the South. He wanted northerners to admit that southern slaveholders had the right to reclaim their "property."

If the North would not agree to the South's demands, Calhoun told the Senate, "let the states . . . agree to part in peace. If you are unwilling that we should part in peace, tell us so, and we shall know what to do." Everyone knew what Calhoun meant. If an agreement could not be reached, the South would secede from the Union.

Webster calls for unity

Daniel Webster of Massachusetts spoke next. He supported Clay's plea to save the Union. Webster stated his position clearly:

> 66 I speak today not as a Massachusetts man, nor as a northern man, but as an American. . . . I speak today for the preservation of the Union. . . . There can be no such thing as a peaceable secession. Peaceable secession is an utter impossibility. 99

Webster feared that the states could not separate without a **civil war.** A civil war is a war between people of the same country.

Like many northerners, Webster viewed slavery as evil. Disunion, however, he believed was worse. To save the Union, Webster was willing to compromise with the South. He would support its demand that northerners be required to return fugitive slaves.

Compromise of 1850

In 1850, as the debate raged, Calhoun died. His last words reportedly were "The South! The South! God knows what will become of her!" President Taylor also died in 1850. The new President was Millard Fillmore. Unlike Taylor, he supported Clay's compromise plan. An agreement finally seemed possible.

Henry Clay gave more than 70 speeches in favor of a compromise. At last, however, he became too sick to continue. **Stephen Douglas,** an energetic senator from Illinois, took up the fight for him. Douglas tirelessly guided each part of Clay's plan, called the **Compromise of 1850,** through Congress.

The Compromise of 1850 had five parts. First, it allowed California to enter the Union as a free state. Second, it divided the rest of the Mexican Cession into the territories of New Mexico and Utah. Voters in each would decide the slavery question according to popular sovereignty. Third, it ended the slave trade in Washington, D.C., the nation's capital. Congress, however, declared that it had no power to ban slave trade between slave states. Fourth, it included a strict fugitive slave law. Fifth, it settled a border dispute between Texas and New Mexico.

Fugitive Slave Law of 1850

Most northerners had ignored the Fugitive Slave Law of 1793. As a result, fugitive slaves often lived as free citizens in northern cities. The **Fugitive Slave Law of 1850** was harder to ignore. It required all citizens to help catch runaway slaves. People who let fugitives escape could be fined $1,000 and jailed for six months.

The new law also set up special courts to handle the cases of runaways. Judges received $10 for sending an accused runaway to the South. They received only $5 for setting someone free. Lured by the extra money, some judges sent African Americans to the South whether or not they were runaways.

The Fugitive Slave Law enraged antislavery northerners. By forcing them to catch runaways, the law made northerners feel they were part of the slave system. In several northern cities, crowds tried to rescue fugitive slaves from their captors.

Martin R. Delany, an African American newspaper editor, spoke for many northerners, black and white:

66 My house is my castle.... If any man approaches that house in search of a slave—I care not who he may be, whether constable or sheriff, magistrate or even judge of the Supreme Court...if he crosses the threshold of my door, and I do not lay him a lifeless corpse at my feet, I hope the grave may refuse my body a resting place. 99

The North and South had reached a compromise. Still, tensions remained because neither side got everything that it wanted. The new Fugitive Slave Law was especially hard for northerners to accept. Each time the law was enforced, it convinced more northerners that slavery was evil.

★ Section 1 Review ★

Recall

1. **Locate** (a) Missouri, (b) Maine, (c) Missouri Compromise Line, (d) California, (e) New Mexico Territory, (f) Utah Territory.
2. **Identify** (a) Missouri Compromise, (b) Wilmot Proviso, (c) Free Soil party, (d) Zachary Taylor, (e) Stephen Douglas, (f) Compromise of 1850, (g) Fugitive Slave Law of 1850.
3. **Define** (a) sectionalism, (b) popular sovereignty, (c) secede, (d) fugitive, (e) civil war.

Comprehension

4. Describe three different views on the issue of slavery in the West.

5. Why did some people leave the Whig and Democratic parties and create the Free Soil party?
6. Explain the five parts of the Compromise of 1850.

Critical Thinking and Writing

7. **Analyzing Ideas** Why might the goals of the Free Soil party have pleased some northerners but not others?
8. **Analyzing Visual Evidence** Based on your understanding of the painting on page 428, how did the Compromise of 1850 create new conflict over the slavery issue?

Activity **Making a Decision** You are a northerner of the 1850s. There is a knock at your door. It's a fugitive slave! Will you help the runaway or will you turn the person in to the authorities? Write a brief statement explaining the reasons for your decision.

The Crisis Turns Violent

As You Read

Explore These Questions
- How did *Uncle Tom's Cabin* affect attitudes toward slavery?
- Why did a civil war break out in Kansas?
- How did the Dred Scott decision divide the nation?

Define
- repeal
- guerrilla warfare
- lawsuit

Identify
- Harriet Beecher Stowe
- *Uncle Tom's Cabin*
- Kansas-Nebraska Act
- Franklin Pierce
- Border Ruffians
- John Brown
- Bleeding Kansas
- Charles Sumner
- Dred Scott decision

SETTING the Scene In the mid-1850s, proslavery and antislavery forces battled for control of the territory of Kansas. An observer described election day in one Kansas district in 1855:

66 On the morning of the election, before the polls were opened, some 300 or 400 Missourians and others were collected in the yard...where the election was to be held, armed with bowie-knives, revolvers, and clubs. They said they came to vote, and whip the...Yankees, and would vote without being sworn. Some said they came to have a fight, and wanted one. 99

Hearing of events in Kansas, Abraham Lincoln, then a young lawyer in Illinois, predicted that "the contest will come to blows, and bloodshed." Once again, the issue of slavery in the territories divided the nation.

An Antislavery Bestseller

An event in 1852 added to the growing antislavery mood of the North. That year, **Harriet Beecher Stowe** published a novel called ***Uncle Tom's Cabin.*** Stowe wrote the novel to show the evils of slavery and the injustice of the Fugitive Slave Law. She had originally published the story as a serial in an abolitionist newspaper.

A powerful story

Stowe told the story of Uncle Tom, an enslaved African American noted for his kindness and his devotion to his religion. Tom is bought by Simon Legree, a cruel planter who treats his slaves brutally. In the end, Uncle Tom refuses to obey Legree's order to whip another slave. Legree then whips Uncle Tom to death.

Uncle Tom's Cabin had wide appeal in the North. The first 5,000 copies that were printed sold out in two days. In its first year, Stowe's novel sold 300,000 copies. The book was also published in many different languages. Soon, a play based on the novel appeared in cities not only in the North but around the world.

Nationwide reaction

Although *Uncle Tom's Cabin* was popular in the North, southerners objected to the book. They claimed that it did not give a true picture of slave life. Indeed, Stowe had seen little of slavery firsthand.

Even so, the book helped to change the way northerners felt about slavery. No longer could they ignore slavery as a political problem for Congress to settle. They now saw the slavery issue as a moral problem facing every American. For this reason, *Uncle Tom's Cabin* was one of the most important books in American history.

Kansas-Nebraska Act

Americans had hoped that the Compromise of 1850 would end debate over slavery in the West. In 1854, however, the issue of slavery in the territories surfaced yet again.

In January 1854, Senator Stephen Douglas introduced a bill to set up a government for the Nebraska Territory. This territory stretched from Texas north to Canada, and from Missouri west to the Rockies.

Douglas knew that white southerners did not want to add another free state to the Union. He proposed that the Nebraska Territory be divided into two territories, Kansas and Nebraska. (See the map below.) The settlers living in each territory would decide the issue of slavery by popular sovereignty. Douglas's bill was known as the **Kansas-Nebraska Act.**

Support for the act

The Kansas-Nebraska Act seemed fair to many people. After all, the Compromise of 1850 had applied popular sovereignty in New Mexico and Utah.

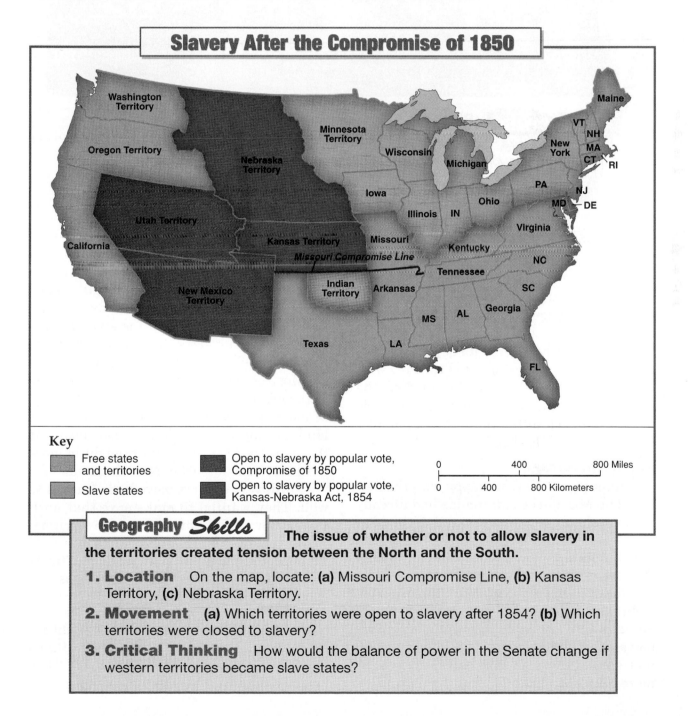

Slavery After the Compromise of 1850

Key

- Free states and territories
- Slave states
- Open to slavery by popular vote, Compromise of 1850
- Open to slavery by popular vote, Kansas-Nebraska Act, 1854

0 · 400 · 800 Miles
0 · 400 · 800 Kilometers

Geography Skills The issue of whether or not to allow slavery in the territories created tension between the North and the South.

1. Location On the map, locate: **(a)** Missouri Compromise Line, **(b)** Kansas Territory, **(c)** Nebraska Territory.

2. Movement **(a)** Which territories were open to slavery after 1854? **(b)** Which territories were closed to slavery?

3. Critical Thinking How would the balance of power in the Senate change if western territories became slave states?

Viewing History

Bleeding Kansas

In 1856, a bloody civil war broke out in Kansas. Proslavery and antislavery forces fought for control of the territory. The battle depicted here took place at Hickory Point, 25 miles north of Lawrence. ★ **How was the violence in Kansas related to the Kansas-Nebraska Act?**

Southern leaders especially supported the Kansas-Nebraska Act. They were sure that slave owners from neighboring Missouri would move across the border into Kansas. In time, they hoped, Kansas would become a slave state.

President **Franklin Pierce,** a Democrat elected in 1852, also supported the bill. With the President's help, Douglas pushed the Kansas-Nebraska Act through Congress. He did not realize it at the time, but he had lit a fire under a powder keg.

Northern outrage

Other people were unhappy with the new law. The Missouri Compromise had already banned slavery in Kansas and Nebraska, they insisted. In effect, the Kansas-Nebraska Act would **repeal,** or undo, the Missouri Compromise.

The northern reaction to the Kansas-Nebraska Act was swift and angry. Opponents of slavery called the act a "criminal betrayal of precious rights." Slavery could now spread to areas that had been free for more than 30 years.

Bleeding Kansas

Kansas now became a testing ground for popular sovereignty. Stephen Douglas hoped that settlers would decide the slavery issue peacefully on election day. Instead, proslavery and antislavery forces sent settlers to Kansas to fight for control of the territory.

Most of the new arrivals were farmers from neighboring states. Their main interest in moving to Kansas was to acquire cheap land. Few of these settlers owned slaves. At the same time, abolitionists brought in more than 1,000 settlers from New England.

Proslavery settlers moved into Kansas as well. They wanted to make sure that antislavery forces did not overrun the territory. Proslavery bands from Missouri often rode across the border. These **Border Ruffians** battled the antislavery forces in Kansas.

Two governments

In 1855, Kansas held elections to choose lawmakers. Hundreds of Border Ruffians crossed into Kansas and voted illegally. They helped to elect a proslavery legislature.

The new legislature quickly passed laws to support slavery. One law said that people could be put to death for helping slaves escape. Another made speaking out against slavery a crime punishable by two years of hard labor.

Antislavery settlers refused to accept these laws. They elected their own governor and legislature. With two rival governments, Kansas was in chaos. Armed gangs roamed the land looking for trouble.

A bloody battleground

In 1856, a band of proslavery men raided the town of Lawrence, an antislavery stronghold. The attackers destroyed homes and smashed the press of a Free Soil newspaper.

John Brown, an abolitionist, decided to strike back. Brown had moved to Kansas to help make it a free state. He claimed that God had sent him to punish supporters of slavery.

Brown rode with his four sons and two other men to the town of Pottawatomie (paht uh WAHT uh mee) Creek. In the middle of the night, they dragged five proslavery settlers from their beds and murdered them.

The killings at Pottawatomie Creek led to more violence. Both sides fought fiercely and engaged in **guerrilla warfare,** or the use of hit-and-run tactics. By late 1856, more than 200 people had been killed. Newspapers called the territory **Bleeding Kansas.**

Violence in the Senate

Even before John Brown's attack, the battle over Kansas had spilled into the Senate. **Charles Sumner** of Massachusetts was the leading abolitionist senator. In one speech, the sharp-tongued Sumner denounced the proslavery legislature of Kansas. He then viciously criticized his southern foes, singling out Andrew Butler, an elderly senator from South Carolina.

Butler was not in the Senate on the day Sumner spoke. A few days later, however, Butler's nephew, Congressman Preston Brooks, marched into the Senate chamber. Using a heavy cane, Brooks beat Sumner until he fell down, bloody and unconscious, to the floor.

Many southerners felt that Sumner got what he deserved for his verbal abuse of another senator. Hundreds of people sent canes to Brooks to show their support. To northerners, however, the brutal act was just more evidence that slavery led to violence.

The Dred Scott Case

With Congress in an uproar, many Americans looked to the Supreme Court to settle the slavery issue and restore peace. In 1857, the Court ruled on a case involving a slave named Dred Scott. Instead of bringing harmony, however, the Court's decision further divided North and South.

Dred Scott had lived for many years in Missouri. Later, he moved with his owner to Illinois and then to the Wisconsin Territory,

 **Dred Scott**

Dred Scott filed a lawsuit for his freedom. He argued that he should be a free man because he had lived in a free territory. The Supreme Court, however, ruled that he had no right to sue because he was property and not a citizen. After the decision, Scott's new owner granted freedom to Scott and his family. Just one year later, Scott died of consumption. ★ **How did the Dred Scott decision overturn the Missouri Compromise?**

Chapter 17

The Civil War

1861–1865

For more than four years, Americans fought Americans in the Civil War. The South wanted to exist as an independent nation. The North wanted to force the South back into the Union. The war was also linked closely to the question of slavery. President Lincoln made this clear when he issued the Emancipation Proclamation.

Throughout the North and the South, both soldiers and civilians experienced much suffering. The Union's armies struggled in the early years of the war. However, the North's superior resources wore heavily on the South. By the end of 1863, the South was in retreat. In 1865, the South surrendered and the Civil War came to an end.

Why Study History?

During the Civil War, millions of northerners and southerners served their nation well. Their efforts, as both soldiers and civilians, affected the course of the war. To see an example of how one person can affect the course of history, see this chapter's *Why Study History?* feature, "One Person Can Make a Difference." The feature focuses on the achievements of Clara Barton.

American Events

●1861
Civil War begins with attack on Fort Sumter

●1862
Union gunboats capture New Orleans and Memphis

1863 ●
Abraham Lincoln issues Emancipation Proclamation

1861   **1862**   **1863**

World Events

 1861 World Event
Russian czar frees serfs

 1862 World Event
Britain refuses to recognize the Confederacy

The Soldiers of the Civil War

In A Rainy Day in Camp by Winslow Homer, Civil War soldiers find time to gather around a campfire. It is estimated that more than 2,500,000 men served as soldiers in the Civil War. Over 600,000 of them died—more than in any other American war. ★ **What emotions do you think soldiers felt on the eve of a battle? Explain.**

●**1863**
Battle of Gettysburg ends Confederate drive into the North

●**1864**
General Grant becomes commander of Union army

●**1865**
General Lee surrenders at Appomattox Courthouse

1863   **1864**   **1865**

 1863 World Event
First Red Cross societies established in Europe

The Conflict Takes Shape

As You Read

Explore These Questions
- What strengths and weaknesses did the Confederacy have?
- What strengths and weaknesses did the Union have?
- What special qualities did Presidents Abraham Lincoln and Jefferson Davis possess?

Define
- racism
- martial law

Identify
- border states
- Robert E. Lee

Confederate canteen

SETTING the Scene In April 1861, President Abraham Lincoln called for 75,000 volunteers to serve as soldiers for 90 days in a campaign against the South. The response was overwhelming. Throughout the North, crowds cheered the Stars and Stripes and booed the southern "traitors."

Southerners were just as enthusiastic for the war. They rallied to the Stars and Bars, as they called the new Confederate flag. Volunteers flooded into the Confederate army.

With flags held high, both northerners and southerners marched off to war. Most felt certain that a single, gallant battle would bring a quick end to the conflict. Few suspected that the Civil War would last four terrible years and be the most destructive war in the nation's history.

A Nation Divided

As the war began, each side was convinced that its cause was just. Southerners believed that they had the right to leave the Union. In fact, they called the conflict the War for Southern Independence. Southerners wanted independence so that they could keep their traditional way of life—including the institution of slavery.

Northerners, meanwhile, believed that they had to fight to save the Union. At the outset of the war, abolishing slavery was not an official goal of the North. In fact, many northerners, guided by feelings of racism, approved of slavery. **Racism** is the belief that one race is superior to another.

In April 1861, eight slave states were still in the Union. They had to make the difficult decision of which side to join. Virginia,* North Carolina, Tennessee, and Arkansas joined the Confederacy. The four **border states** of Delaware, Kentucky, Missouri, and Maryland remained in the Union. (See the map on page 449.)

Still, some citizens of the border states supported the South. For example, in April 1861, pro-Confederate mobs attacked Union troops in Baltimore, Maryland. In response, President Lincoln declared **martial law,** or rule by the army instead of the elected government. Many people who sided with the South were arrested.

Strengths and Weaknesses

Both sides in the conflict had strengths and weaknesses as the war began. The South had the strong advantage of fighting a defensive war. It was up to the North to go on the offensive, to attack and defeat the South. If the North did not move its forces into the South, the Confederacy would remain a separate country.

---

*Many people in western Virginia supported the Union. When Virginia seceded, westerners formed their own government. West Virginia became a state of the Union in 1863.

The South

Southerners believed that they were fighting a war for independence, similar to the American Revolution. Defending their homeland and their way of life gave them a strong reason to fight bravely. "Our men must prevail in combat," one Confederate said, "or they will lose their property, country, freedom—in short, everything."

Also, many southerners had skills that made them good soldiers. Hunting was an important part of southern life. From an early age, boys learned to ride horses and use guns. Wealthy young men often went to military school. Before the Civil War, many of the best officers in the United States Army were from the South.

The South, however, had serious economic weaknesses. (See the chart on page 450.) It had few factories to produce weapons and other vital supplies. It also had few railroads to move troops and supplies. The railroads that it did have often did not connect to one another. The South also had political problems. The Confederate constitution favored states' rights and limited the authority

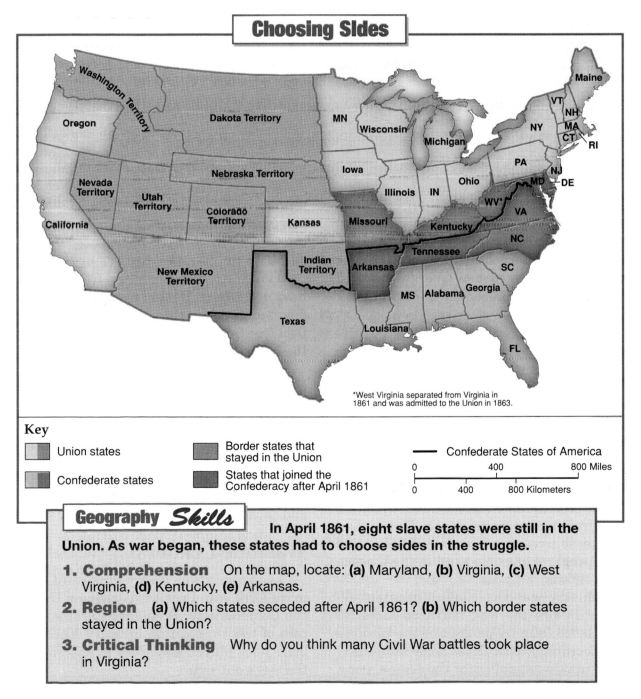

Choosing Sides

*West Virginia separated from Virginia in 1861 and was admitted to the Union in 1863.

Key

■ Union states

■ Confederate states

■ Border states that stayed in the Union

■ States that joined the Confederacy after April 1861

— Confederate States of America

0   400   800 Miles

0   400   800 Kilometers

Geography *Skills*

In April 1861, eight slave states were still in the Union. As war began, these states had to choose sides in the struggle.

1. **Comprehension** On the map, locate: **(a)** Maryland, **(b)** Virginia, **(c)** West Virginia, **(d)** Kentucky, **(e)** Arkansas.

2. **Region** **(a)** Which states seceded after April 1861? **(b)** Which border states stayed in the Union?

3. **Critical Thinking** Why do you think many Civil War battles took place in Virginia?

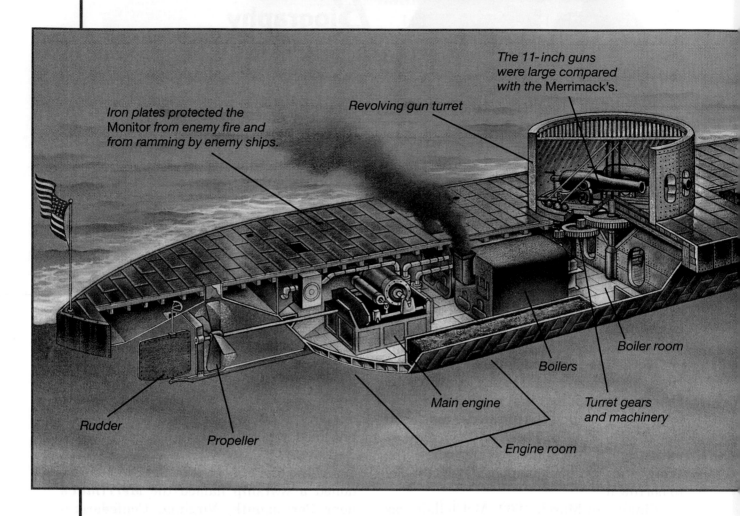

Iron plates protected the Monitor from enemy fire and from ramming by enemy ships.

Revolving gun turret

The 11- inch guns were large compared with the Merrimack's.

Rudder

Propeller

Main engine

Boilers

Boiler room

Turret gears and machinery

Engine room

Antietam

In September 1862, General Lee took the offensive and marched his troops north into Maryland. He believed that a southern victory on northern soil would be a great blow to northern morale.

Luck was against Lee, however. A Confederate messenger lost Lee's battle plans. Two Union soldiers found them and turned them over to General McClellan.

Even with Lee's battle plan before him, however, McClellan was slow to act. After waiting a few days, he finally attacked Lee's main force at Antietam (an TEE tuhm) on September 17. In the day-long battle that fol-

lowed, more than 23,000 Union and Confederate soldiers were killed or wounded.

On the night of September 18, Lee ordered his troops to slip back into Virginia. The Confederates breathed a sigh of relief when they saw that McClellan was not pursuing them.

Neither side was a clear winner at the **Battle of Antietam.** The North was able to claim victory, though, because Lee had ordered his forces to withdraw. As a result, northern morale increased. Still, President Lincoln was keenly disappointed. The Union army had suffered huge numbers of dead and wounded. Furthermore, General McClellan had failed to follow up his victory by pursuing

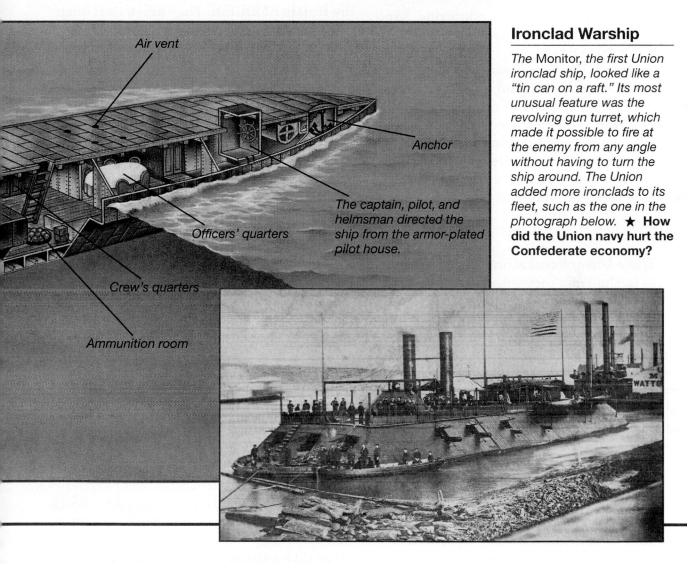

Ironclad Warship

The Monitor, *the first Union ironclad ship, looked like a "tin can on a raft." Its most unusual feature was the revolving gun turret, which made it possible to fire at the enemy from any angle without having to turn the ship around. The Union added more ironclads to its fleet, such as the one in the photograph below.* ★ **How did the Union navy hurt the Confederate economy?**

Air vent

Anchor

The captain, pilot, and helmsman directed the ship from the armor-plated pilot house.

Officers' quarters

Crew's quarters

Ammunition room

the Confederates. In November, Lincoln appointed General Ambrose Burnside to replace McClellan as commander of the Army of the Potomac.

Confederate Victories

Two stunning victories for the Confederacy came in late 1862 and 1863. (See the map on page 454.) General Robert E. Lee won by outsmarting the Union generals who fought against him.

Fredericksburg

In December 1862, Union forces set out once again toward Richmond. This time, they were led by General Ambrose Burnside.

Meeting Lee's army outside Fredericksburg, Virginia, Burnside ordered his troops to attack. Lee pulled back and left the town to Burnside. The Confederates dug in at the crest of a treeless hill above Fredericksburg. There, in a strong defensive position, they waited for the Union attack.

As the Union soldiers advanced, Confederate guns mowed them down by the thousands. Six times Burnside ordered his men to charge. Six times the rebels drove them back. "We forgot they were fighting us," one southerner wrote, "and cheer after cheer at their fearlessness went up along our lines." **The Battle of Fredericksburg** was one of the Union's worst defeats.

Chancellorsville

In May 1863, Lee, aided by Stonewall Jackson, again outwitted the Union army. This time, the battle took place on thickly wooded ground near Chancellorsville, Virginia. Lee and Jackson defeated the Union troops in three days.

Although the South won the **Battle of Chancellorsville,** it paid a high price for the victory. At the end of one day, nervous Confederate sentries fired at what they thought was an approaching Union soldier. The "Union soldier" was General Stonewall Jackson. Jackson died as a result of his injuries several days later.

The War in the West

While Union forces struggled in the East, those in the West met with success. As you have read, the Union strategy was to seize control of the Mississippi River. General **Ulysses S. Grant** began moving toward that goal. (See the map on page 470.) In February 1862, Grant attacked and captured Fort Henry and Fort Donelson in Tennessee. These Confederate forts guarded two important tributaries of the Mississippi.

Grant now pushed south to Shiloh, a village on the Tennessee River. At Shiloh, on April 6, he was surprised by Confederate forces. The Confederates won the first day of the **Battle of Shiloh.** They drove the Union troops back toward the river.

Grant now showed the toughness and determination that would enable him to win many battles in the future. "Retreat?" he replied to his doubting officers after that first day. "No. I propose to attack at daylight and whip them."

With the aid of reinforcements, Grant was able to win his victory and beat back the Confederates. However, the Battle of Shiloh was one of the bloodiest encounters of the Civil War. More Americans were killed or wounded at Shiloh than in the American Revolution, the War of 1812, and the Mexican War combined.

While Grant was fighting at Shiloh, the Union navy moved to gain control of the Mississippi River. In April 1862, Union gunboats captured New Orleans. Other ships seized Memphis, Tennessee. By capturing these two cities, the Union controlled both ends of the Mississippi. No longer could the South use the river as a supply line.

★ Section 2 Review ★

Recall

1. **Locate** (a) Richmond, (b) Washington, D.C., (c) Potomac River, (d) Fort Henry, (e) Fort Donelson, (f) New Orleans, (g) Memphis.
2. **Identify** (a) Stonewall Jackson, (b) Battle of Bull Run, (c) George McClellan, (d) *Merrimack,* (e) *Monitor,* (f) Battle of Antietam, (g) Battle of Fredericksburg, (h) Battle of Chancellorsville, (i) Ulysses S. Grant, (j) Battle of Shiloh.

Comprehension

3. (a) Describe the North's three-part plan for defeating the South. (b) Which part of the plan did the North achieve first?

4. Why was President Lincoln unhappy with General McClellan's performance as commander of the Union armies?
5. How did the loss of New Orleans and Memphis affect the South?

Critical Thinking and Writing

6. **Analyzing Primary Sources** In response to Stonewall Jackson's death, General Lee said, "I have lost my right arm." What did Lee mean by this statement?
7. **Analyzing Visual Evidence** Study the ironclad ships on pages 456–457. Explain how such ships were superior to wooden sailing ships.

★ ★

Activity **Making a Map** You are the chief cartographer for the Union army. Your assignment is to make a map illustrating the Union's three-part plan for defeating the South.

3 ★ A Promise of Freedom

As You Read

Explore These Questions
- Why did Lincoln issue the Emancipation Proclamation?
- What were the effects of the Proclamation?
- How did African Americans contribute to the Union war effort?

Define
- emancipate
- discrimination

Identify
- Emancipation Proclamation
- 54th Massachusetts Regiment
- Fort Wagner

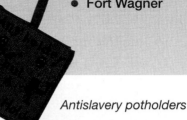

Antislavery potholders

SETTING the Scene At first, the Civil War was not a war against slavery. Yet wherever Union troops went, enslaved African Americans eagerly rushed to them, expecting to be freed. Most were sorely disappointed. Union officers often held these runaways until their masters arrived to take them back to slavery.

Some northerners began to raise questions. Was slavery not the root of the conflict between North and South? Were tens of thousands of men dying so that a slaveholding South would come back into the Union? Questions like these led Northerners to wonder what the real aim of the war should be.

Lincoln Was Cautious

The Civil War began as a war to restore the Union, not to end the institution of slavery. President Lincoln made this clear in the following statement.

> 66 If I could save the Union without freeing any slave, I would do it; and if I could save it by freeing all the slaves, I would do it; and if I could do it by freeing some and leaving others alone, I would also do that. 99

Lincoln had a reason for handling the slavery issue cautiously. As you have read, four slave states remained in the Union. The President did not want to do anything that might cause these states to shift their loyalty to the Confederacy. The resources of the border states might allow the South to turn the tide of the war.

The Emancipation Proclamation

By mid-1862, however, Lincoln came to believe that he could save the Union only by broadening the goals of the war. He decided to **emancipate,** or free, enslaved African Americans living in the Confederacy. In the four loyal slave states, however, slaves would not be freed. Nor would slaves be freed in Confederate lands that had already been captured by the Union, such as the city of New Orleans.

Motives and timing

Lincoln had practical reasons for his emancipation plan. At the start of the Civil War, more than 3 million enslaved people labored for the Confederacy. They helped grow the food that fed Confederate soldiers. They also worked in iron and lead mines that were vital to the South's war effort. Some served as nurses and cooks for the army. Lincoln knew that emancipation would weaken the Confederacy's ability to carry on the war.

However, Lincoln did not want to anger slave owners in the Union. Also, he knew that many northerners opposed freedom for

Freedom proclaimed

On September 22, 1862, five days after the Union victory at Antietam, Lincoln issued a preliminary proclamation. It warned that on January 1, 1863, anyone held as a slave in a state still in rebellion against the United States would be emancipated.

Then, on January 1, 1863, Lincoln issued the formal Emancipation Proclamation. The **Emancipation Proclamation** declared:

❝ On the 1st day of January, in the year of our Lord 1863, all persons held as slaves within any state or...part of a state [whose] people...shall then be in rebellion against the United States, shall be then, thenceforward, and forever free. ❞

Impact of the Proclamation

Because the rebelling states were not under Union control, no slaves actually gained their freedom on January 1, 1863. Nevertheless, as a result of the Emancipation Proclamation, the purpose of the war changed. Now, Union troops were fighting to end slavery as well as to save the Union.

The opponents of slavery greeted the proclamation with joy. In Boston, African American abolitionist Frederick Douglass witnessed one of the many emotional celebrations that took place:

❝ The effect of this announcement was startling...and the scene was wild and grand....My old friend Rue, a Negro preacher,...expressed the heartfelt emotion of the hour, when he led all voices in the anthem, 'Sound the loud timbrel o'er Egypt's dark sea, Jehovah hath triumphed, his people are free!' ❞

Connections With Arts

Many northerners greeted the Emancipation Proclamation with music and song. At Boston's Music Hall, people celebrated with performances of Mendelssohn's *Hymn of Praise,* and Handel's *Hallelujah Chorus*.

enslaved African Americans. Lincoln therefore hoped to introduce the idea of emancipation slowly, by limiting it to territory controlled by the Confederacy.

The President had another very important motive, too. As you read in Chapter 16, Lincoln believed that slavery was wrong. When he felt that he could act to free slaves without threatening the Union, he did so.

Lincoln was concerned about the timing of his announcement. The war was not going well for the Union. He did not want Americans to think he was freeing slaves as a desperate effort to save a losing cause. He waited for a victory to announce his plan.

The Proclamation won the Union the sympathy of people in Europe, especially workers. As a result, it became less likely that Britain or any other European country would come to the aid of the South.

African Americans Help

When the war began, thousands of free blacks volunteered to fight for the Union. At first, federal law forbade African Americans to serve as soldiers. When Congress repealed that law in 1862, however, both free African Americans and escaped slaves enlisted in the Union army.

In the Union army

The army assigned these volunteers to all-black units, commanded by white officers. At first, the black troops served only as laborers. They performed noncombat duties such as building roads and guarding supplies. Black troops received only half the pay of white soldiers.

African American soldiers protested against this policy of **discrimination** that denied them the same rights and treatment as other soldiers. Gradually, conditions changed. By 1863, African American troops were fighting in major battles against the Confederates. In 1864, the United States War Department announced that all soldiers would receive equal pay. By the end of the war, about 200,000 African Americans had fought for the Union. Nearly 40,000 lost their lives.

Acts of bravery

One of the most famous African American units in the Union army was the **54th Massachusetts Regiment.** The 54th accepted African Americans from all across the

Viewing HISTORY **Assault on Fort Wagner**

In this painting by Tom Lovell, African American soldiers of the 54th Massachussetts Regiment charge against Confederate troops at Fort Wagner. Nearly half the regiment died in the failed attack, including the regiment's commander, Colonel Robert Gould Shaw. ★ **Why do you think the Union army was reluctant to appoint African American officers?**

North. Frederick Douglass helped recruit troops for the regiment, and two of his sons served in it.

On July 18, 1863, the 54th Massachusetts Regiment led an attack on **Fort Wagner** near Charleston. Under heavy fire, troops fought their way into the fort before being forced to withdraw. In the desperate fighting, almost half the regiment, including its young commander, Robert Shaw, were killed.

The courage of the 54th Massachusetts and other regiments helped to win respect for African American soldiers. Sergeant William Carney of the 54th Massachusetts was awarded the Congressional Medal of Honor for acts of bravery. He was the first of 16 African American soldiers to be so honored during the Civil War. In a letter to President Lincoln, Secretary of War Stanton praised African American soldiers.

❝ [They] have proved themselves among the bravest of the brave, performing deeds of daring and shedding their blood with a heroism unsurpassed by soldiers of any race. ❞

Behind Confederate lines

In the South, despite the Emancipation Proclamation, African Americans still had to work as slaves on plantations. However, many enslaved African Americans slowed down their work. Others refused to work at all or to submit to punishment. In so doing, they knew they were helping to weaken the South's war effort. They knew that when victorious Union troops arrived in their area, they would be free.

Throughout the South, thousands of enslaved African Americans also took direct action to free themselves. Whenever a Union army appeared in an area, the slaves from all around would flee their former masters. They crossed over to the Union lines and to freedom. By the end of the war, about one fourth of the enslaved population in the South had escaped to freedom.

The former slaves helped Union armies achieve victory in a variety of ways. They used their knowledge of the local terrain to serve as guides and spies. Many more enlisted in African American regiments of the Union army.

★ Section 3 Review ★

Recall

1. **Identify** (a) Emancipation Proclamation, (b) 54th Massachusetts Regiment, (c) Fort Wagner.
2. **Define** (a) emancipate, (b) discrimination.

Comprehension

3. (a) Why was President Lincoln cautious about making emancipation a goal of the war? (b) Why did he finally decide to issue the Emancipation Proclamation?
4. Why were no slaves actually freed when the Proclamation was issued?
5. (a) How did the 54th Massachussetts Regiment's attack on Fort Wagner affect public opinion about enslaved African American soldiers?

(b) How did African Americans help to weaken the Confederacy?

Critical Thinking and Writing

6. **Drawing Conclusions** What did the Union army's policy toward all-black regiments reveal about northern attitudes toward African Americans? Explain.
7. **Analyzing Primary Sources** In 1861, Frederick Douglass said, "This is no time to fight with one hand when both hands are needed. This is no time to fight with only your white hand, and allow your black hand to remain tied!" (a) What did Douglass mean by this statement? (b) Did the United States Congress agree with Douglass? Explain.

★ ★

Activity **Writing a Poem** A monument is being built to honor the courageous African American soldiers of the Civil War. Write a poem to be engraved on the monument, mentioning some of the facts you have learned in this section.

Hardships of War

As You Read

Explore These Questions
- What was life like for soldiers in the Civil War?
- How did women contribute to the war effort?
- What problems did each side face during the war?

Define
- civilians
- draft
- habeas corpus
- income tax
- inflation
- profiteer

Identify
- Copperheads
- Loreta Janeta Velazquez
- Rose Greenhow
- Dorothea Dix
- Clara Barton
- Sojourner Truth
- Sally Tompkins

SETTING the Scene The Civil War caused hardships not only for soldiers but for people at home as well. Southerners, especially, suffered from the war, because most of the fighting took place in the South.

On both sides, **civilians,** or people who were not in the army, worked on farms and labored in factories to support the war effort. They used their mules to move troops and supplies. They tended the wounded. As their hardships increased, so did opposition to the war.

The Hard Life of Soldiers

On both sides, most soldiers were under age 21. However, war quickly turned gentle boys into tough men. Soldiers drilled and marched for long hours. They slept on the ground even in rain and snow. In combat, boys of 18 learned to stand firm as cannon blasts shook the earth and bullets whizzed past their ears.

New technology added to the horror of war. Cone-shaped bullets, which made rifles twice as accurate, replaced round musket balls. New cannons could hurl exploding shells several miles. The new weapons had deadly results. In most battles, one fourth or more of the soldiers were killed or wounded.

Sick and wounded soldiers faced other horrors. Medical care on the battlefield was crude. Surgeons routinely cut off injured

▲ Confederate cap

▲ Union cap

arms and legs. Minor wounds often became infected. With no medicines to fight infection, thousands of wounded died. Diseases like pneumonia and malaria killed more men than guns or cannons did.

On both sides, prisoners of war faced horrifying conditions. At Andersonville, a prison camp in Georgia, more than one Union prisoner out of three died of disease or starvation. One prisoner wrote:

66 There is no such thing as delicacy here.... In the middle of last night I was awakened by being kicked by a dying man. He was soon dead. I got up and moved the body off a few feet, and went to sleep to dream of the hideous sights. 99

Discontent in the North

Some northerners opposed using force to keep the South in the Union. Supporters of the war called these people **Copperheads,** after the poisonous snake. Other northerners supported the war but opposed the way Lincoln was conducting it. In some northern cities, this opposition led to riots.

The Faces of War
Confederate soldiers wore gray uniforms and were sometimes called Johnny Rebs. Union soldiers wore blue and were called Billy Yanks. During the Civil War, about 1 of every 10 soldiers deserted from service. ★ **Why do you think desertion rates were high in both armies?**

The draft law

As the war dragged on, public support dwindled. Soon, not enough men were volunteering to serve in the Union army. The government took action.

In 1863, Congress passed a **draft** law. It required all able-bodied males between the ages of 20 and 45 to serve in the military if they were called.

Under the law, a man could avoid the draft by paying the government $300 or by hiring someone to serve in his place. This angered many people. They began to see the Civil War as "a rich man's war and a poor man's fight."

Riots in the cities

Opposition to the draft law led to riots in several northern cities. The draft law had gone into effect soon after Lincoln issued the Emancipation Proclamation. As a result, some northerners believed that they were being forced to fight to end slavery. This idea angered some white workers, especially recent immigrants in the cities. Like many other northerners, some of these immigrants held racist beliefs. They also feared that free African Americans would be employed at jobs that they needed, too.

The worst riot took place in New York City during July 1863. For four days, white workers attacked free blacks. Rioters also attacked rich New Yorkers who had paid to avoid serving in the army. At least 74 people were killed during the riot.

President Lincoln moved to stop the riots and other "disloyal practices." Several times, he denied **habeas corpus** (HAY bee uhs KOR puhs), the right to have charges filed or a hearing before being jailed. Lincoln defended his actions by saying that the Constitution gave him the right to deny people their rights "when in the cases of rebellion or invasion, the public safety may require it."

Problems in the South

President Davis, meanwhile, struggled to create a strong federal government for the Confederacy. Many southerners were strong supporters of states' rights. They resisted paying taxes to a central government. At one point, Georgia threatened to secede from the Confederacy!

Like the North, the South had to pass a draft law to fill its army. However, men who owned or supervised more than 20 slaves did not have to serve in the army. Southern farmers who owned few or no slaves resented this law.

Near war's end, the South no longer had enough white men to fill the ranks. Robert E. Lee urged that enslaved African Americans be allowed to serve as soldiers. Desperate, the Confederate congress finally agreed. However, the war ended before any enslaved people put on Confederate uniforms.

Why Study History?

Because One Person Can Make a Difference

★ ★

Historical Background

In the early days of the Civil War, Clara Barton and other women provided medical care to wounded soldiers. However, the government required women to stay far from battle. As a result, many soldiers received treatment too late and died of their wounds. Barton therefore sought permission to work directly on the fields of battle.

After some initial refusals, the government gave in. Through the remainder of the war, Clara Barton served as a battlefield nurse. Because of her courageous efforts, she became known as the "Angel of the Battlefield."

Connections to Today

After the Civil War, Barton continued to make a difference. In Europe, she worked with the International Red Cross, an organization that aided victims of war. In 1881, after returning to the United States, she founded the American Red Cross. This new organization served both victims of war and victims of natural disaster.

Today, disaster relief remains a primary service of the Red Cross. The Red Cross helps people recover from natural disasters such as fires, floods, and hurricanes. It provides victims with medical assistance, food, clothing, and shelter.

The American Red Cross provides other services as well. It helps homeless people and seniors in need. It supervises donations of blood and other organs. It also provides instruction in a variety of safety programs.

Connections to You

Like Clara Barton, you too can make a difference. You can learn about first aid and safety procedures in a Red Cross educational course. Courses include first aid, water safety, fire prevention, and even babysitting. Some local Red Cross chapters invite teens to serve as volunteers. You might also organize or participate in a drive to help raise funds for the Red Cross. Red Cross disaster relief services are provided free of charge because of contributions made by caring Americans.

▲ Clara Barton

▲ Red Cross book

1. **Comprehension** How does the American Red Cross help victims of disaster?

2. **Critical Thinking** At the start of the Civil War, why do you think government officials allowed men, but not women, to aid wounded soldiers on the field of battle?

 **Making an Advertisement** Create an advertisement that seeks public support for the Red Cross by informing people about the many services the Red Cross provides.

The Northern Economy

The Civil War cost far more than any earlier war. The Union had to use several strategies to raise money. In some ways, though, war helped the North's economy.

Taxation and inflation

In 1861, to pay for the war, Congress established the nation's first **income tax** on people's earnings. In addition, the Union issued bonds worth millions of dollars. Still, taxes and bonds did not raise enough money. To get the funds it needed, the North printed more than $400 million in paper money.

As the money supply increased, each dollar was worth less. In response, businesses charged more for their goods. The North was experiencing **inflation,** a rise in prices and a decrease in the value of money. During the war, prices for goods nearly doubled in the North.

Economic benefits

In some ways, the war helped the North's economy. Because many farmers went off to fight, more machines were used to plant and harvest crops. As a result, farm production actually went up during the war.

The wartime demand for clothing, shoes, guns, and other goods helped many northern industries. Some manufacturers made fortunes by profiteering. **Profiteers** charged excessive prices for goods the government desperately needed for the war.

The Southern Economy

For the South, war brought economic ruin. The South had to struggle with the cost of the war, the loss of the cotton trade, and severe shortages brought on by the Union blockade.

The economy suffers

To raise money, the Confederacy imposed an income tax and a tax-in-kind. The tax-in-kind required farmers to turn over one tenth of their crops to the government. The government took crops because it knew that southern farmers had little money.

Like the North, the South printed paper money. It printed so much, in fact, that wild inflation set in. By 1865, one Confederate dollar was worth only two cents in gold.

The war did serious damage to the cotton trade, the South's main source of income. Early in the war, President Davis halted cotton shipments to Britain. He hoped that Britain would side with the South in order to get cotton. The tactic backfired. Britain simply bought more cotton from Egypt and

$ Connections With Economics

As inflation in the South worsened, it became more and more difficult to feed and clothe a family. Near the end of the war, a barrel of flour cost $1,000 and a pair of shoes cost $400.

India. Davis succeeded only in cutting the South's income.

Effects of the blockade

The Union blockade created severe shortages in the South. Confederate armies sometimes had to wait weeks for supplies of food and clothing. Guns and ammunition were also in short supply. With few factories of its own, the South bought many of its weapons in Europe. However, the blockade cut off most deliveries from Europe.

For civilians, the blockade brought food shortages. Even the wealthy went hungry. "I had a little piece of bread and a little molasses today for my dinner," wrote plantation mistress Mary Chesnut in her diary. By 1865, there was widespread famine in the Confederacy.

Women at War

Women of both the North and South played vital roles during the war. As men left for the battlefields, women took jobs in industry, in teaching, and on farms.

Women and the military

Women's aid societies helped supply the troops with food, bedding, clothing, and medicine. Throughout the North, women held fairs and other fund-raising events to pay for the supplies. They succeeded in raising millions of dollars.

A few women disguised themselves so they could serve as soldiers. **Loreta Janeta Velazquez,** for example, fought for the South at Bull Run and Shiloh. Other women worked as spies. **Rose Greenhow** gathered information for the South while entertaining Union leaders in her Washington, D.C., home. She was caught, convicted of treason, and exiled.

Nursing the wounded

Women on both sides worked as nurses. Doctors were unwilling at first to permit even trained nurses to work in military hospitals. When wounded men began to swamp army hospitals, however, this attitude soon changed.

Dorothea Dix, famous for her work reforming prisons and mental hospitals, became superintendent of nurses for the Union army. **Clara Barton** earned fame as a Civil War nurse. She later founded the American Red Cross. **Sojourner Truth,** the African American antislavery leader, worked in Union hospitals and in camps for freed slaves. In the South, **Sally Tompkins** set up a hospital in Richmond, Virginia.

★ Section 4 Review ★

Recall

1. **Identify** (a) Copperheads, (b) Loreta Janeta Velazquez, (c) Rose Greenhow, (d) Dorothea Dix, (e) Clara Barton, (f) Sojourner Truth, (g) Sally Tompkins.
2. **Define** (a) civilians, (b) draft, (c) habeas corpus, (d) income tax, (e) inflation, (f) profiteer.

Comprehension

3. Describe three hardships faced by soldiers during the Civil War.

4. Describe three ways women contributed to the war effort.
5. How did the Union blockade affect the South?

Critical Thinking and Writing

6. **Linking Past and Present** (a) What advances in technology made Civil War battles deadly? (b) In what ways would a war today be even more deadly?
7. **Defending a Position** What facts support the charge that the Civil War was "a rich man's war and a poor man's fight"?

Activity **Making a Chart** You are the graphic illustrator for an economics magazine. Create a flowchart or cause-and-effect chart to illustrate how the high cost of the Civil War led to high inflation.

The War Ends

As You Read

Explore These Questions
- What was the significance of the Union victories at Vicksburg and Gettysburg?
- What ideals did Lincoln express in the Gettysburg Address?
- How did Union generals use a new type of war to defeat the Confederacy?

Define
- siege
- total war

Identify
- Battle of Gettysburg
- Gettysburg Address
- Ulysses S. Grant
- Philip Sheridan
- William Tecumseh Sherman

SETTING the Scene As you have read, Confederate armies won major battles at Fredericksburg in December 1862 and at Chancellorsville in May 1863. These were gloomy days for the North.

Then, in July 1863, the tide of war turned against the South. In the West, the Union extended its control of the Mississippi River and cut the South in two. At the Battle of Gettysburg, in Pennsylvania, both Union and Confederate forces suffered terrible losses. However, as President Davis later explained, "Theirs could be repaired, ours could not."

The following year, President Lincoln would appoint Ulysses S. Grant commander in chief of the Union army. In Grant, Lincoln had found the general who could lead the Union to victory.

The Fall of Vicksburg

After capturing New Orleans and Memphis, the Union controlled both ends of the Mississippi River. Still, the North could not safely use the river because Confederates held Vicksburg, Mississippi. Vicksburg sat on a cliff high above the river. Cannons there could shell boats traveling between New Orleans and Memphis.

Early in 1863, Grant's forces tried again and again to seize Vicksburg. The Confederates held out bravely. At last, Grant devised a brilliant plan. Marching his troops inland, he launched a surprise attack on Jackson, Mississippi. Then, he turned west and attacked Vicksburg from the rear. (See the map on page 470.)

For over six weeks, Grant's forces lay siege to Vicksburg. A **siege** is a military blockade of an enemy town or position in order to force it to surrender. Day after day, the Union soldiers pushed their lines closer to the town. Union artillery and gunboats on the Mississippi bombarded the besieged soldiers and inhabitants. As their food supplies ran out, the southerners began to use mules and rats as food. Finally, on July 4, 1863, the Confederates surrendered Vicksburg.

On July 9, Union forces also captured Port Hudson, Louisiana. The entire Mississippi was now under Union control. The Confederacy was split into two parts. Texas, Arkansas, and Louisiana were cut off from the rest of the Confederacy.

Union Victory at Gettysburg

In the East, after his victory at Chancellorsville, General Lee moved his army north into Pennsylvania. He hoped to take the Yankees by surprise. If he was successful, Lee planned to then swing south and capture Washington, D.C.

Vicksburg National Military Park

You can learn about the siege of Vicksburg, Mississippi, by touring the actual battle site. The park includes a museum, miles of defensive earthworks, and more than 125 cannons. You can even walk the deck of a Union ironclad gunboat, raised from the Mississippi River in the 1960s. Throughout the park, numerous monuments honor the soldiers who fought and died for control of this small Mississippi River town.

★ **To learn more about this historic site, write:** Vicksburg National Military Park, 3201 Clay Street, Vicksburg, MS 39180.

◀ *Ohio regiment monument*

On June 30, 1863, a Union force under General George C. Meade met part of Lee's army at the small town of Gettysburg, Pennsylvania. Both sides quickly sent in reinforcements. The three-day Battle of Gettysburg that followed was one of the most important battles of the Civil War.

At the start of the battle, the Confederates drove the Union forces out of Gettysburg. The Yankees took up strong positions on Cemetery Ridge, overlooking the town. On July 2, a Confederate attack failed with heavy casualties. Nevertheless, Lee decided to launch another attack. On July 3, he ordered General George Pickett to lead 15,000 men in a daring charge against the center of the Union line. To reach the Yankees, Pickett's men had to cross an open field and run up a steep slope.

Pickett gave the order to charge and the Union guns opened fire. Row after row of soldiers fell to the ground, bleeding. Still, the Confederate troops continued to rush forward against a rain of bullets and shells. Few were able to reach the Union lines. A Union soldier described the fighting at the crest of the ridge:

> 66 Men fire into each other's faces not five feet apart. There are bayonet thrusts, saber strokes, pistol shots, men going down on their hands and knees... gulping blood, falling, legless, armless, headless. 99

Pickett's charge failed. As the survivors limped back, Lee rode among them. "It's all my fault," he admitted humbly. Lee had no choice but to retreat. After their defeat at the **Battle of Gettysburg,** the Confederates would never again invade the North.

The Union victories at Vicksburg and Gettysburg marked the turning point of the Civil War. On July 4, 1863, northerners had good reason to celebrate.

The Gettysburg Address

The Battle of Gettysburg left more than 40,000 dead or wounded. When the soldiers who died there were buried, their graves stretched as far as the eye could see. On November 19, 1863, northerners held a ceremony to dedicate this cemetery.

President Lincoln attended the ceremony, but he was not the main speaker. At the time, his popularity was quite low. Lincoln sat with his hands folded as another speaker talked for two hours. When it was his turn, the President rose and spoke for about three minutes.

In his **Gettysburg Address,** Lincoln said that the Civil War was a test of whether or not a democratic nation could survive. He reminded Americans that their nation was founded on the belief that "all men are created equal." Looking out at the thousands of graves, Lincoln told the audience:

66 We here highly resolve that these dead shall not have died in vain— that this nation, under God, shall have a new birth of freedom—and that government of the people, by the people, for the people, shall not perish from the earth. **99**

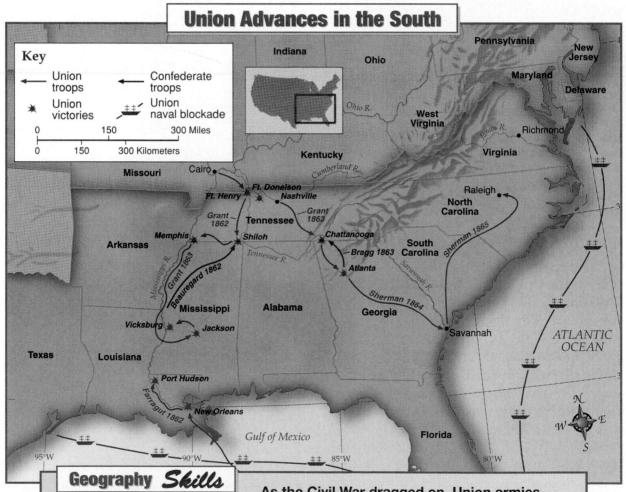

Union Advances in the South

Key

← Union troops ← Confederate troops

✱ Union victories ⚓ Union naval blockade

0 — 150 — 300 Miles
0 — 150 — 300 Kilometers

Geography Skills

As the Civil War dragged on, Union armies advanced deeper and deeper into the South. General Sherman marched his troops through Georgia and the Carolinas.

1. Location On the map, locate: **(a)** Vicksburg, **(b)** Atlanta, **(c)** Savannah.

2. Place What three Confederate states were cut off from the rest of the Confederacy after Union forces gained control of the Mississippi River?

3. Critical Thinking Based on the map, why would the South be hurt more than the North—no matter who won the war?

Few people listened to Lincoln that day. Newspapers gave his speech little attention. Later generations, however, have honored Lincoln's brief address as a profound statement of American ideals.

The Union Wages Total War

For three years, Lincoln had searched for a general who could lead the Union to victory. More and more, he thought of **Ulysses S. Grant.** After capturing Vicksburg, Grant continued to win battles in the West. In 1864, Lincoln appointed him commander of the Union forces.

Some questioned the choice, but President Lincoln felt that "Unconditional Surrender" Grant was the general who would lead the Union to victory. "I can't spare this man," Lincoln said. "He fights."

Grant and other Union generals began to wage **total war** against the South. In total war, civilians as well as soldiers are affected. The Union army waged total war by destroying food and equipment that might be useful to the enemy. Civilians in the South suffered the same hardships as soldiers.

Sheridan in the Shenandoah

Grant had a plan for ending the war. He wanted to destroy the South's ability to fight. Grant sent General **Philip Sheridan** and his cavalry into the rich farmland of Virginia's Shenandoah Valley. He instructed Sheridan:

66 Leave nothing to invite the enemy to return. Destroy whatever cannot be consumed. Let the valley be left so that crows flying over it will have to carry their rations along with them. 99

Sheridan obeyed. In the summer and fall of 1864, he marched through the valley, destroying farms and livestock.

Sherman's march to the sea

Grant also ordered General **William Tecumseh Sherman** to capture Atlanta, Georgia, and then march to the Atlantic coast. Like Sheridan, Sherman had orders to destroy everything useful to the South.

Cause and Effect

Causes

- Issue of slavery in the territories divides the North and South
- Abolitionists want slavery to end
- South fears it will lose power in the national government
- Southern states secede after Lincoln's election
- Confederates bombard Fort Sumter

The Civil War

Effects

- Lincoln issues the Emancipation Proclamation
- Northern economy booms
- South loses its cotton trade with Britain
- Total war destroys the South's economy
- Hundreds of thousands of Americans killed

Effects Today

- Sectionalism is less of a force in American life and politics
- African Americans have equal protection under the Constitution
- Millions of Americans visit Civil War battlefields each year

Graphic Organizer *Skills*

The Civil War was a major turning point in the history of the United States.

1. **Comprehension** How did the war affect the northern and southern economies differently?
2. **Critical Thinking** Describe another cause or effect that could be added to this chart.

Sherman's troops captured Atlanta in September 1864. They burned the city in November. Then Sherman began his "march to the sea."

Sherman's troops ripped up railroad tracks, built bonfires from the ties, then heated and twisted the rails. They killed livestock and tore up fields. They burned barns, homes, and factories.

Lincoln Is Reelected

In 1864, Lincoln ran for reelection. At first, his defeat seemed, in his own words, "extremely probable." Before the capture of Atlanta, Union chances for victory looked bleak. Lincoln knew that many northerners were unhappy with his handling of the war. He thought that this might cost him the election.

The Democrats nominated General George McClellan to oppose Lincoln. Although he had commanded the Union army, McClellan was more willing than Lincoln to compromise with the South. If peace could be achieved, he was ready to restore slavery.

When Sherman took Atlanta in September, the North rallied around Lincoln. Sheridan's smashing victories in the Shenandoah Valley in October further increased Lincoln's popular support. In the election in November, the vote was close, but Lincoln remained President.

In his second Inaugural Address, Lincoln looked forward to the coming of peace:

> 66 With malice toward none, with charity for all...let us strive...to bind up the nation's wounds...to do all which may achieve a just and a lasting peace among ourselves and with all nations. 99

The War Ends

Grant had begun a drive to capture Richmond in May 1864. Throughout the spring and summer, he and Lee fought a series of costly battles.

Northerners read with horror that Grant had lost 60,000 dead and wounded in a single month at the battles of the Wilderness,

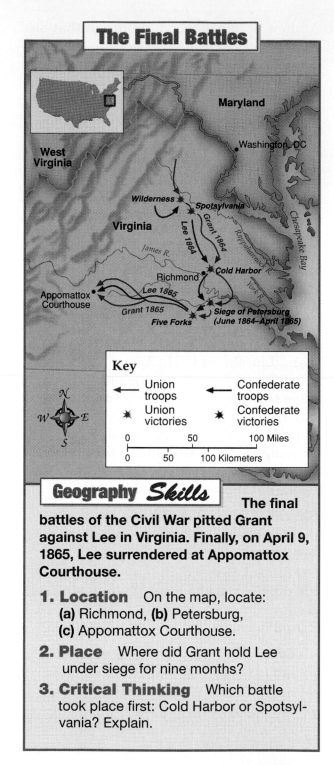

The Final Battles

Geography Skills The final battles of the Civil War pitted Grant against Lee in Virginia. Finally, on April 9, 1865, Lee surrendered at Appomattox Courthouse.

1. **Location** On the map, locate:
   (a) Richmond, (b) Petersburg,
   (c) Appomattox Courthouse.

2. **Place** Where did Grant hold Lee under siege for nine months?

3. **Critical Thinking** Which battle took place first: Cold Harbor or Spotsylvania? Explain.

Spotsylvania, and Cold Harbor. Still, Grant pressed on. He knew that the Union could replace men and supplies. The South could not.

Lee dug in at Petersburg, near Richmond. Here, Grant kept Lee under siege for nine months. At last, with a fresh supply of troops, Grant took Petersburg on April 2, 1865. The same day, Richmond fell.

General Lee surrenders to General Grant at Appomattox Courthouse.

Lee and his army withdrew to a small Virginia town called Appomattox Courthouse. There, a week later, they were trapped by Union troops. Lee knew that his men would be slaughtered if he kept fighting. On April 9, 1865, Lee surrendered.

At Appomattox Courthouse, Grant offered generous terms of surrender to the defeated Confederate army. Soldiers were required to turn over their rifles, but officers were allowed to keep their pistols. Soldiers who had horses could keep them. Grant knew that southerners would need the animals for spring plowing.

As the Confederates surrendered, Union soldiers began to cheer. Grant ordered them to be silent. "The war is over," he said. "The rebels are our countrymen again."

Effects of the War

More than 360,000 Union soldiers and 250,000 Confederate soldiers lost their lives in the Civil War. No war has ever resulted in more American deaths. As a result, feelings of bitterness remained among both northerners and southerners.

Southerners had special reasons to view the North with resentment. They had lost their struggle for independence. Their way of life had been forcibly changed. Union armies had destroyed much of their land. In addition, many southerners feared that the North would seek revenge against the South after the war.

Finally, the Civil War was a major turning point in American history. The Union was secure. States' rights had suffered a terrible blow. As a result, the power of the federal government grew. The war also brought freedom to millions of African Americans. Still, a long and difficult struggle for equality lay ahead.

★ Section 5 Review ★

Recall

1. **Locate** (a) Vicksburg, (b) Port Hudson, (c) Gettysburg, (d) Atlanta, (e) Petersburg, (f) Appomattox Courthouse.
2. **Identify** (a) Battle of Gettysburg, (b) Gettysburg Address, (c) Ulysses S. Grant, (d) Philip Sheridan, (e) William Tecumseh Sherman.
3. **Define** (a) siege, (b) total war.

Comprehension

4. Why did the Union victories at Vicksburg and Gettysburg mark a turning point in the war?

5. What ideals did Lincoln express in his Gettysburg Address and Second Inaugural Address?
6. How did Sheridan and Sherman use total war to destroy the South's ability to fight?

Critical Thinking and Writing

7. **Predicting Consequences** If Sherman and Sheridan had not won victories just before the election of 1864, how might the election and the war have turned out differently?
8. **Defending a Position** Some people have condemned Grant's decision to wage total war. Do you agree or disagree with this position? Explain.

★ ★

Activity **Writing a Speech** It is a sad day for the South. You are a member of the Confederate Congress and you have just heard of Lee's surrender. Write a speech in which you reflect on the hardships of the war and offer hope for the future.

Chapter 17 Review and Activities

★ Sum It Up ★

Section 1 The Conflict Takes Shape
▶ The Union's advantages included a greater population and superior industrial resources.
▶ The Confederacy's advantages included better military leaders and its position of defending the homeland.

Section 2 A Long, Difficult Struggle
▶ The Union navy blockaded southern ports. Union armies tried to take Richmond and the Mississippi Valley.
▶ The Confederates won major battles in the East. Union armies were more successful in the West.

Section 3 A Promise of Freedom
▶ The Emancipation Proclamation made the end of slavery a goal of the war.
▶ African Americans worked, fought, and died in the effort to preserve the Union and end slavery.

Section 4 Hardships of War
▶ Both men and women suffered hardships in their efforts to win the war.
▶ During the war, the Union and Confederacy both struggled with political and economic problems.

Section 5 The War Ends
▶ The North waged total war deep into the South, disrupting civilian lives and inflicting great losses.
▶ Lee surrendered his army at Appomattox Courthouse, Virginia, on April 9, 1865.

For additional review of the major ideas of Chapter 17, see **Guide to the Essentials of American History** or **Interactive Student Tutorial CD-ROM,** which contains interactive review activities, graphic organizers, and practice tests.

📖 Reviewing the Chapter

Define These Terms
Match each term with the correct definition.

Column 1	Column 2
1. emancipate	**a.** rule by the army
2. martial law	**b.** set free
3. draft	**c.** people who overcharge for desperately needed goods
4. profiteers	**d.** a rise in prices
5. inflation	**e.** a law requiring people to serve in the military

Explore the Main Ideas
1. What advantages did the United States have over the Confederate States?
2. Why were Confederate armies in the East often victorious in the early years of the war?
3. What were the results of the Emancipation Proclamation?
4. How did women support the war effort?
5. Explain how total war affected the South.

📊 Chart Activity

Use the chart below to answer the following questions:
1. How many members of Company D were captured and imprisoned by the Union? **2.** How many soldiers were in Company D at the start of the war? **Critical Thinking** Why do you think so many soldiers died from disease?

Seventh Virginia Infantry, Company D	
Original members	122
Killed in battle or died of wounds	17
Died of disease	14
Discharged	29
Transferred	6
Prisoners of war	27
On leave, hospitalized, or at home	8
Deserted	12
Surrendered at Appomattox	9

Source: David E. Johnston, *The Story of a Confederate Boy in the Civil War*

🔲 Critical Thinking and Writing

1. **Understanding Chronology** For each pair of events that follow, select the event that happened first: **(a)** Battle of Bull Run, Battle of Gettysburg; **(b)** fall of Richmond, Emancipation Proclamation; **(c)** Sherman's march to the sea, fall of Vicksburg.

2. **Linking Past and Present** How do you think Americans would react today if a general lost 60,000 soldiers in one month as General Grant once did? Explain your answer.

3. **Identifying Alternatives** Should African American men have volunteered to serve in the Union army in 1862? Explain two reasons for volunteering and two reasons for not volunteering.

4. **Exploring Unit Themes** **Sectionalism** Do you think sectional differences and conflicts continued even after the end of the Civil War? Explain the reasons for your answer.

🔲 Using Primary Sources

Confederate General John B. Gordon described how his troops felt at Appomattox Courthouse as General Lee was about to surrender:

> ❝ The men cried like children. Worn, starved, and bleeding as they were, they had rather have died than have surrendered.... But I could not permit it.... That these men should have wept at surrendering so unequal a fight, at being taken out of this constant [bloodshed] and storm, at being sent back to their families... was [proof of bravery] and patriotism that might set an example. ❞

Source: *Reminiscences of the Civil War* by John B. Gordon, 1903.

Recognizing Points of View **(a)** Why did General Gordon's troops cry? **(b)** How did Gordon feel about the behavior of the soldiers? **(c)** How do you think Confederate veterans felt about northern soldiers occupying southern lands after the war?

ACTIVITY BANK

▶ Interdisciplinary Activity

Exploring Science Research and prepare a report on medical care during the Civil War. Include information on battlefield hospitals, common diseases, and people who cared for the sick and wounded.

Career Skills Activity

Cartographer Choose a Civil War battle and make a map showing the positions and movements of troops in the battle. Do research to find the information you need.

Citizenship Activity

Writing a Speech In the late 1860s, Memorial Day emerged as a day to honor soldiers who had died in the Civil War. Today, the holiday honors those whose lives were sacrificed in all American wars. Write a brief speech explaining why it is important to honor those who have died in American wars.

Internet Activity

On the Internet, find sites dealing with the Civil War. Choose a specific Civil War topic and prepare a five-minute presentation to give to the class. Possible topics include: a specific battle, a particular military or political leader, or the poetry and music of the Civil War.

EYEWITNESS Journal

Assume the role of an enslaved African American living in the Confederacy or an enslaved African American living in the Union. In your EYEWITNESS JOURNAL, describe your thoughts and feelings on January 1, 1863, the day the Emancipation Proclamation took effect.

Chapter 18

The Reconstruction Era

1864–1877

After the Civil War, rebuilding the ruined South was a tremendous job. Just as troubling was the task of bringing the former Confederate states back into the Union. Should southerners who had fought against the United States government be welcomed back or treated harshly? How could the nation protect the newly won rights of freed African Americans?

During a period called Reconstruction, North and South slowly reunited. At the same time, the economy of the South slowly recovered, and African Americans in the South gained several important rights and freedoms. However, in the years following Reconstruction, many of these rights were lost.

Why Study History?

During Reconstruction and after, many African Americans became victims of violence. Groups like the Ku Klux Klan used terror to prevent black citizens from voting. Today, Americans continue to battle "hate crimes" and encourage tolerance, or acceptance of all people. To focus on this connection, see the *Why Study History?* feature in this chapter, "Tolerance Begins With You."

American Events

1865
Abraham
Lincoln is
assassinated

1867
Reconstruction Act
imposes strict
measures on
southern states

1868
House of Representatives
votes to impeach
President Johnson

| 1864 | 1866 | 1868 | 1870 |

World Events

1864 World Event
Maximillian becomes
Emperor of Mexico

1867 World Event
Dominion of Canada
is formed

 Viewing HISTORY **Reunion Begins**

*This painting by Dennis Malone Carter shows Abraham Lincoln arriv-
ing in Richmond, Virginia. The President visited the captured Confederate capital
during the final days of the Civil War. The painting shows Lincoln receiving a hero's
welcome. In fact, though, many Richmond residents resented the visit by the leader
of the victorious North. The reunion of the nation would not be easy.* ★ **Predict two
problems that the nation would face as the North and South reunited.**

●1870
Fifteenth Amendment
guarantees voting
rights for African
American men

●1872
Congress pardons
former Confederate
officials

1877 ●
Rutherford B. Hayes
becomes President;
Reconstruction ends

1870   **1872**   **1874**   **1876**

▲
1870 World Event
Italy is unified

▲
1873 World Event
Abolition of slave markets
in Zanzibar

Both old and young were eager to learn. Grandparents and grandchildren sat side by side in the classroom. One bureau agent in South Carolina observed that freedmen "will starve themselves, and go without clothes, in order to send their children to school." Charlotte Forten, an African American woman from Philadelphia, came south as a volunteer teacher. She wrote of her students:

> **66** I never before saw children so eager to learn.... It is wonderful how a people who have been so long crushed to the earth...can have so great a desire for knowledge, and such a capacity for attaining it. **99**

The Freedmen's Bureau laid the foundation for the South's public school system. It set up more than 4,300 grade schools. It also created colleges for African American students, including Howard, Morehouse, and Fisk. Many graduates of these schools became teachers themselves. By the 1870s, African Americans were teaching in grade schools throughout the South.

Lincoln Is Assassinated

President Lincoln hoped to persuade Congress to accept his Reconstruction plan. However, he never got the chance.

On April 14, 1865, just five days after Lee's surrender, the President attended a play at Ford's Theater in Washington, D.C. As Lincoln watched the play, **John Wilkes Booth,** a popular actor from the South, crept into the President's box and shot Lincoln in the head. Within a few hours, the President was dead. Booth was later caught and killed in a barn outside the city.

Biography — Charlotte Forten

Charlotte Forten came from a wealthy Philadelphia family. A strong abolitionist, she devoted her life to helping other African Americans improve their lives through education. When she was 25, she helped set up a school on the Sea Islands off South Carolina. Later, she helped recruit other teachers for the Freedmen's Bureau. ★ **Why do you think education was so important to freedmen?**

surrendered, Congress passed a bill creating the **Freedmen's Bureau.** Lincoln signed it.

The Freedmen's Bureau gave food and clothing to former slaves. It also tried to find jobs for freedmen. The bureau helped poor whites as well. It provided medical care for more than one million people. One former Confederate was amazed to see "a Government which was lately fighting us with fire, and sword, and shell, now generously feeding our poor and distressed."

One of the bureau's most important tasks was to set up schools for freed slaves in the South. By 1869, about 300,000 African Americans attended bureau schools. Most of the teachers were volunteers, often women, from the North.

Connections With Arts

Walt Whitman's famous poem "O Captain! My Captain!" expresses his grief at the death of Lincoln. It begins, "O Captain! my Captain! our fearful trip is done, / The ship has weather'd every rack, the prize we sought is won." You can find this and other Civil War poems in Whitman's collection *Leaves of Grass.*

The nation plunged into grief. Millions who had been celebrating the war's end now mourned Lincoln's death. "Now he belongs to the ages," commented Secretary of War Edwin Stanton.

A New President

Vice President **Andrew Johnson** became President when Lincoln died. Johnson had served as governor of Tennessee and had represented that state in Congress. When Tennessee seceded, Johnson had remained loyal to the Union.

At first, many Republicans in Congress were pleased when Johnson became President. They believed that he would support a strict Reconstruction plan. As it turned out, Johnson's plan was much milder than expected.

Johnson called for a majority of voters in each southern state to pledge loyalty to the United States. He also demanded that each state ratify the **Thirteenth Amendment,** which banned slavery throughout the nation. (As you have read, Lincoln's Emancipation Proclamation did not free slaves in states that remained loyal to the Union.) Congress

Playbill from Ford's Theater on the night Lincoln was shot

had approved the Thirteenth Amendment in January 1865.

Rebellion in Congress

The southern states quickly met Johnson's conditions. As a result, the President approved their new state governments in late 1865. Voters in the South then elected representatives to Congress. Many of those elected had held office in the Confederacy. For example, Alexander Stephens, the former vice president of the Confederacy, was elected senator from Georgia.

Republicans in Congress were outraged. The men who had led the South out of the Union were being elected to the House and Senate. Also, no southern state allowed African Americans to vote.

When Congress met in December 1865, Republicans refused to let southern representatives take their seats. Instead, they set up a Joint Committee on Reconstruction to draw up a new plan for the South. The stage was set for a showdown between Congress and the President.

★ Section 1 Review ★

Recall

1. **Identify** (a) Reconstruction, (b) Ten Percent Plan, (c) Wade-Davis Bill, (d) Freedmen's Bureau, (e) John Wilkes Booth, (f) Andrew Johnson, (g) Thirteenth Amendment.
2. **Define** (a) freedmen, (b) amnesty.

Comprehension

3. Describe two problems the South faced after the Civil War.
4. (a) What was President Lincoln's Reconstruction plan? (b) How did it differ from the Wade-Davis Bill?

5. (a) What was President Johnson's plan for readmitting the former Confederate states to the Union? (b) How did Republicans in Congress react to Johnson's plan?

Critical Thinking and Writing

6. **Analyzing Information** The North lost more soldiers in the Civil War than the South did. Why was it easier for the North to recover from the war?
7. **Ranking** (a) What services did the Freedmen's Bureau provide? (b) Which do you think was most important? Explain.

Activity Writing a Poem President Lincoln has been shot! Taking the viewpoint of a northerner or southerner, write a poem about the death of Lincoln. If you like, you may set your poem to music.

Radical Reconstruction

As You Read

Explore These Questions
- What were the goals of the Radical Republicans?
- Why did Congress try to remove President Johnson from office?
- What were the Fourteenth and Fifteenth Amendments?

Define
- black codes
- radical
- impeach

Identify
- Radical Republicans
- Thaddeus Stevens
- Charles Sumner
- Fourteenth Amendment
- Radical Reconstruction
- Reconstruction Act
- Fifteenth Amendment

SETTING the Scene In the spring of 1866, disturbing reports trickled into Congress. In some southern cities, peddlers were openly selling Confederate flags. Throughout the South, people sang a new song, "I'm a good old rebel / And I don't want no pardon for anything I done."

These reports confirmed what many Republicans had suspected. "The rebellion has not ended," declared one angry Republican. "It has only changed its weapons!"

Black Codes

After the war, most southern states had promptly ratified the Thirteenth Amendment, which banned slavery. At the same time, however, Southern legislatures passed **black codes,** laws that severely limited the rights of freedmen.

Black codes forbade African Americans to vote, own guns, or serve on juries. In some states, African Americans were permitted to work only as servants or farm laborers. In others, the codes required freedmen to sign contracts for a year's work. Those without contracts could be arrested and sentenced to work on a plantation.

Black codes did give African Americans some rights they did not have before the Civil War. For example, the codes permitted African Americans to marry legally and to own some kinds of property. Still, the codes were clearly meant to keep freedmen from gaining political or economic power.

The North Reacts

Republicans were angered by the black codes, as well as by the election of former Confederate leaders to Congress. The Joint Committee on Reconstruction sent the President a report accusing the South of trying to "preserve slavery in its original form as much and as long as possible." When Johnson ignored the report, members of Congress vowed to take Reconstruction out of the President's hands.

Those who led the opposition to President Johnson were called **Radical Republicans,** or Radicals. A **radical** wants to make drastic changes in society. **Thaddeus Stevens** of Pennsylvania led the Radicals in the House. **Charles Sumner** of Massachusetts was the chief Radical Republican in the Senate.

Radicals had two main goals. First, they wanted to break the power of wealthy planters who had long ruled the South. Radicals blamed these "aristocrats" for the Civil War. Second, Radicals wanted to ensure that freedmen received the right to vote.

Radical Republicans did not control Congress. To accomplish their goals, they needed the support of moderate Republicans, the largest group in Congress. Moderates and Radicals disagreed on many issues. However, they shared a strong political motive for endorsing strict treatment of the South. Most southerners were Democrats. With southerners barred from Congress, Republicans easily controlled both houses.

The President vs. Congress

The conflict between the President and Congress came to a head in 1866. In April, Congress passed the Civil Rights Act, giving citizenship to African Americans. Congress hoped to combat the black codes and secure basic rights for African Americans. When Johnson vetoed the bill, Congress overrode the veto.

The Fourteenth Amendment

Congressional Republicans worried that the Supreme Court might declare the Civil Rights Act unconstitutional. In the Dred Scott decision of 1857, the Court had ruled that African Americans were not citizens. Hoping to avoid a similar ruling, Republicans proposed the Fourteenth Amendment.

The **Fourteenth Amendment** granted citizenship to all persons born in the United States. This included nearly all African Americans. It also guaranteed all citizens "equal protection of the laws" and declared that no state could "deprive any person of life, liberty, or property without due process of law." This provision made it illegal for states to discriminate against an individual on unreasonable grounds, such as skin color.

The Fourteenth Amendment also provided that any state that denied African Americans the right to vote would have its representation in Congress reduced. Republicans believed that freedmen would be able to defend their rights if they could vote.

With the Fourteenth Amendment, Republicans hoped to secure basic political rights for African Americans in the South. In fact, the nation had far to go before all Americans achieved equality. Over the next 100 years, citizens would seek to obtain their rights by asking the courts to enforce the Fourteenth Amendment.

Election of 1866

President Johnson urged the former Confederate states to reject the Fourteenth Amendment. He also decided to make the amendment an issue in the November 1866 congressional elections. Traveling through the North, the President called on voters to reject the Radical Republicans.

Viewing HISTORY New Rights for Freedmen

Under the black codes, former slaves gained some new rights, such as the right to marry legally. Forms like this one helped freedmen keep their marriage and family records. ★ **Why were family records so valuable to freedmen?**

In many towns, audiences heckled the President. One heckler shouted that Johnson should hang Jefferson Davis. Losing his temper, Johnson yelled back, "Why not hang Thad Stevens?" Many northerners criticized Johnson for acting in an undignified manner.

In July, white mobs in New Orleans, Louisiana, killed 34 African Americans. This convinced many northerners that stronger measures were needed to protect freedmen.

In the end, the election results were a disaster for Johnson. Republicans won majorities in both houses of Congress. They also won every northern governorship and majorities in every northern state legislature.

The Radical Program

In 1867, Republicans in Congress prepared to take charge of Reconstruction. The period that followed is often called **Radical Reconstruction.** With huge majorities in

Rival Plans for Reconstruction

Plan	Ten Percent Plan	Wade-Davis Bill	Johnson Plan	Reconstruction Act
Proposed by	President Abraham Lincoln (1863)	Republicans in Congress (1864)	President Andrew Johnson (1865)	Radical Republicans (1867)
Conditions for former Confederate states to rejoin Union	■ 10 percent of voters must swear loyalty to Union ■ Must abolish slavery	■ Majority of white men must swear loyalty ■ Former Confederate volunteers cannot vote or hold office	■ Majority of white men must swear loyalty ■ Must ratify Thirteenth Amendment ■ Former Confederate officials may vote and hold office	■ Must disband state governments ■ Must write new constitutions ■ Must ratify Fourteenth Amendment ■ African American men must be allowed to vote

Graphic Organizer *Skills*   **In the early years of Reconstruction, federal leaders debated several plans for readmitting southern states.**

1. **Comprehension** (a) Identify one similarity between the Wade-Davis Bill and President Johnson's plan. (b) Identify one difference.
2. **Critical Thinking** If Lincoln had lived, do you think he would have supported the 1867 Reconstruction Act? Explain.

Civics

both the House and the Senate, Congress could easily override a presidential veto.

First Reconstruction Act

In March 1867, Congress passed the first **Reconstruction Act** over Johnson's veto. The Reconstruction Act threw out the southern state governments that had refused to ratify the Fourteenth Amendment—all the former Confederate states except Tennessee. The act also divided the South into five military districts under army control.

The Reconstruction Act required the former Confederate states to write new constitutions and to ratify the Fourteenth Amendment before rejoining the Union. Most important, the act stated that African Americans must be allowed to vote in all southern states.

Further Republican victories

Once the new constitutions were in place, the reconstructed states held elections to set up new state governments. To show their disgust with Radical Reconstruction policies, many white southerners stayed away from the polls. Freedmen, on the other hand, proudly turned out to exercise their new right to vote. As a result, Republicans gained control of all of the new southern state governments.

Congress passed several more Reconstruction acts. Each time, the Republicans easily overrode Johnson's veto.

Johnson Is Impeached

It was Johnson's duty, as President, to enforce the new Reconstruction laws. However, many Republicans feared he would not do so. Republicans in Congress decided to remove the President from office.

On February 24, 1868, the House of Representatives voted to impeach President Johnson. To **impeach** means to bring formal charges of wrongdoing against an elected official. According to the Constitution, the House can impeach the President only for "high crimes and misdemeanors." The Senate tries the case. The President is removed from office only if found guilty by two thirds of the senators.

During Johnson's trial, it became clear that he was not guilty of high crimes and misdemeanors. Even Charles Sumner, the President's bitter foe, admitted that the charges were "political in character."

Despite intense pressure, seven Republican senators refused to vote for conviction. The Constitution, they believed, did not allow a President to be removed from office simply because he disagreed with Congress. In the end, the Senate vote was 35 for and 19 against impeachment—one vote short of the two-thirds majority needed to remove the President from office. Johnson served out the few remaining months of his term.

A New President

In 1868, Republicans nominated General Ulysses S. Grant as their candidate for President. Grant was the Union's greatest hero in the Civil War.

By election day, most of the southern states had rejoined the Union. As Congress demanded, the new southern governments allowed African Americans to vote. About 500,000 blacks went to the polls in the 1868 election. Nearly all cast their votes for Grant. He easily defeated his opponent, Horatio Seymour.

The Fifteenth Amendment

In 1869, Republicans in Congress proposed another amendment to the Constitution. The **Fifteenth Amendment** forbade any state to deny African Americans the right to vote because of their race.

Many Republicans had moral reasons for supporting the Fifteenth Amendment. They remembered the great sacrifices that were made by African American soldiers in the Civil War. They also felt it was wrong to let African Americans vote in the South but not in the North.

Some Republicans also supported the Fifteenth Amendment for political reasons. African American votes had brought Republicans victory in the South. If African Americans could also vote in the North, they would help Republicans to win elections there, too.

The Fifteenth Amendment was ratified in 1870. At last, all African American men over age 21 had the right to vote.

★ Section 2 Review ★

Recall

1. **Identify** (a) Radical Republicans, (b) Thaddeus Stevens, (c) Charles Sumner, (d) Fourteenth Amendment, (e) Radical Reconstruction, (f) Reconstruction Act, (g) Fifteenth Amendment.
2. **Define** (a) black codes, (b) radical, (c) impeach.

Comprehension

3. Describe the Reconstruction plan enacted by Congress in 1867.
4. (a) Why did Congress impeach President Johnson? (b) What was the result?

5. Describe the goals of: (a) the Fourteenth Amendment; (b) the Fifteenth Amendment.

Critical Thinking and Writing

6. **Defending a Position** (a) Compare Johnson's plan for Reconstruction with the Radical Reconstruction plan. (b) Which plan would you have supported? Defend your position.
7. **Analyzing Ideas** A senator who voted against the removal of President Johnson later said that he did not vote in favor of Johnson but in favor of the presidency. What do you think he meant?

Activity **Writing a Speech** Write a speech from the point of view of a radical or moderate Republican. Present your position on Reconstruction and give reasons for your opinion.

Changes in the South

As You Read

Explore These Questions
- What groups dominated southern politics during Reconstruction?
- What did Reconstruction governments do to rebuild the South?
- Why did many southerners sink into a cycle of poverty?

Define
- scalawag
- carpetbagger
- sharecropper

Identify
- Hiram Revels
- Blanche K. Bruce
- Conservatives
- Ku Klux Klan

SETTING the Scene By 1867, life in the South had changed dramatically. African Americans were free to work for themselves, to vote, and to run for office. In Alabama, a political convention of freedmen drew up this ringing declaration:

66 We claim exactly the same rights, privileges and immunities as are enjoyed by white men. We ask nothing more and will be content with nothing less. 99

Before the Civil War, a small group of rich planters controlled southern politics. During Reconstruction, however, new groups dominated state governments in the South. They tried to reshape southern politics. At the same time, others were taking strong action to reverse the gains made by African Americans.

New Forces in Southern Politics

The state governments created during Radical Reconstruction were different from any governments the South had known before. The old leaders had lost much of their influence. Three groups stepped in to replace them. These new groups were white southerners who supported the Republicans, northerners who moved south after the war, and African Americans.

Scalawags

Some white southerners supported the new Republican governments. Many were business people who had opposed secession in 1860. They wanted to forget the war and get on with rebuilding the South.

Many whites in the South felt that any southerner who helped the Republicans was a traitor. They called white southern Republicans **scalawags,** a word used for small, scruffy horses.

Carpetbaggers

Northerners who came south after the war were another important force. To white southerners, the new arrivals from the North were **carpetbaggers**—fortune hunters hoping to profit from the South's misery. Southerners claimed that these northerners were in such a hurry they had time only to fling a few clothes into cheap suitcases, or carpetbags.

In fact, northerners went south for a number of reasons. A few were fortune hunters who hoped to profit as the South was being rebuilt. Many more, however, were Union soldiers who had grown to love the South's rich land. Others, both white and

To many southerners, the carpetbag became a hated symbol of Reconstruction.

During Reconstruction, several African Americans won election to Congress. Here, Robert Brown Elliott of South Carolina stands in the House of Representatives to argue for a civil rights bill. Words from his speech appear on the banner above. "What you give to one class, you must give to all. What you deny to one class, you shall deny to all." ★ **Summarize Elliott's main point in your own words.**

black, were teachers, ministers, and reformers who sincerely wanted to improve the lives of the freedmen.

African Americans

Freedmen and other African Americans were the third major new group in southern politics. Before the war, African Americans had no voice in southern government. During Reconstruction, they not only voted in large numbers, but they also ran for and were elected to public office in the South.

African Americans became sheriffs, mayors, and legislators in the new state and local governments. Between 1869 and 1880, 16 African Americans were elected to Congress.

Two African Americans, both representing Mississippi, served in the Senate. **Hiram Revels,** a clergyman and teacher, became the nation's first black senator in 1870. He completed the unfinished term of former Confederate president Jefferson Davis. In 1874, **Blanche K. Bruce** became the first African American to serve a full term in the Senate. Born into slavery, Bruce escaped to freedom when the Civil War began and later served as a country sheriff.

Freedmen had less political influence than many whites claimed, however. Only in South Carolina did African Americans win a majority in one house of the state legislature. No state elected a black governor.

Conservatives Resist

From the start, most prominent white southerners resisted Reconstruction. These **Conservatives** wanted the South to change as little as possible. They were willing to let African Americans vote and hold a few offices. Still, they were determined that real power would remain in the hands of whites.

A few wealthy planters tried to force African Americans back onto plantations. Many small farmers and laborers wanted the government to take action against the millions of freedmen who now competed with them for land and power.

Most of these white southerners were Democrats. They declared war on anyone who cooperated with the Republicans. "This is a white man's country," they cried, "and white men must govern it."

Spreading terror

White southerners formed secret societies to help them regain power. The most dangerous was the **Ku Klux Klan,** or KKK. The Klan worked to keep blacks and white Republicans out of office.

Congress tried to end Klan violence. In 1870, Congress made it a crime to use force to keep people from voting. As a result, Klan activities decreased. Yet the threat of violence lingered. Some African Americans continued to vote and hold office despite the risk. Many others were frightened away from the ballot box.

The Task of Rebuilding

Despite political problems, Reconstruction governments tried to rebuild the South. They built public schools for both black and white children. Many states gave women the right to own property. In addition, Reconstruction governments rebuilt railroads, telegraph lines, bridges, and roads. Between 1865 and 1879, the South put down 7,000 miles of railroad track.

Rebuilding cost money. Before the war, southerners paid very low taxes. Reconstruction governments raised taxes sharply. This created discontent among many southern whites.

Southerners were further angered by widespread corruption in the Reconstruction governments. One state legislature, for example, voted $1,000 to cover a member's bet on a horse race. Other items billed to the state included hams, perfume, and a coffin.

Corruption was not limited to the South. After the Civil War, dishonesty plagued northern governments as well. In fact, most southern officeholders served their states honestly.

A Cycle of Poverty

In the first months after the war, freedmen left the plantations on which they had

Dressed in white robes and hoods to hide their identity, Klansmen rode at night to the homes of African American voters, shouting threats and burning wooden crosses. When threats did not work, the Klan turned to violence. Klan members murdered hundreds of African Americans and their white allies.

Congress responds

Many moderate southerners condemned the violence of the Klan. Yet they could do little to stop the Klan's reign of terror. Freedmen turned to the federal government for help. In Kentucky, African American voters wrote to Congress:

66 We believe you are not familiar with the Ku Klux Klan's riding nightly over the country spreading terror wherever they go by robbing, whipping, and killing our people without provocation. 99

$ Connections With Economics

While the Ku Klux Klan carried out its program of violence, others used economic weapons to intimidate African Americans. Planters refused to rent land to blacks. Employers refused to hire them, and storekeepers denied them credit. What effect do you think such pressures had?

| Critical Thinking | Managing Information | Communication | Maps, Charts, and Graphs |

Interpreting a Political Cartoon

How Will I Use This Skill?

Almost every newspaper today includes political cartoons. Cartoonists comment on current events through both visual imagery and words. Their pictures often use symbols and exaggeration to make their point. Learning to analyze cartoons can help you better understand views on current issues.

LEARN the Skill

❶ Identify the characters and symbols used in the cartoon. Remember that a symbol is an object that represents something beyond itself. The eagle, for example, is often used as a symbol for the United States.

❷ Note details in the drawing. Are some details larger or smaller than normal? Are any facial features or actions in the cartoon exaggerated?

❸ Analyze the relationship between the pictures and any words in the cartoon.

❹ Identify the cartoonist's point of view. Try to identify policies or actions that the cartoonist wants readers to support.

PRACTICE the Skill

The cartoon on the right appeared in a northern newspaper in the 1870s. Use the steps above to analyze the cartoon.

❶ The figure at the top of the cartoon is President Grant. Explain what these other symbols represent: (a) the woman; (b) the soldiers; (c) the carpetbag.

❷ (a) Note the size of the details in this

drawing. Are any larger than normal? Why? (b) What do Grant's facial expression and the position of his arms suggest about his attitude toward the South?

❸ (a) What words are written on the paper sticking out of the carpetbag? What do they mean? (b) What is the woman doing? (c) Is her task easy or difficult?

❹ (a) How do you think this cartoonist felt about Radical Reconstruction? Explain. (b) What policy do you think the cartoonist would want his readers to support?

APPLY the Skill

Find a current political cartoon in the editorial section of a newspaper. Using the skills you have learned in this section, write a paragraph explaining the cartoon.

lived and worked. They found few opportunities, however.

"Nothing but freedom"

Some Radical Republicans talked about giving each freedman "40 acres and a mule." Thaddeus Stevens suggested breaking up big plantations and distributing the land. Most Americans opposed the plan, however. In the end, former slaves received—in the words of a freedman—"nothing but freedom."

Through hard work or good luck, some freedmen were able to become landowners. Most, however, had little choice but to return to where they had lived in slavery.

Sharecropping

Some large planters had held onto their land and wealth through the war. Now, they had land but no slaves to work it. During Reconstruction, many freedmen and poor whites went to work on the large plantations. These **sharecroppers** farmed the land, using seed, fertilizer, and tools provided by the planters. In return, the planters got a share of the crop at harvest time. Sharecroppers hoped to have their own land one day. Meanwhile, they were lucky to have enough food for themselves and their families.

Even farmers who owned land faced hard times. Each spring, the farmers received supplies on credit. In the fall, they had to repay what they had borrowed. Often, the harvest did not cover the debt. Unable to pay, many farmers lost their land and became sharecroppers themselves. Many southerners became locked in a cycle of poverty.

Sharecroppers growing cotton behind their cabin

★ Section 3 Review ★

Recall

1. **Identify** (a) Hiram Revels, (b) Blanche K. Bruce, (c) Conservatives, (d) Ku Klux Klan.
2. **Define** (a) scalawag, (b) carpetbagger, (c) sharecropper.

Comprehension

3. (a) What role did freedmen play in Reconstruction governments? (b) How was this different from the role of African Americans before the Civil War?
4. (a) What were two accomplishments of Reconstruction governments? (b) What were two problems?

5. Why did many freedmen and poor whites become sharecroppers?

Critical Thinking and Writing

6. **Understanding Causes and Effects** During Reconstruction, freedmen proved that, given the chance, they could do the same jobs as whites. Do you think this made southern Conservatives more willing or less willing to accept African Americans as equals? Explain.
7. **Linking Past and Present** Many southerners were angered by high taxes imposed by Reconstruction governments. (a) How do voters today feel about paying high taxes? (b) Do you think some services should be provided even if they require high taxes? Explain.

★ ★

Activity Drawing a Political Cartoon Draw a political cartoon expressing your opinion about scalawags, carpetbaggers, the Ku Klux Klan, or another aspect of Reconstruction in the South.

Reconstruction Ends

As You Read

Explore These Questions
- Why did Reconstruction end?
- How did the southern economy expand after Reconstruction?
- How did African Americans in the South lose rights?

Define
- poll tax
- literacy test
- grandfather clause
- segregation
- lynching

Identify
- Rutherford B. Hayes
- Henry Grady
- James Duke
- Jim Crow laws
- *Plessy* v. *Ferguson*

SETTING the Scene In 1876, millions of Americans visited a great Centennial Exposition held in Philadelphia. The fair celebrated the first hundred years of the United States. Visitors gazed at the latest wonders of modern industry—the elevator, the telephone, a giant steam engine.

As Americans looked to the future, they lost interest in Reconstruction. By the late 1870s, white Conservatives had regained control of the South.

Radicals in Decline

By the 1870s, Radical Republicans were losing power in Congress. Many northerners grew weary of trying to reform the South. It was time to forget the Civil War, they believed, and let southerners run their own governments—even if that meant African Americans might lose their rights.

Republicans were also hurt by disclosure of widespread corruption in the government of President Grant. The President had appointed many friends to office. Some used their position to steal large sums of money from the government. Grant won reelection in 1872, but many northerners had lost faith in Republican leaders and their policies.

Congress reflected the new mood of the North. In May 1872, it passed the Amnesty Act, which restored the right to vote to nearly all white southerners. As expected, they voted solidly Democratic. At the same time, southern whites terrorized African Americans who tried to vote.

White Conservatives were firmly in control once more. One by one, the Republican governments in the South fell. By 1876, only three southern states—Louisiana, South Carolina, and Florida—were still controlled by Republicans.

Election of 1876

The end of Reconstruction came with the election of 1876. The Democrats nominated Samuel Tilden, governor of New York, for President. Tilden was known for fighting corruption. The Republican candidate was **Rutherford B. Hayes,** governor of Ohio. Like Tilden, Hayes vowed to fight dishonesty in government.

Tilden won 250,000 more popular votes than Hayes. However, Tilden had only 184 electoral votes—one vote short of the number needed to win. Twenty other votes were in dispute. The outcome of the election hung on these votes. All but one of the disputed votes came from Florida, Louisiana, and South Carolina—the three southern states still controlled by Republicans.

As inauguration day drew near, the nation still had no one to swear in as President. Congress set up a special commission to settle the crisis. A majority of the commission members were Republicans. The commission decided to give all the disputed electoral votes to Hayes.

Southern Democrats could have fought the election of Hayes. Hayes, however, had privately agreed to end Reconstruction. Once in office, he removed all remaining federal troops from South Carolina, Louisiana, and Florida. Reconstruction was over.

Industry and the "New South"

During Reconstruction, the South made some progress toward rebuilding its economy. Cotton production, long the basis of the South's economy, slowly recovered. By 1880, planters were growing as much cotton as they had in 1860.

After Reconstruction, a new generation of southern leaders worked to expand the economy. **Henry Grady,** editor of the *Atlanta Constitution,* made stirring speeches calling for the growth of a "New South." Grady argued that the South should use its vast natural resources to build up its own industry, instead of depending on the North.

Agricultural industries

Southerners agreed that the best way to begin industrializing was to process the region's agricultural goods. Investors built textile mills to turn cotton into cloth. By 1880, the entire South was still producing fewer textiles than Massachusetts. In the next decade, though, more and more communities started building textile mills.

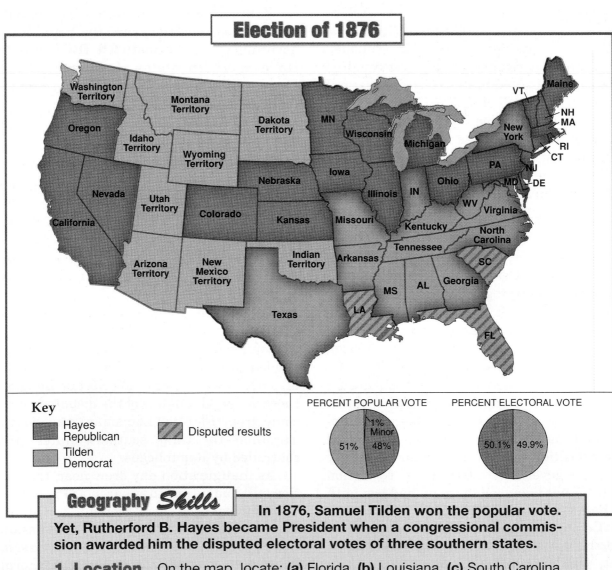

Election of 1876

Key

- Hayes Republican
- Tilden Democrat
- Disputed results

PERCENT POPULAR VOTE

51% | 48% | 1% Minor

PERCENT ELECTORAL VOTE

50.1% | 49.9%

Geography Skills

In 1876, Samuel Tilden won the popular vote. Yet, Rutherford B. Hayes became President when a congressional commission awarded him the disputed electoral votes of three southern states.

1. Location On the map, locate: **(a)** Florida, **(b)** Louisiana, **(c)** South Carolina.

2. Movement Which candidate carried the undisputed southern vote?

3. Critical Thinking Based on the map, do you think the Civil War ended sectionalism in the United States? Explain.

The tobacco industry also grew rapidly. In North Carolina, **James Duke** used new machinery to revolutionize production of tobacco products. In 1890, he bought out several competitors to form the American Tobacco Company. Duke eventually controlled 90 percent of the nation's tobacco industry.

New industries

The South also tapped its mineral resources. Local deposits of iron ore and coal, as well as low wages for workers, made steel production cheaper in Alabama than in Pennsylvania. Oil refineries developed in Louisiana and Texas. Other states became leading producers of coal, copper, granite, and marble.

By the 1890s, many northern forests had been cut down. The southern yellow pine was competing with the northwestern white pine as a lumber source. Some southern factories began to make cypress shingles and hardwood furniture.

A visitor from New England described what he found on a visit to the South in 1887:

66 We find a South wide awake with business, excited and even astonished at the development of its own immense resources in metals, marbles, coal, timber, fertilizers, eagerly laying lines of communication, rapidly opening mines, building furnaces, foundries, and all sorts of shops for utilizing the native riches. 99

By 1900, the South had developed a more balanced economy. Still, it failed to keep up with even more rapid growth in the North and the West.

Restricting the Rights of African Americans

The years after Reconstruction brought prosperity to some southerners. For African Americans, though, the end of Reconstruction had tragic effects.

With the North out of southern affairs, white Conservatives tightened their grip on southern governments. Some groups continued to use violence to keep African Ameri-

Viewing HISTORY **Rise of the New South**

From Darkness to Light *by Grant Hamilton* shows the New South rising from the ruins of war. Hamilton created this picture for one of several industrial expositions held in Atlanta, Georgia, in the late 1800s. ★ **According to this picture, what products helped the southern economy grow?**

cans from voting. Southern states also found new ways to keep African Americans from exercising their rights.

Voting restrictions

In the 1880s, many southern states began passing new laws that restricted the right to vote. **Poll taxes** required voters to pay a fee each time they voted. As a result, poor freedmen could rarely afford to vote. **Literacy tests** required voters to read and explain a section of the Constitution. Since most freedmen had little education, such tests kept them away from the polls.

Many poor southern whites also could not pass the literacy test. To increase the number of eligible white voters, states passed **grandfather clauses.** If a voter's father or grandfather had been eligible to vote on January 1, 1867, the voter did not have to take

Why Study History?

Because Tolerance Begins With You

* *

Historical Background

During and after Reconstruction, hate groups like the Ku Klux Klan used violence and terror to keep African Americans from voting or holding any political office. Angry mobs set fire to African American homes, churches, and schools. They even lynched people. Often, these tactics worked. Yet many whites and African Americans continued to speak out against injustice.

Artist Jim Osborn created this painting to encourage respect and tolerance.

Connections to Today

Discrimination and hate crimes have not been limited to African Americans in the South in the 1800s. Almost every group in this nation has suffered the pain of senseless hatred. People feel the sting of prejudice for many reasons: religion, race, economic status, age, or physical or mental abilities.

Acts of prejudice continue today. In recent years, Jewish cemeteries have been vandalized. African American churches have been burned. Asian American stores have been covered in racist graffiti. Mexican American or Arab American businesses have been attacked. In some areas, police have set up special "hate crime" units to investigate actions such as these.

Connections to You

Tolerance begins with you. You can fight prejudice by respecting and appreciating people's differences. Everyone in your class has different talents and experiences. You can get to know your classmates for who they are, rather than on the basis of what you think you know about them. You will find that you have much in common with students who seem different.

Many schools provide opportunities for you to increase your ability to get along with others. Human relations clubs promote understanding of diverse groups. Peer-mediation programs can teach you how to deal with anger and conflict. By keeping an open mind and educating yourself, you can help end discrimination and prejudice.

1. **Comprehension** **(a)** What tactics did hate groups use against African Americans in the South? **(b)** Identify two kinds of discrimination some people face today.

2. **Critical Thinking** How do prejudice and discrimination begin?

 **Making a Poster** Make a list of three things that you could do to promote tolerance. Create a poster illustrating one of them.

a literacy test. Since no African Americans in the South could vote before 1868, grandfather clauses were a way to ensure that only white men could vote.

Racial segregation

Southern blacks lost more than the right to vote. After 1877, segregation became the law of the South. **Segregation** means separating people of different races in public places. Southern states passed laws that separated blacks and whites in schools, restaurants, theaters, trains, streetcars, playgrounds, hospitals, and even cemeteries. **Jim Crow laws,** as they were known, trapped southern blacks in a hopeless situation. In 1885, the Louisiana novelist George Washington Cable described segregation as:

> **66** ...a system of oppression so rank that nothing could make it seem small except the fact that [African Americans] had already been ground under it for a century and a half. **99**

African Americans brought lawsuits to challenge segregation. In 1896, in the case of **Plessy v. Ferguson,** the Supreme Court ruled that segregation was legal so long as facilities for blacks and whites were equal. In fact, facilities were rarely equal. For example, southern states spent much less on schools for blacks than for whites.

Violence

When Reconstruction ended, groups like the Ku Klux Klan declined. However, violent acts against African Americans continued. During the 1890s, almost 200 Americans were lynched each year. **Lynching** is the illegal seizure and execution of someone by a mob. Four out of five lynchings took place in the South, and the majority of the victims were African American.

Some lynching victims were accused of crimes. Others were simply considered troublemakers. Victims—including some women and children—were hanged, shot, or burned to death, often after painful torture. Members of lynch mobs rarely faced punishment. By the late 1800s, some reformers began to speak out against lynching.

Results of Reconstruction

Reconstruction was a time of both success and failure. Southerners faced hard times. Still, the South gained a public education system and expanded its rail lines.

As a result of Reconstruction, all African Americans became citizens for the first time. These rights eroded after Reconstruction ended. However, the laws passed during Reconstruction, such as the Fourteenth Amendment, became the basis of the civil rights movement almost 100 years later.

★ Section 4 Review ★

Recall

1. **Identify** (a) Rutherford B. Hayes, (b) Henry Grady, (c) James Duke, (d) Jim Crow laws, (e) *Plessy* v. *Ferguson.*
2. **Define** (a) poll tax, (b) literacy test, (c) grandfather clause, (d) segregation, (e) lynching.

Comprehension

3. Why did Radical Republicans' power decline?
4. How did the economy of the South change?

5. Describe two ways that African Americans lost their rights after Reconstruction ended.

Critical Thinking and Writing

6. **Evaluating Information** Do you think that Reconstruction was successful? Explain.
7. **Predicting Consequences** How do you think *Plessy* v. *Ferguson* affected later efforts to achieve equality for African Americans?

★ ★

Activity **Acting a Scene** With a partner, act out a scene of an African American man trying to vote in the South in the late 1880s. Begin by considering how you might feel if you knew that you had the right to vote, yet someone was able to prevent you from voting.

Chapter 18 **Review and Activities**

★ Sum It Up ★

Section 1 First Steps to Reunion
▶ After the Civil War, the South faced the task of repairing tremendous destruction.
▶ The Freedmen's Bureau helped newly freed African Americans learn to read, and provided food and clothing to the needy.
▶ Presidents Lincoln and Johnson recommended mild plans for Reconstruction, but Congress refused to accept either one.

Section 2 Radical Reconstruction
▶ Radical Republicans wanted to break the power of rich planters in the South and make sure that freedmen could vote.
▶ Congress tried and failed to remove President Johnson from office.
▶ Republicans proposed the Fourteenth and Fifteenth amendments to ensure the civil rights of African Americans.

Section 3 Changes in the South
▶ Southern Republicans, whites from the North, and freed African Americans played important roles in southern governments.
▶ Landless black and white sharecroppers became locked in a cycle of poverty.

Section 4 Reconstruction Ends
▶ Reconstruction ended after presidential candidate Rutherford B. Hayes made a private deal with southern politicians.
▶ After Reconstruction, a new industrial economy began to emerge in the South.
▶ Southern whites passed new laws to deny African Americans equal rights.

 **CD-ROM Review** For additional review of the major ideas of Chapter 18, see *Guide to the Essentials of American History* or *Interactive Student Tutorial CD-ROM,* which contains interactive review activities, graphic organizers, and practice tests.

📖 Reviewing the Chapter

Define These Terms
Match each term with the correct definition.

Column 1
1. freedman
2. black codes
3. scalawag
4. poll tax
5. segregation

Column 2
a. laws that severely limited the rights of freedmen
b. tax required before someone could vote
c. white southern Republican
d. former slave
e. separating people of different races in public places

Explore the Main Ideas
1. Describe the condition of the South after the war.
2. How did Republicans in Congress gain control of Reconstruction?
3. Give two reasons why Republicans supported the Fifteenth Amendment.
4. Describe the economic recovery of the South after the Civil War.
5. Why did most Americans lose interest in Reconstruction in the 1870s?
6. What was the purpose of Jim Crow laws?

📖 Geography Activity

Match the letters on the map with the following places:
1. South Carolina, 2. Florida, 3. Louisiana, 4. Ohio, 5. New York. **Region** Which southern states were under Republican control in 1876?

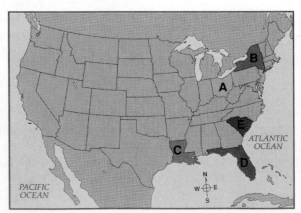

📖 Critical Thinking and Writing

1. **Understanding Chronology** **(a)** Put the following in the order in which they were first proposed: the Reconstruction Acts; the Wade-Davis Bill; the Ten Percent Plan; Jim Crow laws. **(b)** Why did Lincoln have so little influence on Reconstruction?

2. **Exploring Unit Themes** **Sectionalism** Briefly state your own plan for repairing the bitter feelings between North and South.

3. **Analyzing Ideas** Most people call groups such as the Ku Klux Klan "un-American." Explain the reasons for this belief.

4. **Predicting Consequences** After the Civil War, the United States entered a period of industrial growth that made it the richest nation in the world. How do you think the South's experiences during Reconstruction affected its share in this industrial boom?

📖 Using Primary Sources

Born into slavery, Booker T. Washington became a leading educator. Here, he describes one of the problems that came with emancipation:

> 66 Was it any wonder that within a few hours the wild rejoicing ceased and a feeling of deep gloom seemed to pervade the slave quarters? To some it seemed that, now that they were in actual possession of it, freedom was a more serious thing than they expected to find it. Some of the slaves were seventy or eighty years old; their best days were gone. They had no strength with which to earn a living in a strange place and among strange people, even if they had been sure where to find a new place of abode. 99

Source: *Up From Slavery,* Booker T. Washington, 1901.

Recognizing Points of View **(a)** What caused the "wild rejoicing" Washington mentions? **(b)** Why did the rejoicing end so quickly? **(c)** Why do you think many African Americans were unprepared for the realities of freedom?

ACTIVITY BANK

▶ Interdisciplinary Activity

Connections With Arts Review the goals of the Freedmen's Bureau. Then create a poster advertising the Bureau's work and encouraging volunteers to participate.

▶ Career Skills Activity

Playwrights and Actors Find out more about the events and issues leading up to the trial of President Andrew Johnson. Then prepare a skit in which you act out Johnson's trial in the United States Senate.

▶ Citizenship Activity

Understanding the Constitution Study the text of the Fourteenth and Fifteenth amendments printed in the Reference Section. Create a graphic organizer for each amendment. Include the main ideas of each amendment and show how it affects the daily lives of Americans today. You may illustrate your work with original drawings or clippings.

Internet Activity

Use the Internet to find primary sources on Reconstruction. Then use the primary source to create a newspaper interview with the person who wrote the material you have found. Create questions that are answered by quotations taken from the primary source.

EYEWITNESS Journal

You are a freedman, a Radical Republican, a Conservative southern planter, or a northerner who went south during Reconstruction. In your EYEWITNESS JOURNAL, describe your reaction to three important events of the Reconstruction era.

History Through Literature

The Red Badge of Courage

Stephen Crane

Introduction

Stephen Crane was born six years after the Civil War ended. He spent many hours reading about the war and talking to veterans. In 1895, he published his great Civil War novel, *The Red Badge of Courage*. It tells the story of Henry Fleming, a young volunteer in the Union Army. The following passage describes Henry's departure from home and his early days in the army.

Vocabulary

Before you read the selection, find the meaning of these words in a dictionary: **doggedly, shirking, monotonous, province, pickets, philosophical, reflectively, reproached, infantile, assurance.**

When [Henry] had stood in the doorway with his soldier's clothes on his back, and with the light of excitement and expectancy in his eyes almost defeating the glow of regret for the home bonds, he had seen two tears leaving their trails on his mother's scarred cheeks.

Still, she had disappointed him by saying nothing whatever about returning with his shield or on it.* He had privately primed himself for a beautiful scene. He had prepared certain sentences which he thought could be used with touching effect. But her words destroyed his plans. She had doggedly peeled potatoes and addressed him as follows: "You watch out, Henry, an' take good care of yerself in this here fighting business —you watch out, an' take good care of yerself. Don't go a-thinkin' you can lick the hull rebel army at the start, because yeh can't. Yer jest one little feller amongst a hull lot of others, and yeh've got to keep quiet an' do what they tell yeh. I know how you are, Henry.

"I've knet yeh eight pair of socks, Henry, and I've put in all yer best shirts, because I want my boy to be jest as warm and comf'able as anybody in the army. Whenever they get holes in 'em, I want yeh to send 'em rightaway back to me, so's I kin dern 'em.

"An' allus be careful an' choose yer comp'ny. There's lots of bad men in the army, Henry. The army makes 'em wild, and they like nothing better than the job of leading off a young feller like you, as ain't never been away from home much and has allus had a mother, an' a-learning 'em to drink and swear. Keep clear of them folks, Henry....

"I don't know what else to tell yeh, Henry, excepting that yeh must never do no shirking, child, on my account. If so be a time comes when yeh have to be kilt or do a mean thing, why, Henry, don't think of anything 'cept what's right, because there's many a woman has to bear up 'ginst sech things these times, and the Lord'll take keer of us all.

"Don' forget about the socks and the shirts, child; and I've put a cup of blackberry jam with yer bundle, because I know yeh like it

---

* The Spartan people of ancient Greece carried home their dead warriors on their shields.

This anonymous painting, Off to the Front, 1861, *is owned by the museum of the United States Military Academy at West Point, New York. It shows a young soldier saying goodbye to his family in the first year of the Civil War. Scenes like this were common in homes throughout the North and South.* ★ **Choose one of the people in this painting. What do you think are that person's thoughts and feelings?**

above all things. Good-by, Henry. Watch out, and be a good boy."

He had, of course, been impatient under the ordeal of this speech. It had not been quite what he expected, and he had borne it with an air of irritation. He departed feeling vague relief.

Still, when he had looked back from the gate, he had seen his mother kneeling among the potato parings. Her brown face, upraised, was stained with tears, and her spare form was quivering. He bowed his head and went on, feeling suddenly ashamed. . . .

After complicated journeyings with many pauses, there had come months of monotonous life in a camp. He had had the belief that real war was a series of death struggles with small time in between for sleep and meals; but since his regiment had come to the field the army had done little but sit still and try to keep warm. . . .

He had grown to regard himself merely as a part of a vast blue demonstration. His province was to look out, as far as he could, for his personal comfort. For recreation he could twiddle his thumbs and speculate on the thoughts which must agitate the minds of the generals. Also, he was drilled and drilled and reviewed, and drilled and drilled and reviewed.

The only foes he had seen were some pickets along the river bank. They were a suntanned, philosophical lot, who sometimes shot reflectively at the blue pickets. When reproached for this afterward, they usually expressed sorrow, and swore by their gods that the guns had exploded without their permission. The youth, on guard duty one night, conversed across the stream with one of them. He was a slightly ragged man, who spat skillfully between his shoes and possessed a great fund of bland and infantile assurance. The youth liked him personally.

"Yank," the other had informed him, "yer a right dum good feller." This sentiment, floating to him upon the still air, had made him temporarily regret war.

Analyzing Literature

1. What advice did Henry's mother give him?
2. How was a soldier's life different than what Henry expected?
3. **Making Generalizations** What does Henry's experience with the enemy picket suggest about the special problems of fighting a civil war?

Unit 6 Transforming the Nation

Viewing UNIT THEMES — A Triumph of Technology

On May 24, 1883, New Yorkers celebrated the opening of the Brooklyn Bridge with fireworks and a boat parade. The bridge was one of the greatest feats of American engineering. At first, the Brooklyn Bridge carried pedestrians and horse-drawn carriages. Soon after, a new invention—the automobile—would appear.
★ **Name two earlier inventions that improved transportation in the United States.**

Unit Theme Industrialization

After the Civil War, the United States underwent a great transformation. Industrialists opened thousands of new factories. Shrewd business leaders made fortunes building railroads, manufacturing steel, or drilling for oil. New inventions, from the light bulb to the automobile, changed daily life. Industrialization fueled the rapid growth of cities.

How did people of the time feel about industrialization? They can tell you in their own words.

★ ★

VIEWPOINTS ON INDUSTRIALIZATION

❝ In factories where labor-saving machinery has reached its most wonderful development, little children are at work. **❞**
Henry George, economist and journalist (1879)

❝ Better morals, better sanitary conditions, better health, better wages, these are the practical results of the factory system. **❞**
Carroll D. Wright, United States labor commissioner (1882)

❝ Law, I reckon I was born to work in a mill. I started when I was ten years old and I aim to keep right on just as long as I'm able. I'd a-heap rather do it than housework. **❞**
Alice Caudle, textile worker, recalling her childhood (1938)

★ ★

Activity Writing to Learn Industrialization transformed the way people worked. You are a young American of the late 1800s. You grew up in the country, working on the family farm. You have just moved to a big city where you are about to begin your new job in a factory making lawnmowers. Make a list of the ways in which your new job differs from your old one.

Chapter 19

An Era of Change in the West 1865–1914

After the Civil War, settlers flooded the West. Miners sought gold and silver. Railroad builders spanned the continent with rail lines. Ranchers raised great herds of cattle. Farmers changed grasslands into fields of wheat and corn. As these westerners gained political influence, they urged government leaders to address their needs and concerns.

Native Americans, meanwhile, were driven from their homelands. The Indians struggled to keep their way of life. In the end, however, they were defeated. On reservations, they were forced to learn new ways. Native Americans suffered greatly from the changes that swept the West.

Why Study History?

According to most historians, the cowhand was an important figure in the American West for only a short time. Nevertheless, the cowboy entered American culture as an enduring mythic hero. The image of the cowboy still speaks to people today. To learn more about this topic, see this chapter's *Why Study History?* feature, "The Cowboy Is Part of Our Culture."

American Events

●1869
Nation's first transcontinental railroad is completed

●1876
Sitting Bull defeats Custer during the Sioux War

1887 ●
Dawes Act encourages Native Americans to change their lifestyle

1865   1870   1875   1880   1885   1890

World Events

1869 World Event
Suez canal opens in Egypt

1879 World Event
British and Zulus go to war in southern Africa

 Viewing HISTORY **Cold Morning on the Range**

In the late 1800s, the West and its wide-open spaces captured the imagination of adventurers, settlers, business people, writers, and artists. They all saw the frontiers of the West as places of opportunity. Sadly, few people were concerned with the Native Americans who already lived there. In this colorful painting by Frederic Remington, a cowhand tries to ride a bucking bronco. ★ **How do you think this and similar paintings affected people's ideas about the West? Explain.**

●1891
Farmers and labor unions join to form Populist Party

●1897
William McKinley becomes President

●1913
States ratify income tax amendment to the Constitution

| 1890 | 1895 | 1900 | 1905 | 1910 | 1915 |

▲ **1891 World Event**
Work begins on Trans-Siberian railroad to connect Moscow to Pacific coast

▲ **1910 World Event**
China abolishes slavery

 503

The Plains Indians

As You Read

Explore These Questions
- How did Plains Indians rely on the horse and the buffalo?
- What traditions were important to the Plains Indians?
- How did the roles of women and men differ?

Define
- tepee
- travois
- corral
- jerky

Identify
- Sun Dance

SETTING the Scene Standing Bear, a Lakota, or Sioux* Indian, recalled the buffalo-rib sled his father made for him when he was a boy living on the Plains:

66 After all the meat had been cleaned from the bones, my father took six of the ribs and placed them together. He then split a piece of cherry wood and put the ends of the bones between the pieces of wood. The whole affair was then laced together with rawhide rope. 99

Standing Bear's rib sled is only one example of the many uses that Plains Indians had for the buffalo that roamed their homeland. Indians had been living for centuries on the Great Plains. They developed ways of life that were well suited to the region.

Way of Life

Many different Native American nations lived on the Great Plains. (See the map on page 31.) A number of nations, such as the Arikaras, had lived on the Plains for hundreds of years. Others, like the Lakotas, did not move to the Plains until the 1700s.

Plains Indians had rich and varied cultures. They had well-organized religions, made fine handicrafts, and created much poetry. Each nation had its own language. People from different nations used sign language to talk to one another.

At one time, most Plains Indians were farmers who lived in semipermanent villages. From there, they sent out hunting parties that pursued herds of buffalo and other animals on foot. Agriculture, however, was their main source of food.

During the 1600s, the Plains Indians' way of life changed as they captured and tamed wild horses. These horses were descended from animals that the Spanish had brought to the Americas. On horseback, the Indians could travel farther and faster. As a result, buffalo hunting replaced farming as the basis of life for many Plains people.

Following the buffalo

Plains Indians followed the huge herds of buffalo that roamed the Plains. They began to live in **tepees** (TEE pees), or tents made by stretching buffalo skins on tall poles. The tepees could easily be carried on a **travois** (trə VOI), or sled pulled by a dog or horse.

Connections With Science

Plains Indians rubbed buffalo fat on their skin to protect themselves from the weather and from insects. They used paints made from clay, charred wood, and copper ore to decorate their faces.

*Sioux was the French name for these Indians. In fact, the Sioux included many different groups who had their own names for themselves, including Lakota, Dakota, and Nakota.

Viewing History

Following the Buffalo Run

During buffalo hunts, Plains women packed, moved, and unpacked the group's possessions. In this painting by Charles M. Russell, women have loaded their belongings on a travois. They are following the buffalo to a new location, where they will set up camp. ★ **Do you think Plains Indians had many personal possessions? Why or why not?**

▲ *Kiowa baby carrier*

The migration of the Plains Indians mirrored the movement of the buffalo. In winter, small groups of buffalo moved off the Plains to protected valleys and forests. In summer, huge buffalo herds gathered on the Plains where the grass was growing high. In the same way, Plains Indians spent the winter in small bands and gathered in large groups during the summers. The people worked together and owned many things in common.

These groups often staged buffalo drives. Shouting and waving colored robes, hunters drove a herd of buffalo into a **corral,** or enclosure. There, they killed the trapped buffalo. After a kill, the band celebrated with a feast of roasted buffalo meat.

Uses of the buffalo

Plains Indians depended on the buffalo for food, clothing, and shelter. Buffalo meat, rich in protein, was a main item in the Indians' diet. Women cut up and dried the meat on racks. The dried meat was called **jerky.**

Women also tanned buffalo hides to make leather. They wove buffalo fur into coarse, warm cloth. Buffalo horns and bones were carved into tools and toys. The sinews of the buffalo could be used as thread or bowstrings.

Traditions

In summer, many Native American groups met on the Plains. They hunted together, played games, and staged foot and horse races.

Summer gatherings were also the time for councils. At the councils, leaders consulted with elders about problems that affected the whole nation. Indian doctors treated the sick.

One of the most important events was a religious ceremony known as the **Sun Dance.** Thousands of people attended the four-day ceremony to thank the Great Spirit for help in times of trouble.

The Sun Dance took place in a lodge made of tree branches. A sacred tree stood in the middle, and people hung their offerings from it. Dancers circled the tree and asked the Great Spirit for good fortune in the coming year.

A Well-Ordered Society

Women oversaw life in the home. They gathered foods and prepared meals for their families. They also performed such heavy work as raising and taking down tepees. Women cared for the children and taught them the traditions of their people.

Women also engaged in many crafts. They sewed animal hides to make clothing and tepees. They made the baskets, pottery, and blankets that were essential to the community. Their work often displayed great artistic skill and design. In fact, a woman's ability in crafts established her rank in society. The woman who made the most beautiful clothing or prepared the greatest number of baskets gained much the same honor as a man who performed bravely in battle.

Cheyenne war shield

In some of the tribes, women helped men with the duties of hunting and governing. A Blackfoot woman, Running Eagle, led many hunting parties herself. In other bands, a woman respected for her wisdom made the final decisions about important matters.

The men of the Plains Indians had important responsibilities too. They hunted and traded. They passed on their valuable skills and knowledge to the boys. They supervised the spiritual life of the community by leading religious ceremonies. Men with special skills provided medical care for the sick and injured.

Another important responsibility of the men was to provide military leadership. They waged war to defend or extend territory, to gain horses and other riches, or to seek revenge. More than anything else, however, men waged war to protect their people and to prove their bravery and ability. The most successful warriors gained great respect and status among their nation.

★ Section 1 Review ★

Recall

1. **Identify** Sun Dance.
2. **Define** (a) tepee, (b) travois, (c) corral, (d) jerky.

Comprehension

3. **(a)** How did the use of horses change the way Plains Indians lived? **(b)** Why did Plains Indians live in different places at different times of the year?
4. Describe three ways in which Native Americans made use of buffalo.

5. What activities took place at the summer gatherings of Plains Indians?

Critical Thinking and Writing

6. **Making Inferences** How did the dependence on hunting buffalo affect the roles of Indian women and men on the Plains?
7. **Making Generalizations** Based on what you know about the Sun Dance ceremony, what were some religious beliefs of the Plains Indians?

★ ★

Activity **Making a Graphic Organizer** Based on what you have learned in this section, make a graphic organizer to show the different ways in which the Plains Indians relied on the buffalo.

Miners and Railroaders

As You Read

Explore These Questions
- How did mining change the West?
- What was life like for miners and railroad workers?
- How did railroads help the West develop?

Define
- vigilante
- subsidy
- transcontinental railroad

Identify
- Comstock Lode
- Union Pacific Railroad
- Central Pacific Railroad
- Leland Stanford

SETTING the Scene Many Americans were lured west by the chance to strike it rich mining gold and silver. "What a clover-field is to a steer, the sky to the lark, a mudhole to a hog, such are new diggings to a miner," wrote one observer in 1862.

Miners reversed the traditional pattern of expansion. Instead of moving from east to west as the earlier pioneers had done, many journeyed from west to east. From the California coast, they fanned out eastward, ever in search of new ways to make their fortune.

The Mining Boom

The western mining boom had begun with the California Gold Rush of 1849. When the Gold Rush ended, miners looked for new opportunities. The merest rumor sent them racing east in search of new strikes.

Gold and silver strikes

In 1859, two young prospectors struck gold in the Sierra Nevada. Suddenly, another miner, Henry Comstock, appeared. "The land is mine," he cried, and demanded to be made a partner. From then on, Comstock boasted about "his" mine. The strike became known as the **Comstock Lode.** A lode is a rich vein of gold or silver.

Comstock and his partners often complained about the heavy blue sand that was mixed in with the gold. It clogged the devices used for separating the gold and made the gold hard to reach. When Mexican miners took the "danged blue stuff" to an expert in California, tests showed it was loaded with silver. Comstock had stumbled onto one of the richest silver mines in the world.

Miners moved into many other areas of the West. Some found valuable ore in Montana and Idaho. Others struck it rich in Colorado. In the 1870s, miners discovered gold in the Black Hills of South Dakota. (See the map on page 510.) In the late 1890s, thousands rushed north to Alaska after major gold strikes were made there.

Boom towns and ghost towns

Gold and silver strikes attracted thousands of prospectors. Miners came from across the United States, as well as from Germany, Ireland, Mexico, and China. Towns sprang up near all the major mining sites.

First, miners built a tent city near the diggings. Then, thousands of people came to supply the miners' needs. Traders brought mule teams loaded with tools, food, and clothing. Merchants hauled in wagonloads of supplies and set up stores.

Connections With Arts

After failing as a prospector, Samuel Clemens became a writer for a Nevada newspaper. His amusing articles appeared in papers throughout the West. In 1863, Clemens signed one of his articles with a new name, one well-known to readers today—Mark Twain.

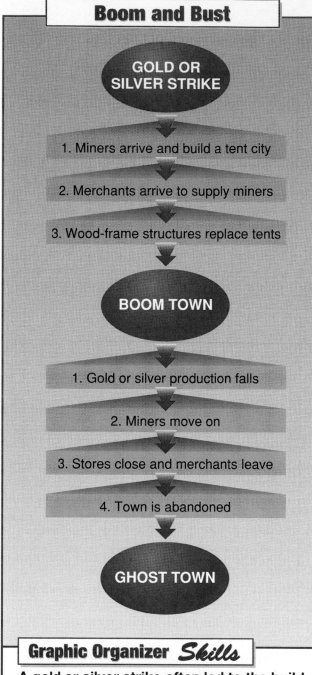

Boom and Bust

GOLD OR SILVER STRIKE

1. Miners arrive and build a tent city

2. Merchants arrive to supply miners

3. Wood-frame structures replace tents

BOOM TOWN

1. Gold or silver production falls

2. Miners move on

3. Stores close and merchants leave

4. Town is abandoned

GHOST TOWN

Graphic Organizer *Skills*

A gold or silver strike often led to the building of a boom town. However, many boom towns quickly became ghost towns.

1. **Comprehension** **(a)** Why did merchants often follow miners? **(b)** What caused large numbers of miners to suddenly leave a boom town?

2. **Critical Thinking** Based on this chart and on the map on page 510, why do you think there are more ghost towns today in Colorado than there are in Texas?

Economics $

Soon, wood frame houses, hotels, restaurants, and stores replaced the tents. For example, it took less than a year for the mining camp at the Comstock Lode to become the boom town of Virginia City, Nevada.

Most settlers in the boom towns of the mining frontier were men. However, enterprising women also found ways to profit. Some women ran boarding houses and laundries. Others opened restaurants, where miners gladly paid high prices for a home-cooked meal.

Many boom towns lasted for only a few years. When the gold or silver ore was gone, miners moved away. Without miners for customers, businesses often had to close. In this way, a boom town could quickly go bust and turn into a ghost town.

Still, some boom towns survived and prospered even after the mines shut down. In these towns, miners stayed and found new ways to make a living.

Impact of the boom

The surge of miners into the West created problems. Mines and towns polluted clear mountain streams. Miners cut down forests to get wood for buildings. As you will read, they also forced Native Americans from the land.

Foreign miners were often treated unfairly. In many camps, mobs drove Mexicans from their claims. Chinese miners were heavily taxed or forced to work claims abandoned by others.

Few miners got rich quickly. Much of the gold and silver lay deep underground. It could be reached only with costly machinery. Eventually, most mining in the West was taken over by large companies that could afford to buy this equipment.

Governing the mining frontier

Lawlessness and disorder often accompanied the rapid growth of a town. In response, miners sometimes resorted to organizing groups of **vigilantes.** These self-appointed law enforcers tracked down outlaws and punished them, usually without a trial. A common punishment used by vigilantes was lynching.

HISTORY HAPPENED HERE

Bannack State Park

In 1862, gold was found along Grasshopper Creek in Montana. The boom town of Bannack grew up at the site and became Montana's first territorial capital. Bannack was a wild frontier town, complete with saloons, gambling, and gunfights. But, when the gold disappeared, so did the people. Today, the ghost town is Bannack State Park. Visitors can walk among the remains of more than 50 buildings, including the Montana Territorial Capitol, the Hotel Meade, and the town jail.

★ **To learn more about this historic site, write:** Bannack State Park, 4200 Bannack Road, Dillon, MT 59725.

Informal methods of government gradually gave way to more formal arrangements. In 1861, Colorado, Dakota, and Nevada were organized into territories. Idaho and Arizona followed in 1863 and Montana in 1864. The process of more permanent settlement and government had begun.

The Railroads

The people of the mining towns needed large amounts of supplies. They also needed to transport their gold and silver. As a result, railroad companies raced to lay track to the mines and boom towns.

Spanning the continent

The federal government helped the railroad companies because it felt that rail lines in the West would benefit the entire nation. The government's aid came in the form of subsidies. A **subsidy** is financial aid or a land grant from the government. Congress lent money to the railroad companies and gave them land. Often, both business and government ignored the fact that Native Americans lived on the land.

In 1863, two companies began a race to build the first transcontinental railroad. A **transcontinental railroad** is one that stretches across a continent from coast to coast. The **Union Pacific** started building a rail line from Omaha, Nebraska, westward. The **Central Pacific** began in Sacramento, California, and built eastward. The *Sacramento Union* of January 8, 1863, reported:

❝ With rites appropriate to the occasion ... ground was formally broken at noon for the commencement of the Central Pacific Railroad—the California link of the continental chain that is to unite American communities now divided by thousands of miles of trackless wilderness. ❞

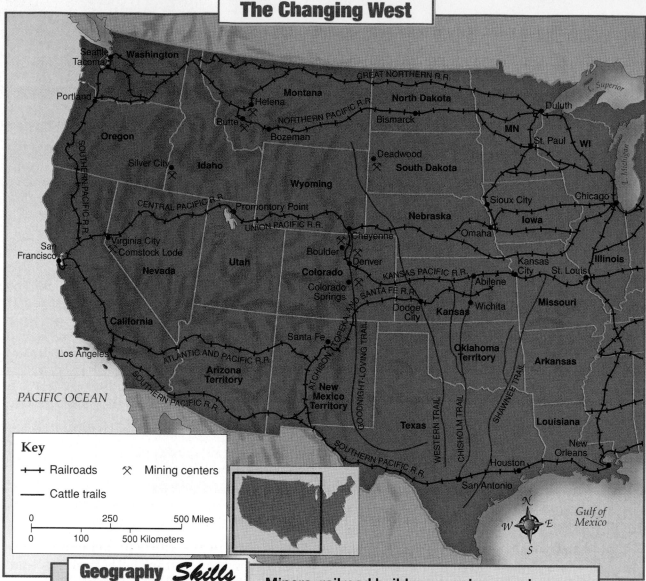

The Changing West

Key
- ┼┼ Railroads
- ⚒ Mining centers
- ── Cattle trails

0 ... 250 ... 500 Miles
0 ... 100 ... 500 Kilometers

Geography *Skills*

Miners, railroad builders, ranchers, and cowhands all played a major role in changing the West.

1. **Location** On the map, locate: **(a)** Comstock Lode, **(b)** Central Pacific Railroad, **(c)** Promontory Point, **(d)** Chisholm Trail.

2. **Interaction** How did mining affect nearby soil, water, and other natural resources?

3. **Critical Thinking** Why did most railroad lines in the West run east-west rather than north-south?

Immigrant workers

Both companies had trouble getting workers. Labor was scarce during the Civil War. Also, the work was backbreaking and dangerous and the pay low.

The railroad companies hired immigrant workers, who accepted the low wages. The Central Pacific brought in thousands of workers from China. The Union Pacific hired new-comers from Ireland. African Americans and Mexican Americans also worked for each line.

The workers faced a tough task. The Central Pacific had to carve a path through the rugged Sierra Nevada. The Union Pacific had to cut through the towering Rockies. Snowstorms and avalanches killed workers and slowed progress. At times, crews advanced only a few inches a day.

Chinese and European immigrants worked together to complete the transcontinental railroad. ★ **What dangers and hardships did the workers face?**

Impact of the railroads

The Central Pacific and Union Pacific met at Promontory Point, Utah, on May 10, 1869. **Leland Stanford,** president of the Central Pacific, hammered a golden spike into the rail that joined the two tracks and united the country. The nation's first transcontinental railroad was completed.

With the Civil War fresh in their minds, people cheered this new symbol of unity. The words that were engraved on the golden spike expressed their feelings:

66 May God continue the unity of our Country as the Railroad unites the two great Oceans of the world. 99

Before long, other major rail lines linked the West and the East. The railroads brought growth and new settlement all across the West. They enabled people, supplies, and mail to move quickly and cheaply across the plains and mountains. Wherever rail lines went, settlements sprang up along the tracks. The largest towns and cities developed where major railroad lines met.

Because of their rapid growth, western territories began to apply for statehood. Nevada became a state in 1864, Colorado in 1876, North Dakota, South Dakota, Montana, and Washington in 1889. Idaho and Wyoming entered the Union in 1890.

★ Section 2 Review ★

Recall

1. **Locate** **(a)** Virginia City, **(b)** Idaho, **(c)** Montana, **(d)** Colorado, **(e)** South Dakota, **(f)** Promontory Point.

2. **Identify** **(a)** Comstock Lode, **(b)** Union Pacific Railroad, **(c)** Central Pacific Railroad, **(d)** Leland Stanford.

3. **Define** **(a)** vigilantes, **(b)** subsidy, **(c)** transcontinental railroad.

Comprehension

4. How did mining encourage the growth of towns?

5. Describe two problems that immigrants faced as miners or railroad workers.

6. How did transcontinental railroads help to bring more states into the Union?

Critical Thinking and Writing

7. **Understanding Causes and Effects** Why did railroad companies hire immigrants to build the first transcontinental railroad?

8. **Linking Past and Present** Are railroads as important today as they were in the late 1800s? Explain.

Activity **Writing a Speech** You are a railroad official in 1869. Write a short speech to celebrate the completion of the first transcontinental railroad. In your speech, explain how you think the railroad will benefit the entire nation.

Ranchers and Cowhands

As You Read

Explore These Questions
- Why were there cattle drives?
- What was the life of a cowhand like?
- Why did the Cattle Kingdom end?

Define
- cattle drive
- cowhand
- vaquero
- cow town

Identify
- Chisholm Trail
- Cattle Kingdom

SETTING the Scene In the 1860s, a new group of Americans arrived in the West. These riders on horseback came from Texas, leading dusty lines of bellowing cattle. As they rode along, these cattle herders passed the time by singing songs like this one:

66 Well, come along, boys, and listen to my tale;
I'll tell you of my troubles on the old Chisholm Trail.
With a ten dollar horse and a forty dollar saddle,
I started in herding these Texas cattle. 99

The Cattle Drives

Before the arrival of settlers from the United States, the Spanish and then the Mexicans set up cattle ranches in the Southwest. Over the years, strays from these ranches grew into large herds of wild cattle, known as longhorns. They roamed freely across the grassy plains of Texas.

After the Civil War, the demand for beef increased. Growing cities in the East needed more meat. Miners, railroad crews, and soldiers in the West added to the demand.

In response, Texas ranchers began rounding up herds of longhorns. They drove the animals hundreds of miles north to railroad lines in Kansas and Missouri. The long trips were called **cattle drives.**

Jesse Chisholm blazed one of the most famous cattle trails. Chisholm was half Scottish and half Cherokee. In the late 1860s, he began hauling goods by wagon between Texas and the Kansas Pacific Railroad. His route crossed rivers at the best places and passed by water holes. Ranchers began using the **Chisholm Trail** in 1867. Within five years, more than one million head of cattle had walked the road. (See the map on page 510.)

The Cowhands

Ranchers employed **cowhands** to tend their cattle and drive herds to market. These hard workers rode alongside the huge herds in good and bad weather. They kept the cattle moving and rounded up strays. It is estimated that nearly one in three cowhands was either Mexican American or African American.

Spanish heritage

American cowhands learned much about riding, roping, and branding from Spanish and Mexican **vaqueros** (vah KEHR ohs). Vaqueros were skilled riders who herded cattle on ranches in Mexico, California, and the Southwest.

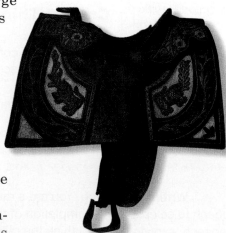

Saddle used by a Mexican vaquero

Viewing HISTORY California Vaqueros

Mexican American vaqueros were very important to the cattle industry of California, Texas, and the entire Southwest. The American artist James Walker painted this scene in the 1870s. ★ **Why did vaqueros and cowhands wear wide-brimmed hats?**

The gear used by American cowhands was modeled on the tools of the vaquero. Cowhands used the lariat—a leather rope—to catch runaway cattle. *Lariat* comes from the Spanish word for rope. Cowhands wore wide-brimmed hats like the Spanish sombrero. Their leather leggings, called chaps, were modeled on Spanish chaparreras (chap ah RAY rahs). Chaps protected a rider's legs from the thorny plants that grow in the Southwest.

On the trail

A cattle drive was hot, dirty, tiring work. Cowhands worked in all kinds of weather and faced many dangers. They had to prevent nervous cattle from drowning while crossing a fast-flowing river. They had to fight raging grass fires. They also faced attacks from cattle thieves who roamed the countryside.

One of the cowhand's worst fears on a cattle drive was a stampede. A clap of thunder or a gunshot could set thousands of longhorns off at a run. Cowhands had to ride into the crush of hoofs and horns. They slowed the stampeding herd by turning the cattle in a wide circle.

Most cowhands did not work for themselves. Instead, they were hired hands for the owners of large ranches. For all their hard work, cowhands were lucky to earn $1 a day! Even in the 1870s, this was low pay.

The Cow Towns

Cattle drives ended in **cow towns** that had sprung up along the railroad lines. The Chisholm Trail, for example, ended in Abilene, Kansas. (See the map on page 510.) In cow towns, cattle were held in great pens until they could be loaded on railroad cars and shipped to markets in the East.

In Abilene and other busy cow towns, dance halls, saloons, hotels, and restaurants catered to the cowhands. Sheriffs often had a hard time keeping the peace. Some cowhands spent wild nights drinking, dancing, and gambling.

Cow towns also attracted settlers who wanted to build stable communities where families could thrive. Doctors, barbers, artisans, bankers, and merchants helped to establish the cow towns.

The main street of a town was where people conducted business. Almost every town

Why Study History?

Because the Cowboy Is Part of Our Culture

★ ★

Historical Background

In the late 1800s, writers and artists created the popular image of the American cowboy. The mythic and heroic cowboy was a hard worker—brave, dependable, and self-reliant. He helped the weak, fought for justice, and punished wrongdoers. He was a man of action.

People throughout the nation were captivated by the exciting adventures of this new American folk hero. They read about him in dime novels and magazines. They admired him in paintings and sculptures. They saw him in Wild West shows entertaining audiences with trick riding, fancy roping, and mock gunfights. In the early 1900s, people began watching their favorite cowboy stars in the motion pictures.

Pawnee Bill, shown here, is the popular cowboy star of a Wild West Show.

Connections to Today

Today, the cowboy remains an important part of American culture. Wild West shows are still popular, and rodeos are enjoying increasing attention. Some men and women try to take part in the action by vacationing on a dude ranch. Also, the heroic cowboy still rides the range in film and television. Sometimes, though, the cowboy is an "intergalactic starfighter," the West is outer space, and the outlaws are aliens bent on destroying the Earth.

Connections to You

The heroic cowboy image seems to capture the imagination of each new generation. Many young people enjoy listening to country-western music. Others like to wear western jeans and boots. Cowboys and western scenes often appear in commercial advertisements for a variety of products.

The heroic cowboy remains a popular figure in American culture today because of the ideals that are often associated with him. These ideals include independence, courage, hard work, and justice. The cowboy will probably remain an enduring American symbol as long as Americans cherish those values.

1. **Comprehension** **(a)** How was the heroic cowboy image created? **(b)** What were the key characteristics of the heroic cowboy?

2. **Critical Thinking** How are science-fiction films such as those of the *Star Wars* and *Star Trek* series similar to traditional movie westerns?

★*Activity*  **Interviewing** Interview several people of different generations. Ask them to describe some ideals that they associate with the cowboy heroes of literature, film, and television. Share your findings in a report to the class.

had a general store that sold groceries, tools, clothing, and all sorts of goods. The general store also served as a social center where people could talk and exchange the latest news. As a town grew, more and more specialty shops lined its main street. These included drug stores, hardware stores, and even ice cream parlors.

Religion also played an important role for the townspeople. Throughout the West, places of worship grew in number and membership. They served as spiritual and social centers, and as symbols of progress and stability. "A church does as much to build up a town as a school, a railroad, or a fair," noted one New Mexico newspaper.

The Cattle Boom

In the 1870s, ranching spread north from Texas across the grassy Plains. Soon, cattle grazed from Kansas to present-day Montana. Ranchers had built a **Cattle Kingdom** in the West.

The open range

Ranchers let their cattle run wild on the open range. To identify cattle, each ranch had its own brand that was burned into the cattle's hide. Twice a year, young calves were rounded up and branded.

Sometimes, there were conflicts on the range. Since water was scarce, ranchers battled over rights to water holes and streams. When sheepherders moved onto the Plains, ranchers tried to drive them out. The ranchers complained that sheep nibbled the grass so low that cattle could not eat it.

End of an era

In the 1870s, farmers began moving onto the range. They fenced their fields with barbed wire. Sharp barbs kept cattle and sheep from pushing over fences and trampling plowed fields. As more farmers bought land and strung barbed wire, the open range began to disappear.

Bad weather on the Great Plains speeded the end of the Cattle Kingdom. The bitterly cold winters of 1886 and 1887 killed millions of cattle. By the spring of 1887, nine out of ten head of cattle on the northern Plains had frozen to death.

Cattle owners began to buy land and fence it in. Soon, farmers and ranchers divided the open range into a patchwork of large fenced plots. The days of the Cattle Kingdom were over.

★ Section 3 Review ★

Recall

1. **Locate** (a) Texas, (b) Kansas, (c) Abilene, (d) Dodge City, (e) Montana.
2. **Identify** (a) Chisholm Trail, (b) Cattle Kingdom.
3. **Define** (a) cattle drive, (b) cowhand, (c) vaquero, (d) cow town.

Comprehension

4. After the Civil War, why did Texas ranchers drive cattle herds to Kansas?
5. Describe some of the dangers that cowhands faced.

6. Explain two reasons why the Cattle Kingdom came to an end.

Critical Thinking and Writing

7. **Analyzing Visual Evidence** Study the painting of California vaqueros on p. 513. Then, identify and describe some of the equipment used by both vaqueros and cowhands.
8. **Predicting Consequences** How do you think the growth of the Cattle Kingdom affected the Plains Indians? Explain.

★ ★

Activity **Writing a Song** Round 'em up! Move 'em out! You are driving cattle along the old Chisholm Trail. Review the song verse at the start of this section. Then, based on what you have learned about a cowhand's life, write a second verse to the song.

4 ★ A Way of Life Ends

As You Read

Explore These Questions
- Why did Native Americans and settlers come into conflict?
- How did Native Americans try to preserve their way of life?
- How did government policies affect Native American culture?

Define
- reservation

Identify
- Sitting Bull
- Fort Laramie Treaty
- Chivington Massacre
- Battle of Little Bighorn
- Chief Joseph
- Geronimo
- Ghost Dance
- Susette La Flesche
- Helen Hunt Jackson
- Dawes Act

 SETTING the Scene In 1876, **Sitting Bull,** a Lakota chief, wrote to the commander of United States Army troops, who had been sent to force him off his land:

66 I want to know what you are doing on this road. You scare all the buffalo away. I want to hunt in this place. I want you to turn back from here. If you don't, I will fight you. 99

After the Civil War, many Americans moved west. At first, the United States government promised to protect Indian hunting grounds. However, as settlers pushed westward, the government broke its promises. When Indians resisted the arrival of settlers, wars spread across the West. For Native Americans, tragedy was the result.

Broken Promises

Conflict began as early as the 1840s when settlers and miners began to cross Indian hunting grounds. The settlers and miners asked for government protection from the Indians.

Fort Laramie Treaty

In 1851, federal government officials met with Indian nations near Fort Laramie in Wyoming. The officials asked each nation to keep to a limited area. In return, they promised money, domestic animals, agricultural tools, and other goods. Officials told the Native Americans that the lands that were reserved for them would be theirs forever.

Native American leaders agreed to the terms in the **Fort Laramie Treaty.** However, in 1858, gold was discovered at Pikes Peak in Colorado. A wave of miners rushed to land that the government had promised to the Cheyennes and Arapahos.

Federal officials forced Indian leaders to sign a new treaty giving up the land around Pikes Peak. Some Native Americans refused to accept the agreement. They attacked white settlers.

The Chivington Massacre

The settlers struck back. In 1864, Colonel John Chivington led his militia against a peaceful Cheyenne village that the government had promised to protect. When Chivington attacked, the Indians raised a white flag of surrender. Chivington ignored the flag. He ordered his men to destroy the village and take no prisoners. In the **Chivington Massacre,** the militia slaughtered more than 100 men, women, and children.

People throughout the United States were outraged. "When the white man comes in my country he leaves a trail of blood behind him," said Lakota War Chief Red Cloud. Across the Plains, soldiers and Indians went to war.

Learning "American" ways

In 1867, federal officials established a peace commission. The commission wanted to end the wars on the Plains so that railroad builders and miners would be safe. The commission urged Native Americans to settle down and live as white farmers did. It also urged them to send their children to white schools to learn "American" ways.

At one white school in Indiana, Lakota children were horrified to hear that their hair would be cut short. Among the Lakotas, only cowards had short hair. One girl described her distress:

> 66 I cried aloud... I felt the cold blades of the scissors against my neck, and heard them gnaw off one of my thick braids. Then I lost my spirit. 99

Forced onto reservations

In 1867, the Kiowas, Comanches, and other southern Plains Indians signed a new treaty with the government. They promised to move to Indian Territory in present-day Oklahoma. The soil there was poor. Also, most Plains Indians were hunters, not farmers. The Indians did not like the treaty but knew they had no choice.

The Lakotas and Arapahos of the northern Plains also signed a treaty. They agreed to live on reservations in present-day South Dakota. A **reservation** is a limited area set aside for Native Americans.

End of the Buffalo

The Plains Indians suffered from lost battles and broken treaties. Even worse for them, however, was the destruction of the buffalo.

As the railroads moved west, buffalo hunting became a fashionable sport. Trainloads of easterners shot the animals from the comfort of railroad cars. Then, in the 1870s, buffalo hide blankets became popular in the East. Commercial hunters began shooting

Linking United States and the World

United States

New Zealand

Surrendering Their Land

In 1868, Sioux leaders met with United States government officials at Fort Laramie. The Indians signed a treaty agreeing to live on a reservation. In 1840, on the other side of the world, the Maori people of New Zealand signed the Treaty of Waitangi. By this treaty, the Maori leaders gave Great Britain control over New Zealand. ★ **Why do you think the United States and Britain both wanted more land?**

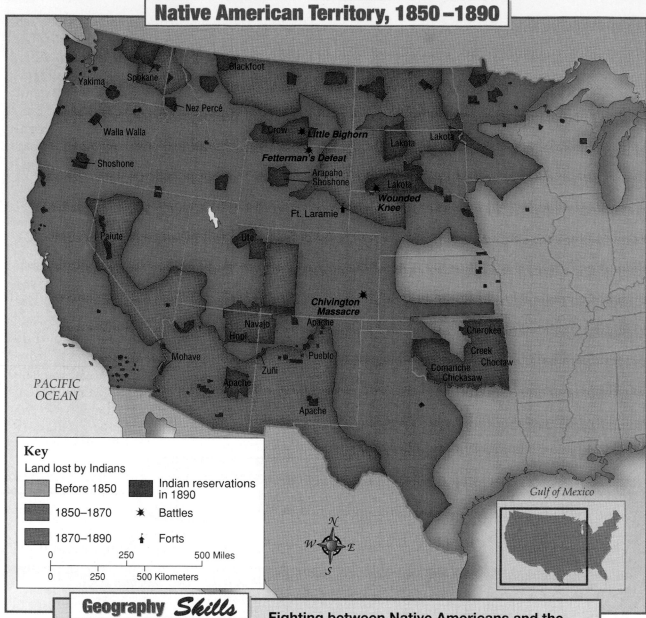

Native American Territory, 1850–1890

Yakima
Spokane
Blackfoot
Nez Percé
Walla Walla
Crow
★ **Little Bighorn**
Lakota
Lakota
Shoshone
★ **Fetterman's Defeat**
Arapaho
Shoshone
★ Lakota
Wounded Knee
Ft. Laramie
Paiute
Ute
★ **Chivington Massacre**
Navajo
Hopi
Apache
Cherokee
Mohave
Pueblo
Creek
Choctaw
Zuñi
Comanche
Chickasaw
Apache

PACIFIC OCEAN

Apache

Gulf of Mexico

Key

Land lost by Indians

▨ Before 1850	▨ Indian reservations in 1890	
▨ 1850–1870	★ Battles	
▨ 1870–1890	⚑ Forts	

0   250   500 Miles

0   250   500 Kilometers

N W E S

Geography *Skills*

Fighting between Native Americans and the United States government went on for years until most Indians were forced onto reservations.

1. **Location** On the map, locate: **(a)** Fort Laramie, **(b)** Little Bighorn, **(c)** Apache reservations, **(d)** Wounded Knee.

2. **Region** In which areas of the country did Native Americans still retain much of their land in 1870?

3. **Critical Thinking** Why do you think the Apaches of the desert Southwest were one of the last Indian nations to lose their land?

2 to 3 million buffalo every year. The number of buffalo fell from 13 million in 1860 to a few hundred in 1900.

Facing starvation, the Plains Indians had to struggle simply to survive. As the buffalo disappeared, so did the Plains Indians' way of life. Years later, Pretty Shield, a woman of the Crow nation, sadly recalled the tragedy. "When the buffalo went away the hearts of my people fell to the ground, and they could not lift them up again.... I [saw] dead buffalo scattered all over our beautiful country."

The Final Battles

Settlers and miners continued to move into the West. They wanted more and more land for themselves. Even on reservations, the Indians were not left in peace.

Sioux War of 1876

In 1874, prospectors found gold in the Black Hills region of the Lakota, or Sioux, reservation. Thousands of miners rushed to the area. Led by Sitting Bull and Crazy Horse, another Lakota chief, the Indians fought back in what became known as the Sioux War of 1876.

In June 1876, Colonel George A. Custer led a column of soldiers into the Little Bighorn Valley. Indian scouts warned Custer that there were many Lakotas and Cheyennes camped ahead. Custer did not wait for more soldiers. Instead, he attacked with only 225 men. Custer and all his men died in the **Battle of Little Bighorn.**

The Indian victory at the Little Bighorn was shortlived. The army soon defeated the Lakotas and Cheyennes. Then, Congress ordered that no food rations be distributed to the Indians until they agreed to the government's demands. To avoid starvation, the Lakotas gave up all claims to the Black Hills and other territory. In this way, they surrendered about one third of the lands that the United States government had guaranteed them by the Fort Laramie Treaty.

Chief Joseph

The Nez Percés lived in the Snake River valley, at a place where Oregon, Washington, and Idaho meet. In the 1860s, gold strikes brought miners onto Nez Percé land. The government ordered the Nez Percés to move to a reservation in Idaho.

At first, **Chief Joseph,** a Nez Percé leader, refused to leave. Then, in 1877, he and his people, including women and children, fled north toward Canada. Army troops followed close behind.

In the months that followed, Chief Joseph earned the respect and admiration of many. Again and again, he fought off or eluded pursuing army units. He set high standards for his soldiers, warning them not to injure women or children as the white soldiers did. He also made sure that his soldiers paid settlers for any supplies that they took.

Finally, after a tragic journey of more than 1,000 miles, Chief Joseph decided that he must surrender. Of the approximately 700 Nez Percés who had set out with him, fewer than 450 remained. As he lay down his weapons, he sadly said:

> 66 It is cold, and we have no blankets. The little children are freezing to death.... Hear me, my chiefs! I am tired. My heart is sick and sad. From where the sun now stands, I will fight no more forever. 99

The Apache wars

In the arid lands of the Southwest, the Apaches fiercely resisted the loss of their lands. One leader, **Geronimo,** continued fighting the longest. In 1876, he assumed leadership of a band of Apache warriors when the government tried to force his people onto a reservation.

Geronimo waged war off and on for the next ten years. From Mexico, he led frequent raids into Arizona and New Mexico. In the end, 5,000 United States soldiers were trying to capture Geronimo, who, by this time, had fewer than forty followers. Geronimo finally surrendered in 1886. His capture marked the end of formal warfare between Indians and whites.

A Way of Life Lost

Many Indians longed for their lost way of life. On the reservations, the Lakotas and other Plains Indians turned to a religious ceremony called the **Ghost Dance.** It celebrated the time when Native Americans lived freely on the Plains.

The Ghost Dance

In 1889, word spread that a prophet named Wovoka had appeared among the Paiute people of the southern Plains. Wovoka said that the Great Spirit would make a new world for his people, free from whites and filled with plenty. To bring about this new

Biography — Geronimo

For many years, Geronimo (on horseback) fought against both Mexico and the United States. He paid a high price for his fierce resistance. At a peace conference in the 1850s, Mexican soldiers murdered his mother, wife, and three children. After he surrendered to the United States Army, he was imprisoned for two years. ★ **Why do you think Geronimo refused to surrender for so long?**

world, all the Indians had to do was to dance the Ghost Dance.

Across the Plains, many Indians began preparing for the new world. Ghost Dancers painted their faces red and put on the sacred Ghost Dance shirt. Some believed that the shirt protected them from harm, even from the bullets of soldiers' guns.

In their ceremonies, Ghost Dancers joined hands in a large, spinning circle. As they danced, they all cried and laughed. A "growing happiness" filled them, said one. They saw a glowing vision of a new and perfect world.

Settlers react

Many settlers grew alarmed. The Ghost Dancers, they said, were preparing for war.

The settlers persuaded the government to outlaw the Ghost Dance.

In December 1890, police officers entered a Lakota reservation to arrest Sitting Bull, who had returned from Canada and was living on the reservation. They claimed that he was spreading the Ghost Dance among the Lakotas. In the struggle that followed, Sitting Bull was accidentally shot and killed.

Wounded Knee

Upset by Sitting Bull's death, groups of Lakotas fled the reservations. Army troops pursued them to Wounded Knee Creek, in present-day South Dakota. On December 29, the Indians were preparing to surrender. As nervous troops watched, they began to give up their guns.

Suddenly, a shot rang out. The army opened fire with rifles and artillery. By the time the shooting stopped, nearly 300 Native American men, women, and children lay dead. About 25 soldiers also died.

The fighting at Wounded Knee marked the end of the Ghost Dance religion. Years later, Black Elk, a former Ghost Dancer, remembered the events at Wounded Knee:

66 When I look back now from this high hill of my old age, I can still see the . . . women and children lying [on the ground there]. . . . And I can see that something else died there. . . . A people's dream died there. 99

Failed Reforms

The Native Americans were no longer able to resist the government. During the late 1800s, the army forced more Indians onto reservations every year.

Reformers speak out

Many people—Indian and white—spoke out against the tragedy that was occurring. **Susette La Flesche,** daughter of an Omaha chief, wrote and lectured about the destruction of the Native American way of life. Her work led others to take up the Indian cause.

One reformer influenced by La Flesche was **Helen Hunt Jackson.** In 1881, Jackson published *A Century of Dishonor.* The book vividly recounted the long history of broken treaties between the United States and the Native Americans. In her book, Jackson urged the United States government to end its policy of "cheating, robbing, [and] breaking promises."

Alice Fletcher was another reformer who worked for the Indians. She became an agent of the Indian Bureau, the government department that handled Indian affairs. To better understand Native American culture, Fletcher lived for a time with various Indian nations, including the Omahas and Winnebagos of Nebraska.

The Dawes Act

Calls for reform led Congress to pass the **Dawes Act** in 1887. The act encouraged Native Americans to become farmers. Some tribal lands were divided up and given to individual Native American families.

Ghost Dance shirt

The Dawes Act worked poorly. To Native Americans, land was an open place for riding and hunting—not something to divide into small parcels. As a result, Indians often sold their parcels to whites for low prices. In the end, Native Americans lost more than one half of the land that they had owned before the passage of the Dawes Act.

Life on the reservations changed Native American culture. The federal government took away the power of Indian leaders. In their place, it appointed government agents to make most decisions. These agents believed that Native Americans should give up their old ways, including their language, religion, and traditional customs.

Because Native Americans could no longer hunt buffalo, many had to depend on food and supplies guaranteed by treaties. Few Indians were content with life on the reservations.

★ Section 4 Review ★

Recall

1. **Locate** (a) Wyoming, (b) Colorado, (c) Oklahoma, (d) South Dakota, (e) Little Bighorn, (f) Wounded Knee.
2. **Identify** (a) Sitting Bull, (b) Fort Laramie Treaty, (c) Chivington Massacre, (d) Battle of Little Bighorn, (e) Chief Joseph, (f) Geronimo, (g) Ghost Dance, (h) Susette La Flesche, (i) Helen Hunt Jackson, (j) Dawes Act.
3. **Define** reservation.

Comprehension

4. Why did treaties between Native Americans and the United States fail to bring peace to the Plains?

5. Why were many Plains Indians attracted to Wovoka's teachings about the Ghost Dance?
6. How did each of the following affect Native Americans: (a) peace commission of 1867, (b) destruction of the buffalo, (c) establishment of reservations?

Critical Thinking and Writing

7. **Recognizing Points of View** Why do you think the government wanted Plains Indians to settle down and become farmers?
8. **Solving Problems** What do you think the federal government could have done to avoid wars with Native Americans in the West?

Activity **Writing a Poem** You are a Native American looking back at the changes that have occurred between 1865 and 1890. Write a poem describing your thoughts and feelings about those changes.

The Farmers

As You Read

Explore These Questions
- What were the different origins of western farmers?
- Why was life hard for Plains farmers?
- Why did farmers unite in the late 1800s?

Define
- sod house
- sodbuster
- cooperative
- wholesale

Identify
- Mary Elizabeth Lease
- Homestead Act
- Exodusters
- Hispanic-American Alliance
- National Grange
- Farmers' Alliance
- Populist party
- William Jennings Bryan
- William McKinley

SETTING the Scene Like miners and ranchers who arrived before them, farmers dreamed of a new life in the West. Mary Zimmerman and her family were among the first farmers on the Great Plains. She recalled their early struggle:

66 The soil was [new]. It had to be broken, turned, stirred, and taught to produce. With the simple means of the time, the process was slow, but...I helped my father on the farm and learned to do the work pretty well. 99

Later, western farmers would face other challenges. In the 1890s, **Mary Elizabeth Lease,** a fiery Kansas reformer, spoke bitterly of a struggle against low prices:

66 We raised the big crop...and what came of it? Eight-cent corn, ten-cent oats, two-cent beef....Then the politicians told us we suffered from overproduction. 99

Farmers Settle in the West

Congress passed the **Homestead Act** in 1862. The law promised 160 acres of land to anyone who farmed it for five years. The government was encouraging farmers to settle the West. It also wanted to give poor easterners a chance to own a farm.

Homesteaders

Many easterners rushed to accept the offer of free land. They planted their 160 acres with wheat and corn. By 1900, half a million Americans had set up farms under the Homestead Act.

The Homestead Act had its problems. The land was free, but poor people did not have the money to move west and start a farm. Also, only about 20 percent of the homestead land went directly to small farmers. Land-owning companies took large areas of land illegally. They divided the land and resold it to farmers at a high price.

Exodusters

African Americans joined the rush for homestead land. The largest group moved west at the end of Reconstruction. At this time in the South, blacks were seeing many of their hard-won freedoms slip away.

In 1879, a group of African Americans moved to Kansas. They called themselves **Exodusters.** They took the name from Exodus, the book of the Bible that tells about the Jews escaping slavery in Egypt.

Some white southerners did not want to lose the cheap labor supplied by African Americans. They used force to stop boats from carrying Exodusters up the Mississippi. Nevertheless, between 40,000 and 70,000 African Americans moved to Kansas by 1881.

Mexicanos

Easterners who moved to the Southwest met a large Spanish-speaking population there. As you recall, the United States had gained the Southwest through the Mexican War. Spanish-speaking southwesterners called themselves Mexicanos. White Americans who lived in the region were known as Anglos.

Most Mexicanos lived in small villages. They farmed and raised sheep for themselves and their families. A few wealthy Mexicanos were large landowners and merchants.

As growing numbers of Anglos settled in the Southwest, they acquired the best jobs and land. Often, Mexicanos found themselves working as low-paid laborers on Anglo farms. Many Mexicanos ended up living in poverty.

Some Mexicanos fought back. In New Mexico, in the 1880s, angry farmers known as "Las Gorras Blancas," or "White Caps," demanded fair treatment. They protested the fencing of their grazing lands by cutting the barbed wire fences of Anglo cattle ranchers.

Other Mexicanos united in political organizations. In 1894, Mexicanos in Arizona founded the **Hispanic-American Alliance.** It vowed "to protect and fight for the rights of Spanish Americans" through political action.

A Final Rush for Land

As settlers spread across the West, free land began to disappear. The last major land rush took place in Oklahoma. Several Indian nations lived there, but the government forced them to sell their land. The government then announced that farmers could claim free homesteads in Oklahoma. They could not stake their claims, however, until noon on April 22, 1889.

On the appointed day, as many as 100,000 land seekers lined up at the Oklahoma border. At noon, a gunshot rang out. The "boomers" charged into Oklahoma, but they found that others were already there.

Viewing HISTORY: Exodusters

In this photograph, Exodusters await the arrival of a steamboat to take them up the Mississippi River. Most Exodusters settled in Kansas. African American homesteaders also settled in Nebraska, Oklahoma, and other western states. ★ **Why did some white southerners try to prevent African Americans from moving west?**

These homesteaders posed for a family picture in front of their sod house. ★ **Why did people on the Plains build sod houses rather than wood houses?**

"Sooners" had sneaked into Oklahoma before the official opening and had staked out much of the best land.

Hard Life on the Plains

Farmers on the western plains faced many hardships. The first problem was shelter. Since wood was scarce on the Great Plains, many farmers built houses of sod—soil held together by grass roots. Rain was a serious problem for **sod houses.** One pioneer woman complained that her sod roof "leaked two days before a rain and for three days after."

Sodbusting

The fertile soil of the Great Plains was covered with a layer of thick sod that could crack wood or iron plows. A new sodbusting plow made of steel reached the market by 1877. It enabled **sodbusters,** as Plains farmers were called, to cut through the sod to the soil below.

Technology helped farmers in other ways. On the Great Plains, water often lay hundreds of feet underground. Farmers built windmills to pump the water to the surface. New reapers, threshing machines, and binders helped farmers to harvest crops.

Battling the climate

The dry climate was a constant threat. When too little rain fell, the crops shriveled and died. Dry weather also brought the threat of fire. In the strong winds that whipped across the land, a grass fire traveled "as fast as a horse could run."

The summers often brought swarms of grasshoppers that darkened the sky like a storm. Grasshoppers ate everything in their path—crops, food, tree bark, even clothing.

Pioneers dreaded the winters most. With few trees or hills to block the wind, icy gusts built huge snowdrifts. The deep snow buried farm animals and trapped families inside their homes. Wise sodbusters kept enough food on hand to help them survive during a long blizzard.

Women on the Plains

Women had to be strong to survive the hardships of life on the Great Plains. Since there were few stores, women made clothing, soap, candles, and other goods by hand. They also cooked and preserved food needed through the long winter.

Women served their families and their communities in many ways. They often helped with planting and harvesting. Most schoolteachers were women. When there were no doctors nearby, women treated the sick and injured.

Pioneer families usually lived miles apart. They relaxed by visiting with neighbors and gathering for church services. Picnics, dances, and weddings were eagerly awaited events. "Don't think that all of our time and thoughts were taken up with the problems of living," one woman wrote. "We were a social people."

FOR LIFE

| Critical Thinking | Managing Information | Communication | Maps, Charts, and Graphs |

Working in Teams

How Will I Use This Skill ?

By forming a team, you bring together the skills, knowledge, and experience of a number of people. A team can often produce better results in less time than an individual. In the classroom, on the playing field, or in the workplace, people often work together on a team to achieve some common goal.

LEARN the Skill

You can work as a member of a team by following these four steps:

❶ Organize a team and identify your goal.

❷ Identify the tasks needed to complete the goal. Sometimes, team members work together for the entire project. Other times, they divide the tasks, work separately, and then come together to share their results.

❸ The team members complete their tasks by working together, individually, or in smaller groups or committees.

❹ The team develops a presentation to share their work with others.

A marching band relies on teamwork.

PRACTICE the Skill

Using the information on pages 526–527, work in teams to learn about efforts to help farmers in the late 1800s.

❶ Organize three teams. One team will focus on the Grange, a second team will learn about the Farmers' Alliance, and a third team will study the Populist Party.

❷ The members of each team should read and take notes on their assigned topic.

❸ Each team should come together to discuss their findings and to make sure that everyone understands the material.

❹ Each team should prepare a presentation that includes a poster and a speech. Some members should prepare the poster, while others prepare the speech. Finally, one member will present and explain the poster to the class. Another team member will make the speech.

APPLY the Skill

Organize a team to research and present information on a current issue. Use newspapers, magazines, or the Internet as sources.

Biography — Mary Elizabeth Lease

Kansas lawyer Mary Elizabeth Lease won fame as an activist for the Farmers' Alliance and Populist party. She was a stirring, dynamic speaker. The way to fight falling grain prices, she told Kansan farmers, was to "raise less corn and more hell."
★ **Why were grain prices falling in the late 1800s?**

Crisis for farmers

Despite the harsh conditions, farmers began to thrive in the West. Before long, they were selling huge amounts of wheat and corn in the nation's growing cities and even in Europe.

Then, however, farmers faced a strange problem. The more they harvested, the less they earned. In 1881, a bushel of wheat sold for $1.19. By 1894, the price had plunged to 49 cents.

Western farmers were hurt most by low grain prices. They had borrowed money during good times to buy land and machinery. When wheat prices fell, they could not repay their debts. In the South, cotton farmers faced the same problem when the price of cotton dropped.

Farmers Take Action

As early as the 1860s, farmers began to work together. They learned that they could improve their condition through economic cooperation and political action.

The Grange

In 1867, farmers formed the **National Grange.** Grangers wanted to boost farm profits. They also wanted to reduce the rates that railroads charged for shipping grain.

Grangers helped farmers set up cooperatives. In a **cooperative,** a group of farmers pooled their money to buy seeds and tools wholesale. **Wholesale** means buying or selling something in large quantities at lower prices. Grangers built cooperative warehouses so that farmers could store grain cheaply while waiting for better selling prices.

Leaders of the Grange urged farmers to use their vote. In 1873, western and southern Grangers pledged to vote only for candidates who supported their aims. They elected officials who understood the farmers' problems.

As a result, several states passed laws limiting what could be charged for grain shipment and storage. Nevertheless, crop prices continued to drop. Farmers sank deeper and deeper into debt.

Farmers' Alliance

Another group, the **Farmers' Alliance,** joined the struggle in the 1870s. Like the Grange, the Alliance set up cooperatives and warehouses. The Farmers' Alliance spread from Texas through the South and into the Plains states. In the South, the Alliance tried to bring black and white farmers together. Alliance leaders also tried to join with factory workers and miners who were angry about their treatment by employers.

The Populist Party

In 1891, farmers and labor unions joined together to form the **Populist party.** At their first national convention, the Populists demanded government help with falling farm prices and regulation of railroad rates. They also called for an income tax, an eight-hour workday, and limits on immigration.

Another Populist party demand was "free silver." Populists wanted all silver mined in the West to be coined into money. They said that farm prices dropped because there was not enough money in circulation. Free silver would increase the money supply and make it easier for farmers to repay their debts.

Eastern bankers and factory owners disagreed. They argued that increasing the money supply would cause inflation, or runaway prices. Business people feared that inflation would wreck the economy.

Rise and Fall of the Populists

The Populist candidate for President in 1892 won one million votes. The next year, a severe depression brought the Populists new support. In 1894, they elected six senators and seven representatives to Congress.

Election of 1896

The Populists looked toward the election of 1896 with high hopes. Their program had been endorsed by one of the great orators of the age—**William Jennings Bryan.**

Bryan was a young Democratic congressman from Nebraska. He was called the "Great Commoner," because he championed the cause of common people. Like the Pop-

ulists, he believed that the nation needed to increase the supply of money. He often spoke out on behalf of the farmers.

At the Democratic convention in 1896, Bryan made a powerful speech. Delegates cheered wildly as he thundered against the rich and powerful and for free silver.

Both Democrats and Populists supported Bryan for President. However, bankers and business people feared that Bryan would ruin the economy. They supported **William McKinley,** the Republican candidate.

Bryan narrowly lost the election of 1896. He carried the South and West, but McKinley won the heavily populated states of the East.

Populist Party Fades

The Populist party broke up after 1896. One reason was that the Democrats adopted several Populist causes. Also, prosperity returned in the late 1890s. People worried less about railroad rates and free silver.

Still, the influence of the Populists lived on. In the years ahead, the eight-hour workday became standard for American workers. In 1913, the states ratified an income tax amendment. Perhaps most important, the Populists had helped to tie the West more tightly to the politics of the nation.

★ Section 5 Review ★

Recall
1. **Identify** (a) Mary Elizabeth Lease, (b) Homestead Act, (c) Exodusters, (d) Hispanic-American Alliance, (e) National Grange, (f) Farmers' Alliance, (g) Populist party, (h) William Jennings Bryan, (i) William McKinley.
2. **Define** (a) sod house, (b) sodbuster, (c) cooperative, (d) wholesale.

Comprehension
3. (a) Why did Exodusters move to the Plains? (b) How did the arrival of white settlers affect Mexicano farmers in the Southwest?

4. Describe three hardships that farmers faced on the Great Plains.
5. Identify and explain two goals that the National Grange and Populist party shared.

Critical Thinking and Writing
6. **Analyzing Primary Sources** An army general wrote to President Hayes, "Every river landing is blockaded by white enemies of the colored exodus." Explain in fuller detail the event to which the general was referring.
7. **Understanding Causes and Effects** How did the amount of grain that farmers produced affect the price of that grain? Explain.

★ ★

Activity Drawing a Political Cartoon You are a political commentator of the late 1800s. Draw a political cartoon to illustrate one of the problems that farmers faced during this period.

Chapter 19 Review and Activities

★ Sum It Up ★

Section 1 The Plains Indians
▶ On the Great Plains, Native American nations depended on the buffalo for survival.
▶ Plains Indians had a rich religious life and a well-ordered society.

Section 2 Miners and Railroaders
▶ With gold and silver strikes came a rush of miners and the building of boom towns.
▶ Transcontinental railroads brought rapid growth to the West.

Section 3 Ranchers and Cowhands
▶ In the 1860s and 1870s, cattle ranching spread across the Great Plains.
▶ The life of the cowhand was difficult and dangerous.

Section 4 A Way of Life Ends
▶ Native Americans struggled to keep their lands and their way of life.
▶ The United States government forced Indians to move onto reservations and to adopt new ways of life.

Section 5 The Farmers
▶ By 1900, despite many hardships, half a million farmers had settled on the Great Plains.
▶ To improve their condition, farmers united to form several economic and political organizations.

CD-ROM Review For additional review of the major ideas of Chapter 19, see **Guide to the Essentials of American History** or **Interactive Student Tutorial CD-ROM,** which contains interactive review activities, graphic organizers, and practice tests.

🗂 Reviewing the Chapter

Define These Terms
Match each term with the correct definition.

Column 1	Column 2
1. travois	a. a limited area set aside for a group of people
2. corral	b. an enclosure for livestock
3. reservation	c. early farmers on the Great Plains
4. sodbusters	d. sled pulled by a dog or horse
5. cooperative	e. an organization in which people pool their resources for more buying power

Explore the Main Ideas
1. Why was the buffalo very important to the Plains Indians?
2. How did the mining boom lead to the growth of western towns?
3. **(a)** What caused the cattle boom of the 1870s? **(b)** Why did the Cattle Kingdom decline in the 1880s?
4. How did life change for the Plains Indians between the 1860s and 1880s?
5. **(a)** What problems did sodbusters and other farmers face? **(b)** How did the Grange help farmers?

🗂 Geography Activity

Match the letters on the map with the following places:
1. Texas, **2.** Colorado, **3.** Nevada, **4.** Promontory Point, **5.** Omaha, **6.** San Francisco. **Interaction** What natural obstacles slowed the building of the first transcontinental railroad?

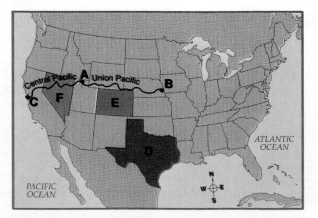

Critical Thinking and Writing

1. Understanding Chronology Place the following events in chronological order: **(a)** Dawes Act, **(b)** Fort Laramie Treaty, **(c)** Battle of Little Bighorn, **(d)** discovery of gold on Lakota land, **(e)** death of Sitting Bull, **(f)** fighting at Wounded Knee.

2. Linking Past and Present **(a)** What places are considered frontiers today? **(b)** How do these frontiers compare with the American frontiers of the 1800s?

3. Evaluating Information **(a)** What is inaccurate in the way movie westerns depict the life of the American cowhand? **(b)** Why do you think these inaccuracies exist?

4. Exploring Unit Themes Industrialization Why were easterners and westerners both eager to build transcontinental railroads?

Using Primary Sources

Hamilton Wicks was a "boomer" who staked a land claim during the Oklahoma land rush of April 1889. Years later, Wicks recalled the early days of Guthrie, Oklahoma—the town where he settled:

> **66** All that there was of Guthrie . . . on April 22, at 1:30 P.M., . . . was a water tank, a small station house, a shanty for the Wells Fargo Express, and a Government Land Office. . . . [By day's end] ten thousand people had [settled] upon a square mile of virgin prairie . . . and . . . [thousands] of white tents [had] suddenly appeared upon the face of the country. . . . Here indeed was a city laid out and populated in half a day. **99**

Source: "The Opening of Oklahoma" by Hamilton Wicks, 1889, in *Voices of America*, 1963.

Recognizing Points of View **(a)** What happened to Guthrie, Oklahoma, on April 22, 1889? **(b)** Why did the town change so suddenly?

ACTIVITY BANK

Interdisciplinary Activity

Exploring the Arts Working with other students, prepare a skit about the hopes and dreams of the Exodusters. Perform the skit for the class.

Career Skills Activity

Farmer Do research to find out about the challenges facing farmers today. In a written report, compare conditions that exist today with those of the 1890s.

Citizenship Activity

Writing a Petition Citizens can bring about change by submitting petitions with many signatures to government leaders. Write a petition that Helen Hunt Jackson might have composed in the 1880s. In your petition, list the actions that you would like the government to take to improve conditions for Native Americans.

Internet Activity

Use the Internet to find sites dealing with one of the Native American nations discussed in this chapter. Gather information related to these questions: **(a)** How do Native Americans work to preserve their culture today? **(b)** What special problems still face Native Americans? Present your findings in a written or oral presentation.

EYEWITNESS Journal

Write three different eyewitness reports of what happened at Wounded Knee on December 29, 1890. Write one description as a United States soldier, a second description as a Lakota Ghost Dancer, and a third description as a white settler in South Dakota. You may wish to do additional research before completing this assignment.

Chapter 20

The Rise of Industry and Unions 1865–1914

After the Civil War, American industry boomed. One reason for this tremendous growth was the rapid increase in the number of railways in the nation. Shrewd, energetic (and sometimes ruthless) business leaders created vast companies. A constant stream of new inventions also helped industry grow.

In the new economy, workers often faced long hours, unsafe conditions, and low pay. They soon banded together to win improvements in their lives. Slowly, organized labor became a powerful new force in American society.

Why Study History?

In 1859, Americans discovered a valuable new natural resource—oil! This "black gold" became a major source of fuel, and a major source of wealth for those individuals who controlled it. Today, we use oil and oil products every day. Limits on the world's oil supply make it an even more valuable resource. To focus on this connection, see the *Why Study History?* feature, "The Need for Oil Affects You," in this chapter.

American Events

1876
Alexander Graham Bell develops first telephone

1882
Standard Oil trust controls oil industry

1886
American Federation of Labor is formed

1865 1870 1875 1880 1885 1890

World Events

1871 World Event
Britain makes labor unions legal

1886 World Event
Electricity is introduced to Japan

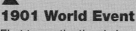

Viewing HISTORY

Business Was Booming!

In the 1880s, William Henry Jackson used a secret chemical process to create early colored photographs like this one. It shows a glass-roofed shopping arcade in Cleveland, Ohio. There, shoppers could buy anything from the latest fashions to new products such as the phonograph. In the late 1800s, new inventions, new industries, and new business practices helped the American economy to boom.

★ **Based on this picture, how was this arcade similar to a modern shopping mall? How was it different?**

●1894
Federal court rules
Pullman strike illegal

1911●
Triangle Shirtwaist
fire shows need for
safety measures

●1913
Henry Ford uses
assembly line to
mass produce
automobiles

1890	1895	1900	1905	1910	1915

▲
1901 World Event
First transatlantic wireless
message is sent

▲
1909 World Event
French aviator makes
first flight across English
Channel

Railroads and Industry

As You Read

Explore These Questions
- How did railroads expand after the Civil War?
- What effects did competition have on the railroad industry?
- How did railroads spur the growth of industry?

Define
- network
- consolidate
- rebate
- pool

Identify
- George Westinghouse
- George Pullman
- Cornelius Vanderbilt
- James Hill

SETTING the Scene In 1873, Americans began singing a new folk song. "John Henry" tells the story of a legendary African American railroad worker who drives steel spikes into rock with a hammer. When the boss introduces a steam-powered drill, John Henry vows:

> 66 Before I'll let that steam drill beat me down
> I'll die with my hammer in my hand. 99

True to his word, John Henry dies after beating the steam drill in a contest.

Railroad workers loved singing of John Henry's victory over the machine. Still, nothing could slow down the nation's amazing industrial growth. Of the many factors spurring this growth, none was more important than the railroad.

A Railroad Network

The Civil War showed the importance of railroads. Railroads carried troops and supplies to the battlefields. They also moved raw materials to factories. After the war, railroad companies began to build new lines all over the country. (See page 509.)

Connecting lines

Early railroads were short lines that served local communities. Many lines ran for no more than 50 miles (80 km). When passengers and freight reached the end of one line, they had to move to a train on a different line to continue their journey.

Even if the lines had been connected, the problem would not have been solved. Different lines used rails of different gauges, or widths. As a result, the trains from one line could not run on the tracks of another line. In general, the tracks of northern and southern rail lines used different gauges .

In 1886, railroads in the South decided to adopt the northern gauge. On May 30, southern railroads stopped running so that work could begin. Using crowbars and sledgehammers, crews worked from dawn to dusk to move the rails a few inches farther apart. When they had finished, some 13,000 miles (20,800 km) of track had been changed.

Once the track was standardized, American railroads formed a **network,** or system of connected lines. The creation of a rail network brought benefits to shippers. Often, rail companies arranged for freight cars on one line to use the tracks of another. For example, goods loaded in Chicago could stay on the same car all the way to New York, instead of being transferred from one car to another. As a result, the shipper had to pay only one fare for the whole distance.

New rails knit the sprawling nation together. By 1900, there were more miles of tracks in the United States than in Europe and Russia combined.

Other improvements

To simplify train schedules, the railroad companies set up a system of standard time zones in 1883. Before that, each town kept its own time, based on the position of the sun. Towns in Illinois, for example, had 27 different local times! The new system divided the nation into four time zones: Eastern, Central, Mountain, and Pacific. Every place within the same time zone observed the same time.

New inventions helped make railway travel safer and faster. In 1869, **George Westinghouse** began selling his new air brake. On early trains, each railroad car had its own brakes and its own brake operator. If different cars stopped at different times, serious accidents could result. Westinghouse's air brake allowed a locomotive engineer to stop all the railroad cars at once.

The air brake increased safety and allowed for longer, faster trains. By 1900, a passenger could travel from New York to San Francisco in only six days, rather than months.

Long distance travel also became more comfortable. In 1864, **George Pullman** de-

signed a railroad sleeping car. Pullman cars had convertible berths as well as lavatories. Rail lines also added dining cars. Porters, conductors, and waiters attended to the needs of passengers. A national magazine described the comforts of a rail trip in 1872:

66 From Chicago to Omaha your train will carry a dining car. . . . You sit at little tables which comfortably accommodate four persons; you order your breakfast, dinner, or supper from a bill of fare which contains a surprising number of dishes; you eat from snow-white linen . . . admirable cooked food, and pay a modest price. 99

Consolidation

As railroads grew, they looked for ways to operate more efficiently. Many companies began to **consolidate,** or combine. Larger

Viewing HISTORY — A Nation Linked by Rail

By the late 1800s, a complex network of rail lines linked the nation. Freight trains, like the one below, hauled tons of coal and other resources needed by industry. Passenger lines advertised a new level of elegance and comfort (right).
★ How were the nation's local rail lines transformed into a network?

Viewing HISTORY · Farmers vs. Railroads

In this 1873 cartoon, Thomas Nast portrayed railroads as a monster snaking through American farmland. A bearded farmer bravely opposes the monster. ★ **The building shown in the background is the Capitol building. Why do you think Nast showed the Capitol in the monster's coils?**

Building New Lines

Railroad builders raced to create thousands of miles of new tracks. In the years after Leland Stanford hammered in the golden spike in 1869, Americans built three more transcontinental railroads. **James Hill,** a Canadian-born railroad baron, finished the last major cross-country line in 1893. (See the map on page 510.) His Great Northern Railway wound from Duluth, Minnesota, to Everett, Washington.

Unlike other rail lines, the Great Northern was built without financial aid from Congress. To make his railroad succeed, Hill had to turn a profit from the start. He encouraged farmers and ranchers to settle near his railroad. He gave seed to farmers and helped them buy equipment. He even imported special bulls to breed hardier cattle. Not only was Hill's policy generous, it made good business sense.

Abuses

With builders rushing to share in the profits of the railroad boom, overbuilding occurred. Soon, there were too many rail lines in some parts of the country. Between Atlanta and St. Louis, for example, 20 different lines competed for business. There was not nearly enough rail traffic to keep all these lines busy.

Reducing competition

In the West, especially, there were too few people for the railroads to make a profit. Competition was fierce. Rate wars broke out as rival railroads slashed their fares to win customers. Usually, all the companies lost money as a result.

To win new business or keep old business, big railroads secretly offered **rebates,** or discounts, to their biggest customers. This

companies bought up smaller ones or forced them out of business. The Pennsylvania Railroad, for example, consolidated 73 companies into its system.

Tough-minded business people led the drive for consolidation. The most powerful of these "railroad barons" was **Cornelius Vanderbilt.** The son of a poor farmer, Vanderbilt earned his fortune in steamship lines. He then began to buy up railroad lines in New York State.

Vanderbilt sometimes used ruthless tactics to force smaller owners to sell to him. In the early 1860s, he decided to buy the New York Central Railroad. The owners refused to sell. Vanderbilt then announced that New York Central passengers would not be allowed to transfer to his trains. With their passengers stranded and business dropping sharply, the New York Central owners gave in and sold their line to Vanderbilt.

Vanderbilt then bought up most of the lines between Chicago and Buffalo. By the time of his death in 1877, his companies controlled 4,500 miles (7,200 km) of track and linked New York City to the Great Lakes region.

Other consolidations were soon underway. Before long, the major railroads of the nation were organized into systems directed by a handful of powerful men.

practice forced many small companies out of business. It also hurt small shippers, such as farmers, who still had to pay the full price.

Railroad barons soon realized that cut-throat competition was hurting even their large lines. They looked for ways to end the competition. One method was pooling. In a **pool,** several railroad companies agreed to divide up business in an area. They then fixed their prices at a high level.

High prices for farmers

Railroad rebates and pools angered small farmers in the South and the West. Both practices kept shipping prices high for them. Indeed, rates were so high that at times farmers burned their crop for fuel rather than ship it to market.

As you read in Chapter 19, many farmers joined the Populist party. Populists called for government regulation of rail rates. Congress and several states passed laws regulating railroad companies. However, the laws did not end abuses. Railroad barons bribed officials to keep the laws from being enforced.

Spurring Economic Growth

Despite their problems, railroads made possible the rapid growth of industry after 1865. As railroads expanded, they stimulated the whole economy.

Building rail lines created thousands of jobs. Steelworkers turned millions of tons of iron into steel for tracks and engines. Lumberjacks cut down whole forests to supply wood for railroad ties. Miners sweated in dusty mine shafts digging coal to fuel railroad engines. The railroad companies themselves employed thousands of workers. They laid tracks, built trestles across rivers, and carved tunnels through mountains.

Because they were so large, railroads also pioneered new ways of managing business. Rail companies created special departments for shipping and accounting and for servicing equipment. Expert managers headed each department, while chains of command ensured that the organization ran smoothly. Other big businesses soon copied these management techniques.

Railroads opened every corner of the country to settlement and growth. They brought people together, especially in the West. New businesses sprang up, and towns sprouted where rail lines crossed. With rail lines in place, the United States was ready to become the greatest industrial nation the world had ever seen.

★ Section 1 Review ★

Recall

1. **Identify** (a) George Westinghouse, (b) George Pullman, (c) Cornelius Vanderbilt, (d) James Hill.

2. **Define** (a) network, (b) consolidate, (c) rebate, (d) pool.

Comprehension

3. Describe three changes that took place in the railroad industry after the Civil War.

4. (a) What methods did big railroads use to win and keep business? (b) How did these practices affect small businesses and farmers?

5. List three ways that railroads spurred the growth of industry.

Critical Thinking and Writing

6. **Synthesizing Information** After the Civil War, railroads consolidated as large railroad companies took over smaller ones. (a) What were the advantages of consolidation? (b) What were the disadvantages?

7. **Linking Past and Present** Are railroads as important today as they were in the 1800s? Why or why not?

Activity **Asking Questions** "Tonight's special guest: railroad baron Cornelius Vanderbilt. The phone lines are now open." Jot down three or four questions you would ask Vanderbilt if he appeared on a talk show. The questions may concern his goals, his business practices, and his achievements.

Big Business

★★

As You Read

Explore These Questions
- Why did the steel industry become important after the Civil War?
- What new ways of doing business did Americans develop?
- What were the arguments for and against the growth of giant corporations?

Define
- vertical integration
- corporation
- stock
- dividend
- trust
- monopoly
- free enterprise system

Identify
- John D. Rockefeller
- Bessemer process
- Andrew Carnegie
- J. Pierpont Morgan
- Standard Oil Company
- Sherman Antitrust Act

SETTING the Scene On a February day in 1865, an unusual auction was held. The owners of an Ohio oil refinery stood toe to toe, the only two people in the room. Each was bidding to buy the other's share in the company.

Bidding opened at $500. The price swiftly jumped higher and higher. Finally, the bid reached $72,500. "I'll go no higher, John," said one of the men. "The business is yours." John paid the $72,500 and became sole owner of the company. It was a smart buy. When he died more than 70 years later, **John D. Rockefeller** was a multimillionaire who dominated the entire American oil industry.

Rockefeller was one of a new breed of American business leaders in the late 1800s. They were bold, imaginative—and sometimes ruthless. During the next 50 years, these leaders shaped the nation's emerging businesses and industries.

Growth of the American Steel Industry

The growth of railroads after the Civil War fueled the growth of the steel industry. Early trains ran on iron rails that wore out quickly. Railroad owners knew that steel rails were much stronger and not as likely to rust as iron. Steel, however, was costly and difficult to make.

A new way to make steel

In the 1850s, William Kelly in the United States and Henry Bessemer in England each discovered a new way to make steel. The **Bessemer process,** as it came to be called, enabled steelmakers to produce strong steel at a lower cost. As a result, railroads began to lay steel rails.

Other industries also took advantage of the cheaper steel. Manufacturers made steel nails, screws, needles, and other items. Steel girders supported the great weight of the new "skyscrapers."

Steel mills spring up

Steel mills sprang up in cities throughout the Midwest. Pittsburgh became the steel-making capital of the nation. Nearby coal mines and good transportation helped Pittsburgh's steel mills to thrive.

The thriving steel mills brought jobs and prosperity to Pittsburgh and other steel-towns. They also caused problems. The mills belched thick black smoke that turned the air gray. Soot blanketed houses, trees, and streets. Waste polluted local rivers.

Andrew Carnegie

Many Americans made fortunes in the steel industry. Richest of all was a Scottish immigrant, **Andrew Carnegie.** Carnegie's ideas on how to make money—and how to spend it—had a wide influence.

Carnegie's career reads like a history of American industry. As a child, he went to work in a textile mill. Later, he became a telegraph operator. When the railroad boom started, Carnegie got a job with the Pennsylvania Railroad.

Traveling in England in the 1870s, Carnegie visited a factory and saw the Bessemer process at work. When he returned to the United States, he built a steel mill at Homestead, Pennsylvania, south of Pittsburgh. His friendships with railroad owners helped him win contracts for the steel he manufactured.

Controlling the steel industry

Within a short time, Carnegie was earning huge profits from his steel mill. He used the money to buy out rivals. He also bought iron mines, railroad and steamship lines, and warehouses.

Soon, Carnegie controlled all phases of the steel industry—from mining iron ore to shipping finished steel. Acquiring control of all the steps required to change raw materials into finished products is called **vertical integration.** Vertical integration gave Carnegie a great advantage over other steel companies.

In 1892, Carnegie combined all of his businesses into the Carnegie Steel Company. By 1900, it was turning out more steel than all of Great Britain.

The "gospel of wealth"

Like other business owners, Carnegie drove his workers hard, Still, he believed that the rich had a duty to help the poor and improve society. He called this idea the "gospel of wealth." He wrote:

> 66 Wealth, passing through the hands of the few, can be made a much more powerful force for the elevation of our race than if it had been distributed in small sums to the people themselves. 99

Carnegie himself gave millions to charities. He donated $60 million to build public libraries in towns all over the country. After selling Carnegie Steel in 1901, he spent his time and money helping people.

Rise of Corporations

Before the railroad boom, nearly every American town had its own small factories. They produced goods for people in the area. By the late 1800s, however, big factories were producing goods more cheaply than small factories could. Railroads distributed these goods to nationwide markets. As demand for local goods fell, many small factories closed. Big factories then increased their output.

Expanding factories needed capital, or money, for investment. Factory owners used the capital to buy raw materials, pay workers, and cover shipping and advertising costs. To raise capital, Americans adopted new ways of organizing their businesses.

Biography   Andrew Carnegie

As a teenager, Andrew Carnegie worked in a textile mill for $1.20 a week. By the age of 50, he was the nation's "Steel King." Carnegie believed that the rich had a right to make money, and a duty to spend it for the public good. He gave away millions to schools, libraries, and the cause of world peace.
★ **What business methods did Carnegie use to build his steel company?**

Many expanding businesses became corporations. A **corporation** is a business that is owned by investors. A corporation sells **stock,** or shares in the business, to investors, who are known as stockholders. The corporation can use the money invested by stockholders to build a new factory or buy new machines.

In return for their investment, stockholders hope to receive **dividends,** or shares of a corporation's profit. To protect their investment, stockholders elect a board of directors to run the corporation.

Thousands of people bought stock in corporations. Stockholders faced fewer risks than owners of private businesses. If a private business goes bankrupt, the owner must pay all the debts of the business. By law, stockholders cannot be held responsible for a corporation's debts.

Banks and Industry

In the years after the Civil War, corporations attracted large amounts of capital from American investors. Corporations also borrowed millions of dollars from banks. These loans helped American industry grow at a rapid pace. At the same time, the banks made huge profits.

The most powerful banker of the late 1800s was **J. Pierpont Morgan.** Morgan's influence was not limited to banking. He used his banking profits to gain control of major corporations.

During economic hard times in the 1890s, Morgan and other bankers invested in the stock of troubled corporations. As large stockholders, they easily won seats on the boards of directors. They then adopted policies that reduced competition and ensured big profits. "I like a little competition, but I like combination more," Morgan used to say.

Between 1894 and 1898, Morgan gained control of most of the nation's major rail lines. He then began to buy up steel companies, including Carnegie Steel, and merge them into a single large corporation. By 1901, Morgan had become head of United States Steel Company. It was the first American business worth more than $1 billion.

The Oil Industry

Industry could not have expanded so quickly in the United States without the nation's rich supply of natural resources. Iron ore was plentiful, especially in the Mesabi Range of Minnesota. Pennsylvania, West Virginia, and the Rocky Mountains had large deposits of coal. The Rockies also contained minerals such as gold, silver, and copper. Vast forests provided lumber for building.

In 1859, Americans discovered a valuable new resource—oil. Drillers near Titusville, Pennsylvania, made the nation's first oil strike. An oil boom quickly followed. Hundreds of prospectors rushed to western Pennsylvania ready to drill wells in search of a "gusher."

Rockefeller and Standard Oil

Among those who came to the Pennsylvania oil fields was young John D. Rockefeller. Rockefeller, however, did not rush to drill for oil. He knew that oil had little value until it was refined, or purified, to make kerosene. Kerosene was used as a fuel in stoves and lamps.

The son of a humble New York peddler, Rockefeller moved with his family to Ohio when he was 14. At 23, he invested in his first oil refinery.

Rockefeller believed that competition was wasteful. He used the profits from his refinery to buy up other refineries. He then combined the companies into the **Standard Oil Company** of Ohio.

Rockefeller was a shrewd businessman. He was always trying to improve the quality of his oil. He also did whatever he could to get rid of competition. Standard Oil slashed

Connections With Arts

J. Pierpont Morgan used much of his wealth to collect manuscripts and rare books—some of them more than 400 years old. By 1906, his collection could no longer fit into his private library. Morgan then had a separate building constructed. After Morgan's death, the Pierpont Morgan Library in New York City was opened to the public.

Why Study History?

Because the Need for Oil Affects You

★ ★

Historical Background

In 1859, drillers struck oil in Pennsylvania. At the time, most refined oil ended up as kerosene for lamps. Factories also used oil to lubricate machines.

By the early 1900s, new inventions like the automobile created a demand for gasoline—another oil product. Before long, filling stations sprang up in cities and towns. Oil was fueling a growing nation.

Connections to Today

You know that we use oil as fuel for cars, buses, airplanes, lawn mowers, and heaters. Did you also know that manufacturers use petroleum to make plastics, cloth, paints, and medicines? Oil also fuels generators that supply electricity.

This valuable resource is also limited. The world's supply of petroleum could eventually run out. Scientists are working to develop alternate sources of energy.

Connections to You

How would your future change if the use of oil was restricted? High fuel costs might limit your ability to travel. Expensive heating oil might force you to live in a colder home. Prices for other items would rise, too, as factories paid higher prices for oil.

Such extreme shortages are not likely to happen soon. However, saving energy in small ways can help stretch our precious oil resources. Here are some things you can do:
- Recycle plastics and other products.
- Turn off lights when you leave a room.
- Avoid wasting hot water.
- Whenever possible, take the bus or train.

1. **Comprehension** **(a)** How was oil used in the late 1800s? **(b)** List three ways you use oil and petroleum products.
2. **Critical Thinking** Today, the United States imports much of its oil supply from other countries. Why do you think many Americans worry about dependence on foreign oil?

★Activity **Writing an Advertisement** List the qualities that you would want a new fuel source to have. Then, create a name and write an advertisement for your new fuel.

Petroleum is used to make hundreds of products, from plastic combs to pool floats.

Past

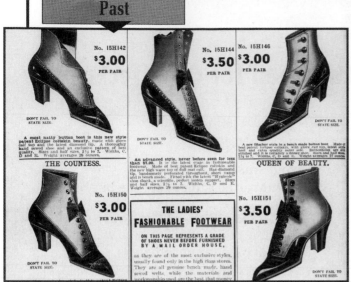

Present

Shopping at Home

In the late 1800s, manufacturers pioneered new ways to sell their products nationwide. Companies like Sears, Roebuck used mail order catalogs (left) to sell goods to isolated western farmers. Today, Americans can turn on their televisions and instantly order anything from jewelry to cookware (right). ★ **What are the advantages and disadvantages of shopping at home?**

its prices to drive rivals out of business. It pressured its customers not to deal with other oil companies. Rockefeller even persuaded railroad companies eager for his business to grant rebates to Standard Oil. Lower shipping costs gave Rockefeller an important edge over his competitors.

Creating a trust

To tighten his hold over the oil industry, Rockefeller formed the Standard Oil trust in 1882. A **trust** is a group of corporations run by a single board of directors.

Stockholders in dozens of smaller oil companies turned over their stock to Standard Oil. In return, they got stock in the newly created trust. The trust stock paid the stockholders high dividends. However, the stockholders gave up their right to choose the board of directors. The board of Standard Oil, headed by Rockefeller, managed all the companies, which before had been rivals.

The Standard Oil trust created a monopoly in the oil industry. A **monopoly** controls all or nearly all the business of an industry. The Standard Oil trust controlled 95 percent of all oil refining in the United States.

Other businesses followed Rockefeller's lead. They set up trusts and tried to build monopolies. By the late 1890s, monopolies and trusts controlled some of the nation's most important industries.

Big Business: Two Viewpoints

Some Americans charged that the leaders of giant corporations were abusing the free enterprise system. In a **free enterprise system,** businesses are owned by private citizens. Owners decide what products to make, how much to produce, where to sell products, and what prices to charge. Companies compete to win customers by making the best product at the lowest price.

Opposition to trusts

Critics argued that trusts and monopolies reduced competition. Without competition, there was no reason for companies to keep prices low or to improve their products. It was also hard for new companies to start up and compete against powerful trusts. Workers, moreover, often felt that large corporations treated them badly.

Critics were also upset about the political influence of trusts. Leaders of big business were richer than Americans had ever been before. Some people worried that millionaires were using their wealth to buy favors from elected officials. The *Chicago Tribune* warned that "liberty and monopoly cannot live together." John Reagan, a member of Congress from Texas, said:

> 66 There were no beggars till Vanderbilts and . . . Morgans . . . shaped the actions of Congress and molded the purposes of government. Then the few became fabulously wealthy, the many wretchedly poor. 99

Under pressure from the public, the government slowly moved toward controlling giant corporations. Congress approved the **Sherman Antitrust Act** in 1890. The act banned the formation of trusts and monopolies. However, it was too weak to be effective. Some state governments passed laws to regulate business, but the corporations usually sidestepped them. Later reformers began to demand even stronger measures.

Support for trusts

Naturally, business leaders defended trusts. Andrew Carnegie published articles arguing that too much competition ruined businesses and put people out of work. In an article titled "Wealth and Its Uses," he wrote:

> 66 It will be a great mistake for the community to shoot the millionaires, for they are the bees that make the most honey, and contribute most to the hive even after they have gorged themselves full. 99

Defenders of big business argued that the growth of giant corporations brought lower production costs, lower prices, higher wages, and a better quality of life for millions of Americans. By 1900, Americans enjoyed the highest standard of living in the world. Innovative business leaders also helped usher in a new age of technology and invention that revolutionized American life.

★ Section 2 Review ★

Recall

1. **Identify** (a) John D. Rockefeller, (b) Bessemer process, (c) Andrew Carnegie, (d) J. Pierpont Morgan, (e) Standard Oil Company, (f) Sherman Antitrust Act.
2. **Define** (a) vertical integration, (b) corporation, (c) stock, (d) dividend, (e) trust, (f) monopoly, (g) free enterprise system.

Comprehension

3. Name three uses for cheap steel in the 1800s.
4. Why did many American businesses become corporations?

5. Why did some Americans think that big business threatened the free enterprise system?

Critical Thinking and Writing

6. **Understanding Causes and Effects** (a) What were two causes of the growth of the steel industry? (b) What were two effects?
7. **Applying Information** Andrew Carnegie once said of people who held onto their fortunes, "The man who dies thus rich, dies disgraced." (a) Restate Carnegie's meaning in your own words. (b) Did Carnegie carry out this philosophy in his own life? Explain.

★ ★

Activity Creating a Business Plan You are a clever business owner in the late 1800s. Describe the business you would choose to build. Then, outline a plan showing how you would go about doing it.

3 A Flood of Inventions

As You Read

Explore These Questions
- What inventions improved communication in the 1800s?
- Why was Menlo Park called an "invention factory"?
- How did Henry Ford revolutionize the automobile industry?

Define
- assembly line
- mass production

Identify
- Cyrus Field
- Alexander Graham Bell
- Thomas Edison
- Jan Matzeliger
- Gustavus Swift
- George Eastman
- Henry Ford
- Orville and Wilbur Wright

 SETTING the Scene Josephine Cochrane was annoyed. The wife of an Illinois politician, she hosted many elegant dinners. Her fine china, though, often broke when being washed.

Cochrane took a hose, some wire, a motor, and a large copper boiler to the woodshed. There, she built the first automatic dishwasher. Soon, Cochrane was selling her machine to restaurants. She patented her invention in 1886.

A flood of invention swept the United States in the late 1800s. By the 1890s, Americans were patenting 21,000 new inventions a year. These inventions helped industry to grow and become more efficient. New devices also made daily life easier in many American homes.

Advanced Communication

Some remarkable new devices filled the need for faster communication. The telegraph had been in use since 1844. (See Chapter 14.) It helped people around the nation stay in touch. It also helped business. For example, a steelmaker in Pittsburgh could instantly order iron ore from a mine in Minnesota.

Transatlantic cable

The telegraph speeded communication within the United States. It still took weeks, however, for news from Europe to arrive by boat.

In 1866, **Cyrus Field** ran an underwater telegraph cable across the Atlantic Ocean. Field marveled at his success:

66 In five months...the cable had been manufactured, shipped... stretched across the Atlantic, and was sending messages...swift as lightning from continent to continent. 99

Field's transatlantic cable brought the United States and Europe closer together.

The telephone

Morse and Field used a dot and dash code to send messages over telegraph wires. Meanwhile, **Alexander Graham Bell,** a Scottish-born teacher of the deaf, was trying to transmit sound.

In March 1876, Bell was ready to test his "talking machine." Before the test, Bell accidentally spilled battery acid on himself. His assistant, Thomas Watson, was in another

Alexander Graham Bell's telephone

room. Bell spoke into the machine, "Watson, come here, I want you!" Watson rushed to Bell's side. "Mr. Bell," he cried, "I heard every word you said, distinctly!" The telephone worked.

Bell's telephone aroused little interest at first. Scientists praised the invention. Most people, however, saw it as a toy. Bell offered to sell the telephone to the Western Union Telegraph Company for $100,000. The company refused—a costly mistake. In the end, the telephone earned Bell millions.

Bell formed the Bell Telephone Company in 1877. By 1885, he had sold more than 300,000 phones, mostly to businesses. The telephone speeded up the pace of business even more. Instead of having to go to a telegraph office, people could find out about prices or supplies simply by talking on the telephone.

Thomas Edison

In an age of invention, **Thomas Edison** was right at home. In 1876, he opened a research laboratory in Menlo Park, New Jersey. There, Edison boasted that he and his 15 co-workers set out to create "minor" inventions every 10 days and "a big thing every 6 months or so."

The "invention factory"

The key to Edison's success lay in his approach. He turned inventing into a system. Teams of experts refined Edison's ideas and translated them into practical inventions. Menlo Park became an "invention factory."

The results were amazing. Edison became known as the "Wizard of Menlo Park" for inventing the light bulb, the phonograph, and hundreds of other devices.

One invention from Edison's laboratory launched a new industry—the movies. In 1893, Edison introduced his first machine for showing moving pictures. Viewers watched short films by looking through a peephole in a cabinet. Later, Edison developed a motion picture projector, making it possible for many people to watch a film at the same time. By 1905, thousands of silent movie houses called nickelodeons were opening in cities across the United States.

▲ Electric light bulb   ▲ Phonograph

*B*iography — Thomas Alva Edison

A poor student, Thomas Edison grew up to invent the light bulb, the phonograph and dozens of other devices. The photo above was taken after Edison went without sleep for three days working on his phonograph. At last, he heard his own voice reciting "Mary Had a Little Lamb." ★ **Edison said, "Genius is one percent inspiration and ninety-nine percent perspiration." What do you think he meant?**

Electric power

One of Edison's most important creations was the electric power plant. Edison built the first power plant in New York City in 1882. He wired the business district first in hopes of attracting investors. With the flip of a switch, Edison set the district ablaze in light.

Within a year, Edison's power plant was supplying electricity to homes as well as businesses. Soon, more power plants were built. Factories replaced steam-powered engines with safer, quieter electric engines. Electric energy powered streetcars in cities and lighted countless homes. The modern age of electricity had begun.

Skills FOR LIFE

Critical Thinking	Managing Information	Communication	Maps, Charts, and Graphs

Using a Computerized Card Catalog

How Will I Use This Skill?

Whether you are hunting for information on the development of the automobile, or the newest bestseller, you may find yourself searching in a library. Today, most libraries are equipped with computerized catalogs to assist you during your search.

LEARN the Skill

❶ Decide whether your search should start with a specific author, a title of a publication, or a subject.

❷ Use the main menu to start your search. The main menu presents you with a list of options. From this list, choose the path to begin your search: Author, Title, or Subject.

❸ Narrow your search. Follow the instructions on the computer screen to locate the books you need.

❹ Select books that might be helpful. Write down the call numbers, titles, and authors of the books. The call numbers will allow you to find the books on the library shelves.

PRACTICE the Skill

Using the sample screens to the right, practice searching a typical library computer catalog.

❶ Review screens 1 and 2. Which option has been chosen to begin the library search: Author, Title, or Subject?

❷ Look at Screen 1, Main Menu. Which number would you type to begin the search documented on these diagrams?

❸ Look at Screens 2 and 3. Identify the topic chosen for research. On Screen 3, note the books available on this topic.

❹ Look at Screen 4. What are the title and call number of the chosen book?

APPLY the Skill

Use the computerized catalog in your school or community library to research the history of any invention discussed in this chapter.

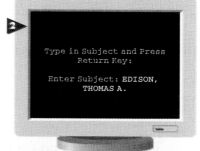

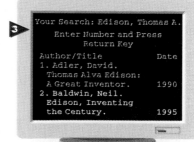

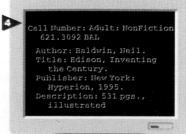

A Rush of Technology

Almost every day, it seemed, American inventors were creating new devices that made business more efficient and life more pleasant. The United States became known as the land of invention.

Inventions by African Americans

African Americans contributed to the flood of inventions. In 1872, Elijah McCoy created a special device that oiled engines automatically. It was widely used on railroad engines and in factories. Granville T. Woods found a way to send telegraph messages between moving railroad trains.

Jan Matzeliger invented a machine that could perform almost all the steps in shoemaking that had been done before by hand. Patented in 1883, Matzeliger's machine was eventually used in shoe factories everywhere.

Many African American inventors had trouble getting patents for their inventions. Even so, in 1900, an assistant in the patent office compiled a list of patents issued to African American inventors. The list, together with drawings and plans of all the inventions, filled four huge volumes.

Refrigeration

In the 1880s, **Gustavus Swift** came up with an idea that transformed the American diet. Swift introduced refrigeration to the meatpacking industry. In the past, cattle, pigs, and chickens had been raised and sold

A Time of Invention

Inventor	Date	Invention
Elisha Otis	1852	passenger elevator brake
George Pullman	1864	sleeping car
George Westinghouse	1869	air brake
Elijah McCoy	1872	automatic engine-oiling machine
Andrew S. Hallidie	1873	cable streetcar
Stephen Dudley Field	1874	electric streetcar
Alexander Graham Bell	1876	telephone
Thomas Alva Edison	1877	phonograph
Anna Baldwin	1878	milking machine
Thomas Alva Edison	1879	first practical incandescent light bulb
James Ritty	1879	cash register
Jan E. Matzeliger	1883	shoemaking machine
Lewis E. Waterman	1884	fountain pen
Granville T. Woods	1887	automatic air brake
Charles and J. Frank Duryea	1893	gasoline-powered car
King C. Gillette	1895	safety razor with throwaway blades
John Thurman	1899	motor-driven vacuum cleaner
Leo H. Baekeland	1909	improved plastic

Chart Skills New inventions transformed daily life in the United States. They also helped the American economy grow.

1. **Comprehension** (a) What did George Westinghouse invent? In what year? (b) Who improved on Westinghouse's invention? In what year?

2. **Critical Thinking** (a) Which of these inventions made transportation easier? (b) Which of these inventions might be found in a home today?

The Henry Ford Museum

Not far from his Detroit auto plant, Henry Ford built a place to display "every household article, every kind of vehicle, every sort of tool." Today at the Henry Ford Museum, you can explore the world's largest transportation collection, from canoes to giant locomotives to classic cars. You can also see devices you might have had in your home 100 years ago.

★ **To learn more about this historic site, write:** Henry Ford Museum, P.O. Box 1970, Dearborn, MI 48121.

Early American washing machine ➤

locally. Meat spoiled quickly, so it could not be shipped over distances.

Swift set up a meatpacking plant in Chicago, a railroad hub midway between the cattle ranches of the West and the cities of the East. Cattle were shipped by train to Chicago. At Swift's plant, the animals were slaughtered and carved up into sides of beef. The fresh beef was quickly loaded onto refrigerated railroad cars and carried to market. Even in summer, Swift sent fresh meat to eastern cities. As a result, Americans began to eat more meat.

Inventions for home and office

New inventions also affected life at home and in the office. Christopher Sholes perfected the typewriter in 1868. This invention made office work easier.

In 1888, **George Eastman** introduced the lightweight Kodak camera. No longer did photography require bulky equipment and chemicals. The cost was only $25, including a roll of film. After 100 snaps of the shutter, the owner returned the camera to Kodak. The company developed the pictures and sent them back, along with a reloaded camera. Taking pictures became a popular pastime.

The Automobile

No single person invented the automobile. Europeans had produced motorized vehicles as early as the 1860s. Several Americans began building cars in the 1890s. Still, only the wealthy could afford them.

Ford and mass production

It was **Henry Ford,** with his "motor car for the multitude," who made the auto a part of everyday American life. In 1913, Ford introduced the **assembly line.** In this method of production, workers are stationed in one place as products edge along on a moving belt. At Ford's auto plant, one group of workers would bolt seats onto a passing car frame, the next would add the roof, and so on. The assembly line greatly reduced the time needed to build a car. Other industries soon adopted it.

Ford's assembly line allowed mass production of cars. **Mass production** means making large quantities of a product quickly and cheaply. Because of mass production, Ford could sell his cars at a lower price than other auto makers.

Cars become popular

At first, most people laughed at the "horseless carriage." Some thought automobiles were dangerous. A backfiring auto engine could scare a horse right off the road. Towns and villages across the nation posted signs: "No horseless carriages allowed."

Slowly, attitudes toward the automobile changed. No other means of travel offered such freedom. As prices dropped, more people could afford to buy cars. In 1900, only 8,000 Americans owned cars. By 1917, more than 4.5 million autos were chugging along American roads.

Automobiles were at first regarded as machines for men only. Auto makers soon realized, however, that women could drive—and buy—cars. Companies began to direct advertisements to women, stressing the comfort and usefulness of automobiles. Driving gave women greater independence.

A hit song from 1905 shows the growing popularity of the automobile. "In My Merry Oldsmobile" is a love story about a boy, a girl, and a car:

> 66 Johnnie Steel has an Oldsmobile;
>   He loves a dear little girl:
> She is the queen of his gas machine;
>   She has his heart in a whirl.
> Now when they go for a spin, you know,
>   She tries to learn the auto, so
> He lets her steer while he gets her ear
>   And whispers soft and low:
>
> 'Come away with me Lucile,
>   In my merry Oldsmobile....' 99

The Airplane

Meanwhile, two Ohio bicycle mechanics, **Orville and Wilbur Wright,** were experimenting with another new method of transportation—flying. After trying out hundreds of designs, the Wright brothers tested their first "flying machine" on December 17, 1903. At Kitty Hawk, North Carolina, Orville took off. The plane, powered by a small gasoline engine, stayed in the air for 12 seconds and flew a distance of 120 feet (37m).

The Wrights' flight did not attract much attention. Most people saw little use for flying machines. Slowly, however, air pioneers built better planes and made longer flights. In time, the airplane changed the world.

★ Section 3 Review ★

Recall

1. **Identify** (a) Cyrus Field, (b) Alexander Graham Bell, (c) Thomas Edison, (d) Jan Matzeliger, (e) Gustavus Swift, (f) George Eastman, (g) Henry Ford, (h) Orville and Wilbur Wright.
2. **Define** (a) assembly line, (b) mass production.

Comprehension

3. Describe two inventions that transformed communication in the 1800s.

4. Why was Edison's electric power plant important?
5. How did the assembly line change auto making?

Critical Thinking and Writing

6. **Drawing Conclusions** Why might inventors be more creative working in an "invention factory" than working on their own?
7. **Ranking** Which invention discussed in this section had the greatest impact on American life? Explain your answer.

Activity **Playing a Role** Which invention mentioned in this section would have amazed you the most if you lived at that time? In a brief skit, play the role of a person seeing that invention for the first time.

4 ★ Labor in the Age of Industry

As You Read

Explore These Questions
- How did the role of the worker change in the new industrial age?
- What were the goals of early unions?
- Why was progress slow for labor?

Define
- sweatshop
- strikebreaker
- anarchist
- collective bargaining
- injunction

Identify
- Knights of Labor
- Terence Powderly
- Haymarket Riot
- Samuel Gompers
- American Federation of Labor
- Mother Jones
- International Ladies' Garment Workers Union
- Triangle Fire
- Western Federation of Miners

SETTING the Scene In 1896, Frederick Taylor observed workers at a steel plant. He wrote down the number of times a worker picked up a shovel and the amount of time he took to swing it. Taylor then redesigned the shovels and work pattern in order to make the workers more productive.

Many factory owners adopted Taylor's system of "scientific management." Workers, however, often complained that they were being treated as parts of the machinery.

The rise of industry changed the workplace. By the late 1800s, harsh new conditions led workers to organize.

A Changing Workplace

Factories drew workers from many different backgrounds. Most workers were native-born white men. Many had left farms to take jobs in large cities.

Some northern factory workers were African Americans who had migrated from the South. Large numbers of immigrants from Europe, Asia, and Mexico also found jobs in factories. Women and children worked in factories, too. All of these groups earned lower wages than native-born white men.

Workers and employers

Workers had to adjust to the new kinds of factories of the late 1800s. Before the Civil War, most factories were small and family-run. Bosses knew their workers by name and chatted with them about their families. Because most workers had skills that the factory needed, they could bargain with the boss for wages.

By the 1880s, the relationship between worker and boss declined. Workers stood all day tending machines in a large, crowded, noisy room. Their skills were no longer needed, and they worked for wages fixed by their bosses. In the garment trade and other industries, sweatshops became common. A **sweatshop** is a workplace where people labor long hours in poor conditions for low pay. Most sweatshop workers were immigrants, young women, or children.

Child labor

The 1900 census reported nearly 2 million children under age 15 at work through-

The American Federation of Labor and other unions fought to win workers an eight-hour day.

Children—many of them from immigrant families—labored in the nation's industries. "Breaker boys" hand-sorted slate from coal in grimy mines (right). Young girls operated heavy machinery in textile mills (left). ★ **How do you think the lives of these children were affected by having to go to work at an early age?**

out the country. Boys and girls labored in hazardous textile mills, tobacco factories, and garment sweatshops. In coal mines, they picked stones out of the coal for 12 hours a day, 6 days a week.

Working children had little time for schooling. Lack of education reduced their chance to build a better life as adults.

Many Americans believed that child labor was wrong. However, as long as factory owners could hire children at low pay, and as long as their families needed the money, child labor continued.

Dangerous conditions

Factories brimmed with hazards. Lung-damaging dust filled the air of textile mills. Cave-ins and gas explosions plagued mines. In steel mills, vats of red-hot metal spilled without warning.

Owners were more concerned with profits than with worker safety. They spent little to improve working conditions. Some workers had their health destroyed. Others were severely injured or killed in industrial accidents. In one year, 195 workers died in the steel mills of Pittsburgh.

Workers Organize

Low pay, long hours, and unhealthful conditions threatened the well-being of workers. Many found ways to fight back. Some workers took days off or slowed their work pace. Others went on strike. Strikes were usually informal, organized by workers in individual factories.

Sometimes, workers banded together to win better conditions. Most early efforts to form unions failed, however. (See page 379.)

Knights of Labor

In 1869, workers formed the **Knights of Labor.** At first, the union was open to skilled workers only. Members held meetings in secret because employers fired workers who joined unions.

In 1879, the Knights of Labor selected **Terence Powderly** as their president. Powderly worked to strengthen the union by opening membership to immigrants, blacks, women, and unskilled workers.

Powderly wanted the Knights to make the world a better place for both workers and employers. He did not believe in strikes.

Rather, he relied on rallies and meetings to win public support. Goals of the Knights included a shorter workday, an end to child labor, and equal pay for men and women.

In 1885, some Knights of Labor launched a strike that forced the Missouri Pacific Railroad to restore wage cuts. The Knights did not officially support the strike. Still, workers everywhere saw the strike as a victory for the union. Membership soared to 700,000, including 60,000 African Americans.

Haymarket Riot

The following year, the Knights of Labor ran into serious trouble. Workers at the Mc-

Cormick Harvester Company in Chicago went on strike. Again, the Knights did not endorse the strike.

Like many companies at the time, the McCormick company hired **strikebreakers,** or replacements for striking workers. On May 3, 1886, workers clashed with strikebreakers outside the factory. Police opened fire. Four workers were killed.

The next day, thousands of workers gathered in Haymarket Square to protest the killings. The rally was led by **anarchists,** people who oppose all forms of organized government. Suddenly, a bomb exploded, killing one police officer and wounding others. Police peppered the crowd with bullets, killing or wounding many more people.

Eight anarchists were arrested for their part in the **Haymarket Riot,** as the incident was called. No real evidence linked these men to the bombing, but four were tried, convicted, and hanged. A wave of anti-labor feeling swept the nation. Membership in the Knights of Labor dropped sharply.

American Federation of Labor

Despite the failure of the Knights of Labor, the labor movement continued to grow. In 1886, a British-born cigarmaker named **Samuel Gompers** organized a new union in Columbus, Ohio. The **American Federation of Labor,** or AFL, was open to skilled workers only.

Workers did not join the AFL directly. Rather, they joined a trade union, a union of persons working at the same trade. For example, a typesetter would join a typesetter's union. The union then joined the AFL. In effect, the AFL was a union made up of other unions.

Limited goals

Unlike the Knights of Labor, the AFL did not set out to change the world. It stressed practical goals. As one AFL leader said:

66 Our organization does not consist of idealists. We are going on from day to day. We are fighting only for immediate objects—objects that can be realized in a few years. 99

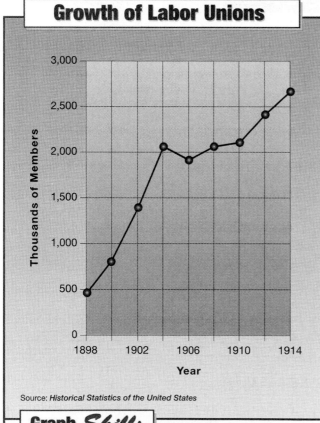

Growth of Labor Unions

Source: *Historical Statistics of the United States*

Graph Skills   A growing number of workers joined unions in the late 1800s and early 1900s.

1. **Comprehension**   (a) How much did union membership increase between 1898 and 1914? (b) What years showed a decrease in membership?

2. **Critical Thinking**   Why did membership in unions grow so much?

Economics $

The AFL stressed higher wages, shorter hours, and improved working conditions. It led the fight for **collective bargaining,** the right of unions to negotiate with management for workers as a group.

A powerful union

Unlike the Knights of Labor, the AFL supported the use of strikes to achieve its goals. The AFL collected money from its member unions. Some of it went into a strike fund. When AFL members went on strike, they were paid from the fund so that they could still feed their families.

Its practical approach helped the AFL become the most powerful union in the nation. Between 1886 and 1910, membership in the AFL swelled from 150,000 to more than one and a half million. However, because African Americans, immigrants, and unskilled workers were barred from most trade unions, they could not join the AFL.

Women in the Labor Movement

By 1890, one million women worked in American factories. In the textile mills of New England and the tobacco factories of the South, women formed the majority of workers. In New York City, women outnumbered men in the garment industry.

During the 1800s, women formed their own unions. A few, like the all-black Washerwomen's Association of Atlanta, struck for higher wages. None of these unions succeeded, however.

Mother Jones

The best-known woman in the labor movement was Irish-born Mary Harris Jones, known as **Mother Jones.** Jones worked as a

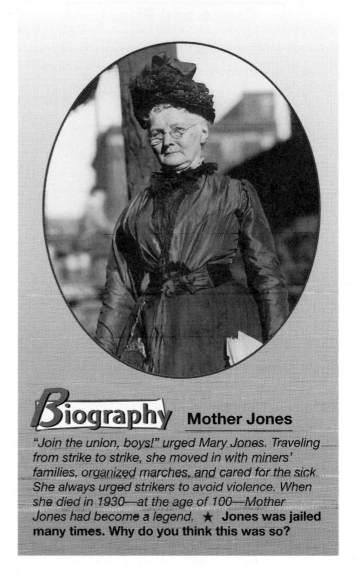

Biography   Mother Jones

"Join the union, boys!" urged Mary Jones. Traveling from strike to strike, she moved in with miners' families, organized marches, and cared for the sick. She always urged strikers to avoid violence. When she died in 1930—at the age of 100—Mother Jones had become a legend. ★ **Jones was jailed many times. Why do you think this was so?**

dressmaker in Chicago until the Chicago fire of 1871 destroyed her business. Faced with the need to start all over again, she devoted the rest of her life to the cause of workers.

In 1877, Jones supported striking railroad workers in Pittsburgh. Later, she traveled around the country, organizing coal miners and campaigning for improved working conditions.

Jones spoke out about the hard lives of children in textile mills, "barefoot...reaching thin little hands into the machinery." By calling attention to such abuses, Mother Jones helped pave the way for reform.

Organizing garment workers

In 1900, garment workers organized the **International Ladies' Garment Workers Union,** or ILGWU. More than 20,000 women and men in the ILGWU walked off their jobs

$ Connections With Economics

Some immigrant workers banded together to demand higher wages. In 1903, Mexican and Japanese farm workers in Oxnard, California, organized the Japanese-Mexican Labor Association. Their strike forced farmers to pay them $5 per acre for thinning beets.

Cause and Effect

Causes

- Railroad boom spurs business
- Businesses become corporations
- Nation has rich supply of natural resources
- New inventions make business more efficient

The Rise of Industry

Effects

- Steel and oil become giant industries
- Monopolies and trusts dominate important industries
- Factory workers face harsh conditions
- Membership in labor unions grows

Effects Today

- United States is world's leading economic power
- American corporations do business around the world
- Government laws regulate monopolies

Graphic Organizer Skills

American industry boomed after the Civil War. The effects of industrial growth are still being felt today.

1. Comprehension List two causes for the rise of industry.

2. Critical Thinking Why do you think the government now tries to regulate monopolies?

Economics $

in 1910. After a few weeks, employers met union demands for better pay and shorter hours. The ILGWU became a key member of the AFL.

Despite the efforts of the ILGWU and other labor groups, most women with factory jobs did not join unions. They continued to work long hours for low pay. Many labored under unsafe conditions. Then, a tragic event focused attention on the dangers faced by women workers.

The Triangle Fire

In 1911, a fire broke out in the Triangle Shirtwaist Factory, a sweatshop in New York City. Within minutes, the upper stories were ablaze. Hundreds of workers raced for the exits, only to find them locked. The company had locked the doors to keep workers at their jobs. In their panic, workers ran headlong into the doors, blocking them with their bodies.

Fire trucks arrived almost immediately, but their ladders could not reach the upper floors. One after another, workers trying to escape the flames leaped to their deaths. One reporter wrote:

> 66 As I looked up...there, at a window, a young man was helping girls to leap out. Suddenly one of them put her arms around him and kiss[ed] him. Then he held her into space and dropped her. He jumped next. Thud...dead. Thud...dead. 99

Nearly 150 people, mostly young women, lost their lives in the **Triangle Fire.** The deaths shocked the public. As a result, New York and other states approved new safety laws to help protect factory workers.

Slow Progress for Labor

The new era of industry led to vast economic growth. At the same time, it created economic strain. In the rush for profits, many industries overexpanded. As goods flooded the market, prices dropped. To cover their losses, factory owners often fired workers. In time, factories geared up again, and the cycle was repeated.

The economy swung wildly between good times and bad. Between 1870 and 1900, two major depressions and three smaller recessions rocked the country. Workers lost their jobs or faced pay cuts. Often, they had no money to pay rent or buy food.

Violent strikes

During a severe depression in the 1870s, railroad workers were forced to take several cuts in pay. In July 1877, workers went on strike, shutting down rail lines across the country. Riots erupted in many cities as workers burned rail yards and ripped track from the ground. In Pittsburgh, a battle between strikebreakers and strikers left more than 20 people dead.

Violent strikes also broke out in the West. In the 1870s, miners in Idaho tried to shut down two large mines. Violence flared until the territorial governor threatened to bring in troops. In 1893, after another bitter strike, miners formed the **Western Federation of Miners.** This militant union gained great strength in the Rocky Mountain states. Between 1894 and 1904, it organized strike after strike when owners refused to negotiate.

A major setback

The federal government usually sided with factory owners. Several Presidents sent in troops to end strikes. Courts ruled against strikers, too.

In 1894, a Chicago court dealt a serious blow to unions. A year earlier, George Pullman had cut the pay of workers at his railroad car factory. Yet, he did not reduce the rents he charged them for company-owned houses. Workers walked off the job in protest.

A federal judge issued an injunction against the strikers. An **injunction** is a court order to do or not to do something. The judge ordered the Pullman workers to stop their strike. Leaders of the strike were jailed for violating the Sherman Antitrust Act. This act had been meant to keep trusts from limiting free trade. The courts, however, said that the strikers were limiting free trade. This decision was a major setback for unions.

Small gains

Union workers staged thousands of strikes during the late 1800s. Strikers won little sympathy at first. Few Americans supported unions. They believed that individuals who worked hard would be rewarded. Many were afraid that unions were run by foreign-born radicals. Because unions were unpopular, owners felt free to crush them.

Workers did make some gains. Skilled workers in the AFL won better conditions and higher pay. Overall, wages for workers rose slightly between 1870 and 1900. Still, progress was slow. In 1910, only one worker in 20 belonged to a union. Some 30 years would pass before large numbers of unskilled workers were able to join unions.

★ Section 4 Review ★

Recall

1. **Identify** (a) Knights of Labor, (b) Terence Powderly, (c) Haymarket Riot, (d) Samuel Gompers, (e) American Federation of Labor, (f) Mother Jones, (g) International Ladies' Garment Workers Union, (h) Triangle Fire, (i) Western Federation of Miners.
2. **Define** (a) sweatshop, (b) strikebreaker, (c) anarchist, (d) collective bargaining, (e) injunction.

Comprehension

3. How did factory work change in the late 1800s?

4. What were the goals of (a) the Knights of Labor? (b) the AFL?
5. How did the public view labor unions in the late 1800s?

Critical Thinking and Writing

6. **Making Inferences** Why did machines make some workers' skills useless?
7. **Drawing Conclusions** Why do you think workers gained so little from strikes in the late 1800s and early 1900s?

Activity Drawing a Cartoon Choose one of the events or issues you have read about in this section. Draw a political cartoon illustrating the topic you have chosen.

Chapter 20 Review and Activities

★ Sum It Up ★

Section 1 Railroads and Industry
▶ After the Civil War, thousands of miles of new railway lines were built, creating a nationwide rail network.
▶ Despite many abuses by large railroads, the growth of railroads stimulated the nation's economy.

Section 2 Big Business
▶ In the late 1800s, steelmaking became a huge source of wealth and power for American companies.
▶ Large corporations formed trusts and monopolies to control competition and maximize profit.

Section 3 A Flood of Inventions
▶ Advances in communication in the late 1800s included the laying of the first transatlantic telegraph cable and the invention of the telephone.
▶ At his research laboratory, Thomas Edison invented the light bulb, the phonograph, and hundreds of other useful devices.
▶ Through his use of the assembly line, Henry Ford made it possible for millions of Americans to afford automobiles.

Section 4 Labor in the Age of Industry
▶ Though various labor unions had differing ideals and methods, they all worked to improve conditions and pay for workers.
▶ Labor unions made slow progress at first because few Americans supported their goals.

 For additional review of the major ideas of Chapter 20, see *Guide to the Essentials of American History* or *Interactive Student Tutorial CD-ROM,* which contains interactive review activities, graphic organizers, and practice tests.

Reviewing the Chapter

Define These Terms
Match each term in Column 1 with the correct definition in Column 2.

Column 1	Column 2
1. trust	a. discount
2. rebate	b. business owned by investors
3. corporation	c. court order
4. stock	d. share in a business
5. injunction	e. group of corporations run by a single board of directors

Explore the Main Ideas
1. What tactics did railroads use to fight competition?
2. What methods did American businesses use to raise capital in the late 1800s?
3. Summarize the arguments for and against monopolies.
4. Why was Edison's research laboratory an important development?
5. How did the Triangle Fire influence public opinion?

Chart Activity

Look at the table below and answer the following questions:
1. During what five-year period did the government issue the most patents? **2.** How many patents were issued between 1881 and 1890? **Critical Thinking** Make two generalizations about American technology in the late 1800s.

United States Patents, 1861–1900

Five-Year Periods	Number of Patents
1861–1865	20,725
1866–1870	58,734
1871–1875	60,976
1876–1880	64,462
1881–1885	97,156
1886–1890	110,358
1891–1895	108,420
1896–1900	112,188

Source: *Historical Statistics of the United States*

Critical Thinking and Writing

1. **Understanding Chronology** Suppose you were asked to create a graphic organizer in the shape of a pyramid showing the growth of American industry. At the bottom you plan to place three items that began that growth. What three items would you choose?

2. **Linking Past and Present** Today, airlines often have "price wars" to attract customers. Judging from what you know about railroad competition, what do you think might be the long-term result of these "wars"?

3. **Exploring Unit Themes Industrialization** Describe one way each of the following transformed the nation: **(a)** steel, **(b)** new sources of power, **(c)** advances in communication, **(d)** new forms of transportation.

4. **Analyzing a Quotation** Jay Gould, a railroad owner, once said, "I can hire one half of the working class to kill the other half." **(a)** What do you think he meant? **(b)** Based on the statement, what do you think was Gould's opinion of unions? Explain.

Using Primary Sources

James J. Davis began working in the iron mills of Pittsburgh when he was twelve. He later described his job:

> **❝** I had iron biscuits to bake; my forge fire must be hot as a volcano. There were five bakings every day and this meant the shoveling in of nearly two tons of coal. In summer I was stripped to the waist and panting while sweat poured down across my heaving muscles. My palms and fingers, scorched by the heat, became hardened like goat hoofs.... Do [weight-lifting exercises] ten hours in a room so hot it melts your eyebrows and you will know what it is like to be [an ironworker]. **❞**

Source: *The Life of an Iron Puddler*, James W. Davis, 1922.

Recognizing Points of View (a) To what did Davis compare the work of an ironworker? **(b)** How do you think Mother Jones would have reacted to this description? Explain.

ACTIVITY BANK

Interdisciplinary Activity

Exploring Economics Review the material on railroads and the growth of industry. Then make a concept map to show the industries that resulted from or were related to the growth of a railroad network in the United States.

Career Skills Activity

Advertising Writers Create advertisements for a mail-order catalog selling the new inventions discussed in the chapter. Write text and use pictures in your ads. Then organize your ads into a catalog.

Citizenship Activity

Learning About Corporate Citizenship Many corporations today make an effort to be good citizens in their communities. Interview the public relations officer at a large local corporation to find out what that company has done to help your community. Write up your interview and prepare a report.

Internet Activity

Use the Internet to find sites dealing with the Carnegie Foundation. After learning about the work of the foundation, write a proposal for a project that you would like to see the foundation support.

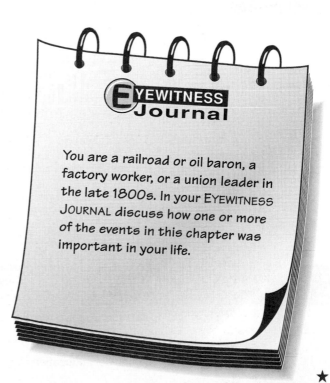

EYEWITNESS Journal

You are a railroad or oil baron, a factory worker, or a union leader in the late 1800s. In your EYEWITNESS JOURNAL discuss how one or more of the events in this chapter was important in your life.

Chapter 21

Immigration and the Growth of Cities

1865–1914

In the 50 years after the Civil War, 25 million immigrants poured into the United States. Most were driven by hunger and poverty and drawn by hope of a better life. They came from places such as Italy, Eastern Europe, Armenia, China, and Mexico. During this time, American cities grew rapidly.

Population growth brought problems including poor housing and strained city services. At the same time, it led to a rich mix of cultures. Cities fostered new leisure-time activities, such as sports. As education improved, newspapers, magazines, and new American fiction gained a larger audience.

Why Study History?

In the late 1800s, educators made vast improvements in public education. Today, Americans continue to stress the role of education in producing good citizens and preparing them for a changing future. To focus on this connection, see the *Why Study History?* feature, "You Have a Right to an Education," in this chapter.

American Events				
●**Mid-1800s** Immigrants from Northern Europe flock to United States		**1882** ● Chinese Exclusion Act bars Chinese immigrants		●**1886** Statue of Liberty is dedicated
1865	**1870**	**1875**	**1880**	**1885**	**1890**

 1870 World Event
Britain establishes compulsory education

 1881 World Event
Russia increases violent pogroms against Jews

World Events

Viewing History A Busy City Street

In his painting Houston Street, *George Benjamin Luks captured the bustle of a crowded New York City street. Many of these pushcart vendors, shopping housewives, or playing children probably spoke Italian, Russian, or other foreign languages. In the late 1800s and early 1900s, a boom in immigration fed the rapid growth of American cities.* ★ **Why do you think many immigrants wanted to come to the United States at this time?**

●**1889**
Jane Addams
founds Hull House
to help poor
immigrants

1902 ●
Macy's department
store opens nine-
story building

●**1904**
New York opens
its subway system

| **1890** | **1895** | **1900** | **1905** | **1910** | **1915** |

▲ **1891 World Event**
Arthur Conan Doyle
publishes *Adventures
of Sherlock Holmes*

▲ **1905 World Event**
Chinese in Shanghai boy-
cott American goods to
protest exclusion laws

The New Immigrants

Explore These Questions
- Why did immigration boom in the late 1800s?
- How did immigrants adjust to life in their new land?
- Why did anti-immigrant feeling grow?

Define
- push factor
- pull factor
- pogrom
- steerage
- ethnic group
- assimilation
- nativist

Identify
- Statue of Liberty
- Emma Lazarus
- Ellis Island
- Angel Island
- Chinese Exclusion Act

 In 1884, Rosa Cristoforo left her village in Italy to join her husband in "l'America." After two weeks on a cramped steamship, she finally caught sight of land:

66 America! The country where everyone could find work! Where wages were so high no one had to go hungry! Where all men were free and equal and where even the poor could own land! But now we were so near it seemed too much to believe. 99

Millions of immigrants flooded into the United States after the Civil War. Most came from eastern and southern Europe. Latin Americans and Asians came, too. All left homelands that offered them little hope for a better future. The United States, they heard, was a land of opportunity.

Reasons for Immigration

Between 1866 and 1915, more than 25 million immigrants poured into the United States. Both push and pull factors played a part in this vast migration. **Push factors** are conditions that drive people from their homes. **Pull factors** are conditions that attract immigrants to a new area.

Push factors

Many immigrants were small farmers or landless farm workers. As European populations grew, land became scarce. Small farms could barely support the families who worked them. In some areas, new farm machines replaced farm workers.

Political and religious persecution pushed many people to leave their homes. In the late 1800s, the Russian government supported **pogroms** (poh GRAHMZ), or organized attacks on Jewish villages. "Every night," recalled a Jewish girl who fled Russia, "they were chasing after us, to kill everyone." Millions of Jews fled Russia and Eastern Europe to settle in American cities.

Persecution was also a push factor for Armenian immigrants. The Armenians lived in the Ottoman Empire (present-day Turkey). Between the 1890s and the 1920s, the Ottoman government killed a million or more Armenians. Many fled, eventually settling in California and elsewhere.

After 1910, a revolution led thousands of Mexicans to cross the border into the Southwest. For the Chinese, poverty and hardship at home acted as push factors, driving them to make new homes across the Pacific.

Pull factors

The promise of freedom and hopes for a better life attracted poor and oppressed people from Europe, Asia, and Latin America. Often, one bold family member—usually a young single male—set off for the United States. Before long, he would write home with news of the rich land across the ocean or across the border. Once settled, he would send for family members to join him.

Once settled, the newcomers helped pull neighbors from the "old country" to the United States. In the late 1800s, one out of every ten Greeks left their homes for the United States. Thousands of Italians, Poles, and Eastern European Jews also sailed to the Americas.

Jobs were another pull factor. American factories needed workers. Factory owners sent agents to Europe and Asia to hire workers at low wages. Steamship companies competed to offer low fares for the ocean crossing. Railroads posted notices in Europe advertising cheap land in the American West.

The Long Voyage

Leaving home required great courage. The voyage across the Atlantic or Pacific was often miserable. Most immigrants could afford only the cheapest berths. Ship owners jammed up to 2,000 people in **steerage,** as the airless rooms below deck were called. On the return voyage, cattle and cargo filled those same spaces.

In such close quarters, diseases spread rapidly. An outbreak of measles infected every child on a German immigrant ship. The dead were thrown into the water "like cattle," reported a horrified passenger.

A "golden door" in New York

For most European immigrants, the voyage ended in New York City. There, after 1886, they saw the giant **Statue of Liberty** in the harbor. The statue was a gift from France to the United States.

The Statue of Liberty became a symbol of the hope and freedom offered by the United States. **Emma Lazarus** wrote a poem, "The New Colossus," that was carved at the base of the statue. It welcomes all newcomers and ends with these lines:

> **66** Give me your tired, your poor,
> Your huddled masses yearning to
>   breathe free,
> The wretched refuse of your teeming
>   shore.
> Send these, the homeless, tempest-
>   tossed to me:
> I lift my lamp beside the golden
>   door! **99**

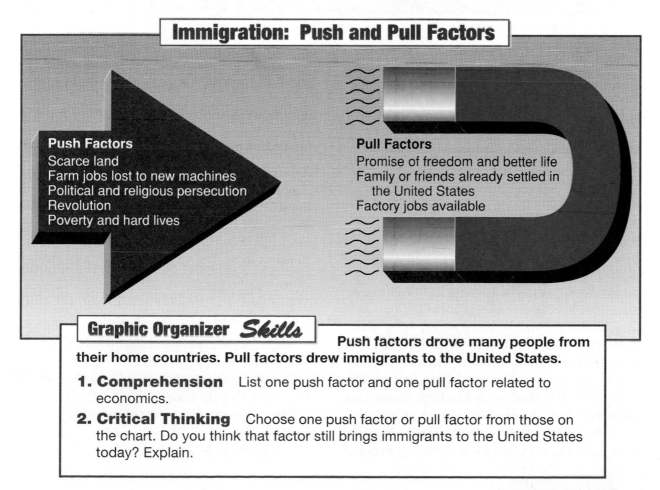

Immigration: Push and Pull Factors

Push Factors
Scarce land
Farm jobs lost to new machines
Political and religious persecution
Revolution
Poverty and hard lives

Pull Factors
Promise of freedom and better life
Family or friends already settled in
    the United States
Factory jobs available

Graphic Organizer *Skills*

Push factors drove many people from their home countries. Pull factors drew immigrants to the United States.

1. **Comprehension** List one push factor and one pull factor related to economics.
2. **Critical Thinking** Choose one push factor or pull factor from those on the chart. Do you think that factor still brings immigrants to the United States today? Explain.

Ellis Island

In the harbor between New York and New Jersey, Ellis Island was the gateway for millions of European immigrants. Hopeful newcomers were crowded into pens in the main hall (left), nervously awaiting interviews with immigration officials. For years, Ellis Island fell into disrepair. In the 1980s, it was restored and is now a museum devoted to the immigrant experience. You can see hundreds of items carried by immigrants, like the ones shown here.

★ **To learn more about this historic site, write:** Ellis Island National Monument, New York, NY 10004.

▲ *Czechoslovakian vest*   *Italian pasta pot* ▲

Ellis Island

After 1892, ships entering New York harbor stopped at the new receiving station on **Ellis Island.** Here, immigrants faced a last hurdle, the dreaded medical inspection.

Doctors watched the newcomers climb a long flight of stairs. Anyone who appeared out of breath or walked with a limp might be stopped. Doctors also examined eyes, ears, and throats. The sick had to stay on Ellis Island until they got well. Those who failed to regain full health were sent home.

With hundreds of immigrants to process each day, officials had only minutes to check each new arrival. To save time, they often changed names that they found difficult to spell. Krzeznewski became Kramer. Smargiaso ended up as Smarga. One Italian immigrant found that even his first name had been changed—from Bartolomeo to Bill.

A few lucky immigrants went directly from Ellis Island into the welcoming arms of friends and relatives. Most, however, stepped into a terrifying new land whose language and customs they did not know.

Angel Island

On the West Coast, immigrants from China, and later from Japan, faced even harsher experiences than the Europeans in the East. By the early 1900s, many Asians were processed on **Angel Island** in San Francisco Bay.

Because Americans wanted to discourage Asian immigration, new arrivals often faced long delays. One immigrant from China scratched these lines on the wall:

> 66 Why do I have to languish in this jail?
> It is because my country is weak and my family poor.
> My parents wait in vain for news;
> My wife and child, wrapped in their quilt, sigh with loneliness. 99

Changing Patterns of Immigration

Before 1885, most new immigrants to the United States were Protestants from Northern and Western Europe. Those from England and Ireland already spoke English. The Irish, English, Germans, and Scandinavians became known as "old immigrants." At first, the old immigrants faced some discrimination. As the nation grew, though, they were drawn into American life.

In the late 1800s, the patterns of immigration changed. Large numbers of people arrived from Southern and Eastern Europe. Millions of Italians, Poles, Greeks, Russians, and Hungarians landed in the eastern United States. On the West Coast, a smaller but growing number of Asian immigrants arrived, first from China, then from Japan. There were also a few immigrants from Korea, India, and the Philippines.

Few of these "new immigrants" spoke English. Many of the Europeans were Catholic, Eastern Orthodox, or Jewish. Immigrants from Asia might be Buddhist or Daoist. Their languages and religions set the new immigrants apart. As a result, they found it harder to adapt to a new life.

Adjusting to a New Land

Many immigrants had heard stories that the streets in the United States were paved with gold. Once in the United States, the newcomers had to adjust their dreams to reality. They immediately set out to find work. European peasants living on the land had little need for money, but it took cash to survive in the United States. Through friends, relatives, labor contractors, and employment agencies, the new arrivals found jobs.

Most immigrants stayed in the cities where they landed. The slums of cities soon became packed with poor immigrants. By 1900, one such neighborhood on the lower east side of New York City had become the most crowded place in the world.

Ethnic neighborhoods

Immigrants adjusted to their new lives by settling in neighborhoods with their own ethnic group. An **ethnic group** is a group of people who share a common culture. Across the United States, cities were patchworks of Italian, Irish, Polish, Hungarian, German, Jewish, and Chinese neighborhoods.

Within these ethnic neighborhoods, newcomers spoke their own language and celebrated special holidays with foods prepared as in the old country. Italians joined ethnic clubs such as the Sons of Italy. Hungarians bought and read Hungarian newspapers.

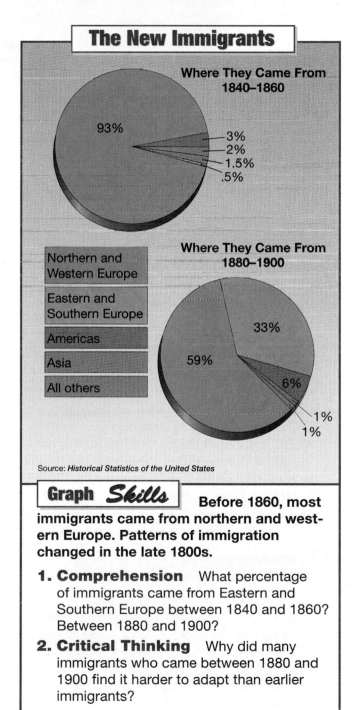

The New Immigrants

Where They Came From 1840–1860

93%
3%
2%
1.5%
.5%

Northern and Western Europe

Eastern and Southern Europe

Americas

Asia

All others

Where They Came From 1880–1900

33%
59%
6%
1%
1%

Source: *Historical Statistics of the United States*

Graph Skills Before 1860, most immigrants came from northern and western Europe. Patterns of immigration changed in the late 1800s.

1. **Comprehension** What percentage of immigrants came from Eastern and Southern Europe between 1840 and 1860? Between 1880 and 1900?
2. **Critical Thinking** Why did many immigrants who came between 1880 and 1900 find it harder to adapt than earlier immigrants?

This photograph shows Chinese children sitting on a stoop in San Francisco's Chinatown. For many immigrants like these, learning English was important. Books of useful phrases helped immigrants get through shopping and other activities of day-to-day life. ★ **Do you think these children had already assimilated into American culture when this picture was taken? How can you tell?**

◀ *Phrase book for Chinese immigrants*

Religion stood at the center of immigrant family life. Houses of worship sprang up in most neighborhoods. They brought ethnic groups together but also separated them. Catholics from Italy worshipped in Italian neighborhood parishes. Those from Poland worshipped in Polish parishes. Jewish communities divided into the older orthodox branch and the newer conservative wing.

Becoming Americans

Often, newcomers were torn between old traditions and American ways. Still, many struggled to learn the language of their new nation. Learning English was an important step toward becoming a citizen.

In their effort to adapt, immigrants sometimes blended their native tongues with English. Italians, for example, called the Fourth of July *"Il Forte Gelato,"* an Italian phrase that sounds like the holiday name but means "the great freeze." In El Paso, Texas, Mexican immigrants developed *Chuco,* a language that blended English and Spanish.

The process of becoming part of another culture is called **assimilation.** Children assimilated more quickly than their parents. They learned English in school and then helped their families learn to speak it. Because children wanted to be seen as Americans, they often gave up customs their parents honored. They played American games and dressed in American-style clothes.

A New Surge of Nativism

Many Americans opposed the increase in immigration. They felt the newcomers would not assimilate because their languages, religions, and customs were too different.

Even before the Civil War, **nativists** had wanted to limit immigration and preserve the country for native-born white Protestants. In the late 1800s, nativist feelings reached a new peak. Many workers resented the new immigrants because they took jobs for low pay. One newspaper complained:

❝ The Poles, Slavs, Huns, and Italians come over without any ambition to live as Americans live and... accept work at any wages at all, thereby lowering the tone of American labor as a whole. ❞

Connections With Arts

One Russian Jewish immigrant became the nation's most popular songwriter. Israel Baline came to New York in 1893, when he was five years old. Under the name Irving Berlin, he went on to write such familiar tunes as "Easter Parade," "White Christmas," and "God Bless America."

Nativist pressure grew wherever new immigrants settled. Nativists targeted Jews and Italians in the Northeast and Mexicans in the Southwest. On the West Coast, nativists worked to end immigration from China.

Chinese exclusion

Since the California Gold Rush and the building of the railroads, Chinese immigrants had helped build the West. Most lived in cities, in tight-knit communities called "Chinatowns." Others made their living as farmers.

Most Americans did not understand Chinese customs. Also, some Chinese did not try to learn American ways. Like many other immigrants, they planned to stay only until they made a lot of money. They then hoped to return home, to live out their lives as rich and respected members of Chinese society. When that dream failed, many Chinese settled in the United States permanently.

As the numbers of Chinese grew, so did the prejudice and violence against them. Gangs attacked and sometimes killed Chinese people, especially during hard times.

Congress responded to this anti-Chinese feeling by passing the **Chinese Exclusion Act** in 1882. Under it, no Chinese laborer could enter the United States. In addition, no Chinese living in the United States could return once they left the country.

The Chinese Exclusion Act was the first law to exclude a specific national group from immigrating to the United States. Congress renewed the original 10-year ban several times. It was finally repealed in 1943.

Other limits

In 1887, nativists formed the American Protective Association. It soon had a million members. The group campaigned for laws to restrict immigration. Congress responded by passing a bill that denied entry to people who could not read their own language.

President Grover Cleveland vetoed the bill. It was wrong, he said, to keep out peasants just because they had never gone to school. Congress passed the bill again and again. Three more presidents vetoed it. In 1917, Congress overrode President Woodrow Wilson's veto, and the bill became law.

★ Section 1 Review ★

Recall

1. **Locate** (a) Italy, (b) Russia, (c) Armenia, (d) Greece, (e) China.
2. **Identify** (a) Statue of Liberty, (b) Emma Lazarus, (c) Ellis Island, (d) Angel Island, (e) Chinese Exclusion Act.
3. **Define** (a) push factor, (b) pull factor, (c) pogrom, (d) steerage, (e) ethnic group, (f) assimilation, (g) nativist.

Comprehension

4. Identify one push factor and one pull factor that caused people to come to the United States.
5. Why did children adjust more easily to the United States than their parents?

6. (a) Why did many Americans resent the new immigrants? (b) What steps did they take to limit immigration?

Critical Thinking and Writing

7. **Making Inferences** (a) How did the "old immigrants" differ from the "new immigrants"? (b) Why do you think the new immigrants faced greater problems when they first arrived in the United States than the old immigrants had?
8. **Distinguishing Facts From Opinions** Read the following statement: "Immigrants work for almost nothing and seem to be able to live on wind." (a) Is this a fact or an opinion? How do you know? (b) Who would most likely have made a statement like this? Explain.

Activity Writing a Handbook You are an immigrant to the United States in the 1880s. Write at least one page for a handbook for future immigrants from your country. Tell them what problems they should expect to have and how they can overcome those problems.

Booming Cities

As You Read

Explore These Questions
- Why did cities grow in the late 1800s?
- What hazards did city dwellers face?
- How did reformers help to improve city life?

Define
- urbanization
- tenement
- building code
- settlement house

Identify
- Jane Addams
- Hull House
- Mother Cabrini
- Social Gospel
- Salvation Army
- Young Men's Hebrew Association

Chicago street in the late 1800s

 A small fire started in the barn behind the O'Leary cottage. Within hours, dry winds had whipped the blaze into an inferno that raged across Chicago. A survivor described how panicked residents fled their homes:

66 Everybody was running north. People were carrying all kinds of crazy things. A woman was carrying a pot of soup, which was spilling all over her dress. People were carrying cats, dogs, and goats. In the great excitement, people saved worthless things and left behind good things. 99

Fire was a constant danger in cities. However, Americans agreed they had never seen anything like the great Chicago Fire of 1871. The blaze killed nearly 300 people, left almost 100,000 homeless, and destroyed the entire downtown.

Yet from the ashes, a new city rose. By the end of the century, Chicago was the fastest growing city in the world, with a population of over one million. Other American cities, too, underwent a population explosion. For new and old Americans alike, the golden door of opportunity opened into the city.

City Populations Grow

"We cannot all live in cities," declared the newspaper publisher Horace Greeley, "yet nearly all seem determined to do so." **Urbanization,** the movement of population from farms to cities, began slowly in the early 1800s. As the nation industrialized after the Civil War, urbanization became much more rapid. In 1860, only one American in five lived in a city. By 1890, one in three did.

Jobs drew people to cities. As industries grew, so did the need for workers. New city dwellers took jobs in steel mills, meatpacking plants, and garment factories. They worked as sales clerks, waiters, barbers, bank tellers, and secretaries.

Immigrants and farmers

The flood of immigrants swelled city populations. Also, by the 1890s, most land in the West had been divided into farms and ranches. As a result, fewer pioneers went there to homestead. In fact, many Americans left farms to find a better life in the city. A young man in a story by western writer Hamlin Garland summed up the feelings of many farmers:

66 I'm sick of farm life... it's nothing but fret, fret, and work the whole time, never going any place, never seeing *anybody*. 99

African Americans migrate

African Americans, too, moved to cities to improve their lives. Most African Americans lived in the rural South. When hard times hit or prejudice led to violence, some blacks headed to northern cities. By the 1890s, the south side of Chicago had a thriving African American community. Detroit, New York, Philadelphia, and other northern cities also had growing African American neighborhoods. The migration to the north began gradually, but increased rapidly after 1915.

As with immigrants from overseas, black migration usually began with one family member moving north. Later, relatives and friends joined the bold pioneer. Like immigrants from rural areas in Europe, many African Americans faced the challenge of adjusting to urban life.

City Life

Cities grew outward from their old downtown sections. Before long, many took on a similar shape.

Poor families crowded into the city's center, the oldest section. Middle-class people lived farther out in row houses or new apartment buildings. Beyond them, the rich built fine homes with green lawns and trees.

The poor

Poor families struggled to survive in crowded slums. The streets were jammed with people, horses, pushcarts, and garbage.

Because space was so limited, builders devised a new kind of house to hold more people. They put up buildings six or seven stories high. They divided the buildings into small apartments, called **tenements.** Many tenements had no windows, heat, or indoor bathrooms. Often, 10 people shared a single room.

Typhoid and cholera raged through the tenements. Tuberculosis, a lung disease, was the biggest killer, accounting for thousands of deaths each year. Babies, especially, fell victim to disease. In one Chicago slum, more than half of all babies died before they were one year old.

Despite the poor conditions, the population of slums grew rapidly. Factory owners moved in to take advantage of low rents and cheap labor. They took over buildings for use as factories, thus forcing more and more people into fewer and fewer apartments.

The middle class

Beyond the slums stood the homes of the new middle class, including doctors, lawyers, business managers, skilled machinists, and office workers. Rows of neat houses lined tree-shaded streets. Here, disease broke out less frequently than in the crowded slums.

The Growth of Cities

Population Growth in Ten Selected Cities

City	Population in 1870	Population in 1900
New York	1,478,103	3,437,202
Chicago	298,977	1,698,575
Philadelphia	674,022	1,293,697
St. Louis	351,189	575,238
Boston	250,526	560,892
San Francisco	149,473	342,782
New Orleans	191,418	287,104
Denver	4,759	133,859
Los Angeles	5,728	102,479
Memphis	40,226	102,320

Rural and Urban Population in the United States, 1860–1920

Year	Rural	Urban
1860	80%	20%
1870	74%	26%
1880	72%	28%
1890	65%	35%
1900	60%	40%
1910	54%	46%
1920	49%	51%

Rural Population   Urban Population

Source: *United States Census Bureau*

Graph Skills City populations grew rapidly in the United States in the decades following the Civil War.

1. **Comprehension** Between 1870 and 1900, which cities on the chart above more than doubled in population?

2. **Critical Thinking** Study the bar graphs above. Make one generalization about the population of the United States after 1870.

◀ Tiffany lamp

The Brown Family, *a painting by East-man Johnson, suggests the elegance and fine manners of a wealthy American family. Many of the furnishings in this home, such as the crystal chandelier, were probably imported from Europe. Later, American manufacturers like Louis Tiffany produced fine glassware and other items for the rich.* ★ **In a typical American city, where did the rich live?**

Middle-class people joined singing societies, bowling leagues, and charitable organizations. Such activities gave them a sense of community and purpose. As one writer said, the clubs "bring together many people who are striving upward, trying to uplift themselves."

The wealthy

On the outskirts of the city, behind brick walls or iron gates, lay the mansions of the very rich. In New York, huge homes dotted Fifth Avenue, which was still on the city's outskirts. In Chicago, by the 1880s, 200 millionaires lived along the exclusive lake front. In San Francisco, wealthy residents lived nearer the center of the city, but they built their mansions in the exclusive Nob Hill area. ("Nob" is British slang for a person of wealth and position.)

Rich Americans modeled their lives on European royalty. They filled their mansions with priceless artworks and gave lavish parties. At one banquet, the host handed out cigarettes rolled in hundred-dollar bills.

Cleaning Up the Cities

As more and more people crowded into cities, problems grew. Tenement buildings were deathtraps if fires broke out. One magazine reporter in 1888 wrote:

    66 It would be impossible for the occupants of the crowded rooms to escape by the narrow stairways, and the flimsy fire-escapes ... are so laden with broken furniture, bales, and boxes that they would be worse than useless. **99**

Garbage rotted in the streets. Factories polluted the air. Crime flourished. Thieves and pickpockets haunted lonely alleys, especially at night.

By the 1880s, reformers were demanding change. They forced city governments to pass **building codes**—laws that set standards for how structures should be built. The codes required new buildings to have fire escapes and decent plumbing. Cities also hired workers to collect garbage and sweep the streets. To reduce pollution, zoning laws kept factories out of neighborhoods where people lived.

Safety improved when cities set up professional fire companies and trained police forces. Gas—and later electric—lights made streets less dangerous at night. As you will read, many cities built new systems of public transportation as well.

Pushed by reformers, city governments hired engineers and architects to design new water systems. New York City, for example,

Skills FOR LIFE

Critical Thinking | **Managing Information** | **Communication** | **Maps, Charts, and Graphs**

Synthesizing Information

How Will I Use This Skill?

Most of the things we learn about in life do not come to us from just one source. When something happens in your community, you may see a report on local television, read an account in a newspaper, and hear what friends say about it. Then, you put together and analyze the different pieces of information to form a complete picture. This process is called synthesizing.

LEARN the Skill

❶ Identify the different sources of information and the facts and ideas in each.

❷ Compare the evidence from each source. Do the pieces support one another? Is there any contradictory evidence?

❸ Synthesize the evidence so that you can draw conclusions.

PRACTICE the Skill

To practice the skill, use the following pieces of information: the photograph on this page; the painting on page 566; the quotation to the right; the information in your textbook.

❶ (a) What is the subject of the photograph?
(b) What does the painting show?
(c) What topic is Riis talking about?

❷ (a) How does the family in the painting differ from that in the photograph? List three details that show the differences. (b) Does the quotation describe the photograph or the painting? (c) What information in the text is supported by the painting? The photograph?

❸ Based on the evidence, make two generalizations about city life in the late 1800s.

Tenement family in New York City

“ In this house, where a case of smallpox was reported, there were fifty-eight babies and thirty-eight children...over five years of age. ”

—Journalist Jacob Riis, describing a Jewish community in New York City

APPLY the Skill

Research a current topic in a newsmagazine or newspaper. Synthesize the written information with evidence from a photograph.

Singing class at
Hull House ▶

Biography Jane Addams

A wealthy woman, Jane Addams dedicated her life to serving the poor. She founded Hull House in Chicago, which provided many services to immigrants and others. Above, neighbors enjoy a singing class at Hull House. Addams also worked for world peace. In 1931, she became the first American woman to win the Nobel Peace Prize.

★ **Addams insisted on living at Hull House herself. What does this tell you about her?**

dug underground tunnels to the Catskill Mountains—100 miles to the north. The tunnels brought a clean water supply to the city every day.

The Settlement House Movement

Some people looked for ways to help the poor. By the late 1800s, individuals began to organize settlement houses. A **settlement house** is a community center that offers services to the poor. The leading figure of the settlement house movement was a Chicago woman named **Jane Addams.**

Connections With Civics

Most settlement houses did not admit African Americans, so some black women opened their own settlement houses. In New York City, Victoria Earle Matthews started the White Rose Mission and Verna Morton-Jones opened Lincoln House. They offered shelter, child care, and classes to their communities.

Hull House

Addams came from a well-to-do family but had strong convictions about helping the poor. After college, she moved into one of the poorest slums in Chicago. There, in an old mansion, she opened a settlement house in 1889. She called it **Hull House.**

Other idealistic young women soon joined Addams. They took up residence in Hull House so that they could experience firsthand some of the hardships of the slum community in which they worked. These women dedicated their lives to service and to sacrifice—"like the early Christians," in the words of one volunteer.

The Hull House volunteers provided day nurseries for children whose mothers worked outside the home. They organized sports and a theater for young people. They taught English to immigrants and gave classes in health care. They also launched investigations into social and economic conditions in the city.

Over the years, the settlement house movement spread. By 1900, about 100 such centers had opened in cities across the United States.

Working for reform

Jane Addams and her Hull House staff were an important influence in bringing about reform legislation to improve the living and working conditions of the poor. They studied the slum neighborhoods where they worked and lived. They realized that the problems were too big for any one person or group, and they urged the government to act.

Alice Hamilton, a Hull House doctor, campaigned for better health laws. Florence Kelley worked to ban child labor. Jane Addams herself believed that reform legislation would be speeded if women could vote. She campaigned tirelessly for women's suffrage.

Religious Organizations Help the Poor

Religious groups also provided services to the poor. The Catholic Church ministered to the needs of Irish, Polish, and Italian immigrants. An Italian nun, **Mother Cabrini,** helped found more than 70 hospitals in North and South America. These hospitals treated people who could not afford doctors.

In cities, Protestant ministers began preaching a new **Social Gospel.** They called on their well-to-do members to do their duty as Christians by helping society's poor. One minister urged merchants and industrialists to pay their workers enough to enable them to marry and have families. He also proposed that they grant their workers a half day off on Saturdays.

Protestant groups set up programs for needy slum dwellers. In 1865, a Methodist minister named William Booth created the **Salvation Army** in London. By 1880, it expanded to the United States. In addition to spreading Christian teachings, the Salvation Army offered food and shelter to the poor.

In Jewish neighborhoods, too, religious organizations provided community services. The first **Young Men's Hebrew Association** (YMHA) began in Baltimore in 1854. The YMHA provided social activities, encouraged good citizenship, and helped Jewish families preserve their culture. In the 1880s, the Young Women's Hebrew Association (YWHA) grew out of the YMHA.

Other groups—like the YMCA (Young Men's Christian Association) and the YWCA (Young Women's Christian Association)— taught classes, organized team sports, and held dances. Such activities offered young people a brief escape from the problems of slum life.

★ Section 2 Review ★

Recall

1. **Identify** (a) Jane Addams, (b) Hull House, (c) Mother Cabrini, (d) Social Gospel, (e) Salvation Army, (f) Young Men's Hebrew Association
2. **Define** (a) urbanization, (b) tenement, (c) building code, (d) settlement house.

Comprehension

3. Name three causes for the growth of city populations in the late 1800s.

4. What problems did cities face as their populations grew?
5. What reforms did cities make?

Critical Thinking and Writing

6. **Comparing** Compare and contrast the lives of the rich, the middle class, and the poor in American cities in the late 1800s.
7. **Linking Past and Present** How do the problems of city dwellers today compare to those of city dwellers in the late 1800s?

★ ★

Activity **Writing a Grant Proposal** You are a modern-day reformer who wants to start a settlement house somewhere in a nearby city or town. Choose a good location. Then write a proposal in which you ask a charitable foundation for funds to start your settlement house. Explain why the settlement is needed and what kind of services you plan to offer.

City Life Transformed

As You Read

Explore These Questions
- How did cities change in the late 1800s?
- Why did newspapers grow in number and importance?
- How did Americans spend their leisure time?

Define
- yellow journalism
- vaudeville
- ragtime

Identify
- Joseph Pulitzer
- William Randolph Hearst
- Nellie Bly
- Will Rogers
- Scott Joplin
- John Philip Sousa
- James Naismith

 Bells rang. Cannons thundered. Fireworks crackled in the afternoon sky. New Yorkers were celebrating the opening of the Brooklyn Bridge. In 1883, its soaring arches were a triumph of modern engineering. Linking Manhattan Island and Brooklyn, the bridge was soon carrying 33 million people each year across New York City's East River.

The Brooklyn Bridge was only one sign of the changing face of New York. Other American cities, too, underwent vast changes that transformed their appearance and their way of life.

A New Look for Cities

A building boom changed the face of American cities in the late 1800s. Cities like Chicago and New York ran out of space in their downtown areas. Resourceful city planners and architects decided to build up instead of out.

Skyscrapers

After fire leveled downtown Chicago, planners tried out many new building ideas. Using new technology, they designed tall buildings with many floors. Called skyscrapers, these high-rise buildings had frames of lightweight steel to hold the weight of the structure.

Newly invented electric elevators carried workers to upper floors. Elevators moved so quickly, according to one rider, that "the passenger seems to feel his stomach pass into his shoes."

Public transportation

As skyscrapers crowded more people into smaller spaces, cities began to face a new problem: the traffic jam. Downtown streets were choked with horse-drawn buses, carriages, and carts.

Electricity offered one solution. In 1887, Frank Sprague, an engineer from Richmond, Virginia, designed the first electric streetcar system. Streetcars, or trolleys, were fast, clean, and quiet. Many trolley lines ran out from the center of a city to the outlying countryside.

Other cities, such as New York, built steam-driven passenger trains on overhead tracks. In 1897, Boston led the way in building the first American subway, or underground electric railway. In 1904, New York opened the first section of its subway system. These trains carried workers rapidly to and from their jobs.

Open spaces

While cities grew up and out, some planners wanted to preserve open spaces. They believed that open land would calm busy city dwellers.

In the 1850s, architect Frederick Law Olmsted planned Central Park in New York City. Other cities followed this model. They

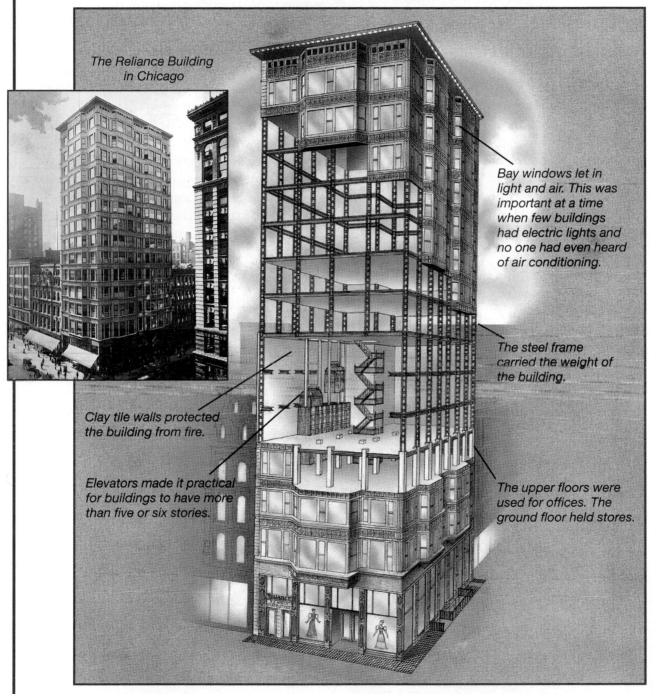

The Reliance Building in Chicago

Bay windows let in light and air. This was important at a time when few buildings had electric lights and no one had even heard of air conditioning.

The steel frame carried the weight of the building.

Clay tile walls protected the building from fire.

Elevators made it practical for buildings to have more than five or six stories.

The upper floors were used for offices. The ground floor held stores.

Skyscaper

As people crowded into American cities, architects began building up instead of out. Today, the Reliance Building in Chicago, shown here, does not look very tall. When it was built in the 1890s, however, its 16 stories made it a "skyscraper." ★ **Based on this drawing, what new kinds of technology made skyscrapers possible?**

set aside land for zoos and gardens so that city people could enjoy green grass and trees during their leisure time.

Department stores

Shopping areas also got a new look. In the late 1800s, department stores sprang up. In the past, people had bought shoes in one store, socks in another, and dishes in a third. The new department stores sold all kinds of goods in one building.

In 1902, R. H. Macy opened a nine-story building in New York. It had 33 elevators and a motto that became famous: "We sell goods cheaper than any house in the world." Soon, other cities had department stores. Shopping became a popular pastime. People browsed each floor, looking at clothes, furniture, and jewelry. On the street, "window shoppers" paused to enjoy elaborate window displays.

The Daily Newspaper

"Read all about it!" cried newsboys on city street corners. The number of newspapers grew dramatically after 1880. By 1900, half the newspapers in the world were printed in the United States.

The rapid growth in the number of newspapers was linked to the growth of cities. In towns and villages, neighbors shared news when they met. In the city, people had thousands of "neighbors." Also, there was so much news that people needed newspapers to be informed.

Newspapers reported on major events of the day. Most featured stories about local government, business, fashion, and sports. Many immigrants learned to read English by spelling their way through a daily paper. At the same time, they learned about life in the United States.

Two newspaper giants

Joseph Pulitzer created the first modern, mass-circulation newspaper. Pulitzer was a Hungarian immigrant. In 1883, he bought the New York *World*. He set out to make it lively and "truly democratic."

To win readers, Pulitzer slashed prices and added comic strips. He introduced bold "scare" headlines to attract reader attention and used pictures to illustrate stories. The *World* splashed crimes and political scandals across its front page. The paper's circulation jumped from 20,000 to one million.

William Randolph Hearst, who came to New York City from San Francisco, challenged Pulitzer. Hearst's New York *Journal* began to outdo the *World* in presenting scandals, crime stories, and gossip. Critics coined the term **yellow journalism** for the sensational reporting style of the *World* and the *Journal*. They complained that the papers offered less news and more scandal every day.

Women journalists

Newspapers competed for women readers. They added special sections on fashion, social events, health, homemaking, and family mat-

Viewing HISTORY · **A Popular Newspaper**

This 1880 advertisement for the New York Sun *shows the growing popularity of newspapers. The ad suggests that* The Sun *covered everything from politics and shipping news to horse races and weddings. Readers could buy from a corner newsboy or get home delivery.* ★ **Why did newspapers become more important as cities grew?**

ters. Newspapers rarely pushed for women's rights, however. Most were afraid to take bold positions that might anger some readers.

A few women worked as reporters, like **Nellie Bly** of the *World*. Once, Bly pretended to be insane in order to find out about treatment of the mentally ill. Her articles about cruelty in mental hospitals led to reforms.

A World of Entertainment

By the late 1800s, American cities supported a wide variety of cultural activities. Talented Italian, German, Jewish, and other immigrants contributed to a new world of music and theater.

Music and other kinds of entertainment brought Americans together. People from different cultures sang the same songs and enjoyed the same shows. As railroads grew, circuses, acting companies, and "Wild West" shows toured the country. These traveling groups helped spread American culture beyond the cities to small towns throughout the United States.

Vaudeville

Many large cities organized symphony orchestras and opera companies. Generally, only the wealthy attended the symphony or the opera. For other city dwellers, an evening out often meant a trip to a vaudeville house. **Vaudeville** (VAWD vihl) was a variety show that included comedians, song-and-dance routines, and acrobats.

Vaudeville provided opportunities for people from many ethnic backgrounds, such as Irish American dancer-singer George M. Cohan and Jewish comedians like the Marx Brothers. **Will Rogers,** a performer of Cherokee descent, was one of the best-loved performers in the nation. Wearing a cowboy hat and twirling a rope, Rogers used gentle wit to comment about American life.

Popular music

Songwriters produced many popular tunes, such as "Shine On, Harvest Moon." Later, Thomas Edison's phonograph sparked a new industry. By 1900, millions of phonograph records had been sold.

Biography Scott Joplin

Fingers flying swiftly over the piano keys, Scott Joplin was the "King of Ragtime." By the age of 14, he was already making a living as a piano player. He went on to compose more than 60 pieces of music, including his popular "Maple Leaf Rag." Joplin also wrote an opera, Treemonisha, *which was not performed until more than 60 years after his death.* ★ **How did popular music styles like ragtime spread across the country?**

Ragtime was a new kind of music with a lively, rhythmic sound. **Scott Joplin,** an African American composer, helped make ragtime popular. His "Maple Leaf Rag" was a nationwide hit.

In towns and cities, marching bands played the military music of **John Philip Sousa.** Sousa wrote more than 100 marches, including "The Stars and Stripes Forever." His marches became favorites at Fourth of July celebrations.

Sports and Leisure

The rise of the factory split the worlds of work and play more sharply than ever. With less chance to socialize on the job, there was more interest in leisure. In sports, Americans found a great escape from factories, stores, and offices.

Baseball: the national pastime

Baseball was the most popular sport in the nation. The game was first played in New York in the 1840s. During the Civil War, New York soldiers showed other Union troops how to play the game. By the 1870s, the country had several professional teams and its first league.

Early baseball was very different from today's game. Pitchers threw underhanded. Catchers caught the ball after one bounce. Fielders did not wear gloves. As a result, high scores were common. One championship game ended with a score of 103 to 8!

At first, African Americans played professional baseball. In the 1880s, however, the major leagues barred black players. In 1885, Frank Thompson organized a group of waiters into one of the first African American professional teams, the Cuban Giants of Long Island.

Football

Football grew out of soccer, which Americans had played since colonial times. Early football called for lots of muscle and little skill. On every play, the opposing teams crashed into each other like fighting rams. The quarterback ran or jumped over the tangle of bodies.

Players did not wear helmets and were often hurt. In one brutal season, 44 college football players died from injuries. Some colleges banned the sport or drew up stricter rules of play for the game.

This toy bank shows three unhelmeted football players. If you drop in a coin, the players turn and collide.

Basketball

In 1891, **James Naismith** invented a new sport: basketball. Naismith was teaching physical education at a YMCA in Springfield, Massachusetts. He wanted to find a sport that could be played indoors in winter. Naismith had two bushel baskets nailed to the gym walls. Players tried to throw a soccer ball into the baskets.

Basketball caught on quickly. It spread to other YMCAs and then to schools and colleges around the country.

★ Section 3 Review ★

Recall

1. **Identify** (a) Joseph Pulitzer, (b) William Randolph Hearst, (c) Nellie Bly, (d) Will Rogers, (e) Scott Joplin, (f) John Philip Sousa, (g) James Naismith.
2. **Define** (a) yellow journalism, (b) vaudeville, (c) ragtime.

Comprehension

3. How did new technology change the face of American cities?
4. Describe newspapers of the late 1800s.

5. (a) How did entertainment unite Americans? (b) What sports were popular in the late 1800s?

Critical Thinking and Writing

6. **Understanding Cause and Effect** Describe the cause-and-effect relationship between population growth and development of the skyscraper.
7. **Identifying Alternatives** Some journalists defend sensational stories by saying they are giving the public what it wants. What types of stories do you think newspapers and other media should provide? Explain your answer.

★ ★

Activity Creating a Poster You are a printer in the early 1900s. Create an illustrated poster advertising one of the following: a new department store; a sporting event; a vaudeville show.

Education and Culture

As You Read

Explore These Questions
- How did public education improve in the late 1800s?
- How did American reading habits change?
- What themes did American writers and painters explore?

Define
- dime novel
- realist
- local color

Identify
- Chautauqua Society
- Horatio Alger
- Stephen Crane
- Paul Laurence Dunbar
- Mark Twain
- Winslow Homer
- Henry Tanner
- Mary Cassatt

SETTING the Scene The writer Mark Twain felt sure that the new mechanical typesetter would revolutionize publishing. The machine could do the work of four people. He invested $5,000 in it—a huge sum in 1880. "Very much the best investment I have ever made," he concluded.

In fact, Twain lost his investment. The company that he backed was a failure. The mechanical typesetter, however, did change publishing. It made printing easier and cheaper. Mass-produced, affordable books helped spread American culture.

Public Education

Before 1870, fewer than half of American children went to school. Many who did attended one-room schoolhouses, with only one teacher. Often, several students shared a single book.

Growth of schools

As industry grew after the Civil War, the nation needed an educated work force. As a result, states improved public schools at all levels. St. Louis created the first kindergarten in the United States in 1873. By 1900, there were 4,000 such programs serving children from ages 3 through 7 across the nation.

In the North, most states passed laws that required children to attend school, usually through sixth grade. In the South, the Freedmen's Bureau built grade schools for both African American and white students.

However, most schools in the South were segregated.

In cities such as Boston and New York, public schools taught English to young immigrants. Native-born and immigrant children also learned about the duties and rights of citizens. In the 1880s, Catholic immigrants became worried that public schools stressed Protestant teachings. They opened their own, church-sponsored schools.

The school day

The typical school day lasted from 8:00 A.M. to 4:00 P.M. Pupils learned the "three Rs": reading, 'riting, and 'rithmetic. The most widely used textbook was *McGuffey's Eclectic Reader*. Students memorized and recited passages from *McGuffey's Reader*. With titles like "Waste Not, Want Not," the poems and stories taught not only reading but religion, ethics, and values.

Schools emphasized discipline and obedience. A 13-year-old boy complained:

> **66** They hits ye if yer don't learn and they hits ye if ye whisper, . . . and they hits ye if yer seat squeaks, and they hits ye if ye don't stan' up in time, and they hits ye if yer late, and they hits ye if ye ferget the page. **99**

High schools and colleges

After 1870, many cities and towns built public high schools. By 1900, the United States had 6,000 high schools.

Why Study History?

Because You Have a Right to an Education

★ ★

Historical Background

Today, it is easy to take education for granted. This was not true 150 years ago. Many states did not require children to go to school. If you were from a poor family, your chances of getting an education were slim. Then, reformers expanded American public education. They insisted that every child had a right to an education.

Schooling was especially valuable to young immigrants. Most had little opportunity for schooling in their homelands. Few could speak English. However, free public schools gave immigrant children the opportunity to succeed in their new homeland. They learned not only English, but American customs, laws, and history.

Graduation day

Connections to Today

In today's information age, education is more important than ever before. The modern world depends on advanced electronics, rapid communication, and computer technology. There are fewer and fewer good-paying, steady jobs for people who do not have at least a high school education.

Schools develop skills employers seek, such as creative thinking, organization, and public speaking. Schools also stress values like responsibility, self-discipline, and teamwork. Perhaps most important, schools prepare Americans for the duties of citizenship. Today, as in the past, democracy depends on an informed public.

Connections to You

It is your responsibility to get the most out of your education. The variety of classes you take give you an opportunity to explore your talents. A subject or activity may interest you enough for you to pursue a career in that field.

In addition, school gives you the opportunity to know and work with people who have different backgrounds and viewpoints. By taking advantage of what your school has to offer, you will prepare yourself for whatever your future brings.

1. **Comprehension** **(a)** How did immigrant children benefit from public schools? **(b)** List three skills that employers look for today.
2. **Critical Thinking** List three qualities that you need to do well in your classes. Write a sentence explaining how each quality can be important outside of school.

★ *Activity* **Making a Poster** With a partner, create a poster that encourages students to stay in school. Use a catchy slogan as well as images.

To help meet the need for trained workers, the Chicago Manual Training School opened in 1884. It offered courses in "shop work" as well as a few academic subjects. Within a decade, almost every public school in the nation had programs aimed at educating students for jobs in business and industry.

Higher education also expanded. New private colleges for both women and men opened. Many states built universities that offered free or low-cost education. However, for women, African Americans and others, opportunities for a college education were often limited.

Adult education

A new form of family education grew up along Lake Chautauqua in New York State. There, in 1874, a Methodist minister opened a summer school for Bible teachers. So many people enrolled that the next year the camp was opened to the general public and nonreligious subjects were introduced.

By the 1880s, some 75,000 people gathered at Lake Chautauqua each summer not only for spiritual guidance but for lectures about art, politics, philosophy, and other subjects. Reformers, religious leaders, and seven American presidents spoke there. In the restful setting, the mostly middle-class audiences discovered that education could be fun as well as uplifting.

In 1903, the **Chautauqua Society** began to send out traveling companies. Before long, Chautauquas were reaching as many as 5 million people in 10,000 American towns every year.

New Reading Habits

As more Americans learned to read in the late 1880s, they read not only newspapers but also more books and magazines. New printing methods lowered the cost of magazines. Magazines also added eye-catching pictures to attract readers.

Each magazine had its special audience. The *Ladies' Home Journal* appealed mostly to middle-class women with articles about famous people and stories by well-known authors. By 1900, it had one million readers.

Other magazines, such as *Harper's Monthly* and *The Nation,* specialized in politics and current events.

Dime novels

In the late 1800s, paperback books became popular. Bestsellers were often **dime novels.** These low-priced paperbacks offered thrilling adventure stories. Many told about the "Wild West." Young people loved dime novels, but parents often disapproved of the stories. One critic complained:

> 66 Stories for children used to begin, 'Once upon a time there lived—.' Now they begin, 'Vengeance, blood, death,' shouted Rattlesnake Jim. 99

Horatio Alger, a popular writer, produced more than 100 dime novels for children. Most told the story of a poor boy who became rich and respected through hard work, luck, and honesty. Americans snapped up these rags-to-riches stories. They offered

Biography Horatio Alger, Jr.

In the novels of Horatio Alger, virtue and hard work were always rewarded. Alger published more than 130 "rags-to-riches" tales, with titles such as Tattered Tom, Phil the Fiddler, and Paul the Peddler. Alger devoted many of the profits from his books to a New York home for orphans and runaways.
★ **How did Alger's books reflect an optimistic view of the United States?**

Mothers and children were a favorite theme of Mary Cassatt. This 1880 painting is titled Mother About to Wash Her Sleepy Child. *Cassatt was influenced by new French styles as well as by Japanese prints, which were becoming popular in Europe.*
★ **Describe the work of one other American painter of the late 1800s.**

the hope that even the poorest person could become rich and successful in the United States.

New American writers

In the 1880s, a new crop of writers appeared. For the first time, Americans read more books by American authors than by British authors. One group of writers, known as **realists,** tried to show the harsh side of life as it was. Many realists had worked as newspaper reporters. They had seen the poverty and the growth of cities created by the Industrial Revolution.

Stephen Crane was best known for his Civil War novel *The Red Badge of Courage.*

(See page 498.) Crane also wrote about the hard lives of young city slum dwellers in novels like *Maggie: A Girl of the Streets.* Hamlin Garland described the harsh lives of farmers in the 1890s. Jack London, born in California, wrote about the hardships of miners and sailors on the West Coast.

Kate Chopin found an audience for short stories about New Orleans life in women's magazines. Chopin's stories showed women breaking out of traditional roles.

Paul Laurence Dunbar was the first African American to make a living as a writer. He wrote poems, such as "We Wear the Mask," in a serious, elegant style. In other poems, short stories, and novels, he used everyday language to express the feelings of African Americans of the time.

Mark Twain

The most famous and popular author of this period was Samuel Clemens, better known by his pen name, **Mark Twain.** As a young man, Clemens worked on a Mississippi River steamboat. There, he heard the boatman's cry "Mark twain," meaning that the river was two "marks," or 12 feet, deep. He took it as his name when he sent out his first story.

Popular stories

Like many other American writers, Twain used local color to make his stories more realistic. **Local color** refers to the speech and habits of a particular region. Twain's novels captured the speech patterns of Southerners who lived and worked along the Mississippi. Twain used homespun, nononsense characters to poke fun at serious issues. Novels like *The Adventures of Tom Sawyer* and short stories like "The Celebrated Jumping Frog of Calaveras County" became so well known that people often quoted them to win arguments.

Huckleberry Finn

Twain's greatest work was probably *The Adventures of Huckleberry Finn.* The novel takes place along the Mississippi River before the Civil War. Huck is a country boy who helps an escaped slave named Jim. The two become good friends as they raft down the river together.

Twain filled his novel with humor and adventure to entertain his readers. At the same time, he made a serious point. In the beginning, Huck Finn accepts slavery. During the novel, Huck comes to respect Jim and decides that their friendship is more important than the unjust laws that enslaved Jim. In the following passage, Huck tells of Jim's longing to be reunited with his family:

66 He was saying how the first thing he would do when he got to a free state he would go to saving up money,... and when he got enough he would buy his wife, which was owned on a farm close to where Miss Watson lived; and then they would both work to buy the two children, and if their master wouldn't sell them, they'd get an Ab'litionist to go and steal them. 99

Although *Huckleberry Finn* became a classic American novel, some schools and libraries refused to buy the book. They claimed that Huck was a crude character who would have a bad influence on "our pure-minded lads and lasses."

Realism in Art

Like writers of the period, many artists sought to capture local color and the gritty side of modern life. In the late 1800s, leading artists painted realistic everyday scenes.

As a young man during the Civil War, **Winslow Homer** drew scenes of brutal battles for magazines. Later, he gained fame for realistic scenes of the New England coast. Painter Thomas Eakins learned anatomy and dissected dead bodies to be able to portray the human form accurately. Many of his paintings depicted sports scenes or medical operations. **Henry Tanner,** an African American student of Eakins, won fame for pictures of black sharecroppers. Later, Tanner moved to Paris to enjoy greater freedom.

Other American artists preferred to work in Europe, too. James Whistler left Massachusetts for Paris and London, where his use of color and light influenced young European artists. John Singer Sargent made money painting portraits of wealthy Europeans.

The painter **Mary Cassatt** (kuh SAT) was born in Pennsylvania but settled in Paris. She carved out a place for herself in the French art world. Cassatt painted bright, colorful scenes of people in everyday situations, especially mothers with their children.

★ Section 4 Review ★

Recall

1. **Identify**   (a) Chautauqua Society, (b) Horatio Alger, (c) Stephen Crane, (d) Paul Laurence Dunbar, (e) Mark Twain, (f) Winslow Homer, (g) Henry Tanner, (h) Mary Cassatt.
2. **Define**   (a) dime novel, (b) realist, (c) local color.

Comprehension

3. How did public education change after the Civil War?

4. Describe two new kinds of reading matter that became popular in the late 1800s.
5. What was Mark Twain's goal in *Huckleberry Finn*?

Critical Thinking and Writing

6. **Understanding Causes and Effects**   How do you think the growth of public education was related to the popularity of newspapers, magazines, and books in the late 1800s?
7. **Drawing Conclusions**   Why do you think many American artists and writers turned to realism in the late 1800s?

★ ★

Activity   **Writing a Short Story**   Horatio Alger lives! Write the outline and first page for a "rags-to-riches" dime novel. Make your story begin with a thrilling "hook" that captures the attention of the reader.

Review and Activities

★ Sum It Up ★

Section 1 The New Immigrants
▶ Immigrants from southern and eastern Europe, Asia, and Latin America poured into the United States after the Civil War.
▶ Most immigrants settled in ethnic neighborhoods in cities while they assimilated into American culture.
▶ A new surge of nativism arose in response to the so-called new immigrants.

Section 2 Booming Cities
▶ Cities grew rapidly in the late 1800s, and many poor people lived in crowded slums.
▶ Under pressure from reformers, cities passed building codes and improved city services.
▶ Church groups, along with idealistic reformers like Jane Addams, worked to improve the life of poor city residents.

Section 3 City Life Transformed
▶ Skyscrapers, public transportation, and public parks became a part of the city scene in the late 1800s.
▶ Newspaper circulation grew as publishers introduced new features, comics, and sensational "yellow journalism."
▶ Leisure activities such as sports and entertainment helped unite Americans.

Section 4 Education and Culture
▶ In the late 1800s, education improved in the United States.
▶ American literature and art ranged from dime novels to new works of realism.

 For additional review of the major ideas of Chapter 21, see *Guide to the Essentials of American History* or *Interactive Student Tutorial CD-ROM,* which contains interactive review activities, graphic organizers, and practice tests.

🖵 Reviewing the Chapter

Define These Terms
Match each term with the correct definition.

Column 1	Column 2
1. ethnic group	**a.** process of becoming part of another culture
2. assimilation	
3. tenement	**b.** apartment in a slum building
4. vaudeville	**c.** variety show
5. dime novel	**d.** group of people who share a common culture
	e. low-priced paperback, usually offering thrilling adventure stories

Explore the Main Ideas
1. Why did many Armenians and Russian Jews immigrate to the United States in the late 1800s?
2. How did nativist reaction to immigration vary by region?
3. Describe the three sections of cities in the late 1800s.
4. How did church programs help the poor?
5. How did cities cope with traffic problems?

🖵 Chart Activity

Look at the graph below and answer the following questions:
1. About how many daily newspapers were printed in the United States in 1860? in 1900? **2.** During what 10-year period did the number of newspapers increase the most?
Critical Thinking List two causes for the rapid increase in the number of newspapers.

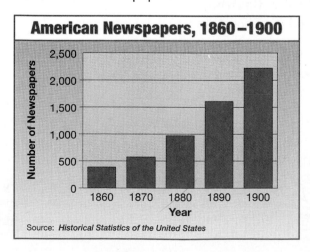

American Newspapers, 1860–1900

Source: *Historical Statistics of the United States*

☐ Critical Thinking and Writing

1. **Exploring Unit Themes Industrialization** What effect do you think the increased supply of immigrant workers in industry had on American industrial output?

2. **Understanding Chronology** Place the following events in their proper order: American cities boomed; city governments did not adequately serve their citizens; immigrants moved to the United States; reforms helped cities work better; Europeans and Asians were looking for economic opportunities.

3. **Linking Past and Present (a)** What did city dwellers in the 1800s do to escape the pressures of city life? **(b)** How do people in cities today relax?

4. **Making Decisions** If you had been alive in the late 1800s, would you have preferred to live in a large city like New York or Chicago, or on a ranch or farm in the West? Explain.

☐ Using Primary Sources

A New York journalist reporting on Chicago in 1893 told his readers:

> **66** I do not know how many very tall buildings Chicago contains, but they must number nearly two dozen.... The best of them are very elegantly and completely [decorated], and the communities of men inside them might almost live their lives within their walls, so [varied] are the occupations and services of the tenants.... It is a great mistake to think that we in New York possess all the elegant, rich, and ornamental [products] of taste. **99**

Source: *Harper's Chicago and the World's Fair,* Julian Ralph, 1893.

Recognizing Points of View (a) Does the reporter approve or disapprove of Chicago's buildings? **(b)** How does the writer think Chicago's buildings compare with those of New York?

ACTIVITY BANK

▶ Interdisciplinary Activity

Exploring Geography Research population figures for San Francisco, Chicago, and New York between 1865 and 1910. Create a line graph that shows how the population of these cities grew during this period.

▶ Career Skills Activity

Architects Find out more about the layout and the buildings of a city in the late 1800s. Then create a model of a city. Include skyscrapers, tenements, stores, theaters, parks, and other features.

▶ Citizenship Activity

Understanding Reform Look for a problem in your community that is similar to the problems faced by reformers like Jane Addams. Consult with officials and action groups in your area. Then, work out a proposal for reform of the problem.

Internet Activity

Use the Internet to find sites dealing with Angel Island. Use the information you find to write a poem like the one on page 560. In your poem, refer to specific conditions described by sites you visited.

EYEWITNESS Journal

You are an immigrant living in an American city in the 1880s or 1890s. In your EYEWITNESS JOURNAL, describe a typical day in your life. You might describe work, education, the importance of family and religion, neighborhood life, and leisure activities.

History Through Literature

My Ántonia

Willa Cather

Introduction

Willa Cather was one of the greatest American novelists. When she was nine, her family moved to Nebraska. Cather's experiences on the frontier inspired her 1918 novel *My Ántonia*. It tells the story of two young people growing up in Nebraska: the narrator, Jim, and his immigrant friend, Ántonia. In this passage, Jim describes a Nebraska winter on his family's farm.

Vocabulary

Before you read the selection, find the meaning of these words in a dictionary: **boisterously, bile, mottled.**

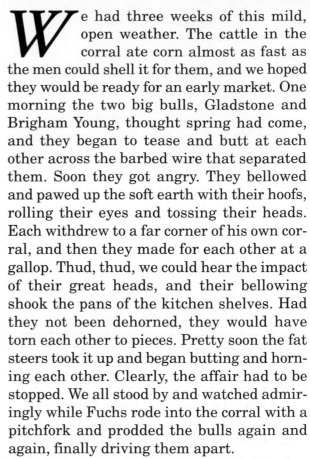

We had three weeks of this mild, open weather. The cattle in the corral ate corn almost as fast as the men could shell it for them, and we hoped they would be ready for an early market. One morning the two big bulls, Gladstone and Brigham Young, thought spring had come, and they began to tease and butt at each other across the barbed wire that separated them. Soon they got angry. They bellowed and pawed up the soft earth with their hoofs, rolling their eyes and tossing their heads. Each withdrew to a far corner of his own corral, and then they made for each other at a gallop. Thud, thud, we could hear the impact of their great heads, and their bellowing shook the pans of the kitchen shelves. Had they not been dehorned, they would have torn each other to pieces. Pretty soon the fat steers took it up and began butting and horning each other. Clearly, the affair had to be stopped. We all stood by and watched admiringly while Fuchs rode into the corral with a pitchfork and prodded the bulls again and again, finally driving them apart.

The big storm of the winter began on my eleventh birthday, the twentieth of January. When I went down to breakfast that morning, Jake and Otto came in white as snowmen, beating their hands and stamping their feet. They began to laugh boisterously when they saw me, calling:

"You've got a birthday present this time, Jim, and no mistake. They was a full-grown blizzard ordered for you."

All day the storm went on. The snow did not fall this time, it simply spilled out of heaven, like thousands of feather-beds being emptied. That afternoon the kitchen was a carpenter-shop; the men brought in their tools and made two great wooden shovels with long handles. Neither grandmother nor I could go out in the storm, so Jake fed the chickens and brought in a pitiful contribution of eggs.

Next day our men had to shovel until noon to reach the barn—and the snow was still falling! There had not been such a storm in the ten years my grandfather had lived in Nebraska. He said at dinner that we would

Like Willa Cather, Sallie Cover grew up in rural Nebraska. In her painting Homestead of Ellsworth L. Ball, *Cover shows a neighboring farm in the 1880s. Mrs. Ball tends to her baby in the doorway of the house. Her husband works with a team of horses in the field.*

★ **Compare this painting to the photograph on page 524. What differences can you see between the two homesteads?**

not try to reach the cattle—they were fat enough to go without their corn for a day or two; but to-morrow we must feed them and thaw out their water-tap so that they could drink. We could not so much as see the corrals, but we knew the steers were over there, huddled together under the north bank. Our ferocious bulls, subdued enough by this time, were probably warming each other's backs. "This'll take the bile out of 'em!" Fuchs remarked gleefully.

At noon that day the hens had not been heard from. After dinner Jake and Otto, their damp clothes now dried on them, stretched their stiff arms and plunged again into the drifts. They made a tunnel through the snow to the hen-house, with walls so solid that grandmother and I could walk back and forth in it. We found the chickens asleep; perhaps they thought night had come to stay. One old rooster was stirring about, pecking at the solid lump of ice in their water-tin. When we flashed the lantern in their eyes, the hens set up a great cackling and flew about clumsily, scattering down-feathers. The mottled, pin-headed guinea-hens, always resentful of captivity, ran screeching out into the tunnel and tried to poke their ugly, painted faces through the snow walls. By five o'clock the chores were done—just when it was time to begin them all over again! That was a strange, unnatural sort of day.

Analyzing Literature

1. How does Cather show that the blizzard was unusually harsh? Give two examples.
2. **(a)** Identify two extra chores that had to be done because of the blizzard. **(b)** What chore is Jim unable to do?
3. **Making Inferences** **(a)** What attitude do the men seem to have toward the storm? **(b)** What does this suggest about the people who settled the Plains?

Unit 7

A New Role for the Nation

ALL NATIONS ARE WELCOME TO THE WORLD'S COLUMBIAN EXPOS...

Viewing UNIT THEMES — Becoming a World Power

J.R. Campbell created this poster to celebrate a giant industrial fair in Chicago. At left are Uncle Sam and Columbia, two symbols of the United States. They welcome representatives of many lands—from Britain and Turkey to Mexico and China. By the late 1800s, the United States was becoming a major force in world trade and politics. ★ **How does this poster express national pride?**

Unit Theme Global Interaction

George Washington had advised the United States to limit its involvement with other nations. By the late 1800s, however, many Americans wanted the country to become more involved in world affairs. American industry, they said, needed new markets for its products. National pride also led some Americans to push for overseas colonies and a stronger military.

How did Americans of the time feel about global interaction? They can tell you in their own words.

★ ★

VIEWPOINTS ON GLOBAL INTERACTION

66 Whether they will or no, Americans must begin to look outward. The growing production of the country demands it. **99**
Alfred Thayer Mahan, naval officer (1897)

66 You cannot govern a foreign territory, a foreign people, another people than your own…you cannot [conquer] them and govern them against their will, because you think it is for their good. **99**
George Hoar, representative from Massachusetts (1899)

66 This is the divine mission of America…. American law, American order, American civilization, and the American flag will plant themselves on shores hitherto bloody and [ignorant]. **99**
Albert Beveridge, senator from Indiana (1900)

★ ★

Activity Writing to Learn Americans still disagree about how involved our country should be in global affairs. Conduct a survey of ten adults you know outside of school. Ask: "Do you think the United States should be more involved or less involved in foreign affairs?" Tally the responses in writing and share them with the class.

Chapter 22

Progressives and Reformers
1876–1914

A period of reform known as the Progressive Era took shape in the late 1800s. During this time, Americans worked to fight corruption in government, reduce the power of big business, and improve society. Government became more democratic as people in many states gained the power to pass laws directly. After years of effort, American women finally won the right to vote. From 1901 to 1921, three Presidents played a leading role in reform efforts.

African Americans and other minorities also took action against discrimination during the Progressive Era. Despite many setbacks, they laid the groundwork for future progress in civil rights.

Why Study History?

During the Progressive Era, journalists helped expose a variety of social ills, from child labor to lynching. Today, investigative reporters still play an important role in society. Yet their methods are often subject to criticism. To explore this connection, see the *Why Study History?* feature, "Journalists Keep Us Informed," in this chapter.

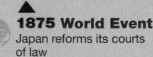

American Events

1881 Booker T. Washington founds Tuskegee Institute

1887 Interstate Commerce Act bans some railroad practices

1890 Wyoming is first state with women's suffrage admitted to union

1875   1880   1885   1890   1895

World Events

1875 World Event
Japan reforms its courts of law

1893 World Event
New Zealand gives vote to women

 Viewing HISTORY — **Fighting the Power of Trusts**

Horace Taylor created this cartoon, The Trust Giant's Point of View, *in 1900. Taylor was one of several cartoonists who used his art to protest against the power of giant corporations. Here, oil tycoon John D. Rockefeller holds the White House in his hand.* ★ **What do the buildings in the background represent? Why do you think Taylor put smokestacks on top of them?**

1901 ●
Theodore Roosevelt
becomes President

●1906
Pure Food and Drug
Act bans use of impure
ingredients

●1913
Federal Reserve Act
regulates banks

1895   1900   1905   1910   1915

 1900 World Event
Chinese rebels seek to
expel foreigners

 1910 World Event
Revolution begins in Mexico

Early Reforms

As You Read

Explore These Questions
- What was American politics like in the 1870s and 1880s?
- Why did many Americans oppose the spoils system?
- How did the government try to regulate business?

Define
- patronage
- civil service

Identify
- Gilded Age
- James Garfield
- Chester Arthur
- Grover Cleveland
- Interstate Commerce Commission
- Benjamin Harrison
- Sherman Antitrust Act

SETTING the Scene In the 1870s, Mark Twain and Charles Dudley Warner wrote *The Gilded Age.* ("Gilded" means coated with a thin layer of gold paint.) The novel poked fun at greed and political corruption. In one scene, a land speculator describes how he gets funds from Congress:

> **❝** A majority of the House committee, say, $10,000 apiece—$40,000; a majority of the Senate committee, the same each—say $40,000;... a lot of dinners to members—say $10,000 altogether; lot of [gifts] for Congressmen's wives and children—those go a long way.... **❞**

Of course, Twain and Warner were exaggerating. Still, for many Americans, the novel captured the spirit of the time. Before long, the decades between the 1870s and 1890s became known as the **Gilded Age.** During this period, reformers began to take steps to combat political corruption.

Gilded Age Politics

During the Gilded Age, political power was split between the two major parties. By and large, the North and Far West voted Republican, the South Democrat. In national elections, margins of victory were often paper-thin. Neither party could win control

The Gilded Age
by Twain and Warner

of Congress for more than a term or two. The Republican party did hold on to the White House for nearly 25 years. However, Presidents during the Gilded Age generally had less power than Congress.

For Americans of the Gilded Age, politics was mass entertainment. Campaigns featured brass bands, torchlight parades, free picnics, and three-hour speeches. Millions turned out to march, eat, drink, and listen. Voter turnout in presidential elections was higher than at any other time before or since: almost 80 percent.

Two concerns shaped the politics of the Gilded Age. Many Americans worried over the growing power of "special interests." Americans feared that bankers, industrialists, and other men of wealth were gaining control of politics and overpowering the interests of the public. A second worry was political corruption. Bribery and voter fraud angered voters. Reformers especially targeted the corrupt spoils system, the practice of rewarding supporters with government jobs.

Taming the Spoils System

Since the days of Andrew Jackson, the spoils system had grown. When a new President entered the White House, thousands of job seekers swarmed into Washington. They sought government jobs as rewards for their political support. Giving jobs to loyal supporters is called **patronage.** By handing out jobs, politicians cemented ties with their supporters and increased their control of government.

Patronage often led to corruption. Some officeholders helped themselves to public money. Many people appointed to government jobs had no skills for those jobs. For example, one man appointed as a court reporter in New York could not read or write.

Early reform efforts

Calls for reform slowly brought change. In 1877, President Rutherford Hayes took steps toward ending the spoils system. He refused to appoint his own supporters to office unless they were qualified for the job. Hayes also launched an investigation of the New York customs house. Investigators found that more than 200 appointed officials received high salaries for doing no work. Despite the protests of leading Republicans, Hayes dismissed two senior customs house officials.

James Garfield entered the White House in 1881. He thought that people should get government jobs on the basis of merit, or ability, rather than as a political reward. However, like other Presidents, Garfield found himself swamped by people seeking patronage.

One disappointed office seeker, Charles Guiteau, blamed Garfield for his failure. In July 1881, Guiteau shot the President in a train station. Two months later, Garfield died. The assassination outraged Americans and sparked new efforts to end the spoils system.

Exams for federal jobs

Upon Garfield's death, Vice President **Chester Arthur** became President. As a New York politician, Arthur had used the spoils system. In fact, he was one of the customs house officials dismissed by President Hayes only a few years earlier! "Elegant Arthur" was better known for his fine wardrobe than his political ideals. Yet, as President, he prosecuted corrupt politicians and worked with Congress to reform the spoils system.

In 1883, Congress passed the Pendleton Act. It created a Civil Service Commission to conduct exams for federal jobs. The **civil service** includes all federal jobs except elected positions and the armed forces. The aim of the civil service was to fill jobs on the basis of merit. People who scored highest on the civil service exams earned the posts.

At first, the Civil Service Commission controlled only a few federal jobs. Under pressure from reformers, however, later Presidents added more jobs to the civil service list. By 1900, the commission controlled about 40 percent of all federal jobs.

 Wealthy Americans in a Gilded Age

This painting by William T. Smedley shows a golf tournament at a country club near Washington, D.C. The Gilded Age was a time of great luxury for wealthy Americans like these. They built great mansions, dressed in the latest fashions, and enjoyed leisure activities like tennis and polo. Some also used their fortunes to buy political influence. ★ **Why were many Americans concerned about the power of the rich?**

Skills
FOR LIFE

| Critical Thinking | Managing Information | Communication | Maps, Charts, and Graphs |

Solving Problems

How Will I Use This Skill?

Every day, you face problems and make decisions about how to solve them. Sometimes, the problem is so simple the solution is automatic. When the issue is more complex, you have to put more effort into considering possible solutions and the consequences of each alternative. In the community, leaders and citizens try to come up with practical solutions that not only solve problems but eliminate their causes as well.

LEARN the Skill

To solve a problem, you first have to define what the problem is. Use the following steps to help you in this process:

❶ Identify the problem.

❷ Determine the impact of the problem.

❸ Identify alternate solutions to the problem.

❹ Determine the effectiveness of the solution.

PRACTICE the Skill

Reread what you have learned about the spoils system. Then, answer the following questions:

❶ Reformers during the Gilded Age considered the spoils system to be a problem. Describe how the spoils system worked.

❷ (a) How did the spoils system lead to corruption? (b) Do you think the spoils system made government more or less efficient? Explain.

❸ (a) What actions did Congress take to tame the spoils system? (b) Jot down two or three other alternatives you might have considered if you had been in Congress at the time.

❹ How effective was Congressional action in solving the negative effects of the spoils system? Explain.

APPLY the Skill

Think about some problem that you or your classmates faced in school recently. Describe the problem. Give as many alternatives as you can to resolve the issue. Which do you think is the best solution? Explain your answer.

President Grover Cleveland supported reforms to expand the civil service.

Regulating Big Business

In 1877, Collis Huntington, builder of the Central Pacific Railroad, faced a problem. A bill before Congress aimed at breaking his control of rail routes to southern California. To Huntington, the solution was simple—bribe members of Congress to kill the bill. "It costs money to fix things," he explained.

The behavior of men like Huntington convinced many Americans that big businesses controlled the government. Public outcry against monopolies grew.

Interstate Commerce Act

The government responded by taking steps to regulate railroads and other large businesses. In 1887, President **Grover Cleveland** signed the Interstate Commerce Act. The new law forbade practices such as pools and rebates. (See pages 534–535.) It also set up the **Interstate Commerce Commission,** or ICC, to oversee the railroads.

At first, the ICC was weak. Richard Olney, an attorney for one of the railroad owners, explained:

66 The Commission...satisfies the popular clamor for a government supervision of the railroads, at the same time that supervision is almost entirely [ineffective]. **99**

In court challenges, most judges ruled in favor of the railroads. Still, Congress had shown that it was ready to regulate big business. Later laws made the Interstate Commerce Commission more effective.

Sherman Antitrust Act

In 1888, President Cleveland lost his bid for reelection. **Benjamin Harrison** became President. In 1890, Harrison signed the **Sherman Antitrust Act.** The act prohibited trusts or other businesses from limiting competition.

The Sherman Antitrust Act sounded strong, but in practice trusts used the courts to block enforcement. Judges ruled that the law was an illegal attempt by government to control private property.

Instead of regulating trusts, the Sherman Antitrust Act was first used to stop labor unions. The courts said union strikes blocked free trade and thereby threatened competition. As the reform spirit spread, however, courts began to use the Sherman Act against monopolies.

★ Section 1 Review ★

Recall

1. **Identify** (a) Gilded Age, (b) James Garfield, (c) Chester Arthur, (d) Grover Cleveland, (e) Interstate Commerce Commission, (f) Benjamin Harrison, (g) Sherman Antitrust Act.
2. **Define** (a) patronage, (b) civil service.

Comprehension

3. What two concerns dominated Gilded Age politics?
4. Why did many Americans favor creation of a civil service?

5. **(a)** Why did Congress create the ICC? **(b)** Was the ICC effective? Explain.

Critical Thinking and Writing

6. **Making Inferences** The term "golden age" is used to describe a period of great progress and achievement. What point do you think Twain and Warner were making by calling the 1870s the Gilded Age?
7. **Synthesizing Information** Why do you think early efforts to regulate big business had little success?

★ ★

Activity **Writing an Editorial** You are a newspaper editor in 1881. Write an editorial on President James Garfield's death. Explain the circumstances and tell why the assassination shows the need to reform the spoils system.

2 ★ The Progressives and Their Goals

As You Read

Explore These Questions
- Why did reformers attack city governments?
- How did the press contribute to reform efforts?
- What new practices gave more power to voters?

Define
- muckraker
- public interest
- primary
- initiative
- referendum
- recall
- graduated income tax

Identify
- William Tweed
- Ida Tarbell
- Upton Sinclair
- Progressives
- John Dewey
- Robert La Follette
- Wisconsin Idea
- Sixteenth Amendment

SETTING the Scene Joseph Folk, city prosecutor of St. Louis, was furious. Local politicians had just ordered him to hire men he felt were dishonest.

"I and my office, the criminal law, was to be run by—criminals!" he complained to reporter Lincoln Steffens. Instead, Folk led a crusade against dishonest politicians and businessmen. Elsewhere, other reformers fought to oust corrupt politicians and to give voters greater power.

Reforming City Government

How had city governments become so corrupt? Growing cities needed many improvements, such as new sewers, better garbage collection, and more roads. In many cities, politicians traded these jobs for money. In some places, bribes and corruption became a way of life.

Boss rule

Powerful politicians, known as bosses, came to rule many cities. They controlled all work done in the city and demanded payoffs from businesses. Often, bosses did not hold office. Instead, they worked behind the scenes to influence officeholders. In California, for example, Abraham Ruef was the Republican boss for northern San Francisco. At one time, Boss Ruef controlled enough delegates to choose his party's nominee for governor.

City bosses were popular with the poor, especially with immigrants. Bosses provided jobs and made loans to the needy. They handed out extra coal in winter and turkeys at Thanksgiving. In exchange, the poor voted for the boss or his candidate.

Boss Tweed

In New York City, Boss **William Tweed** carried corruption to new heights. During the 1860s and 1870s, Tweed cheated New York out of more than $100 million. Reformers tried to have him jailed.

Journalists exposed Tweed's wrongdoings. Cartoonist Thomas Nast showed Boss Tweed as a vulture destroying the city. Nast's attacks upset Tweed. He complained that his supporters might be unable to read, but they could understand pictures.

Faced with prison, Tweed fled to Spain. There, local police arrested him when they recognized him from a Nast cartoon. Tweed died in jail in 1878. Thousands of poor New Yorkers mourned his death.

Good government leagues

Reformers in many cities formed good government leagues. Their goal was to replace corrupt officials with honest leaders.

The leagues met with some success. The good government league in Minneapolis sent a corrupt mayor to jail. In Cleveland, reformers elected Tom Johnson as mayor. Johnson improved garbage collection and sewage systems in the city. He also set up services to help the poor of Cleveland.

Muckrakers Rouse Public Opinion

To bring about change, reformers first had to ignite public anger. A major weapon was the press. Newspaper reporters visited the slums. They described burned-out tenements and exposed how corruption led to inadequate fire protection. They talked to mothers whose babies were dying of tuberculosis, a lung disease. Photographer Jacob Riis provided shocking images of slum life.

Crusading journalists like Riis became known as **muckrakers.** People said they raked the dirt, or muck, and exposed it to public view. One muckraker, **Ida Tarbell,** targeted the unfair practices of big business. Her articles about the Standard Oil Company led to demands for tighter controls on trusts.

In 1906, **Upton Sinclair** shocked the nation when he published *The Jungle.* This novel revealed gruesome details about the meatpacking industry in Chicago. Although the book was fiction, it was based on things Sinclair had seen. One passage described the rats in a meatpacking house:

> 66 These rats were nuisances, and the packers would put poisoned bread out for them: they would die, and then rats, bread, and meat would go into the hoppers together. 99

Muckrakers helped change public opinion. For years, middle-class people had ignored the need for reform. When they saw

Viewing HISTORY **Rousing Public Anger**

Danish-born muckraker Jacob Riis used a powerful weapon—the camera—to influence public opinion. In books like How the Other Half Lives, *he showed middle-class readers what poverty really looked like. This Riis photograph shows an Italian ragpicker and her baby in a New York City tenement.*
★ **How do you think photographs like this encouraged reform?**

Camera of the 1890s

how corruption menaced the nation, they joined with muckrakers to demand change.

The Progressives

By 1900, reformers were calling themselves **Progressives.** By that, they meant they were forward-thinking people who wanted to improve American life. They won many changes from 1898 to 1917. This period is often called the Progressive Era.

Progressives were never a single group with a single aim. They backed various causes. What united them was their faith that the problems of society could be solved.

Progressive beliefs

Progressives drew inspiration from two sources. One was religion. In the late 1800s, Protestant ministers had begun preaching a social gospel. (See page 569.) It stressed the duty of Christians to improve society.

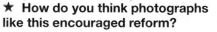

Connections *With* **Civics**

Mayor Tom Johnson of Cleveland fought to make public parks more open to the public. Upper-class people protested, especially when Johnson ordered the removal of "Keep Off the Grass" signs. Eventually, Johnson created a citywide system of parks with hundreds of playgrounds and baseball fields.

Why Study History?

Because Journalists Keep Us Informed

★ ★

Historical Background

During the Progressive Era, Josiah Flynt wrote about crime in American cities. His reports were accurate because Flynt had gone undercover. He had assumed the role of an urban thug and joined criminal gangs. To blend in, he committed crimes himself.

Some people found Flynt's methods inexcusable. Nevertheless, Flynt's muckraking articles exposed illegal gang activities and corruption among police and political officials. His work helped spark needed reforms.

Connections to Today

Today, investigative journalists are everywhere, from your local paper to national news programs such as *60 Minutes*. Like muckrakers of the past, today's reporters continue to provide information that can benefit the public. Some critics, though, say that reporters go too far.

In 1992, a television station used undercover reporters with hidden cameras to show unsanitary conditions at a supermarket. The reporters lied in order to be hired. They also took pictures without the store's permission. After the report aired, the supermarket sued. A jury found that reporters had trespassed and engaged in fraud to get their story. The court ordered the network to pay the supermarket $5.5 million.

Connections to You

We may disagree about the methods investigative journalists use. Yet these muck-

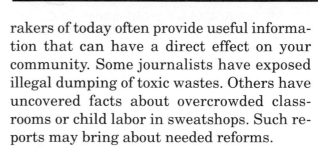

Television news teams have exposed many public health violations, such as illegal dumping of dangerous chemicals.

rakers of today often provide useful information that can have a direct effect on your community. Some journalists have exposed illegal dumping of toxic wastes. Others have uncovered facts about overcrowded classrooms or child labor in sweatshops. Such reports may bring about needed reforms.

1. **Comprehension**   How did Josiah Flynt get the information to write his stories?

2. **Critical Thinking**   Do you think journalists should be allowed to break some laws to expose wrongdoing? Explain.

 **Exploring Local News**
Read a local newspaper or watch a local television news program to find an example of investigative journalism. Write a brief summary of the story.

Advances in science also inspired Progressives. Like scientists, Progressives made use of careful analysis and statistics.

Progressive reformers believed that the **public interest,** or the good of the people, should guide government actions. The public interest, they said, must not be sacrificed to the greed of a few trusts and city bosses.

Progressives stressed the importance of education. **John Dewey,** a Progressive educator, wanted schools to promote reform. They must not only teach democratic values, he argued, but reflect them. Dewey encouraged students to ask questions and work together to solve problems. On college campuses, Progressive educators stressed the need to teach skills to help society. Colleges offered new courses in areas such as social work.

Women played leading roles in the Progressive Era. In the mid-1800s, a new view of women emerged. Many Americans believed that women were morally superior to men. In a world of corruption, they said, women had the moral force to bring about change. This view encouraged many women to work for reform. To increase their social influence, they also sought the right to vote.

The Wisconsin Idea

Progressivism got its start in the states of the Midwest. Among the leading Progressives was **Robert La Follette** of Wisconsin. "The will of the people shall be the law of the land," was his motto. His fighting spirit won him the nickname "Battling Bob."

In 1900, La Follette was elected governor. He introduced a statewide program of Progressive reforms, called the **Wisconsin Idea.** For example, he lowered railroad rates. The result was increased rail traffic, which helped both railroad owners and customers.

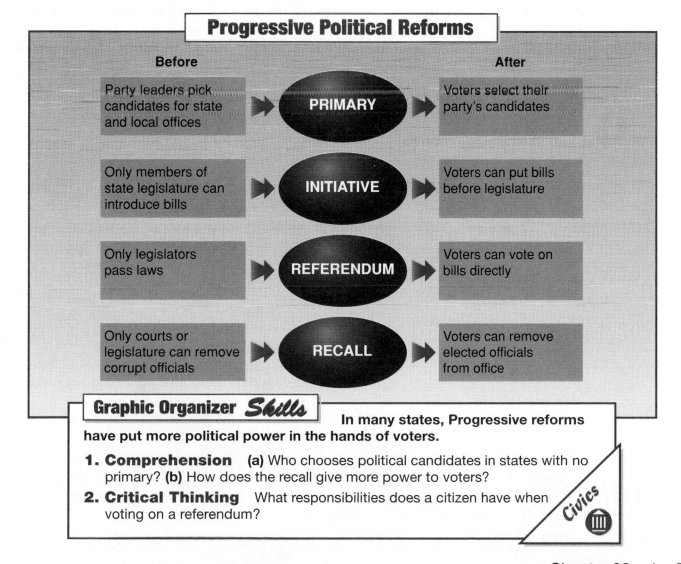

Progressive Political Reforms

Before		After
Party leaders pick candidates for state and local offices	**PRIMARY**	Voters select their party's candidates
Only members of state legislature can introduce bills	**INITIATIVE**	Voters can put bills before legislature
Only legislators pass laws	**REFERENDUM**	Voters can vote on bills directly
Only courts or legislature can remove corrupt officials	**RECALL**	Voters can remove elected officials from office

Graphic Organizer Skills

In many states, Progressive reforms have put more political power in the hands of voters.

1. **Comprehension** (a) Who chooses political candidates in states with no primary? (b) How does the recall give more power to voters?
2. **Critical Thinking** What responsibilities does a citizen have when voting on a referendum?

Civics

Progressives from other states visited Wisconsin to study La Follette's system. Before long, voters in California, Indiana, Arkansas, Oregon, and New York were talking about the Wisconsin Idea. They, too, elected Progressive governors who introduced far-reaching changes.

The will of the people

LaFollette and other Progressives believed that the people would make the right decisions if given the chance. As a result, they pressed for reforms to give voters more power.

Since Andrew Jackson's time, party leaders had picked candidates for local and state offices. Instead, Progressives pressed for **primaries,** in which voters choose their party's candidate for the general election. In 1903, Wisconsin was the first state to adopt the primary. By 1917, all but four states had done so.

Progressives also urged states to adopt measures that allowed voters to participate directly in lawmaking. The **initiative** gave voters the right to put a bill directly before the state legislature. The **referendum** allowed them to vote the bill into law at the next election.

Another Progressive measure was the **recall.** The recall allowed voters to remove an elected official in the middle of his or her term. This gave ordinary people a chance to get rid of corrupt officials.

Other Reforms

Other Progressive reforms required federal action. Most Progressives supported a **graduated income tax,** which taxes people from different income levels at different rates. The wealthy pay taxes at a higher rate than the poor or the middle class.

In 1895, the Supreme Court had ruled that a federal income tax was unconstitutional. In response, Progressives campaigned to amend the Constitution. In 1913, the states ratified the **Sixteenth Amendment.** It gave Congress the power to impose an income tax.

Progressives backed another amendment. Since 1789, senators had been elected by state legislatures, rather than directly by voters. Special interests sometimes bribed lawmakers to vote for certain candidates. Progressives wanted to end such abuses. In 1913, the states ratified the Seventeenth Amendment for the direct election of senators.

★ Section 2 Review ★

Recall

1. **Identify:** (a) William Tweed, (b) Ida Tarbell, (c) Upton Sinclair, (d) Progressives, (e) John Dewey, (f) Robert La Follette, (g) Wisconsin Idea, (h) Sixteenth Amendment.
2. **Define** (a) muckraker, (b) public interest, (c) primary, (d) initiative, (e) referendum, (f) recall, (g) graduated income tax.

Comprehension

3. (a) How did city bosses win the support of the poor? (b) Why did reformers oppose bosses?

4. How did muckrakers help change public attitudes?
5. Describe two ways the Progressives increased the power of voters.

Critical Thinking and Writing

6. **Analyzing Ideas** Dewey thought school classes should reflect democratic values. What did he mean?
7. **Defending a Position** Do you agree with La Follette and other Progressives that the people will make the right decisions if given the chance? Why or why not?

Activity **Drawing a Political Cartoon** You are Thomas Nast. Boss Tweed and his pals are stealing millions from the city you love. Draw a political cartoon commenting on Tweed's corruption.

3 Presidents Support Reforms

As You Read

Explore These Questions
- How did Theodore Roosevelt try to control trusts?
- What other reforms did Roosevelt support?
- What were Woodrow Wilson's goals as President?

Define
- trustbuster
- conservation
- national park

Identify
- Theodore Roosevelt
- Square Deal
- Pure Food and Drug Act
- William Howard Taft
- Bull Moose party
- Woodrow Wilson
- New Freedom
- Federal Reserve Act
- Federal Trade Commission

SETTING the Scene In 1900, Republicans needed a reform-minded candidate to run with President William McKinley. They offered the job to **Theodore Roosevelt,** a New York politician. However, Roosevelt was not interested in serving as Vice President. "I will not accept under any circumstances," he replied.

As a loyal Republican, Roosevelt finally did accept the nomination. A year later, McKinley was shot and Roosevelt became President.

By 1901, Progressives were having success in many states. With Roosevelt in the White House, they hoped to push national reforms and turn the federal government into a protector of the people.

Teddy Roosevelt

Teddy Roosevelt—or "TR," as he was called—belonged to an old, wealthy New York family. As a child, he suffered from asthma and was often sick. To build his strength, he lifted weights, ran, and boxed.

Early career

The children of wealthy, old families were expected to live lives of ease and privilege. Instead, TR entered politics after college, determined to end corruption and protect the public interest.

Roosevelt's friends mocked his political ambitions. He later recalled:

66 They assured me that the men I met would be rough and brutal and unpleasant to deal with. I answered that I certainly would not quit until I...found out whether I was really too weak to hold my own in the rough and tumble. 99

By age 26, Roosevelt was serving in the New York state legislature. Then tragedy almost ended his political career. In 1884, his mother and his young wife died on the same day. Overcome by grief, Roosevelt quit the legislature. He went west to work on a cattle ranch in present-day North Dakota.

After two years, Roosevelt returned to the East and to politics. He served on the Civil Service Commission. Later on, he held posts as head of the New York City police department and as assistant secretary of the navy.

In 1898, when the United States went to war against Spain, Roosevelt fought in Cuba. He returned home to a hero's welcome. That same year, he was elected governor of New York.

Pitcher in the likeness of Theodore Roosevelt

TR on the Campaign Trail

▲
*Teddy bear
of the early 1900s*

This photograph shows Theodore Roosevelt campaigning in Wyoming in 1903. TR put tremendous energy into his speeches, pounding his fists into the air as he spoke. Roosevelt's activities as an outdoorsman also helped his public image. After he refused to shoot a small captured bear, a toy company named a new product after the President: the Teddy bear. ★ **How did Roosevelt's actions as President support his image as an energetic fighter?**

A progressive governor

Since his days in the legislature, Roosevelt had pushed for reform. Other legislators called him a "goo goo," a mocking name for someone who wanted good government. As governor, Roosevelt worked for Progressive reforms.

New York Republican bosses were relieved when Roosevelt became Vice President. Then, in September 1901, an assassin shot President McKinley. At age 42, Roosevelt became the nation's youngest President.

TR and Big Business

Roosevelt promised to continue McKinley's pro-business policies. Still, many business people worried about the new President's Progressive ideas.

Roosevelt believed that giant corporations were here to stay. He thought, however, that there were good trusts and bad trusts. Good trusts were efficient and fair and should be left alone, TR said. Bad trusts took advantage of their workers and cheated the public. The government should either control them or break them up.

Taking on the trusts

Roosevelt wanted to test the power of the government to break up bad trusts. In 1902, he ordered the Attorney General, the government's chief lawyer, to bring a lawsuit against the Northern Securities Company. Roosevelt argued that Northern Securities used unfair business practices in violation of the Sherman Act.

Stock prices on Wall Street, the New York center of business and finance, fell at news of the lawsuit. One newspaper editor noted:

❝ Wall Street is paralyzed at the thought that a President of the United States would sink so low as to try to enforce the law. ❞

While business leaders worried, ordinary people supported the President.

In 1904, the Supreme Court ruled that Northern Securities had violated the Sherman Antitrust Act by limiting trade. It ordered the trust to be broken up. The decision showed the effects of Progressive reform. In the 1890s, the Sherman Antitrust Act had been used to break up unions, not trusts.

President Roosevelt hailed the case as a victory. He then ordered the Attorney General to file suit against other trusts, including Standard Oil and the American Tobacco Company. The courts later ordered both trusts to be broken up on the grounds that they blocked free trade.

Some business leaders called Roosevelt a **trustbuster** who wanted to destroy all trusts. "Certainly not," replied Roosevelt, only those that "have done something we regard as wrong." He preferred to control or regulate trusts, not "bust" them.

Support for labor

Roosevelt also clashed with the nation's mine owners. In 1902, Pennsylvania coal miners went on strike. They wanted better pay and a shorter workday. Mine owners refused to talk to the miners' union.

As winter approached, schools and hospitals around the country ran out of coal. Furious at the stubbornness of mine owners, Roosevelt threatened to send in troops to run the mines. In response, owners sat down with the union and reached an agreement.

Working men and women around the country cheered. Earlier Presidents had used federal troops to break strikes. Roosevelt was the first to side with labor.

The Square Deal

In 1904, Roosevelt ran for President in his own right. During the campaign, he promised Americans a **Square Deal.** By this, he meant that many different groups—farmers and consumers, workers and owners—should have an equal opportunity to succeed. The promise of a Square Deal helped Roosevelt win a landslide victory.

Railroads were a key target of the Square Deal. Roosevelt knew that the Interstate Commerce Act of 1887 had done little to end rebates and other abuses. He urged Congress to pass the Elkins Act in 1903. It outlawed rebates. In 1906, Congress gave the ICC the power to set railroad rates.

Protecting consumers

Roosevelt had read Upton Sinclair's shocking novel, *The Jungle.* In response, he sent more government inspectors to meatpacking houses. The owners refused to let the inspectors in.

Roosevelt fought back. He gave the newspapers copies of a government report that supported Sinclair's picture of the meatpacking industry. As public rage mounted, Congress passed the Meat Inspection Act of 1906. It forced packers to open their doors to more inspectors.

Roosevelt supported other reforms to protect consumers. Muckrakers had revealed that the drug companies made false claims about their medicines. They also found that

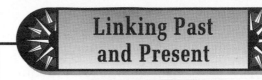

Linking Past and Present

Past

Present

Protecting the Consumer

Before the Progressive Era, drug manufacturers were not controlled by the law. Advertisers often made wild, exotic claims for medicines that actually did nothing. Today, every medicine label must include a list of ingredients, exact directions for use, and warnings about possible side effects. ★ **How is the advertisement at the top different from a medicine ad you might see in a magazine today?**

the food industry added dangerous chemicals to canned foods. In 1906, Congress passed the **Pure Food and Drug Act.** It required food and drug makers to list ingredients on their packages. It also tried to end false advertising and the use of impure ingredients.

Protecting resources

Roosevelt grew alarmed about the destruction of the American wilderness. To fuel the nation's industrial growth, lumber companies were cutting down whole forests. Miners were taking iron and coal from the earth at a frantic pace and leaving gaping holes.

Roosevelt loved the outdoors and objected to this destruction of the land. He believed in **conservation,** the protection of natural resources. "The rights of the public to natural resources outweigh private rights," he said.

Roosevelt thought that natural resources could serve both the public interest and private companies. Some forest and mountain areas, he said, should be left as wilderness. Others could supply wood for lumber. He wanted lumber companies to replant trees in the forests they were clearing. Mining, too, should be controlled.

Under Roosevelt, the government created some 170,000 acres of national parkland. A **national park** is an area set aside and run by the federal government for people to visit.

Taft and the Reformers

In 1908, Roosevelt decided not to run for reelection. Instead, he threw his support behind **William Howard Taft,** his Secretary of War. With Roosevelt's backing, Taft won an easy victory. A confident Roosevelt said:

Connections With Geography

Theodore Roosevelt's conservation efforts encouraged Mexican immigration. In 1902, Congress passed the Newlands Act to finance construction of irrigation projects in arid states. The law created millions of acres of new farmland in California, Texas, and Arizona. As a result, many Mexicans entered the United States in search of work.

66 Taft will carry on the work ... as I have. His policies, principles, purposes, and ideals are the same as mine. The Roosevelt policies will not go out with Roosevelt. 99

Roosevelt then set off for Africa to hunt big game for a year. He left behind an impressive record as a reformer. He also left the presidency more powerful than it had been at any time since the Civil War.

Taft was different from Roosevelt. Unlike the hard-driving, energetic Roosevelt, Taft was quiet and careful. Roosevelt loved power. Taft feared it.

Nevertheless, Taft supported many Progressive causes. He broke up even more trusts than TR. He supported the graduated income tax, approved new safety regulations for mines, and signed laws setting an eight-hour day for government employees. Under Taft, the Department of Labor set up a bureau to deal with the problems of working children.

Despite such successes, Taft lost Progressive support. In 1909, Taft signed a bill that raised most tariffs. Progressives opposed high tariffs because they felt tariffs raised prices for consumers. Also, Taft fired the chief of the United States Forest Service during a dispute over the sale of wilderness areas in Alaska. Progressives accused Taft of blocking conservation efforts.

Election of 1912

When Roosevelt returned from Africa, he found that reformers felt Taft had betrayed them. Roosevelt declared that Taft was "a flub-dub with a streak of the second-rate." TR decided to run against Taft for the Republican nomination in 1912.

The Bull Moose party

Roosevelt won wide public support. He won almost every state primary he entered. Still, many Republican business leaders distrusted Roosevelt. Also, Taft still controlled the party leadership. At the Republican convention, the party nominated Taft.

Right in the middle of Taft's nomination, angry Progressive Republicans stormed out

Yosemite National Park

Almost 100 years ago, President Theodore Roosevelt camped out in the Yosemite Valley in California. He viewed its majestic mountains and walked beneath its towering sequoia trees—the oldest living things on Earth. Today, thanks to the work of conservationists like Roosevelt, you can still enjoy Yosemite and other natural beauties. In fact, you can even see the very same redwoods Roosevelt saw!

★ *To learn more about this historic site, write: Yosemite National Park, PO Box 577, Yosemite, CA 95389.*

◄ *This sign welcomes you to Yosemite's sequoia forest.*

of the convention. They set up a new Progressive party and chose Roosevelt as their candidate. He eagerly accepted. "I feel as strong as a bull moose," he boasted. Roosevelt and his supporters became known as the **Bull Moose party.**

A Democratic victory

Democrats picked **Woodrow Wilson,** a Progressive, as their candidate. Born in Virginia, Wilson was the son of a Presbyterian minister. His father taught him that the world was strictly divided between good and evil. As a boy, Wilson made up his mind always to fight for what he thought was right. Wilson had served as president of Princeton University and as governor of New Jersey. He was known as a brilliant scholar and a cautious reformer.

Together, Taft and Roosevelt won more votes than Wilson. However, they split the Republican vote. Their quarrel helped Wilson win the election of 1912.

President Wilson

Wilson took the oath of office in March 1913. His inaugural address reflected his strong, unbending sense of morality:

❝ The nation has been deeply stirred, stirred by a solemn passion, stirred by the knowledge of wrong, of ideals lost, of government too often... made an instrument of evil. The feelings with which we face this new age of right and opportunity sweep across our heart-strings like some air out of God's own presence. ❞

Wilson asked honest, forward-looking Americans to stand at his side. "God helping me," he pledged, "I will not fail them."

The New Freedom

At first, Wilson's goal was to break up trusts into smaller companies. By doing so, he hoped to restore the competition that had once existed in the American economy. "If America is not to have free enterprise, then she can have freedom of no sort whatever," he said. Wilson called his program the **New Freedom.**

Wilson worked with Congress for laws to spur competition. He pushed first for a lower tariff to create more competition from imports. After a struggle, Congress lowered the tariff. It also imposed a graduated income tax to make up for lost revenues.

To regulate banking, Congress passed the **Federal Reserve Act** in 1913. The act set up a nationwide system of federal banks. The system gave the government the power to raise or lower interest rates and control the money supply.

I THINK WE'VE GOT ANOTHER WASHINGTON AND WILSON IS HIS NAME

Campaign song for Woodrow Wilson

Regulating competition

To ensure fair competition, President Wilson persuaded Congress to create the **Federal Trade Commission** (FTC) in 1914. The FTC had power to investigate companies and order them to stop using business practices that destroyed all competitors.

That same year, Wilson signed the Clayton Antitrust Act. The law was weaker than he wanted. However, it did ban some business practices that limited free enterprise. It also barred antitrust laws from being used against unions—a major victory for labor.

Despite Wilson's successes, the Progressive movement slowed after 1914. By then, the Progressives had achieved many of their goals. In addition, the outbreak of war in Europe seized public attention. Americans became concerned that the fighting in Europe might soon involve the United States.

★ Section 3 Review ★

Recall

1. **Identify** (a) Theodore Roosevelt, (b) Square Deal, (c) Pure Food and Drug Act, (d) William Howard Taft, (e) Bull Moose party, (f) Woodrow Wilson, (g) New Freedom, (h) Federal Reserve Act, (i) Federal Trade Commission.
2. **Define** (a) trustbuster, (b) conservation, (c) national park.

Comprehension

3. (a) How did Roosevelt feel about trusts? (b) What action did he take in the Northern Securities case?
4. Describe one action Roosevelt took to achieve each of the following goals: (a) consumer protection, (b) protection of natural resources.

5. Describe two actions Wilson took to ensure competition.

Critical Thinking and Writing

6. **Analyzing Ideas** Reread the comment of the newspaper editor on page 598. (a) Why were many business leaders surprised by Roosevelt's actions in the Northern Securities case? (b) What point was the editor making about the role of the President?
7. **Making Inferences** "I'm glad to be going," commented William Howard Taft as he left the White House in 1913. "This is the lonesomest place in the world." Why do you think Taft might have felt this way?

Activity Expressing an Opinion You are the owner of a large area of wilderness. Theodore Roosevelt wants to use your land for a park. Write him a letter in which you explain your reaction to his proposal.

Progress for Women

4

As You Read

Explore These Questions
- How did women work for suffrage in the Progressive Era?
- What new opportunities did women earn?
- How did the temperance movement gain strength?

Define
- suffragist
- temperance movement

Identify
- Carrie Chapman Catt
- Alice Paul
- Nineteenth Amendment
- Florence Kelley
- Frances Willard
- Carry Nation
- Eighteenth Amendment

SETTING the Scene Susan B. Anthony had broken the law. Her crime was voting. Along with 15 other women, Anthony registered to vote in her home town of Rochester, New York, in 1872. When she cast her ballot, she was arrested.

At her trial, the judge directed that Anthony be found guilty. The judge then asked if she had anything to say. Anthony responded defiantly:

> 66 Yes, your honor, I have many things to say; for in your ordered verdict of guilty, you have trampled underfoot every vital principle of our government. My natural rights, my civil rights, my political rights, are all alike ignored. Robbed of the fundamental privilege of citizenship, I am degraded from the status of a citizen to that of a subject; and not only myself individually, but all of my sex, are...doomed to political subjection. 99

Anthony refused to quiet down or to ask for mercy. The judge then ordered her to pay a fine of $100. "May it please your honor," Anthony replied, "I shall never pay a dollar of your unjust penalty." Anthony never did pay the fine. Her courageous stand won her many new followers.

Porcelain figure of a women's suffrage campaigner

During the Progressive Era, women continued their long battle to win the right to vote. They also worked for many other reforms. Women spoke out against trusts, supported pure food laws, and called for an end to child labor. They also led a renewed effort to ban the sale of alcohol.

Working for the Vote

The struggle to grant women the vote, or suffrage, went back many years. As you read in Chapter 15, the Seneca Falls Convention in 1848 was the start of an organized women's rights movement in the United States. Delegates at the convention called for many reforms, including women's suffrage.

After the Civil War, Elizabeth Cady Stanton and Susan B. Anthony led a renewed drive to win the vote. In 1869, they formed the National Woman Suffrage Association. This group worked to amend the Constitution to give women the vote. Stanton and Anthony opposed the Fifteenth Amendment because it gave the vote to African American men but not to women.

Women vote in the West

Few politicians favored women's suffrage. Still, in the late 1800s, women gained the right to vote in four western states: Wyoming, Utah, Colorado, and Idaho. Pioneer women had worked alongside men

By 1906, Elizabeth Cady Stanton and Susan B. Anthony had died. A new generation of leaders took up their cause. **Carrie Chapman Catt** spoke powerfully in favor of suffrage. Catt had worked as a school principal and a reporter. Later, she became head of the National American Woman Suffrage Association.

Catt was an inspired speaker and a brilliant organizer. She devised a detailed battle plan for fighting the war for suffrage, state by state. Around the country, **suffragists,** or people who campaigned for women's right to vote, followed her strategy.

Slowly, the efforts of Catt and other suffragists succeeded. Year by year, more states in the West and Midwest gave women the vote. For the most part, women in these states were allowed to vote only in state elections. In time, more and more women called for an amendment to the Constitution to give them a voice in national elections.

Amending the Constitution

Some suffragists took strong measures to achieve their goal. **Alice Paul** was one of them. In 1907, Paul had gone to England. There, she had marched with suffragists in London. She had been jailed and gone on hunger strikes—all to help British women win the vote. Later, Paul returned home to support the cause of suffrage for American women.

Protest at the White House

Paul and other suffragists met with President Wilson soon after he took office in 1913. Wilson was not opposed to women's suffrage. He did not, however, support a constitutional amendment. Paul told the President what suffragists wanted:

❦ We said we're going to try and get [a constitutional amendment] through Congress, that we would like to have his help and needed his support very much. And then we sent him another delegation and another and another and another and another and another and another—every type of women's group we could get. ❧

to build the farms and cities of the West. By giving women the vote, these states recognized women's contributions.

When Wyoming applied for statehood in 1890, many members of Congress wanted the state to change its voting law. During the debate, Wyoming lawmakers wired Congress: "We may stay out of the Union for 100 years, but we will come in with our women." Wyoming barely won admission.

Suffragists

In the early 1900s, the women's suffrage movement gained strength. More than 5 million women were earning wages outside the home. Although women were paid less than men, wages gave women a sense of power. Many demanded a say in making the laws that governed them.

In January 1917, Paul and other women stopped sending delegations and began to picket at the White House. After several months of these silent demonstrations, police began arresting the protesters. Paul received a seven-month jail sentence for obstructing the sidewalk. To protest their arrest, Paul and others went on a hunger strike. Prison officials force fed the women in an attempt to end the strike. Upon release, Paul and the other women resumed their picketing.

Victory at last

By early 1918, the tide began to turn in favor of the suffrage cause. The tireless work of Catt, Paul, and others began to pay off. President Wilson agreed to support the suffrage amendment.

Finally, in 1919, Congress passed the **Nineteenth Amendment** guaranteeing women the right to vote. By August 1920, three fourths of the states had ratified the Nineteenth Amendment. The amendment doubled the number of eligible voters in the United States.

Women Win New Opportunities

For years, women struggled to open doors to jobs and education. Most states refused to grant women licenses to practice in professions such as law, medicine, or college teaching. Myra Bradwell taught herself law, just as Abraham Lincoln had done. Still, Illinois denied her a license in 1869 because she was a woman. In 1890, Illinois at last let Bradwell practice law.

Higher education

Despite obstacles, a few women managed to get the higher education needed to enter the professions. In 1877, Boston University granted the first Ph.D. to a woman. In the next decades, women made important advances. By 1900, about 1,000 women lawyers and 7,000 women doctors were in practice.

Women entered the sciences, too. Mary Engle Pennington earned a degree in chemistry. She became the nation's top expert on preserving foods.

Viewing HISTORY — Suffragists on the March

Suffragists parading for the right to vote were a common sight in many cities and towns. These women, along with their children, are marching down a New York City street in 1912. ★ **Why do you think these suffragists carried American flags as they marched?**

▲ Window banner from 1915

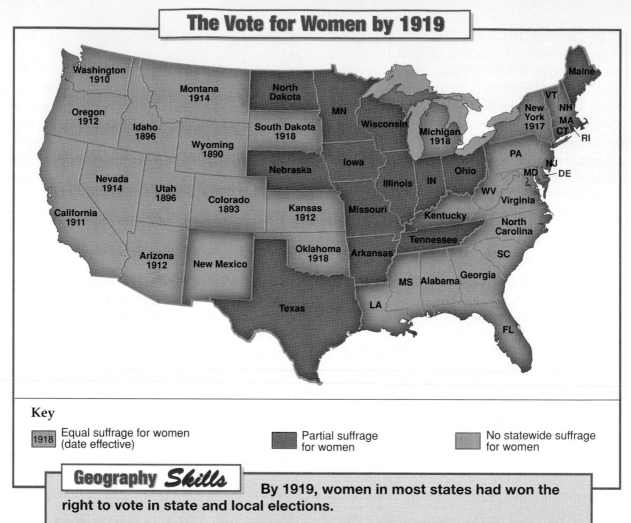

The Vote for Women by 1919

Key

1918	Equal suffrage for women (date effective)
	Partial suffrage for women
	No statewide suffrage for women

Geography *Skills*

By 1919, women in most states had won the right to vote in state and local elections.

1. Location On the map, locate: **(a)** Wyoming, **(b)** Colorado, **(c)** Idaho, **(d)** Utah.

2. Region In what region of the country did women gain equal suffrage first?

3. Critical Thinking **(a)** What was unusual about the state of New Mexico? **(b)** What was unusual about New York and Michigan?

Commitment to reform

Women in the Progressive Era were committed to reform. Some entered the new profession of social work. Others worked to call attention to social ills. **Florence Kelley** investigated conditions in sweatshops. She became the first chief factory inspector for the state of Illinois.

Kelley's chief concern was child labor. As secretary of the National Consumer's League (NCL), she organized a boycott of products made with child labor. The NCL published a list of manufacturers whose factories met their approval. By 1907, many businesses vied to get the NCL "white label" of approval on their products.

Many women joined the women's clubs that had sprung up in the late 1800s. At first, clubwomen read books, went to plays, and sought other ways to improve their minds. By the early 1900s, they were caught up in the reform spirit. Clubwomen raised money for libraries, schools, and parks. They fought for laws to protect women and children, for pure food and drug laws, and for the right to vote.

Faced with racial barriers, African American women formed their own clubs, such as the National Association of Colored Women. These members crusaded against lynching and racial separation, as well as for suffrage and other causes.

The Temperance Crusade

The **temperance movement** against the use of alcoholic beverages began in the early 1800s. By the end of the century, the temperance movement was gaining strength.

Women reformers were the major force in the crusade against alcohol. Many wives and mothers recognized alcohol as a threat to their families. Drinking was a frequent cause of violence and economic hardship in the home. Other women campaigned against the saloon for political reasons. In saloons, male political bosses often decided matters of politics far from the reach of women. Most saloons refused entry to women.

Willard and Nation

In 1874, a group of women founded the Women's Christian Temperance Union, or WCTU. **Frances Willard** became a leader of the WCTU. Willard recalled joining temperance leaders as they entered a saloon in Pittsburgh:

> 66 The tall, stately lady who led us placed her Bible on the bar and read a psalm.... Then we sang "Rock of Ages" as I thought I had never sung it before.... This was my Crusade baptism. The next day I went on to the West. 99

In 1880, Willard became president of the WCTU. She worked to educate people about the evils of alcohol. She urged states to pass laws banning the sale of liquor. She also worked to outlaw saloons as a step toward strengthening democracy. Later, Willard joined the suffrage movement, bringing many WCTU members along with her.

A more radical temperance crusader was **Carry Nation.** After her husband died from heavy drinking, Nation dedicated her life to fighting "demon rum." Swinging a hatchet, she stormed into saloons where she smashed beer kegs and liquor bottles. Nation won publicity, but her actions embarrassed many WCTU members.

The Eighteenth Amendment

Temperance crusaders wanted to amend the Constitution to prohibit the sale of liquor. After 1917, support for such an amendment grew. In that year the United States entered World War I. Temperance forces argued that grain used to make liquor should go to feed American soldiers instead.

Temperance leaders finally persuaded Congress to pass the **Eighteenth Amendment** in 1917. By 1919, three fourths of the states had ratified the amendment. The amendment made it illegal to sell alcoholic drinks anywhere in the United States.

★ Section 4 Review ★

Recall

1. **Identify** (a) Carrie Chapman Catt, (b) Alice Paul, (c) Nineteenth Amendment, (d) Florence Kelley, (e) Frances Willard, (f) Carry Nation, (g) Eighteenth Amendment.
2. **Define** (a) suffragist, (b) temperance movement.

Comprehension

3. Describe two methods suffragists used to achieve their goal.

4. Describe two opportunities women gained during the Progressive Era.
5. Why did many women support temperance?

Critical Thinking and Writing

6. **Defending a Position** Do you think Alice Paul's tactics to win suffrage for women were necessary? Explain your position.
7. **Linking Past and Present** Frances Willard considered alcohol a threat to society. What threats does alcohol abuse pose today?

Activity Writing a Song You have worked for passage of the Nineteenth Amendment, and finally it has become law. Using a tune you know, write a song celebrating your success.

As You Read

Explore These Questions
- What problems did African Americans face during the Progressive Era?
- How did African American leaders try to fight discrimination?
- What challenges faced other minorities?

Define
- barrio
- mutualista

Identify
- Ida B. Wells
- Booker T. Washington
- W.E.B. Du Bois
- NAACP
- George Washington Carver
- Society of American Indians
- Gentlemen's Agreement

SETTING the Scene The Thirteenth Amendment abolished slavery in 1865. Yet, 50 years later, life for many African Americans had not changed for the better. One woman declared:

66 Whether in the cook kitchen, at the washtub, over the sewing machine, behind the baby carriage, or at the ironing board, we are but little more than pack horses, beasts of burden, slaves! 99

In general, white Progressives did little for the needs of nonwhites. It was up to African Americans to help themselves. Mexican Americans, Native Americans, and Asian Americans, too, had to fight for justice.

African Americans

After the end of Reconstruction, African Americans in the South lost their hard-won political rights. Jim Crow laws led to segregation in schools, trains, and other public places. (See Chapter 18.)

Northern blacks also faced prejudice. Landlords in white neighborhoods refused to rent homes to African Americans. Many hotels and restaurants would not serve blacks. In the North and the South, African Americans were hired only for low-paying jobs.

In the 1890s, life grew worse for African Americans. The depression of 1893 threw many people out of work. In some areas, mainly in the South, unemployed whites took out their anger on blacks. In the 1890s, lynch mobs murdered more than 1,000 blacks.

Such violence outraged the African American journalist **Ida B. Wells.** In her newspaper, *Free Speech,* Wells published shocking statistics about lynching. She urged African Americans to protest by refusing to ride the streetcars or shop in white-owned stores. Wells spoke out despite threats to her life.

Washington's solution

Booker T. Washington offered one answer to the question of how to fight discrimination. In his autobiography, *Up From Slavery,* Washington told how he had succeeded. Born into slavery, he taught himself to read. In 1881, he founded Tuskegee Institute in Alabama. It became a center for black higher education.

Washington stressed living in harmony with whites. He urged African Americans to work patiently and move upward slowly. First, learn trades and earn money, advised Washington. Only then would African Americans have the power to insist on political and social equality.

In the meantime, Washington accepted segregation. "In all things that are purely social," he said, "we can be as separate as the fingers, yet one as the hand in all things essential to mutual progress."

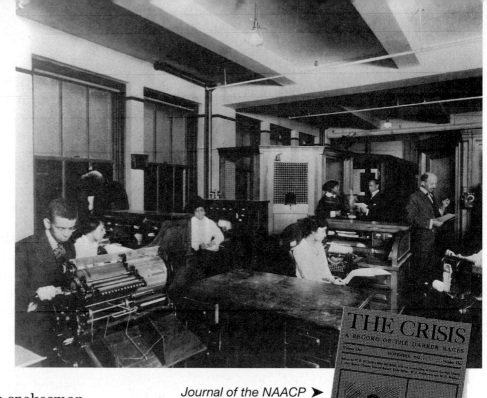

W.E.B. Du Bois refused to accept discrimination. As editor of The Crisis, *the journal of the NAACP, he spoke out against injustice and demanded equal rights for African Americans. Here, Du Bois is shown standing at right in the offices of* The Crisis. ★ **How did the view of Du Bois differ from those of Booker T. Washington?**

Journal of the NAACP ➤

Booker T. Washington was a spokesman for many African Americans. Business tycoons such as Andrew Carnegie and John D. Rockefeller gave him money to build trade schools for African Americans. Several Presidents sought his advice on racial issues.

Du Bois disagrees

Other African Americans disagreed with Washington. How could blacks move ahead, they asked, when whites denied them advanced education and jobs? Racial harmony was impossible when whites were lynching blacks and denying them the right to vote.

W.E.B. Du Bois (doo BOYS) was one leader who took this view. Du Bois was a professor, author, and public speaker. In 1895, he became the first African American to earn a Ph.D. from Harvard University.

Du Bois agreed with Booker T. Washington on the need for "thrift, patience, and industrial training." However, he added, "So far as Mr. Washington apologizes for injustice, we must firmly oppose him." Instead, Du Bois urged blacks to fight discrimination actively.

In 1909, Du Bois joined with Jane Addams, Lincoln Steffens, and other reformers to form the National Association for the Advancement of Colored People, or **NAACP.** Blacks and whites in the NAACP worked to gain equal rights for African Americans.

Obstacles and successes

Still, most Progressives thought little about the problems of African Americans. When black soldiers were accused of rioting in Brownsville, Texas, President Roosevelt ordered their whole regiment to be dishonorably discharged. Later, President Wilson ordered the segregation of black and white government workers. When black leaders protested, Wilson replied that "segregation is not humiliating, but a benefit." His action led hotels, restaurants, and stores in the nation's capital to enforce segregation.

Some African Americans succeeded despite huge obstacles. **George Washington Carver** discovered hundreds of new uses for peanuts and other crops grown in the South.

⚛ Connections With Science

George Washington Carver established a "school on wheels." In this traveling classroom, he taught Alabama farmers how intensive cultivation of cotton and tobacco depleted the soil, while growing peanuts and sweet potatoes helped to enrich it.

Mexican Americans

In 1910, revolution and famine swept Mexico. To escape the disorder, thousands of Mexicans crossed the border into the American Southwest. Many were poor farmers forced off their land. Others were soldiers or political leaders who had supported the losing side. Although many later returned to Mexico, some remained.

Living in the Southwest

Many of the poor Mexican immigrants worked in the fields, harvesting crops. They built highways and dug irrigation ditches. Some lived in shacks alongside the railroads they had helped to construct. Others moved to cities.

Like other immigrant groups, Mexicans created ethnic neighborhoods, or **barrios.** There, they preserved their language and much of their culture. Los Angeles had the largest barrio in the United States. From 1910 to 1920, the Mexican population of Los Angeles almost tripled.

Need for mutual aid

Some Americans in the Southwest responded with violence to the flood of immigrants from Mexico. Nativists often attacked citizens as well as newcomers.

In defense, Mexican Americans formed **mutualistas,** or mutual aid groups. The constitution of one mutualista defined its goals:

66 To bring closer together…the relations of the Mexicanos…in order that they extend to each other the hand of brotherly love for their protection [and] mutual benefits. 99

Members of mutualistas pooled money to buy insurance and pay for legal advice. They also collected money for the sick.

Native Americans

The Dawes Act had granted Native Americans plots on reservation lands. With these lands, Indians were supposed to become farmers and enter the mainstream of American life. Instead, Indians were swindled out of millions of acres of land.

His writings about crop rotation changed southern farming practices. Sarah Walker, better known as Madame C. J. Walker, created a line of hair care products for African American women. She became the first American woman to earn over $1 million.

Ordinary African Americans felt a sense of pride in their communities. Churches like the African Methodist Episcopal Church offered a strong foundation for religious and family life. They were also training grounds for African American leaders. Black colleges and universities trained young people to enter the professions. Black-owned insurance companies, banks, and other businesses served community needs.

In the early 1900s, a new generation of Native American leaders emerged. One group set up the **Society of American Indians.** It included artists, writers, Christian ministers, lawyers, and doctors from many Native American groups. The Society worked for social justice and tried to educate other Americans about Indian life.

Japanese farmers in California

Asian Americans

As you have read, anti-Chinese feelings led Congress to pass the Chinese Exclusion Act of 1882. With new immigration cut off, the Chinese population slowly declined.

Japanese immigration increases

Americans on the West Coast then turned to other Asian lands for cheap labor. They hired Filipino and Japanese workers, mostly young men. More than 100,000 Japanese entered the United States in the early 1900s.

Many Japanese were farmers. They settled on dry, barren land that other western farmers thought was useless. Through hard work and careful management, the Japanese made their farms profitable. Other Japanese immigrants went to work in canneries, lumber mills, and mines.

San Francisco school crisis

Many Americans mistrusted the Asian newcomers because they competed for jobs and had an unfamiliar culture. In 1906, the San Francisco Board of Education placed the city's 93 Asian pupils, including some adults, in a separate school. Japan protested the insult.

Eager to soothe Japanese feelings, President Roosevelt denounced the school board's action. He persuaded the school board to accept a compromise. If the board would return Asian children of proper age to regular schools, he would take steps to restrict further Japanese immigration.

President Roosevelt reached a **Gentlemen's Agreement** with Japan in 1907. Japan agreed to curb the number of workers coming to the United States. In exchange, Roosevelt agreed to allow the wives of Japanese men already living in the United States to join them.

★ **Section 5 Review** ★

Recall

1. **Identify** (a) Ida B. Wells, (b) Booker T. Washington, (c) W.E.B. Du Bois, (d) NAACP, (e) George Washington Carver, (f) Society of American Indians, (g) Gentlemen's Agreement.
2. **Define** (a) barrio, (b) mutualista.

Comprehension

3. (a) How did Booker T. Washington and W.E.B. Du Bois agree in their views? (b) How did they disagree?

4. How did Mexican Americans protect their rights?
5. (a) How did the Chinese Exclusion Act affect Japanese immigration to the United States? (b) How were Japanese immigrants greeted?

Critical Thinking and Writing

6. **Applying Information** Would you consider Ida B. Wells a muckraker? Why or why not?
7. **Comparing** How were the situations of African Americans and Mexican Americans similar during the Progressive Era?

Activity Listing Pros and Cons It is 1912. You are a Mexican American who escaped from revolution and famine in Mexico and made a life in the United States. Make two lists—one of the good qualities of your new life, and one of the problems you face in your new country.

Chapter 22 — Review **and** Activities

★ Sum It Up ★

Section 1 Early Reforms
▶ During the Gilded Age, reformers worked to end the spoils system.
▶ Early laws intended to break up monopolies were weak and had little effect.

Section 2 The Progressives and Their Goals
▶ Journalists brought the problems of society to the attention of the middle class.
▶ In the early 1900s, Progressives pushed to limit trusts, reform city governments, and give more power to voters.

Section 3 Presidents Support Reforms
▶ President Theodore Roosevelt supported programs to break up some trusts, conserve resources, and protect consumers.
▶ Under President Woodrow Wilson, Congress pushed to preserve competition in American businesses.

Section 4 Progress for Women
▶ The long campaign for women's suffrage finally succeeded with the passage of the Nineteenth Amendment.
▶ During the Progressive Era, women took a leading role in promoting social reforms including temperance.

Section 5 Fighting for Equality
▶ African American leaders pursued different paths to improve their lives.
▶ Faced with discrimination, Asian Americans and Mexican Americans carved a place in society.

CD-ROM Review For additional review of the major ideas of Chapter 22, see *Guide to the Essentials of American History* or *Interactive Student Tutorial CD-ROM,* which contains interactive review activities, graphic organizers, and practice tests.

🔲 Reviewing the Chapter

Define These Terms
Match each term with the correct definition.

Column 1	Column 2
1. patronage	**a.** vote to make a bill a law
2. referendum	**b.** crusading journalist
3. muckraker	**c.** Mexican American neighborhood
4. public interest	**d.** giving of jobs to loyal supporters
5. barrio	**e.** good of the people

Explore the Main Ideas
1. How did Congress try to regulate railroads and big business in the late 1800s?
2. What was the goal of good government leagues?
3. Explain the goal of the following: **(a)** Elkins Act, **(b)** Meat Inspection Act, **(c)** Federal Reserve Act.
4. Why did the women's suffrage movement gain strength?
5. What were the goals of the NAACP?

🔲 Graph Activity

Look at the graph and answer the following questions:
1. How many women were enrolled in higher education in 1880? **2.** How much did enrollment increase from 1910 to 1920? **Critical Thinking** Do you think education helped the suffragist movement? Explain.

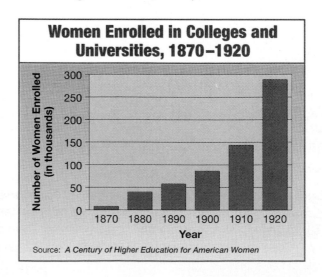

Women Enrolled in Colleges and Universities, 1870–1920

Number of Women Enrolled (in thousands)

Year

Source: *A Century of Higher Education for American Women*

▢ Critical Thinking and Writing

1. **Understanding Chronology** **(a)** List one event that resulted from each of the following: Nast publishes cartoons attacking Boss Tweed; Sinclair publishes *The Jungle;* Tarbell reveals business practices of Standard Oil. **(b)** Make one generalization about the role of the press in bringing about reform.

2. **Linking Past and Present** Congress passed the Pure Food and Drug Act in 1906. **(a)** What does the law provide? **(b)** How does the government protect consumers today?

3. **Recognizing Points of View** "The way for people to gain their reasonable rights is not by voluntarily throwing them away." Who do you think made this statement: Booker T. Washington or W.E.B. Du Bois? Explain your reasoning.

4. **Exploring Unit Themes** **Global Interaction** **(a)** What was the purpose of the Gentlemen's Agreement between the United States and Japan? **(b)** Why do you think Roosevelt wanted the cooperation of the Japanese government?

▢ Using Primary Sources

A 1905 book explained the work of a "district leader" in the corrupt political organization of New York City:

> **❝** Nearly everybody goes to him for assistance of one sort or another, especially the poor of the tenements. He is always obliging. He will go to the police courts to put in a good word for the 'drunks and disorderlies' or pay their fines, if a good word is not effective. He will attend christenings, weddings, and funerals. He will feed the hungry and help bury the dead. A philanthropist? Not at all. He is playing politics all the time. **❞**

Source: *Plunkitt of Tammany Hall,* William L. Riordon, 1905.

Recognizing Points of View **(a)** What kind of work does the district leader do? **(b)** A philanthropist is someone who helps others out of sheer kindness. Why does the writer insist that the district leader is not a philanthropist?

ACTIVITY BANK

▶ Interdisciplinary Activity

Exploring Geography Research and prepare a report on methods used to preserve land and water resources in Theodore Roosevelt's day. You may wish to focus on the work of an important conservationist such as John Muir or Gifford Pinchot.

▶ Career Skills Activity

Political Strategist Review the steps necessary to pass an amendment to the Constitution. Prepare a flowchart for display in the class, using the Eighteenth or Nineteenth Amendment as an example.

▶ Citizenship Activity

Learning About Democracy Does your state allow initiatives or referendums? If so, find out about some recent examples. Working with other class members, prepare for a debate or panel discussion of one of these issues.

Internet Activity

Use the Internet to find sites dealing with George Washington Carver. When you locate the sites, use them to find the titles of books about Carver. Then find the books in a library and do research for a biography about Carver. Your biography should include a list of some of Carver's many inventions.

EYEWITNESS Journal

It is the Progressive Era. You are a Progressive President, a muckraker, a city boss, a suffragist, the president of a railroad, or a member of a minority group. Choose the one event during the Progressive Era that was most important to you and describe it and your reaction to it in your EYEWITNESS JOURNAL.

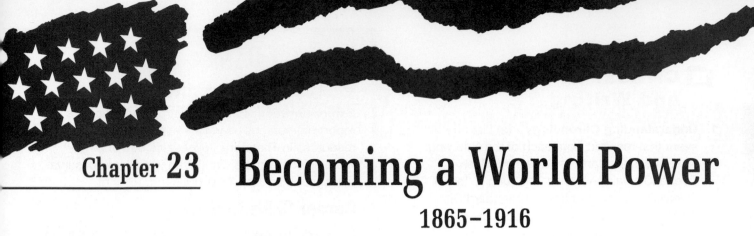

Chapter 23

Becoming a World Power

1865–1916

The United States increased its role in world affairs throughout the second half of the nineteenth century. As the nation became an industrial and commercial power, American leaders sought new trade opportunities in Asia. Alaska, Hawaii, and other overseas territories came under United States control.

As a result of the Spanish-American War of 1898, the United States acquired an overseas empire. After the war, the United States played an increasing role in the affairs of Latin America. As a result, many Latin Americans began to view the United States with distrust and anger.

Why Study History?

In 1898, the United States sent soldiers to Cuba to help Cubans gain independence from Spain. Today, the United States continues to send American soldiers to troubled spots around the world. To study some of the reasons for these actions, see this chapter's *Why Study History?* feature, "Americans Are Involved in World Affairs."

American Events

•1867
United States buys Alaska from Russia

1898 •
United States defeats Spain in Spanish-American War

•1899
Open Door Policy keeps trade with China open to all nations

| 1865 | 1890 | 1895 | 1900 |

World Events

1870s World Event
Age of Imperialism begins

1895 World Event
Cubans rebel against Spain

 Viewing HISTORY   **The Great White Fleet**

In this painting by Henry Reuterdahl, the "Great White Fleet" of the United States steams into the harbor of San Francisco. The fleet, named for the fact that its ships were painted white, proclaimed the new role of the United States in the world. In his autobiography, President Theodore Roosevelt referred to the fleet as "the most important service that I rendered to peace." ★ **What do you think Roosevelt meant by his statement?**

●1900
Hawaii becomes territory of United States

●1904
President Roosevelt declares right of United States to intervene in Latin America

1914 ●
Panama Canal opens

1900	1905	1910	1915

▲
1904 World Event
Russo-Japanese war begins

▲
1911 World Event
Revolution in China begins

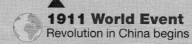 ★ **615**

Across the Pacific

As You Read

Explore These Questions
- How did treaties with Japan and Russia benefit the United States?
- Why did some Americans favor imperialism in the late 1800s?
- How did United States policy concerning Hawaii differ from American policy in China?

Define
- isolationism
- expansionism
- annex
- imperialism
- sphere of influence

Identify
- Matthew Perry
- Treaty of Kanagawa
- William Seward
- Alfred Mahan
- Great White Fleet
- Liliuokalani
- John Hay
- Open Door Policy
- Boxer Rebellion

SETTING the Scene In 1880, the ruler of the Turkish empire thought of a way to save his country money. He would shut down his nation's embassies in "minor" countries. One of these minor countries was the United States, a nation known to play only a small role in world affairs.

Turkey's plan was badly timed. By 1880, the United States was making moves to increase its diplomatic contacts with the rest of the world. In fact, it was on the verge of becoming a world power.

Isolationism and Expansionism

In his Farewell Address, as you recall, George Washington had advised the nation to "steer clear of permanent alliances." He urged Americans to have "as little political connection as possible" with foreign nations. Later Presidents continued this policy of **isolationism,** or having little to do with the political affairs of other nations. Americans had no wish to be dragged into Europe's frequent wars.

Earlier in his career, however, Washington had also called the United States a "rising empire." Indeed, from its earliest existence, the American republic followed a policy of **expansionism,** or extending its national boundaries. The people of the United States were constantly pressing westward across the continent.

At the same time, Americans conducted a lively foreign trade. From the early 1700s, sailing ships carried American goods to Europe. American traders also traveled to Asia, including China and the Philippines. The Asian nation of Japan, however, refused to open its doors to American trade.

Opening Trade With Japan

Japan was a small island nation. Fearing outsiders, the Japanese had cut themselves off from the world in the 1600s. They expelled all Westerners* and allowed only one ship a year—from the Dutch East India Company—to trade at the port of Nagasaki. Foreign sailors wrecked on the shores of Japan were not allowed to leave.

Perry's mission

American merchants wanted to open Japan to trade. They also wanted the Japanese to help shipwrecked sailors who washed up on their shores. To achieve these goals, President Millard Fillmore sent Commodore **Matthew Perry** to Japan in the early 1850s.

With four warships, Perry entered Tokyo Bay in July 1853. The Japanese had never seen steam-powered ships. They denounced the Americans as "barbarians in floating volcanoes" and ordered them to leave.

---

* To the Japanese, Westerners were white people from Europe and North America.

Before departing, Perry presented Japanese officials with a letter from President Fillmore. In it, the President asked the Japanese to open trading relations with the United States. Perry said he would return the following year for an answer.

A new treaty

Perry returned in February 1854, this time with seven warships. Impressed by this show of strength, the Japanese emperor signed the **Treaty of Kanagawa.** The treaty accepted American demands to help ship-wrecked sailors. It also opened two Japanese ports to trade.

Perry's visit had important effects. First, it launched trade between Japan and the West. Second, it made the Japanese aware of the power of the Western industrial nations. As a result, Japan soon set out to become a modern, industrial nation itself, with the United States as one of its models.

The Purchase of Alaska

American interest in Asia and the Pacific continued. In the 1860s, Secretary of State **William Seward** wanted the United States to dominate trade in the Pacific. In 1867, he persuaded Congress to **annex** Midway Island, in the middle of the Pacific Ocean. In this way, the island became part of the United States. In that same year, Seward made a deal to buy the vast territory of Alaska.

An amazing land deal

In the 1800s, Alaska belonged to Russia. The Russians, however, were eager to get rid of the territory, which was too far away to govern effectively. Seward saw Alaska as an important stepping stone for increasing United States commerce in Asia and the Pacific.

One night in 1867, Seward was playing cards in Washington, D.C. He was interrupted by a message from the Russian ambassador. The czar of Russia, said the ambassador, was willing to sell Alaska to the United States for $7.2 million. Seward did not hesitate. He agreed to buy the land then and there.

Viewing HISTORY — Opening Trade With Japan

Perry's mission to Japan in 1853 is portrayed in the painting Perry's First Landing in Japan at Kurihama *by Gessan Ogata. Perry gave the Japanese many gifts, including several clocks, a telescope, and a toy train.* ★ **Why did the United States government send Perry to Japan?**

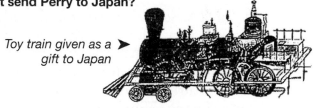

Toy train given as a ➤ gift to Japan

"But your Department is closed," said the ambassador. "Never mind that," Seward replied. "Before midnight you will find me at the Department, which will be open and ready for business."

Next morning, Seward completed the deal. The cost came to 2 cents an acre. The purchase of Alaska increased the area of the United States by almost one fifth.

"Seward's Folly"

To most Americans, the purchase of Alaska—which they thought of as a barren land of icy mountains and frozen fish— seemed foolish. They mockingly called Alaska "Seward's Ice Box" and referred to the purchase as "Seward's Folly."

HISTORY HAPPENED HERE

White Pass and Yukon Railroad

This rail line was built during the mad gold rush of 1898. It carried miners and supplies from Skagway, Alaska, to the rich Klondike goldfields in Canada. Today, tourists can ride the train along the very trail that the miners used in 1898. As you view the spectacular natural beauty of Alaska's mountains, you pass Bridal Veil Falls, Inspiration Point, and Dead Horse Gulch.

★ *To learn more about this historic site, write: White Pass and Yukon Railroad, P.O. Box 435, Skagway, AK 99840.*

In fact, Seward was correct in considering Alaska a very valuable territory. The lowlands of southern Alaska are well suited to farming. The land is also rich in timber, copper, and other natural resources. In the 1890s, miners rushed to the territory after prospectors found gold in Alaska and nearby Canada. In 1959, Alaska was admitted as the forty-ninth state. Today, the state is a very important source of petroleum and natural gas.

Age of Imperialism

The period between 1870 and 1914 has often been called the Age of Imperialism. **Imperialism** is the policy of powerful countries seeking to control the economic and political affairs of weaker countries or regions. Between 1870 and 1914, European nations seized control of almost the entire continent of Africa and much of southern Asia. During this period, the United States and Japan also became imperial powers.

Reasons for imperialism

One reason for the growth of imperialism in the 1800s was economic. The industrial nations of Europe wanted raw materials from Africa and Asia. European factories would use the raw materials to manufacture goods. Some of these goods would then be sold to people in Africa and Asia.

Imperialism had other causes. Many Europeans believed that they had a duty to spread their religion and culture to people whom they considered to be less civilized. British writer Rudyard Kipling called this responsibility "the white man's burden." Such thinking ignored the fact that Africans and Asians already had rich cultures of their own.

A third cause was competition. When a European country colonized an area, it often closed the area's markets to other countries. A European nation might take over an area just to keep a rival nation from gaining control of it.

American interests in empire

Americans could not ignore Europe's race for colonies. By the 1890s, the United States was a world leader in both industry and agriculture. American factories turned out huge amounts of steel and other goods. American farms grew bumper crops of corn, wheat, and cotton. The nation was growing rapidly, and arguments in favor of expansion held great appeal.

Many people believed that the American economy would collapse unless the United States gained new foreign markets for its products. Albert Beveridge, campaigning for the Senate from Indiana in 1898, summed up the arguments for commercial expansion:

66 Today we are raising more than we can consume. Today we are making more than we can use. Today our industrial society is congested; there are more workers than there is work.... Therefore we must find new markets for our produce, new occupations for our capital, new work for our labor. 99

Expansionists also argued that Americans had a right and a duty to bring Western culture to the "uncivilized" peoples of the world. Josiah Strong, a Congregational minister, declared that Americans were "divinely commissioned" to spread democracy and Christianity "down upon Mexico, down upon Central and South America, out upon the islands of the sea."

Other expansionists stressed the need to offset the vanishing frontier. For 100 years, the economy had boomed as Americans settled the western frontier. The 1890 census said, however, that the frontier was gone. People in crowded eastern cities had no new land to settle. The solution, said some, was to take new land overseas.

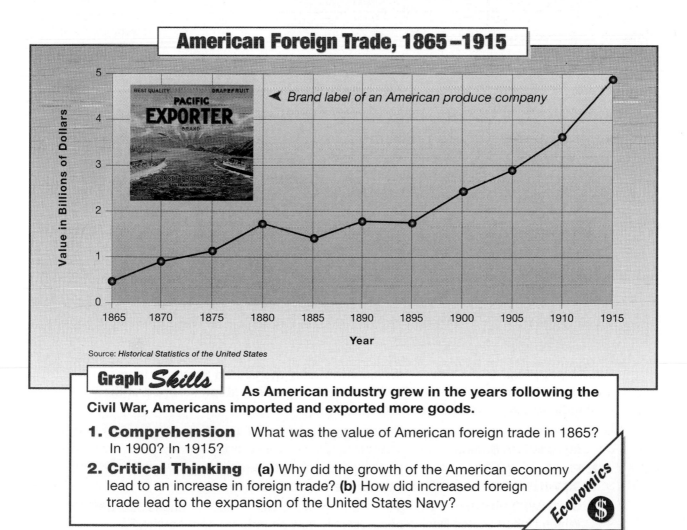

American Foreign Trade, 1865–1915

◄ Brand label of an American produce company

Value in Billions of Dollars

Year

Source: *Historical Statistics of the United States*

Graph *Skills* As American industry grew in the years following the Civil War, Americans imported and exported more goods.

1. **Comprehension** What was the value of American foreign trade in 1865? In 1900? In 1915?

2. **Critical Thinking** **(a)** Why did the growth of the American economy lead to an increase in foreign trade? **(b)** How did increased foreign trade lead to the expansion of the United States Navy?

Economics $

American naval power

One leading supporter of American imperialism was Captain **Alfred Mahan** of the United States Navy. He argued that the prosperity of the United States depended on foreign trade. Furthermore, he said a bigger navy was needed to protect American merchant ships. "When a question arises of control over distant regions," Mahan wrote, "it must ultimately be decided by naval power."

In Mahan's view, the United States could not expand its navy unless it acquired overseas territories A bigger navy would need bases throughout the world. Mahan was especially interested in acquiring harbors in the Caribbean and the Pacific as stepping stones to Latin America and Asia.

Even before Mahan's appeal, Congress had begun to enlarge and modernize the navy. New steam-powered warships with steel hulls were already being built in the 1880s. By the late 1890s, a large and powerful American navy was ready for action. Its ships were called the **Great White Fleet** because they were all painted white.

A Naval Base in Samoa

As naval power grew, the United States showed increasing interest in Samoa, a chain

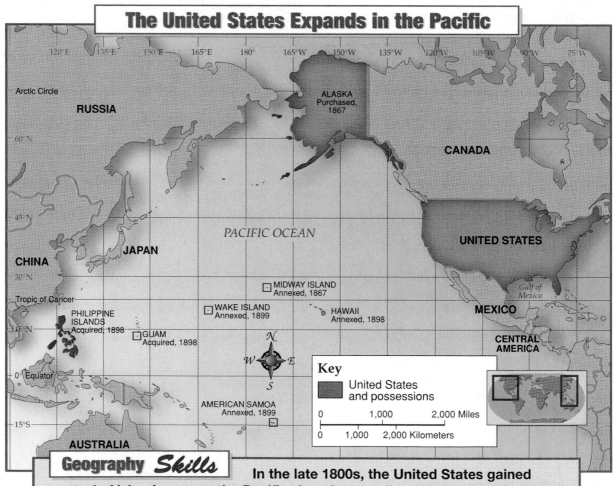

The United States Expands in the Pacific

Geography Skills   In the late 1800s, the United States gained control of islands across the Pacific. American trading ships stopped at these islands on their way to China and Japan.

1. **Location**   On the map, locate: **(a)** Japan, **(b)** China, **(c)** Alaska, **(d)** Hawaii, **(e)** American Samoa.

2. **Region**   **(a)** Which Pacific island did the United States acquire first? **(b)** Which territory was farthest from the United States mainland?

3. **Critical Thinking**   Compare this map to the world map on pages 898–899. Which United States Pacific possession is now an independent country?

of islands in the South Pacific. Samoa had a fine harbor that could serve as a naval base and commercial port. Germany and Great Britain also realized the value of the harbor. As a result, the three nations competed for control of the islands.

In 1889, a military clash seemed very likely. German ships had fired upon Samoan villages that were friendly to the Americans. For months, German and American sailors eyed each other nervously from their warships. Then, just as tensions were at their highest, a powerful storm struck and sank ships of both countries.

Later, the three nations arranged a peaceful settlement. The United States and Germany divided Samoa, while Britain received territories elsewhere in the Pacific. The people of Samoa, meanwhile, had little say in the matter. The United States had demonstrated that it would assert its power in the Pacific Ocean.

Annexing Hawaii

Another territory that had long interested the United States was Hawaii. Hawaii is a chain of eight large islands and more than 100 smaller islands. They are located in the Pacific Ocean, about 2,400 miles (3,800 km) southwest of California. The islands have rich soil, a warm climate, and plenty of rainfall. These conditions make it possible to grow crops all year round.

About 2,000 years ago, people from Polynesia—islands in the Central and South Pacific—first settled Hawaii. Europeans and Americans first learned about Hawaii in 1778. That year, a British sea captain, James Cook, stopped at the islands for water on his way to China. In the early 1800s, American ships bound for China began stopping in Hawaii, and a few American sailors and traders settled there.

Missionaries and planters

In 1820, the first American missionaries arrived. Their goal was to convert the Hawaiians to Christianity. The missionaries and other Americans advised the rulers of Hawaii from the 1830s on. Americans also helped write Hawaii's first constitution in 1840.

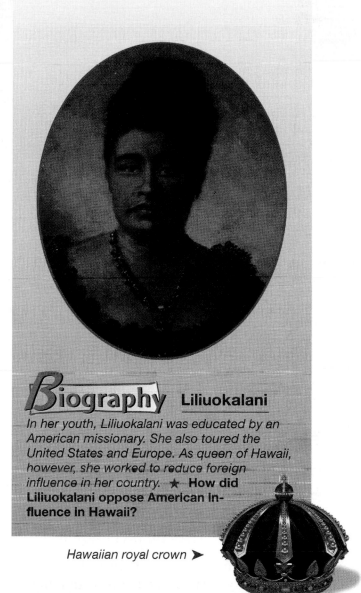

Biography Liliuokalani

In her youth, Liliuokalani was educated by an American missionary. She also toured the United States and Europe. As queen of Hawaii, however, she worked to reduce foreign influence in her country. ★ **How did Liliuokalani oppose American Influence in Hawaii?**

Hawaiian royal crown ➤

By the mid-1800s, Americans had set up large sugar plantations in Hawaii. The planters wanted cheap labor. They brought thousands of workers from China, Korea, the Philippines, and Japan. By 1900, one fourth of Hawaii's population had been born in Japan.

As the sugar industry grew, so did the power of American planters. In 1887, they forced the Hawaiian king, Kalakaua, to accept a new constitution. It reduced the king's power and increased the planters' influence.

Planters stage a revolt

In 1891, Kalakaua died, and his sister **Liliuokalani** (lih lee oo oh kah LAH nee) came to the throne. The new queen cherished Hawaiian independence and deeply resented the growing power of American planters. She

therefore rejected the new constitution. She hoped to reduce the influence and privileges of foreign merchants.

In early 1893, the American planters rebelled against the queen's attempt to limit their power. The American ambassador called for United States marines to land on Hawaii and protect American lives. In fact, the marines helped topple the queen.

Faced with American guns, Liliuokalani gave up her throne. However, she wrote a protest to the United States government:

> 66 I, Liliuokalani, ... do hereby solemnly protest against any and all acts done against myself and the constitutional Government of the Hawaiian Kingdom....
>
> I yield to the superior force of the United States of America, whose [ambassador] ... has caused United States troops to be landed [on Hawaii]....

Connections With Civics

Liliuokalani later sued the United States government for losses totaling $450,000. The lawsuit was unsuccessful. However, the Hawaiian territorial government granted her a pension of $4,000 per year and allowed her some income from a sugar plantation.

Now, to avoid any collision of armed forces and perhaps the loss of life, I do this under protest, and impelled by said force, yield my authority. 99

A United States territory

With Liliuokalani gone, the planters quickly set up a republic and asked the United States to annex Hawaii. A debate raged in Congress for months. President Grover Cleveland blocked moves to take over the islands. "Our interference in the Hawaiian Revolution of 1893 was disgraceful," he later said. "I am ashamed of the whole affair."

Congress finally annexed Hawaii in 1898, after Cleveland left office. Two years later, Hawaii became a United States territory. In 1959, Hawaii became the fiftieth state.

Rivalry in China

By acquiring Hawaii and Samoa, the United States gained important footholds in the Pacific. Still, the United States was a latecomer in the race for Pacific and Asian territory. Britain, Germany, Japan, and other nations were already competing for colonies in Asia. Rivalry among the industrial nations was especially fierce in China.

China had once been the most advanced empire in the world. However, years of civil war had weakened the empire. In addition, China had failed to industrialize as other nations had in the 1800s. As a result, it was unable to fight off industrial nations that wanted to reap profits from its vast resources and markets.

The Open Door Policy

In the late 1800s, Britain, France, Germany, Russia, and Japan carved spheres of influence in China. A **sphere of influence** was an area, usually around a seaport, where a nation had special trading privileges. Each nation made laws for its own citizens in its own sphere.

American leaders feared that the Europeans and Japanese would try to bar the United States from trading in China. In 1899, therefore, Secretary of State **John Hay** sent a letter to all the nations that had spheres of influence in China. He urged them to follow an **Open Door Policy** in China. Under the policy, any nation could trade in the spheres of others.

Reluctantly, the imperialist powers accepted the Open Door Policy. The agreement allowed the United States to trade freely with the Chinese without interference from the foreign powers in China.

The Boxer Rebellion

Many Chinese opposed foreign influence in their country. Some belonged to a secret society called the Righteous Fists of Harmony, or Boxers. The Boxers wanted to rid China of "foreign devils."

In 1900, the Boxers rebelled. They attacked foreigners all over China, killing more than 200. The Boxers trapped hundreds of foreigners in Beijing, the Chinese capital. Foreign governments quickly organized an international army that included 2,500 Americans. Armed with modern weapons, the international army fought its way into Beijing. They freed the trapped foreigners and crushed the rebellion.

Several nations saw the **Boxer Rebellion** as an excuse to seize more land in China. Secretary of State Hay sent another Open Door letter, urging all nations to respect China's independence. Britain, France, and Germany accepted Hay's letter. Japan and Russia, fearing that any attempt to divide China might lead to war, quietly observed Hay's policy. Hay's Open Door letters showed that the United States was playing a new role in world affairs.

★ Section 1 Review ★

Recall

1. **Locate** (a) Japan, (b) Alaska, (c) Samoa, (d) Hawaii, (e) China.
2. **Identify** (a) Matthew Perry, (b) Treaty of Kanagawa, (c) William Seward, (d) Alfred Mahan, (e) Great White Fleet, (f) Liliuokalani, (g) John Hay, (h) Open Door Policy, (i) Boxer Rebellion.
3. **Define** (a) isolationism, (b) expansionism, (c) annex, (d) imperialism, (e) sphere of influence.

Comprehension

4. How did the United States benefit from: (a) the Treaty of Kanagawa; (b) the purchase of Alaska?

5. In the late 1800s, why did some Americans favor a policy of imperialism?
6. (a) How did United States policy concerning Hawaii differ from the policy concerning China? (b) Why did the United States pursue these different policies?

Critical Thinking and Writing

7. **Understanding Causes and Effects** What were the causes and effects of the 1893 rebellion against Hawaii's Queen Liliuokalani?
8. **Linking Past and Present** Do you think that the United States could follow a policy of isolationism today? Explain.

★ ★

Activity **Summarizing Ideas** You are Secretary of State William Seward. Write a brief telegram to Congress and the President summarizing your reasons for buying Alaska and annexing Midway Island.

The Spanish-American War

Explore These Questions
- What were the causes of the Spanish-American War?
- What were the major events of the war?
- What were the results of the war?

Define
- yellow journalism
- armistice
- protectorate

Identify
- Lola Rodríguez de Tió
- José Martí
- George Dewey
- Emilio Aguinaldo
- Rough Riders
- Battle of San Juan Hill
- Platt Amendment
- Foraker Act

As You Read

Replica of 1890s ➤ United States Army hat

SETTING the Scene In the late 1890s, Americans opened their daily newspapers to find shocking tales of violence. The reports told about a revolution in Cuba, a Spanish-owned island just 90 miles off the Florida coast. A typical story cried out against Spanish actions toward the Cuban people:

66 Blood on the roadsides, blood in the fields, blood on the doorsteps, blood, blood, blood! 99

Such sensational reports were often inaccurate or one-sided. Yet they succeeded in stirring American anger against Spain. In 1898, the United States put aside its long policy of neutrality to intervene in the Cuban revolution. In the process, American power grew in the Caribbean and across the Pacific.

Trouble in Cuba

For many years, Americans had looked longingly at Cuba. In 1823, Secretary of State John Quincy Adams compared Cuba to a ripe apple. A storm, he said, might tear that apple "from its native tree"—the Spanish empire—and drop it into American hands.

By the 1890s, Spain's once-vast empire in the Western Hemisphere had shrunk to two islands in the Caribbean, Cuba and Puerto Rico. Then, Cuban rebels created the storm that Adams had hoped for.

Revolts against Spain

In 1868, the Cuban people had rebelled against Spanish rule. The revolution was finally crushed after 10 years of fighting. Some of the revolutionaries fled to New York where they kept up the battle for freedom. **Lola Rodríguez de Tió** wrote patriotic poems in support of Cuban independence. **José Martí** told of the Cuban struggle for freedom in his newspaper, *Patria*.

In 1895, Martí returned to Cuba. With cries of *Cuba Libre!*—Free Cuba!—rebels launched a new fight against Spain. Martí died early in the fighting, but the rebels won control of much of the island.

The rebels burned sugar cane fields and sugar mills all over Cuba. They hoped that this would make the island unprofitable for Spain, and convince the Spanish to leave. The rebels killed workers who opposed them. They even blew up some passenger trains.

In response, Spain sent a new governor to Cuba, General Valeriano Weyler (WAY ee lair). Weyler used brutal tactics to crush the revolt.

$ Connections With Economics

An American tariff helped cause the Cuban Revolution. The Wilson-Gorman Tariff of 1894 placed a high tariff on imported sugar. As Americans bought less Cuban sugar, the island's economy declined. Increasing poverty contributed to popular discontent.

His men moved about half a million Cubans into detention camps so they could not aid the rebels. At least 100,000 died from starvation and disease.

Americans react

In the United States, people watched the revolt in nearby Cuba with growing concern. Americans had invested about $50 million in the island. The money was invested in sugar and rice plantations, railroads, tobacco, and iron mines. American trade with Cuba was worth about $100 million a year.

Opinion split over whether the United States should intervene in Cuba. Many business leaders opposed American involvement. They thought that it might hurt trade. Other Americans sympathized with Cuban desires for freedom and wanted the government to take action.

War Fever

The press whipped up American sympathies for Cuba. Two New York newspapers—Joseph Pulitzer's *World* and William Randolph Hearst's *Journal*—competed to print the most grisly stories about Spanish cruelty. The publishers knew that war with Spain would boost sales of their newspapers.

Yellow journalism

To attract readers, Hearst and Pulitzer used **yellow journalism,** or sensational stories that were often biased or untrue. "You supply the pictures," Hearst supposedly told a photographer bound for Cuba. "I'll supply the war." News stories described events in Cuba in graphic and horrifying detail.

President Cleveland wanted to avoid war with Spain. He called the war fever in the United States an "epidemic of insanity." Stories in the press, he grumbled, were nonsense. When William McKinley became President in 1897, he also tried to keep the country neutral.

Sinking of the *Maine*

In 1898, fighting broke out in Havana, the Cuban capital. Acting promptly, President McKinley sent the battleship *Maine* to Havana to protect American citizens and property there.

On the night of February 15, the *Maine* lay at anchor. Just after the bugler played taps, a huge explosion ripped through the ship. The explosion killed at least 260 of the 350 sailors and officers on board.

The yellow press quickly pounced on the tragedy. "DESTRUCTION OF THE WARSHIP *MAINE* WAS THE WORK OF AN ENEMY," screamed one New York newspaper. "THE WARSHIP *MAINE* SPLIT IN TWO BY AN ENEMY'S SECRET INFERNAL MACHINE?" suggested another.

The real cause of the explosion remains a mystery. Most historians believe it was an accident. But Americans, urged on by Pulitzer and Hearst, clamored for war with Spain. "Remember the *Maine!*" they cried.

Viewing HISTORY — Yellow Journalism

The front page of the New York Journal and Advertiser *shouted that an enemy had sunk the* Maine. *To the reading public, that enemy was Spain. Today, most historians believe that the explosion was accidental.* ★ **Why did newspaper publishers favor sensationalist headlines such as this?**

Still hoping to avoid war, McKinley tried to get Spain to talk with the Cuban rebels. In the end, however, he gave in to war fever. On April 25, 1898, Congress declared war on Spain.

The Spanish-American War

The Spanish-American War lasted only four months. The battlefront stretched from the nearby Caribbean to the distant Philippine Islands.

Fighting in the Philippines

Two months earlier, Assistant Secretary of the Navy Theodore Roosevelt had begun making preparations for a possible war with Spain. Roosevelt realized that a conflict with Spain would be fought, not only in the Caribbean, but wherever Spanish sea power lay. The Philippine Islands, a Spanish colony

and Spain's main naval base in the Pacific, would be a major objective.

Roosevelt believed it was important to attack the Spanish in the Philippines as soon as war began. He wired secret orders to Commodore **George Dewey,** commander of the Pacific fleet:

> 66 Order the squadron . . . to Hong Kong. . . . [I]n the event of declaration of war [with] Spain, your duty will be to see that the Spanish squadron does not leave the Asiatic coast. And then [begin] offensive operations in Philippine Islands. 99

Dewey followed Roosevelt's instructions. Immediately after war was declared, the Commodore sailed his fleet swiftly to Manila, the main city of the Philippines. On April 30, 1898, Dewey's ships slipped into Manila

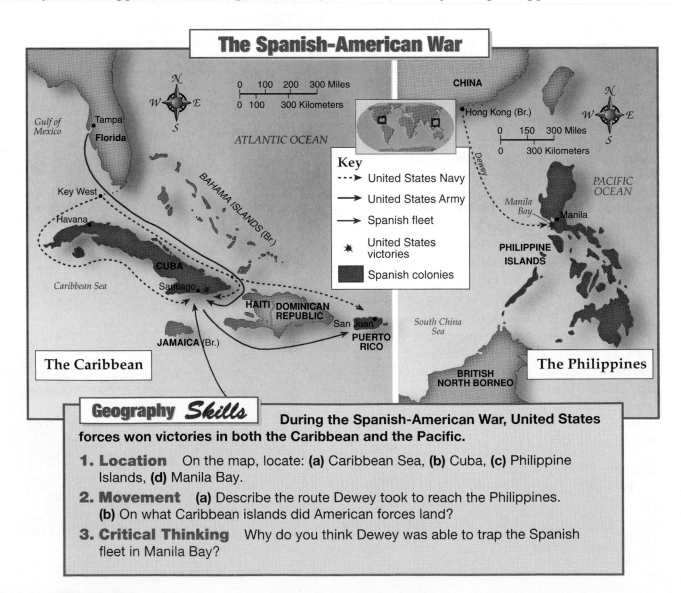

The Spanish-American War

Geography Skills During the Spanish-American War, United States forces won victories in both the Caribbean and the Pacific.

1. **Location** On the map, locate: **(a)** Caribbean Sea, **(b)** Cuba, **(c)** Philippine Islands, **(d)** Manila Bay.

2. **Movement** **(a)** Describe the route Dewey took to reach the Philippines. **(b)** On what Caribbean islands did American forces land?

3. **Critical Thinking** Why do you think Dewey was able to trap the Spanish fleet in Manila Bay?

harbor under cover of darkness. There lay the Spanish fleet.

At dawn, Dewey told his flagship commander, Charles Gridley, "You may fire when you are ready, Gridley." Taking their cue, the Americans bombarded the surprised Spanish ships. By noon, the Spanish fleet had been destroyed.

By July, American troops had landed in the Philippines. As in Cuba, local people had been fighting for independence from Spain for years. With the help of the rebels, led by **Emilio Aguinaldo** (ah gwee NAHL doh), the Americans captured Manila.

Fighting in the Caribbean

Meanwhile, American troops had also landed in Cuba. The expedition was badly organized. Soldiers wore heavy woolen uniforms in the tropical heat, and they often had to eat spoiled food. Yet, most were eager for battle.

None was more eager than Theodore Roosevelt. When the war broke out, Roosevelt resigned his position as Assistant Secretary of the Navy. He then organized the First Volunteer Cavalry Regiment, later called the **Rough Riders.** The Rough Riders were a mixed crew—ranging from cowboys to college students and adventurers.

During the battle for the key Cuban city of Santiago, Roosevelt led the Rough Riders in a charge up San Juan Hill. They were joined by African American soldiers of the 9th and 10th Cavalries. Under withering fire, American troops took the hill. John J. Pershing, commander of the 10th Cavalry, described how the troops united in the **Battle of San Juan Hill:**

> 66 White regiments, black regiments, regulars and Rough Riders, representing the young manhood of the North and South, fought shoulder to shoulder...mindful of their common duty as Americans. 99

Two days later, the Americans destroyed the Spanish fleet in Santiago Bay. The Spanish army in Cuba surrendered. American troops then landed on Puerto Rico and claimed the island.

Biography — Emilio Aguinaldo

"Filipino citizens! Now is the occasion for shedding our blood for the last time, that we may achieve our beloved freedom." With these words, Aguinaldo urged Filipinos to throw off Spanish rule. Later, he led an unsuccessful revolt against United States rule. The Philippines did not become an independent nation until 1946. ★ **Was Aguinaldo an imperialist or an anti-imperialist? Explain.**

Spain was defeated. On August 12, Spain and the United States agreed to sign an **armistice,** thus ending the fighting. American losses in battle were fairly light—379 killed. However, more than 5,000 Americans died of other causes, such as yellow fever, typhoid, and malaria.

John Hay, who was soon to become Secretary of State, summed up American enthusiasm for the war. "It's been a splendid little war," he wrote. A malaria-ridden veteran of the war had a different view: "I was lucky—I survived."

American Soldiers in Cuba

This United States Army cavalry unit served in Cuba during the Spanish-American War. A number of African American cavalry units also fought against Native Americans in the American West.
★ **How do you think these soldiers felt about fighting in Cuba?**

▲ *Army bugle*

The Fruits of Victory

In a peace treaty signed in Paris in December 1898, Spain agreed to grant Cuba its freedom. Spain also gave the United States two islands: Puerto Rico in the Caribbean and Guam in the Pacific. Finally, in return for $20 million, Spain handed over the Philippines to the United States.

Before the Senate approved the treaty, a great debate occurred. Many Americans objected to the treaty. They said it violated American principles of democracy by turning the United States into a colonial power.

Expansionists favored the treaty. They said that the navy needed bases in the Caribbean and the Pacific. They pointed out that the Philippines and Puerto Rico offered new territory for American businesses. Also, many Americans agreed with President McKinley, who said that the United States would "uplift and civilize and Christianize [the Filipinos]." In fact, most Filipinos already were Christians.

Urged on by McKinley, the Senate narrowly approved the treaty in early 1899. At last, the United States had an empire.

Ruling Cuba and Puerto Rico

Americans had to decide how to rule their new territories. When the war with Spain began, the United States had pledged to "leave the government and control of [Cuba] to its people." That promise was not kept.

After the war, American soldiers remained in Cuba while the nation debated. Many in Congress believed that Cuba was not ready for independence. American business leaders feared that an independent Cuba might threaten their investments there.

In the end, the United States let the Cuban people write their own constitution. However, Cuba had to accept the **Platt Amendment.** The amendment allowed the United States to intervene in Cuba and gave the United States control of the naval base at Guantanamo Bay.

Why Study History?

Because Americans Are Involved in World Affairs

★ ★

Historical Background

In 1897, American observer William Calhoun described the terrible situation in Cuba. "Every house had been burned... and everything in the shape of food destroyed. ... The country was wrapped in the stillness of death."

Both Cuban rebels and Spanish soldiers were responsible for the destruction. All over the island, rebels had burned sugar fields so that Cuba would not yield a profit for Spain. To prevent people from aiding the rebels, the Spanish moved 500,000 Cubans into detention camps. One hundred thousand people, including women and children, died from lack of food, shelter, and medicine.

Economic and humanitarian concerns fueled the drive for the United States to get involved. On April 19, 1898, the United States Congress recognized Cuban independence and authorized President McKinley to use military force to end the fighting in Cuba. On April 24, Spain declared war on the United States.

Connections to Today

When should the United States intervene in conflicts within or between other nations? Some say only when vital American interests are at stake. Such was the case when Iraq invaded Kuwait and threat-

An American soldier in Somalia

ened the United States oil supply. In the Persian Gulf War that followed, American and United Nations military forces defeated Iraq.

Other people think that the United States should also intervene for humanitarian reasons. American peacekeeping forces were sent to Somalia in Africa to help the innocent victims of a civil war. The war itself did not provide a direct threat to the United States in this case.

Connections to You

What do you think? Under what circumstances should the United States commit American soldiers to foreign military conflicts? The question is one that each generation of Americans must answer for themselves by weighing the benefits of a policy against its costs. The answer is not always easy.

1. **Comprehension** Why did the United States get involved in the war in Cuba?
2. **Critical Thinking** How can American voters influence United States foreign policy decisions?

★*Activity* **Writing an Editorial** Do research to learn about a current or recent military intervention by the United States. Then write an editorial in which you agree or disagree with the use of American military power in this case.

In effect, the amendment made Cuba an American **protectorate,** a nation whose independence is limited by the control of a more powerful country. The United States pulled its army out of Cuba in 1902. However, American soldiers would return to Cuba in 1906 and again in 1917.

In Puerto Rico, the United States set up a new government under the **Foraker Act** of 1900. The act gave Puerto Ricans only a limited say in their own affairs. In 1917, Puerto Ricans were made citizens of the United States. Americans set up schools, improved health care, and built roads on the island. Even so, many Puerto Ricans wanted to be free of foreign rule.

Filipino War for Independence

Filipino nationalists had begun fighting for independence long before the Spanish-American War. When the United States took over their land after the war, Filipinos felt betrayed. Led by Emilio Aguinaldo, they now fought for freedom against a new imperial power—the United States.

Aguinaldo, who had fought beside the Americans against Spain, accused the United States of forgetting its beginnings. The United States, he said, was using military force to keep the Filipinos from attaining "the same rights that the American people proclaimed more than a century ago."

The war in the Philippines dragged on for years. At one point, about 60,000 American troops were fighting there. Aguinaldo was captured in 1901, and the war finally came to an end.

The war against Aguinaldo's nationalists was longer and more costly than the original war against Spain in 1898. More than 4,000 Americans died in the Philippines. Nearly 20,000 Filipino soldiers were killed. Another 200,000 civilians died from shelling, famine, and disease.

In 1902, the United States set up a government in the Philippines similar to the one in Puerto Rico. Filipinos, however, were not made American citizens because the United States planned to give them independence in the future. It was not until 1946, however, that the United States allowed Filipinos to govern themselves.

★ Section 2 Review ★

Recall

1. **Locate** (a) Cuba, (b) Philippine Islands, (c) Puerto Rico.
2. **Identify** (a) Lola Rodríguez de Tió (b) José Martí, (c) George Dewey, (d) Emilio Aguinaldo, (e) Rough Riders, (f) Battle of San Juan Hill, (g) Platt Amendment, (h) Foraker Act.
3. **Define** (a) yellow journalism, (b) armistice, (c) protectorate.

Comprehension

4. Explain one long-term cause and one immediate cause of the Spanish-American War.
5. (a) How did the United States Navy help win the war? (b) How did Theodore Roosevelt contribute to American victory? (c) What role did African American soldiers play in the war?
6. How did the war affect the relationship between the United States and each of the following? (a) Cuba, (b) Puerto Rico, (c) Philippines

Critical Thinking and Writing

7. **Analyzing Primary Sources** Review the newspaper headlines that reported the sinking of the *Maine.* How are they examples of yellow journalism?
8. **Analyzing Ideas** Why did Emilio Aguinaldo fight alongside American soldiers as an ally, but later fight against them?

★ ★

Activity **Drawing a Political Cartoon** You are a journalist covering international affairs after the Spanish-American War. Draw a cartoon about some topic related to the results of the war.

3 Relations With Latin America

Explore These Questions
- Why did the United States build the Panama Canal?
- What policies did the United States adopt toward Latin America?
- Why did the United States invade Mexico in 1916?

Define
- isthmus
- dollar diplomacy
- moral diplomacy

Identify
- William Gorgas
- George Goethals
- Roosevelt Corollary
- Francisco "Pancho" Villa
- John J. Pershing

As You Read

SETTING the Scene In 1889, Secretary of State James G. Blaine invited Latin American nations to a conference in Washington, D.C. He wanted to remove trade barriers between the United States and Latin America. He also wanted to ease concerns that the United States might extend its growing power across the Western Hemisphere.

The conference failed to remove the fears. The Latin American states refused to open their borders to trade with the United States for fear that a flood of American imports would ruin their own industries. Cuban patriot and writer José Martí charged that the real purpose of the conference was to achieve "an era of United States dominion over the nations of America."

Roosevelt and the Panama Canal

When Theodore Roosevelt became President in 1901, he was determined to build a canal through the Isthmus of Panama. (See the map on page 632.) An **isthmus** is a narrow strip of land connecting two larger bodies of land. Panama was a perfect place for a canal because of its location between the Caribbean Sea and the Pacific Ocean. Also,

U.S. postage stamp honoring the Panama Canal

the isthmus was narrow—only about 50 miles (80 km) wide.

Roosevelt knew that a canal through the isthmus would greatly benefit American commerce and military capability. By avoiding the long trip around South America, ships could shorten the journey from New York City to San Francisco by nearly 8,000 miles (12,800 km). Thus, a canal would reduce the cost of shipping goods. In addition, in the event of a war, naval ships could move back and forth between the Pacific Ocean and Atlantic Ocean more quickly than ever before.

A failed deal

In order to build the canal, Roosevelt had to deal with Colombia, the Latin American country to which Panama belonged. Roosevelt asked Secretary of State John Hay to approach Colombia. Hay offered $10 million cash plus $250,000 a year to rent a strip of land across Panama. Colombian officials turned down the offer.

President Roosevelt was furious. He exclaimed to Secretary of State Hay:

66 I do not think the [Colombian] lot of obstructionists should be allowed permanently to bar one of the future highways of civilization. 99

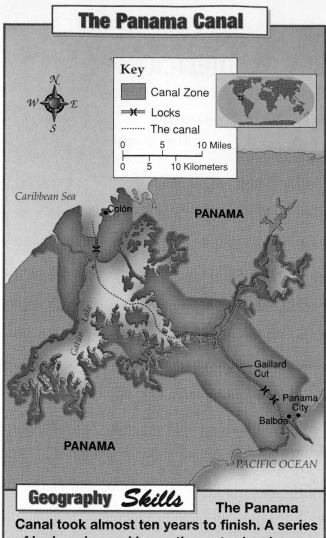

Key
- Canal Zone
- ⟶⤫⟵ Locks
- .... The canal

| 0 | 5 | 10 Miles |
| 0 | 5 | 10 Kilometers |

Caribbean Sea

Colón

PANAMA

Gatún Lake

Gaillard Cut

Panama City

Balboa

PANAMA

PACIFIC OCEAN

Geography *Skills*

The Panama Canal took almost ten years to finish. A series of locks raise and lower the water level so that ships can move through the canal.

1. **Location** On the map, locate: **(a)** Panama, **(b)** Canal Zone, **(c)** Panama City.

2. **Movement** In what direction do ships travel to get from the Caribbean Sea to the Pacific Ocean?

3. **Critical Thinking** **(a)** Describe the location of the Canal Zone in relation to the country of Panama. **(b)** How do you think Panamanians felt about United States control of the zone?

At times like this, Roosevelt often quoted an African proverb: "Speak softly and carry a big stick, and you will go far." He meant that words should be supported by strong action.

Revolution in Panama

Roosevelt knew that some Panamanians wanted to rebel and break away from Colombia. He made it known that he would not help Colombia suppress the rebels. In fact, he might even support the rebellion.

On November 2, 1903, the American warship *Nashville* dropped anchor in the port of Colón, Panama. The next day, the people of Panama rebelled against Colombia. American forces stopped Colombian troops from crushing the revolt. On November 3, Panama declared itself an independent republic.

The United States recognized the new nation at once. Panama then agreed to let the United States build a canal on terms similar to those it had offered to Colombia.

Roosevelt's high-handed action in Panama angered many Latin Americans. It also upset some members of the United States Congress. The President, however, was proud of his action. "I took the Canal Zone," he said later, "and let Congress debate."

Battling disease

With its tropical heat, heavy rainfall, and plentiful swamps, Panama was a "mosquito paradise." This presented serious difficulties for the canal builders. Mosquitoes carry two of the deadliest tropical diseases: malaria and yellow fever.

Dr. **William Gorgas,** an army physician who had helped wipe out yellow fever in Cuba, arrived in Panama to help control the mosquitoes and the spread of disease. He ordered workers to locate all pools of water, where mosquitoes laid their eggs. Day after day, the workers drained swamps, sprayed tons of insecticide, and spread oil on stagnant water to kill mosquito eggs.

By 1906, Gorgas had won his battle. Yellow fever had disappeared from Panama. Malaria cases dropped dramatically. Work on the Panama Canal could proceed.

Digging the canal

Under the supervision of army engineer Colonel **George Goethals,** more than 40,000 workers struggled to dig the canal. Most were blacks from the West Indies. They blasted a path through mountains and carved out the largest artificial lake in the world up to that time. In all, they removed more than 200 million cubic yards of earth. Then, they built gigantic locks to raise and lower ships as they

Skills FOR LIFE

Critical Thinking	Managing Information	Communication	Maps, Charts, and Graphs

Using the Internet

How Will I Use This Skill?

The Internet is a global computer network. By "surfing the Net," you can link to millions of computer sites sponsored by businesses, governments, educational groups, and individuals all over the world. The Internet provides many services, including information, electronic mail, and on-line shopping.

Students using the Internet ➤

LEARN the Skill

You can search the Internet by using an on-line search engine such as Yahoo, Lycos, or Excite, and by following these steps:

❶ Choose a search engine and type in key words to describe your research topic.

❷ Scan the site descriptions that the search engine provides and click on one that seems to apply best to your topic.

❸ At each Internet site, you can take notes on the on-screen information. Usually, you can also print the information or copy and import it to your own computer. You can also click on highlighted hyperlinks to take you to other related Internet sites.

❹ Return to the search engine. Continue your search by scanning more site descriptions, or start a new search by typing in new key words.

PRACTICE the Skill

Use these steps to learn about the economic importance of the Panama Canal today.

❶ Choose a search engine. What key words should you type?

❷ Based on the site descriptions you see, which site seems most pertinent to your topic? Go to the site by clicking on the description.

❸ Look for information on the volume of goods and ships that travel through the canal. When you find the information, take notes, print, or import the data. What hyperlinks does the site provide to other sites?

❹ Return to the search engine and continue scanning site descriptions. How could you start a new search on the history of the canal?

APPLY the Skill

Use a search engine to see if your state's department of education provides an Internet site. If it does, visit and explore the site. What kinds of useful information and hyperlinks do you find there? Do you have any ideas for improving the site? Perhaps, you could E-mail your suggestions directly to the department of education.

Colombia

United States

Trading Partners

During the early 1900s, trade increased between the United States and Latin America. At left, young Colombian farm workers display a harvest of coffee beans. At right, an American coffee company advertises the finished product: packaged, ground coffee.
★ **Does Colombia import coffee or export coffee?**

passed through the canal. Finally, in 1914, the first ocean-going steamship traveled through the Panama Canal.

The new waterway helped the trade of many nations. American merchants and manufacturers benefited most. They could now ship goods cheaply to South America and Asia. However, many Latin American nations remained bitter about the way in which the United States had gained control of the canal.

Policing Latin America

The Panama Canal involved the United States more than ever in Latin America. Gradually, President Roosevelt and succeeding Presidents established a policy of intervening in Latin America to settle disputes and disturbances. The United States was especially concerned when disturbances threatened American lives, property, and interests in Latin America.

The Roosevelt Corollary

In 1902, several European countries sent warships to force Venezuela to repay its debts. The United States did not want Europeans to interfere in Latin America. President Roosevelt decided that the United States must step in to keep Europeans out. Roosevelt declared that it was the responsibility of the United States to prevent disorder and lawlessness in Latin America:

&& If we intend to say hands off to the powers of Europe, then sooner or later we must keep order ourselves. &&

In 1904, Roosevelt announced an important addition to the Monroe Doctrine. In the **Roosevelt Corollary,** he claimed the right of the United States to intervene in Latin America to preserve law and order. By using this "international police power," the United States could force Latin Americans to pay their debts to foreign nations. It would also keep those nations from meddling in Latin American affairs.

Over the next 20 years, several Presidents, including Roosevelt, used this police power. Most Latin Americans strongly resented this interference in their affairs.

Dollar diplomacy

Roosevelt's successor, William Howard Taft, also favored a strong American role in Latin America. Taft, however, wanted to "substitute dollars for bullets." He urged American bankers to invest in Latin America. It was better to use trade than warships to expand American influence in Latin America, he said. This policy of building strong economic ties to Latin America became known as **dollar diplomacy.**

American investors responded eagerly. They helped build roads, railroads, and harbors in Latin America. These improvements increased trade, benefiting both Americans and local governments. The new railroads, for example, brought minerals and other resources to Latin American ports. From there, they were shipped all over the world.

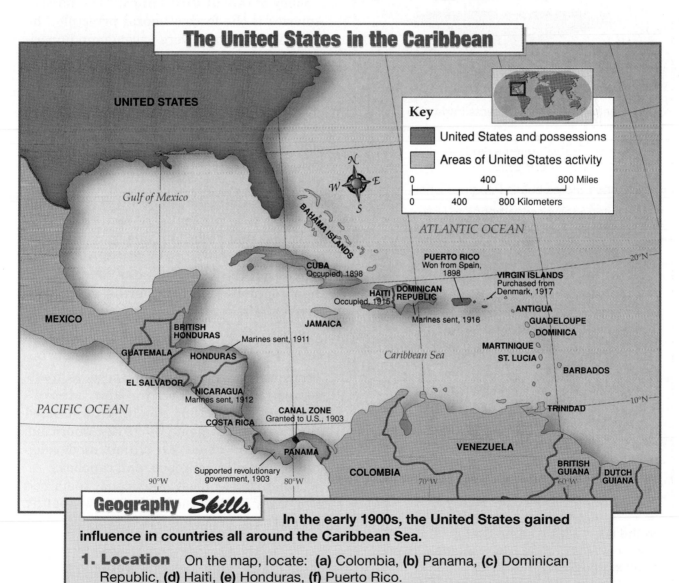

The United States in the Caribbean

Key
- United States and possessions
- Areas of United States activity

UNITED STATES

Gulf of Mexico

BAHAMA ISLANDS

ATLANTIC OCEAN

CUBA
Occupied, 1898

PUERTO RICO
Won from Spain, 1898

VIRGIN ISLANDS
Purchased from Denmark, 1917

HAITI
Occupied, 1915

DOMINICAN REPUBLIC

ANTIGUA

Marines sent, 1916

GUADELOUPE

DOMINICA

MARTINIQUE

ST. LUCIA

BARBADOS

MEXICO

BRITISH HONDURAS

Marines sent, 1911

JAMAICA

Caribbean Sea

GUATEMALA

HONDURAS

EL SALVADOR

NICARAGUA
Marines sent, 1912

PACIFIC OCEAN

CANAL ZONE
Granted to U.S., 1903

COSTA RICA

TRINIDAD

VENEZUELA

PANAMA

Supported revolutionary government, 1903

COLOMBIA

BRITISH GUIANA

DUTCH GUIANA

90°W   80°W   70°W   60°W

20°N

10°N

Geography Skills

In the early 1900s, the United States gained influence in countries all around the Caribbean Sea.

1. **Location** On the map, locate: **(a)** Colombia, **(b)** Panama, **(c)** Dominican Republic, **(d)** Haiti, **(e)** Honduras, **(f)** Puerto Rico.

2. **Region** What areas shown on the map were governed directly by the United States?

3. **Critical Thinking** Review what you have learned about the Roosevelt Corollary. Identify three areas on the map where Presidents used the Roosevelt Corollary.

Causes

- Western frontier closes
- Businesses seek raw materials and new markets
- European nations compete for resources and markets

Overseas Expansion

Effects

- United States develops strong navy
- Open Door Policy protects trade with China
- United States governs lands in Caribbean and Pacific
- United States builds Panama Canal
- United States sends troops to Latin American nations to protect its interests

Effects Today

- United States is global superpower
- Alaska and Hawaii are 49th and 50th states
- Puerto Rico, American Samoa, Guam, and U.S. Virgin Islands remain United States territories
- United States has close economic ties with Latin America and Pacific Rim

Graphic Organizer *Skills*

In the late 1800s, United States foreign policy slowly shifted from isolation to overseas expansion.

1. **Comprehension** List three effects of expansion on Latin America.

2. **Critical Thinking** Which of the Effects Today listed here do you think is most important? Explain.

Dollar diplomacy created problems, too. American businesses, such as the United Fruit Company, often meddled in the political affairs of host countries. Sometimes, the United States used military force to keep order. In 1912, when a revolution erupted in Nicaragua, the United States sent in marines to protect American investments.

Wilson and moral diplomacy

Woodrow Wilson, elected President in 1912, disliked the heavy-handed foreign policy of his predecessors. He proposed instead a policy of **moral diplomacy.** "The force of America is the force of moral principle," he said. Wilson's goals were to condemn imperialism, spread democracy, and promote peace.

Nevertheless, Wilson ordered military intervention in Latin America more than any prior President. When disturbances erupted in Haiti in 1915 and in the Dominican Republic in 1916, Wilson sent in the marines. American troops remained in Haiti until 1934.

Again and again, the United States declared that its troops were restoring peace and order and guarding American lives and property. However, many Latin Americans denounced the United States for invading their countries and interfering in their internal affairs.

Relations With Mexico

Wilson's moral diplomacy faced its greatest test in Mexico. Porfirio Díaz, Mexico's president from 1884 to 1911, welcomed American investment. By 1912, Americans had invested about $1 billion to develop mines, oil wells, railroads, and ranches.

Meanwhile, most Mexicans remained poor. They worked the land of a few wealthy families and they received very little for their labor. These harsh conditions led to widespread discontent.

The Mexican Revolution

In 1910, Mexicans rebelled against Díaz. The new leader, Francisco Madero, promised democratic reform. Then, in 1913, Madero was himself overthrown and killed by General Victoriano Huerta (WEHR tuh). As civil war raged in Mexico, Wilson vowed that he would never recognize this "government of butchers."

Wilson tried to stay neutral. He hoped that Mexico would develop a democratic government without American interference. However, Huerta's dictatorship grew more brutal. In response, Wilson authorized the sale of arms to Huerta's rival, Venustiano Carranza.

Finally, a minor incident led to American intervention. In 1914, Huerta's troops arrested several American sailors. The sailors were quickly released and an apology issued. Still, Wilson ordered the United States Navy to occupy the Mexican port of Veracruz. Rallied by the American show of strength, Carranza's forces drove Huerta from power. The United States troops withdrew.

American soldiers in Mexico

Still, civil war continued in Mexico. Now, General **Francisco "Pancho" Villa** hoped to overthrow Carranza. The United States, meanwhile, supported Carranza.

In January 1916, Villa's soldiers removed 17 American citizens from a train in Mexico and shot them. In March, Villa raided the town of Columbus, New Mexico, killing 19 Americans. He hoped that his actions would weaken relations between the United States and the Carranza government. Villa's plan backfired.

To capture Villa, President Wilson sent General **John J. Pershing** with an army of several thousand soldiers into Mexico. When Mexico demanded that the "invasion" be halted, the United States refused. There were some calls for war, but both Wilson and Carranza opposed the idea. In 1917, after failing to capture Villa, Wilson ordered Pershing's army to withdraw.

Once again, the United States had demonstrated its willingness to use force to protect its interests. However, there was a cost. Like many other Latin Americans, Mexicans became more resentful of their powerful neighbor to the North.

As United States troops headed home from Mexico, many Americans realized that their nation's role in world affairs had dramatically changed over the years. Now the United States kept troops and ships in both Asia and Latin America. American business interests spanned the globe. It would be very difficult for the United States to ignore the war that had been raging in Europe since 1914.

★ Section 3 Review ★

Recall

1. **Locate** **(a)** Colombia, **(b)** Panama, **(c)** Panama Canal, **(d)** Venezuela, **(e)** Mexico.

2. **Identify** **(a)** William Gorgas, **(b)** George Goethals, **(c)** Roosevelt Corollary, **(d)** Francisco "Pancho" Villa, **(e)** John J. Pershing.

3. **Define** **(a)** isthmus, **(b)** dollar diplomacy, **(c)** moral diplomacy.

Comprehension

4. Why did President Roosevelt think it was important for the United States to build the Panama Canal?

5. How were the foreign policies of Roosevelt, Taft, and Wilson similar?

6. **(a)** Why did Mexicans rebel against their government in 1910? **(b)** Why did President Wilson send General Pershing into Mexico?

Critical Thinking and Writing

7. **Understanding Causes and Effects** How did geographic conditions in Panama make it difficult to build a canal there?

8. **Thinking Creatively** What do you think President Wilson could have done to help bring the Mexican Revolution to a peaceful end?

Activity **Preparing for an Interview** You are a historian about to interview President Theodore Roosevelt concerning his policy in Latin American countries. Write three questions you would ask him.

Review and Activities

★ Sum It Up ★

Section 1   Across the Pacific
▶ In the mid-1800s, the United States increased its influence in the Pacific by opening trade with Japan and by buying Alaska from Russia.
▶ Americans began to favor imperialism because they wanted raw materials and markets in other regions.
▶ After American planters rebelled against the Hawaiian government, the United States annexed Hawaii.
▶ To protect American trading rights in China, the United States established the Open Door Policy.

Section 2   The Spanish-American War
▶ The Cuban revolt against Spain led to war between the United States and Spain.
▶ United States forces defeated the Spanish in Cuba, Puerto Rico, and the Philippines.
▶ After the war, the United States took control of Spain's former colonies in the Caribbean Sea and the Pacific Ocean.
▶ Filipino nationalists fought unsuccessfully against the United States Army.

Section 3   Relations With Latin America
▶ The United States built the Panama Canal through Central America.
▶ Roosevelt and succeeding Presidents intervened repeatedly in Latin American affairs.
▶ In response to events of the Mexican Revolution, President Wilson sent United States troops into Mexico.

CD-ROM Review For additional review of the major ideas of Chapter 23, see *Guide to the Essentials of American History* or *Interactive Student Tutorial CD-ROM,* which contains interactive review activities, graphic organizers, and practice tests.

📕 Reviewing the Chapter

Define These Terms
Match each term with the correct definition.

Column 1	Column 2
1. isolationism	a. policy of having little to do with foreign nations
2. sphere of influence	b. agreement to end fighting
3. isthmus	c. part of a nation where another nation has special trading privileges
4. yellow journalism	d. sensational news reporting
5. armistice	e. narrow strip of land connecting two larger areas of land

Explore the Main Ideas
1. Why did many Americans favor imperialism in the late 1800s?
2. How did the United States extend its interests in Asia and the Pacific?
3. **(a)** What was one cause of the Spanish-American War? **(b)** What was one effect of the war?
4. How did the United States acquire the rights to build a canal in Panama?
5. Explain each of the following: **(a)** Roosevelt Corollary, **(b)** dollar diplomacy, **(c)** moral diplomacy.

📕 Geography Activity

Match the letters on the map with the following places:
1. United States, **2.** Puerto Rico, **3.** Panama Canal, **4.** Cuba, **5.** Nicaragua, **6.** Dominican Republic. **Place** Why was the Isthmus of Panama a good place to build a canal?

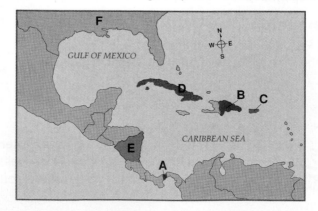

📷 Critical Thinking and Writing

1. **Understanding Chronology** List the following events in chronological order: **(a)** Filipino War for Independence, **(b)** Spanish-American War, **(c)** Cuban rebellion against Spain, **(d)** the sinking of the battleship *Maine.*

2. **Linking Past and Present** What national projects today present challenges similar to those overcome in building the Panama Canal? Explain.

3. **Making Inferences** In the quotation on page 555, Pershing described the American forces at San Juan as being made up of men "of North and South." Why did he choose this way of describing the military?

4. **Exploring Unit Themes   Global Interaction** Captain Mahan insisted that the navy was the decisive power that would control events in distant regions. **(a)** Give evidence to prove or disprove that his view was correct in his time. **(b)** Does his view hold true today?

📷 Using Primary Sources

Naval Lieutenant John Blandin was on the *Maine* when it exploded. He later made this statement about the event:

> 66 I have no theories as to the cause of the explosion. I cannot form any. I, with others, had heard that the Havana harbor was full of [explosive mines], but the officers whose duty it was to examine into that reported that they found no signs of any. Personally, I do not believe that the Spanish had anything to do with the disaster. Time may tell. I hope so. 99

Source: *Memories of Two Wars: Cuban and Philippine Experiences,* Frederick Funston, 1911.

Recognizing Points of View   (a) According to Blandin, what evidence was there that the Spanish were to blame for the sinking of the *Maine*? **(b)** Why did the views of Blandin and other witnesses have little effect on American public opinion about the explosion?

ACTIVITY BANK

▶ Interdisciplinary Activity

Exploring Geography Choose one of the lands the United States acquired during its period of foreign expansion. Prepare a geographic fact sheet on its geography. Then, write a short essay explaining why the geography of the place you have chosen made it a target for American imperialists.

▶ Career Skills Activity

Cartographers On a large sheet of paper, draw a map of the world. Indicate the following on the map: **(a)** the territory of the United States in 1850, **(b)** the territory gained by the United States between 1850 and 1914.

▶ Citizenship Activity

Writing an Editorial The question of whether the United States should act as the police officer of the world arose many times during the early 1900s. Write an editorial in which you either support or oppose the use of United States military forces to settle disputes and disturbances in other parts of the world.

▶ Internet Activity

Use the Internet to find sites dealing with the Spanish-American War. Gather information on a single event of the war. Then, write a newspaper story as it might have appeared in the yellow press of the time. How do the facts and your story differ?

EYEWITNESS Journal

You are an American farmer, industrialist, missionary, or naval officer during the Age of Imperialism. In your EYEWITNESS JOURNAL, describe your thoughts on the increasing role of the United States in world affairs.

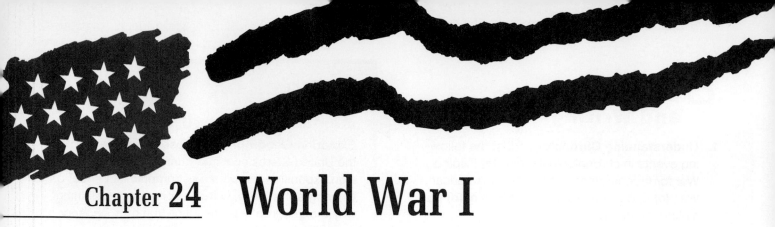

Chapter 24

World War I

1914–1919

In 1914, long-standing rivalries among European nations exploded into war. At first, President Woodrow Wilson tried to keep the United States neutral. However, after several of Germany's actions affected American citizens, the United States entered the war against Germany in 1917.

World War I, as the war is now called, cost millions of lives. After the war ended, Wilson worked hard to build a lasting peace. However, because of conflicts at the peace conference and at home, he was unable to achieve all of his goals.

Why Study History?

World War I ended on November 11, 1918. Today, Americans celebrate November 11 as Veterans Day. On this day, we remember and honor all the men and women who have served the nation in the armed services. To focus on this connection, see the *Why Study History?* feature, "We Honor Our Veterans," in this chapter.

American Events

1915
Americans die when Germany sinks the *Lusitania*

1916
Avoiding war helps President Wilson win reelection

1917
United States enters World War I

1914   1915   1916   1917

World Events

 1914 World Event
World War I begins in Europe

 1916 World Event
Hundreds of thousands die in Battle of Verdun

Viewing HISTORY

Americans Fight in Europe

During World War I, the government sent artists to the battleground in Europe. This painting, 18 on the Trail of the San Mihiel, *is by W. J. Aylward. It shows American troops in 1918 moving equipment to the front.* ★ **Why do you think the government sent artists to the front lines?**

1918 ●	1919 ●	1921 ●
Armistice ends World War I fighting	Senate rejects Treaty of Versailles	United States signs peace treaty with Germany

1917	**1918**	**1919**	**1920**

▲ **1917 World Event**
Russian Revolution begins

▲ **1918 World Event**
Influenza epidemic kills millions

War Erupts in Europe

As You Read

Explore These Questions
- Why were tensions high in Europe in 1914?
- What event triggered World War I?
- How did Americans react to the outbreak of war in Europe?

Define
- nationalism
- militarism
- mobilize
- kaiser
- stalemate
- trench warfare
- propaganda
- U-boat

Identify
- Triple Alliance
- Triple Entente
- Franz Ferdinand
- World War I
- Central Powers
- Allied Powers
- *Lusitania*

SETTING the Scene President Woodrow Wilson's friend and adviser Colonel Edward House visited Europe in May 1914. He quickly saw that tensions among the continent's nations threatened the peace. "The situation is extraordinary," he noted. "There is too much hatred, too many jealousies."

It was not long before events proved House correct. Three months after the colonel returned home, Europe exploded into war.

Tensions in Europe

The fact that war erupted in August 1914 did not surprise many Europeans. After all, tensions had torn Europe for years.

Extreme nationalism

Extreme feelings of **nationalism,** or pride in one's nation, fueled the tension. In the 1870s, European nationalists demanded freedom and self-government. They believed that people with a common language and culture should throw off foreign rule and form their own countries.

While nationalism encouraged unity, it also created mistrust and bitter rivalry between nations. For example, France and Germany had gone to war in 1870. As a result of that war, France had to give Germany the iron-rich territory of Alsace-Lorraine. The French never forgot this blow to their national pride. They hoped for an opportunity to regain their lost territory.

In Eastern Europe, nationalism deepened hostility between Austria-Hungary and Russia. Russia encouraged Serbs and other minorities in Austria-Hungary to rise up against their rulers.

Imperialism and militarism

Imperialism fueled rivalries between powerful nations. Between 1870 and 1914, Britain, France, Germany, Italy, and Russia scrambled for colonies in Africa, Asia, and the Pacific. Often, several nations competed for power in the same region. This competition sometimes led to wars in places far from Europe.

Militarism was a third source of tension. **Militarism** is the policy of building up strong armed forces to prepare for war. European nations expanded their armies and navies, creating new stresses. For example, Germany built up its navy. Britain responded by adding more ships to its fleet. This race for naval dominance strained relations between the two nations.

Rival alliances

To protect themselves, European powers formed rival alliances. Germany organized the **Triple Alliance** with Austria-Hungary and Italy. France responded by linking itself to Russia and Britain in the **Triple Entente** (ahn TAHNT).

The alliance system posed a new danger. Allies agreed to support one another in case of an attack. Thus, a crisis involving one member of an alliance affected that nation's allies. This meant that a minor incident could spark a major war. On June 28, 1914, that incident finally took place.

War Breaks Out

For years, nationalism had caused turmoil in the Balkan peninsula in southeastern Europe. (See the map on page 646.) There, the rival nations of Albania, Bulgaria, Greece, Montenegro, Romania, and Serbia battled for territory. At the same time, Balkan nationalists called on related people in Austria-Hungary to free themselves of Austrian rule.

Assassination in Serbia

In June 1914, a new crisis struck the region. Archduke **Franz Ferdinand,** heir to the throne of Austria-Hungary, was visiting Sarajevo, the capital of Bosnia. At the time, Bosnia was part of the Eastern European empire ruled by Austria-Hungary. Franz Ferdinand's visit angered members of the Black Hand, a Serbian terrorist group. The Black Hand wanted Bosnia to break away from Austria-Hungary and join Serbia.

On June 28, the archduke and his wife, Sophie, rode through Sarajevo in an open car. Suddenly, a young terrorist named Gavrilo Princip stepped from the curb, waving a pistol. Taking aim, he fatally shot Franz Ferdinand and Sophie.

Alliances lead to war

In the days that followed, Austria-Hungary accused the Serbian government of organizing the archduke's assassination. When Austria-Hungary threatened war, Russia moved to protect Serbia. Diplomats rushed to ease tensions, but they could not stop the system of alliances from running its fateful course.

On July 28, Austria-Hungary declared war on Serbia. The next day, Russia ordered its forces to **mobilize,** or prepare for war. Austria-Hungary's ally, Germany, called on Russia to cancel the order to mobilize. When it received no reply, Germany declared war on Russia on August 1.

On August 2, the American ambassador to Britain, Walter Page, wrote:

66 The Grand Smash is come....I walked out in the night a while ago. The stars are bright, the night is silent, the country quiet—as quiet as peace itself. Millions of men are in camp and on warships. Will they all have to fight and many of them die—to untangle this network of treaties and alliances...so that the world may start again? 99

The answer came the next day. On August 3, Germany declared war on Russia's ally France. When German armies sliced through neutral Belgium on their march to

Alliances Lead to War

Distressed Americans looked on as World War I unfolded in Europe. This cartoon appeared in an American newspaper in the summer of 1914.
★ What does the woman in the background represent? What are the nations of Europe doing in the cartoon?

France, Britain declared war on Germany. Long before, Britain had promised to defend Belgium if it were attacked.

In this way, what began as a local crisis in Bosnia exploded into a major war. For years, Europeans had expected war. When it came, many welcomed the chance to show their power and strength. Others, however, feared what war might bring.

On the Battlefront

"You will be home before the leaves have fallen from the trees," the **kaiser,** or German emperor, promised his troops as they marched to war. Europeans on both sides of the conflict thought the war would end soon. Sadly, they were mistaken. The war dragged on for four blood-soaked years, from 1914 to 1918. At the time, the conflict was called the Great War. Later, it became known as **World War I.**

The war pitted the **Central Powers**—Germany, Austria-Hungary, and the Ottoman or Turkish Empire—against the **Allied Powers**—France, Britain, and Russia. In time, 21 other nations, including Italy, joined the Allies.

By November 1914, a German advance and an Allied counterattack had produced nothing but a deadly stalemate. A **stalemate** is a deadlock in which neither side is strong enough to defeat the other. For three years, the two armies fought huge battles, but with little to show for it. While thousands of young Europeans lost their lives, neither side gained much territory.

Both sides dug in, creating a maze of trenches protected by mines and barbed wire. Soldiers spent weeks in these muddy, rat-infested holes in the ground. One soldier later recalled: "The men slept in mud, washed in mud, ate mud, and dreamed mud." Some trenches were shallow ditches. Others were elaborate tunnels that served as headquarters and first-aid stations. Between the front-line trenches of each side lay a "no man's land" of barbed wire and deadly land mines.

In **trench warfare,** soldiers spent day after day shelling the enemy. Then, on orders from an officer, the troops charged bravely "over the top" of the trenches. Soldiers raced across "no man's land" to attack the enemy.

Most offensives were long and deadly. The Battle of Verdun in 1916 lasted 10 months. The Germans lost some 400,000 men trying to overrun French lines. The French lost even more lives defending their position.

In the meanwhile, in the east, the vast armies of Germany and Austria-Hungary faced off against those of Russia and Serbia. Stalemate and trench warfare brought mounting tolls there as well. By mid-1916, the Russians had lost more than one million soldiers. Yet, neither side could win a decisive victory.

The United States Remains Neutral

When war broke out in Europe, the United States was determined to avoid being dragged into the conflict. The government adopted an official position of neutrality. President Woodrow Wilson called on Americans to "be neutral in fact as well as in name."

Public opinion, however, was divided, often along ethnic lines. Most Americans favored the Allies because of long-standing ties of language, history, and culture to Britain. The United States and France had been allies in the American Revolution.

On the other hand, many of the 8 million Americans of German or Austrian descent favored the Central Powers. Millions of Irish Americans also sympathized with the Central Powers. They hated Britain, which had ruled Ireland for centuries. Many American Jews favored Germany against Russia. Some of them had fled persecution in Russia only a few years earlier.

Impact of the war

The war had several immediate effects on the United States. First, the economy boomed. American farmers and manufacturers rushed to fill orders for war goods. By 1917, trade with the Allies had grown seven times in value and by a smaller amount with

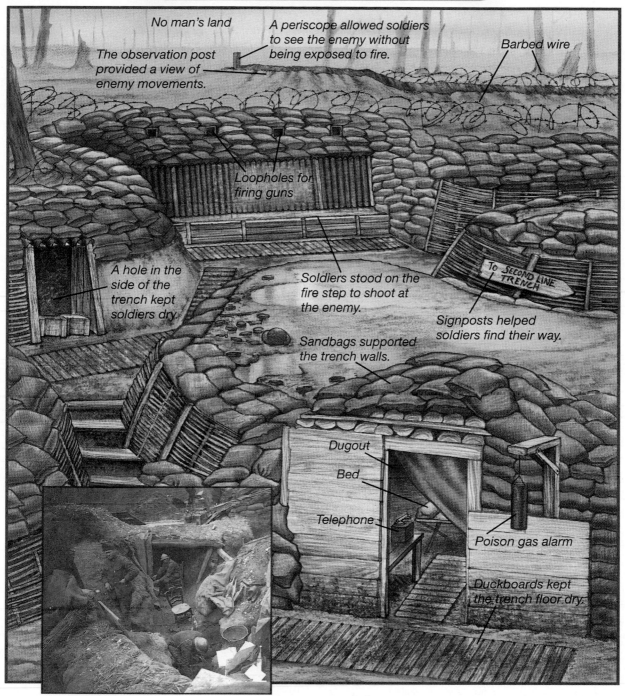

No man's land

A periscope allowed soldiers to see the enemy without being exposed to fire.

Barbed wire

The observation post provided a view of enemy movements.

Loopholes for firing guns

A hole in the side of the trench kept soldiers dry.

Soldiers stood on the fire step to shoot at the enemy.

To Second Line Trench

Signposts helped soldiers find their way.

Sandbags supported the trench walls.

Dugout

Bed

Telephone

Poison gas alarm

Duckboards kept the trench floor dry.

Trench Warfare

During World War I, soldiers on both sides dug networks of trenches. The typical trench was about 6 to 8 feet (1.8 to 2.4 m) deep and just wide enough for two men to pass. "No man's land," a stretch of barren ground protected by barbed wire and land mines, lay between enemy trenches. ★ **How do you think trench warfare affected the land and resources of the surrounding environment?**

Europe in World War I

Key
- Allies
- Central Powers
- Neutral nations

0 300 600 Miles
0 300 600 Kilometers

Geography Skills World War I was fought on many fronts. The Central Powers clashed with the Allies in France, Belgium, Russia, Italy, and the Ottoman Empire.

1. **Location**   On the map, locate: **(a)** Sarajevo, **(b)** Serbia, **(c)** Austria-Hungary, **(d)** Germany, **(e)** Russia, **(f)** France, **(g)** Great Britain.

2. **Movement**   Through which country did German troops march on their way to France?

3. **Critical Thinking**   Judging from the map, why was the alliance between France and Russia a threat to Germany?

the Central Powers. This trade imbalance meant that the United States was not strictly neutral.

Both sides waged a propaganda war in the United States. **Propaganda** is the spreading of ideas that help a cause or hurt an opposing cause. Each side pictured the other as savage beasts who killed innocent civilians. Anti-German propaganda often referred to the Germans as "Huns," the name of a tribe of ancient barbarians.

Submarine warfare

In the end, it was not propaganda that brought the United States into the war against Germany. Rather, anti-German feeling hardened when Germany interfered with what Americans saw as their freedom of the seas.

As a neutral nation, the United States claimed the right to trade with either side in the conflict. Early in the war, however, Britain blockaded German ports, hoping to starve Germany into surrender. In response, Germany set up a blockade around Britain. To enforce the blockade, Germany used a powerful new weapon—a fleet of submarines known as **U-boats.** German U-boats attacked any ship that entered or left British ports.

U-boat attacks on neutral shipping raised a storm of protest. Under international law, a country at war could stop and search a neutral ship suspected of carrying war goods. But German submarines were not equipped to conduct a search. After surfacing, they simply torpedoed enemy and neutral ships, often killing scores of civilians.

Germany warned the United States and other neutral nations to keep their ships out of the blockade zone. President Wilson rejected this limit on neutral shipping. He vowed to hold Germany responsible if its U-boats caused any loss of American life or property.

The New York Times *headline of May 8, 1915*

Sinking of the *Lusitania*

Germany ignored Wilson's threat. On May 7, 1915, a German submarine torpedoed the *Lusitania,* a British passenger ship, off the coast of Ireland. Nearly 1,200 people died, including 128 Americans.

An outraged Wilson called the sinking of the *Lusitania* "murder on the high seas." He threatened to break off diplomatic relations if Germany did not stop sinking passenger ships. Germany was not ready to risk war with the United States. It agreed to stop attacking neutral ships without warning.

★ Section 1 Review ★

Recall

1. **Locate** (a) France, (b) Germany, (c) Austria-Hungary, (d) Russia, (e) Britain, (f) Italy, (g) Serbia.
2. **Identify** (a) Triple Alliance, (b) Triple Entente, (c) Franz Ferdinand, (d) World War I, (e) Central Powers, (f) Allied Powers, (g) *Lusitania.*
3. **Define** (a) nationalism, (b) militarism, (c) mobilize, (d) kaiser, (e) stalemate, (f) trench warfare, (g) propaganda, (h) U-boat.

Comprehension

4. List three causes for tension in Europe in 1914.

5. What was the immediate cause of World War I?
6. (a) How did war in Europe affect the American economy? (b) Why did anti-German feeling grow in the United States?

Critical Thinking and Writing

7. **Analyzing Ideas** How did the alliance system help bring about war?
8. **Predicting Consequences** Based on what you have read in Section 1, do you think that the United States stayed out of World War I? Explain.

★ ★

Activity **Writing a Letter** You are a soldier in one of the European armies. Write a letter home describing your feelings about the conflict. Be sure to date your letter. Your feelings in 1914 might be different than your feelings two years later.

The United States Enters the War

As You Read

Explore These Questions
- Why did the United States enter the war in 1917?
- How did the nation organize its war effort?
- How did the government respond to critics of the war?

Define
- warmonger
- czar
- draft
- illiterate
- bureaucracy
- pacifist
- socialist

Identify
- Zimmermann telegram
- Jeannette Rankin
- Selective Service Act
- Herbert Hoover
- Liberty Bonds

SETTING the Scene The outbreak of war in Europe horrified American automaker Henry Ford. In December of 1915, Ford sailed on a mission to Europe. His goal was to bring the warring powers to the peace table. "We're going to have the boys out of the trenches by Christmas," Ford confidently announced.

Christmas passed, yet the war went on. Ford's mission had failed. Still, his efforts for a negotiated peace reflected the American belief that an end to the fighting could be achieved with words instead of guns.

Wilson Tries to Bring Peace

President Wilson, too, tried to bring both sides to peace talks. He believed that the United States, as a neutral, could lead warring nations to a fair peace, a "peace without victory." But Wilson's peace efforts, like Ford's, failed.

Even as he was trying to make peace, Wilson knew that the United States might be drawn into the war. Thus, the President began to lobby for a stronger army and navy.

In 1916, Wilson ran for reelection against Republican Charles Evans Hughes, a Supreme Court Justice. Although Hughes also favored neutrality, Democrats were able to portray him as a **warmonger,** or person who tries to stir up war. At the same time, they boosted Wilson's image with the slogan "He kept us out of war!"

The race was close. On election night, Hughes went to bed believing he had won. Just after midnight, his telephone rang. "The President cannot be disturbed," a friend told the caller. "Well, when he wakes up," the caller replied, "just tell him he isn't President." Late returns from California had given Wilson the election.

Moving Toward War

In January 1917, Wilson issued what proved to be his final plea for peace. It was too late. In a desperate effort to break the Allied blockade, Germany had already decided to renew submarine warfare. Germany warned neutral nations that after February 1, 1917, its U-boats would have orders to sink any ship nearing Britain.

German leaders knew that renewed U-boat attacks would probably bring the United States into the war. They gambled that they would defeat the Allies before American troops could reach Europe. To protest Germany's action, Wilson broke off diplo-

This Wilson campaign button stressed military readiness.

Should the United States Declare War on Germany?

NO

- United States has tradition of neutrality
- Some Americans sympathize with Central Powers
- Wilson opposes alliance with Russian czar
- Pacifists oppose war

United States in 1917

YES

- Americans outraged by German submarine warfare
- Many Americans favor Britain and France
- Zimmermann telegram angers Americans
- American trade with Allies grows

Graphic Organizer *Skills*   As World War I progressed, the United States found it harder and harder to maintain neutrality.

1. **Comprehension** (a) List two factors that led the United States government to try to remain neutral. (b) List two factors that pushed the nation toward war.

2. **Critical Thinking** Review what you have learned about President George Washington's Farewell Address. (See page 252.) What policy do you think Washington would have favored during World War I? Explain.

---

matic relations with Germany. Even so, the President still hoped to maintain neutrality.

The Zimmermann telegram

A few weeks later, a startling discovery moved the United States closer to war. In February, Wilson learned that Arthur Zimmermann, Germany's foreign secretary, had sent a secret note to the German minister in Mexico. The **Zimmermann telegram** instructed the minister to urge Mexico to attack the United States if the United States declared war on Germany. In return, Germany would help Mexico win back its "lost provinces" in the American Southwest.*

When Americans heard about the Zimmermann telegram, anti-German feeling soared. They were furious that the alliance system that had plunged Europe into war was spreading to the Americas.

---

*The "lost provinces" referred to land that the United States gained as a result of the Mexican War. See Chapter 13.

The Russian Revolution

Two other events in early 1917 pushed the country still closer to war. First, German submarines sank several American merchant ships. Second, a revolution in Russia drove Czar Nicholas II from power.

For hundreds of years, **czars,** or Russian emperors, had ruled with absolute power. Several times in the 1800s and early 1900s, Russians had revolted against czarist rule. Their efforts all ended in failure.

When the war in Europe began in 1914, Russians united behind the czar. However, as the war brought heavy losses at the front and economic hardship at home, discontent resurfaced. In March 1917, riots protesting the shortage of food turned into a revolution. The czar was forced to step down. Revolutionaries then set up the Provisional Government and called for democratic reforms.

President Wilson welcomed the Russian Revolution. He was a firm believer in democracy, and it was against his principles to be

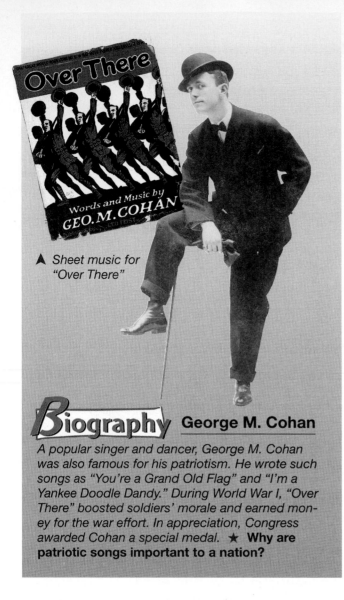

▲ Sheet music for "Over There"

Biography — George M. Cohan

A popular singer and dancer, George M. Cohan was also famous for his patriotism. He wrote such songs as "You're a Grand Old Flag" and "I'm a Yankee Doodle Dandy." During World War I, "Over There" boosted soldiers' morale and earned money for the war effort. In appreciation, Congress awarded Cohan a special medal. ★ **Why are patriotic songs important to a nation?**

an ally of an absolute ruler. Without the czar, it would be easier for Wilson to support the Allied cause.

Declaration of war

On April 2, President Wilson went before Congress to ask for a declaration of war. "The world must be made safe for democracy," he declared. His war message assured the American people that entering the war was not only just, it was noble. He concluded:

> ❝ It is a fearful thing to lead this great peaceful people into war, into the most terrible and disastrous of all wars, civilization itself seeming to be in the balance. But the right is more precious than peace, and we shall fight for the thing which we have always carried nearest our hearts—for democracy. ❞

Congress voted for war 455 to 56. Among those who voted against the declaration was **Jeannette Rankin** of Montana, the first woman elected to Congress. She hated war as much as she loved her country. "I want to stand by my country, but I cannot vote for war. I vote no!" she said.

On April 6, the President signed the declaration of war. It thrust Americans into the deadliest war the world had yet seen.

The Nation at War

The day after Congress declared war, George M. Cohan wrote a new song, "Over There." The patriotic tune swept the nation. Its opening lines expressed the confidence that Americans felt :

> ❝ Over there, over there,
> Send the word, send the word, over there,
> That the Yanks are coming... ❞

Its closing message promised, "We'll be over, we're coming over, And we won't come back till it's over over there."

Americans had to do more than sing patriotic tunes, however. They had to prepare to fight—and quickly. The Allies needed everything from food to arms. Britain and France were on the verge of collapse. In Russia, soldiers at the front were deserting to join the revolution.

Building an army

Before it could fight, the United States needed an army. On May 18, Congress passed the **Selective Service Act.** It required all young men from age 21 to 30 to register for the military draft. A **draft** is a law requiring people of a certain age to serve in the military.

In the next 18 months, 4 million men and women joined the armed forces. People from every ethnic group enlisted. About 20,000 Puerto Ricans served in the armed forces, as did many Filipinos. Scores of soldiers were immigrants who had recently arrived in the United States.

Many Native Americans were not citizens, so they could not be drafted. Large numbers of Native Americans enlisted anyway. One family of Winnebago Indians provided 35 volunteers! They served together in the same unit.

At first, the armed forces did not allow African Americans in combat. When the government abandoned this policy, more than 2 million African Americans registered for the draft. Nearly 400,000 were accepted for duty. They were forced into segregated "black-only" units that were commanded mostly by white officers.

Still, African Americans rallied behind the war effort. Blacks like W.E.B. Du Bois voiced strong support for the war's goals:

66 Let us, while the war lasts, forget our special grievances and close ranks ... with our fellow citizens and the allied nations that are fighting for democracy. 99

In training

While men drilled for combat, women served as radio operators, clerks, and stenographers. At training camps, there were not always enough weapons for everyone. Until supplies increased, some recruits trained using broomsticks for guns.

Despite long hours of drill, soldiers got caught up in the war spirit. A young recruit wrote, "We don't know where we are going, but the band plays 'Over There' every day, and they can't send us any too soon." To many, the war seemed like a great adventure. "Here was our one great chance for excitement and risk," wrote a volunteer. "We could not afford to pass it up."

Educating the recruits

For many recruits, especially African Americans, southerners, and immigrants, the Army offered several firsts. It was their first exposure to military authority and discipline. It was the first time most had ventured outside their farms and villages, let alone outside their country. Some had never taken regular baths or eaten regular meals before. Others had never used indoor plumbing. About 25 percent were **illiterate,** that is, unable to read or write.

The Army became a great educator. It taught millions of young Americans not only how to fight but also how to read, how to eat nutritious meals, and how to care for their daily health needs.

Shocking rates of illiteracy and other low test scores among recruits fueled a drive to reform public education. State and local school boards lengthened the school day and

 **Building an Army**

The Selective Service Act required young men between the ages of 21 and 30 to register for the draft. In this photograph, a blindfolded woman selects the numbers of men to be called for duty. ★ **Do you think a draft is a fair way to raise an army? Explain.**

required students to spend more years in school. They raised teacher training standards. More truancy officers patrolled the streets. By 1920, 75 percent of all school-age children were enrolled in school.

Organizing the War Effort

The United States reorganized its economy to produce food, arms, and other goods needed to fight the war. President Wilson set up government agencies to oversee the effort. A huge bureaucracy (byoo ROK ruh see) emerged to manage the war effort. A **bureaucracy** is a system of managing government through departments run by appointed officials.

"Food will win the war"

Wilson chose **Herbert Hoover** to head the Food Administration. Hoover's job was to boost food production. The nation had to feed its troops and help the Allies.

In keeping with the nation's democratic traditions, Hoover relied on cooperation rather than force. He tried to win support for his programs with publicity campaigns that encouraged Americans to act voluntarily. "Food Will Win the War," proclaimed one Food Administration poster. A magazine urged:

66 Do not permit your child to take a bite or two from an apple and throw the rest away; nowadays even children must be taught to be patriotic to the core.99

Encouraged by rising food prices, farmers grew more crops. Families planted "victory gardens." People went without wheat on "wheatless Mondays," and without meat on "meatless Tuesdays." The food they saved helped the men in the trenches.

Wartime industry

War caught the nation short of supplies. The military had on hand only around 600,000 rifles, 2,000 machine guns, and fewer than 1,000 pieces of artillery. Disorder threatened as the military competed with private industry to buy scarce materials.

To meet this crisis, President Wilson set up a new government agency, the War Industries Board. It told factories what they had to produce. It also divided up limited resources.

Without the support of workers, industry could not mobilize. In 1918, Wilson created the War Labor Board. It settled disputes over working hours and wages and tried to prevent strikes. With workers in short supply, unions were able to win better pay and working conditions. With the President supporting workers, union membership rose sharply.

The Home Front

Americans on the home front united behind the war effort. Movie stars, such as Charlie Chaplin and Mary Pickford, helped sell **Liberty Bonds.** By buying bonds, American citizens were lending money to the government to pay for the war. The sale of Liberty Bonds raised $21 billion, just over half of what the United States spent on the war.

To rally public support for the war, the government sent out 75,000 speakers known as "Four-Minute Men." Their name reminded people of the heroic Minutemen of 1776. It also referred to the four-minute speeches the men gave at public events, movies, and theaters. The speakers urged Americans to make sacrifices for the goals of freedom and democracy.

Women at work

As men joined the armed forces, women stepped into their jobs. Women received better pay in war industries than they had in peacetime. Still, they earned less than the men they replaced.

In factories, women assembled weapons and airplane parts. Some women drove trol-

---

$ Connections With Economics

President Wilson also did his part for the war effort. He kept a herd of sheep to trim the White House lawn. The sheep replaced gardeners who had been drafted. In addition, Wilson raised $100,000 for the Red Cross by selling the wool of the White House sheep.

Viewing History

Women Support the War Effort

Whether in uniform or on the job, American women rallied behind the war effort. The poster at right urged support for women serving in the military. The shipyard workers above hold the tongs and buckets they used to work with red-hot steel rivets. ★ **How do you think wartime work helped women win the right to vote?**

Back our girls over there Y.W.C.A.
United War Work Campaign

---

ley cars and delivered the mail. Others served as police officers. By performing well in jobs once reserved for men, women helped change the view that they were fit only for "women's work." Unfortunately, most of the gains made by women disappeared when the men returned to the work force at the end of the war.

Anti-German feelings

German Americans endured suspicion and intolerance during the war. Newspapers questioned their loyalty. Mobs attacked them on the streets. In 1918, a mob lynched Robert Prager, whose only crime was that he had been born in Germany. A jury later refused to convict the mob leaders.

Anti-German prejudice led some families to change their names. Schools stopped teaching the German language. Concert halls banned works by German composers. Americans began referring to German measles as "liberty measles" and sauerkraut as "liberty cabbage."

Other ethnic tensions

During the war, almost a half million African Americans and thousands of Mexican Americans embarked on a great migration. They left the South and Southwest for cities in the North, hoping to escape poverty and discrimination.

In northern cities, many blacks found better-paying jobs in war industries. At the

Skills FOR LIFE

Critical Thinking	Managing Information	Communication	Maps, Charts, and Graphs

Recognizing Propaganda

How Will I Use This Skill?

Propaganda is an attempt to spread ideas that support a particular cause or hurt an opposing cause. In our everyday lives, propaganda can be found in advertisements, in political posters and speeches, even in movies and television shows. Being aware of propaganda techniques can help us evaluate the messages we receive and make reasoned judgments.

LEARN the Skill

Propaganda often stresses emotional appeals. It may use half-truths, stressing some truths but ignoring others. In extreme cases, propaganda may even use outright lies. Other common propaganda techniques include name-calling and using symbols and words that show the opposition in the worst light. To recognize propaganda, look for these points:

❶ Identify factual information, exaggerations, or misinformation.

❷ Analyze the type of emotion the propaganda wants the reader to feel. Look for name-calling and the use of emotional symbols and words.

❸ Try to determine the source of the propaganda. Identify the action or opinion the propaganda is trying to support or oppose.

❹ Judge whether the propaganda is effective.

PRACTICE the Skill

The propaganda poster above appeared after the United States declared war on Germany

in 1917. Look at the poster and answer the following questions.

❶ Is any factual information about the war included in this poster? Explain.

❷ (a) What image of the enemy do the words and picture convey? (b) What emotions is the poster trying to stir?

❸ (a) Who do you think produced this poster? (b) What action do they want to encourage?

❹ Do you think this poster was effective propaganda at the time? Why or why not?

APPLY the Skill

Advertisements, like propaganda, use emotions and facts to persuade us to perform certain actions. Choose an advertisement from a newspaper or magazine. Using the steps given above, analyze the advertisement as propaganda.

same time, they ran into prejudice and even violence. Competition for housing and jobs sometimes led to race riots. In 1917, 39 African Americans were killed during a riot in East St. Louis, Illinois. A New York parade protested the deaths. Marchers carried signs demanding, "Mr. President, Why Not Make AMERICA Safe for Democracy?"

In the Southwest, ranchers pressed the government to let more Mexicans cross the border. Almost 100,000 Mexicans entered the United States to work on farms, mostly in California and Texas. By 1920, Mexicans were the leading foreign-born group in California. Some Mexicans moved on to northern cities, where they worked in factories.

Throughout the war, Mexicans worked in cotton and beet fields, in copper mines, and in steel mills. All these jobs were important to the war effort. Yet after the war, when veterans returned and unemployment grew, the United States tried to force Mexican workers to return to Mexico.

Silencing protest

Some Americans opposed the war. Among them were Progressives such as Jane Addams. Many of these critics were **pacifists,** people who refuse to fight in any war because they believe war is evil.

Antiwar feeling also ran high among socialists and radical labor groups. A **socialist** believes that the people as a whole rather than private individuals should own all property and share the profits from all businesses. Socialists argued that the war benefited factory owners but not workers.

To encourage unity, Congress passed laws making it a crime to criticize the government or to interfere with the war. Nearly 1,600 men and women were arrested for breaking these laws. Eugene V. Debs, Socialist candidate for President five times, was jailed for protesting the draft. The government also jailed "Big Bill" Haywood, head of the Industrial Workers of the World (IWW), a radical union. Using special powers granted under the wartime laws, government authorities ransacked the IWW's offices.

A few people questioned these laws. They argued that silencing critics violated the Constitution's guarantee of freedom of speech. Most Americans, however, felt that the laws were necessary in wartime.

★ Section 2 Review ★

Recall

1. **Identify** **(a)** Zimmermann telegram, **(b)** Jeannette Rankin, **(c)** Selective Service Act, **(d)** Herbert Hoover, **(e)** Liberty Bonds.
2. **Define** **(a)** warmonger, **(b)** czar, **(c)** draft, **(d)** illiterate, **(e)** bureaucracy, **(f)** pacifist, **(g)** socialist.

Comprehension

3. Identify three events that moved the United States toward war.
4. **(a)** List three government agencies that were set up to organize the war effort. **(b)** What did each agency do?

5. What steps did the government take to silence critics of the war?

Critical Thinking and Writing

6. **Synthesizing Information** Review the account of the East St. Louis race riot on page 655. Why did the marchers carry signs demanding: "Mr. President, Why Not Make AMERICA Safe for Democracy?"
7. **Defending a Position** Do you think that the government should have the right to silence critics during wartime? Defend your position.

★ ★

Activity **Preparing a Speech** You have only four minutes. *GO!* As one of Wilson's "Four-Minute Men," you must give a speech urging Americans to make sacrifices for the war effort. Be sure to think about what kind of arguments would most appeal to your listeners.

Winning the War

★ ★

As You Read

Explore These Questions
- Why did the Allies face hard times in 1917?
- How did Americans help defeat Germany?
- What were the human costs of the war?

Define
- armistice
- abdicate
- epidemic

Identify
- Bolsheviks
- V. I. Lenin
- Treaty of Brest-Litovsk
- John J. Pershing
- Harlem Hell Fighters
- Battle of Belleau Wood
- Ferdinand Foch
- Alvin York
- Battle of the Argonne Forest

American soldiers carried shaving kits like this one to the trenches in France.

SETTING the Scene Soon after war was declared, an official at the War Department asked the Senate for $3 billion for arms and other supplies. "And we may have to have an army in France," he added. "Good grief!" sputtered one senator. "You're not going to send soldiers over there, are you?"

The United States would send more than 2 million soldiers to France. The buildup took time. First, troops had to be trained and armed. By March 1918, fewer than 300,000 American troops had reached France. Then they poured in. Fresh and eager to fight, they gave the Allies a much-needed boost.

Hard Times for the Allies

The first American troops reached France in June 1917. They quickly saw the desperate situation of the Allies. The Allies had lost millions of soldiers. Troops in the trenches were exhausted and ill. Many civilians in Britain and France were near starvation.

Russia withdraws from the war

To make matters worse, Russia withdrew from the war. In November 1917, a group known as the **Bolsheviks** seized power from the Provisional Government. Under the leadership of **V. I. Lenin,** the Bolsheviks wanted to bring a communist revolution to Russia.

Lenin embraced the ideas of Karl Marx, a German thinker of the 1800s. Marx had predicted that workers around the world would unite to overthrow the ruling class. After the workers revolted, they would end private property and set up a classless society. Lenin was determined to lead such a revolution in Russia.

Once in power, Lenin opened talks with Germany. He had opposed the war, arguing that it benefited only the ruling class. In March 1918, Russia and Germany signed the **Treaty of Brest-Litovsk.** Although Russia had to give up land to Germany, Lenin welcomed peace. With war ended, he could focus on the communist revolution.

The Allies saw the treaty as a betrayal. It gave Germany coal mines and other resources in Russia. More important, with Russia out of the way, Germany could move its armies away from the Russian front and into France. In early 1918, Germany used these troops in an all-out attack on the Allies.

A new German offensive

By March 21, German forces had massed near the French town of Amiens. (See the map at right.) The Germans called this move a "peace offensive." They hoped that a final push would end the war.

Dozens of German divisions massed up against a small British force. Late at night, 6,000 German cannons began pounding the British troops camped at Amiens. Despite the heavy fire, the British held on. The battle lasted for two weeks. At last, on April 4, the Germans gave up their attack.

The Germans continued their offensive elsewhere. By late May, they had smashed through Allied lines along the Aisne (EHN) River. On May 30, they reached the Marne River, just east of Château-Thierry (sha TOH tee ER ee). Paris lay only 50 miles (80 km) away. At this point, American troops entered the war in force.

Americans in France

By June 1918, American troops were reaching France in record numbers. Commanding the American Expeditionary Force (AEF) was General **John J. Pershing.** Pershing was already well known at home for leading American troops into Mexico in 1916 to hunt for Mexican rebel leader Francisco "Pancho" Villa. (See page 637.)

Allied generals wanted the fresh troops to reinforce their own war-weary soldiers. Pershing refused. He insisted that American troops operate as separate units. The United States wanted to have an independent role in shaping the peace. Only by playing "a definite and distinct part" in the war would it win power at the peace table.

In the end, Pershing agreed to let some Americans fight with the British and French. At the same time, he set up an American operation to fight on its own.

Harlem Hell Fighters

Among the first American units attached to the French Army was the 369th United States Infantry. This African American unit became known as the **Harlem Hell Fighters.** Although the United States allowed few African Americans to train for combat, the French respected the bravery of African American soldiers and were glad to fight side by side with them.

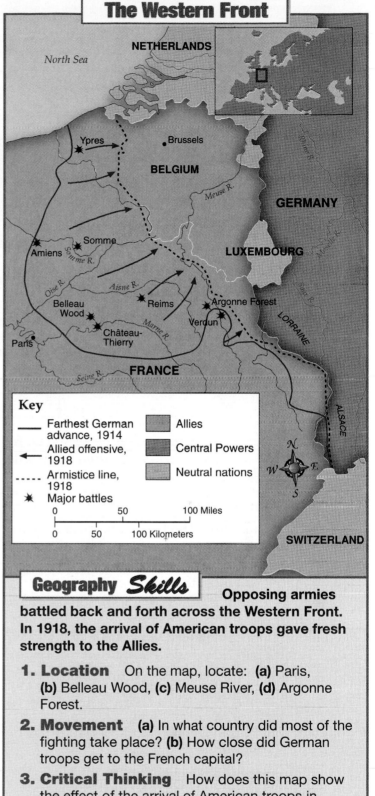

The Western Front

Geography *Skills* Opposing armies battled back and forth across the Western Front. In 1918, the arrival of American troops gave fresh strength to the Allies.

1. **Location** On the map, locate: **(a)** Paris, **(b)** Belleau Wood, **(c)** Meuse River, **(d)** Argonne Forest.
2. **Movement** **(a)** In what country did most of the fighting take place? **(b)** How close did German troops get to the French capital?
3. **Critical Thinking** How does this map show the effect of the arrival of American troops in 1918?

In the end, the Harlem Hell Fighters spent more time under fire than any other American unit. For their bravery, the French awarded them the Croix de Guerre, or Cross

Viewing HISTORY   Victims of Poison Gas

Gassed, by John Singer Sargent, shows troops disabled by poison gas in 1918. Gas was one of the most feared weapons of World War I. Various gases caused choking, blindness, or severe skin blisters.
★ **Why do you think nations later agreed to ban the use of poison gas?**

◄ *World War I gas mask*

of War, and numerous other decorations. After the war, New Yorkers greeted them with a huge parade.

Belleau Wood

Meanwhile, the Germans were continuing their "peace offensive." As Germans rolled across the Aisne River, the French prepared to evacuate Paris.

In June 1918, American troops plunged into their first major battle in Belleau (BEH loh) Wood, outside Paris. A French general sent General James Harbord of the United States a message: "Have your men prepare entrenchments some hundreds of yards to the rear in case of need." Harbord sent back a firm reply:

Connections With Arts

John Singer Sargent, who painted *Gassed* (above), was one of the leading American artists of his time. Sargent gained fame for his portraits of elegant society women. Wealthy American and European women flocked to his Paris studio. Sargent was over 60 years old when he volunteered to serve as a war artist.

❝ We dig no trenches to fall back on. The marines will hold where they stand. ❞

The **Battle of Belleau Wood** raged for three weeks. At last, on June 25, General Harbord passed along the good news: "Wood now exclusively U.S. Marine Corps."

Final Battles

In mid-July, the Germans launched another drive to take Paris. They pushed the Allies back until they came up against American troops. Within three days, the Allies had forced the Germans to retreat.

The Allies now took the offensive. French Marshal **Ferdinand Foch** (FOHSH), commander of the Allied forces, ordered attacks along a line from Verdun to the North Sea. American forces stormed the area between the Meuse (MYOOZ) River and the Argonne Forest. (See the map on page 657.)

Into the Argonne Forest

On September 26, 1918, more than one million American soldiers pushed into the Argonne Forest. Years of fierce fighting had left the land scarred with trenches and shell

Why Study History?

Because We Honor Our Veterans

★ ★

Historical Background

In 1919, on the first anniversary of the end of World War I, President Wilson proclaimed a new holiday. November 11 would be celebrated as Armistice Day. In 1954, the holiday was renamed Veterans Day—the day we honor all men and women who have served in the nation's armed forces.

To honor the dead of World War I, the United States also dedicated the Tomb of the Unknown Soldier. In 1921, the body of an unidentified American soldier was brought from an unmarked grave in France to a military cemetery in Arlington, Virginia. Above his grave, a marble monument bears the inscription: "Here rests in honored glory an American soldier known but to God." Since then, unknown soldiers from three later wars have joined him.

VFW members salute as a Veterans Day parade passes.

Connections to Today

Today, the government and private organizations continue to honor and serve veterans. The Department for Veterans Affairs oversees veterans' pensions and benefits and runs veterans' hospitals. The Veterans of Foreign Wars (VFW), a nonprofit organization, offers support to veterans, as well as sponsoring community projects.

Each year, tourists visit the Tomb of the Unknown Soldier, the Vietnam War Memorial, and other monuments. Many families fly the flag on Veterans Day and Memorial Day.

Connections to You

How can you honor veterans? You might attend a parade or put flowers on a war memorial. Your local VFW post can supply a list of monuments in your area. You can enter the VFW's annual essay contest for seventh, eighth, and ninth graders. As you get older, you may do volunteer work in a veterans' hospital.

Mostly, you can honor veterans by remembering the past. As the Secretary of the Army said on Veterans Day 1996:

❝ American veterans all … your nation and your Army honor you for your sacrifice and continuing selfless service. ❞

1. **Comprehension** List three ways that Americans honor veterans.

2. **Critical Thinking** Why do you think groups like the VFW urge young people to learn more about American history?

 **Creating a Memory Book** With your classmates, interview veterans in your community. Some students can write questions, while others set up the interviews. Write up your interviews and compile them in an illustrated binder. Ask your school or library to display your memory book on Veterans Day.

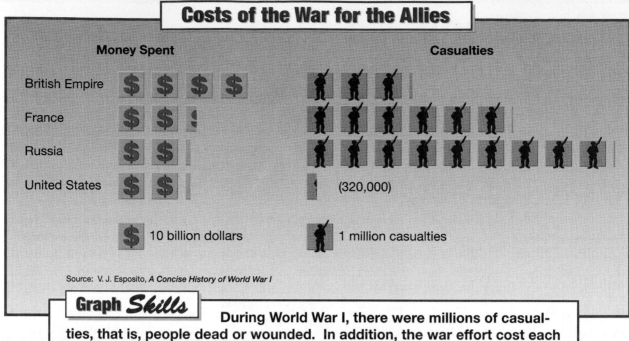

Costs of the War for the Allies

Money Spent   **Casualties**

British Empire

France

Russia

United States   (320,000)

$ 10 billion dollars   1 million casualties

Source: V. J. Esposito, *A Concise History of World War I*

Graph *Skills*

During World War I, there were millions of casualties, that is, people dead or wounded. In addition, the war effort cost each side billions of dollars.

1. Comprehension **(a)** Which Allied nation had the greatest number of casualties in World War I? **(b)** How much money did the United States spend on the war effort?

2. Critical Thinking **(a)** Which nation shown here had the fewest casualties? **(b)** Why was this so?

---

holes. The air still smelled of poison gas from earlier battles.

At first, the Americans advanced despite heavy German fire. Then, rains and the thick woods slowed their movement. Small units drove forward to capture deadly German positions. Armed with a single rifle, Sergeant **Alvin York** of Tennessee wiped out a nest of German machine gunners. His bravery helped clear the way for advancing American troops. York became the most decorated American soldier of the war.

Finally, after 47 days, the Americans broke through the German defense. They had won the **Battle of the Argonne Forest.** The cost was high on both sides. Americans and Germans each suffered more than 100,000 casualties in the battle.

British, French, and Belgian forces also smashed through the German lines in their areas. By November, German forces were in retreat. After more than four years of fighting, the Great War was finally nearing its end.

The war ends

In September, German generals told the kaiser that the war could not be won. On October 4, Prince Max of Baden, head of the German cabinet, secretly cabled President Wilson:

66 To avoid further bloodshed, the German government requests the President to arrange the immediate conclusion of an armistice on land, by sea, and in the air. 99

An **armistice** is an agreement to stop fighting. Wilson set two conditions for an armistice. First, Germany must accept his plan for peace. Second, the German emperor must **abdicate,** that is, give up power.

While German leaders debated a response, rebellion simmered in the ranks. Daily, the German army lost ground. Morale plunged among the troops. German sailors mutinied. Several German cities threatened to revolt.

On November 9, the German emperor was forced to resign. He and his son fled to Holland, and Germany became a republic. The new German leaders agreed to the armistice terms. At 11 A.M. on November 11, 1918—the eleventh hour of the eleventh day of the eleventh month—World War I ended at last.

The costs of war

The costs of the war were staggering. A generation of young Europeans lost their lives. Between 8 million and 9 million people died in battle. Germany, alone, lost close to 2 million men. Almost 4 million Russian, French, and British soldiers were killed. The United States lost over 50,000 men. Many more died of diseases. More than 20 million soldiers on both sides were wounded.

Much of northern France lay in ruins. Millions of Germans were near starvation. In France and other nations, many children were left orphaned and homeless.

In 1918, a new disaster struck. A terrible influenza epidemic spread around the world. An **epidemic** is the rapid spread of a conta-gious disease among large numbers of people. Between 1918 and 1919, more than half a million Americans died in the flu epidemic. The death toll in other countries was even higher. All told, the epidemic killed more than 20 million people—twice as many as the war itself!

A wounded veteran and his family

★ Section 3 Review ★

Recall

1. **Locate** (a) Amiens, (b) Marne River, (c) Château Thierry, (d) Belleau Wood, (e) Argonne Forest.
2. **Identify** (a) Bolsheviks, (b) V. I. Lenin, (c) Treaty of Brest-Litovsk, (d) John J. Pershing, (e) Harlem Hell Fighters, (f) Battle of Belleau Wood, (g) Ferdinand Foch, (h) Alvin York, (i) Battle of the Argonne Forest.
3. **Define** (a) armistice, (b) abdicate, (c) epidemic.

Comprehension

4. Describe the situation of the Allies when the Americans arrived in June 1917.
5. What role did the Americans play in ending the war?

6. What conditions did Europeans face at the end of the war?

Critical Thinking and Writing

7. **Making Inferences** Why do you think General Pershing wanted American troops to fight as independent units rather than alongside the British and French?
8. **Analyzing Visual Evidence** Study the paintings on pages 641 and 658. (a) Describe what each painting shows. (b) How is the mood of the first picture different from that of the second picture?

★ ★

History AND YOU

Activity **Planning a Celebration** It is November 11, 1918. The armistice has just been signed. You have been asked to plan a community celebration in honor of the event. Prepare a schedule for the celebration, including at least four meaningful events.

Wilson and the Peace

As You Read

Explore These Questions
- What was Wilson's plan for peace?
- How did Wilson's goals for peace differ from those of the other Allies?
- Why did the Senate reject the Versailles Treaty?

Define
- self-determination
- reparation
- isolationist

Identify
- Fourteen Points
- League of Nations
- Big Four
- Treaty of Versailles
- Henry Cabot Lodge

SETTING the Scene Huge crowds cheered Woodrow Wilson when he arrived in France in December 1918. Some people cried with joy to see the American leader. After years of suffering, Europeans saw Wilson as a symbol of hope. He was the man who had promised to make the world "safe for democracy."

Wilson went to France determined to achieve a just and lasting peace. He believed that most Europeans shared his views. He soon learned, however, that his goals were often at odds with those of the other Allies.

Wilson's Peace Plan

In Europe, Wilson visited Paris, London, Milan, and Rome. Everywhere, cheering crowds welcomed him. To Wilson, this was a sign that Europeans supported his goal of "peace without victory." In fact, he was wrong. The people who greeted Wilson so warmly scoffed at his high-minded proposals. They and their leaders were determined to punish the Germans for the war.

In January 1918, even before the war ended, Wilson outlined his peace plan. Known as the **Fourteen Points,** it was

President Woodrow Wilson

meant to prevent international problems from causing another war.

The first point in Wilson's plan called for an end to secret agreements. Secrecy, Wilson felt, had created the rival alliances that had helped lead to war. Next, he called for freedom of the seas, free trade, and a limit on arms. He urged peaceful settlement of disputes over colonies. He also supported the principle of national **self-determination,** that is, the right of national groups to their own territory and forms of government.

For Wilson, however, the fourteenth point was the most important. It called for a "general association of nations," or **League of Nations.** Its job would be to protect the independence of all countries— large or small. The goal was simple, he noted:

> **❝**...justice to all peoples and nationalities, and their right to live on equal terms of liberty and safety with one another, whether weak or strong. **❞**

Wilson persuaded the Allies to accept the Fourteen Points as the basis for making peace. However, the plan soon ran into trouble. Some goals were too vague. Others conflicted with reality. In Paris,

Wilson faced a constant battle to save his Fourteen Points. He discovered that the Allies were more concerned with protecting their own interests.

The Peace Treaty

Diplomats from more than 30 nations met in Paris and Versailles (vuhr SI), hoping to make a lasting peace. Key issues were decided by the **Big Four**—Woodrow Wilson of the United States, David Lloyd George of Britain, Georges Clemenceau (kleh mahn SOH) of France, and Vittorio Orlando of Italy.

Conflicting goals

Each leader had his own aims. Wilson had called for "peace without victory." He opposed punishing the defeated powers.

The other Allies, however, ached for revenge. Germany must pay, they said. They insisted on large **reparations,** or cash payments, for the losses they had suffered during the war. Further, they wanted Germany to accept responsibility for the war.

The Allies were also determined to prevent Germany from rebuilding its military strength. In particular, Clemenceau wanted to weaken Germany so that it could never again threaten France. During the months of haggling, Wilson had to compromise on his Fourteen Points in order to save his key goals, especially the League of Nations.

The final treaty

By June 1919, the **Treaty of Versailles** was ready. None of the Allies was satisfied with it. Germany, which had not even been allowed to send delegates to the peace talks, was horrified by the terms of the treaty. Still, it had no choice but to sign.

Under the treaty, Germany had to take full blame for the war. It had to pay the Allies huge reparations, including the cost of pensions for Allied soldiers or their widows and children. The total cost of German reparations would come to over $300 billion.

Other provisions of the Treaty of Versailles were aimed at weakening Germany. The treaty severely limited the size of the German military. It returned Alsace-Lorraine to France. In addition, the treaty

 **Wilson at the Peace Conference**

British artist William Orpen painted this scene at the 1919 Paris peace conference. The Big Four, including Woodrow Wilson, are seated center. Facing them, two German representatives read the treaty.
★ **How do you think the Germans responded to the Treaty of Versailles?**

stripped Germany of its overseas colonies. However, instead of gaining independence, the colonies were put under the control of Britain or France.

Wilson's successes

Wilson had his way on a few issues, however. In Eastern Europe, the Allies provided for several new nations to be formed on the principle of national self-determination. They included Poland, Czechoslovakia, and Yugoslavia. They were created out of lands once ruled by Germany, Russia, and Austria-Hungary. (See the map on page 664.)

Still, some people were dissatisfied with the new boundaries. Many Germans, for example, had settled in Poland and Czechoslovakia. Before long, Germany would seek to

Europe After World War I

Geography Skills A series of treaties ended World War I. The treaties created several new nations in Eastern Europe.

1. Location On the map, locate: **(a)** Poland, **(b)** Czechoslovakia, **(c)** Yugoslavia.

2. Region **(a)** In what region of Europe were most of the new nations created? **(b)** Which new nations bordered Russia?

3. Critical Thinking Compare this map to the map on page 646. **(a)** What happened to Austria-Hungary? **(b)** What happened to Serbia? **(c)** What happened to the city of Sarajevo?

regain control of German-speaking peoples in Eastern Europe.

To Wilson, however, his greatest achievement was persuading the Allies to include the League of Nations in the treaty. Wilson was certain that the League would prevent future wars by allowing nations to talk over their problems. If talk failed, members would join together to fight aggressors. "A living thing is born," he declared. The League "is definitely a guarantee of peace."

Battle Over the Treaty

When President Wilson returned home, he faced a new battle. He had to persuade the Senate to approve the Versailles Treaty.

Opposition to the League

Most Americans favored the treaty. A vocal minority opposed it, however. Some said that it was too soft on the defeated powers. Many German Americans felt that it was too harsh. Some Republicans hoped to embarrass

President Wilson, a Democrat, by rewriting or defeating the treaty. **Isolationists,** people who wanted the United States to stay out of world affairs, opposed the League of Nations.

Critics of the treaty found a leader in **Henry Cabot Lodge** of Massachusetts. Lodge, a Republican, was chairman of the powerful Senate Foreign Relations Committee. Lodge accepted the idea of the League of Nations. However, he wanted changes in some provisions relating to the League.

Specifically, Lodge objected to Article 10 of the treaty. It called for the League to protect any member whose independence or territory was threatened. Lodge argued that Article 10 could involve the United States in future European wars. He wanted changes in the treaty that would ensure that the United States remained independent of the League. He also wanted Congress to have the power to decide whether the United States would follow League policy.

Wilson believed that Lodge's changes would weaken the League. Advisers urged the President to compromise, giving up some of his demands in order to save the League. Wilson replied, "Let Lodge compromise." He refused to make any changes.

A defeat for Wilson

As the battle grew hotter, the President took his case to the people. In early September 1919, Wilson set out across the country, making 37 speeches in 29 cities. He urged Americans to let their senators know that they supported the treaty.

Wilson kept up a killing pace. On September 25, the exhausted President complained of a headache. His doctors canceled the rest of the trip. Wilson returned to Washington. A week later, his wife found him unconscious. He had suffered a stroke that left him bedridden for weeks.

In November 1919, the Senate rejected the Versailles Treaty. "It is dead," Wilson mourned, "[and] every morning I put flowers on its grave." Gone, too, was Wilson's cherished goal—American membership in the League of Nations.

The United States did not sign a peace treaty with Germany until 1921. Many nations had already joined the League of Nations. Without the United States, though, the League failed to live up to its goals of protecting members against aggression. Wilson's dream of a world "safe for democracy" would have to wait.

★ Section 4 Review ★

Recall

1. **Identify** (a) Fourteen Points, (b) League of Nations, (c) Big Four, (d) Treaty of Versailles, (e) Henry Cabot Lodge.
2. **Define** (a) self-determination, (b) reparation, (c) isolationist.

Comprehension

3. (a) Describe the major points of Wilson's peace plan. (b) Which point did Wilson consider most important? Why?
4. Why did Wilson's peace plan run into trouble at Versailles?

5. (a) What changes did critics want to make in the peace treaty? (b) How did the President respond to their demands?

Critical Thinking and Writing

6. **Predicting Consequences** (a) List three ways that the Treaty of Versailles punished Germany. (b) What do you think the effects of this harsh treatment might be?
7. **Defending a Position** Many historians blame Wilson for the defeat of the Versailles Treaty in Congress. What reasons can you give to support this position?

Activity Drawing a Political Cartoon Draw a political cartoon expressing your feelings about the conflict over the League of Nations. If possible, include figures representing Henry Cabot Lodge and Woodrow Wilson.

Review and Activities

★ Sum It Up ★

Section 1   War Erupts in Europe

▶ Nationalism, imperialism, and militarism increased tensions in Europe in the early years of the 1900s.

▶ After Austria-Hungary declared war on Serbia in 1914, the alliance system drew other nations into the conflict.

▶ While the United States remained neutral, German submarine warfare outraged Americans.

Section 2   The United States Enters the War

▶ After declaring war on Germany in 1917, the United States set up a military draft.

▶ A huge government bureaucracy built support for the war effort.

▶ The government silenced protests against the war by arresting people who criticized the government.

Section 3   Winning the War

▶ In the final battles of the war, American troops helped defeat German forces at Belleau Wood and the Argonne Forest.

▶ World War I was a costly war, with some 30 million people killed or wounded.

Section 4   Wilson and the Peace

▶ Wilson's plan for peace included a call for a League of Nations to settle disputes between nations.

▶ The Senate rejected the peace treaty because critics believed that the League of Nations might draw the United States into future wars.

For additional review of the major ideas of Chapter 24, see **Guide to the Essentials of American History** or **Interactive Student Tutorial CD-ROM,** which contains interactive review activities, graphic organizers, and practice tests.

🗋 Reviewing the Chapter

Define These Terms

Match each term with the correct definition.

Column 1

1. nationalism
2. militarism
3. bureaucracy
4. armistice
5. self-determination

Column 2

a. system of managing government though departments

b. pride in one's country

c. right of a national group to its own territory and own form of government

d. policy of building up armed forces to prepare for war

e. agreement to stop fighting

Explore the Main Ideas

1. How did the alliance system help lead to World War I?
2. **(a)** What nations formed the Central Powers? **(b)** What nations formed the Allied powers?
3. How did the Russian Revolution affect the war?
4. **(a)** Describe the German "peace offensive" of 1918. **(b)** What were the results?
5. How did Britain and France feel about Germany during the Paris peace conference?

🗋 Geography Activity

Match the letters on the map with the following places:
1. Allied Powers, **2.** Central Powers, **3.** Sarajevo, **4.** Great Britain, **5.** France, **6.** Russia, **7.** Germany, **8.** Austria-Hungary.
Movement Why did European nations seek colonies in Asia and Africa?

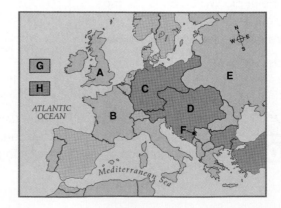

Critical Thinking and Writing

1. **Understanding Chronology** **(a)** List the following events in chronological order: Zimmermann telegram is discovered; U-boats sink the *Lusitania;* Archduke Franz Ferdinand is assassinated; United States declares war on Germany; armistice is signed. **(b)** Describe the relationship between any two events on the list.

2. **Linking Past and Present** During World War I, inventions such as submarines and machine guns changed the nature of the fighting. List two kinds of technology that are important in warfare today.

3. **Analyzing Ideas** Why do you think Americans accepted government controls on the economy during World War I?

4. **Exploring Unit Themes   Global Interaction** Based on what you have learned, make two generalizations about American isolationism and global interaction before, during, and after World War I.

Using Primary Sources

President Wilson toured the nation in 1919, hoping to gain support for the Versailles Treaty. In one speech, he talked about how the sight of American soldiers impressed him:

> **❝** I saw many fine sights in Paris, many gallant sights, many sights that quickened the pulse; but my pulse never beat so fast as when I saw groups of our boys [marching] along the street. They looked as if they owned something, and they did. They owned the finest thing in the world. . . . They owned the ideals . . . that will govern the world. **❞**

Source: "The Destiny of America," Woodrow Wilson, *Senate Document 120,* 1919–1920.

Recognizing Points of View **(a)** Why was Wilson thrilled to see American soldiers in Paris? **(b)** What did Wilson mean by his statement that American ideals would "govern the world"? **(c)** Do you think Georges Clemenceau would have agreed with Wilson's statement?

ACTIVITY BANK

▶ Interdisciplinary Activity

Exploring the Arts   Learn the song "Over There" by George M. Cohan. Write an additional stanza for the song or write a new song of your own. Perform the song for the class.

▶ Career Skills Activity

Economists   Find out more about the effects that the war had on the nation's economy. Then make a concept map showing these effects.

▶ Citizenship Activity

Organizing a Debate   Organize a classroom debate about freedom of speech during wartime. One team of students will argue that the government should be allowed to silence protests during wartime. The other team will argue that the government does not have the right to silence protests. Assign one student to act as moderator. After the debate, write a paragraph explaining your position.

Internet Activity
Use the Internet to find sites dealing with the causes of World War I. Then, use the results of your research to write a short essay on whether you think the war could have been avoided.

EYEWITNESS Journal

You are one of the following: an American isolationist in 1914; a Mexican immigrant working in America for the war effort; a German American; a woman working in a factory; an American soldier in Europe; President Wilson. In your EYEWITNESS JOURNAL, describe the events of the war years that had the greatest impact on you.

History Through Literature

Picture Bride

Yoshiko Uchida

Introduction

In the early 1900s, many Japanese women who came to the United States were "picture brides." The marriages were arranged by relatives, with the bride and bridegroom seeing each other only through pictures. Yoshiko Uchida tells the story of one of these immigrants in her novel *Picture Bride*. Here, young Hana Omiya looks back on her decision to go to the United States.

Vocabulary

Before you read the selection, find the meaning of these words in a dictionary: **samurai, conscientious, affluence, latitude, tuberculosis.**

*I*t was she who had first planted in her uncle's mind the thought that she would make a good wife for Taro Takeda, the lonely man who had gone to America to make his fortune in Oakland, California.

It all began one day when her uncle had come to visit her mother.

"I must find a nice young bride," he had said, startling Hana with this blunt talk of marriage in her presence. She blushed and was ready to leave the room when her uncle quickly added, "My good friend Takeda has a son in America. I must find someone willing to travel to that far land."

This last remark was intended to indicate to Hana and her mother that he didn't consider this a suitable prospect for Hana who was the youngest daughter of what once had been a fine family. Her father, until his death fifteen years ago, had been the largest land-holder of the village and one its last *samurai*. They had once had many servants and field hands, but now all that was changed. Their money was gone. . . .

Her uncle spoke freely of Taro Takeda only because he was so sure Hana would never consider him. "He is a conscientious, hard-working man who has been in the United States for almost ten years. He is thirty-one, operates a small shop and rents some rooms above the shop where he lives." Her uncle rubbed his chin thoughtfully. "He could provide well for a wife," he added.

"Ah," Hana's mother said softly.

"You say he is successful in this business?" Hana's sister inquired.

"His father tells me he sells many things in his shop—clothing, stockings, needles, thread and buttons—such things as that. He also sells bean paste, pickled radish, bean cake and soy sauce. A wife of his would not go cold or hungry."

They all nodded, each of them picturing this merchant in varying degrees of success and affluence. There were many Japanese emigrating to America these days, and Hana had heard of the picture brides who went with nothing more than an exchange of photographs to bind them to a strange man.

Viewing HISTORY : A Workshop in Japan

This 1897 woodblock print shows young women working in a Japanese clothing factory. The machinery and the clothing worn by the workers show the influence of American ways. ★ **Why were many young Japanese women permitted to come to the United States after 1907?**

Almost before she realized what she was doing, Hana spoke to her uncle. "Oji San, perhaps I should go to America to make this lonely man a good wife."

"You, Hana Chan?" Her uncle observed her with startled curiosity. "You would go all alone to a foreign land so far away from your mother and family?"

"I would not allow it." Her mother spoke fiercely. Hana was her youngest and she had lavished upon her the attention and latitude that often befall the last child. How could she permit her to travel so far, even to marry the son of Takeda who was known to her brother.

But now, a notion that had seemed quite impossible a moment before was lodged in his receptive mind, and Hana's uncle grasped it with pleasure that comes from an unexpected discovery....

"You know," he said looking at Hana, "it might be a very good life in America."

Hana felt a faint fluttering in her heart. Perhaps this lonely man in America was her means of escaping....

Her uncle spoke with increasing enthusiasm of sending Hana to become Taro's wife. And the husband of Hana's sister, who was head of their household, spoke with equal eagerness. Although he never said so, Hana guessed he would be pleased to be rid of her, the spirited younger sister who stirred up his placid life with what he considered radical ideas about life and the role of women. He often claimed that Hana had too much schooling for a girl.

A man's word carried much weight for Hana's mother.... Finally, she agreed to an exchange of family histories and an investigation was begun into Taro Takeda's family, his education and his health, so they would be assured there was no insanity or tuberculosis or police records concealed in his family's past.

Analyzing Literature

1. What did Hana know about Taro Takeda before she left Japan?
2. Why did Hana's mother agree to let her go?
3. **Making Inferences** Give two reasons why Hana might have wanted to go to the United States.

Unit 8

Prosperity, Depression, and War

Viewing UNIT THEMES — A Growing Role for the Federal Government

In the 1930s, the nation was in the midst of an economic depression. President Franklin Roosevelt used the power of government to help the needy. This mural shows Roosevelt signing a bill to build dams in the Tennessee Valley. However, critics argued the federal government was growing too large and costly. ★ **According-ing to this mural, who would benefit from the bill Roosevelt is signing?**

Unit Theme Role of Government

In 1849, author Henry David Thoreau wrote, "that government is best which governs least." Most early American leaders would have agreed. In the 1920s, Presidents like Calvin Coolidge and Herbert Hoover were especially opposed to government regulation of the economy. Soon after, though, the nation faced two major crises: a massive economic depression, followed by the largest war the world had ever seen. As a result, the federal government began to take on a vast new role.

How did Americans of the time feel about the role of government? They can tell you in their own words.

★ ★

VIEWPOINTS ON THE ROLE OF GOVERNMENT

❝ You cannot extend the mastery of the government over the daily working life of a people without at the same time making it master of the people's souls and thoughts. ❞

President Herbert Hoover (1932)

❝ A government that could not care for its old and sick, that could not provide work for the strong… was not a government that could endure…. ❞

Franklin Roosevelt, Candidate for President (1932)

❝ In a country as vast as the United States, with its range of physical and economic variations, power cannot be administered entirely from the national capital. ❞

David E. Lilienthal, government official (1940)

★ ★

Activity Writing to Learn Make a chart with two columns. Label one column Advantages and the other column Disadvantages. Then, list as many as you can of the advantages and disadvantages associated with having a big federal government that gets involved in many areas of people's lives.

Chapter 25

The Roaring Twenties

1919–1929

In the decade after World War I, Presidents Harding and Coolidge encouraged business growth. The economy grew rapidly as factories churned out new consumer goods, and stock prices soared. American society also changed dramatically. Inexpensive cars and a wide variety of new products for the home became available for the first time. Manners became freer. Young people danced to a wild, new music called jazz.

Not all Americans shared in the good times of the boom years. Even for those Americans who seemed fortunate, trouble loomed ahead.

Why Study History?

In the 1920s, going to the movies was one of the most popular American pastimes. Silent films united audiences all over the nation. Still, some people worried about the effects of movies on young audiences. Today, movies are just as popular—and as controversial. To explore this connection, see this chapter's *Why Study History?* feature, "Movies Have a Powerful Effect on Us."

★ ★

American Events

●1919
Eighteenth Amendment bans making or selling of alcohol

●1921
Emergency Quota Act limits immigration to the United States

●1923
Teapot Dome scandal reveals government corruption

1918   1920   1922   1924

World Events

 1919 World Event
Treaty of Versailles is signed

 1922 World Event
Union of Soviet Socialist Republics is formed

Life

FEBRUARY 15, 1926 Teaching old Dogs new tricks PRICE 15 CENTS

Viewing HISTORY An Image of the Roaring Twenties

In magazine covers like this one, artist John Held, Jr., poked fun at the new fashions, dances, and attitudes of the 1920s. American life was not always as carefree as Held showed it to be. Still, his drawings helped create a popular image of the "Roaring Twenties." ★ **Do you think most Americans of the time dressed and danced like the people in Held's illustration? Explain.**

1926
Langston Hughes publishes his first volume of poetry

1927
Charles Lindbergh flies alone across the Atlantic Ocean

1929
Great Depression begins

1924 | **1926** | **1928** | **1930**

▲
1926 World Event
United States intervenes in Nicaragua

▲
1928 World Event
Kellogg-Briand Pact outlaws war

Politics and Prosperity

As You Read

Explore These Questions
- What problems faced the Harding administration?
- How did the economy grow in the 1920s?
- What role did the United States play in world affairs?

Define
- recession
- installment buying
- stock
- bull market
- on margin
- communism
- disarmament

Identify
- Warren G. Harding
- Teapot Dome Scandal
- Calvin Coolidge
- Kellogg-Briand Pact

SETTING the Scene The word on the page was plain as day: "normality." Yet **Warren G. Harding,** an Ohio Republican who was running for President in 1920, got it wrong. What the country needs is "normalcy," he declared.

Still, the crowd knew what Harding meant. Normalcy suggested a welcome return to calm after years of war and reform. Harding's slip of the tongue soon became his campaign slogan: "Back to Normalcy."

Returning to Normalcy

World War I had helped the economy. Europeans ordered vast amounts of supplies from American factories. After the United States entered the war in 1917, American factories expanded rapidly to meet the demand for military supplies.

When the war ended, more than 2 million soldiers came home and began to look for jobs. At the same time, factories stopped turning out war materials. The result was a sharp **recession,** or economic slump.

Harding takes office

The recession fed voter discontent with the Democrats, who had held power for eight years. In the 1920 election, Warren Harding swamped his Democratic opponent.

For the top Cabinet posts, Harding chose able men who followed strongly pro-business policies. Andrew Mellon, a wealthy financier, became secretary of the treasury. Mellon balanced the budget and lowered taxes.

Herbert Hoover became the new secretary of commerce. During World War I, Hoover had earned the world's admiration by organizing efforts to supply food to millions of starving Belgians. As secretary of commerce, he worked to help American businesses expand overseas.

Harding campaign button

Political scandals

To fill most other Cabinet posts, however, Harding brought in his old friends. They became known as the "Ohio Gang." Harding himself was honest and hard-working, but the Ohio Gang saw government service as a way to enrich themselves. A series of scandals resulted. For example, Harding made Charles Forbes head of the Veterans Bureau. Forbes was later convicted of stealing millions of dollars from the bureau.

Harding looked on Forbes's crime as a betrayal. When rumors of new scandals surfaced, he grew even more distressed. "I can take care of my enemies all right," he said, "but my... friends, they're the ones that keep me walking the floors nights!" In August 1923, Harding died of a heart attack. Many believed that the scandals contributed to his sudden death.

Scandals Rock Washington

© N. Y. "Tribune."

· The First Good Laugh They've Had in Years.

After Harding died, new scandals came to light. The most serious involved Secretary of the Interior Albert Fall. Two oil executives had bribed Fall. In return, he secretly leased them government land in California and at Teapot Dome, Wyoming. As a result of the **Teapot Dome Scandal,** Fall became the first Cabinet official ever sent to prison.

Coolidge takes office

On the day Harding died, Vice President **Calvin Coolidge** was visiting his father's farm in Vermont. Coolidge recalled, "I was awakened by my father.... I noticed that his voice trembled." Coolidge's father, a justice of the peace, used the family Bible to swear his son in as President. The simple ceremony reassured Americans.

"Silent Cal" Coolidge was very different from Harding. Harding loved throwing parties and making long speeches. Coolidge was tight with both money and words. A woman reportedly told Coolidge she had bet that she could get him to say more than three words. "You lose," Coolidge replied.

Coolidge set out to repair the damage caused by the scandals. He forced the officials involved in scandals to resign. In 1924, Coolidge ran against Democrat John Davis and Progressive Robert La Follette. Voters chose to "Keep Cool With Coolidge" and returned the cautious New Englander to office.

Coolidge Prosperity

Like Harding, Coolidge believed that prosperity for all Americans depended on business prosperity. He told reporters:

66 The business of America is business. The man who builds a factory builds a temple. The man who works there worships there. 99

True to this philosophy, Coolidge cut regulations on business. He also named business leaders to head government agencies.

Industry booms

Coolidge's pro-business policies contributed to a period of rapid economic growth. People referred to this boom as "Coolidge prosperity." As factories switched to consumer goods, the postwar recession ended. From 1923 to 1929, the quantity of goods made by industry almost doubled.

For most Americans, incomes rose. As a result, they were able to buy a flood of new consumer products. Electric refrigerators, radios, phonographs, vacuum cleaners, and many other appliances took their place in American homes.

Businesses used advertising to boost sales of consumer goods. Advertisements encouraged people to think that their happiness depended on owning a wealth of shiny, new products.

Faced with so many goods, people often wanted to buy things they could not afford. In response, businesses allowed **installment buying,** or buying on credit. For example, buyers could take home a new refrigerator by paying down just a few dollars. Each month, they paid an installment until they had paid the full price, plus interest.

The new policy of "buy now, pay later" increased the demand for goods. At the same time, however, consumer debt jumped. By the end of the decade, consumers owed more than the amount of the federal budget. The comedian Will Rogers joked:

> 66 If we want anything, all we have to do is go and buy it on credit. So that leaves us without any economic problems whatsoever, except perhaps some day to have to pay for them. 99

A soaring stock market

The economic boom of the 1920s gave the stock market a giant boost. As you read in Chapter 20, corporations sold **stocks,** or shares of ownership, to investors. Investors made or lost money depending upon whether the price of the shares went up or down.

By the later 1920s, more people were investing in the stock market than ever before. Stock prices rose so fast that some people made fortunes almost overnight. Stories of ordinary people becoming rich drew others into the stock market. Such a period of increased stock trading and rising stock prices is known as a **bull market.**

Many people bought stocks **on margin.** Under this system, an investor bought a stock for just a 10 percent down payment.

The buyer held the stock until the price rose and then sold it at a profit. Margin buying worked as long as stock prices kept going up.

In 1928 and 1929, however, the prices of many stocks rose faster than the value of the companies themselves. A few experts warned that the bull market could not last forever. Still, most investors ignored the warnings.

Foreign Affairs

After World War I, the United States was the world's leading economic power. Europeans expected the United States to take a major role in world affairs.

Presidents Harding and Coolidge wanted to keep the hard-won peace in Europe. However, they did not want to commit the United States to the job of keeping world peace. The United States sent observers to the League of Nations but refused to join. Most Americans supported this return to prewar isolationism. However, one American diplomat warned:

> 66 We feel that we can stand outside all international organizations and that our prosperity is such that it cannot be touched by external events. We are profoundly mistaken. 99

Latin America

During the war, Latin American nations had been cut off from Europe. As a result, United States trade and investment in the region increased. This trend continued after the war.

At times, the United States intervened to protect its economic interests in Latin America. In 1926, for example, a revolution broke

ONE perfected feature—the MOTOR DRIVEN BRUSH—is alone worth to you the entire price of the Electric SWEEPER-VAC. This efficient, soft brush (motor driven) revolves 1350 times per minute. It gets ALL lint, threads, hairs and embedded dirt, and, with Powerful Suction, draws them into the dust bag. Ask your dealer for the "Electric SWEEPER-VAC" (don't accept a substitute.) Give it a thorough test on your own rugs.

Pneuvac Company—156 Fremont Street—Worcester, Mass.

Electric SWEEPER-VAC
With Motor Driven Brush

Viewing HISTORY Advertising New Products

Advertising fed the business boom of the 1920s. This ad from a 1921 magazine encourages women to buy an amazing new product—an electric vacuum cleaner. ★ **What message does this advertisement try to give to homemakers?**

Skills

FOR LIFE

| Critical Thinking | Managing Information | Communication | Maps, Charts, and Graphs |

Decision Making

How Will I Use This Skill?

You make dozens of decisions each day. Some are as simple as deciding what to wear. Others might be very important, such as choosing what career you want to follow. Decision making involves reviewing many possible choices and picking the best one.

LEARN the Skill

To make a decision, you have to recognize your goal and evaluate the many possible ways of reaching it. Use the following steps to make a decision:

❶ Identify the goal or purpose.

❷ Review possible options to achieve the goal.

❸ Predict the probable results of each alternative.

❹ Select the choice whose probable results best meet your needs with the fewest negative consequences.

PRACTICE the Skill

Review the subsection Foreign Affairs. Answer the following questions:

❶ What was the goal of the United States in Latin America after World War I?

❷ (a) What option did the United States choose to achieve its goal in Nicaragua? (b) What option did the United States choose to achieve its goal in Mexico?

❸ Predict the possible positive and negative effects of (a) military intervention and (b) diplomacy.

❹ Which of these two options do you think was better? Explain your answer.

APPLY the Skill

Think about what you would like to do for summer vacation. List the possibilities for young people. Review the positive and negative aspects for each choice. Then, write a paragraph explaining your decision.

When revolution broke out in Nicaragua in 1926, President Coolidge sent in the marines.

out in Nicaragua, where Americans owned plantations and railroads. Coolidge sent marines to oversee new elections.

In 1927, Mexico announced plans to take over foreign-owned oil and mining companies. American investors called on President Coolidge to send in troops. Instead, Coolidge sent a diplomat, Dwight Morrow, to Mexico. After much hard bargaining, Morrow was able to work out a compromise with the Mexican government.

The Soviet Union

Meanwhile, in the Soviet Union, V. I. Lenin was creating the world's first communist state.* **Communism** is an economic system in which all wealth and property is owned by the community as a whole.

The United States refused to recognize Lenin's government. Most Americans disliked communism. It shocked them when the Soviet government did away with private property and attacked religion.

Despite disapproval of the Soviet government, Congress voted $20 million in aid when famine threatened Russia in 1921.

---

* In 1922, Russia became the most important state in the newly created Union of Soviet Socialist Republics, or Soviet Union.

American aid may have saved as many as 10 million Russians from starvation.

Disarmament

An arms race in Europe had helped cause World War I. For this reason, many people in the 1920s favored **disarmament,** or the reduction of armed forces and weapons of war. Pacifist groups such as the Woman's International League for Peace and Freedom, founded by Jane Addams, led the call for disarmament in the United States and Europe.

Presidents Harding and Coolidge also backed peace efforts. At the Washington Conference of 1921, the United States, Britain, and Japan agreed to limit the size of their navies. Seven years later, the United States and 61 other nations signed the **Kellogg-Briand Pact.** This treaty outlawed war. Secretary of State Frank Kellogg signed the treaty with a foot-long pen made of gold. "Peace is proclaimed," he said.

The treaty had a fatal flaw. It did not set up any means for keeping the peace. One nation could still use force against another without fear of punishment. Still, many hailed the Kellogg-Briand pact as the beginning of a new age of peace.

★ Section 1 Review ★

Recall

1. **Identify** (a) Warren G. Harding, (b) Teapot Dome Scandal, (c) Calvin Coolidge, (d) Kellogg-Briand Pact.
2. **Define** (a) recession, (b) installment buying, (c) stock, (d) bull market, (e) on margin, (f) communism, (g) disarmament.

Comprehension

3. What problems did the Ohio Gang cause?
4. (a) What policies did Harding and Coolidge adopt toward business? (b) Give two examples of how the economy grew in the 1920s.

5. How did most Americans in the 1920s view the nation's role in world affairs?

Critical Thinking and Writing

6. **Analyzing Ideas** President Harding once complained: "I listen to one side and they seem right. . . . I talk to the other side and they seem just as right, and here I am where I started." What does this statement tell you about the problems faced by a President?
7. **Predicting Consequences** The Kellogg-Briand Pact outlawed war. Do you think it could succeed in achieving its goal? Why or why not?

★ ★

Activity Writing Persuasively Buy now, pay later! You are a teenager in the 1920s. Write a list of arguments you might use to persuade your parents to purchase your family's first electric refrigerator on installment.

New Ways of Life

As You Read

Explore These Questions
- What was Prohibition?
- How did women's lives change in the 1920s?
- How did a mass culture begin to emerge in the 1920s?

Define
- bootlegger
- speakeasy
- repeal
- suburb

Identify
- Prohibition
- League of Women Voters
- Ana Roqué de Duprey
- Equal Rights Amendment
- Henry Ford
- Charlie Chaplin

SETTING the Scene At the stroke of midnight on the morning of January 16, 1920, church bells rang all across the United States. What some people called the "noble experiment" had begun. The experiment was **Prohibition,** a ban on the manufacture, sale, and transportation of liquor anywhere in the United States.

Supporters of Prohibition were overjoyed. Popular preacher Billy Sunday predicted that the ban on alcohol would cure a wide variety of social ills:

66 The slums will soon be only a memory. We will turn our prisons into factories and our jails into storehouses and corncribs. Men will walk upright now. Women will smile and children will laugh. 99

Only time would tell if the "noble experiment" would succeed or fail.

Prohibition was one of many developments that had a dramatic impact on society in the 1920s. New ideas, new products, and new forms of entertainment were rapidly changing the American way of life.

A Ban on Alcohol

For nearly a century, reformers like the Women's Christian Temperance Union had

Button supporting the Eighteenth Amendment

worked to ban alcoholic beverages. They achieved their triumph when the states ratified the Eighteenth Amendment in January 1919. (See page 607.) One year later, Prohibition went into effect.

In 1920, as today, alcohol abuse was a serious problem. Many Americans hoped the ban on liquor would improve American life. In fact, the ban did have some positive effects. Alcoholism declined during Prohibition. So did liver diseases caused by liquor. In the end, however, the ban did not work.

Getting around the law

One reason Prohibition failed was that many Americans found ways to get around the law. Some people manufactured their own alcohol in homemade stills. Others smuggled in liquor from Canada and the Caribbean. Because these smugglers sometimes hid bottles of liquor in their boots, they became known as **bootleggers.**

Illegal bars, called **speakeasies,** opened in nearly every city and town. A visitor to Pittsburgh reported that it took him only 11 minutes to find a speakeasy. In some ways, speakeasies made drinking liquor even more popular than ever. Before Prohibition, it was not considered proper for a woman to go into a saloon. Speakeasies, however, welcomed women as well as men.

Viewing HISTORY **Enforcing the Ban on Alcohol**

During Prohibition, federal agents like these destroyed hundreds of barrels of illegal liquor. Still, both bootleggers and "respectable" citizens kept finding ways around the law. ★ **What effect did Prohibition have on crime?**

To enforce the ban, the government sent out federal prohibition agents. These "g-men" traveled across the United States, shutting down speakeasies, breaking up illegal stills, and stopping smugglers. Still, the lawbreaking was too widespread for just 1,500 federal agents to control.

Rise of organized crime

Prohibition gave a huge boost to organized crime. Every speakeasy needed a steady supply of liquor. Professional criminals, or gangsters, took over the job of meeting this need. As bootleggers earned big profits, crime became a big business. "Ours is a business nation," said one official. "Our criminals apply business methods."

Connections With Science

Prohibition laws allowed manufacturers to produce alcohol for industrial uses. Some bootleggers took advantage of this loophole by converting industrial alcohol to liquor. Unfortunately, most bootleggers lacked knowledge of chemistry. Their illegal product often caused blindness, paralysis, or even death.

Gangsters divided up cities and forced speakeasy owners in their "territories" to buy liquor from them. Sometimes, gangsters gunned down their rivals in battles for control. Newspapers played up alarming tales of gangland violence. Journalists also showed the public how gangsters broke the law and got away with it. Gangsters used some of their profits to bribe police officers, public officials, and judges.

Repeal of Prohibition

Gradually, more and more Americans came to think that Prohibition was a mistake. The ban reduced drinking but never stopped it. Even worse, argued critics, Prohibition was undermining respect for the law. Every day, millions of Americans were buying liquor in speakeasies. By the mid-1920s, almost half of all federal arrests were for Prohibition crimes.

By the end of the decade, many Americans were calling for the **repeal,** or cancellation, of Prohibition. In 1933, the states ratified the Twenty-first Amendment, which repealed the Eighteenth Amendment.* The noble experiment was over.

New Rights for Women

Another constitutional amendment also changed American life, but in a very different way. The Nineteenth Amendment, ratified in 1920, gave women the right to vote. (See page 605.)

Women voters

Women went to the polls nationwide for the first time in November 1920. Their votes helped elect Warren Harding as President.

---

* To date, the Eighteenth Amendment is the only constitutional amendment that has ever been repealed.

Women did not vote as a group, however, as some people had predicted. Like men, some women voted for Republicans, some for Democrats, and many did not vote at all.

In 1920, Carrie Chapman Catt, head of the National Woman Suffrage Association, set up the **League of Women Voters.** The organization worked to educate voters, as it still does today. It also worked to guarantee other rights, such as the right of women to serve on juries.

As women in the United States voted for the first time, women in Puerto Rico asked if the new law applied to them. They were told that it did not. Led by **Ana Roqué de Duprey,** an educator and writer, Puerto Rican women crusaded for the vote. In 1929, their crusade finally succeeded.

Fighting for equal rights

Leaders in the suffrage movement also worked for other goals. Alice Paul, who had been a leading suffragist, pointed out that women still lacked many legal rights. For example, many professional schools still barred women, and many states gave husbands legal control over their wives' earnings. Paul called for a new constitutional amendment in 1923. Paul's proposed **Equal Rights Amendment** (ERA) stated that "equality of rights under the law shall not be denied or abridged by the United States or by any State on account of sex."

Many people feared that the ERA went too far. Some even argued that women would *lose* some legal safeguards, such as laws that protected women in factories. Paul worked vigorously for the ERA until her death in 1977, but the amendment never passed.

Women's work

Women's lives changed in other ways in the 1920s. During World War I, thousands of women had worked outside the home for the first time. They filled the jobs of men who had gone off to war. When the troops came home, many women were forced to give up their jobs. Still, some remained in the work force.

For some women, working outside the home was nothing new. Poor women and working-class women had been cooks, ser-

vants, and seamstresses for many years. In the 1920s, they were joined by middle-class women who worked as teachers, typists, secretaries, and store clerks. A few women even managed to become doctors and lawyers, despite discrimination.

Life at home also changed for women. More of them bought ready-made clothes instead of sewing for the whole family as in the past. Electric appliances such as refrigerators, washers, irons, and vacuum cleaners made housework easier. On the other hand, such conveniences also encouraged some women to spend even more time on housework. Even women who worked outside the home found they had to work a second shift when they came home. Most husbands expected their wives to cook, clean, and care for children even if they held full-time jobs.

Biography   Nellie Tayloe Ross

The first state to allow women to vote, Wyoming was also the first to have a woman as governor. In 1924, Nellie Tayloe Ross was elected to succeed her late husband. In office, Governor Ross supported tax relief for farmers and better funding for schools. She later served for 20 years as director of the United States Mint. ★ **Why do you think no state elected a woman governor before the 1920s?**

Impact of the Automobile

"Why on earth do you need to study what's changing this country?" one man asked the experts. "I can tell you what's happening in just four letters: A-U-T-O." In the 1920s, Americans traveled to more places and moved more quickly than ever before—all because of the automobile.

The auto industry played a central role in the business boom of the 1920s. Car sales grew rapidly during the decade. The auto boom spurred growth in related fields such as steel and rubber.

Affordable cars

Lower prices sparked the auto boom. By 1924, the cost of a Model T had dropped from $850 to $290. As a result, an American did not have to be rich to buy a car.

Car prices fell because factories became more efficient. As you have read, **Henry Ford** introduced the assembly line in his automobile factory in 1913. (See page 546.) The goal, Ford said, was to make the cars identical, "just like one pin is like another pin." Before the assembly line, it took 14 hours to put together a Model T. In Ford's new factory, workers could assemble a Model T in 93 minutes!

Linking History and Technology

Ford Assembly Line

Henry Ford transformed manufacturing and daily life with the automobile assembly line. Workers stood at their stations while unfinished cars moved past them on a conveyor belt. Each worker performed one task on each car as it passed by. ★ **What disadvantages might there be to working on an assembly line?**

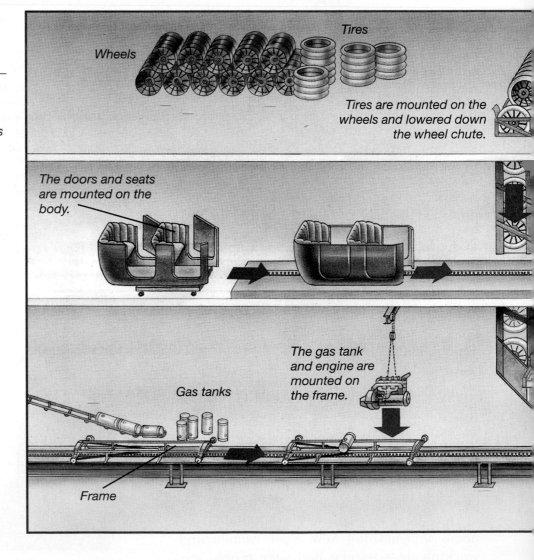

Wheels

Tires

Tires are mounted on the wheels and lowered down the wheel chute.

The doors and seats are mounted on the body.

The gas tank and engine are mounted on the frame.

Gas tanks

Frame

Other companies copied Ford's methods. In 1927, General Motors passed Ford as the top auto maker. Unlike Ford, General Motors sold cars in a variety of models and colors. Henry Ford had once boasted that people could have his cars in "any color so long as it's black." Faced with the success of General Motors, he changed his mind. His next car, the Model A, came in different colors. Before long, car companies were offering new makes and models every year.

Economic effects

Car sales spurred growth in other parts of the economy. By 1929, some four million Americans owed their jobs to the automobile, directly or indirectly. Tens of thousands of people worked in steel mills, producing metal parts for cars. Others made tires, paint, and glass for cars. Some drilled for oil in the Southwest or worked in the oil refineries where crude petroleum was converted into usable gasoline.

The car boom had other effects. States and towns paved more roads and built new highways. In 1925, the Bronx River Parkway in New York was the first of many highways in parklike settings.

Gas stations, tourist camps, and roadside restaurants sprang up across the country to

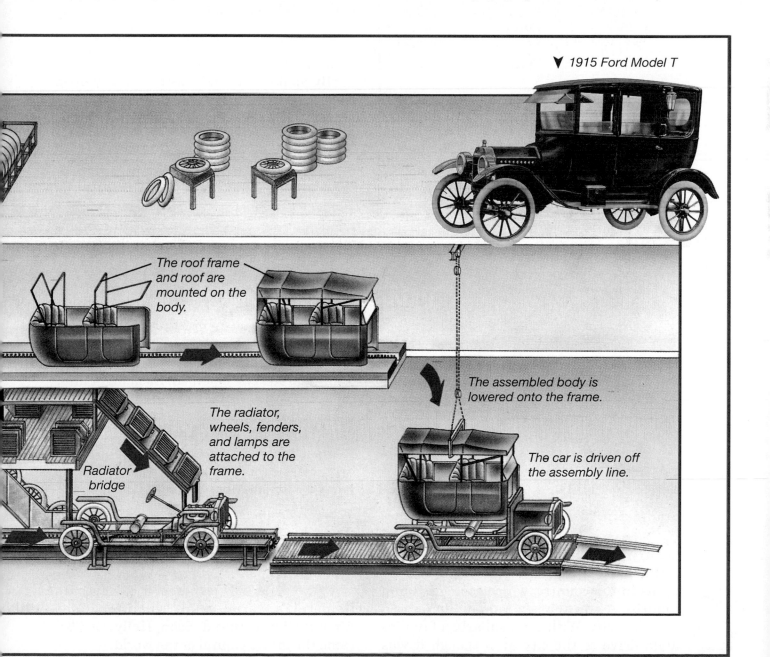

▼ 1915 Ford Model T

The roof frame and roof are mounted on the body.

The radiator, wheels, fenders, and lamps are attached to the frame.

Radiator bridge

The assembled body is lowered onto the frame.

The car is driven off the assembly line.

Families With Radios

Millions of Families With Radios (y-axis: 0–11)
Year (x-axis): 1922, 1923, 1924, 1925, 1926, 1927, 1928, 1929

Source: *Historical Statistics of the United States*

Graph *Skills*

The 1920s could be called the age of radio. Millions of American families bought radios and listened to popular programs.

1. **Comprehension** About how many families owned radios in 1924? In 1929?

2. **Critical Thinking** Do you think radio is as important today as it was in the 1920s? Why or why not?

Radio of the 1920s

serve the millions who traveled by car. In 1920, there were only about 1,500 filling stations in the entire United States. By 1929, there were more than 120,000.

Social effects

Cars shaped life in the city and in the country. Many city dwellers wanted to escape crowded conditions. They moved to nearby towns in the country, which soon grew into suburbs. A **suburb** is a community located outside a city. With cars, suburban families could drive to the city even though it was

many miles away. They could also drive to stores, schools, or work. No longer did people have to live where they could walk or take a trolley to work.

Another major shift came when suburban housewives refused to be confined to the passenger seat. Instead, they took their place behind the wheels of their own automobiles. As they did, they broke down still another barrier that separated the worlds of men and women.

In the country, cars brought people closer to towns, shops, and the movies. Such trips had taken several hours by horse and buggy. One farm woman bought a car before she got indoor plumbing. "You can't go to town in a bathtub," she explained.

Creating a Mass Culture

By making travel easier, cars helped Americans from different parts of the country learn more about one another. They thus played a role in creating a new, national culture that crossed state lines.

New forms of entertainment also contributed to the rise of a mass culture. In the 1920s, rising wages and labor-saving appliances gave families more money to spend—and more leisure time in which to spend it.

Radio

Radio became very popular in the 1920s. The country's first radio station, KDKA, started broadcasting in Pittsburgh in 1920. By 1929, more than 10 million American families owned radios.

A new lifestyle emerged. Each night after dinner, families gathered around the radio to tune in to shows such as "Roxy and His Gang" or "Jack Frost's Melody Moments." Radio listeners enjoyed comedies and westerns, classical music and jazz, news reports and play-by-play sports broadcasts.

The movies

In the late 1800s, Thomas Edison and George Eastman had helped to develop the first moving picture cameras. In the 1920s, the movie industry came of age. Southern California's warm, sunny climate allowed filming all year round. Soon, Hollywood became the movie capital of the world.

Why Study History?

Because Movies Have a Powerful Effect on Us

★ ★

Historical Background

He galloped across the desert on a white horse, his long Arabian robes flowing behind him. In darkened theaters from coast to coast, millions of viewers felt a thrill. In movies like *The Sheik* (1921), Rudolph Valentino became the most popular romantic star of his day.

Then, in 1926, came the shocking news. Valentino was dead! More than 100,000 weeping fans mobbed the funeral home to say goodbye to their favorite star.

The reaction to Valentino's death showed the enormous popularity of movies and movie stars. At the same time, it raised concerns about the unhealthy effects of movies, especially on young people. Critics warned that movie stars were being worshipped like gods.

Connections to Today

Today, movies continue to enjoy tremendous popularity. Large audiences watched movies ranging from cartoons like *The Lion King* to serious dramas like *Schindler's List*. In 1998, the romantic epic *Titanic* broke the all-time box office record. Every spring, hundreds of millions of television viewers around the world tune in to watch their favorite stars at the Academy Awards.

Connections to You

What role do movies play in your life? The chances are that you have seen a movie recently and that you have favorite stars. Movies entertain us, stir our imaginations, and can teach us about unfamiliar people and places. Yet today, as in the past, some critics worry about the effects of movies on young people.

One area of concern is violence. Many experts believe that watching violent movies encourages violent behavior in some younger viewers. The debate about movies will probably continue for a long time to come.

1. Comprehension **(a)** How did movie fans in the 1920s react to the death of Rudolph Valentino? **(b)** Why did this reaction worry some people?

2. Critical Thinking Do you think that viewers under a certain age should be prevented from watching violent movies? Why or why not?

 **Writing a Movie Review** Select a movie that you think would have a positive effect on viewers. Prepare and deliver a one-minute review explaining why you recommend this film.

Moviemakers today spend millions of dollars creating films for the profitable "teen market."

In the 1920s, millions of Americans went to the movies at least once a week. They thrilled to westerns, romances, adventures, and comedies. In small towns, theaters were bare rooms with hard chairs. In cities, they were huge palaces with red velvet seats.

The first movies had no sound. Audiences followed the plot by reading "title cards" that appeared on the screen. A pianist played music that went with the action. Sometimes the audience also provided sound effects. As one movie-house musician recalled:

Charlie Chaplin

66 To provide sound for Western or battle scenes, the older [children] would fire cap pistols. The younger ones, identifying with the hero as he was being stalked, would blurt hysterical warnings: 'Look out! He's behind the door!' There were always children reading aloud to their immigrant parents....They supplied...translations into Italian, Yiddish, or German. 99

Fans adored Hollywood movie stars. Cowboy stars like Tom Mix thrilled audiences with their heroic adventures. Clara Bow won fame playing restless, fun-seeking young women. The most popular star of all was comedian **Charlie Chaplin,** nicknamed "The Little Tramp." In his tiny derby hat and baggy pants, Chaplin presented a comical figure. His attempts to triumph over the problems of everyday life moved audiences to both laughter and tears.

In 1927, Hollywood caused a sensation when it produced *The Jazz Singer.* The film was a "talkie"—a movie with a sound track. Audiences were thrilled when singer Al Jolson looked down from the screen and promised, "You ain't heard nothin' yet!" Soon, all new movies were talkies.

Movies contributed to the new mass culture. When a Chaplin comedy opened, people from coast to coast rushed to see it. Immigrants and native-born Americans laughed together. Movies, said a Hollywood executive, reached "audiences speaking twenty different languages but understanding in common the universal language of pictures."

★ Section 2 Review ★

Recall

1. **Identify** (a) Prohibition, (b) League of Women Voters, (c) Ana Roqué de Duprey, (d) Equal Rights Amendment, (e) Henry Ford, (f) Charlie Chaplin.
2. **Define** (a) bootlegger, (b) speakeasy, (c) repeal, (d) suburb.

Comprehension

3. Why did a national ban on alcohol fail?
4. How did the Nineteenth Amendment change women's lives?

5. Describe one way each of the following affected American life: (a) the automobile, (b) radio, (c) movies.

Critical Thinking and Writing

6. **Linking Past and Present** Cars transformed American life in the 1920s. Are cars just as important in American life today? Explain.
7. **Analyzing Ideas** A mass culture began to emerge in the 1920s. (a) What advantages does a mass culture bring? (b) What disadvantages?

Activity **Writing Title Cards** You are a moviemaker producing a silent film about the Roaring Twenties. Write ten title cards for scenes that show what the decade was like.

The Jazz Age

As You Read

Explore These Questions

- Why were the 1920s called the Roaring Twenties and the Jazz Age?
- Why did some writers criticize American society?
- Who were the leading figures of the Harlem Renaissance?

Define

- fad
- flapper
- jazz
- expatriate

Identify

- Louis Armstrong
- Ernest Hemingway
- F. Scott Fitzgerald
- Harlem Renaissance
- Langston Hughes
- Zora Neale Hurston
- Babe Ruth
- Charles A. Lindbergh

SETTING the Scene When asked about her favorite pastime, one young woman of the 1920s promptly replied, "I adore dancing. Who doesn't?" New dance crazes such as the Charleston, the Lindy Hop, and the Shimmy forever marked the decade as the "Jazz Age" and the "Roaring Twenties."

During the 1920s, new dances, new music, new games, and other new ways to have fun swept the country. For all the serious business of the 1920s, the decade also roared with laughter. At the same time, a new generation of writers were taking a critical look at American society.

An Era of Changing Fashions

"Ev'ry morning, ev'ry evening, ain't we got fun?" went a hit song of 1921. During the "Era of Wonderful Nonsense"—yet another nickname for the 1920s—fun came in many forms.

Dress and beads worn by a flapper

Following the latest fads

Fads caught on, then quickly disappeared. A **fad** is an activity or a fashion that is taken up with great passion for a short time. Flagpole sitting was one fad of the 1920s. Young people would perch on top of flagpoles for hours, or even days. Another fad was the dance marathon, where couples danced for hundreds of hours at a time to see who could last the longest. Crossword puzzles and mah-jongg, a Chinese game, were other popular fads of the 1920s.

Dance crazes came and went rapidly. The most popular new dance was probably the Charleston. First performed by African Americans in southern cities like Charleston, South Carolina, the dance became a national craze after 1923. To a quick beat, dancers pivoted their feet while kicking out first one leg, then the other, backward and forward.

Flappers set the style

Perhaps no one pursued the latest fads more intensely than the **flappers.** These young women rebelled against traditional ways of thinking and acting. Flappers wore their hair bobbed, or cut short. They wore their dresses short, too—shorter than Americans had ever seen before. Flappers shocked their parents by wearing bright red lipstick.

To many older Americans, the way flappers behaved was even more shocking than the way they looked. Flappers smoked cigarettes in public, drank bootleg alcohol in

New Music

Another innovation of the 1920s was jazz. Born in New Orleans, **jazz** combined West African rhythms, African American work songs and spirituals, and European harmonies. Jazz also had roots in the ragtime rhythms of composers like Scott Joplin. (See page 573.)

Louis Armstrong was one of the brilliant young African American musicians who helped create jazz. Armstrong learned to play the trumpet in the New Orleans orphanage where he grew up. Too young to play in clubs, Armstrong made his debut at a picnic. One musician remembers, "Everyone in the park went wild over this boy in knee trousers who could play so great." Armstrong had the ability to take a simple melody and experiment with the notes and the rhythm. This allowed his listeners to hear many different sides of the basic tune. Other great early jazz players included "Jelly Roll" Morton and singer Bessie Smith.

Jazz quickly spread from New Orleans to Chicago, Kansas City, and the African American section of New York known as Harlem. White musicians, such as trumpeter Bix Beiderbecke, also began to adopt the new style. Before long, the popularity of jazz spread to Europe as well.

Many older Americans worried that jazz and the new dances were a bad influence on the nation's young people. Despite their complaints, jazz continued to grow more popular. Today, jazz is recognized as a uniquely American art form created by African Americans. It is considered one of the most important cultural achievements of the United States.

Biography — Louis Armstrong

As a child, Louis "Satchmo" Armstrong liked to follow brass bands around the streets of New Orleans. After coming to Chicago in 1922, he quickly became the most popular jazz musician of his day. His recordings, such as "Potato Head Blues," brought jazz to a nationwide audience. "Satchmo" also pioneered a new form of jazz singing, called scat. ★ **What were the origins of jazz?**

speakeasies, and drove fast cars. "Is 'the old-fashioned girl,' with all that she stands for in sweetness, modesty, and innocence, in danger of becoming extinct?" wondered one magazine in 1921.

The flappers defiantly mocked such criticism. A song from a 1925 musical comedy became an informal flapper anthem:

    66 Flappers are we
    Flappers and fly and free.
    Never too slow
    All on the go....
    Dizzy with dangerous glee. 99

Only a few young women were flappers. Still, they set a style for others. Slowly, older women began to cut their hair and wear makeup and shorter skirts. For many Americans, the bold fashions pioneered by the flappers symbolized a new sense of freedom.

Connections With Arts

One unique feature of jazz was its free style. Generally, the written melody was only a framework. Musicians would improvise, playing with the tune and encouraging one another to take the mood a step farther. When a group of jazz musicians improvised together, it was known as a jam session.

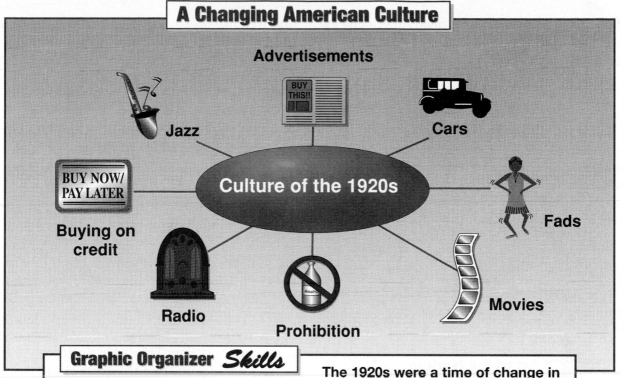

A Changing American Culture

Advertisements

Jazz

Cars

BUY NOW/ PAY LATER

Buying on credit

Culture of the 1920s

Fads

Radio

Prohibition

Movies

Graphic Organizer *Skills* The 1920s were a time of change in the United States. A number of new inventions, ideas, and practices contributed to this change.

1. Comprehension Identify two items on this graphic organizer that were linked to the economic boom of the 1920s.

2. Critical Thinking **(a)** Which items shown here affected American leisure activities? **(b)** Of these, which are still popular today?

A New Generation of Writers

A new generation of American writers earned worldwide fame in the 1920s. Many of them were horrified by their experiences in World War I. They criticized Americans for caring too much about money and fun. Some became so unhappy with life in the United States that they moved to Paris, France. There, they lived as **expatriates,** people who leave their own country to live in a foreign land.

Hemingway and Fitzgerald

Ernest Hemingway was one of the writers who lived for a time in Paris. Still a teenager at the outbreak of World War I, he traveled to Europe to drive an ambulance on the Italian front. Hemingway drew on his war experiences in *A Farewell to Arms,* a novel about a young man's growing disgust with war. In *The Sun Also Rises,* he exam-

ined the lives of American expatriates in Europe. They travel from Paris to Spain and back, searching for momentary pleasure without any plans or hopes for the future.

Hemingway became one of the most popular writers of the 1920s. His simple but powerful style influenced many other writers.

The young writer who best captured the mood of the Roaring Twenties was Hemingway's friend **F. Scott Fitzgerald.** In *The Great Gatsby* and other novels, Fitzgerald told about wealthy young people who attended endless parties but could not find happiness. His characters included flappers, bootleggers, and movie makers. Fitzgerald became a hero to college students and flappers, among others.

Other writers

Sinclair Lewis grew up in a small town in Minnesota and later moved to New York City. In novels such as *Babbitt* and *Main*

Street, he presented small-town Americans as dull and narrow-minded. Lewis reflected the attitude of many city dwellers toward rural Americans. In fact, the word *babbitt* became a popular nickname for a smug businessman uninterested in literature or the arts.

Edna St. Vincent Millay, a poet, was enormously popular. She expressed the frantic pace of the 1920s in her verse, such as her short poem "First Fig":

66 My candle burns at both ends;
It will not last the night;
But ah, my foes, and oh, my friends—
It gives a lovely light. 99

Another writer, Eugene O'Neill, revolutionized the American theater. Most earlier playwrights presented romantic, unrealistic stories. O'Neill shocked audiences with powerful, realistic dramas based on his years at sea. In other plays, he used experimental methods to expose the inner thoughts of tortured young people.

Harlem Renaissance

In the 1920s, large numbers of African American musicians, artists, and writers settled in Harlem, in New York City. "Harlem was like a great magnet for the Negro intellectual," said one black writer. This gathering of black artists and musicians led to the **Harlem Renaissance,** a rebirth of African American culture.

During the Harlem Renaissance, young black writers celebrated their African and American heritage. They also protested prejudice and racism. For the first time, too, a large number of white Americans took notice of the achievements of black artists and writers.

Langston Hughes

Probably the best-known poet of the Harlem Renaissance was **Langston Hughes.** He published his first poem, "The Negro Speaks of Rivers," soon after graduating from high school. The poem connected the experiences of black Americans living along the Mississippi River with those of ancient Africans living along the Nile and Niger rivers. (See page 758.)

Like other writers of the Harlem Renaissance, Hughes encouraged African Americans to be proud of their heritage. In "My People," he wrote:

66 The night is beautiful,
So the faces of my people.
The stars are beautiful,
So the eyes of my people.
Beautiful, also, is the sun.
Beautiful, also, are the souls of
   my people. 99

In other poems, Hughes protested racism and acts of violence against African Americans. In addition to his poems, Hughes wrote plays, short stories, and essays about the black experience.

Viewing HISTORY — Art of the Harlem Renaissance

Writers and artists of the Harlem Renaissance often stressed the African heritage of black Americans. In The Ascent of Ethiopia, *painter Lois Mailou Jones links the Egyptian pharaoh (front) to the modern urban skyscraper in the background.* ★ **What point do you think Jones is making in this painting?**

Viewing HISTORY — Sports Heroes of the 1920s

In the 1920s, as today, Americans loved to follow the triumphs of famous athletes. The photograph at left shows Helen Wills at age 19, when she won the second of her seven United States tennis championships. She also won the Wimbledon title eight times. The mighty hitting of Babe Ruth, right, helped the New York Yankees win seven World Series in 13 years. ★ **Why do you think sports stars attract so much admiration?**

Other writers

Other poets such as Countee Cullen and Claude McKay also wrote of the experiences of African Americans. A graduate of New York University and Harvard, Cullen taught in a Harlem high school. In the 1920s, he won prizes for his books of poetry.

McKay came to the United States from Jamaica. In his poem "If We Must Die," he condemned the lynchings and other mob violence that black Americans suffered after World War I. The poem concludes with the lines "Like men we'll face the murderous, cowardly pack, / Pressed to the wall, dying but fighting back!"

Zora Neale Hurston, who grew up in Florida, wrote novels, essays, and short stories. Hurston grew concerned that African American folklore "was disappearing without the world realizing it had ever been." In 1928, she set out alone to travel through the South in a battered car. For two years, she collected the folk tales, songs, and prayers of black southerners. She later published these in her book *Mules and Men.*

Heroes of the Roaring Twenties

Radio, movies, and newspapers created heroes and heroines known across the country. Americans followed the exploits of individuals whose achievements made them stand out from the crowd.

Athletes

Some of the best-loved heroes of the decade were athletes. Each sport had its stars. Bobby Jones won almost every golf championship. Bill Tilden and Helen Wills ruled the tennis courts. Jack Dempsey reigned as world heavyweight boxing champion for seven years. At the age of 19, Gertrude Ederle awed the world when she became the first woman to swim across the English Channel.

College football also drew huge crowds. Many Americans who had never attended college rooted for college teams. Flappers and their dates paraded in the stands wearing the latest fashion—thick, bulky raccoon

▲ Medal honoring Charles A. Lindbergh

coats. They thrilled to the exploits of football stars like Red Grange, the "Galloping Ghost" of the University of Illinois.

Americans loved football, but baseball was their real passion. The most popular player of the 1920s was **Babe Ruth.** Ruth had grown up in an orphanage and was often in trouble as a boy. Through talent and hard work, he became the star of the New York Yankees. Fans flocked to games to see "the Sultan of Swat" hit home runs. The 60 home runs he hit in one season set a record that lasted more than 30 years. His lifetime record of 714 home runs was not broken until 1974.

Charles Lindbergh

The greatest hero of the decade, however, was not an athlete but an aviator. On a gray morning in May 1927, **Charles A. Lindbergh** took off from an airport in New York. A shy young man from Minnesota, Lindbergh planned to be the first person to fly nonstop across the Atlantic Ocean—alone.

For 33½ hours, Lindbergh piloted his tiny single-engine plane, *The Spirit of St. Louis,* over the stormy Atlantic. He carried no map, no parachute, and no radio. Lindbergh later described how he battled his worst problem, fatigue:

66 Sleeping is winning. My whole body argues dully that nothing, nothing life can attain, is quite so desirable as sleep. My mind is losing resolution and control. 99

Still, Lindbergh flew on. At last, he landed in Paris, France. The cheering crowd lifted him on their shoulders and carried him across the airfield. Back home, headlines announced LINDY DOES IT! "Lucky Lindy" returned to the United States as the hero of the decade.

★ Section 3 Review ★

Recall

1. **Identify** (a) Louis Armstrong, (b) Ernest Hemingway, (c) F. Scott Fitzgerald, (d) Harlem Renaissance, (e) Langston Hughes, (f) Zora Neale Hurston, (g) Babe Ruth, (h) Charles A. Lindbergh.
2. **Define** (a) fad, (b) flapper, (c) jazz, (d) expatriate.

Comprehension

3. How did flappers reflect changes in American culture?
4. What aspects of American life did writers criticize?

5. What themes did the writers of the Harlem Renaissance address in their works?

Critical Thinking and Writing

6. **Analyzing Ideas** Review Edna St. Vincent Millay's poem on page 690. How does it reflect the spirit of the 1920s?
7. **Linking Past and Present** (a) What new kinds of music and dancing are popular among young people today? (b) How do most older Americans respond to these new forms? (c) Is this response similar to or different from attitudes toward flappers and jazz in the 1920s? Explain.

★ ★

Activity Using Flashcards Make a set of flashcards about the important people of the 1920s. On the front of each card, write the name of one of the heroes, writers, artists, or leaders of the times. On the back, write key facts about that person. Use the cards to review what you have learned about the 1920s.

4 ★ Trouble Below the Surface

★ ★

As You Read

Explore These Questions
- Which Americans did not share in the prosperity of the 1920s?
- Why did many Americans want to limit immigration?
- What obstacles did African Americans face in northern cities?

Define
- company union
- sabotage
- anarchist
- deport
- nativism
- quota system

Identify
- Red Scare
- Sacco and Vanzetti trial
- Emergency Quota Act
- Jones Act
- Scopes trial
- Marcus Garvey
- Herbert Hoover
- Alfred E. Smith

SETTING the Scene Writing in the magazine *The Nation,* Oswald Garrison Villard warned Americans that the high living of the Roaring Twenties could not last. Under the surface, millions "were steadily sinking...worse housed and fed than any peasants in Europe."

Villard knew that no one wanted to listen. "Nobody wanted anything but to be left alone to make money," he complained. Still, he was right. Even at its height, "Coolidge prosperity" never included everyone.

Uneven Prosperity

As Villard pointed out, many Americans did not share in the boom of the 1920s. Workers in the clothing industry, for example, were hurt by changes in women's fashions. Shorter skirts meant that less cloth was needed to make dresses. Coal miners also faced hard times as oil replaced coal as the major source of energy. Railroads slashed jobs because trains were losing business to cars and trucks.

Farmers suffer

Farmers were hit the hardest. During World War I, Europeans had bought American farm products, sending prices up. Farmers borrowed money to buy more land and tractors. They planned to pay off these loans with profits from increased production.

When the war ended, however, European farmers were again able to produce for their own needs. As a result, prices for American farm products dropped sharply throughout the 1920s. Farmers were unable to pay their debts. By the end of the decade, the farmers' share of national income had shrunk by almost half.

Setbacks for labor

For labor unions, too, the 1920s were a disaster. During the war, unions had worked with the government to keep production high. Labor's cooperation contributed to victory. In return, union leaders expected the government to support labor.

During the war, wages had not kept up with prices. Now, with the war over, workers demanded higher pay. When employers refused, unions launched a wave of strikes. Management moved quickly to crush the strikes. Because the government did not step in to help them, workers felt betrayed.

The strikes turned the public against labor. One strike in particular angered Americans. In 1919, the city of Boston fired 19 police officers who had tried to join the American Federation of Labor (AFL). Boston police struck in protest. The sight of police leaving their posts shocked the country.

The later 1920s saw even more setbacks for labor. In one court case after another, judges limited the rights of unions. At the

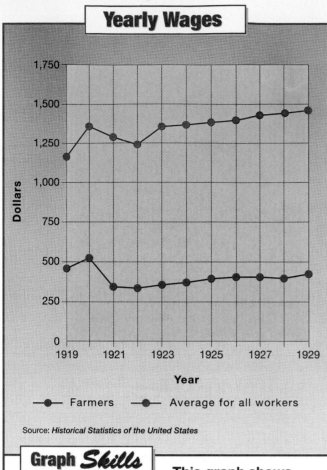

Yearly Wages

Dollars (y-axis): 1,750, 1,500, 1,250, 1,000, 750, 500, 250, 0

Year (x-axis): 1919, 1921, 1923, 1925, 1927, 1929

⬤— Farmers ⬤— Average for all workers

Source: *Historical Statistics of the United States*

Graph *Skills*

This graph shows the average yearly wage for all American workers and for farmers in the 1920s. Generally, farmers earned less than most other workers.

1. **Comprehension** **(a)** What was the average yearly wage for all American workers in 1925? **(b)** How far below the average were farmers' wages that year?

2. **Critical Thinking** Do you think farmers were able to buy many of the new goods available in the 1920s?

---

same time, employers created **company unions,** labor organizations that were actually controlled by management. As a result, union membership dropped from 5 million in 1920 to 3.4 million by 1929.

The Red Scare

During the war, Americans had been on the alert for enemy spies and **sabotage**—secret destruction of property or interference with work in factories. These wartime worries led to a growing fear of foreigners.

The rise of communism in the Soviet Union fanned that fear. Lenin, the communist leader, called on workers everywhere to overthrow their governments. Many Americans saw the strikes that swept the nation as the start of a communist revolution.

Rounding up radicals

The actions of **anarchists,** or people who oppose organized government, added to the sense of danger. One group of anarchists plotted to kill well-known Americans, including John D. Rockefeller, the head of Standard Oil. Because many anarchists were foreign born, their attacks led to an outcry against all foreigners.

The government took harsh actions against both communists, or "Reds," and anarchists. During the **Red Scare,** thousands of radicals were arrested and jailed. Many foreigners were **deported,** or expelled from the country.

Sacco and Vanzetti

The trial of two Italian immigrants in Massachusetts came to symbolize the anti-foreign feeling of the 1920s. Nicola Sacco and Bartolomeo Vanzetti were arrested for robbery and murder in 1920. The two men admitted that they were anarchists but insisted they had committed no crime. A jury convicted them, however. Sacco and Vanzetti were then sentenced to death.

The **Sacco and Vanzetti trial** created a furor across the nation. The evidence against the two men was limited. The judge was openly prejudiced against the two immigrants. Many Americans thought that Sacco and Vanzetti were convicted, not because they were guilty, but because they were immigrants and radicals. The two men waited in jail during a six-year fight to overturn their convictions. Their appeals were turned down. In 1927, they were executed.

The issue of whether Sacco and Vanzetti received a fair trial has been debated ever since. In the meantime, many Americans felt the case proved that the United States had to keep out dangerous radicals.

Did Sacco and Vanzetti get a fair trial? Many Americans did not think so. One artist created this poster calling for a new trial. Writers such as Edna St. Vincent Millay and Countee Cullen also supported the two Italian-born anarchists. In spite of protests, Sacco and Vanzetti were executed in 1927. ★ **Why did some people question the verdict in the Sacco and Vanzetti trial?**

cut immigration, especially from Eastern Europe, which was seen as a center of anarchism and communism. In addition, Japanese were added to the list of Asians denied entry to the country.

Newcomers from Latin America

Latin Americans and Canadians were not included in the quota system. As a result, Mexican immigrants continued to move to the United States. Farms and factories in the Southwest depended on Mexican workers. By 1930, a million or more Mexicans had crossed the border. Most came to work in the vegetable fields, orchards, and factories of the Southwest. The pay was low and the housing was poor. Still, the chance to earn more money was a very powerful lure.

Puerto Ricans also moved to the mainland in large numbers. In 1917, the **Jones Act** granted American citizenship to Puerto Ricans. Poverty on the island led to a great migration to the north. In 1910, only 1,500 Puerto Ricans lived on the mainland. By 1930, there were 53,000.

The Scopes Trial

In the 1920s, cities drew thousands of people from farms and small towns. Those who stayed in rural areas often feared that new ways of life in the city were a threat to traditional values.

The clash between old and new values erupted in the small town of Dayton, Tennessee. At the center of the controversy was Charles Darwin's theory of evolution. Darwin, a British scientist, had claimed that all life had evolved, or developed, from simpler forms over a long period of time.

Limiting Immigration

In the end, the Red Scare died down. Yet anger against foreigners led to a new move to limit immigration. As you recall, this kind of antiforeign feeling is known as **nativism.**

The quota system

After years of war, millions of Europeans hoped to find a better life in the United States. American workers feared that a flood of newcomers would force wages down. Others worried that communists and anarchists would invade the United States.

Congress responded by passing the **Emergency Quota Act** in 1921. The act set up a **quota system** that allowed only a certain number of people from each country to enter the United States. "America must be kept American," said Calvin Coolidge.

The quota system favored immigrants from Northern Europe, especially Britain. In 1924, Congress passed new laws that further

Some churches condemned Darwin's theory, saying it denied the teachings of the Bible. Tennessee, Mississippi, and Arkansas passed laws that banned the teaching of Darwin's theory. In 1925, John Scopes, a biology teacher in Dayton, taught evolution to his class. Scopes was arrested and tried.

Two of the nation's best-known figures opposed each other in the **Scopes trial.** William Jennings Bryan, who had run for President three times, argued the state's case against Scopes. Clarence Darrow, a Chicago lawyer who had helped unions and radicals, defended Scopes.

As the trial began, the nation's attention was riveted on Dayton. Reporters recorded every word of the battle between Darrow and Bryan. "Scopes isn't on trial," Darrow thundered at one point, "civilization is on trial." Darrow even put Bryan on the witness stand to show how little he knew about science. Bryan firmly defended his belief in the Bible.

In the end, Scopes was convicted and fined. The law against teaching evolution remained on the books, although it was rarely enforced.

The New Klan

Fear of change gave new life to an old organization. In 1915, a group of white men in Georgia declared the rebirth of the Ku Klux Klan. The original Klan had used terror to keep African Americans from voting after the Civil War. (See page 487.) The new Klan had a broader aim: to preserve the United States for white, native-born Protestants.

The new Klan waged a campaign against immigrants, especially Catholics and Jews. Klan members burned crosses outside people's homes. They used whippings and lynchings to terrorize immigrants and African Americans. The Klan strongly supported efforts to limit immigration.

Because of its large membership, the Klan gained political influence. In the mid-1920s, however, many Americans became alarmed at the Klan's growing power. At the same time, scandals surfaced that showed Klan leaders had stolen money from members. Klan membership dropped sharply.

Fighting Racism

African Americans had hoped that their service during World War I would weaken racism at home. However, returning black soldiers found that the South was still a segregated society. In the North, too, racial prejudice was widespread.

Racial tensions in the North

Many African Americans moved north during and after the war. They took factory jobs in Chicago, Detroit, New York, Philadelphia, and other large cities. The newcomers often found that only the lowest-paying jobs were open to them. Also, in many neighborhoods, whites refused to rent apartments to blacks.

Viewing HISTORY ★ **Rebirth of the Ku Klux Klan**

This photo shows members of the Ku Klux Klan parading in front of the Capitol Building in Washington, D.C. Many Americans were alarmed by the rebirth of the Klan. Journalist William Allen White warned, "To make a case against a birthplace, a religion, or a race is wickedly un-American and cowardly." ★ **Why do you think White described the Klan as "un-American"?**

At the same time, many blacks newly arrived from the South wanted to live near one another. As a result, areas with large black populations grew in many northern cities.

Many northern white workers felt threatened by the arrival of so many African Americans. Racial tension grew. In 1919, race riots broke out in several cities. The worst took place in Chicago, leaving 38 dead.

Marcus Garvey

Shocked by the racism they found, African Americans looked for new ways to cope. **Marcus Garvey** became one of the most popular black leaders. Garvey organized the Universal Negro Improvement Association. He hoped to promote unity and pride among African Americans. "I am the equal of any white man," Garvey said.

Garvey urged African Americans to seek their roots in Africa. Although few black Americans actually went to Africa, Garvey's "Back to Africa" movement built racial pride.

Election of 1928

By 1928, Republicans had led the nation for eight years. They pointed to prosperity as their outstanding achievement. Still, when asked about the upcoming election, President Coolidge said tersely, "I do not choose to run." Instead, Secretary of Commerce **Herbert Hoover** easily won the Republican nomination. The Democrats chose as their candidate **Alfred E. Smith,** a former governor of New York.

The contrast between the candidates revealed the tensions lurking below the surface of American life. Smith, the son of Irish immigrants, was the first Catholic to run for President. City dwellers, including many immigrants and Catholics, rallied around Smith. Hoover was a self-made millionaire from the Midwest. He won votes from rural Americans and big business. Supporters of Prohibition also supported Hoover because Smith favored repeal.

In the election, Smith won the country's 12 largest cities. Rural and small-town voters, however, supported Hoover. He won by a landslide.

Americans hoped Hoover would keep the country prosperous. Less than a year after Hoover took office, however, the economy would come crashing down.

★ Section 4 Review ★

Recall

1. **Identify** (a) Red Scare, (b) Sacco and Vanzetti trial, (c) Emergency Quota Act, (d) Jones Act, (e) Scopes trial, (f) Marcus Garvey, (g) Herbert Hoover, (h) Alfred E. Smith.
2. **Define** (a) company union, (b) sabotage, (c) anarchist, (d) deport, (e) nativism, (f) quota system.

Comprehension

3. Describe the problems each of the following faced in the 1920s: (a) farmers, (b) labor unions.
4. Why did the Red Scare lead Americans to demand limits on immigration?

5. (a) What did African American soldiers expect when they returned home after World War I? (b) What conditions did they face?

Critical Thinking and Writing

6. **Linking Past and Present** (a) Does anti-immigration sentiment exist in the United States today? (b) At which groups is it directed? (c) What might be some reasons people give for resenting those groups?
7. **Defending a Position** "Groups such as the Ku Klux Klan have a right to exist under the Constitution." Do you agree or disagree with this statement? Defend your position.

★ ★

Activity Drawing a Political Cartoon You are one of the great newspaper cartoonists of the 1920s. Choose one of the issues or events described in this section and draw a political cartoon expressing your own view about it.

Review and Activities

Section 1 Politics and Prosperity
► President Harding's administration was marred by scandals.
► The economy boomed in the 1920s as industries produced new goods and the stock market soared.
► After World War I, many Americans favored a return to prewar isolationism.

Section 2 New Ways of Life
► During Prohibition, the manufacture and sale of alcoholic beverages was banned, but many Americans ignored the law.
► After winning the vote, women enjoyed new opportunities.
► A mass culture emerged as people began to watch movies, listen to radio, and travel in cars.

Section 3 The Jazz Age
► The 1920s were a time of changing fashions, including the popularity of jazz.
► Many writers of the 1920s criticized American life.
► African American writers and artists brought about a rebirth of black arts and literature.

Section 4 Trouble Below the Surface
► Many farmers and workers did not share in the prosperity of the 1920s.
► Fearing foreign radicals, the United States acted to limit immigration.

 For additional review of the major ideas of Chapter 25, see *Guide to the Essentials of American History* or *Interactive Student Tutorial CD-ROM,* which contains interactive review activities, graphic organizers, and practice tests.

🗔 Reviewing the Chapter

Define These Terms
Match each term with the correct definition.

Column 1	Column 2
1. disarmament	a. period of rising stock prices
2. recession	b. reduction of armed forces and weapons of war
3. bull market	c. illegal bar
4. speakeasy	d. person opposed to organized government
5. anarchist	e. economic slump

Explore the Main Ideas
1. What happened in the Teapot Dome Scandal?
2. How did the process of buying on margin work?
3. How did women's lives change during the 1920s?
4. Describe the themes explored by two American writers of the 1920s.
5. What was the Red Scare?

🗔 Graph Activity

Look at the graph below and answer the following questions. **1.** In which year were the most cars sold? **2.** About how many cars were purchased in 1923? **Critical Thinking** Do you think car sales would have increased if Ford had not introduced the assembly line? Explain.

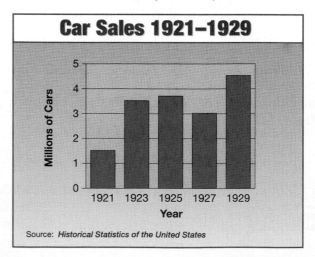

Car Sales 1921–1929

Source: *Historical Statistics of the United States*

🗐 Critical Thinking and Writing

1. **Exploring Unit Themes Role of Government** What role did the United States government play in the economy during the 1920s?

2. **Predicting Consequences** During the 1920s, many Americans bought consumer goods on credit and stocks on margin. How would this make economic conditions worse after the economy began to slow down?

3. **Linking Past and Present** People sometimes compare today's war on drugs with Prohibition. **(a)** How are the two similar? **(b)** How are they different?

4. **Understanding Chronology (a)** Which came first, the rise of communism in Russia or the Red Scare in the United States? **(b)** How did one event follow from the other?

🗐 Using Primary Sources

Reporter Louis Stark gave this account of the final words of Bartolomeo Vanzetti just before he was executed:

> 66 Vanzetti spoke in English. His voice was calm throughout. There was not the slightest tremor or quaver.... He said ... 'I am innocent of all crime, not only of this, but all. I am an innocent man.' Then he spoke his last words: 'I wish to forgive some people for what they are doing to me.' 99

Source: *The New York Times*, August 23, 1927.

Recognizing Points of View (a) What was Vanzetti's manner as he faced death? **(b)** What was Vanzetti's attitude toward those who were executing him? **(c)** If you had no other evidence about Vanzetti except his last words, would you think he was innocent or guilty? Explain.

ACTIVITY BANK

▶ Interdisciplinary Activity

Exploring Economics A few experts predicted that the United States economy was headed for trouble in the 1920s. Find out what economists are predicting about today's economy. Then, write a report in which you explain the experts' predictions.

▶ Career Skills Activity

Poets Write a poem in which you try to capture the mood of the 1920s. Remember that it was a complicated time in which some people had great wealth and fun and others struggled with poverty and racism. Try to reflect both sides of the times in your poem.

▶ Citizenship Activity

Examining Immigration Do research in current sources to find out about the main issues surrounding immigration today. Create an illustrated poster in which you state your own view on immigration issues or explore different viewpoints.

Internet Activity

Use the Internet to find sites dealing with some aspect of jazz in the 1920s. For instance, you might focus on a famous musician or singer, a well-known jazz club, or a dance such as the Charleston. Then, do further research both on and off the Internet for a class presentation. Try to include a recording of jazz.

EYEWITNESS Journal

Choose one of the following important figures of the 1920s: a flapper; an African American writer; a woman moving into the world of work while also taking care of a family; a bootlegger; an Italian immigrant; or a business leader. In your EYEWITNESS JOURNAL, describe the key events of the 1920s from your point of view.

Chapter 26

The Great Depression
1929–1941

In October 1929, a stock market crash brought the prosperity of the Roaring Twenties to a sudden end. The period that followed, known as the Great Depression, was the worst economic disaster in United States history. Poverty, hunger, and joblessness became widespread. Believing the government should not interfere too much with the economy, President Herbert Hoover took only limited action.

Seeking bolder action, Americans elected Franklin Delano Roosevelt as President in 1932. Roosevelt started a large number of programs to restart the economy. Though Roosevelt's programs provided help for many Americans, other people criticized him for expanding the size and role of the government.

Why Study History?

Few people saw the depression coming. Afterward, experts asked: What did we do wrong? By carefully studying the mistakes of the past, they hoped to prevent such a disaster from happening again. To focus on this connection, see this chapter's *Why Study History?* feature, "The Past Provides Lessons for Today."

American Events

●1929
Stock market crash sets off Great Depression

1933 ●
President Franklin Roosevelt begins New Deal

●1935
Social Security Act sets up pensions for elderly and unemployed

1929 1931 1933 1935

World Events

 1930 World Event
Effects of depression are felt worldwide

 1933 World Event
Economic problems lead to rise of dictator in Germany

![Viewing History logo] **Out of Work**

Millions of Americans were thrown out of work during the nation's worst economic depression. Isaac Soyer's painting Employment Agency *captures the despair felt by many Americans who lost their jobs.* ★ **How does this painting convey a mood of hopelessness?**

1935 ●	●1937	●1941
Wagner Act gives unions right to collective bargaining	President Roosevelt tries to increase number of Supreme Court justices	United States enters World War II

1935 **1937** **1939** **1941**

 1939 World Event
World War II begins in Europe

The Economy Crashes

As You Read

Explore These Questions
- Why did the stock market crash?
- How did the Great Depression affect the nation?
- How did Hoover try to end the crisis?

Define
- capital
- bankrupt
- relief program
- soup kitchen
- public works
- bonus

Identify
- Black Tuesday
- Great Depression
- Reconstruction Finance Corporation
- Bonus Army

 **SETTING the Scene** Herbert Hoover was confident as he campaigned for election in 1928. Pointing to the booming economy, Hoover declared:

66 We in America are nearer to the final triumph over poverty than ever before in the history of any land. The poorhouse is vanishing from among us. 99

Hoover took office in March 1929. Only seven months later, a stock market crash signaled the start of the worst economic crisis in the nation's history.

An Economy in Trouble

Hoover did realize that some Americans had not shared in the prosperity of the 1920s. Farmers, especially, faced hard times. Once in office, Hoover persuaded Congress to create the Federal Farm Board. It helped farmers market their products and worked to keep prices stable. Farmers, however, did not reduce production. As a result, prices for farm products stayed low.

Low farm prices were only one sign of trouble. The economy was slowing down. The demand for new homes and office buildings fell. Consumers were buying less. Wealth was distributed unevenly, with less than 1 percent of the population controlling a third of the nation's resources. However, the government kept few detailed records, so most Americans were unaware of the problems.

Stock Market Crash

By August 1929, a few investors had begun selling their stocks. They felt the boom might end soon. In September, more people decided to sell. The rash of selling caused stock prices to fall. Hoover reassured investors that the "business of the country is on a sound and prosperous basis." Still, the selling continued and stock prices tumbled.

Many investors had bought stocks on margin. (See page 676.) Now, with prices falling, brokers asked investors to pay what they owed. Investors who could not pay had to sell their stock. A panic quickly set in. Between October 24 and October 29, desperate people tried to unload millions of shares. As a result, stock prices dropped even more.

On Tuesday, October 29, a stampede of selling hit the New York Stock Exchange. Prices plunged because there were no buyers. People who thought they owned valuable stocks were left with worthless paper. Millionaires lost their fortunes overnight.

Connections With Science

First Lady Lou Henry Hoover was the first American woman to earn a degree in geology. Along with her husband, she won honors for translating a 1556 textbook on mining from Latin into English. She also published many scientific articles and founded the Women's Amateur Athletic Federation.

BROOKLYN DAILY EAGLE
And Complete Long Island News

WALL ST. IN PANIC AS STOCKS CRASH

Attempt Made to Kill Italy's Crown Prince

V̄iewing HISTORY | The Stock Market Crashes

After the dizzying prosperity of the Roaring Twenties, the stock market crash caught the nation by surprise. In the panic that followed, many people who had made fortunes lost them overnight. Here, a well-dressed New Yorker tries to sell the expensive car he bought when times were good. ★ **What effect did panic have on stock prices?**

After **Black Tuesday,** as it became known, business leaders tried to restore confidence in the economy. John D. Rockefeller told reporters, "My son and I have for some days been purchasing some common stocks." Replied comedian Eddie Cantor, "Sure, who else has any money left?"

Onset of the Depression

The period of economic hard times that followed the crash is known as the **Great Depression.** It lasted until 1941.

The stock market crash did not cause the Great Depression, but it did shake people's confidence in the economy. As the depression worsened, people tried to understand how the prosperity of the 1920s had vanished.

Causes

Among the chief causes of the Great Depression was overproduction. American factories and farms produced vast amounts of goods in the 1920s. Yet, because wages did not keep up with prices, workers could not afford to buy luxury goods. Farmers also had little money for cars and other items. Soon, factories and farms were producing more goods than people were buying. As orders slowed, factories closed or laid off workers.

Another cause of the depression was weakness in the banking system. During the 1920s, banks made unwise loans. For exam-ple, banks lent money to struggling farmers and people who invested in the stock market. When the stock market crashed, borrowers could not repay their loans. Without the money from the loans, the banks could not give depositors their money when they asked for it. Many banks were forced to close.

More than 5,000 banks closed between 1929 and 1932. When a bank closed, depositors lost the money they had in the bank. A family's savings could disappear overnight.

A cycle of disaster

After the stock market crash, the economy skidded downhill. One disaster triggered another. The stock market crash, for example, ruined many investors. Without **capital,** or money, from investors, businesses could no longer grow and expand. Businesses could not turn to banks for capital, since the banks were in trouble, too.

As factories cut back on production, they cut wages and laid off workers. Unemployed workers, in turn, had little money to spend, so demand for goods fell. In the end, many businesses declared that they had gone **bankrupt,** or unable to pay their debts. As bankrupt businesses closed their doors, even more people were thrown out of work.

The Great Depression led to a worldwide economic crisis. In the 1920s, the United States had loaned large sums to European

Why Study History?

Because the Past Provides Lessons for Today

★ ★

Historical Background

The stock market crash of 1929 ended the prosperity and optimism of the 1920s. In the disaster that followed, everyone looked for reasons why. Economists and historians examined the evidence to find out what had gone wrong—and why no one had seen it coming.

There was more than one answer. Wild speculation, risky loans, margin buying, and in the end, panic selling all contributed to the crash. (See page 703.) Unequal distribution of wealth and income, overproduction, and widespread bank failures fueled the depression that followed.

Connections to Today

Government and business leaders took steps to prevent another depression. Today, the federal government carefully regulates banking practices to avoid a repeat of the 1929 crash. The Federal Deposit Insurance Corporation (FDIC) insures bank deposits up to $100,000. If a bank fails, depositors can still get their money. The Securities and Exchange Commission (SEC) protects investors by watching for signs of illegal activities in the stock market.

A less serious stock crash in 1987 led the government to increase the power of the SEC. Today, SEC regulators can temporarily stop trading if average prices drop too greatly and too suddenly. By doing so, regulators hope to avoid the kind of panic that contributed to the great crash.

Connections to You

Since 1929, no stock market crash has been so severe. Because we learned from the mistakes of the past, you can face a safer future.

You, too, can learn from the past—what to avoid and what to copy. As historian Gerda Lerner noted, "Human beings have always used history in order to find their direction toward the future: to repeat the past or depart from it."

1. **Comprehension** (a) How does the FDIC protect bank depositors today? (b) How does the SEC protect stock investors?
2. **Critical Thinking** Describe two things that people could have done in the 1920s to help avoid the Great Depression.

 **Collecting Primary Sources** Put together a collection of primary sources on the Great Depression. Include the words of people who experienced hard times firsthand. You might also include copies of photographs.

The New York Stock Exchange is still an active center of American business.

nations. When American banks stopped making loans or demanded repayment of existing loans, European banks began to fail.

Hard Times

The United States had suffered other economic depressions. None, however, was as severe or lasted as long as the Great Depression. In earlier times, most Americans lived on farms and grew their own food. In the 1930s, millions of Americans lived in cities and worked in factories. When factories closed, the jobless had no money for food and no land on which to grow it.

Unemployment

As the depression spread, the unemployment rate soared. By the early 1930s, one in every four workers was jobless. Millions more worked shortened hours or took pay cuts. Many of the jobless lost their homes.

The chance of finding work was small. On an average day, one New York job agency had 5,000 people looking for work. Only about 300 found jobs. In another city, police had to keep order as 15,000 women pushed and shoved to apply for six jobs cleaning offices. Some of the jobless sold apples or shined shoes on street corners.

Human suffering

During the depression, families suffered. Marriage and birth rates dropped. Hungry parents and children searched through city dumps and restaurant garbage cans. In one school, a teacher ordered a thin little girl to go home to eat. "I can't," replied the girl. "This is my sister's day to eat."

The pressure of hard times led some families to split up. Fathers and even children as young as 13 or 14 years old left home to hunt for work. Their leaving meant the family had fewer people to feed.

Jobless men and women drifted from town to town looking for work. Some lived in railroad cars and hitched rides on freight trains. Louis Banks, a young black man, later described what it was like to "ride the rails":

66 Twenty-five or thirty would be out on the side of the rail, white and colored. They didn't have no mothers or

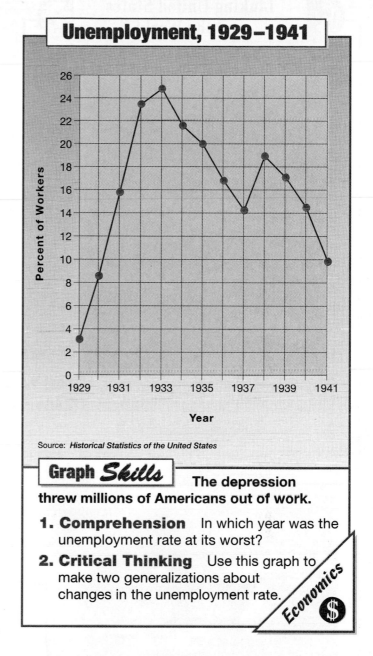

Unemployment, 1929–1941

Percent of Workers

Year

Source: *Historical Statistics of the United States*

Graph *Skills*

The depression threw millions of Americans out of work.

1. **Comprehension**   In which year was the unemployment rate at its worst?
2. **Critical Thinking**   Use this graph to make two generalizations about changes in the unemployment rate.

Economics $

sisters, they didn't have no home, they were dirty, they had overalls on, they didn't have no food, they didn't have anything. 99

Americans did their best to cope. Neighbors shared what little they had or exchanged services free of charge. Some families doubled up, taking in aunts, uncles, and cousins. Women began to grow vegetables and can foods instead of shopping in stores.

Still, the Great Depression shook Americans' belief in themselves. "No matter that others suffered the same fate, the inner voice whispered, 'I'm a failure,'" one unemployed man wrote.

United States

Austria

A Worldwide Depression

The Great Depression caused misery throughout the industrialized world. From Europe to Japan, the jobless struggled desperately to survive. At top, unemployed, homeless New Yorkers camp out in rickety shacks in Central Park. At bottom, Austrians line up for hot soup on a city street. ★ **How did the depression spread from the United States to other countries?**

Hoover Responds

President Hoover expressed deep concern about the suffering of the jobless. He tried to restore confidence in the economy by predicting better times ahead. However, Hoover did not believe that government should become directly involved in helping to end the business crisis. It was up to businesses, he felt, to work together to end the downslide.

Relief programs

At first, Hoover also opposed government **relief programs**—programs to help the needy. Instead, the President urged business leaders to keep workers employed and to maintain wages.

Hoover also called on private charities to help the needy. Churches set up **soup kitchens,** places where the hungry could get a free meal. Ethnic communities organized their own relief efforts. In San Francisco's Chinatown, the Six Companies gave out food and clothing. Father Divine, an African American religious leader in New York's Harlem, fed 3,000 hungry people a day. Mexican Americans and Puerto Ricans turned to mutualistas, or aid societies. Still, the numbers of needy soon overwhelmed private charities.

Hoover realized he had to take other steps. He set up public works programs. **Public works** are projects built by the government for public use. The government hired workers to build schools, construct dams, and pave highways.

By providing jobs, government programs enabled people to earn money. Workers could then spend their wages on goods. Hoover hoped that the increased demand for goods would lead to business recovery.

Hoover also approved the **Reconstruction Finance Corporation,** or RFC. The RFC loaned money to railroads, banks, and insurance companies to help them stay in business. Saving these businesses, Hoover hoped, would also save workers' jobs.

The depression deepens

Hoover did more to reverse hard times than any previous President. Still, his efforts had little effect. In 1931, as the third winter of the depression approached, more and more people joined the ranks of the hungry and homeless.

Many people blamed the President for doing too little. They called the shacks where the homeless lived Hoovervilles. The newspapers that the homeless covered themselves with to keep warm were called "Hoover blankets." The unemployed staged hunger marches against the government.

The Bonus Army

Veterans of World War I also took action. After the war, Congress had voted to give veterans a **bonus,** or additional sum of money, to be paid in 1945. In 1932, more than 20,000 jobless veterans marched to Washington to demand the bonus right away.

The **Bonus Army,** as the veterans were called, traveled to the capital as cheaply as possible. One decorated soldier walked from New Jersey. "I done it all by my feet—shoe leather," he told Congress. "I come to show you people that we need our bonus." Some veterans brought their wives and children. For two months, the Bonus Army camped in a tent city along the Potomac River.

In the end, the Senate rejected a bill to pay the bonus immediately. Senators thought that the cost would destroy any hope for the country's recovery. Many of the veterans went home. Thousands of others remained, vowing to stay until 1945 if necessary.

Local police tried to force the veterans to leave. Battles with police left four people dead. Hoover then ordered General Douglas MacArthur to clear out the veterans. Using cavalry, tanks, machine guns, and tear gas, MacArthur moved into the camp and burned it to the ground. An editorial in the *Washington News* expressed the shock many Americans felt:

66 What a pitiful spectacle is that of the great American Government, mightiest in the world, chasing unarmed men, women, and children with Army tanks.... If the Army must be called out to make war on unarmed citizens, this is no longer America. 99

After the attack on the Bonus Army, the President lost what little support he still had. Convinced that the country needed a change, Americans turned to a new leader.

★ Section 1 Review ★

Recall

1. **Identify** (a) Black Tuesday, (b) Great Depression, (c) Reconstruction Finance Corporation, (d) Bonus Army.
2. **Define** (a) capital, (b) bankrupt, (c) relief program, (d) soup kitchen, (e) public works, (f) bonus.

Comprehension

3. Why did stock prices drop in October 1929?
4. What problems did Americans face during the Great Depression?

5. What steps did Hoover take to ease the economic crisis?

Critical Thinking and Writing

6. **Understanding Causes and Effects** Describe how each of the following contributed to the Great Depression: (a) stock market crash, (b) overproduction, (c) bank closings.
7. **Identifying Main Ideas** Review the subsection Hoover Responds on page 706. (a) What is the main idea of the subsection? (b) State two facts that support the main idea.

★ ★

Activity **Formulating Questions** You're a reporter for a newspaper in 1932. It's up to you to explain President Hoover's policies to the American people. Write five questions you would like to ask Hoover during an interview.

The New Deal

As You Read

Explore These Questions
- Why did Americans elect Roosevelt in 1932?
- How did FDR restore faith in the banks?
- What programs made up the New Deal?

Define
- fireside chat
- surplus
- speculation

Identify
- Franklin Roosevelt
- Eleanor Roosevelt
- Frances Perkins
- Hundred Days
- New Deal
- Works Progress Administration
- Tennessee Valley Authority
- Federal Deposit Insurance Corporation

1932 campaign button

SETTING the Scene As the impact of the depression deepened, many Americans despaired. The government seemed helpless. In 1932, Democrats chose New York governor **Franklin Roosevelt** to run for President. Roosevelt seemed to respond to people's suffering. He told a friend:

> 66 I have looked into the faces of thousands of Americans. They have the frightened look of lost children ....They are saying: 'We're caught in something we don't understand; perhaps this fellow can help us out.' 99

Franklin D. Roosevelt

Franklin Delano Roosevelt, known as FDR, came from a wealthy, influential family. He attended Harvard University and Columbia Law School. In 1905, he married a distant cousin, Anna Eleanor Roosevelt, a niece of former President Theodore Roosevelt. Together, Franklin and **Eleanor Roosevelt** forged a powerful partnership.

During World War I, FDR served as assistant secretary of the navy. In 1920, he was the Democratic candidate for Vice President.

Then, in the summer of 1921, Roosevelt was stricken with a severe case of polio. The disease left his legs paralyzed. With his wife's help, FDR struggled to rebuild his strength. The battle taught him patience and courage. Roosevelt once joked that, after a person had spent two years just trying to wiggle his small toe, everything else seemed easy. In the end, he was able to walk with the aid of heavy leg braces and crutches.

In time, Roosevelt returned to public life. In 1928, he was elected governor of New York. Then, in 1932, the Democrats named him their presidential candidate. The Republicans again nominated Hoover, even though they knew he had little chance of winning.

A Call to Action

Roosevelt set a new tone right from the start. He broke tradition by taking a plane to the Democratic convention to accept the nomination in person. Standing before the delegates, he declared: "I pledge myself to a new deal for the American people."

FDR did not spell out what he meant by "a new deal." Still, he sounded a hopeful note. In campaign speeches, he promised to help the jobless, poor farmers, and the elderly.

Voters responded to FDR's confident manner and personal charm. On election day, he won a landslide victory. Democrats also gained many seats in Congress. On inauguration day, the new President addressed the American people with optimism:

66 This great nation will endure as it has endured, will revive and will prosper. So, first of all, let me assert my firm belief that the only thing we have to fear is fear itself—nameless, unreasoning, unjustified terror which paralyzes needed efforts to convert retreat into advance. 99

FDR then issued a call to action. "The nation asks for action and action now," he said. Many Americans welcomed this energetic new President, especially since Hoover's more cautious approach had failed to end the nation's economic crisis.

The Hundred Days

During his campaign for the presidency, FDR had sought advice on how to fight the depression. He turned to a number of college professors who were experts on economic issues. These experts, nicknamed the Brain Trust, helped Roosevelt to plan bold new programs.

Once in office, President Roosevelt chose able advisers. Harold Ickes (IH keez), a Republican reformer from Chicago, became secretary of the interior. FDR named social worker **Frances Perkins** as secretary of labor. Perkins was the first woman to hold a Cabinet post.

The new President moved forward on many fronts. He urged his staff to "take a method and try it. If it fails, admit it and try another. But above all try something."

Starting with the banks

Roosevelt's first challenge was the nation's crumbling banking system. Many banks had closed. Fearful depositors had withdrawn their savings from others. People hid their money under mattresses or buried it in their yards.

FDR knew that without sound banks, the economy could not recover. On his second day in office, he declared a "bank holiday." He closed every bank in the country for eight days. He then asked Congress to pass the Emergency Banking Relief Act. Under this act, only those banks with enough funds to meet depositors' demands could reopen. Others had to stay closed.

A week after taking office, President Roosevelt spoke to Americans by radio. Under the new law, the President told the people, "it

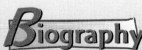 **Franklin and Eleanor Roosevelt**

Franklin and Eleanor Roosevelt belonged to a leading New York family. Both believed that the wealthy had a duty to help those less fortunate. As President, FDR put this belief into action. Eleanor used her position as First Lady to speak out on issues ranging from conditions in coal mines to justice for African Americans. She also acted as the President's "eyes and ears," traveling about the country and reporting back to him. He would often begin press conferences with the words: "My Missus says...". ★ **FDR told Americans that "the only thing we have to fear is fear itself." What do you think he meant?**

Skills
FOR LIFE

Critical Thinking	Managing Information	Communication	Maps, Charts, and Graphs

Public Speaking

A middle school student gives a speech.

How Will I Use This Skill?

Knowing how to prepare and deliver a speech is a skill that you will find useful throughout your life. Some speeches are informative, such as an oral report in school or a presentation at the workplace. Other speeches may be persuasive. In a job interview, for example, you will speak about yourself and your skills to persuade an employer that you are the right person for the job.

LEARN the Skill

You can prepare and deliver a speech by following these steps:

❶ Determine the topic and purpose of your speech. Some speeches are meant to be entertaining, while others may be informative or persuasive.

❷ Understand the nature of your audience so that you can decide the appropriate content and style for your speech. For example, you would not speak to children the same way you would speak to adults. You would not address people who agree with you the same way you would address people with opposing ideas.

❸ Prepare your speech. Do research to collect supporting information. Decide the style you will use. For example, will you be serious at all times or will you use some humor? Write your speech and practice it several times.

❹ Deliver your speech. Speak clearly. If your audience is in front of you, remember to establish eye contact and use appropriate gestures. You might invite questions after the speech.

PRACTICE the Skill

Review the material about President Roosevelt's fireside chats on page 711. Then, answer the following questions:

❶ (a) What was the topic of FDR's first fireside chat? (b) Why did he think it was necessary to give the speech?

❷ (a) Who was Roosevelt's audience? (b) Why did his speeches need to be both informative and persuasive?

❸ (a) What factual information did FDR need to support his first fireside chat? (b) What style of speaking did he use?

❹ Do you think the chats might have been more effective if people could have seen the President speaking? Explain.

APPLY the Skill

Choose a topic that interests you. Then, follow the steps above to prepare and deliver a three-minute speech to the class. Afterward, invite comments from classmates as to how you might improve your presentation.

Viewing HISTORY — Recruiting for the CCC

Posters like this one encouraged young men to join the Civilian Conservation Corps. The government provided "CCC boys" with housing, clothes, and food. This allowed them to send most of their earnings home to their families. After a hard day's work, the young men could play sports, go to dances, or attend self-improvement classes. ★ **How did the CCC benefit the country?**

is safer to keep your money in a reopened bank than under your mattress."

The radio broadcast worked. FDR explained things so clearly, said humorist Will Rogers, that even the bankers understood it. Reassured by the President, depositors returned their money to banks, and the banking system grew stronger.

FDR gave 30 radio speeches while in office. He called them **fireside chats** because he spoke from a chair near a fireplace in the White House. All across the nation, families gathered around their radios to listen. Many felt the President understood their problems.

A flood of new laws

The bank bill was the first of many bills FDR sent to Congress during his first three months in office. Between March 9 and June 16, 1933, Congress passed 15 major new laws. Even the President admitted he was "a bit shell-shocked" by the **Hundred Days,** as this period was called.

The bills covered programs from job relief to planning for economic recovery. Together, they made up Roosevelt's **New Deal.** The New Deal had three main goals: relief for the unemployed, plans for recovery, and reforms to prevent another depression.

Providing Relief

In 1933, when Roosevelt took office, 13 million Americans were out of work. The President asked Congress for a variety of programs to help the jobless.

CCC and FERA

Among the earliest New Deal programs was the Civilian Conservation Corps (CCC). The CCC hired unemployed single men between the ages of 18 and 25. For $1 a day, they planted trees, built bridges, worked on flood control projects, and developed new parks. The CCC served a double purpose. It conserved natural resources, and it gave jobs to young people.

The Federal Emergency Relief Administration (FERA) gave federal money to state and local agencies. These agencies then distributed the money to the unemployed.

WPA

In 1935, the Emergency Relief Appropriations Act set up the **Works Progress Administration** (WPA). The WPA put the jobless to work building hospitals, schools, parks, playgrounds, and airports.

The WPA also hired artists, photographers, actors, writers, and composers. Artists painted murals on public buildings. The Federal Theatre put on new plays for adults and children, as well as classics by writers such as Shakespeare.

Writers collected information about American life, folklore, and traditions. Some WPA writers interviewed African Americans who had lived under slavery. Today, scholars still use these "slave narratives" to learn firsthand about slave life.

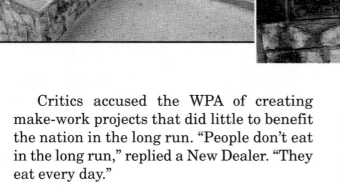

HISTORY HAPPENED HERE

San Antonio River Walk

You may ride down a highway, cross a bridge, or enter a post office—and never know you are seeing a piece of history. Hundreds of projects like these were built during the depression by the Works Progress Administration. On the San Antonio River in Texas, WPA workers constructed a network of concrete walkways, bridges, and stairs. Today, tourists from around the world enjoy the hotels, shops, and restaurants along the San Antonio River Walk, or Paseo del Rio.

★ *To learn more about this historic site, write: San Antonio Visitors Bureau, P.O. Box 2277, San Antonio, TX 78298-2277.*

◀ *WPA plaque on the River Walk*

Critics accused the WPA of creating make-work projects that did little to benefit the nation in the long run. "People don't eat in the long run," replied a New Dealer. "They eat every day."

Promoting Recovery

To bring about recovery, the President had to boost both industry and farming. He called for programs that greatly expanded the government's role in the economy.

Help for industry

To help industry, New Dealers drew up plans to control production, stabilize prices, and keep workers on the job. A key new law was the National Industrial Recovery Act (NIRA). Under this law, each industry wrote a code, or set of rules and standards, for production, wages, prices, and working conditions. The NIRA tried to end price cutting and worker layoffs.

To enforce the new codes, Congress set up the National Recovery Administration (NRA). Companies that followed the NRA codes stamped a blue eagle on their products. The government encouraged people to do business only with companies displaying the NRA eagle. The NRA soon ran into trouble, however. Many companies ignored the codes. Also, small businesses felt that the codes favored the biggest firms.

The NIRA also set up the Public Works Administration (PWA). It promoted recovery by hiring workers for thousands of public works projects. PWA workers built the Grand Coulee Dam in Washington, public schools in Los Angeles, and two aircraft carriers for the navy. Despite these efforts, the PWA did little to bring about recovery.

Help for farmers

On farms, overproduction remained the main problem. Surpluses kept prices and farmers' incomes low. A **surplus** occurs when farmers produce more than they can sell.

To help farmers, the President asked Congress to pass the Agricultural Adjustment Act (AAA). Under the AAA, the government paid farmers not to grow certain crops. Roosevelt hoped that with smaller harvests, prices would rise.

The government also paid farmers to plow surplus crops under the soil and to dispose of surplus cows and pigs. Many Americans were outraged that crops and livestock were being destroyed when people in the cities were going hungry. Yet the plan seemed necessary to help farmers recover.

The Rural Electrification Administration (REA) provided money to extend electric lines to rural areas. The number of farms with electricity rose from 10 percent to 25 percent. A farm woman recalled, "I just turned on the light and kept looking at Paw. It was the first time I'd ever seen him after dark." Electricity helped save many farms from ruin. For example, refrigeration meant that dairy farmers did not have to worry about milk going sour before it could be sent to market.

TVA

Perhaps the boldest program of the Hundred Days was the **Tennessee Valley Authority** (TVA). It set out to remake the Tennessee River valley. This vast region often suffered terrible floods. Because the farmland was so poor, more than half the region's families were on relief.

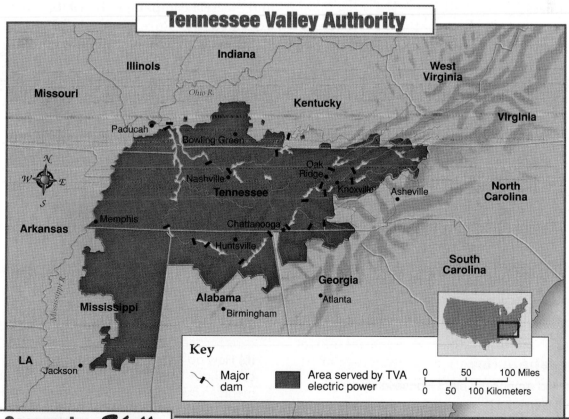

Tennessee Valley Authority

Key

⌇ Major dam

▮ Area served by TVA electric power

Geography *Skills* The Tennessee Valley Authority directed projects that helped millions of people in the South.

1. **Location** On the map, locate: **(a)** Tennessee River, **(b)** Cumberland River, **(c)** Nashville, **(d)** Knoxville.

2. **Interaction** What did the Tennessee Valley Authority do to control flooding of the Tennessee and Cumberland rivers?

3. **Critical Thinking** Based on this map, why was the Tennessee River valley a good area in which to develop hydroelectric power?

The TVA was a daring experiment in regional planning. To control flooding, TVA engineers built 40 dams in seven states. (See the map on page 713.) The dams also produced cheap electric power. In addition to building dams, the TVA deepened river channels for shipping. It planted new forests to conserve soil and developed new fertilizers to improve farmland. The agency also set up schools and health centers.

The TVA sparked a furious debate. Critics argued that the government had no right to interfere in the economy of the region. Power companies in the Tennessee River valley were especially outraged. They pointed out that the government could supply electrical power more cheaply than a private company could. Having to compete with the government, they said, might force them out of business.

Supporters replied that the TVA showed how the government could use its resources to help private enterprise. In the end, the program transformed a region of poor farms into a rich and productive area.

Long-Term Reforms

The third New Deal goal was to prevent another depression. During the Hundred Days, Congress passed laws regulating the stock market and the banking system. The Truth-in-Securities Act was designed to end wild **speculation**—risky buying and selling of stocks in the hope of making a quick profit. Experts agreed that uncontrolled speculation was a leading cause of the 1929 crash.

The **Federal Deposit Insurance Corporation** (FDIC) insured savings accounts in banks approved by the government. If a bank insured by the FDIC failed, the government would make sure depositors received their money.

Later New Deal laws strengthened government regulations. Laws regulated gas and electric companies. In 1938, a new law extended the Pure Food and Drug Act of 1906. It protected consumers by requiring manufacturers to list the ingredients of certain products. Medicines also had to undergo strict tests before they could be sold.

★ Section 2 Review ★

Recall

1. **Locate** Tennessee River.
2. **Identify** (a) Franklin Roosevelt, (b) Eleanor Roosevelt, (c) Frances Perkins, (d) Hundred Days, (e) New Deal, (f) Works Progress Administration, (g) Tennessee Valley Authority, (h) Federal Deposit Insurance Corporation.
3. **Define** (a) fireside chat, (b) surplus, (c) speculation.

Comprehension

4. Why did Americans elect Roosevelt in 1932?
5. What steps did Roosevelt take to end the banking crisis?
6. (a) What were the three main goals of the New Deal? (b) Describe one law aimed at achieving each goal.

Critical Thinking and Writing

7. **Making Inferences** Roosevelt promised the nation a "new deal," but he never spelled out exactly what he meant by that. Why do you think Americans responded to him so strongly?
8. **Linking Past and Present** (a) How did Americans respond to Roosevelt's fireside chats? (b) How do Presidents communicate with Americans today? (c) How do you think the use of mass media to communicate with the public has affected the way Americans view their Presidents?

★ ★

Activity **Writing Persuasively** Do you have the "gift of gab"? You are a speechwriter for FDR. Write a radio speech in which you explain to ordinary Americans one of the programs of the New Deal. Remember, your goal is to be both reassuring and informative.

3 ★ Reaction to the New Deal

As You Read

Explore These Questions
- Why did some Americans object to the New Deal?
- How did New Deal programs help workers and the elderly?
- Why was the New Deal a turning point in American history?

Define
- pension
- collective bargaining
- sitdown strike
- unemployment insurance
- laissez faire
- deficit spending
- national debt

Identify
- Huey Long
- Francis Townsend
- Charles Coughlin
- Liberty League
- Wagner Act
- John L. Lewis
- Social Security Act

SETTING the Scene The first hundred days of the New Deal encouraged a sense of hope among Americans. As noted political columnist Walter Lippmann commented:

❝ At the end of February, we were a [group] of disorderly panic-stricken mobs and factions. In the hundred days from March to June, we became again an organized nation confident of our power to provide for our own security and control our own destiny. ❞

Still, the New Deal failed to end the depression. As hard times lingered, critics of FDR and his policies grew louder.

Critics of the New Deal

From the beginning, a number of Americans had opposed the New Deal. Many of these critics wanted the government to do more. Others wanted it to do less.

Senator **Huey Long** of Louisiana had supported Roosevelt in 1932. However, Long soon turned on the President. The Kingfish, as Long was nicknamed, believed that FDR had not gone far enough to help the poor. Adopting the motto "Share Our Wealth," Long called for heavy taxes on the rich. He

Huey Long

promised to use the tax money to provide every family with a house, a car, and a decent annual income. Millions of people, especially the poor, cheered Long's idea. They overlooked the fact that he had used bribery and threats to win political power.

A California doctor, **Francis Townsend,** also had a plan. The government, he said, had turned its back on older citizens. Townsend wanted everyone over age 60 to get a pension of $200 a month. A **pension** is a sum of money paid to people on a regular basis after they retire. People receiving the pension would have to retire, thus freeing a job for someone else. They would also agree to spend the pension money at once to boost the economy.

Like Long and Townsend, **Charles Coughlin** (KAWG lihn), a Roman Catholic priest, felt the New Deal did not go far enough. Father Coughlin spoke over the radio each week to almost 10 million listeners. The popular "radio priest" criticized Roosevelt for not taking strong action against bankers and rich investors.

On the other hand, many conservative political and business leaders felt the New Deal went too far. They formed the **Liberty League** to combat FDR's actions. The League complained that the New Deal interfered too

much with business and with people's lives. The government, they warned, was taking away basic American freedoms.

FDR and the Supreme Court

In 1935, the Supreme Court entered the debate. Roosevelt and his advisers defended the New Deal by comparing the depression to a national emergency. The government had to increase its powers, they said, just as it had during World War I. The Supreme Court disagreed.

In 1935, the Supreme Court ruled that the National Industrial Recovery Act was unconstitutional. The NIRA, said the Court, gave too much power to the President and to the federal government. A year later, the Court struck down the Agricultural Adjustment Act. Then it overturned nine other New Deal laws. To Roosevelt, the Supreme Court rulings threatened not only the New Deal but his ability to lead the nation.

A plan to expand the Court

Roosevelt waited until after the 1936 election to take action. He easily beat his Republican opponent. FDR thought the election results showed that Americans favored his programs.

Soon after his inauguration in January 1937, Roosevelt put forward a plan to reshape the federal courts. He called for raising the number of Justices on the Supreme Court from 9 to 15. The change would make it possible for him to appoint six new Justices who supported his programs.

A defeat and a victory

The President's move raised a loud outcry. Both supporters and critics of the New Deal accused him of trying to "pack" the Court with Justices who supported his views. They saw his move as a threat to the separation of powers set up by the Constitution.

For six months, the President fought for his plan. Even his allies in Congress deserted him. Finally, he withdrew his proposal.

Still, in the end, Roosevelt got the Supreme Court majority he wanted without a battle. One Justice who had voted against many New Deal laws changed his views. Another retired. FDR filled his place with a new Justice who was favorable to his programs. During his years in office, FDR had the chance to appoint nine new Justices—more than any President since Washington.

Labor Reforms

During the New Deal, FDR supported programs to help workers. In 1935, Congress passed the National Labor Relations Act, or **Wagner Act.** Senator Robert Wagner, the act's sponsor, was a strong supporter of labor.

Unions grow stronger

The Wagner Act protected American workers from unfair management practices, such as firing a worker for joining a union. It also guaranteed workers the right to collec-

New Deal Programs

Program	Initials	Begun	Purpose
Civilian Conservation Corps	CCC	1933	Provided jobs for young men to plant trees, build bridges and parks, and set up flood control projects
Tennessee Valley Authority	TVA	1933	Built dams to provide cheap electric power to seven southern states; set up schools and health centers
Federal Emergency Relief Administration	FERA	1933	Gave relief to unemployed and needy
Agricultural Adjustment Administration	AAA	1933	Paid farmers not to grow certain crops
National Recovery Administration	NRA	1933	Enforced codes that regulated wages, prices, and working conditions
Public Works Administration	PWA	1933	Built ports, schools, and aircraft carriers
Federal Deposit Insurance Corporation	FDIC	1933	Insured savings accounts in banks approved by the government
Rural Electrification Administration	REA	1935	Loaned money to extend electricity to rural areas
Works Progress Administration	WPA	1935	Employed men and women to build hospitals, schools, parks, and airports; employed artists, writers, and musicians
Social Security Act	SSA	1935	Set up a system of pensions for the elderly, unemployed, and people with disabilities

Graph Skills Congress passed dozens of new laws as part of FDR's New Deal. This chart describes 10 major New Deal programs.

1. **Comprehension** (a) Which programs provided work for the unemployed? (b) Which provided financial aid?
2. **Critical Thinking** Which of the New Deal programs do you consider to be most important today? Explain.

Economics $

tive bargaining. **Collective bargaining** is the process in which a union representing a group of workers negotiates with management for a contract. Workers had fought for this right since the late 1800s.

The Wagner Act helped union membership grow from 3 million to 9 million during the 1930s. Union membership got a further boost when **John L. Lewis** set up the Congress of Industrial Organizations (CIO). The CIO represented workers in whole industries, such as steel, automobiles, and textiles.

With more members, unions increased their bargaining power. They also became a powerful force in politics.

Struggles and victories

Despite the Wagner Act, employers tried to stop workers from joining unions. Violent confrontations often resulted.

Workers then tried a new strategy. At the Goodyear Tire Factory in Akron, Ohio, workers staged a **sitdown strike.** They stopped all machines and refused to leave the factory until Goodyear recognized their union. The sitdown strike worked. Workers at other factories made use of this method until the Supreme Court outlawed it in 1939.

Roosevelt persuaded Congress to help nonunion workers, too. The Fair Labor Standards Act of 1938 set a minimum wage of 40

A monthly check to you —

FOR THE REST
OF YOUR LIFE
- - BEGINNING
WHEN YOU ARE
65

GET YOUR
SOCIAL SECURITY
ACCOUNT NUMBER
promptly

Your monthly
Social Security
check

WHO IS ELIGIBLE

HOW TO RETURN APPLICATION

Social Security Board

INFORMATION MAY BE OBTAINED AT ANY POST OFFICE

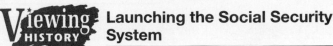

Posters like these encouraged workers to sign up for the new Social Security system. Today, Social Security continues to provide income for retired or disabled Americans.
★ **How does the government get the money to pay Social Security benefits?**

cents an hour. The act also set maximum hours—44 a week—for workers in a number of industries. At the same time, it banned children under the age of 16 from working in these industries.

Social Security

On another front, the President sought to help the elderly. In the 1930s, the United States was the only major industrial nation that did not have a formal pension program. FDR and Secretary of Labor Perkins pushed to enact an old-age pension program.

In September 1935, Congress passed the **Social Security Act.** The new law had three parts. First, it set up a system of pensions for older people. Payments from employers and employees supported this system.

Second, the new act set up the nation's first system of **unemployment insurance.** People who lost their jobs received small payments until they found work again. Third, the act gave states money to support dependent children and people with disabilities.

Critics condemned Social Security. Some argued that it did too little for the elderly and unemployed. Others pointed out that it

did not include farm workers, domestic servants, or the self-employed—many of whom were women or members of minority groups. Conservatives, on the other hand, saw Social Security as another way for the government to meddle in people's lives.

Despite these attacks, the Social Security system survived. It has been expanded over the years. Today, it provides medical benefits to older Americans as well as pensions and unemployment insurance.

The New Deal: Good or Bad?

The New Deal changed American government forever. Ever since, Americans have debated whether the change was good or bad for the country.

Arguments against the New Deal

Before the 1930s, most Americans had little contact with the federal government. New Deal programs, however, touched almost every citizen. The federal government grew in size and power. It took on new jobs—from helping the needy to ensuring that the economy prospered.

Many people worried about the increased power of government. They complained that the government was intruding into people's lives, threatening both individual freedoms and private property. These critics called for a return to the traditional policy of **laissez faire**—a policy based on the idea that government should play as small a role as possible in the economy. Former President Hoover warned:

66 Either we shall have a society based upon ordered liberty and the initiative of the individual, or we shall have a planned society that means dictation no matter what you

call it or who does it. There is no half-way ground. **99**

Critics also expressed alarm because the government was spending more than it took in. This practice of **deficit spending** was creating a huge increase in the **national debt,** or the total sum of money the government owes.

Finally, despite its vast spending, the New Deal had not achieved its major goal—ending the depression. In fact, full economic recovery did not come until 1941. By then, the United States was producing goods for nations fighting in World War II.

Arguments for the New Deal

Supporters of the New Deal noted that FDR had steered the nation through the worst days of the depression. New Deal legislation had ended the banking crisis, protected farmers, and found work for millions of unemployed.

Supporters also argued that the government had a responsibility to use its power to help all its citizens, not just business and the wealthy. Programs like Social Security, New Dealers said, were necessary for national survival.

Most important of all, supporters argued, the New Deal had saved the nation's democratic system. Elsewhere in the world, people were turning to dictators to lead them out of hard times. President Roosevelt, on the other hand, worked to use the powers of the federal government to restore the nation to economic health while preserving its liberties. Roosevelt declared:

> **66** I believe in my heart that...here in America we are waging a great and successful war. It is not alone a war against want and destitution and economic demoralization....It is a war for the survival of democracy. **99**

Over the years, Americans have continued to debate the expanded role of government that began during the New Deal. The question of whether government management of the economy will harm the free enterprise system remains a lively one today.

★ Section 3 Review ★

Recall

1. **Identify** (a) Huey Long, (b) Francis Townsend, (c) Charles Coughlin, (d) Liberty League, (e) Wagner Act, (f) John L. Lewis, (g) Social Security Act.
2. **Define** (a) pension, (b) collective bargaining, (c) sitdown strike, (d) unemployment insurance, (e) laissez faire, (f) deficit spending, (g) national debt.

Comprehension

3. Describe why each of the following criticized the New Deal: (a) Huey Long, (b) Francis Townsend, (c) the Liberty League.
4. How did the Wagner Act help workers?

5. (a) How did the New Deal change the role of the government? (b) State one argument for and one argument against the New Deal.

Critical Thinking and Writing

6. **Defending a Position** (a) Why did many Americans oppose Roosevelt's plan to increase the size of the Supreme Court? (b) Do you agree or disagree with these critics? Explain.
7. **Linking Past and Present** (a) Describe three ways in which the federal government directly affects your life today. (b) Do you think you are better off or worse off as a result? Explain.

★ ★

Activity Writing an Editorial Which side are you on? Write an editorial in which you agree or disagree with one of the critics of the New Deal—Huey Long, Francis Townsend, Charles Coughlin, or the Liberty League. Give reasons for the position you take.

Surviving Hard Times

As You Read

Explore These Questions
- What was the Dust Bowl?
- How did the Great Depression affect women and minorities?
- How did Americans find escape from the hardships of the depression?

Define
- migrant worker
- civil rights
- repatriate

Identify
- Dust Bowl
- Black Cabinet
- Mary McLeod Bethune
- Indian New Deal
- John Steinbeck
- Richard Wright
- Dorothea Lange

SETTING the Scene A cotton picker in Texas sat by the road as others worked in nearby fields. "I picked all week and made 85 cents," the man said in a hopeless voice. "I can starve sitting down a lot easier than I can picking cotton."

Across the country, Americans struggled to survive. New Deal programs helped some. Others made ends meet as best they could.

The Dust Bowl

During much of the 1930s, states from Texas to the Dakotas suffered a severe drought. One region—including parts of Oklahoma, Kansas, Colorado, New Mexico, and Texas—was especially hard hit. The topsoil dried out. High winds carried the soil away in blinding dust storms. As a result, this area of the Great Plains became known as the **Dust Bowl.**

Black blizzards

Dust storms, called black blizzards, buried farmhouses, fences, and even trees. People put shutters over doors and windows, but the dust blew in anyway. Even food crunched when it was chewed.

Dust storms were widespread. One storm blew dust from Oklahoma to Albany, New York, and out into the Atlantic Ocean. When the dry winds came, a third of the Great Plains just blew away. A Kansas farmer sadly reported that he sat by his window counting the farms going by.

What caused the disaster? Years of overgrazing by cattle and plowing by farmers destroyed the grasses that once held the soil in place. The drought of the 1930s and high winds did the rest.

Migrant workers

Hardest hit by the drought and dust storms were poor farmers in Oklahoma and Arkansas. Hundreds of these "Okies" and "Arkies" packed their belongings into cars and trucks and headed west. They became **migrant workers**—people who move from one region to another in search of work. They hoped to find jobs in the orchards and farms of California, Oregon, or Washington.

Once they reached the West Coast, the migrants faced a new disaster—they were not wanted. Local citizens feared that the newcomers would take away jobs from people already living in the West. Sometimes, angry crowds blocked the highways and sent the migrants away. Those who did find work were paid little. They lived in tents and cardboard shacks without any water or electricity.

Working Women

Working women faced special problems during the depression. If jobs were available, employers hired men before they would hire women. Even the federal government refused to hire a woman if her husband had a job. Some New Deal programs, such as the CCC, were not open to women at all.

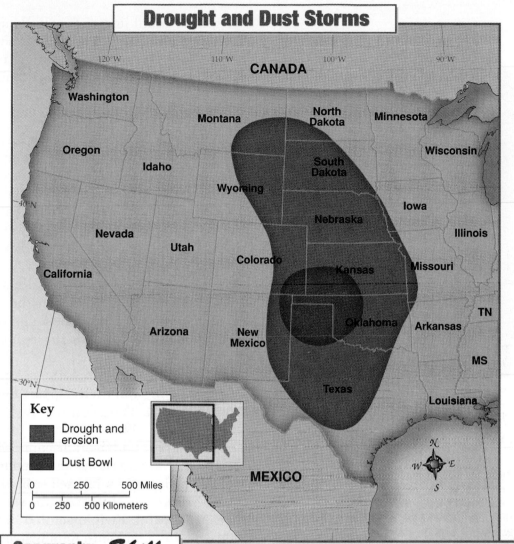

Drought and Dust Storms

Key

Drought and erosion

Dust Bowl

0 250 500 Miles
0 250 500 Kilometers

Geography Skills In the 1930s, drought and wind erosion ruined farmlands across much of the Great Plains. The hardest hit area became known as the Dust Bowl.

1. **Location** On the map, locate: **(a)** Kansas, **(b)** Oklahoma, **(c)** Texas, **(d)** Nebraska, **(e)** South Dakota.

2. **Region** According to the map, which three states were most affected by severe drought and erosion?

3. **Critical Thinking** Why did many farmers migrate from the Great Plains to California in the 1930s?

Women in the workplace

Despite such obstacles, millions of women earned wages in order to support themselves and their families. During the 1930s, the number of married women in the workforce increased by 52 percent. Educated women took jobs as secretaries, school teachers, and social workers. Other women earned a living as maids, factory workers, and seamstresses.

Some women workers struck for better pay. In San Antonio, Texas, at least 80 percent of the pecan shellers were Mexican American women. When employers lowered their pay, a young worker, Emma Tenayuca, organized the shellers and led them off the job. Tenayuca said later, "I had a basic faith in the American idea of freedom and fairness. I felt something had to be done."

Biography · Marian Anderson

In 1939, Marian Anderson was already a world-famous singer. Yet she was refused permission to sing at a private hall in Washington. Outraged, Eleanor Roosevelt arranged for Anderson to give a concert at the Lincoln Memorial. On Easter, some 75,000 people gathered to hear Anderson. Anderson later became the first African American to sing at the Metropolitan Opera in New York. ★ **Why was the Lincoln Memorial a fitting place for Anderson's concert?**

An active First Lady

Eleanor Roosevelt created a new role for herself as First Lady. Acting as the "eyes and ears" of the President, she toured the nation—traveling 40,000 miles in one year alone. She visited farms and Indian reservations and even traveled deep down into a coal mine. She talked to homemakers, observing the condition of their clothing on the washline. Back in Washington, she told the President what she had seen and heard.

The First Lady did more than just aid the President. She used her position to speak out for women's rights, as well as other issues. She gave press conferences for women reporters only. In her newspaper column, "My Day," she called on Americans to live up to the goal of equal justice for all. By speaking out on social issues, Eleanor Roosevelt angered some people. However, many other Americans admired her strong stands.

African Americans

When the Great Depression hit, African American workers were often the first to lose their jobs. Many times, they were denied public works jobs. At relief centers, young African American men were threatened or beaten when they signed up for work. Some charities even refused to serve blacks at centers giving out food to the needy.

Eleanor Roosevelt and others close to the President urged him to improve the situation of African Americans. Thousands of young black men learned a trade through the CCC, for example.

FDR reached out to African Americans. In doing so, he won their support for the Democratic party. The President invited black leaders to the White House to advise him. These unofficial advisers became known as the **Black Cabinet.** They included Robert C. Weaver, a Harvard-educated economist, and **Mary McLeod Bethune,** a well-known Florida educator. FDR appointed Bethune to head the National Youth Administration's Division of Negro Affairs. She was the first African American to head a government agency.

Often, Roosevelt followed the advice of the Black Cabinet. However, when African American leaders pressed the President to support an antilynching law, he refused. He feared that by doing so he would lose the support of southerners in Congress for his New Deal programs.

Connections With Civics

Arthur W. Mitchell of Chicago was the first black Democrat elected to Congress. In 1937, a railroad conductor ejected Representative Mitchell from a Pullman car because Arkansas state law prohibited blacks from riding in the same car as whites. Mitchell took his case to the Supreme Court and won.

Many black leaders called on African Americans to unite to achieve **civil rights**— the rights due to all citizens. They used their votes, won higher-level government jobs, and kept up pressure for equal treatment. Slowly, they made a few gains. However, the struggle for civil rights would take many more years.

Mexican Americans

By the 1930s, Mexican Americans worked in cities around the country. A large number, however, were farm workers in the West and Southwest. There, they faced discrimination in education, jobs, and at the polls.

In good times, employers had encouraged Mexicans to move north and take jobs. When hard times struck, however, many Americans wanted Mexicans to be **repatriated,** that is, sent back to their original country. More than 400,000 people were rounded up and sent to Mexico. Some of them were citizens who had been born in the United States.

Asian Americans

Asian Americans also faced discrimination. They were often refused service at barber shops, restaurants, and other public places. White Americans resented Chinese, Japanese, and Filipino workers who competed with them for scarce jobs. Sometimes violence against Asians erupted.

Responding to pressure, the government sought to reduce the number of Asians in the United States. In 1935, FDR signed the Repatriation Act. This law provided free transportation for Filipinos who agreed to return to the Philippines and not come back. Many took advantage of this offer.

Native Americans

In 1924, Congress had granted all Native Americans citizenship. Still, most Native Americans lived in terrible poverty. President Roosevelt encouraged new policies toward Native Americans.

In the 1930s, Congress passed a series of laws that have been called the **Indian New Deal.** The laws gave Native American nations greater control over their own affairs.

Cause and Effect

Causes

- Great Depression deepens
- Banking system nears collapse
- Millions of people are jobless
- Many businesses are bankrupt
- FDR becomes President

The New Deal

Effects

- Role of government in the economy increases
- Social Security gives pensions to retired people
- People who lose their jobs can receive money from unemployment insurance
- Savings accounts in banks are insured by government
- Government pays for building projects, such as highways, schools, and dams

Effects Today

- Increased government spending contributes to national debt
- Congress debates how to reform Social Security system
- People disagree about proper size of government

Graphic Organizer *Skills*

The New Deal eased the impact of the depression. Its effects are still felt today.

1. **Comprehension** What problems did the New Deal try to solve?
2. **Critical Thinking** Do you think the New Deal led to lower or higher taxes? Explain.

Economics $

Portraits of the Rural Poor

Photographer Dorothea Lange gained fame for pictures like this one that showed the despair of rural Americans during the depression. Commenting on her work, Lange said, "We don't see what's right before us. We don't see it until someone tells us." ★ **Why do you think the government hired photographers like Dorothea Lange?**

The President chose John Collier, a longtime defender of Indian rights, to head the Bureau of Indian Affairs. He ended the government policy of breaking up Indian land holdings. In 1934, Congress passed the Indian Reorganization Act (IRA). It protected and even expanded land holdings of Native American reservations.

The government also ended its efforts to wipe out Native American religions. Rather, it supported the right of Native Americans to live according to their own traditions. It also strengthened Native American governments by letting reservations organize corporations and develop their own economic projects.

To provide jobs during the depression, the government set up the Indian Emergency Conservation Work Group. It employed Native Americans in programs of soil-erosion control, irrigation, and land development. In 1935, Congress launched the Indian Arts and Craft Board. It promoted the creation and sale of Native American art.

Arts of the Depression

Creative artists recorded images of depression life. Many writers depicted the hard times Americans faced across the country. In *The Grapes of Wrath,* **John Steinbeck** told the heartbreaking story of the Okies:

> 66 Carloads, caravans, homeless and hungry.... They streamed over the mountains, hungry and restless—restless as ants, scurrying to find work to do...anything, any burden to bear, for food. 99

Black writers of the Harlem Renaissance continued to create new works. In *Uncle Tom's Children,* **Richard Wright** described racial violence against black southerners.

Many painters turned to familiar themes. The huge murals of Thomas Hart Benton brought the history of the frontier to life. In *American Gothic,* Grant Wood painted an Iowa farmer and his daughter who look determined enough to survive any hardship.

The government sent out photographers to create a lasting record of American life during the Great Depression. The vivid photographs of **Dorothea Lange** showed the suffering of Dust Bowl farm families. Margaret Bourke-White photographed poor tenant farmers in the South.

Escaping Hard Times

Americans found ways to escape the hard times of the 1930s. Among their favorite pastimes were listening to the radio and going to the movies.

Radio

Every night, millions of Americans tuned in to their favorite radio programs. Comedians such as George Burns and Gracie Allen made people forget their troubles for a time. Classical music broadcasts let Americans enjoy music that they could not have heard otherwise.

With so many people out of work, daytime radio shows became popular. People listened to dramas like "Ma Perkins" that told a story over weeks or months. Because many of these serials were sponsored by soap companies, they became known as soap operas.

Perhaps the most famous broadcast took place in 1938. On Halloween night, actor Orson Welles presented a newscast based on a science fiction novel, *The War of the Worlds*. Welles grimly reported the landing of invaders from the planet Mars. People who tuned in late mistook the program for a real newscast. Thousands of terrified people ran into the streets, seeking ways to escape the Martian invasion.

Movies

In the 1930s, moviemakers tried to restore people's faith in the United States. Movies told optimistic stories about happy families or people finding love and success. Shirley Temple became a hugely popular star at the age of five. When Temple sang "On the Good Ship Lollipop" or danced with popular black entertainer Bill "Bojangles" Robinson, her upbeat spirit cheered up audiences.

One of the most popular movies was Walt Disney's *Snow White and the Seven Dwarfs*.

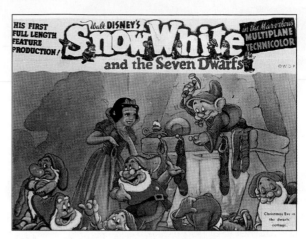

1937 movie poster

It was the first full-length animated film. In 1939, Judy Garland won American hearts in *The Wizard of Oz*. The movie told of a young girl's escape from a bleak life in depression-era Kansas to the magical land of Oz.

The most expensive and most popular movie of the 1930s was *Gone With the Wind*. It showed the Civil War in a romantic light. For more than three hours, many Americans forgot their worries as they watched the story of love and loss in the old South. The movie also encouraged many Americans. They had survived hard times before. They would do so again.

★ Section 4 Review ★

Recall

1. **Identify** (a) Dust Bowl, (b) Black Cabinet, (c) Mary McLeod Bethune, (d) Indian New Deal, (e) John Steinbeck, (f) Richard Wright, (g) Dorothea Lange.
2. **Define** (a) migrant worker, (b) civil rights, (c) repatriate.

Comprehension

3. (a) Give two causes of the dust storms of the 1930s. (b) What problems did farmers in the Dust Bowl region face?
4. Explain how each of these people tried to improve life for others during the depression:

(a) Eleanor Roosevelt, (b) Emma Tenayuca, (c) Robert C. Weaver, (d) John Collier.

5. Why were movies and radio important to Americans during the depression?

Critical Thinking and Writing

6. **Understanding Causes and Effects** Why do you think minorities suffered greater discrimination during the depression than during good times?
7. **Making Inferences** Why do you think movies that told stories about good times were popular during the depression?

★ ★

Activity **Writing a Diary** You are one of the people shown in the Dorothea Lange photograph on page 724. Write a diary entry about what was happening in your life at the time the photograph was taken.

Chapter 26 Review and Activities

★ Sum It Up ★

Section 1 The Economy Crashes
► The stock market crashed in 1929, partly because of unhealthy investment practices.
► The stock crash triggered a slide into a severe economic depression, made worse by overproduction and a weak banking system.
► President Hoover eventually began relief and public works programs.

Section 2 The New Deal
► Hoping for a bold new approach to the depression, Americans elected Franklin Roosevelt as President in 1932.
► The goals of Roosevelt's New Deal were to help the unemployed, promote recovery, and prevent another depression.

Section 3 Reaction to the New Deal
► Some critics argued that the New Deal did not do enough to help the poor, while others argued that it went too far.
► Roosevelt met with strong criticism when he tried to "pack" the Supreme Court.
► Later New Deal measures strengthened labor unions and set up Social Security to help the elderly and disabled.

Section 4 Surviving Hard Times
► Dust storms destroyed many farms in the Great Plains region.
► Women and members of minority groups faced particular problems during the Great Depression.
► Americans frequently turned to radio and movies to escape from their troubles.

For additional review of the major ideas of Chapter 26, see *Guide to the Essentials of American History* or *Interactive Student Tutorial CD-ROM,* which contains interactive review activities, graphic organizers, and practice tests.

🖺 Reviewing the Chapter

Define These Terms
Match each term with the correct definition.

Column 1	Column 2
1. public works	a. amount owed by the government
2. speculation	b. rights due to citizens
3. national debt	c. sum paid to people after they retire
4. pension	d. government-funded projects for public use
5. civil rights	e. risky buying and selling

Explore the Main Ideas
1. Why did Hoover start public works programs?
2. Describe one way the New Deal helped each of the following groups: **(a)** the unemployed, **(b)** farmers, **(c)** factory workers.
3. Why was the TVA controversial?
4. Why did the Supreme Court rule that the NIRA was unconstitutional?
5. How did FDR reach out to African Americans and Native Americans?

🖺 Geography Activity

Match the letters on the map with the following locations:
1. Tennessee Valley Authority, **2.** Dust Bowl, **3.** Oklahoma, **4.** Arkansas, **5.** California, **6.** Washington, D.C. **Interaction** How did the TVA solve the problem of flooding in the Tennessee River valley?

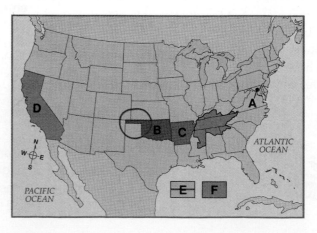

Critical Thinking and Writing

1. **Thinking Creatively** If you were President and a Great Depression struck today, what would you do?

2. **Understanding Chronology** (a) What problem did FDR tackle first? (b) Why did he target this problem?

3. **Linking Past and Present** (a) Identify a major ecological problem in the world today. (b) How is it similar to, and how is it different from, the Dust Bowl problem of the 1930s?

4. **Exploring Unit Themes Role of Government** Many Americans during the Great Depression feared that, under the New Deal, the government was gaining too much power. Do you think this fear was justified? Explain your answer.

Using Primary Sources

Evalyn Walsh McLean, a wealthy Washingtonian, helped feed the starving men of the Bonus Army. She later wrote:

> **66** Nothing I had seen before in my whole life touched me as deeply as what I had seen in the faces of those men. . . . Their way of righting things was wrong—oh, yes; but it is not the only wrong. . . . I was out in California when the United States army was used to drive them out of Washington. In a moving-picture show I saw in a news reel the tanks, the cavalry, and the gas-bomb throwers running those wretched Americans out of our capital. I was so raging mad I could have torn the theater down. They could not be allowed to stay, of course; but even so I felt myself one of them. **99**

Source: *Father Struck It Rich,* Evalyn Walsh McLean, 1936.

Recognizing Points of View (a) Describe McLean's opinion of the Bonus Army. (b) Why was she outraged by the government's actions?

ACTIVITY BANK

► Interdisciplinary Activity

Exploring Economics Find out more about the steps taken by FDR to resolve the banking crisis. Prepare a presentation for a class of younger students, such as third graders, that explains the banking crisis and how FDR's actions ended it. Use charts and graphs to illustrate your presentation.

► Career Skills Activity

Musicians In songs such as "Roll On, Columbia," folksinger Woody Guthrie celebrated some of the programs of the New Deal. Find out more about Guthrie's songs. Then, write a song of your own either celebrating or criticizing a New Deal action.

► Citizenship Activity

Understanding the Role of Charities The question of who should take care of needy Americans is still controversial. Working with a classmate, locate an organization in your community that helps people in need. Interview the leaders of the organization about what they do and where they get funds. Report what you have learned to the class.

Internet Activity

Use the Internet to find sites dealing with the Tennessee Valley Authority. Do research in the sites to create a data sheet of fascinating facts about the TVA. If possible, include images.

EYEWITNESS Journal

You are an investor in the stock market, a member of FDR's Brain Trust, a worker employed by the CCC or WPA, a farmer, or a business leader who opposes the New Deal. In your EYEWITNESS JOURNAL, describe your reaction to one of the key events of the Great Depression.

Chapter 27

World War II

1935–1945

After World War I, most Americans wanted to avoid involvement in international conflicts. However, during the 1930s, Germany, Italy, and Japan increased their military power and invaded other nations. The United States responded by gradually abandoning its policy of neutrality. After the Japanese attacked Pearl Harbor in 1941, the United States entered World War II.

Millions of Americans joined with troops from Britain and other allies to fight for victory. At home, civilians worked hard to support the soldiers. First, Italy was defeated, and then Germany. Finally, in 1945, the United States defeated Japan by using a new weapon—the atomic bomb.

Why Study History?

During World War II, millions of innocent men, women, and children were executed. Today we know this tragic event as the Holocaust. To learn more about the Holocaust and why it is important to study, see this chapter's *Why Study History?* feature, "We Must Never Forget."

	American Events			
	●**1935** Congress passes first of three Neutrality Acts	●**1936** Roosevelt visits Argentina as part of Good Neighbor Policy		**1940** ● United States establishes its first peacetime draft

1934   **1936**   **1938**   **1940**

World Events

 1937 World Event
Japan launches full-scale war against China

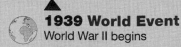 **1939 World Event**
World War II begins

Battle of the Coral Sea

World War II was fought all over the world—on land, at sea, and in the air. In the Battle of the Coral Sea, shown above in a dramatic painting by Robert Benney, American ships and planes forced a large Japanese fleet to turn away. The battle was one of the first American victories in the war. ★ **How do you think new technology affected the way World War II was fought?**

 1941
Attack on Pearl Harbor
brings United States
into World War II

1944 ●
Allied troops
invade Europe on
D-Day

1945
World War II ends

1940   **1942**   **1944**   **1946**

1940 World Event
France surrenders to Axis
powers

1943 World Event
Soviet armies defeat Germans
at Stalingrad and Leningrad

Dictatorship and Aggression

Explore These Questions

- How did dictators take away people's freedoms?
- How did dictators threaten world peace in the 1930s?
- How did the United States respond to the rise of dictators?

Define

- dictator
- totalitarian state
- collective farm
- nationalism
- aggression
- concentration camp

Identify

- Joseph Stalin
- Benito Mussolini
- Fascist party
- Haile Selassie
- Adolf Hitler
- Nazis
- Final Solution
- Neutrality Acts
- Good Neighbor Policy

As You Read

SETTING the Scene After World War I, many Americans believed that the nation should never again become involved in a war. As one writer noted:

> 66 Humanity is not helpless. This is God's world! We can outlaw this war system just as we outlawed slavery and the saloon. 99

"Bread through work," says this Soviet poster

In the 1930s, however, war clouds again gathered. In Europe and Asia, ambitious rulers gained power and set out to conquer neighboring lands. When other nations did not act to stop their expansion, the rulers became bolder.

A Dictator in the Soviet Union

In the Soviet Union, as you recall, communists under V. I. Lenin had staged a revolution in Russia in 1917. Later, they set up the Soviet Union.

After Lenin's death in 1924, **Joseph Stalin** came to power and soon ruled as a dictator. A **dictator** is a ruler who has complete power over a country. Stalin used all the weapons of the totalitarian state. In a **totalitarian state,** a single party controls the government and every aspect of people's lives. Citizens must obey the government without question. Criticism of the government is severely punished.

To strengthen the Soviet economy, Stalin launched a series of five-year plans. His goal was to modernize Soviet industry and farming. In the 1930s, the government ordered peasants to hand over their land and farm animals and to join **collective farms**—farms run by the government. When farmers resisted, millions were executed or sent to labor camps.

Under Stalin's harsh rule, Soviet industry expanded. Steel and oil production rose. Stalin knew that these materials were important for building a modern military force.

Fascists in Italy

Meanwhile, in Western Europe, dictators came to power in both Italy and Germany. These dictators won support by exploiting people's fears about the economy and feelings of extreme nationalism. **Nationalism,** as you recall, is a feeling of patriotic pride and devotion to one's country.

Mussolini becomes dictator

In 1922, **Benito Mussolini** seized power in Italy. He played on Italian anger about the Versailles Treaty ending World War I. Many

Italians felt cheated by the treaty because it did not grant Italy the territory it wanted. Mussolini also used economic unrest and fears of a communist revolution to win support for himself and his **Fascist party.**

Once in power, Mussolini outlawed all political parties except his own. He controlled the press and banned criticism of the government. In schools, children recited the motto "Mussolini is always right." They learned total obedience to "Il Duce" (ihl DOO chay)—the leader—as Mussolini was called.

Invading Ethiopia

In the 1930s, Mussolini used foreign conquest to distract Italians from economic problems at home. Remembering the glories of ancient Rome, he promised to restore Italy to greatness. Under Mussolini's leadership, Italy committed several acts of aggression. **Aggression** is any warlike act by one country against another without just cause.

As a first step to building a new Roman empire, Mussolini invaded Ethiopia, in North Africa, in 1935. The Ethiopians fought bravely. However, their cavalry and outdated rifles were no match for the tanks and airplanes of Mussolini's modern army.

Emperor **Haile Selassie** (HI lee suh LAS ee) of Ethiopia called on the League of Nations for help. The League responded weakly. The democratic powers Britain and France were concentrating on their own economic problems. Also, grim memories of World War I made the British and French unwilling to risk another war. Unable to secure help, Ethiopia fell to the invaders.

Rise of Nazi Germany

Like Mussolini, Germany's **Adolf Hitler** took advantage of anger about the Versailles Treaty. Germans bitterly resented the treaty because it blamed their country for World War I and saddled them with heavy war costs. Hitler organized a political party—the National Socialist German Workers' Party, or **Nazis**—to help him win power.

Hitler becomes dictator

Germany had not lost the war, he said. Rather, Jews and other traitors had "stabbed Germany in the back" in 1918. The argument was false, but in troubled times, people welcomed a scapegoat on which to blame their problems.

Hitler was a powerful speaker and skillful leader. By the late 1920s, a growing number of Germans had accepted his ideas. When the depression struck, many Germans turned to Hitler as a strong leader with answers to their problems.

In 1933, Hitler became chancellor, or head, of the German government. Within two years, he ended democratic government. In Hitler's Nazi Germany, the government controlled the press, schools, and religion. Hitler crushed all rivals and created a militaristic totalitarian state.

American reporter William Shirer visited Nazi Germany in 1934. At Nuremberg, he watched a week-long rally organized by

Viewing HISTORY Two Dictators

In full military uniform, Italian dictator Benito Mussolini (left) and German dictator Adolf Hitler stand together to view parading soldiers. The swastika on Hitler's armband was a symbol of the Nazi party. ★ **Why do you think many Italians and Germans supported these dictators?**

In the 1930s, in Nuremberg, thousands of Germans attended massive Nazi rallies. The crowds viewed Germany's military might and listened to Hitler's hypnotic speeches. They also chanted slogans, such as "We want one leader! Nothing for us! Everything for Germany! Heil Hitler!"

★ How do you think people in nearby countries felt about the rallies?

Hitler. The rally was an unforgettable display. Germans marched in endless parades and chanted slogans praising Hitler and the Nazi party. One day, the army staged a mock battle. Shirer noted in his diary:

> ❝ It is difficult to exaggerate the frenzy of the three hundred thousand German spectators when they saw their soldiers go into action, heard the thunder of the guns, and smelt the powder. ❞

Attacks on Jews

Hitler and the Nazis preached a message of racial and religious hatred. Hitler claimed that Germans belonged to a superior "Aryan" race. He blamed Jews, Gypsies, communists, and others for Germany's troubles.

The Nazi government singled out the Jews for special persecution. It passed many laws against Jews. Jews were deprived of their citizenship, forbidden to use public facilities, and driven out of almost every type of work.

As Nazi power grew, attacks on Jews increased. The government rounded up thousands of Jews and sent them to concentration camps. A **concentration camp** is a prison camp for civilians who are considered enemies of the state. In time, Hitler would unleash a plan to kill all the Jews in Europe. He called the plan the **Final Solution.** (See pages 754–755).

German military buildup

Under Hitler, Germany built up its armed forces in violation of the Versailles Treaty. Hitler also claimed that Germany had the right to expand to the east.

In response, the League of Nations condemned Hitler's actions. Still, Hitler moved ahead with his plans. The rest of Europe will "never act," he boasted. "They'll just protest. And they will always be too late."

In the meantime, Hitler pressed ahead with plans for conquest. In 1936, he moved troops into the Rhineland, near the border of France and Belgium. His action violated the terms of the Versailles Treaty. France and Britain protested, but they took no action.

Military Rule in Japan

Japan's economy suffered severely in the Great Depression. Trade slowed, and businesses failed. As the economic crisis worsened, many Japanese grew impatient with their democratic government.

In the early 1930s, military leaders took power. The new leaders believed that Japan, like Britain and France, had the right to win an overseas empire. They set out to expand into Asia.

In 1931, Japanese forces seized Manchuria in northeastern China. The Japanese wanted Manchuria because it was rich in coal and iron. As a small island nation, Japan lacked adequate supplies of these important resources. Japan set up a state in Manchuria, and called it Manchukuo.

China called on the League of Nations for assistance. The League condemned Japanese aggression but did little else. Similarly, the United States refused to recognize the state of Manchukuo, but took no other action against Japan.

American Foreign Policy

During the depression, Americans had too many economic worries to care much about events overseas. A strong isolationist mood gripped the country. As threats of war in Europe and Asia grew, Americans were determined to keep the United States from becoming involved.

Isolationists in Congress pressed for a series of **Neutrality Acts.** These laws banned arms sales or loans to countries at war. They also warned Americans not to travel on ships of countries at war. By limiting economic ties with warring nations, the United States hoped to stay out of any foreign conflict.

Closer to home, the United States tried to improve relations with Latin American nations. In 1930, President Hoover rejected the Roosevelt Corollary. (See page 634.) The United States, he declared, no longer claimed the right to intervene in the affairs of Latin American nations.

When Franklin Roosevelt took office, he announced a **Good Neighbor Policy** of establishing friendlier relations with Latin American countries. He withdrew American troops from Nicaragua and from Haiti. He also canceled the Platt Amendment, which had limited the independence of Cuba. (See page 628.)

As tensions increased in other parts of the world, the need to build friendly relations with the nations of the Western Hemisphere became more pressing. On a visit to Argentina in 1936, President Roosevelt said,

66 [Nations seeking] to commit acts of aggression against us will find a hemisphere wholly prepared to consult together for our mutual safety and our mutual good. 99

★ Section 1 Review ★

Recall

1. **Identify** (a) Joseph Stalin, (b) Benito Mussolini, (c) Fascist party, (d) Haile Selassie, (e) Adolf Hitler, (f) Nazis, (g) Final Solution, (h) Neutrality Acts, (i) Good Neighbor Policy.

2. **Define** (a) dictator, (b) totalitarian state, (c) collective farm, (d) nationalism, (e) aggression, (f) concentration camp.

Comprehension

3. Describe the totalitarian state that Adolf Hitler established in Germany.

4. Describe one way that each of the following nations threatened world peace in the 1930s: (a) Italy, (b) Germany, (c) Japan.

5. Why did the United States Congress pass a series of Neutrality Acts?

Critical Thinking and Writing

6. **Making Generalizations** (a) Make a generalization about how democratic nations responded to aggression in the 1930s. (b) Give two examples to support your generalization.

7. **Predicting Consequences** Do you think United States isolationism encouraged or discouraged future acts of aggression by dictators? Explain.

★ ★

Activity Identifying Alternatives You are a foreign policy adviser to the President of the United States. Japan has just seized Manchuria. The President wants you to identify and describe the various ways in which the United States might respond. The President also wants you to explain the benefits and drawbacks of each possible response.

The War Begins

As You Read

Explore These Questions
- How did World War II begin?
- How did the United States respond to the outbreak of World War II?
- Why did the United States enter the war?

Define
- annex
- appeasement
- blitzkrieg

Identify
- Munich Conference
- Nazi-Soviet Pact
- Axis
- Allies
- Winston Churchill
- Battle of Britain
- Edward R. Murrow
- Lend-Lease Act
- Atlantic Charter

SETTING the Scene "I hate war," FDR had told an audience as he campaigned for the presidency in 1936.

❛❛ I have passed unnumbered hours, I shall pass unnumbered hours, thinking and planning how war may be kept from this nation. ❝❝

During the late 1930s, Italy, Japan, and Germany continued their policies of aggression. The United States and the European democracies did little in response. Americans and Europeans hoped to avoid another bloody conflict like the world war that had ended only 20 years before.

War in Asia

In 1937, Japan began an all-out war against China. Japanese planes bombed China's major cities. Thousands of civilians were killed. Japanese troops defeated Chinese armies and occupied northern and central China.

The Japanese advance into China alarmed American leaders. They felt it undermined the Open Door Policy, which promised equal access to trade in China. It also threatened the Philippines, which the United States controlled. Nevertheless, isolationist feelings remained strong among the American people and kept the United States from taking a firm stand against the Japanese.

War in Europe

In Europe, Hitler continued his plans for German expansion. In 1938, just two years after occupying the Rhineland, Hitler **annexed,** or took over, Austria. By this action, he once again violated the Treaty of Versailles.

Later that year, Hitler claimed the Sudetenland, the western part of Czechoslovakia. He justified his demand by claiming that the Sudetenland contained many people of German heritage.

The Munich Conference

Britain and France had signed treaties to protect Czechoslovakia, but were reluctant to go to war. The two nations sought a peaceful solution to the crisis. In September 1938, the leaders of Britain, France, Italy, and Germany met in Munich, Germany.

At the **Munich Conference,** Hitler promised that Germany would seek no further territory once it acquired the Sudetenland. To preserve peace, Britain and France gave in. They agreed that Germany should have the Sudetenland. This practice of giving in to aggression in order to avoid war is known as **appeasement.**

The policy of appeasement failed. Nazi Germany seized the rest of Czechoslovakia the very next year. Only then did Britain and France realize that they had to take action to stop further Nazi aggression.

Invasion of Poland

Hitler's next target was Poland. To achieve his goal, he made an alliance with the Soviet Union. In August 1939, Hitler and Stalin signed the **Nazi-Soviet Pact.** The two agreed not to attack each other. Secretly, they also agreed to divide Poland and other parts of Eastern Europe between them.

In September 1939, Hitler launched Germany's military might in a swift attack against Poland. The Germans used planes and tanks, while the Poles used cavalry and old rifles. Unable to withstand the German **blitzkrieg,** or lightning war, the Poles soon surrendered.

Meanwhile, the Soviet Union seized eastern Poland. Stalin's forces also invaded Finland and later annexed Estonia, Lithuania, and Latvia. Stalin claimed that these steps were needed to build Soviet defenses.

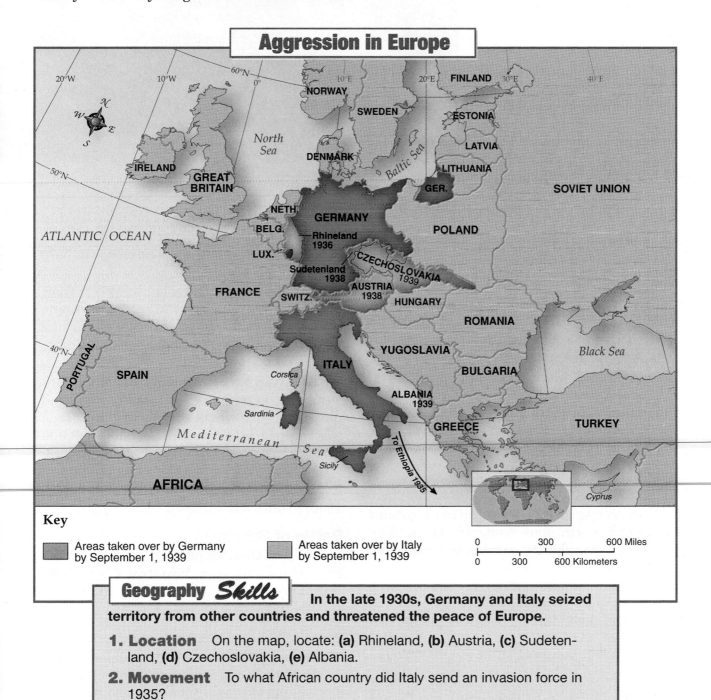

Aggression in Europe

Key

Areas taken over by Germany by September 1, 1939

Areas taken over by Italy by September 1, 1939

0 300 600 Miles
0 300 600 Kilometers

Geography *Skills*

In the late 1930s, Germany and Italy seized territory from other countries and threatened the peace of Europe.

1. **Location**   On the map, locate: **(a)** Rhineland, **(b)** Austria, **(c)** Sudetenland, **(d)** Czechoslovakia, **(e)** Albania.

2. **Movement**   To what African country did Italy send an invasion force in 1935?

3. **Critical Thinking**   Why did Poland have much to fear from an alliance between Nazi Germany and the Soviet Union?

Battle of Britain

In the Battle of Britain, German planes bombed London and other English cities such as Dover, shown here. During World War II, both the Axis and Allies bombed major population centers. ★ **Do you think German bombings weakened or strengthened the morale of the English people? Explain.**

A Global Conflict

Britain and France declared war on Germany two days after the invasion of Poland. In time, Italy, Japan, and six other nations would join Germany to form the **Axis** powers. Opposing the Axis powers were the **Allies.** Before World War II was over, the Allies would include Britain, France, the Soviet Union, the United States, China, and 45 other countries.

World War II was a global conflict. Military forces fought all over the world. Many millions of people were killed. When it finally ended, cities across Europe and Asia lay in ruins.

France surrenders

In the spring of 1940, Hitler's armies marched north and west. In April, they smashed through Denmark and Norway. In May, they overran Holland and Belgium and pushed into France. Hitler's ally, Italy, also attacked France. Britain sent troops to help France resist the assault.

The British and French, however, were quickly overpowered. By May, the Germans had forced them to retreat to Dunkirk, a French port on the English Channel. There, they were trapped.

In a bold action, the British sent every available merchant ship, fishing boat, and pleasure craft across the channel to rescue the trapped soldiers. They carried 338,000 soldiers to safety in England.

Unhindered, German armies marched on to Paris, the French capital. On June 22, 1940, France surrendered.

Battle of Britain

Britain then stood alone. Even so, the new prime minister, **Winston Churchill,** was confident. He informed the world that the British people would stand firm:

> 66 We shall defend our island, whatever the cost may be, we shall fight on the beaches, we shall fight on the landing grounds, we shall fight in the fields and in the streets . . . we shall never surrender. 99

Connections With Science

Britain used the new invention of radar to detect incoming German planes. Radar works because radio waves bounce off things. When radio waves bounce off an airplane in the sky, a blip appears on a screen.

German planes dropped bombs on London and other British cities during the **Battle of Britain.** British fighter pilots fought back, gunning down nearly 2,000 German planes. By late 1940, after months of bombing, Hitler gave up his planned invasion of Britain.

In the United States, people listened to the radio reports of **Edward R. Murrow** and other war correspondents who saw the fighting firsthand. As they listened, Americans wondered how much longer the United States could stay out of the war.

FDR and American Policy

After the invasion of Poland, President Roosevelt announced that the United States would remain neutral. He realized that most Americans sympathized with the Allies but did not want to enter the war.

Helping the Allies

Roosevelt sought ways to help the Allies. He asked Congress to repeal the neutrality law that banned the sale of arms to warring nations. Isolationists blocked the move, but FDR won a compromise. The United States could sell arms to the Allies under a "cash-and-carry" plan. The Allies had to pay cash for the goods and carry them away in their own ships.

By 1940, German submarines had sunk many British ships. Churchill asked the United States for ships. Roosevelt agreed to give Britain 50 old American destroyers. In exchange, Britain gave the United States 99-year leases on military bases in Newfoundland and the Caribbean.

Preparing for war

The United States also took several steps to prepare for war. Congress approved greater spending for the army and navy. In September 1940, it passed a law that set up the first peacetime draft in American history.

Isolationists opposed these moves, especially aid for Britain. Many other Americans, however, felt that the United States had no choice. If Britain fell, Hitler might control the Atlantic Ocean.

FDR wins a third term

The threat of war persuaded FDR to run for a third term in 1940. His decision broke the precedent set by George Washington of serving only two terms as President.

Republicans nominated Wendell Willkie. Willkie and Roosevelt agreed on many issues. Like Roosevelt, Willkie favored sending aid to Britain. Both candidates also pledged not to send Americans into any foreign wars.

Republicans—and some Democrats—criticized Roosevelt for breaking the two-term tradition. Still, the voters gave FDR a clear victory. They seemed to agree with a slogan used by Roosevelt in his campaign: "Don't change horses in mid-stream."

Biography — Edward R. Murrow

After attending Washington State College, Murrow traveled abroad and served as assistant director of the Institute of International Education. As director of the European bureau of CBS, he personally described the Nazi takeover of Austria for radio audiences. His broadcasts from London during German bombing raids made him famous. After the war, Murrow hosted influential news programs for both radio and TV. ★ **How did Murrow's experience prepare him for a journalism career?**

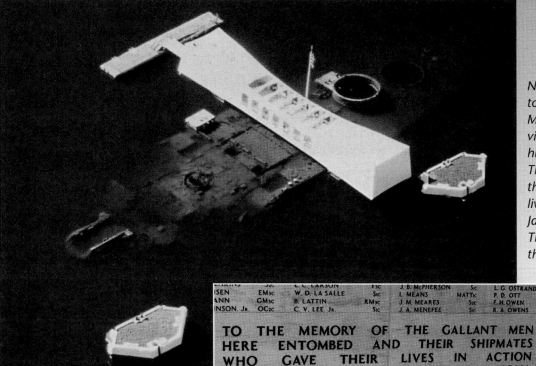

USS *Arizona* Memorial

Navy shuttle crafts take visitors to and from the USS Arizona *Memorial. There, visitors can view beneath them the sunken hull of the battleship* Arizona. *The Memorial commemorates those Americans who lost their lives in the December 7, 1941, Japanese attack on Pearl Harbor. The USS* Arizona *was sunk in that attack with 1,102 sailors trapped inside.*

★ *To learn more about this historic site, write: USS* Arizona *Memorial, 1 Arizona Memorial Place, Honolulu, HI 96818.*

TO THE MEMORY OF THE GALLANT MEN HERE ENTOMBED AND THEIR SHIPMATES WHO GAVE THEIR LIVES IN ACTION ON DECEMBER 7, 1941 ON THE U.S.S. ARIZONA

THIS MEMORIAL WALL WAS INSTALLED AND REDEDICATED BY AMVETS APRIL 4, 1984

▲ *The "remembrance exhibit" names all who died in the attack on Pearl Harbor.*

"Arsenal of democracy"

By late 1940, Britain was running out of cash to buy arms. Roosevelt boldly suggested lending supplies to Britain. Isolationists were outraged.

Roosevelt proclaimed that Britain was defending democracy against totalitarian forces. The United States, he declared, "must be the great arsenal of democracy." He urged Americans to defend "Four Freedoms"—freedom of speech, freedom of worship, freedom from want, and freedom from fear.

In March 1941, Congress passed the **Lend-Lease Act.** It allowed sales or loans of war materials to "any country whose defense the President deems vital to the defense of the United States." Under Lend-Lease, the United States sent airplanes, tanks, guns, and ammunition to Britain. British merchant ships transported the goods, with escorts of American warships providing protection as far as Iceland.

In June 1941, Hitler launched a surprise invasion of the Soviet Union. The Soviets were now fighting on the Allied side. Although Roosevelt condemned Stalin's totalitarian rule, he extended Lend-Lease aid to the Soviet Union.

The Atlantic Charter

In August 1941, Roosevelt and Churchill issued the **Atlantic Charter,** which set goals for the postwar world. The two leaders agreed to seek no territorial gain from the war. They pledged to support "the right of all peoples to choose the form of government under which they will live." The charter also called for a "permanent system of general security," such as an organization like the League of Nations.

The United States Enters the War

To Roosevelt, Japanese aggressions in Asia were as alarming as Germany's advance through Europe. The Japanese had seized much of China. After Germany defeated France in 1940, Japan took control of French colonies in Southeast Asia. (See the map on page 752.) In September 1940, the Japanese signed an alliance with Germany and Italy.

Opposing Japanese aggression

The United States tried to stop Japanese aggression by refusing to sell oil and scrap metal to Japan. This move angered the Japanese because they badly needed these resources. "Sparks will fly before long," predicted an American diplomat.

Japanese and American officials held talks in November 1941. Japan asked the United States to lift the embargo on oil and scrap metal. The United States called on Japan to withdraw its armies from China and Southeast Asia. Neither side would compromise. As the talks limped along, Japan completed plans for a secret attack on the United States.

Japan attacks

On Sunday, December 7, 1941, Japanese planes swept through the skies in a surprise attack on Pearl Harbor, Hawaii. There, the American Pacific fleet rode peacefully at anchor. In less than two hours, the Japanese sank or seriously damaged 19 American ships, destroyed almost 200 American planes, and killed about 2,400 people.

Americans were stunned by the attack. The next day, President Roosevelt asked Congress to declare war on Japan.

66 Yesterday, December 7, 1941—a date which will live in infamy—the United States of America was suddenly and deliberately attacked by naval and air forces of the Empire of Japan. . . . No matter how long it may take us to overcome this premeditated invasion, the American people, in their righteous might, will win through to absolute victory. 99

Congress declared war on Japan. In response, Germany and Italy declared war on the United States. Americans were now united in the cause of freedom. Even isolationists backed the war effort.

★ Section 2 Review ★

Recall

1. **Locate** (a) Czechoslovakia, (b) Poland, (c) France, (d) Britain, (e) Pearl Harbor.
2. **Identify** (a) Munich Conference, (b) Nazi-Soviet Pact, (c) Axis, (d) Allies, (e) Winston Churchill, (f) Battle of Britain, (g) Edward R. Murrow, (h) Lend-Lease Act, (i) Atlantic Charter.
3. **Define** (a) annex, (b) appeasement, (c) blitzkrieg.

Comprehension

4. What nations did Hitler conquer in 1939 and 1940?

5. What did Roosevelt mean when he called the United States the "arsenal of democracy"?
6. (a) Why did Japan attack Pearl Harbor? (b) How did Americans respond to the attack?

Critical Thinking and Writing

7. **Analyzing Ideas** At the start of World War II, the official policy of the United States was neutrality. Do you think the United States was truly neutral in its actions toward the Axis and Allies? Explain.
8. **Recognizing Points of View** Why did Roosevelt urge Americans to support the Lend-Lease Act?

Activity Drawing a Cartoon You are a political cartoonist for an American newspaper during the 1930s. Your assignment is to draw a cartoon criticizing German aggression and British and French appeasement. The title of your cartoon is "Hitler Is a Spoiled Child!"

The Home Front

Explore These Questions

- How did Americans mobilize for war?
- How did American women and minorities contribute to the war effort?
- How were some Americans treated unjustly during the war?

Define

- ration
- segregation

Identify

- victory garden
- A. Philip Randolph
- Tuskegee airmen
- bracero program
- Navajo code-talkers

Poster showing a strong and confident factory worker

SETTING the Scene The Japanese attack on Pearl Harbor plunged the United States into World War II. Isolationism died almost overnight as the nation mobilized all its resources to fight the enemy. As one woman recalled:

66 There was a great coming together of people, working as a team, being proud of what you were doing because you knew it was contributing something to the war effort. Everybody did their share, from the oldest gentleman on the street...to little children who saved things that were crucial at that time—paper, tin cans, scrap, anything that could be reused for the war. 99

Mobilizing for Victory

During World War II, more than 15 million American men and women served in the military. Many millions more spent the war years at home, far from the battlefields. Winning the war depended on military victories and on mobilizing the home front to support and supply the armed forces.

Training for combat

In 1941, the military's first task was to train forces for combat. Army, navy, and air bases were built all over the country. Recruits were trained to fight in the jungles of the Pacific, the deserts of North Africa, and the towns and farmlands of Europe.

Women joined all the armed services. Women pilots logged 60 million air miles ferrying bombers from base to base, towing targets, and teaching men to fly. Although women were not allowed in combat, many served close to the front lines.

Organizing the economy

Even more than in World War I, the government controlled the economy during World War II. Government agencies set the prices of goods and negotiated with labor unions. They also decided what products should be produced.

The War Production Board helped factories shift from making consumer goods to making guns, ships, aircraft, and other materials needed to win the war. Auto makers, for example, switched from turning out cars to producing tanks and trucks. A Nazi leader once scoffed that "Americans can't build planes, only electric iceboxes and razor blades." He was wrong. Americans performed a miracle of production. In 1942 alone, American workers produced more than 60,000 planes and shipped more than 8 million tons of goods.

As production of war materials grew, consumer goods became scarcer. The government **rationed,** or limited, the amount of certain goods that Americans could buy. Americans used ration coupons issued by the government to purchase all sorts of goods, including coffee, sugar, meat, shoes, gasoline, and tires. When people ran out of coupons, they could not buy the rationed items until new coupons were issued.

To combat food shortages, many Americans planted **victory gardens.** At the height of the war, there were more than 20 million victory gardens in the country. They produced 40 percent of all vegetables grown in the country during World War II.

To pay for the war, the government raised taxes. It also borrowed huge amounts of money by selling war bonds to millions of American citizens. Movie stars and other celebrities took part in drives to sell bonds and boost patriotic spirit.

The war quickly ended the Great Depression. Unemployment fell as millions of jobs opened up in factories. Minority workers found jobs where they had been rejected in the past.

Jobs for Women

"If you can drive a car," the government told American women, "you can run a machine." Newspapers and magazines echoed this call to American women to work for victory. "Why do we need women workers?" asked a radio announcer. The answer: "You can't build ships, planes, and guns without them."

During World War II, women responded to the urgent demand for their labor. Almost 5 million women entered the work force. They replaced men who joined the armed services. Many women worked in offices. Millions more kept the nation's factories operating around

Linking Past and Present

Past

Present

National Defense

During World War II, American workers achieved a miracle of production by turning out all the equipment needed to win the war. Today, American workers continue to build the military hardware needed for national defense. The photos above show a B-29 bomber of World War II and a modern stealth bomber. ★ **Why does the United States spend massive amounts of money on military equipment even during peacetime?**

Skills FOR LIFE

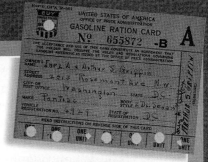

| Critical Thinking | **Managing Information** | Communication | Maps, Charts, and Graphs |

Managing Resources

How Will I Use This Skill?

A common economic problem is providing what is needed or desired with a limited amount of resources. As a family member, you may have to balance the family's income and expenses. In business, you may have to figure out how to get the job done with a limited budget and number of workers. Whatever the situation, knowing how to manage resources will help you get the most out of what you have.

▲ *During World War II, Americans used ration cards and coupons.*

LEARN the Skill

To manage resources, use the following plan:

❶ List the goods and services that are needed or wanted.

❷ Rank the items on the list according to importance. Remember that basic needs are most important and cannot be disregarded. Luxuries make life more enjoyable, but you can live without them.

❸ List your available resources. These include things like materials, time, money, and people.

❹ Figure out what goods and services you can afford. Be sure to take care of basic needs first and luxuries last.

❺ Try to increase your resources and save some resources for later needs.

PRACTICE the Skill

Review pages 740 and 741. Then, answer the following questions.

❶ Before the United States entered World War II, what two different types of goods did American factories produce?

❷ After the United States entered World War II, which type of goods did the government consider more important than any other? Why?

❸ Why were there shortages of workers and food?

❹ What did the government do to make sure that there were enough goods for the soldiers overseas?

❺ How did the government try to raise money to pay for the war?

APPLY the Skill

Make a monthly budget for yourself. Start by estimating your total income from all sources, such as work, allowances, and gifts. List what you must pay for or buy and what you would like to buy. Complete your budget, or resource management plan, by continuing to follow the steps that you learned above.

the clock. Some welded, ran huge cranes, and tended blast furnaces. Others became bus drivers, police officers, and gas station attendants.

Because women were badly needed in industry, they were able to win better pay and working conditions. The government agreed that women and men should get the same pay for the same job. Many employers, however, found ways to avoid equal pay.

The war changed fashions for women. Instead of wearing skirts on the job, many women dressed in trousers. They wore overalls and tied scarves around their hair.

More important, war work gave many women a new opinion of themselves. One woman noted how her confidence increased:

66 I never could handle the simplest can openers, or drive a nail without getting hurt, and now I put in half my nights armed with hammers and wrenches handling the insides of giant machines. **99**

African Americans

When the war began, African Americans rallied to their nation's cause. The war helped end some of the worst discrimination against African Americans. Still, the struggle for equality was not easy.

Discrimination at home

As industry geared up for war, factories replaced "No Help Wanted" signs with "Help Wanted, White" signs. Such discrimination angered African Americans.

In 1941, **A. Philip Randolph,** head of the Brotherhood of Sleeping Car Porters, called for a protest march on Washington. The government, he said, "will never give the Negro justice until they see masses— ten, twenty, fifty thousand Negroes on the White House lawn."

Government officials worried that such a march would feed Hitler's propaganda machine. "What will Berlin say?" they asked. After meeting with Randolph, FDR ordered employers doing business with the government to end discrimination in hiring. As a result, the employment of skilled black craftsworkers doubled during the war.

However, as black employment increased, so did racial tension. Thousands of Americans—blacks and whites—moved to cities to work in industry. Competition for scarce housing led to angry incidents and even violence. In 1943, race riots broke out in Detroit, New York, and other American cities.

Heroism in the military

While FDR acted against discrimination in hiring, he refused to end **segregation,** or separation, of the races in the military. Nearly a million African Americans enlisted or were drafted. They had to serve in all-black units commanded by white officers.

Despite such treatment, blacks served heroically. The **Tuskegee airmen** were African American fighter pilots who trained

Viewing HISTORY **Tuskegee Airmen**

After training at Tuskegee, African American combat pilots compiled an enviable combat record in action over North Africa and Europe. None of the bombers they escorted was shot down. Here, Colonel Benjamin O. Davis gives advice to Lieutenant Charles Dryden. ★ **How did prejudice affect African Americans in the military?**

Viewing HISTORY

Tragedy for Japanese Americans

By order of the United States government, troops moved Japanese American families from their homes to relocation camps. "Herd 'em up, pack 'em off," was the recommendation of one newspaper columnist.
★ **What reason did the government give for this relocation policy?**

at Tuskegee, Alabama. By the end of the war, the Tuskegee airmen had destroyed or damaged about 400 enemy aircraft.

African Americans served heroically in all branches of the armed forces. In the army, African American combat units included artillery and tank units. African Americans in the navy served as gunner's mates and helped build bases in the Pacific. African American marines helped defend American posts against Japanese attacks.

One of the earliest heroes of World War II was Dorie Miller, an African American sailor serving on the battleship *West Virginia* during the attack on Pearl Harbor. As the battle raged. Miller dragged his wounded captain to safety. Then, though he had no training as a gunner, Miller manned a machine gun and shot down four enemy planes. For heroism in action, Miller was awarded the Navy Cross.

Tragedy for Japanese Americans

The war brought suffering to many Japanese Americans. Most Japanese Americans lived on the West Coast or in Hawaii. Many of those on the West Coast were successful farmers and business people. For years, they had faced prejudice, in part because of their success.

Following the attack on Pearl Harbor, many people on the West Coast questioned the loyalty of Japanese Americans. Japanese Americans, they said, might act as spies and help Japan invade the United States. No evidence of disloyalty existed. Yet the President agreed to move Japanese Americans from their homes to "relocation" camps.

About 110,000 Japanese Americans were forced to sell their homes and businesses at great loss. In the relocation camps, Japanese Americans lived in crowded barracks behind barbed wire. They could not understand why they were singled out for such treatment.

Even though they and their families were treated unfairly, thousands of Japanese

Connections With Civics

Italian immigrants also suffered during the war. Hundreds were held in government camps for up to two years. Thousands more were forbidden to travel more than 5 miles from home and were forced to turn in cameras and shortwave radios.

American men served in the armed forces. Most were put in segregated units and sent to fight in Europe. There, they won many honors for bravery. The 442nd Nisei Regimental Combat Team became the most highly decorated military unit in United States history.

Years later, in 1988, Congress apologized to Japanese Americans who had been driven from their homes in World War II. They also approved a payment of $20,000 to every survivor of the camps.

Latinos

Many Puerto Rican Americans and Mexican Americans served in the military during World War II. In fact, Latinos—people of Latin American origin or descent—won many awards for bravery, including 17 Congressional Medals of Honor. Guy Gabaldon, a Marine Corps private, received a Silver Star for capturing 1,000 Japanese.

Because of the need for workers during the war, the United States signed a treaty with Mexico in 1942. The agreement allowed the recruitment of Mexican laborers to work in the United States. The program was called the **bracero program.** During the war, many Mexicans arrived in the United States to work on farms and railroads.

Despite their contribution to the war effort, Latinos still faced prejudice. In June 1943, for example, white sailors on leave from their ships savagely attacked a group of young Mexican Americans, beating and clubbing them on the streets. The incident sparked several days of rioting in Los Angeles.

Newspapers blamed the violence on the Mexican Americans. Eleanor Roosevelt disagreed. In her newspaper column, she noted that the riots were the result of "longstanding discrimination against the Mexicans in the Southwest."

Native Americans

Native Americans supplied the highest proportion of servicemen of any ethnic group. More than one out of three able-bodied Native American men were in uniform.

Navajo soldiers in the Pacific made an unusual contribution. They used their own language as a code for sending vital messages. Although the Japanese intercepted the messages, they could not understand these **Navajo code-talkers.**

★ Section 3 Review ★

Recall

1. **Identify** (a) victory garden, (b) A. Philip Randolph, (c) Tuskegee airmen, (d) bracero program, (e) Navajo code-talkers.
2. **Define** (a) ration, (b) segregation.

Comprehension

3. Describe two economic policies that helped the United States produce the military equipment needed to win the war.
4. Why did job opportunities for women expand during the war?

5. Describe one way the war affected each of these groups: (a) African Americans, (b) Japanese Americans, (c) Latinos, (d) Native Americans.

Critical Thinking and Writing

6. **Analyzing Ideas** How did prejudice affect the organization of units in the United States army?
7. **Making Inferences** Why do you think Japanese Americans were the only group forced to live in relocation camps?

★ ★

Activity **Researching** What role did your community play in the effort to win World War II? In the local library, consult news articles that appeared in your town's newspaper during the war years. You might also interview people who lived in your community during the war.

The Allies Advance

Explore These Questions

- Why was 1942 a difficult year for the Allies?
- What victories turned the war in favor of the Allies?
- How did the Allies force Germany to surrender?

Identify

- Douglas MacArthur
- Battle of Midway
- Dwight D. Eisenhower
- Operation Overlord
- D-Day
- Battle of the Bulge
- Harry S Truman

 When British Prime Minister Winston Churchill heard about the attack on Pearl Harbor, he rejoiced. "We have won the war," he remarked. Churchill felt sure that the United States would lead the Allies to victory.

Despite Churchill's optimism, Allied prospects seemed grim in December 1941. Hitler's armies occupied most of Europe and much of North Africa. Japan was advancing across Asia and the Pacific. As 1942 began, the Allies faced the bleakest days of the war.

A Time of Peril

In early 1942, the Germans seemed unbeatable. German submarines were sinking ships faster than the Allies could replace them. Most of Europe was in German hands. German armies were closing in on Moscow, Leningrad, and Stalingrad in the Soviet Union.

The Soviets resisted heroically. They burned crops and destroyed farm equipment so that the Germans could not use them. In Leningrad and elsewhere, people suffered terrible hardships. More than one million Russian men, women, and children died during the 900-day siege of Leningrad.

Meanwhile, Japanese forces were on the move in the Pacific. After Pearl Harbor, they seized Guam, Wake Island, Hong Kong, and Singapore. (See the map on page 752.)

General **Douglas MacArthur,** commander of United States forces in the Pacific, faced a difficult task. With few troops, he had to defend a huge area. MacArthur directed American and Filipino troops in the defense of the Philippines. They fought bravely against enormous odds. In the end, however, MacArthur was forced to withdraw. "I shall return," he vowed. A Filipino described the defeat in these words:

66 Besieged on land and blockaded
by sea,
We have done all that human
endurance can bear....
Our defeat is our victory. 99

The Japanese pressed on. They captured Malaya, Burma, and the Dutch East Indies. They threatened India to the west and Australia and New Zealand to the south.

Turning the Tide

The Allied leaders had to agree on a strategy if they were to succeed against the Axis powers. Even before Pearl Harbor, American and British planners had decided that the Allies must defeat Germany and Italy first. Then, they would send their combined forces to fight Japan.

Victories in the Pacific

The adoption of the "beat Hitler first" strategy did not mean abandoning the war in the Pacific. Luckily, the United States's aircraft carriers in the Pacific had survived the attack on Pearl Harbor. Relying on the carriers, a naval task force engaged a Japanese fleet in the Coral Sea near Java in May 1942. After a three-day battle, the Japanese fleet turned back.

One month later, the United States Navy won a stunning victory at the **Battle of Midway.** American planes sank four Japanese aircraft carriers. The battle severely ham-

pered the Japanese offensive. It also kept Japan from attacking Hawaii again.

Success in North Africa

British and American forces began to push back the Germans in North Africa. In October 1942, the British won an important victory at El Alamein in Egypt. German

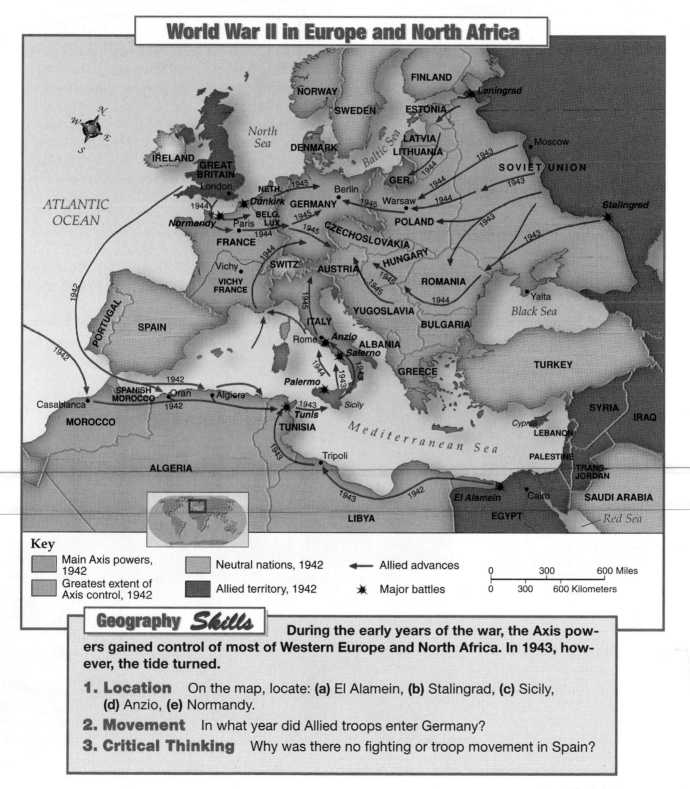

World War II in Europe and North Africa

Key
- Main Axis powers, 1942
- Greatest extent of Axis control, 1942
- Neutral nations, 1942
- Allied territory, 1942
- ← Allied advances
- ✳ Major battles

0   300   600 Miles
0   300   600 Kilometers

Geography Skills During the early years of the war, the Axis powers gained control of most of Western Europe and North Africa. In 1943, however, the tide turned.

1. **Location** On the map, locate: **(a)** El Alamein, **(b)** Stalingrad, **(c)** Sicily, **(d)** Anzio, **(e)** Normandy.

2. **Movement** In what year did Allied troops enter Germany?

3. **Critical Thinking** Why was there no fighting or troop movement in Spain?

forces under General Erwin Rommel were driven west into Tunisia.

Meanwhile, American troops landed in North Africa. Under the command of General **Dwight D. Eisenhower,** they occupied Morocco and Algeria. The Allied armies trapped Rommel's forces in Tunisia. In May 1943, his army had to surrender.

Allied advances in Europe

From bases in North Africa, the Allies organized the invasion of Italy. They used paratroopers, or airborne troops, and soldiers brought by sea to capture Sicily. In early September 1943, the Allies crossed from Sicily to the mainland of Italy.

By then, the Italians had overthrown Mussolini. The new Italian government sided with the Allies. The Germans, however, still occupied much of the country. In a series of bloody battles, the Allies slowly fought their way up the Italian peninsula. On June 4, 1944, Allied troops marched into Rome. It was the first European capital to be freed from Nazi control.

Despite the massive German assault on the Soviet front, the Russians held their ground. In 1943, the Soviet army pushed the Germans back from Leningrad. At Stalingrad, after months of fierce house-to-house fighting, Soviet soldiers forced the German army to surrender. Slowly, the Soviet army pushed the Germans westward through Eastern Europe.

D-Day Invasion at Normandy

Soon after Hitler invaded the Soviet Union in 1941, Stalin had urged Britain and the United States to send armies across the English Channel into France. Such an attack would create a second front and ease pressure on the Soviet Union. However, Churchill and Roosevelt were not prepared to attempt it until 1944.

Years of planning went into **Operation Overlord,** the code name for the invasion of Europe. General Eisenhower was appointed commander of Allied forces in Europe. He would direct the invasion.

Eisenhower faced an enormous task. He had to organize a huge army, ferry it across the English Channel, and provide it with ammunition, food, and other supplies. By June 1944, almost 3 million troops were ready for the invasion.

The Germans knew that an attack was coming. They did not know when or where.

Viewing HISTORY **D-Day Invasion at Normandy**

American, British, and Canadian forces opened the long-awaited second front against Germany on June 6, 1944, known as D-Day. Tens of thousands of troops landed on the beaches of Normandy in France. ★ **Why had Stalin urged such an invasion?**

They had built a strong "Atlantic wall" against an Allied invasion. They had mined beaches and strung barbed wire. Machine guns and concrete antitank walls stood ready to stop an advance.

On June 6, 1944—**D-Day,** as it was known—a fleet of 4,000 Allied ships carried the invasion force to France. Allied troops scrambled ashore at Normandy. Despite intense German gunfire and heavy losses, they pushed on. Every day, more soldiers landed to reinforce the advance.

On August 25, 1944, the Allies entered Paris. After four years under Nazi rule, the Parisians greeted their liberators with joy. Within a month, all of France was free.

Advancing on Germany

By September, the Allies were moving east toward Germany. However, a shortage of truck fuel hindered their efforts to supply the troops. The advance slowed.

On December 16, 1944, German forces began a fierce counterattack. They pushed the Allies back, creating a bulge in the front lines. The **Battle of the Bulge,** as it was later called, slowed the Allies but did not stop them.

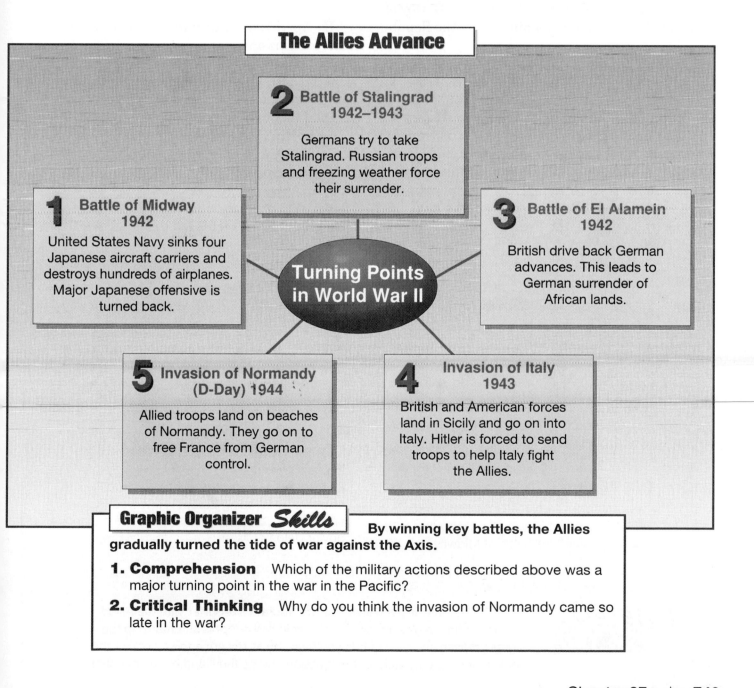

The Allies Advance

2 **Battle of Stalingrad 1942–1943**

Germans try to take Stalingrad. Russian troops and freezing weather force their surrender.

1 **Battle of Midway 1942**

United States Navy sinks four Japanese aircraft carriers and destroys hundreds of airplanes. Major Japanese offensive is turned back.

Turning Points in World War II

3 **Battle of El Alamein 1942**

British drive back German advances. This leads to German surrender of African lands.

5 **Invasion of Normandy (D-Day) 1944**

Allied troops land on beaches of Normandy. They go on to free France from German control.

4 **Invasion of Italy 1943**

British and American forces land in Sicily and go on into Italy. Hitler is forced to send troops to help Italy fight the Allies.

Graphic Organizer *Skills* By winning key battles, the Allies gradually turned the tide of war against the Axis.

1. **Comprehension**   Which of the military actions described above was a major turning point in the war in the Pacific?
2. **Critical Thinking**   Why do you think the invasion of Normandy came so late in the war?

While Allied armies advanced on the ground, Allied planes bombed Germany. At night, British airmen dropped tons of bombs on German cities. By day, the Americans bombed factories and oil refineries. The bombing caused severe fuel shortages in Germany and reduced the nation's ability to produce war goods.

A New President

By mid-1944, the Allied advance shared headlines in American newspapers with the upcoming election. Breaking all tradition, President Roosevelt ran for a fourth term. His opponent was Governor Thomas E. Dewey of New York, who was nominated by the Republican Party.

"All that is within me cries to go back to my home on the Hudson," FDR wrote in 1944. Roosevelt was tired and ill. Still, he and his running mate, Senator **Harry S Truman** of Missouri, campaigned strongly. Their efforts paid off. Roosevelt won more than 54 percent of the vote.

In early April 1945, FDR was on vacation in Georgia. While he was sitting to have his portrait painted, the President complained of a headache. Within hours, he was dead.

Franklin D. Roosevelt was mourned by people all over the world. His death especially shocked Americans. Roosevelt had been President for 12 years. Many Americans could hardly remember anyone else as their leader.

Vice President Harry S Truman had to take over a country in the midst of war. Truman described his reaction:

> ❝ I felt like the moon, the stars, and all the planets had fallen on me. I've got the most terribly responsible job a man ever had. ❞

Victory in Europe

By April 1945, Germany was collapsing. American troops were closing in on Berlin from the west. Soviet troops were advancing from the east. On April 25, American and Soviet troops met at Torgau, 60 miles (96 km) south of Berlin.

In Berlin, Hitler hid in his underground bunker as Allied air raids pounded the city. Unwilling to accept defeat, he committed suicide on April 30. A week later, on May 7, 1945, Germany surrendered to the Allies. On May 8, the Allies celebrated the long-awaited V-E Day—Victory in Europe.

★ Section 4 Review ★

Recall

1. **Locate (a)** Leningrad, **(b)** Philippines, **(c)** El Alamein, **(d)** Sicily, **(e)** Stalingrad, **(f)** Normandy, **(g)** Paris.
2. **Identify (a)** Douglas MacArthur, **(b)** Battle of Midway, **(c)** Dwight D. Eisenhower, **(d)** Operation Overlord, **(e)** D-Day, **(f)** Battle of the Bulge, **(g)** Harry S Truman.

Comprehension

3. Why was early 1942 a bleak time for the Allies?
4. How did each of the following help the Allies to turn the tide of war? **(a)** Battle of Midway, **(b)** Battle of El Alamein, **(c)** invasion of Italy, **(d)** Battle of Stalingrad
5. How did the D-Day invasion contribute to the eventual defeat of Germany?

Critical Thinking and Writing

6. **Solving Problems** Why was it important for the Allied leaders to cooperate in the defeat of the Axis powers?
7. **Making Inferences** Stalin asked the Allies to help him by invading Europe. How would a second front in Europe help ease pressure on the Soviet Union?

★ ★

Activity **Writing a News Report** You are a reporter with the Allied troops landing at Normandy. Write a radio news report summarizing the sights you see and the sounds you hear. Try to describe the emotions the soldiers feel as they wait for the invasion and as they land on the beaches.

Final Victory

Explore These Questions
- What strategy did the United States follow in the Pacific war?
- Why did the United States use the atomic bomb on Japan?
- Why was World War II the deadliest war in history?

Define
- island hopping
- kamikaze
- atomic bomb

Identify
- Potsdam Declaration
- Bataan Death March
- Holocaust
- Nuremberg Trials

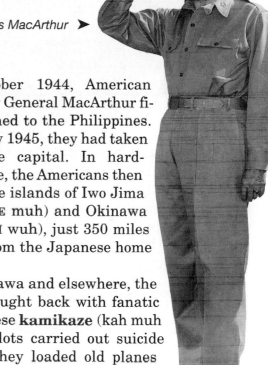

General Douglas MacArthur ➤

 SETTING the Scene Soon after FDR's death, a reporter addressed Harry Truman. "Mr. President..." he began. "I wish you didn't have to call me that," Truman interrupted.

As Vice President, Truman had met with Roosevelt fewer than 10 times. He knew little about the plans that had been made for ending the war and keeping the postwar peace. As President, Truman had to learn quickly. Just weeks after he took office, Germany surrendered. The Allies then turned their full attention to defeating Japan.

Campaign in the Pacific

Even while the war raged in Europe, the Allies kept up pressure on Japan. By mid-1942, the United States had two main goals in the Pacific war: to regain the Philippines and to invade Japan.

For its plan to work, the United States had to control the Pacific Ocean. American forces conducted an **island hopping** campaign, capturing some Japanese-held islands and going around others. The Americans used the islands they won as stepping stones toward Japan.

The strategy of island hopping became a deadly routine. First, American ships shelled a Japanese-held island. Next, troops waded ashore under heavy gunfire. Then, in hand-to-hand fighting, Americans overcame fierce Japanese resistance.

In October 1944, American forces under General MacArthur finally returned to the Philippines. By February 1945, they had taken Manila, the capital. In hard-fought battle, the Americans then captured the islands of Iwo Jima (EE woh JEE muh) and Okinawa (oh kuh NAH wuh), just 350 miles (563 km) from the Japanese home islands.

At Okinawa and elsewhere, the Japanese fought back with fanatic zeal. Japanese **kamikaze** (kah muh KAH zee) pilots carried out suicide missions. They loaded old planes with bombs and then deliberately crashed them into Allied ships.

By April 1945, United States forces were close enough to launch repeated attacks against the Japanese home islands. American bombers pounded Japanese factories and cities. American warships bombarded the coast and sank ships. The Japanese people were suffering terribly. Still, their leaders talked about winning a glorious victory over the Allies.

United States military leaders made plans to invade Japan in the autumn. They warned that the invasion might cost between 150,000 and 250,000 American casualties.

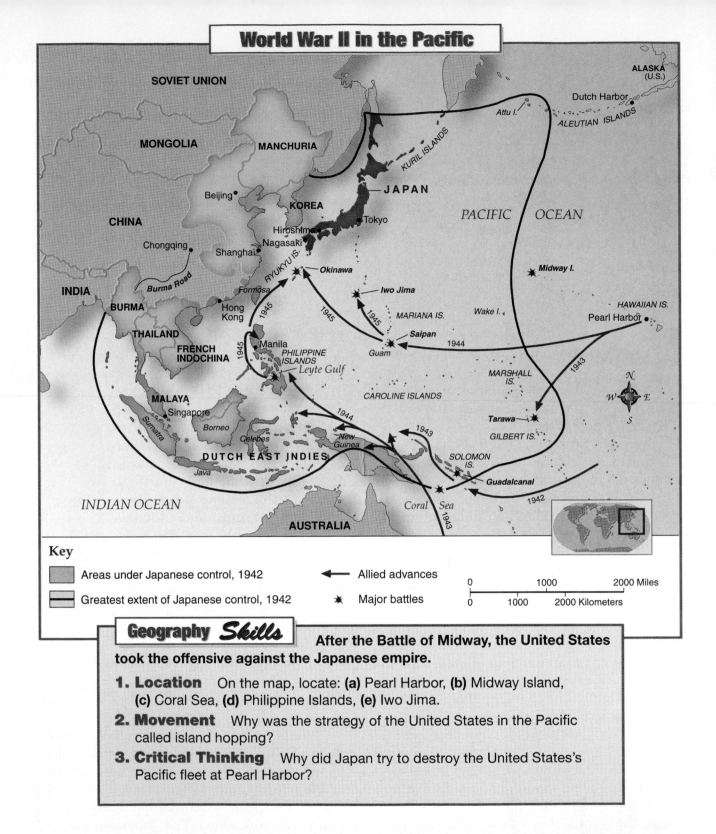

World War II in the Pacific

Key

- Areas under Japanese control, 1942
- Greatest extent of Japanese control, 1942
- ← Allied advances
- ✴ Major battles

0   1000   2000 Miles
0 1000 2000 Kilometers

Geography Skills After the Battle of Midway, the United States took the offensive against the Japanese empire.

1. **Location** On the map, locate: **(a)** Pearl Harbor, **(b)** Midway Island, **(c)** Coral Sea, **(d)** Philippine Islands, **(e)** Iwo Jima.
2. **Movement** Why was the strategy of the United States in the Pacific called island hopping?
3. **Critical Thinking** Why did Japan try to destroy the United States's Pacific fleet at Pearl Harbor?

Defeat of Japan

In late July 1945, the Allied leaders—Truman, Churchill, and Stalin—met at Potsdam, Germany. While there, Truman received startling news from home. American scientists had successfully tested a secret new weapon—the **atomic bomb.** The new weapon was so powerful that a single bomb could destroy an entire city. Some scientists believed that it was too dangerous to use.

From Potsdam, the Allied leaders sent a message warning Japan to surrender or face "prompt and utter destruction." Japanese leaders did not know about the atomic bomb. They ignored the **Potsdam Declaration.**

On August 6, 1945, the *Enola Gay,* an American bomber, dropped an atomic bomb on Hiroshima, Japan. The blast killed at least 70,000 people and injured an equal number. It destroyed most of the city.

On August 9, the United States dropped a second atomic bomb—this time on Nagasaki. About 40,000 residents died instantly. Later, many more people in both Nagasaki and Hiroshima died from the effects of atomic radiation—deadly particles released by the bombs.

After a furious debate in the Japanese cabinet, the emperor of Japan announced that his nation would surrender on August 14, 1945. The formal surrender took place on September 2 aboard the USS *Missouri* in Tokyo Bay. The warship flew the same American flag that had waved over Washington, D.C., on the day Japan bombed Pearl Harbor.

News of Japan's surrender sparked wild celebrations across the United States. People honked their car horns. Soldiers and sailors danced in victory parades. Workers in tall office buildings showered confetti on people in the streets below.

Costs of the War

After the celebrations, people began to count the costs of the war—the deadliest in human history. The exact number of casualties will probably never be known. However, historians estimate that somewhere between 30 million and 60 million people were killed in battle or behind the lines. (See the chart on page 756.)

World War II was different from World War I, which had been fought mainly in trenches. During World War II, aircraft bombed cities and towns and destroyed houses, factories, and farms. By 1945, millions were homeless and had no way to earn a living.

During the war, stories trickled out about the mistreatment of prisoners. Afterward, Americans learned horrifying details about brutal events such as the **Bataan Death March.** After the Japanese captured the Philippines in 1942, they forced about 75,000

Viewing **Bombing of Hiroshima**
HISTORY
"We had seen the city when we went in," said the pilot of the Enola Gay. *"There was nothing to see when we came back."* In the photo, below, two Japanese passersby view the blasted landscape. ★ **Why do you think President Truman decided to use atomic bombs?**

Atomic mushroom cloud over
▼ *Hiroshima*

Why Study History?

Because We Must Never Forget

★ ★

Historical Background

More than one million children—Jews and non-Jews—were victims of Hitler's "Final Solution." Those who were not sent to concentration camps were left to suffer malnutrition and disease in Jewish ghettoes. Age was no protection from the horrors of the Holocaust.

Connections to Today

Today, young people are encouraged to learn about the Holocaust. It is hoped that by understanding the causes of the Holocaust we can ensure it never happens again. Many cities have museums that commemorate the victims and their suffering. These museums serve as a reminder that we must guard against history repeating itself.

Connections to You

Could a state like Nazi Germany ever exist again? Could people once again follow a leader like Adolf Hitler? Some years ago, with questions like these in mind, a social studies teacher taught his class a special lesson.

The California teacher re-created elements of Nazism in his high school classroom. He selected "gifted students" to join a special youth group. Other students were left out because they were "not gifted." The teacher set up a strict system where obedience was rewarded. The system depended on the cooperation of student informers.

To the teacher's surprise, students eagerly participated. In fact, many liked the system and earned higher grades. Most alarming was that "gifted students" were willing to follow instructions and turn in fellow students.

The teacher ended the lesson with a film about the Holocaust. The students grew silent as they understood. They had given up freedoms and followed a leader. They had turned on others. They had embraced ideas that had led to the Holocaust.

1. **Comprehension** Why is it important for students to learn about the Holocaust?
2. **Critical Thinking** Why do you think some people have been willing to follow the orders of a dictator?

 **Using the Internet** On the Internet, visit one of the many Holocaust museums that exist in the United States. Gather information and write a report about one young person who was a victim of the Holocaust.

Starving prisoners in a Nazi concentration camp

American and Filipino prisoners to march 65 miles (105 km) with little food or water. About 10,000 of the prisoners died or were killed during the march.

The Holocaust

In the last months of the European war, the Allied forces uncovered other horrors. The Allies had heard about Nazi death camps. As they advanced into Germany and Eastern Europe, they discovered the full extent of the **Holocaust**—the slaughter of Europe's Jews by the Nazis.

During the war, the Nazis imprisoned Jews from Germany and the nations they conquered. In prison camps, they tortured and murdered more than 6 million Jews. When Allied troops reached the death camps, they saw the gas chambers the Nazis had used to murder hundreds of thousands. The battle-hardened veterans wept at the sight of the dead and dying human beings.

Photographer Margaret Bourke-White made a record of the horrors. She worked "with a veil over my mind. . . . I hardly knew what I had taken until I saw prints of my own photographs." After touring one death camp, General Omar Bradley wrote:

66 The smell of death overwhelmed us even before we passed through the stockade. . . . More than 3,200 naked, emaciated bodies had been flung into shallow graves. 99

The Nazis murdered other groups as well as Jews. Nearly 6 million Poles, Slavs, and Gypsies were also victims of the death camps. Nazis killed prisoners of war and people they considered unfit because of physical or mental disabilities.

As the full horror of the Holocaust was revealed, the Allies decided to put Nazi leaders on trial. In 1945 and 1946, they conducted war crimes trials in Nuremberg, Germany. As a result of the **Nuremberg Trials,** 12 Nazi leaders were sentenced to death. Thousands of other Nazis were found guilty of war crimes and imprisoned. The Allies also tried and executed Japanese leaders accused of war crimes.

★ Section 5 Review ★

Recall

1. **Locate** (a) Philippines, (b) Iwo Jima, (c) Okinawa, (d) Hiroshima, (e) Nagasaki.
2. **Identify** (a) Potsdam Declaration, (b) Bataan Death March, (c) Holocaust, (d) Nuremberg Trials.
3. **Define** (a) island hopping, (b) kamikaze, (c) atomic bomb.

Comprehension

4. (a) What two goals did the United States set for the war in the Pacific? (b) What strategy did it adopt to achieve these goals?
5. How did the United States force Japan to surrender?

6. Why was World War II more deadly than World War I?

Critical Thinking and Writing

7. **Analyzing Ideas** The Allies did not try enemy leaders as war criminals after World War I. (a) Why do you think they conducted war crimes trials after World War II? (b) Do you think they were right to do so?
8. **Defending a Position** After the war, President Truman said he had agreed to the use of the atomic bomb "to shorten the agony of war [and] save the lives of thousands of young Americans." Do you think he made the right decision? Defend your position.

Activity Linking Past and Present Write a brief essay on how World War II affects your life today. Consider in your essay the following points: (a) the defeat of the Axis dictatorships, (b) the threat of nuclear weapons, (c) the Holocaust.

Chapter 27 Review and Activities

★ Sum It Up ★

Section 1   Dictatorship and Aggression
▶ Rulers in the Soviet Union, Germany, Italy, and Japan established dictatorships and threatened world peace.
▶ The League of Nations and the leading democracies did little to stop international aggression.

Section 2   The War Begins
▶ As World War II began, the Axis powers overran much of China and Europe.
▶ Although officially neutral, the United States offered aid to the Allies.
▶ After the Japanese attack on Pearl Harbor, the United States entered the war.

Section 3   The Home Front
▶ The United States mobilized its military and economic strength.
▶ Women and minorities made important contributions to the war effort.
▶ Prejudice and segregation affected many Americans.

Section 4   The Allies Advance
▶ The Allies won key victories in the Pacific, in North Africa, and in Italy.
▶ After the D-Day Invasion, Allied troops advanced into Germany and forced its surrender.

Section 5   Final Victory
▶ The United States used atomic bombs to defeat Japan.
▶ World War II was the deadliest war in history.
▶ Millions of Jews died in the Holocaust.

 **CD-ROM Review** For additional review of the major ideas of Chapter 27, see *Guide to the Essentials of American History* or *Interactive Student Tutorial CD-ROM,* which contains interactive review activities, graphic organizers, and practice tests.

▢ Reviewing the Chapter

Define These Terms

Match each term with the correct definition.

Column 1
1. dictator
2. blitzkrieg
3. ration
4. annex
5. kamikaze

Column 2
a. a suicide soldier or pilot
b. limit the availability of goods
c. take over a land
d. lightning war
e. one who has total power over a country

Explore the Main Ideas

1. What policies did dictators and military rulers follow in the 1930s?
2. What were the effects of isolationism and appeasement?
3. **(a)** How did American civilians contribute to the war effort? **(b)** How did some American civilians suffer unjustly during the war?
4. Identify and describe some of the major turning points of World War II.
5. Describe the terrible costs of World War. II

▢ Chart Activity

Use the table below to answer the following questions:
1. Which country suffered the most deaths? **2.** Which Axis state had the most civilian deaths? **Critical Thinking**   Why did the United States have very few civilian deaths?

World War II Deaths		
	Military Dead	**Civilian Dead**
Britain	389,000	65,000
France	211,000	108,000
Soviet Union	7,500,000	15,000,000
United States	292,000	*
Germany	2,850,000	5,000,000
Italy	77,500	100,000
Japan	1,576,000	300,000

* Very small number
All figures are estimates

Source: Henri Michel, *The Second World War*

Critical Thinking and Writing

1. **Linking Past and Present** **(a)** Why do you think George Washington chose to retire after two terms? **(b)** Why do you think FDR broke this precedent?

2. **Drawing Conclusions** Why do you think Japanese Americans volunteered to serve in the army even though the government was treating Japanese Americans unjustly?

3. **Understanding Chronology** Create a time line illustrating the major events in Europe leading to the start of war in 1939.

4. **Exploring Unit Themes** **Role of Government** **(a)** How did the government control the United States economy during the war? **(b)** Do you think many people complained about the government's economic laws? Explain.

Using Primary Sources

A reporter filed this report after flying with the team of planes that dropped the second atomic bomb on Japan:

> 66 Observers in the tail of our ship saw a giant ball of fire rise as though from the bowels of the earth, belching forth enormous white smoke rings. Next they saw a giant pillar of purple fire, ten thousand feet high, shooting skyward with enormous speed.... Awe-struck, we watched it...become ever more alive as it climbed skyward through the white clouds. It was no longer smoke, or dust, or even a cloud of fire. It was a living thing, a new species of being, born right before our incredulous eyes. 99

Source: William L. Laurence, *The New York Times,* September 9, 1945.

Recognizing Points of View **(a)** What emotions do you sense in the reporter's words? **(b)** Does the reporter seem to liken the aftermath of the atomic bomb explosion to some terrible monster? Explain.

ACTIVITY BANK

▶ Interdisciplinary Activity

Exploring Geography Find out more about one land or sea battle in World War II. Then, prepare a map showing the locations and movements of the opposing forces in the battle.

▶ Career Skills Activity

Statistician Study the casualty statistics that appear in the table on page 756. Use the statistics to create a bar graph or pie graph showing the same information.

▶ Citizenship Activity

Creating a Poster Create a poster that urges American citizens to support the war effort in some way. Your poster could illustrate the idea of joining the military, working in a factory, buying war bonds, planting a victory garden, rationing, or some other idea.

Internet Activity

Use the Internet to find sites that contain images of World War II, such as art, photographs, and posters. Select a topic having to do with the war. Then, print out images pertaining to the topic. Write a brief caption to go with each image. Display your work in a folder or on a bulletin board.

EYEWITNESS Journal

Choose one of the following: a soldier in France on D-Day; a woman factory worker; a Tuskegee airman; a Navajo code-talker; a Mexican American in California; a Japanese American on the West Coast. In your EYEWITNESS JOURNAL, describe how the person contributed to World War II or was affected by it.

History Through Literature

Poems of the Harlem Renaissance

Various authors

Introduction

Injustice, pride in African heritage, hope for the future—these were some of the major themes of the Harlem Renaissance. In the 1920s, New York City's Harlem was the center of a great flowering of African American art, music, and literature. The many poets who added their voices to the Harlem Renaissance included Langston Hughes, Countee Cullen, and Georgia Douglas Johnson.

Vocabulary

Before you read the selection, find the meaning of these words in a dictionary: **tableau, sable, indignant, oblivious, discerning.**

The Negro Speaks of Rivers

Langston Hughes

I've known rivers:
I've known rivers ancient as the world and
    older than the flow of human blood in
    human veins.

I bathed in the Euphrates when dawns
    were young.
I built my hut near the Congo and it lulled
    me to sleep.
I looked upon the Nile and raised the
    pyramids above it.*
I heard the singing of the Mississippi when
    Abe Lincoln went down to New Orleans,
    and I've seen its muddy bosom turn all
    golden in the sunset.

I've known rivers:
Ancient dusky rivers.

My soul has grown deep like the rivers.

Mother to Son

Langston Hughes

Well, son, I'll tell you:
Life for me ain't been no crystal stair.
It's had tacks in it,
And splinters,
And boards torn up,
And places with no carpet on the floor—
Bare.
But all the time
I'se been a-climbin' on,
And reachin' landin's.
And turnin' corners,
And sometimes going in the dark
Where there ain't been no light.
So boy, don't you turn back.
Don't you set down on the steps
'Cause you finds it's kinder hard.
Don't you fall now—
For I'se still goin', honey,
I'se still climbin',
And life for me ain't been no crystal stair.

---

* The Euphrates is a river in the Middle East. The Nile and Congo are rivers in Africa.

Tableau

Countee Cullen

Locked arm in arm they cross the
    way,
    The black boy and the white,
The golden splendor of the day,
    The sable pride of night.

From lowered blinds the dark folk
    stare,
    And here the fair folk talk,
Indignant that these two should dare
    In unison to walk.

Oblivious to look and word
    They pass, and see no wonder
That lightning brilliant as a sword
    Should blaze the path of thunder.

Common Dust

Georgia Douglas Johnson

And who shall separate the dust
Which later we shall be:
Whose keen discerning eye will scan
And solve the mystery?

The high, the low, the rich, the poor,
The black, the white, the red,
And all the chromatique* between,
Of whom shall it be said:

---

* Chromatique refers to the range of colors from
darkest to lightest.

Viewing HISTORY — A Painter of the Harlem Renaissance

Aaron Douglas was one of the many black artists who came to New York during the Harlem Renaissance. In works like his 1936 painting Aspiration *(above), he celebrated the African American experience. Douglas also illustrated books of poetry by Langston Hughes and Countee Cullen.* ★ **Summarize the theme of this painting.**

Here lies the dust of Africa;
Here are the sons of Rome;
Here lies one unlabeled
The world at large his home!

Can one then separate the dust,
Will mankind lie apart,
When life has settled back again
The same as from the start?

Analyzing Literature

1. **(a)** In "Mother to Son," what kind of life has the mother had? **(b)** What advice does she give her son?
2. **(a)** In "Tableau," what sight upsets both the blacks and the whites in the neighborhood? **(b)** How do the two children react?
3. **Critical Thinking Summarizing** Summarize what you think are the main points of: **(a)** "The Negro Speaks of Rivers"; **(b)** "Common Dust."

The Nation Today and Tomorrow

Viewing UNIT THEMES **A Leader in a Changing World**

In Modern Business World, *Boris Lyubner shows the United States at the center of a busy global economy. Technology and free enterprise have contributed to American economic leadership. Since World War II, the United States has also become the world's leading military power.* ★ **Identify three examples of advanced technology in this picture. Which do you think is most important to the economy?**

Unit Theme World Leadership

As World War II ended, the United States entered a long rivalry with its former ally, the Soviet Union. Conflict between these two "superpowers" influenced events all over the world. Then, in 1991, the Soviet Union broke up. The United States stood alone as the leading military, political, and economic power in the world.

Still, Americans often disagreed on how to use that power. Should the United States stay out of the affairs of other nations? Or should we take the lead in keeping peace around the world?

How did Americans of the time feel about their role in the world? They can tell you in their own words.

★ ★

VIEWPOINTS ON WORLD LEADERSHIP

❝The free peoples of the world look to us for support in maintaining their freedom. If we falter in our leadership, we may endanger the peace of the world.❞

President Harry S Truman (1947)

❝Leadership does come with a price tag, and there is an eagerness to let someone else pick up the tab. But it is a price worth paying.❞

Senator Robert Dole of Kansas (1995)

❝The United States is still acting as the world's policeman, rushing armed forces to any place on the globe where conflict erupts.... Why not help ourselves first?❞

A North Carolina high school student (1996)

★ ★

Activity **Writing to Learn** War has broken out between two small countries thousands of miles away. Hundreds of people are being killed, including children. The United States could send in troops to keep the peace, but it would cost money and some American soldiers might lose their lives. Write a letter to the President expressing what you think the United States should do.

Chapter 28

The Cold War Era

1945–1991

Soon after World War II, a new kind of struggle developed. As the Soviet Union sought to expand its influence around the world, the United States tried to protect non-communist governments. Both superpowers built many atomic weapons. Tensions during the Cold War, as the conflict became known, led to several crises and military conflicts. However, Soviet and American forces never faced each other directly in battle.

For more than 40 years, the Cold War divided the world into opposing camps. This state of tensions continued until the 1990s, when the breakup of the Soviet Union brought an end to the Cold War.

Why Study History?

During the Cold War, both sides armed themselves with powerful atomic weapons. However, American and Soviet leaders were able to avoid a full-scale nuclear war. The lesson of how to resolve dangerous conflict can also be applied to everyday life. To examine this connection, see the *Why Study History?* feature, "We Can Learn to Ease Conflict."

American Events	1950 ● Korean War begins		1962 ● Cuban missile crisis almost begins a nuclear war	●1964 Gulf of Tonkin Resolution increases United States role in Vietnam War
1945	**1951**	**1957**	**1963**	**1969**

World Events	▲ **1949 World Event** Chinese Communists set up People's Republic of China	▲ **1957 World Event** Soviet Union launches first artificial satellite into space

Military and Industrial Power

This painting, Preparedness, *by artist Roy Lichtenstein reflects the growing power of the United States during the Cold War years. For over four decades, the Soviet Union and United States competed in many ways. Each tried to have greater political, economic, and military strength than the other.* ★ **Identify two images that Lichtenstein uses to symbolize American might.**

1972 ●
President Nixon visits China and the Soviet Union

●**1973**
United States withdraws troops from Vietnam

●**1987**
President Reagan signs arms reduction treaty with Soviet Union

1969   **1975**   **1981**   **1987**   **1993**

▲
1975 World Event
North Vietnam defeats South Vietnam

▲
1985 World Event
Mikhail Gorbachev becomes leader of Soviet Union

The Nation Faces a Cold War

As You Read

Explore These Questions
- How did the United States and the Soviet Union become rivals?
- What steps did the United States take to prevent the spread of communism in Europe?
- Why did Berlin become a focus of Cold War tension?

Define
- satellite nation
- containment

Identify
- Cold War
- Truman Doctrine
- George Marshall
- Marshall Plan
- Berlin Wall
- Chiang Kai-shek
- Mao Zedong
- United Nations
- North Atlantic Treaty Organization
- Warsaw Pact

SETTING the Scene On March 5, 1946, Winston Churchill gave a speech in Fulton, Missouri. In the audience was President Harry Truman. He nodded as Churchill warned of the growing power of the Soviet Union in Europe:

66 From Stettin in the Baltic to Trieste in the Adriatic, an iron curtain has descended across the Continent.... Warsaw, Berlin, Prague, Vienna, Budapest, Belgrade, Bucharest, and Sofia, all these famous cities and populations around them lie in what I must call the Soviet sphere and all are subject to a very high and, in many cases, increasing measure of control from Moscow. 99

To Churchill, the Iron Curtain was a barrier cutting off Eastern Europe from the rest of the world. Behind that barrier, the Soviet Union was setting up harsh governments. Churchill urged Americans to stand firm against the Soviet dictator Joseph Stalin.

The United States heeded that plea. For the next half century, it remained locked in a new kind of war with the Soviet Union. The two powers competed for influence around the world, but did not face each other directly in battle. This long, bitter rivalry became known as the **Cold War.**

Roots of the Conflict

During World War II, the Allies had worked together. Yet, even before the war ended, divisions developed. On one side were the United States and Britain; on the other, the Soviet Union.

Growing distrust

The United States and Britain had long distrusted the Soviet Union and its communist government. Communists openly rejected religion and the idea of private property. Soviet leaders boasted that they would spread their revolutionary ideas throughout the world.

For their part, the Soviets distrusted the western powers.* In both world wars, Germany had invaded Russia. For many Russians, invasion from the West remained a deadly threat. The Soviets also accused the United States of trying to gain control over the economies of Europe after World War II.

Soviet expansion

By the end of the war, the Soviets had driven German forces out of the Soviet Union and back to Germany. As a result, Soviet troops occupied much of Eastern Europe.

---

* The Cold War pitted the West (the United States and its allies) against the East (the Soviet Union and its allies).

HISTORY HAPPENED HERE

Harry S Truman National Historic Site

President Truman's home in Independence, Missouri, was far removed from Cold War tensions. At his "Missouri White House," Truman could think quietly about crucial decisions. Today, you can visit the house and the nearby Truman Library. It contains papers, photographs, and even a sign he kept on his desk. Its message—"The Buck Stops Here"—suggested that United States Presidents cannot pass their responsibilities to others.

★ *To learn more about this historic site, write: Harry S Truman National Historic Site, 223 North Main Street, Independence, MO 64050.*

◀ *Truman's desk sign*

▲ *Harry Truman*

Stalin promised the other Allies that he would hold "free elections as soon as possible" in the Eastern European nations.

After the war, however, Stalin went back on his promise. "A freely elected government in any of the Eastern European countries would be anti-Soviet," he said, "and that we cannot allow." By 1948, the government of every Eastern European country was under communist control.

Except for Yugoslavia, all of these communist nations remained satellites of the Soviet Union. A **satellite nation** is one that is dominated politically and economically by a more powerful nation. In each satellite nation, the Soviets supported harsh governments. Citizens who protested were imprisoned or killed.

Communist parties supported by the Soviets enjoyed success in other nations. After the war, the Italian Communist party won 104 out of 556 seats in the Italian parliament. In Greece, communist rebels fought a civil war to overthrow the king. Neighboring Turkey felt Soviet pressure, too, when Stalin canceled a treaty of friendship between the two nations.

American Response

Truman decided that a show of strength was needed to stop Soviet expansion. Like Churchill, he saw danger in letting communist governments take power in other countries. He was determined to keep Soviet influence contained within existing boundaries. This Cold War policy was known as **containment.**

The Truman Doctrine

In March 1947, President Truman asked Congress for $400 million in military and economic assistance for Greece and Turkey.

With American aid, both countries were able to put down communist revolts.

The President's program of helping nations threatened by communist expansion became known as the **Truman Doctrine.** Truman explained why the policy was needed:

> 66 The free peoples of the world look to us for support in maintaining their freedoms. If we falter in our leadership, we may endanger the peace of the world—and we shall surely endanger the welfare of our own nation. 99

The Marshall Plan

Other European nations needed aid, too. The war had left homes, roads, and factories in ruins. When Secretary of State **George Marshall** toured Europe, he saw thousands of refugees without homes or struggling to find food.

Marshall feared that hungry, homeless people might support communist revolu-

Viewing HISTORY **Stalin and the Marshall Plan**

Under the Marshall Plan, the United States spent billions of dollars to help Europe recover from World War II. This 1947 cartoon shows Soviet dictator Joseph Stalin attempting to block the plan. On the back of his uniform are the hammer and sickle, symbols of the Soviet Union. ★ **Why did Stalin oppose the Marshall Plan?**

tions. As a result, in June 1947, he proposed a large-scale plan to help Europe rebuild its economy. The President and Congress accepted the **Marshall Plan.**

Stalin angrily rejected the Marshall Plan. He saw it as a plot to weaken Soviet influence. Under pressure from the Soviet Union, Eastern European nations refused to accept American aid.

Between 1948 and 1952, the Marshall Plan provided more than $12 billion in aid to Western European countries. By helping these nations recover, the Marshall Plan lessened the chance of communist revolutions in Western Europe.

Focus on Berlin

In 1948, a crisis developed over Berlin, the former capital of Germany. After the war, the Allies had divided Germany into four zones. American, British, French, and Soviet troops each occupied a zone. Berlin was also divided among the Allies, even though it lay deep inside the Soviet zone.

By 1948, the United States, Britain, and France were ready to allow Germans to reunite into a single nation. Stalin, on the other hand, opposed a unified Germany. He feared that if Germany became too strong, it might again threaten the Soviet Union. Also, he wanted to preserve Soviet influence in the eastern part of Germany.

In June 1948, the United States, Britain, and France announced that they would join their zones into the German Federal Republic, or West Germany. In response, Stalin closed all the roads, railway lines, and river routes connecting Berlin with West Germany. The blockade cut off West Berlin from the rest of the world.

Berlin airlift

President Truman did not want to let West Berlin fall into Soviet hands. At the same time, he feared ordering American troops to open a path to West Berlin through the Soviet-occupied zone. Such an action might lead to a new war.

In the end, Truman decided to set up a huge airlift. Day after day, planes flew in food, fuel, and other supplies to 2 million

Past

Present

Americans to the Rescue

During the Berlin Airlift, the United States sent tons of food to the people of West Berlin. On the left, Berliners watch eagerly as an American cargo plane brings needed supplies. Today, Americans continue to respond generously to needy people around the world, such as these refugees from the war-torn African nation of Rwanda (right). ★ **Why do you think many Americans are willing to help people in faraway lands?**

West Berliners. At the height of the Berlin Airlift, hundreds of planes carried more than 5,000 tons of supplies into West Berlin each day.

For nearly a year, the airlift continued. Stalin became convinced that the western powers were determined to keep Berlin open. In May 1949, he lifted the blockade.

Berlin Wall

Both Germany and Berlin remained divided, however. With aid from the United States, West Germany rebuilt its economy. The Soviet zone became the German Democratic Republic, or East Germany.

Over the next 12 years, 3 million East Germans, discontented with life under communism, fled to West Berlin. They then continued on to West Germany. The flight of so many people embarrassed East Germany and the Soviet Union.

Suddenly, in August 1961, East German soldiers began building a wall of concrete and barbed wire all across Berlin. Within days, the wall sealed off East Berlin from West Berlin—and from the rest of the noncommunist world. East Berliners who tried to escape to the West risked being shot by border guards. The **Berlin Wall** became a symbol of the Cold War that divided Europe.

The Shocks of 1949

Until 1949, many Americans felt confident that they could restrain the Soviet Union. After all, only the United States had the powerful atomic bomb.

Then, on September 3, 1949, an American B-29 aircraft brought back startling news. On patrol in the North Pacific, it had detected radioactivity high in the atmosphere. This could mean only that the Soviet Union had exploded its own atomic bomb. Suddenly, the threat of communism loomed larger. "This is now a different world," warned Senator Arthur Vandenberg of Michigan.

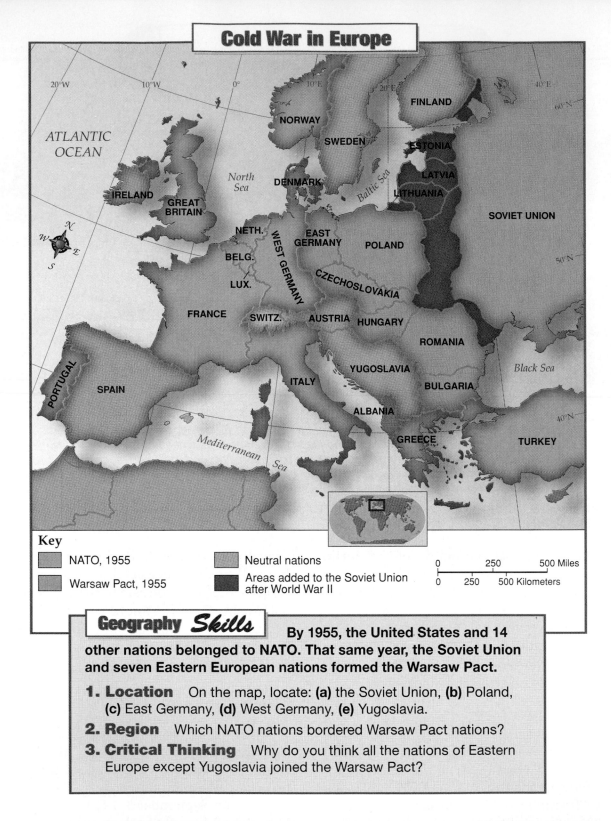

Cold War in Europe

Key

- NATO, 1955
- Warsaw Pact, 1955
- Neutral nations
- Areas added to the Soviet Union after World War II

Geography Skills By 1955, the United States and 14 other nations belonged to NATO. That same year, the Soviet Union and seven Eastern European nations formed the Warsaw Pact.

1. Location On the map, locate: **(a)** the Soviet Union, **(b)** Poland, **(c)** East Germany, **(d)** West Germany, **(e)** Yugoslavia.

2. Region Which NATO nations bordered Warsaw Pact nations?

3. Critical Thinking Why do you think all the nations of Eastern Europe except Yugoslavia joined the Warsaw Pact?

Soon after, Americans received a second shock when communists took over the government in China. For years, **Chiang Kai-shek** (chang ki SHEHK) had ruled China. Chiang's government was corrupt, however, and over the years, he lost most of his support. Beginning in the 1930s, communist forces led by **Mao Zedong** (mow dzuh DOONG) fought to overthrow Chiang. In October 1949, Mao set up the People's Republic of China. By December, the communists had driven all of Chiang's forces from the Chinese mainland.

Mao Zedong's victory meant that the largest nation in Asia had become communist. The Chinese communists often disagreed with the Soviet Union. Yet, between them, these two communist nations controlled almost one quarter of the Earth's surface. Many Americans worried that communist forces might take over all of Asia.

Striving for Peace

Many of the disputes in the Cold War were debated in a new international peacekeeping organization, known as the **United Nations** (UN). The UN came into being in October 1945, when 51 original members ratified its charter.

The United Nations

Under the United Nations charter, member nations agreed to bring disputes before the UN for peaceful settlement. Every member had a seat in the General Assembly, where problems could be discussed. A smaller Security Council conferred on conflicts that threatened the peace.

Over the years, the UN's greatest successes have been in fighting hunger and disease and improving education. United Nations health officers have vaccinated millions of children. UN relief programs have pro-

vided tons of food, clothing, and medicine to victims of disasters.

Preventing wars has proved more difficult. Sometimes, nations have refused to go along with United Nations decisions. In other cases, UN negotiators or troops have kept crises from becoming full-scale wars. As you will read, the UN played an active part in the Korean War.

Competing alliances

As another way of keeping international peace, the United States created alliances with friendly nations. In 1949, it joined with many Western European countries to form the **North Atlantic Treaty Organization,** or NATO. By joining NATO, the United States made it clear that it would help to defend the nations of Western Europe against any Soviet aggression.

In 1955, the Soviet Union formed its own military alliance, called the **Warsaw Pact.** The Soviet Union demanded complete loyalty from its Warsaw Pact neighbors. The Iron Curtain that Winston Churchill had warned about was now firmly in place.

★ Section 1 Review ★

Recall

1. **Locate** (a) Greece, (b) Turkey, (c) Berlin, (d) China.
2. **Identify** (a) Cold War, (b) Truman Doctrine, (c) George Marshall, (d) Marshall Plan, (e) Berlin Wall, (f) Chiang Kai-shek, (g) Mao Zedong, (h) United Nations, (i) North Atlantic Treaty Organization, (j) Warsaw Pact.
3. **Define** (a) satellite nation, (b) containment.

Comprehension

4. Why did tensions develop among the Allied powers?
5. How did the Marshall Plan help prevent the spread of communism?

6. (a) Describe the events leading up to the Berlin Airlift. (b) What were the results of the airlift?

Critical Thinking and Writing

7. **Identifying Alternatives** (a) What alternatives did President Truman consider for dealing with the Soviet blockade of Berlin? (b) Which alternative did he adopt? (c) Do you think he made a wise choice? Why or why not?
8. **Making Inferences** After World War I, the United States refused to join the League of Nations. Why do you think Americans were willing to join the United Nations after World War II?

Activity **Writing a Letter** You are a teenager in East or West Berlin. Write a letter to your cousin in the United States telling her about the building of the Berlin Wall. Describe how you feel about the wall.

The Cold War Heats Up

As You Read

Explore These Questions
- Why did the United States become involved in the Korean War?
- How did Cold War tensions feed fears of communism at home?
- How did the United States react to the rise of communism in Cuba?

Define
- censure
- superpower
- exile

Identify
- Joseph McCarthy
- Nikita Khrushchev
- National Aeronautics and Space Administration
- Fidel Castro
- John F. Kennedy
- Bay of Pigs
- Cuban missile crisis

 SETTING the Scene "For me, it was a typical Sunday night in Japan," recalled Sergeant Bill Menninger. In June 1950, Menninger was one of the American troops stationed in Japan after World War II.

66 My wife was giving the kids a bath prior to putting them to bed, and I was reading a book . . . when the call came for me to report at once to headquarters! The wife wanted to know what the call was about. 'Something must be wrong with next week's training schedule,' I answered. 'I'll be back as soon as I can.' 99

Dogtags of an American soldier in Korea

As it turned out, Menninger did not return for 11 months. When he got to headquarters, he learned that communist North Korea had invaded South Korea. The Cold War was turning hot.

War in Korea

The Korean peninsula borders Russia and China in northeastern Asia. From 1910 to 1945, Korea had been a Japanese colony. After World War II, it was divided at the 38th parallel of latitude. North Korea was governed by communists supported by the Soviet Union. The United States backed a noncommunist government in South Korea.

In June 1950, North Korean soldiers swept across the 38th parallel into South Korea. President Truman acted quickly. He asked the United Nations to send armed forces to Korea to stop the invasion. The Security Council agreed to set up a force, under the command of a general chosen by Truman. The President named Douglas MacArthur. About 80 percent of the UN force was American.

Advances and retreats

At first, UN forces were outnumbered and poorly supplied. Armed with new Soviet tanks, the North Koreans pushed steadily southward. By August 1950, communist troops controlled almost all of South Korea.

MacArthur launched a daring counterattack. He landed by sea at Inchon, behind North Korean lines. Caught by surprise, the North Koreans were forced to retreat back across the 38th parallel. (See the map on page 771.)

MacArthur's original orders called for him to drive the North Koreans out of South Korea. Truman and his advisers, however, wanted to punish North Korea for its aggression. They also wanted to unite Korea. With these goals in mind, they won UN approval for MacArthur to cross into North Korea.

As MacArthur advanced, the Chinese warned that they would not "sit back with folded hands" if the United States invaded North Korea. When UN forces neared the Chinese border, thousands of Chinese troops rushed across the Yalu River into North Korea. Once again, MacArthur was forced to retreat deep into South Korea.

Truman versus MacArthur

By March 1951, UN troops had regained control of the south. MacArthur argued that, to win, the UN had to attack China. Truman, though, feared that an attack on China might start a new world war. He preferred to limit the war and restore the boundary between North and South Korea.

MacArthur complained publicly that politicians in Washington were holding him back. "There is no substitute for victory," he insisted. Angry that MacArthur was defying orders, Truman fired the general.

Many Americans were furious. They gave MacArthur a hero's welcome when he returned home. Truman, however, successfully defended his action. Under the Constitution, he pointed out, the President is commander in chief, responsible for key decisions about war and peace. MacArthur's statements, said Truman, undermined attempts to reach a peace settlement.

Declaring a cease-fire

Peace talks began in July 1951. At first, there was little progress. Then, in 1952, the popular World War II General Dwight D. Eisenhower was elected President. To fulfill a campaign promise, he journeyed to Korea to get the stalled peace talks moving.

In July 1953, the two sides finally signed a cease-fire agreement. It set the border between North and South Korea near the 38th parallel, where it had been before. In this sense, the Korean War changed nothing. Still, the UN had pushed back North Korea's invasion. The United States and its allies showed that they were ready to go to war to prevent communist expansion.

The human cost of the Korean War was high. About 54,000 Americans, as well as 2 million Koreans and Chinese, lost their lives.

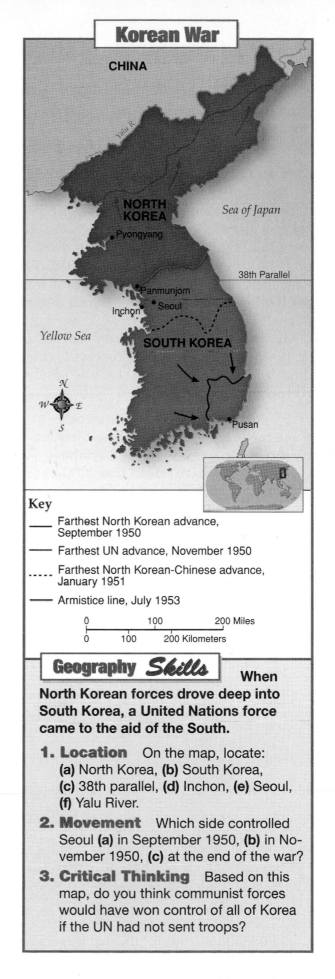

Korean War

Key

—— Farthest North Korean advance, September 1950

—— Farthest UN advance, November 1950

····· Farthest North Korean-Chinese advance, January 1951

—— Armistice line, July 1953

| 0 | 100 | 200 Miles |

| 0 | 100 | 200 Kilometers |

Geography *Skills*

When North Korean forces drove deep into South Korea, a United Nations force came to the aid of the South.

1. **Location** On the map, locate: **(a)** North Korea, **(b)** South Korea, **(c)** 38th parallel, **(d)** Inchon, **(e)** Seoul, **(f)** Yalu River.

2. **Movement** Which side controlled Seoul **(a)** in September 1950, **(b)** in November 1950, **(c)** at the end of the war?

3. **Critical Thinking** Based on this map, do you think communist forces would have won control of all of Korea if the UN had not sent troops?

Hunting Communists at Home

Many Americans worried that communists might be working secretly within the United States to overthrow the government. Such fears inspired a "Red Scare" like the one that followed World War I. (See page 694.)

Search for Soviet spies

Between 1946 and 1950, several people in the United States were arrested as Soviet spies. Ethel and Julius Rosenberg were convicted of stealing nuclear secrets. Despite protests, they were executed in 1953. The Rosenberg case made many Americans wonder if other Soviet spies were posing as ordinary citizens.

In 1947, President Truman ordered investigations of government workers to determine if they were loyal to the United States. His attorney general warned:

    66 American Reds are everywhere—in factories, offices, butcher stores, on street corners, in private businesses—and each carries in himself the germ of death for society. **99**

Thousands of government employees underwent questioning. Nearly 3,000 people were forced to resign, even though little evidence of communist activity was found.

McCarthy's campaign

In 1950, Senator **Joseph McCarthy** of Wisconsin announced that he had a list of 57 State Department employees who were Communist party members. McCarthy was never able to prove his claims. Yet his dramatic charges won him national attention.

During the next four years, McCarthy's campaign spread fear and suspicion across the nation. Businesses and colleges questioned employees. Many people were fired. Others, afraid of losing their own jobs, refused to defend accused co-workers.

In 1954, the Senate held televised hearings to investigate McCarthy's charges that there were communists in the United States Army. Under the glare of the television lights, McCarthy came across to the public as a bully, not a hero. His popularity plunged.

In December 1954, the Senate passed a resolution to **censure,** or officially condemn, McCarthy for "conduct unbecoming a member." As a result, McCarthy lost power. By the time he died, three years later, the worst of the Red Scare was over.

The Arms Race

Meanwhile, the United States and the Soviet Union embarked on an arms race. Each side built up its supply of missiles and atomic weapons. Each wanted to have enough weapons to withstand an attack by the other. By 1953, both nations had tested powerful new hydrogen bombs.

In 1957, a Soviet rocket launched *Sputnik,* the world's first artificial satellite. **Nikita Khrushchev** (KROO shawf), who had become Soviet leader after Stalin's death in

Viewing HISTORY **Hunting Communists in Entertainment**

In 1947, the House Committee on Un-American Activities held hearings to see if movie makers were affected by communist infiltration. As a result, studios denied work to many writers, directors, and actors. The publication Red Channels, *at left, listed suspected communists in radio and television.* ★ **Why do you think some Americans feared communist influence in movies, radio, and television?**

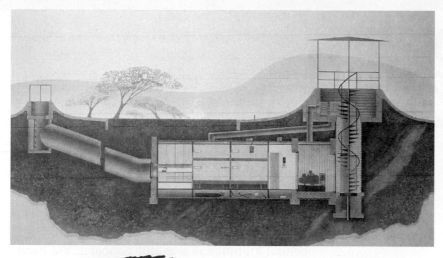

Viewing HISTORY — Responding to the Arms Race

During the 1950s, Americans responded in many ways to the threat of nuclear war. Some families and communities built "fallout shelters" (left). These underground hideaways were designed to protect against the radiation of an atomic blast. At right, school children learn to "duck and cover" in case of an atomic missile attack.

★ **Do schools conduct air raid drills today? Why or why not?**

1953, boasted that Soviet factories were turning out new rockets "like sausages." Americans were stunned. If the Soviets could launch a satellite, their atomic missiles could reach the United States as well.

Many Americans worried that the United States faced a "missile gap." In fact, the United States remained well ahead of the Soviet Union in the arms race. Between 1958 and 1960, the number of atomic weapons stockpiled by the United States tripled—from 6,000 to 18,000. Both sides spent billions of dollars on weapons and missiles.

In response to the launching of *Sputnik,* the government also created the **National Aeronautics and Space Administration** (NASA) in 1958. The goal of this agency was to establish an American space program to compete with that of the Soviets. The United States quickly moved ahead in the "space race."

Conflicts in Cuba

By the 1960s, the United States and the Soviet Union were **superpowers**—nations with enough military, political, and economic strength to influence events in many areas around the globe. One place where the superpowers clashed was Cuba.

In 1959, **Fidel Castro** led a revolution that set up a socialist state in Cuba. Castro's government took over private companies, including many owned by American businesses. Thousands of Cubans, especially those from the middle and upper classes, fled to the United States.

Bay of Pigs invasion

Castro's actions worried American leaders. Cuba was located just 90 miles (145 km) off the coast of Florida. The Soviet Union had begun supplying the new socialist state with large amounts of economic aid. In response, President Eisenhower approved a secret plan to train an army of Cuban exiles to invade Cuba. **Exiles** are people who have been forced to leave their own country.

⚛ Connections With Science

The arms race stimulated a uranium mining rush in the West. Uranium was needed to produce atomic weapons. In the early 1950s, prospectors with Geiger counters swarmed through the mountains and canyons of Colorado and Utah in search of uranium.

Why Study History?

Because We Can Learn to Ease Conflict

★ ★

Historical Background

The Cuban missile crisis of 1962 sticks in the memory of everyone who lived through it. (See page 775.) One American recalled, "I went to bed that night thinking that if there would ever be a World War III, it would probably be now."

Despite such fears, war was avoided. As the conflict eased, the United States and the Soviet Union set up a direct telephone link so their leaders could communicate instantly. The famous "hot line" symbolized the willingness of two enemies to resolve any conflicts that might lead to nuclear war.

Connections to Today

The Cold War ended in 1991 with the breakup of the Soviet Union. Today, schoolchildren no longer have to interrupt classes to take part in air raid drills. Families do not build underground nuclear fallout shelters in the backyard.

Still, dangerous conflicts continue to exist throughout the world. As in the Cold War, communication can be the key to easing tensions. Often, the United States plays the role of mediator, bringing enemies together to find solutions. American negotiators have helped hammer out peace agreements in the Middle East, Yugoslavia, Northern Ireland, and other trouble spots.

Connections to You

Today, few young Americans dread the outbreak of nuclear war. Yet you may face other kinds of fears and tensions. For some, school violence is a major concern. We have all heard of cases where simple arguments have had tragic outcomes.

For many schools, "peer mediation" programs are part of the solution to violence. Volunteers train to act as negotiators between other students. The mediator listens to both sides and tries to get them to reach an agreement. Both parties then sign a copy of the agreement. In schools, as in the world, communication can be the key to easing tension and reducing violence.

1. **Comprehension** **(a)** What was the purpose of the "hot line" between the United States and the Soviet Union? **(b)** What is the goal of peer mediation programs today?

2. **Critical Thinking** Some people think dress codes are one way to curb gang violence. Why might such a solution be effective?

 **Writing a Speech** You are running for office on the platform of ending school violence. Write a speech explaining how you would solve the problem. Include a catchy slogan that could be used on posters or buttons.

These students are learning to become "peer mediators" to resolve conflicts in their schools.

In 1961, **John F. Kennedy** became President. A few months later, on April 17, about 1,200 Cuban exiles landed at the **Bay of Pigs** on the southern coast of Cuba. They hoped other Cubans who opposed Castro would join them. The landing, however, was badly planned. Also, Kennedy canceled air support for the attack. Castro's forces quickly rounded up the invaders. In the end, the Bay of Pigs incident strengthened Castro in Cuba and embarrassed the United States.

Cuban missile crisis

After the Bay of Pigs invasion, the Soviet Union decided to give Cuba more weapons. In October 1962, President Kennedy learned that the Soviets were secretly building missile bases on the island. If the bases were completed, atomic missiles could reach American cities within minutes.

For a week, Kennedy and his advisers debated in secret. Then, in a dramatic television statement, the President told Americans about the missile sites. He announced that the navy would begin a "strict quarantine" of Cuba. American warships would turn back any Soviet ship carrying missiles.

A tense week followed as Soviet ships steamed toward Cuba. Attorney General Robert Kennedy, the President's brother, recalled one grim moment at the White House during the crisis:

66 Was the world on the brink of a holocaust?...[The President's] hand went up to his face and covered his mouth. He opened and closed his fist. His face seemed drawn, his eyes pained, almost gray. We stared at each other across the table. 99

At the last minute, the Soviet ships turned back. "We're eyeball to eyeball," said Secretary of State Dean Rusk, "and I think the other fellow just blinked."

Kennedy's strong stand led the Soviets to compromise. Khrushchev agreed to take the missiles out of Cuba. In turn, the United States agreed not to invade the island. Kennedy also promised to dismantle American missiles in Turkey.

The **Cuban missile crisis** had shaken both American and Soviet officials. In all the years of the Cold War, the world never came closer to a full-scale nuclear war.

★ Section 2 Review ★

Recall

1. **Locate** (a) North Korea, (b) South Korea, (c) Cuba.
2. **Identify** (a) Joseph McCarthy, (b) Nikita Khrushchev, (c) National Aeronautics and Space Administration, (d) Fidel Castro, (e) John F. Kennedy, (f) Bay of Pigs, (g) Cuban missile crisis.
3. **Define** (a) censure, (b) superpower, (c) exile.

Comprehension

4. (a) What action led to the Korean War? (b) Why did the Chinese join the fighting? (c) How did the war end?
5. (a) What steps did President Truman take to fight communism at home? (b) How did Senator Joseph McCarthy come to national attention?
6. Why did Castro's revolution in Cuba worry the United States?

Critical Thinking and Writing

7. **Analyzing Ideas** Why do you think the Constitution made the President commander in chief of the military?
8. **Linking Past and Present** Television played a major role in the downfall of Senator Joseph McCarthy. Does television influence public opinion today? Give an example to support your answer.

Activity **Understanding Psychology** You are a psychologist who views history in terms of people's feelings. Give three examples of how fear affected American history between 1950 and 1962. (Remember, fear is not always a weakness. Sometimes, it can even save your life!)

Cold War Battlegrounds

Explore These Questions
- Why did many new nations emerge after World War II?
- Why did the Cold War spread to Asia and Africa?
- What policies did the United States follow in Latin America?

Identify
- Alliance for Progress
- Peace Corps
- Organization of American States
- Ronald Reagan
- Iran-Contra deal

SETTING the Scene In September 1959, Soviet premier Nikita Khrushchev arrived in New York. He had come to address the United Nations. At first, Khrushchev spoke calmly, expressing hopes that the Cold War between the United States and the Soviet Union would end. Soon, however, Khrushchev's manner changed. Twice, he became so angry that he took off his shoe and pounded it on the table.

Khrushchev's visit symbolized the calms and storms of the continuing Cold War. As the two superpowers confronted each other, the nations of Africa, Asia, and Latin America became battlegrounds in the struggle.

Emerging Nations

After World War II, people in Asia and Africa began to demand independence. For years, they had been governed as colonies of European and other foreign powers. In the postwar years, many new nations emerged.

In the colonies, communist rebels often campaigned to overthrow foreign control. Khrushchev promised support for what he called "wars of national liberation." Both openly and secretly, the Soviets gave economic and military aid to rebel forces.

The West tried to prevent the Soviets from expanding their influence. In doing so, American leaders faced difficult choices. Should the United States provide aid to a nation even if that meant helping a military dictator? Should Americans use secret aid to counter the Soviets? Should they send troops into other nations to influence their internal affairs? In the end, the United States used all these tactics at one time or another to contain communism and win the Cold War.

The Philippines

The United States also had to address the issue of its own colonies. On July 4, 1946, it granted independence to the Philippines. Crowds in Manila braved heavy rains to attend the independence ceremony. They cheered as the American flag was lowered and the Filipino flag hoisted high.

Still, the transition to independence was not easy. A few wealthy Filipinos owned most of the land. Many Filipinos wanted to divide the land more equally among the peasant farmers. When the government did not act quickly to make changes, fighting broke out. Some of the rebels were communists. By 1954, the government defeated the rebels. It also made some land reforms.

In 1965, Ferdinand Marcos became president of the Philippines. Under Marcos, the government became less democratic. In the years that followed, both noncommunists and communists pushed for reforms.

India and Southeast Asia

In 1947, the people of India won independence from Britain. The land was divided into two nations—India and Pakistan. Both the United States and the Soviet Union tried to win the support of these giant new nations. Feeling threatened by the Soviet Union to its north, Pakistan became an ally of the United States. India accepted both American and Soviet economic aid, but remained neutral in the Cold War. India also led other neutral nations in calling on the superpowers to stop their arms race.

In Southeast Asia, Burma, Malaysia, and Singapore became independent from Britain. Indonesia won freedom from the Netherlands. In Indochina, nationalists fought for independence from France.* The war in Indochina lasted for almost 30 years and eventually involved the United States, as you will read in Section 4.

African Nations

During the 1950s and 1960s, Africans worked to win independence from European colonial rule. By 1970, more than 30 independent states had been formed. Most political divisions within emerging African nations were based on tribal loyalties.

As part of the Cold War, both the United States and Soviet Union sought allies among Africa's new states. To achieve this goal, the superpowers offered economic and military aid to nations or tribal groups within nations.

The Cold War fueled international conflicts and civil wars in Africa. In East Africa, the superpowers were involved in a long war between Somalia and Ethiopia. The United States backed Somalia, while the Soviet Union backed Ethiopia. In southern Africa, the Cold War intensified a civil war in Angola. Angola's communist government was aided by Soviet finances and by more than

---

* Indochina included the present-day countries of Laos, Cambodia, and Vietnam.

50,000 Cuban troops. The United States, meanwhile, supported anticommunist rebel groups.

Latin America and the Cold War

Closer to home, American leaders focused on Latin America. In the early 1900s, the United States had frequently intervened in the internal affairs of Latin American nations. Now, Cold War tensions led the United States to resume its active role. As you have read, American efforts to keep Soviet missiles out of Cuba nearly resulted in nuclear war. As the Cold War continued, American leaders worked to contain communism in other Latin American nations as well.

Economic issues

Latin America had long faced severe social and economic problems. As populations grew, governments found it impossible to provide enough jobs, schools, and hospitals. Poor people migrated to cities, seeking work. There, they often lived in tin or cardboard shacks, without heat, light, or water.

Many poor Latin Americans saw communism as a solution to their problems. Communists pointed out that a small number of wealthy citizens owned most of the land in Latin America. They called for land to be divided more equally. Some noncommunists also supported this view.

The economies of many Latin American nations depended on American corporations.

 Fear of World Communism

This panel appeared in an American anticommunist comic book during the 1950s. The man standing is Soviet premier Nikita Khrushchev. He is shown plotting to spread the communist ideas of Marx and Lenin throughout the world. ★ **Why do you think foes of communism published this comic book?**

Vice President Richard Nixon got a stormy welcome when he visited Venezuela in 1958. Here, an angry mob throws rocks and eggs at Nixon's limousine. At one point, Nixon faced protesters directly and challenged them to a debate. ★ **Why did some people in Latin America distrust the United States?**

◀ Vice President Richard Nixon

These businesses made large profits from their Latin American investments, yet they paid workers very low wages. Reformers called for stronger regulation of foreign corporations. Communists demanded that such companies be taken over by the state.

American aid

Many American leaders agreed with the need for reform. They hoped that American aid would help make Latin American nations more democratic, ease the lives of the people, and lessen communist influence.

President Kennedy worked to strengthen ties to Latin America. In 1961, he set up a program called the **Alliance for Progress.** The Alliance tried to help the people of Latin America build schools and hospitals, improve farming, and win economic and social reform.

Kennedy also formed the **Peace Corps.** Under this program, thousands of American volunteers went to Latin America or other developing areas. Volunteers lived with the local people for two years, teaching or giving technical advice. One volunteer later said:

66 Just imagine a person thinking he can actually do something about world hunger, poverty, illiteracy, or disease. Those are not 'just' problems, but problems the size of mountains, yet the average Peace Corps volunteer believes he can do his part by chipping away at those mountains ...one person at a time. 99

The United States also backed the **Organization of American States,** or OAS. Through the OAS, it encouraged economic progress in Latin America by investing in transportation and industry.

Military intervention

At other times, the United States sent troops or military aid to Latin American countries. In doing so, it often supported military dictators because they were strongly anticommunist. Between 1950 and 1990, American forces were sent to Guatemala, the Dominican Republic, Panama, and Grenada.

Many Latin Americans complained that the United States had begun using its "big stick" again in foreign policy. When Vice President Richard Nixon toured eight Latin American nations in 1958, angry mobs pelted his car with eggs and stones.

Through the years, American Presidents defended their actions. The United States would intervene in Latin America, said President Lyndon Johnson, whenever "the object [of rebels] is the establishment of a Communist dictatorship."

Nicaragua

American actions in Latin America increased during the 1980s. President **Ronald Reagan** took office in 1981. As a strong anticommunist, he provided aid to friendly forces in both Nicaragua and El Salvador.

In Nicaragua, a revolutionary group called the Sandinistas had taken power in 1979 and set up a socialist government. The Sandinistas later won an election in 1984. Their opponents were known as Contras, from the Spanish word meaning "against." President Reagan supported the efforts of Contra rebels to overthrow the Sandinistas.

Many members of Congress disagreed with President Reagan's policy in Nicaragua. They passed laws banning military aid to the Contras. Even so, some people on the President's staff provided military aid secretly. To finance their program, the officials used profits from illegal weapons sales to Iran, a country in the Middle East.

In 1986, news reporters discovered the details of the secret **Iran-Contra deal.** The news stirred a great deal of debate because officials working for the President had lied to Congress about their actions. After an investigation, several members of the President's staff were put on trial. The President, however, said he did not know his staff had done anything to break the law.

In 1987, the president of Costa Rica helped arrange a peace plan for Nicaragua. In elections in 1990, Nicaraguans rejected the Sandinistas and voted in new leaders.

El Salvador

In El Salvador, Reagan sent arms and military advisers to help the government in a civil war that raged there. The United States supported the government even though it was often brutal and oppressive. Fighting between rebels and the government lasted 12 years and cost more than 50,000 lives.

Finally, through the efforts of the United Nations, a cease-fire agreement was reached in early 1992. "This is a new country," said one former rebel leader. Two years later, El Salvador held democratic elections. Many hoped the elections would lead to greater democracy and stability in the country.

★ Section 3 Review ★

Recall

1. **Locate** (a) the Philippines, (b) India, (c) Pakistan, (d) Nicaragua, (e) El Salvador.
2. **Identify** (a) Alliance for Progress, (b) Peace Corps, (c) Organization of American States, (d) Ronald Reagan, (e) Iran-Contra deal.

Comprehension

3. What major changes took place in Asia and Africa after World War II?
4. How did the Soviet Union try to win support from emerging nations?

5. Describe two ways that the United States tried to influence Latin America during the Cold War.

Critical Thinking and Writing

6. **Understanding Causes and Effects** Why might the competition between the United States and the Soviet Union have hindered development in the new nations of Asia and Africa?
7. **Recognizing Points of View** Why do you think that relations between the United States and Latin America were often strained?

★ ★

Activity **Writing a Position Statement** You are an adviser to an American President during the Cold War. The President is trying to decide whether the United States should or should not support an anticommunist dictator in an African nation. Write a brief statement in which you explain your position.

4

The Vietnam War

As You Read

Explore These Questions
- Why did the United States send troops to Vietnam?
- Why did many Americans oppose United States involvement in the Vietnam War?
- What were the results of the war?

Define
- guerrilla
- domino theory
- escalate

Identify
- Ho Chi Minh
- Vietcong
- Lyndon Johnson
- Gulf of Tonkin Resolution
- Vietnam War
- Tet Offensive
- Richard Nixon
- Khmer Rouge

SETTING the Scene In 1961, journalist Stanley Karnow stopped by the White House to talk with Attorney General Robert Kennedy. Karnow had been reporting from Southeast Asia for several years. He wanted to warn Kennedy that the nation of Vietnam was becoming a serious trouble spot.

Kennedy was not convinced. "We've got 20 Vietnams a day to handle," he said. Karnow turned out to be right, though. During the 1960s, a small conflict in Asia grew steadily into the longest war in American history.

The Two Vietnams

Vietnam is a narrow country that stretches 1,000 miles (1600 km) along the South China Sea. Since the late 1800s, it had been ruled by France as a colony.

After World War II, a Vietnamese communist named **Ho Chi Minh** (HOH CHEE MIHN) led a war for independence. Ho's army finally defeated the French in 1954. An international peace conference divided Vietnam into two nations. North Vietnam, led by Ho Chi Minh, received aid from the Soviet Union. South Vietnam, under Ngo Dinh Diem (NOH DIN dee EHM), was backed by the United States.

Vietnamese peasant

By the time President John Kennedy took office in 1961, many South Vietnamese had come to distrust Diem. They felt that he favored the nation's few wealthy landowners and ignored the problems of its peasants.

As discontent grew, many peasants joined the **Vietcong**—guerrillas who opposed Diem. **Guerrillas** (guh RIHL uhz) are fighters who use hit-and-run attacks. They do not wear uniforms or fight in large forces. In time, the Vietcong became communist and were supported by North Vietnam. Vietcong influence quickly spread, especially in the small villages of South Vietnam.

Growing American Involvement

The successes of the Vietcong worried American leaders. They reasoned that, if South Vietnam fell to the communists, neighboring countries in Southeast Asia would follow—like a row of falling dominoes. This idea became known as the **domino theory.** The goal of the United States was to prevent the first domino from falling.

President Kennedy strongly believed in the domino theory. In 1961, he sent military advisers to help Diem fight the Vietcong.

These advisers were not to take part in combat. Their mission was to help organize and train the South Vietnamese army. Meanwhile, Diem continued to lose support. In November 1963, he was assassinated.

In 1963, **Lyndon Johnson** became President. Like Kennedy, Johnson believed that the United States could not allow the Vietcong to take over South Vietnam. Johnson increased aid to South Vietnam. Still, the Vietcong continued to gain influence.

Americans in combat

Then, in August 1964, North Vietnamese torpedo boats attacked an American ship patrolling in the Gulf of Tonkin. A second attack was reported but never confirmed. North Vietnam claimed that the American ships were spying in North Vietnamese waters.

At Johnson's urging, Congress passed the **Gulf of Tonkin Resolution.** It allowed the President "to take all necessary measures to repel any armed attack or to prevent further aggression." Johnson used the resolution to order the bombing of North Vietnam, as well as some targets in South Vietnam.

As a result of the Gulf of Tonkin Resolution, the role of Americans in Vietnam changed from military advisers to active fighters. Across South Vietnam, American troops battled against North Vietnamese and Vietcong communist forces. By 1968, President Johnson had sent more than 500,000 troops to fight in the **Vietnam War.**

Fighting a jungle war

As the war **escalated,** or expanded, Johnson used the draft to raise troops. The draft affected American youths unequally. Many young men from wealthy or middle-class families found legal ways to avoid being drafted. As a result, a high percentage of the troops in Vietnam were poor, including many African Americans and Latinos.

American soldiers quickly discovered that the Vietnam War was different from other wars. Rather than trying to gain ground, Americans were sent on "search and destroy" missions. The goal was to search for Vietcong strongholds and destroy them. Then, the Americans moved on.

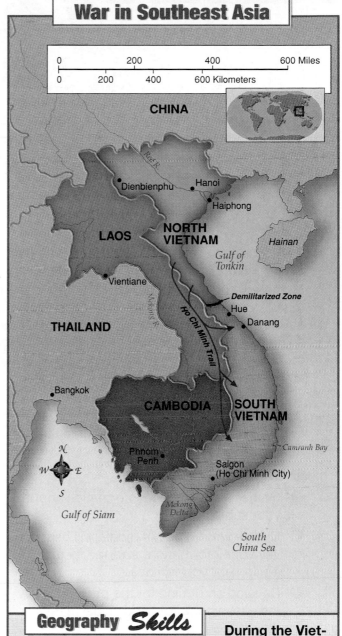

War in Southeast Asia

Geography Skills   During the Vietnam War, North Vietnam supplied arms to communist guerrillas in the South. The system of supply routes from the North was known as the Ho Chi Minh Trail.

1. **Location**   On the map, locate: **(a)** North Vietnam, **(b)** South Vietnam, **(c)** Gulf of Tonkin, **(d)** Saigon, **(e)** Cambodia.
2. **Movement**   Through which countries did the Ho Chi Minh Trail run?
3. **Critical Thinking**   According to the domino theory, what nations would be threatened if the communists won control of South Vietnam?

Skills FOR LIFE

| Critical Thinking | Managing Information | Communication | Maps, Charts, and Graphs |

Planning a Multimedia Presentation

How Will I Use This Skill?

Multimedia presentations combine both audio and visual formats, including music, moving and still pictures, and printed material. They are effective because most people remember what they see better than what they hear. By using a variety of methods, you can communicate your ideas clearly and more forcefully. Multimedia presentations are used not only in class but in government and the business world as well.

LEARN the Skill

Follow these steps to prepare your multimedia presentation:

❶ Choose your topic.

❷ Gather materials and information about your subject.

❸ Decide what types of media will best convey your information. Arrange for any equipment you will need.

❹ Develop an outline for the presentation. Indicate what audio and visual materials you will use, and when.

❺ Practice and give your multimedia presentation.

You can use tools like these to create a multimedia presentation.

PRACTICE the Skill

❶ Focus your presentation on this topic: What was life like in the United States during the Vietnam War era?

❷ Research the topic. What books or videos are available on this topic? What kinds of music can you use for background? Are there any Internet sites related to the Vietnam War? What people might you interview in your family or community?

❸ List answers to these questions: Will visuals include videotapes, overheads, interactive computer displays? Will audio include taped interviews, music, CD-ROMs? What equipment will you need?

❹ Complete your outline, indicating where and how you will use audio and visual materials.

❺ Make your presentation.

APPLY the Skill

Use the steps you have learned to create a multimedia presentation about your family history or cultural background. Consider using photos, taped interviews, family mementos, or antiques.

Vietcong forces were hard to pin down, however. When Americans took an area, the Vietcong retreated into dense jungle forests. After the Americans moved on, the Vietcong returned and reclaimed the territory. As a result, Americans found themselves going back again and again to fight in the same areas with the same uncertain results.

American soldiers faced an even more frustrating problem in Vietnam. Often, they could not tell which villagers were Vietcong. The enemy might be the old woman cooking rice outside her hut or the man walking down the village path to the market. As one American soldier explained:

> 66 The farmer you waved to from your jeep in the day...would be the guy with the gun out looking for you at night. 99

In such an uncertain situation, it was difficult to win clear victories.

Divisions at Home

When Congress approved the Gulf of Tonkin Resolution, President Johnson received overwhelming support. However, as casualties mounted, more and more people began to question American involvement in the war.

Television reports increased this growing sense of doubt. For the first time, Americans could sit in their own living rooms and witness the sights and sounds of warfare. They watched villages burn and saw wounded soldiers, children, and old people.

Hawks and doves

The country soon divided into two camps. Those who supported the war became known as hawks. Hawks argued that North Vietnamese aggression had forced Americans into war. Therefore, the United States should do whatever was necessary to win.

Doves—those who opposed the war—saw the conflict in Vietnam as a civil war. They believed that the United States had no right to interfere in it. Further, doves noted that the billions spent on the war could have been better spent on social programs at home.

Protesting the war

Many doves took part in antiwar protests. Protests were especially strong on college campuses. Students staged marches and sit-ins. Young men burned their draft cards and counseled others to avoid the draft. At some universities, militant protesters took over buildings and destroyed property.

The protesters charged that American lives and money were being wasted on an unjust war. The government of South Vietnam, they said, was no better than the Vietcong or the North Vietnamese.

Antiwar protests fed a widespread spirit of rebellion. Some young people of the 1960s

 The Vietnam War, at Home and Overseas

At left, two American soldiers on patrol wade through muddy waters in the jungles of South Vietnam. While some young Americans fought, others protested. At right, college students march to demonstrate their opposition to the war.
★ **How did television affect public support for the war effort?**

Antiwar medallion ➤

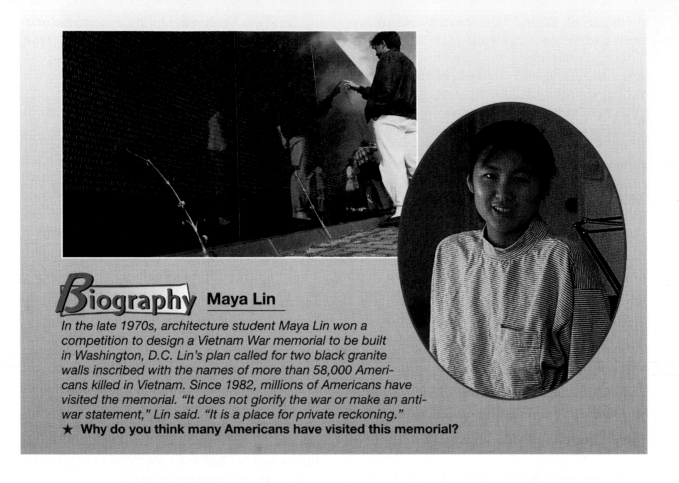

Biography — Maya Lin

In the late 1970s, architecture student Maya Lin won a competition to design a Vietnam War memorial to be built in Washington, D.C. Lin's plan called for two black granite walls inscribed with the names of more than 58,000 Americans killed in Vietnam. Since 1982, millions of Americans have visited the memorial. "It does not glorify the war or make an anti-war statement," Lin said. "It is a place for private reckoning."

★ **Why do you think many Americans have visited this memorial?**

and early 1970s rejected traditional American values and culture. They experimented with clothing, music, and ways of life that shocked their parents. Unfortunately, many young rebels also experimented with illegal drugs. Drug abuse became a growing social problem in the United States.

A Turning Point

In January 1968, the Vietcong launched surprise attacks on cities throughout South Vietnam. Vietcong guerrillas even stormed the walls of the American embassy in Saigon, the capital of South Vietnam. The attack became known as the **Tet Offensive** because it took place during Tet, the Vietnamese New Year's holiday.

In the end, American and South Vietnamese forces pushed back the enemy. Still, the Vietcong had won a major political victory. The Tet Offensive showed that even with half a million American troops, no part of Vietnam was safe from Vietcong attack.

Hoping to bring calm to the nation, a weary President Johnson announced that he would not seek reelection in 1968. That year, Republican **Richard Nixon** was elected President in a close race. During the campaign, he had pledged to end the war.

The War Winds Down

At first, President Nixon escalated the war. Protests grew, especially after Nixon ordered the bombing of Cambodia, Vietnam's neighbor to the west.

Bombing of Cambodia

Throughout the war, North Vietnamese soldiers carried supplies and arms into South Vietnam along trails in Cambodia. They also used Cambodia as a place where they could escape from American and South Vietnamese forces.

In 1969, Nixon secretly ordered the bombing of communist bases in Cambodia. American and South Vietnamese forces also made ground attacks on the bases in 1970. As Cambodians took sides in the struggle, their nation was plunged into a civil war.

End of the war

Meanwhile, the President gradually began to bring troops home from Vietnam. At the same time, peace talks were held in Paris. In January 1973, Henry Kissinger, Nixon's national security adviser, reached a cease-fire agreement. The following year, the last American troops left Vietnam.

The United States continued to send billions of dollars in aid to South Vietnam. Even so, the South Vietnamese were unable to stop the North Vietnamese advance. In April 1975, communist forces captured Saigon and renamed it Ho Chi Minh City. Soon after, Vietnam was reunited.

Tragedy in Cambodia

That year, the civil war in Cambodia was won by the communist **Khmer Rouge** (kuh MER ROOJ). For the next few years, Cambodians suffered under a brutal reign of terror. The Khmer Rouge forced millions of people to work in the fields from dawn to dark. More than a million Cambodians were killed or starved to death.

In 1979, Vietnam invaded Cambodia and set up a new communist government. It was less harsh than the Khmer Rouge, but it could not end the fighting.

Vietnam Balance Sheet

For all concerned, the Vietnam War was a costly conflict. Between 1961 and 1973, more than 58,000 American soldiers lost their lives. For the Vietnamese, the statistics were even more grim. More than a million Vietnamese soldiers and perhaps half a million civilians died. The destruction caused by the war shattered the Vietnamese economy.

After 1975, hundreds of thousands of people fled Vietnam and Cambodia. Refugees from Vietnam escaped in small boats. Many of these "boat people" drowned or died of hunger and thirst. The United States took in many refugees.

The Vietnam War era was one of the most painful periods in American history. The government spent vast amounts of money on the war. Beyond that, the war had divided the nation in an often-bitter debate. In the Cold War, it was not easy to decide how far Americans should go to fight communism.

★ Section 4 Review ★

Recall

1. **Locate** (a) Vietnam, (b) Cambodia.
2. **Identify** (a) Ho Chi Minh, (b) Vietcong, (c) Lyndon Johnson, (d) Gulf of Tonkin Resolution, (e) Vietnam War, (f) Tet Offensive, (g) Richard Nixon, (h) Khmer Rouge.
3. **Define** (a) guerrilla, (b) domino theory, (c) escalate.

Comprehension

4. (a) Why did President Kennedy send advisers to Vietnam? (b) How did President Johnson increase American involvement in Vietnam?

5. What arguments did protesters use against the Vietnam War?
6. (a) Why did civil war break out in Cambodia? (b) What were the results of the war?

Critical Thinking and Writing

7. **Synthesizing Information** How did the Cold War affect American policy in Vietnam?
8. **Comparing** (a) Compare American attitudes about fighting in World War II with those about the Vietnam War. (b) How might you explain the difference?

★ ★

Activity **Summarizing** Write a series of newspaper headlines that summarize the history of the Vietnam War. Include headlines that describe events in Vietnam, Southeast Asia as a whole, and the United States. Be sure to write headlines that would have caught your attention if you had been an American teenager at that time!

The End of the Cold War

As You Read

Explore These Questions
- How did President Nixon ease tensions with the communist world?
- What events led to the breakup of the Soviet Union?
- What steps did Americans take to help the people of the former Soviet Union?

Define
- détente
- martial law
- glasnost
- summit meeting
- free market

Identify
- SALT Agreement
- Gerald Ford
- Jimmy Carter
- Star Wars
- Solidarity
- Mikhail Gorbachev
- INF Treaty
- Boris Yeltsin

SETTING the Scene It was November 1989, and the world was witnessing one of the strangest celebrations it had ever seen. In Berlin, far into the night, cheering people wielded pickaxes and sledgehammers against barbed wire and concrete. After nearly 30 years, the wall between East and West was coming down.

As you read, communist East German troops had put up the wall dividing East and West Berlin in 1961. Those who tried to escape to the West were often shot on sight by East German border guards. The Berlin Wall stood as a symbol of tensions between the communist and noncommunist worlds.

By the late 1980s, however, the Cold War was coming to an end. One East German woman described her visit to West Berlin:

66 One day last week, I took my bike and—just went over. I had to stop and laugh! I felt so strange. For 40 years we couldn't do something so simple. I just had to stop and laugh! 99

Berlin was only one of many places where citizens celebrated their release from communist oppression.

A Temporary Thaw

The first hopes that the Cold War might end came in 1971. In that year, American troops were still fighting communists in Vietnam. Even so, President Richard Nixon looked for ways to ease world tension. His first move was to seek improved relations with the People's Republic of China.

Recognizing China

Since 1949, the United States had refused to recognize Mao Zedong's communist government in China. Richard Nixon had been one of the most outspoken opponents of recognizing communist China. As President, however, in 1971, Nixon began secret talks to consider closer ties with China. To show its good will, China invited the American ping-pong team to a competition in Beijing.

To the surprise of many Americans, President Nixon himself visited the People's Republic of China in February 1972. Television cameras captured the President walking along the Great Wall of China and attending state dinners with Chinese leaders.

The visit was a triumph for Nixon and the start of a new era in relations with China. As tensions continued to ease, the United States established formal diplomatic relations with China in 1979.

A policy of détente

President Nixon followed his visit to China with another historic trip. In May 1972, he became the first American President to visit the Soviet Union since the Cold

War began. The trip was part of Nixon's effort to reduce tensions between the superpowers. This policy was known as **détente** (day TAHNT).

Détente eased the Cold War by allowing more trade and other contacts between the United States and the Soviet Union. More important, the two nations signed a treaty agreeing to limit the number of nuclear warheads and missiles that they built. This treaty was known as the **SALT Agreement.** (SALT stands for Strategic Arms Limitation Talks.)

Détente continued under the next two Presidents—**Gerald Ford,** who served from 1974 to 1977, and **Jimmy Carter,** who served from 1977 to 1981. Trade between the United States and the Soviet Union increased. The Soviets bought tons of American wheat. In 1975, Soviet and American astronauts conducted a joint space mission. In June 1979, President Carter met with Soviet leader Leonid Brezhnev (BREHZH nehf). They worked out the details of a SALT II Treaty.

New Tensions

Before the Senate could ratify the new SALT treaty, hopes for détente faded. In 1979, the world entered another decade of Cold War tensions.

Soviet invasion of Afghanistan

In December 1979, Soviet troops invaded Afghanistan, a mountainous nation along the Soviet Union's southern border. Soviet forces seized major cities and gave military support to a pro-Soviet government that had seized power there.

Aleksandr Solzhenitsyn, a major Russian writer of the twentieth century, won the Nobel Prize for literature in 1970. His novels present vivid accounts of the struggle for freedom against Soviet repression. After the Soviet government exiled him in 1974, Solzhenitsyn and his family moved to a town in Vermont.

Biography — Henry Kissinger

At the age of 15, Henry Kissinger fled Germany to escape Nazi persecution of Jews. A brilliant student of history, he became a college professor. In the 1970s, Dr. Kissinger was President Nixon's closest adviser on foreign policy, working tirelessly to bring about détente. Kissinger was also known for "shuttle diplomacy"—traveling back and forth between nations in an attempt to ease conflicts.
★ **How did Kissinger and Nixon change American policy toward China?**

"The Soviet Union must pay a price for its aggression," President Carter declared. He withdrew the SALT II Treaty from the Senate. He also announced that American athletes would not compete in the 1980 summer Olympic Games in Moscow.

Despite the tough American response, Soviet troops remained in Afghanistan for eight years. They suffered heavy losses as Afghan rebels, supplied by the United States, battled the communist government. The war in Afghanistan became so costly for the Soviets in the long run that it eventually contributed to the downfall of the Soviet Union. For the time being, however, the invasion marked the end of détente.

Reagan's strong stand

When Ronald Reagan took office in 1981, he firmly believed that the Soviet Union was "the focus of evil in the modern world." He called on Americans to "oppose it with all our might." As you read, Reagan strongly supported anticommunist forces in Latin America.

Reagan wanted to deal with the Soviets from a position of strength. He told the American people that "we must find peace through strength." He persuaded Congress to increase military spending by more than $100 billion during his first five years in office. His defense program included research on weapons that he hoped could shoot down Soviet missiles from space. The system was nicknamed **Star Wars.**

Throughout Reagan's first term, the two superpowers viewed each other with deep mistrust. During Reagan's first year in office, an event in Eastern Europe set the tone for new tensions.

In December 1981, Poland's communist government cracked down on **Solidarity,** an independent labor union. The Polish government, with the backing of the Soviet Union, declared **martial law,** or emergency military rule.

President Reagan quickly condemned what he called the police-state tactics of Poland's communist government. He urged the Soviets to permit the restoration of basic human rights in Poland. He also put economic pressure on Poland to end martial law.

Reforms and Cooperation

Cracks in the Soviet empire began to appear in the mid-1980s. Growing economic problems plagued the Soviet Union as it continued to spend large sums of money on military production. One major problem was that consumer products were in short supply. Soviet citizens spent hours waiting in lines for poorly made goods. The time was ripe for reform.

Reforms in the Soviet Union

In 1985, a new Soviet leader, **Mikhail Gorbachev** (mee kah EEL GOR buh chawf),

Cause and Effect

Causes

- Soviet Union takes control of Eastern European nations
- Communism gains influence in Western Europe, the Middle East, and Asia
- Western powers fear Soviet expansion

The Cold War

Effects

- Arms race between United States and Soviet Union results in heavy military spending
- Western powers and Soviet Union create separate military alliances
- Armed conflicts erupt in Korea and Vietnam
- United States and Soviet Union compete for influence in developing nations

Effects Today

- United States is world's greatest military power
- Eastern European countries are struggling to create democratic governments
- Southeast Asian countries are still recovering from war

Graphic Organizer *Skills*

For 45 years, the Cold War pitted the United States against the Soviet Union.

1. **Comprehension** (a) What event in Europe helped spark the Cold War? (b) Which effects of the Cold War involved Americans in actual fighting?

2. **Critical Thinking** How did the Cold War help the United States become the world's greatest military power?

came to power. Only 54 years old, Gorbachev was younger and more energetic than the leaders who had come before him. He believed that he had to take bold steps to improve the failing Soviet economy.

Gorbachev called for **glasnost,** a policy of speaking out honestly and openly. Earlier leaders had cracked down on anyone who criticized their policies or exposed problems in Soviet life. Now, under Gorbachev, Soviet newspapers could write about poor harvests, crime, and corruption. Gorbachev hoped that allowing public discussion of problems would help the nation find solutions.

Reagan and Gorbachev cooperate

Gorbachev also decided that he had to cut military spending sharply in order to solve the Soviet Union's economic problems. To achieve this goal, he tried to improve relations with the United States.

President Reagan agreed to meet with Gorbachev in several summit meetings. A **summit meeting** is a conference between the highest-ranking officials of different nations. Reagan's own staff members were stunned by his willingness to meet with Gorbachev. The President, however, explained that Gorbachev was unlike earlier Soviet leaders and that glasnost was very different from the bad old days of the "evil empire."

In 1987, Reagan and Gorbachev signed an arms control pact called the **Intermediate Nuclear Force (INF) Treaty.** In the treaty, the United States and Soviet Union agreed to get rid of short-range and medium-range missiles. President Reagan signed the agreement despite strong objections from officials in the Defense Department.

In 1989, Gorbachev withdrew Soviet troops from Afghanistan. This action removed another barrier to cooperation between the superpowers.

Communist governments fall in Eastern Europe

For nearly 50 years, the communist governments of Eastern Europe had crushed independent political parties or open debate. Sometimes, the Soviet Union intervened militarily in its satellite nations. In 1956, Soviet tanks had helped crush a revolt in Hungary. In 1968, Soviet tanks had again rolled when a new leader tried to reform the communist government of Czechoslovakia.

Now, Eastern Europeans greeted news of Gorbachev's reforms with demands of their own. To everyone's surprise, Gorbachev viewed the Eastern European protests as signs of needed change. Encouraged by this response, reformers pressed their demands. With opposition so widespread, most Eastern European governments did not dare use military force to block change.

Viewing HISTORY **The Berlin Wall**

For nearly 30 years, the grim concrete and barbed wire barrier of the Berlin Wall divided the city. Then, in 1989, the wall was opened. At left, joyful Berliners climb over and through the wall before tearing it down completely. ★ **How did the fall of the Berlin Wall mark a turning point in the Cold War?**

In 1989, Poland's communist government held the nation's first free elections in 50 years. Rejecting communism, the Poles voted into office all the candidates put up by Solidarity, the trade union. Solidarity leader Lech Walesa, who had been thrown in jail eight years earlier, became head of the new Polish government.

In Romania, demonstrators overthrew and executed a brutal dictator. Communist governments also fell in Hungary, Czechoslovakia, Bulgaria, and Albania.

In 1989, peaceful protests swept major cities in East Germany. The communist government was forced out and replaced with reformers who promised democratic changes. East and West Berliners demolished the wall that had divided their city since 1961. Within a year, Germany was reunited under a democratic government.

Breakup of the Soviet Union

The Soviet Union itself was made up of 15 republics held together by a strong central government. The republics enjoyed few freedoms. By 1990, unrest led to a flare-up of ancient rivalries among some of the nation's 120 ethnic groups. Some groups, including Lithuanians, Latvians, and Estonians, boldly demanded self-rule.

Democratic reforms

Amid the turmoil, Gorbachev announced new moves toward democracy. For nearly 70 years, the Soviet Union had been a one-party state. Under Gorbachev's reforms, new political parties were allowed to form. For the first time, groups could openly oppose the communists.

In August 1991, some desperate communist officials tried to overturn the new reforms. Holding Gorbachev captive, they sent military forces to surround the parliament building in Moscow.

To the surprise of the plotters, thousands of Russians turned out to block the soldiers. Led by a politician named **Boris Yeltsin,** the reformers turned the tide. Standing on top of a tank that the crowd had surrounded, Yeltsin shouted his defiance to the plotters and his belief in democracy:

   66 By their criminal actions, they have confronted the country with the danger of terror, and have placed themselves outside the law.... Aggression will not go forward! Only democracy will win! **99**

In the months that followed, republic after republic declared its independence from the Union of Soviet Socialist Republics. In December 1991, Gorbachev resigned and the Soviet Union ceased to exist.

Economic reforms and American aid

Eventually, the Soviet Union broke up into 15 separate nations. Of these, Russia was the largest and most powerful. With

Yeltsin as its president, Russia began the difficult task of rebuilding its economy and introducing a free-market system. In a **free market,** individuals decide what to produce and sell. Under communism, the government had made such economic decisions.

Most Americans agreed that it was important for the new republics to succeed with their reforms. Along with Western European nations, the United States provided economic aid to Russia. American experts advised business leaders in the former republics and in Eastern Europe about the shift to a free-market system. The United States hoped that the former communist states would in time become profitable trading partners.

Half a Century of Cold War

For nearly half a century, the shadow of the Cold War touched every corner of American life. Students in the 1950s practiced hiding in fallout shelters in case an atomic war broke out. Millions of young Americans went off to fight in Korea and Vietnam. From 1946 to 1990, the United States spent over 6 trillion dollars on national defense.

Most Americans were happy to claim victory in the Cold War. President Truman's policy of containment had been followed by eight other American Presidents, both Republicans and Democrats. The United States had slowed down or stopped communist expansion in Asia and Africa as well as in Europe and the Americas. Free elections had come to many nations for the first time in decades.

Victory did not come without its price. During the 1950s, exaggerated fears of communists led many loyal Americans to lose their jobs. The threat of nuclear war demanded caution from both American and Soviet leaders. Even one mistake could plunge the world into an atomic war that might destroy civilization.

Americans also debated how to contain communism effectively. Some criticized military aid to anticommunist dictators. Hundreds of thousands of citizens protested against the war in Vietnam.

No matter what their individual opinions, Americans viewed their freedom to debate as a precious heritage. Though many argued over how the Cold War was fought, they could agree that freedom was worth fighting for.

★ Section 5 Review ★

Recall

1. **Locate** (a) China, (b) the Soviet Union, (c) Afghanistan, (d) Poland, (e) Russia.
2. **Identify** (a) SALT Agreement, (b) Gerald Ford, (c) Jimmy Carter, (d) Star Wars, (e) Solidarity, (f) Mikhail Gorbachev, (g) INF Treaty, (h) Boris Yeltsin.
3. **Define** (a) détente, (b) martial law, (c) glasnost, (d) summit meeting, (e) free market.

Comprehension

4. (a) How did United States relations with China and the Soviet Union change in the 1970s? (b) Why did détente end?

5. (a) Why did the Soviet Union cease to exist? (b) How did the Soviet collapse affect the nations of Eastern Europe?
6. How did the United States respond to the breakup of the Soviet Union?

Critical Thinking and Writing

7. **Thinking Creatively** (a) Describe one way the United States could help the former communist nations make the shift to democracy and a free-market economy. (b) Do you think that the United States should provide that help? Why?
8. **Linking Past and Present** List two ways that the end of the Cold War has affected your life.

Activity Writing a News Dispatch You are a foreign correspondent for a major American newspaper. Write three reports to send to your paper, dated in 1985, 1989, and 1991. In each report, describe the events leading to the collapse of the Soviet Union.

Chapter 28 Review and Activities

★ Sum It Up ★

Section 1   The Nation Faces a Cold War
▶ After World War II, Soviet expansion and growing distrust between the United States and the Soviet Union led to the Cold War.
▶ The United States followed a policy of containing communism to the countries where it already existed.

Section 2   The Cold War Heats Up
▶ The United States reacted forcefully to communist expansion in Korea and Cuba.
▶ Fear of communism at home led to a Red Scare that cost thousands of Americans their jobs.

Section 3   Cold War Battlegrounds
▶ The Soviet Union sought to gain influence in newly independent nations.
▶ The United States supported anticommunist governments and rebels in Asia and Latin America.

Section 4   The Vietnam War
▶ The United States sent troops to Southeast Asia to prevent a communist takeover of South Vietnam.
▶ Many people in the United States protested American involvement in Vietnam.

Section 5   The End of the Cold War
▶ In the 1970s, efforts to ease tensions with the Soviet Union ended with the Soviet invasion of Afghanistan.
▶ Economic problems and growing demands for democracy contributed to the breakup of the Soviet Union.

CD-ROM Review For additional review of the major ideas of Chapter 28, see *Guide to the Essentials of American History* or *Interactive Student Tutorial CD-ROM,* which contains interactive review activities, graphic organizers, and practice tests.

▢ Reviewing the Chapter

Define These Terms
Match each term with the correct definition.

Column 1
1. exile
2. guerrilla
3. glasnost
4. détente
5. martial law

Column 2
a. emergency military rule
b. person who has been forced to leave his or her country
c. policy of reducing tension
d. fighter who uses hit-and-run tactics
e. policy of allowing open and honest public speech

Explore the Main Ideas
1. What was the Iron Curtain?
2. How did the Cuban missile crisis end?
3. What was the goal of the Peace Corps?
4. Describe three results of the Vietnam War.
5. What efforts at détente were made in the 1970s?

▢ Geography Activity

Match the letters on the map with the following places: **1.** Soviet Union, **2.** Cuba, **3.** China, **4.** South Korea, **5.** Vietnam, **6.** West Germany.   **Movement**   Why do you think many Cubans fled to the United States in the 1960s?

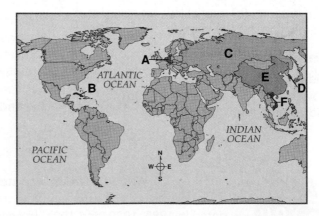

Critical Thinking and Writing

1. **Linking Past and Present** Do you think people feel the same way about nuclear war today as they did during the Cold War? Explain.
2. **Comparing** Compare and contrast the Korean War with the Vietnam War in terms of **(a)** American goals and **(b)** results.
3. **Understanding Chronology** **(a)** Which began first, glasnost or the breakup of the Soviet Union? **(b)** Explain why these two events occurred in the order in which they did rather than the other way around.
4. **Exploring Unit Themes World Leadership** With the breakup of the Soviet Union, the United States became the only superpower. Explain whether you think this will increase or decrease tensions in the world.

Using Primary Sources

In October 1962, President John F. Kennedy appeared on television to tell the American people that the Soviets were shipping missiles to Cuba:

> **66** I have directed the Armed Forces to prepare for any eventualities. ...We will not prematurely or unnecessarily risk the costs of worldwide nuclear war in which even the fruits of victory would be ashes in our mouths, but neither will we shrink from that risk at any time it must be faced. **99**

Source: Television address, October 22, 1962.

Recognizing Points of View (a) According to Kennedy, would he be willing to risk the possibility of nuclear war? **(b)** How do you think American viewers responded to Kennedy's message? **(c)** How do you think Nikita Khrushchev responded?

ACTIVITY BANK

Interdisciplinary Activity

Exploring Economics   Research the economies of the United States and the Soviet Union during the 1980s. Create a display of graphs to show how both the communist system and the free-market system provided goods and services for people. Present your graphs to the class, explaining their meaning.

Career Skills Activity

Travel Agent   You are planning a trip for a client who wants to see sights that were important during the Cold War. Gather material on tourist travel in Russia, Eastern Europe, China, Korea, and Vietnam today. Plan a tour, using the information you have gathered. Include an explanation of why you have included each site on the trip.

Citizenship Activity

Debating National Security Issues   Do further research on the search for communists in the United States government during the 1940s and 1950s. Then, organize a mock debate between those who are in favor of investigating the political beliefs of citizens and those who oppose it.

Internet Activity

Use the Internet to find sites dealing with the Vietnam War. Drawing on the information you find, write an essay on the personal impact of the war on Americans, both during the war and in the present.

EYEWITNESS Journal

You are an American teenager growing up in either the 1950s, the 1960s, the 1970s, or the 1980s. In your EYEWITNESS JOURNAL, describe three Cold War events that have had the most impact on your life.

Chapter 29 Prosperity and Reform

1945–1980

In the 1950s, as the United States struggled with the Cold War, the nation entered an era of remarkable economic growth. Prosperity made many Americans feel secure and comfortable. As a result, many wanted to follow a course of political conservatism. Most Americans opposed any form of radical change.

In the 1960s and 1970s, however, American politics went through upheaval. One President was assassinated and another resigned. Citizens disagreed over the war in Vietnam. Women and minorities struggled for justice and equality with protests and demonstrations. By the 1980s, they had won increased recognition for their rights.

Why Study History?

Dr. Martin Luther King, Jr., was a leading figure in the struggle for justice and equality. Today, King's birthday is a federal holiday. Some Americans celebrate the day by participating in community service. To learn more about this, see this chapter's *Why Study History?* feature, "You Can Learn About Helping Others."

American Events			
1950s Baby boom increases United States population	**1954** Supreme Court rules that school segregation is unconstitutional		**1963** Civil rights supporters march on Washington, D.C., to end discrimination

1945	1951	1957	1963

World Events

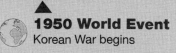 **1950 World Event**
Korean War begins

 1960s World Event
Nations gain independence across Africa

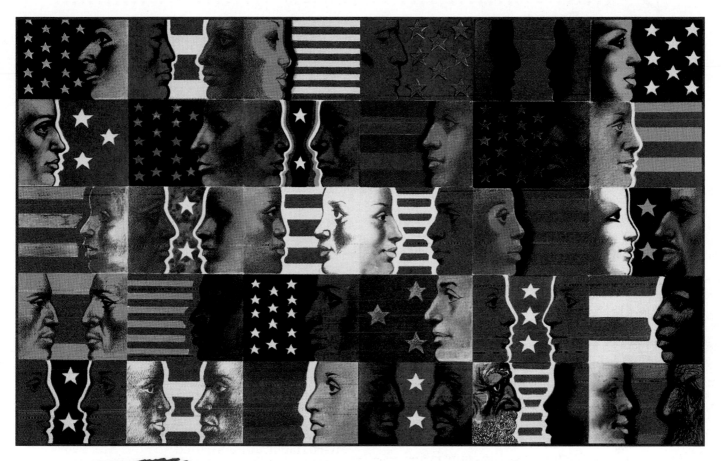

Viewing HISTORY — Many People, One Nation

Colleen Browning celebrated the diversity of the United States in her lithograph Union Mixer. *It shows a wide mix of Americans—male and female, young and old, of many races and nationalities. Behind them are the stars and stripes of the flag that unites them all into a single people.* ★ **How can diversity be a source of both strength and conflict?**

1966
National Organization for Women (NOW) is formed

1974
Watergate Scandal leads to resignation of President Nixon

1963   1969   1975   1981

1960s World Event
United States involvement in the Vietnam War grows

1975 World Event
Helsinki Agreement defines basic human rights

The Booming Postwar World

★ ★

As You Read

Explore These Questions

- What domestic policies did Presidents Truman and Eisenhower follow?
- What factors contributed to the economic prosperity of the 1950s?
- How did American lifestyles change in the 1950s?

Define

- inflation
- birth rate
- baby boom
- productivity
- standard of living
- affluence
- suburb

Identify

- GI Bill of Rights
- Fair Deal
- Dwight D. Eisenhower
- Levittown
- Sunbelt
- Interstate Highway Act
- Elvis Presley
- beatnik

SETTING the Scene After World War II, Americans resumed their lives. Veterans went back to peacetime jobs. Many hoped to buy a home and start a family. Now that rationing was over, Americans wanted to purchase a host of new products. *Life* magazine made an exciting boast:

    ❝ The year 1946 finds the U.S. on the threshold of marvels, ranging from runless stockings and shineless serge suits to jet-propelled airplanes that will flash across the country in just a little less than the speed of sound. **❞**

Life magazine had made an accurate prediction. For the United States, the Cold War era after World War II was a time of strong economic growth. Many Americans enjoyed the period of prosperity.

The Truman Years

Following World War II, President Harry Truman tried to help the society and the economy return to peacetime conditions.

Economic difficulties

Even before the war ended and Truman was President, Congress aided returning soldiers by passing what became known as the **GI Bill of Rights.*** Under this law, the gov-

---

*GI stands for "government issue." During World War II, GI came to mean any member of the United States armed forces.

ernment spent billions of dollars to help veterans set up farms and businesses. Many GIs received loans to pay for college or a new home. The GI Bill's many aid programs helped the economy to expand.

Inflation, or rising prices, was a major postwar problem. After the war, the government removed wage and price controls. The cost of food, clothing, and other goods soared.

To help pay these increased prices, workers demanded more pay. When employers refused, labor unions called strikes. Steelworkers, meatpackers, auto workers, coal miners, and railroad workers all walked off the job.

Truman agreed that workers deserved higher wages, but he feared such increases would add to inflation. Truman pressured strikers to return to work. He even threatened to draft some striking workers into the army.

Election of 1948

In 1948, the prospects for President Truman and his Democratic party were poor. Labor strikes and soaring prices had helped Republicans win a majority in both the House and the Senate for the first time since the 1920s. The Republicans confidently nominated Governor Thomas Dewey of New York as their candidate for President.

Truman fought back, crisscrossing the country by train. At every stop, he made hard-hitting speeches warning that Republicans were "all set to do a hatchet job on the New Deal." Crowds warmed to his scrappy style and encouraged him with cries of "Give 'em hell, Harry." When all the votes were counted, Truman won a stunning surprise victory over Dewey.

The Fair Deal

During his presidency, Truman introduced a 21-point program of proposed reforms known as the **Fair Deal.** The goal was to extend New Deal policies. Truman, however, faced heavy opposition from a coalition of conservative Democrats and Republicans in Congress.

Only a few of the proposed reforms were passed by Congress. Congress raised the minimum wage, expanded Social Security benefits, and provided loans for people to buy low-cost houses. Among the ideas rejected by Congress was a plan to provide health insurance financed by the government.

The Eisenhower Years

Truman did not run for reelection in 1952. The Democratic presidential candidate was Adlai Stevenson of Illinois. Republicans chose General **Dwight D. Eisenhower.** They thought that "Ike" could win the conflict in Korea and lead Americans through the Cold War. The voters liked Eisenhower's military experience and foreign policy skills. They gave Ike a landslide victory.

President Eisenhower said his political course was "that straight road down the middle." He considered himself "conservative when it comes to money and liberal when it comes to human beings." Like most Republicans, Eisenhower believed that the federal government should limit its spending and its involvement in the economy. Still, he agreed to expand the benefits of Social Security and some other New Deal programs.

Most Americans supported Eisenhower's middle-of-the-road approach. In the 1956 presidential election, American voters reelected Ike to a second term of office.

The Baby Boom

In the late 1940s and 1950s, the **birth rate**—or number of children being born relative to the total population—soared. Population experts called the phenomenon a **baby boom.** In the 1950s, the population of the United States grew by 29 million, compared with 19 million in the 1940s and only 9 million in the 1930s.

In part, American families were growing in order to make up for lost time. During the hard years of the Great Depression, it was

"I Like Ike" ➤ campaign button

Viewing HISTORY **We Like Ike**

In 1952, women from the Republican National Committee were eager to show support for presidential candidate Dwight D. Eisenhower. Americans liked "Ike" well enough to elect him to two terms as President. ★ **How do you think Eisenhower's role in World War II affected the election results?**

difficult to support a large family. Also, many couples who married during World War II did not have children until after the war.

Improvements in health care also contributed to the baby boom. Better care for pregnant women and newborn infants meant that more babies survived. Fewer children died from childhood diseases than in the past.

Economic Prosperity

In addition to a baby boom, there was an economic boom. In the mid-1950s, the United States accounted for about 35 percent of total world production. Corporate profits rose, as did average wages for workers.

The baby boom was in fact a major reason for the economic boom. Newspaper columnist Sylvia Porter was amazed by the census figures that reported more than 3,548,000 babies born in 1950. Porter predicted the baby boom would lead to economic expansion:

66 Just imagine how much these extra people...will absorb—in food, in clothing, in gadgets, in housing, in services. Our factories must expand just to keep pace. 99

Federal projects also increased output from factories. The government provided money to build new roads, houses, and schools. Government spending on Cold War military production spurred the economy, too.

New technology was another factor that contributed to economic growth. Improved methods of production led to steady rises in **productivity,** or the average output per worker. Corporations began using computers to perform calculations and keep records. In 1957, Navy captain Hyman G. Rickover oversaw the development of the first commercial nuclear plant in Shippingport, Pennsylvania.

The economic boom raised Americans' **standard of living,** an index based on the amount of goods, services, and leisure time people have. Many people celebrated their **affluence,** or wealth, by going on a spending spree. Americans bought large numbers of washing machines, vacuum cleaners, televisions, and automobiles.

Life in the 1950s

With the changes in the economy came changes in lifestyle. Americans were eager to enjoy the fruits of their economic success.

The suburbs

As families and economic opportunities grew, so did the demand for new housing. Many people moved to the **suburbs**—communities outside the cities. During the 1950s,

Skills FOR LIFE

| Critical Thinking | Managing Information | Communication | Maps, Charts, and Graphs |

Using a Special-Purpose Map

How Will I Use This Skill?
Special-purpose maps communicate information on a particular topic or theme. Some examples are a road map, a map of your school, and a map showing the layout of a shopping mall. Whatever kind of work you do in the future, you will probably use special-purpose maps.

LEARN the Skill
The following steps will help you read special-purpose maps.

❶ Read the map title and key to identify the topic and region that the map deals with.

❷ Analyze the map key. Make sure you understand the meaning of all terms. Determine the purpose of colors and symbols.

❸ Locate and study each symbol and color on the map itself.

❹ Use the map and your critical thinking skills to draw conclusions.

PRACTICE the Skill
Study the special-purpose map on this page. It shows the Syracuse area of New York. Use the steps you have learned to answer the following questions.

❶ (a) What is the topic of the map? (b) On what region does the map focus?

❷ (a) Define the terms *residential* and *industrial.* (b) What different types of land use are indicated by color? (c) What do the two symbols represent?

❸ Identify one region of the Syracuse area that was occupied mostly by (a) businesses, (b) homes, (c) fields and woods.

❹ How do you think the economic boom of the 1950s affected the development of Syracuse and nearby towns?

APPLY the Skill
Construct a special-purpose map to communicate information about one of the following: (a) land use in your neighborhood or town, (b) the location of books on various subjects in your school or local library, (c) the location of different types of shops in a nearby mall.

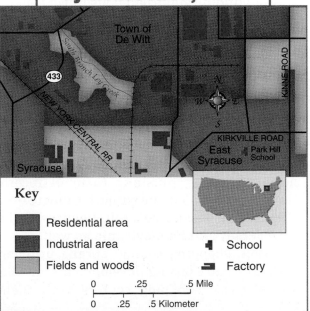

Syracuse Area, 1957

Town of De Witt

South Branch Ley Creek

433

NEW YORK CENTRAL RR

KINNE ROAD

KIRKVILLE ROAD

East Syracuse — Park Hill School

Syracuse

Key
- Residential area
- Industrial area
- Fields and woods
- ◀ School
- ◀ Factory

0   .25   .5 Mile

0   .25   .5 Kilometer

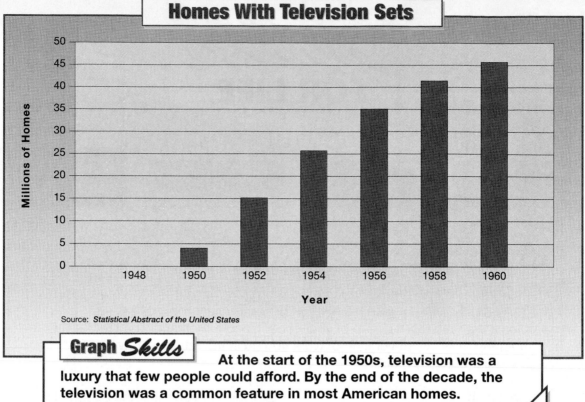

Homes With Television Sets

Millions of Homes

Year

Source: *Statistical Abstract of the United States*

Graph Skills At the start of the 1950s, television was a luxury that few people could afford. By the end of the decade, the television was a common feature in most American homes.

1. **Comprehension** How many homes had television sets in 1960?

2. **Critical Thinking** How does television affect your life today?

Economics $

suburbs grew 40 times faster than cities. The GI Bill encouraged home building in the suburbs by offering low-interest loans to veterans.

Builder William Levitt pioneered a new way of building suburban houses. He bought large tracts of land and then divided them into small lots. On each lot, he built an identical house. Because these houses were mass produced, they cost much less to build than custom-made houses.

Levitt began his first big project in 1947. On Long Island, outside New York City, he put up 17,000 new homes. Teams of carpenters, plumbers, and electricians moved from house to house, finishing them in record time. Levitt called the project **Levittown.** During the 1950s, he built Levittowns in New Jersey and Pennsylvania as well.

Soon, shopping centers sprang up near the suburban housing developments. In the 1950s, these shopping centers with their modern department stores were an exciting novelty.

The Sunbelt

While millions of people were moving to the suburbs, millions more were moving into the South and West. The populations of California, Texas, and Florida grew rapidly. In time, the region to which so many people were moving came to be known as the

$ **Connections With Economics**

American teenagers shared in the affluence that the nation was enjoying. In 1959, *Life* magazine summarized the buying power of teens: "Counting only what is spent to satisfy their special teenage demands, the youngsters and their parents will shell out about $10 billion this year, a billion more than the total sales of General Motors."

Sunbelt. The Sunbelt stretches across the southern part of the nation from Florida to California.

There were several reasons for migrating to the Sunbelt. Some people liked the warm climate that could be found through much of the region. Others were looking for better jobs. They were attracted by the Sunbelt's prosperous economy, based on agriculture, oil, electronics, and national defense industries.

Businesses also moved to the region. They liked the low taxes commonly found in Sunbelt states. Companies were also attracted by the Sunbelt's growing workforce. The workforce included many recent immigrants from Latin America and Asia.

The automobile

Unlike people in the older cities of the East, suburbanites and residents of the Sunbelt often needed a car to commute to work or drive to a store. During the 1950s, cars became more important to daily life. By 1960, 9 out of 10 families living in the suburbs owned a car.

The federal government encouraged the growing dependence on automobiles by building thousands of miles of highways. In 1956, Congress passed the **Interstate Highway Act.** It called for a network of high-speed roads linking the nation. The project would cost more than $250 billion.

The interstate highway system was partly a result of Cold War fears. It was designed so that troops and military equipment could move quickly across the country. The new roads would also enable people to leave major cities rapidly in case of a Soviet attack.

Television

Television was another product that had a great effect on American life. In 1946, only about 17,000 television sets existed in the entire country. In the 1950s, nearly 7 million sets were sold each year.

Television offered something for everyone. Children enjoyed a puppet show called *Howdy Doody.* Parents watched variety specials, quiz shows, dramas, and westerns. The husband-and-wife team of Desi Arnaz and Lucille Ball starred in a zany comedy series,

I Love Lucy. Millions of Americans also tuned in to nightly news programs.

Television affected American culture in several ways. It brought news and entertainment into people's homes. Its commercials encouraged spending and buying. Television also helped to make the 1950s a time when people wanted to look and act the same. Many programs presented a single view of the ideal middle-class family. However, not all families were like the ones that appeared on television.

Rock 'n' roll

A new music style burst onto the scene in the mid-1950s. Rock 'n' roll combined the sounds of rhythm, blues, country, and gospel.

 Elvis Presley

Elvis Presley did not invent rock 'n' roll, but he probably did more than anyone to popularize it. From the mid-1950s, the "King's" attitude, vocal mannerisms, sideburns, and gyrating movements made him an international star of the young. The U.S. Postal Service honored Presley in 1993 by releasing a stamp with his image. ★ **Why do you think many older Americans disliked Presley's style?**

It provided an opportunity for younger Americans to show their independence. Many teenagers embraced rock 'n' roll, rejecting the sweetly tuneful "pop" music of their parents' generation. African American singers Chuck Berry and Little Richard gained national fame. Out of the south came Buddy Holly and Elvis Presley. Latino singer Richie Valens also picked up the beat.

Of all the rock 'n' roll stars of the era, **Elvis Presley** gained the greatest fame—a fame that has endured even years after his death. In 1956, millions of young Americans across the country would wait eagerly for one of his television appearances. Teenagers dressed like him, bought his records, and nicknamed him "the King." Many parents, however, disapproved of Presley's long hair, sideburns, music, and dance style.

Hints of Change

Not everyone was swept up in the optimism of the 1950s. As the expanding economy encouraged increased spending, some Americans opposed what they saw as the growing materialism of American society. To them, people seemed more interested in material goods than in spiritual values.

Some writers and artists criticized American society for its devotion to business and its lack of individuality. A popular novel of the day, *The Man in the Gray Flannel Suit,* painted a bleak picture of business people working for large, faceless corporations. Novelist Jack Kerouac coined the term *Beat,* meaning "weariness with all forms of the modern industrial state." Middle-class observers called Kerouac and others like him **beatniks.** Kerouac's best-selling novel *On the Road* influenced many young Americans.

Challenges to the mainstream, however, were not very common in the 1950s. Millions of Americans enjoyed the comforts and prosperity of the period after World War II. They hoped that the "good life" would continue.

Still, in some corners, a growing outcry could be heard. It came from the Americans who were denied an equal share in the American dream. More and more, these Americans would struggle for change.

★ Section 1 Review ★

Recall

1. **Identify** (a) GI Bill of Rights, (b) Fair Deal, (c) Dwight D. Eisenhower, (d) Levittown, (e) Sunbelt, (f) Interstate Highway Act, (g) Elvis Presley, (h) beatnik

2. **Define** (a) inflation, (b) birth rate, (c) baby boom, (d) productivity, (e) standard of living, (f) affluence, (g) suburb.

Comprehension

3. (a) What reforms did Congress pass as part of Truman's Fair Deal? (b) How did Eisenhower follow a middle-of-the-road policy?

4. Describe two factors that helped the economy to expand after World War II.

5. Describe one way in which each of the following changed the way some Americans lived: (a) growth of suburbs, (b) Interstate Highway Act, (c) television, (d) rock 'n' roll.

Critical Thinking and Writing

6. **Recognizing Points of View** Why did some people dislike the cultural changes that were occurring in the 1950s?

7. **Linking Past and Present** Today, some people are concerned about the type of programming on television. Others fear that young Americans watch too much television. Do you agree or disagree with these concerns? Explain the reasons for your opinion.

★ ★

Activity **Formulating Questions** You are a news reporter writing an article on how the United States changed during the 1950s. Write five questions you would ask someone who lived during those years. Each question should be based on one of the headings in this section.

The Civil Rights Movement Begins

As You Read

Explore These Questions
- What kinds of discrimination did minorities face?
- What advances were made in the fight for equality?
- What methods did Martin Luther King, Jr., use to fight for equal rights?

Define
- segregation
- integration
- boycott
- civil disobedience

Identify
- NAACP
- Thurgood Marshall
- civil rights movement
- *Brown* v. *Board of Education of Topeka*
- *Hernández* v. *Texas*
- Martin Luther King, Jr.
- Mohandas Gandhi
- Southern Christian Leadership Conference
- Ralph Abernathy

SETTING the Scene In 1957, William Myers, Jr., went looking for a house. He and his wife were expecting a baby, and they needed more living space. Myers, a World War II veteran, liked the look of Levittown, Pennsylvania, a new suburban community of about 60,000 people.

Myers and his family were African Americans. When they moved into their Levittown home, a hostile white resident threw a rock through their window. Others made threatening telephone calls. It took a judge's court order to restore calm.

Throughout the United States, African Americans and other minority groups faced discrimination in jobs, housing, and education. After World War II, their struggle for equality and civil rights intensified.

Patterns of Discrimination

Discrimination existed throughout the nation. In the North, many qualified African Americans could not get decent jobs. In the South, Jim Crow laws enforced strict separation, or **segregation,** of the races in schools, theaters, restaurants, and other public places. Signs even identified restrooms and drinking fountains for "colored" users only.

Mexican Americans and other Latinos also faced discrimination. Although they were not subject to Jim Crow laws, other laws—as well as traditions—worked against them.

Mexican Americans were prevented from attending neighborhood schools. Instead, they had to attend poorly equipped "Mexican schools." Custom kept them from living in certain neighborhoods or using some hotels or restaurants. Often, better-paying jobs were not open to them.

Early Successes

Those opposed to segregation applauded two historic "firsts" in the 1940s. In 1947, Jackie Robinson became the first African American to play on a major league baseball team. Playing for the Brooklyn Dodgers, he was honored with the rookie-of-the-year award. The following year, President Truman ordered **integration,** or the mixing of different ethnic groups, in the armed forces.

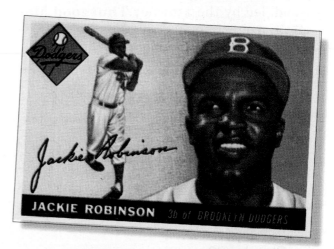

Jackie Robinson baseball card

Biography — Thurgood Marshall

After earning a law degree from Howard University in 1933, and graduating first in his class, Thurgood Marshall became chief of the legal-defense section of the NAACP. Seeking equality under the law for African Americans, Marshall brought 32 cases before the Supreme Court. He won 29 of them. Marshall later became the first African American Supreme Court Justice. ★ **How did Marshall help African Americans gain equality in education?**

During the Korean War, black and white soldiers fought together in the same units.

During World War II, membership in the **NAACP** (National Association for the Advancement of Colored People) jumped from about 50,000 to 500,000. The NAACP conducted voter registration drives and fought against discrimination in housing and employment. Its Legal Defense and Education Fund, led by the attorney **Thurgood Marshall,** mounted a number of legal challenges to segregation.

After serving in World War II and the Korean War, veterans were in the forefront in efforts to win equal rights. These soldiers had risked their lives for their country. They were no longer willing to remain silent when they faced discrimination. Such veterans "have acquired a new courage, have become more vocal in protesting inequalities," reported one observer.

Struggle for Equality

During the 1950s, African Americans, Latinos, and others stepped up the struggle for equality. Their efforts became known as the **civil rights movement.**

In the schools

In 1896, the U.S. Supreme Court had decided in *Plessy* v. *Ferguson* that "separate but equal" facilities for blacks and whites were constitutional. (See page 495.) The NAACP had challenged this idea with some success in the 1940s. Yet in the early 1950s, laws in 21 states and the District of Columbia still allowed segregated public schools.

Oliver Brown of Topeka, Kansas, decided to challenge the Kansas law. He asked the local school board to let his daughter, Linda, attend the all-white school near their home rather than the distant, segregated school where she had been assigned. The school board refused.

With the help of the NAACP, Brown filed a suit against the school board. The case of ***Brown* v. *Board of Education of Topeka*** reached the Supreme Court.

Brown's lawyer, Thurgood Marshall, argued that "separate" could never be "equal." Segregated schools, he said, could never provide equal education. By their very nature, said Marshall, segregated schools violated the Fourteenth Amendment, which gave "equal protection" to all citizens.

The Supreme Court ruled in Brown's favor in 1954. In writing the decision, Chief Justice Earl Warren noted that segregation affected the "hearts and minds" of black students "in a way unlikely ever to be undone." A year later, the Court ordered the schools to

Connections With Arts

In 1959, Lorraine Hansberry wrote a play about an African American family in Chicago that buys a house in an all-white suburban neighborhood. The play, *A Raisin in the Sun,* became the first play by a black woman to be produced on Broadway.

be desegregated "with all deliberate speed." In a few places, schools were integrated fairly smoothly. In many others, officials resisted.

In Little Rock, Arkansas, Governor Orval Faubus opposed integration. In 1957, he called out the National Guard to keep African American students from attending Central High School. President Eisenhower stepped in because the Arkansas governor was defying a federal law. Eisenhower sent troops to Little Rock. Under their protection, black students entered Central High.

Eisenhower was the first President since the days of Reconstruction to use armed federal troops in support of African American rights. The action showed that the federal government could make significant efforts in the protection of people's civil rights.

In the courts

In the same year as *Brown* v. *Board of Education,* the Supreme Court decided another case, **Hernández v. Texas.** That case had been brought by Mexican Americans seeking their own civil rights.

James DeAnda, a Mexican American, was one of the lawyers who helped bring the Hernández case before the Supreme Court. DeAnda had previously worked to desegregate areas of Corpus Christi, Texas, where Mexican Americans were not allowed to buy houses.

In the case of *Hernández* v. *Texas,* DeAnda and other lawyers argued that Mexican Americans in Texas were denied equal protection under the law in that they were prevented from serving on juries. The Supreme Court agreed and ended the exclusion of Mexican Americans from Texas jury lists. In future years, other minority groups would use this decision to help them claim their civil rights.

Montgomery Bus Boycott

In December 1955, Rosa Parks was riding home from work on a crowded bus in Montgomery, Alabama. The driver ordered her to give up her seat so that a white man could sit down, as Alabama's Jim Crow laws required. Parks, a well-known activist and secretary of the local chapter of the NAACP, refused to leave her seat. She was arrested, fingerprinted, and sent to jail.

Organized protest

In response, a number of women from the NAACP composed a letter asking all African Americans to **boycott,** or refuse to use, the buses. The women hoped that the boycott would financially hurt the city and force it to end segregation on the buses. The women made thousands of copies of the letter and distributed them to the African American people of Montgomery.

To support the protest, Montgomery's black leaders formed a new organization, the Montgomery Improvement Association (MIA). They chose Dr. **Martin Luther King, Jr.,** a Baptist minister, to head the organization.

Viewing HISTORY Ending Segregated Schools

In 1957, the governor and many citizens of Arkansas opposed a federal court order to integrate Central High School in Little Rock. In the end, President Eisenhower had to send soldiers to protect students going to and from school. ★ **How do you think the students in this photograph felt as they went to school each day?**

India

United States

Peaceful Protest

Martin Luther King, Jr., shown above right in a 1965 protest march, believed that African Americans should use civil disobedience and other peaceful protest methods to gain justice and equality. King admired Mohandas Gandhi (above left), who used peaceful protest methods to help India gain independence from Great Britain in the 1940s. ★ **How do you think religious beliefs affected King's strategy for gaining civil rights?**

Dr. King spoke at a meeting in the Holt Street Baptist Church. Hundreds were in the church, and thousands more stood outside. Upon his arrival, it took King 15 minutes to work his way through the crowd.

"We are here this evening—for serious business," King began. "Yes, yes!" the crowd shouted. As the crowd cheered him on, King continued:

❝ You know, my friends, there comes a time when people get tired of being trampled over by the iron feet of oppression.... [W]e are determined here in Montgomery—to work and fight until justice runs down like water, and righteousness like a mighty stream! ❞

The boycott succeeds

The boycott went on for just over a year. The MIA organized a system of car pools to get African Americans to and from their workplaces. Each day, as many as 20,000 rides

were provided. Many people simply walked. One elderly woman made a remark that became a common response of boycotters: "My feets is tired, but my soul is rested."

Some members of the white community fought back. Police harassed boycotters by giving them numerous traffic tickets. King and others were arrested. King's house was bombed. Still, Montgomery's blacks persisted.

King insisted that his followers limit their actions to **civil disobedience,** or nonviolent protests against unjust laws. He said, "We must use the weapon of love. We must have compassion and understanding for those who hate us."

Throughout the bus boycott struggle, African Americans held mass meetings in local churches. These church meetings helped keep morale high. The boycotters sang together, prayed together, and listened to individual stories of sacrifice. By coming together in this way, they gave courage and inspiration to one another.

To end bus segregation in Montgomery, the MIA filed a lawsuit in federal court. In 1956, almost a year after the boycott started, the Supreme Court ruled that segregation of riders on Alabama buses was unconstitutional. The Montgomery bus company agreed to integrate the buses and to hire black bus drivers.

National significance

The Montgomery bus boycott had several lasting effects. The boycott gained national attention for the civil rights movement. It also introduced nonviolent protest as an important method in the struggle for social equality. The boycott made clear that a new generation of African American leaders was emerging. One of the most prominent of these new national figures was Martin Luther King, Jr.

Martin Luther King, Jr.

Martin Luther King, Jr., was an educated and religious man. He was the son of a prominent Baptist minister. King graduated from Morehouse College, a prestigious all-black school. He later earned a Ph.D. in theology from Boston University.

King's education had introduced him to a wide range of philosophers and political thinkers. He studied the philosophy of ancient Greece and the European Enlightenment. Above all, King came to admire **Mohandas Gandhi,** a lawyer and spiritual man who had led a successful nonviolent movement against British rule in India.

Following the Montgomery victory, King and other African American leaders founded the **Southern Christian Leadership Conference** (SCLC) to carry on the struggle for equal rights. The group, consisting of nearly 100 black ministers, elected King president and the Reverend **Ralph Abernathy** treasurer. The SCLC urged African Americans to fight injustice by using civil disobedience:

66 Understand that nonviolence is not a symbol of weakness or cowardice, but as Jesus demonstrated, nonviolent resistance transforms weakness into strength and breeds courage in the face of danger. 99

Still, segregation remained widespread. The protests of the 1950s would soon grow into much larger protests in cities and towns all across the United States.

★ Section 2 Review ★

Recall

1. **Identify** (a) NAACP, (b) Thurgood Marshall, (c) civil rights movement, (d) *Brown* v. *Board of Education of Topeka,* (e) *Hernández* v. *Texas,* (f) Martin Luther King, Jr., (g) Mohandas Gandhi, (h) Southern Christian Leadership Conference, (i) Ralph Abernathy.

2. **Define** (a) segregation, (b) integration, (c) boycott, (d) civil disobedience.

Comprehension

3. Describe three forms of discrimination faced by minorities.

4. Describe three victories made by the civil rights movement in the 1950s.

5. What methods did Martin Luther King, Jr., support in the struggle for equality?

Critical Thinking and Writing

6. **Making Decisions** If you were an African American in Montgomery in the 1950s, would you have decided to participate in the bus boycott? Explain the reasons for your decision.

7. **Solving Problems** Do you think that civil disobedience is an effective method of protest? Explain.

Activity **Writing an Editorial** It is the 1950s and you are a newspaper editor in the American Southwest. You are upset about discrimination against Mexican Americans. Write an editorial protesting the treatment of Mexican Americans in the 1950s.

Years of Crisis and Change

As You Read

Explore These Questions
- What goals did Presidents Kennedy and Johnson set for the nation?
- What problems did President Nixon face?
- What principles guided President Carter?

Define
- counterculture
- "silent majority"
- stagflation
- deficit

Identify
- Warren Commission
- Great Society
- Medicare
- Medicaid
- Neil Armstrong
- Watergate Affair
- Gerald R. Ford
- Jimmy Carter
- Helsinki Agreement

SETTING the Scene At age 43, John F. Kennedy was the youngest man ever elected President of the United States. During his campaign, he had inspired Americans with his youthful ideals and high hopes for the future. In his inaugural address, on January 20, 1961, Kennedy captured the imagination of many with these words:

> 66 Now the trumpet summons us again...to bear the burden of a long twilight struggle...against the common enemies of man: tyranny, poverty, disease, and war itself. 99

As it turned out, Kennedy and the Presidents who followed him faced very difficult challenges. For American Presidents—and for the nation as a whole—the 1960s and 1970s were years of uncertainty and turmoil.

The Kennedy Years

In 1960, the Republicans chose Vice President Richard Nixon to run for President. The Democrats chose Senator John F. Kennedy of Massachusetts. Kennedy was Irish American and Roman Catholic. After serving heroically in World War II, he had been elected to the House and the Senate.

Nixon led through much of the campaign. One reason was that no Catholic had ever been President. Many Americans feared that Kennedy's first loyalty might be to the Roman Catholic Church rather than the country. Kennedy responded by stressing his belief in separation of church and state.

The first televised debates ever held in a presidential campaign constituted a turning point in the campaign. Kennedy appeared youthful and confident. Nixon, recovering from a recent illness, looked tired and nervous. In the election that soon followed, Kennedy won by a narrow margin.

Economic and social policies

As President, Kennedy urged Congress to pass laws to help the millions of Americans living in poverty. In his travels as a candidate, he had been shocked to find hungry families in the United States. Visiting a poor area in West Virginia, Kennedy exclaimed, "Just imagine, kids who never drink milk!"

Congress did not support the President's poverty programs. It did, however, approve funds to explore the "new frontier" of space. It also funded the Peace Corps—as you recall, volunteers sent to teach or provide technical help in developing nations of the world.

Kennedy proposed many other programs. Before these could be enacted, however, a tragic event shattered the nation.

Kennedy assassinated

On November 22, 1963, Kennedy was in Dallas, Texas, on a political tour. As he rode in an open car past cheering crowds, shots rang out. The President slumped back in his seat. The car raced to a nearby hospital, but it was too late. President Kennedy was dead. That afternoon, Vice President Lyndon Johnson was sworn in as President.

Dallas police arrested Lee Harvey Oswald for the murder. Two days later, as police escorted Oswald to a more secure jail, Jack Ruby shot and killed him.

There were many questions. Did Oswald act alone? How was Ruby able to get near him? Chief Justice Earl Warren led an investigation. The **Warren Commission** concluded that Oswald had acted alone. Today, most historians agree with the Warren Commission's conclusion.

Johnson and the Great Society

President Johnson continued many of Kennedy's programs. In November 1964, voters chose to keep him in the White House. Johnson defeated Republican senator Barry Goldwater of Arizona in a landslide victory.

Johnson developed a plan he called the **Great Society.** Its ambitious goal was to improve the standard of living of every American. To achieve his Great Society, Johnson asked the nation to join him in a "war on poverty."

Congress had been unwilling to support such a plan under Kennedy. Johnson, however, used his strong persuasive powers to make Congress act. One senator recalled the "Johnson treatment" as being like "a great overpowering thunderstorm that consumed you as it closed in around you." During his first two years in office, Johnson persuaded Congress to pass more than 50 new laws.

One important Great Society program was **Medicare.** Under this plan, the government helped pay the hospital bills of citizens over age 65. Another program, **Medicaid,** gave states money to help poor people of all ages with their medical bills.

At Johnson's urging, Congress passed the Economic Opportunity Act in 1964. The act set up job-training programs for the poor. It

Viewing HISTORY — Kennedy Assassinated

Millions of stunned Americans watched President Kennedy's funeral procession on television. Later, a Life *magazine cover showed a mournful Jacqueline Kennedy and her children during the funeral.* ★ **How do you think the assassination affected the mood of the nation?**

also gave loans to poor farmers and to businesses in poor sections of cities.

The government also set up programs to build housing for low-income and middle-income families. To carry out these programs, Congress created the Department of Housing and Urban Development, or HUD. Robert Weaver was named to head the department. He became the first African American to serve in a Cabinet post.

An Era of Protest

Despite these social reforms, the 1960s was an era of protest. The civil rights movement was gaining strength. More and more people opposed the Vietnam War. Many young Americans questioned the way of life they had grown up with.

The counterculture

Many young Americans became involved in the **counterculture** movement. Like the Beat Generation of the 1950s, members of the counterculture rejected traditional customs and ideas.

Young people protested against the lifestyle of their parents by trying to be different. They developed their own lifestyle. They liked to wear torn, faded jeans and simple work clothes. Women wore miniskirts. Men often wore beards and let their hair grow long. Many listened to new forms of rock music. Some experimented with illegal drugs.

Members of the counterculture adopted new attitudes and values. They criticized competition and the drive for personal success. They questioned some aspects of traditional family life. Inspired by the civil rights movement, protesters called for peace, justice, and social equality.

The antiwar movement

During the Johnson presidency, many youthful protesters focused their attention on the Vietnam War. Antiwar protesters staged rallies, burned draft cards, and refused to serve in the military. Many of the largest demonstrations took place on college campuses.

By 1968, the antiwar movement was in full swing. As a result, President Johnson's popularity rapidly declined. To avoid being confronted by angry crowds of protesters, Johnson stayed in the White House more and more. He decided not to seek reelection.

The election of 1968

Several Democrats sought their party's nomination in 1968. One was New York senator Robert Kennedy, brother of the late President. While campaigning in Los Angeles, Kennedy was shot and killed by a Palestinian who opposed the senator's support for the nation of Israel. (See page 838.)

In Chicago, the Democrats selected Vice President Hubert Humphrey as their candidate. Humphrey's chances for success were

Kennedy Space Center

The history of United States space exploration is on display at the Kennedy Space Center in Florida. Visitors can view IMAX movies, walk among actual rockets, explore a simulated space station, and climb aboard a full-sized replica of a space shuttle. Exhibits honor the past achievements of American astronauts and highlight goals for the future. On some days, visitors might even view a space-shuttle launch.

★ *To learn more about this historic site, write: NASA Visitor Services, Kennedy Space Center, FL 32899.*

At the Space Center, an entry ➤ sign advises visitors about the next shuttle launch.

hurt, however, by antiwar demonstrations outside the convention hall.

The Republicans again nominated former Vice President Richard Nixon to run for President. He promised to win "peace with honor" in Vietnam and restore "law and order" at home. Alabama governor George Wallace entered the race as a third-party candidate. Helped by this and by divisions in the Democratic party, Nixon won the election.

The Nixon Era

During his years as President, Nixon took steps to fulfill his campaign promises. He also wanted to reduce the involvement of the federal government in people's lives.

Helping the "silent majority"

The new President considered himself to be the leader of a group of Americans that he called the **"silent majority."** These were people who were disturbed by the unrest of the 1960s. Nixon defined these people as the "great majority of Americans, the nonshouters, the nondemonstraters."

As part of a "law-and-order" program, he used federal funds to help local police departments. He also named four Justices to the Supreme Court. The new Justices were more conservative than those who had retired.

Success in space

One of the greatest successes of the Nixon years occurred in the space program that Nixon inherited from Kennedy and Johnson. (See page 773.) In 1969, astronauts **Neil Armstrong** and Buzz Aldrin piloted a small craft onto the moon's surface. With millions of television viewers around the world watching, Armstrong became the first person to step onto the moon. "That's one small step for

After resigning as President, Richard Nixon bid a final farewell as he left Washington, D.C., in August 1974. Nixon was so entangled in the Watergate scandal that his impeachment seemed certain. ★ **Who succeeded Nixon as President?**

man, one giant leap for mankind," he radioed back to Earth. American astronauts visited the moon five more times.

Economic policies

Nixon opposed some programs of the Great Society. He thought that they were too costly and that they contributed to inflation. As a result, Nixon backed off from many of the reforms of the Johnson years. He cut federal funds for education and low-income housing.

During the Nixon era, the economy was afflicted by what some called **stagflation,** a combination of rising prices, high unemployment, and slow economic growth. Nixon tried several remedies. To battle inflation, he established a temporary freeze on wages and prices. To stimulate the economy, he increased federal spending.

Despite Nixon's efforts, economic problems remained. Increased federal spending caused federal budget **deficits,** in which the government spent more than it received in revenues. Early in Nixon's second term, an oil embargo put added pressure on the economy. (See page 838.) Higher energy prices caused the price of goods to rise even more.

Scandal and resignation

During his second term of office, Nixon faced a scandal arising out of a burglary in Washington, D.C. On June 17, 1972, while Nixon was campaigning for reelection, police caught five men breaking into Democratic party headquarters in the Watergate apartment building. Evidence suggested that the burglars were linked to Nixon's reelection committee. The President assured the public that no one in the White House was involved in the **Watergate Affair.**

New evidence, however, soon linked the burglars to the White House. In May 1973, a Senate committee began public hearings. The hearings revealed that Nixon had made secret tape recordings of conversations in his office. These tapes showed that the President and several close advisers had tried to cover up the truth about the Watergate break-in.

In the midst of the Watergate Affair, another scandal erupted. Vice President Spiro Agnew was accused of taking bribes and was forced to resign. Under the Twenty-fifth Amendment, the President had to choose a new Vice President. Nixon selected Representative **Gerald R. Ford** of Michigan, who had served in Congress for 25 years. Congress approved the appointment.

The Watergate crisis came to a head in July 1974. A House of Representatives committee passed articles of impeachment against the President. One charge was obstructing, or blocking, justice. Even the President's strongest defenders found the evidence to be convincing.

The scandal completely overshadowed Nixon's foreign policy successes. The President who had brought the troops home from Vietnam, established relations with communist China, and achieved détente with the Soviet Union, was finished. (See pages 784, 786.) In August 1974, before an impeachment trial could begin, Richard Nixon became the first President to resign from office.

Ford Takes Office

Gerald Ford, the new President, added to the controversy. Soon after taking office, Ford granted Nixon a "full, free, and absolute pardon." Some felt that Nixon should have been brought to trial. Ford, however, wanted to save the country from a long and bitter debate over Watergate.

The Carter White House

In 1976, Ford won the Republican nomination for President. To run against him, the Democrats chose **Jimmy Carter,** a former governor of Georgia.

Carter used the fact that he had no experience in Washington to his advantage. He admitted to being a Washington outsider, but claimed that "the vast majority of Americans ...are also outsiders." Carter promised a change from Washington politics and scandals. In the 1976 election, he defeated Ford by a narrow margin.

Carter's term began with hope for a fresh approach. During his first year in office, the new President sent Congress almost a dozen major bills. They included reforms in the Social Security system and in the tax code. Carter, however, could not win congressional support for his legislation.

Another problem the President faced was inflation rates of 10 percent or higher. The government tried to slow inflation, yet prices kept rising. Many families had a hard time paying for food, clothing, and rent.

Carter took a firm stand on human rights. In 1975, the United States had signed the **Helsinki Agreement.** In it, 35 nations pledged to respect basic rights such as religious freedom and freedom of thought. Carter took this pledge seriously. The United States, he said, should not aid countries that violated human rights.

★ Section 3 Review ★

Recall

1. **Identify** (a) Warren Commission, (b) Great Society, (c) Medicare, (d) Medicaid, (e) Neil Armstrong, (f) Watergate Affair, (g) Gerald R. Ford, (h) Jimmy Carter, (i) Helsinki Agreement.
2. **Define** (a) counterculture, (b) "silent majority," (c) stagflation, (d) deficit.

Comprehension

3. (a) What did President Kennedy think should be the role of the government in the economy? (b) Describe two Great Society programs that became law.
4. Explain how Nixon tried to deal with each of the following: (a) stagflation, (b) Watergate Affair.

5. (a) What were the goals of Carter's domestic program? (b) Did he achieve them? Why or why not?

Critical Thinking and Writing

6. **Analyzing Ideas** Referring to the Watergate Affair, President Ford said, "The Constitution works." What do you think he meant?
7. **Comparing** (a) Compare the ability of the following four Presidents in getting Congress to pass their domestic programs: Kennedy, Johnson, Nixon, Carter. (b) How might you explain the success or failure of each?

★ ★

Activity **Interviewing** To learn more about the difficult times you have read about, interview several older friends and relatives who lived through the turbulent times of the 1960s and 1970s. Prepare a list of questions. Keep a written or audio record of the interviews. What similarities and differences do you find in the responses?

4 ★ The Civil Rights Movement Expands

★ ★

As You Read

Explore These Questions
- What were the major goals of the civil rights movement?
- How did civil rights groups bring about change?
- What civil rights laws were passed in the 1960s and 1970s?

Define
- sit-in
- affirmative action
- migrant worker
- bilingual

Identify
- Freedom Rider
- Civil Rights Act of 1964
- Voting Rights Act
- Black Panthers
- Malcolm X
- National Organization for Women
- César Chávez
- Voting Rights Act of 1975
- Asian American Political Alliance
- American Indian Movement

SETTING the Scene One day in 1960, four college students sat talking in their dorm room. The students, all African Americans, went to college in Greensboro, North Carolina. Downtown, the "whites only" lunch counters refused to serve blacks. The students were angry at the unjust laws that limited the rights of black Americans.

The more they talked, the more the students felt that they ought to do something to change things. They went to a local department store and sat down at a segregated lunch counter. When the waitress would not serve them, they refused to leave.

News of the **sit-in,** a form of protest in which people sit and refuse to leave, spread rapidly. In the months ahead, thousands of blacks and whites conducted sit-ins at public places across the South. The protests signaled a new determination to bring about equality for all Americans.

African Americans Seek Change

Segregated lunch counters were only one example of racial discrimination in the South in 1960. As you read in Section 2 of this chapter, segregation laws also restricted blacks to separate facilities in bus stations, restrooms,

and other public places. The Greensboro sit-ins inspired African American leaders to press harder for change.

Peaceful protests

Several civil rights organizations led the struggle. The NAACP brought cases of discrimination before the courts. The Southern Christian Leadership Conference, led by Martin Luther King, Jr., taught African Americans about various methods of peaceful protest. The Congress of Racial Equality (CORE) organized "Freedom Rides." **Freedom Riders** rode buses from town to town throughout the South, trying to integrate bus terminals.

These early civil rights groups held firmly to the tactics of peaceful civil disobedience. They used sit-ins, boycotts, marches, and other peaceful methods to achieve their goals.

It took courage to participate in acts of civil disobedience and other methods of peaceful protest. Police sometimes used attack dogs or water hoses against protesters. More than once, mobs bombed the houses and churches of black leaders. Many civil rights workers, black and white, were injured or killed.

In 1963, more than 200,000 Americans marched on Washington, D.C. They wanted Congress to pass laws to end discrimination and help the poor. Among the speakers that day was Martin Luther King, Jr. In a now-famous speech, he proclaimed:

> 66 When we let freedom ring...we will be able to speed up that day when all of God's children, black men and white men, Jews and Gentiles, Protestants and Catholics, will be able to join hands and sing in the words of the old Negro spiritual, 'Free at last! Free at last! Thank God Almighty, we are free at last!' 99

Civil rights laws

The demonstrations spurred Presidents Kennedy and Johnson to push for strong civil rights laws. The **Civil Rights Act of 1964** protected the right of all citizens to vote. It outlawed discrimination in hiring and ended segregation in public places.

Other laws soon followed. In 1964, the Twenty-fourth Amendment was ratified. It banned poll taxes, which prevented African Americans from voting. In 1965, the **Voting Rights Act** ended literacy tests. It also allowed federal officials to register voters in states where local officials practiced discrimination. Thanks to these laws, tens of thousands of African Americans voted for the first time.

Despite new civil rights laws, discrimination remained a problem. Northern states had no formal system of segregation. Informally, though, housing in certain neighborhoods and employment in many companies remained closed to African Americans. Millions of blacks lived in rundown areas of cities. Many were unemployed or could get only low-paying jobs.

New voices and views

Some African Americans thought nonviolent protest was not working. Radical groups such as the **Black Panthers** urged African Americans to arm themselves. The Panthers argued that blacks must be prepared to fight for their rights if necessary.

Black Muslims, such as **Malcolm X,** argued that African Americans could succeed only if they separated from white society. Malcolm X later modified his views. Before he was assassinated in 1965, he called for "a society in which there could exist honest white-black brotherhood."

Both moderates and radicals talked about "black power." They urged African Americans to achieve economic independence by starting their own businesses and shopping in black-owned stores. Leaders also called for "black pride," encouraging African Americans to learn more about their heritage.

Violent protests

In crowded city neighborhoods, many blacks were angry about discrimination, the

Viewing HISTORY Freedom Riders

In 1961, black and white protesters rode together on buses through the South. They were protesting segregation on buses and in bus terminals. Some freedom riders were assaulted, while others were arrested. ★ **Why did it take a special kind of courage to engage in nonviolent protest?**

In the 1960s, riots became all too common in American cities. Here, National Guard troops help put out the fires after the 1965 riot in the Watts section of Los Angeles.

★ **What were the causes of the urban riots of the 1960s?**

lack of jobs, and poverty. In several cities, their anger exploded into violence. One of the most violent riots took place in Watts, a black neighborhood in Los Angeles. During six days in August 1965, rioters set fire to buildings and looted stores. Some 4,000 people were arrested, 34 were killed, and 1,000 were injured.

In the summers of 1966 and 1967, much more violence occurred. More than 40 cities experienced rioting in 1966. In July 1967, days of rioting in Newark, New Jersey, resulted in the deaths of 23 people and millions of dollars in damaged property. Just one week later, rioting broke out in Detroit. Before order was restored, 43 people died and blocks of buildings were burned.

King assassinated

During the years of riots, Martin Luther King, Jr., remained committed to nonviolence. In April 1968, he went to Memphis, Tennessee, to support black sanitation workers who were on strike. When he stepped outside his motel room, a white gunman shot and killed him.

King was buried in Atlanta, Georgia. His life has continued to inspire Americans to work for peaceful change. In 1986, his birthday was made a national holiday.

Progress is made

During the 1970s, the civil rights movement began to show results. African Americans won public offices in small towns and large cities. Atlanta, Cleveland, Detroit, New Orleans, and Los Angeles all had black mayors by 1979. African Americans made gains in the federal government as well. In 1967, Edward Brooke of Massachusetts became the first black senator since Reconstruction. A year later, President Johnson appointed Thurgood Marshall to the Supreme Court.

Businesses and universities provided more opportunities for African Americans. **Affirmative action** programs were set up to hire and promote minorities, women, and others who had faced discrimination. By the 1970s, more African Americans were entering professions such as medicine and law. Still, many blacks faced discrimination in receiving promotions and advancement in their jobs.

Rights for Women

Like African Americans, women struggled to win equal rights. Since the 1960s, women's struggle for equality has been known as the women's rights movement.

Women faced discrimination in many areas. Many employers refused to hire women for certain jobs even though the women were qualified. When women were hired, they were not treated the same as men. A female steelworker complained:

66 One woman... worked in the masonry department. She could carry two buckets when most of the men carried only one. She got fired because she was too short and they said it was unsafe for her. 99

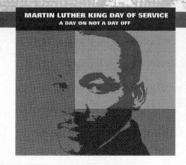

MARTIN LUTHER KING DAY OF SERVICE
A DAY ON NOT A DAY OFF

Why Study History?

Because You Can Learn About Helping Others

★ ★

Historical Background

In 1986, Martin Luther King, Jr.'s, birthday was declared a federal holiday. Since then, many schools and businesses have observed the day just as they observe other federal holidays. They close and give their students and employees a day off.

Some people, however, thought that this was not the best way to honor Martin Luther King, Jr. As a civil rights leader, King had stressed the importance of helping people. He once said, "Life's most persistent and urgent question is, What are you doing for others?" Inspired by words such as these, Congress passed the Martin Luther King Day of Service Act. Its purpose was to urge Americans to turn a day away from school or work into a day of community service.

Connections to Today

Philadelphia was one of the first communities to embrace the spirit of the new law. Each year, the city celebrates King's birthday through a program of community service. Thousands of Philadelphians of all ages work together to help others. They volunteer their time and energy in more than 100 projects. These include cleaning up parks, visiting senior citizens, renovating people's homes, tutoring children, and much more.

Connections to You

What can you do to celebrate the birthday of Martin Luther King, Jr.? As in Philadelphia, students in every city and community can create their own tradition of helping others. To get started, just look around your community and see what needs to be done.

According to Coretta Scott King, serving others is an ideal way to honor her husband. As she put it, "Our goal is to change the way Americans think about the holiday, from seeing it as a day off to a day on."

These middle school students are packing donated clothes to help those in need.

1. Comprehension Why did Congress create the Martin Luther King Day of Service Act?

2. Critical Thinking How can service projects make a community a better place to live and work?

 ★*Activity* **Make a list** of service projects that could help people in your community. Choose one and develop an action plan for carrying out the project. Your plan should outline the materials needed, the number of people needed, the amount of time the project will take, and the benefits of the project.

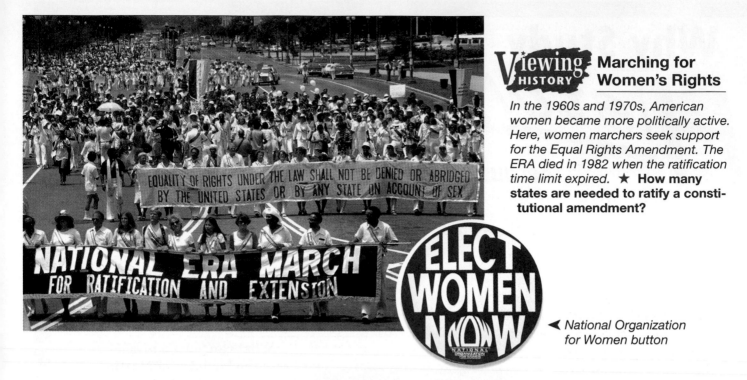

EQUALITY OF RIGHTS UNDER THE LAW SHALL NOT BE DENIED OR ABRIDGED BY THE UNITED STATES OR BY ANY STATE ON ACCOUNT OF SEX

NATIONAL ERA MARCH FOR RATIFICATION AND EXTENSION

ELECT WOMEN NOW

In the 1960s and 1970s, American women became more politically active. Here, women marchers seek support for the Equal Rights Amendment. The ERA died in 1982 when the ratification time limit expired. ★ **How many states are needed to ratify a constitutional amendment?**

◄ National Organization for Women button

When men and women held the same job, women were often paid less. Also, women were seldom promoted as fast as men. Many law schools and medical schools gave preference to male applicants.

In 1966, Betty Friedan helped to set up the **National Organization for Women** (NOW). It worked for equal rights for women in jobs, pay, and education. The NOW helped women bring discrimination cases to court. It campaigned for maternity leave and child care centers and urged women to become more politically active.

Women made some gains through new laws. The Equal Pay Act of 1963 required equal pay for equal work. The Civil Rights Act of 1964 outlawed discrimination in hiring based on gender as well as on race.

In the 1970s, the women's movement suffered a major defeat. In 1972, Congress passed a proposal for the Equal Rights Amendment (ERA) to the Constitution. The amendment would ban discrimination based on gender. However, Phyllis Schlafly and other conservative women led a successful campaign against the amendment.

Schlafly and other opponents of the ERA argued that the amendment would lead to undesired changes. One of these, they said, would be the drafting of women into the armed forces. They also charged that the ERA would cause the decline of the traditional family. In the end, the amendment failed to be ratified in enough states.

Despite this defeat, the decades of reform brought women more power and equality. The leaders of the women's movement promised that they would continue the fight for equal opportunity.

Latinos

By the end of the 1970s, more than 10 million Latinos lived in the United States. Like African Americans, women, and other groups, they joined in the struggle for equality and civil rights.

Mexican Americans

Mexican Americans are the largest group of Latinos. Large numbers of Mexicans were living in the Southwest when the United States annexed the region after the Mexican War. Since then, Mexicans have continued to immigrate to the United States. From 1960 to 1980, the largest number of immigrants to the United States came from Mexico.

Many Mexican Americans lived and worked in urban areas. Many others were **migrant workers** who traveled from farm to farm looking for work.

In both the cities and rural areas, life was difficult for Mexican Americans. They received low wages and their working conditions were poor. Few schools offered programs for children whose first language was Spanish. Migrants had little chance to get an education because families moved often, and it was hard for children to attend school.

Puerto Rican Americans

Many Latinos in the eastern United States trace their origins to Puerto Rico. Since 1898, Puerto Rico has been governed by the United States. As you recall, Puerto Ricans became American citizens in 1917. In 1952, the island became a self-governing commonwealth. This gave the people more say over their own affairs. Many Puerto Ricans have been happy to remain a commonwealth. Others have called for independence.

In the 1950s, thousands of people left Puerto Rico and headed to the mainland United States in search of work. Many took jobs in the factories of New York City, New Jersey, Connecticut, and Pennsylvania. Others settled in cities such as Boston, Chicago, and San Francisco. Many Puerto Ricans faced discrimination in housing and jobs.

Cuban Americans

Another major Latino group came from Cuba. After Fidel Castro set up a communist government in Cuba in 1959, more than 200,000 Cubans fled to the United States. (See page 773.) Most settled in southern Florida. Many of the immigrants were well educated and they adapted quickly to their new home.

In 1980, a new wave of Cubans arrived when Castro allowed thousands of people to leave the country. Most of the new refugees were unskilled workers who found it difficult to make a living.

As their numbers grew, Cuban Americans became an important force in southern Florida. Miami took on a new look. Shop windows displayed signs in Spanish. Cuban restaurants and shops opened. Cubans published Spanish-language newspapers and operated radio and television stations.

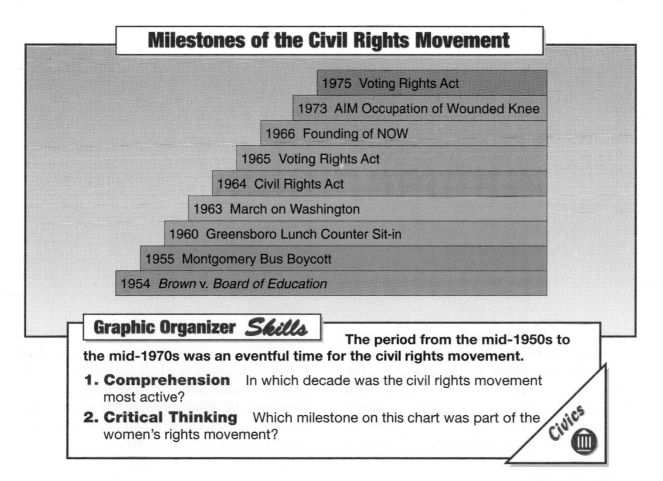

Milestones of the Civil Rights Movement

1975 Voting Rights Act
1973 AIM Occupation of Wounded Knee
1966 Founding of NOW
1965 Voting Rights Act
1964 Civil Rights Act
1963 March on Washington
1960 Greensboro Lunch Counter Sit-in
1955 Montgomery Bus Boycott
1954 *Brown* v. *Board of Education*

Graphic Organizer *Skills*

The period from the mid-1950s to the mid-1970s was an eventful time for the civil rights movement.

1. **Comprehension** In which decade was the civil rights movement most active?

2. **Critical Thinking** Which milestone on this chart was part of the women's rights movement?

Civics

Biography   César Chávez

The son of a migrant farm worker, César Chávez attended more than 30 elementary schools. In 1965, he organized the United Farm Workers among California farm workers. He used nationwide boycotts of grapes, wine, and lettuce to pressure California growers into raising wages and improving working conditions. ★ **Why is it difficult for migrant workers to get a good education?**

Symbol urging people ➤ *to boycott grapes*

Organizing for reform

In the 1960s, Latinos organized to seek a variety of reforms. **César Chávez** formed a migrant workers' union, the United Farm Workers. At first, owners refused to talk to the union. Chávez called for a nationwide boycott of grapes, lettuce, and other farm products. In the end, farm owners recognized the union, and workers won higher wages.

By the mid-1960s, Latinos began to take increased pride in their history and culture. Mexican Americans expressed this pride by calling themselves Chicanos, a name that comes from the Spanish word *Mexicano*.

Latino groups registered voters and made sure that voting laws were enforced. As a result, voters elected more Latino officials to represent their interests.

One result of these efforts was the **Voting Rights Act of 1975.** This law required areas with large numbers of non-English-speaking citizens to hold bilingual elections. **Bilingual** means in two languages. In a bilingual election, information is provided in more than one language. With a ballot that was written in Spanish, it was easier for Latinos to vote.

Other important laws were the Bilingual Education Acts of 1968 and 1973. These laws promoted bilingual programs in public schools with Spanish-speaking and Asian students.

Asian Americans

Asian Americans also took part in the civil rights movement of the 1960s and 1970s. In 1968, students at the University of California at Berkeley founded the **Asian American Political Alliance** (AAPA). Students of Chinese, Japanese, Filipino, and other Asian descent worked together to promote the rights and cultural heritage of Asian Americans. Their work resulted in some success. Between 1968 and 1973, major universities across the United States established programs in Asian American studies.

Young Asian Americans participated in public protests. In 1968, for example, activists presented the San Francisco city government with a list of grievances about unjust conditions in Chinatown. They cited problems such as poor housing and medical facilities. When the city failed to take action, the Asian Americans organized protest marches.

Native Americans

Native Americans also worked to achieve full rights under the law. In their case, they claimed rights not only as individuals but as members of tribal groups. Over the years, the federal government had recognized tribal governments by signing treaties with them.

During the late 1940s and the 1950s, the federal government sought to break up tribal governments. They also encouraged Indians to leave their reservations. By the late 1960s, more than half of all Native Americans lived off the reservations, mainly in urban areas. Gradually, city life weakened traditional tribal ties and customs.

Native Americans organized to counter the government's policies. The National Congress of American Indians regularly sent delegations to Washington to defend Indian rights.

Another organization, the Native American Rights Fund, stressed legal action. Its members worked to regain title to lands or to mineral and fishing rights that had been given to them in earlier treaties. In some cases, courts awarded Native Americans money for lands that had been taken illegally in the past.

The **American Indian Movement** (AIM) actively protested the treatment of Indians. In 1973, AIM members occupied Wounded Knee, South Dakota, for several weeks. As you may recall, the United States Army had killed nearly 300 Indians at Wounded Knee in 1890. (See page 520.) AIM wanted to remind people of the government's failure to deal fairly with Native Americans.

Protests and court cases have won sympathy for Indian causes. They have also won more rights for Native Americans. Today, Native Americans continue to speak out forcefully to achieve their goals.

Indian rights ➤ poster

★ Section 4 Review ★

Recall

1. **Identify** **(a)** Freedom Rider, **(b)** Civil Rights Act of 1964, **(c)** Voting Rights Act, **(d)** Black Panthers, **(e)** Malcolm X, **(f)** National Organization for Women, **(g)** César Chávez, **(h)** Voting Rights Act of 1975, **(i)** Asian American Political Alliance, **(j)** American Indian Movement.

2. **Define** **(a)** sit-in, **(b)** affirmative action, **(c)** migrant worker, **(d)** bilingual.

Comprehension

3. Describe three forms of injustice that some Americans experienced in the 1960s.

4. **(a)** Describe three peaceful methods used in the struggle for civil rights. **(b)** Give two examples of the violence that afflicted American society in the 1960s and 1970s.

5. Describe any three laws or developments that established more justice and equal rights in the United States.

Critical Thinking and Writing

6. **Linking Past and Present** Many schools and businesses began affirmative action programs in the 1960s. Today, some Americans charge that affirmative action gives minorities an unfair advantage. What is your opinion? Explain.

7. **Understanding Causes and Effects** How did the civil rights movement begun by African Americans in the 1950s help other groups in their struggle for equality?

★ ★

Activity **Writing a Speech** You are a leader of one of the civil rights movements described in this section. Write a speech to inspire other Americans to support your cause.

★ Sum It Up ★

Section 1   The Booming Postwar World
▶ Growing numbers of people moved to the suburbs and the Sunbelt.
▶ The automobile and television helped shape American life.

Section 2   The Civil Rights Movement Begins
▶ African Americans and other minorities faced discrimination and inequality.
▶ Martin Luther King, Jr., urged African Americans to use nonviolent methods in their struggle for equality.

Section 3   Years of Crisis and Change
▶ Kennedy and Johnson supported government programs to help Americans living in poverty.
▶ Political and economic troubles weakened the effectiveness of several Presidents in the late 1960s and 1970s.

Section 4   The Civil Rights Movement Expands
▶ By using a variety of methods, African Americans won greater equality.
▶ Women sought equal opportunities in government and in the workplace.
▶ In the 1960s and 1970s, American minorities of many different backgrounds worked to end social, political, and economic injustices.

 For additional review of the major ideas of Chapter 29, see *Guide to the Essentials of American History* or *Interactive Student Tutorial CD-ROM,* which contains interactive review activities, graphic organizers, and practice tests.

🗐 Reviewing the Chapter

Define These Terms
Match each term with the correct definition.

Column 1	Column 2
1. baby boom	**a.** nonviolent protests against unjust laws
2. civil disobedience	
3. stagflation	**b.** inflation and slow economic growth
4. segregation	**c.** expenditures are greater than revenues
5. deficit	**d.** large increase in the birth rate
	e. separation of people of different backgrounds

Explore the Main Ideas

1. Describe three characteristics of American life in the 1950s.
2. How did Martin Luther King, Jr., rise to national prominence?
3. What domestic problems did Richard Nixon face as President?
4. What gains did African Americans make in the 1960s and 1970s?
5. Describe one way in which each of the following groups fought against injustice: **(a)** women, **(b)** Latino Americans, **(c)** Asian Americans, **(d)** Native Americans.

🗐 Graph Activity

Use the graph below to answer the following questions: **1.** About how much money did the federal government spend on highways in 1950? **2.** In which two-year period did spending increase the most? **Critical Thinking**   How do you think the building of highways affected where Americans lived? Explain.

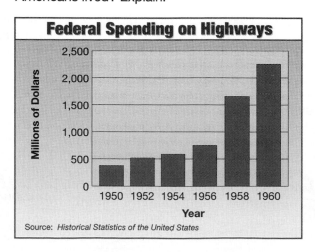

Federal Spending on Highways

Source: *Historical Statistics of the United States*

☐ Critical Thinking and Writing

1. **Comparing** Compare the Great Society programs of the 1960s with the New Deal programs of the 1930s. **(a)** How were they similar? **(b)** How were they different?

2. **Linking Past and Present** One of the reforms of the civil rights era was the establishment of bilingual education. Today, some people question the benefits of that program. What is your opinion? Explain.

3. **Understanding Chronology** Why did the baby boom occur after World War II rather than before or during the war?

4. **Exploring Unit Themes** **World Leadership** How do you think events in the United States during the 1960s and 1970s affected the way nations around the world viewed the United States?

☐ Using Primary Sources

In 1957, during the troubles over school desegregation in Little Rock, Arkansas, one of the students commented:

> **❝** I think [that opposition to African Americans entering the white high school] is downright un-American. I think it's the most terrible thing ever seen in America. I mean, I guess I'm sounding too patriotic or something, but I always thought all men were created equal. **❞**

Source: *Eyes on the Prize: America's Civil Rights Years, 1954–1965* by Juan Williams.

Recognizing Points of View **(a)** What did the student believe about opposition to African Americans entering the high school in Little Rock? **(b)** Do you agree with the student? Explain your thinking.

ACTIVITY BANK

▶ Interdisciplinary Activity

Exploring the Arts Learn some songs that were used in the civil rights movement. Perform these songs for the class. Then, hold a discussion with other class members to explore why the songs were so important for the movement.

▶ Career Skills Activity

Historians Research one of the Presidents you have read about in this chapter. Explore in depth the President's policy goals and how well he achieved them. Then, present a report to the class.

▶ Citizenship Activity

Creating an Action Plan Every citizen in a democracy can have an influence on current issues. Choose a problem or issue in your community and create a plan showing ways that you would go about having an influence on that issue.

Internet Activity

On the Internet, find sites dealing with any one of the interesting personalities discussed in this chapter. Use the information to write a brief biography of the person.

EYEWITNESS Journal

You are a foreign correspondent from Britain covering the news in the United States. What do you think are the two most important events or developments in the United States in the 1950s? Explain the reasons for your choices in your EYEWITNESS JOURNAL. Do the same for the 1960s and the 1970s.

Chapter 30

New Directions

1980–Present

In the 1980s, the nation entered a new political era. President Ronald Reagan, a conservative Republican, vowed to cut taxes and reduce the size of government. The nation entered a period of economic growth. After a brief recession, growth continued in the 1990s under Democratic President Bill Clinton. Clinton also worked with a Republican Congress to bring government spending under control.

With the Cold War over, Americans debated the role of the United States in the world. The environment, foreign competition, and greater diversity brought their own challenges. Still, Americans faced a new century with hopes for a bright future.

Why Study History?

You have learned a lot about American history this year.
Studying history can help you become an informed, responsible citizen. Did you know that a background in history also prepares you for many jobs? To focus on this connection, see the *Why Study History?* feature, "Knowing History May Help Your Career," in this chapter.

American Events

●1981
Ronald Reagan becomes President

1986 ●
Immigration Reform and Control Act reduces illegal immigration

1990 ●
Americans With Disabilities Act outlaws discrimination against disabled people

1980   **1985**   **1990**

World Events

1979 World Event
Revolution in Iran overthrows the shah

1989 World Event
China crushes pro-democracy demonstrations

 Viewing HISTORY : **Celebrating Liberty**

As they entered a new century, Americans sometimes disagreed on the best ways to protect their precious rights. Yet the nation still worked to preserve liberty at home and support democracy in other lands. In his painting Liberty States, *Taiwanese-born artist Tsing-fang Chen used familiar images to stress the continuing value of liberty.* ★ **What do you think are the two greatest challenges facing the United States in the future?**

1991
United Nations
allies defeat Iraq in
Persian Gulf War

1996
Welfare reform
limits federal aid
to the poor

1999
Senate acquits
President Clinton
of impeachment

1990   **1995**   **Present**

▲ **1994 World Event**
South Africa holds first
multiracial elections

▲ **1998 World Events**
India and Pakistan conduct
nuclear tests; peace accord
in Northern Ireland

A Conservative Tide

Explore These Questions

- What goals did conservatives have in the 1980s and 1990s?
- What domestic policies did Presidents Reagan and Bush pursue?
- What successes and failures did President Clinton have?

Define

- deregulation
- balanced budget
- downsizing
- recession

Identify

- Barry Goldwater
- Moral Majority
- Reaganomics
- George Bush
- Sandra Day O'Connor
- Bill Clinton
- Hillary Rodham Clinton
- Newt Gingrich

SETTING the Scene "Government is not the solution to our problem, government is the problem." Ronald Reagan spoke those words in 1981 after being sworn in as President of the United States. The new President called for a conservative revolution that would change the direction of the federal government.

Conservative Goals

Ronald Reagan swept into office on a rising conservative tide. A growing number of Americans were beginning to view conservative ideas and values as the answer to the nation's problems. These ideas contrasted sharply with the political thinking that had prevailed in the 1960s and 1970s.

Limiting the role of government

Since the time of President Franklin Roosevelt's New Deal, the size of the federal government had grown steadily. (See Chapter 26.) Later Presidents followed FDR's lead. John F. Kennedy and Lyndon Johnson believed that the federal government should take an active role in managing the economy and providing for the welfare of its citizens. Such a position came to be known as liberal.* Kennedy and Johnson sponsored federal pro-

grams to erase poverty, build low-income housing, or provide medical care to those who could not afford it.

Kennedy and Johnson were both Democrats. Many Republicans, however, also expanded the role of the federal government. President Richard Nixon created agencies to set safety standards for workers and to protect the environment.

Against this liberal trend, a new conservative movement began to take shape in the 1960s. Its leading voice was Arizona senator **Barry Goldwater.** Early on, Goldwater warned against growing federal power:

> 66 None of us here in Washington knows all or even half of the answers. You people out there in the 50 states had better understand that.
> ...If you cherish your freedom, don't leave it all up to big government. 99

Goldwater lost the presidential election to Johnson in 1964. Still, his ideas influenced a new generation of conservatives, including Ronald Reagan.

By the 1980s, these conservative critics of "big government" dominated the Republican party. Reagan and others argued that federal social programs had become too costly, driving taxes up. Another concern was that government regulations kept businesses from growing. State and local governments, conservatives said, should decide what regulations were needed.

---

* Generally, the term *liberal* refers to people who favor change, while the term *conservative* refers to people who want to preserve or return to established traditions. However, both terms have taken on different political meanings at different times in history.

Religion and values

Many conservatives also called for a return to traditional values after decades of social change. These conservatives praised family life, religion, and patriotism.

Growing church membership reflected the renewed emphasis on traditional values. During the 1970s and 1980s, evangelical Christian churches grew rapidly. Evangelicals stress a personal conversion experience. Leading evangelical ministers used television to reach a wider audience.

Not all conservatives were evangelicals, and not all evangelicals supported the new conservative movement. Still, many evangelicals took an active role in conservative political causes. In 1979, the Reverend Jerry Falwell founded the **Moral Majority.** The group aided political candidates who favored conservative religious goals, such as a constitutional amendment allowing prayer in the public schools. With other conservative religious organizations, the Moral Majority strongly supported Reagan in 1980.

The Reagan Years

Ruggedly handsome, Ronald Reagan had been a popular movie star. After entering politics, he was elected governor of California. His skill at presenting ideas in terms ordinary people could understand won him the nickname the Great Communicator.

In 1980, Reagan defeated Jimmy Carter for President. After the protests of the 1960s and the high inflation of the 1970s, voters responded to Reagan's reassuring promise to "Make America Great Again." Reagan was reelected in 1984 by an even greater margin.

Economic policies

Once in office, Reagan began to put his economic program—often called **Reaganomics**—into effect. He persuaded Congress to cut taxes in an effort to stimulate the economy. Reagan hoped that taxpayers would use the extra money to buy more. That would benefit businesses selling goods and services. The President also expected taxpayers to save more. Increasing the amount of

money in savings accounts would allow banks to invest in new ventures.

With less tax revenue coming in, Reagan sought ways to cut government spending. He called on Congress to reduce spending on social programs such as welfare and aid to education. Critics charged that such spending cuts hurt the poor, the elderly, and children. Supporters responded that Reagan was just trimming programs that did not work.

Reagan also supported **deregulation,** or reduction of restrictions on businesses. Earlier Presidents had deregulated certain industries. For example, Jimmy Carter had reduced regulations on airlines, railroads, and truckers. Reagan increased the pace of

Viewing HISTORY **Reagan, a Popular President**

His relaxed, good-humored manner and unshakable patriotism made Ronald Reagan a popular President. His policies brought a conservative revolution to government. Here, Reagan greets young fans on a campaign stop. ★ **How did Ronald Reagan try to change the direction of the federal government?**

▲ *1980 campaign button*

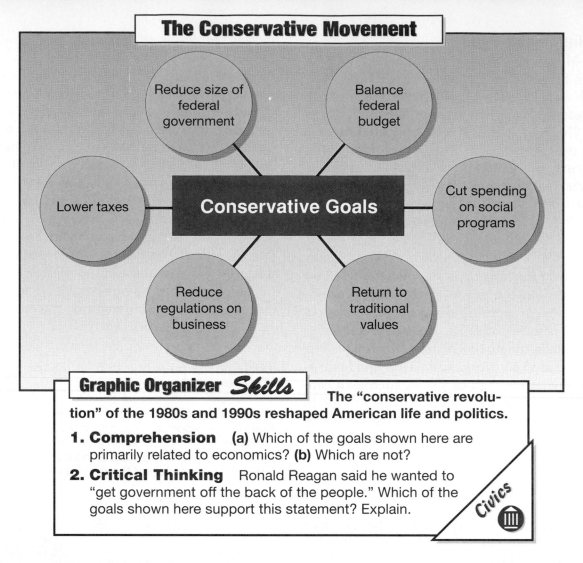

The Conservative Movement

Conservative Goals

- Reduce size of federal government
- Balance federal budget
- Lower taxes
- Cut spending on social programs
- Reduce regulations on business
- Return to traditional values

Graphic Organizer *Skills* The "conservative revolution" of the 1980s and 1990s reshaped American life and politics.

1. **Comprehension** (a) Which of the goals shown here are primarily related to economics? (b) Which are not?

2. **Critical Thinking** Ronald Reagan said he wanted to "get government off the back of the people." Which of the goals shown here support this statement? Explain.

Civics

deregulation. He opposed laws that required industries to install expensive antipollution devices.

Mixed results

At first, Reagan's program slowed the economy. Many people lost their jobs. By late 1982, however, the economy was booming. Many businesses opened or grew. When Reagan left office, there were 16 million more jobs, while inflation had been kept in check.

Another Reagan goal—balancing the budget—proved more difficult to achieve. With a **balanced budget,** the government spends only as much as it takes in. Although Reagan worked to cut back social programs, he sharply increased military spending. When Reagan took office, Cold War tensions were high due to the Soviet invasion of Afghanistan. (See page 787.) To oppose the Soviet "evil empire," Reagan said, the United States needed a stronger military.

With military spending rising and taxes cut, the budget deficit soared. The deficit for 1986 was $240 billion—nearly 10 times higher than under any other President. Still, as the economy expanded, Reagan remained popular.

The Economy Under Bush

Prosperity helped Reagan's Vice President, **George Bush,** win a landslide victory in 1988. Bush sought to carry on the policies of the Reagan years. In a dramatic campaign speech, he promised to cut the deficit without raising taxes. "Read my lips," he proclaimed boldly. "No new taxes."

It was a promise Bush was unable to keep. Democrats and Republicans could not agree on which government programs to cut in order to reduce the deficit. By 1990, Congress and the President were deadlocked. Finally, Bush agreed to raise taxes in order to save some popular programs. Many conservatives felt betrayed.

At the same time, the nation's economy slowed down. As businesses scrambled to avoid losing money, they cut costs by using fewer people to do the same work. This practice is known as **downsizing.** While downsizing increased businesses' profits, it also left more people out of work.

These conditions combined to create a recession. A **recession** is an economic slump that is milder than a depression. The recession continued for more than a year.

A More Conservative Supreme Court

Both Bush and Reagan had a chance to extend the conservative revolution to the Supreme Court. Between them, they appointed five Supreme Court Justices. The new Justices were more conservative than the ones they replaced. One of Reagan's choices was **Sandra Day O'Connor,** the first woman to serve on the Supreme Court.

In several major decisions, the Court showed its more conservative bent. During the 1960s, the Court had expanded the rights of people accused of crimes. In the 1980s, the Court placed new limits on the rights of suspected criminals. It also limited the rights of prisoners to appeal their convictions.

The Court also became more conservative in the area of civil rights. Since the 1960s, many communities had tried to achieve school integration by busing black or white students to schools outside their own communities. In the 1980s, the Supreme Court cut back on busing. It also made it harder for workers to win job discrimination cases.

Clinton Takes Office

Running for reelection in 1992, President Bush faced a stiff challenge. The recession continued. Unemployment had risen to 7.8 percent—the highest level in eight years. In addition, many Americans were dissatisfied with the government. They charged that the President and Congress seemed unable to work together to solve the nation's problems.

A dissatisfied vote

The Democrats nominated **Bill Clinton,** governor of Arkansas, as their candidate for President. His running mate was Tennessee Senator Albert Gore. At ages 46 and 44, Clinton and Gore were the youngest ticket in American history. They promised to involve the government more actively in areas that had been ignored by Reagan and Bush.

On election day, voters sent a clear signal that they were dissatisfied. Only 38 percent voted for Bush. Clinton received 43 percent. The remaining 19 percent went to Ross

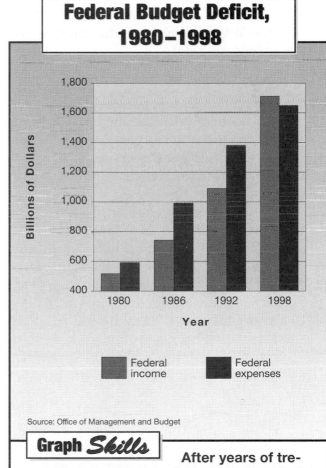

Federal Budget Deficit, 1980–1998

Source: Office of Management and Budget

Graph Skills After years of tremendous growth, the federal budget deficit finally began to drop in the 1990s. To calculate the size of the deficit, subtract income from expenses.

1. **Comprehension** (a) What was the budget deficit in 1980? In 1992? (b) What happened to the deficit between 1992 and 1998?

2. **Critical Thinking** Why did the deficit increase during the 1980s?

Economics

In 2000, George W. Bush (far left) and Al Gore were the Republican and Democratic candidates in a history-making presidential election. An extraordinary series of events left the outcome of the race uncertain long after Election Day.
★ **How did this election highlight the role of the electoral college?**

Perot, a Texas billionaire who ran as an independent candidate.

A moderate course

President Clinton pursued a middle-of-the-road course. On the one hand, he persuaded Congress to increase some taxes and reduce spending. For the first time in over 40 years, the federal deficit began a steady downward trend.

The President pushed hardest to reform the American health care system. In 1994, some 37 million Americans had no health insurance. Even those with insurance faced sharply rising costs for medical care. Clinton appointed a team headed by his wife, Hillary Rodham Clinton, to draw up reforms. The First Lady had been a prominent lawyer.

The Clinton plan called for a national system guaranteeing health insurance for almost all Americans. After heated debate, however, Congress defeated the President's proposals. Many Americans worried that the plan would prove too costly and involve the government too deeply in people's lives.

Conservatives at High Tide

The health care debate fueled voter discontent. Critics of the plan charged that the Clintons were trying to expand "big government." Supporters, on the other hand, were frustrated that a Democratic President and a Democratic Congress had not been able to pass a key program.

When voters went to the polls in November 1994, they gave the Republicans a resounding victory. For the first time since the 1950s, the Republicans held a majority in both the Senate and the House of Representatives. "It was a revolution," cheered Toby Roth, a Wisconsin Republican.

The Republican program

Republican Newt Gingrich of Georgia became Speaker of the House. Under his leadership, the House quickly drew up legislation designed to reduce social welfare programs, such as food stamps. Other bills cut back on environmental regulations, to make it easier for businesses to expand. At the same time, Republicans proposed a $245 billion tax cut.

President Clinton attacked many of the proposals as unfair to poor and middle-class Americans. He vetoed the Republican budget. Angrily, Republicans cut off funds, forcing government agencies to close for several weeks. As the government remained shut down, public opinion turned against Congress.

In the end, Congress compromised with the President. It agreed on a spending plan to balance the federal budget by the year 2002. In fact, the economy grew so strongly that the federal government reported a budget surplus in 1998. That surplus grew even larger over the next two years.

Congress and Clinton also agreed on a major overhaul of the welfare system. The government limited the amount of welfare benefits available. In this way, it hoped to encourage unemployed Americans to find jobs.

Critics complained that the welfare reform bill failed to guarantee aid to poor children and cut spending on food stamps. Most Americans, however, were willing to try the new system.

Impeachment

In 1996, Clinton easily won reelection against former Senator Robert Dole. Yet controversy engulfed Clinton's second term.

Kenneth Starr, a federal prosecutor, had been investigating the real estate dealings of the Clintons as well as a number of other matters. Starr found no evidence to charge the President with wrongdoing in these matters. He did, however, accuse Clinton of lying under oath about an improper personal relationship with a White House intern.

Amid heated debate, the House of Representatives voted to impeach the President. For only the second time in history, the Senate held a trial to decide the issue. In February 1999, Clinton was acquitted. The vote was along party lines, with all 45 Democratic senators supporting the President. All but five Republicans voted to convict.

The Election of 2000

The impeachment controversy affected the election of 2000. The Republicans nominated **George W. Bush,** the governor of Texas and also the son of former President George Bush. Along with vice presidential nominee Richard Cheney, Bush campaigned to return "honor and decency" to the White House.

Vice President **Al Gore** ran for the Democrats, taking credit for the nation's booming economy. For his running mate he chose Senator Joseph Lieberman of Connecticut. Lieberman was the first Jewish candidate nominated for Vice President by a major party.

Gore won the popular vote by a narrow margin. It was not clear, however, which candidate would receive a majority of votes in the electoral college. Whoever won Florida's election would be the victor. Bush clung to a slim lead there.

Because the Florida vote was so close, Gore asked for a hand recount in several key counties. Bush opposed that request. While the votes were being counted, both sides took the dispute to court. Eventually, the Supreme Court issued a ruling that discontinued all recounts in Florida. George W. Bush was declared the winner.

★Section 1 Review ★

Recall

1. **Identify** (a) Barry Goldwater, (b) Moral Majority, (c) Reaganomics, (d) George Bush, (e) Sandra Day O'Connor, (f) Bill Clinton, (g) George W. Bush, (h) Al Gore.
2. **Define** (a) deregulation, (b) balanced budget, (c) downsizing, (d) recession.

Comprehension

3. Describe two ideas or values of the conservatives of the 1980s.
4. (a) Describe Reagan's economic policies. (b) What were the results of these policies?

5. (a) Why did the House of Representatives impeach President Clinton? (b) What was the result of the Senate trial?

Critical Thinking and Writing

6. **Applying Information** (a) How did Reagan and Bush affect the Supreme Court? (b) Why is naming Supreme Court Justices one of the President's most important powers?
7. **Synthesizing Information** Why are President Reagan's years in office called a "conservative revolution"?

★ ★

Activity Composing Slogans You want to be a campaign consultant during the next presidential election. When you apply for the job, you are asked to demonstrate your skills. Do so by writing slogans that could have been used in the campaigns of the last four Presidents.

The Post–Cold War World

As You Read

Explore These Questions
- How did the United States become involved in Bosnia?
- What attempts were made to limit nuclear arms?
- How did the end of the Cold War affect the role of the United States in the world?

Define
- sanctions
- apartheid

Identify
- Dayton Accord
- Nelson Mandela
- George Mitchell

SETTING the Scene On a wintry day in January 1998, Staff Sergeant Paul Correale patrolled the streets of Olovo. The village, in the Eastern European nation of Bosnia, was thousands of miles from Correale's home in Ohio. All around him, he saw scenes of horrifying destruction. Nearly every home and store had been damaged or destroyed by shelling.

Unlike other American military actions of the past 50 years, Correale's mission was not part of the Cold War. Instead of fighting communist guerrillas, he was helping keep the peace after a bloody civil war. In Olovo, American troops had helped to reopen the village's only hospital.

As the Cold War faded, conflicts in many areas of the globe still threatened the peace. During the 1990s, the United States worked with many nations in an effort to create a more stable, more democratic world.

Eastern Europe and the Former Soviet Union

As you read, the Soviet Union split apart in 1991. American leaders anxiously watched the former Soviet republics and the nations of Eastern Europe. How would these nations adapt to their new freedom?

Under communism, governments had owned all major businesses and industries. The transition to a free-market economy was not easy. As governments gradually sold off businesses to private enterprise, inflation and unemployment rose.

In Russia, hard times and ethnic unrest unsettled the nation. President Clinton supported Russian president Boris Yeltsin in his efforts to build a stable democracy. Yeltsin, however, lost popularity when he failed to put down a rebellion in the Russian province of Chechnya. Rebels there battled to set up an independent republic.

In 2000, Yeltsin resigned before his term in office was finished. He was replaced by Vladimir Putin, a former communist official. Putin appeared less interested in promoting a democratic system of government.

Civil war in Bosnia

In Eastern Europe, Yugoslavia faced the most serious crisis. Yugoslavia was made up of several republics, including Croatia, Serbia, and Bosnia-Herzegovina. After the fall of communism, rivalries stirred among the nation's many ethnic groups. In 1991, Croatia and Bosnia declared their independence. However, Serbs in Croatia and Bosnia wanted to remain part of Yugoslavia. With help from Serbia, they began fighting to prevent the new governments from splitting away.

The civil war dragged on for four years. Cities were destroyed and two million people were forced to flee their homes. More than 250,000 people died. Zlata Filipovic, an 11-year-old native of Serbia, wrote in her diary:

66 Today a shell fell on the park in front of my house, the park where I used to play and sit with my girlfriends. A lot of people were

The United States joined UN efforts to end the bloody civil war in Bosnia. Above, American soldiers patrol a bombed-out town. Later, another crisis erupted In Kosovo. ★ **How did the fall of communism contribute to the outbreak of civil war?**

▼ *Bosnian women and children at a refugee camp*

hurt ... AND NINA IS DEAD.... She was such a nice, sweet girl. **99**

Beginning in 1992, Serbs forced tens of thousands of Bosnian Muslims into detention camps. They called this practice "ethnic cleansing." Other reports, however, claimed that the Serbs were carrying out mass executions. The War Crimes Tribunal, located in the Netherlands, charged more than 50 Serbs with murder, torture, and other "crimes against humanity."

In November 1995, the United States hosted peace talks at an air base in Dayton, Ohio. The **Dayton Accord** called for Bosnia to remain a single nation, but to be governed as two separate republics.

To help guarantee the peace, President Clinton sent about 20,000 American ground troops to Bosnia. There, they joined NATO and Russian forces in a peacekeeping mission. The troops helped to restore order.

Crisis in Kosovo

The Dayton Accord did not end the troubles in former Yugoslavia. Kosovo, a province within Serbia, also sought greater independence. The Albanians living there were in the majority and resented Serbian rule.

In 1998, Serbs launched a series of attacks against Albanian rebels in Kosovo. For nearly a year, the Serbs tried to uproot Albanians and drive them from Kosovo. Hundreds of thousands of refugees fled the province.

President Clinton condemned the attacks as "feeding the flames of ethnic and religious division." In March 1999, American forces joined NATO in bombing Serbia. The War Crimes Tribunal charged the president of Serbia, Slobodan Milosevic, with crimes against humanity.

Serbia removed its troops from Kosovo in return for an end to the bombing. A NATO peacekeeping mission entered the province. The rebuilding has gone slowly, however.

Limiting Nuclear Arms

The end of the Cold War presented other challenges. One major issue involved the thousands of missiles that the Soviet Union and the United States had stockpiled.

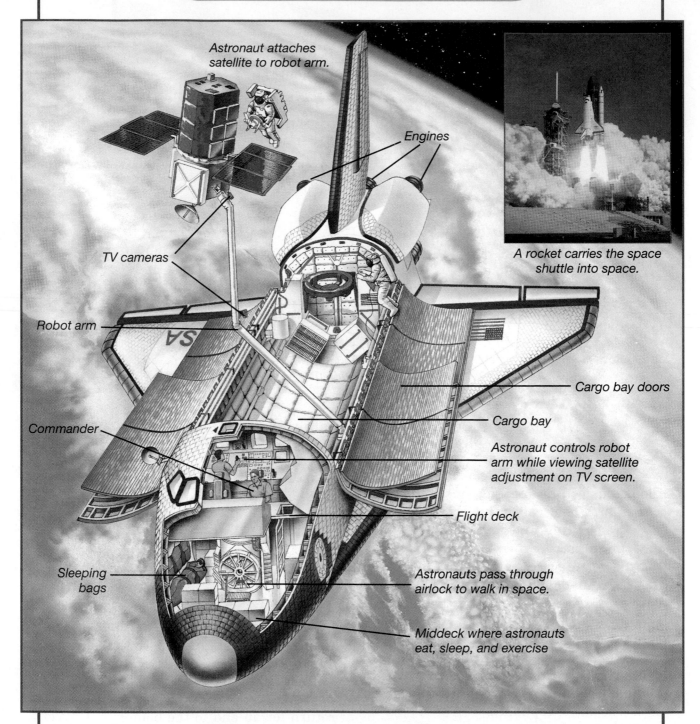

Astronaut attaches satellite to robot arm.

Engines

TV cameras

A rocket carries the space shuttle into space.

Robot arm

Cargo bay doors

Cargo bay

Commander

Astronaut controls robot arm while viewing satellite adjustment on TV screen.

Flight deck

Sleeping bags

Astronauts pass through airlock to walk in space.

Middeck where astronauts eat, sleep, and exercise

The Space Shuttle

During the Cold War, the United States developed space technology to win a "space race" with the Soviet Union. Today, American space shuttles perform a variety of peaceful tasks, from medical testing to launching communication satellites. After each mission, the shuttle returns to Earth, landing on a giant runway. ★ **Early space capsules "splashed down" in the ocean, where they were retrieved by ships. What are the advantages of a reusable spacecraft that can travel on its own power?**

Ending the arms race

Before the Soviet Union disbanded, it had already agreed to several treaties with the United States to reduce nuclear arms. The most important was the Strategic Arms Reduction Treaty, or START. The two powers signed START in 1991.

Russia later agreed to even greater reductions. The START II Treaty of 1993 cut the number of American and Russian missiles by one third. Both nations began destroying weapons, as inspection teams looked on.

New threats

Despite such progress, some other nations had begun to develop nuclear weapons. Britain, France, and China had all developed nuclear weapons during the Cold War. American intelligence agencies believed that Israel, Iran, Iraq, and North Korea also had atomic weapons programs.

Yet ending the arms race was not easy. In 1996, the Clinton administration helped to draft the **Comprehensive Test Ban Treaty.** Its goal was to ban further testing of nuclear weapons.

Many nations, however, were not eager to give up nuclear testing. Russia and China made no move to adopt the treaty. President Clinton signed it, but the Senate delayed a vote to ratify it.

Then, in 1998, the nuclear arms race spread to South Asia. India announced that it had conducted five nuclear tests. A few weeks later, India's neighbor and rival Pakistan exploded five of its own nuclear devices. "Today, we have evened the score with India," boasted Pakistan's prime minister.

Other world leaders saw the tests as the beginning of a dangerous new arms race. President Clinton called for economic sanctions against both India and Pakistan. **Sanctions** are actions taken against a country in an effort to force a change in its policy.

The test ban treaty received a further blow in 1999 when the Senate voted to reject it. Its provisions were "unenforceable" and "even dangerous," warned Senate Majority Leader Trent Lott. The vote marked the first time that a major treaty had been rejected since the Senate voted down the Versailles agreement ending World War I.

The Spread of Freedom

During the Cold War, the United States and its allies called themselves "the free world." The name referred to political freedom. It also referred to economic freedom, where companies and individuals could compete with less interference from the state.

In the 1980s and 1990s, more nations followed the path toward greater freedom. The United States encouraged this trend.

South Africa

In 1948, the government of South Africa began enforcing a policy of **apartheid** (uh PAHR tayt), or strict separation of races. The nation's nonwhite majority was segregated and allowed no voice in the government.

In 1986, Congress approved economic sanctions against South Africa. The law forbade American companies to invest in South Africa or import South African products. The

Viewing HISTORY   The Spread of Freedom

By 1990, democratic reforms were shaking the Soviet Union and Eastern Europe. At the same time, South Africa was taking steps to end its system of racial separation. This cartoon from a Kentucky newspaper comments on these two victories for freedom. ★ **Why does the cartoonist show apartheid and communism as dinosaurs?**

In 1989, young demonstrators like these rallied to demand democratic reforms in China. An estimated one million people took to the streets of Beijing, the Chinese capital. ★ **How did the Chinese communist government respond to the prodemocracy demonstrations?**

United Nations also pressured South Africa to end apartheid.

In the 1990s, South Africa moved to end white-minority rule. Under a new constitution, elections were held in 1994. All races were permitted to vote. **Nelson Mandela,** a black who had spent 27 years in prison for his opposition to apartheid, became president. In 1999, Mandela retired. The nation held its second all-race elections.

Asian nations

Democracy also made headway in the Philippines. In 1986, thousands of Filipinos protested the rule of dictator Ferdinand Marcos. They accused Marcos of fraud in a recent election. Proclaiming "people power," they refused to recognize Marcos as president. When the army supported the people, Marcos fled. The United States backed Corazon Aquino, the woman who had run against him. During the 1990s, the United States continued to provide economic aid for the young Filipino democracy.

Other nations in Asia had mixed success with political reforms. During the 1970s, South Korea developed a booming economy, but its government remained undemocratic. In 1987, after fierce protests by students and other citizens, the government allowed more democratic elections.

In May 1998, violent protests shook Indonesia when its economy faltered. Many Indonesians resented widespread corruption.

Under pressure, Indonesia's president resigned. In 1999, Indonesians voted in the first free elections in more than 40 years.

China's struggle

During the 1980s, the communist government of China took some steps to build a free-market economy. However, Chinese leaders refused to accept political reforms.

In 1989, students and workers launched a bold campaign to bring democracy to China. Hundreds of thousands gathered at Tiananmen Square in the nation's capital, Beijing. However, the army crushed the demonstrations. Many people were killed or arrested.

President Bush disapproved of the crackdown, but he did not take strong action against the Chinese government. Instead, he hoped to influence China by keeping communication open. President Clinton followed a similar policy. On a 1998 visit to China, he pledged to strengthen ties between the two nations. At the same time, he publicly debated human rights issues with China's president.

Other communist nations

Other communist nations that refused to reform their systems faced hard times. North Korea's people faced severe famine during the 1990s. To encourage North Korea to make reforms, the United States and the UN provided famine relief.

In Cuba, Fidel Castro remained as president more than 40 years after coming to power. During that time, the United States had enforced a trade embargo against Cuba. With the fall of the Soviet Union, Cuba lost its main source of trade and economic aid. As the Cuban economy worsened, more than 30,000 Cubans fled by boat to the United States.

In 1994, the United States signed an agreement with Cuba to allow Cubans to emigrate more freely. The United States continued to enforce its embargo, but Americans debated whether to open up trade with Cuba.

The Last Superpower

With the Soviet Union gone, the United States became the world's remaining superpower. Some Americans hoped the country would take the opportunity to reduce its role in world affairs. "In the post–Cold War world, we will no longer require our people to carry an unfair burden for the rest of humanity," said Representative Dana Rohrabacher.

Others argued that the nation had a responsibility to use its power when needed. "The U.S. must lead, period," declared Speaker Gingrich. President Clinton said:

66 If we are going to...lead abroad, we have to overcome a dangerous and growing temptation in our own land to focus solely on the problems we face here in America. The new isolationists must not be allowed to pull America out of the game. **99**

Both President Bush and President Clinton used United States influence to help bring stability to war-torn regions, such as Bosnia. In 1992, American forces led a United Nations mission to Somalia in eastern Africa. They distributed food during a famine caused by civil war. In 1994, American troops joined a UN mission to the Caribbean nation of Haiti. They forced out military dictators who had seized power. The UN then restored an elected president.

The United States also used diplomacy to bring about peace. In Northern Ireland, religious strife divided the land. Many Catholics wanted the region to be reunited with the rest of Ireland. Most Protestants wanted to remain under British rule. From 1969 to 1998, more than 3,000 people were killed by police, rival armies, and terrorist bombings. To help with peace talks, President Clinton sent former Senator **George Mitchell** of Maine to Ireland. Mitchell's negotiations helped produce a peace agreement in April 1998.

★ Section 2 Review ★

Recall

1. **Locate** (a) Bosnia-Herzegovina, (b) India, (c) Pakistan, (d) South Africa, (e) the Philippines, (f) China, (g) Cuba, (h) Northern Ireland.
2. **Identify** (a) Dayton Accord, (b) Comprehensive Test Ban Treaty, (c) Nelson Mandela, (d) George Mitchell.
3. **Define** (a) sanctions, (b) apartheid.

Comprehension

4. (a) What role did American troops play in Bosnia? (b) What action did the United States take in the Kosovo crisis?

5. What agreements did the United States and Russia make regarding nuclear weapons?
6. Give two examples of how the United States used its power to promote democracy and stability.

Critical Thinking and Writing

7. **Identifying Alternatives** (a) How did President Bush respond when China crushed the prodemocracy movement? (b) What other actions might he have taken?
8. **Linking Past and Present** Review pages 664–665. How was the debate on foreign policy after World War I similar to that after the Cold War?

Activity **Writing a Letter** Write a letter to Zlata Filipovic (see page 832) to express your sympathy for her suffering. In your letter, explain what the United States might do to end the conflict in her region, and why.

3 ★ War and Peace in the Middle East

As You Read

Explore These Questions
- Why did an oil shortage occur in the United States in 1973?
- How did the United States help promote peace between Israel and Palestinian Arabs?
- Why did the United States go to war against Iraq?

Identify
- OPEC
- Camp David Accords
- Palestine Liberation Organization
- Yasir Arafat
- Saddam Hussein
- Persian Gulf War

 In the fall of 1973, American motorists got a shock. Signs in front of many service stations announced, "Sorry, No Gas Today." At stations that did have gas, cars lined up for blocks.

The gas lines came about when nations in the Middle East cut back on the amount of oil they exported. Americans suddenly discovered how much events in faraway lands could affect their lives. In many different ways, conflicts in the Middle East have posed a challenge for American foreign policy.

A Vital Region

The Middle East has long been one of the "crossroads of the world," linking Africa, Asia, and Europe. The region was the birthplace of three major religions: Judaism, Christianity, and Islam. Over the centuries, tensions among various religious groups have often led to violence. The Middle East is also the focus of world attention because it has large oil reserves.

In dealing with the Middle East, the United States has had to balance conflicting interests. It has strongly supported Israel, the Jewish state created in 1948. Yet it has also tried to maintain ties with the Arab states that have opposed Israel.

Israel and Its Arab Neighbors

In the late 1800s, European Jews began to arrive in Palestine, a region along the Mediterranean coast. They hoped to create a Jewish state in the ancient home of their people. The number of Jewish settlers increased in the 1930s as European Jews fled Nazi persecution. (See page 732.)

In 1948, Jewish residents of Palestine announced the creation of the state of Israel. The United Nations recognized the new state. So did the United States and other nations.

Arab-Israeli Wars

The Arabs who lived in Palestine and the Arab nations bordering Israel refused to recognize Israel. To do so would have meant giving up Arab claims to the land. Determined to resist, they attacked the new state.

Israel won the 1948 war. It even added to its territory. After 1948, more than 500,000 Arabs fled Palestine. These Palestinians gathered in refugee camps in Jordan, Lebanon, and Syria. (See the map on page 839.)

Israel again defeated its Arab neighbors in 1967 and in 1973. As a result of these wars, Israel won control of lands from Egypt, Jordan, and Syria. Arabs referred to these lands as the "occupied territories."

The United States supported Israel with arms and supplies in the 1973 war. In response, Arab members of **OPEC,** the Organization of Petroleum Exporting Countries, cut off oil shipments to the United States. They also slowed down oil production. This caused oil shortages and higher oil prices all over the world. The oil embargo showed that the Arab states were willing to use oil as an economic weapon. The Arab nations lifted the oil embargo in 1974.

Camp David Accords

In 1977, Egyptian president Anwar el-Sadat became the first Arab head of state ever to visit Israel. His visit led to a series of peace talks between the two nations.

When talks threatened to break down, President Jimmy Carter stepped in. He invited Sadat and Israeli Prime Minister Menachem Begin (muh NAHK uhm BAY gihn) to Camp David, the President's retreat in Maryland. After nearly two weeks, Israel agreed to a timetable to return the Sinai Peninsula to Egypt. In turn, Egypt agreed to recognize the state of Israel. As a result of the **Camp David Accords,** Sadat and Begin signed a peace treaty in 1979.

The Palestinians

Palestinian Arabs continued to wage a guerrilla war against Israel. Most Palestinians lived in the occupied territories or in

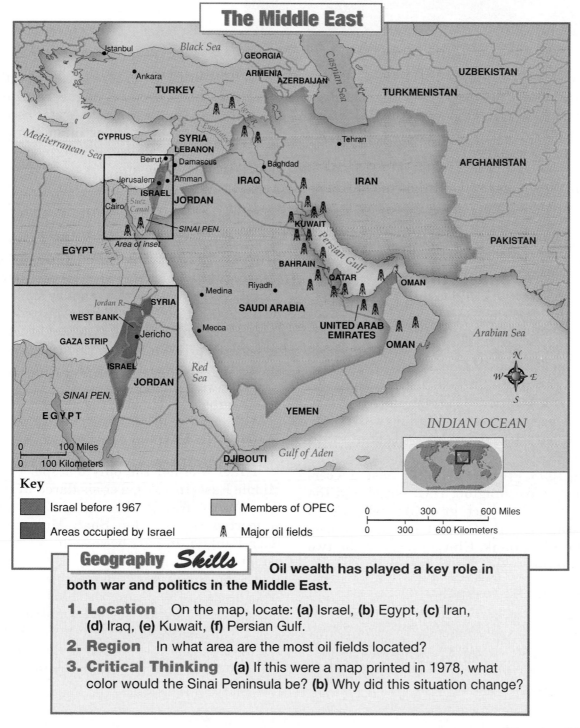

The Middle East

Key

Israel before 1967

Areas occupied by Israel

Members of OPEC

Major oil fields

Geography *Skills* Oil wealth has played a key role in both war and politics in the Middle East.

1. **Location** On the map, locate: (a) Israel, (b) Egypt, (c) Iran, (d) Iraq, (e) Kuwait, (f) Persian Gulf.

2. **Region** In what area are the most oil fields located?

3. **Critical Thinking** (a) If this were a map printed in 1978, what color would the Sinai Peninsula be? (b) Why did this situation change?

refugee camps outside Israel. They wanted to live in their homeland under a Palestinian government. Many supported the **Palestine Liberation Organization,** or PLO. Its leader, **Yasir Arafat,** announced that the PLO's goal was to destroy Israel.

In 1987, Palestinians in the occupied territories took to the streets to protest Israeli rule. The unrest called attention to the need for solutions to the Palestinian issue.

The road toward peace

In 1991, the United States finally persuaded the two sides to sit down together at the bargaining table. After two years of meetings, Israel and the PLO reached a peace agreement. The PLO agreed to recognize "the right of the State of Israel to exist in peace and security." It also promised to give up violence as a means of dealing with Israel. For its part, Israel agreed to negotiate with the PLO.

In 1993, President Clinton hosted a ceremony in Washington, D.C. Israel and the PLO signed a pact granting self-rule to Palestinians in the Gaza Strip and in Jericho on the West Bank. Clinton praised the two sides for making a "brave gamble."

Progress and setbacks

As the peace process continued, it brought new achievements. In 1994, Israel signed a peace treaty with its neighbor Jordan. The two nations had been in a formal state of war for 46 years.

The following year, Israel granted Palestinians the right to set up a government in some areas of the West Bank. Arafat became the leader of the new Palestinian National Authority. Eager Palestinians elected a council to administer the area.

Radicals on both sides tried to disrupt the peace process. Arab groups launched a series of suicide bombings in Israeli cities. In 1995, a Jewish student assassinated Israeli prime minister Yitzhak Rabin, who had signed the treaty with the PLO. Such incidents showed that the road to peace would not be smooth.

In 2000, President Clinton hosted new talks at Camp David between Arafat and a new Israeli prime minister, Ehud Barak. Despite several weeks of hard negotiation, the two sides were unable to resolve all of the differences that remained between them.

Tensions With Iran

Israel was not the only hot spot in the Middle East. In 1979, a crisis flared in Iran. Since World War II, the United States had supported Iran's ruler, Shah Muhammad Reza Pahlavi, in part because he was anti-communist. Many Iranians, however, opposed the shah's harsh, undemocratic rule. Also, devout Muslims opposed his efforts to make Iran more like Western countries.

In 1979, a revolution forced the shah to flee. A religious leader, the Ayatollah Khomeini (i yuh TOH luh koh MAYN ee), took command. The new ruler wanted Iranians to return to the strict traditions of Islam. He also led a strong anti-American campaign.

In November 1979, President Carter let the shah enter the United States for medical treatment. Iranian revolutionaries responded by seizing the American embassy in Tehran, the Iranian capital. They took 53 American hostages. The hostages were not freed until January 1981.

Conflict With Iraq

In August 1990, **Saddam Hussein,** the dictator of Iraq, sent 100,000 troops to invade neighboring Kuwait. Kuwait is one of the richest oil producers in the Middle East. Before long, Iraqi forces were in control of Kuwait and its oil wells.

Persian Gulf War

President George Bush feared that the invasion was the start of a larger plan to gain control of the Middle East's oil. To prevent further Iraqi aggression, he sent American forces to Saudi Arabia. He also persuaded the UN to impose a trade boycott on Iraq.

The United States and its allies set January 15, 1991, as the deadline for Iraq to withdraw from Kuwait. Hussein ignored the demand.

One day after the deadline passed, the UN allies launched an air attack on Iraq. In an operation dubbed "Desert Storm," troops from 28 nations—including Saudi Arabia, Syria, and Egypt—joined Americans in bombing missions against the Iraqi capital of Baghdad. Within 24 hours, the Iraqi air-defense missile systems and the Iraqi air force had been rendered all but useless.

By the end of February, UN troops had driven the Iraqis out of Kuwait. The **Persian Gulf War** lasted only six weeks.

Aftermath of the war

UN economic sanctions against Iraq continued. The goal was to force Saddam Hussein to stop his chemical and biological weapons programs. Hussein, however, failed to cooperate with UN arms inspectors. In late 1998, American and British planes launched a four-day air strike against Iraq. Although the attacks did considerable damage, Hussein remained defiant.

Meanwhile, the sanctions took their toll on the Iraqi people. The UN had set up an oil-for-food program in the late 1990s. It allowed Iraq to sell some oil on the world market and use the profits to buy food and medicine. Still, the Iraqi people suffered great hardships.

★ Section 3 Review ★

Recall

1. **Locate**   (a) Israel, (b) Iran, (c) Iraq, (d) Kuwait.
2. **Identify**   (a) OPEC, (b) Camp David Accords, (c) Palestine Liberation Organization, (d) Yasir Arafat, (e) Saddam Hussein, (f) Persian Gulf War.

Comprehension

3. (a) Why did Arab nations cut off oil shipments to the United States in 1973? (b) What were the effects of the embargo?
4. What progress has been made toward peace between Israel and the Palestinian Arabs?

5. Describe the causes of the Persian Gulf War.

Critical Thinking and Writing

6. **Understanding Causes and Effects**   How do you think the Middle East's large supplies of oil affect the way the United States responds to events there?
7. **Making Generalizations**   Based on what you have read, make a generalization about the role of Saddam Hussein in Middle Eastern affairs. Give two facts to support your generalization.

Activity   **Creating a Time Line**   Make a time line of events in the Middle East starting in 1948. Use your time line to review the events discussed in this section. Include a symbol for events that involved the United States.

4 The Environment and the World Economy

As You Read

Explore These Questions
- What are the goals of the environmental movement?
- How have Americans tried to save energy?
- Why has the United States had to compete in a world economy?

Define
- environmentalist
- solar energy
- renewable resource
- global warming
- trade deficit

Identify
- Rachel Carson
- Environmental Protection Agency
- Earth Summit
- North American Free Trade Agreement

 One night in May 1998, Elena Marin's son woke up coughing. Marin, a doctor in Texas, recognized the symptoms of asthma, a lung disease. She also knew the cause of the attack: the heavy smoke drifting across the border from Mexico.

After two years of drought, nearly 10,000 uncontrolled forest fires blazed in Mexico. Mexican officials urged residents to stay indoors. Texas authorities declared the air quality unhealthy across the entire state.

Some scientists warned that the drought might signal a dangerous change in the Earth's climate. Said one:

> 66 This may be a wake-up call.... Is it some kind of isolated event? I don't think so. It seems to be part of something much, much bigger. 99

Whatever the cause, the sooty clouds were a sober reminder that the United States and other nations needed to pay attention to the quality of the natural environment.

The Environmental Movement

In the early 1900s, a few Americans like Theodore Roosevelt stressed the need to protect the land and conserve natural resources. (See page 600.) By the 1960s, concern for the environment was growing stronger.

Marine biologist **Rachel Carson** helped focus attention on environmental dangers. In her 1962 book, *Silent Spring,* she charged that chemical pesticides were poisoning the land and water. Carson pictured a bleak future:

> 66 It was a spring without voices. On the mornings that had once throbbed with the dawn chorus of robins, catbirds, doves, jays, wrens ... there was now no sound; only silence lay over the fields and woods and marsh. 99

Reformers known as **environmentalists** began calling attention to a wide variety of environmental dangers. Chemical wastes turned rivers into sewers. Factory smokestacks belched foul-smelling fumes. People tossed litter along roads. Massive tankers ran aground, spilling oil into the sea.

The federal government responded to environmental concerns. In 1970, the Nixon administration created the **Environmental Protection Agency** (EPA) to lead the attack on pollution. The same year, Congress passed the Clean Air Act. It required automakers to clean up car exhausts. The Clean Water Act of 1972 fought pollution in rivers and lakes. The Waste Cleanup Act of 1980 created a "superfund" to clean up chemical dumps.

Local governments also took action to clean up the environment. Many communities required residents to recycle materials such as aluminum, glass, and paper. Recycling helped the environment in two ways. It reduced the amount of garbage that had to be buried or burned. It also slowed down the rate at which resources such as aluminum and trees were used up.

Still, the environmental movement has faced opposition. In the 1980s, President Reagan sought to ease environmental laws. He argued that overregulation placed too great a financial burden on American businesses. Often, environmental concerns must be balanced against economic needs. For example, environmentalists have sought to preserve forestland in Alaska and the Pacific Northwest from logging. Loggers, however, point out that forest products are vital to the nation's economy. Also, restrictions on logging may cost many people their jobs.

Energy Use

Environmentalists also directed attention to energy use in the United States. Americans make up only 5 percent of the total population of the world, yet they consume more than one fourth of its energy supply.

Conserving energy

The 1973 Arab oil embargo made Americans realize that the United States depended heavily on foreign energy sources. When oil shipments resumed, prices skyrocketed. Within 10 years, the fuel used by homes and industries cost four times as much as before the embargo. To cover added fuel costs, businesses increased the prices they charged for goods and services.

Americans tried to use less energy. Under government pressure, carmakers made autos that burned less gasoline. Homeowners added insulation to reduce the amount of fuel needed to heat or cool their homes. Environmentalists pointed out that conserving energy did more than save money. It also cut down on pollution.

▼ An American blue jay

iography **Rachel Carson**

Rachel Carson shocked the nation with her 1962 book, Silent Spring. *Carson warned that the pesticide DDT remained in the environment, killing birds and fish, and might eventually contaminate human food supplies. The book's popularity led President Kennedy to appoint a commission to study pesticides. Shortly after Carson died, Congress passed laws that restricted the use of DDT.* ★ **Review pages 593 and 599. How was** *Silent Spring* **similar to** *The Jungle?*

Connections With Science

In the 1990s, automobile manufacturers began producing cars that ran on fuels other than gasoline. Alternative fuels included natural gas and methanol. Other experimental automobiles were powered by solar energy.

New energy sources

Since the 1970s, Americans have sought to develop other sources of energy. Many factories have switched from oil to coal. The United States has nearly one fifth of the world's coal reserves. However, compared to oil, coal is a dirty fuel. Coal-burning plants must use "scrubbers" and other devices to reduce the smoke and acids they emit into the air. That adds to the cost of using coal.

Today, nuclear plants generate about one fifth of the nation's electric power. Still, nuclear power is costly, and it produces long-lasting radioactive wastes. An accident at a nuclear power plant could release harmful radioactive gases into the air. Carried by the wind, these gases could endanger people living hundreds of miles away.

Skills FOR LIFE

Critical Thinking	Managing Information	Communication	Maps, Charts, and Graphs

Using E-Mail

How Will I Use This Skill

The Internet allows us to have instant communication with people around the world. With its system of electronic mail, or e-mail, you can write to friends, newspapers, government officials, or even your favorite movie stars. In addition, more and more jobs today require the efficient use of e-mail.

LEARN the Skill

To send or receive messages by e-mail, use the following steps:

❶ Click on the electronic mail icon. Sign on, or log in, with your password.

❷ Address your message by typing in the e-mail address of the recipient. You may also give your message a title.

❸ Write your message. Attach any document you may want to send. After you have written your message, read it over to make sure it says what you want it to say.

❹ When you are satisfied with your message, click the Send icon. After the message is sent, you cannot change it.

PRACTICE the Skill

Use e-mail to gather information about energy use in your area.

❶ Open the e-mail application on your computer and log in.

❷ Type in the e-mail address of a local energy supplier, such as an electric or gas

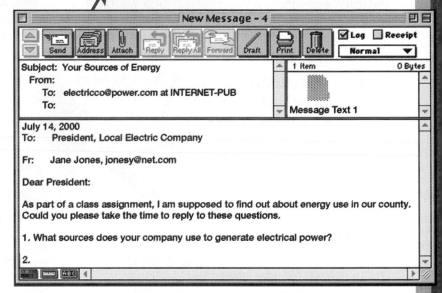

```
New Message - 4                                    ☑ Log  ☐ Receipt
Send  Address  Attach  Reply  Reply All  Forward  Draft  Print  Delete    Normal ▼
Subject: Your Sources of Energy               1 Item                0 Bytes
From:
    To:  electricco@power.com at INTERNET-PUB
    To:                                        Message Text 1

July 14, 2000
To:      President, Local Electric Company

Fr:      Jane Jones, jonesy@net.com

Dear President:

As part of a class assignment, I am supposed to find out about energy use in our county.
Could you please take the time to reply to these questions.

1. What sources does your company use to generate electrical power?

2.
```

company. The address may be found on company advertisements, pamphlets, or bills. Give your message a title that describes the subject matter.

❸ Ask questions about energy use. For example, you may want to find out what sources of energy the company uses, how the company sets a price for its use, or what the company is doing to safeguard the environment. Think of issues important to your household or community.

❹ Make sure you check your message before it is sent. Include your e-mail address for a prompt reply.

APPLY the Skill

Use e-mail to make contact with a school in another part of the country. Form a team with two or three other students to select a school and create a list of questions about life in that state or city.

Scientists are working to harness **solar energy,** or power from the sun. Solar energy is appealing because it is renewable and clean. A **renewable resource** is one that can be quickly replaced by nature. However, for many uses solar energy remains expensive.

Wind is another renewable resource. Rows of windmills in the California hills create electricity for thousands of homes.

International Cooperation

Environmental problems do not stop at national borders. In 1992, world leaders met at the **Earth Summit** in Brazil. They focused on a number of key problems.

Global warming

In the 1980s and 1990s, a prolonged period of warmer-than-usual weather caused problems in many parts of the world. African countries suffered deadly droughts. China received unusually heavy rains.

Some scientists thought that the Earth's atmosphere was warming up. They concluded that human activities, such as driving cars and operating factories, were adding carbon dioxide to the atmosphere. Carbon dioxide holds in heat that would otherwise escape into space. The scientists predicted a slow but steady rise in the world's average temperature. **Global warming** might one day turn green fields into deserts!

Not all scientists agreed with the global warming theory. They pointed out that the Earth had gone through many cold and warm cycles in the past. Still, leaders at the Earth Summit pledged to reduce the amounts of carbon dioxide their countries released into the atmosphere. That goal, however, was hard to reach. In the late 1990s, American carbon dioxide levels continued to rise.

Holes in the ozone layer

Miles above the Earth's surface is a layer of ozone gas. This ozone layer blocks out ultraviolet rays from the sun. Such rays can cause health problems such as skin cancer.

In the 1980s, scientists warned that gases used in homes and industries were creating holes in the ozone layer. The scientists pointed especially to gases used in aerosol cans, refrigerators, and air conditioners. Nations all over the world agreed to phase out the use of the dangerous gases.

Competing in a World Economy

The environment is only one area in which Americans have had to think beyond the borders of the United States. More than ever, American businesses sell products in a world marketplace. In 1970, foreign trade

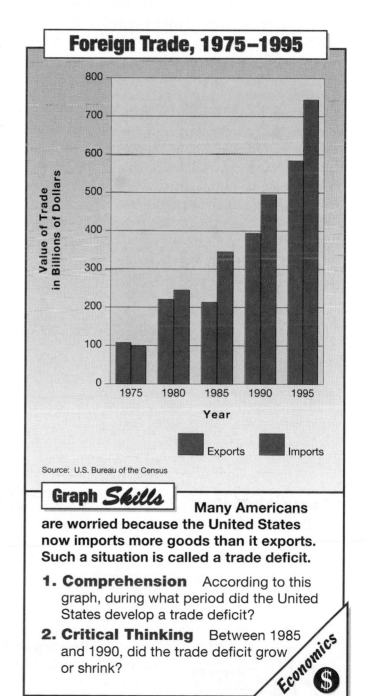

Foreign Trade, 1975–1995

Value of Trade in Billions of Dollars

Year

Exports ■ Imports ■

Source: U.S. Bureau of the Census

Graph Skills **Many Americans are worried because the United States now imports more goods than it exports. Such a situation is called a trade deficit.**

1. **Comprehension** According to this graph, during what period did the United States develop a trade deficit?
2. **Critical Thinking** Between 1985 and 1990, did the trade deficit grow or shrink?

Economics $

made up only about 10 percent of the American economy. By 1997, foreign trade amounted to nearly 25 percent.

A growing trade deficit

In this growing world economy, the United States must compete with economic powers in Europe and Asia. Competition has posed some problems. For example, American companies pay their workers higher wages than companies in most other countries. As a result, many foreign products cost less than similar American products.

Foreign competition has caused a trade deficit for the United States. A **trade deficit** occurs when a nation buys more goods and services from foreign countries than it sells to them. To combat this deficit, many American firms have built more efficient factories. They also tried to attract overseas customers by offering superior products.

Today, as in the past, the government can protect some American industries by raising tariffs. (See page 310.) Opponents of tariffs, however, argue that they are harmful in the

This symbol shows how NAFTA links the United States, Canada, and Mexico.

long term. Other nations respond with their own tariffs, leading to costly "trade wars."

Removing trade barriers

In 1993, after months of bitter debate, Congress ratified the **North American Free Trade Agreement** (NAFTA). The purpose of this treaty was to do away gradually with tariffs and other trade barriers among the United States and its neighbors, Canada and Mexico.

Overall, NAFTA encouraged new trade. Most economists agree that growing foreign trade created jobs and benefited the American economy.

However, critics pointed out that NAFTA hurt some industries. For example, carmakers moved many auto parts factories to Mexico, where wages were lower. Also, foreign countries did not enforce the same strict antipollution laws as the United States did.

In 1997, Congress refused to give President Clinton extra powers to negotiate more free-trade agreements. The debate over foreign trade continued into a new century.

★ Section 4 Review ★

Recall

1. **Identify** (a) Rachel Carson, (b) Environmental Protection Agency, (c) Earth Summit, (d) North American Free Trade Agreement.
2. **Define** (a) environmentalist, (b) solar energy, (c) renewable resource, (d) global warming, (e) trade deficit.

Comprehension

3. Describe two changes that came about as a result of the environmental movement.
4. (a) How did the oil embargo affect American attitudes toward energy use? (b) Identify two ways Americans tried to reduce dependence on foreign oil.
5. (a) What problems have American businesses faced in the world marketplace? (b) What steps have they taken to address these problems?

Critical Thinking and Writing

6. **Solving Problems** Why would many environmental problems be hard to solve without international cooperation? Give two examples.
7. **Understanding Causes and Effects** How did the United States develop a trade deficit?

★ ★

Activity **Creating an Action Plan** Your community has asked you to join an environmental task force. To start off, list three actions that individual citizens like you can take to improve the environment.

5 A Diverse Nation

As You Read

Explore These Questions
- How have Americans worked to win greater opportunities for all?
- How have immigration patterns changed in recent years?
- What challenges do Americans face as they move toward a new century?

Define
- mainstream
- refugee
- illegal alien

Identify
- American Indian Religious Freedom Act
- Colin Powell
- Jesse Jackson
- Madeleine Albright
- Americans With Disabilities Act
- Amy Tan
- Immigration Reform and Control Act

SETTING the Scene During the great wave of immigration in the early 1900s, many Americans proudly described their country as a "melting pot." They meant that people of different backgrounds blended into a single American culture.

Today, the United States is still one of the most diverse nations in the world. Civil rights leader Jesse Jackson commented:

66 America is not like a blanket—one piece of unbroken cloth, the same color, the same texture, the same size. America is more like a quilt—many patches, many pieces, many colors, many sizes, all woven and held together by a common thread. **99**

Such diversity has brought its share of challenges. Various groups have sometimes had to struggle to protect their rights as citizens. At the same time, diversity has been a major source of pride for Americans.

Native Americans

After centuries of decline, the nation's Native American population is growing. By the year 2000, it was about 2.4 million people. More than half live in urban areas. Another third live on reservations.

By 1970, the federal government had abandoned its policy of encouraging Indians to leave their reservations. (See page 821.) Instead, Native American tribes and organizations have won greater power to govern their own ways of life.

The Indian Education Act of 1972 focused attention on the unique educational needs of American Indians. Under the law, Indian parents became more involved in developing programs for their children in schools both on and off reservations. By taking courses on their history and traditions, said one parent, "our kids will grow up proud to be Indians."

In 1978, Congress passed the **American Indian Religious Freedom Act.** It directed federal agencies not to interfere with Native American religious practices. For example, the navy now allows Shoshone Indians to visit traditional healing springs on the China Lake Naval Weapons Center.

Connections With Arts

Many people have learned about life on Navajo reservation lands through the award-winning mystery novels of Tony Hillerman. The main characters in Hillerman's novels are Navajo tribal police officers. For his respectful portrayal of Indian life and customs, Hillerman was awarded the Navajo Tribe's Special Friend Award.

Biography — Colin Powell

"I remember the feeling that you can't make it," Colin Powell told young people. *"But you can."* Powell was born in New York City's Harlem, the son of garment workers. Joining the army, he won a Purple Heart in Vietnam and eventually rose to be chairman of the Joint Chiefs of Staff. After retiring from the army, he headed a campaign to encourage Americans to volunteer for public service.

★ **A poll named Colin Powell as one of the most admired Americans among both blacks and whites. Why do you think this was so?**

Congress has also responded to Native American demands for control over artifacts from their past. A 1990 law requires museums to catalog the Indian objects in their collections. They must then give Indian groups a chance to reclaim such items as human remains and religious objects.

Indian groups have worked to develop economic independence. Many reservations set up banks, factories, and other businesses. As a result of the Tribal College Movement, a number of tribes opened their own colleges and universities.

African Americans

The civil rights movement of the 1950s and 1960s toppled many barriers. At the same time, many African Americans still work to win full equality in American society.

Success stories

In the 1980s and 1990s, African Americans made notable advances in politics and government. In 1989, Douglas Wilder of Virginia became the first black to be elected governor of a state. That same year, **Colin Powell** became chairman of the Joint Chiefs of Staff. General Powell helped plan the victory over Iraq in the Persian Gulf War.

Civil rights leader **Jesse Jackson** was a key contender for the Democratic presidential nomination in 1988. Jackson's Rainbow Coalition—made up of people of all colors working together for the good of all people—stressed the needs of the cities, nonwhites, farmers, and the unemployed.

The civil rights movement opened new jobs and educational opportunities to African Americans. As a result, by the 1990s, the black middle class was steadily growing. Some African Americans earned great success in the business world. Reginald Lewis, a Wall Street financier, became one of the nation's richest men.

Continuing issues

Despite such successes, many African Americans struggled against economic hardship. The wages of African Americans lagged behind those of whites. The unemployment rate for blacks was more than twice that for whites. At the same time, the number of African American students attending college dropped during the 1980s.

Poverty and lack of education trapped many African Americans in urban slums. During the 1980s and 1990s, black and white leaders alike warned of a growing "underclass" of poorly educated, jobless blacks with few prospects of a better future.

As the economy expanded during the 1990s, however, many African Americans took advantage of the prosperity. By 1998, 92 percent of black Americans seeking jobs found employment, compared with 87 percent in 1980.

In addition, more African Americans were attending college than ever before. Fewer were living below the poverty level, and more were living longer. By 1998, 46 percent of African Americans owned their own home—a record high.

Women Today

The women's rights movement has continued to press for equal treatment of women. It claims many successes.

In government

In government, women have taken increasingly prominent roles, especially on the local level. Across the nation, women became mayors or school board presidents or served on county commissions.

On the national level, more women won election to Congress. By the late 1990s, two of the nine Supreme Court Justices were women: Sandra Day O'Connor and Ruth Bader Ginsburg. In 1997, **Madeleine Albright** became the first woman to serve as secretary of state, the highest-ranking Cabinet post. Albright played a major role in shaping post–Cold War foreign policy.

In the workplace

By the year 2000, about 60 percent of American women worked outside the home. Women held a wide range of jobs once closed to them, from police officers and firefighters to sportscasters and professional basketball players. Prodded by affirmative action programs, businesses hired and promoted many talented women. For the first time, women held large numbers of managerial and professional jobs.

Overall, women's incomes rose. The gap between women's and men's wages narrowed, but did not close. On average, women earned less than 75 percent of what men earned. In many companies, women complained that a "glass ceiling" of invisible discrimination kept them out of the highest-paying positions.

At the same time, more and more households were headed by single women. Such households were likely to be poor. More than half the children in families headed by women lived below the poverty line. Working mothers also had the problem of finding affordable, adequate day care.

Americans With Disabilities

Americans with disabilities waged their own struggle for equal rights. In the past, people in wheelchairs had limited access to public transportation or buildings. Disabled rights organizations backed laws requiring reserved parking spaces, ramped curbs, and wheelchair lifts on buses.

Much of the support for disabled rights came from veterans of Vietnam or other wars. Many had lost limbs or become paralyzed serving their country. Now, they insisted on their right to make a living.

A 1975 law ensured access to public schools for children with disabilities. Some of these children have been **mainstreamed,** or placed in regular classes. Others attend small classes with specialized help.

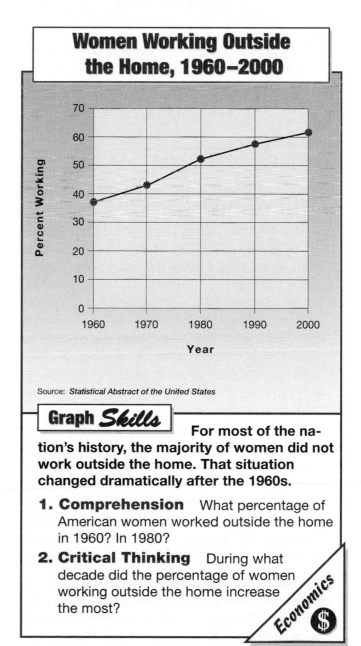

Women Working Outside the Home, 1960–2000

Source: *Statistical Abstract of the United States*

Graph Skills For most of the nation's history, the majority of women did not work outside the home. That situation changed dramatically after the 1960s.

1. **Comprehension** What percentage of American women worked outside the home in 1960? In 1980?

2. **Critical Thinking** During what decade did the percentage of women working outside the home increase the most?

Economics $

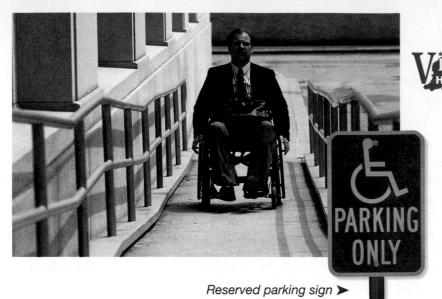

Today, many laws require employers and public buildings to provide access for people with disabilities. These accommodations include reserved parking spaces and wheelchair ramps. Here, a worker in Cleveland, Ohio, goes to his office. ★ **How could ramps and parking spaces help people with disabilities achieve economic independence?**

Reserved parking sign ➤

In 1990, Congress passed the **Americans With Disabilities Act.** It outlawed discrimination in hiring people with physical or mental impairments. The law also required employers to make "reasonable accommodations," such as building ramps for workers in wheelchairs.

Immigration Continues

Since the 1970s, immigrants have been arriving in the United States at a faster rate than at any time since the start of the 1900s. Like earlier immigrants, the new arrivals are helping to reshape the nation.

As in the past, immigrants left home for many reasons. Some sought economic opportunity. Others fled harsh governments or religious persecution. An increasing number of immigrants were refugees from civil wars. **Refugees** are people who flee their homelands to seek safety elsewhere. Most refugees were women and children.

In 1965, Congress ended the quota system that began in the 1920s. (See page 695.) The old laws favored Europeans. New laws made it easier for non-Europeans to enter the country. Today, most immigrants come from Asia, Latin America, or the Caribbean.

Immigrants from Latin America

New immigrants arrived from Latin America. Some were refugees from civil wars in Nicaragua, El Salvador, and Guatemala during the 1980s. Others fled harsh governments in such places as Cuba and Chile. Still others came to escape rural poverty in Mexico, Brazil, and other nations. By the year 2000, people from Latin America and their descendants were on their way to becoming the largest ethnic minority in the United States.

Hundreds of thousands of immigrants have also come from the islands of the Caribbean, such as Jamaica, the Dominican Republic, and Haiti. These people bring a rich mixture of African, European, Native American, and other backgrounds.

Immigrants from Asia

Wars and famines pushed many Asians to seek new homes in other parts of the world. As you read, after the Vietnam War, "boat people" from Southeast Asia sought refuge in the United States. (See page 785.) Other immigrants came from such places as the Philippines, India, and Korea. Asian Americans are now the nation's fastest-growing ethnic group.

New immigration patterns have fueled a debate over what it means to be American. Should immigrants assimilate into American society? How much should they preserve of their own cultures? Author **Amy Tan** depicted such mixed feelings in *The Joy Luck Club*. The novel looks at the lives and attitudes of Chinese-born mothers and their American-born daughters. Many are eager to adopt American ways, but do not want to abandon the traditions of their homeland.

New immigration policy

People who want to immigrate to the United States must apply for admission. Those with relatives in the United States or with valuable job skills are most likely to be accepted. Thousands of others, however, are turned down. Still others enter the nation without permission, becoming **illegal aliens.**

In 1986, Congress tried to reduce illegal immigration by passing the **Immigration Reform and Control Act.** The act allowed people who had arrived illegally before 1982 to remain and apply for citizenship. To discourage further illegal immigration, the act imposed stiff fines on employers who hire undocumented, or illegal, workers.

States with large immigrant populations found it increasingly expensive to provide education, medical care, and other services to illegal immigrants. In 1994, voters in California adopted a controversial law that banned schooling and most health services for illegal immigrants. The law faced a stiff challenge in the courts.

Two years later, Congress passed a new law that allowed local police to arrest illegal immigrants. It also nearly doubled the number of officials who patrol the borders where people try to enter illegally.

Challenges for Today and Tomorrow

As the twenty-first century begins, Americans face both opportunities and challenges. They are adjusting to a changing world. At the same time, they are grappling with new challenges.

Substance abuse

One of the most serious social problems of the 1990s was the use and abuse of illegal drugs. Schools are still in the front lines in the war against drug abuse. They are trying to protect students from dangerous substances like cocaine and heroin.

Americans have been torn between two approaches to fighting illegal drugs. Some emphasize social problems that may lead to drug abuse. They favor setting up treatment centers to help drug users end their addictions. Other Americans see drug abuse as a criminal problem. They want stiffer penalties for drug dealers and users. Since 1980, the United States has spent billions of dollars pursuing drug smugglers and dealers. Yet drug abuse remains widespread.

One legal substance that has come under attack is nicotine, found in tobacco. In the 1990s, several states sued the large tobacco companies to recover money spent on treating smoking-related illnesses. The states

Sources of Immigration to the United States, 1900–1990

Source: *Statistical Abstract of the United States; Historical Statistics of the United States*

Graph Skills The United States has often been called a nation of immigrants. Since 1900, patterns of immigration have shifted dramatically.

1. **Comprehension** Where did the largest number of immigrants come from in 1900? In 1990?
2. **Critical Thinking** Why did immigration from Asia increase sharply after the 1960s?

Why Study History?

Because Knowing History May Help Your Career

★ ★

Historical Background

"Those who cannot remember the past are condemned to repeat it." With these words, Spanish American philosopher George Santayana stressed the need to understand history. Yet not all Americans have placed the same value on the study of our past. Automaker Henry Ford proclaimed, "History is more or less bunk." Since 1957, when the Soviet Union launched the first artificial satellite, American schools have often emphasized science and mathematics.

To become an archaeologist, you need more than a shovel—you need a knowledge of history!

Connections to Today

Can history be helpful in today's job market? The answer is yes! The United States Department of Labor lists more than 30 careers for people with a background in history, including:

- Antiques
- Banking
- Insurance
- Journalism
- Law
- Library science
- Museum operations
- Publishing
- Research
- Teaching
- Tourism

Connections to You

Current statistics say that in the next century, people will change jobs at least five to seven times. This means that your education must prepare you for change. You will have to be adaptable, flexible, and creative. The skills you need to study history—researching, creative thinking, understanding causes and effects, recognizing other viewpoints—can be valuable no matter what career you finally choose.

1. Comprehension Identify two skills that the study of history can help you develop.

2. Critical Thinking Choose one career from the Department of Labor list above. Explain why you think knowledge of history might be helpful in that career.

 **Investigating Careers** Do further research into one of the careers listed above. (Your school librarian can suggest resources.) Prepare a fact sheet summarizing the responsibilities of the job, the average pay range, and future opportunities in that field.

uncovered evidence that tobacco executives deliberately hid scientific studies showing that nicotine was addictive. Other evidence suggested that the companies targeted teenagers in marketing cigarettes.

In 1998, four tobacco companies accepted a $206 billion settlement. The states agreed to drop their lawsuits in exchange for millions of dollars. The companies agreed to change how they marketed their products. They also promised to pay for advertising and educational programs to discourage teen smoking.

Terrorism and violence

Starting in the 1960s, terrorist bombings, kidnappings, and hijackings became increasingly common in Europe, the Middle East, and elsewhere. Americans were sometimes the victims of such acts. However, not until the 1990s did terrorism seem a real threat within the United States.

In 1993, a bomb rocked the World Trade Center in New York City. Two years later, a blast at a federal building in Oklahoma City killed 168 people, including 15 preschool children. A young man who resented the government was later convicted and sentenced to death for the Oklahoma City bombing.

In 1999, a different kind of terror shocked the nation. Two students at Columbine High School in Littleton, Colorado, opened fire on fellow students. Fifteen people died. The Columbine incident was one of several school shootings that led Americans to debate how such violence could be prevented.

Moving toward the future

The United States faces complex issues in the future. Yet Americans have met such challenges before. In 1776, the problems were so great that many believed the new nation would not survive. Instead, it grew to become a superpower and a model for democratic nations everywhere.

From the beginning, the motto of the United States has been *E pluribus unum*—"Out of many, one." This motto reflects the nation's many regions, peoples, and cultures. This diversity is and has always been a major source of the nation's strength.

Today, the bold experiment continues. As we begin the new century, Americans continue to celebrate freedom: the freedom to be ourselves, to respect one another, and to work together, using one another's strengths to build a better nation.

★ Section 5 Review ★

Recall

1. **Identify** **(a)** American Indian Religious Freedom Act, **(b)** Colin Powell, **(c)** Jesse Jackson, **(d)** Madeleine Albright, **(e)** Americans With Disabilities Act, **(f)** Amy Tan, **(g)** Immigration Reform and Control Act.
2. **Define** **(a)** mainstream, **(b)** refugee, **(a)** illegal alien.

Comprehension

3. Describe one success each of the following groups has had: **(a)** Native Americans, **(b)** African Americans, **(c)** women, **(d)** Americans with disabilities.

4. **(a)** How have sources of immigration changed in recent years? **(b)** What is the reason for the change?
5. What two approaches have Americans taken to combat drug abuse?

Critical Thinking and Writing

6. **Making Inferences** How can individual success stories like those of Colin Powell, Reginald Lewis, or Madeline Albright inspire others?
7. **Defending a Position** Would you be willing to give up some of your personal freedom in order to protect against possible terrorism? Why or why not?

Activity **Writing a Speech** You have been selected to welcome a group of new immigrants. In your speech, describe what will be expected of them as Americans and how diversity has contributed to the nation's strength.

Chapter 30 · **Review and Activities**

★ Sum It Up ★

Section 1   A Conservative Tide
▶ The conservative goals of President Ronald Reagan included reducing taxes and limiting the role of the federal government.
▶ President Bill Clinton generally followed middle-of-the-road policies.

Section 2   The Post–Cold War World
▶ After the Cold War ended, the United States reached agreements with Russia to reduce nuclear arms.
▶ As the last remaining superpower, the United States took a major role in promoting democracy and stability.

Section 3   War and Peace in the Middle East
▶ In the Middle East, the United States has supported Israel while trying to improve relations with Arab nations.
▶ In the Persian Gulf War, American forces helped drive Iraqi invaders out of Kuwait.

Section 4   The Environment and the World Economy
▶ The government and individuals have taken steps to protect the environment.
▶ The United States sought ways to compete in a global marketplace.

Section 5   A Diverse Nation
▶ Although many problems remained, groups such as Native Americans, African Americans, women, and people with disabilities have made many advances.
▶ Continuing challenges for the future include combating drug abuse and terrorism.

CD-ROM Review For additional review of the major ideas of Chapter 30, see *Guide to the Essentials of American History* or *Interactive Student Tutorial CD-ROM,* which contains interactive review activities, graphic organizers, and practice tests.

🗔 Reviewing the Chapter

Define These Terms
Match each term with the correct definition.

Column 1
1. apartheid
2. downsizing
3. renewable resource
4. trade deficit
5. solar energy

Column 2
a. raw material that can be readily replaced by nature
b. gap that occurs when a nation imports more than it exports
c. strict separation of races
d. power from the sun
e. using fewer people to do the same work

Explore the Main Ideas
1. How did Ronald Reagan and other conservatives view the federal government?
2. What caused the recession of the early 1990s?
3. How did the United States try to bring peace to Northern Ireland?
4. List one cause and two effects of the Arab oil embargo of 1973.
5. What changes occurred for women in the job market?

🗔 Chart Activity

Look at the table below and answer the following questions:
1. How many tons of garbage did the United States burn or dump in 1980? **2.** What percentage of the total amount of garbage was recycled or composted in 1970? In 1990?
Critical Thinking Why do environmentalists favor recycling?

Garbage Disposal in the United States				
	1970	1980	1990	2000
Total Generated *	121	152	197	222
Recycled or Composted *	8	15	34	67
Burned or Dumped *	113	137	163	155

* In millions of tons
Source: Environmental Protection Agency

🗂 Critical Thinking and Writing

1. **Understanding Chronology** Why was the United States able to balance its budget after the Cold War ended, but not before?

2. **Exploring Unit Themes World Leadership** Reread the statements by Dana Rohrabacher and Newt Gingrich on page 837. **(a)** What do you think Rohrabacher meant by "an unfair burden"? **(b)** Has the United States continued to "lead," as Gingrich suggested? Explain.

3. **Linking Past and Present**   **(a)** How was the Persian Gulf War similar to World War II? **(b)** How was it different?

4. **Ranking**   What would you consider the three most important events described in this chapter? Give reasons for your choices.

🗂 Using Primary Sources

In 1996, President Bill Clinton addressed a group of American business leaders:

> ❝ Every day all you have to do is pick up the paper or watch the evening news to see that differences among people—racial, ethnic, religious, and other differences— are tearing the heart out of societies and regions all around the world. In America we're turning all those differences to our advantage. And I think more and more we're getting comfortable with the fact that we are more than ever still a nation of immigrants. ❞

Source: M2 PressWIRE, October 1, 1996.

Recognizing Points of View (a) According to Clinton, what has torn apart many societies around the world? Give three examples from this chapter that support this view. **(b)** According to Clinton, how does the United States differ from these other places?

ACTIVITY BANK

▶ Interdisciplinary Activity

Exploring Sciences   Find out more about the various energy sources available today. Make a chart showing the advantages and disadvantages of each. Accompany your chart with diagrams that show how each energy source creates power.

▶ Career Skills Activity

Architects   Find out how a public building in your area has provided access for people in wheelchairs. Create a diagram or model showing the kinds of improvements that have been made.

▶ Citizenship Activity

Creating Posters   Focus on an environmental problem in your community, such as littering or improper disposal of toxic household waste. Make educational posters to teach members of your community about the problem and possible solutions.

Internet Activity

Use the Internet to find a Web site for a national or local news agency, newspaper, or television station. Report on what kinds of news you can get from that site, and how you can use that site to keep informed about current and future issues.

EYEWITNESS Journal

You are yourself, a young student attending an American school right now. In your EYEWITNESS JOURNAL, describe three events of the past 25 years that have had the biggest impact on your life. You may write as if you had the ability to go back in time to witness these events.

History Through Literature

The Circuit

by Francisco Jiménez

Introduction

As a child, Francisco Jiménez labored in the fields of California. He later became a writer and university teacher. Many of his stories describe "the joys and disappointments of growing up in a migrant setting." In his short story "The Circuit," Jiménez describes how being constantly on the move affects Panchito, a young migrant worker.

Vocabulary

Before you read the selection, find the meaning of these words in a dictionary: **savoring, instinct, enthusiastically.**

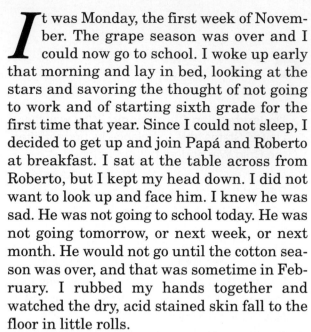

It was Monday, the first week of November. The grape season was over and I could now go to school. I woke up early that morning and lay in bed, looking at the stars and savoring the thought of not going to work and of starting sixth grade for the first time that year. Since I could not sleep, I decided to get up and join Papá and Roberto at breakfast. I sat at the table across from Roberto, but I kept my head down. I did not want to look up and face him. I knew he was sad. He was not going to school today. He was not going tomorrow, or next week, or next month. He would not go until the cotton season was over, and that was sometime in February. I rubbed my hands together and watched the dry, acid stained skin fall to the floor in little rolls.

When Papá and Roberto left for work, I felt relief. I walked to the top of a small grade next to the shack and watched the car disappear in the distance in a cloud of dust.

Two hours later, around eight o'clock, I stood by the side of the road waiting for school bus number twenty. When it arrived I climbed in. Everyone was busy either talking or yelling. I sat in an empty seat in the back.

When the bus stopped in front of the school, I felt very nervous. I looked out the bus window and saw boys and girls carrying books under their arms. I put my hands in my pant pockets and walked to the principal's office. When I entered I heard a woman's voice say: "May I help you?" I was startled. I had not heard English for months. For a few seconds I remained speechless. I looked at the lady who waited for an answer. My first instinct was to answer her in Spanish, but I held back. Finally, after struggling for English words, I managed to tell her that I wanted to enroll in the sixth grade. After answering many questions, I was led to the classroom.

Mr. Lema, the sixth grade teacher, greeted me and assigned me a desk. He then introduced me to the class. I was so nervous and scared at that moment when everyone's eyes were on me that I wished I were with Papá and Roberto picking cotton. After taking roll, Mr. Lema gave the class the assignment for

Tony Ortega painted Los Jovenes con Bicicleta *(Young People With Bicycle) in 1991. Ortega's use of bright colors shows the influence of Mexican artistic style. Art from many different cultures has enriched American culture.* ★ **How would you describe the mood of this painting? Explain.**

the first hour. "The first thing we have to do this morning is finish reading the story we began yesterday," he said enthusiastically. He walked up to me, handed me an English book, and asked me to read. "We are on page 125," he said politely. When I heard this, I felt my blood rush to my head; I felt dizzy. "Would you like to read?" he asked hesitantly. I opened the book to page 125. My mouth was dry. My eyes began to water. I could not begin. "You can read later," Mr. Lema said understandingly.

For the rest of the reading period I kept getting angrier and angrier with myself. I should have read, I thought to myself.

During recess I went into the restroom and opened my English book to page 125. I began to read in a low voice, pretending I was in class. There were many words I did not know. I closed the book and headed back to the classroom.

Mr. Lema was sitting at his desk correcting papers. When I entered he looked up at me and smiled. I felt better. I walked up to

him and asked if he could help me with the new words. "Gladly," he said.

The rest of the month I spent my lunch hours working on English with Mr. Lema, my best friend at school.

One Friday during lunch hour Mr. Lema asked me to take a walk with him to the music room. "Do you like music?" he asked me as we entered the building. "Yes, I like corridos,"* I answered. He then picked up a trumpet, blew on it and handed it to me. The sound gave me goose bumps. I knew that sound. I had heard it in many corridos. "How would you like to learn how to play it?" he asked. He must have read my face because before I could answer, he added: "I'll teach you how to play it during our lunch hours."

That day I could hardly wait to get home to tell Papá and Mamá the great news. As I got off the bus, my little brothers and sisters ran up to meet me. They were yelling and screaming. I thought they were happy to see me, but when I opened the door to our shack, I saw that everything we owned was neatly packed in cardboard boxes.

---

*Corridos refers to a form of dance music popular in Mexico.

Analyzing Literature

1. Why was Panchito unable to go to school before November?

2. How does Mr. Lema win Panchito's freindship?

3. **Making Inferences** **(a)** At the end of the story, what emotions do you think Panchito feels when he sees the packed boxes? **(b)** What is Jiménez suggesting about the education of young migrant workers?

Reference Section

The Mayflower Compact

UNIT 1

Introduction In 1620, the *Mayflower* anchored in what is now Provincetown Harbor off Cape Cod, Massachusetts. Before the landing, 41 male passengers on the ship signed a binding agreement that set up, a basis for self-government. This document became known as the Mayflower Compact.

Vocabulary Before you read the selection, find the meaning of these words in a dictionary: **sovereign, covenant, furtherance, ordinances.**

Document in Brief

The signers of this document promise to join together to create a government for the Plymouth colony and to make laws for the good of the community.

In the name of God Amen, We whose names are underwritten, the loyal subjects of the dread sovereign Lord King James by the grace of God, of Great Britain, France, and Ireland king, defender of the faith, etc.

Having undertaken for the glory of God, and advancements of the Christian faith and honor of our King and country, a voyage to plant the first colony in the northern parts of Virginia, do by these presents solemnly and mutually in the presence of God, and one of another, covenant and combine ourselves together into a civil body politic; for our better ordering and preservation and furtherance of the ends afore said; and by virtue hereof to enact, constitute, and frame such just and equal laws, ordinances, acts, constitutions, and offices, from time to time, as shall be thought most meet and convenient for the general good of the colony: unto which we promise all due submission and obedience.

In witness whereof we have here under subscribed our names at Cape Cod the 11 of November, in the year the reign of our sovereign Lord King James of England, France, and Ireland, the eighteenth and of Scotland the fifty-fourth Anno Domini 1620

▲ *Colonial Boston in the 1660s*

Analyzing Primary Sources

1. The purpose of the Mayflower Compact was to
   A. elect church members.
   B. separate from England.
   C. establish a governing body.
   D. honor the English king.

2. The signers promised to submit themselves to
   F. King James.
   G. the governor of the colony.
   H. the common good.
   J. the Church.

3. **Critical Thinking Linking Past and Present** How are the ideas in the Mayflower Compact reflected in the form of government that exists in the United States today?

UNIT 2 "Give Me Liberty or Give Me Death"
Patrick Henry

Introduction   Patrick Henry gave his most famous speech in Richmond, Virginia, on March 23, 1775. Less than a month later, the battles of Lexington and Concord marked the start of the American Revolution. Portions of Henry's speech are printed below.

Vocabulary   Before you read the selection, find the meaning of these words in a dictionary: **remonstrated, supplicated, prostrated, inviolate, inestimable, resounding.**

Document in Brief

In this speech, Henry argues that it is already too late for the 13 colonies to settle their differences with England.

Let us not, I beseech you, sir, deceive ourselves any longer. Sir, we have done everything that could be done to avert the storm which is now coming on. We have petitioned; we have remonstrated; we have supplicated; we have prostrated ourselves before the tyrannical hands of the ministry and parliament. Our petitions have been slighted; our remonstrances have produced additional violence and insult; our supplications have been disregarded; and we have been spurned, with contempt, from the foot of the throne. In vain, after these things, may we indulge the fond hope of peace and reconciliation. There is no longer any room for hope. If we wish to be free—if we mean to preserve inviolate those inestimable privileges for which we have been so long contending—if we mean not basely to abandon the noble struggle in which we have been so long engaged, and which we pledged ourselves never to abandon until the glorious object of our contest shall be obtained, we must fight! . . .

It is in vain, sir, to extenuate the matter. Gentlemen may cry peace, peace—but there is no peace. The war is actually begun! The next gale that sweeps from the North will bring to our ears the clash of resounding arms! Our brethren are already in the field! Why stand we here idle? What is it that gentlemen wish? What would they have? Is life so dear, or peace so sweet, as to be purchased at the price of chains and slavery? Forbid it, Almighty God! I know not what course others may take; but as for me, give me liberty, or give me death!

▲ *Colonial tax protest*

Analyzing Primary Sources

1. According to Henry, England has responded to the colonists' complaints by
   A. debating them in Parliament.
   B. ignoring them.
   C. calling a Congress.
   D. declaring war.

2. What is more important to Henry than life?

F. slavery
G. freedom
H. democracy
J. victory

3. **Critical Thinking   Recognizing Points of View** How does Henry feel about people who want to restore peace with England?

UNIT 3 Farewell Address
George Washington

Introduction   In 1796, as he neared the end of his second term, President George Washington wrote his famous Farewell Address. In it, he gave his views on the best policies for the young republic to follow. The following excerpt is from Washington's Farewell Address.

Vocabulary   Before you read the selection, find the meaning of these words in a dictionary: **intimated, baneful, enfeeble, animosity, foments, insurrection, infidelity, maxim.**

Document in Brief

As he leaves office, Washington warns Americans of the dangers of forming political parties and of getting involved in the affairs of other nations.

I have already intimated to you the danger of parties in the State, with particular reference to the founding of them on geographical [bases]. Let me now take a more comprehensive view, and warn you in the most solemn manner against the baneful effects of the spirit of party, generally....

It serves always to distract the public councils and enfeeble the public administration. It agitates the community with ill-founded jealousies and false alarms, kindles the animosity of one part against another, foments occasionally riot and insurrection. It opens the door to foreign influence and corruption....

The great rule of conduct for us in regard to foreign nations is, in extending our commercial relations to have with them as little political connection as possible. So far as we have already formed engagements let them be fulfilled, with perfect good faith. Here let us stop....

It is our true policy to steer clear of permanent alliances with any portion of the foreign world, so far, I mean as we are now at liberty to do it; for let me not be understood as capable of [supporting] infidelity to existing engagements. I hold the maxim no less applicable to public than to private affairs that honesty is always the best policy. I repeat, therefore, let those engagements be observed in their genuine sense. But in my opinion it is unnecessary and would be unwise to extend them.

Taking care always to keep ourselves by suitable establishments on a respectable defensive posture, we may safely trust to temporary alliances for extraordinary emergencies.

▲ *Mug honoring President Washington*

Analyzing Primary Sources

1. What is Washington's view of political parties?

   A. They cost too much money.
   B. They cause dangerous divisions within the nation.
   C. They often lead to the rise of monarchs.
   D. They lead to war.

2. What advice about foreign policy did Washington give?

   F. Seek trade but avoid other links with Europe.
   G. Have no contact with Europe.
   H. Cancel all treaties with European countries.
   J. Build up a strong army and navy.

3. **Critical Thinking   Making Inferences**
   Under what circumstances do you think Washington would approve of making an alliance with another country?

UNIT 4 Seneca Falls Declaration of Sentiments

Introduction In 1848, Elizabeth Cady Stanton and Lucretia Mott led a women's rights convention in Seneca Falls, New York. The convention adopted the following Declaration of Sentiments, based partly on the Declaration of Independence.

Vocabulary Before you read the selection, find the meaning of these words in a dictionary: **endowed, inalienable, allegiance, usurpations, franchise.**

Document in Brief

The leaders of the Seneca Falls women's rights convention declare that women and men should have equal rights.

We hold these truths to be self-evident that all men and women are created equal; that they are endowed by their Creator with certain inalienable rights; that among these are life, liberty, and the pursuit of happiness; that to secure these rights governments are instituted, deriving their just powers from the consent of the governed. Whenever any form of government becomes destructive of these ends, it is the right of those who suffer from it to refuse allegiance to it, and to insist upon the institution of a new government, laying its foundation on such principles, and organizing its powers in such form, as to them shall seem most likely to effect their safety and happiness....

The history of mankind is a history of repeated injuries and usurpations on the part of man toward woman, having in direct object the establishment of an absolute tyranny over her. To prove this, let facts be submitted to a candid world....

He has compelled her to submit to laws, in the formation of which she had no voice....

Having deprived her of this first right of a citizen, the elective franchise, thereby leaving her without representation in the halls of legislation, he has oppressed her on all sides....

He has taken from her all right in property, even to the wages she earns....

He has denied her the facilities for obtaining a thorough education—all colleges being closed against her.

▲ *Elizabeth Cady Stanton*

Analyzing Primary Sources

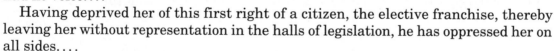

1. What is the main point of this document?
  A. Men should have more rights than women.
  B. Women should have more rights than men.
  C. Women should have the same rights as men.
  D. Women should be paid more.

2. According to this document, women did not have the right to

  F. vote.
  G. keep their earnings.
  H. attend college.
  J. all of the above.

3. Critical Thinking   Making Inferences
Why do you think that the writers of this document echoed the wording of the Declaration of Independence?

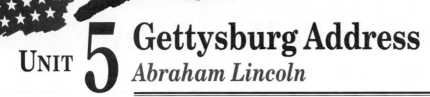

UNIT 5 Gettysburg Address
Abraham Lincoln

Introduction   At the Battle of Gettysburg in July 1863, both the North and the South suffered heavy casualties. On November 19, 1863, President Abraham Lincoln visited Gettysburg to dedicate the battlefield cemetery. The brief but stirring speech Lincoln gave on that day became known as "The Gettysburg Address."

Vocabulary   Before you read the selection, find the meaning of these words in a dictionary: **score, proposition, consecrate, hallow, detract, vain, perish.**

Document in Brief

In this speech, Lincoln says the best way to honor the Union dead is to keep alive the principles of democracy for which they died.

Four score and seven years ago our fathers brought forth on this continent, a new nation, conceived in liberty, and dedicated to the proposition that all men are created equal. Now we are engaged in a great civil war, testing whether that nation, or any nation so conceived and so dedicated, can long endure. We are met on a great battlefield of that war. We have come to dedicate a portion of that field, as a final resting place for those who here gave their lives that that nation might live. It is altogether fitting and proper that we should do this. But, in a larger sense, we can not dedicate—we can not consecrate—we can not hallow—this ground. The brave men, living and dead, who struggled here, have consecrated it, far above our poor power to add or detract. The world will little note, nor long remember what we say here, but it can never forget what they did here. It is for us the living, rather, to be dedicated here to the unfinished work which they who fought here have thus far so nobly advanced. It is rather for us to be here dedicated to the great task remaining before us—that from these honored dead we take increased devotion to that cause for which they gave the last full measure of devotion—that we here highly resolve that these dead shall not have died in vain—that this nation, under God, shall have a new birth of freedom—and that government of the people, by the people, for the people, shall not perish from the earth.

▲ *Lincoln Memorial*

Analyzing Primary Sources

1. Lincoln believes the Civil War will show that
   A. slavery is wrong.
   B. the North is stronger than the South.
   C. a democratic nation can survive.
   D. Americans are brave fighters.

2. Lincoln says the world will soon forget
   F. the sacrifices of the soldiers at Gettysburg.
   G. his speech.
   H. the principles of liberty and justice.
   J. the Civil War.

3. **Critical Thinking   Analyzing Ideas**
   Give examples of how Lincoln uses this speech to try to remind people of the ideals upon which the United States was founded.

UNIT 6 "I Will Fight No More Forever"
Chief Joseph

Introduction In 1877, the United States government tried to force the Nez Percé Indians onto a reservation. Chief Joseph led a band of Nez Percés from their home in western Oregon on a flight toward Canada. They traveled over 1,000 miles before finally surrendering. The following is Chief Joseph's surrender to the army.

Document in Brief

In this speech, Chief Joseph announces that he can no longer carry on his fight against the United States government.

Tell General Howard that I know his heart. What he told me before I have in my heart. I am tired of fighting. Our chiefs are killed. Looking Glass is dead, Tu-hul-hil-sote is dead, the old men are all dead. It is the young men who now say yes or no. He who led the young men* is dead. It is cold and we have no blankets. The little children are freezing to death. My people—some of them have run away to the hills and have no blankets and no food. No one knows where they are—perhaps freezing to death. I want to have time to look for my children and see how many of them I can find. Maybe I shall find them among the dead. Hear me, my chiefs, my heart is sick and sad. From where the sun now stands I will fight no more forever.

_____
*Chief Joseph is referring to his own brother, Alikut.

▲ *Sioux leaders surrendering to the government*

Analyzing Primary Sources

1. How would you describe Chief Joseph's mood in this speech?
   A. angry
   B. mournful
   C. hopeful
   D. proud

2. What is Chief Joseph's main concern?
   F. getting food and blankets
   G. keeping his authority over his people
   H. achieving peace
   J. restoring of Indian lands

3. **Critical Thinking Linking Past and Present** Why do you think Chief Joseph's speech is so well remembered today?

UNIT **7** # The Fourteen Points
Woodrow Wilson

Introduction In January 1918, World War I was still raging in Europe. President Woodrow Wilson outlined to Congress his hopes for the peace settlement. He included a list of specific goals, which came to be known as the Fourteen Points. Six of these goals are listed below.

Vocabulary Before you read the selection, find the meaning of these words in a dictionary: **covenants, maintenance, impartial, sovereignty, equitable, integrity.**

Document in Brief

President Wilson's goals for the world after World War I include an end to secret diplomacy, arms reduction, and the formation of the League of Nations.

1. Open covenants of peace, openly arrived at, after which there shall be no private international understandings of any kind, but diplomacy shall proceed always frankly and in public view.

2. Absolute freedom of navigation upon the seas, outside territorial waters, alike in peace and in war, except as the seas may be closed in whole or in part by international action for the enforcement of international covenants.

3. The removal, so far as possible, of all economic barriers and the establishment of an equality of trade conditions among all the nations consenting to the peace and associating themselves for its maintenance.

4. Adequate guarantees given and taken that national armaments will be reduced to the lowest points consistent with domestic safety.

5. A free, open-minded and absolutely impartial adjustment of all colonial claims based upon a strict observance of the principle that in determining all such questions of sovereignty, the interests of the populations concerned must have equal weight with the equitable claims of the government whose title is to be determined. . . .

14. A general association of nations must be formed under specific covenants for the purpose of affording mutual guarantees of political independence and territorial integrity to great and small [states] alike.

▲ *Versailles peace conference*

Analyzing Primary Sources

1. In Point 1, Wilson hopes to do away with
   A. secret treaties.
   B. colonial disputes.
   C. open covenants.
   D. war.

2. Which of the Fourteen Points concerns imperialism?
   F. Point 2
   G. Point 3
   H. Point 4
   J. Point 5

3. **Critical Thinking Making Inferences** Point 14 was probably the most important to Wilson. **(a)** Why do you think this was so? **(b)** Why do you think he put it last on his list?

UNIT **8** # First Inaugural Address
Franklin D. Roosevelt

Introduction   On March 4, 1933, Franklin Delano Roosevelt took the oath of office as President. In his inaugural speech, FDR tried to build confidence while promising to do whatever was necessary to combat the Great Depression.

Vocabulary   Before you read the selection, find the meaning of these words in a dictionary: **induction, candor, impels, preeminently.**

Document in Brief

President Roosevelt tells Americans that together they can combat the Great Depression.

I am certain that my fellow Americans expect that on my induction into the Presidency I will address them with a candor and a decision which the present situation of our Nation impels. This is preeminently the time to speak the truth, the whole truth, frankly and boldly. Nor need we shrink from honestly facing conditions in our country today. This great Nation will endure as it has endured, will revive and will prosper. So, first of all, let me assert my firm belief that the only thing we have to fear is fear itself—nameless, unreasoning, unjustified terror which paralyzes needed efforts to convert retreat into advance....

Our greatest primary task is to put people to work. This is no unsolvable problem if we face it wisely and courageously. It can be accomplished in part by direct recruiting by the Government itself, treating the task as we would treat the emergency of a war, but at the same time, through this employment, accomplishing greatly needed projects to stimulate and reorganize the use of our natural resources....

[I]n our progress toward a resumption of work we require... safeguards against a return of the evils of the old order: there must be a strict supervision of all banking and credits and investments; there must be an end to speculation with other people's money; and there must be provision for an adequate but sound currency.

There are the lines of attack. I shall presently urge upon a new Congress in special session detailed measures for their fulfillment, and I shall seek the immediate assistance of the several States. Through this program of action we address ourselves to putting our own national house in order and making income balance outgo....

▲ *Franklin and Eleanor Roosevelt*

Analyzing Primary Sources

1. What does Roosevelt say is the greatest danger facing the country?
  A. unemployment
  B. bank failures
  C. war
  D. fear

2. FDR says his top priority is to
  F. end the Depression.
  G. put people to work.
  H. stop speculation.
  J. save natural resources.

3. Critical Thinking   Applying Information Describe how each of the following programs met one of the goals outlined in FDR's speech: **(a)** Civilian Conservation Corps; **(b)** Truth-in-Securities Act.

UNIT 9 "I Have a Dream"
Martin Luther King, Jr.

Introduction In August 1963, more than 200,000 Americans marched to Washington, D.C., in support of civil rights. Martin Luther King, Jr., gave a ringing speech in front of the Lincoln Memorial. Portions of King's "I Have a Dream" speech are printed below.

Vocabulary Before you read the selection, find the meaning of these words in a dictionary: **creed, Gentiles.**

Document in Brief

Dr. King describes a future where all Americans can live together in harmony.

I have a dream that one day, this nation will rise up and live out the true meaning of its creed: "We hold these truths to be self-evident; that all men are created equal. . . ."

I have a dream that my four little children will one day live in a nation where they will not be judged by the color of their skin but by the content of their character.

I have a dream today!

I have a dream that one day the state of Alabama . . . will be transformed into a situation where little black boys and black girls will be able to join hands with little white boys and white girls as sisters and brothers. . . .

With this faith we will be able to work together, to pray together, to struggle together, to go to jail together, to stand up for freedom together, knowing that we will be free one day. This will be the day when all of God's children will be able to sing with new meaning—"my country 'tis of thee; sweet land of liberty; of thee I sing; land where my fathers died, land of the pilgrim's pride, from every mountain side, let freedom ring"—and if America is to be a great nation, this must become true. . . .

Let freedom ring from Lookout Mountain of Tennessee.

Let freedom ring from every hill and molehill of Mississippi. From every mountainside, let freedom ring.

When we let freedom ring, when we let it ring from every village and every hamlet, from every state and every city, we will be able to speed up that day when all of God's children, black men and white men, Jews and Gentiles, Protestants and Catholics, will be able to join hands and sing in the words of the old Negro spiritual: "Free at last! free at last! thank God almighty, we are free at last!"

▲ *King leading a civil rights march*

Analyzing Primary Sources

1. King wants people to be judged by
   A. their race.
   B. their religious faith.
   C. their character.
   D. their commitment to civil rights.

2. In the selection above, King quotes from

   F. "The Star-Spangled Banner."
   G. the Declaration of Independence.
   H. "America the Beautiful."
   J. the Pledge of Allegiance.

3. **Critical Thinking** **Identifying the Main Idea** What is King's main idea?

★ The Declaration of Independence ★

On June 7, 1776, the Continental Congress approved the resolution that "these United Colonies are, and of right ought to be, free and independent States." Congress then appointed a committee to write a declaration of independence. The committee members were John Adams, Benjamin Franklin, Robert Livingston, Roger Sherman, and Thomas Jefferson.

Jefferson actually wrote the Declaration, but he got advice from the others. On July 2, Congress discussed the Declaration and made some changes. On July 4, 1776, it adopted the Declaration of Independence in its final form.

The Declaration is printed in black. The headings have been added to show the parts of the Declaration. They are not part of the original text. Annotations, or explanations, are on the tan side of the page. Page numbers in the annotations show where a subject is discussed in the text. Difficult words are defined.

dissolve: break *powers of the earth:* other nations *station:* place *impel:* force

The colonists feel that they must explain to the world the reasons why they are breaking away from England.

When in the course of human events it becomes necessary for one people to dissolve the political bands which have connected them with another and to assume, among the powers of the earth, the separate and equal station to which the laws of nature and of nature's God entitle them, a decent respect to the opinions of mankind requires that they should declare the causes which impel them to the separation.

The Purpose of Government Is to Protect Basic Rights

endowed: given *unalienable rights:* so basic that they cannot be taken away *secure:* protect *instituted:* set up *deriving:* getting *alter:* change *effect:* bring about

People set up governments to protect their basic rights. Governments get their power from the consent of the governed. If a government takes away the basic rights of the people, the people have the right to change the government.

prudence: wisdom *transient:* temporary, passing *disposed:* likely *usurpations:* taking and using powers that do not belong to a person *invariably:* always *evinces a design to reduce them under absolute despotism:* makes a clear plan to put them under complete and unjust control *sufferance:* endurance

We hold these truths to be self-evident, that all men are created equal; that they are endowed by their Creator with certain unalienable rights; that among these are life, liberty, and the pursuit of happiness. That, to secure these rights, governments are instituted among men, deriving their just powers from the consent of the governed; that, whenever any form of government becomes destructive of these ends, it is the right of the people to alter or to abolish it, and to institute a new government, laying its foundation on such principles and organizing its powers in such form, as to them shall seem most likely to effect their safety and happiness. Prudence, indeed, will dictate that governments long established should not be changed for light and transient causes; and, accordingly, all experience hath shown that mankind are more disposed to suffer, while evils are sufferable, than to right themselves by abolishing the forms to which they are accustomed. But when a long train of abuses and usurpations, pursuing invariably the same object, evinces a design to reduce them under absolute despotism, it is their right, it is their duty, to throw off such government and to provide new guards for their future security. Such has been the patient sufferance of these colonies, and such is now the necessity which constrains them to alter their former systems of government. The history of the present King of Great Britain is a history of repeated injuries and usurpations, all having, in direct object, the establishment of an absolute tyranny over these States. To prove this, let facts be submitted to a candid world:

Wrongs Done by the King

He has refused his assent to laws the most wholesome and necessary for the public good.

He has forbidden his governors to pass laws of immediate and pressing importance, unless suspended in their operation till his assent should be obtained; and, when so suspended, he has utterly neglected to attend to them.

He has refused to pass other laws for the accommodation of the large districts of people, unless those people would relinquish the right of representation in the legislature; a right inestimable to them and formidable to tyrants only.

He has called together legislative bodies at places unusual, uncomfortable, and distant from the depository of their public records, for the sole purpose of fatiguing them into compliance with his measures.

He has dissolved representative houses, repeatedly for opposing, with manly firmness, his invasions on the rights of the people.

He has refused, for a long time after such dissolutions, to cause others to be elected: whereby the legislative powers, incapable of annihilation, have returned to the people at large for their exercise; the state remaining, in the meantime, exposed to all the danger of invasion from without and convulsions within.

He has endeavored to prevent the population of these States; for that purpose, obstructing the laws for naturalization of foreigners, refusing to pass others to encourage their migration hither, and raising the conditions of new appropriations of lands.

He has obstructed the administration of justice by refusing his assent to laws for establishing judiciary powers.

He has made judges dependent on his will alone for the tenure of their offices and the amount and payment of their salaries.

He has erected a multitude of new offices and sent hither swarms of officers to harass our people and eat out their substance.

He has kept among us, in time of peace, standing armies, without the consent of our legislatures.

He has affected to render the military independent of, and superior to, the civil power.

He has combined with others to subject us to a jurisdiction foreign to our Constitution and unacknowledged by our laws, giving his assent to their acts of pretended legislation—

For quartering large bodies of armed troops among us;

constrains: forces **absolute tyranny:** harsh and unjust government **candid:** free from prejudice

People do not change governments for slight reasons. But they are forced to do so when a government becomes tyrannical. King George III has a long record of abusing his power.

assent: approval **relinquish:** give up **inestimable:** too great a value to be measured **formidable:** causing fear

This part of the Declaration spells out three sets of wrongs that led the colonists to break with Britain.
  The first set of wrongs is the king's unjust use of power. The king refused to approve laws that are needed. He has tried to control the colonial legislatures.

depository: storehouse **fatiguing:** tiring out **compliance:** giving in **dissolved:** broken up **annihilation:** total destruction **convulsions:** disturbances

The king has tried to force colonial legislatures into doing his will by wearing them out. He has dissolved legislatures (such as those of Massachusetts). (See page 90.)

endeavored: tried **obstructing:** blocking **naturalization:** process of becoming a citizen **migration:** moving **hither:** here **appropriations:** grants **obstructed the administration of justice:** prevented justice from being done **judiciary powers:** system of law courts **tenure:** term (of office) **erected:** set up **multitude:** large number **swarms:** huge crowds **harass:** cause trouble **render:** make

Among other wrongs, he has refused to let settlers move west to take up new land. He has prevented justice from being done. Also, he has sent large numbers of customs officials to cause problems for the colonists.

jurisdiction: authority

quartering: housing

mock: false

The king has joined with others, meaning Parliament, to make laws for the colonies. The Declaration then lists the second set of wrongs—unjust acts of Parliament.

imposing: forcing   **depriving:** taking away   **transporting us beyond seas:** sending colonists to England for trial   **neighboring province:** Quebec   **arbitrary government:** unjust rule   **fit instrument:** suitable tool   **invested with power:** having the power

During the years leading up to 1776, the colonists claimed that Parliament had no right to make laws for them because they were not represented in Parliament. Here, the colonists object to recent laws of Parliament, such as the Quartering Act and the blockade of colonial ports (page 90), which cut off their trade. They also object to Parliament's claim that it had the right to tax them without their consent.

abdicated: given up   **plundered:** robbed   **ravaged:** attacked   **mercenaries:** hired soldiers   **desolation:** misery   **perfidy:** falseness   **barbarous:** uncivilized   **constrained:** forced   **brethren:** brothers   **domestic insurrections:** internal revolts

Here, the Declaration lists the third set of wrongs—warlike acts of the king. Instead of listening to the colonists, the king has made war on them. He has hired soldiers to fight in America.

oppressions: harsh rule   **petitioned:** asked   **redress:** relief   **unwarrantable jurisdiction over:** unfair authority   **magnanimity:** generosity   **conjured:** called upon   **common kindred:** relatives   **disavow:** turn away from   **consanguinity:** blood relationships, kinship   **acquiesce:** agree   **denounces:** speaks out against

During this time, colonists have repeatedly asked for relief. But their requests have brought only more suffering. They have appealed to the British people but received no help. So they are forced to separate.

For protecting them by a mock trial from punishment for any murders which they should commit on the inhabitants of these States;

For cutting off our trade with all parts of the world;

For imposing taxes on us without our consent;

For depriving us, in many cases, of the benefit of trial by jury;

For transporting us beyond seas to be tried for pretended offences;

For abolishing the free system of English laws in a neighboring province, establishing therein an arbitrary government, and enlarging its boundaries, so as to render it at once an example and fit instrument for introducing the same absolute rule into these colonies;

For taking away our charters, abolishing our most valuable laws, and altering, fundamentally, the powers of our governments;

For suspending our own legislatures and declaring themselves invested with power to legislate for us in all cases whatsoever.

He has abdicated government here by declaring us out of his protection and waging war against us.

He has plundered our seas, ravaged our coasts, burnt out towns, and destroyed the lives of our people.

He is, at this time, transporting large armies of foreign mercenaries to complete the works of death, desolation, and tyranny already begun with circumstances of cruelty and perfidy scarcely paralleled in the most barbarous ages, and totally unworthy, the head of a civilized nation.

He has constrained our fellow citizens, taken captive on the high seas, to bear arms against their country, to become the executioners of their friends and brethren, or to fall themselves by their hands.

He has excited domestic insurrections amongst us and has endeavored to bring on the inhabitants of our frontiers, the merciless Indian savages, whose known rule of warfare is an undistinguished destruction of all ages, sexes, and conditions.

In every state of these oppressions, we have petitioned for redress in the most humble terms; our repeated petitions have been answered only by repeated injury. A prince whose character is thus marked by every act which may define a tyrant is unfit to be the ruler of a free people.

Nor have we been wanting in attention to our British brethren. We have warned them, from time to time, of attempts made by their legislature to extend an unwarrantable jurisdiction over us. We have reminded them of the circumstances of our emigration and settlement here. We have appealed to their native justice and magnanimity, and we have conjured them, by the ties of our common kindred, to disavow these usurpations, which would inevitably interrupt our connections and correspondence. They, too, have been deaf to the voice of justice and consanguinity. We must, therefore, acquiesce in the necessity which denounces our separation, and hold them, as we hold the rest of mankind, enemies in war, in peace, friends.

Colonies Declare Independence

We, therefore, the representatives of the United States of America, in general Congress assembled, appealing to the Supreme Judge of the world for the rectitude of our intentions, do, in the name and by the authority of the good people of these colonies, solemnly publish and declare, that these united colonies are, and of right ought to be, free and independent states: that they are absolved from all allegiance to the British Crown, and that all political connection between them and the state of Great Britain is, and ought to be, totally dissolved; and that, as free and independent states, they have full power to levy war, conclude peace, contract alliances, establish commerce, and to do all other acts and things which independent states may of right do. And, for the support of this declaration, with a firm reliance on the protection of Divine Providence, we mutually pledge to each other our lives, our fortunes, and our sacred honor.

appealing: calling on **rectitude of our intentions:** moral rightness of our plans **absolved from all allegiance:** freed from loyalty **levy war:** declare war **contract alliances:** make treaties

As the representatives of the United States, they declare that the colonies are free and independent states.

The states need no longer be loyal to the British king. They are an independent nation that can make war and sign treaties.

Relying on help from Divine Providence, the signers of the Declaration promise their lives, money, and honor to fight for independence.

★ Signers of the Declaration of Independence ★

John Hancock, President
Charles Thomson, Secretary

New Hampshire
Josiah Bartlett
William Whipple
Matthew Thornton

Massachusetts
Samuel Adams
John Adams
Robert Treat Paine
Elbridge Gerry

Rhode Island
Stephen Hopkins
William Ellery

Connecticut
Roger Sherman
Samuel Huntington
William Williams
Oliver Wolcott

Delaware
Caesar Rodney
George Read
Thomas McKean

New York
William Floyd
Philip Livingston
Francis Lewis
Lewis Morris

New Jersey
Richard Stockton
John Witherspoon
Francis Hopkinson
John Hart
Abraham Clark

Georgia
Button Gwinnett
Lyman Hall
George Walton

Maryland
Samuel Chase
William Paca
Thomas Stone
Charles Carroll

North Carolina
William Hooper
Joseph Hewes
John Penn

Virginia
George Wythe
Richard Henry Lee
Thomas Jefferson
Benjamin Harrison
Thomas Nelson, Jr.
Francis Lightfoot Lee
Carter Braxton

South Carolina
Edward Rutledge
Thomas Heyward, Jr.
Thomas Lynch, Jr.
Arthur Middleton

Pennsylvania
Robert Morris
Benjamin Rush
Benjamin Franklin
John Morton
George Clymer
James Smith
George Taylor
James Wilson
George Ross

★ The Constitution ★
of the United States of America

T he Constitution is printed in black. The titles of articles, sections, and clauses are not part of the original document. They have been added to help you find information in the Constitution. Some words or lines are crossed out because they have been changed by amendments or no longer apply. Annotations, or explanations, are on the tan side of the page. Page numbers in the annotations show where a subject is discussed in the text. Difficult words are defined.

★ THE CONSTITUTION ★

The Preamble describes the purpose of the government set up by the Constitution. Americans expect their government to defend justice and liberty and provide peace and safety from foreign enemies.

The Constitution gives Congress the power to make laws. Congress is divided into the Senate and the House of Representatives.

Clause 1 *Electors* refers to voters. Members of the House of Representatives are elected every two years. Any citizen allowed to vote for members of the larger house of the state legislature can also vote for members of the House.

Clause 2 A member of the House of Representatives must be at least 25 years old, an American citizen for 7 years, and a resident of the state he or she represents.

Clause 3 The number of representatives each state elects is based on its population. An *enumeration,* or census, must be taken every 10 years to determine population. Today, the number of representatives in the House is fixed at 435.

This is the famous Three-Fifths Compromise worked out at the Constitutional Convention (page 124). *Persons bound to service* meant indentured servants. *All other persons* meant slaves. All free people in a state were counted. However, only three fifths of the slaves were included in the population count. This three-fifths clause became meaningless when slaves were freed by the Thirteenth Amendment.

Preamble

We the people of the United States, in order to form a more perfect Union, establish justice, insure domestic tranquillity, provide for the common defense, promote the general welfare, and secure the blessings of liberty to ourselves and our posterity, do ordain and establish this Constitution for the United States of America.

Article 1. The Legislative Branch

Section 1. A Two-House Legislature

All legislative powers herein granted shall be vested in a Congress of the United States, which shall consist of a Senate and House of Representatives.

Section 2. House of Representatives

1. Election of Members The House of Representatives shall be composed of members chosen every second year by the people of the several states, and the electors in each state shall have the qualifications requisite for electors of the most numerous branch of the state legislature.

2. Qualifications No person shall be a Representative who shall not have attained to the age of twenty-five years, and been seven years a citizen of the United States, and who shall not, when elected, be an inhabitant of that state in which he shall be chosen.

3. Determining Representation Representatives and direct taxes shall be apportioned among the several states which may be included within this Union, according to their respective numbers which shall be determined by adding to the whole number of free persons, including those bound to service for a term of years, and excluding Indians not taxed, three-fifths of all other persons. The actual enumeration shall be made within three years after the first meeting of the Congress of the United States, and within every subsequent term of ten years, in such manner as they shall by law direct. The number of Representatives shall not exceed one for every 30,000, but each state shall have at least one Representative; and until such enumeration shall be made, the state of New Hampshire shall be entitled to choose three; Massachusetts, eight; Rhode Island and Providence Plantations, one; Connecticut, five; New York, six; New Jersey, four; Pennsylvania, eight; Delaware, one; Maryland, six; Virginia, ten; North Carolina, five; South Carolina, five; and Georgia, three.

4. Filling Vacancies   When vacancies happen in the representation from any state, the executive authority thereof shall issue writs of election to fill such vacancies.

5. Selection of Officers; Power of Impeachment   The House of Representatives shall choose their Speaker and other officers; and shall have the sole power of impeachment.

Section 3. The Senate

1. Selection of Members   The Senate of the United States shall be composed of two Senators from each state chosen by the legislature thereof, for six years, and each Senator shall have one vote.

2. Alternating Terms; Filling Vacancies   Immediately after they shall be assembled in consequence of the first election, they shall be divided as equally as may be into three classes. The seats of the Senators of the first class shall be vacated at the expiration of the second year, of the second class at the expiration of the fourth year, and of the third class at the expiration of the sixth year, so that one-third may be chosen every second year; and if vacancies happen by resignation, or otherwise, during the recess of the legislature of any state, the executive thereof may make temporary appointments until the next meeting of the legislature, which shall then fill such vacancies.

3. Qualifications   No person shall be a Senator who shall not have attained to the age of thirty years, and been nine years a citizen of the United States, and who shall not, when elected, be an inhabitant of that state for which he shall be chosen.

4. President of the Senate   The Vice-President of the United States shall be president of the Senate, but shall have no vote, unless they be equally divided.

5. Election of Senate Officers   The Senate shall choose their other officers, and also a president *pro tempore,* in the absence of the Vice-President, or when he shall exercise the office of the President of the United States.

6. Impeachment Trials   The Senate shall have the sole power to try all impeachments. When sitting for that purpose, they shall be on oath or affirmation. When the President of the United States is tried, the Chief Justice shall preside; and no person shall be convicted without the concurrence of two-thirds of the members present.

Clause 4   *Executive authority* means the governor of a state. If a member of the House leaves office before his or her term ends, the governor must call a special election to fill the seat.

Clause 5   The House elects a speaker. Today, the speaker is usually chosen by the party that has a majority in the House. Also, only the House has the power to *impeach,* or accuse, a federal official of wrongdoing.

Clause 1   Each state has two senators. Senators serve for six-year terms. The Seventeenth Amendment changed the way senators were elected.

Clause 2   Every two years, one third of the senators run for reelection. Thus, the makeup of the Senate is never totally changed by any one election. The Seventeenth Amendment changed the way of filling *vacancies,* or empty seats. Today, the governor of a state must choose a senator to fill a vacancy that occurs between elections.

Clause 3   A senator must be at least 30 years old, an American citizen for 9 years, and a resident of the state he or she represents.

Clause 4   The Vice President presides over Senate meetings, but he or she can vote only to break a tie.

Clause 5   *Pro tempore* means temporary. The Senate chooses one of its members to serve as president pro tempore when the Vice President is absent.

Clause 6   The Senate acts as a jury if the House impeaches a federal official. The Chief Justice of the Supreme Court presides if the President is on trial. Two thirds of all senators present must vote for *conviction,* or finding the accused guilty. No President has ever been convicted. The House impeached President Andrew Johnson in 1868, but the Senate acquitted him of the charges (page 413). President Bill Clinton was impeached by the House in December 1998. His Senate trial also ended in acquittal (page 831). In 1974, President Richard Nixon resigned before he could be impeached.

Clause 7 If an official is found guilty by the Senate, he or she can be removed from office and barred from holding federal office in the future. These are the only punishments the Senate can impose. However, the convicted official can still be tried in a criminal court.

7. Penalties Upon Conviction Judgment in cases of impeachment shall not extend further than to removal from office, and disqualification to hold and enjoy any office of honor, trust, or profit under the United States; but the party convicted shall nevertheless be liable and subject to indictment, trial, judgment, and punishment, according to law.

Clause 1 Each state legislature can decide when and how congressional elections take place, but Congress can overrule these decisions. In 1842, Congress required each state to set up congressional districts with one representative elected from each district. In 1872, Congress decided that congressional elections must be held in every state on the same date in even-numbered years.

Clause 2 Congress must meet at least once a year. The Twentieth Amendment moved the opening date of Congress to January 3.

Section 4. Elections and Meetings

1. Election of Congress The times, places, and manner of holding elections for Senators and Representatives shall be prescribed in each state by the legislature thereof; but the Congress may at any time by law make or alter such regulations, except as to the places of choosing Senators.

2. Annual Sessions The Congress shall assemble at least once in every year, ~~and such meeting shall be on the first Monday in December, unless they shall by law appoint a different day.~~

Clause 1 Each house decides whether a member has the qualifications for office set by the Constitution. A *quorum* is the smallest number of members who must be present for business to be conducted. Each house can set its own rules about absent members.

Clause 2 Each house can make rules for the conduct of members. It can only expel a member by a two-thirds vote.

Clause 3 Each house keeps a record of its meetings. *The Congressional Record* is published every day with excerpts from speeches made in each house. It also records the votes of each member.

Section 5. Rules for the Conduct of Business

1. Organization Each house shall be the judge of the elections, returns, and qualifications of its own members, and a majority of each shall constitute a quorum to do business; but a smaller number may adjourn from day to day, and may be authorized to compel the attendance of absent members, in such manner, and under such penalties, as each house may provide.

2. Procedures Each house may determine the rules of its proceedings, punish its members for disorderly behavior, and with the concurrence of two-thirds, expel a member.

3. A Written Record Each house shall keep a journal of its proceedings, and from time to time publish the same, excepting such parts as may in their judgment require secrecy; and the yeas and nays of the members of either house on any question shall, at the desire of one-fifth of those present, be entered on the journal.

Clause 4 Neither house can *adjourn,* or stop meeting, for more than three days unless the other house approves. Both houses of Congress must meet in the same city.

4. Rules for Adjournment Neither house, during the session of Congress, shall, without the consent of the other, adjourn for more than three days, nor to any other place than that in which the two houses shall be sitting.

Section 6. Privileges and Restrictions

Clause 1 *Compensation* means salary. Congress decides the salary for its members. While Congress is in session, a member is free from arrest in civil cases and cannot be sued for anything he or she says on the floor of Congress. This allows for freedom of debate. However, a member can be arrested for a criminal offense.

1. Salaries and Immunities The Senators and Representatives shall receive a compensation for their services, to be ascertained by law and paid out of the Treasury of the United States. They shall in all cases, except treason, felony, and breach of the peace, be privileged from arrest during their attendance at the session of their respective houses, and in going to and returning from the same; and for any speech or debate in either house, they shall not be questioned in any other place.

2. Restrictions on Other Employment No Senator or Representative shall, during the time for which he was elected, be appointed to any civil office under the authority of the United States, which shall have been created, or the emoluments whereof shall have been increased, during such time; and no person holding any office under the United States shall be a member of either house during his continuance in office.

Section 7. Law-Making Process

1. Tax Bills All bills for raising revenue shall originate in the House of Representatives; but the Senate may propose or concur with amendments as on other bills.

2. How a Bill Becomes a Law Every bill which shall have passed the House of Representatives and the Senate shall, before it become a law, be presented to the President of the United States; if he approve, he shall sign it, but if not, he shall return it, with his objections, to that house in which it shall have originated, who shall enter the objections at large on their journal, and proceed to reconsider it. If after such reconsideration two-thirds of that house shall agree to pass the bill, it shall be sent, together with the objections, to the other house, by which it shall likewise be reconsidered, and, if approved by two-thirds of that house, it shall become a law. But in all such cases the votes of both houses shall be determined by yeas and nays, and the names of the persons voting for and against the bill shall be entered on the journal of each house respectively. If any bill shall not be returned by the President within ten days (Sundays excepted) after it shall have been presented to him, the same bill shall be a law, in like manner as if he had signed it, unless the Congress by their adjournment prevent its return, in which case it shall not be a law.

3. Resolutions Passed by Congress Every order, resolution, or vote to which the concurrence of the Senate and House of Representatives may be necessary (except on a question of adjournment) shall be presented to the President of the United States; and before the same shall take effect, shall be approved by him, or being disapproved by him, shall be repassed by two-thirds of the Senate and House of Representatives, according to the rules and limitations prescribed in the case of a bill.

Section 8. Powers Delegated to Congress

The Congress shall have the power

1. Taxes To lay and collect taxes, duties, imposts, and excises, to pay the debts and provide for the common defense and general welfare of the United States; but all duties, imposts, and excises shall be uniform throughout the United States;

2. Borrowing To borrow money on the credit of the United States;

Clause 2 *Emolument* also means salary. A member of Congress cannot hold another federal office during his or her term. A former member of Congress cannot hold an office created while he or she was in Congress. An official in another branch of government cannot serve at the same time in Congress. This strengthens the separation of powers.

Clause 1 *Revenue* is money raised by the government through taxes. Tax bills must be introduced in the House. The Senate, however, can make changes in tax bills. This clause protects the principle that people can be taxed only with their consent.

Clause 2 A *bill,* or proposed law, that is passed by a majority of the House and Senate is sent to the President. If the President signs the bill, it becomes law.

A bill can also become law without the President's signature. The President can refuse to act on a bill. If Congress is in session at the time, the bill becomes law 10 days after the President receives it.

The President can *veto,* or reject, a bill by sending it back to the house where it was introduced. Or if the President refuses to act on a bill and Congress adjourns within 10 days, then the bill dies. This way of killing a bill without taking action is called the *pocket veto.*

Congress can override the President's veto if each house of Congress passes the bill again by a two-thirds vote. This clause is an important part of the system of checks and balances (page 130).

Clause 3 Congress can pass resolutions or orders that have the same force as laws. Any such resolution or order must be signed by the President (except on questions of adjournment). Thus, this clause prevents Congress from bypassing the President simply by calling a bill by another name.

Clause 1 *Duties* are tariffs. *Imposts* are taxes in general. *Excises* are taxes on the production or sale of certain goods. Congress has the power to tax and spend tax money. Taxes must be the same in all parts of the country.

Clause 2 Congress can borrow money for the United States. The government often borrows money by selling *bonds,* or certificates that promise to pay the holder a certain sum of money on a certain date (page 174).

Clause 3 Only Congress has the power to regulate foreign and *interstate trade,* or trade between states. Disagreement over interstate trade was a major problem with the Articles of Confederation (pages 117–118).

Clause 4 *Naturalization* is the process whereby a foreigner becomes a citizen. *Bankruptcy* is the condition in which a person or business cannot pay its debts. Congress has the power to pass laws on these two issues. The laws must be the same in all parts of the country.

Clause 5 Congress has the power to coin money and set its value. Congress has set up the National Bureau of Standards to regulate weights and measures.

Clause 6 *Counterfeiting* is the making of imitation money. *Securities* are bonds. Congress can make laws to punish counterfeiters.

Clause 7 Congress has the power to set up and control the delivery of mail.

Clause 8 Congress may pass copyright and patent laws. A *copyright* protects an author. A patent makes an inventor the sole owner of his or her work for a limited time.

Clause 9 Congress has the power to set up *inferior,* or lower, federal courts under the Supreme Court.

Clause 10 Congress can punish *piracy,* or the robbing of ships at sea.

Clause 11 Only Congress can declare war. Declarations of war are granted at the request of the President. *Letters of marque and reprisal* were documents issued by a government allowing merchant ships to arm themselves and attack ships of an enemy nation. They are no longer issued.

Clauses 12, 13, 14 These clauses place the army and navy under the control of Congress. Congress decides on the size of the armed forces and the amount of money to spend on the army and navy. It also has the power to write rules governing the armed forces.

Clauses 15, 16 The *militia* is a body of citizen soldiers. Congress can call up the militia to put down rebellions or fight foreign invaders. Each state has its own militia, today called the National Guard. Normally, the militia is under the command of a state's governor. However, it can be placed under the command of the President.

3. Commerce To regulate commerce with foreign nations, and among the several states, and with the Indian tribes;

4. Naturalization; Bankruptcy To establish a uniform rule of naturalization, and uniform laws on the subject of bankruptcies throughout the United States;

5. Coins; Weights; Measures To coin money, regulate the value thereof, and of foreign coin, and fix the standard of weights and measures;

6. Counterfeiting To provide for the punishment of counterfeiting the securities and current coin of the United States;

7. Post Offices To establish post offices and post roads;

8. Copyrights; Patents To promote the progress of science and useful arts by securing for limited times to authors and inventors the exclusive right to their respective writings and discoveries;

9. Federal Courts To constitute tribunals inferior to the Supreme Court;

10. Piracy To define and punish piracies and felonies committed on the high seas and offenses against the law of nations;

11. Declarations of War To declare war, ~~grant letters of marque and reprisal,~~ and make rules concerning captures on land and water;

12. Army To raise and support armies, but no appropriation of money to that use shall be for a longer term than two years;

13. Navy To provide and maintain a navy;

14. Rules for the Military To make rules for the government and regulation of the land and naval forces;

15. Militia To provide for calling forth the militia to execute the laws of the Union, suppress insurrections, and repel invasions;

16. Rules for the Militia To provide for organizing, arming, and disciplining the militia, and for governing such part of them as may be employed in the service of the United States, reserving to the states, respectively, the appointment of the officers, and the authority of training the militia according to the discipline prescribed by Congress;

17. National Capital   To exercise exclusive legislation in all cases whatsoever, over such district (not exceeding ten miles square) as may, by cession of particular states, and the acceptance of Congress, become the seat of government of the United States, and to exercise like authority over all places purchased by the consent of the legislature of the state in which the same shall be, for the erection of forts, magazines, arsenals, dock-yards, and other needful buildings;—and

18. Necessary Laws   To make all laws which shall be necessary and proper for carrying into execution the foregoing powers, and all other powers vested by this Constitution in the government of the United States, or in any department or officer thereof.

Section 9. Powers Denied to the Federal Government

1. The Slave Trade   ~~The migration or importation of such persons as any of the states now existing shall think proper to admit shall not be prohibited by the Congress prior to the year 1808; but a tax or duty may be imposed on such importation, not exceeding $10 for each person.~~

2. Writ of Habeas Corpus   The privilege of the writ of habeas corpus shall not be suspended, unless when in cases of rebellion or invasion the public safety may require it.

3. Bills of Attainder and Ex Post Facto Laws   No bill of attainder or *ex post facto* law shall be passed.

4. Apportionment of Direct Taxes   ~~No capitation or other direct tax shall be laid, unless in proportion to the census or enumeration herein before directed to be taken.~~

5. Taxes on Exports   No tax or duty shall be laid on articles exported from any state.

6. Special Preference for Trade   No preference shall be given any regulation of commerce or revenue to the ports of one state over those of another; nor shall vessels bound to, or from, one state, be obliged to enter, clear, or pay duties in another.

7. Spending   No money shall be drawn from the Treasury, but in consequence of appropriations made by law; and a regular statement and account of the receipts and expenditures of all public money shall be published from time to time.

Clause 17   Congress controls the district around the national capital. In 1790, Congress made Washington, D.C., the nation's capital (page 175). In 1973, it gave residents of the District the right to elect local officials.

Clause 18   Clauses 1–17 list the powers delegated to Congress. The writers of the Constitution added Clause 18 so that Congress could deal with the changing needs of the nation. It gives Congress the power to make laws as needed to carry out the first 17 clauses. Clause 18 is sometimes called the elastic clause because it lets Congress stretch the meaning of its power.

Clause 1   *Such persons* means slaves. This clause resulted from a compromise between the supporters and the opponents of the slave trade (page 125). In 1808, as soon as Congress was permitted to abolish the slave trade, it did so. The $10 import tax was never imposed.

Clause 2   A *writ of habeas corpus* is a court order requiring government officials to bring a prisoner to court and explain why he or she is being held. A writ of habeas corpus protects people from unlawful imprisonment. The government cannot suspend this right except in times of rebellion or invasion.

Clause 3   A *bill of attainder* is a law declaring that a person is guilty of a particular crime. An *ex post facto law* punishes an act which was not illegal when it was committed. Congress cannot pass a bill of attainder or *ex post facto* laws.

Clause 4   A *capitation tax* is a tax placed directly on each person. **Direct taxes** are taxes on people or on land. They can be passed only if they are divided among the states according to population. The Sixteenth Amendment allowed Congress to tax income without regard to the population of the states.

Clause 5   This clause forbids Congress to tax exports. In 1787, southerners insisted on this clause because their economy depended on exports.

Clause 6   Congress cannot make laws that favor one state over another in trade and commerce. Also, states cannot place tariffs on interstate trade.

Clause 7   The federal government cannot spend money unless Congress **appropriates** it, or passes a law allowing it. This clause gives Congress an important check on the President by controlling the money he or she can spend. The government must publish a statement showing how it spends public funds.

Clause 8 The government cannot award titles of nobility, such as Duke or Duchess. American citizens cannot accept titles of nobility from foreign governments without the consent of Congress.

Clause 1 The writers of the Constitution did not want the states to act like separate nations. So they prohibited states from making treaties or coining money. Some powers denied to the federal government are also denied to the states. For example, states cannot pass *ex post facto* laws.

Clauses 2, 3 Powers listed here are forbidden to the states, but Congress can lift these prohibitions by passing laws that give these powers to the states.

Clause 2 forbids states from taxing imports and exports without the consent of Congress. States may charge inspection fees on goods entering the states. Any profit from these fees must be turned over to the United States Treasury.

Clause 3 forbids states from keeping an army or navy without the consent of Congress. States cannot make treaties or declare war unless an enemy invades or is about to invade.

Clause 1 The President is responsible for *executing,* or carrying out, laws passed by Congress.

Clauses 2, 3 Some writers of the Constitution were afraid to allow the people to elect the President directly (page 130). Therefore, the Constitutional Convention set up the electoral college. Clause 2 directs each state to choose electors, or delegates to the electoral college, to vote for President. A state's electoral vote is equal to the combined number of senators and representatives. Each state may decide how to choose its electors. Members of Congress and federal officeholders may not serve as electors. This much of the original electoral college system is still in effect.

Clause 3 called upon each elector to vote for two candidates. The candidate who received a majority of the electoral votes would become President. The runner-up would become Vice President. If no candidate won a majority, the House would choose the President. The Senate would choose the Vice President.

The election of 1800 showed a problem with the original electoral college system (page 189). Thomas Jefferson was the Republican candidate

8. Creation of Titles of Nobility   No title of nobility shall be granted by the United States; and no person holding any office of profit or trust under them, shall, without the consent of the Congress, accept of any present, emolument, office, or title, of any kind whatever, from any king, prince, or foreign state.

Section 10. Powers Denied to the States

1. Unconditional Prohibitions   No state shall enter into any treaty, alliance, or confederation; grant letters of marque and reprisal; coin money; emit bills of credit; make anything but gold and silver coin a tender in payment of debts; pass any bill of attainder, *ex post facto* law, or law impairing the obligation of contracts, or grant any title of nobility.

2. Powers Conditionally Denied   No state shall, without the consent of the Congress, lay any imposts or duties on imports or exports, except what may be absolutely necessary for executing its inspection laws; and the net produce of all duties and imposts, laid by any state on imports or exports, shall be for the use of the Treasury of the United States; and all such laws shall be subject to the revision and control of the Congress.

3. Other Denied Powers   No state shall, without the consent of Congress, lay any duty of tonnage, keep troops, or ships of war in time of peace, enter into any agreement or compact with another state, or with a foreign power, or engage in war, unless actually invaded, or in such imminent danger as will not admit of delay.

Article 2. The Executive Branch

Section 1. President and Vice-President

1. Chief Executive   The executive power shall be vested in a President of the United States of America. He shall hold his office during the term of four years, and together with the Vice-President, chosen for the same term, be elected as follows:

2. Selection of Electors   Each state shall appoint, in such manner as the legislature thereof may direct, a number of electors, equal to the whole number of Senators and Representatives to which the state may be entitled in the Congress; but no Senator or Representative, or person holding an office or trust or profit under the United States, shall be appointed an elector.

3. Electoral College Procedures   The electors shall meet in their respective states, and vote by ballot for two persons, of whom one at least shall not be an inhabitant of the same state with themselves. And they shall make a list of all the persons voted for, and of the number of votes for each; which list they shall sign and certify, and transmit sealed to the seat of the government of the United States, directed to the president of the Senate. The president of the Senate shall, in the presence of the Senate and House of Representatives, open all the certificates, and the votes shall then be counted. The person having the greatest number of votes shall be President, if such number be a majority of the whole number of electors appointed; and if there be more than one who have such majority, and have an equal number of votes, then the House of Representatives shall immediately choose by ballot one of them for President; and if no person have a majority, then from the five highest on the list the said House shall in like manner choose the President. But in choosing the President the votes shall be taken by states, the representation from each state having one vote. A quorum for this purpose shall consist of a member or members from two-thirds of the states, and a majority of all the states shall be necessary to a choice. In every case, after the choice of the President, the person having the greatest number of votes of the electors shall be the Vice-President. But if there should remain two or more who have equal votes, the Senate shall choose from them by ballot the Vice-President.

4. Time of Elections The Congress may determine the time of choosing the electors, and the day on which they shall give their votes; which day shall be the same throughout the United States.

5. Qualifications for President No person except a natural-born citizen or a citizen of the United States, at the time of the adoption of this Constitution, shall be eligible to the office of the President; neither shall any person be eligible to that office who shall not have attained to the age of thirty-five years, and been fourteen years a resident within the United States.

6. Presidential Succession In case of the removal of the President from office, or of his death, resignation, or inability to discharge the powers and duties of the said office, the same shall devolve on the Vice-President, and the Congress may by law provide for the case of removal, death, resignation, or inability, both of the President and Vice-President, declaring what officer shall then act as President, and such officer shall act accordingly, until the disability be removed, or a President shall be elected.

7. Salary The President shall, at stated times, receive for his services, a compensation, which shall neither be increased nor diminished during the period for which he shall have been elected, and he shall not receive within that period any other emolument from the United States, or any of them.

8. Oath of Office Before he enter on the execution of his office, he shall take the following oath or affirmation:—"I do solemnly swear (or affirm) that I will faithfully execute the office of President of the United States, and will to the best of my ability, preserve, protect, and defend the Constitution of the United States."

for President, and Aaron Burr was the Republican candidate for Vice President. In the electoral college, the vote ended in a tie. The election was finally decided in the House, where Jefferson was chosen President. The Twelfth Amendment changed the electoral college system so that this could not happen again.

Clause 4 By a law passed in 1792, electors are chosen on the Tuesday after the first Monday of November every four years. Electors from each state meet to vote in December.

Today, voters in each state choose **slates,** or groups, of electors who are pledged to a candidate for President. The candidate for President who wins the popular vote in each state wins that state's electoral vote.

Clause 5 The President must be a citizen of the United States from birth, at least 35 years old, and a resident of the country for 14 years. The first seven Presidents of the United States were born under British rule, but they were allowed to hold office because they were citizens at the time the Constitution was adopted.

Clause 6 The powers of the President pass to the Vice President if the President leaves office or cannot discharge his or her duties. The wording of this clause caused confusion the first time a President died in office. When President William Henry Harrison died, it was uncertain whether Vice President John Tyler should remain Vice President and act as President or whether he should be sworn in as President. Tyler persuaded a federal judge to swear him in. So he set the precedent that the Vice President assumes the office of President when it becomes vacant. The Twenty-fifth Amendment replaced this clause.

Clause 7 The President is paid a salary. It cannot be raised or lowered during his or her term of office. The President is not allowed to hold any other federal or state position while in office. Today, the President's salary is $200,000 a year.

Clause 8 Before taking office, the President must promise to protect and defend the Constitution. Usually, the Chief Justice of the Supreme Court gives the oath of office to the President.

Clause 1 The President is head of the armed forces and the state militias when they are called into national service. So the military is under *civilian,* or nonmilitary, control.

The President can get advice from the heads of executive departments. In most cases, the President has the power to grant a reprieve or pardon. A *reprieve* suspends punishment ordered by law. A *pardon* prevents prosecution for a crime or overrides the judgment of a court.

Clause 2 The President has the power to make treaties with other nations. Under the system of checks and balances, all treaties must be approved by two thirds of the Senate. Today, the President also makes agreements with foreign governments. These executive agreements do not need Senate approval.

The President has the power to appoint ambassadors to foreign countries and to appoint other high officials. The Senate must *confirm,* or approve, these appointments.

Clause 3 If the Senate is in *recess,* or not meeting, the President may fill vacant government posts by making temporary appointments.

The President must give Congress a report on the condition of the nation every year. This report is now called the State of the Union Address. Since 1913, the President has given this speech in person each January.

The President can call a special session of Congress and can adjourn Congress if necessary. The President has the power to receive, or recognize, foreign ambassadors.

The President must carry out the laws. Today, many government agencies oversee the execution of laws.

Civil officers include federal judges and members of the Cabinet. *High crimes* are major crimes. *Misdemeanors* are lesser crimes. The President, Vice President, and others can be forced out of office if impeached and found guilty of certain crimes.

Judicial power is the right of the courts to decide legal cases. The Constitution creates the Supreme Court but lets Congress decide the size of the Supreme Court. Congress has the power to set up inferior, or lower, courts. The Judiciary Act of 1789 (page 173) set up district and circuit courts, or courts of appeal. Today, there are 94 district courts and 13 courts of appeal. All federal judges serve for life.

Section 2. Powers of the President

1. Commander in Chief of the Armed Forces The President shall be Commander in Chief of the Army and Navy of the United States, and of the militia of the several states, when called into the actual service of the United States; he may require the opinion, in writing, of the principal officer in each of the executive departments, upon any subject relating to the duties of their respective offices, and he shall have power to grant reprieves and pardons for offenses against the United States, except in cases of impeachment.

2. Making Treaties and Nominations He shall have power, by and with the advice and consent of the Senate, to make treaties, provided two-thirds of the Senators present concur; and he shall nominate, and by and with the advice and consent of the Senate, shall appoint ambassadors, other public ministers and consuls, judges of the Supreme Court, and all other officers of the United States, whose appointments are not herein otherwise provided for, and which shall be established by law; but the Congress may by law vest the appointment of such inferior officers, as they think proper, in the President alone, in the courts of law, or in the heads of departments.

3. Temporary Appointments The President shall have power to fill up all vacancies that may happen during the recess of the Senate, by granting commissions which shall expire at the end of their next session.

Section 3. Duties

He shall from time to time give to the Congress information of the state of the Union, and recommend to their consideration such measures as he shall judge necessary and expedient; he may, on extraordinary occasions, convene both houses, or either of them, and in case of disagreement between them, with respect to the time of adjournment, he may adjourn them to such time as he shall think proper; he shall receive ambassadors and other public ministers; he shall take care that the laws be faithfully executed, and shall commission all the officers of the United States.

Section 4. Impeachment and Removal From Office

The President, Vice-President, and all civil officers of the United States, shall be removed from office on impeachment for, and conviction of, treason, bribery, or other high crimes or misdemeanors.

Article 3. The Judicial Branch

Section 1. Federal Courts

The judicial power of the United States shall be vested in one Supreme Court, and in such inferior courts as the Congress may from time to time ordain and establish. The judges, both of the Supreme and inferior courts, shall hold their offices during good behavior, and shall, at stated times, receive for their services a compensation, which shall not be diminished during their continuance in office.

Section 2. Jurisdiction of Federal Courts

1. Scope of Judicial Power   The judicial power shall extend to all cases, in law and equity, arising under this Constitution, the laws of the United States, and treaties made or which shall be made, under their authority; to all cases affecting ambassadors, other public ministers and consuls; to all cases of admiralty and maritime jurisdiction; to controversies to which the United States shall be a party; to controversies between two or more states; ~~between a state and citizens of another state;~~ between citizens of the same state claiming lands under grants of different states, and between a state or the citizens thereof, and foreign states, citizens, or subjects.

2. The Supreme Court   In all cases affecting ambassadors, other public ministers and consuls, and those in which a state shall be a party, the Supreme Court shall have original jurisdiction. In all the other cases before mentioned, the Supreme Court shall have appellate jurisdiction, both as to law and fact, with such exceptions, and under such regulations as the Congress shall make.

3. Trial by Jury   The trial of all crimes, except in cases of impeachment, shall be by jury; and such trial shall be held in the state where the said crimes shall have been committed; but when not committed within any state, the trial shall be at such place or places as the Congress may by law have directed.

Section 3. Treason

1. Definition   Treason against the United States shall consist only in levying war against them, or in adhering to their enemies, giving them aid and comfort. No person shall be convicted of treason unless on the testimony of two witnesses to the same overt act, or on confession in open court.

2. Punishment   The Congress shall have power to declare the punishment of treason, but no attainder of treason shall work corruption of blood or forfeiture except during the life of the person attainted.

Article 4. Relations Among the States

Section 1. Official Records and Acts

Full faith and credit shall be given in each state to the public acts, records, and judicial proceedings of every other state. And the Congress may by general laws prescribe the manner in which such acts, records, and proceedings shall be proved, and the effect thereof.

Section 2. Privileges of Citizens

1. Privileges   The citizens of each state shall be entitled to all privileges and immunities of citizens in the several states.

Clause 1   *Jurisdiction* refers to the right of a court to hear a case. Federal courts have jurisdiction over cases that involve the Constitution, federal laws, treaties, foreign ambassadors and diplomats, naval and maritime laws, disagreements between states or between citizens from different states, and disputes between a state or citizen and a foreign state or citizen.

In *Marbury* v. *Madison,* the Supreme Court established the right to judge whether a law is constitutional (page 197).

Clause 2   *Original jurisdiction* means the power of a court to hear a case where it first arises. The Supreme Court has original jurisdiction over only a few cases, such as those involving foreign diplomats. More often, the Supreme Court acts as an appellate court. An *appellate court* does not decide guilt. It decides whether the lower court trial was properly conducted and reviews the lower court's decision.

Clause 3   This clause guarantees the right to a jury trial for anyone accused of a federal crime. The only exceptions are impeachment cases. The trial must be held in the state where the crime was committed.

Clause 1   Treason is clearly defined. An *overt act* is an actual action. A person cannot be convicted of treason for what he or she thinks. A person can be convicted of treason only if he or she confesses or two witnesses testify to it.

Clause 2   Congress has the power to set the punishment for traitors. Congress may not punish the children of convicted traitors by taking away their civil rights or property.

Each state must recognize the official acts and records of any other state. For example, each state must recognize marriage certificates issued by another state. Congress can pass laws to ensure this.

Clause 1   All states must treat citizens of another state in the same way it treats its own citizens. However, the courts have allowed states to give residents certain privileges, such as lower tuition rates.

Clause 2 Extradition means the act of returning a suspected criminal or escaped prisoner to a state where he or she is wanted. State governors must return a suspect to another state. However, the Supreme Court has ruled that a governor cannot be forced to do so if he or she feels that justice will not be done.

Clause 3 *Persons held to service or labor* refers to slaves or indentured servants. This clause required states to return runaway slaves to their owners. The Thirteenth Amendment replaces this clause.

Clause 1 Congress has the power to admit new states to the Union. Existing states cannot be split up or joined together to form new states unless both Congress and the state legislatures approve. New states are equal to all other states.

Clause 2 Congress can make rules for managing and governing land owned by the United States. This includes territories not organized into states, such as Puerto Rico and Guam, and federal lands within a state.

In a ***republic,*** voters choose representatives to govern them. The federal government must protect the states from foreign invasion and from ***domestic,*** or internal, disorder if asked to do so by a state.

The Constitution can be ***amended,*** or changed, if necessary. An amendment can be proposed by (1) a two-thirds vote of both houses of Congress or (2) a national convention called by Congress at the request of two thirds of the state legislatures. (This second method has never been used.) An amendment must be ***ratified,*** or approved, by (1) three fourths of the state legislatures or (2) special conventions in three fourths of the states. Congress decides which method will be used.

The United States government promised to pay all debts and honor all agreements made under the Articles of Confederation.

2. Extradition A person charged in any state with treason, felony, or other crime, who shall flee from justice, and be found in another state, shall on demand of the executive authority of the state from which he fled, be delivered up, to be removed to the state having jurisdiction of the crime.

3. Return of Fugitive Slaves ~~No person held to service or labor in one state, under the laws thereof, escaping into another, shall in consequence of any law or regulation therein, be discharged from such service or labor, but shall be delivered up on claim of the party to whom such service or labor may be due.~~

Section 3. New States and Territories

1. New States New states may be admitted by the Congress into this Union; but no new state shall be formed or erected within the jurisdiction of any other state; nor any state be formed by the junction of two of more states, or parts of states, without the consent of the legislatures of the states concerned as well as of the Congress.

2. Federal Lands The Congress shall have power to dispose of and make all needful rules and regulations respecting the territory or other property belonging to the United States; and nothing in this Constitution shall be so construed as to prejudice any claims of the United States, or of any particular state.

Section 4. Guarantees to the States

The United States shall guarantee to every state in this Union a republican form of government, and shall protect each of them against invasion; and on application of the legislature, or of the executive (when the legislature cannot be convened) against domestic violence.

Article 5. Amending the Constitution

The Congress, whenever two-thirds of both houses shall deem it necessary, shall propose amendments to this Constitution, or, on the application of the legislatures of two-thirds of the several states, shall call a convention for proposing amendments, which, in either case, shall be valid to all intents and purposes, as part of this Constitution, when ratified by the legislatures of three-fourths of the several states, or by conventions in three-fourths thereof, as the one or the other mode of ratification may be proposed by the Congress; provided that ~~no amendments which may be made prior to the year 1808 shall in any manner affect the first and fourth clauses in the Ninth Section of the First Article; and that~~ no state, without its consent, shall be deprived of its equal suffrage in the Senate.

Article 6. National Supremacy

Section 1. Prior Public Debts

All debts contracted and engagements entered into, before the adoption of this Constitution, shall be as valid against the United States under this Constitution, as under the Confederation.

Section 2. Supreme Law of the Land

This Constitution, and the laws of the United States which shall be made in pursuance thereof, and all treaties made, or which shall be made, under the authority of the United States, shall be the supreme law of the land; and the judges in every state shall be bound thereby, anything in the constitution or laws of any state to the contrary notwithstanding.

The Constitution, federal laws, and treaties that the Senate has ratified are the supreme, or highest, law of the land. Thus, they outweigh state laws. A state judge must overturn a state law that conflicts with the Constitution or with a federal law.

Section 3. Oaths of Office

The Senators and Representatives before mentioned, and the members of the several state legislatures, and all executive and judicial officers, both of the United States and of the several states, shall be bound by oath or affirmation, to support this Constitution; but no religious test shall ever be required as a qualification to any office or public trust under the United States.

State and federal officeholders take an oath, or solemn promise, to support the Constitution. However, this clause forbids the use of religious tests for officeholders. During the colonial period, every colony except Rhode Island required a religious test for officeholders.

Article 7. Ratification

The ratification of the convention of nine states shall be sufficient for the establishment of the Constitution between the states so ratifying the same.

During 1787 and 1788, states held special conventions. By October 1788, the required nine states had ratified the Constitution.

Done in convention, by the unanimous consent of the states present, the seventeenth day of September, in the year of our Lord one thousand seven hundred and eighty-seven, and of the independence of the United States of America the twelfth. In Witness whereof, we have hereunto subscribed our names.

Attest: William Jackson
Secretary

George Washington
President and deputy from Virginia

New Hampshire
John Langdon
Nicholas Gilman

Massachussetts
Nathaniel Gorham
Rufus King

Connecticut
William Samuel Johnson
Roger Sherman

New York
Alexander Hamilton

New Jersey
William Livingston
David Brearley
William Paterson
Jonathan Dayton

Pennsylvania
Benjamin Franklin
Thomas Mifflin
Robert Morris
George Clymer
Thomas FitzSimons
Jared Ingersoll
James Wilson
Gouverneur Morris

Delaware
George Read
Gunning Bedford, Jr.
John Dickinson
Richard Bassett
Jacob Broom

Maryland
James McHenry
Dan of St. Thomas Jennifer
Daniel Carroll

Virginia
John Blair
James Madison, Jr.

North Carolina
William Blount
Richard Dobbs Spaight
Hugh Williamson

South Carolina
John Rutledge
Charles Cotesworth Pinckney
Charles Pinckney
Pierce Butler

Georgia
William Few
Abraham Baldwin

★ Amendments to the Constitution ★

The first 10 amendments, which were added to the Constitution in 1791, are called the Bill of Rights. Originally, the Bill of Rights applied only to actions of the federal government. However, the Supreme Court has used the due process clause of the Fourteenth Amendment to extend many of the rights to protect individuals against action by the states.

Amendment 1

Freedoms of Religion, Speech, Press, Assembly, and Petition

Congress shall make no law respecting an establishment of religion, or prohibiting the free exercise thereof; or abridging the freedom of speech, or of the press; or the right of the people peaceably to assemble, and to petition the government for a redress of grievances.

Congress cannot set up an established, or official, church or religion for the nation. During the colonial period, most colonies had established churches. However, the authors of the First Amendment wanted to keep government and religion separate.

Congress may not *abridge,* or limit, the freedom to speak and write freely. The government may not censor, or review, books and newspapers before they are printed. This amendment also protects the right to assemble, or hold public meetings. *Petition* means ask. *Redress* means to correct. *Grievances* are wrongs. The people have the right to ask the government for wrongs to be corrected.

Amendment 2

Right to Bear Arms

A well-regulated militia, being necessary to the security of a free state, the right of the people to keep and bear arms shall not be infringed.

State militias, such as the National Guard, have the right to bear arms, or keep weapons. Courts have generally ruled that the government can regulate the ownership of guns by private citizens.

Amendment 3

Lodging Troops in Private Homes

No soldier shall, in time of peace, be quartered in any house, without the consent of the owner; nor in time of war, but in a manner to be prescribed by law.

During the colonial period, the British quartered, or housed, soldiers in private homes without the permission of the owners (page 90). This amendment limits the government's right to use private homes to house soldiers.

Amendment 4

Search and Seizure

The right of the people to be secure in their persons, houses, papers, and effects, against unreasonable searches and seizures, shall not be violated; and no warrants shall issue but upon probable cause, supported by oath or affirmation, and particularly describing the place to be searched, and the persons or things to be seized.

This amendment protects Americans from unreasonable searches and seizures. Search and seizure are permitted only if a judge has issued a *warrant,* or written court order. A warrant is issued only if there is probable cause. This means an officer must show that it is probable, or likely, that the search will produce evidence of a crime. A search warrant must name the exact place to be searched and the things to be seized. In some cases, courts have ruled that searches can take place without a warrant. For example, police may search a person who is under arrest. However, evidence found during an unlawful search cannot be used in a trial.

Amendment 5

Rights of the Accused

No person shall be held to answer for a capital, or otherwise infamous, crime, unless on a presentment or indictment of a grand jury, except in cases arising in the land or naval forces, or in the militia, when in actual service in time of war or public danger; nor shall any person be subject for the same offense to be twice put in jeopardy of life and limb; nor shall be compelled, in any criminal case, to be a witness against himself; nor be

This amendment protects the rights of the accused. *Capital crimes* are those that can be punished with death. *Infamous crimes* are those that can be punished with prison or loss of rights. The federal government must obtain an *indictment,* or formal accusation, from a grand jury to prosecute anyone for such crimes. A *grand jury* is a panel of between 12 and 23 citizens who

deprived of life, liberty, or property, without due process of law; nor shall private property be taken for public use, without just compensation.

Amendment 6

Right to Speedy Trial by Jury

In all criminal prosecutions, the accused shall enjoy the right to a speedy and public trial, by an impartial jury of the state and district wherein the crime shall have been committed, which district shall have been previously ascertained by law, and to be informed of the nature and cause of the accusation; to be confronted with the witnesses against him; to have compulsory process for obtaining witnesses in his favor, and to have the assistance of counsel for his defense.

Amendment 7

Jury Trial in Civil Cases

In suits at common law, where the value in controversy shall exceed $20, the right of trial by jury shall be preserved, and no fact tried by a jury shall be otherwise re-examined in any court of the United States than according to the rules of the common law.

Amendment 8

Bail and Punishment

Excessive bail shall not be required, nor excessive fines imposed, nor cruel and unusual punishments inflicted.

Amendment 9

Powers Reserved to the People

The enumeration in the Constitution, of certain rights, shall not be construed to deny or disparage others retained by the people.

Amendment 10

Powers Reserved to the States

The powers not delegated to the United States by the Constitution, nor prohibited by it to the states, are reserved to the states respectively, or to the people.

Amendment 11

Suits Against States

Passed by Congress on March 4, 1794. Ratified on January 23, 1795.

The judicial power of the United States shall not be construed to extend to any suit in law or equity, commenced or prosecuted against one of the United States, by citizens of another state, or by citizens or subjects of any foreign state.

decide if the government has enough evidence to justify a trial. This procedure prevents prosecution with little or no evidence of guilt. (Soldiers and the militia in wartime are not covered by this rule.)

Double jeopardy is forbidden. This means that a person cannot be tried twice for the same crime—unless a court sets aside a conviction because of a legal error. A person on trial cannot be forced to testify, or give evidence, against himself or herself. A person accused of a crime is entitled to **due process of law,** or a fair hearing or trial. Finally, the government cannot seize private property for public use without paying the owner a fair price for it.

In criminal cases, the jury must be **impartial,** or not favor either side. The accused is guaranteed the right to a trial by jury. The trial must be speedy. If the government purposely postpones the trial so that it becomes hard for the person to get a fair hearing, the charge may be dismissed. The accused must be told the charges against him or her and be allowed to question prosecution witnesses. Witnesses who can help the accused can be ordered to appear in court.

The accused must be allowed a lawyer. Since 1942, the federal government has been required to provide a lawyer if the accused cannot afford one. In 1963, the Supreme Court decided that states must also provide lawyers for a defendant too poor to pay for one.

Common law refers to rules of law established by judges in past cases. This amendment guarantees the right to a jury trial in lawsuits where the sum of money at stake is more than $20. An appeals court cannot change a verdict because it disagrees with the decision of the jury. It can set aside a verdict only if legal errors made the trial unfair.

Bail is money the accused leaves with the court as a pledge to appear for trial. If the accused does not appear for trial, the court keeps the money. **Excessive** means too high. This amendment forbids courts to set unreasonably high bail. The amount of bail usually depends on the seriousness of the charge and whether the accused is likely to appear for the trial. The amendment also forbids cruel and unusual punishments such as mental and physical abuse.

People have rights not listed in the Constitution. This amendment was added because some people feared that the Bill of Rights would be used to limit rights to those actually listed.

This amendment limits the power of the federal government. Powers that are not given to the federal government belong to the states. The powers reserved to the states are not listed in the Constitution.

This amendment changed part of Article 3, Section 2, Clause 1. As a result, a private citizen from one state cannot sue the government of another state in federal court. However, a citizen can sue a state government in a state court.

Amendment 12

Election of President and Vice-President

Passed by Congress on December 9, 1803. Ratified on June 15, 1804.

This amendment changed the way the electoral college voted. Before the amendment was adopted, each elector simply voted for two people. The candidate with the most votes became President. The runner-up became Vice President. In the election of 1800, however, a tie vote resulted between Thomas Jefferson and Aaron Burr (page 189).

In such a case, the Constitution required the House of Representatives to elect the President. Federalists had a majority in the House. They tried to keep Jefferson out of office by voting for Burr. It took 35 ballots in the House before Jefferson was elected President.

To keep this from happening again, the Twelfth Amendment was passed and ratified in time for the election of 1804.

This amendment provides that each elector choose one candidate for President and one candidate for Vice President. If no candidate for President receives a majority of electoral votes, the House of Representatives chooses the President. If no candidate for Vice President receives a majority, the Senate elects the Vice President. The Vice President must be a person who is eligible to be President.

This system is still in use today. However, it is possible for a candidate to win the popular vote and lose in the electoral college. This happened in 1876 (pages 419–420).

The electors shall meet in their respective states, and vote by ballot for President and Vice-President, one of whom, at least, shall not be an inhabitant of the same state with themselves; they shall name in their ballots the person voted for as President, and in distinct ballots the person voted for as Vice-President, and they shall make distinct lists of all persons voted for as President, and of all persons voted for as Vice-President, and of the number of votes for each, which lists they shall sign and certify, and transmit, sealed, to the seat of government of the United States, directed to the President of the Senate; the President of the Senate shall, in the presence of the Senate and House of Representatives, open all the certificates and the votes shall then be counted; the person having the greatest number of votes for President shall be the President, if such number be a majority of the whole number of electors appointed; and if no person have such majority, then from the persons having the highest numbers not exceeding three on the list of those voted for as President, the House of Representatives shall choose immediately, by ballot, the President. But in choosing the President, the votes shall be taken by the states, the representation from each state having one vote; a quorum for this purpose shall consist of a member or members from two-thirds of the states, and a majority of all the states shall be necessary to a choice. And if the House of Representatives shall not choose a President whenever the right of choice shall devolve upon them, before the fourth day of March next following, then the Vice-President shall act as President, as in the case of the death or other constitutional disability of the President. The person having the greatest number of votes as Vice-President, shall be the Vice-President, if such number be a majority of the whole number of electors appointed, and if no person have a majority, then, from the two highest numbers on the list, the Senate shall choose the Vice-President; a quorum for the purpose shall consist of two-thirds of the whole number of Senators, and a majority of the whole number shall be necessary to a choice. But no person constitutionally ineligible to the office of President shall be eligible to that of Vice-President of the United States.

Amendment 13

Abolition of Slavery

Passed by Congress on January 31, 1865. Ratified on December 6, 1865.

The Emancipation Proclamation (1863) freed slaves only in areas controlled by the Confederacy (pages 387–388). This amendment freed all slaves. It also forbids *involuntary servitude,* or labor done against one's will. However, it does not prevent prison wardens from making prisoners work.

Section 2 says that Congress can pass laws to carry out this amendment.

Section 1. Neither slavery nor involuntary servitude, except as a punishment for crime whereof the party shall have been duly convicted, shall exist within the United States, or any place subject to their jurisdiction.

Section 2. Congress shall have power to enforce this article by appropriate legislation.

Amendment 14

Rights of Citizens

Passed by Congress on June 13, 1866. Ratified on July 9, 1868.

Section 1 defines citizenship for the first time in the Constitution, and it extends citizenship to

Section 1. Citizenship All persons born or naturalized in the United States and subject to the jurisdiction thereof, are citizens of the United States and of the state wherein they reside. No state shall make or enforce any law which shall abridge the privileges or immunities of citizens of the United States; nor shall any state deprive any person of life, liberty, or property, without due process of law; nor deny to any person within its jurisdiction the equal protection of the laws.

Section 2. Apportionment of Representatives

Representatives shall be apportioned among the several states according to their respective numbers, counting the whole number of persons in each state, excluding Indians not taxed. But when the right to vote at any election for the choice of electors for President and Vice-President of the United States, Representatives in Congress, the executive and judicial officers of a state, or the members of the legislature thereof, is denied to any of the male inhabitants of such state, being twenty-one years of age and citizens of the United States, or in any way abridged, except for participation in rebellion, or other crime, the basis of representation therein shall be reduced in the proportion which the number of such male citizens shall bear to the whole number of male citizens twenty-one years of age in such state.

Section 3. Former Confederate Officials

No person shall be a Senator or Representative in Congress, or elector of President and Vice-President, or hold any office, civil or military, under the United States, or under any state, who, having previously taken an oath, as a member of Congress, or as an officer of the United States, or as a member of any state legislature, or as an executive or judicial officer of any state, to support the Constitution of the United States, shall have engaged in insurrection or rebellion against the same, or given aid or comfort to the enemies thereof. But Congress may, by vote of two-thirds of each house, remove such disability.

Section 4. Government Debt

The validity of the public debt of the United States, authorized by law, including debts incurred for payment of pensions and bounties for services in suppressing insurrection or rebellion, shall not be questioned. But neither the United States nor any state shall assume or pay any debt or obligation incurred in aid of insurrection or rebellion against the United States or any claim for the loss or emancipation of any slave; but all such debts, obligations, and claims shall be held illegal and void.

Section 5. Enforcement

The Congress shall have power to enforce, by appropriate legislation, the provisions of this article.

Amendment 15

Voting Rights

Passed by Congress on February 26, 1869. Ratified on February 2, 1870.

Section 1. Extending the Right to Vote

The right of citizens of the United States to vote shall not be denied or abridged by the United States or any state on account of race, color, or previous condition of servitude.

---

blacks. It also prohibits states from denying the rights and privileges of citizenship to any citizen. This section also forbids states to deny due process of law.

Section 1 guarantees all citizens "equal protection under the law." For a long time, however, the Fourteenth Amendment did not protect blacks from discrimination. After Reconstruction, separate facilities for blacks and whites sprang up (page 423). In 1954, the Supreme Court ruled that separate facilities for blacks and whites were by their nature unequal. This ruling, in the case of *Brown* v. *Board of Education,* made school segregation illegal.

Section 2 replaced the three-fifths clause. It provides that representation in the House of Representatives is decided on the basis of the number of people in the state. It also provides that states which deny the vote to male citizens over age 21 will be punished by losing part of their representation in the House. This provision has never been enforced.

Despite this clause, black citizens were often prevented from voting. In the 1960s, federal laws were passed to end voting discrimination.

This section prohibited people who had been federal or state officials before the Civil War and who had joined the Confederate cause from serving again as government officials. In 1872, Congress restored the rights of former Confederate officials.

This section recognized that the United States must repay its debts from the Civil War. However, it forbade the repayment of debts of the Confederacy. This meant that people who had loaned money to the Confederacy would not be repaid. Also, states were not allowed to pay former slave owners for the loss of slaves.

Congress can pass laws to carry out this amendment.

Previous condition of servitude refers to slavery. This amendment gave blacks, both former slaves and free blacks, the right to vote. In the late 1800s, southern states used grandfather clauses, literacy tests, and poll taxes to keep blacks from voting (pages 421–422).

Congress can pass laws to carry out this amendment. The Twenty-fourth Amendment barred the use of poll taxes in national elections. The Voting Rights Act of 1965 gave federal officials the power to register voters in places where there was voting discrimination.

Congress has the power to collect taxes on people's income. An income tax can be collected without regard to a state's population. This amendment changed Article 1, Section 9, Clause 4.

This amendment replaced Article 1, Section 3, Clause 1. Before it was adopted, state legislatures chose senators. This amendment provides that senators are directly elected by the people of each state.

When a Senate seat becomes vacant, the governor of the state must order an election to fill the seat. The state legislature can give the governor power to fill the seat until an election is held.

Senators who had already been elected by the state legislatures were not affected by this amendment.

This amendment, known as **Prohibition,** banned the making, selling, or transporting of alcoholic beverages in the United States. Later, the Twenty-first Amendment **repealed,** or canceled, this amendment.

Both the states and the federal government had the power to pass laws to enforce this amendment.

This amendment had to be approved within seven years. The Eighteenth Amendment was the first amendment to include a time limit for ratification.

Neither the federal government nor state governments can deny the right to vote on account of sex. Thus, women won **suffrage,** or the right to vote. Before 1920, some states had allowed women to vote in state elections.

Congress can pass laws to carry out this amendment.

Section 2. Enforcement   The Congress shall have power to enforce this article by appropriate legislation.

Amendment 16

The Income Tax

Passed by Congress on July 12, 1909. Ratified on February 3, 1913.

The Congress shall have power to lay and collect taxes on incomes, from whatever source derived, without apportionment among the several states, and without regard to any census or enumeration.

Amendment 17

Direct Election of Senators

Passed by Congress on May 13, 1912. Ratified on April 8, 1913.

Section 1. Method of Election   The Senate of the United States shall be composed of two Senators from each state, elected by the people thereof, for six years; and each Senator shall have one vote. The electors in each state shall have the qualifications requisite for electors of the most numerous branch of the state legislatures.

Section 2. Vacancies   When vacancies happen in the representation of any state in the Senate, the executive authority of such state shall issue writs of election to fill such vacancies: *Provided* that the legislature of any state may empower the executive thereof to make temporary appointments until the people fill the vacancies by election as the legislature may direct.

Section 3. Exception   This amendment shall not be so construed as to affect the election or term of any Senator chosen before it becomes valid as part of the Constitution.

Amendment 18

Prohibition of Alcoholic Beverages

Passed by Congress on December 18, 1917. Ratified on January 16, 1919.

Section 1. Ban on Alcohol   After one year from the ratification of this article the manufacture, sale, or transportation of intoxicating liquors within, the importation thereof into, or the exportation thereof from, the United States and all territory subject to the jurisdiction thereof for beverage purposes is hereby prohibited.

Section 2. Enforcement   The Congress and the several states shall have concurrent power to enforce this article by appropriate legislation.

Section 3. Method of Ratification   This article shall be inoperative unless it shall have been ratified as an amendment to the Constitution by the legislatures of the several states, as provided in the Constitution, within seven years from the date of the submission hereof to the states by the Congress.

Amendment 19

Women's Suffrage

Passed by Congress on June 4, 1919. Ratified on August 18, 1920.

Section 1. The Right to Vote   The right of citizens of the United States to vote shall not be denied or abridged by the United States or by any state on account of sex.

Section 2. Enforcement   Congress shall have power to enforce this article by appropriate legislation.

Amendment 20

Presidential Terms; Sessions of Congress

Passed by Congress on March 2, 1932. Ratified on January 23, 1933.

Section 1. Beginning of Term The terms of the President and Vice-President shall end at noon on the 20th day of January, and the terms of Senators and Representatives at noon on the 3rd day of January, of the years in which such terms would have ended if this article had not been ratified; and the terms of their successors shall then begin.

The date for the President and Vice President to take office is January 20. Members of Congress begin their terms of office on January 3. Before this amendment was adopted, these terms of office began on March 4.

Section 2. Congressional Sessions The Congress shall assemble at least once in every year, and such meeting shall begin at noon on the 3rd day of January, unless they shall by law appoint a different day.

Congress must meet at least once a year. The new session of Congress begins on January 3. Before this amendment, members of Congress who had been defeated in November continued to hold office until the following March. Such members were known as *lame ducks.*

Section 3. Presidential Succession If at the time fixed for the beginning of the term of the President, the President-elect shall have died, the Vice-President-elect shall become President. If a President shall not have been chosen before the time fixed for the beginning of his term, or if the President-elect shall have failed to qualify, then the Vice-President-elect shall act as President until a President shall have qualified; and the Congress may by law provide for the case wherein neither a President-elect nor a Vice-President-elect shall have qualified, declaring who shall then act as President, or the manner in which one who is to act shall be selected, and such person shall act accordingly until a President or Vice-President shall have qualified.

By Section 3, if the President-elect dies before taking office, the Vice President-elect becomes President. If no President has been chosen by January 20 or if the elected candidate fails to qualify for office, the Vice President-elect acts as President, but only until a qualified President is chosen.

Finally, Congress can choose a person to act as President if neither the President-elect nor Vice President-elect is qualified to take office.

Section 4. Elections Decided by Congress The Congress may by law provide for the case of the death of any of the persons from whom the House of Representatives may choose a President whenever the right of choice shall have devolved upon them, and for the case of the death of any of the persons from whom the Senate may choose a Vice-President whenever the right of choice shall have devolved upon them.

Congress can pass laws in cases where a presidential candidate dies while an election is being decided in the House. Congress has similar power in cases where a candidate for Vice President dies while an election is being decided in the Senate.

Section 5. Date of Effect ~~Sections 1 and 2 shall take effect on the 15th day of October following the ratification of this article.~~

Section 5 sets the date for the amendment to become effective.

Section 6. Ratification Period ~~This article shall be inoperative unless it shall have been ratified as an amendment to the Constitution by the legislatures of three-fourths of the several states within seven years from the date of its submission.~~

Section 6 sets a time limit for ratification.

Amendment 21

Repeal of Prohibition

Passed by Congress on February 20, 1933. Ratified on December 5, 1933.

Section 1. Repeal of National Prohibition The eighteenth article of amendment to the Constitution of the United States is hereby repealed.

The Eighteenth Amendment is repealed, making it legal to make and sell alcoholic beverages. Prohibition ended December 5, 1933.

Section 2. State Laws The transportation or importation into any state, territory, or possession of the United States for delivery or use therein of intoxicating liquors, in violation of the laws thereof, is hereby prohibited.

Each state was free to ban the making and selling of alcoholic drink within its borders. This section makes bringing liquor into a "dry" state a federal offense.

Section 3. Ratification Period ~~This article shall be inoperative unless it shall have been ratified as an amendment to the Constitution by conventions in the several states, as provided in the Constitution, within seven years from the date of the submission hereof to the states by the Congress.~~

Special state conventions were called to ratify this amendment. This is the only time an amendment was ratified by state conventions rather than state legislatures.

Before Franklin Roosevelt became President, no President served more than two terms in office. Roosevelt broke with this custom and was elected to four terms. This amendment provides that no President may serve more than two terms. A President who has already served more than half of someone else's term can serve only one more full term. However, the amendment did not apply to Harry Truman, who had become President after Franklin Roosevelt's death in 1945.

A seven-year time limit is set for ratification.

Amendment 22

Limit on Number of President's Terms

Passed by Congress on March 12, 1947. Ratified on March 1, 1951.

Section 1. Two-Term Limit No person shall be elected to the office of the President more than twice, and no person who has held the office of President, or acted as President, for more than two years of a term to which some other person was elected President shall be elected to the office of the President more than once. ~~But this Article shall not apply to any person holding the office of President when this Article was proposed by the Congress, and shall not prevent any person who may be holding the office of President, or acting as President, during the term within which this Article becomes operative from holding the office of President or acting as President during the remainder of such term.~~

Section 2. Ratification Period ~~This Article shall be inoperative unless it shall have been ratified as an amendment to the Constitution by the legislatures of three-fourths of the several states within seven years from the date of its submission to the states by the Congress.~~

This amendment gives residents of Washington, D.C., the right to vote in presidential elections. Until this amendment was adopted, people living in Washington, D.C., could not vote for President because the Constitution had made no provision for choosing electors from the nation's capital. Washington, D.C., has three electoral votes.

Amendment 23

Presidential Electors for District of Columbia

Passed by Congress on June 16, 1960. Ratified on April 3, 1961.

Section 1. Determining the Number of Electors The District constituting the seat of Government of the United States shall appoint in such manner as the Congress may direct: A number of electors of President and Vice-President equal to the whole number of Senators and Representatives in Congress to which the District would be entitled if it were a State, but in no event more than the least populous State; they shall be in addition to those appointed by the States, but they shall be considered, for the purposes of the election of President and Vice-President, to be electors appointed by a State; and they shall meet in the District and perform such duties as provided by the twelfth article of amendment.

Congress can pass laws to carry out this amendment.

Section 2. Enforcement The Congress shall have power to enforce this article by appropriate legislation.

A *poll tax* is a tax on voters. This amendment bans poll taxes in national elections. Some states used poll taxes to keep blacks from voting. In 1966, the Supreme Court struck down poll taxes in state elections, also.

Amendment 24

Abolition of Poll Tax in National Elections

Passed by Congress on August 27, 1962. Ratified on January 23, 1964.

Section 1. Poll Tax Banned The right of citizens of the United States to vote in any primary or other election for President or Vice-President, for electors for President or Vice-President, or for Senator or Representative in Congress, shall not be denied or abridged by the United States or any state by reason of failure to pay any poll tax or other tax.

Congress can pass laws to carry out this amendment.

Section 2. Enforcement The Congress shall have the power to enforce this article by appropriate legislation.

Amendment 25

Presidential Succession and Disability

Passed by Congress on July 6, 1965. Ratified on February 11, 1967.

Section 1. President's Death or Resignation In case of the removal of the President from office or his death or resignation, the Vice-President shall become President.

If the President dies or resigns, the Vice-President becomes President. This section clarifies Article 2, Section 1, Clause 6.

Section 2. Vacancies in Vice-Presidency Whenever there is a vacancy in the office of the Vice-President, the President shall nominate a Vice-President who shall take the office upon confirmation by a majority vote of both houses of Congress.

Section 3. Disability of the President Whenever the President transmits to the President pro tempore of the Senate and the Speaker of the House of Representatives his written declaration that he is unable to discharge the powers and duties of his office, and until he transmits to them a written declaration to the contrary, such powers and duties shall be discharged by the Vice-President as Acting President.

Section 4. Whenever the Vice-President and a majority of either the principal officers of the executive departments or of such other body as Congress may by law provide, transmit to the President *pro tempore* of the Senate and the Speaker of the House of Representatives their written declaration that the President is unable to discharge the powers and duties of his office, the Vice-President shall immediately assume the powers and duties of the office as Acting President.

Thereafter, when the President transmits to the President *pro tempore* of the Senate and the Speaker of the House of Representatives his written declaration that no inability exists, he shall resume the powers and duties of his office unless the Vice-President and a majority of either the principal officers of the executive department or of such other body as Congress may by law provide, transmit within four days to the President *as* of the Senate and the Speaker of the House of Representatives their written declaration that the President is unable to discharge the powers and duties of his office. Thereupon Congress shall decide the issue, assembling within 48 hours for that purpose if not in session. If the Congress, within 21 days after receipt of the latter written declaration, or, if Congress is not in session, within 21 days after Congress is required to assemble, determines by two-thirds vote of both houses that the President is unable to discharge the powers and duties of his office, the Vice-President shall continue to discharge the same as Acting President; otherwise, the President shall assume the powers and duties of his office.

Amendment 26
Voting Age
Passed by Congress on March 23, 1971. Ratified on July 1, 1971.

Section 1. Lowering of Voting Age The right of citizens of the United States, who are 18 years of age or older, to vote shall not be denied or abridged by the United States or any state on account of age.

Section 2. Enforcement The Congress shall have the power to enforce this article by appropriate legislation.

Amendment 27
Congressional Pay Increases
Ratified on May 7, 1992.

No law varying the compensation for the services of the Senators and Representatives shall take effect, until an election of Representatives shall have intervened.

When a Vice President takes over the office of President, he or she appoints a Vice President who must be approved by a majority vote of both houses of Congress. This section was first applied after Vice President Spiro Agnew resigned in 1973. President Richard Nixon appointed Gerald Ford as Vice President.

If the President declares in writing that he or she is unable to perform the duties of office, the Vice President serves as Acting President until the President recovers.

Two Presidents, Woodrow Wilson and Dwight Eisenhower, have fallen gravely ill while in office. The Constitution contained no provision for this kind of emergency.

Section 3 provided that the President can inform Congress that he or she is too sick to perform the duties of office. However, if the President is unconscious or refuses to admit to a disabling illness, Section 4 provides that the Vice President and Cabinet may declare the President disabled. The Vice President becomes Acting President until the President can return to the duties of office. In case of a disagreement between the President and the Vice President and Cabinet over the President's ability to perform the duties of office, Congress must decide the issue. A two-thirds vote of both houses is needed to decide that the President is disabled or unable to fulfill the duties of office.

In 1970, Congress passed a law allowing 18-year-olds to vote. However, the Supreme Court decided that Congress could not set a minimum age for state elections. So this amendment was passed and ratified.

Congress can pass laws to carry out this amendment.

If members of Congress vote themselves a pay increase, it cannot go into effect until after the next congressional election.

THE CONSTITUTION

PRESIDENTS OF THE UNITED STATES ★

1 George Washington
(1732–1799)

Years in office:
1789–1797
Party:
none
Elected from:
Virginia
Vice President:
John Adams

2 John Adams
(1735–1826)

Years in office:
1797–1801
Party:
Federalist
Elected from:
Massachusetts
Vice President:
Thomas Jefferson

3 Thomas Jefferson
(1743–1826)

Years in office:
1801–1809
Party:
Democratic
  Republican
Elected from:
Virginia
Vice President:
1) Aaron Burr,
2) George Clinton

4 James Madison
(1751–1836)

Years in office:
1809–1817
Party:
Democratic
  Republican
Elected from:
Virginia
Vice President:
1) George Clinton,
2) Elbridge Gerry

5 James Monroe
(1758–1831)

Years in office:
1817–1825
Party:
Democratic
  Republican
Elected from:
Virginia
Vice President:
Daniel Tompkins

6 John Quincy Adams
(1767–1848)

Years in office:
1825–1829
Party:
National
  Republican
Elected from:
Massachusetts
Vice President:
John Calhoun

7 Andrew Jackson
(1767–1845)

Years in office:
1829–1837
Party:
Democratic
Elected from:
Tennessee
Vice President:
1) John Calhoun,
2) Martin Van
  Buren

8 Martin Van Buren
(1782–1862)

Years in office:
1837–1841
Party:
Democratic
Elected from:
New York
Vice President:
Richard Johnson

9 William Henry Harrison*
(1773–1841)

Years in office:
1841
Party:
Whig
Elected from:
Ohio
Vice President:
John Tyler

10 John Tyler
(1790–1862)

Years in office:
1841–1845
Party:
Whig
Elected from:
Virginia
Vice President:
none

11 James K. Polk
(1795–1849)

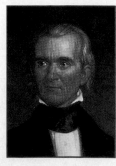

Years in Office:
1845–1849
Party:
Democratic
Elected from:
Tennessee
Vice President:
George Dallas

12 Zachary Taylor*
(1784–1850)

Years in office:
1849–1850
Party:
Whig
Elected from:
Louisiana
Vice President:
Millard Fillmore

*Died in office

13 Millard Fillmore
(1800–1874)

Years in office:
1850–1853
Party:
Whig
Elected from:
New York
Vice President:
none

14 Franklin Pierce
(1804–1869)

Years in office:
1853–1857
Party:
Democratic
Elected from:
New Hampshire
Vice President:
William King

15 James Buchanan
(1791–1868)

Years in office:
1857–1861
Party:
Democratic
Elected from:
Pennsylvania
Vice President:
John Breckinridge

16 Abraham Lincoln**
(1809–1865)

Years in office:
1861–1865
Party:
Republican
Elected from:
Illinois
Vice President:
1) Hannibal
   Hamlin,
2) Andrew
   Johnson

17 Andrew Johnson
(1808–1875)

Years in office:
1865–1869
Party:
Republican
Elected from:
Tennessee
Vice President:
none

18 Ulysses S. Grant
(1822–1885)

Years in office:
1869–1877
Party:
Republican
Elected from:
Illinois
Vice President:
1) Schuyler
   Colfax,
2) Henry Wilson

19 Rutherford B. Hayes
(1822–1893)

Years in office:
1877–1881
Party:
Republican
Elected from:
Ohio
Vice President:
William Wheeler

20 James A. Garfield**
(1831–1881)

Years in office:
1881
Party:
Republican
Elected from:
Ohio
Vice President:
Chester A. Arthur

21 Chester A. Arthur
(1829–1886)

Years in office:
1881–1885
Party:
Republican
Elected from:
New York
Vice President:
none

22 Grover Cleveland
(1837–1908)

Years in office:
1885–1889
Party:
Democratic
Elected from:
New York
Vice President:
Thomas
   Hendricks

23 Benjamin Harrison
(1833–1901)

Years in office:
1889–1893
Party:
Republican
Elected from:
Indiana
Vice President:
Levi Morton

24 Grover Cleveland
(1837–1908)

Years in office:
1893–1897
Party:
Democratic
Elected from:
New York
Vice President:
Adlai Stevenson

**Assassinated

25 William McKinley**
(1843–1901)

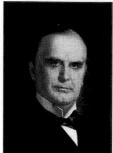

Years in office:
1897–1901
Party:
Republican
Elected from:
Ohio
Vice President:
1) Garret Hobart,
2) Theodore
   Roosevelt

26 Theodore Roosevelt
(1858–1919)

Years in office:
1901–1909
Party:
Republican
Elected from:
New York
Vice President:
Charles Fairbanks

27 William Howard Taft
(1857–1930)

Years in office:
1909–1913
Party:
Republican
Elected from:
Ohio
Vice President:
James Sherman

28 Woodrow Wilson
(1856–1924)

Years in office:
1913–1921
Party:
Democratic
Elected from:
New Jersey
Vice President:
Thomas Marshall

29 Warren G. Harding*
(1865–1923)

Years in office:
1921–1923
Party:
Republican
Elected from:
Ohio
Vice President:
Calvin Coolidge

30 Calvin Coolidge
(1872–1933)

Years in office:
1923–1929
Party:
Republican
Elected from:
Massachusetts
Vice President:
Charles Dawes

31 Herbert C. Hoover
(1874–1964)

Years in office:
1929–1933
Party:
Republican
Elected from:
California
Vice President:
Charles Curtis

32 Franklin D. Roosevelt*
(1882–1945)

Years in office:
1933–1945
Party:
Democratic
Elected from:
New York
Vice President:
1) John Garner,
2) Henry Wallace,
3) Harry S Truman

33 Harry S Truman
(1884–1972)

Years in office:
1945–1953
Party:
Democratic
Elected from:
Missouri
Vice President:
Alben Barkley

34 Dwight D. Eisenhower
(1890–1969)

Years in office:
1953–1961
Party:
Republican
Elected from:
New York
Vice President:
Richard M.
Nixon

35 John F. Kennedy**
(1917–1963)

Years in office:
1961–1963
Party:
Democratic
Elected from:
Massachusetts
Vice President:
Lyndon B.
Johnson

36 Lyndon B. Johnson
(1908–1973)

Years in office:
1963–1969
Party:
Democratic
Elected from:
Texas
Vice President:
Hubert
Humphrey

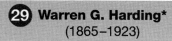

*Died in office
**Assassinated

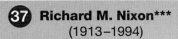

37 Richard M. Nixon***
(1913–1994)

Years in office:
1969–1974
Party:
Republican
Elected from:
New York
Vice President:
1) Spiro Agnew,
2) Gerald R. Ford

38 Gerald R. Ford
(1913–   )

Years in office:
1974–1977
Party:
Republican
Appointed from:
Michigan
Vice President:
Nelson
  Rockefeller

39 Jimmy Carter
(1924–   )

Years in office:
1977–1981
Party:
Democratic
Elected from:
Georgia
Vice President:
Walter Mondale

40 Ronald W. Reagan
(1911–   )

Years in office:
1981–1989
Party:
Republican
Elected from:
California
Vice President:
George H.W.
  Bush

41 George H.W. Bush
(1924–   )

Years in office:
1989–1993
Party:
Republican
Elected from:
Texas
Vice President:
J. Danforth
  Quayle

42 William J. Clinton
(1946–   )

Years in office:
1993–2001
Party:
Democratic
Elected from:
Arkansas
Vice President:
Albert Gore, Jr.

43 George W. Bush
(1946–   )

Years in office:
2001–
Party:
Republican
Elected from:
Texas
Vice President:
Richard Cheney

PRESIDENTS OF THE UNITED STATES

***Resigned

★ The Fifty States ★

State	Date of Entry to Union (Order of Entry)	Land Area in Square Miles	Population (In Thousands)	Number of Representatives in House	Capital	Largest City
Alabama	1819 (22)	50,750	4,219	7	Montgomery	Birmingham
Alaska	1959 (49)	570,374	606	1	Juneau	Anchorage
Arizona	1912 (48)	113,642	4,075	6	Phoenix	Phoenix
Arkansas	1836 (25)	52,075	2,453	4	Little Rock	Little Rock
California	1850 (31)	155,973	31,431	52	Sacramento	Los Angeles
Colorado	1876 (38)	103,730	3,656	6	Denver	Denver
Connecticut	1788 (5)	4,845	3,275	6	Hartford	Bridgeport
Delaware	1787 (1)	1,955	706	1	Dover	Wilmington
Florida	1845 (27)	53,997	13,953	23	Tallahassee	Jacksonville
Georgia	1788 (4)	57,919	7,055	11	Atlanta	Atlanta
Hawaii	1959 (50)	6,423	1,179	2	Honolulu	Honolulu
Idaho	1890 (43)	82,751	1,133	2	Boise	Boise
Illinois	1818 (21)	55,593	11,752	20	Springfield	Chicago
Indiana	1816 (19)	35,870	5,752	10	Indianapolis	Indianapolis
Iowa	1846 (29)	55,875	2,829	5	Des Moines	Des Moines
Kansas	1861 (34)	81,823	2,554	4	Topeka	Wichita
Kentucky	1792 (15)	39,732	3,827	6	Frankfort	Louisville
Louisiana	1812 (18)	43,566	4,315	7	Baton Rouge	New Orleans
Maine	1820 (23)	30,865	1,240	2	Augusta	Portland
Maryland	1788 (7)	9,775	5,006	8	Annapolis	Baltimore
Massachusetts	1788 (6)	7,838	6,041	10	Boston	Boston
Michigan	1837 (26)	56,809	9,496	16	Lansing	Detroit
Minnesota	1858 (32)	79,617	4,567	8	St. Paul	Minneapolis
Mississippi	1817 (20)	46,914	2,669	5	Jackson	Jackson
Missouri	1821 (24)	68,898	5,278	9	Jefferson City	Kansas City
Montana	1889 (41)	145,556	856	1	Helena	Billings
Nebraska	1867 (37)	76,878	1,623	3	Lincoln	Omaha
Nevada	1864 (36)	109,806	1,457	2	Carson City	Las Vegas
New Hampshire	1788 (9)	8,969	1,137	2	Concord	Manchester
New Jersey	1787 (3)	7,419	7,904	13	Trenton	Newark
New Mexico	1912 (47)	121,365	1,654	3	Santa Fe	Albuquerque
New York	1788 (11)	47,224	18,169	31	Albany	New York
North Carolina	1789 (12)	48,718	7,070	12	Raleigh	Charlotte
North Dakota	1889 (39)	68,994	638	1	Bismarck	Fargo
Ohio	1803 (17)	40,953	11,102	19	Columbus	Columbus
Oklahoma	1907 (46)	68,679	3,258	6	Oklahoma City	Oklahoma City
Oregon	1859 (33)	96,003	3,086	5	Salem	Portland
Pennsylvania	1787 (2)	44,820	12,052	21	Harrisburg	Philadelphia
Rhode Island	1790 (13)	1,045	997	2	Providence	Providence
South Carolina	1788 (8)	30,111	3,664	6	Columbia	Columbia
South Dakota	1889 (40)	75,898	721	1	Pierre	Sioux Falls
Tennessee	1796 (16)	41,220	5,175	9	Nashville	Memphis
Texas	1845 (28)	261,914	18,378	30	Austin	Houston
Utah	1896 (45)	82,168	1,908	3	Salt Lake City	Salt Lake City
Vermont	1791 (14)	9,249	580	1	Montpelier	Burlington
Virginia	1788 (10)	39,598	6,552	11	Richmond	Virginia Beach
Washington	1889 (42)	66,582	5,343	9	Olympia	Seattle
West Virginia	1863 (35)	24,087	1,822	3	Charleston	Charleston
Wisconsin	1848 (30)	54,314	5,082	9	Madison	Milwaukee
Wyoming	1890 (44)	97,105	476	1	Cheyenne	Cheyenne
District of Columbia		61	570	1 (nonvoting)		

Self-Governing Areas, Possessions, and Dependencies	Land Area in Square Miles	Population (In Thousands)	Capital
Puerto Rico	3,515	3,522	San Juan
Guam	209	133	Agana
U.S. Virgin Islands	132	102	Charlotte Amalie
American Samoa	77	52	Pago Pago

Sources: *Department of Commerce, Bureau of the Census, 1997 Information Please Almanac*

★ State Flags ★

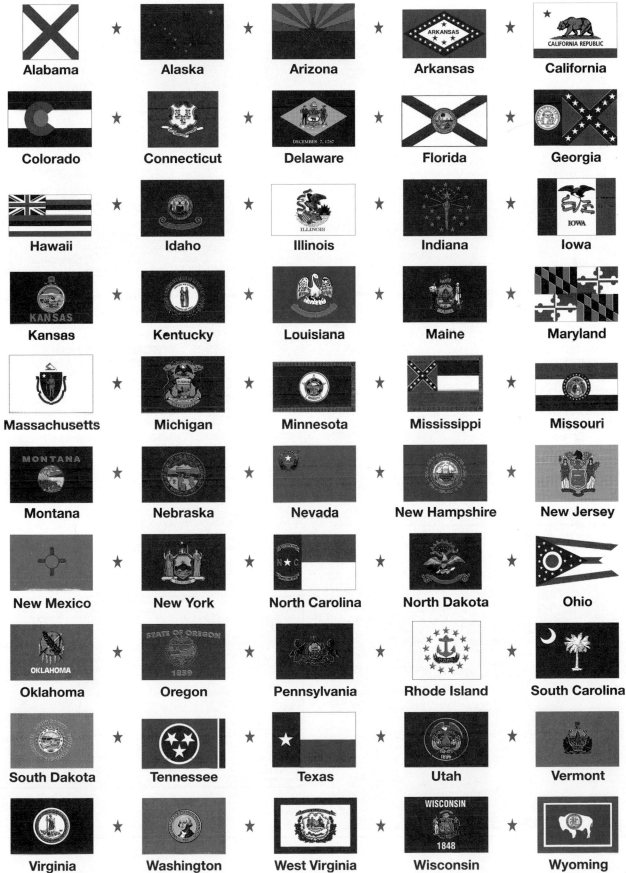

Alabama   Alaska   Arizona   Arkansas   California

Colorado   Connecticut   Delaware   Florida   Georgia

Hawaii   Idaho   Illinois   Indiana   Iowa

Kansas   Kentucky   Louisiana   Maine   Maryland

Massachusetts   Michigan   Minnesota   Mississippi   Missouri

Montana   Nebraska   Nevada   New Hampshire   New Jersey

New Mexico   New York   North Carolina   North Dakota   Ohio

Oklahoma   Oregon   Pennsylvania   Rhode Island   South Carolina

South Dakota   Tennessee   Texas   Utah   Vermont

Virginia   Washington   West Virginia   Wisconsin   Wyoming

★ THE FIFTY STATES ★

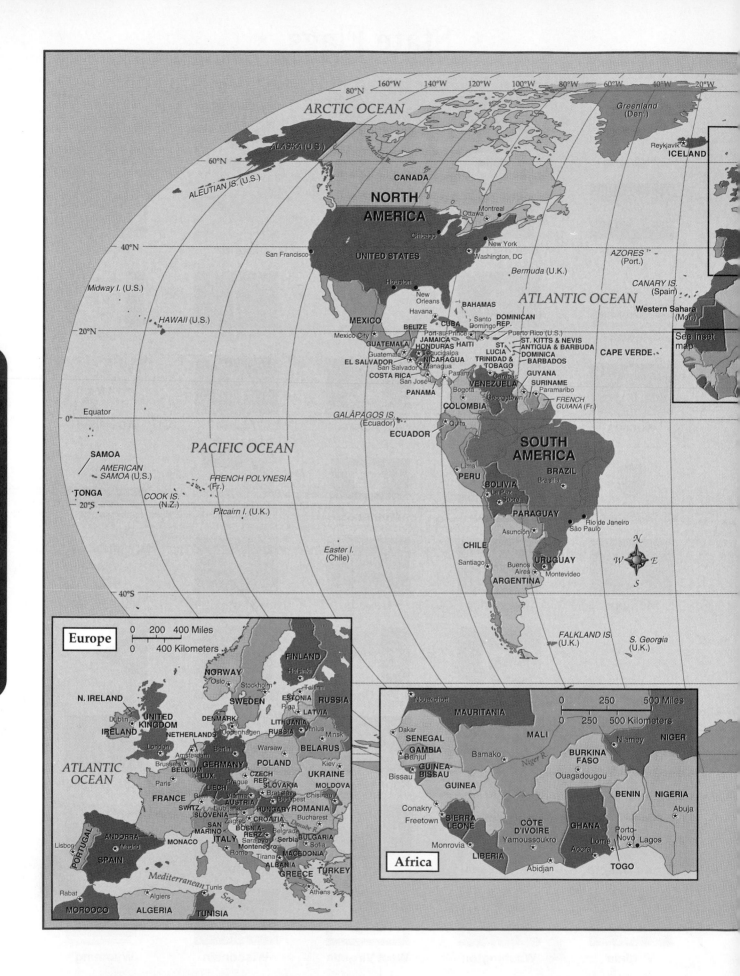

ARCTIC OCEAN

160°W 140°W 120°W 100°W 80°W 60°W 40°W 20°W

80°N

Greenland (Den.)

ALASKA (U.S.)

Reykjavik
ICELAND

60°N

ALEUTIAN IS. (U.S.)

CANADA

NORTH AMERICA

Ottawa
Montreal

40°N

Chicago

New York

San Francisco

UNITED STATES

Washington, DC

AZORES (Port.)

Houston

Bermuda (U.K.)

ATLANTIC OCEAN

CANARY IS. (Spain)

Midway I. (U.S.)

New Orleans

BAHAMAS

Havana

Western Sahara (Mor.)

20°N

HAWAII (U.S.)

MEXICO

CUBA

Santo Domingo

DOMINICAN REP.

Puerto Rico (U.S.)

See inset map

CAPE VERDE

Mexico City

BELIZE

Port-au-Prince

JAMAICA

ST. KITTS & NEVIS
ANTIGUA & BARBUDA

Guatemala

GUATEMALA

HAITI

HONDURAS

ST. LUCIA

DOMINICA
BARBADOS

Tegucigalpa

NICARAGUA

TRINIDAD & TOBAGO

EL SALVADOR

San Salvador

Managua

Panama

COSTA RICA

San José

VENEZUELA

Caracas

GUYANA

SURINAME
Paramaribo

PANAMA

Bogotá

Georgetown

FRENCH GUIANA (Fr.)

Equator 0°

GALÁPAGOS IS. (Ecuador)

COLOMBIA

Quito

ECUADOR

PACIFIC OCEAN

SOUTH AMERICA

Lima

BRAZIL

SAMOA

PERU

Brasília

AMERICAN SAMOA (U.S.)

BOLIVIA

La Paz

FRENCH POLYNESIA (Fr.)

TONGA

Sucre

COOK IS. (N.Z.)

PARAGUAY

20°S

Pitcairn I. (U.K.)

Rio de Janeiro

São Paulo

Asunción

N

Easter I. (Chile)

CHILE

W   E

Santiago

Buenos Aires

URUGUAY

S

Montevideo

40°S

ARGENTINA

FALKLAND IS. (U.K.)

S. Georgia (U.K.)

Europe

0   200   400 Miles

0   400 Kilometers

FINLAND

NORWAY

Helsinki

N. IRELAND

Oslo

Stockholm

Tallinn

RUSSIA

SWEDEN

ESTONIA

Riga

LATVIA

UNITED KINGDOM

DENMARK

LITHUANIA

Vilnius

RUSSIA

Dublin

Minsk

IRELAND

NETHERLANDS

Copenhagen

Berlin

BELARUS

London

Amsterdam

Warsaw

Kiev

ATLANTIC OCEAN

Brussels

GERMANY

POLAND

UKRAINE

BELGIUM

LUX.

CZECH REP.

Nouakchott

0   250   500 Miles

Paris

LIECH.

Prague

SLOVAKIA

MOLDOVA

MAURITANIA

0   250   500 Kilometers

FRANCE

Bern

Vienna

Bratislava

Budapest

Chisinau

Dakar

MALI

SWITZ.

AUSTRIA

HUNGARY

ROMANIA

SENEGAL

Niamey

NIGER

SLOVENIA

Ljubljana

Zagreb

CROATIA

Bucharest

GAMBIA

Bamako

BURKINA FASO

SAN MARINO

BOSNIA-HERZ.

Belgrade

Banjul

GUINEA-BISSAU

ANDORRA

MONACO

ITALY

Sarajevo

Serbia

BULGARIA

Bissau

Ouagadougou

Lisbon

Madrid

Rome

Montenegro

Sofia

GUINEA

BENIN

NIGERIA

PORTUGAL

Tirana

MACEDONIA

Conakry

Abuja

SPAIN

ALBANIA

GREECE

TURKEY

Freetown

SIERRA LEONE

CÔTE D'IVOIRE

GHANA

Porto-Novo

Lagos

Rabat

Mediterranean Sea

Tunis

Athens

Monrovia

Yamoussoukro

Lomé

Accra

MOROCCO

Algiers

LIBERIA

Abidjan

TOGO

ALGERIA

TUNISIA

Africa

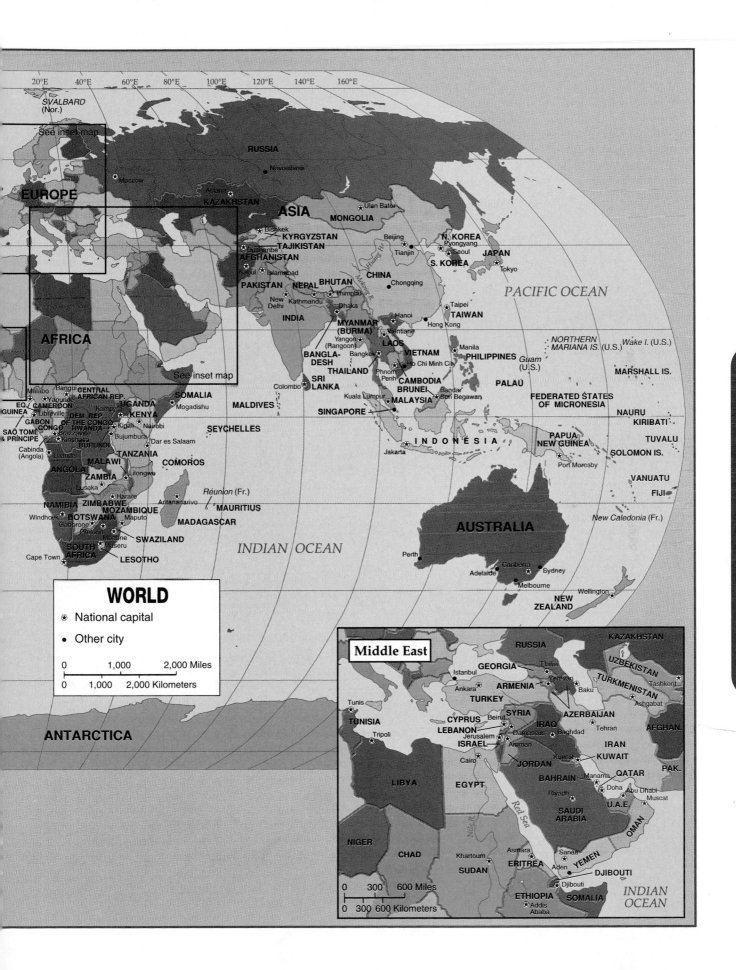

WORLD

⊛ National capital

• Other city

| 0 | 1,000 | 2,000 Miles |
| 0 | 1,000 | 2,000 Kilometers |

Middle East

| 0 | 300 | 600 Miles |
| 0 | 300 600 Kilometers |

GEOGRAPHIC ATLAS

GEOGRAPHIC ATLAS ★

130°W · 125°W · 120°W · 115°W · 110°W · 105°W · 100°W · 95°W

50°N

CANADA

Pacific Time Zone

Mountain Time Zone

Central Time Zone

Seattle
Spokane
Olympia ★
Washington 1889

Great Falls
Helena ★
Montana 1889
Billings

Minot
Grand Forks
North Dakota 1889
★ Bismarck

45°N

Portland
Salem ★
Eugene
Oregon 1859

Boise ★ **Idaho 1890**
Pocatello

Wyoming 1890
Casper
Cheyenne

South Dakota 1889
★ Pierre
Rapid City
Sioux Falls

Sioux City

40°N

San Francisco
Oakland
San Jose
Sacramento ★
Reno
★ Carson City
Nevada 1864
Las Vegas

Ogden
★ Salt Lake City
Utah 1896

★ Denver
Colorado Springs
Colorado 1876

Nebraska 1867
Omaha
Lincoln

Topeka ★
Kansas 1861
Wichita

35°N

California 1850

Los Angeles
Long Beach
San Diego
Salton Sea

Arizona 1912
★ Phoenix
Tucson

Santa Fe ★
Albuquerque
New Mexico 1912
Las Cruces
El Paso

Tulsa
Oklahoma 1907
Oklahoma City ★

Dallas
Fort Worth

30°N

*PACIFIC
OCEAN*

Texas 1845
Austin ★
San Antonio

120°W · 110°W · 115°W

MEXICO

100°W

160°W · 155°W
Hawaii–Aleutian Time Zone
Hawaii 1959
Honolulu ★
PACIFIC OCEAN
20°N
0 50 100 Miles
0 50 100 Kilometers
160°E · 170°E
50°N
Hawaii–Aleutian Time Zone
PACIFIC OCEAN

180° · 70°N · 170°W · 160°W · 150°W
RUSSIA
140°W
130°W
Alaska Time Zone
Alaska 1959
Fairbanks
Anchorage
Juneau
Bering Sea
Gulf of Alaska
60°N
Pacific Time Zone
Mountain Time Zone
CANADA
0 200 400 Miles
0 200 400 Kilometers

900 ★ Reference Section

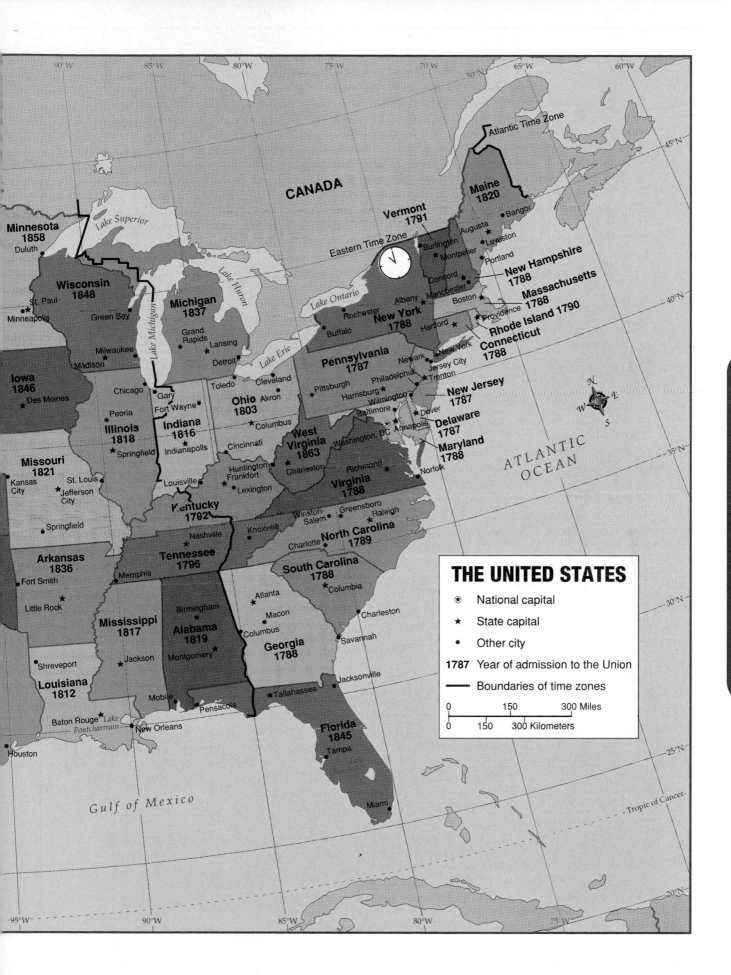

THE UNITED STATES

⊛ National capital

★ State capital

• Other city

1787 Year of admission to the Union

— Boundaries of time zones

0	150	300 Miles
0	150	300 Kilometers

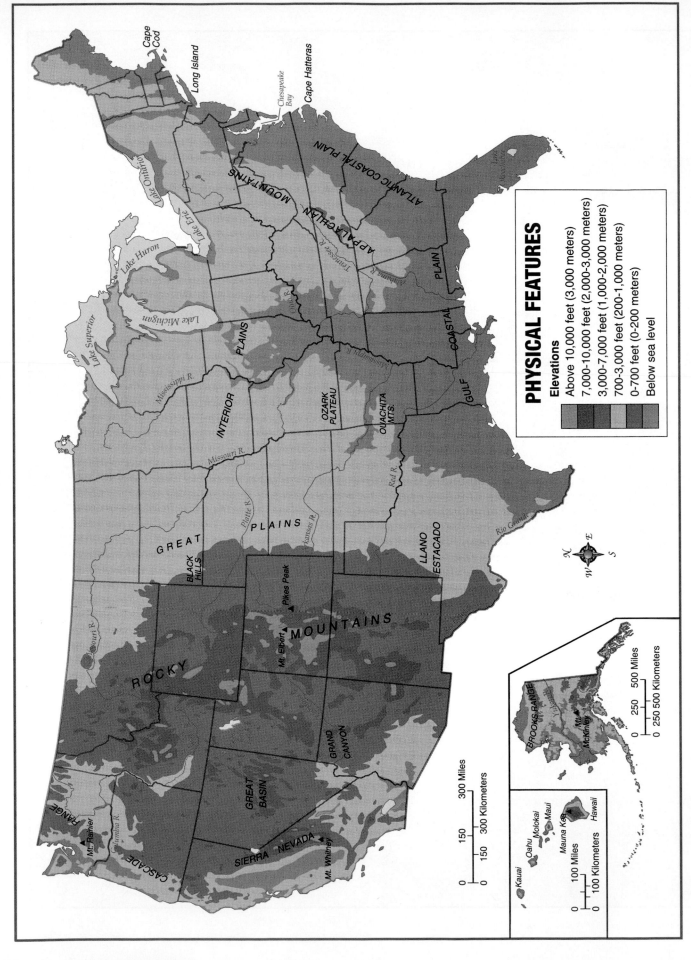

PHYSICAL FEATURES

Elevations

- Above 10,000 feet (3,000 meters)
- 7,000-10,000 feet (2,000-3,000 meters)
- 3,000-7,000 feet (1,000-2,000 meters)
- 700-3,000 feet (200-1,000 meters)
- 0-700 feet (0-200 meters)
- Below sea level

Cape Cod

Long Island

Chesapeake Bay

Cape Hatteras

ATLANTIC COASTAL PLAIN

APPALACHIAN MOUNTAINS

PLAIN

COASTAL

GULF

Lake Ontario

Lake Erie

Lake Huron

Lake Michigan

Lake Superior

Tennessee R.

Cumberland R.

Ohio R.

Mississippi R.

INTERIOR PLAINS

OZARK PLATEAU

OUACHITA MTS.

Mississippi R.

Missouri R.

Red R.

Rio Grande

Kansas R.

Platte R.

GREAT PLAINS

BLACK HILLS

Pikes Peak

Mt. Elbert

LLANO ESTACADO

ROCKY MOUNTAINS

Missouri R.

GRAND CANYON

Columbia R.

GREAT BASIN

CASCADE RANGE

Mt. Rainier

SIERRA NEVADA

Mt. Whitney

N
W E
S

300 Miles
150
0
300 Kilometers
150
0

BROOKS RANGE

Yukon R.

Mt. McKinley

500 Miles
250
0
500 Kilometers
250
0

Kauai

Oahu
Molokai
Maui

Mauna Kea

Hawaii

100 Miles
0
100 Kilometers
0

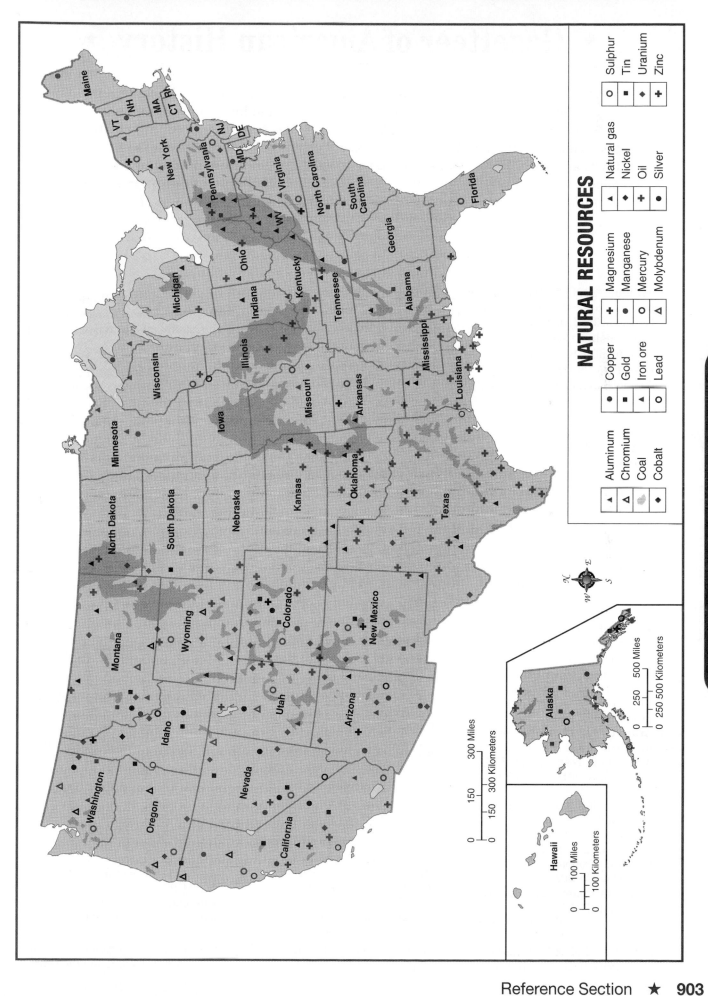

NATURAL RESOURCES

◄	Aluminum	●	Copper	+	Magnesium	◄	Natural gas	○	Sulphur
◁	Chromium	■	Gold	●	Manganese	◆	Nickel	■	Tin
	Coal	◄	Iron ore	○	Mercury	+	Oil	◆	Uranium
◆	Cobalt	○	Lead	◄	Molybdenum	●	Silver	+	Zinc

★ GEOGRAPHIC ATLAS ★

★ Gazetteer of American History ★

This gazetteer, or geographic dictionary, lists places that are important in American history. The approximate latitude and longitude are given for cities, towns, and other specific locations. See text page 10 for information about latitude and longitude. In the Gazetteer, after the description of each place, there are usually two numbers in parentheses. The first number refers to the text page where you can find out more about the place. The second appears in slanted, or *italic,* type and refers to a map *(m)* where the place is shown.

A

Abilene (39°N/97°W) Former cow town in Kansas at the end of the Chisholm Trail. (p. 513, *m510*)

Afghanistan Country in South Asia. Invaded by the Soviet Union in 1979. (p. 787, *m898–899*)

Africa Second largest continent in the world. (p. 12, *m10*)

Alabama 22nd state. Nicknamed the Heart of Dixie or the Cotton State. (p. 896, *m900–901*)

Alamo (29°N/99°W) Mission in San Antonio, Texas, where 255 rebels died during the Texas war for independence. (p. 352, *m352*)

Alaska 49th state. Purchased from Russia in 1867. (p. 896, *m900–901*)

Albany (43°N/74°W) Capital of New York. (p. 171, *m170*)

Andes Rugged mountain chain in South America. (p. 50, *m47*)

Appalachian Mountains Mountain chain that stretches from Georgia to Canada. (p. 16, *m19*)

Appomattox Courthouse (37°N/79°W) Town in Virginia where Lee surrendered to Grant. (p. 473, *m472*)

Argentina Country in South America. (p. 313, *m314*)

Argonne Forest (49°N/6°E) World War I battle site in France (p. 660, *m657*)

Arizona 48th state. Nicknamed the Grand Canyon State. (p. 896, *m900–901*)

Arkansas 25th state. Nicknamed the Land of Opportunity. (p. 896, *m900–901*)

Armenia Country in southwest Europe. (p. 558, *m898–899*)

Asia Largest of the world's continents. (p. 12, *m10*)

Atlanta (34°N/84°W) Capital and largest city of Georgia. Burned by Sherman during the Civil War. (p. 472, *m460*)

Atlantic Ocean World's second largest ocean. (p. 14, *m10*)

Austria-Hungary One of the Central Powers in World War I. Divided into several countries after 1918. (p. 642, *m646*)

B

Baltimore (39°N/77°W) Port city in Maryland. (p. 287, *m286*)

Beijing (40°N/116°E) Capital of China. (p. 623, *m752*)

Belleau Wood (49°N/3°E) World War I battle site in France. (p. 658, *m657*)

Bering Sea Narrow sea between Asia and North America. Scientists think a land bridge was here during the last ice age. *(m31)*

Berlin (53°N/13°E) City in Germany divided during the Cold War. (p. 766, *m767*)

Bosnia Country in southeastern Europe. Broke from Yugoslavia in 1991. Plagued by civil war. (p. 832, *m898–899*)

Boston (42°N/71°W) Seaport and industrial city in Massachusetts. (p. 17, *m96*)

Brazil Largest country in South America. (p. 313, *m314*)

Breed's Hill (42°N/71°W) Overlooks Boston harbor. Site of fighting during the Battle of Bunker Hill. (p. 162)

Buena Vista (26°N/101°W) City in Mexico. Site of an American victory in the Mexican War. (p. 362, *m361*)

Buffalo (43°N/79°W) City in New York State on Lake Erie. (p. 307, *m306*)

Bunker Hill (42°N/71°W) Overlooks Boston harbor. Site of first major battle of the Revolution. (p. 162)

C

Cahokia (39°N/90°W) British fort captured by George Rogers Clark during the American Revolution. (p. 174, *m175*)

California 31st state. Nicknamed the Golden State. Ceded to the United States by Mexico in 1848. (p. 896, *m900–901*)

Cambodia Nation in Southeast Asia. (p. 784, *m781*)

Canada Northern neighbor of the United States. Second largest nation in the world. (p. 141, *m898–899*)

Canadian Shield Lowland region that lies mostly in eastern Canada. (p. 17, *m19*)

Caribbean Sea Tropical sea in the Western Hemisphere. (p. 65, *m67*)

Chancellorsville (38°N/78°W) Site of a Confederate victory in 1863. (p. 458, *m454*)

Charleston (33°N/80°W) City in South Carolina. Site of battles in both the American Revolution and the Civil War. (p. 108, *m107*)

Chesapeake Bay Large inlet of the Atlantic Ocean in Virginia and Maryland. (p. 287, *m286*)

Chicago (42°N/88°W) City in Illinois on Lake Michigan. (p. 5, *m900–901*)

China Country in East Asia. (p. 560, *m898–899*)

Chisholm Trail Cattle trail from Texas to the railroad at Abilene, Kansas. (p. 512, *m510*)

Cincinnati (39°N/84°W) City in southern Ohio on the Ohio River. *(m900–901)*

Cleveland (41°N/82°W) City in northern Ohio on Lake Erie. (p. 520, *m303*)

Coastal Plains Region consisting of the Atlantic Plain and the Gulf

Plain along the Gulf of Mexico.
(p. 17, *m19*)

Colombia Country in South America. (p. 631, *m635*)

Colorado 38th state. Nicknamed the Centennial State.
(p. 896, *m900–901*)

Colorado River Begins in Rocky Mountains and flows into Gulf of California. (p. 18, *m19*)

Columbia River Chief river of the Pacific Northwest.
(p. 275, *m273*)

Concord (43°N/71°W) Village in Massachusetts where battle occurred between the British and Americans at the start of the American Revolution. (p. 154, *m162*)

Connecticut One of the original 13 states. Nicknamed the Constitution State or the Nutmeg State.
(p. 896, *m900–901*)

Cowpens (35°N/82°W) In South Carolina, site of an American victory in the Revolutionary War.
(p. 179, *m179*)

Cuba (22°N/79°W) Island nation in the Caribbean. (p. 624, *m626*)

Cumberland Gap (37°N/84°W) Pass in the Appalachian Mountains near the border of Virginia, Kentucky, and Tennessee.
(p. 143, *m303*)

Cuzco (14°S/72°W) Capital of the Incan empire. (p. 50, *m47*)

Czechoslovakia Country in Eastern Europe. Created after World War I; split into two separate countries in 1992.
(p. 663, *m664*)

D

Dallas (33°N/97°W) Major city in north central Texas. (*m900–901*)

Delaware One of the original 13 states. Nicknamed the First State or the Diamond State.
(p. 896, *m900–901*)

Delaware River Flows into the Atlantic Ocean through Delaware Bay. (p. 82, *m88*)

Denver (40°N/105°W) City in Colorado. (*m510*)

Detroit (42°N/83°W) Largest city in Michigan. (p. 285, *m286*)

District of Columbia Located on the Potomac River. Seat of the federal government of the United States. (p. 247, *m900–901*)

Dominican Republic Country in the Caribbean. (p. 636, *m635*)

Dunkirk (51°N/2°E) French port on the English Channel where Allied troops were trapped by the Germans during World War II.
(p. 736, *m756*)

Dust Bowl During the 1930s, name for an area of the Great Plains afflicted by drought and wind erosion. (p. 720, *m721*)

E

Egypt Country in the Middle East. (p. 838, *m839*)

El Alamein (31°N/29°E) In northern Egypt, site of a British victory in World War II. (p.747, *m747*)

El Salvador Country in Central America. (p. 779, *m898–899*)

England Part of Great Britain.
(p. 78, *m79*)

English Channel Narrow body of water separating Britain from the European mainland.
(p. 736)

Equator Line of latitude labeled 0°. Separates the Northern and Southern hemispheres.
(p. 10, *m10*)

Erie Canal Linked the Hudson and Mohawk rivers with Buffalo and Lake Erie. Built between 1817 and 1825. (p. 306, *m306*)

Europe World's second smallest continent. (p. 12, *m10*)

F

Florida 27th state. Nicknamed the Sunshine State.
(p. 896, *m900–901*)

Fort Donelson (37°N/88°W) Located in Tennessee. Captured by Grant in 1862. (p. 458, *m470*)

Fort Henry (37°N/88°W) Located in Tennessee. Captured by Grant in 1862. (p. 458, *m470*)

Fort McHenry (39°N/77°W) Located in Baltimore harbor. British bombardment there in 1814 inspired Francis Scott Key to write "The Star-Spangled Banner."
(p. 287)

Fort Necessity (40°N/79°W) British fort during the French and Indian War. (p. 136, *m138*)

Fort Pitt (40°N/80°W) British fort in the 1700s on the site of present-day Pittsburgh.
(p. 140, *m175*)

Fort Sumter (33°N/80°W) Guarded Charleston harbor in South Carolina. First shots of the Civil War fired there in 1861.
(p. 443, *m470*)

Fort Ticonderoga (44°N/74°W) Fort at the south end of Lake Champlain. Captured from the British by Ethan Allen in 1775.
(p. 140, *m138*)

France Country in Western Europe. (p. 81, *m898–899*)

Fredericksburg (38°N/78°W) Located in eastern Virginia. Site of a Confederate victory in 1862.
(p. 457, *m454*)

G

Gadsden Purchase Land purchased from Mexico in 1853. Now part of Arizona and New Mexico.
(p. 363, *m363*)

Gaza Strip (31°N/34°E) Strip of land between Israel and the Mediterranean Sea. Palestinians were granted self-rule of the territory in 1993. (p. 840, *m839*)

Georgia One of the original 13 states. Nicknamed the Peach State or the Empire State of the South.
(p. 896, *m900–901*)

Germany Country in central Europe. (p. 642, *m646*)

Gettysburg (40°N/77°W) Town in southern Pennsylvania. Site of a Union victory in 1863 and Lincoln's Gettysburg Address.
(p. 469, *m454*)

Goliad (29°N//97°W) Texas town where Mexicans killed several hundred Texans during the Texas war for independence.
(p. 355, *m355*)

Gonzales (29°N/97°W) City in Texas near San Antonio. Site of the first Texan victory over Mexico in 1835. (p. 352, *m355*)

Great Britain Island nation of Western Europe. Includes England, Scotland, Wales, and Northern Ireland. (p. 135, *m898–899*)

Great Lakes Chain of five lakes in central North America. Lakes Superior, Michigan, Huron, Ontario, and Erie. (p. 18, *m19*)

Great Plains Western part of the Interior Plains. (p. 16, *m19*)

GAZETTEER

Great Salt Lake (41°N/113°W) Lake in northern Utah with highly saline water. (p. 365, *m366*)

Great Wagon Road Early pioneer route across the Appalachians. (p. 105, *m102*)

Greensboro (36°N/80°W) City in North Carolina where sit-ins to protest segregation occurred in the 1960s. (p. 814, *m900–901*)

Guam (14°N/143°E) Territory of the United States. Acquired from Spain in 1898. (p. 628, *m620*)

Guatemala Country in Central America. Mayas built a civilization there about 3,000 years ago. (p. 46, *m898–899*)

Gulf of Mexico Body of water along the southern coast of the United States. (p. 17, *m19*)

H

Haiti Country in the West Indies. The nation won independence from France in the early 1800s. (p. 270, *m898–899*)

Harlem (41°N/74°W) Neighborhood in New York City known as a center of African American culture. (p. 690)

Harpers Ferry (39°N/78°W) Town in West Virginia. John Brown raided the arsenal there in 1859. (p. 438, *m454*)

Hawaii Newest of the 50 states. Nicknamed the Aloha State. (p. 896, *m900–901*)

Hawaiian Islands Region in the Pacific Ocean composed of a group of eight large islands and many small islands. (p. 17, *m19*)

Hiroshima (34°N/133°E) Japanese city. The United States dropped an atomic bomb there during World War II. (p. 753, *m752*)

Hudson River Largest river in New York State. (p. 78, *m88*)

I

Idaho 43rd state. Nicknamed the Gem State. Acquired as part of the Oregon Territory. (p. 896, *m900–901*)

Illinois 21st state. Nicknamed the Inland Empire. Settled as part of the Northwest Territory. (p. 896, *m900–901*)

India Country in south Asia. World's second most populous country. (p. 776, *m898–899*)

Indiana 19th state. Nicknamed the Hoosier State. Settled as part of the Northwest Territory. (p. 896, *m900–901*)

Interior Plains Region of the central United States that stretches from the Rockies to the Appalachians. (p. 16, *m19*)

Intermountain Region Rugged region from the Rocky Mountains to the Sierra Nevada and coastal mountains of the western United States. (p. 15, *m19*)

Iowa 29th state. Nicknamed the Hawkeye State. Acquired as part of the Louisiana Purchase. (p. 896, *m900–901*)

Iran Oil-producing country in the Middle East. Since 1979, often had tense relations with the United States. (p. 840, *m839*)

Iraq Oil-producing country in the Middle East. Fought United Nations forces in Persian Gulf War of 1991. (p. 841, *m839*)

Israel Country in the Middle East. Set up as a Jewish homeland in 1948. (p. 838, *m839*)

Isthmus of Panama Narrow strip of land in Central America joining North and South America. (p. 631, *m632*)

Italy Country in southern Europe. (p. 561, *m898–899*)

J

Jamestown (37°N/77°W) First successful English colony in North America. (p. 85, *m88*)

Japan Island nation in East Asia. (p. 616, *m620*)

K

Kansas 34th state. Nicknamed the Sunflower State. Acquired as part of the Louisiana Purchase. (p. 896, *m900–901*)

Kaskaskia (38°N/90°W) British fort on the Mississippi River captured by George Rogers Clark during the American Revolution. (p. 174, *m175*)

Kentucky 15th state. Nicknamed the Bluegrass State. (p. 896, *m900–901*)

Kilwa (8°S/39°E) East African trading state in the 1400s. (p. 73, *m75*)

King's Mountain (35°N/81°W) In South Carolina, site of an American victory in the Revolutionary War. (p. 178, *m179*)

Korea Asian nation divided in two after World War II. Site of a Cold War conflict. (p. 770, *m771*)

Kuwait Oil-producing country in the Middle East. Invaded by Iraq in 1990. (p. 841, *m839*)

L

Lancaster Turnpike Road built in the 1790s linking Philadelphia and Lancaster, Pennsylvania. (p. 302, *m303*)

Latin America Name for those parts of the Western Hemisphere where Latin languages such as Spanish, French, and Portuguese are spoken. Includes Mexico, Central and South America, and the West Indies. (p. 312, *m314*)

Lexington (42°N/71°W) Village in Massachusetts. Site of the first clash between minutemen and British troops in 1775. (p. 155, *m162*)

Liberia Country in West Africa. Set up in 1822 as a colony for free African Americans. (p. 403, *m898–899*)

Little Bighorn Site of a Lakota and Cheyenne victory over Custer in 1876. (p. 519, *m518*)

Little Rock (35°N/92°W) Capital of Arkansas. Site of 1957 school integration conflict. (p. 805, *m900–901*)

London (51°N/0°) Capital of United Kingdom. (*m898–899*)

Long Island Located in New York. Site of a British victory in the Revolution. (p. 169, *m170*)

Los Angeles (34°N/118°W) City in southern California. First settled by Spanish missionaries. (p. 15, *m67*)

Louisbourg (46°N/60°W) Fort in eastern Canada that played a major role in the French and Indian War. (p. 140, *m138*)

Louisiana 18th state. Nicknamed the Pelican State. First state created out of the Louisiana Purchase. (p. 896, *m900–901*)

GAZETTEER

Lowell (43°N/83°W) City in Massachusetts. Important site of Industrial Revolution. (p. 296)

M

Maine 23rd state. Nicknamed the Pine Tree State. Originally part of Massachusetts. (p. 896, *m900–901*)

Mali Kingdom in West Africa. Reached its peak between 1200 and 1400. (p. 73, *m75*)

Manchuria (48°N/125°E) Region of China. Seized by Japan in the 1930s. Returned to China after World War II. (p. 732, *m752*)

Maryland One of the original 13 states. Nicknamed the Old Line State or the Free State. (p. 896, *m900–901*)

Mason-Dixon Line Boundary between Pennsylvania and Maryland surveyed and marked in the 1760s. (p. 106)

Massachusetts One of the original 13 states. Nicknamed the Bay State or the Old Colony. (p. 896, *m900–901*)

Memphis (35°N/90°W) City in Tennessee on the Mississippi River. Captured by Union forces in 1862. (p. 458, *m470*)

Mexican Cession Lands acquired by the United States from Mexico under the Treaty of Guadalupe Hidalgo in 1848. (p. 363, *m363*)

Mexico Southern neighbor of the United States. Gained independence from Spain in 1821. (p. 312, *m898–899*)

Mexico City (19°N/99°W) Capital of Mexico. (p. 434, *m433*)

Michigan 26th state. Nicknamed the Great Lake State or the Wolverine State. Settled as part of the Northwest Territory. (p. 896, *m900–901*)

Middle East Region at the eastern end of the Mediterranean Sea. (p. 60, *m898–899*)

Midway Island (28°N/179°W) Pacific island. In World War II, site of a decisive American victory over Japanese forces. (p. 747, *m752*)

Minnesota 32nd state. Nicknamed the Gopher State. Most of

it was acquired as part of the Louisiana Purchase from France. (p. 896, *m900–901*)

Mississippi 20th state. Nicknamed the Magnolia State. (p. 896, *m900–901*)

Mississippi River Longest river in the United States. Links the Great Lakes with the Gulf of Mexico. (p. 17, *m19*)

Missouri 24th state. Nicknamed the Show Me State. Acquired as part of the Louisiana Purchase. (p. 896, *m900–901*)

Missouri River Second longest river in the United States. Rises in the northern Rocky Mountains and joins the Mississippi River near St. Louis. (p. 17, *m19*)

Mogadishu (2°N/45°E) East African trading state in the 1400s. (p. 73, *m75*)

Montana 41st state. Nicknamed the Treasure State. Acquired in part through the Louisiana Purchase. (p. 896, *m900–901*)

Montgomery (32°N/86°W) City in Alabama. Site of bus boycott during the civil rights movement. (p. 805, *m900–901*)

Montreal (46°N/74°W) Major city in Canada. Located in the province of Quebec. (p. 141, *m138*)

Moscow (56°N/37°E) Capital of Russia and former Soviet Union. (*m898–899*)

N

Nagasaki (33°N/130°E) Japanese city. The United States dropped an atomic bomb there during World War II. (p. 753, *m752*)

National Road Early road to the West that began in Cumberland, Maryland. (p. 303, *m303*)

Nauvoo (41°N/91°W) Town founded by the Mormons in Illinois in the 1840s. (p. 365, *m366*)

Nebraska 37th state. Nicknamed the Cornhusker State. Acquired as part of the Louisiana Purchase. (p. 896, *m900–901*)

Nevada 36th state. Nicknamed the Sagebrush State or the Battle Born State. Acquired at the end of the Mexican War. (p. 896, *m900–901*)

New Amsterdam (41°N/74°W) Town established by Dutch settlers on Manhattan Island in the early 1600s. Renamed New York by the British. (p. 82)

New France Colony established by France in North America. (p. 81, *m79*)

New Hampshire One of the original 13 states. Nicknamed the Granite State. (p. 896, *m900–901*)

New Jersey One of the original 13 states. Nicknamed the Garden State. (p. 896, *m900–901*)

New Mexico 47th state. Nicknamed the Land of Enchantment. Acquired at the end of the Mexican War. (p. 896, *m900–901*)

New Netherland Dutch colony on the Hudson River. Seized by the English and renamed New York in 1664. (p. 82)

New Orleans (30°N/90°W) Port city in Louisiana near the mouth of the Mississippi River. Settled by the French in the 1600s. (p. 82, *m79*)

New Spain Area in the Americas ruled by Spain for some 300 years. Included much of present-day western United States. (p. 68, *m68*)

New York One of the original 13 states. Nicknamed the Empire State. (p. 896, *m900–901*)

New York City (41°N/74°W) Port city at the mouth of the Hudson River. (p. 101, *m102*)

Nicaragua Country in Central America. (p. 779, *m898–899*)

Normandy Region in northwest France. Allied forces landed there on D-Day in World War II. (p. 749, *m747*)

North America World's third largest continent. (p. 14, *m10*)

North Carolina One of the original 13 states. Nicknamed the Tar Heel State or the Old North State. (p. 896, *m900–901*)

North Dakota 39th state. Nicknamed the Sioux State or the Flickertail State. Acquired as part of the Louisiana Purchase. (p. 896, *m900–901*)

Northwest Territory Name for lands north of the Ohio River. Acquired by the Treaty of Paris in 1783. (p. 190, *m191*)

Nueces River Claimed by Mexico in the Mexican War as the southern border of Texas. (p. 361, *m361*)

O

Ohio 17th state. Nicknamed the Buckeye State. Settled as part of the Northwest Territory. (p. 896, *m900–901*)

Ohio River Important transportation route. Begins at Pittsburgh and flows to the Mississippi River. (p. 133, *m133*)

Oklahoma 46th State. Nicknamed the Sooner State. Acquired as part of the Louisiana Purchase. (p. 896, *m900–901*)

Oregon 33rd state. Nicknamed the Beaver State. Acquired as part of the Oregon Territory. (p. 896, *m900–901*)

Oregon Trail Overland route from Independence, Missouri, to the Columbia River valley. (p. 349, *m347*)

P

Pacific Coast Highest and most rugged region of the United States. Includes the Cascades and the Sierra Nevada. (p. 15, *m19*)

Pacific Ocean World's largest ocean. (p. 14, *m10*)

Pakistan Country in South Asia. (p. 776, *m898–899*)

Panama Country on the isthmus separating North and South America. Gained independence from Colombia in 1903. (p. 631, *m635*)

Panama Canal Canal dug through the Isthmus of Panama to link the Atlantic and Pacific oceans. (p. 632, *m632*)

Paris (49°N/2°E) Capital of France. (p. 172, *m646*)

Pearl Harbor (21°N/158°W) United States naval base in Hawaii. Site of Japanese surprise attack December 7, 1941. (p. 739, *m752*)

Pennsylvania One of the original 13 states. Nicknamed the Keystone State. (p. 896, *m900–901*)

Persian Gulf Body of water in the Middle East. Important for transportation of oil. (p. 841, *m839*)

Petersburg (37°N/78°W) City in Virginia. Union forces kept the city under siege for nine months during the Civil War. (p. 472, *m472*)

Philadelphia (40°N/75°W) Major port and chief city in Pennsylvania. (p. 247, *m102*)

Philippine Islands Group of islands in the Pacific Ocean. Acquired by the United States in 1898. Gained independence in 1946. (p. 626, *m626*)

Pikes Peak (39°N/105°W) Mountain located in the Rocky Mountains of central Colorado. (p. 275, *m273*)

Plymouth (42°N/71°W) New England colony founded in 1620 by Pilgrims. (p. 89, *m88*)

Poland Country in Eastern Europe. (p. 735, *m735*)

Portugal Country in Western Europe. (p. 61, *m75*)

Potomac River Forms part of the Maryland-Virginia border. Flows through Washington, D.C., and into Chesapeake Bay. (p. 455, *m455*)

Prime Meridian Line of longitude labeled 0°. (p. 10, *m10*)

Princeton (40°N/75°W) City in New Jersey. Site of an American victory during the Revolution. (p. 170, *m170*)

Promontory Point (42°N/112°W) Place where the Central Pacific and Union Pacific railroads were joined to form the first transcontinental railroad. (p. 511, *m520*)

Puerto Rico (18°N/67°W) Island in the Caribbean Sea. A self-governing commonwealth of the United States. (p. 624, *m626*)

Q

Quebec (47°N/71°W) City in eastern Canada. (p. 81, *m79*)

R

Rhode Island One of the original 13 states. Nicknamed Little Rhody or the Ocean State. (p. 896, *m900–901*)

Richmond (38°N/78°W) Capital of Virginia. Capital of the Confederate States of America during the Civil War. (p. 453, *m454*)

Rio Grande River that forms the border between the United States and Mexico. (p. 18, *m19*)

Roanoke Island (36°N/76°W) Island off North Carolina. Site of English "lost colony" founded in 1587. (p. 84, *m88*)

Rocky Mountains Mountains extending through the western United States and Canada. (p. 16, *m19*)

Russia Largest country in the world, spanning Europe and Asia. Part of the communist Soviet Union until 1991. (p. 558, *m898–899*)

S

Sacramento (39°N/122°W) Capital of California. Developed as a gold rush boom town. (p. 367, *m366*)

St. Augustine (30°N/81°W) City in Florida. Founded by Spain in 1565. Oldest European settlement in the United States. (p. 69, *m67*)

St. Lawrence River Waterway from the Great Lakes to the Atlantic Ocean. Forms part of the border between the United States and Canada. (p. 18, *m79*)

St. Louis (38°N/90°W) City in Missouri on the Mississippi River. Lewis and Clark began their expedition there. (p. 272, *m273*)

Salt Lake City (41°N/112°W) Largest city in Utah. Founded in 1847 by Mormons. (p. 366, *m366*)

San Antonio (29°N/99°W) City in southern Texas. Site of the Alamo. (p. 352, *m352*)

San Diego (33°N/117°W) City in southern California. Founded as the first Spanish mission in California. (p. 357, *m366*)

San Francisco (38°N/122°W) City in northern California. Boom town of the California gold rush. (p. 359, *m366*)

★ GAZETTEER ★

Santa Fe (35°N/106°W) Capital of New Mexico. First settled by the Spanish. (p.69, *m67*)

Santa Fe Trail Overland trail from Independence to Santa Fe. Opened in 1821. (p. 356, *m366*)

Saratoga (43°N/75°W) City in eastern New York. The American victory there in 1777 was a turning point in the Revolution. (p. 172, *m170*)

Savannah (32°N/81°W) Oldest city in Georgia, founded in 1733. (p. 108, *m107*)

Serbia Balkan country in southeastern Europe. Involved in the beginning of World War I. (p. 643, *m646*)

Sierra Nevada Mountain range mostly in California. (p. 15, *m19*)

Songhai West African kingdom in the 1400s. (p. 74, *m75*)

South Africa Country in southern Africa where apartheid existed. (p. 835, *m898–899*)

South America World's fourth largest continent. (p. 12, *m10*)

South Carolina One of the original 13 states. Nicknamed the Palmetto State. (p. 896, *m900–901*)

South Dakota 40th state. Nicknamed the Coyote State or the Sunshine State. Acquired as part of the Louisiana Purchase. (p. 896, *m900–901*)

Soviet Union Short name for the Union of Soviet Socialist Republics. Broke up in 1991. (p. 730, *m735*)

Spain Country in southwestern Europe. (p. 61, *m79*)

Spanish Florida Part of New Spain. Purchased by the United States in 1821. (p. 282, *m283*)

Stalingrad (49°N/45°E) During World War II, city in the Soviet Union where Russians won a decisive victory over German forces. (p. 748, *m747*)

Sudetenland Region of Czechoslovakia given to Germany by the Munich Conference in 1938. (p. 734, *m735*)

T

Tennessee 16th state. Nicknamed the Volunteer State. Gained statehood after North Carolina ceded its western lands to the United States. (p. 896, *m900–901*)

Tenochtitlán (19°N/99°W) Capital of the Aztec empire. Now part of Mexico City. (p. 48, *m47*)

Texas 28th state. Nicknamed the Lone Star State. Proclaimed independence from Mexico in 1836. Was a separate republic until 1845. (p. 896, *m900–901*)

Tikal (17°N/90°W) Ancient Mayan city. (p. 47, *m47*)

Timbuktu (17°N/3°W) City on the Niger River in Africa. (p. 74, *m75*)

Trenton (41°N/74°W) Capital of New Jersey. Site of an American victory in the Revolution. (p. 170, *m170*)

U

Utah 45th state. Nicknamed the Beehive State. Settled by Mormons. (p. 896, *m900–901*)

V

Valley Forge (40°N/76°W) Winter headquarters for the Continental Army in 1777–1778. Located near Philadelphia. (p. 173, *m170*)

Veracruz (19°N/96°W) Port city in Mexico on the Gulf of Mexico. (p. 362, *m361*)

Vermont 14th state. Nicknamed the Green Mountain State. (p. 896, *m900–901*)

Vicksburg (42°N/86°W) City in Mississippi. Site of a Union victory in 1863. (p. 468, *m470*)

Vietnam Country in Southeast Asia. Site of a war involving the United States during the Cold War. (p. 780, *m781*)

Vincennes (39°N/88°W) City in Indiana. British fort there was captured by George Rogers Clark in 1779. (p. 174, *m175*)

Virgin Islands (18°N/64°W) Territory of the United States. Purchased from Denmark in 1917. (p. 896, *m898–899*)

Virginia One of the original 13 states. Nicknamed the Old Dominion. (p. 896, *m900–901*)

Virginia City (39°N/120°W) City in Nevada. Boom town in 1800s because of Comstock Lode mines. (p. 508, *m510*)

W

Washington 42nd state. Nicknamed the Evergreen State. Acquired as part of Oregon Territory. (p. 896, *m900–901*)

Washington, D.C. (39°N/77°W) Capital of the United States since 1800. (p. 287, *m214*)

West Indies Islands in the Caribbean Sea. Explored by Columbus. (p. 62, *m68*)

West Virginia 35th state. Nicknamed the Mountain State. Separated from Virginia early in the Civil War. (p. 896, *m900–901*)

Western Hemisphere Western half of the world. Includes North and South America. (p. 12, *m10*)

Wisconsin 30th state. Nicknamed the Badger State. Settled as part of the Northwest Territory. (p. 896, *m900–901*)

Wounded Knee (43°N/102°W) Site of a massacre of Indians in 1890. Located in what is now South Dakota. (p. 520, *m518*)

Wyoming 44th state. Nicknamed the Equality State. (p. 896, *m900–901*)

Y

Yalu River River along the border between North Korea and China. (p. 771, *m771*)

Yorktown (37°N/76°W) Town in Virginia. Site of the British surrender in 1781. (p. 180, *m179*)

Yugoslavia Eastern European country created after World War I. Torn by civil war after the fall of communism in the 1990s. (p. 832, *m664*)

★ **GAZETTEER** ★

★ Glossary ★

This glossary defines all vocabulary words and many important historical terms and phrases. These words and terms appear in blue or boldfaced type the first time that they are used in the text. The page number(s) after each definition refers to the page(s) on which the word or phrase is defined in the text. For other references, see the index.

Pronunciation Key

When difficult names or terms first appear in the text, they are respelled to help you with pronunciation. A syllable printed in SMALL CAPITAL LETTERS receives the greatest stress. The pronunciation key below lists the letters and symbols that will help you pronounce the word. It also includes examples of words using each sound and showing how they would be pronounced.

Symbol	Example	Respelling
a	hat	(hat)
ay	pay, late	(pay), (layt)
ah	star, hot	(stahr), (haht)
ai	air, dare	(air), (dair)
aw	law, all	(law), (awl)
eh	met	(meht)
ee	bee, eat	(bee), (eet)
er	learn, sir, fur	(lern), (ser), (fer)
ih	fit	(fiht)
i	mile	(mīl)
ir	ear	(ir)
oh	no	(noh)
oi	soil, boy	(soil), (boi)
oo	root, rule	(root), (rool)
or	born, door	(born), (dor)
ow	plow, out	(plow), (owt)

Symbol	Example	Respelling
u	put, book	(put), (buk)
uh	fun	(fuhn)
yoo	few, use	(fyoo), (yooz)
ch	chill, reach	(chihl), (reech)
g	go, dig	(goh), (dihg)
j	jet, gently bridge	(jeht), (JEHNT lee), (brihj)
k	kite, cup	(kīt), (kuhp)
ks	mix	(mihks)
kw	quick	(kwihk)
ng	bring	(brihng)
s	say, cent	(say), (sehnt)
sh	she, crash	(shee), (krash)
th	three	(three)
y	yet, onion	(yeht), (UHN yuhn)
z	zip, always	(zihp), (AWL wayz)
zh	treasure	(TREH zher)

A

abdicate to give up power (p. 660)

abolitionist person who wanted to end slavery in the United States (p. 404)

absolute power total authority by a ruler over the people (p. 49)

adobe sun-dried clay brick (p. 35)

affirmative action program in areas such as employment and education to provide more opportunities for members of groups that faced discrimination in the past (p. 816)

affluence wealth (p. 798)

aggression any warlike act by one country against another without just cause (p. 731)

ally nation that works with another nation for a common purpose (p. 172)

altitude height above sea level (p. 19)

amend to change (p. 208)

amendment formal written change (p. 222)

amnesty government pardon (p. 479)

anarchist person who opposes organized government (pp. 550, 694)

annex to add on (pp. 355, 617)

apartheid South African government policy of separation of the races enforced by law (p. 835)

appeal to ask that a decision be reviewed by a higher court (p. 230)

appeasement practice of giving in to an aggressor nation's demands in order to keep peace (p. 734)

apprentice (uh PREHN tihs) person who learns a trade or craft from a master (p. 120)

appropriate to set aside money for a special purpose (p. 226)

aqueduct channel for carrying water (p. 50)

archaeology (ahr kee AHL uh jee) study of evidence left by early people in order to find out about their culture (p. 32)

armistice agreement to stop fighting (pp. 627, 660)

arsenal warehouse for guns and ammunition (p. 438)

Articles of Confederation first constitution of the United States (p. 189)

artifact (AHRT uh fakt) object made by humans and used by archaeologists to learn about past human cultures (p. 32)

artisan worker who has learned a trade, such as carpentry (p. 379)

assembly line method of production in which workers add

parts to a product as it moves along on a belt (p. 546)

assimilation process of becoming part of another culture (p. 562)

astrolabe (AS troh layb) instrument to measure the positions of stars and figure out latitude (p. 61)

atomic bomb powerful nuclear weapon that could destroy an entire city with one bomb (p. 752)

B

baby boom increased birth rate in United States during the late 1940s and 1950s (p. 797)

backcountry area of land along the eastern slopes of the Appalachian Mountains. (p. 105)

balanced budget condition that exists when the government spends only as much as it takes in (p. 828)

bankrupt unable to pay debts (p. 703)

barrio neighborhood of Spanish-speaking people (p. 610)

beatnik one who criticized American culture for its conformity and devotion to business in the 1950s (p. 802)

bilingual in two languages (p. 820)

bill proposed law (pp. 203, 221)

bill of rights list of freedoms that a government promises to protect (p. 116)

Bill of Rights first 10 amendments to the Constitution (p. 208)

birth rate number of births per year for every thousand, or other number, of a population (p. 797)

black codes laws that severely limited the rights of freedmen after the Civil War (p. 482)

blitzkrieg German word meaning lightning war; the swift attacks launched by Germany in World War II (p. 735)

blockade shutting off a port by positioning ships to keep people or supplies from moving in or out (p. 164)

bond certificate that promises to repay money loaned, plus interest, on a certain date (p. 246)

bonus additional sum of money (p. 707)

bootlegger person who smuggled liquor into the United States during Prohibition (p. 679)

Boston Massacre (1770) shooting of five colonists by British soldiers (p. 148)

Boston Tea Party (1773) protest in which colonists dressed as Indians dumped British tea into Boston harbor (p. 151)

boycott to refuse to buy certain goods or services (pp. 144, 805)

bracero program program that allowed Mexican laborers to work in the United States (p. 745)

buffer land between two other lands that reduces the possibility of conflict between the other two (p. 109)

building code laws regulating the building of new structures in order to improve the health and safety of residents (p. 566)

bull market rising stock market (p. 676)

bureaucracy system of managing government through departments run by appointed officials (p. 652)

C

Cabinet group of officials who head government departments and advise the President (pp. 224, 245)

canal artificial channel filled with water to allow boats to cross a stretch of land (p. 305)

capital money raised for a business venture (p. 703)

capitalist person who invests in a business to make a profit (p. 296)

caravel (KAR uh vehl) ship with a steering rudder and triangular sails (p. 62)

carpetbagger name for a northerner who came south after the Civil War seeking personal gain (p. 486)

cartographer person who makes maps (p. 8)

cash crop crop sold for money (p. 103)

cattle drive herding and moving of cattle, usually to railroad lines (p. 512)

caucus private meeting of political party leaders to choose a candidate (p. 327)

causeway raised road across a stretch of water (p. 48)

cavalry troops on horseback (p. 173)

cede to give up, as land (p. 363)

censure to officially condemn (p. 772)

charter legal document giving certain rights to a person or company (p. 85)

checks and balances system by which each branch of government can check, or control, the actions of the other branches (p. 202)

chinampa Aztec floating garden (p. 49)

city-state town that has its own independent government (p. 73)

civil disobedience nonviolent opposition to a government policy or law by refusing to comply with it (p. 806)

civil rights the constitutional rights due all citizens (p. 723)

civil rights movement the efforts of African Americans and others who worked for equality (p. 804)

civil service all federal jobs except elected positions and the armed forces (p. 589)

civil war war between people of the same country (p. 428)

civilian person not in the military (p. 463)

civilization advanced culture (p. 46)

clan group of related families (p. 45)

climate average weather of a place over a period of 20 to 30 years (p. 19)

clipper ship fast-sailing ship of the mid-1800s (p. 377)

Cold War after World War II, long period of conflict between the Soviet Union and the United States that never erupted into war between the two (p. 764)

collective bargaining right of unions to negotiate with management for workers as a group (pp. 551, 717)

collective farm a farm or group of farms run by the government, as in a communist state (p. 730)

colony group of people who move to a new land and are ruled by the government of their native land (p. 64)

Columbian Exchange worldwide exchange of goods and ideas that began with Columbus's voyages to the Americas (p. 53)

committee of correspondence group of colonists who wrote letters and pamphlets reporting on British actions (p. 149)

common open field where cattle grazed (p. 98)

GLOSSARY ★

communism economic system in which all property is owned by the community (p. 678)

company union labor organization that was controlled by the company owners (p. 694)

compensation repayment for losses (p. 815)

compromise settlement in which each side gives up some of its demands in order to reach an agreement (p. 194)

Compromise of 1850 agreement over slavery under which California joined the Union as a free state and a strict fugitive slave law was passed (p. 428)

concentration camp prison camp for persons who are considered enemies of the state (p. 732)

Confederate States of America nation formed in 1861 by the southern states that seceded from the Union (p. 442)

confederation alliance of independent states (p. 189)

conquistador (kahn KEES tuh dor) Spanish word for conqueror (p. 65)

conservation protection of natural resources (p. 600)

conservative person who wants to keep conditions as they are or return them to the way they used to be (p. 487)

consolidate to combine, such as businesses (p. 533)

constituent person who elected a representative to office (p. 228)

constitution document that sets out the laws and principles of a government (p. 188)

Constitutional Convention (1787) meeting of delegates from 12 states who wrote the United States Constitution (p. 193)

containment in the Cold War, the policy of trying to prevent the spread of Soviet or communist influence beyond where it already existed (p. 765)

Continental Army army established by the Second Continental Congress to fight the British (p. 160)

continental divide mountain ridge that separates river systems flowing toward opposite sides of a continent (p. 274)

cooperative group in which individuals pool their money to buy goods at lower prices (p. 526)

Copperheads northerners who opposed using force to keep the southern states in the Union (p. 463)

corduroy road road made of logs (p. 302)

corporation business that is owned by investors (p. 538)

corral enclosure for animals (p. 505)

cottonocracy name for the wealthy planters who made their money from cotton in the mid-1800s (p. 388)

counterculture rejection of traditional American values and culture (p. 810)

coureur de bois (koo ruhr duh BWAH) phrase meaning runner of the woods; trapper or trader in New France (p. 81)

cow town settlement that grew up at the end of a cattle trail (p. 513)

cowhand worker who tended cattle and drove herds (p. 512)

creole person born in Spain's American colonies to Spanish parents (pp. 70, 312)

Crusades wars fought by Christians in the Middle Ages to gain control of the Middle East (p. 60)

culture entire way of life developed by a people (p. 32)

culture area region in which people share a similar way of life (p. 36)

czar Russian emperor (p. 649)

D

dame school private school for girls in the New England colonies (p. 121)

debtor person who owes money (p. 108)

Declaration of Independence (1776) document stating that the colonies were a free and independent nation (p. 166)

deficit condition of spending more money than the amount received in income (p. 812)

deficit spending government practice of spending more than it takes in from taxes (p. 719)

democratic ensuring that all people have the same rights (p. 266)

deport to expel from a country (p. 694)

depression period when business slows, prices and wages fall, and unemployment rises (pp. 192, 338)

deregulation reduction of government restrictions on businesses (p. 827)

détente easing of tensions between nations (p. 787)

dictator ruler who has complete power (p.730)

dime novels in the late 1800s, low-priced paperback books offering adventure stories (p. 577)

disarmament reduction of nation's armed forces or weapons (p. 678)

discrimination policy or attitude that denies equal rights and treatment to certain groups of people (pp. 381, 461)

dissenting opinion statement explaining why a Supreme Court Justice disagrees with the opinion of the majority (p. 231)

dividend share of a corporation's profits (p. 538)

dollar diplomacy policy of building economic ties to Latin America in the early 1900s (p. 635)

domestic tranquillity peace at home (p. 215)

domino theory in the Cold War, belief that if South Vietnam became communist, other countries in Southeast Asia would become communist, too (p. 780)

downsizing practice of trying to cut costs by using fewer people to do the same work (p. 829)

draft law requiring certain people to serve in the military (pp. 464, 650)

drought long dry spell (p. 35)

due process principle that government must follow the same fair rules in all cases brought to trial (pp. 209, 232)

dumping selling of goods in another country at very low prices (p. 310)

E

electoral college group of electors from every state who meet every four years to vote for the President and Vice President of the United States (p. 202)

elevation height above sea level (p. 14)

emancipate to set free (p. 459)

Emancipation Proclamation (1863) President Lincoln's declaration freeing slaves in the Confederacy (p. 460)

embargo ban on trade with another country (p. 278)

encomienda (ehn koh mee EHN dah) right given by Spanish government to Spanish settlers to demand labor or taxes from Native Americans (p. 70)

English Bill of Rights (1689) document guaranteeing the rights of English citizens (pp. 116, 199)

Enlightenment movement in Europe in the late 1600s and 1700s that emphasized the use of reason (pp. 121, 199)

environmentalist person who works to reduce pollution and protect the natural environment (p. 842)

epidemic rapid spread of a contagious disease among large numbers of people (p. 661)

Equator imaginary line that lies at 0° latitude (p. 10)

escalate to build up, increase, or expand activity (p. 781)

ethnic group people who share a common culture (p. 561)

execute to carry out (p. 188)

executive agreement informal agreement made by the President with another head of state (p. 229)

executive branch branch of government that carries out laws (p. 194)

exile person forced to leave his or her country (p. 773)

expansionism policy of extending a nation's boundaries (p. 616)

expatriate person who leaves his or her country and lives in a foreign land (p. 689)

expedition long journey or voyage of exploration (p. 272)

export trade product sent to markets outside a country (p. 112)

extended family close-knit family group that includes grandparents, parents, children, aunts, uncles, and cousins (p. 393)

F

faction group inside a political party or other group (p. 253)

factory system method of producing goods that brought workers and machinery together in one place (p. 296)

fad style or fashion popular for a short time (p. 687)

Fair Deal program of President Truman to extend New Deal policies (p. 797)

famine severe food shortage and starvation (p. 381)

federal having to do with the national government (p. 215)

federalism division of power between the states and the national government (p. 201)

feudalism (FYOOD 'l ihz uhm) rule by lords who owe loyalty to a monarch (p. 60)

fireside chat radio speeches given by President Franklin Roosevelt (p. 711)

First Continental Congress (1774) meeting of delegates from 12 colonies in Philadelphia (p. 154)

flapper young woman in the 1920s who rebelled against traditional ways of thinking and acting (p. 687)

foreign policy actions that a nation takes in relation to other nations (p. 251)

forty-niner person who headed to California in search of gold during the Gold Rush of 1849 (p. 367)

Fourteen Points President Wilson's goals for peace after World War I (p. 662)

free enterprise system economic system in which businesses are owned by private citizens (p. 540)

free market economic system in which individuals decide for themselves what to produce and sell (p. 791)

freedmen men and women who had been slaves (p. 479)

fugitive runaway (p. 428)

G

general welfare well-being of all the people (p. 216)

gentry highest social class in the 13 English colonies (p. 117)

geography the study of people, their environments, and their resources (p. 4)

Gettysburg Address (1863) speech by President Lincoln after the Battle of Gettysburg (p. 470)

Ghost Dance religious ceremony that celebrated the time when Native Americans lived freely on the Plains (p. 519)

glacier thick sheet of ice (p. 30)

glasnost Mikhail Gorbachev's policy of speaking out openly and honestly about problems in the Soviet Union (p. 789)

global warming theory that Earth's atmosphere is warming up as a result of air pollution (p. 845)

globe sphere with a map of Earth printed on it (p. 8)

Glorious Revolution (1688) movement that brought William and Mary to the throne of England and strengthened the rights of English citizens (p. 116)

Good Neighbor policy President Franklin Roosevelt's policy intended to strengthen friendly relations with Latin America (p. 733)

graduated income tax tax on earnings that charges different rates for different income levels (p. 596)

grandfather clause law that excused a voter from a literacy test if his grandfather had been eligible to vote on January 1, 1867—protected the voting rights of southern whites but not those of southern blacks (p. 493)

Great Awakening religious movement in the English colonies in the early 1700s (p. 119)

Great Compromise plan at the Constitutional Convention that settled the differences between large and small states (p. 196)

Great Depression worst period of economic decline in United States history, beginning in 1929 and lasting until World War II (p. 703)

Great Society President Lyndon Johnson's plan to improve the standard of living of every American (p. 809)

guerrilla soldier who uses hit-and-run tactics (pp. 179, 780)

H

habeas corpus right to have charges filed or a hearing before being jailed (p. 464)

Harlem Renaissance "rebirth" of African American culture in the 1920s (p. 690)

hemisphere half of the Earth (p. 10)

hieroglyphics system of writing that uses pictures to represent words and ideas (p. 47)

hill area of raised land that is lower and more rounded than a mountain (p. 14)

history account of what has happened in the lives of different peoples (p. 4)

hogan house made of mud plaster over a framework of wooden poles (p. 41)

Holocaust murder of millions of European Jews and others by officials of Nazi Germany and its allies (p. 755)

House of Burgesses representative assembly in colonial Virginia (pp. 86, 199)

House of Representatives larger house of Congress, in which each state is represented according to its population (p. 225)

Hudson River School group of American artists who painted landscapes of New York's Hudson River region in the mid-1800s (p. 415)

I

igloo house of snow and ice, developed by the Inuits (p. 37)

illegal alien someone who enters a country without legal permission (p. 851)

illiterate unable to read or write (p. 651)

immigrant person who enters a country in order to settle there (p. 259)

impeach to bring a formal charge of wrongdoing against the President or another public official (pp. 203, 228, 484)

imperialism policy of powerful countries seeking to control the economic and political affairs of weaker countries or regions (p. 618)

import trade product brought into a country (p. 112)

impressment act of forcing someone to serve in the navy (p. 277)

inauguration ceremony at which the President officially takes the oath of office (p. 244)

income tax tax on people's earnings (p. 466)

indentured servant person who agreed to work without wages for some time in exchange for passage to the colonies (p. 117)

Industrial Revolution process by which machines replaced hand tools, and steam and other new sources of power replaced human and animal power (p. 294)

inflation rise in prices and decrease in the value of money (pp. 466, 796)

initiative process by which voters can put a bill directly before the state legislature by collecting signatures on a petition (p. 596)

injunction court order to do or not to do something (p. 553)

installment buying method of buying on credit (p. 675)

integration bringing together people of different races or ethnic groups (p. 803)

interchangeable parts identical, machine-made parts for a tool or instrument (p. 299)

intern to detain or confine, usually in a compound (p. 628)

interstate commerce trade between different states (p. 311)

intervention direct involvement in another country (p. 315)

irrigate to bring water to an area (p. 6)

island hopping strategy of Allies in World War II of capturing some Japanese-held islands and going around others (p. 751)

isolationism policy of having little to do with the political affairs of foreign nations (p. 616)

isthmus narrow strip of land (pp. 14, 631)

J

jazz music style that developed from blues, ragtime, and other earlier styles (p. 688)

jerky dried meat (p. 505)

Jim Crow laws laws that separated people of different races in public places in the South (p. 495)

joint committee congressional committee that includes both House and Senate members (p. 226)

judicial branch branch of government that decides if laws are carried out fairly (p. 194)

judicial review power of the Supreme Court to decide whether acts of a President or laws passed by Congress are constitutional (pp. 224, 269)

justice fairness (p. 215)

K

kachina masked dancer at religious ceremonies of the Southwest Indians (p. 41)

kaiser German emperor (p. 644)

kamikaze in World War II, a Japanese pilot who carried out a suicidal attack on a target (p. 751)

kayak (KI ak) small boat made of animal skins (p. 37)

kinship network close ties among family members (p. 74)

kitchen cabinet group of unofficial advisers to President Andrew Jackson (p. 331)

kiva underground chamber where Pueblo men held religious ceremonies (p. 41)

L

laissez faire (lehs ay FAYR) idea that government should play as small a role as possible in economic affairs (pp. 267, 339, 718)

latitude distance north or south from the Equator (p. 4)

lawsuit legal case brought by one person or group against another to settle a dispute (p. 434)

League of Nations association of nations formed after World War I (p. 662)

legislative branch branch of government that passes laws (p. 194)

legislature group of people who have the power to make laws (p. 114)

Lend Lease Act during World War II, law that allowed the United States to sell arms and equipment to Britain (p. 738)

libel publishing a statement that unjustly damages a person's reputation (p. 123)

liberty freedom to live as you please provided you obey the laws and respect the rights of others (p. 217)

literacy test examination to see if a person can read and write, used in the past to restrict voting rights (p. 493)

local color speech and habits of a particular region (p. 578)

locomotive engine that pulls a railroad train (p. 376)

long house Native American home built of wood poles and bark (p. 44)

longitude distance east or west from the Prime Meridian (p. 4)
Louisiana Purchase (1803) vast territory west of the Mississippi purchased from France (p. 272)
Loyalist colonist who remained loyal to Britain (p.162)
lynching illegal seizure and execution of someone by a mob (p. 495)

M

Magna Carta (1215) document that guaranteed rights to English nobles (pp. 86, 198)
magnetic compass device that shows which direction is North (p. 61)
mainstream to place children with disabilities in regular school classes (p. 849)
majority more than half (p. 324)
Manifest Destiny belief that the United States had the right and the duty to expand to the Pacific (p. 359)
manor district ruled by a lord, including the lord's castle, peasants' huts, and surrounding fields (p. 60)
map projection way of drawing the Earth on a flat surface (p. 8)
Marshall Plan American plan to help European nations rebuild their economies after World War II (p. 766)
martial law rule by the army instead of the elected government (pp. 448, 788)
martyr person who dies for his or her beliefs (p. 438)
mass production making large quantities of a product quickly and cheaply (p. 547)
Mayflower Compact (1620) agreement for ruling the Plymouth Colony, signed by Pilgrims before they landed at Plymouth (pp. 88, 199)
Medicaid government program of helping poor people pay medical bills (p. 809)
Medicare government program of helping older Americans pay medical and hospital bills (p. 809)
mercantilism (MER kuhn tihl ihz uhm) economic theory that a nation's strength came from building up its gold supplies and expanding its trade (p. 112)

mercenary soldier who fights merely for pay, often for a foreign country (p. 164)
mestizo in Spanish colonies, person of mixed Spanish and Indian background (p. 70)
Middle Ages period of time in European history from about 500 to 1350 (p, 60)
middle class in the 13 English colonies, class that included skilled craftsworkers, farmers, and some tradespeople (p. 117)
Middle Passage ocean trip from Africa to the Americas in which thousands of enslaved Africans died (p. 77)
migrant worker agricultural worker who moves with the seasons, planting or harvesting crops (pp. 720, 818)
militarism policy of building up strong armed forces to prepare for war (p. 642)
militia army of citizens who serve as soldiers in an emergency (p. 154)
minuteman colonial volunteer who trained to fight the British (p. 154)
mission religious settlement run by Catholic priests and friars (p. 69)
missionary person who tries to spread certain religious beliefs among a group of people (p. 81)
Missouri Compromise (1819) plan proposed by Henry Clay to keep the number of slave and free states equal (p. 424)
mobilize to prepare for war (p. 643)
monarch king or queen (p. 60)
monopoly company that controls all or nearly all the business of an industry (p. 540)
Monroe Doctrine (1823) President Monroe's foreign policy statement warning European nations not to interfere in Latin America (p. 315)
moral diplomacy foreign policy proposed by President Wilson to condemn imperialism, spread democracy, and promote peace (p. 636)
mountain high, steep, rugged land, usually at least 1,000 feet (372 m) above the surrounding land (p. 14)
mountain man fur trapper who lived in the western mountains in the early 1800s (p. 347)

muckraker journalist who exposed corruption and other problems of the late 1800s and early 1900s (p. 593)
mudslinging political tactic of using insults to attack an opponent's reputation (p. 341)
mutualista Mexican American mutual aid group (p. 610)

N

national debt total sum of money a government owes (pp. 245, 719)
national park natural or historic area set aside and run by the federal government for people to visit (p. 600)
nationalism pride in one's nation (pp. 282, 642, 730)
nativist person who wanted to limit immigration and preserve the United States for native-born white Protestants (pp. 381, 562)
natural rights rights that belong to all people from birth (p. 168)
network system of connected lines, as in a network of railroad lines (p. 532)
neutral not taking sides in a war (pp. 174, 282)
New Deal program of President Franklin D. Roosevelt to end the Great Depression (p. 711)
nominating convention meeting at which a political party chooses a candidate (p. 327)
North American Free Trade Agreement (NAFTA) treaty among the United States, Canada, and Mexico to gradually remove tariffs and other trade barriers (p. 846)
North Atlantic Treaty Organization (NATO) alliance formed in 1949 by the United States and Western European nations to fight Soviet aggression (p. 769)
nullification idea that a state had the right to cancel a federal law it considered unconstitutional (p. 333)
nullify to cancel (p. 260)

O

on margin practice that allowed people to buy stock with a down payment of 10 percent of the full value (p. 676)

GLOSSARY

OPEC (Organization of Petroleum Exporting Countries) league of oil-producing nations (p. 838)

Open Door Policy (1899) policy toward China that allowed a nation to trade in any other nation's sphere of influence (p. 623)

opinion a judge's official statement regarding the laws bearing on a case (p. 231)

ordinance law (p. 190)

Organization of American States association of American countries working for collective defense, cooperation, and peaceful settlement of disputes (p. 778)

override to overrule or set aside (pp. 203, 221)

P

pacifist person who opposes all wars (p. 655)

Parliament representative assembly in England (p. 86)

Patriot colonist who supported independence from British rule (p. 161)

patronage practice of giving jobs to loyal supporters (p. 589)

patroon owner of a huge estate in a Dutch colony (p. 100)

penal system system of prisons (p. 399)

peninsulare (puh nihn suh LAH ray) person from Spain who held a position of power in a Spanish colony (p. 70)

pension sum of money paid to people on a regular basis after they retire (p. 715)

pet bank state bank in which President Jackson and Secretary of the Treasury Taney deposited federal money (p. 332)

petition formal request to someone in authority, usually written and signed by a group of people (p. 144)

Pilgrims in the 1600s, English settlers who sought religious freedom in the Americas (p. 88)

plain broad area of fairly level land (p. 14)

plantation large estate farmed by many workers (pp. 72, 109)

plateau raised plain (p. 14)

pogrom in Eastern Europe, an organized attack on a Jewish community (p. 558)

poll tax tax required before a person can vote (p. 493)

pool group of companies that divided up business in an area and fixed prices (p. 535)

popular sovereignty idea that the people hold the final authority in government (p. 218), allowing each territory to decide whether to allow slavery (p. 426)

potlatch ceremonial dinner among some Native Americans of the Northwest Coast (p. 38)

preamble opening statement of a declaration, constitution, or other official document (pp. 168, 214)

precedent (PREHS uh dehnt) act or decision that sets an example for others to follow (pp. 224, 244)

precipitation (pree sihp uh TAY shuhn) water that falls as rain, sleet, hail, or snow (p. 19)

predestination belief that God decided in advance which people will gain salvation in heaven (p. 398)

presidio (prih SIHD ee oh) fort where soldiers lived in the Spanish colonies (p. 69)

primary election in which voters choose their party's candidate for the general election (p. 596)

Prime Meridian imaginary line that lies at 0° longitude (p. 10)

productivity measure of how much a given number of workers can produce in a given time (p. 798)

profiteer person who takes advantage of a crisis to make money (p. 466)

Progressives reformers who wanted to improve American life in the late 1800s and early 1900s (p. 593)

Prohibition ban on manufacture, sale, and transportation of liquor anywhere in the United States from 1920 to 1933 (p. 679)

propaganda spreading of ideas that help a cause or hurt an opposing cause (p. 646)

proprietary colony English colony in which the king gave land to proprietors in exchange for a yearly payment (p. 101)

proprietor owner of a proprietary colony (p. 101)

protective tariff tax on imported goods to protect a country's industry from foreign competition (p. 247)

protectorate nation whose independence is limited by the control of a more powerful country (p. 630)

Protestant Reformation movement to reform the Roman Catholic Church in the 1500s; led to creation of many different Christian churches (p. 79)

public interest the good of the people (p. 595)

public school school supported by taxes (p. 120)

public works projects built by the government for public use (p. 706)

pueblo adobe dwelling of the Anasazis (p. 35); town in the Spanish colonies (p. 69)

pull factor condition that attracts people to move to a new area (p. 558)

Puritans group of English Protestants who settled the Massachusetts Bay Colony (p. 94)

push factor condition that encourages people to move away from their homeland (p. 558)

Q

quota system system that limited immigration by allowing only a certain number of people from each country to immigrate to the United States (p. 695)

R

racism belief that one race is superior to another (pp. 111, 448)

radical person who wants to make drastic changes in society (p. 482)

ragtime popular music of the late 1800s that had a lively, rhythmic sound (p. 573)

ratify to approve (pp. 182, 204)

ration to limit the amount of goods people can buy (p. 741)

Reaganomics program of President Ronald Reagan to cut taxes in an effort to stimulate the economy (p. 827)

realist writer or artist who shows life as it really is (p. 578)

rebate discount on services or merchandise (p. 534)

recall process by which voters can remove an elected official from office (p. 596)

recession mild depression in which business slows and some workers lose their jobs (pp. 674, 829)

★ GLOSSARY ★

Reconstruction rebuilding of the South after the Civil War (p. 479)

referendum process by which people vote directly on a bill (p. 596)

refugee person who flees his or her homeland to seek safety elsewhere (p. 164)

relief program government program to help the needy (p. 706)

Renaissance (REHN uh sahns) French word meaning rebirth; burst of learning in Europe from the late 1300s to about 1600 (p. 61)

rendezvous (RAHN day voo) yearly meeting where mountain men traded furs (p. 348)

renewable resource natural resource that can be quickly replaced by nature (p. 845)

reparations after a war, payments from a defeated nation to a victorious nation to pay for losses suffered during the war (p. 663)

repatriate to send back to one's own country (p. 723)

repeal to cancel or undo (pp. 144, 680)

representative government government in which voters elect representatives to make laws for them (pp. 86, 218)

republic nation in which voters elect representatives to govern them (p. 198)

reservation limited area set aside for Native Americans by the government (p. 517)

revival huge meeting held to stir religious feelings (p. 398)

Roosevelt Corollary (1904) President Theodore Roosevelt's addition to the Monroe Doctrine, claiming the right of the United States to intervene in Latin America to preserve law and order (p. 634)

royal colony colony under the control of the English crown (p. 101)

S

Sabbath holy day of rest in some religions (p. 98)

sabotage secret destruction of property or interference with production in a factory or other workplace (p. 694)

sachem tribal chief of an Eastern Woodlands Native American people (p. 45)

sanction action taken against a country in an effort to force a change in its policy (p. 835)

satellite nation country that is dominated by a more powerful nation (p. 765)

scalawag white southerner who supported the Republicans during Reconstruction (p. 486)

secede to withdraw from membership in a group (pp. 335, 427)

Second Great Awakening religious movement that swept the United States in the early 1800s (p. 398)

sectionalism loyalty to a state or section rather than to the whole country (pp. 310, 425)

sedition stirring up rebellion against a government (p. 259)

segregation separation of people based on racial, ethnic, or other differences (pp. 495, 743)

self-determination right of national groups to their own territory and forms of government (p. 662)

Senate smaller house of Congress, in which each state has two senators (p. 225)

Seneca Falls Convention (1848) meeting at which leaders of the women's rights movement called for equality for women (p. 409)

separation of powers principle by which the powers of government are divided among separate branches (p. 200)

serf peasant who worked for a lord and could not leave without the lord's permission (p. 60)

settlement house community center that offers services to the poor (p. 568)

sharecropper person who farms land owned by another in exchange for a share of the crops (p. 490)

siege military blockade of an enemy town or position in order to force it to surrender (pp. 180, 354)

silent majority President Nixon's term for Americans who were disturbed by the unrest of the 1960s (p. 811)

sit-in protest in which people sit and refuse to leave (p. 814)

sitdown strike work stoppage in which workers refuse to leave a factory (p. 717)

slave code laws that controlled the lives of enslaved African Americans and denied them basic rights (pp. 111, 390)

smuggler person who violates trade laws by illegally taking goods into or out of a country (p. 278)

social reform organized attempt to improve what is unjust or imperfect in society (p. 398)

Social Security federal program begun in the 1930s to provide aid for the elderly and unemployed; the program was later expanded (p. 718)

socialist person who supports community ownership of property and the sharing of all profits (p. 655)

sod house house built of soil held together by grass roots (p. 524)

sodbuster nickname for a Plains farmer (p. 524)

solar energy power from the sun (p. 845)

soup kitchen place where food is provided to the needy at little or no charge (p. 706)

speakeasy illegal bar that served liquor during Prohibition (p. 679)

speculator person who invests in a risky venture in the hope of making a large profit (pp. 246, 338)

sphere of influence area in which a foreign nation had special trading privileges and made laws for its own citizens (p. 623)

spinning jenny machine developed in the 1760s that could spin several threads at once (p. 294)

spoils system practice of rewarding supporters with government jobs (p. 331)

Square Deal Theodore Roosevelt's promise that all groups should have an equal opportunity to succeed (p. 599)

stagflation combination of rising prices, high unemployment, and slow economic growth (p. 812)

stalemate deadlock in which neither side is strong enough to defeat the other (p. 644)

standard of living an index based on the amount of goods, services, education, and leisure time that people have (p. 798)

standard time zone one of 24 divisions of the Earth, each an hour apart (p. 12)

standing committee permanent congressional committee assigned to study a specific issue (p. 226)

states' rights idea that states have the right to limit the power of the federal government (p. 333)

steerage on a ship, the cramped quarters for passengers paying the lowest fares (p. 559)

stock share in a corporation (pp. 538, 676)

strike refusal by workers to do their jobs until their demands are met (p. 379)

strikebreaker worker hired as a replacement for a striking worker (p. 550)

subsidy financial aid or a land grant from the government (p. 509)

suburb community located within commuting distance of a city (pp. 684, 798)

suffrage right to vote (p. 326)

suffragist person who campaigned for women's right to vote (p. 604)

summit meeting conference between the highest-ranking officials of different nations (p. 789)

Sun Dance religious ceremony of the Plains Indians (p. 505)

Sunbelt name for the southern part of the United States from Florida to southern California (p. 801)

superpower nation with enough strength to influence events in many areas around the world (p. 773)

Supreme Court highest court in the United States (p. 231)

surplus an extra amount, more than is needed (pp. 50, 713)

sweatshop workplace where people labor long hours in poor conditions for low pay (p. 548)

T

tariff tax on foreign goods brought into a country (p. 247)

telegraph communication device that sends electrical signals along a wire (p. 375)

temperance movement campaign against the sale or drinking of alcohol (pp. 401, 607)

tenement small apartment in a city slum building (p. 565)

tepee (TEE pee) tent made by stretching animal skins on tall poles (pp. 42, 504)

terrace level strip of land carved into the side of a hill or mountain for farming (p. 50)

Three-Fifths Compromise agreement at the Constitutional Convention that three fifths of the slaves in any state be counted in its population (p. 196)

toleration willingness to let others practice their own customs and beliefs (p. 96)

total war all-out war that affects civilians at home as well as soldiers in combat (p. 471)

totalitarian state country where a single party controls the government and every aspect of the lives of the people (p. 730)

town meeting session in which citizens discuss and vote on local community issues (p. 98)

trade deficit when a nation buys more goods and services from foreign countries than it sells to them (p. 846)

trade union association of trade workers formed to gain higher wages and better working conditions (p. 379)

traitor person who betrays his or her country (p. 166)

transcendentalism belief that the most important truths in life go beyond human reason (p. 413)

transcontinental railroad railroad that stretches across a continent (p. 509)

travois (truh VOI) sled used by Plains people and pulled by a dog or horse (pp. 41, 504)

trench warfare type of fighting in which both sides dig trenches and attempt to overrun the enemy's trenches (p. 644)

triangular trade colonial trade route between New England, the West Indies, and Africa (p. 112)

tribe group of Native American people sharing the same customs, languages, and rituals (p. 36)

tributary stream or smaller river that flows into a bigger river (p. 17)

Truman Doctrine President Truman's policy of giving American aid to nations threatened by communism (p. 766)

trust group of corporations run by a single board of directors (p. 540)

trustbuster person who wanted to end all trusts (p. 598)

turnpike road built by a private company that charges a toll to use it (p. 302)

tutor private teacher (p. 120)

U

U-boat German submarine (p. 647)

unconstitutional not permitted by the Constitution (pp. 221, 254)

underground railroad network of abolitionists who helped runaway slaves reach freedom in the North or Canada (p. 405)

unemployment insurance program that gives payments to people who have lost their jobs until they find work again (p. 718)

United Nations international organization formed in 1945 to help solve conflicts between nations (p. 769)

urbanization movement of population from farms to cities (pp. 300, 564)

V

vaquero (vah KEHR oh) Spanish or Mexican cowhand (p. 512)

vaudeville variety show that included comedians, song-and-dance performers, and acrobats (p. 573)

vertical integration control of all phases of an industry, from raw materials to finished product (p. 537)

veto to reject (pp. 203, 221)

vigilante (vihj uh LAN tee) self-appointed law enforcer who deals out punishment without a trial (pp. 368, 508)

W

warmonger person who tries to stir up war (p. 648)

Warsaw Pact military alliance of Soviet Union and other communist states in Europe (p.769)

weather condition of the Earth's atmosphere at any given time and place (p. 19)

wholesale buying or selling of goods in large quantities at lower prices (p. 526)

women's rights movement campaign to win equality for women (p. 410)

writ of assistance legal document that let a British customs officer inspect a ship's cargo without giving any reason for the search (p. 145)

Y

yellow journalism sensational style of reporting used by some newspapers in the late 1800s (pp. 572, 625)

★ Index ★

INDEX

INDEX ★

★ INDEX ★

★ Credits ★

Acknowledgments

Art and Design: Kathryn Foot, Karen Vignola, Patty Rodriguez, Rui Camarinha, Anthony Barone, Ernest Albanese, Robert Aleman, Penny Baker, Paul Delsignore, Frances Medico, Doreen Mazur **Editorial:** Mary Aldridge, Gaynor Ellis, Marian Manners, Jeremy Naidus, Andrew Roney **Photo Research:** *PhotoSearch,* Inc., Lashonda Williams, Vickie Menanteaux, Katarina Gavilanes, Diane Alimena

Text Credits

Grateful acknowledgment is made to the following for copyrighted material:

Page 126 From *American Indian Myths and Legends,* edited by Richard Erdoes and Alfonso Ortiz (New York: Pantheon Books, a division of Random House, 1984). Copyright 1984 by Richard Erdoes and Alfonso Ortiz. **Page 238** Excerpts from "Valley Forge" by Maxwell Anderson from *America on Stage,* edited by Stanley Richards. Copyright ©1976. **Page 346** From *Nightjohn* by Gary Paulsen. Copyright ©1993 by Gary Paulsen. Used by permission of Delacorte Press, a division of Bantam Doubleday Dell Publishing Group, Inc. **Page 510** From *My Antonia* by Willa Cather, published by Houghton Mifflin Company. **Page 596** From *The Picture Bride* by Yoshiko Uchida. Copyright ©1987 by Yoshiko Uchida. Published by Northland Press, 1987. Reprinted courtesy of The Bancroft Library, University of California, Berkeley. **Page 632** From "The Circuit" by Francisco Jiménez. Copyright by Francisco Jiménez. Reprinted by permission of the author. **Page 758** "The Negro Speaks of Rivers" from *Selected Poems* by Langston Hughes. Copyright 1926 by Alfred A. Knopf, Inc. and renewed 1954 by Langston Hughes. Reprinted by permission of Alfred A. Knopf, Inc. "Mother to Son" from *Collected Poems* by Langston Hughes. Copyright ©1994 by the Estate of Langston Hughes. Reprinted by permission of Alfred A. Knopf, Inc. **Page 759** "Tableau" by Countee Cullen. Copyrights held by the Amistad Research Center, Tulane University, New Orleans, Louisiana, administered by Thompson and Thompson, New York, NY. "Common Dust" by Georgia Douglas Johnson, from *3000 Years of Black Poetry,* edited by Alan Lomax and Raoul Abdual (New York: Dodd, Mead & Co., 1970).

Note: Every effort has been made to locate the copyright owner of material used in this textbook. Omissions brought to our attention will be corrected in subsequent editions.

Illustration Credits

Cover and Title Page Wolfgang Kaehler; Day Williams/Photo Researchers, Inc. **iv** *t* Jerry Jacka Photography; *m* The Granger Collection, New York; *b The Puritan,* Augustus Saint-Gaudens, All Rights Reserved, The Metropolitan Museum of Art, Bequest of Jacob Ruppart, 1939 (39.65.53) **v** *t* Copyright © 1996 By the Metropolitan Museum of Art; *m* Gallery of the Republic; *b* Courtesy, Independence National Historical Park Collection **vi** *b* O.C. Seltzer, *Lewis and Clark with Sacajawea at the Great Falls of the Missouri,* From the Collection of Gilcrease Museum, Tulsa; *t* Rembrandt Peale, *Thomas Jefferson,* detail, Collection of The New-York Historical Society; *m* American Textile History Museum, Lowell, MA **vii** *mt* Dean Beason, *Settlers' Wagon,* National Gallery of Art, Washington; *m* National Museum of History and Technology, Smithsonian Institution, Photo no. 90-4210; *b* Museum of Art, Rhode Island School of Design, Gift of Miss Lucy T. Aldrich **viii** *m* Courtesy of the Library of Congress; *t* Photography by Larry Sherer/High Impact Photography, Time-Life Books, Inc.; *m t* Photography by Larry Sherer/High Impact Photography, Time-Life Books, Inc.; *b* Richard Norris Brooke, *Furling the Flag,* West Point Museum Collections, United States Military Academy, West Point, New York **ix** *t* Denver Art Museum; *m* © 1999 Michael Freeman; *b* The George Meany Memorial Archives **x** *t* The Granger Collection, New York; *m* The Museum of American Political Life, University of Hartford; photo by Sally Andersen-Bruce; *b* The Imperial War Museum, London, John Singer Sargent, *Gassed* **xi** *t* Culver Pictures, Inc.; *m* Brown Brothers; *b* Naval Combat Art Collection, Washington, D.C. **xii** *t* Matthew Frost/CORBIS-BETTMANN; *b* Corporation for National Service, Washington D.C., 1998 **xiii** Courtesy Erie Canal Village **xiv** *b* Myrleen Ferguson/PhotoEdit; *t* Carolyn Schaefer/Gamma Liaison **xv** Lynn Saville **xx** George Catlin, *LaSalle Claiming Louisiana for France, April 9, 1682,* 1847/1848, Paul Mellon Collection, ©1998 Board of Trustees, National Gallery of Art, Washington **3** NOAA **6** Vito Palmisano/Tony Stone Images **8** Silver Burdett Ginn **12** Map Divison, New York Public Library. Astor, Lenox and Tilden Foundation **14** Daniel J. Cox/Gamma Liaison **15** Jeff Gnass Photography **16** *r* Robert Farber/The Image Bank; *l* ©Francois Gohier/Photo Researchers, Inc. **17** *l* Siegfried Layda/Tony Stone Images; *r* ©Jeff LePore/Photo Researchers, Inc. **18** *r* UPI/Corbis-Bettmann; *l* Courtesy National Archives, photo no. NWDNS-79-AA_F09 **20** East Bay Municipal Utility District **21** *l* Duricux/SIPA; *r* Weather Graphics Courtesy of AccuWeather, Inc., 619 West College Avenue, State College, PA 16801, (814) 237-0309; Other Educational Weather Products Available © 1997 **29** Courtesy of the Wheelwright Museum of the American Indian **30** National Museum of American Art, Smithsonian Institution **33** *l* Tom Till/International Stock Photography, Ltd.; *r* Peabody Museum of Archaeology and Ethnology, Harvard University **34** *r* National Park Service; *l* ©Richard J. Green/Photo Researchers, Inc. **35** Jerry Jacka Photography **37** *r* Lee Boltin Picture Library; *l* Grove/Zuckerman/Index Stock Photography, Inc. **41** *l Kachina Doll,* The Brooklyn Museum, 05.588.7193, Museum Expedition 1905, Museum Collection Fund; *r Butterfly Maiden, Kachina,* Courtesy of the Denver Art Museum, Denver Art Museum, Denver, CO **42** National Museum of American Art, Smithsonian Institution **43** Courtesy of The New York State Museum, Albany, NY, Lewis Henry Morgan collection **44** Neg./Trans. no. K 10302. Courtesy Department of Library Services, American Museum of Natural History **46** The Granger Collection, New York **48** Laurie Platt Winfrey, Inc. **50** Museo Nacional de Arqueologia, Antropologia E Historia del Peru **51** Loren Mcintyre/Woodfin Camp & Associates **52** ©University Museum of National Antiquities, Oslo, Norway. Photo: Eirik Irgens Johnsen **53** The Granger Collection, New York **54** ©Index Stock Photography, Inc. **59** New York Public Library, Rare Book Division; Astor, Lenox and Tilden Foundations **61** Erich Lessing/Art Resource, NY **62** *l Christopher Columbus,* Sebastiano del Piombo, All rights reserved, The Metropolitan Museum of Art; The Metropolitian Museum of Art, The Edward C. Moore Collection, Bequest of Edward C. Moore, 1891, Copyright ©The Metropolitian Museum of Art **63** Colin Fisher for Prentice Hall **65** Victoria & Albert Museum, London/The Bridgeman Art Library, London **66** *t* The Granger Collection, New York; *b* The Metropolitan Museum of Art, Bashford Dean Memorial Collection, Purchase, 1929.(29.158.142) **69** *t* Luis Castañeda/The Image Bank; *b* ©Brent Winebrenner/International Stock Photography, Ltd. **70** Ampliaciones y Reproducciones MAS (Arxiu Mas) **73** All rights reserved, The Metropolitan Museum of Art, Louis V. Bell and Rogers Funds, 1972 (1972.63ab) **74** *r* Merrit Vincent/PhotoEdit; *l* The Granger Collection, New York **76** *l* Photo Bibliothèque Nationale, Paris; *r Sugar Harvest in Louisiana & Texas,* 1856–1860, #65.39.120, Collection: Glenbow Museum, Calgary, Alberta **81** *t* North Wind Picture Archives; *b* Minnesota Historical Society **82** New York Public Library, Rare Book Division; Astor, Lenox and Tilden Foundations **85** detail, National Portrait Gallery, Smithsonian Institution/Art Resource, NY **86** State Capitol, Commonwealth of Virginia. Courtesy The Library of Virginia

89 Courtesy of the Pilgrim Society, Plymouth, Massachusetts 93 Stephen & Carol Huber 95 *l* Eliot Elisofon/LIFE Magazine©TIME Inc.; *r The Puritan,* Augustus Saint-Gaudens, All Rights Reserved, The Metropolitan Museum of Art, Bequest of Jacob Ruppart, 1939 (39.65.53) 97 Courtesy of the Library of Congress 98 *r* Courtesy of the Peabody Essex Museum, Salem, MA. Photo by Mark Sexton; *l* North Wind Picture Archives 100 Museum of the City of New York, Museum purchase, Mrs. Elon Huntington Hooker Fund 101 Collection of The New-York Historical Society 103 *l* Courtesy of the Library of Congress; *r* Kelly Mooney/Corbis 105 New York State Historical Association, Cooperstown 108 The Granger Collection, New York 109 *l* North Wind Picture Archives; *r* The Granger Collection, New York 110 *l* Courtesy, American Antiquarian Society; *r* Gibbes Museum of Art, Carolina Art Association 115 John Lei/Omni-Photo Communications, Inc. for Prentice Hall 117 John Lewis Stage 118 *l Mrs. Elizabeth Freake and Baby Mary,* unknown artist, Worcester Art Museum, Worcester, Massachusetts, Gift of Mr. and Mrs. Albert W. Rice; *r* Breton Littlehales ©National Geographic Society 120 *George Whitefield,* 1742, John Wollaston, By Courtesy of the National Portrait Gallery, London 121 *l* Yale University Art Gallery; *r* New York Public Library, Rare Book Division; Astor, Lenox and Tilden Foundations 122 *r* Richard T. Nowitz/Corbis 127 Courtesy of W. E. Channing & Co., Santa Fe, NM 128 From the collections of Henry Ford Museum & Greenfield Village, MI/#63.41 131 detail, The Granger Collection, New York 134 National Gallery of Canada, Ottawa 136 The West Point Museum, United States Military Academy, West Point, New York, Photo by Paul Warchol 137 *l* The Historical Society of Pennsylvania; *r* Giraudon/Art Resource, NY 143 The Granger Collection, New York 145 *l* Courtesy of the Library of Congress; Colorized by Marilynn Hawkridge; *br* Colonial Williamsburg Foundation; *tr* Courtesy of the Library of Congress 146 *t* Chuck Nacke/Woodfin Camp & Associates; *b* Corel Professional Photos CD-ROM™ 147 Bequest of Winslow Warren, Courtesy, Museum of Fine Arts, Boston 148 Courtesy American Antiquarian Society 149 *Samuel Adams,* detail, John Singleton Copley. Deposited by the City of Boston. Courtesy Museum of Fine Arts, Boston 151 *l* Courtesy of the Library of Congress; *r* Courtesy of The Bostonian Society Old State House 152 National Museum of American History, Smithsonian Institution, Photo No. 86-4091 154 *r* Ivan Massar/Black Star; *l* Kevin Fleming/Corbis 159 *Surrender of Lord Cornwallis at Yorktown,* John Trumbull, Yale University Art Gallery 161 Fort Ticonderoga Museum 163 *t Attack on Bunker's Hill, with the Burning of Charles Town,* Gift of Edgar William and Bernice Chrysler Garbisch, ©Board of Trustees, National Gallery of Art, Washington; *b* Courtesy of The Bostonian Society Old State House 165 Boston Athenaeum 166 United States Capitol Historical Society 167 ©Darryl Heikes/Stock South,1992/PNI 169 West Point Museum Collections, United States Military Academy, West Point, New York 171 The Historical Society of Pennsylvania 176 *l* Fraunces Tavern Museum, New York City; *r* ©Les Stone/Sygma 178 Copyright ©1996 By the Metropolitan Museum of Art 180 Collections of The Virginia State Historical Society, Richmond, VA 183 Gallery of the Republic 187 Architect of the Capitol 188 *The National Archives of the United States* by Herman Viola. Publisher, Harry N. Abrams, Inc. Photograph by Jonathan Wallen 190 *l* The Granger Collection, New York; *b* The Granger Collection, New York 193 Leif Skoogfors/Woodfin Camp & Associates 194 Yale University Art Gallery, gift of Roger Sherman White, B. A. 1859, M.A. 195 Courtesy, Independence National Historical Park Collection 196 *l* Leif Skoogfors/Corbis; *r* Michael Bryant/Woodfin Camp & Associates 199 Bulloz/Art Resource, NY 205 Courtesy of the Library of Congress 206 The Granger Collection, New York 207 *l* John Ficara/Woodfin Camp & Associates; *r* Pat & Tom Leeson/Photo Researchers, Inc. 208 *l* Virginia Historical Society, Richmond, VA; *r* Alan Klehr/Tony Stone Images 213 Mark Hess/The Image Bank 214 Joseph Sohm/ChromoSohm, Inc./Corbis 216 Food and Drug Administration 218 ©Copyright 1997 PhotoDisc, Inc. 219 George Hall/Woodfin Camp & Associates 225 U.S. House of Representatives 228 *t* C.L. Chryslin/The Image Bank; *b* Corel Professional Photos CD-ROM™ 229 *r* Wally McNamee/Woodfin Camp & Associ-

ates; *l* Dirck Halstead/Gamma Liaison 230 Collection, The Supreme Court of the United States, courtesy The Supreme Court Historical Society. Photo by Richard Strauss, Smithsonian Institution 232 Corbis 233 *m* ©Alon Reininger/Contact/Stock Market; *l* Jack Bender/Waterloo Courier/Rothco; *r* ©Alon Reininger/Contact/The Stock Market 234 PEOPLE weekly ©1997 Andrew Kaufman 239 Courtesy of The Valley Forge Historical Society 240 John Lewis Krimmel, *Election Day in Philadelphia,* 1815, Courtesy, The Henry Francis du Pont Winterthur Museum 243 Courtesy, The Henry Francis du Pont Winterthur Museum 245 *t* Private Collection; *b* The Museum of American Political Life, University of Hartford; photo by Sally Anderson-Bruce 246 Courtesy of the Art Commission of the City of New York 248 David Young Wolff/Tony Stone Images 251 *t* Giraudon/Art Resource, NY; *b* Roger Viollet 252 Courtesy of The Mount Vernon Ladies' Association 254 *l* Unknown, American, Pennsylvania, *He That Tilleth His Land Shall be Satisfied,* detail, Philadelphia Museum of Art: The Edgar William and Bernice Chrysler Garbisch Collection; *r* John Neagle, *Pat Lyon at the Forge,* Henry M. and Zoë Oliver Sherman Fund, Courtesy, Museum of Fine Arts, Boston 255 Corel Professional Photos CD-ROM™ 259 *r* The Granger Collection, New York; *l* The Huntington Library, San Marino, California 260 *r John Adams,* c. 1800, James Sharples, The Museum of Fine Arts, Houston; The Bayou Bend Collection, gift of Miss Ima Hogg; *m* Gilbert Stuart, *Abigail Smith Adams (Mrs. John Adams),* detail, Gift of Mrs. Robert Homans, ©1997 Board of Trustees, National Gallery of Art, Washington, Photo by: Richard Carafelli; *l* National Park Service, Adams National Historic Site 265 *Lewis and Clark on the Lower Columbia,* Charles M. Russell, 1905, 1961.195, gouache, watercolor and graphite on paper, Amon Carter Museum, Forth Worth 267 *r* Rembrandt Peale, *Thomas Jefferson,* detail, Collection of The New York Historical Society; *l* Robert Llewellyn Photography 268 *t* Silver Burdett Ginn; *b* ©Junebug Clark/Photo Researchers, Inc. 270 Missouri Historical Society, St. Louis 271 Chicago Historical Society 274 *l* John Woodhouse Audubon, *Antelope Americana,* detail, Neg./Trans. no._3267 (2) (Photo by: P. Hollembeak/ Bauer) Courtesy Department of Library Services, American Museum of Natural History; *r* O.C. Seltzer, *Lewis and Clark with Sacajawea at the Great Falls of the Missouri,* From the Collection of Gilcrease Museum, Tulsa 276 The Granger Collection, New York 279 Ohio State Historical Society, Jim Roese, photographer, courtesy Historic Waynesborough 280 Collection of Cranbrook Institute of Science, #CIS 2207. ©Robert Hensleigh, Photographer 281 *r* Courtesy of the Library of Congress; *l* The Field Museum, Neg.# A93851.1c, Chicago 283 Courtesy Scott Baker, Ohio Society War of 1812 285 U.S. Navy Photos 287 *l* From the collection of Mac G. and Janelle C. Morris; *r* Ted Baker/The Image Bank 288 Courtesy of the Library of Congress 293 Leon Pomarede, *View of St. Louis,* 1835, The Saint Louis Art Museum, Private collection of Dorothy Ziern Hanon & Joseph B. Hanon 295 *r* James Higgins; Use courtesy of Lowell National Historical Park 297 American Textile History Museum, Lowell, MA 298 Reprinted with permission of the News-Press of Fort Myers 301 Dean Beason, *Settlers' Wagon,* National Gallery of Art, Washington 302 Pavel Petrovich Svinin, *Travel by Stagecoach near Trenton, New Jersey,* All rights reserved, The Metropolitan Museum of Art, Rogers Fund, 1942. (42.95.11) 304 Silver Burdett Ginn and Colonial Williamsburg Foundation 305 Courtesy Erie Canal Village 309 *l* Architect of the Capitol; *m* Francis Alexander, Daniel Webster, 1835, Hood Museum of Art, Dartmouth College, Hanover, New Hampshire; gift of Dr. George C. Shattuck, Class of 1803; *r* Charles Bird King, John Caldwell Calhoun, National Portrait Gallery, Smithsonian Institution, Transfer from the National Gallery of Art; Gift of Andrew W. Mellon, 1942 313 *t* Anne S.K. Brown Military Collection; *b* Coleccion Museo Nacional de Colombia, Bogotá 319 John Quidor, *Return of Rip Van Winkle,* 1829, Andrew W. Mellon Collection, ©1998 Board of Trustees, National Gallery of Art, Washington 320 Scotts Bluff National Monument 323 George Caleb Bingham, *The County Election,* 1851–52, oil on canvas, The Saint Louis Art Museum 326 Eunice Pinney, *Two Women,* c. 1815, New York State Historical Association, Cooperstown 327 *l* Courtesy of the Library of Congress; *r* D.

Stop the Presses

Not so long ago, publishers had to stop the presses to get late-breaking information into their books. Today, Prentice Hall can use the Internet to update you quickly and easily on the most recent developments in Social Studies.

Visit Prentice Hall on the Internet at

http://www.phschool.com

for the Prentice Hall Social Studies Update.

There you will find periodic updates in the following areas:

★ **United States History**

★ **World Studies**

★ **American Government**

Each update topic provides you with background information as well as carefully selected links to guide you to related content on the Internet.